The Fleet Fee Michigan's High School State Championships In Track & Field

1895-2018

By Jim Moyes & Jeff Hollobaugh

Table of Contents

Front cover: Donavan Brazier winning the D1 800 in 2015 (Peter Draugalis).
Back cover: 1) Onsted's Naheed Irani edging Peggy Evans of Detroit Country Day in the 100 hurdles at the 1990 Class B Finals (MHSAA photo); 2)Khance Meyers winning the D1 200 in 2017 (Peter Draugalis).

ISBN: 9781092934299

Preface

Why would one begin such an enormous project of tracking down the thousands of high school athletes who could carry the label as a Michigan High School State Track Champion for more than a century? More than 6,000 state championships have been decided in the Lower Peninsula, including a number of state champs from the Upper Peninsula who tested their skills against downstate opponents.

We have also tracked down more than 4,000 Upper Peninsula individual champions beginning with the 1940 season. After spending many years forced to spend their time on the sidelines, the girls finally got a chance to compete in the early 1970s. Since then we have seen more than 3,000 females win a state individual title.

Each one of these more than 24,446 champions has a story. Obviously, no one person can hope to live long enough to write a biography for every one of them, but we were fortunate to find many stories that will be interesting reading to sports fans statewide.

After many years of research, countless roads trips to town libraries, phone calls, letters, and now with the advent of the Internet and countless emails, this project approached its end. However, there was one humongous problem: How do I get this story published and who should I turn to for help?

I decided to shoot for the top and seek out help ("plead" might be a better word) to finalize this endeavor. I sought out a man I consider to be the foremost expert on this great sport, a gifted writer, the 'voice' of many state championships, and an editor of *Track & Field News*, the Bible of this sport: Jeff Hollobaugh.

There was a huge sigh of relief when Jeff consented to jump on board to assist with this publication. After spinning my wheels and going nowhere, I had now found the perfect person to turn this dream into a reality.

Why write a story on track and not the more visible sports that have captured most of the headlines over the years? The reasons are many and varied. Perhaps the number one reason for me was the excitement of head-to-head competition. Another would be track's long history of documented competition. Unlike other major sports that have had a relatively short history of state championship competition, high school track has been contested since the latter part of the nineteenth century.

As you take the time to pore over the contents of this publication, you will quickly find that we have given much of our attention to the athletes from long ago. Unlike today's youths, who have a myriad of sports to choose from, prep sports in the early days was limited to just four sports: football, basketball, baseball and track & field. And unlike today's age of specialization, with its festering of AAU teams that take away one's ability to maximize participation, the first 70 or so years of high school competition saw most high school athletes take part in more than one sport, and oftentimes three or four during the course of a school year.

One who had the speed and strength to excel in football was often encouraged to take part in a spring sports, with most choosing either baseball or track and field. It was common practice during the early years for the football and the track coach to be one and the same.

Another compelling truth has drawn me to this sport. In a state that has too often seen ugly racism rear up, our sport has played a huge role in fostering better race relationships. Nobody explained it better than one of our early pioneers in track and field, and a person who played a huge role in the writing of this publication, 1928 Class A high jump champ Bob Sampson:

> The thrill of competing in track & field in its earlier days was especially appealing to the Black Americans. For on the track, prejudice had no boundaries. Unlike football, where a biased quarterback might not call one's number, or basketball, where a black might not receive a pass from a white teammate weaned on racial bigotry. In baseball, blacks were not even permitted to play at the professional level until Branch Rickey finally opened the door with his signing of Jackie Robinson in 1947. Even then, a black had to be constantly on the alert for beanballs or flashing spikes.
>
> But there were no barriers in track and field. It was almost as if black Americans were finally free at last. The only opponent was the clock and the string that served as a finish line; or a bar to be cleared or a distance to be attained with a

throw. Those were the barriers blacks, as well as all track athletes, had to cross in order to be successful in track and field."

Unlike many of the professional sports there were no known racial barriers or "quotas" at the high school level here in the state of Michigan. As far back as 1911 an African-American won a state championship. That honor went to miler Fred Cooper from Alma.

In addition, track in the early days was big—to the point that modern fans would be stunned if they somehow traveled back in time. In Detroit back in 1930, 17 heats were necessary at the PSL meet in the 100 and 220-yard dashes. An unheard of five heats were needed for the mile run! With the proliferation of other sports currently available for today's athletes, the turnout for track & field has sadly diminished to its current levels.

Similarly, interest (and certainly media coverage) has waned in recent years. However, the talent has not disappeared. The quality of our current meets continues to amaze.

What has been especially interesting in tracking those that experienced the honor of participating in state track meets is what many have accomplished after their high school careers. Many have gone on to further athletic glory, in college, as professionals, as Olympians. Others have excelled in the worlds of business, academics and politics; a countless number of former stars have given back to sport by becoming coaches.

Many former track stars have given the supreme sacrifice for this country in the numerous wars that have been fought on foreign soils for more than a century. One former state finalist, Gerald R. Ford, served our country as the 38th President. Former Michigan Governor Bill Milliken was himself a high jumper of note. Most have gone on to bigger and better things after their high school careers came to a close; an unfortunate few went on the dark side. Our emphasis will focus on the bright side of the spectrum.

-Jim Moyes

Foreward

It must be more than 20 years ago that I first became aware that Jim Moyes was writing this book. He shared chunks of it with me that I have found to be an invaluable reference for my own work. And as the years flew by, I kept wondering when I would finally get a chance to see the whole thing! More than any other book, I needed it on my shelf and I wished that Jim would hurry up.

Be careful what you wish for! When he called and asked me to help edit the book and get it across the finish line, I could not have been more honored. But the project, I soon discovered, was absolutely massive. Jim had spent decades on this—thousands and thousands of hours in all. And as he has said on more than one occasion, he knew that I could appreciate the importance of this work, because both of us can be accused of "not having both of our oars in the water" when it comes to this sport.

For me, the state finals have always been magical. I still vividly remember my first, the 1976 edition at Houseman Field in Grand Rapids, watching my older brother run the two-mile. As a child I professed to hate all sports, but something about track & field got to me, got in my blood, and I've never been able to shake it loose. I've been lucky to carve out a tremendously fulfilling career in this sport as a writer, an announcer and a coach. As a reporter, I've traveled all over the world and covered seven Olympic Games and 14 World Championships. When other fans ask me what it's like to see track & field at that level, I tell them quite honestly it doesn't match the excitement of announcing the high school state finals. For me, there is no better day in track & field.

For me to pitch in on this project, that was a no-brainer. And while my name is mentioned as a co-author, make no mistake, this amazing book is Jim's baby. I wrote a few chunks here and there, but primarily I edited and did layout and photo selection and am proud to say that any mistakes are mine. All the recognition and praise for this incredible effort belongs to Jim Moyes and his unwavering commitment to the young people who have suited up for this sport every spring. To him I say, thank you.

-Jeff Hollobaugh

Acknowledgements

So many people contributed to this work that it is probably impossible for us to remember them all. Consider this, then, a partial list to the many who have helped us along the way. Consider this also to be a heartfelt appreciation to the countless names that we have neglected to include: athletes, coaches, officials, librarians and friends who have answered our questions and guided our efforts. We are forever appreciative.

Gale Adams, Norb Badar, Elmer Ball, Kevin Bell, Jim Benjamin, Lyle Bennett, Russ Biefer, Janet Bleisch. Richard Bohl, Dolores Buffenbarger, David Carpenedo, Marty Crane, Joe Droski, Heather Dunlop, Shelly Els, Gretchen Emerson, Wayne Falan, Paul Falzone, Steven Flayer, George Forrester, Andy Frushour, Norma Gilbertson, Bob Glavich, Hank Gowdy, Arlene Green, Mark Grueneberg, Aloha Hodges, Fred Hunt, John Ingles, Charlie Janke, David Jesperson, Hayes Jones, Orlin Jones, Mike Jurasek, Barb Kaftan, Pam Karberry, Diane Keller, Eileen Kern, Jeanette Kipp, Ed Kozloff, Phil Langford, Gigi Lincoln, Jane MacDonald, Dawn Marysik, William McElhone, Greg Miller, Peter Morris, Roger Morrison, Joan Mulder, Kathy Nist, Mark Nixon, Marc Okkonen, John Osler, Kathy Pardon, Ron Pesch, Phyllis Petty, Leonard Pikkering, Sue Poll, Mike Roell, Shawn Ruppert, Terry Saari, Robert Sampson, Stu Sanders, Peter Sandman, Dale Schielhorn, Beth Shoemaker, Joy Shoemaker, Jim Short, Steve Sims, Ben Tampas, John Telford, Jim Tobin, Linda Tompkins, Randy VanderVeen, Marion VanLoo, Coleeta Vesper, Bob Watkins, Bill Wehrwein, Erich Ziegler.

The staff of the following libraries deserve extra credit for responding helpfully to our requests: Allegan, Alma, Ann Arbor, Bath, Battle Creek Central, Bear Lake, Berrien Springs, Birmingham, Bloomfield Hills Andover, Centreville, Charlotte, Comstock Park, Detroit Cass Tech, Detroit Central, Dowagiac, Ecorse, Farmington, Fenton, Fowlerville, Grand Rapids Central, Grandville, Greenville, Hastings, Lansign Eastern, Lawton, Mancelona, Marine City, Marshall, Mesick, Milan, Morenci, Mt. Morris, Mt. Pleasant, Niles, Northville, Onekama, Oscoda, Paw Paw, Petoskey, Portage, Richland Gull Lake, Royal Oak, South Haven, Sparta, St. Charles, St. Clair Shores Lake Shore, Three Rivers, Traverse City Central, Vassar.

Kudos to our volunteer editorial staff: David Mitchell, Michael Smith and George Tilt.

A special thank you to John Johnson and the rest of the staff of the Michigan High School Athletic Association for their help and encouragement over the decades. This truly would not have been possible otherwise!

Cover photos – as well as many of the photos throughout the text – have been provided by Peter Draugalis. Thank you for helping this look great!

From high school portraits to sports photography:

https://www.draugalisphotography.com

Notes to the reader

Corrections wanted! Any mistakes you spot, please let us know. The plan, at least for now, is to update the book with the current year's state finals on an annual basis. So please email any corrections or comments to jeffhollobaugh@gmail.com. Thanks!

School Names: Are all states this complicated? While we have tried to be consistent in our usage of school names, it's harder than one might imagine. Between name changes, closures, relocations, consolidations, charterizations, etc., some of the names of schools have been tough to clarify. We put a lot of research into figuring out many of the tougher cases, but local knowledge is often so much better. If you see an issue with nomenclature, let us know.

Timing: In the early days, times were often recorded in fractions of a second. You will see a smattering of them reflected here for various reasons, but in cases where we could easily translate the time to tenths of a second, we have done so (ie. 10 2/5 seconds = 10.4). The only instances where times are shown to the hundredth of a second are when the performance was timed automatically. The first use of automatic timing happened at the 1932 Los Angeles Olympics, but it did not become standard in international and collegiate track until the 1970s. The first use at a Michigan high school championship came at the 1984 Lower Peninsula Class D Finals.

Wind Readings: Contrary to popular belief in some quarters, wind readings were taken at the state finals long before one of your authors started bringing his own wind gauge! In fact, years before high school track even started in Michigan, one Detroiter lost World Record recognition in the 220 because of excess wind—in 1889! From the 1930s through the '60s at the state finals, readings were regularly taken in the sprints, high hurdles and long jump, the events that the rulebook says don't count for records without a legal wind reading. We've noted them where pertinent, but for the sake of consistency—and meaningfulness to modern readers—we have converted them all to meters-per-second from the original miles-per-hour. The legal limit for wind in a record event has always been 2.0mps. That is 4.47mph, which really isn't much at all, once you think about it. It's nowhere near what it takes for a gust to blow down a team tent, a benchmark one coach told us is the "true" deciding point on whether or not races are wind-aided (!).

Distances: From the first days of the sport in Michigan until the late 1970s, all races were run at imperial distances (100 yards, 220, 440, etc.). From 1979 to 1982, the state finals were split, with some running imperial distances while others were on metric tracks. For those years, we have specified distances exactly. Otherwise, prior to 1979, even if we don't specify, we mean yards. From 1983-on, we mean meters.

State Records: The authors themselves have debated this over the years, but in the interests of clarity, have decided to use uniform terminology throughout. We old-timers remember the old chestnut that "state records can only be set at the state finals." We're not sure if other states labored under similar rules, which had the effect of denying athletes credit for all-time bests that they set in other competitions. Throughout the rest of the sport, a record that can only be set at a certain meet is a "meet record" or "championship record." In recent years, the MHSAA has adopted this usage in its meet programs, and has made it clear that it is not in the business of rendering judgment on all-time state records set in other meets. Those, since 1996, have been monitored by Michtrack.org, and the terms have been used in this way in the announcing of the Lower Peninsula D1 Finals. In this book, we'll use "state record" to denote the best performance ever by a Michigan high schooler in any legitimate track meet. (And where we use terms like "D2 record", we are referring to a Division 2 finals meet record, as no one we know has ever kept track of all-time bests by class/division outside of the state finals.)

National Records: Unfortunately, in our sport we have two different sets of national prep records in track & field. The "official" set is maintained by the National Federation of State High School Associations (which is officially abbreviated to NFHS). However, it is very restrictive and includes a number of marks that are questionable, while disallowing other notable marks for reasons that are often head-scratching. The most reliable set of national prep records over the years has been compiled by *Track & Field News* and its high school editor, Jack Shepard, who has spent decades researching the evolution of those marks since the sport's beginnings. When we refer to national prep records being set by Michigan athletes, we are pointing to the T&FN/Shepard listing. When we need to refer to the NFHS records (as in the 2012 Division 1 girls 4x8), we will be specific about that.

STEWART RAMAGE   OTIS COLE, Captain
FORD McCARRICK   T. P. HICKEY, Manager
CLARENCE CHRISTOPHER   CHAS. LESHER   CHANDLER TOMPKINS   HAROLD CHILDS

Lansing won the first state title in track in 1895, and in 1897 the Lansing squad above recaptured the crown from Detroit. At bottom left is Clarence Christopher, our state's first notable high school star.

The Early Days

Organized track and field began in Michigan in the post-Civil War era. Popularly known as "field days," these were the beginnings of college track & field. Some of the field days, such as the well-documented annual event at the University of Michigan, were very well-attended. Coverage in the newspapers was terrific and thousands of fans would turn out to watch what was essentially an intermural track meet, with scoring by class. Many communities hosted field days on the 4th of July, open to all ages. Some were hosted by the YMCA. In Detroit, many events were hosted by the Detroit Athletic Club.

In many places, cash prizes were given to the winners. It wasn't hard to find a field day in the late 1800s that didn't offer money. Even in 1869, a group called the "Father Mathew Total Abstinence & Benevolence Society" dedicated to prohibition of alcohol, sponsored a field day event in Ann Arbor which offered a $5 prize to the winner of the 100-yard dash, as well as to the winners of the high jump, "three horizontal jumps" (i.e. triple jump). "Climbing greasy pole" was only worth $1.50. By the way, $5 back then is worth $88 now.

In 1877, the Scottish Games were held at Detroit's Belle Isle. Prizes went as high as $10 to the winner of an event in what was mostly a recognizable track meet (high jump, long jump, hurdles, hammer throw, pole vault, triple jump) but also a few events that are outmoded now (3-legged race, standing high leap, and putting the stone, both heavy and light).

It was natural that eventually the high school crowd would emulate the collegians (and the community groups) and start hosting their own field days. A few of the larger schools hosted events as early as 1883. Each school would have its own field days that would include, in addition to the usual events for track and field, other activities such as the "sack race," "potato race," "baseball throw," and "drop kick of football." One known result had Walter Brooks of Detroit booming the football dropkick style a whopping 202 feet.

The earliest known meet between competing schools was back in 1894 when the high schools of Lansing and Battle Creek met for a joint field day on May 29. Not long after, on June 22, Saginaw, Bay City and two other area high schools competed in a field day. Like many of the early field days, it included bicycle races.

1895

The success of Lansing-Battle Creek meet was so impressive that during the following winter of 1894-95, school representatives from Battle Creek, Lansing, Grand Rapids, Jackson and Ann Arbor met and formed The Michigan Inter-School Athletic Association. This organization would oversee and orchestrate future interscholastic competition. The inter-school organization was made up mostly of students representing each of the schools, sprinkled in with a faculty member or two.

The above schools met in Jackson for the first state meet—or certainly the first precursor of the state meet. In 1950 the MHSAA published Athletics in Michigan High Schools: The First Hundred Years by Lewis L. Forsythe, and the author—who had been president of the MISAA for 2 terms and later president of the MHSAA's Representative Council—had little doubt, describing the event as the first official state meet. The budget for the event was substantial, with $300 being spent on medals and $200 on other awards. That $500 equates to $15,000 in 2018 dollars! Some 33 gold medals were crafted—actual gold back then. And the best overall athlete would be given a diamond medal.

The field day, conducted on May 30-31, was held at the Jackson County Fairgrounds with the running events taking place on the half-mile horse track (it later became known as the Jackson Harness Raceway and was bulldozed in 2018). Track events included (in the terminology of the time):

    100-yard dash
    220-yard dash
    440-yard dash
    Mile run
    Half-mile walk
    120-yard hurdles
    Running high jump

    Standing high jump
    Pole vault
    Running broad jump
    Standing broad jump
    Running hop, step and jump
    Standing hop step and jump
    Putting 16-pound shot
    Throwing hammer
    Half-mile bicycle race
    Mile bicycle race
    3-mile bicycle race

Lansing won the team score handily with 81 points. The first star of early Michigan High School Track had to be Lansing's Clarence Christopher. He set records in the 100 (10.4), 220 (25.0), 440 (53.6), PV (8-10), LJ (18-7½), TJ (42-1) and standing TJ (27-7). That earned him the diamond medal as the meet's top all-around athlete. A second-place all-around medal—with sapphires on it—went to Vernon Eddy of Jackson, winner of the hammer (57-5½), the walk and the heavy-weight wrestling bout at the opera house, in addition to his 2nd in the pole vault and 3rd in the hurdles.

1896

The second state championships was held in Lansing at the state fairgrounds on May 30. (The fairgrounds, on the banks of the Grand River, were demolished in 1901 to make way for the Olds Motor Works, which later became the General Motors plant.) Sunny skies greeted the athletes and 300 spectators at the start of the day, but by 11 a.m. the clouds had moved in. Heavy rain hit at noon after four events had been completed and caused the remainder of the events to be postponed until the next weekend.

Chandler Tompkins of Lansing won the 16-pound shot at 32-9, but was a distant third in the hammer to Detroit's Leroy King (78-3) and Waldo Avery (72-11). According to the Detroit Free Press, "The Detroit boys were in fine form, and they repeatedly called forth applause as they threw. They outclassed their opponents." Social events were planned for the evening. "The girls of Lansing have a reception to the visiting athletes last night after the indoor events at the armory, which was decorated for the occasion." They "tripped the light fantastic until an early hour." Alas, the Detroit athletes could not attend, because team chaperones insisted they be in their hotel rooms by 9 p.m.

On June 6 the meet was concluded, and Detroit (admitted to the association that spring) won the team score with 72 points, beating Lansing (52), Grand

Rapids (47), Ann Arbor (27) and Jackson (8). Once again Clarence Christopher won the all-around award, narrowly edging (18 points to 17) Hazen S. "Joe" Pingree of Detroit, the son and namesake of the popular Republican mayor of Detroit (and later governor) who made his fame by fighting the big corporations. The younger Pingree would later play football for the University of Michigan.

Christopher's all-around lead would have been bigger but he and teammate Tompkins were disqualified in the 100 for putting Detroit's Kittleman "in a pocket"—apparently boxing him in. The notion of sprinters staying in their lanes apparently was not as prevalent as it is now. The meet also saw a disqualification for showboating, as Ulp of Ann Arbor crossed the line first in the 440y bicycle race but was disqualified for removing his hands from the handlebars after the finish.

The day's most notable performances came from Christopher in the long jump, beating Pingree with an impressive 21-6½ (at a time when the national high school record was 22-6). Pingree turned the tables in the 440, winning at 54.4. Tompkins came back from his shot win to take the triple jump with a 43-11—which bettered the national high school record (by Leon Adcock of Macomb, Illinois) by 5 inches.

Multi-talented Chandler Tompkins of Lansing was the first Michigan athlete to break a national record in track & field, in the hop-step and jump, now known as the triple jump. His 43-11 would still be a winner most years at the MITS Indoor Finals.

1897

The directors of the Michigan Inter-High School Athletic Association had wanted to hold the championship meet in Detroit, but ran into a road block when the principals of the schools involved refused to sanction the meet anywhere but Ann Arbor. On the track they added the 40-yard dash and 40 hurdles. The meet was set for June 4-5, and about 80 athletes participated in track & field at Regents Field, the original Michigan football stadium along State Street, where Schembechler Hall is currently located.

"Perfect weather, a large and enthusiastic crowd and hotly contested events" highlighted the meet according to the Detroit Free Press. Even though Detroit dominated the sprints and the bicycle events, Lansing managed to win the team title, scoring 76 ahead of Detroit (56), Ann Arbor (47), Grand Rapids (41), Jackson (10) and Adrian (0). Detroit's W.W. Kittleman won a sprint double in 10.8/24.0. Lansing's Otis Cole won both hurdle races, hitting 18.0 in the highs (42-inches) and the 220 (30-inch hurdles, 28.2), and also captured the broad jump (20-7) and standing broad jump (9-11).

Clarence Christopher of Lansing won his third-straight pole vault at 9-1 (landing in sand) and also leaped 43-5½ to take back the hop, step and jump title that he had first won in '95.

The biggest spectacle was probably the half-mile race walk, where Detroit's Colburn Standish went so fast that "the other six contestants had to run to keep up with him and were disqualified without delay."

1898

In 1898 the University of Michigan again hosted, but the Interscholastic Meet of the State of Michigan was greatly expanded, with up to 25 schools participating in the May 28 event. Only seven schools figured in the team scoring, topped by defending champion Lansing with 49 points. Detroit High School (forerunner of Detroit Central) was a close runner-up with 47 points. If track events alone had figured into the scoring for the meet, then the edge would have gone to the Motor City lads as Ford McCarrick of Lansing won both the quarter mile and mile bicycle races held at the fairgrounds earlier in the morning. The track and field events were staged at Regents Field in Ann Arbor with showers throughout the afternoon making for slow times.

Lansing, Pontiac and Ann Arbor High Schools got a jump on the rest of their competitors by participating in an additional meet the previous evening. Waterman Gymnasium on the U of M campus hosted a variety of events that included three divisions of wrestling along with a 40-yard dash and a 40-yard hurdles race. These events did not count in scoring for the state team title the following day. All of the competitors, including the wrestlers, would bed down for the night on the Ann Arbor campus and compete on the track the following afternoon.

Clarence Christopher won three events, and was runner-up in two other disciplines, to lead Lansing to the narrow victory. At the time, there were no limits on the number of events an athlete could contest. Roy Ellis of Detroit Central won the 100 and 220-yard dashes and placed first in the 'broad jump' with a respectable leap of 20-6. Christopher, captain of the Lansing team, took home the Brackett trophy for the fourth-straight year as the all-around individual track champion. Sixty years later, at the annual Lansing Central/Sexton alumni banquet, he presented the trophy to officials of the MHSAA.

Waldo Avery of Detroit put the shot only 31-3; however, prior to 1900, high school athletes had to use the much heavier 16 lb. ball. Avery would also set school records in the discus and hammer throw, as well as performing on the football team as a student at the University of Michigan. Just a few months after winning the state shot put championship for Detroit High School, Avery, as an 18-year-old freshman gridder, would be on the field to witness a most memorable moment in Wolverine history.

Charles Widman, a former teammate of Avery's at Detroit Central, raced 65 yards for a touchdown in Michigan's thrilling 12-11 victory at the University of Chicago. While riding the train on the way back to Ann Arbor, Charles Ebel, inspired by Widman's breathtaking run, composed the now legendary fight song "Hail to the Victors." A few years down the road Widman's brothers, Art and George, would be dominant sprinters for Central High. There was also one other historical moment for the Widman clan. George Widman (1905-07) and his son John (1925) were in all likelihood the first father/son combination to win state track titles.

Gold, silver and bronze medals were awarded the top three finishers in each event. The meet was such a hopping success that the athletic association would award a trophy cup to the team champion in 1899.

Legendary University of Michigan Track Coach Keene Fitzpatrick certainly helped insure the success of the meet by taking an active role as the meet's starter and referee. However, in the coming years dissatisfaction would grow as the University of Michigan invited private and out-of-state schools that some Michigan high schools felt were almost capable of being classed among the colleges. Chicago University School and Detroit University School were private schools that monopolized the podium in the early years.

1899

In 1899, the State Athletic Committee and the University of Michigan Athletic Association entered upon a joint sponsorship of the annual track and field meet, an arrangement that was to continue until the

break came in 1912. In the May 28 meet which was delayed by rain, Roy Ellis of Detroit high school pulled off a feat that would never be duplicated in Class A. By repeating as champion in the broad jump (20-8), 100-yard dash (11.6) and 220-yard dash (23.0), Ellis added an additional first in the high jump (5-3). His four solo event first-place finishes have been matched at the lower classifications on a few rare occasions, but not at the Class A level.

Ellis's marks in the broad jump and 220 were especially noteworthy as all the events were staged on a water-soaked track. Water so inundated the track that at one point earlier in the day the meet was announced as postponed. After various disagreements among meet management, and the bailing out of much of the track, the dispute was resolved and the meet continued.

Another star performer of this meet was Chester Barlow of Greenville. The 10th grader captured his school's first-ever state championship in the mile run (5:04.4) and added second-place finishes in the 880-yard run and the high jump. Barlow alone placed Greenville sixth overall in the competition, won by Detroit High with 43 points, with Ann Arbor runner-up with 38 points.

Following the medal presentation at the close of the meet, the Detroit delegation escorted their favorites up from the field to the accompaniment of their "well-known school yell." Most of the 200 athletes participating in the meet were housed at fraternity homes on campus. Among the large group of followers from Detroit High School was the presence of a dozen young ladies under the most careful watch of chaperones. They were the center of attraction for much of the afternoon. This would be the last year the blue and white would be known as Detroit High School. As the 20th century approached the school would henceforth be known as Detroit Central.

1900

The first state-meet of the 20th century produced the first two-way tie for the championship, and would be the first meet contested on a dry track at Regents Field. Grand Rapids High and Ann Arbor High totaled 20 points apiece in a meet that was a see-saw affair all afternoon.

The year of 1900 also saw the first out-of-state school make an appearance (Cleveland, Ohio). This was undoubtedly a harbinger of things to come and would eventually lead to an All-Michigan meet in East Lansing as early as 1906. Good weather produced much swifter performances in 1900, the best of which belonged to Lyman Bennett of the Michigan Military

Academy, the winner of the 220-yard dash in 22.8. Bennett, a native of Phoenix, Arizona, also won the 100-yard dash in 10.4 to become a double winner. Abbott Widdicomb of Grand Rapids also won two events, winning the 880 in 2:10.6 and the mile in 4:55.0.

The show-stopping performer of the meet was Gilkey of Plainwell, winner of the kicking and punting contest held on Regents Field during the morning.

George Haller took honors in the high jump with a modest winning leap of 5-2. Haller's victory was Detroit School for the Boys only state title ever. At the turn of the century the Motor City had but five high schools: Central, School for Boys, University School, Eastern and Western. At the end of the 1900-01 school year, School For Boys was closed, with the expanding University School agreeing to purchase it as well as hire many of its teachers. The School for Boys could boast of producing the first six-foot high jumper in Michigan. Alkman Armstrong, an 1897 graduate, sailed over the bar at 6-0 while competing for the University of Michigan in 1901.

Bob Dawson of Pontiac, winner of the 220-yard low hurdles in 1899, won a first-place medal in the 120-yard highs. Earlier in the fall Dawson kicked the winning extra point in Pontiac's 6-5 state football championship victory over Plainwell. Dawson would later make his mark as a top ranked golfer. At the age of 65, Dawson won the U.S. Senior's championship held in New York.

The first 'City Meet' was held in Detroit with Detroit University High taking the championship held on the D.A.C. grounds with Detroit School for the Boys a close second. Conspicuous with its absence was Detroit Central High, perhaps a move depicted as a forerunner of bitter feelings that would develop with Detroit University School. Although Central would enter the D.I.A.L. (Detroit Interscholastic Athletic League) the following year, Central was none too thrilled with the recruiting of its athletes by the DUS.

1901

The Interscholastic Meet, as it was simply called in Ann Arbor, continued to expand with entries sent in from high schools not only within the state of Michigan but also from schools in Ohio, Indiana, Illinois and Wisconsin. Fifty-six entrants toed the line for the start of the mile, with Martin Daane from Grand Rapids the first to cross the tape in 4:48.4.

The team trophy was another tight battle for first, as Detroit Central edged Ann Arbor by a single point, 34 to 33. Merl Vail from Cleveland, Ohio won the low hurdles to become the first performer from outside the

state of Michigan to claim championship honors. Many more competitors from other states would win first-place honors before the meet was discontinued some 30 years later. In all cases, our policy is to consider the top Michigan finisher the state champion in events where an out-of-stater was the overall winner.

John H. James from Detroit University School finished second to Vail. Later that afternoon Charles Curtis of Wayne High School was second to Fred Spelk from Chicago Northwest Division High School.

As a junior in 1901, Martin Daane of Grand Rapids was the first Michigan prep to break 4:50 for the mile.

Once again, a drizzling rain and a brisk wind throughout the day precluded any outstanding performances, but perhaps Raymond Stewart from Ann Arbor turned in the day's best showing with his win in the 120-yard high hurdles. The future four-time track letter winner at the University of Michigan skimmed the hurdles in 16.6 seconds, with the hurdles at the college and international 42-inch setting.

Ralph Keeler and H.A. Osborne paced the victorious Detroit Central squad with double victories. Keeler won the 100 and 220-yard dashes, with Osborne the winner in the long jump and pole vault. Keeler would repeat his double the following year, but not before making the transfer to nearby Detroit University School.

Chester Barlow of Greenville returned to Regents field to win the two-mile run in 10:52.0. This event would be contested off and on until 1910, when it was deemed by the 'experts' as "too difficult for training."

More than a half a century would elapse before the two-mile run was reinstated for the 1967 season.

1902

Good weather finally arrived for a group reported by the *Detroit News* as "the best bunch of secondary school athletes brought together that The West has ever seen." Every record from the previous four meets went by the wayside with the exception of the mile and two-mile run.

Detroit University School defeated rival Detroit Central 38 to 34 to add the Michigan Interscholastic hardware to its trophy case. Coach Stewart McComber's thinclads had earlier won the Ohio Interscholastic state meet held in Cleveland.

Frank Nicol from Detroit Central was the meet's only double winner, taking both the high and low hurdles. Ralph Keeler sprinted the 100 in 10.2 while his brother Fred Keeler won the 440-yard dash in 53.4. In 1903 Nicol would follow his ex-teammate Keeler from Detroit Central to Detroit University School, a move that would initiate irreparable hard feelings between the two schools.

John N. "Pinky" Patterson, a D.U.S. 9th grader, gave the 2,000 spectators a glimpse of his future stardom by taking second in the high jump.

Athletes attending this meet were guests of U of M undergrads. Students that housed an athlete received free admission for their generosity and were not included in the total attendance. One of the real workhorses of the meet was Detroit Central's Edward Hayes. The Central standout was extremely busy in winning the 880 run, placing second to Henry Nancrede of Ann Arbor in the mile, and taking third in the 440-yard dash.

The winner of the discus was Detroit Central's John Garrels with just a modest winning heave of 101-10 using the college/international 2kg platter. By 1905 Garrels improved greatly, breaking the World Record by 3-feet with his 140-3 while representing Michigan at the Western Conference Championships (now the Big 10 meet). He also won the 220-yard low hurdles that day. In 1906 and 1907 he bettered World Records at the 120-yard hurdles, both times clocking 15.2. However, the first was disallowed by the AAU because he hit and displaced two hurdles. The second because he had a wind at his back.

Garrels would eventually become the state's second Olympic medalist. Following a great football and track career at Michigan, Garrels took the silver in the 120-yard high hurdles at the 1908 Olympics. He added the bronze medal with a third-place finish in the shot put and further displayed his amazing versatility in

making the team (although not placing) in the discus event. Garrels was held in such high esteem that he had the honor of being a flag bearer for the United States team.

1903

Lewis High School of Chicago, Illinois, became the first out-of-state school to win the championship, thanks, in large part, to an incredible performance by future Olympian William Hogenson. Hogenson, who would win bronze medals in the 100 and 200 meters at the 1904 Olympics, captured three events. The Chicago speedster also anchored the winning relay team and, for good measure, took second place in the hammer throw.

Michigan high schoolers were able to win only seven first-place medals out of the fifteen events. Detroit University School's Frank Nicol won both hurdles, leading his squad to a distant second-place finish behind Chicago Lewis. Oddly enough, Nicol won these same two events in 1902, while competing for Detroit Central. Nicol's transfer did not make the powers that be from rival Detroit Central happy campers. From this point on, competition with DUS would be frowned upon by many of the public schools.

The following year Nicol would clinch the Big 10 championship while running for the University of Michigan, taking third place in the meet's final event, the 220-yard low hurdles. Nicol's points gave Michigan a narrow team title over Alonzo Stagg's University of Chicago Maroons.

Floyd Rowe

Floyd Rowe of Battle Creek defended his two-mile run title in the slowest winning time in history, 11:10.0. The time, however, was in no way indicative of Rowe's talents. The Battle Creek star would return the following year to win his third state prep two-mile title (10:29.0) and follow that effort with a spectacular career at the University of Michigan.

At Michigan, Rowe matched his prep feat at the higher level by winning three consecutive Big 10 championships. The distance ace from the Cereal City capped his career by winning his specialty at the National Intercollegiate championship (a forerunner of the NCAA) in a school record 9:34 in 1907. It would be another eleven years before another Michigan athlete would win a conference track title. The Wolverines bolted from the Big 10 following the 1907 school year before returning to the conference beginning with the 1918 season.

Reports circulating out of Ann Arbor had Hogenson enrolling at Michigan in the fall but the Windy City speedster still had a year of eligibility remaining. The Chicago speedster decided to stay home, however, and enrolled at the University of Chicago where he became the Big 10's premier sprinter.

Murray Wendell of Detroit University School brought to light one of the challenges connected with the hammer throw. While winning the event at Detroit's city championships on May 10, Wendell sent the hammer so high that it twisted around a telephone wire, delaying the event for upwards of thirty minutes while meet officials performed the delicate task of working the hammer loose.

Ishpeming High ran off with the Upper Peninsula team track title before 2,000 fans in Ishpeming. Many of the same athletes who played on the state championship Ishpeming football squad were also on the track team.

1904

One would ponder that a team that had already won a major meet on the East Coast (Princeton Invitational) and would feature not one, but two, Olympians, would have an easy time repeating as champs in Ann Arbor. Not only did William Hogenson appear later that summer and medal in the 1904 Olympics, but his Chicago Lewis teammate, William Varnell, would take fourth in the 200 and 400-meter hurdles.

Varnell, however, did not make the trip to Ann Arbor due to unacceptable schoolwork at Chicago Lewis. Hogenson did his part, defending his 100 and 220-yard dash championships, the latter in a very quick 21.8. He finished a respectable second in the long jump behind teammate Edward French and added a third in the discus.

With only the 880-yard relay remaining, heavily favored Lewis High had but a half point lead over

Detroit University School. With the great Hogenson on the anchor, Chicago Lewis was 'doped' by the experts as a cinch winner in the relay. However, Detroit University got great efforts from its first three runners and, when University High's Ralph Sparling was 'touched' for the final leg, he had a huge 20-yard lead. Coming from far behind, Hogenson narrowed the gap on Sparling, who had already won the 440-yard dash. As they crossed the finish line, Sparling held off Hogenson by a scant 18 inches and jubilant Detroit fans stormed the track to celebrate. So many fans mobbed the track that Detroit Central and Saginaw were unable to finish the race. Only after the crowd had cleared the track would the two schools have a run-off to determine the medal for third place.

Although Hogenson, who was reputed to be 21 years of age (he actually would turn 20 on October 26 of that year), won both sprints, a brother tandem from nearby Chelsea would be declared the best from the Wolverine State. Clayton Shenk, in placing second behind the much older Hogenson, would forever be labeled the Michigan state champion, while brother Herb would have the same distinction in the 220. In over 100 years of track and field, the Shenks would be one of only two brother combos who would share state titles in the short sprints (the other was Ray and Robert Branch of Hastings in 1947).

Detroit University's victory in the meet's final event gave the Motor City crew a 36 to 35½ victory over Lewis. John Evvard from Pontiac, Illinois, won all three-weight events to score 15 points. Evvard would later in the season lead Pontiac to the Illinois State Championship.

Floyd Rowe returned to Ann Arbor to capture his third-straight two-mile title in 10:29.0. After his great career at Michigan (see 1903), the Battle Creek distance ace became prominent in state administrative circles as well. Rowe went on to become the director of the High School Athletic Association and kept his interest in track as the starter and referee for many state meets and other major invitationals.

Walter Cole from Cedar Springs placed behind Evvard in the shot put with a heave of 40-7, becoming the state champion. It would be an even 100 years before Cedar Springs would win its next track title; the 4 x 800-meter relay in 2004.

1905

No such team dramatics graced the 1905 meet in Ann Arbor as Detroit University School captured its third outright title in the eighth running of the Michigan interscholastic. Motor City rival Detroit Central placed second with 35¼ points. By scoring 50 points, DUS, percentage wise, earned the highest total in the history of the meet. The Motor City powerhouses were so dominant that they combined to score better than half of all points awarded.

DUS, crippled somewhat with a few nagging injuries, had earlier been nipped by Chicago Lewis at the National Scholastic meet in Chicago. Lewis High, which was only able to place third behind DUS and Detroit Central in Ann Arbor, edged DUS by but two points to earn the national title. John "Pinky" Patterson won the high jump in Ann Arbor as well as Chicago to lead all Detroiters.

Will Ben'O'Liel of Ann Arbor High began his dominance in the two-mile run, equaling Patterson's feat of winning both in Ann Arbor and Chicago. Kenneth Arthur of DUS duplicated John Evvard's feat from the preceding year by winning all three-weight events, including a record-breaking toss of 44-9 in the shot put.

However, Edward Cooke from Chillicothe, Ohio, turned in the most impressive performance. Cooke broke the long jump record with a leap of 22-7½ and tied John Patterson of D.U.S. for first in the high jump. Patterson, later in the day, set a record in the 120-yard high hurdles with a time of 16.1.

Jose Malcomson shattered the 220-yard low hurdle mark in 25.8, and teamed with Ernie Vaughn, Percy Dumphy, and DeForest Candler to win the 880-yard relay in a record-breaking effort of 1:34.0. Malcomson would later win the national AAU championship in the 220-yard low hurdles. D.U.S. won 8 of the 15 events, a feat never surpassed in prep history.

Detroit University School's record-beaking 4 x 220 relay, from left: Percy Dunphy, Ernest Vaughn, DeForest Chandler, Jose Malcomson (photo courtesy of Phil Langford)

Detroit Central's Eddie Hanavan became the first ninth grader ever to capture a state title by defeating all comers in winning the mile in 4:51.4. Hanavan's

teammate, George Widman, paced runner-up Detroit Central by capturing both dashes (10.2/23.8).

1906

Nineteen-ought-six became a breakthrough year for track & field in the state of Michigan. Records were commonplace at the ninth annual Michigan interscholastic meet in Ann Arbor with twelve meet records falling by the wayside. In addition, there was a new kid on the block with Michigan Agricultural College (later renamed MSC and currently MSU) hosting a meet that in two years would become the official state meet.

Fifteen schools from the Central Michigan area competed in East Lansing with Lansing High besting runner-up Freeport. The competition the following week in Ann Arbor was decidedly superior to the first annual meet at MAC. Only Findlay from Battle Creek, who captured the mile run in East Lansing, was able to even place in the top four in Ann Arbor.

One national prep record was set. Ohio's Edward Cook leaped 23-5½ to better his mark set a year earlier, and also posted meet records in the pole vault (11-0) and 100-yard dash (10.0). Had Cook leaped as far at the 1908 Olympics, the Chillicothe sensation would have won the gold medal. Instead, Cook's best jump of 22-10½ was only good for a fourth-place finish at the London Olympics. The future intercollegiate champion at Cornell did earn an Olympic gold medal in the pole vault, tying for first place with an Olympic record vault of 12-2.

Cook might have also broken the 220-yard record at Ann Arbor, but the 220 trials were run off at the same time as the pole vault. Cook's only non-winning performance was in the high jump, placing second behind John "Pinky" Patterson of Detroit University School. Cook cleared 6-¼, pushing Patterson to a meet record in the high jump with a clearance at 6-1¼. Patterson's mark was hailed as a "world's interscholastic record," but that was from a time when journalists weren't able to readily check such facts. In fact, it wasn't even a national prep record, as the best at the time was 6-2¾ Garrett Servis of Brooklyn, New York, set in 1899. Even so, Patterson racked up solid credentials as a national class jumper, jumping 5-11½ to beat a field of collegians and beyond to win the AAU national title a few months later.

Detroit University School moved following a fateful fire to the school in 1916. In 1928 DUS moved again to Grosse Pointe, and in 1969 it merged with the Liggett School to became what it is known as today--Grosse Pointe University Liggett. More than one hundred years have passed and Pinky Patterson still holds the school record.

The team title in 1906 went to Chicago University with 36½ points, edging perennial power DUS by 3½ points. Lewis also won the prestigious National Scholastic meet in Chicago with DUS and Detroit Central placing second and third.

Dana Torrey defeated a pair of future Olympians with a record-setting clocking of 16.0 for the 120-yard high hurdles. Ralph Craig from Detroit Central took second and defending champ Patterson had to settle for third. Craig would win a pair of gold medals six years later in the 100 and 200-meter dash in Stockholm.

Torey duplicated his victory in Chicago with DUS teammate Patterson close behind in second place. Patterson also notched a first-place tie in the high jump. Will Ben O'Liel of Ann Arbor successfully defended his two-mile crown with dual wins in Ann Arbor and Chicago.

George Widman, second to Cook in Ann Arbor in the 100-yard dash, also won in Chicago. Schools representing eleven states throughout the Midwest again gathered in the Windy City for the fifteenth year. The DUS threesome of Jose Malcomson, Ernie Vaughn, and and Bob Woodcock won the quarter mile relay in 46.4 seconds. This trio, with the addition of L.H. White, earlier won the more conventional half mile relay at the U of M meet in 1:33.8.

Ernie Vaughn had a busy week for the Elmwood Avenue School. On June 6 Vaughn pitched and batted DUS to the Detroit Interscholastic championship, a 3-1 win over arch rival Detroit Central. The rivalry was more than just intense. Upset with DUS raiding its star athletes, Central canceled all contests with DUS. This also marked the end of the D.I.A.L. meet, not to be resurrected again until 1921 with DUS never again a member.

Detroit University School: Killed by Its Own Success?

A school that may have drowned in its own pool of success, Detroit University School (DUS) was an educational institution at the turn of the century that produced top-notch athletic teams. However, DUS's enthusiasm to continue its dominance over other Michigan schools may eventually have contributed to its own athletic downfall.

Athletic fans have babbled about innuendoes and charges of recruiting by schools for many years. As far as schools in the Wolverine State allegedly adding to their pool of athletic talent in an indiscreet fashion, DUS undoubtedly precipitated the era. No one, however, could dispute the dominance the institution on Elmwood Avenue in Detroit imposed on its competitors during the first decade of the twentieth century.

In track alone, DUS posted five state titles, finished runner-up twice, and may have been denied yet another title, as it was not issued an invite to the 1908 state meet in East Lansing. The athletes of DUS also excelled in other sports. The football eleven of 1906 became one of only a handful of Michigan High Schools to post an undefeated, untied, and unscored upon season. DUS fielded powerful baseball squads, and even fielded a high school hockey team, perhaps the first in Michigan schoolboy history to lace up the skates.

In the spring of 1899, Frederick Leroy Bliss, then principle of Detroit Central High School, and Henry Gray Sherrard, head of the classical department, began investigating the possibility of organizing a private school for boys in Detroit. Each educator favored small classes, high academic standards, with emphasis on thorough preparation for college. In addition, athletic participation in a sport would be a requirement of all boys.

A building located on Elmwood between Larned and Congress was purchased from the Michigan Athletic Association. The site came equipped not only with the necessary classrooms, but also housed a large athletic field and gymnasium. A number of the students came from schools outside of Detroit, but most of the enrollees came from nearby Detroit Central. After a rather peaceful start, friction soon developed between DUS and Central.

Detroit Western, Detroit Eastern and Detroit School for Boys soon joined DUS and Central as charter members of the Detroit Interscholastic Athletic League (DIAL). Bad blood between DUS and Central led to the league's demise following the 1906 school year. It would be another 15 years before the metro schools from Detroit would form what is today known as the Detroit Public School League. During this era, a fire in 1916 had destroyed the original building housing DUS, leading to the eventual move to the suburban area of Grosse Pointe.

DUS eventually was taken over by such economical bellwethers of the era as Henry Ford, and was transformed into a magnificent facility, known today as Grosse Pointe University Liggett. Liggett track coach, and DUS historian, Phil Langford has diligently researched the colorful past of DUS. "Today, we sometimes get accused of recruiting, and we don't, but back in the early days we certainly did," says Langford. "While looking into the history of DUS track I couldn't believe the incredible array of talent."

Long before anyone did the Fosbury Flop, John Patterson was the nation's top high jumper while still in high school. Two years after his prep best of 6-1¼, he placed 7th in the Olympics. (photo courtesy of Phil Langford)

Perhaps the most talented of all was John "Pinky" Patterson. Patterson was the preeminent high jumper in the early 1900's not only in Michigan but in the entire country. He was so dominant during his era that he not only won the prestigious Penn Relays in the open division, but also captured the National Senior AAU championship, while still in high school. He also annexed the state title three consecutive years, capped by a leap of 6-1¼ at the 1906 state meet, a mark that would stand as the meet record for 23 years. Patterson also was a standout hurdler for DUS, good enough to win the state championship over the tall 42-inch timbers in 1905.

"Pinky" earned his nickname in an unenviable fashion. Before Patterson began his sophomore school year in the fall of 1902, he came down with scarlet fever and sat out the entire school year. Thus, by acquiring the nickname "Pinky," Patterson became perhaps the first "redshirt" in Michigan prep history.

While documenting school records at Liggett, dating back to the 1900 school year, Langford was amazed to find that Patterson still held the school record in the high jump, a school record that may be the oldest of any prep record in the state of Michigan. Two years following his graduation from DUS, Patterson was the youngest athlete on the US roster at the Olympic games in 1908. John was off form, however, during the high jump competition in London and settled for seventh place.

Following his graduation from the University of Michigan, Patterson became a heavyweight in automobile transportation. He pioneered the Lincoln Highway (Route 66) back in 1913 and was probably the first tourist who ever crossed the continent on this heavily traveled highway. He went from San Francisco to New York, carrying with him a jug of water from the Pacific Ocean that he poured into the Atlantic Ocean upon arrival on the east coast. Patterson passed away in 1948 at age 63 in Los Angeles, California. As of this writing his school record still stands, more than a half century after his death.

Track at DUS was an immediate success. In its first year as a school in 1900, under the direction of coach Stuart McComber, DUS managed to place third at the state meet. McComber, who was a graduate from the Detroit School of Medicine with a MD degree, coached four of the state championship squads. Eddie Ryan took over the reigns from McComber in time to guide the Red & White to its last state title in 1906. In 1902 DUS began a dynasty that would propel the red-white-and blue to five-straight state titles. DUS also had the unique experience of also traveling south to Ohio where it won the Ohio state crown. Quality was so deep at DUS that Milton Woodward, not even a member of the track team, set a school record during an inter class scrimmage, leaping 20-8½ inches in the broad jump.

Playing a major role in winning the first of those state titles for DUS was Ralph Keeler. Keeler repeated as state sprint champion by taking first in the 100 and 220-yard dashes. However, a year earlier Keeler had won the sprint double while a student at Detroit Central. Keeler became the first of many transfer athletes who would play a major role in turning DUS into a track powerhouse.

The following season Frank Nicol would duplicate Keeler's double, winning both hurdle races while competing for DUS, a year after he had turned the feat while performing for Central High. Transfer students arrived at DUS from throughout the Midwest, but it was Detroit Central who would feel the crunch in athletics more than any other school.

Other future state champions who would transfer to DUS from Central would include Eddie Hanavan and Roger Hawkins. Hanavan displayed his awesome talent in the mile in his freshman year at Central High by taking the 1905 mile state crown. The future University of Michigan distance ace repeated as the state champion the following year in 4:43.0, a very fast time for the early 1900's. He transferred to DUS in time for his junior and senior years, and again repeated as Michigan's best in the mile at the 1907 state meet. Hawkins joined his former Detroit Central classmate at DUS in 1908, after tying for first in the high jump while a student at Central in 1907.

Neither Hanavan nor Hawkins would win state

The DUS crew that set the 4 x 220 record of 1:33.8 in 1906: from left: Robert Woodcock, Lysle White, Ernest Vaughn, Jose Malcomson. (photo courtesy o Phil Langford)

titles in 1908. The Michigan Interscholastic Athletic Association denied DUS's entry into the state championship, now being held on the campus of Michigan Agricultural College in East Lansing. DUS's recruiting powers had escalated to the point where two star performers from Morgan Park, Illinois, appeared on the Elmwood campus for the 1908 track season. Romulo Mills and Alfred Tilley had led Morgan Park to the University of Michigan Invitational team title the

previous season. Mills, in fact, had won three events in Ann Arbor, scoring but one point less than the legendary Joe Horner of Grand Rapids tallied.

The feud between Central and DUS had now escalated to the point where there was no longer a Detroit City League. Not only had Central ceased competing against DUS in all athletic events, but it had encouraged most of the other state schools to join it in a boycott of the Detroit prep school. Pressure was put on Central by Detroit newspapers to drop the feud, but these words fell on deaf ears to Central administrators. DUS remained very competitive for the next few years, but it had to travel many thousands of miles on the railroad to fulfill a competitive schedule. There is little doubt that if DUS had been allowed to participate at the 1908 state meet in East Lansing that the team would have emerged as state champs. Coach Ryan's crew took its show on the road as far away as Cornell University, where it easily won the East coast's major invitational. In late May, DUS traveled to the windy city of Chicago where it readily captured the Northwestern University Invitational. Included among the distant runner-ups was Oak Park High School, Illinois state champion in 1908.

Never has a team dominated a state more than the Detroit University School track team of 1905. Dr. McComber's thinclads won 8 out of the 15 events contested outright and technically garnered another state champion when Cullen Corliss, although placing a distant fourth, was the top Michigan place winner in the long jump. Using today's formula for tabulating team scores, DUS would have totaled well more than 100 points. The Detroit prep school accomplished this feat with less than 30 seniors in the graduating class. It would be another 50 years before a Class A team would score more than 50 points at a state meet.

If not for the graduation ceremonies taking place on the same day as the National Interscholastic meet in Chicago, DUS in all likelihood would have also walked away with the national prep title. Joining Olympian John Patterson as mainstays on the 1905 powerhouse squad were Jose Malcomson and Kenneth Arthur. Arthur swept all three-weight events in 1905 while Malcomson raced to the 220-yard low hurdles championship.

Malcomson, the USA champion in the low hurdles in 1909, also teamed up with Ernie Vaughn, Percy Dunphy, and DeForest Candler to set a USA prep record for the mile relay, one of two national records set by DUS in 1906. The other record set was in the 880 relay. With a clocking of 1:33.8 seconds, the foursome of Malcomson, Vaughn, Lysle White, and Bob Woodcock set a meet record at the University of Michigan state meet.

After winning its fifth-straight state championship in 1906, DUS would never again win a state team track title. Feelings had become so strong by 1910 that DUS was unable to schedule a dual meet with any public school in Michigan or Ohio.

Although DUS remained a strong athletic power in the early 1910's, failure to find competition locally had a profound impact on its athletic future. Following the fatal fire to its magnificent downtown campus in 1916 DUS would never again emerge as the force it was at the turn of the century.

1907

The most versatile athlete in the first decade of the early 1900s, and maybe the most talented, was Joe Horner from Grand Rapids. Horner stole the show in 1907 in Ann Arbor by scoring points in six events but it wasn't enough to overtake Morgan Park Academy of Chicago for the team title. Horner's Furniture City crew finished a scant one and a half points behind the 1907 champions.

Horner set two meet records on the first day of competition with victories in the pole vault (11-1½) and the shot put (50-4). In his "spare time" he finished third in the discus and was the leading qualifier in both the high and low hurdles. The following day Horner captured third in the hammer and second in both hurdles to future Olympic gold medalist Ralph Craig of Detroit Central. Hard luck cost Horner a first in the low hurdles: he stumbled as he crossed the last flight and was caught at the finish line by Craig. Grand Rapids would have won the team title if not for that.

However, since Grand Rapids was the top team from within the state of Michigan, the Furniture City crew has been dubbed team state champions. Likewise, because only out-of-state competitors placed above Horner in the discus and hammer throws, one has to acknowledge Horner as the Michigan state champion in those events. The star would end his day with four state titles and two second places, the highest point total in state track annals.

Craig, Horner, and Allan Garrels of Detroit Central placed 1-2-3 in the 220 low hurdles at Ann Arbor. This trio then traveled to the National Interscholastic in Chicago to challenge the best timber toppers in the nation. Again, they finished in the same 1-2-3 order.

Craig joined Horner on the University of Michigan team where both would win national championships. Craig would go on to greater glory as the world's premier sprinter. The Detroit speedster became the first gold medal winner out of the state of Michigan, capturing wins in the 100 and 200 meters at the 1912 Olympiad in Stockholm, Sweden.

One also has to wonder what Horner might have done if he had not suffered an injury while preparing for the decathlon. The author feels that a healthy Horner could possibly have defeated the immortal Jim Thorpe in Stockholm to make the controversy over Jim Thorpe's medal a moot point.

A teammate of Horner at Grand Rapids Central began a three-year dominance in the 880-yard run, defeating a stellar field. Tenth grader Henry Sullivan finished ahead of runner-up Scotty Smith of Detroit Central. The following week Smith challenged the nation's best at the National Interscholastic meet in Chicago and in the absence of Sullivan was able to win the 880-yard run.

Joining Smith and Craig as national champions in Chicago was Will BenO'Liel of Ann Arbor in the two-mile run. BenO'Liel of Ann Arbor High also won the interscholastic two-mile run for the third consecutive year, a feat never again matched in Class A or B. Not until 1995 would a runner duplicate Ben-O'Liel's three peat. BenO'Liel was also the only athlete to win an event both at the 1907 East Lansing meet and the Ann Arbor meet.

Ann Arbor easily won team honors at the Central Michigan interscholastic meet in East Lansing, outscoring 17 other schools. This meet would become the "official" state meet the following year, attracting all schools within the state of Michigan. Although the meet in Ann Arbor would attract quality athletes from throughout the Midwest up to the 1931 season, the stage had been set for a state meet limited to only Michigan athletes.

Joe Horner - The Furniture City Strongboy

The State of Michigan can reach back to its earliest years to find arguably the most versatile performer in state high school history. There perhaps have been faster and stronger athletes to grace the Michigan Track scene for the past hundred years, but none other than perhaps the great William Watson could match the all-around talents of Joe Horner.

If Horner had been born a year later, or had taken the sport of track & field more seriously, it is very likely that the native of Grand Rapids would have made Jim Thorpe's controversial winning performance in the 1912 Olympics a moot point. Horner retired from the sport in 1911 following a sensational high school and collegiate career. Horner's retirement was but a short year before an event called the decathlon would become an Olympic event, a discipline for which it is likely Horner would have had no peers. The furniture city strongboy would run virtually his own decathlon during his high school career at Grand Rapids High. Invariably, the talented Horner would win most events he would enter. This period of time was well before present day rules limited participation to four events.

Early in his junior season of 1906 Horner displayed his awesome combination of power and speed at the 20th annual field day for Grand Rapids area schools. Horner entered six out of the nine events offered on the card and romped home victorious in all six. Horner bested three Grand Rapids High records in the process by blazing the 100-yard dash in 10.2 seconds, high jumping 5-6, and putting the shot a modest (for Horner's future standards) 44-10. Horner also copped the pole vault, discus and hammer titles and would undoubtedly have added the hurdles to his laurels if only they had been a part of the program.

It took only a short week for Horner to improve his own records with another laborious display of speed and power at the Western Michigan interscholastic meet held in Howard City. Horner took part in eight events during the afternoon of May 19, 1906, and captured six firsts and two seconds against the best talent offered on the west side of the state. Horner improved his best mark in the shot put to 47-8 but it was in the 100-yard dash where the Grand Rapids muscle man raised most eyebrows. Horner was clocked in 10 seconds flat, equaling the national high school record in the 100-yard dash.

There was still enough energy left in the tireless Horner to take honors a week later at the Michigan Invitational in the shot put and the pole vault. The following year Horner would put on an individual show that has been unmatched during the twentieth century in Michigan High School track.

Early in the season of 1907 Horner, as well as teammates Ord Page and Henry Sullivan, traveled to Evanston, Illinois, where they captured the Northwestern University Invitational over 32 other Midwestern institutions. Horner alone amassed enough points to give his Grand Rapids school a

Joe Horner

second-place finish, but Page and Sullivan came through with valuable points in their specialties to bring home the team championship trophy. Page and Horner teamed up for a one-two sweep in the pole vault, while the tenth grader Sullivan, a three-time Michigan state champ in the 880-yard run, chipped in with a point.

On May 18, 1907, nearly a thousand enthusiastic rooters gathered at Muskegon's Hackley Athletic Field for a much-anticipated dual meet between Grand Rapids and Muskegon High. Although Muskegon easily won the dual meet, it was Captain Joe Horner who stole the show.

Horner, in the space of but a couple of hours, participated in an unheard-of nine events, winning seven and placing second in two others. He had an inauspicious start, however, placing second in the 100-yard dash. Clifton Dick of Muskegon edged Horner by inches in the time of 10.2 seconds. This time might actually had been faster but both runners were guilty of a false start and penalized one yard at the starting line.

It was no disgrace to lose to a runner of the ability of Clifton Dick, who would finish behind only three-time state champion George Widman of Detroit Central at the state finals. Dick also handed Horner his other defeat in Muskegon with a first in the high jump, an event which Dick would be crowned the state champion the following week in Ann Arbor.

The rest of the afternoon found Horner invincible. He won the 120 high hurdles in 16.8, the 220 low hurdles in 27.4, pole vaulted 10-3, hurled the discus 108 feet and the hammer 145-2, put the shot out to 47-10, and completed his day by making up 10 yards in his final leg of the 880-yard relay to take yet another first. Horner had come within one event of running a full decathlon in just a few hours, setting 5 school records in the process.

Horner and his mates traveled to Ann Arbor the next week to take on all comers in the prestigious Michigan Interscholastic Meet. This meet, run over a period of two days, would be the only meet that would bring together all the competing schools from the state of Michigan as well as other powerhouse track squads from surrounding states. It would not be until 1908 that the state of Michigan would have a meet that it could call its own, limited only to high schools from the Wolverine State.

Horner's opening day performance on Friday appeared to have his Grand Rapids school headed to an easy meet championship. Finals on Friday in the field events saw Horner become the first Michigan prepster to surpass two historical barriers. Joe bettered the 11-foot mark in the pole vault with a measured leap of 11-1½ inches, only three and a half inches from the national high school record.

The future University of Michigan star then gave his collegiate coaches a preview of what was to come as a Wolverine by putting the shot 50-4 to set yet another state all-time best. This mark would only last three years until Lansing's Arthur Kohler bettered it with a prodigious throw of 51-6¾ inches. It would be more than a quarter of a century before another state athlete would better fifty feet in the shot put.

Horner set these records while competing in three other events. He qualified for Saturday's hurdle finals by running the fastest qualifier of the day in both the high and low hurdles. He somehow still found time to wander over to the discus ring where he unleashed a throw of 109 feet that was good enough for an overall third place. The first two place winners were from

Illinois, leaving Horner as the Michigan state champion.

It appeared that he would lead Grand Rapids Central to the meet championship after points were tabulated for the opening day, but Friday's grueling schedule took its toll. Morgan Park of Chicago came from back in the pack to nip Horner and his mates by a scant point and a half for the team trophy. However, because Grand Rapids placed ahead of all the other Michigan schools, coach Thomas Wanty's crew would be dubbed the state champs.

Hard luck befell Horner during Saturday's finals or it would have been Grand Rapids bringing home the big championship trophy. Horner had the lead in the 220-yard low hurdles as he approached the final barrier. Perhaps fatigue had set in as he hit the final hurdle, stumbled, and by the time he had regained his balance, had fallen back to second place. A win would have given Horner's squad the team title but to lose to Ralph Craig was no disgrace.

Craig, a future teammate of Horner's at the University of Michigan, also edged Joe in the 120-yard high hurdles. Following his graduation from the U of M in 1912 Craig would become a gold medal winner in the 100 and 200-meter dashes in Stockholm.

Horner added further laurels by flinging the hammer throw past the 145-foot marker, good for a third-place finish behind two out-of-state competitors. Again, since Horner was the highest Michigan place winner, he earned a fourth state title. In the 880-yard relay his teammates left him with too much ground to make up and Grand Rapids finished out of the money. When all the totals were added together, Horner had taken four firsts and placed second in two other events, a feat never again matched in state history.

The seemingly indefatigable senior returned to Muskegon the following weekend and bettered his previous port city performance in a triangular meet with Muskegon and Shelby. This time Horner and his Grand Rapids mates placed ahead of Bob Zuppke's Muskegon squad with Captain Joe winning eight of the nine events he entered. His only loss came when he tripped on the eighth hurdle in the 120-yard highs, opening the door for Harold "Pinky" Shaffer of Muskegon. Shaffer, only a ninth grader, would become a record holder in the high hurdles in 1910.

The grueling season finally took its toll on Horner when he was shut out of any first-place medals at the National Interscholastic in Chicago. The final prep meet in Horner's brilliant career still saw him place in three events against the best in the nation. The editor-in-chief of the Grand Rapids High Yearbook took second in shot put and low hurdles, and earned a fourth in the pole vault with performances below his standards set earlier in the campaign.

Horner picked the University of Michigan over the University of Chicago to pursue a degree in journalism and continue his track career. Although not having to take on as big of a load for the Wolverines, he still showed his amazing blend of power and speed. Often he would run the short sprints, as well as compete in the weight events with amazing success. Only his future Olympic champion teammate Ralph Craig was faster in a Wolverine uniform.

Horner set a new intercollegiate and U of M record in the shot put while winning the national championship in 1911. His record of 48-3 topped the former mark set by two-time Olympic shot put champion Ralph Rose of Michigan and would not be bettered at Michigan for more than 25 years.

Although the javelin was not contested at the University of Michigan, Horner took a fling at this unique event in a meet in San Francisco on August 23, 1909. "All " Joe did in his initial trial in the javelin was hurl the spear 149 feet, five feet farther than the listed American Record, but his implement was ruled not legal.

While at the University of Michigan Horner competed in all the events comprising the decathlon with the exception of the 400 and the 1500m run. There is little doubt that Horner would have been an accomplished 400-meter runner based on his efforts over the 220-yard low hurdles. Listed below are Horner's marks at the U of M as compared with Jim Thorpe's efforts at the 1912 Olympiad in Stockholm.

PRs: Thorpe vs Horner

Day 1	100	LJ	SP	HJ	400
THORPE	11.2	22-3½	42-3½	6-1½	52.2
HORNER	10.9c	23-9	48-3	5-11	nm

Day 2	110H	DT	PV	JT	1500
THORPE	15.6	121-4	10-8	147-1	4:40.1
HORNER	16.0	139-?	11-9	149-0	nm

Whether Horner could have matched his PRs in Stockholm is purely speculative but there is very little doubt that a battle between these two superstars would have been most interesting. Why didn't Horner continue his athletic career behind 1912?

Perhaps the most convincing reason had to be due to Horner's scholastic success at the University of Michigan. The 1911 U of M track captain parlayed his prep interests as a journalist into an instant career following his graduation from the University. Horner was quickly accepted as the circulation manager for the Saginaw News where he would than devote himself full-time to his profession. The decathlon was in its infancy in 1912 and little would Horner know at the time what kind of impact he would have made for future historians to ponder.

Horner's talents did not stop with his journalistic and track achievements. He also made a name for himself in his Grand Rapids neighborhood with his "hands" as well as his feet. Although an accomplished pianist, it was with his "dukes" that he was also admired by his Grand Rapids track teammates. During high school, the track team worked out in a vacant lot about a half mile east of the high school, a site now known as Houseman Field. Following practice session, a hard-boiled group of area youngsters from the district would annoy and harass the tracksters seemingly every afternoon. One certain evening, after their daily workout, the tracksters were hiking back to school when a gang of youths attempted to start a free-for-all.

The leader of the gang was none other than future middle weight boxing champion of the world, Stanley Ketchel. Ketchel made it his business to initiate an argument with the taciturn and likable Horner, the indisputable leader of the young trackmen. This would turn out to be one of the few beatings that Ketchel ever took in his pugilistic career. The fist fight ended with Ketchel sprawled on the road.

Unlike today's professional possibilities in track and field, the early 1900s offered no such rewards. Horne's career ultimately landed him in Green Bay, Wisconsin. There he become general manager and vice president of the Green Bay Press Gazette. Joe served his country as a pilot during World War I and for 17 years served on the Wisconsin aeronautics board. He is also credited with co-founding the community chest and was a past president of several civic and fraternal organizations in the city.

Remembered as one of the all-time track greats, he passed away in September of 1960 at the age of 72.

1908

Finally! A meet that could be called a true Michigan State Championship, held under the auspices of Michigan Agricultural College in East Lansing. While the University of Michigan Interscholastic continued (and remained important), from this point the authors consider the East Lansing meet to be the true state championship, since it was restricted to Michigan schools.

Twenty-five of the finest high school track teams in the state invaded East Lansing on May 16 for the event. Competition was so keen on the Michigan Agricultural College track that only the 440-yard meet record set in 1906 by Lansing's Chester Griffin remained standing after 1908.

Perennial power Detroit Central edged legendary coach Bob Zuppke's Muskegon thinclads 29½ to 20½ for team laurels.

Will Runner of Shelby had the best performance by a state athlete in the discus in taking second place. It was his tie for second in the long jump; however, with a leap of 21-7½ that bears special mention. This mark still remains, as of this printing, a Shelby High School record. Runner lost the coin toss with Roger Hawkins of DUS and had to settle for the third-place medal.

Eddie Hanavan, now running for Detroit University School, lost his unique opportunity to become the first athlete in Michigan schoolboy history to win an event four consecutive years. DUS, however, was not invited to the state meet in East Lansing and instead competed in a major meet on the east coast.

Hanavan was one of a trio of premier milers that the Wolverine state produced in 1908. Mark Kennedy upset Muskegon's George Cowley, the runner-up at the U of M invitational, to become the first state champion from Stockbridge. With the absence of Hanavan and Kennedy in Chicago, Cowley became the "National Mile Champion" although rated only the third-best miler in the state of Michigan.

Allen Garrels of Detroit Central won the 120-yard low hurdles at MAC in 15.0. With the departure to the graduation ranks of 1907 rivals Ralph Craig and Joe Horner, Garrels returned to the Windy City and captured the 220-yard low hurdles against the nation's best. Later in the summer his brother John Garrels took the silver medal in the 110-meter high hurdles at the Olympic Games in London. Lansing Central 10th grader Arthur Kohler shattered the hammer record with a throw of 161-0, the first of the six state championships the future U of M track captain would win in his prep career.

Henry Sullivan repeated as the state's best in the 880-yard run. The Grand Rapids Central junior circled the track two times in 2:03.8, a MAC meet record that would last for fifteen years. Detroit Central assembled a foursome composed of Russell Stoddard, Don James, Art Widman and Allen Garrels that won the state's first running of the mile relay in 3:48.2 seconds. Meet officials perhaps were none too thrilled with two relays being contested on the same date. The mile relay would not be a part of the meet agenda until 1961, more than half of a century following the 1908 meet.

Ann Arbor: Two titles were decided at the Michigan Interscholastic the following week, as the meet in East Lansing ran without competition in the two-mile run and discus. These two events certainly deserve not to be overlooked, as they created a couple of real oddities.

It is a rarity at the state meet to have a tie occur in a running event for a race held in one section. In 1908 a tie did take place in perhaps the unlikeliest running event of all, the two-mile run. Muskegon's Bill Mann and Ann Arbor's Charles Henderson ran stride for stride for the last quarter mile.

Here is how the Grand Rapids Herald described the race: "Around the second turn and the back stretch the competitors raced like quarter-milers. Every spectator was on his feet yelling like mad. This was no two-mile run but a mad dash. Into the home stretch came the runners, tearing wildly. Mann seemed to be so nearly exhausted that the crowd expected to see him fall behind any moment. His arms were swinging crazily, thumping Henderson on the breast and left arm with every swing.

"Still he pounded on and as the two struck the tape it seemed he had won. A big dispute arose among the officials as to whether or not Mann had fouled Henderson. The decision was right--a tie."

1909

A new organization was formed to oversee high school athletics. Originally known as the Michigan Interscholastic Athletic Association (MIAA), this group of administrators would serve Michigan High Schools through 1924 when it would give way to the present-day Michigan High School Athletic Association (MHSAA).

Future University of Illinois football coaching legend Bob Zuppke returned to the May 15 MAC meet to lead his Muskegon team to a commanding win in a meet held in a driving rain. Zuppke had two of his protégés advance to coach state championship teams. Although unable to win a state individual title, Dinnie Upton would turn his talents to coaching, capturing three state team championships as a coach at Grand Rapids

Win Spiegel of DUS won the 100 yards in 10.2.

Central. Ken Coutchie, winner of the 440-yard dash, also turned to coaching and guided Champaign High in Illinois to the 1921 Illinois state Class A title. Following his brief four-year coaching reign at Muskegon, Zuppke directed Illinois' Oak Park High School to the state title in 1913.

George Cowley of Muskegon won the mile run in 4:43.6 on the sloppy track, a great time for the era when track conditions had to be taken into consideration. Crowley had earlier won the Michigan interscholastic and two years in succession captured the national high school championship with back-to-back wins at the National Interscholastic in Chicago. Cowley's mile record of 4:33.1 would stand as a Greater Muskegon all-time best for better than half a century.

Muskegon's powerhouse squad tallied 43½ points to defeat perennial powerhouse Detroit University School. DUS opted to enter the Eastern Invitational hosted by Cornell University rather than compete in the Ann Arbor meet, again won by Zuppke's men. DUS made the right decision as it easily polished off the competition from the East. DUS could boast of having the nation's top sprinter in 1909 as Win Spiegel won the 100 and 220-yard dash titles in Chicago. Speed certainly ran in the family as his brother John placed third in the same races.

The 1909 meet saw an additional twelve teams enter the competition, increasing the total to 37 high schools now competing for medals and trophies. Once again Bill Mann and Charles Henderson battled in the two-mile (this time at East Lansing) with Muskegon's Mann winning outright at the finish.

Detroit Central's Jimmie Craig won both hurdle events to duplicate the double victory earned by his legendary brother Ralph in 1907. Jimmy Craig found his own niche at the University of Michigan by making Walter Camp's All-American Football team in 1913.

Muskegon's George Shaw set a pole vault record of 11-2 despite the torrential rains. Later, while enrolled at MAC, Shaw would become one of the first vaulters in the West to clear 12-0.

Another Detroit Central brother combination also excelled in this meet. With Art Widman's victory in the 220, 1909 would mark the fifth-straight year that a Widman brother would capture the first-place medal for the furlong race. Art's brother George Widman took first-place honors for this event from 1905 through 1907.

Lansing's Arthur Kohler padded his hammer record and won the shot put to become a double winner.

Traverse City captured the Class B 880-yard relay, a prelude of class divisions in the future. This was the first time a race had been held solely for the smaller schools.

Ann Arbor: The track team from Shelby surprised the bigger schools by taking a third-place finish at the U of M meet. The tiny school from Oceana County couldn't come up with the funding to travel to East Lansing the previous week, but the junior-dominated team certainly served notice that it would be a force to be reckoned with in 1910.

In the hammer, Kohler launched a 170-3 heave that shattered the state record. By the time it finally fell in 2018 to Portage Northern soph Josh DeVries' 174-3, it had been recognized as the oldest existing state record in any of the 50 states at 109 years.

1910

The 1910 carnival of athletes saw Muskegon win its second-straight (and last) championship. This meet produced a couple of performances worthy of special mention. One had to be the team runner-up showing of little Shelby High School, which led the much larger school from Muskegon up to the final event.

The other highlight in 1910 that bears mention was the performance of Lansing's Arthur W. Kohler. As Halley's Comet flashed through the skies, Kohler capped his brilliant high school career with three firsts, including a state record in the shot put of 51-6 that stood for 18 years. In addition, Kohler won both the discus and hammer throws with ease. His toss of 119-8 with the discus shattered the previous meet record by nearly 10 feet. The two-time winner of the prestigious National Interscholastic meet took but one throw in the hammer, donned his sweater and retired for the day.

The burly Lansing lad's six individual championships trails only Detroit's Roy Ellis and Benton Harbor's Bert Copeland in Class A history. Kohler later set Western Conference records in the shot put and hammer throw for the University of Michigan.

Serving as a marshal at the state meet was John Owen. Before the turn of the century the Detroit native was one of the nation's premier sprinters, winning the 1890 national title in the 100-yard dash with a World Record of 9.8 seconds.

Leland Wesley from Adrian nearly pulled off the distance triple. He captured first in the 880 and mile runs but finished second in the two-mile, a race he would win the following week in Ann Arbor.

Pacing the Muskegon victory was workhorse Harold Schaffer. "Pinky" finished first in the high hurdles, second in the low hurdles, won by Detroit Central's Jimmie Craig, and third in the broad jump, won by Paul Kress of Alma. A first-place effort by Muskegon's Claude Cross in the pole vault, the day's final event, clinched the title for Zuppke's men.

Shelby's Warren Sergeant, who would later place in the collegiate nationals while performing for the University of Michigan track team, captured runner-up Shelby's only individual first with a win in the high jump.

Norman Bassett of Grand Rapids central reigned supreme in the 440-yard dash, taking first-place honors at the MAC meet (54.0) and the following Saturday in Ann Arbor (52.4).

The other star of the 1910 meet had to be Thomas Toumy of Detroit University School, a double winner in the 100 and 220-yard dashes. Only a bout with the flu kept him from repeating the following week in Ann Arbor, opening the door for Shelby's Steve Lyttle to match Toumy's feat and lead the small West Michigan school to the U of M Interscholastic title.

Ann Arbor: The six-man crew from West Michigan kept its momentum going the following weekend and nipped Muskegon 35 to 29 to capture the Michigan Invitational. A large delegation of the Shelby faithful gathered at the train station to welcome their victorious heroes home from Ann Arbor. Never again would a school this small ever challenge the big schools for a state title.

Shelby's Magical Year with The Big Boys

The State of Michigan had its own version of the fictional city Hickory, popularized in the hit movie "Hoosiers." The tiny West Michigan community of Shelby took on the big boys in 1910 and became the only small school in Michigan prep history to win a

major state title. What was especially noteworthy about the Shelby effort was its total team participation. It has not been uncommon in track lore to have a one, or even a two-man track team, win a state championship. Although the 1910 Shelby track squad certainly had more than its fair share of individual stars, eight out of the nine members of the Tiger's team figured into the scoring at the two big statewide meets in East Lansing and Ann Arbor.

Orin Kaye was the only member of the Shelby powerhouse that failed to score, although Kaye placed just out of the money with a fifth-place finish in the 880-yard run.

Shelby opened more than a few eyes a year earlier when it finished a surprising third at the University of Michigan Invitational. With all members of the 1909 contingent being underclassmen, 1910 would provide Shelby a golden opportunity to earn a bundle of hardware.

Coached by J.J. Nufer, the Tigers began their season with a highly publicized dual meet against the defending state champions from Muskegon. Shelby displayed its incredible team depth by pulling out a 68-58 win in front of a shocked crowd in Muskegon. Legendary Muskegon Coach Bob Zuppke threw in the towel before the last event was to be run, conceding the 880-yard relay to the visiting Shelby squad.

Shelby High School was so small that it occupied just a few rooms in the schoolhouse, which went from K-12.

Just days before the heralded dual with Muskegon, Shelby suffered a big blow when ace pole-vaulter Stanley Sargeant broke his hip during practice. Sargeant had already vaulted over the 10-foot mark, a respectable height during the early part of the century.

Muskegon did regroup to successfully defend its state championship in East Lansing the following week. Zuppke's crew tallied 28 points, with its rivals from Shelby taking home the runner-up trophy with 22 points. Feelings ran high between Shelby and Muskegon. Muskegon's annual, the "Said & Done", clearly depicted the growing animosity between the two west side schools. Following Muskegon's triumph in East Lansing, the annual wrote: "It was a lot of satisfaction to step on Shelby High School."

However, when the tables were turned and Shelby won the Michigan Interscholastic the following week in Ann Arbor, the annual marched to the tune of a different drummer. "Luck was surely against the local team (Muskegon), while Shelby was covered with horseshoes," reported the Muskegon periodical. The Tigers, not content with a runner-up trophy, defeated Muskegon as well as other schools from throughout the Midwest at the prestigious invitational.

In the very early years of state high school competition the meet at the University of Michigan was most coveted by state track powers. The state meet in East Lansing was limited primarily to public schools from within the Wolverine state. The meet held in Ann Arbor attracted schools from throughout the Midwest, public and private schools alike vying for a share of the impressive hardware served up by the university.

Placing in 10 out of the 15 events offered, Shelby compiled 35 points to defeat Muskegon and more than forty other schools to win the much sought-after cup. Leading the way for the Tigers were sprint stars Steve Lyttle and Vern Souter. Lyttle upset the form chart by winning the 100 and 220-yard dashes with Souter also piling up valuable sprint points. Souter placed fourth in the 100, second in the 220 and 440-yard dashes, and teamed up with Lyttle, Clifford Harrison and Erwin Anderson to place third in the 880-yard relay, behind Detroit Central and Grand Rapids Central.

Warren Sargeant, brother of the injured Stanley Sargeant, took home a first-place medal by winning the high jump, defending his first-place title earned a year earlier in Ann Arbor. George Rider earned a fourth place in the hammer throw, Andrew Beam took fourth in the two-mile run and Charles Wright became the eighth Shelby team member to place with a fourth in a strong mile field.

When news of Shelby's victory reached the homefolks back in West Michigan, the celebrations began. Steve Lyttle recounted his memories of the Ann Arbor meet in an interview with Lewis L. Forsythe in 1949:

"Thirty-nine years is quite a while to remember, but my impressions were so vivid of that year that I couldn't forget them if I wanted to. It just happens that I was the captain of the team for the little town that made the big scoop. I still have the gold medals for winning the 100 and 220-yard dash. Well, it was quite an experience because we traveled by train and of course, the Muskegon boys were on the train with us and Bob Zuppke, who was the coach there, was very friendly to us. We stayed at the same fraternity but just where or what, I don't recall. The businessmen of Shelby furnished the funds for traveling and the fraternity cared for us while at Ann Arbor."

Shelby's fans were enthusiastic, and as was the style then, the women wore fancy hats. This photo is from a 1909 dual meet against Grand Rapids.

Continued Lyttle, "the meet lasted two days, Friday and Saturday. The schools were not divided into classes as they are now and as you know we competed with the Detroit high schools, Scott-Toledo High School and the University of Chicago High School. The boys from the latter school all seemed to be tall slender fellows. The townspeople of Shelby were very excited and enthused when we won the meet. The night we returned home (the train got in about 7:00) a great gathering was at the station to meet us. I am sorry to report that my timidity caused a fellow trackman and myself to get off at the back end of the train and hide ourselves so we wouldn't have to make a speech at the celebration and bonfire they had planned for us. Not a nice way for a captain to act, but I was just a green country kid and didn't realize my responsibility.

"During high school I lived with a Doctor Griffin and the week of the meet I had been sick with a sore throat and had never had my track shoes on until the preliminaries on Friday. I remember the doctor gave me condensed milk tablets to eat en route to Ann Arbor."

Many of these same athletes excelled outside the track oval and became very prominent citizens. By 1910 the little school near the shores of Lake Michigan boasted of 26 of its past graduates attending college, a very high percentage for the era. Steve Lyttle, following his college days, moved to Saginaw where he was the principal of Saginaw High School for many years. Lyttle, in 1939, was in the stands at MSC watching his son Bob run a leg on the winning 880-yard relay, making the Lyttle family one of the first father/son combinations to win state titles.

The Shelby class of 1910 consisted of 21 students, the largest class in school history. In addition to that surprising third-place finish at the state track championship in 1909, the football team posted a fine 6 and 1 record the following fall. Only a season-opening loss to the Muskegon Reserves prevented Shelby from posting a perfect record.

Although many of the members of the Shelby championship team would participate in track in college, it was in the classroom and off the track where the champs of 1910 would make their best marks. Warren Sargeant placed fourth at the collegiate nationals in 1912 while performing for the University of Michigan and became the second high jumper in Michigan to surpass the six-foot barrier. His leap of 6-3 in a meet vs. Cornell in 1913 was at that time the best jump ever for a state athlete. Sargeant was no slouch on the track either as he ran a 4:37 mile the same year after earlier clearing 6-2 in the high jump.

After earning his degree from dental school at Michigan, the two-time state high jump champion became a dentist for many years in Kalamazoo. Vern Souter likewise became a dentist, beginning his career in Detroit. Dr. Souter retuned to his hometown of Shelby in 1940 to continue his practice until his death in 1954.

In 1913 Vern Souter lost his younger brother Hal, who drowned while rescuing a young lady. The heroic act earned him the Carnegie Medal for heroism posthumously.

George Rider took his talents to Olivet College and excelled in the classroom as well as on the track. Rider eventually became a college president in Kansas before enjoying his retirement. Rider's brother, Seymour, was becoming a legend back in his hometown of Shelby. Seymour was a hunter held in great esteem in the northern continent. The younger Rider's most legendary feat occurred in the northwoods of Canada where he bagged a moose that tipped the scales at 1,800 pounds, the biggest moose shot in Canadian history. He celebrated his 100th birthday by going hunting.

Many years later the tiny town of Shelby would be one of but two state schools to boast of a state track champion as well an alumnus of the National Basketball Association (Pontiac Central being the other). After leading Shelby to its second-straight Class C basketball championship, Paul Griffin in 1972 ran a leg on the Tiger's state championship mile relay team. He later had a great career in the NBA as a rugged rebounder for the New Orleans Jazz and the San Antonio Spurs.

Griffin wasn't the only former Shelby track state champion to have a successful professional career. Dave Whitsell, the Class C long jump champion in 1954, had a brilliant career as a defensive back in the National Football League. Elected into the New Orleans Saints Hall of Fame in 1996, Whitsell led the NFL in interceptions with 10 during the 1967 season and had five out of his 46 career interceptions returned for touchdowns. Whitsell's crowning moment as an NFL star came late in the 1963 season. Dave intercepted a pass against the Detroit Lions and returned it for a TD to clinch the Western conference championship. Whitsell earned a world championship ring on December 29, 1963 as a starter in the Bears' 14-10 title victory over the New York Giants.

There is very little question that little Shelby High School has had more than its fair share of outstanding athletes. But as a team, none shone more brightly than the state champions of 1910, both on and off the track.

1911

Detroit Central won the final event of the day to tie unheralded Alma for the championship. This meet was run on May 13, with the early date hindering any noteworthy record performances. Alma had to settle for a second-place finish in the B division of the 880-yard relay and stood by with hopes of Detroit Central being upset in the next heat.

Central's foursome of Harold Holland, Austin Chambers, John Bruce, and Frederick Lumley won the relay, scoring the five points needed to tie Alma for the team title.

Another pivotal race in the MAC meet had to be the 880-yard run. Detroit Central team captain Fred Lumley edged Alma's Fred Cooper by a narrow margin in 2:10.8 with the team championship very much at stake.

Two-time state champion Muskegon was a close third as the local Muskegon paper bemoaned the "Sawdust" city's bad fate. The T.B. Rayl cup, annually given to the champion of the meet, had to be shared between the co-champs, with the trophy resting during the first six months in Detroit. Alma then proudly displayed the Rayl cup in its trophy case for the next six months.

A crowded field of 30 milers had toed the starting line under ideal conditions on the MAC track. Fred Cooper of Alma won the race after Burr Osborn from Kalamazoo, who had sprinted past Cooper on the final stretch, was disqualified for interfering with another runner. Cooper's win gave Alma the necessary points to tie the heavily favored Detroiters. It is also likely that the Alma distance ace achieved a milestone most significant in the proud history of high school track and field for the state of Michigan; he became the first of a long line of African-Americans to win a first-place medal at the state meet.

Paul Kress also contributed for Alma, winning the 220-yard dash, taking second in the broad jump, and also scoring points in the 100-yard dash and pole vault for the Scots. The half point that Kress earned with a 2-way tie for fourth in the pole vault, moved Alma into a tie for team honors with Detroit Central.

Another small school was in the spotlight when William Howard from Croswell became the meet's only double winner. His winning leap of 21-½ established the only meet record for the MAC meet, surpassing the mark set a year earlier by Kress of Alma. Howard's teammate Frank Quail won the hammer, giving Croswell three winning performances. Quail some six years later would use his burly stature to become the Sargeant-at-Arms of his law class at the University of Michigan. Howard proved his performance was not a fluke as he again won the 440-yard dash and broad jump at the Michigan invitational the following week.

A standout at the East Lansing site was Joseph Comstock of Alpena. He won the 100 in a meet record equaling time of 10.2, ran a leg on the winning Class B relay team, added a second in the 220, and a third in the broad jump for the Wildcats.

Ann Arbor: The Michigan Invitational, run under a bright sun that reached a sultry 90 degrees plus on the track, demonstrated that taunting didn't originate recently. Team champion Toledo Central's 220-yard dash victor Earl Vail drew the wrath of the crowd, and the press, by "hot dogging" to the crowd near the finish line. Vail turned and exploited his prowess to his luckless pursuers about ten yards from the tape.

Burr Osborne made amends for his mile disqualification in East Lansing by capturing the 880-yard run in the fast time of 2:02.8.

1912

A statewide championship nearly didn't happen in 1912 because of political infighting. The Michigan Schoolmasters Club—made up primarily of school principals—objected to the inclusion of Detroit University School in the Ann Arbor meet, as well as the inclusion of athletes that some felt should be ineligible at both the Ann Arbor and East Lansing meets. The Schoolmasters demanded that the meet directors restrict the meets to members of the interscholastic association (many small schools throughout the state did not belong).

According to the Lansing State Journal, "To this end an attempt was made to use M.A.C. and the university as clubs to compel the minor schools to join, which Macklin refused to do, holding that it was not fair to the minor schools." John Macklin was the athletic director of MAC at the time, as well as the coach of track, football, basketball and baseball.

In April, the Schoolmasters played their trump card, saying they would pass a rule that forbid any member school from competing at a meet against non-members. "Inasmuch as this would keep all the best competitors out of the meets, it was decided to call them off and wait a year or two to see what the results of the meet run by the high schools themselves would be."

The Schoolmasters decided to put on their own state meet in the Detroit area, selecting a worn bicycle track on Bois Blanc Island or "Boblo" as it is popularly called. The site of the meet is worthy of being a trivia question: it was the only state finals in Michigan history to be held in a foreign country. Bois Blanc Island—though just a mile from Grosse Ile, Michigan—is in Ontario, Canada.

While the Schoolmasters did not follow through on their threat to ban any schools that competed against non-members, the door was open for the University of Michigan to again host its interscholastic meet. However, as 28 schools had pledged to compete in the Detroit meet—and most could not afford two out-of-town competitions, Philip Bartelme, Michigan's athletic director, cancelled the Ann Arbor meet, saying he was "glad to get rid of it."

The Ann Arbor News reported the meet was moved to Boblo because "the Michigan Schoolmasters Club thought that the young athletes were subjected to unfavorable influences in Ann Arbor while attending the meet." The Alma Record echoed that, saying that the arrangement of having the athletes stay with fraternities led to "much criticism on the way high school lads were entertained at the fraternity house in Ann Arbor." It is hard to determine whether these "moral" concerns played as big a role as the politics did in the relocation of the meet.

Thirty-seven schools came to Boblo from all areas of the state. With the meet of 1911 being contested at the earliest date on record, 1912 saw the other extreme. June 8 was the date and one can only imagine how this makeshift bicycle track would look in comparison to today's high-tech facilities. Reports given on this meet pointed out numerous incidents, including spectators inadvertently interfering with runners as they circled a slow track laced with odd angles and banks on the turns. Reportedly, the 220-yard hurdlers were particularly challenged in hurdling on a banked surface. This would prove to be the first, and only time, that the meet was held in the Motor City area.

Bay City Eastern's Carman Smith put on a one-man show with three victories, nearly single handedly leading his team to an 18-15 win over second-place Wayne High School. It appeared for a moment that another one-man team, thrower J. D. Cross of Wayne, would win the team title. Cross would meet an untimely death in the 1920s when his automobile crashed into a viaduct in the Detroit area.

Although overshadowed by Carman Smith, another Smith would go on to make a name for himself as a collegiate champion. Harold Smith from Ann Arbor High, who placed second to Carman in the 100 and low hurdles, won the intercollegiate championships in the 100 and 220 in 1916 for the University of Michigan.

Cross' sweep of the weight events put enormous pressure on Smith to produce in the meet's final event-the broad jump. Three jumps were the allowable limit back in the early part of the 20th century. Smith's first jump was just fair. His next attempt was a little better, but on the third he came though with a winning effort of 20-1½, taking first place and winning the meet for Bay City Eastern (now Bay City Central). Captain Smith somehow found time between training and academics to compose the school song for the class of 1912.

Only William Howard from Croswell repeated from the 1911 meet. The future World War I pilot competed in the 220 in 1912 and came away with the win, earning Howard three golds in two years. The meet's biggest upset came when Earl Sheldon of West Branch defeated Muskegon's Hoyt Miller from Muskegon in the

mile. In an earlier meet in Chicago, Miller covered the distance in an impressive 4:31.4. Sheldon dominated the distance events the next two years and eventually set a Ferry Field record while attending Michigan Agricultural College.

Forrest Bailey of Morenci and Harold Wilson of Detroit Central waged a terrific battle in the pole vault. Both cleared 11-0, as high as the standards would go in 1912. A box was then used to elevate each standard with Bailey clearing a remeasured 11-2½ to account for the only meet record. Wilson would place in the 1916 national intercollegiate championships while competing for the University of Michigan.

1913

After a one-year absence, the two meets returned to their familiar haunts. The Detroit Free Press reported that at the fall meeting of the Michigan Schoolmasters Club, it was decided "that it would be better to accept the invitation for Michigan and the Aggies as many features of the Detroit meet did not quite come up to the expectations of the teachers."

A compromise was reached and the Schoolmasters offered a discounted associate membership to smaller schools, thus allowing all schools that participated in the official meet at East Lansing to become members. The championship would remain at Michigan Agriculture College for nearly 40 years (with the exception of 1934).

The University of Michigan Interscholastic, open to all schools in the U.S. as long as they adhered to Michigan's eligibility rules, headed back to Ann Arbor for the 1913 school year. The previously reported moral objections to the entertainment of the young athletes on the Ann Arbor campus were determined to be mostly rumor and exaggeration, according to the Free Press: "It was claimed that the college men entertained them not wisely but too well and the rumor grew with each repetition until it was claimed that the entire affair resembled a Roman holiday, to put it mildly." An adult observer attested that "the rumors were unfounded."

In East Lansing on June 7, Dinnie Upton's Grand Rapids Central team took home the first-place trophy with 19 2/3 points, just edging out the runners-up from Detroit Eastern and Coldwater. The individual standout of the meet had to be Earl Sheldon from West Branch. He repeated as champion in both the half mile and mile runs. His time of 4:33.6, in capturing his second-straight mile championship, would stand for nearly 20 years. What made Sheldon's feat especially amazing was that he had to run against a cold raw wind, and a track made heavy from the previous night's rain.

Sheldon, however, did not score the most points in the meet. That honor went to Hugh Blacklock of the winning Grand Rapids team, taking home a gold watch for his efforts. Blacklock took first in the shot put and hammer throw, grabbed a third in the high hurdles, and also earned a fraction of a point in the high jump. He most likely became the first Michigan state champ to ever play in the annual New Year's Day Rose Bowl classic. Blacklock began his collegiate football career at MAC but played in the Rose Bowl for the winning Great Lakes Naval Station team. He later became one of the early pioneers in the National Football League as a member of the Chicago Bears.

Warner Van Acken of Coldwater set a new record in the 440-yard dash in the winning time of 52.4, shattering the former mark shared by William Howard of Croswell and Norman Bassett of Grand Rapids Central. The Coldwater quarter miler romped to a margin of victory of better than 10 yards over his closest pursuers, and nearly upset Sheldon in the half mile. Van Acken's teammate, Alfred Gamble, gave Coldwater three first-place medals with his sprint double. Gamble's winning time of 10.2 seconds also gave him a share of the meet record.

Ann Arbor: West Branch boasted a pair of milers that would make even today's lads envious. Earl Sheldon won the 880 in 2:02.2, one of the fastest posted in state history. Then his teammate, McKay (first name unknown), topped him in the mile, giving West Branch a 1-2 sweep. After reviewing Sheldon's past and future successes, one would wonder if perhaps the West Branch distance ace intentionally let his lesser known teammate bring home the championship medal.

It's worth noting Frank Foss of team champion Chicago University High was the winner of the pole vault at the Ann Arbor meet. Foss broke Joe Horner's 1907 interscholastic record by clearing 12-½ and would break the World Record four years later, winning the 1920 Olympic gold medal at 13-5½.

1914

Detroit Eastern used a record-setting 10.0 clocking by Herbert Henry in the 100-yard dash to win the 1914 state championship, topping Bay City Eastern 25 to 22. Henry and his mates finished first in five events, accounting for 20 of their 25 points. Elmer Reich won the pole vault for the second-straight year for the victors. Reich, who would become the collegiate record holder in this event for Washington and Jefferson, sailed 10-9 for his repeat victory.

Scoring used in the early part of the century was as follows: five points for first; three points for second, two

for third place, and one for fourth. This system was used from 1898 until 1931 (with the exception of 1920 when, for one year only, five places were counted). Henry set the meet's only record, while teammate Clarence Kretzschmar added valuable points to the champion's cause, placing second to Henry in the 100. Kretzschmar returned to the track later in the afternoon to win the 220-yard dash on the brand-new straightaway. In previous editions, the 220-yard events had been held on a curve. Strong winds blowing out of the East prevented any additional records from toppling.

Misfortune struck John Donovan of Alpena, as Donovan suffered a broken wrist while participating in the high jump. Another mishap occurred when the bleachers collapsed as the athletes were getting their pictures taken. Fortunately, no injuries occurred.

Individual laurels for the meet were won by Pat Smith of runner-up Bay City Eastern. Smith placed first in the discus and shot put and fourth in the hammer throw, earning 11 points. The burly Smith joined Hugh Blacklock as one of the early pioneers of the National Football League, scoring three touchdowns as a fullback during a three-year career with the Buffalo All-Americans.

Ann Arbor: Pat Smith was the only performer from the state of Michigan that was able to win at both MAC and Ann Arbor, with the University of Michigan meet dominated by out-of-state athletes. Grand Rapids Central placed a distant fourth, ahead of Detroit Eastern and Bay City Eastern in Ann Arbor, but well behind teams from Chicago and Wisconsin.

The champion Chicago University School squad repeated, led by the day's best performer, Phil Spink. The first half-miler to crack the two-minute barrier at the Illinois state meet, Spink shattered the interscholastic and Ferry Field record with a spectacular time of 1:56.0. That made him the No. 2 prep in U.S. history, behind only Ted Meredith, the Pennsylvania schoolboy who won the 1912 Olympics in a then-World Record of 1:52.5.

1915

Detroit Eastern came back in 1915 to post an even more impressive showing, scoring 30 points to lead runner-up Muskegon by 9 at the June 5 meet. Muskegon's George Kimball won a rare triple with victories in the shot put (47-4), discus (116-1) and the 12-pound hammer (168-0). The Muskegon ace took his hammer throwing talents to the National Interscholastic Meet in Chicago, where he won his specialty against the top prep throwers in the country.

Eastern's star sprinter, Herbert Henry, had wins in the 100 and 220-yard dashes and also anchored his 880-yard relay team to victory.

Roy Workman was the only man at the meet representing Plainwell, but he alone earned 10 points, placing second in the 220, second in the 440, and tying Miles Casteel from St Johns for first in the pole vault. Casteel became a 12-letter winner for Kalamazoo College before becoming an assistant football and track coach at Michigan State. Casteel was also an early pioneer of the National Football League, playing one year for the Rock Island team in 1922.

One record was broken, with Vernon Parks of St. Johns doing the trick in the broad jump with a distance of 21-3. Oddly enough Parks wasn't credited as the outright champion in this event. Glen Thompson of Rockford matched Park's distance of 21-¾ during the competition, necessitating a jump-off to determine the winner. Reports from this meet had Park's breaking the record with a leap of 21-3 during the jump-off, taking home the first-place medal. Thompson, curiously, was credited as a co-champion in the broad jump, although the future high school coach at Escanaba would have to settle for the second-place medal.

Eastern's margin could have been greater had not two-time defending champion Fred Williams taken a spill in the 220-low hurdle preliminaries.

Perhaps the most significant note to emerge from that meet was a partially separated competition for the smaller Class B schools. At this meet, as well as previous year's championships, the athletes were enticed to excel with offerings of medals, cups, and even a gold Elgin watch for the highest individual point winner. Close to 100 assorted prizes awaited the lucky place winners, a practice that would now be frowned upon by the state's athletic association.

Ann Arbor: At the previous week's meet at the U of M interscholastic (May 22-23), out-of-state foes so dominated the Michiganders that only two individuals came away with championships. Muskegon's George Kimball again won the rare triple in the weights and Scott Burke of Richmond took honors in the 440-yard dash. Kimball added to his laurels by winning the hammer throw at the prestigious National Interscholastic meet in Chicago.

1916

Grand Rapids Central returned to the winner's circle in 1916 (June 10) with a convincing 22-point margin over second-place St Joseph. Coach Dinnie Upton's crew went to the winner's circle seven times, including a double win by hurdler Rod MacKenzie. For his efforts, MacKenzie was awarded a $35 gold watch. Grand Rapids brought back to the Furniture City six silver loving cups, four of which the school would keep permanently.

Grand Rapids initially was credited with 44½ points, a whopping 30 ahead of runner-up St. Joseph. Teams opposing Grand Rapids protested at the outset of the meet against Upton's entering Jack Belknap, but he competed anyway. Belknap was initially declared the winner of the discus but was dropped from the results due to an apparent violation of the eight-semester ruling. When it became apparent, however, Upton's team had the meet cinched, he withdrew Belknap, cutting Grand Rapids' score down to 37 points.

Lansing's Lawrence Bishop was then declared the discus champion following the withdrawal of Belknap from the meet. Grand Rapids won permanent possession of the prestigious Harvard cup, awarded to the team scoring the most points over a five-year period.

One of the greatest athletes never to become a state champion in Michigan: Loren Murchison at age 15 won 7 of 10 events in the "decathlon" at the Detroit schools field day in 1915. After a brief stint at Detroit Eastern, he moved to Missouri. He won Olympic gold on the 4 x 100 in 1920 and 1924, and was a 3-time Olympic sprint finalist. Stricken by cerebrospinal meningitis at age 27, he spent the rest of his life in a wheelchair.

Equaling the meet record in the 440 was Grand Rapids Central's Guy Houston. Inducted into the Michigan Sports Hall of Fame in 1963, Houston was known primarily for his accomplishments as a high school football coach. While coaching football at Flint Northern for 24 years, Houston posted a .783 winning percentage that included 10 undefeated seasons. Houston, who retired as Northern's high school principal in 1963, would be noted in the future as having Flint Northwestern's stadium, home to many state championship meets, named in his honor.

Central won every race contested at 440-yards or longer, including wins by Dave Forbes in the 880-yard run (2:04.0) and Jake VanderVisse in the mile (4:42.4). VanderVisse displayed his versatility by teaming up with McKenzie, Houston, and Wendell Bacon on the Rams' winning 880-yard relay team.

Conspicuous with their unusual poor showing were the tracksters from the city of Detroit. In no event would any athlete from Michigan's largest city muster anything better than a third place. It was apparent that a lack of a city league, dating back to the squabble between Detroit Central and Detroit University School in 1908, had a negative effect on the sport in the Motor City. It would not be until 1921 that the current Detroit Public School League would be formed.

Future Big 10 champ Arthur Cross of Muskegon took honors in the pole vault at 10-9.

The high jump pit at MAC was again the site of an unfortunate injury. Newaygo's Clarence Fessenden, who earlier won the shot put and finished third in the hammer throw, fell while competing in the high jump and fractured both bones in his right forearm. Following a stint in World War I, Fessenden would later captain the MAC Aggies in basketball and track. While performing at MAC, Fessenden, who would possess the shot put and discus records, also won the state intercollegiate title three straight years in the discus.

One record fell when Leonard Merchant of St Joseph sprinted 220-yards in 22.6 seconds.

Ann Arbor: Other than Class B wins--Leonard Merchant took both sprints—no Michigan prep was able to bring home a gold medal at Michigan's meet (June 2-3). Out-of-state schools so dominated that Grand Rapids Central with its third-place finish would be the only state school to place in the top ten.

A two-man team from Oregon, Illinois won. The dynamic duo of Sherman Landers and Frank Loomis traveled to and easily won many big meets in the Midwest that season. Oddly enough, these two future Olympians failed to win their own Illinois State meet. Loomis, who went on to capture the gold medal at the 1920 Olympics in the 440-yard hurdles in world record time, was not eligible according to Illinois High School rules.

Landers won both sprints, the pole vault, and was runner-up in the high hurdles and the broad jump. His 21.6 in the 220 was disallowed as wind-aided. He and Loomis so dominated in Ann Arbor that their performance led to an important rule change. From this point forward, all athletes entered in the University of Michigan Interscholastic would not be permitted to enter more than three events.

Shelby returned to the site of its run to glory back in 1910 by winning the Class B team championship. This became the first time in state history where the class system to determine a team champion was implemented.

1917

Coach Dinnie Upton's last year as coach was another huge success. The Furniture City lads brought home the James Rayle Cup by repeating as state champs. Other valuable hardware garnered by the victors included the Albion Cup and the Larrabee Cup. Earlier in the season the Rams had captured the win at the third annual Kalamazoo College interscholastic track and field meet.

This year's state championship was much more difficult to win as Grand Rapids had to overtake Detroit Central in the final two events of the program to emerge as winners. Upton's boys won the meet despite the loss of Rod McKenzie, the leading scorer of the 1916 meet. The Furniture City meet record holder in the high hurdles was injured the previous week at the Kalamazoo invitational but Grand Rapids Central had more than enough depth to compensate for the loss of McKenzie.

World War I forced cancellation of the University of Michigan Interscholastic and would also bring about the cancellation of the entire 1918 season. The first World War signaled perhaps the darkest era for high school sports in the state of Michigan. A very limited schedule, at best, took place in all sports, and the war would mean the cancellation of the entire season for many schools.

At the state meet in East Lansing a brisk wind was blowing during most of the afternoon and for an hour in the middle of the competition, the program had to be halted while a rain and hail storm worked its way out of the area. The slow track created by the heavy rains made any new records virtually impossible. Competition was extremely balanced with not a double winner produced for the first time since 1908.

Kalamazoo's Lloyd Kurtz edged William Brown of Detroit Central for individual point honors. Both athletes were extremely busy on the MAC cinders with Kurtz taking a first in the 220 low hurdles, second in the high hurdles and high jump, and placed third in the broad jump. Brown scored only a point less than the Kalamazoo star with a first in the 100-yard dash, and seconds in the 220-yard dash and the discus. Brown lost his chance for the tie with Kurtz by taking only a fourth in the shot put.

Jake VanderVisse and Guy Houston from Grand Rapids Central joined Pontiac's Russell Cowan in defending titles won in 1916. Charles Gleason, winner of the 120-yard hurdles from Detroit Eastern, would return to the MAC track in 1918 and win this same event at the 4th annual Intercollegiate state meet, a long-time affair open to all state colleges other than the University of Michigan. Gleason would win the 120-yard high hurdles while competing for Detroit Junior College.

Kalamazoo: The city of Kalamazoo would help take up the slack from the lack of track competitions, offering two major invitationals. In addition to the traditional meet hosted for the previous three years by Kalamazoo College, Western Normal (WMU) College opened up its 2,000-seat track facility to 26 schools from around the state. The latter meet broke the competition into classes. Schools from cities with populations totaling under 10,000 would be permitted to display their wares against schools of near equal size. Chelsea took home the honors in Class B, besting the other 15 Class B schools entered, with 29 points.

Grand Rapids Central and Kalamazoo took turns winning the team championships at each celery city meet, with Detroit Central placing second to Kazoo at the Western Normal Invitational.

1918

In the 100 years of track & field the year of 1918 would lead to the most hardships for Michigan high school athletes. With the world entangled in the Great War, scholastic spring sports not only took a back seat, but also nearly disappeared, with any form of athletic competition being a rarity.

The MIAA, in March of 1918, voted unanimously to discontinue spring sports to "allow the boys to go on the farms early in the spring to make up the deficit of labor in the fields." This edict, coupled with a national influenza epidemic, not only eliminated the 20th running of a state championship track & field meet, but virtually brought sports to a standstill.

Especially hard-hit were the youths from the larger cities. Many of the Detroit athletes moved to neighboring farm communities where they grabbed a hoe instead of a ball and bat. Ernie Wuesthoff, a popular all-around coach at Detroit Eastern High

School, would provide a great example. Wuesthoff, who coached Eastern to the state track & field state championships in 1914 and 1915, took on the additional duty of chief farm enrolling office for his school.

Neighboring Macomb County was the district assigned to Eastern High School. Many other major metropolitan schools did the same before sports returned to their normal pattern in the fall of 1918.

The camaraderie developed while tilling the soil might have been beneficial for Wuesthoff's athletes, as Eastern again returned to the winner's circle and brought home the championship team trophy in 1919.

Newspaper accounts from rural Michigan did show a scattering of athletic events that took place in the late spring of 1918. It was commonplace for many neighboring communities to gather and put on one big event, often combining local schools into a county meet. After a dearth of sporting events, fans were starved to see their local youths in action. Over 5,000 fans packed the little town of Bangor to witness the annual Van Buren County track and field meet.

George Walker from Gobleville was the individual star of the meet by winning three first-place medals, a prelude of what he would do the following year at the state meet in East Lansing. Many other counties also hosted meets similar to the one hosted by Bangor, but for most athletes, track & field at best was but a one-day affair. It would take another World War (WWII) to again bring about a cancellation of the state championships in 1943.

1919

Detroit Eastern nipped Battle Creek Central by a scant half point to prevent the "Crickets," as they were known in 1919, from winning their first championship.

Eastern trailed Battle Creek up to the last race, when a fourth-place finish in the 880-relay gave the Motor City team one point and the championship. Leonard "Shunt" Turnbull won the shot put and hammer and placed third in the discus to lead the winning Detroiters.

Only 5½ points separated the top five teams. With Grand Rapids Central coaching legend Dinnie Upton no longer coaching at Central, Grand Rapids South became the dominant team from the Furniture City. Adam Simeons and Herman DeRuiter were major factors for the high school alma mater of future United States President Gerald Ford. Siemons and DeRuiter each ran a leg on South's victorious 880-yard relay foursome. In addition, Simeons won the 440-yard dash, while DeRuiter uncorked the day's longest throw in the discus.

A notable double winner in the sprints was George Walker of Gobleville (now known as Gobles). His victories in the 100 and 220-yard dashes became the only titles won by the small school in southwestern Michigan. It is likely Walker would have been the top Michigan prep placer in the dashes at the University of Michigan Interscholastic, if only he had entered the meet. Ward Platt of Kalamazoo Central, the runner-up to Walker in the 100-yard dash in East Lansing, was the Ann Arbor winner. Walker went on to Western State Teachers College (WMU), where he set records in the 100 and 220.

Edward McCallum of Detroit Central became the third entrant to win a double by capturing both hurdle events.

Winning the pole vault at 10-5 was Kalamazoo's Rudy Miller, who later won a record 15 varsity letters during his collegiate career at Western Michigan. The versatile Miller followed his stint at Western by playing professional baseball, culminating his career with the briefest of major league tenures. The Kalamazoo lad made one big league appearance for Connie Mack's powerful 1929 A's, striking out as a pinch hitter in his only attempt.

Turnbull took first place in the hammer throw with a modest winning heave of 118-0. This was the last year the hammer would be thrown at the state meet. The hammer would continue to be thrown as part of the Detroit City League championships beginning with the 1922 season. After a trial run of seven years, officials in the Motor City deemed the event too dangerous and did away with the hammer throw following the 1929 season.

Ann Arbor: The University of Michigan interscholastic meet resumed after the war with Champaign, Illinois, taking team honors. Once again, Detroit Eastern finished ahead of Battle Creek by taking second place, two points ahead of the lads from the Cereal City.

Five Michigan tracksters were able to win in Ann Arbor the week following the MAC meet. Repeat champions included Jeff Siemons of Grand Rapids South in the 440-yard dash, William Weekes of Battle Creek in the 880-yard run, Charles Cooper of Detroit Central in the mile run, while Leroy Niesch and Leonard Turnbull of Detroit Eastern repeated as field event victors in the long jump and hammer throw respectively.

1920

A carnival-like atmosphere graced the M.A.C. campus for the 1920 state championships (May 29). Both high schoolers and collegians competed at the

same time. While the tracksters were circling the oval track, a high school band championship was taking place in the infield. Fifty-Six members of the Dowagiac marching band out dueled runner-up Paw Paw for championship honors in the band competition.

A new king was crowned in track & field. Detroit Northwestern edged Grand Rapids Central 29 to 27½, embarking on a reign of eight state championships to be won over the next eleven years. This streak only came to an end in 1931, when Detroit Public Schools refused to compete with out-state prepsters for the next 30 years.

An additional place winner was added to the scrolls in 1920, with medals now given to the first five place winners. Scoring to determine team champions was tabulated on a 5-4-3-2-1 system. This system lasted for but one year, before reverting back to the former method of four medal winners beginning with the 1921 season. It would be another ten years before five place winners would again be declared.

Bill Weekes from Battle Creek became the only repeat champion from the 1919 meet when he won the 880-yard run in 2:04.8. Weekes added the 440 championships to his list of laurels with a time of 53.0. "Hookey" Brooks was a double winner for Chelsea, winning the shot put and discus. Hookey's discus toss was measured at 101 and 3/5 "yards." Other double winners in 1920 included sprinter Carl Blauman, from the championship red & gray Colts, and Harold Price of Grand Rapids Central, the winner of the hurdle events.

The meet was again viewed as a huge success but bigger and better things were planned for the following year when, for the first time in Michigan schoolboy history, the meet would be broken down into three classes: A, B & C. Lloyd Miller of Vassar High got the jump on the smaller schools by winning the Class B 440-yard run at the 1920 meet. This was the first individual Class B event ever contested in state annals other than a relay.

Ann Arbor: Chicago University School had little trouble winning the University of Michigan Interscholastic, nearly doubling the total of the runners-up from Cass City and Kalamazoo. The meet was such a popular event for Midwestern high schools that two other Illinois track powers also competed in Ann Arbor. Hyde Park and LaGrange passed on the Illinois high school state championships, held on the same day, in order to compete against tougher competition on Ferry Field.

Cass City, the little school from Michigan's thumb area, made a very impressive showing. The Red Hawks won three individual championships against the best from the Midwest. James Brooker won the discus and shared first in the pole vault with Kalamazoo's Don

Gainder while Earl Gowen of Cass City sped the 440 in a meet winning time of 52.2.

Brooker was undoubtedly Cass City's most decorated track athlete in the school's history. Brooker not only became a two-time Big 10 pole vault champion at the University of Michigan, but captured the bronze medal at the 1924 Olympics as well. He also once set a collegiate record in the pole vault by scaling 13-0. One has to wonder how Cass City would have fared if the team had elected to enter at the state meet in East Lansing.

The Sprinters of the Roaring Twenties

Although Eddie Tolan became the number one sprinter of the 1920's (and arguably the best Michigan schoolboy sprinter of all time), the early years of the Roaring Twenties presented an incredibly talented group of speedsters.

George "Buck" Hester of Detroit Northern swept the table in the 100 and 220-yard dashes from 1921 thru 1923 and defeated legions of top sprinters.

The future Michigan star produced a pair of times at the 1923 state championships that would stand the test of time for 90 years. The auburn-haired sprinter ran 9.8 in the 100-yard dash, a meet record that would not be erased from the books until Saginaw's Reggie Jones ran 9.6 a half-century later. Later in the day on "Old College Field" in East Lansing, Hester would sprint 220 in 21.7 seconds, a mark that lasted until 1963.

Just as noteworthy as Hester's times were the competitors that he defeated during his three-year reign as the King of Michigan sprinters. In 1923 he was trailed in the 220 by Victor Leschinsky of Detroit Northwestern, Bernard Otto of Jackson, and Lyle Henson of Lansing Central. Hester's time in 1923 lasted for many years but Leschinsky ran just as fast. Both ran shoulder-to-shoulder down the stretch and to many of the spectators gathered at the finish line it looked to be a dead heat. Hester was declared the winner and his name alone would stand in the record books.

In 1924 Leschinsky and Otto would further demonstrate their own talents by coming close to the World Record in the 220. In a Midwest Olympic Trials qualifying meet in Ann Arbor, Leschinsky, a freshman at Michigan, and Otto, a frosh at Michigan Normal

(EMU) each won their heats in 21.1, just two-tenths over the listed World Record.

These two would continue their rivalry as teammates at Michigan. In the 1926 Big Ten championships they ran a dead-heat for first in the 100. Leschinsky would come back and win the 220 outright over Hester.

Lyle Henson proved he was no slouch in the sprints either. The Lansing Central sprinter was able to win the state sprint double in 1924 before embarking on a very successful college career in his own right. While a member of Michigan State College's track squad for three years, Henson placed 3rd in the 220 in the 1928 NCAA championships. In 1948, Lyle's son Dick Henson, while competing for Dearborn Fordson, duplicated his father's sprint double by winning the Class A 100 and 220. Dick Henson also was captain of the 1952 Michigan State College track team, a moniker first earned by his father back in 1929.

The Windsor-born Hester made the Canadian Olympic team in 1924 and 1928. He advanced to the semi finals at the 1924 Olympiad in Paris, losing to the eventual gold medal winner Harold Abrahams of "Chariots of Fire" fame. Following his dead heat finish with Leschinsky at the 1926 Big Ten championships, he lost the NCAA 100 by about an inch. He also won the 100 title at the Penn Relays in 1927 and 1928.

At the 1928 Canadian Olympic Trials, Buck Hester is in the center of the field, arm thrown high. Note the lack of starting blocks. Sprinters used a small shovel to dig a secure placement for their feet.

Track historian Bob Sampson remembered Buck Hester well: "He would always come over to Cass Tech while he was at the University of Michigan. He took a liking to Miss Kelly, who was the girls physical

education teacher at Cass. They eventually got married but their marriage [nearly] cost him a spot on the 1928 Canadian Olympic traveling team. It seems the Canadian Olympic committee felt that Hester wanted to take Miss Kelly with him on a honeymoon to Europe but the Canadians wanted no part of that.

"I can remember Hester would give Eddie Tolan tips on sprinting while visiting with Miss Kelly over at Cass," said Sampson. "He was a wonderful man."

Perhaps the best sprinter not to win a state championship was Lansing's Fred Alderman. Alderman had to take a back seat to Hester during his senior year in high school in 1922, but the capital city dashman made giant strides following his prep career. In many respects Alderman outshone Hester as a collegian.

It doesn't get any better than winning an Olympic gold medal and Alderman can boast of membership in that rare fraternity. Alderman captured his prize as a member of the 4 x 400 relay team that finished first at the 1928 Olympics, setting a World Record in the process.

Alderman won the 220-yard dash in a meet record of 21.0 at the 1925 Big Ten Championships. Although Alderman ran for Michigan State, the University of Michigan media guide for years listed the Spartan flash as running for the Wolverines. His victory so surprised the rest of the Big Ten competitors that it would be years before MSC (now MSU) would again be officially invited to participate.

Alderman became MSC's first NCAA track champion when he captured the 100 (9.9) and 220 (21.1) in Chicago and was the meet's leading scorer. Over his college career he had the state intercollegiate 100 and 220 titles four straight years. In 1927 he won those races in wind-aided times of 9.6 and 20.5.

Following disappointing defeats to Eddie Tolan at the 1928 Midwest Olympic qualifier in Ann Arbor, Alderman attempted to make the USA team in the 400 meters. He demonstrated amazing stamina during the afternoon by winning the 400 in 48.0. This achievement came after running in four previous races and would be the fastest time turned in by a Michigan sprinter until well into the 1940's. Although the Lansing track ace rarely ran the half-mile, he once was clocked in 1:55.0, an amazing time for this early era.

In all, the former Lansing sprint star would lay claim to three World Records. He once ran 300 yards in 31.3, the world's best up to that era, and ran the arcane 175-dash in 17.3.

Another pair of sprinters from this era also bear special mention. Although somewhat overshadowed, Bohn Grim from Sturgis and Leighton Boyd from Detroit Southeastern were stars in their own right. Grim followed his 1921 state championship in the 220 by teaming up with Alderman at MSC. While a collegian in East Lansing Grim was a NCAA finalist in the 220 and became the second runner in state history to break the 49-second barrier in the 440.

Boyd, the 1924 Detroit city 100-yard dash king, became the leading scorer while a member of the Michigan Normal (EMU) track quad. He continued his zest for track by becoming a fixture for many years in the city of Detroit, first as a coach at his alma mater, Southeastern, and later as a longtime starter and referee.

All the above listed sprinters ran the 220 under the 22-second barrier, a time that would win most state championships in today's modern era. One has to wonder what these legends of yesteryear would have accomplished with today's advanced training methods and lightning fast all-weather ovals, along with starting blocks.

1921

The 1921 meet (June 4) was not only hailed as the largest ever, with 63 schools and more than 600 athletes participating, but it was also mentioned as THE principal athletic event of the year in the entire State of Michigan. The 63 schools in East Lansing exceeded by 22 the previous best turnout for past meets. Full competitions were added for Class B and C, and for the first-time competitors in 1921 were limited to two sprint events, the 880-yard relay and any number of field events.

Five former records tumbled by the wayside and one mark was equaled. The Colts from Detroit Northwestern again were easy team victors in Class A. Allegan, behind the magnificent performance of Kent Pritchard, became the State's first champ in Class B. Neighboring Plainwell took home the first trophy awarded in Class C, with the smaller schools making up better than half the total of all athletes.

Pritchard has undoubtedly gone down in Allegan's annals as one of their finest. He broke the long jump record with a leap of 21-6, high jumped a winning 5-9 and captured the 100-yards dash in a respectable 10.4.

Bohn Grim from Sturgis, the first Class C 220 champ, would later become a World Record holder.

Unheralded Bohn Grim, 220-yard dash champ from Class C Sturgis, would later win first place in 1927 at the famed Penn Relays as a member of the Michigan State College 880-yard relay. Grim also would set a World Record in the 75-yard dash (7.5).

The meet also marked the championship debut of sophomore sprinter George "Buck" Hester. The Detroit Northern sprinter captured the first of his six sprint championships during his three-year reign. Hester's meet record in the 100 of 9.8 in 1923 was not surpassed for a record-breaking 40 years, despite running without starting blocks on a cinder track. Hester will certainly go down as one of the all-time great sprinters produced by the state of Michigan; he represented Canada in the 1924 and 1928 Olympics.

George Haggerty of Ypsilanti erased Jimmy Craig's 1909 mark in the 220-yard low hurdles with a clocking of 26.2. In Class A, Detroit Northwestern's George Snider shared the low hurdle title with Harold Belf of Highland Park, producing the only tie in state history in the hurdles. Snider again led the Colts in scoring, winning the high hurdles and placing second in the broad jump behind Muskegon's Paul Cook.

Don Gainder of Kalamazoo repeated as pole vault champion while setting a record at 11-3. Other meet records were by Marshall McCausland of Detroit Eastern in the 440 (51.8) and the 880-relay mark fell to the victorious Colts. Pritchard also anchored Allegan to a new Class B relay record. All other marks, with the exception of the Class B 440-yard dash, would go into the record books, this being the first year for competition in Class B and C.

Although most people felt this was a near perfect meet, Loren M. Post, supervisor of athletics for the Detroit school system, did not share the same enthusiasm. Post felt that a meet conducted in one day was much too hard on the athletes. This message was not the first hint of grumbling from Detroit officials but it may have been the first sign of unrest from the Motor City ranks, ultimately leading to Detroit's break from the rest of the state in 1931. Post threatened to pull the Detroit schools from the 1922 meet if the M.A.C. officials wouldn't make state finals a two-day affair. Post's request was granted and preliminaries for a number of years were conducted on Friday with the finals on Saturday.

Ann Arbor: For the first time in 11 years an in-state school won the University of Michigan Interscholastic meet in Ann Arbor. Northwestern triumphed with ease, outscoring its nearest competitor by a whopping 19 points. Hurdler George Snider led the Colts, winning the pole vault and high jump, placing second to Ypsilanti's George Haggerty in the 120-yard high hurdles and adding further points with a fourth in the long jump.

1922

Detroit high schools staged a party all for themselves in 1922, taking the first four places. Northern won the title in Class A with 21 points, while Eastern finished second with 19. Cass Tech was third and perennial champion Detroit Northwestern trailed in fourth, only five points away from the winning spot.

George Hester again won both sprints, setting the 220 meet record with a time of 22.2 seconds and anchoring the winning 880-relay. In the relay Hester had a handicap of nearly three yards at the start of his anchor leg; however, the little sprinter was equal to the task and led his Northwestern opponent by nearly a foot at the tape. The time of 1:33.5 was the second record set by Northern in the meet.

Hester's closest competition came from Lansing's Fred Alderman in the sprints, who finished 2nd in both dashes. Alderman would go on to bigger things. In 1927 the future Michigan State College Hall of Famer became MSC's first NCAA champion, winning the 100/220 double. He also was MSC's first Olympic track gold medalist, running a leg on the World Record-setting 4 x 400 at the 1928 Olympiad in Amsterdam. He also once owned the World Record in the 300-yard run (31.2).

Despite Hester's heroics, the leading point winner was Dick Doyle of Kalamazoo. Doyle, who earned firsts in the shot put and discus and placed third in the broad jump, went on to stardom at the University of Michigan. The versatile Doyle would not only garner a third-place in the 1926 NCAA discus but would become Michigan's first All-American in basketball.

Lowell Palmer of Grand Rapids Central became the state's first-ever champ in the javelin with a toss of 155-3. This event would only be contested over the next nine years.

Bill Meyers of Cass Tech became the third double winner in Class A, copping the broad jump and the 220-yard low hurdles. Meyers' time of 26.2 was the fastest time posted for the 30-inch hurdles since Jose Malcomson's record race back in 1905.

Ray Hart of Saginaw Arthur Hill edged Loren Brown, Detroit City League champion from Detroit Eastern, in the 880. Brown would later enroll at Michigan State College where, he would not only become a very successful middle-distance runner for the Spartans, but would also serve as MSC's head track coach in the 1930s.

Allegan and Plainwell repeated as Class B and C champs in East Lansing. Allegan proved that it could run with the big boys as it finished fourth overall at the previous week's U of M interscholastic. Once again it was Allegan's Kent Pritchard leading the way with an impressive double victory. Pritchard won the long jump at 21-6 and defeated Class A champ John Huntington of Detroit Eastern in the high jump. Plainwell dominated the team competition with its 48 points. It would stand as the highest point total racked up at the Class C state meet for the next 50 years.

Rockford High School boasted of a double winner with Lyle Bennett winning the Class C discus and high jump. Bennett would later become the long-time head track coach at Central Michigan University. The Chippewa's track would later be named in his honor. Bennett lived for more than 100 years before passing away in 2005.

One of Bennett's peers in the discus at the state meet was Caro High's Glenn Eastman. The discus champ in Class B in 1922 likewise could boast of

Fred Alderman winning at the Penn Relays.

leading a long and active life. Eastham, at 93 years of age, was the oldest active member of the Michigan State University Alumni band, where he would annually strut his stuff on Alumni Band Day in Spartan Stadium.

Ann Arbor: Team honors were shared as Detroit's Northwestern and Eastern highs tied for first place. M.A.C. champ Northern finished third despite another great showing by Hester, who captured the sprint double. Hester was forced to run 101 yards in the century event. By attempting to beat the gun in the prelims, Hester was sent back a yard for the false start. That was the penalty for jumping the gun in sprint events in the early part of the century, but it bothered Hester not in the least as the future Olympian still won the 100 as he pleased.

1923

Detroit Northwestern walked away with the crown with 33½ points, well ahead of runner-up Lansing's 19. Northwestern captured the title in a meet that would feature some of the most talented prep athletes in state history.

Among the many stars for the Colts was Phil Northrup, who won the broad jump title at 21-7½ and would capture three NCAA titles during his collegiate career at the University of Michigan. Oddly enough, none of those titles came in the long jump. The versatile Northrup developed a skill unmatched in collegiate ranks in the javelin, winning NCAA championships in 1925 and 1926. He added another NCAA title in 1925 when he emerged victorious in the pole vault.

George Hester concluded his brilliant prep career by winning the two dashes for the third-straight year, each in record-setting fashion. His 9.8 in Friday's semi-finals was a meet record that would be matched a number of times but not officially erased until 1973. His record in the 220 was in the 'unusual' time of 21.7—unusual, as this was the first meet in state history where the times were recorded in tenths and not fifths of a second. "Buck" Hester's 21.7 time would stand longer than any other individual record in state history, not tied or broken for 40 years.

Northwestern's Victor Leschinsky pressed Hester all the way to the finish line in both dashes. A few years later, running for Michigan, he would win the 1926 Big 10 100 dash.

In East Lansing, Leschinsky would place his name in the record book, along with three of his Colt teammates, with his anchor in the 880-yard relay. The Colt foursome of Stanley Kilpatrick, Lawson Parker, Lowell Blanchard, and Leschinsky posted a winning time of 1:31.8, a mark that might have been recognized as a new meet record. However, only two watches were working as Leschinsky broke the tape just ahead of runner-up Lansing, who also had a time that bettered the previous record. For a record to be ratified it would have been necessary for three watches to be used. Journalists at the time called it a missed national record, but they didn't know that Pasadena, California, had that season thrice broken the old national mark of 1:32.2, with a best of 1:31.4 just four weeks earlier.

The individual point winner for this outstanding meet would be Edward Spence of Detroit Western. The future two-time NCAA champion in the 220-low hurdles took both hurdle events and placed fourth in the broad jump, amassing Detroit Western's entire total of 11 points.

Percy Prout of Detroit Central shattered an 11-year record in the pole vault. The future Michigan vaulter cleared 11-9 to improve the old mark set by Forrest Bailey of Morenci in 1912. Detroit Cass Tech's Dayton Dailey's winning 51.8 time in the 440 also produced an additional record. Saginaw Arthur Hill's Ray Hart

bettered Grand Rapids Central's Henry Sullivan's 15-year-old mark in the 880 with a time of 2:03.1.

Due to the large number of athletes competing over the past two years, the Class A championships were held on June 9, one week after the Class B & C meets in East Lansing. This would be the last state meet held on the old college field oval as a new track & field complex was being constructed on campus—today's present-day site.

Plainwell scored in every event but one to annex its third-straight Class C crown, scoring a whopping 48 points. Alton Vance of Nashville was extremely busy during the field events. He took part in and fared extremely well at these disciplines: placing first in the high jump and broad jump, second in the shot put, and third in the discus, tallying all 15 of Nashville's points. Donald Camp was right behind Vance in the point department, scoring 14 points for the championship Plainwell squad.

Coldwater replaced two-time champion Allegan to win it all in Class B. Harold George of Petoskey scored in five events, including firsts in the high hurdles and long jump to score 17 of his team's 18 points. John Burridge of St. Johns became another double winner in Class B by sweeping the short dashes.

Rule changes were the talk of the day during the meet. Floyd Rowe, head of the state athletic department—and former two-mile state champ at the turn of the century—looked into the compelling age problem of that era. It was proposed by Rowe that competition for high school athletes be limited to those below the age of 20. Reportedly, prior to 1923, many athletes 20 and 21 years of age were still participating in prep sports, particularly football, basketball, and track.

Detroit Central's Olympic Flag Bearers

It is an honor of the highest magnitude to have a member of one's high school carry our nation's flag at the opening ceremonies of the Olympic Games. But to have two athletes from the same high school perform this duty is almost too improbable to comprehend. However, it did indeed happen for a pair of former track greats from Detroit Central High School. In 1908 John Garrels, a 1902 Central graduate, proudly marched into the White City Stadium in London carrying the USA colors. Forty years later Ralph Craig, a 1907 graduate, would follow Garrels.

Craig, a gold medal winner in the 100 and 200-meter dashes at the 1912 Olympic games in Stockholm, carried the USA flag into London Stadium as a member of the 1948 USA Yachting team. The former Central star sprinter would join that rare minority of Olympics athletes who would make the team in two different sports.

Garrels would also have a ubiquitous distinction of medaling at the 1908 in two contrasting events. The versatile future University of Michigan strongman placed second in the high hurdles and took third in the shot put. Garrels also made the USA team in the discus, perhaps his strongest event, but was off form when it counted and did not advance to the finals in Stockholm.

We'll trace these former Trailblazer's careers beginning with Garrels. He won the state discus crown at the 1902 state meet, but his performance would hardly lead one to believe he would one day be the event's World Record holder.

The multi-talented John Garrels could throw and hurdle at a world-class level. He won Olympic medals in both.

Following his prep career for the Blue and White of Detroit Central, Garrels enrolled at the University of Michigan, where he developed into a Maize and Blue legend. Not only was Garrels one of the U of M's all-time track greats, but the 6-1, 205lb dynamo also started three straight years on the football team. During his tenure on Coach Fielding Yost's football

powerhouses of the early 1900s, the Wolverines posted a gaudy overall record of 29 wins, two losses and one tie. In his senior season Garrels dropped kicked a field goal through the uprights to give the Wolverines the points needed to defeat archrival Ohio State.

It was on the track, however, where Garrels made his biggest impact at the University. Just two years after winning the state high school discus title at a distance that barely surpassed 100 feet, Garrels was flinging the platter over the 135-foot marker. He teamed up with Olympic gold medalist Ralph Rose to give the Wolverines a pair of weight performers unmatched in the collegiate ranks of their era.

Rose was a 6-6 native of California who put together back-to-back Olympic shot put gold medal performances at the 1904 and 1908 Olympics. Garrels and Rose gave Michigan a 1-3 finish at the London Olympiad of 1908. Garrels was much more than a shot putter and weightlifter. If the decathlon had been part of the Olympics during Johnny's era, he might have found his best event. Unfortunately, for Garrels and Joe Horner, another Wolverine that followed Garrels at Michigan, the decathlon would not become an Olympic event until 1912.

At the 1905 "Big Nine" conference championships in Chicago, Garrels, with a heave of 140-2, shattered the previous world record in the discus by three feet. Not content with just a discus World Record, Garrels also captured the 220-yard low hurdles crown. He bettered his own showing a year later by nearly winning the Big Nine title all by himself. Garrels took first place honors in the discus, high and low hurdles, and still had enough energy left to place second in the shot put. What was even more amazing was that Garrels had tied another World Record, this time in the hurdles. In the 120-yard high hurdles Garrels tied the mark of 15 and 1/5 seconds. His individual total of 18 points outscored all the other teams entered with the exception of the University of Chicago.

At the intercollegiate championships the following season, the Captain of the 1907 Wolverine track team won both hurdle events and placed second in the shot put. Surprisingly, the intercollegiate did not offer the discus as an event or perhaps Garrels would have won three national championships.

Following the Olympic games of 1908 Garrels made good use of his degree in chemical engineering by becoming the President of the Michigan Alkali Company of Wyandotte before passing away in 1957.

While Garrels was setting World Records at the University of Michigan, young Ralph Craig was making a name for himself back at Detroit Central. Like Garrels, Craig blossomed into a world-renowned track star, even surpassing Johnny's efforts as an Olympian. Craig capped his career by earning the title of "The World's Fastest Human" with gold medal-winning performances at the 1912 Stockholm Olympics.

Craig began his track career in 1903 as a young freshman at Detroit Central, one year after Johnny Garrels graduated from the Blue and the White. At the 1907 interscholastic meet in Ann Arbor, Craig edged his future Michigan teammate Joe Horner in both hurdle events. In addition, Ralph teamed with John Garrel's brother Alan, Tom Stalker, and George Widman to win the 880-yard relay.

Ralph Craig started out as a hurdler at Detroit Central before his college coaches switched him to the sprints. He won the 100 and 200 at the 1912 Olympics.

Although Craig was a decent hurdler as a Wolverine, his career took a decided turn for the better thanks to an injury. In 1910, Ralph had trouble with the arch of his right foot while hurdling and Michigan head track coach Keene Fitzpatrick decided to turn Craig into a sprinter. Ralph made his coach look like a genius by not only winning the national collegiate championships in the 220-yard dash but clocking 21 1/5 second to tie the existing World Record for 200/220 on a straight track. Only a slippage at the start

prevented Craig from also winning the 100-yard dash crown.

The following year Craig took both sprint titles at the intercollegiate championships to establish himself as the USA's best hopes to win the Olympic gold in Stockholm. Craig's backers were certainly not disappointed as the Wolverine bolt of lightning became the second sprinter from the University of Michigan to win the Olympic sprint title, echoing Archie Hahn's feat of 1904.

At the Olympic Trials, a month before the games commenced in Stockholm, Craig had equaled the World 100-meter record of 10.8, but was upset in the finals by Howard Drew. Drew strained a tendon in winning his semi-final heat in Stockholm, eliminating any chance of becoming the first African-American to win an Olympic gold medal. In Stockholm, Craig overcame jitters that were created by eight false starts in the 100-meter finals, and won the title with a convincing victory. In the process, the native Detroiter defeated Donald Lipincott of the US, who had earlier set a new World and Olympic record in winning his semi-final heat in 10.7.

Five days later Craig returned to the Stockholm cinders to make it a clean sweep of the dashes with a win in the 200 meters. He had not been included on the U.S. 4 x 100 relay team, which was just as well. The foursome botched their first exchange in the semis and was disqualified.

In addition to his well-known athletic skills Craig also excelled in the classroom at Michigan. He passed with honors every course that he tackled, with the exception of German, and but for his lack of knowledge of the language of the Fatherland, Craig would have been bestowed Phi Beta Kappa honors.

After the two world wars, Craig would again become an Olympian, this time in yachting. Though he didn't get a chance to actually participate in the London competition, he was named the U.S. flag bearer, 36 years after winning his gold medals in Stockholm. Like Garrels, Craig also put his Michigan degree to good use. Moving to New York, he became the supervisor of finance for the Works Progress Administration of New York and also was very active in real estate in the Albany area. He also became a judge at major dog shows across the United States.

The two Detroit Central alums each had a brother who also became athletic stars at the University of Michigan. Ironically, both of the brothers of the two Olympians fared better at the high school level than either of their famous namesakes.

Allen Garrels won the 220 low hurdles at the 1908 state championships and teamed with Ralph Craig to procure another first-place medal in the 880-yard relay, one more first place than won by his brother John. Allen Garrels also followed in his brother's footsteps by becoming a regular on the Wolverine football squad of 1911.

Jimmy Craig, younger brother of Ralph, in a few cases exceeded his older brother's athletic feats. Jimmy, an all-state football star, won five first-place medals at the interscholastic level while running for Detroit Central, and capped a great track career by winning the 220-yard low hurdles at the intercollegiate championships in 1912. He was better known in Ann Arbor as a football star for Fielding Yost's Wolverines. In 1913 he made Walter Camp's All-American Eleven as a running back, capping his brilliant career by scoring both Wolverine touchdowns in a 13-0 season ending victory over the University of Pennsylvania.

1924

Great weather and perfect conditions on the new Aggie track contributed to six new records in 1924 (June 6). One of those records was set by one of the state's best athletes ever, Bennie Oosterbaan of Muskegon. Oosterbaan, who would later go on to become an All-American at the University of Michigan in three sports, hurled the discus 122-3, erasing the great Arthur Kohler's mark set back in 1910. It should be noted that the discus in the early twentieth century was the two-kilo platter used by today's collegians, not the current 1.6kg hurled by the modern era's prep throwers. Oddly enough, Bennie became a collegiate All-American in football, basketball and baseball, forgoing a promising track career.

It is a certainty that if Oosterbaan had been permitted to play in two spring sports, as was allowed when Charles Hoyt became Michigan's track coach in 1930, he would have been Michigan's only 12 letter-winner. However, Steve Farrell, the varsity track coach in Oosterbaan's time, would not allow the practice, even with an athlete adjudged to be the greatest in university history. It's not that Farrell didn't try to lure Oosterbaan out for track. In the summer of 1927 he sent a postcard to Oosterbaan at a summer camp. It read: "The Olympic boat to Amsterdam leaves next July. Why don't you make the trip?" But Benny, as a senior, remained loyal to baseball and passed up a chance to become an Olympic athlete.

Detroit Northwestern repeated as Class A champ with Kalamazoo Central making a strong showing in second. The Colts' Harry Van Nortwick topped all shot putters with a modest heave of 44-9½. He would continue his love for the sport well into the 1940s, becoming a frequent champion in the hammer throw and the 56-pound weight events at the state AAU championships.

Although Oosterbaan would remain as the biggest "name" competitor of the 1924 state championships, it was Edward Spence of Detroit Western who would earn honors as the star of the meet. Spence won both hurdle events in dazzling fashion. The Cowboy from Western skimmed the 220 lows in 24.6 seconds, smashing the oldest meet record, the 1905 mark of Detroit University's Jose Malcomson, by a full second.

Spence then won the 120-yard highs in 16.0, eclipsing Jimmy Craig's mark set in 1909 that had been matched by Grand Rapid's Rod McKenzie in 1916. Remarkably, Spence was the only member of Detroit Western's track team and competed throughout the season without the benefit of a coach. He concluded his career by winning the hurdle titles two years in a row. Again, it should be pointed out that early high hurdlers were bounding over hurdles at the 42-inch height as opposed to the modern era 39-inch setting.

Harold George put on another superb performance for Petoskey. George, in 1924, received support from teammate Ivan Tillotson in the weight events, helping take the state championship trophy back to the north country. Tillotson, longtime Shelby High track mentor and father of future U of M basketball captain Pete Tillotson, added a second in the shot put and a third in the discus. Plainwell triumphed again in Class C with a narrow three-point win over runner-up Clinton.

Junior miler Leroy Potter of Coldwater turned in the most impressive performance in East Lansing, covering the mile in 4:37.0. He would dominate the event at all levels for the next three years. A week earlier he had taken on, and defeated, all comers at the Ann Arbor meet, running nearly the identical time he posted in East Lansing.

Everett Pauschert from Detroit Northern nipped the previous 440 mark with a time of 51.2 while Raymond Smith of Battle Creek leaped 22-6½ to better the broad jump record set by Kent Pritchard of Allegan in 1921.

Although the hammer throw had been eliminated as one of the disciplines following the 1919 state track meet, this event was still being contested at the Detroit City League championships. Wilford Ketz of Detroit Southwestern won the city title with a modest heave of 126-7 and became the NCAA champion in 1928. In addition, Ketz went on to become the American record holder for the hammer throw while a member of the University of Michigan track team.

Another mainstay of the Detroit City championships was 100 winner Leighton Boyd of Southeastern. Boyd would enter the collegiate ranks at Michigan Normal (EMU) where he became the leading point getter for the Hurons. Following his collegiate career, Boyd would remain active for many years promoting his beloved sport, first as a coach at Detroit Southeastern and then as a long-time referee and starter for many city league championship meets.

1925

"A WORLD RECORD!" "An Individual Winning Four State Championships!" Big headlines came from the 1925 state championships. This meet also marked the first championship run under the sanction of the new Michigan High School Athletic Association. The Class A meet was a 2-day affair with qualifying on Friday in the sprints, hurdles and field events. Finals were the next day on Saturday, May 30. It was highlighted by the speedy 880-relay foursome of Charles "Snitz" Ross, Wallin McMinn, John Widman and Jimmie Tait. The Detroit Northwestern Colts ran 1:31.5 and reportedly eclipsed a long-standing national prep mark, a record of 1:32.4 initially set way back in 1903 by Chicago Institute.

But did they? In another case of the journalists of the time not being clued in, that 1905 record had been bettered many times in the two decades since. Presumably in the pre-Internet age, the reporters did not know about two recent marks, 1:30.6 and 1:30.5, set only weeks earlier by California's San Diego and Los Angeles Manual Arts high schools.

In their state record, Colts had been pressed to the line by Cass Tech's Mechanics, the team that had beaten them by a mere foot in the Detroit City Championships on May 16 in 1:30.4 (in a race that was over 838 yards, so about 4.5 seconds faster than the full distance).

Cass Tech had to be frustrated with its runner-up role in East Lansing as it won six individual championships, the largest haul of hardware ever taken home by a team that did not win the team title.

First-place Northwestern (38 points) and runner-up Detroit Cass Tech (34½) so obliterated the rest of the field that Coldwater finished 3rd with just 8½ points. Five of those points were truly quality points as Leroy

Potter bettered the 12-year old mark in the mile run held by Earl Sheldon of West Branch. Potter, who placed 2nd in the NCAA in the mile while competing for Michigan Normal (now EMU), passed on the Class B meet to move up to 'A' and won in a breeze with a record time of 4:33.0. The previous week he captured the mile title in Ann Arbor with an almost identical time of 4:33.5.

Clifford Robinson posted one of many impressive records set with his winning leap of 22-10½ in the broad jump. A year earlier, the Detroit Northwestern jumper had shattered the Detroit City League all-time best by sailing 22-11½, a mark that would stand the test of time in the talent rich Motor City for 35 years. Robinson, following the state meet, demonstrated he was among the nation's best in his specialty, taking second place at the National Interscholastic meet in Chicago.

Cass Tech's Bill Loving came inches from taking home four first-place medals for runner-up Cass Tech. Loving, in addition to his leg on the 880-yard relay, won both hurdles and shared in a three-way tie for first in the high jump to take high point honors in this talent-loaded meet.

At the Detroit City meet in 1925, Eddie Tolan (right) edged quarter mile legend John Lewis in the 100.

T. Rex Wilson of Ann Arbor joined the record-breaking parade by eliminating the legendary Bennie Oosterbann from the records books with his toss of 126-11 in the discus. Placing second behind Wilson was Detroit Northwestern's Glenn Carlson. Carlson, winner of three events at the Detroit City championships, added additional points toward his team's winning total by also placing second in the shot put. Following the graduation of George Hester in 1923, most track experts were confident that the times set by the former Northern speedster would be unsurpassed for years. These projections were short-lived, however, as Cass Tech's Eddie Tolan began his tenure as one of the greatest sprinters in Michigan schoolboy history. Tolan breezed to wins in both short sprints, seven years before capturing a pair of gold medals and a World Record at the 1932 Olympics.

Don Seeger from Northwestern was heavily favored to defend his record-setting 880-yard title with hopes of finishing his high school career undefeated in the event. However, Milton Kendrick from Mt. Clemens, spoiled those aspirations, handing Seeger his first career loss as a prepster and setting a new record with a time of 2:01.5.

Herman Miethe made the long trek to Southern Michigan a successful venture, capturing the 440-yard dash at the University of Michigan Interscholastic, as well as the state championships in Class A the following weekend in East Lansing. The Escanaba schoolboy became the first athlete from the Upper Peninsula to win a Lower Peninsula state championship with his 51.5.

It is most likely that this meet was the first where a son joined his father in winning a state individual title. John Widman, son of George Widman, who swept the 100 and 220-yard dashes from 1905 thru 1907, copped first place in the javelin.

The Class B and C meets were held the following weekend on June 5-6. Niles dominated in Class B by scoring a whopping 47 points in defeating perennial power Allegan. Lothaire Hall was the big gun for Niles with three firsts and a second. Hall won the 220-yard low hurdles (26.8), the javelin (159-3) and ran a leg on the winning 880-yard relay team. Clare Warner of St. Johns was a double victor with wins in the 100 and 220-yard dashes.

Wayland nipped the one-man crew from Croswell to win its first state championship in Class C. In addition to the championship cup, the Class C team victor was also awarded a "Detroit Michigan Aggie Statue." Croswell's Harold Gilbert became one of only a handful of athletes to win four titles in one year. Only Frank Anderson, the Newaygo shot putter, prevented Gilbert from winning a fifth by copping a first place in the shot put. Gilbert won a "mini" decathlon by taking the 100 and 220 dash, high jump and discus, before settling for second in the shot put.

Future Western Michigan star Myron Smith won the mile run in Class C, the first state champion to emerge from little Woodland High School (the school closed

some 40+ years later, replaced by Lakewood High in Lake Odessa).

1926

Good weather greeted athletes vying for the prestigious Harvard Cup, awarded each year to the Class A state champion. Detroit Cass Tech earned the right to showcase the trophy for one year with its first-ever state championship. Teams could keep permanent possession of it if they could put together three state titles in a row. The trophy moved into the Mechanics' display case next to the national indoor title trophy won by Cass Tech in the winter. Despite the great weather, only one record was matched, Ray Newman of Pontiac equaled the pole vault meet record with a clearance of 11-9.

The Cass Tech team of 1926. Eddie Tolan is bottom, second from left; Bill Loving is top left.

The two-some of Eddie Tolan and hurdler Bill Loving paced the Mechanics by combining for four firsts. Loving captured both hurdle events while Tolan was in the middle year of his three-year sweep in the short dashes. Hart Tolan, brother of Eddie, placed second in the 880-yard run, behind Kalamazoo Central's Ralph Munson, giving the champs more valuable points.

One has to wonder if Hart Tolan might have had the potential to be as nearly as good as his famed brother in the sprints. In school meets for Cass Tech, he primarily ran the 880 for team scoring purposes. However, in the summer he ran for the Detroit Athletic Association, a primarily African-American club that brought together many of the city's prep stars. In the final meet of the summer (against adult talent) he won the 100 in 10.1, edging Eugene Beatty—who the next year would emerge as the fastest prep hurdler in the nation.

A balanced Kalamazoo unit secured second place ahead of Detroit Northwestern. The Giant's best performance came when they ran the "slower" heat in 1:31.7, a full second better than the favored Motor City teams ran in the faster seeded race.

Herb Craig of Flint Central captured the 440-yard dash in 52.6, but more significantly became the first state champion from the city of Flint. Hundreds of state champs from this athletic rich city in future years would follow Craig to the top of the victory stand.

The tightest race of the day came in the mile, with Don Kingsford of Grand Rapids South edging Pontiac's Valden Criger in a respectable time of 4:35.8. Tolan and Loving also swept their events at the University of Michigan interscholastic, pacing the Mechanics to its second big win of the year. While in Ann Arbor the athletes were in awe as workers nearby were putting the finishing touches on the new football stadium. The following year would see huge crowds fill the 70,000-seat structure.

St. Johns made the short trek down to East Lansing a successful jaunt, capturing the Class B crown over second-place St. Joseph. Five different athletes won championships for the victors in a great display of depth. A noted double-winner on the afternoon was Carl Nordberg of the runner-up Bears. Nordberg would return to East Lansing in 1945 to coach the Saginaw Trojans to the Class A state title.

Otsego won Class C with 27 7/12 points. Runner-up Marine City was represented by Milton Jacobi, winner of both short sprints and the broad jump. Jacobi's time of 10.3 in the century was perhaps the best performance during the B & C championships, held once again one week following the 'A' meet.

Winning the Class C shot put was one of Michigan's more colorful athletes, Joe Savoldi from Three Oaks. Savoldi claimed first-place honors in the shot put but would make his claim to fame in other sporting venues.

The muscular Savoldi became a football star for Knute Rockne's Notre Dame powerhouses of the late 1920s. He managed to squeeze in a year as a fullback for the Chicago Bears in 1930. But it was in wrestling where "Jumping Joe" became a household name throughout the world, ruling as the World Heavyweight Wrestling champion. Savoldi's son (Joe Jr.) captained the 1956 Michigan State University track team and took Big 10 honors in the 120-yard high hurdles.

1927

Detroit Northeastern was unable to win the state title, but possessed enough up-front firepower to win the National Interscholastic Track Championships in Chicago. Detroit Cass Tech rode the shoulders of sprinter Eddie Tolan to take third on the Soldier Field oval, with the Michigan Class A state champions from Detroit Northwestern placing seventh. It is doubtful if the state of Michigan could ever surpass the talent that burned the cinders during the 1927 campaign.

Eugene Beatty led the national champs by winning the high and low hurdles and running a leg on Northeastern's winning 880-yard relay team. Beatty's teammate, John Lewis, won the 440-yard dash in 50.2, giving Northeastern four first-place titles. Love Snowden rounded out the scoring by taking a third in the 100-yard dash.

The previous week in East Lansing, Northwestern used its depth to edge Detroit Northeastern for the Class A title by two points. Although Eddie Tolan was again unbeatable, it was Northeastern's Eugene Beatty who rang up the most points. Beatty took both hurdles, sailed 21-8 to win the broad jump and helped his Northeastern team to a new meet record in the 880-relay with a time of 1:30.0.

As a Detroit Northern sophomore in 1927, Bill Bonthron never made the headlines. He transferred to an East Coast prep school his last two years and then went to Princeton where he became one of the world's top milers. In 1934, he won the NCAA finals in that event and broke the World Record for 1500 in capturing the U.S. nationals. According to one story, when reporters went to Northern's coach to get more info, he could barely remember Bonthron being on the team.

Northeastern's relay time would turn out to be the longest standing relay meet record in state history, not equaled or broken for the next 36 years. Anchoring that record-setting foursome was John Lewis, who earlier in the day established a new 440-record at 50.4—a day after he tied the record in the heats with his 51.2. Lewis would go on to a great career running for Detroit City College (now Wayne State). Running the second leg was Snowden, a ten-flat 100-yard sprinter who would win the 100 and 220-yard dashes the following year at the prestigious University of Michigan Invitational. This foursome followed up its record-breaking at the state meet by setting a new meet mark at the National Interscholastic meet in Chicago.

For the first time in history the meet included the present day four-class system. Class D schools were added to the structure in East Lansing with Trenton High School easily taking the championship. For the first time in four years the state championship wasn't divided over a two-week period, as all four classes competed on Saturday, May 28.

Eddie Tolan capped his career at Cass Tech by winning both sprints. His 9.8 in the 100 tied George Hester's record, dubbed by experts as "unbeatable." The future Olympic champion finished undefeated over a three-year period in the 100 and 220.

In the pole vault, Kalamazoo's Baxter Hathaway soared 11-10 record to break the other meet record. Northwestern's only champion was Thad Dennis, who became the first high school prepster to better six feet in the high jump since John Patterson of Detroit University School cleared 6-1¼ in 1906.

St. Joseph won all three short sprint events to take the honors in Class B. Kalamazoo Normal, the only parochial school entered in the carnival, took third.

Ken Barnhill of Charlotte won the only event in the lower classes that bettered any of the Class A standards, hurling the discus 119-10. Plainwell again dominated in Class C with a nine-point margin over runner-up Yale. J. Perry Austin, class valedictorian at Three Oaks, took the Class C mile.

Capturing the pole vault was one of Michigan's finest all-around athletes, Ted Petoskey of St Charles. Petoskey went on to earn eight varsity letters at the University of Michigan and was named to the All-American Football team in 1932 and 1933. Petoskey's best game possibly came against Illinois in 1932 when he galloped for 197 yards. To demonstrate Petoskey's amazing versatility, he had a brief two-year career in the Major Leagues with the Cincinnati Reds, one of only four known state track champions to also play Big League baseball.

It should be noted, however, that a pall was cast over the entire state of Michigan some ten days before the state meet. The public was stunned by the news that a mentally deranged man set off a bomb underneath the school in Bath, snuffing out the lives of 44 innocent people and wounding scores of others. Until the Oklahoma City bombing of 1995, this was the largest mass murder in U.S. history.

1928

Detroit Northeastern, behind a great performance by Eugene Beatty, interrupted the Detroit Northwestern dominance for a year with a championship effort. The Falcons had nipped the Colts by only 1/6 of a point two weeks earlier to capture the University of Michigan interscholastic crown in Ann Arbor.

Beatty contributed to four first-place medals and became the last Class A performer to win as many as six individual gold medals for a career. The 1927 national hurdle champ again won both hurdles and leaped 21-3 to take the long jump for the second year in a row.

Beatty teamed with Love Snowden, Leon Dykas, and Charles Eknovich to easily win the 880-yard relay. Dykas led his teammate Eknovitch to the tape to give the team champs a 1-2 sweep in the 440-yard dash. All four of these athletes would score points at the national championships later in Chicago but the Falcons would be unable to defend their national title.

Lester Nelson of Grand Rapids South upset Northeastern's Snowden to win both short dashes. Snowden had earlier defeated Nelson at the University of Michigan meet but Nelson proved his East Lansing performance was no fluke, placing a very respectable third in the national championships.

Cass Tech's Robert Sampson bettered 6-0 in the high jump, becoming the third Michigander to clear the 6-0 barrier. Sampson during the winter months leaped a state record of 6-2¾ to share first place at the National Indoor Championships. That mark would have been a national record had it come a day or two earlier. The night before Sampson's big jump, a young man named Edwin Lovejoy in Brooklyn, New York, would fly over 6-3 1/8 to claim the High School Record. Lovejoy's mark was buried in history for decades and Sampson understandably believed that he held the record.

In addition to his superior high jumping abilities, Sampson was one of Michigan's all-time ambassadors of track and field. The former "Mechanic" was a valuable contributor to our research for this book.

Ray Swartz of Kalamazoo Central stamped himself as one of Michigan's premier distance runners of all-time, lowering the state record to 4:32.2. Swartz, who became a school record holder during a great collegiate career at Western Michigan, took on all comers at the annual high school national championship meet in Chicago and triumphed in another state record, 4:28.3.

Detroit Western's Rha Arnold became the first runner in state history to break the two-minute barrier in the 880-yard run. Arnold, who captured the 880 in Ann Arbor with a time of 1:59.0, won the state meet in 1:59.9. Edwin Turashoff, representing Detroit Cass Tech, set a new standard in the javelin with a heave of 165-1, but fell short in his quest to eclipse the oldest record in the book, the shot put. Turashoff had put the shot earlier in the season 52-0, but fell far short of Arthur's Kohler's long-standing meet mark of 51-6 set back in 1910.

Both Arnold and Turashoff fared extremely well at the national meet in Chicago. Arnold, who had captured the national indoor 880-title in March, placed second in the 880, while Turashoff finished second in the shot put and javelin. There is little doubt that Robert Sampson would have made an impact in Chicago as well, but tragedy befell the family of the Cass Tech star. Just hours before Sampson would have boarded the train to Chicago, his father passed away, leaving the younger Sampson no choice but to remain home with his grieving family.

The 1928 meet marked the first time where competitors had to qualify by placing in a regional. Detroit athletes advanced the top six finishers from their city meet while the rest of the regions were granted four to qualify in each event.

Dearborn edged defending champ St. Joseph by a point to capture the Class B crown. Moulton Davis of St Joseph won both sprints in impressive fashion for the runner-up Bears. His performances of 10.3 and 22.5 were the fastest times in all classes for the day. The only tie in the mile/1600 run in state history occurred on this day, with judges unable to pick a winner at the tape between Carl Putnam of Caro and Carlton Hoyt of Dowagiac, both clocking 4:49.4.

Ray March had a big day in the field events as the Petoskey star won the high jump (5-6¾), broad jump (21-1¾) and the javelin (149-7) to total 15 of the Northmen's total of 17 points.

Yale, behind the tandem of Joe Salerno and Osborn Slosser, combined for four firsts to lead the school to its first and only state title. Russell Goosen from East Grand Rapids had the best performance in Class C with his record-setting effort of 11-3 in the pole vault, the best vault of the day in all classes. Goosen tied for first at the Ann Arbor meet, becoming the only performer below Class A to win in Ann Arbor against all comers. Just as in Class B, another tie evolved in an unlikely event at the Class C meet. Art Rhody of Kingsford matched Kalamazoo St. Augustine's Johnny

Siwick's best throw at an even 102 feet in the discus, the only tie in that event in state history.

Okemos took home the second-Class D trophy awarded in Class D. Staughton Dalzell from little Muir High School won both sprints in 'D', the only championships in Muir's school history.

Eugene Beatty & the '27-28 Northeastern Falcons

The golden decade that produced more American sports heroes than arguably any other span in sports folklore was undoubtedly the 1920s. Babe Ruth was at his peak in baseball; Red Grange was earning the moniker of the Galloping Ghost with his exploits on the gridiron; Jack Dempsey was the idol of the boxing world, while Bobby Jones became the household name in golf.

The state of Michigan had its heroes in track and field, with Eddie Tolan of Detroit Cass Tech perhaps the most famous thinclad of all. Also making headlines in state track annals was a small band of runners from Detroit Northeastern High School, led by Class A's all-time title holder, Eugene Beatty.

Although small in numbers, it is doubtful if another high school has ever put together so much quality over a two-year span. The Falcons not only interrupted Detroit Northwestern's dominance of the roaring twenties at the state level, but became the first (and only) state school to ever garner an outdoor national high school team title. The Falcons did it twice, annexing the outdoor championships in Chicago in 1927, and grabbed the indoor crown at Northwestern University the following year.

Eugene Beatty was the centerpiece of the green and gold team. New to the school, he was discovered at the end of a gym class when the students raced to the showers. "I wanted to be the first in the shower, and I got in the shower and in came one of the coaches. I didn't know who he was. He said, 'You, I want to see you in my office.' I didn't know what I had done. I knew I hadn't got into any fights."

It turned out that one of the boys that Beatty outsprinted to the showers was the school's fastest sprinter. Beatty's prep career took off.

Although the 1927 Falcons didn't have enough depth to derail the Detroit Northwestern express at the city or state meets, they did possess enough individual

Eugene Beatty (left) and Northeastern teammate Love Snowden.

firepower to win the national team title in the Windy City. Four Falcons made the trip to the National Interscholastic meet in Chicago, and all four were major contributors, led by a record-shattering performance by Eugene Beatty.

John Lewis, Love Snowden, and Norman Schmidt filled out the rest of this speedy foursome. The following year, Leon Dykas, Charles Eknovitch, and weight man Bob Watkins would replace graduates Lewis and Schmidt, maintaining the Falcon's dominance on the cinders. All seven were stars on their own, with five of the seven winning or placing at the national level in individual events.

The incomparable Beatty, leader of what locals called "the Grandy Avenue boys," would not only shine on the track cinders throughout America, but would etch his name in American history as a distinguished educator. At the high school level, Beatty won six individual titles and ran on two winning relay teams to post a perfect eight state championships, one of only two performers among all the legendary track figures in Class A to accomplish this feat. (Benton Harbor's Bert Copeland also won 8 from 1939-41).

At the state meets in 1927 and 1928 Beatty won the 120-yard high hurdles, 220-yard lows, the broad jump, and ran on a leg on Northeastern's victorious 880-yard relay team. Following the 1927 finals, he displayed his skills to the rest of the nation in Chicago by winning both hurdles, setting a national high school record in the lows in the process (24.2). In addition, he also ran a leg on Northeastern's unbeatable 880-yard relay team. This 880-yard relay squad would arguably be the fastest foursome in state high school history. The quartet of Beatty, Snowden, Schmidt and Lewis posted a time of 1:30.0 in East Lansing, establishing a record that would not be tied, or broken, for more than three decades, before Kalamazoo Central was able to finally lower it to 1:29.5 in 1963.

This same quartet had posted a time at the Detroit City championships a week earlier that at first glance was frankly unbelievable. The Falcons clocked 1:26.8 at historic Codd Field, a mark that still drop jaws. However, the newspapers reported that year that the Codd Field track was only 419-yards around, and that relay was actually an 838-yard event. Given that, it was probably worth about a 1:31. (The next year, either the field was reconfigured or the staggers corrected for the distance, because from 1929-on all relays were at the full 880 yards.)

Beatty, the lead runner for the Falcons, passed the baton to Love Snowden, a top sprinter in his own right. He had placed 3rd in the 100-yard dash behind the legendary Eddie Tolan. The following spring, he would come into his own after the graduation of Tolan and walk off with first-place honors at the city meet and the prestigious University of Michigan Invitational. Earlier, at the 1928 indoor nationals in Chicago, Snowden handed future Olympic legend Ralph Metcalf a rare defeat in the 50-yard dash. It was the last time Metcalf tasted defeat in high school or college. The Chicago Tilden superstar is often mentioned as the fastest sprinter in Illinois state history.

Running the third leg was Norman Schmidt, mentioned in newspaper articles of the era as the lone white runner on the squad. Although not as speedy as his three teammates, Schmidt showed he had great credentials of his own by placing third in the 220 at the 1927 city meet. Running the anchor leg for the Falcons was a man who has been mentioned by many old timers as the best quarter miler in Motor City history, John Lewis.

Lewis had the misfortune in his heyday to run in the shadows of Cass Tech's Eddie Tolan, as well as his own Northeastern teammate, Eugene Beatty. Lewis grew tired of always placing second to Tolan in the shorter sprints and decided to move up to the 440 for his senior year. However, it was Lewis, along with Northwestern's John Tait, who handed the legendary Eddie Tolan his only defeat over 100 yards in high school at a PSL meet in 1925.

The decision for the Falcon speedster to concentrate on the 440 proved to be a good move as he set new records at all the 1927 major championships. The Motor City star romped home with easy victories at the city and state meets, each won in the identical time of 50.4 seconds, a mark that would not be broken for another 21 years at either meet. Lewis played a major contribution in garnering Northeastern's national title at the 1927 National Interscholastic. John lowered his own state record and set a meet 440-yard record in the process, with a clocking of 50.2.

Northeastern marched off with the 1928 national indoor championships in Chicago, leading runner-up Detroit Northwestern and third-place Detroit Cass Tech to a 1-2-3 Motor City sweep. Beatty demonstrated his amazing versatility by winning both hurdles, placing less than a yard behind Snowden and Metcalf in the 50-yard dash and showing amazing endurance by placing 3rd in the 880-yard run. In pushing the state of Michigan's first sub two-minute half miler Rha Arnold of Detroit Western to the wire, Beatty showed he had the strength to one day be a world-class 400-meter hurdler.

Leon Dykas and Charles Eknovitch replaced Schmidt and Lewis for the 1928 outdoor campaign and the Falcon machine never lost a beat. The two underclassmen went 1-2 in the 440-yard run to produce valuable points at the city and state championships. They also teamed up with Beatty and Snowden in easily defending their 880-yard relay title. It is too bad that the mile relay had not come onto the scene back in this era, for it's possible that this foursome could have also posted a mark that would have stood the test of time for years to come.

Only Merrill Hershey of Detroit Western prevented Dykas from winning the 440-dash three consecutive years in Class A, a feat accomplished only once in state history. Dykas had defeated Hershey at the 1929 Detroit City championships a week prior to the state meet in East Lansing.

Hershey proved his win was no fluke, however, as he became the second performer in state history to break 49 seconds in the quarter miler as a collegian at Eastern Michigan. Hershey paired up with Northeastern's Beatty, Detroit Western's Rha Arnold, and former Detroit Redford hurdler Red Simmons to form a mile relay team at Eastern Michigan that was among the nation's best in 1932. Simmons went on to become the first women's track coach at the University of Michigan.

Dykas' teammate Charles Ecknovitch captured the state title at the 1929 state meet in the 220-yard low hurdles, giving the Falcons three straight first-place finishes over the lower sticks. Ecknovitch traveled further west than Ypsilanti to pursue his track career, running the lead leg in 1931 for the University of Michigan's record-setting Big 10 mile relay team. Not to be forgotten was the role-played by the quiet "big man" for the 1928 Falcons. Nearly seventy years later Bob Watkins would reminisce about his memorable days. The 6-2, 200lb junior weight event specialist would proudly recall his significant role in leading Northeastern to a couple of major championships. In mid-May in Ann Arbor, Watkins scored but one point at the prestigious University of Michigan invitational. "My fourth place in the shot put was needed as we won the meet by only 1/6 of a point over Detroit Northwestern."

As schools from throughout the Midwest converged on the Wolverine campus, coach Alvin Sandal's lads narrowly squeaked to the first of their three major titles. Watkins fondly remembers the Falcons journey to East Lansing two weeks later. "We all rode in Charles Eknovitch's car for the three-hour journey to the MSC campus," recounted Watkins. "After winning the state championship, we were really in high spirits during the trip home. We were showing off and flirting with a car full of some high school gals when we were pulled over by a policeman. When we showed him our state trophy, he was real kind to us and let us off with a stern warning to be careful for the rest of the journey back to Detroit."

The preceding week Watkins had a more productive showing at the city championships, as Northeastern ended rival Northwestern's four-year string of city titles. Bob placed third in the shot put, and missed by the narrowest of margins in winning the city discus crown. "I missed by 1/8 of an inch from tying Leiphart's best throw in the discus." Watkins third place in the shot put was behind the record-setting performance achieved by Edward Turashoff of Detroit Cass Tech, who hurled the 12-pound iron ball 52-½. "Turashoff wasn't an especially big man but he just knew how to get all his weight behind that shot," said Watkins.

Watkins recalled Eugene Beatty's form in the hurdles. "He was a funny hurdler who appeared to always take a quick step just before going over each of the hurdles." Watkins' third place in the shot was one better than Beatty at the city meet, further emphasizing Beatty's amazing versatility. In 1927 Beatty even took a crack at whirling the hammer at the city championships. With little practice at this highly technical discipline, Beatty still placed fourth.

A cartoon that appeared in newspapers in May 1933.

In 1932, at the NCAA championships, Eugene Beatty and John Lewis pulled off a very rare feat. The former high school teammates, Beatty (Eastern Michigan) and Lewis, running for Detroit City College (now Wayne State), placed 1-2 in the 440

intermediate hurdles. Earlier in the season Beatty set a short-lived American Record of 53.3 in winning the 400IH at the Penn Relays. The former Falcon became the first athlete ever to win an event at this most famous of all relays three straight years.

But for only a stroke of bad luck both of these former Falcons would have made our USA Olympic team. Lewis, in fact, had been selected for the 1928 team based on his performance at the Olympic Trials in Philadelphia. Newspaper articles published in the Detroit papers had announced that Lewis had made the team. But a last-minute decision by the USA coach spelled heartbreak for the Motor City speedster.

Lewis was to have run a leg on the 4 x 400 relay team for Uncle Sam's foursome, but the USA head coach replaced Lewis with Ray Barbuti. One could hardly have second guessed the coach's decision however, as Barbuti won the gold medal in the open 400 meters and anchored the 4 x 400 red, white, and blue team to a World Record.

Beatty and Lewis both qualified to run in the Olympic Trials in 1932, but neither was able to join Detroit buddy Eddie Tolan in Los Angeles. Lewis was 3rd in his heat and just missed his bid to advance to the finals.

Lewis displayed his blazing speed two years out of high school by winning the state collegiates with a time of 9.7 in the 100-yard dash, and a quick 21.9 in the 220. For thirty years Lewis also held the 440-yard dash record at Wayne State (48.6). These two warriors of the track remained active for many years with Lewis finally besting his long-time high school teammate at the 1936 Michigan AAU meet.

Beatty was heavily favored to win the 1932 Olympic Trials in Palo Alto, California, and take the gold medal later that summer. His friend Eddie Tolan tried to impress upon Beatty that the most important thing to accomplish was to make the team, not win the race. A stubborn Beatty had told Tolan "he was going to beat those guys." It certainly appeared that the former Falcon was going to do exactly that as he had a comfortable lead over the field as they approached the final hurdle.

Disaster struck as Beatty caught the last barrier and tumbled to the track. By the time he got back on his feet and finished, he had fallen to fourth place.

Glenn Hardin, who the histories cite as the winner of the Trials, was actually disqualified from the race for leaving his lane. According to Beatty, he started in lane 4 and finished in lane 2.

The DQ of Hardin should have made Beatty the third-place finisher and an Olympic team member. Ray Barbuti, himself the Olympic 400 champion in 1928, had been working for one of the newspapers there. He found Beatty in the locker room and told him that he should talk to Avery Brundage, the president of the American Olympic Committee as well as the AAU, for a ruling. Brundage, incidentally born in Detroit, ruled over the Olympic movement with an iron fist for decades.

Brundage heard Beatty out. He asked him if he actually finished the race. Beatty said yes: "The excuse was that somene had helped me across the finish line. That was not true. I got up and walked across the line myself."

Brundage was an extremely controversial figure. At various times in his career he was accused by newspapers of racism and anti-semitism. He was, reportedly, an admirer of Adolph Hitler. Faced with the choice of putting the disqualified Hardin on the team or Beatty, the actual 3rd-placer, he chose Hardin.

"[Brundage] was a czar, and that's the way that it stood," said Beatty. "That's how I missed out on the Olympic Games."

Hardin, who was white, went on to win the silver medal in the Olympics and the gold four years later. Beatty's track career ended that summer.

Although Beatty rightfully was a legend in the sport, it was in the field of education that he made his biggest mark in history. In 1935, Beatty began teaching in the Ypsilanti public school system. During his 39-year tenure, Beatty spent 27 years as a principal, and enjoyed his experience at Perry Elementary School, where he is credited with initiating the nation's first preschool in 1962. The Perry Preschool Project was the forerunner to the Headstart program that began soon after and is now nationwide.

In appreciation of his work in education a bust of Beatty in bronze, sculptured by John Pappas, was unveiled in 1989 to honor Beatty for his many years of excellence in education. In 1985 Beatty was inducted into Michigan's Education Hall of Fame.

1929

Detroit Northwestern laid claim as the team of the "roaring twenties," as the Colts under coach Warren Hoyt won their seventh state championship.

Northwestern was one of a record 157 schools to compete in East Lansing.

Four Colts captured individual titles, with the highlight being the high jump. Sophomore Willis Ward's leap of 6-1¾ erased the oldest record in the books, John Patterson's record 6-1¼ set back in 1906. Thad Dennis, the runner-up to Ward, had won the event as a sophomore in 1927. Northwestern's Dennis demonstrated his abilities as he captured the long jump with a fine leap of 22-4.

George Huber of Northwestern also produced a record for the Colts with his heave of 127-0 in the discus. That toss in 1929 would remain as the state record until 1987 (the discus was reinstated in 1976 after a hiatus of 45 years, but Huber's record was set throwing the heavier 2-kilo implement, while preps now throw the lighter 1.6-kilo disc and only rarely get the chance to throw the college/international 2k platter). The 6-3 Detroiter would remain active for many years while competing for the Detroit Police team. In 1941 he would be the leading point producer at the state AAU games, scoring 32 points, including a record hammer throw of 166-8.

Muskegon's Morgan Wilson just missed topping the 12-foot barrier in the pole vault as he cleared a record 11-10¼. Jack Hernley of Lansing Eastern, runner-up a week later at the prestigious National Interscholastic meet, bettered the javelin mark with a toss of 171-8. Hernley edged Saginaw Eastern's Ted Petoskey for first-place honors. Petoskey, the 1927 Class C pole vault champion and future Michigan football All-American, had earlier transferred from St. Charles to Saginaw Eastern.

Hernley didn't have to worry about competition coming from the Grand Rapids regional. The event was eliminated from this regional after a student named Andrew Muir was hit with the javelin during a practice session two days before the meet was scheduled at Houseman Field. Three years later the javelin event would be eliminated forever from state meet competition.

The leading point winner in the meet was Charles Eknovich from defending champion Northeastern, with seconds in the high hurdles and long jump and a first-place effort in the low hurdles. Eknovich was long jumping when the finals of the low hurdles were called, but ran to the starting mark and kept on going to win the event. All was not golden for Eknovich, however. The Falcon star dropped the baton while running a leg in the 880-yard relay when a second-place position looked secure. The loss of those valuable points dropped the Falcons into third place behind runner-up Cass Tech.

Defeating Eknovich in the high hurdles was Jack Heston of the championship Colt squad. Heston was the son of Willie Heston, legendary All-American football great during the early Michigan gridiron dynasty of coach Fielding Yost.

Otto Pongrace, who would become the 880-yard record holder at Michigan State College, won the Class A mile in 4:34.6. Earlier in the school year, the Detroit Eastern star captured the national indoor title, the Michigan invitational, and set a Detroit City League record with a time of 4:36.0. Pongrace was the dominant half miler during the early 1930s on the state college circuit, winning the state collegiate invitational 880 three straight years (a meet that all colleges in Michigan participated in except for the University of Michigan).

In the 440-yard dash Merrill Hershey of Detroit Western defeated archrival Leon Dykas of Northeastern in the quick time of 50.7. Hershey, who may have been the fastest Motor City sprinter never to win a city individual championship, would go on to have an outstanding career at Michigan State Normal (EMU). In 1934 Hershey was touted as Michigan's fastest collegiate sprinter. The final state champion from Detroit Western High School won the 220 (21.6) and equaled the meet record with his win in the 440 (48.9).

Detroit Cass Tech's Leroy Oliver was the leading sprinter in the state of Michigan in 1928 by taking both dashes in East Lansing (10.2/22.7). Oliver was second at the University of Michigan Interscholastic to future Olympic great Ralph Metcalfe in the short sprints.

Niles won its first state championship in Class B with a five-point edge over second-place Dearborn. Future Michigan State record holder Ted Bath trimmed the high hurdle meet record down to 16.2 and posted the best mark in all classes with his 44-10 heave in the shot put.

Lowell nipped Kalamazoo State High to win honors in Class C, while Newaygo, in an even tighter battle in Class D, just edged defending champ Okemos by less than a point. Wyandotte Roosevelt's Earl Sonnenberg in the 880-yard run (2:03.5), and East Grand Rapids' pole-vaulter Russell Goosen (11-6) were the only repeat champions from 1928.

Earlier in the season, Edwin Jackson of Dearborn won the broad jump at the University of Michigan meet in Ann Arbor, quickly hopped in an automobile and returned to Dearborn in time to win the broad jump at a big invitational on the Dearborn Fordson track. Two weeks down the road in East Lansing, he would also win the Class B broad jump title at 21-2¾.

Attempting the same unusual double was Jackson's Dearborn teammate, Carl Thiel. Thiel, a two-time state Class B discus champion in East Lansing, placed fourth in Ann Arbor before joining Jackson on the journey back to Dearborn where he finished first in the discus and the shot put. If Thiel could have hurled the discus the same distance in Ann Arbor as he threw at Fordson (121-0), he too would have pulled off a double win.

Eddie Tolan: King of the Sprinters

The Wolverine State has been blessed with great sprinters during the first 100 years of track & field, but Eddie Tolan arguably claims the title as the King of the Sprinters. During Tolan's era of 1925 through 1932, he took part in more than 300 races, placing first in all but seven.

Only once during his prep career would the bespectacled sprinter out of Detroit Cass Tech not hit the finish line first. Eddie's lone defeat as a high school prep came at the University of Michigan Interscholastic Meet in his sophomore year of 1925. Tolan placed third in the 100-yard dash behind winner Jimmie Tait of Detroit Northwestern and runner-up John Lewis of Detroit Northeastern.

The son of a hotel cook who moved his family from Salt Lake City to Detroit to get his children a better education, Tolan led Cass Tech to a state championship in 1926. Earlier in the track season he helped bring the Mechanics (now known as the Technicians) a national indoor prep championship.

Eddie's first love was baseball, and he preferred it to track until coach Vaughn Blanchard saw prospects of future greatness in the young, chunky Tolan and finally prevailed on him to stick with the track game. Some years later, when Tolan was asked what inducement Blanchard offered, Eddie grinned and said: "He told me the track team would take many more out-of-town trips than the baseball team. Right then I became a track man." And travel he did. Tolan's talents in track eventually took him on journeys that ranged from Europe to Australia.

After a sophomore season at Cass Tech, where he was developed into a state champion sprinter by coach Blanchard, Tolan improved even more as a junior under first year coach Bill VanOrden. The Mechanics captured the state title in 1926 with Cass Tech far from a one-man team. Although Tolan would grab most of the headlines during the era, Cass Tech had more than its fair share of talent.

Leading the parade along with Tolan were Eddie Gaines and Bill Loving. Gaines and Loving matriculated to Western Teachers College (Now WMU) where they became the first African Americans to captain a sport for the Broncos. Gaines, who graduated from Cass Tech in 1925, combined speed with endurance, and became a champion broad jumper and high jumper as well as a record-breaking half miler. He propelled the Broncos to the Western Collegiate championships in the late '20s by winning the broad jump (23-1), 440 (50.5), 880 (1:59.9), and tying for first in the high jump (5-11½). His school record time of 1:55.0 for the half mile remained on top of the Bronco leader board for many years.

Bill Loving may even have slightly upstaged his more recognized teammate at the 1926 state championships in East Lansing. Loving won both hurdle events, placed third in the discus and tied for fourth in the high jump as Cass Tech breezed to its first state title.

Tolan became the second high school sprinter to crack the 10 second barrier with his 9.9 clocking for the century, to go along with a quick 22.2 solo win for the 220. One must keep in mind that sprinters, prior to the 1932 Olympics, took off from the starting line without the aid of starting blocks. Consider also the slower cinder surfaces used during the roaring twenties.

Comparing those surfaces to the sleek all-weather ovals used today would make for some interesting musings on just how fast a modern Eddie Tolan could go.

Cass Tech just missed repeating as state champs during Tolan's senior season in 1927. Four times a Mechanic trackster stood atop the awards stand to receive the first-place medal, but the victors from Detroit Northwestern had too much depth for Cass Tech, who had to settle for third place, six points behind the Colts. In his final meet as a prep, Tolan blistered both the 100 and 220-yard dashes in the National Interscholastic meet in Chicago with times of 9.8 and 21.5.

Although Tolan attracted much attention for his national interscholastic sprint double victory in Chicago, it was his showing against the big boys at the Michigan State AAU on Belle Isle in Detroit that really turned some heads. The stocky Motor City sprinter teamed up with many of his Cass Tech teammates and other Detroit prep stars to win the state team title. In the process, Tolan won both the 100 and 220-yard dashes in his first match-up against veteran runners such as George Hester and Victor Lechinsky. Tolan's impeccable credentials as an athlete and a student would earn him a scholarship to the University of Michigan.

Equally as shocking to many at the 1927 AAU state championships was the upset win posted by Tolan's teammate at Cass Tech, Robert Sampson. While still just a junior in high school, the relatively unknown Sampson upset future Olympian Ken Doherty and state high school record holder Thad Dennis in the high jump. Sampson, who sailed over the bar at better than six feet fondly recalled his former teammate: "Eddie was a wonderful, wonderful man," said Sampson. "Since he's a schoolboy teammate of mine he was the greatest in my estimation. My, how he would chew on that gum! When his mother was there he could beat anybody. When she was in the stands watching Eddie run he would put it in another gear. When she wasn't there he would just run to win," recalled Sampson some 70 years later.

Collegiate freshmen were ineligible to compete at the varsity level during Tolan's era but the ruling didn't prevent them from competing at the Olympic trials. While running unattached at a pre-Olympic try out in Detroit in 1928, Tolan shocked local followers by defeating defending NCAA champion Fred Alderman of Michigan State College in both the 100 and 220 dashes. This qualified Tolan to compete the following week in Boston, but he elected to sit 1928 out while awaiting 1932 to roll around.

Tolan's next big breakthrough came at the Big 10 championships on May 25, 1929. Tolan, with his big horn-rimmed glasses firmly taped to his head, electrified the crowd in Evanston, Illinois by winning the 100-yard dash in a new World Record time of 9.5 seconds. Tolan came from behind in the last 20 yards to nip archrival George Simpson of Ohio State by the narrowest of margins. Simpson did have his day in the sun later on in the afternoon by defeating Tolan in the 220-yard dash. Simpson's winning time of 20.6 seconds was fast enough to equal the existing World Record and set up a rivalry that would last for another four years.

Head finish judge Knute Rockne, immortal football coach at Notre Dame, deemed the winds under the allowable to put Tolan and Simpson in the record books. "Other than the race in Illinois, Simpson would beat Eddie for 100 yards," reminisced Sampson, "but over 100 meters it was a different story. That extra 10 meters made the all the difference for Eddie." Tolan backed up Sampson's statement while taking part on a European tour late in the summer of 1929. Five times on that tour Tolan equaled the World Record in the 100 meters at 10.4 seconds.

George Simpson nipped Eddie twice at the tape to win the Big 10 100 and 220-yard dashes at the 1930 Big 10 championships, but Tolan would dominate this heated rivalry hereafter. He concluded his brilliant college career by copping both short sprints at the 1931 Big 10 championships in easy fashion. He had his goals set for the following year.

He wanted to peak at, and not before, the Olympic Games set for Los Angeles in August. He did his graduate work at West Virginia University and continued to train in-between his study sessions. Tolan tuned up for his quest by returning to his alma mater. On June 25, at an Olympic qualifier on historic Ferry Field, Tolan blazed the fastest sprint double in history. Although his times were wind-aided, Tolan was clocked at 10.3 in the 100-meters and 20.7 for the 200-meters, both clockings equal to or under the accepted world records.

Steve Farrell, Tolan's first coach at Michigan acted as the head timer. He said the wind was a little too stiff to allow the record but indicated that Tolan appeared to be running faster than when he was at his peak in college. Tolan finished 15 feet ahead of Love Snowden

of Detroit in the 100 and 10 feet ahead of his closest pursuer in the 200.

Farrell's statement proved true a couple of weeks later at the Final Olympics Trials in Palo Alto, California. Runners had to battle a breeze blowing directly into their faces as they dug into their starting blocks on the Stanford University track. The first heat was won in a plodding time of 10.9 that saw Simpson and Chicago's Ralph Metcalfe advance into Sunday's finals. Tolan toed the starting line against a field that included one-time World Record holder Frank Wykoff.

One of the greatest sportswriters of all-time, Grantland Rice, described Tolan's heat: "The second heat was the big feature. It was a half-second faster than the first heat and it served notice in California that Wykoff, one of the greatest of all sprinters, would have to set a World Record to win in the finals. For Tolan was a black streak — a shot of sable dynamite — as he whirled across the finish line in World Record time, faster than any Olympic 100 meters ever run. When you consider the beating force of the Western wind the Tolan performance was the main act of the afternoon."

Tolan failed to win either the 100 or the 200 meters the following afternoon but did accomplish his primary goal of making the Olympic team. He placed second behind Metcalfe in each race to qualify for the big show two weeks later down the road in Los Angeles.

In one of the closest finishes in Olympic history, Tolan edged Metcalf to capture Olympic gold in the 100 meters. Tolan's time of 10.3 equaled the World Record and naturally set the Olympic record as well. Still photos of the finish showed Tolan's margin over Metcalf to be about one inch. Officials had set up one of the earliest phototiming systems ever and both men were timed in 10.38.

No photo was needed to determine the winner of the 200 meters as Tolan led archrival George Simpson by a yard at the finish line. His time of 21.2 (21.12 FAT) was not only an Olympic Record, but was a new World best for 200-meters on the turn. It gave him his second gold medal, matching fellow Detroiter Ralph Craig's double from the 1912 Olympiad.

He had nearly made a tactical blunder during his semi-final of the 200 meters. Setting a goal to just qualify, thus preserving his strength for the finals, Tolan just coasted along during his heat. He didn't see Harold Wright of Canada pressing him for third place and the final berth in the finals. Officials had to scrutinize the photos closely to be certain that Eddie

Tolan's winning margin in the 200 at the Olympics.
(photo courtesy of Bentley Historical Library)

did indeed nip Wright to qualify for the next day's finals.

Along with Bade Didricksen, Eddie was unquestionably the hero of the Olympiad. Some observers were skeptical of Tolan ever winning the sprint double as he ran with his left knee braced. Tolan's friend Lawson Robertson was asked whether Tolan had hurt his knee. "Tolan always wears the brace around his left knee. He wears it for luck. I don't think he even realizes that he is wearing it until the brace slips down, being loose from so much wear, and he has to pin it up again."

Tolan, using today's methods of picking relay team members, undoubtedly would have garnered yet another gold medal if permitted to run on the 4 x 100 relay. But American coaches, it an effort to get as many members of the USA team involved as possible, were confident they could win the gold without using any of the sprint dash medalists. The USA foursome did indeed win the gold and set a WR in the process. But if Uncle Sam's officials had decided to run Tolan, Metcalf, and Simpson, that record would have been much faster.

Following his Olympic glory, and no more amateur laurels to covet, Tolan turned professional and showed his flying heels to all competitors here and abroad. As a professional Tolan remained undefeated, capping his career by winning the world's professional sprinting championship in Australia. Not only did he contend in athletics, but he battled prejudices along the way. Since the Olympics were restricted to amateurs back then, that prevented him from participating in future Games, and meant that fans would never see him race his successor, the legendary Jesse Owens. Years later

Owens would say that Eddie Tolan was his idol while growing up in Cleveland, Ohio.

Following his retirement from racing in 1935 he became a teacher at Detroit's Goldberg Elementary School. He also enrolled in night law school and later became a clerk in the Wayne County Office of Deeds. Tolan, who suffered from a kidney disorder, died of a heart attack in 1967 at the age of 58. He was named to the Michigan Sports Hall of Fame later that year, the first track athlete ever so enshrined.

1930

On April 27, the news hit. "LOCAL SCHOOLS BAN TOURNEYS" read the headline in the Detroit Free Press. Vaughn Blanchard, the director of athletics for the Detroit schools, announced that Detroit schools would no longer participate in MHSAA state finals after the current school year. This followed rumors that had been circulating for months that Detroit's Metropolitan League would break away from the MHSAA altogether.

The official reason given: "This action is being taken because of the rapid growth of the Metropolitan league." Some 16 schools big at that point, league officials expected it to grow to 20 within a few years. They also passed a second measure, banning any sporting events with schools outside of a 25-mile radius.

It would be more than 30 years before we would again see Detroit city league prepsters competing with out-state schools. Detroit Northwestern made sure its swan song was a good one as it again displayed awesome dominance with its eighth state championship since 1920. Cass Tech, again, played the bridesmaid role with its third runner-up performance in three years.

Northwestern once more was led by Willis Ward, who would go on to political and legal fame as the Probate Judge of Wayne County. Ward won both hurdles events for the Colts, but finished second in the high jump behind Detroit Mackenzie's Arnold DeNeau, in his unsuccessful bid to defend his record-setting performance of 1929. Second to Ward in the high hurdles was Richard Austin from Cass Tech. Austin would go on to launch a brilliant political career of his own, as a long time and innovative Michigan secretary of state.

The political careers of Ward and Austin would perhaps pale in comparison with the fourth-place finisher in the discus. That was Gerald R. Ford of Grand Rapids South, who later became the 38th President of the United States. Jack Fundis of

Northwestern took home the first-place honors in the discus, and became a double winner with his victory in the shot put. William Bryant of Detroit Cass Tech took both short sprints.

Eddie Laskey became Hamtramck's only track & field state champion in prep history with his winning clearance of 11-6 in the pole vault. Class A experimented for one year by running the 880-yard run in two sections, a practice that would be copied beginning with the 1938 season. Raymond Roe of Detroit Northwestern won the first section in 2:00.4 with Detroit Redford's Karl Kahler the next heat winner in a slower clocking of 2:02.6. Roe left little doubt as to who was the best half miler in Class A, as the Colt had earlier defeated Kahler at the Detroit City championships. Kahler proved more than adept at the half-mile distance, setting a freshman record the following spring for Eastern Michigan.

"Tim Quinn, a rugged lad from Ludington competing in Class B, rose to a dizzy height in the greatest achievement of the day when he ran the half mile in the sizzling pace of 1:58.8," wrote the Grand Rapids Herald. Quinn's time was the fastest for all classes and bettered Rha Arnold's meet record of 1:59.9 in Class A, not to mention crushing the old state record.

The Ludington ace took on all comers at the National Interscholastic meet in Chicago the following week and defeated the best in the country. He dusted the competition by 15 yards in the mind-boggling time for the era of 1:57.2. It would be another 32 years before a half-miler in any class would exceed Quinn's time at the state meet.

Monroe began its quest to become a track power with a convincing win in Class B, paced by double sprint victories from future Eastern Michigan ace Fred Schatte. William Stoner won the pole vault for Monroe, keying off a period of dominance for the Trojans, who would win eight state titles in the vault over the next 12 years.

Mt. Clemens produced a state champion of note in the javelin. Wally Weber would go on to the University of Michigan where he became a fixture as an assistant football coach for many years.

Allegan's Bernard McNutt established two records with wins in the shot put and discus. McNutt, future captain and star fullback for MSC, showed speed as well as power by placing second to Schatte in the 100-yard dash.

In the tightest team battle of the day, Kalamazoo St. Augustine edged Otsego by a single point to take honors in Class C. East Grand Rapids' Harry Samrick posted the quickest 100-yard dash time for all classes with his winning time of 10.2. Frank McCrory won the award for the winner coming the longest distance. His

long trek from the western Upper Peninsula town of Ontonagon was an unqualified success, as he won the discus competition in Class C.

Okemos used a record-setting heave by future MSC track star Cleo Beaumont in the javelin to spark the Capitol City area lads to the Class D championship. Beaumont accomplished a rarity by winning the javelin not only in Class D but also at the University of Michigan Interscholastic in Ann Arbor.

The decision by the Detroit Public Schools to eliminate any outside competition after 1930 undoubtedly also signaled the death knoll for the meet in University of Michigan Interscholastic in Ann Arbor. The forerunner of what would become the Mansfield Relays was won by powerful Northwestern, 35 points more than its closest competitor.

Bob Sampson: Gentleman of the High Jump

One of the many rewards in doing the research for this publication was the chance to meet and interview so many great people over the years. Unquestionably, one I will never forget was an elderly gentleman from Detroit, Robert Sampson.

I first met Sampson while attending an annual meeting for the Detroit Old-Timers Club, a resilient group made up of former Motor City track performers from the past who are staunch supporters for preserving the great history of track and field.

What a great treat it was to be introduced to Sampson, the state champion in the high jump way back in 1928. We quickly hit it off and over the years Bob would add much needed information and those invaluable 'nuggets' that would provide some great insight into the lives of many of those track greats from yesteryear.

Over the next few years Bob would be quick to introduce me to some of his old pals from yesteryear as well as supply me with photos and clippings from the years long gone bye. Sampson was not just a source for stories and highlights from the olden days, but was also an outstanding athlete in his own right. And, if not for an untimely passing of his father in his senior year back in 1928, Sampson could very well have claimed two national titles in his specialty.

In the summer before entering his senior season at Cass Tech, Bob Sampson beat Thad Dennis & future Olympian Ken Doherty at the 1927 state AAU games with a jump of 6-0 1/8, only the third high jumper in

Cass Tech, during Sampson's time, had a capacity of 3,600 students, with a lunchroom that served more than 5,000 a day (Commerce High was attached by a walkway). At one point in the mid-1920s, Associated Press reported the school had an enrollment of over 13,000—attending in shifts.

state history to clear six feet.

Then in the winter of his senior season at Cass Tech, Sampson won the National Interscholastics. His winning height of 6-2¾ set a state indoor record.

With his victory in the at the state meet in 1928, he was favored to capture the national outdoor crown in Chicago shortly after the close of the high school season.

"Prior to the nationals I was jumping 6-4 every day in practice and I wanted to jump 6-5 at the nationals. But my dad died the day before the meet and I wasn't able to go. It broke my heart," Sampson said in the late 1990s.

Sampson grew up during an era that would be considered the golden era of sports; it also was a difficult era for many of the African-Americans raised in the Motor City.

For Bob Sampson, there was no better time than growing up in the Detroit Area in the roaring twenties. "I believe I remembered almost every black schoolboy who participated on the various high school track teams during the years 1924 through 1928," related Sampson in a newspaper clipping from 1979.

"No group of teenage athletes had more fun than we did. The spirit, the rivalry, the thrills and the shared experiences of competing in the city, state and national track meets are treasured episodes, trimmed in gold that somehow shines with a new luster with each remembrance," Sampson so eloquently penned.

"While attending high school I frequently didn't have anything to eat. I would kind of saunter into the lunchroom and somebody would generally give me something to eat. But I was OK. I didn't suffer. My brother raised me since my father was pretty old. It was my brother who wouldn't let me go to the Nationals in Chicago," said Sampson during one of our conversations.

Sampson often mentioned old Codd Field, the site of many memorable PSL track meets during this exciting era.

"A short time ago I took my son for a drive over to Codd Field, but it was so dismal that I said you don't know why your Dad would take you over to a place that was nothing but weeds. I was trying to explain where the track was laid out and where the stands stood. I told my son that if I could have talked real good with the powers to be, than I would have a new track laid out just like Codd Field. Everything was where you could see each event. My son was polite and he looked over the field and than looked back at me with that look in his eye... I was disappointed myself."

But what fond memories Sampson had of those years when track and field was much more popular then it is today. He witnessed many city and state track meets over the years which led me to prod Bob on two obvious Detroit prep speedsters, Eddie Tolan and Henry Carr, both Olympic gold medalists.

"Henry Carr & Eddie Tolan could have run with anybody," he said. When asked how they would have fared against one another in their prime, Sampson replied diplomatically, "It would be a tie between Tolan and Carr as my all-time fastest sprinters. And Herb Washington would be right with those guys too," added Sampson.

The incomparable Tolan had a big boost from his biggest fan while running. "When Mrs. Tolan was in the stands then Eddie was the greatest," Sampson said with a chuckle.

Despite the racial tensions of the time, Sampson reserved some of his greatest praises for a number of white athletes and others from the early half of the twentieth century.

"The twenties, to be sure, produced quite a number of white prep stars who had their fair share of track talents," said Sampson. Among them were George "Buck" Hester, Leighton Boyd, Jimmy Tate, Charles 'Snitz' Ross, Everett Pauschert, Phil Cavanaugh, Phil Northrup and hurdling sensation Edward Spence.

Another white sprinter to earn Sampson's respect was Lansing's Fred Alderman, who later won NCAA titles in the 100 and 220 and was a gold medalist in the 1600-meter relay for the USA team in 1928. "I really took a shining to him. He was an engineer who graduated from Michigan State."
Sampson related to me that Hester, some five years younger than Tolan, would take the time to give Tolan some valuable tips. After his graduation from Detroit Northern, Hester was a frequent visitor at Cass Tech High School, and for a very good reason, according to Sampson.

"Hester's future wife, Miss Kelly, coached girls physical education at Cass Tech. Buck was madly in love with Miss Kelly and would come over to Cass Tech a couple of times a week. He would take the time to show Eddie Tolan how to start," said Sampson.
Hester, born across the river in Windsor, made the Canadian Olympic team in 1924 and 1928 but Sampson explained that Hester almost didn't run in the latter Games. Canadian officials weren't wild about him wanting to bring his new wife along for a honeymoon.
Surprisingly, Sampson confessed to me, "I had trouble with school. I did well in English."

If he had come along in a later era there is little doubt that he would have been a top-notch scholar. It should be duly noted that Sampson was the first African-American to have his work published in the Business News.

Although the talented Sampson was not able to afford to attend college in the 1920s, he was proud that his son Robert Jr. was a graduate of Eastern Michigan, while his son Todd went to Kentucky State and became an attorney.

He shared this little tale from his schooldays at Cass Tech. "I had a wonderful teacher in Mrs. Yost. She passed me in biology where I was a little weak and she then would go and cheer for us at the track meets."
Here is a short story Sampson wrote for his many friends who were a part of the Brewsters Old Timers athletic dynasty.

The years were so long ago they may be blurred in the telling.
Were those years as gray as the clouds or were they as golden as the sun?
It's too difficult to say. You and I, after all, were young teenagers at the time.
History suddenly turned into a cyclone during those growing awareness years. Episodes and events---good or bad that aroused your curiosity were like perpetual adventure serial. More and more you and I became enthralled with the movies, the risqué vaudeville shows at the Koppen Theatre and the good night kiss being offered in the Ford Flivver rather than the front porch. The jiving and jumping at the Grey Stone Ballroom to the music of Fletcher Henderson, the McKinney Cotton Pickers and Duke Ellington. The melodious singing of the Ink Spots and the Mill Brothers were episodes beyond comparison.

Detroit's "Purple Gang" was running wild and raising all sorts of hell in the 'boot-legging' racket.
In Chicago, mobster Al Capone engineered the "St. Valentine's Day Massacre," wiping out the "Bugs Moran Gang."
In Alabama, Mississippi, and Georgia, the Klu Klux Klan swelled to 4 million. Sweet-talking Marcus Garvey was touring the big cities, raising money to buy a boat to take us "Back to Africa." Presidents Harding, Coolidge and Hoover took their turns running the country as the "Good Times" rolled on. The Babe hit 60 home runs and made a fortune. Charles Lindberg, the lone eagle, flew solo to Paris and became a millionaire. Ex-heavyweight champion of the world, Jack Johnson was appearing in the neighborhood theatres for 'peanuts.' Turkey Stearns, the greatest centerfielder that ever played baseball, languished in Mack Park, unheralded and unsung by the daily newspapers. In track and field DeHart Hubbard, University of Michigan great, was setting a record in the long jump. Cass Tech's Eddie Tolan, Northeastern's John Lewis and Eugene Beatty, Northwestern's Cliff Robinson were city, state and national champions. The immortal Leon "Toy" Wheeler was busily teaching the Jewish, Italians, and Black youngsters how to box, play basketball and baseball with skill and finesse.

And, you and I who were so close to it all---it did not seem all that unusual at the time. Or that we were living in an exceptional era. Only when we left the twenties and embark into the thirties did it become apparent that we had gone from "Happy Days" to "Brother Can You Spare a Dime?" Nevertheless, you and I survived, partly, I suppose, because we were bred in an atmosphere of church, religion, music and laughter. If this seems corny, a lot of us have survived on philosophy and at times little else.

Although I truly enjoyed the years spent on the west side of the state on the shores of Lake Michigan, I wish I had more time to travel to Detroit and spend time with a man who was a truly classy gentleman and one who I wish I had met years earlier.

1931

Monroe made the move from Class B to Class A successfully as it became the first school to win the championship in the absence of the Detroit schools. For more than 30 years there was always the unanswered question: "Who would win if the City League was here?" From 1931 until Detroit resumed competition with out-state schools in 1962, we also cover the Detroit City Meet.

A strong headwind hurt sprinters and hurdlers in East Lansing. Boyd Pantlind of Grand Rapids Central did lower the meet record in the 120-yard high hurdles, clocking 15.8 in the prelims. This was the only record set in the adverse wind conditions. Pantlind, a future star hurdler at the University of Michigan, fared well at the National Interscholastic meet later in the season, placing a very respectable fourth.

This would mark the final year that the javelin was ever thrown during in state competition. Milford Haveman of Kalamazoo Central, in hurling the spear 176-11, forevermore etched his name in the record book.

The discus would also be eliminated for many years but would come back to the scene 45 years later after better safety precautions were observed. Veteran CMU track coach Lyle Bennett mentioned that a number of times he held his breath as he watched errant javelin spears and discus platters sail dangerously over athletes and spectators' heads. It wasn't until state officials had cages installed for the discus that this discipline would again resurface on the track & field scene in 1976.

Tim Quinn again won the 880 in the second-fastest time ever recorded in the state finals, 1:59.5. Only his own meet record set a year earlier would be better than Quinn's effort in 1930, but strong winds and little competition failed to push the Ludington Oriole ace to a better time. Quinn again proved to be one of the top 880 runners in the country, successfully defending his half mile title in Chicago in 1:57.4.

Quinn's teammate, Charles Dennis, gave Ludington a powerful one-two punch as Dennis lowered the standard in the Class B mile down to 4:36.5. Dennis traveled with Quinn to the national meet in Chicago and placed an impressive fifth. Although the Ludington distance duo were the meet's stars, South Haven defeated Grand Haven 29 to 25½ to take the Class B team title

The Class C scene marked the second year for Caro's Clare McDurman to emerge on the scene. McDurman won the long jump as a freshman in 1930 and, in 1931, set a Class C record in the high jump with a leap of 5-11¼. Before McDurman would cap his brilliant career, he would win a total of nine individual first-place medals, a feat that would last until Tyrone Wheatley would appear more than a half century later to match McDurmon's feat.

Algonac edged Paw Paw 23 to 22 to take the trophy in Class C, while Centreville won by an even a slimmer margin in Class D, winning by less than a point over runner-up South Lake. Frank McCrory again made the long trip down from Ontonagon in the UP even more memorable than the preceding year, winning the shot put and the discus in record-setting fashion.

Detroit: Willis Ward matched his preliminary time of 15.1 in a wind-aided final. This performance would have shattered the existing state meet record had Ward been allowed to compete in East Lansing. One must remember that hurdlers prior to 1935 had to clear the 42-inch hurdles as opposed to the present-day height of 39-inches.

Although competing under less than ideal conditions, Ward finished his incredible prep career at Detroit Northwestern in a blaze of glory. Not only did this sports legend break the high hurdles mark in the Motor City championships, but set new standards in the 120-yard low hurdles and high jump.

In cold conditions, Ward's 6-4 leap would not be topped at the out-state level for nearly 30 years. The next year, even though freshmen weren't allowed to compete at the NCAA level typically, the Wolverine jumper was invited to compete as a guest competitor since the meet was a qualifier to the Olympic Trials. Ward won with a leap of 6-7 1/8, but was not officially regarded as an NCAA champion. At the Final Olympic Trials at Stanford, Ward tied for fourth, just missing the team. Showing his amazing speed, he won the 100-yard dash as a sophomore at the 1933 Big 10 championships in 9.6 seconds. Only a world record in the 120-yard high hurdles by Ohio State's Jack Keller kept Ward from winning that event as well.

The records will clearly show the tremendous accomplishments Ward impacted in sports on the field. However, it might have been a brief speech he made in front of the board of education in April of 1961, where he made his most renowned impact. As seven board of

Willis Ward won Big 10 titles for Michigan in the 100, high jump and long jump.

education members pondered on whether to permit Detroit Athletes to compete with out-state athletes in tournament competition, the Detroit Probate Judge gave a most impressive address that may have swayed the stubborn board into accepting public school league readmittance to out-state competition.

Detroit Northwestern raced to its ninth-straight City League title, and there is very little doubt in this author's mind that the Colts would have snatched up their ninth state title as well, if not for the PSL's withdrawal from out-state tourney competition. The Detroit prepsters posted better marks in all but five events on the cold and windswept Detroit Central athletic field. Ward's teammate, Francis Krug, by winning the 100 and 220-yard dashes, also had a perfect day. Krug, getting the baton on the anchor leg, made up a five-yard deficit in leading the Colts to the 880-yard relay crown. Jack Fundis, Northwestern's stellar weight event specialist, gave the victors their eighth individual first-place medal with wins in the shot put and discus.

Detroit Southwestern star Frank Bolog had the best showing outside the Northwestern contingent. Bolog ran the 440 in 51.0, a good time under the ghastly conditions, and added the long jump title as well with a fine leap of 22-4½.

1932

One big change came in the 1932 state finals. After 9 straight years of it being a two-day event (Friday saw the sprint/hurdle preliminaries—including the 440—and some field event finals), the MHSAA opted to go to a one-day meet "as a gesture toward answering critics charging over-emphasis on the meet."

The highlight of the meet itself had to be the one-man gang from Caro winning the state championship. Clare McDurmon took all four events he entered (both hurdles, 16.9 & 27.5, HJ 5-5½, LJ 20-9½), single-

handedly earning enough points to capture the Class C title. Boyne City, led by sprint star Ham White, finished second with 18 points, two less than McDurmon's 20.

Harold Stein became the first pole vaulter in Michigan prep history to clear 12-0 with his record clearance of 12-¾. His vault mark continued the steady stream of Monroe vaulters who would scale this lofty height for the next decade.

Ed Kalawart led Grand Rapids Ottawa Hills to its first Class A state title. Kalawart won the high hurdles (16.2) and long jump (22-2½) despite the presence of strong winds on a cold day. The Furniture City champs garnered five firsts to withstand a strong showing by runner-up Ann Arbor. Ottawa Hills, trailing Ann Arbor as they approached the final event of the day, delivered a strong win in the 880-relay (1:32.1) to give the Indians a two-point victory.

Kalawart may have received more attention, but one of his hurdler teammates would go on to become an even bigger star in the collegiate ranks. Following a two-year stay at Grand Rapids Junior College, Harvey Woodstra, winner of the 220-low hurdles, would become a star hurdler for Michigan State College. He swept the 120 highs and the 220 lows against many of the nation's best at the IC4A meet in 1938.

St. Joseph used the record-breaking twosome of Kurt Warmbein and Bob Erickson to propel the Bears to a second state championship. Warmbein had the best effort in all classes with his record-setting leap of 5-10 in the Class B high jump. Warmbein also won both hurdle events while Erickson improved the Class B pole vault record to 11-6. Warmbein would later enjoy a great football career while performing for Michigan State.

Future MSC track captain Charles Dennis of Ludington demonstrated he was not only the premier miler in the state, but one of the best in the country. After defending his Class B mile championship in 4:38.3, Dennis journeyed to Chicago where he finished an impressive second against the nation's best. Class A mile champion Lucille Kaiser from Lansing Eastern placed fifth in that same race.

Centreville again showed its heels to its competitors in Class D, becoming the only repeat team champion. James Desy of Mackinaw City defended his title in the Class D shot put with a record-setting heave of 43-5½. Rex Wolf from tiny Prattville High in Hillsdale County won the Class D 100-yard dash, sharing a distinction with Desy as the only athletes to ever win state championships for their schools.

Winning the pole vault in Class D at an even eleven feet was Howard Elzinga. The Ellsworth native went to work for a couple of years following his prep days, earning money for his college education. Elzinga not only earned his degree at Central Michigan University but also somehow found time to earn twelve varsity letters during a brilliant collegiate career, at the time the most letters won in CMU history.

Elzinga became Central's record holder in the pole vault, qualifying for the 1936 Olympic Trials. With the nation in the midst of a deep depression, Elzinga had to hitchhike with his bamboo-vaulting pole to Wisconsin to qualify for the right to advance to the final trials. He won the regional, but couldn't afford the trip to the West Coast to try out for the Olympic team.

Detroit: Much improved weather prevailed at the Detroit City championships, held at Central's Roosevelt Field a week after the state meet. William Bryant, a double sprint winner two years earlier in East Lansing while representing Cass Tech, repeated his double in Detroit after transferring to Hamtramck High School (10.2/21.8w).

Bill Daly of Cass Tech stamped himself as one of Michigan's all-time bests in the mile. He set a new city record in 4:30.2 and later embarked on a great collegiate career. His clocking of 4:16.6 while attending the University of Detroit equaled the Michigan intercollegiate record in 1935. The next year he ran in the Olympic Trials but failed to place.

The best miler Michigan produced in the era was a young man who was so average as a sophomore at Detroit Northern that he never got his name in the paper. Bill Bonthron transferred to prestigious Phillips Exeter Academy to finish high school and didn't start winning acclaim for his running until his junior year at Princeton. That year, 1933, his only loss was to Jack Lovelock's World Record mile; Bonthron, in second, ran an American Record 4:08.7. The following year, he won the NCAA and then defeated the legendary Glenn Cunningham to win the AAU 3national title at 1500m with a World Record 3:48.8. In 1936 he finished fourth at the Olympic Trials.

Starting blocks were used for the first time at the Detroit city meet in June but it would be another couple of years before they caught on statewide. Claude Snarey's Detroit Eastern squad won the team championship, its fifth major title in three years, as perennial power Detroit Northwestern settled for second place.

The quality of the Detroit meet was best illustrated with the spirited competition in the high jump. Arnold Deneau of Mackenzie and Albert King of Detroit Pershing were declared co-champs after each had cleared the bar at 6-2. King, only a junior, qualified for the 1932 Olympic trials at Palo Alto, California. Although he failed to make the Olympic Team, his leap of 6-4 5/8 was good for an eighth-place tie and a state record.

1933

Kalamazoo Central capitalized on a near sweep in the high jump in winning the 1933 Class A title. The Giants went 1-2 and tied for third in this event, their only first-place finish of the competition. Monroe's Harold Stein set the only A record when he raised his own mark in the pole vault up to 12-2¼.

Two speedsters in Class C nearly stole the show in East Lansing. Boyne City's Ham White shattered two meet records and took three individual titles. White's leap of 22-1 in the broad jump was the best in all classes for the day, while his 10.0 clocking in the 100 matched all performers. The future Central Michigan University sprint star was the only sprinter in history to win the Class C 100-yard dash three times.

White was even more impressive at the regionals a week earlier. Ham sped the century in a brisk 9.9, blazed the 220 in 21.8, and sailed an amazing 22-10¼ inches in copping the broad jump.

Clare McDurmon capped a brilliant career by winning both hurdles, placing in a three-way tie for first in the high jump, and finishing second to White in the broad jump. In 1933 his efforts were good "only" for a second place in the team standings for Caro. Buchanan had more depth than the one-man gang from the thumb area as the Southern Michigan school compiled 22 1/6 points.

Birmingham made a strong showing to take the Class B crown. Four individuals teamed up to win five titles for the Detroit metro team, with William Guckelberg winning a pair (100 and 220). John McKee, the Class B broad jump champ a year earlier, won the 120-yard high hurdles. Rex Overbeck shared his first-place medal in the high jump with co-champ Victor Wellwood from Redford Union. Guckelberg and McKee teamed up with Clark Matthews and Don Donaldson to tie Allegan in the 880-yard relay.

Birmingham's Clayton Brelsford led the field in the 880-yard run in 2:01.7, more than two seconds faster than any other half-miler ran during the day. Two years later the first of the running Brelsfords (brother Quinten would win three state titles in the 880) would win the mile run at the Big 10 championships for the University of Michigan, and the next year he would place 4th in the NCAA 1500.

James Wright of Berkley set a "B" mark in the 440 with a 51.9, a mark matched by Carl Lauterhahn from Grand Rapids South in Class A.

The final record to fall came in the mile run with J. Nelson Gardner coasting around the track in 4:34.6. In mid-June Gardner won his mile race at the National Interscholastic in Chicago in 4:28.4, missing the state

Albert King of Detroit Pershing finished 8th in the Olympic Trials high jump while still a high school junior.

record by a tenth of a second.

Centreville made it a three-peat in Class D, edging nearby Portage 23 1/3 to 19. Lester Walters won both hurdle races to pace the victors.

Detroit: Heavy rains preceded the city meet, run a week earlier than the state meet, eliminating any hopes for record-breaking performances. Hamtramck High won its first championship with Pershing's Albert King posting the best performance. The defending champion flew over the bar at 6-2 and just missed in three attempts at a new record height of 6-4 7/8. A few weeks later, King traveled to Chicago to compete in the Junior AAU Nationals. He tied for the win with a leap of 6-5. The next night that would have taken 2nd in the senior competition. (Note the above photo notes 6-5¼ for that meet. All of the available sources report the mark as 6-5. Perhaps the extra fraction was just bad memory at work.)

Winning the long jump was Highland Park's Fran Dittrich. He would further his long jumping career as an undergrad at Michigan State College before taking over as the long-time head coach of the Spartans beginning with the 1950 season. In 1965 Dittrich would coach Michigan State University to its first Big 10 track title.

Bill Watson: Fate's Victim

Of all the great athletes that have donned spikes at Michigan high schools over the past 100 years, it is doubtful if any combined the raw speed and power that belonged to William Watson. Although blessed with unbelievable talent, Watson also met with more than his fair share of hard luck and tragedy. World War II perhaps denied the former Saginaw High and University of Michigan great his proper place among Olympic heroes.

There is very little doubt that if Watson had lived in any other era of the 20th Century he would have joined the likes of Jesse Owens and Carl Lewis as a track and field legend. Watson won nine outdoor Big 10 championships during his three-year varsity career at the University of Michigan. Beginning with his sophomore season in 1937, he would win the broad jump, shot put, and discus events three straight years. The future Detroit policeman set records in the shot put (52-6) and discus (160-10) not to mention a best effort of 25-5½ in the broad jump.

Charley Hoyt, Watson's first coach at Michigan proclaimed Watson a sure bet to win the decathlon at the ill-fated 1940 Olympics slated for Helsinki. "He could make the Olympic team right now in either the shot put or discus, or both, and win one of the events," remarked Hoyt in 1939, "but he's a natural for the decathlon."

The Watson family picked up stakes and moved from Oklahoma to Saginaw in November 1923. The lure of a better education for their children and hopes for gainful employment played a factor in the move. But the promise of a place where they envisioned improved race relations may have been the most compelling reason for the journey north. Blacks for the most part lived in a repressive atmosphere at the time, especially in the South.

In 1933 Watson's talent caught the eye of his first track coach, Chet Stackhouse. "I first met him in a gym class at Saginaw High in his sophomore year," recalled Stackhouse. "In an effort to cull every student who might have track talent we went through all gym classes. On this memorable day in my coaching career we had some 50 boys jumping over a high jump bar placed at three feet. Every boy cleared the bar but when Watson's turn came he bounced over it with feet to spare. When I went home at noon I told my wife I had just seen an Olympic champion. He weighed only 130 pounds at that time---quite a far cry from the 195 pounds he weighed two years later."

In his sophomore year Watson participated in the pole vault, as well as the high jump and shot put. Because of his rapid growth he did not vault again until he graduated from Michigan, Stackhouse told Saginaw's Ed Miller shortly after Watson's untimely death in 1973.

While a junior in 1934 Watson won the first of his five state championships at the Class A meet by capturing the shot at 48-10¼ and high jump (5-11). If not for an injury to sprint favorite Bob Kolbe, it is likely that Coach Stackhouse's Trojans would have captured their first state championship. Watson and his mates left little room for doubt as to who would bring home the state title the following year.

Indeed, the next year the Trojans brought the trophy back to Saginaw, having nearly doubled the score over second-place Monroe. Coach Stackhouse's tracksters could boast of being one of the strongest teams in state prep history.

Although Watson was unquestionably the shining star of the Trojans, ten other members of the Black and Gold figured in the scoring. Pete Fager was the only Trojan other than Watson to win a first-place medal, while Ralph Schwarzkopf and 1936 high hurdles champion Sherman Olmstead would join Bill as teammates at the University of Michigan.

Schwarzkopf, by being elected Captain of the 1940 Wolverines, gave Saginaw back-to-back captains at Michigan, Watson having served in the same capacity in 1939. Fager chose Michigan State to test his track skills and helped the Spartan's mile relay team win the state intercollegiate title in 1938.

The fans that packed the oval at Michigan State College in East Lansing in 1935 were treated to one of the greatest individual performances in state history. Watson's 53-10 3/8 effort in the shot shattered the oldest existing record on the books. Arthur Kohler had set the standard of 51-6 a full quarter of a century earlier, and only Grand Rapids' Joe Horner had been able to break the 50-foot barrier until Watson's achievement.

After winning the high jump at 6-1¼, Watson had the bar raised to 6-4, more than two inches above the met record held at that time by Willis Ward of Detroit Northwestern. Watson's third trial at this lofty height

had him sailing well over the bar. Unfortunately, he dragged one hand, barely tipping over the bar. Watson won his third state title with a respectable leap of 22-4 in the broad jump, but well short of his goal for a new meet record. Trouble at the board saw Bill narrowly foul at jumps estimated at well over 23 feet.

Traditionally, around the first weekend in June, the Michigan AAU State championships would bring together the cream of the crop of track stars. Rarely would a collegiate or open track & field performer miss this chance to vie for medals against the best in the state. Rarely, however, would a high school star win an event against the older collegians.

The more experienced competitors didn't prove to be a formidable obstacle for Watson. Bill surprised even coach Stackhouse by winning the shot (the collegiate 16 pounds) with a toss of 45-10. A brilliant track career at the University of Michigan now loomed ahead.

NCAA regulations of the era prohibited freshman from competing at the varsity level, limiting Watson to open meets. He returned to the State AAU championships in Grand Rapids where he repeated as shot put champ and took the broad jump as well. Big Bill (as he was now known at Michigan) took only one leap to win the broad jump at 23-10. These marks, both state AAU records, were good enough to earn Watson an invite to the regional Semi-Final Olympic trials in Milwaukee. His third-place finish earned him a trip to the final Olympic Trials in New York but Coach Hoyt wanted Watson to further develop his skills as they pointed toward the 1940 Olympiad.

It was at these trials in Milwaukee where Watson observed his first decathlon. Watson was indeed impressed as he watched 1936 gold medalist Glen Morris set a new World Record in the decathlon, further whetting his appetite for the promising future that undoubtedly loomed ahead.

Watson enthusiastically awaited his first season on the Wolverine varsity track squad and he disappointed no one. He wasted no time in demonstrating his skills by setting a new Michigan record in his first appearance in a Wolverine uniform. His put of 51-½ inch was a school record. He capped his first Big 10 meet by winning three events, the shot in a meet record 50-10 3/8, the discus at 153-9, and the broad jump (24-4½).

The Maize and Blue had a powerhouse unit that included Olympian sprinter Sam Stoller, hurdler Bob Osgood, a world record holder, and AAU vault champ

Bob Humm. All took a backseat to Watson's heroics. Watson and John Townsend, an NCAA place winner in 1936, earned Michigan a one-two sweep in the discus. (Townsend, a three-year letter winner in basketball and track, would be the grandfather of future basketball All-American and NBA star Eric Montross.)

Watson jumping at Ferry Field.

Watson continued to improve his marks the following season, including an outstanding performance at the Penn Relays in April of 1938. He placed third in the discus, second in the shot put, and showed his amazing talent by producing the second-best leap in Penn Relays history with his 24-11¾ in the broad jump. He again won his three specialties at the Big 10 meet in Columbus but suffered his only defeat in the high jump. Watson scissored 6-5 in the high jump but placed third. He had improved his own all-time best marks in the shot put (52-11½), discus (154-8¼) and again flirted with the 25-foot barrier (24-11¾). The University of Michigan was ahead of the curve on race relations, as Watson became the school's first African-American captain in any sport.

That summer he got a taste of international competition in a whirlwind tour of Europe. Against the finest array of talent in the world, he responded with nine wins in the 14 events entered. He displayed awesome speed and was selected to run on the winning USA 4 x 100 relay team in Dresden, Germany. During the indoor season of his final year at Michigan, Watson made it a clean sweep as he won the Big 10 indoor shot for the third-straight year. He then tuned up for the Penn Relays by tossing the shot 54-1¾ in a meet against the University of Illinois, a mark second only to Jack Torrence's World Indoor Record.

Coach Hoyt was now pointing Watson towards the decathlon as they boarded the train for Philadelphia. Hoyt thought the Saginaw senior could compile a record number of points in most of the decathlon events to offset weaknesses in others. "He has another year to go and another year of experience will mean the difference between a near-great and a great athlete," Hoyt added. Watson was enthused. "I'm going to work hard to make the trip," he said, "and boy, it's going to be a tough job keeping me at home," he remarked to the Ann Arbor News in April of 1939. War clouds, however, loomed on the horizon.

Watson was befriended at this time by one of the great sports stars of any era in the person of Joe Louis. While being employed as Louis's secretary, Watson had also joined the "Brown Bomber" on many distance runs, further developing his endurance. Rumors had also circulated around Ann Arbor that Watson would also like to perhaps follow in his boss's footsteps and take up boxing.

The Penn Relays played host to some 3,000 track and field athletes on the last weekend of April in 1939. Watson set a meet record in the shot and placed second in the broad jump. As the Big 10 championships drew near, expectations grew for Watson and his Wolverine teammates. In front of thousands of spectators and a large audience that tuned into the meet on WJR in Detroit, Watson and his fellow thinclads disappointed no one.

The Wolverines gave their veteran coach Charles Hoyt a rousing send-off in his final season by easily winning the Big 10 crown. Hoyt would leave to take over the coaching reigns at Yale.

Watson capped a near perfect Big 10 career by placing first in 9 out of the 10 events entered during his career. Adding in his three indoor shot titles, Watson scored an amazing 12 Big 10 wins. His last shot competition came up just short of his own meet record but he displaced a 23-year-old discus mark from the books with his 160-10 toss. Watson hurled the platter 160-10 to shatter the old standard by better than five feet. Only in the broad jump was he unable to set a Big 10 standard. However, his winning 25-5½—the farthest in the world that year—was second in Big 10 history to Jesse Owen's World Record leap of 26-8¼.

Among those in attendance at Ferry Field was Watson's close friend, Joe Louis. It was initially reported that Watson would forgo the NCAA and Big 10/Pacific Coast meets to join the Louis training camp as a secretary, but Louis talked him out of that and thus prolonged his track career.

Watson tuned up for the trip by capturing his three specialties at the state AAU meet. At the NCAA meet in Los Angeles, he set personal records in the shot (54-6½) and the discus (161-9) to win silver medals. Although a disappointment only to Watson, he added a fourth-place in the long jump (24-¼). Though tired, he still managed to place second in his usual three events later that week at the Big 10/Pacific Coast Conference meet.

Rewarded again with a trip to Europe, Watson was unquestionably the USA star of the tour. He won 16 of 19 individual events on the tour, including four gold medals at the World Student Games in Monaco. He also ran a leg on a 4 x 400 winning USA relay team in Paris that clocked a 3:15.6. On the 1st of September Germany invaded Poland. World War II had begun. Watson and teammate Schwarzkopf made their way to Nice, France, with the rest of the American team. On September 5, AAU secretary Dan Ferris reported that that the team was safe and he had wired funds to pay for their return stateside on the Italian liner Rex. Watson's dreams for the 1940 Olympics were now doomed. The Games would be canceled. The World had bigger worries.

Although enrolled for the spring term and working out with the team, Watson never received his degree from Michigan. With the Olympics no longer an option it is doubtful that Bill possessed the same intensity he had while a member of the varsity. He looked forward to competing in his first decathlon, scheduled for mid June of 1940. There were reports that in practice he had bettered the World Record in the 10-eventer.

Publicity for the State AAU meet had Watson entered in six events in preparation for his journey to Cleveland, Ohio. Such was not to be, much to the disappointment of meet organizers as track fans gathered in Kalamazoo. Watson missed most of the meet, as he caught a ride with his former high school coach, Chester Stackhouse, who was now a Michigan assistant. The car broke down just a few short miles

out of Ann Arbor. The new head coach at Michigan, Ken Doherty, came to the rescue and transported Watson to Kalamazoo.

With very little, or no warm up preparation, Big Bill easily defended his shot put and long jump titles and then moved to the javelin area where he needed much work. Winning the javelin, with the nation's second leading throw of 1940, was none other than Lee Bartlett. The three-time Olympian from Union City— who had never competed for his high school team— would have had a real shot at the 1940 Games had they been held.

In Cleveland, rookie decathlete Watson faced two-time defending champion Joe Scott. Watson started auspiciously, sprinting the 100 faster than any American decathlete in history with his 10.8. He long jumped 24-4¼, threw the shot 50-1¾, high jumped a disappointing 5-10, and capped day one by churning the 400 meters in 52.2 seconds. Watson had scored more on the first day than any athlete in history; he stood 99 points ahead of the World Record pace set by Glenn Morris.

Day two saw the former Saginaw great run the high hurdles in 16.5, hurl the discus 151-3 5/8—another decathlon record, and vault 11-8½. With two events remaining Watson was still on World Record pace. Lack of any javelin experience—it was the first time he had ever thrown a javelin in a meet—undid his World Record hopes as he flung the spear but 144-11. A 4:30.4 in the 1500 meters was another decathlon record. Watson won by nearly 600 points. His total of 7523 was the fourth-best total in world history.

Watson's story has been documented in Dr. Frank Zarnowski's book Olympic Glory Denied. The author concluded his chapter on Watson by saying: "Today there is no debate as to whether he would have, at age 23, been the Olympic decathlon favorite in 1940 in Helsinki. Likely, Bill Watson would have won easily. What track authorities do debate is whether he would have repeated the win in 1944."

Watson remained active in track through the 1940s where he still would help area athletes if need be. He passed along shot techniques to Charles Fonville in the late 1940s. The University of Michigan ace used Watson's advice wisely, parlaying those techniques into a World Record in 1948, knocking off Watson's Michigan record in the process.

With Watson among the competitors at the 1948 AAU championships, Fonville eclipsed Watson's 10-year-old state AAU mark in the shot put. Not to be denied, the veteran Watson showed he still had what it takes as he set a new mark in the 56-pound weight throw.

The final chapter in Watson's life was tainted by tragedy. He joined the police force in Detroit in 1941 and remained a patrolman for 25 years, retiring in 1966. During his tenure, he won eight meritorious service citations. He was a personal bodyguard for former Detroit Police Commissioner Edward S. Piggins, and the first African-American officer ever assigned to Detroit Recorders Court on security detail. Incredibly, Watson never once received a promotion during his 25 loyal years on the Detroit Police Force. Longtime track enthusiast Robert Sampson remembered Bill's days as an officer: "He was so nice he hardly ever made an arrest." As an athlete there was no argument. "If it had not been for the war he would have run away with the Olympics. He was the finest athlete in Michigan. He could pole vault, high jump, run the dashes, and he was easy to coach."

The end came suddenly in early March 1973. Watson had been getting psychiatric treatment and was "losing it" according to many of his closest friends. He had joined a private law enforcement agency and had a permit to carry a revolver. Earlier in the week, he had a confrontation with police officers and was taken into the station, where they took away his gun for a time. On the afternoon of March 2, he was driving his car in the Northwest part of Detroit. Two uniformed policemen had pulled over a motorist for a minor traffic violation when Watson pulled up.

According to an eye witness, Watson yelled at the two police officers to "turn the boy loose." Then, according to reports, Watson cursed one patrolman, who was also African-American, and said: "I'm going to kill you." The patrolman saw that Watson had a revolver in his hand and shouted to his partner to duck. Watson, police said, got out of his car, ducked down behind his open car door, stuck the gun through the open window and fired a shot.

The police officers, according to reports, then opened fire. Struck in the chest, Watson was dead on arrival at Detroit General Hospital. He was 56 years old. "William Watson was a fine fellow," reminisced Sampson. "Bill was a real down-to-earth gentleman." Michigan has had more than its share of track greats for the past 100+ years. Of all the champions who went on to greatness, Bill Watson just might have been, if fate hadn't stepped in, the greatest of them all.

1934

Grand Rapids schools finished 1-2, with Ottawa Hills outdueling neighborhood rival Grand Rapids South 35 to 23 7/10. Pre-meet favorite Saginaw's hopes went up in smoke during the morning prelims when defending 100-yard dash champion Bob Kolbe pulled a muscle. A healthy Kolbe could possibly have sent the third-place Trojans home with the championship trophy.

During the Class A regionals held at Flint's Dort field, Kolbe actually jumped out of the landing pit during the competition. Kolbe bettered his own regional record by 3¼ inches, but he would have added possibly another foot or so if not for a too-short landing pit. Kolbe landed on the edge and fell back. The measurement was taken from where he sat back into the sand. Observers estimated his actual jump might have been 23-feet or more.

The win was the second in the past three years for Ottawa Hills coach Lowell Palmer. The 1922 state champion in the javelin while a student at Grand Rapids Central, Palmer became the first former individual champ to also coach a team state champion. Bill Strehl copped both sprints, anchored the winning 880 relay team, and finished fourth in the broad jump while guiding the Indians to victory.

Saginaw's Bill Watson was a double winner for third-place Saginaw, winning the shot put (48-7¾) and tying for first in the high jump, giving the spectators a preview of his exploits to come the following year. Lorimer Miles of Kalamazoo established a new standard in the mile with a time of 4:31.3.

Dowagiac won the Class B state championship in exciting fashion, taking the final event, the 880-relay, to win it all over second-place Dearborn. Art Frontczak anchored after having won both short sprints, to pace Dowagiac's slim one-point victory. Gayle Oldt of River Rouge nearly became the second Michigan pole vaulter to clear the 12-0 barrier, but final measurements had the bar set officially at 11-11¼. Frank Koppitsch of Dearborn had the day's best throw in the Class B shot with a record-setting heave of 48-10½.

Alan Smith of Paw Paw began a streak that was nearly unprecedented in state track history. Smith would win four gold medals two years in a row to lead Paw Paw to the first of its three consecutive state Class C championships. It would be 62 years before Smith's achievements would be matched (John Mack of New Haven in 1995-96). Smith, a future Big 10 champion in the 220-yard dash, captured both short sprints, the long jump and anchored the winning 880-

relay, a feat he would repeat the following year in even more spectacular fashion.

Not to be outdone, Lester Walters was the workhorse for Centreville, leading the Bulldogs to their fourth-straight Class D crown. Walters joined Smith as a four-event winner and would win seven state titles during his varsity career.

Detroit: Bernard Lucas led Detroit Eastern to the city championship with three wins, including a record leap of 6-4¾ in the high jump. To perhaps better appreciate the magnitude of Lucas's high jump effort, this mark would not be bettered at the state track championships for 30 years. He then upset the defending long jump champion (and future MSC head track coach) Fran Dittrich with a winning leap of 21-9. His third win of the day on the University of Detroit track came in the 120-yard high hurdles (16.0).

Eastern had only six athletes qualify, but it proved more than enough to hold off runner-up Hamtramck for the team championship. Hamtramck might have tied Eastern for the crown, but was disqualified after initially winning the 880 relay. Dorsey Gray of Eastern piled up valuable points for the winners by winning the 100 and 220 dashes.

The day's most thrilling race occurred in the 440-yard dash when Central's Sam Schwartz outleaned Hamtramck's James McMillan at the tape in 52.0.

A real oddity occurred during the Motor City meet as Walter Kraft of Cooley was declared the shot winner even though he failed to participate in the finals. Kratt led all qualifiers during the Wednesday preliminaries, but turned 20 years of age a day before Saturday's final. Meet officials counted his prelim mark for the finals, and declared Kratt the winner when all other participants failed to match his qualifying throw.

Alan Smith:
An American Hero

There may have been faster sprinters throughout the many years of track and field in Michigan, but none has captured the essence of our spirit more than Alan Smith. Although his exploits on the cinders rank among the best all-time, it was his melding of athleticism and valor that will live in our hearts forever.

The records will show that Alan Smith led Paw Paw High School to back-to-back state titles in 1934 and 1935. He was one of but three state athletes (Eugene Beatty and John Mack the others) to win four state titles back-to-back.

A Big 10 dash champion, a graduate from the engineering school at the University of Michigan, a husband who would see his wife become a doctor, a heavily decorated pilot—the life of Alan Smith was one that was made for Hollywood moguls to drool over. Unfortunately, it came to an end all too soon. The Smith family settled on a farm just west of Paw Paw when Alan was only a couple of years of age. His father, Ernest Smith, was a mechanical engineer who made the move to Paw Paw for health reasons. The elder Smith's original plan was to reside in the Paw Paw area for a brief period of time, but ultimately their love of southwestern Michigan inspired them to stay.

More than 70 years later Alan's biggest fan would reminisce about the early years in Paw Paw. Miriam Toren, who resided in Cool, California, spoke with unabashed pride about her brother's younger years. "Alan was a very even-tempered boy. I don't think he ever picked a fight. He could handle himself very nicely but he was always under control. When he would come home from school he would occupy his time by reading the family encyclopedia."

Looking back on the spring of 1934, one can't help but think it would have been appropriate if Smith wore Number 16¼ on his track jersey. That's what he scored in every major meet that he ran in his two years on the Redskins track squad. With first place counting 5 points, and each member of a victorious relay team accumulating 1¼, Alan Smith rarely failed to attain the 16¼ points. Only in meets when head coach Bryan Emmert rested him would he fail to garner the maximum.

Smith's older sister Miriam not only attended all of Alan's meets in high school, but also often was called upon to work as a timer. "It was a great thrill to watch Alan run," she recalled. "I saw every meet he ever ran in high school and many of his meets in college. I couldn't sleep at night before a big track meet because I would be so concerned about him."

It didn't take Paw Paw fans long to see that they had a young phenom on their hands. At the prestigious Kalamazoo Relays, despite the biting late April cold, Smith won the broad jump with a school record leap of 21-8¼, and easily dusted the field to takes firsts in the 100 and 220-yard dashes. When the fleet sprinter received the baton in the 880-yard relay he had 20 yards to make up. Naturally, Smith made up the necessary ground, and his usual feat of scoring 16¼ points was again intact.

Smith began his attack on the record books at the

Smith long jumping at Ferry Field.
(photo courtesy of Miriam Toren)

1934 Class C Regional in Kalamazoo. He ran the fastest 100-yard dash ever recorded in any class on the Western State Teachers College cinders. He followed his 100 record by running the 220 in a record-breaking 22.2 and topped it off by easily winning the broad jump. The day ended with another winning 880-yard relay.

Smith and his fellow Redskins took their act to East Lansing where they nipped East Grand Rapids for the Class C championship. Smith accounted for 16¼ of his teams winning total of 26 1/5, just 1 1/5 points more than the runners-up from East. This 1 1/5 point's difference was due to Paw Paw's Eugene Emery ending up in a five-way tie for third in the high jump.

The following fall found Smith utilizing his speed on the gridiron, leading the Redskins to a 7-1 record. Against arch rival Allegan High Smith blazed 70 yards for Paw Paw's only touchdown in a 7-6 win. He capped his season by running for a 79-yard TD against Kalamazoo State High. Following the football campaign he was an easy choice for All-Southwestern Michigan honors.

Early into the 1935 season Smith wasted no time in setting three Van Buren County records in a dual meet with South Haven. He ran the 100-yard dash in 10 seconds flat, and sprinted around the curve and flew down the straightaway to breast the tape in 22.8 for another record in the 220. He then leaped 22-1 in the broad jump to erase yet another old mark.

The following week a much-awaited dual meet took place on Paw Paw's Alumni Field. The contest not only brought together the Class B and Class C team champs from 1934, but also the defending sprint kings as well. Dowagiac's Art Frontczak had matched Smith's feat of winning the 100 and 220-yard state titles in 1934 and area bragging rights were at stake for this eagerly anticipated dual. Running into a stiff wind Smith defeated Frontczak by two yards in the 100 (10.2) and by five yards in the 220.

Smith also copped the broad jump honors as well with a leap over 21 feet in very unfavorable conditions. Placing second to Smith in this event was Dowagiac's Allen Cisco. The Dowagiac jumper would win this event at the Class B state finals but was no match for Alan Smith. In another dual featuring state champions, Smith anchored the Redskins 880-yard relay team to victory over the 1934 state Class B championship team from Dowagiac.

The first week of May saw Coach Emmert take five of his tracksters with him to nearby Kalamazoo, where the Redskins and Alan Smith would go head to head against Class A and B opponents in the Kalamazoo relay carnival. In this meet no team scores were given as the competing schools entered only selected members of their teams, rather than complete squads. A few special events were held in addition to four relay races.

It was Smith who took high point honors. He won the 100-yard dash over a very tough field that, in addition to Dowagiac's Frontczak, featured 18 other sprinters from Class A schools, including the defending Class A champion. On the wet and heavy track Smith powered home first by two yards in 10.3 seconds. He also easily won the broad jump title on the slow runway at 21-5, more than a foot better than his nearest competitor.

In the 880-yard relay Smith found himself in fifth position against a stellar field. He managed to pass three of his competitors to move the Redskins into second place behind only Muskegon, a powerful foursome that featured state hurdles champion Gayle Robinson.

The Redskins utilized this meet to prepare them for the Class C regional that would take place in two weeks. Smith certainly had plenty of help as the defending state and regional Class C champions piled up an unbelievable total of 72¼ points. Paw Paw won 10 of the 13 events and placed in all 13 as ten of the athletes qualified for the trip back to East Lansing. Smith completed his high school career in a fashion in which legends are created. In the morning Smith leaped 22-6¼ in the long jump, breaking the record set by Ham White of Boyne City in 1933. This was the best mark of the day in any class, exceeding even the best jump by Saginaw's William Watson in Class A. Watson would go on to win the Big 10 long jump title three straight years for the University of Michigan.

Smith also ran the day's fastest time in the 100-yard dash and tied White's Class C best of 10.0. In the 220, Smith just ran to win in order to save his strength for the day's final event, the 880-yard relay. It should be noted that his competition in the 220 was not just your ordinary fare. Trailing Smith to the tape in the 220 were Stoddard of Millington and Carl Swingle from Shelby. More than 60 years after those youngsters let the cinders spew behind their flashing spikes, their school records lasted into the next century.

The most thrilling event of the meet was the relay between Paw Paw and Millington. The Redskins had the meet won before this final event, but were eager to break their own record of 1:34.7 set a year earlier. Dave Warner, Paw Paw's leadoff man, ran on even terms with Arnold Smith of Millington, who had placed in the 100-yard dash. Louis Oswalt, who earlier had won the 200-yard low hurdles, kept Paw Paw even but had a bad hand-off to Joe Lula. Though Lula finished well the Redskins still trailed Millington by a few yards as Smith grabbed the baton. William Stoddard, who trailed only Smith in the 220-yard dash finals, made a gallant bid to hold off the fast-charging Smith.

The Redskin ace was forced to run the hardest race of his career as both runners swept into the straightaway for the finish. Smith could not be denied, however, and broke the tape two yards ahead of Stoddard in 1:34.0.

The records Smith set would stay in the record books for a combined 82 years. Only George Hester's remarkable record in the sprints totaling 90 years

outdistanced those marks posted by Smith. If Smith could only have found a way to add an additional half-inch to his broad jump mark, his records would have extended to cover 97 years. It is likely that if Smith had the advantage of today's lightning fast surfaces, one or more of his records may still be in the books today.

Word of Smith's exploits were passed on to University of Michigan head coach Charles Hoyt. It undoubtedly was no coincidence that the head speaker at a year-end banquet honoring the state champs from Paw Paw was Hoyt. Not surprisingly, Smith accepted a track scholarship where he would eventually earn a degree in aeronautical engineering.

After earning his letter M in 1938 Smith then became a major contributor on coach Hoyt's Big 10 championship team of 1939. Although teammate William Watson drew the major share of the headlines with his three victories, the former Paw Paw speedster placed second in the 220 and third in the 100. Following the Big 10 meet, Smith participated in the 16th annual Michigan A.A.U. track and field championships in Ypsilanti. For years, this contest served as the major meet for all track and field performers in the state. All the state universities would send their top athletes, and even young high school phenoms would test their skills against the collegians and open competitors. Alan Smith was unquestionably the king of the sprinters in the Wolverine State during the 1939-40 season.

He sprinted the 100-yard dash on a soggy track in 10 seconds flat to defeat a stellar field that included Wayne State hurdling star Alan Tolmich and 1938 Class A 100-yard dash champ George Doran. Later in the day he earned an even more impressive victory in the 220-yard dash. He bested high school sensation Ronald Mead of East Lansing and others in a meet record time of 21.5, eclipsing the standard set 11 years earlier by Bernard Otto of Michigan Normal. (EMU) The following week saw Smith make the long journey to the West Coast where he made the finals in the 220-yard dash at the NCAA championships.

Smith entered his final year at the University determined to win that elusive Big 10 title and establish himself as the premier sprinter of the Midwest. He was disappointed to lose the Big 10 100 by a whisker to Myron Piker of Northwestern. Both runners were timed in 9.7 seconds with Piker getting the victory from the finish line judges. Smith turned the tables in the 220, however, and romped to victory in 21.0 seconds. His dream of a Big 10 championship had been accomplished.

His final appearance on the cinders in Michigan took place at the AAU meet held in Kalamazoo on June 1, 1940. Returning to the site where he had earlier won regional championships while competing for his beloved Paw Paw High School, he certainly didn't disappoint his legion of followers who made the short trek over from his home town.

After winning the 100 in 9.9 seconds, Smith came back to lower his own mark for the 220 down to 21.2.

With his track career over, he surely suspected, as many did, that the war had begun in Europe would eventually draw in the United States into battle. He entered the service in August of 1941, four months before the Japanese bombed Pearl Harbor. The Michigan speedster would not likely have been drafted later on, as he was married and the father of a child. Smith's wife Dottie, a Michigan grad serving her medical internship at Bellevue Hospital in New York, reluctantly agreed with his decision.

Smith quickly earned his wings as an Army Air Force pilot at Kelly Field, Texas in March of 1942. The upcoming summer saw Lieutenant Alan H. Smith sent to Tunisia to serve in the North Africa campaign. He joined General Bernard Montgomery's Eighth British Army as a pilot for the Black Scorpion squad. On March 4, 1943, Smith became the first U.S. serviceman of his unit to be decorated with the Silver Star for gallantry in action.

The citation said in part: "that even though wounded he continued to engage the enemy when his formation was attacked, and through superior skill managed to damage one of the enemy planes and put shots into another plane for which he made no claim, and that he safely landed his own damaged plane."

Shortly after being released from the hospital, following treatment for his wounds, Smith returned to his base. He had already been cleared to return home but insisted on staying until his replacement was trained. With approximately 5,000 servicemen gathered at the outpost in northern Tunisia, a lone German artillery shell was fired from some distance away. As fate would have it, the shell struck only Alan Smith, where he was killed instantly. The date was April 20, 1943.

Smith's former coach Bryan Emmert spoke at the memorial service eulogizing Paw Paw's town hero a month later. The son of Mr. and Mrs. Ernest C. Smith had been buried near where he gave his life for his

Smith as an Army Air Force pilot; he died in action in 1943.
(photo courtesy of Miriam Toren)

country, in the North AfricaAmerican Cemetery in Carthage, Tunisia.

Hoyt, Smith's college track coach, was also in attendance. Following the service, he confessed to Smith's sister Miriam that he was not fair to him in college. "I should have let Alan run the 440," recalled Hoyt, "but he was the only great sprinter that I had. I had a good 440 runner, who was not as good as Alan, but he could win."

The impact of Smith's death had an impact throughout Paw Paw and adjacent communities. People in nearby Decatur were crying on the streets when they had learned that the popular Smith had lost his life in the line of duty.

It has often been said that time heals all wounds. One of the real tragedies is that Paw Paw High School past administrators have all but forgotten their greatest hero. This author finds it truly hard to believe that there is no honor or awards at his alma mater to help perpetuate his memory. It is but a simple touch for me to rightfully dub Alan Smith as the Captain of the All-time Michigan High School Track & Field All-State Team. It is the least we can do to thank Alan Smith and the other heroes of World War II for giving us the good life, the right to live in the greatest nation in the world, and most importantly, our freedom.

1935

May 26, 1935, will go down as one of the more important dates in track & field history for the state of Michigan. While the annual high school track championship was taking place in East Lansing, just 60 miles away in Ann Arbor, spectators at Ferry Field saw Ohio State's Jesse Owens set three world records and tie yet another at the Big 10 championships. His long jump world record of 26-8¼ would last into the 1960s while his Ferry Field record lasted until the facility was repurposed in 2017.

Meanwhile, in East Lansing, Saginaw High showed off one of the most potent teams in Class A history, nearly doubling the score over runner-up Monroe. The Trojans' William Watson, who would go on to even bigger fame at the University of Michigan, established himself as one of the finest all-around athletes ever. He eclipsed the state's oldest meet record, erasing Lansing's Arthur Kohler's mark from 1910. Watson's record put measured out at 53-10 5/8. A few weeks later at the state AAU games in Grand Rapids, using the 16lb ball, the Saginaw senior defeated a field of mostly collegians with a throw of 45-10.

Watson also captured the high jump and broad jump titles with near record-breaking performances. He high jumped 6-1¼ ands then missed at 6-4, just nicking the bar off on his final trial. In the broad jump, he settled for a winning mark of 22-4 after having narrowly fouled on jumps estimated at better than 23-feet.

Willard Fager helped the Saginaw cause by defeating a stellar field in the mile run. He edged meet record holder Lorimer Miles of Kalamazoo in 4:32.6. Saginaw's depth was so deep that another Trojan middle-distance ace, who finished second in the 880-yard run, would join Watson as a star at the University of Michigan. Ralph Schwarzkopf, runner-up to Harold Davidson of Grand Rapids Ottawa Hills, would go on to captain the Michigan squad in 1940, one year after his Trojan teammate Watson held the position in 1939. Schwarzkopf later finished second in the two-mile run at the 1939 NCAA Championships, and third a year later.

Future distance ace Roy Fehr of Royal Oak took the 440 in a modest 52.6, but it was in the two-mile where Fehr would make his presence felt. While attending Michigan State College, Fehr became the nation's best collegian, winning the NCAA two-mile run in 1940.

This year brought about a major change in the hurdles. No longer would high schoolers have to stretch over the 42-inch highs. Muskegon's Gayle Robinson became the new record holder at the current 39-inch height, winning in 15.6. The future longtime MSC athletic trainer also won the lows over the new distance of 200 yards, automatically becoming the new record holder.

Niles took its third team title in Class B by scoring seven more points than second-place Allegan. Niles' only first place came in the 880-yard relay. Allan Cisco of Dowagiac, with wins in the broad jump and pole vault, and St. Joseph's Vinton Davis, with a double win in the short sprints, were the afternoon's only multiple winners. William F Williams, the Albion High School horseshoe champion, won his school's first-ever state title with his performance in the high jump.

Alan Smith excelled as the day's fastest sprinter. The future Big 10 220 dash champ matched the meet record 10.0 set by Ham White of Boyne City in 1933 and the mark would last 25 years. Smith bettered White's record in the long jump with a leap of 22-6½. This achievement would last an even longer 32 years. Smith, in leading the Redskins to their second-straight Class C championship, capped his brilliant career by sprinting to the 220-yard dash crown (22.7) and again anchoring the victorious 880-yard relay. The Paw Paw foursome of Dave Oswalt, Lewis Oswalt, Joseph Lula and Smith churned out a clocking of 1:34.0, a record that would last into the 1960s.

Roy Breen of Grand Rapids Lee became the first athlete in Class C to scale better than six feet in the high jump with a leap of 6-0 3/8, a record that would last for 23 years.

It was then left for William Weise of Class D Champion Bear Lake to cap a truly historic day. Weise won the broad jump and long jump in Class D, as well as both short sprints. In winning four-individual first-place medals, Weise's feat would not be duplicated at the boys state finals for another 17 years.

Detroit: Nasty weather conditions greeted the prepsters competing for the Detroit City Championships the following week. Two competitor's marks, however, did stand out. Ulysses Amos of Northwestern took the 880-yard run in 2:00.2 and Eastern's Bernard Lucas nearly matched his 1934 effort by soaring 6-3 in the high jump.

Willie Henderson of Southwestern, in defending his title in the 120-yard low hurdles, became the only Detroit prep in the 1931-61 era to win four straight.

Hamtramck, by winning the day's final event, took the city title from defending champion Eastern. James McMillan blazed a great third lap to give the Cosmos a

commanding lead going into the final leg. Eastern, needing a win in the relay to defend its title, gave it everything but finished second.

Morris Barnes won the 100-yard dash in 10.8 on the mucky track, becoming the first of many city champions to emerge from Detroit's first (and only) all-Black high school--Miller High.

1936

For the first time since 1912, when the state meet was held on Bois Blanc Island in Ontario, a change of venue was in order. With a new track being installed on the M.S.C. campus, the state track & field championships were moved to Houseman Field in Grand Rapids.

A blistering sun and high winds hampered the distance races and thwarted any new records in the straight running events. Monroe used its exceptional strength in the hurdles and sprints to defeat the hometown crew from Grand Rapids South to capture the "A" title. Ira Hughes sprinted to a 9.9 win in the 100, and Perry Mason and Willie Campbell placed 1-2 in the low hurdles for the Trojans. These three aces teamed up with Percy Zimmerman to win the 880-yard relay in 1:32.5.

Campbell placed second in the high hurdles to Sherman Olmsted from Saginaw. Olmsted, a future track letter winner at Michigan, would coach St. Louis High to the Class C state championships in basketball and track in the early 1950s.

The headliner event for the afternoon had to be the record-setting performance of Middleton's Tony Mazey in the pole vault. He became the second Class D performer in state history to boast the best performance in an event in all classes, vaulting 11-5. With the nation still gripped in a long economic depression Mazey accomplished this feat while attired in corduroy trousers and canvas sneakers. The mark would not be erased in Class D for 24 years.

Ted Tyrocki from Lansing Central had the best effort in Class A, leaping a state record 22-11¾ in the broad jump. This performance would stand until future Olympic gold medalist Hayes Jones would set a new mark two decades later.

Birmingham placed in all but two events to win the Class B trophy with 37½ points. Sophomore Quentin Brelsford won the first of his three titles in the 880-yard run to lead the Maroons. Dan Kinsey of Plymouth became the first Class B performer to better 50-0 in the shot put with his record heave of 50-8¾.

Despite strong winds, Ed Holderman made his trip down from the UP a success. The Escanaba star had the day's best time in winning the Class B mile in a

record 4:34.3. Holderman would later capture the Big 10 two-mile championship and place second in the mile, while competing for Purdue.

Perennial power Paw Paw notched another state Class C championship, outlasting runner-up Lowell 29 to 23. East Grand Rapids had a double winner in Don Wilber with his 10-10 pole vault and his 22-3½ broad jump, second only to Tyrocki's record in Class A.

Taking honors in the shot put in Class C was Milan's Les Bruckner. He would later have a brief two game stint in the NFL with the Chicago Cardinals in 1945.

Onekama scored in 8 of 12 events to win its only Class D crown ever, edging second-place St. Clair Shores Lakeview 46 to 43. Stan McCrea of Pellston won the Hornets' only title ever by taking the shot put. The class valedictorian went on to letter in football at M.S.C. in the late 1930s.

Detroit: Hamtramck won its third Detroit City championship in four years with a convincing performance at University of Detroit Stadium. The Cosmos won five events and tied for first in another in earning their surprisingly easy victory. Jim Knight swept the hurdles while Walter Radzienda copped both dashes for the victors.

Hamtramck's Jim Knight winning the low hurdles.

Carl Culver gave Detroit Central its only title with his leap of 21-3 in the broad jump. Carl's twin brother Fred garnered the third-place medal for Central and the Culver twins would later earn their varsity letters in track while competing for the University of Michigan.

1937

Monroe made it back-to-back wins in 1937. The Trojans had to survive a scare from Saginaw, and won by only a single point, 26-25. Hurdlers Willie Campbell (15.3) and Perry Mason (22.9) again won their respective specialties in meet records to pace Monroe's victory.

Mud and rain greeted the athletes on the new track surface at M.S.C., but good performances still ruled the day. Ted Tyrocki, future Purdue track star, proved that his record-setting effort in 1936 was no fluke, nearly improving on his own impressive record in winning the broad jump. Tyrocki, who leaped an amazing state record 23-1¾ in winning the Ann Arbor regional, popped a jump of 22-9 in the finals. Burgess Wright from Davis Tech in Grand Rapids finished second to defending champion George Angelson of Royal Oak in the shot put. Wright's second-place heave of 50-7½ however, did eclipse Joe Horner's 30-year old Greater Grand Rapids record.

Saginaw and Monroe went down to the final event, the 880-yard relay, to eventually decide the meet. Monroe finished second to first-place Pontiac while Muskegon's edging of Saginaw for the event's third placing decided the team championship. Saginaw remained in the chase thanks in part to Charles Schmeling's winning performance in the 440 dash. Schmeling placed only third in his regional meet a week earlier.

Birmingham repeated as State B champs with a 15½-point advantage over runner-up Niles. Ron Mead from East Lansing began a three-year reign as the Class B sprint king by winning the 100 and 220-yard dashes. Jim Bekkering of Fremont captured the pole vault at 11-6. Bekkering's son Bill would establish a meet record in the event 29 years later.

Starr Keesler scored 19 points to lead Okemos to the Class C championship. Keesler's victory in the broad jump (21-1½) was the Chief's only individual title of the day, but Okemos possessed enough depth to hold off second-place Plainwell. Bruce Smith of Mancelona placed third in the broad jump, and later captured the low hurdles title for the Ironmen. Earlier in the season he had set a broad jump record that would stand as a Mancelona school record for an even 50 years.

Tom Cherry from St Clair Shores Lake Shore was the only Class D entrant to record a double win as he took both the 100 and 220. Mt. Morris St. Mary's and Bloomfield Hills waged a battle for Class D supremacy before St Mary's prevailed 36½ to 34 to win its only state track team title. Freshman Buck Flarity from Onekama had a near record effort under the sloppy conditions, winning the pole vault at 11-1½.

Detroit: Coach Floyd Slocum's Hamtramck Cosmos again copped the city title. Detroit Redford, with its best showing ever, trailed first-place Hamtramck by eight points. Redford's Bob Abbott was the leading point producer, easily capturing the 100 and 220 and running the anchor leg on the winning 880-yard relay.

In the closest race of the afternoon on the University of Detroit oval, Bob Wingo passed his Hamtramck teammate Jim Bradford in the last stride to win by inches.

Charles Moore from Detroit Cooley was the only city champion to better a performance made in East Lansing, scaling an even 6-0 in the high jump. Redford's Bob McKenna would win the discus with a heave of 122-10, an event that had been eliminated from the MHSAA tournament 6 years earlier. Detroit officials followed suit after this meet, and the discus would be gone from Michigan prep competition for 40 years.

1938

Saginaw High (referred to by many as Saginaw Eastern) began a four-year winning streak in Class A with a come-from-behind 31 3/5 to 30½ win over second-place Flint Central. The Trojan's win did not overshadow a sensational performance by Central's Floyd Bates, winner of three events, two of them in

A half-miler at Birmingham, Quentin Brelsford became an NCAA cross country champion.

meet records. Bates lowered the high hurdle standard down to 15.0 and cleared the high jump at 6-2 7/8. In the 200-yard low hurdles in 22.4 he was pushed by a tailwind, but otherwise might have had a third meet record. He stunned track fans earlier in the season by jumping an all-time state best of 6-5¾ at the CMU Relays, a record that would last into the 1960s.

Charles Schmeling led the Trojan scoring by equaling the 440-yard record in 50.4 and clinching the title by anchoring the 880-yard relay to a runner-up finish. George Doran of Grand Rapids South scored wins in the 100 and 220 and anchored the victorious 880-yard relay team, as he helped his school take third in Class A.

The most outstanding achievement of the day was the performance by Quentin Brelsford of Birmingham in the Class B 880 run. The Maroon sensation concluded his high school career unbeaten in the 880, and his final race was the day's best in any class, 1:57.6. Oddly enough, it would only take but a week before Brelsford would finally taste defeat, placing third in the Michigan AAU meet. Brelsford's brother Clayton took second in the race, finishing behind Lloyd Chappell of Western Michigan, who set a new AAU record of 1:54.9.

Eight years after winning the state 880-yard run in record-setting fashion, Brelsford would win the NCAA cross country championship in 1946 while competing for Ohio Wesleyan University. A year later, except for a spill near the finish line while leading comfortably, Brelsford would have been crowned NCAA champion again.

Longevity of records held true to form in the half mile races contested in 1938. While Brelsford's meet record in Class B would last for 24 years, Howard City's Vincent Butler's winning 2:01.6 in Class C would hold up for a period of 25 years.

East Lansing's Ron Mead was a part of three Class B records. Mead lowered the 220 record in B to 21.9, equaled the 100-yard mark at 10.2 and anchored the Trojan 880 relay team to a 1:32.5

. Algonac captured its first Class C crown as Arthur Cuthbertson won the same triple as Mead. Charlevoix's Dick Bergman won a pair of events for the upstate Red Raiders, while his neighboring school to the east jumped into the record-breaking parade. Boyne City's Elwood Hauser established a new meet mark in the 440 at 50.8, a mark that would last 28 years until being cracked.

Bloomfield Hills just nipped Mt. Morris St. Mary by a single point to earn team honors in Class D. Dick LaBrosseur from Nahma in the Upper Peninsula won both short sprints. With all future UP athletes staying north of the straits during the running of the LP championships, LaBrosseur became the last state champion from the UP.

Detroit: Future Central Michigan University professor Al Thomas led Detroit Cooley to the City championship. Thomas was the meet's leading point winner, while teammate Dave Wall set a new 120-yard

Mac Umstattd went to Texas, where he was the anchor on a sprint medley World Record in 1941. He cut his track career short to become a decorated navigator for a B-17 bomber in World War II.

high hurdles record in 15.0. The decision to wipe out Willis Ward's mark of 15.1 set in 1931 did not go down without a fight from area track leaders. Many felt it was unfair to deprive Ward of a record, as he sailed over the 42" barriers in 1931, compared to Wall's trip over hurdles 39" high.

Other impressive marks in the Motor City championships were turned in by Willie Marsh of Pershing in the high jump and Northwestern's Mac Umstattd in the 880-yard run. Marsh's jump of 6-2¾ exceeded all efforts at MSC while Umstattd's 1:58.8 was only about a second slower than Brelford's mark set in East Lansing.

After posting but one mark at the 1937 city championships that bettered a mark made at MSC, Detroit newspapers boasted of the 1938 Detroit tracksters having an edge in all but two of the events over the lads competing in East Lansing.

However, the following week at the Wayne Relays, Dave Conway of Wyandotte Roosevelt, runner-up to George Doran at the MSC Class A meet, defeated the best sprinters from the Motor City in a special edition of the 100 dash.

1939

Lyman L. Frimodig began his 25th year as meet director as the 1939 championships got under way. Frimodig, a long-time assistant athletic director for his alma mater, won a record 10 letters during his career as a student at East Lansing.

River Rouge became the first Detroit Metro school to win the State A championship since 1930, the year the city schools of Detroit first made a decision not to compete with out-state schools. First-place finishes by the Panthers' Paul White in the high hurdles (15.1) and Otis Wade in the high jump (6-0 3/8), combined with a balanced attack, led River Rouge to a 34½ to 26 victory over runner-up Lansing Central. Wade later improved his best mark in the high jump at the Wayne Relays with a leap of 6-3.

Paul White, after captaining the 1943 University of Michigan football team, joined the Marine Air Corps before finishing his education in Ann Arbor. Following the war, White then returned to Michigan football team, where in 1946, he joined his brother J.T. White as regulars for the Wolverines. White played at the next level, with one year in the NFL for the Pittsburgh Steelers.

Jim Naveaux, one of the vaulting Naveaux brothers from Monroe, set the only record in A when he improved on Harold Stein's former mark, vaulting 12-4¼. Future record holder Forrest Naveaux would have to settle for a tie for second, before eventually setting a record of his own in 1941.

Saginaw's Bob Lyttle anchored Saginaw's 880-yard relay team to victory in 1:34.7. A proud spectator in the stands in East Lansing was Lyttle's father, Steve Lyttle, the principal of Saginaw High School. Back in 1910, the elder Lyttle also anchored Shelby's 880-yard relay team to victory.

Ron Mead capped a brilliant career at East Lansing, winning his third-straight sprint double. Mead's 9.8 was wind-aided but his 21.9 dash for the 220 broke his own mark set in 1938. He entered the AAU state meet on June 10. There Michigan's star sprinter Alan Smith blistered the furlong in a meet record 21.5, with Mead second, but ahead of 1938 Class A state champ George Doran.

Dan Sullivan of Wayne heaved the shot 53-9½, second all-time in Michigan to Saginaw's legendary William Watson, to easily eclipse the Class B shot put standard.

The big surprise in Class B was the showing of the St. Joseph Bears. Coach Arnold Karsten's squad went the entire season without winning a dual meet, but had just enough firepower to squeak by second-place Niles 25 to 24½. Victory was so unexpected that coach

Benton Harbor's 1939 state meet squad. Third from the left is Bert Copeland, who would win three events the next year.

Karsten had even started home without waiting to claim the team trophy.

Algonac repeated as champs in Class C, coached by a man who would become a legend down the road in Grand Rapids. Ted Sowle, long time Grand Rapids Catholic Central football coach, won his first of many state championships as Algonac nearly doubled its winning margin over runner-up Paw Paw. Jim Sutton's 23.7 win in the low hurdles was the Muskrat's only individual title.

Junior Gordon Craig became a member of that special fraternity of four-time winners in one state meet, leading Bloomfield Hills to a convincing win in Class D with victories in the 100 (10.3), 200 lows (23.9), long jump (20-3¾) and relay (1:38.5). Shot putter Ivan Watkins of Osseo, slugger on his school's baseball team, won his school's only state title.

Sophomore Donald Montemore, Lambertville High School's only state champion, won the first of his two pole vault titles at 10-10. Far back in a tie for fifth was Art Holland of Comstock Park. Holland, later on a popular usher at Grand Rapids Old Kent Park, still continued as an active pole vaulter while competing in master meets at the age of seventy-five despite a couple of heart bypass operations.

Detroit: Max Umstattd produced one of the fastest-ever marks in the 880 while winning the Detroit City Championship. Clocked in 1:56.6, he missed Quentin Brelsford's state record of 1:55.4 set the previous June against collegiate and open competition at the Michigan AAU championships. In 1941, his first year running for the University of Texas, he twice anchored world record sprint medleys for the Longhorns and broke the Southwest Conference record in the 880. After only two seasons of collegiate track, he joined the war effort, winning the Distinguished Flying Cross as a bomber navigator on the European front. After the war he returned to Texas with a year of eligibility remaining, but chose to focus on law school instead.

Eugene Hirsh from Southeastern defended his shot title with the second-best put in Detroit City history, 51-10½. Only Edwin Turashoff of Cass Tech, Bill Watson of Saginaw and Dan Sullivan of Wayne had ever thrown farther than Hirsh.

Dave Wall, while defending his City hurdles championships, also had the unusual distinction of winning a state championship in another state. Wall, as a sophomore in Omaha, took first-place medals in the high jump and the hurdles at the 1937 Nebraska State Meet; he transferred to Detroit the following year.

Coach Claude Snarney's Cooley Cardinals took the team title with Henry Lord providing valuable points with his 4:39.2 win in the mile run. Lord would later die in action as a pilot during World War II.

There is arguably very little doubt that if Motor City personnel would have competed at the state meet in East Lansing, the state Class A champ would have come from Detroit. Following the state meet at the Wayne Relays, Class A state champion River Rouge was able to place but 10th in a field made up predominately of PSL teams.

1940

For the first time in four years, it did not rain upon the state championships. The athletes took advantage of the improved conditions, smashing eight records and tying two others. Leading the record breakers were the milers. Only the Class D mark, escaped the onslaught. As it was, Calvin Kelsey, the only state champion ever from Merritt, posted a respectable time of 4:47.9 in winning the Class D crown. It marked the second school that Kelsey represented in winning a state title; he had won the 1939 Class D title for Albion Starr Commonwealth. Once he transferred, it didn't take long for him to make an impression at Merritt. In his first year he was elected president of the student body.

The best performance was turned in by Ralph Brakcrog, 16-year old Mt. Morris senior. Brakcrog won the Class B mile in 4:28.2, the fastest time clocked by a Michigan high school boy. Just ten minutes before Brakcrog ran his spectacular race, Rex Woolsey of Jackson had erased the previous all-class meet record from the books with a 4:30.8 performance in Class A. Woolsey's time, set as he finished an undefeated career as a high school miler, lasted only while Brakcrog warmed up and went about the business of leaving his closest competitor 75 yards behind in the Class B race.

The two top Michigan prep milers of their era then faced one another in a headline match-up a week later at the state AAU championships. Brakcrog handed Woolsey his first defeat as a prep with a time of 4:29.4.

The Class C mile was taken by Ralph Golding of Keego Harbor who lowered the meet record to 4:39.9.

Four new team champions were crowned in East Lansing, with Battle Creek winning the state Class A championship. The Bearcats took the meet's final event, the 880-relay, to clinch the meet. Individual point winner for the day was Benton Harbor's fleet sprinter Bert Copeland, who won all three events he entered to score 18. His heroics kept his team in first place throughout most of the day until Battle Creek won the relay.

Harold Carpenter of Royal Oak won the 880-yard run in 1:59.0, a Class A meet record that would last for 16 years.

East Lansing easily took honors over second-place Kalamazoo State High in Class B. Ironically, neither school would have the honor of winning an individual first place. Fremont's Walter Derby led the points tally, winning both dashes (10.3/22.7) and anchoring the winning 880-yard relay team for third-place Fremont.

A twelve-way tie for 5th developed in the Class B high jump, won by Ed Geisler of Dowagiac. Garnering one of those 5th-place ties was none other than the future Governor of the State of Michigan, William Milliken. The Traverse City star—fittingly the class president—qualified for the meet by sharing first place at the regional with his lifelong close friend, Jack Bensley.

In C, East Grand Rapids won its first state championship, triggering a most successful reign during the 1940s. The Pioneers edged runner-up Leelanau School by just a fraction of a point in Class C. Frank Lee led the Pioneers with wins in both short sprints. Shelby's Lawrence Beckman won the 120 hurdles in 15.6 to set a school record for the Tigers.

Harold Dugan of Romulus set the only record in Class C, winning the 200-yard low hurdles in 23.4.

Bath and Michigan School for the Deaf dominated action in Class D, with Bath the victor. Despite four first-place performances, including William Griswold's record-breaking time of 52.2 in the 440, the Flint school was unable to overcome Bath's superior depth.

Detroit: Further illustrating why 1940 was the year of the miler, Detroit Cooley's Britton Lux lowered the city mark to 4:28.6. Lux, the city cross country champion during the fall, knocked nearly seven seconds off his previous best, pacing Cooley to its third-straight team title.

Leonard Alkon, a muscular 200lb athlete from Detroit Northern, won both sprints in record-breaking fashion, the 100-yard dash in 9.9, and the 220 in 22.1. Earlier in the week, during the city qualifying heats, Alkon broke the previous city all-time best posted by Northwestern's Snitz Ross in 1925 with a time of 10.0. Although former legendary Motor City sprinters Eddie Tolan and George Hester both ran the 100-yard dash in 9.8 at the state meet, conditions were none too favorable when they toed the line at the Detroit city league championships.

Alkon won the 220 by about 10 yards over his closest competitor, shattering the mark set in 1938 by Redford's Bob Sawyer. So impressive was Alkon's performance, it would be another 14 years before a Motor City sprinter would surpass Alkon's 22.1.

Tom Patsalis from Detroit Southeastern had the state's best leap in the broad jump in 1940 (22-1¾), soaring more than a foot farther than the second-place finisher. Southeastern placed second behind Cooley in the team chase, thanks to 21 points scored in the 120-yard high hurdles. Louis Schmidt led three other Jungaleer timber toppers across the finish line as Southeastern placed 1-2-5-6.

Milford Woods garnered Miller High's lone first place with a heave of 49-4 in the shot, bettering any mark set at the state meet in East Lansing. For the first time in ten years, a Detroit high jumper failed to clear the six-foot barrier. Cooley's Glen Mathias cleared 5-10, still higher than anything made in East Lansing.

Upper Peninsula: The first "official" Upper Peninsula track and field finals were contested at Engineer Field on the campus of Michigan Tech College in Houghton. Previously dubbed a regional contest, the meet would now be called the UP Finals and, for better or for worse, UP teams would not compete at the Lower Peninsula state finals for the rest of the twentieth century.

There was one competitor who did not toe the line. Iron River's Eddie Sloden, the premier sprinter in the Upper Peninsula, instead opted to test his speed against the best from below the Straits of Mackinac. Sloden placed a close second to Walter Derby of Fremont in the 100-yard dash, becoming the last track star from the UP to compete in the LP finals. The Iron River speedster than returned to the UP the following week to win the 100-yards dash against all comers in a record-breaking 10.1.

Cold and rainy weather met the athletes in Houghton. Don Kirkpatrick clearly had the day's best mark in winning the 440-yard dash in 53.5, a mark that would not be broken for 23 years.

Ironwood in Class B, L'Anse in Class C, and Rock in Class D became the first official UP Team Champions. However, the question would loom over the many decades since: "How they would have fared against their down-state rivals?"

Winning the mile run for Alpha was Ernest Leonardi, with an impressive mark of 4:46.8, setting a UP Class D record that would last for 16 years. Leonardi would leave tiny Alpha for the much bigger stage at the University of Michigan where he would excel as a distance runner for the Wolverines as a Big 10 place-winner. Like many athletes from this war-torn era, Lombardi's track career was cut short as he left college to serve his country.

1941

Benton Harbor registered a clean sweep during the 1940-41 sports season. Benton Harbor's football team went undefeated during the fall; future Michigan head coach Don Perigo's basketball team won the state Class A basketball crown and the 1941 Class A track championship also went to the Tigers.

Bert Copeland again led Coach Jack Smith's crew. The fleet of foot Tiger had a perfect afternoon with firsts in the 100 (third-straight year), 220, long jump, and an anchor on the winning 880-yard relay. Maurice Hofmeister won the shot to provide Copeland some much needed help, as the Tigers trailed runner-up Monroe going into the final event.

William Cave helped keep Monroe in the hunt for championship honors by taking the 440-yard dash in 51.6. Cave would later coach Flint Northern to a pair of State Class A championships in the early 1950s.

Sophomore hurdler Horace Smith of Jackson twice lowered the state mark in the 120 highs. Smith clicked off a 14.7 in the morning prelims and lowered it to 14.6 in the finals. Following World War II, Smith would go on and earn seven letters at Michigan State in football and track.

Winning the 200-yard low hurdles for the second-straight year was Dearborn High's Russ Reader. After World War II, Reader was the leading passer and scoring leader for Michigan State College. Reader also had a brief stint in the NFL with the Chicago Bears.

As in Class A, the championships in classes B and D were settled in the closing event, the half-mile relay. East Lansing's quartet romped in third ahead of Three Rivers to clinch the B title, while Bear Lake snatched the D title by taking third when Bath's relay lost the team lead by failing to place. Roy Dygert of East

Lansing set a new B record in the pole vault by scaling 12-¼.

The winner of the Class B relay, Mt. Pleasant, did so with a great anchor leg by Terry Carey. His kid brother Paul would become the voice of high school sports for WJR in Detroit. Paul Carey was undoubtedly better known as Ernie Harwell's long-time sidekick in the broadcasting booth for the Detroit Tigers.

St. Clair Shores Lake Shore had little trouble in "C," as it romped to the title by scoring 43 points. Two records fell in Class C. Stan Bocek of Corunna set a new mark in the shot with a toss of 49-2, and Flint Hoover's Harold Flynn negotiated the mile in 4:37.6. A week later at the Michigan AAU Games, Flynn would defeat Class A mile second-place finisher Jim Gibbard of Royal Oak. Gibbard would later be named as the head track coach at Michigan State University.

Native American Francis Miskokomon from Algonac took the Class C 440-yard dash in 51.4, a school record that lasted until broken in 1995.

Rene LaFreniere of Mt. Morris St. Mary set the only mark in Class D, leaping 20-11¼ in taking the broad jump.

Detroit: Southeastern dominated the 1941 championships by amassing nearly 90 points, more than double the tally of Mackenzie. It was a clean sweep for coach Leighton Boyd's Jungleleers, having won the city indoor meet and the Wayne Relays earlier in the season.

The Motor City produced another fine effort in the high jump with Southeastern's Fred Weaver clearing 6-2, six inches higher than his nearest competitor. Detroit leapers seemed to have a virtual monopoly in this event as they went the entire decade of the 1930s with all winners clearing at least six feet.

Northeastern's Elmer Swanson was the meet's only double winner, taking both hurdle races contested over the 120-yard distance. Swanson's 13.1 effort in the 120 lows was especially noteworthy being only one-tenth slower than the meet record set by the legendary Willis Ward eleven years earlier.

No new records were produced, but performances were deemed creditable on a University of Detroit track that was never considered "fast."

Detroit Mackenzie's foursome of Fred Pedlar, Robert Fraser, Edward Keegan, and Richard Drake equaled Benton Harbor's state winning time in the 880-yard relay (1:32.9). Paul Bargowski of Hamtramck also ran the same time that Class A winner Copeland registered in taking the 220 (22.8).

Carl Neych of Hamtramck topped any heave made in East Lansing with his 49-3¼ in the shot put.

Upper Peninsula: George Shomin, Escanaba junior, led the Eskimos to the 1941 UP championship in Class B. Shomin won three events, two in record-setting fashion, but was disqualified after the 200-yard low hurdles. The Escanaba star tripped and fell attempting to clear the final hurdle, returned to his feet and crossed the line first. However, Shomin had left his lane during his spill and was disqualified. Shomin's jump of 21 feet in the broad jump would stand for sixteen years.

Shomin, like most of his peers from this era, entered the service following his graduation from Escanaba High. Following his tour of duty with the U.S. Marine Corps during World War II, Shomin returned. Teammate Bob Dufresne was not as fortunate. A member of the Eskimos' record-setting 880-yard relay team, Dufresne was killed in action in the Philippines.

Wakefield's Eugene Danielson sped to a UP record in the mile. His 4:50.8 would stand as a meet record for 15 years. Joining Escanaba as team champs were Stephenson in Class C and Hermansville in Class D.

1942

World War II whittled down the number of teams offering track & field during the war. Only 162 schools qualified entrants from the regionals for the state championships, 17 fewer than in 1941. In 1942, 690 performers qualified as compared to 711 athletes the preceding year.

Fred Weaver won the 1941 Detroit high jump by 6 inches.

Meet director Lymon Frimodig said it was likely the actual field for the four-class carnival would be much smaller than the numbers eligible to compete. Frimodig said that many coaches would think in terms of tires rather than trophies before embarking on any lengthy journey to the meet. Defending champ Benton Harbor, for example, sent only four to East Lansing, although several more had qualified.

Kalamazoo Central replaced Benton Harbor as ruler of the top division as only one champion, Bear Lake in Class D, successfully defended a team title. Speedy Bob Rogers, who won both dashes (10.5/23.2) and anchored the winning relay (1:33.0), led the Kalamazoo squad. Bob Whitfield won the broad jump with his 21-5 for the Giants and joined Rogers, Neil Clark and Dave Wenzel on the relay. Gordon McMickens also won the 880 (2:02.4) for coach A.E. Stoddard's squad.

Perhaps the best performance was turned in by Forrest Naveaux, who vaulted a record 12-7½, a mark that would last for sixteen years. It was the fourth straight win by one of the Naveaux brothers. One upset took place when Flint Northern's Bill Hamilton defeated record holder Horace Smith of Jackson in the high hurdles. Smith redeemed himself by later capturing the 200-yard low hurdles.

Oddly enough Smith's achievements wouldn't begin to compare with a medal earned by a former Smith classmate at Jackson High. Bill Porter, after leaving Jackson High in 1942 for schooling in Pennsylvania, had transformed into a world-class hurdler by 1948. At the AAU Nationals, he snapped legendary hurdler Harrison Dillard's consecutive win streak at 82. Remarkably, Porter had been the last person to beat Dillard when the streak started. Then he won the gold medal at the 1948 Olympic Games in an Olympic record of 13.9.

It was not a good day for defending champions as five of the returning eight titleholders fell by the wayside. Birmingham took four first places, including a double sprint title by Jack Steelman, to win it all in Class B.

Bill Dale of Wayne was able to repeat with a meet record leap of 6-2 in Class B, a mark not to be bettered for 18 years. He would take his talents to the University of Michigan where he copped the 1944 Big 10 championship in the high jump.

Imlay City notched an easy win in Class C, nearly doubling the score over runner-up Grandville. Fred Johnson of the runner-up Bulldogs won both jumps, including the day's best effort in the broad jump at 21-9¼.

Marine City's Jay DeCou broke his own mark, established back in 1940 in the pole vault, clearing the bar at 11-7½ to improve upon his own Class C record.

Perhaps the most inspirational effort of the entire day belonged to Bob Mosher. Representing the alma mater of longtime Detroit Free Press high school beat writer Hal Schram, Mosher won the 440-yard dash in Class D for the Lansing School for the Blind. The only Class D mark to fall came when the 880-relay

foursome from White Pigeon won in the new record time of 1:36.4.

Colon High School brought its entire team, namely Larry Pratt. The speedster from the "City of Magic" took the 100-yard dash in 10.8. It was the only state track championship in his school's history.

For 1942 champions, such as juniors Bob Rogers, Horace Smith, and Jimmy Gibson of Pontiac, dreams of repeating as state champs the following year would not be possible. World War II would create havoc for all activities and all ways of life, until the long sought-after victory came in 1945. Many promising athletes-turned-soldiers, such as UP 880 champion Fred Babich of Ironwood, paid the ultimate sacrifice.

Detroit: Coach Leighton Boyd, former Eastern Michigan University football and track standout, piloted Southeastern to its second-straight city championship to go along with two cross-country titles. Eastern accounted for the only meet record with its win in the 880-yard relay. The foursome of Don Wines, Bob Knoll, Emille Simonel and Arnold Jones was clocked in 1:32.0, winning by a margin estimated at 25 yards. Wines was the meets only double champion with wins in the 100 (10.3) and 220-yard (22.7) dashes.

It is hard to believe that a young lad from Northeastern High could only place fourth in the shot put, as this athlete would ultimately earn the title of the World's Strongest Man. Norb Schemansky would become an Olympic legend for his feats as a weightlifter, one of the few athletes in any sport to win medals in four different Olympics.

Escanaba and Hermansville successfully defended their UP state titles in Class B and D while Newberry replaced Stephenson as the Class C titlist. John Ludlow, who would become an ace pilot during World War II, led Newberry with record-breaking performances in the shot (43-2) and low hurdles (24.9).

George Shomin capped his career for Escanaba by winning both hurdles (16.1/24.9) and sharing first place in the high jump at 5-9¾ with teammates Bob Stephens and Ron Rouse, all of the performances meet records.

Reno Fochesato of Hermansville earned the honors for the top performance. Although falling short of his 10.0 clocking earlier in season in the 100-yard dash, his 10.2 time would stand as the UP Class D record for 35 years. Fochesato's time was also far superior to any time run at the Lower Peninsula state finals.

1943

Sports certainly suffered a setback during World II, with 1943, easily, being the year hit the hardest. The

MHSAA cancelled all statewide competition. It was eventually decided, however, that high school sports would carry on the following fall and winter because they had proven to be an important part of the physical fitness program for future soldiers.

From Julian W. Smith, state director of athletics came this statement: "We got by our programs this year despite travel restrictions and other difficulties, and should be able to continue." Smith declared that many academic men as well as coaches who had been only lukewarm for athletics in the past were now in favor of them. "I haven't talked to a single school that intends dropping football," responded Smith. The only sports in which there would be little activity for the duration were golf and tennis.

State competition for 1944 would resume in swimming, cross country, basketball and track. Smith, principal at Battle Creek Lakeview, succeeded Charles E. Forsythe as state athletic director when the latter became a lieutenant commander in the Navy.

Despite the fact that the state meets were cancelled for track & field in 1943, various competitions were held throughout the state. Among the highlights, Owosso won the CMU Relays. Howell's Hollis Gehringer doubled at 10.4 and 22.6.

Benton Harbor topped Kalamazoo at the Southwestern Michigan Conference meet in Holland, Bill Dudas winning both the high jump (5-11½) and the pole vault (10-6).

Area meets across the state saw Royal Oak win the only Class A meet. Owosso won a Class B title on its home track, while Alma won at Mt. Pleasant. In Class C, Fenton and Ithaca won, and the Michigan School for the Deaf won the D title at Mt. Pleasant.

At the Wayne Relays, Detroit Cody took the Class A crown by winning the 4 x 880 (8:51.6), 4 x mile (20:01.2), the shuttle hurdles (60.7). Royal Oak's Jim Gibbard anchored a very fast 3:43.6 sprint medley. Birmingham dominated in Class B, winning every event.

Doug Brown of Royal Oak took part in the State AAU meet in early June and won the 220-yard dash from a field of collegians in 22.5. Royal Oak's Gibbard took second in a very fast mile race; with the winner clocking 4:24.5, that raises the possibility that Gibbard might have been under the state high school record of 4:28.2, but with no time reported for him, we'll never know.

Detroit: The city meet, where travel was not a problem, again took place with Cooley taking team honors over runner-up Southeastern. Both teams' head coaches had been teammates at Michigan Normal (EMU). Claude Snarey and Leighton Boyd, in their

undergrad days, ran on EMU's unbeaten relay teams of 1925 and 1926.

Tom Clark of Redford took the broad jump title, while a future Olympic gold medalist would have to settle for fourth place. Clark's leap of 21-11¼ topped, amongst others, Lorenzo Wright from Miller High School. Wright ran a leg on the winning 4 x 100 at the 1948 Olympics, and just missed winning a medal in the broad jump by placing fourth. He eventually became the long-time athletic director for the Detroit Public Schools.

In keeping with the spirit of the times it was appropriate that the only two double winners were just days away from joining the military. Dan Davis of Cooley took first place in the high and low hurdles, and placed second in the broad jump for the victors. Southeastern's David Bernard captured both dashes. Davis soon left to join the Marines with Bernard enlisting in the U.S. Army.

1944

With the war still raging, statewide competition returned to Michigan. Saginaw Arthur Hill, led by one of the state's all-time most versatile athletes, won the Class A crown. Just as he almost single handedly led Arthur Hill to the Basketball A title, Dick Rifenburg was the big noise as his team outclassed the 32-team field with 36 points. Rifenburg earned 17½ points for the victors, winning the shot put, tying for first in the high jump, 2nd in the high hurdles and finishing 5th in the low hurdles.

All-arounder Dick Rifenburg scored in four events, winning the shot and high jump.

Despite his heroics, Rifenburg wasn't the meet's leading point winner. This honor went to Monroe's Garion Campbell, who netted all his team's 19 points, including a record-breaking performance in the 200-yard low hurdles. The Monroe speedster would later become a stellar dashman while competing for Eastern Michigan, clocking 9.6 in the 100 for the Hurons.

Rifenburg would go on to become a more noted football star at the University of Michigan. In 1948 he was a consensus All-American end for the Wolverines, making first team on nine out of the eleven published teams. He later played a year in the NFL. Bill Kelly, the Arthur Hill coach in both track and football, would go on to establish a great football tradition of his own. Shortly after leaving Arthur Hill, he became a very successful head football coach at Central Michigan University.

Campbell's 22.8 clocking in the low hurdles bested the former mark set by Monroe's Perry Mason in the 1937 season. The other record to fall during the day came in the Class C mile when Grant's John Klever ran 4:35.1.

Bob Swain was the hero of a thrilling Class B conquest by East Grand Rapids. Swain, whose triumphs in the 100 and 220 dashes were the fastest performances of the day, anchored the 880-yard relay to victory in the closing event, giving his squad a winning total of 23 1/5 points. A 13 way-tie in the high jump forced officials to furrow their brains in a tussle with fractions that reached a 65th (!). Niles had 22 and 43/65th points for second in Class B. The tension of the close battle was thick: East Grand Rapids was no better than third going into the final race.

The day's best performance in the high jump came as teammates Tom Doland and Harold Townsend from Hastings both leaped 6-¾ to share the title in Class B.

In Class C, Fowlerville rode victories by Marvin Grostic in the 100 and Dean Dingman in the shot to capture its first team state track title.

Only 11 teams scored points in the mysterious Class D battle. Mysterious, in that there were no results published by any of the wire services. Out of nearly 9,000 state titlists dating back to 1895, tracking down the 1944 Class D state champs proved the most difficult. Leelanau School for Boys edged Bloomfield Hills by only a point and a half to earn the crown. Henry Rolike was the meet's only triple winner as he won the shot in addition to both dashes in Class D.

Of the thousands of events contested at the state finals for more than a century, only one event winner remains unknown. This author has devoted a number of hours in attempting to research the winner of the Class D 880-yard run, but the winner is still unknown as of this writing.

None of the public schools representing Flint competed at the state level in 1944, but it had little to do with World War II, unlike some districts. The talented Flint runners were not able to participate because a teachers's strike shut down their schools.

Detroit: Cooley dominated action at the city meet by edging surprising Miller. Cooley trailed Miller by 14 points before the points were tallied in the concluding event of the meet, the pole vault. Cooley placed four in the top six, including a two-way tie for first to win the meet. The best of the many Cooley vaulters was John Harrower. Harrower had the best vault in metro history with his clearance of 11-10½ inches at the Wayne Relays.

A notable double-winner in Detroit was Miller High's Lorenzo Wright. He was only able to produce a modest winning leap of 20-2¼, well below his norm and no hint of what he would accomplish in future years. Wright also ran the lead leg on the victorious 880-yard relay team that included double dash winner Cleo Caldwell, Elmer Coleman and Adam Houghton.

Bill Webb from Detroit Eastern was a prohibitive favorite to win the mile but Lady Luck was not kind. Undefeated for the season, the city indoor champion was forced to take an exam during the running of his event and was unable to compete.

Upper Peninsula: Four records were broken and five others tied at the UP finals in Houghton. Escanaba, Stephenson and Chassell took home the team championships in a meet hailed as the largest and fastest ever held in the UP.

Lorenzo Wright: Miller's Gold Medalist

An Olympic gold medal would be the ultimate high point in a life well-lived, but Detroit's Lorenzo Wright will perhaps most fondly be remembered by native Detroiters for his coaching and administrative deeds.

In May of 1969, the former Miller High School standout became the first African-American to be appointed supervisor of athletics for the Detroit Public School League. He made tremendous improvements in many areas during a tenure that was far too brief.

The son of Robert and Lizzie Mae Wright, he was a lifelong resident of the Motor City, whose crowning athletic achievement, came at the 1948 Olympic Games, the day that Wright called "my biggest day in sports." Records will show that Wright earned his gold medal on Saturday, August 7, 1948. In reality, it was a full three days later, while Wright was sailing home with his teammates, when the USA 4 x 100 relay team was declared the winner of one of the London Olympics' most controversial races.

Initially, the United States foursome crossed the finish line a full seven yards ahead of runner-up Great Britain. Officials in London declared that the U.S. was disqualified when it had allegedly received a baton out of the exchange zone. Barney Ewell, the leadoff, had less than a smooth pass to Wright and the exchange judge reported it as a foul. Moments later, the U.S. team was disqualified. The foursome from Great Britain—reportedly embarrassed—was given the gold on the award stand.

Three days later, once the jury of appeals reviewed the film of the race, the U.S. protest was upheld and Wright and his fellow running mates were adjudged Olympic champions. After competing in a few post-Olympic meets, they received their cherished medals in a special ceremony aboard the S.S. Washington on their way home.

The trail to London began when Wright entered Miller High School for the 1941 school year. It was at Miller where the son of the assistant pastor of the St. John C.M.E. Church at Blaine and Woodward would hone his skills under the expert tutelage of Leroy Dues and Will Robinson. He would win 10 letters as a football, basketball and track star in high school. He placed a nondescript fourth place in the broad jump at the 1943 city championships, hardly a harbinger of great feats to follow. His best effort during the 1944 prep season was a jump slightly over the 22-foot mark. At the 1944 city championships Wright teamed up with Elmore Coleman, Adam Houghton, John Rowan and Cleo Caldwell to win seven of the 12 events contested. Miller High, however, had to settle for second place behind perennial city powerhouse Cooley.

Wright was only the third leading scorer on his own high school squad. Houghton won both hurdle events at the 1944 city championships, while Caldwell had wins in both dashes, including the 220, where Wright settled for second.

It would be in 1945, at nearby Wayne State, where Wright would develop into a full-fledged star. At the state intercollegiate track and field championships that year he took individual honors, winning the 100 (10.0), 220 (22.5), broad jump (23-5¾) and placing second in the low hurdles. He scored 18 of Wayne State's 26 points. It was no disgrace to place second in the lows behind Western Michigan's Bill Porter. The native of Jackson would also win gold at the London Games.

Wright became a world-class performer at Wayne State – and took time off to fight in World War II before making his way to Olympic gold.

A week following his eye-popping performance at MSC, the young 18-year-old freshman would make his final meet in a Wayne State uniform a memorable one. In a dual against the University of Chicago he won five individual events: the 100, 220, 120HH, 220LH, the broad jump and anchor on the winning 880-yard relay team. Four days later, with World War II still being waged in the Pacific Theatre, Wright joined the U.S. Army.

Two years of active duty for Uncle Sam didn't see Wright lose his skills. Enrolling once again at Wayne State in time for the 1947 track season, he led the Tartars to the Mid-America conference championship. Wright won both short dashes, the 220-yard low hurdles, and sailed past the 24-foot barrier in easily winning the conference broad jump crown.

Wright then stole the show at the State AAU meet in Ypsilanti by again winning four events against much stiffer competition. Matched up against former Monroe prep star Garion Campbell, Wright edged the Eastern Michigan record holder in the 100, winning in 9.7 seconds. Earlier in the prelims, Campbell had set a new Huron record with a clocking of 9.6. Wright blazed the 220 in an even 21.0, skimmed over the 220-yard low hurdles in 23.3 and again surpassed the 24-foot mark by leaping 24-1 7/8 inches in the broad jump. At the NCAA meet in the friendly altitude of Salt Lake City, he placed second with a 25-9½ leap, the third-longest jump in the world that year.

In 1948 Wright won the AAU National Indoor broad jump title with his 25-3¾. That made him the second long jumper to surpass the 25-foot mark indoors; Jesse Owens was first. During the outdoor season he captured third in the NCAA (24-5¼). He lost by 2 inches to Michigan State's Fred Johnson at the AAU Nationals in Milwaukee, going 25-2½. Then came the Olympic Trials in Evanston, Illinois. Wright hit 25-¼ in the prelimnary rounds and was not able to improve on that in the final. Under the rules of the time, prelim marks counted in the final standings. Wright's mark held up for third place and a trip to London. The same day Wright also competed in the 100 heats, placing sixth, and the 200 heats, placing fifth. Not even a sprint finalist, he was named to the 4 x 100 squad.

After his Olympic gold, Wright was celebrated in Detroit, with Mayor Eugene Van Antwerp declaring November 13 "Lorenzo Wright Day" and presenting him with a trophy at halftime during Wayne State's final football game of the year.

Refusing to rest on his laurels, Wright and his Wayne State Tartars enjoyed a record-breaking season in 1949. The foursome of Leon Wingo, Irving Petross, Buddy Coleman and Wright were virtually unbeatable. This group caught everyone's fancy in the Penn Relays when they copped a pair of relay victories. In late May they also won the Western (Ontario) Relays, breaking a Canadian all-comers record in the 4 x 220 with their 1:26.7. The same quartet, in winning the 440-yard relay in 42.3, equaled the best time ever run on Canadian soil.

Lorenzo Wright received his diploma from Wayne State in February of 1951, where he would bring his talents into the world of academics and coaching. After a brief teaching stop at Cleveland Junior High School in Detroit, Wright would transfer to his old alma mater.

At Miller High School, as a reserve football and basketball coach, he honed his coaching and administrative skills under the watchful eyes of his old coaches, Will Robinson and Leroy Dues. He stayed four years at Miller before taking over the head swimming and track and field duties at Eastern High in January of 1956. His last venture in coaching track and field, before taking on the role of supervisor of athletics for the entire Detroit Public School system, was at Southwestern High.

On two occasions Wright took leave of absences from his Detroit position to take up adventurous roles in distant territories. In 1961-62 he went to Nigeria to lecture on health and physical education, while doubling as a track coach. Wright teamed up with his former Olympic teammate Harrison Dillard in the African nation to pass along some of their vast knowledge in their favorite sport.

In 1967-68, shortly before taking over his supervisory reigns, he served on the Detroit Committee on the Youth, Recreation and Cultural Affairs Task Force. "I wanted more exposure to current issues that affect our community," he said. "I received that experience by serving on the task force."

The appointment of the 42-year-old Wright was greeted with much enthusiasm when announced in May of 1969. Hailed by the media as the most outstanding athlete from the Detroit Public Schools to return to the school system in the last 25 years, the late 1960's were turbulent times for the PSL and the city of Detroit. Taking charge only a couple of years after the race riots of 1967, Wright faced serious challenges. The city championship football game at historic Briggs Stadium, matching the PSL champ with the winner of the Detroit Catholic League, was but a fleeting memory from the past. The same two leagues had also suspended their matchups for the basketball title because of fan violence. Only one high school football game was allowed in a police precinct in the same day. Crowds at regular season basketball games were limited strictly to students from the competing schools. On three occasions officials were attacked while working local high school basketball games. Lorenzo Wright was clearly not facing an easy task.

In addition, Wright also clearly remembered when he and his fellow public-school league athletes were not permitted to compete outside the Detroit city limits. Wright was determined to play not only Catholic League teams but also suburban and out-state schools. Shortly before Wright's tenure as supervisor of athletics, Detroit prep performers were not permitted to compete outside the city, except during state tournaments sanctioned by the Michigan High School Athletic Association.

For the next three years Wright made good progress in Detroit. The long overdue restrictions imposed on PSL athletes in out-state track events were removed during Wright's administration. Holiday basketball tournaments, sportsmanship, and vastly improved communication with coaches and administrators were just a few of his achievements.

But tragedy struck in late March of 1972. A family dispute between Wright and his wife, 42-year-old Elizabeth—who worked as a counselor at the county youth home—erupted over a possible separation. Mrs. Wright fatally stabbed her husband of 24 years. When arrested her face was bruised; that possibly indicated that the stabbing might have been in self-defense. She was found guilty of involuntary manslaughter and given 5 years probation—a key factor in the sentencing may have been that the couple had six children.

This author had the good fortune while doing research for this book to travel to the Motor City and meet many former metro track athletes. It would take just a few moments before the name of Lorenzo Wright would pop up. Wright's contemporaries remember him not only as a great athlete, but also as a humanitarian who made many lasting contributions to his beloved city.

Hal Schram, long time prep beat writer for the Detroit Free Press, perhaps best depicted Wright for the man he was: "Mild of manner, soft spoken but persuasive, he was the stabilizing influence in the Detroit Public School League in its moment of strife."

Wright is buried in Detroit's Elmwood Cemetery, under a modest plaque that notes he was a private first class in the U.S. Army in World War II. It doesn't mention he was an Olympic gold medalist. The athletic field at King High School is named in his honor.

1945

In Class A, Ann Arbor held the lead entering the final event, but without a qualifying relay team, the Pioneers had to watch their championship hopes slip away. Saginaw High won the 880-yard relay, leaping from third to first, with Flint Central passing Ann Arbor into second place.

Saginaw coach Carl Nordberg capped a perfect year in winning the state championship. His football team won all nine of its games, earning a mythical state title. Nordberg even had further satisfaction as he watched his high school alma mater, St. Joseph, win the Class B track title by five points over defending champion East Grand Rapids. The Saginaw mentor also joined the special fraternity of those who won state titles as a coach and a competitor. He was the pole vault and low hurdles champion back in 1926.

After missing the 1944 meet because of a teacher strike, Flint Central demonstrated that it would have been a serious contender, as the Indians narrowly missed winning the 1946 title by a single point. Central might have taken the Class A championship but for a stroke of fate that deprived it of an entry in the 120-yard high hurdles. Jesse Thomas, who turned in the best time for all the regional meets in that event, arrived too late to compete in his qualifying heat and thus did not advance. He did come back later in the day to win the long jump for the Indians.

Flint Central was dealt another tough break when Jim Adair, fighting for a second place in his section of the 880, tripped and fell about 50 yards from the finish.

Good fortune, however, did fall upon Saginaw. Honest John O'Connell of Battle Creek came to the rescue and helped the Trojans get three points in the mile. John Picard, wearing No 220, finished fourth, but the place judge believed the fourth-place runner was wearing No 20 (O'Connoll's number) and gave those points to Battle Creek. When Picard protested, officials asked O'Connell where he had placed. He admitted he was about 16th or 17th (out of 18). These three points were enough to give Saginaw the title.

Another good gesture took place in the Class A regionals. Bill Bridges of Pontiac intentionally missed in the pole vault after tying with teammate Chuck Richards. Richards had suffered an arm injury and was unable to continue. Bridges made a half-hearted attempt in his three trials at the tied height, as a clearance would have eliminated his teammate from the state meet. Bridges was rewarded for his gracious gesture by winning the state title the following weekend at a height of 11-4½.

Although it finished second behind Class B winner St. Joseph, East Grand Rapids had the day's outstanding performer in Bob Swain. The sprinter not only defended his 100 and 220 championships, but did so in record fashion. He ran the 100-yard dash in 9.9 seconds and the 220 in 21.8. A week earlier he took the regional in 9.7 seconds, a state record. It was a school record that was never broken.

Romulus posted its first track state championship, winning the Class C by a couple of points over second-place St. Clair Shores Lake Shore. It would be another 64 years before Romulus would annex another title, the Class A crown in 2009.

Arlon Dennison led Michigan School for the Deaf to the Class D championship. Dennison won both short dashes in record-setting times (10.3/23.0), took first in the shot put (40-½) and anchored the winning 880-yard relay, becoming a member of the rare circle of athletes to capture four titles at a single meet.

Bob Swain setting a state record 9.7 in the 100 at the Houseman Field Regional. (photo courtesy of Grand Rapids Public Library)

Detroit: Charles Fonville led Miller High to its first-ever city championship. Fonville's put of 51-8 was four inches shy of breaking Ed Turashoff's record set back in 1928. Fonville would win the Big 10 in 1947 as a sophomore at the University of Michigan with a prodigious throw of 54-1, eclipsing Bill Watson's record set in 1939. Arguably the best male shot putter in state history, he then improved that mark to a World Record 58-3/8 while winning the Kansas Relays in 1948.

Much of the credit for Fonville's success would belong to Miller coach Leroy Dues. The veteran tutor himself put the shot 49-9 7/8 in 1933, setting a new state collegiate record for the 16-pound ball.

Miller tallied a whopping 105 1/5 points, scoring in nine of twelve events. Joining Fonville as individual winners from Miller High were George Sayles and Tommy Truss. Sayles won two, taking the pole vault at an even 11-0 and leading defending champ Ralph Rowan of the Trojans to the tape in the 120-yard high hurdles. Truss won the long jump with a 22-1 and

placed second behind Pershing's Charles Jenkins in the 100 and 220 dashes. To show that he had speed, as well as unquestioned power, Fonville took third place in the 220-yard dash.

Upper Peninsula: The Sault Ste. Marie Blue Devils, scoring in all but one event, won their first UP championship by dethroning Escanaba.

Chassell failed to defend its Class D title when its hurdler was disqualified in the 200-yard low sticks. The disqualification cost four points, when one point would have been sufficient to topple the eventual champions. Ewen placed a thin half a point ahead of Chassell.

Bill Eiola of Hancock and Chuck Atkokunis of Stephenson earned individual honors at the meet, contested at the new track at Marquette High School. Eiola and Atkokunis each won three. Jack Holt of the victorious Soo squad broke the only Class B record by taking the 880-yard run in 2:04.7.

1946

Saginaw High School, with virtually no seniors on its squad, repeated as Class A champions in front of 2,500 rain-soaked fans at Michigan State College. The Trojans beat crosstown rival Arthur Hill as the Saginaw Valley dominated the meet.

Due to the heavy rains that soaked the Spartan surface, no records were set. Jesse Thomas concluded a great career for Flint Central as the meet's only double winner. Thomas, who would set the season record for pass interceptions at Michigan State with eight picks, won the high hurdles and the broad jump. Demonstrating his versatility, in 1951 he became Big 10 champion in the 100-yard dash and the high hurdles. The Flint speedster added further laurels to his athletic resume by playing three years for the Baltimore Colts in the National Football League, intercepting four passes and scoring 1 TD during his NFL tenure.

Dick Sundeck, place winner in the low hurdles from Midland, had earlier been expected to push Thomas in the high hurdles. Midland's team bus broke down a week earlier on the way to the Class A Regional. Sundeck arrived five minutes after the qualifying trial in the 120-yard high hurdles, failing to even get an attempt to qualify for the state meet. Sundeck's teammate, Wilson Gay, repeated as the A mile champion but Allen Hosler, running for Class C Milan, posted the day's best time at 4:35.6.

Charlotte won the Class B title decisively over runner-up Fremont, despite picking up but one first place. Ulysses Rogers of Ecorse won both sprints in Class B, and ran a leg on the winning 880-yard relay, to lead the individual point tally. Bill Chesquiere (named Mr. Atlas Michigan in 1946) and Art Marschner took the gold in the shot put and 100-yard dash respectively, becoming Detroit University High's first champions since the early part of the century. Bob Sullivan of Belleville won the Class B pole vault for the third-straight year.

Howard McCants, a 6-7 senior from River Rouge, won the high jump title in Class B. However, McCant's winning effort of 5-7¾ was well below the 6-1 record leap he posted later in the season at the Wayne Relays.

East Grand Rapids coasted to yet another victory in Class C. Runner-up Ypsilanti Roosevelt's Keith Gundrum equaled Roger's three titles in Class B, winning the 100, 120 hurdles and also running a leg on the winning 880-yard relay. Future MSC quarterback Al Dorow won the pole vault in Class C for Imlay City.

Arlon Dennison nearly matched Paw Paw's Allen Smith's feat of four state titles back-to-back, but fell short in the shot put. Dennison was off form in the weight event, finishing far back in sixth place. Dennison did repeat as 100 and 220-dash champ as well as anchoring Michigan School for the Deaf to the 880-yard relay title. The School for the Deaf posted 52 points to take the D crown, five points ahead of Baldwin.

Don Plonta from Bayport was a double winner in the field events in Class D, taking top honors in the high jump and broad jump, the first titles ever for the school.

Detroit: Miller High's George Sayles set the only record at the city championships, taking the high hurdles in 14.8. Not a word was mentioned in meet articles covering the 1946 city championships of Willis Ward's 15.0 clocking over the taller 42" hurdles in 1931, a feat at least equal to Sayles' mark.

Coach Claude Snarey's Cooley Cardinals won their fourth major meet of the season by taking team honors with 50 points. A sweep in the mile run by Snarey's distance corps paved the way for their second-straight city title. Ross Smith, Dave Rice, and Bob Hahn, all members of Cooley's victorious cross-country team in the fall, went 1-2-3. A week earlier Smith was clocked in 4:22.4 for his anchor split during the four-mile relay at the Wayne Relays.

An injury in an informal football game earlier in the week kept Mearl Jones of Northern, the indoor champion, out of the high jump. With Jones watching from the sidelines, Harold Jackson of Northeastern copped the outdoor title with a jump of 6-1. Sophomore Stan McConner of Northwestern, who would eventually become Michigan's first prep runner to run under 50 seconds in the 440-yard dash, took honors in the 880-yard run (2:02.2). Tom Stewart of Denby was the meet's leading scorer, winning the 100-yard dash and

broad jump, and placing third behind Sayles in the 120-yard low hurdles. Hamtramck's Leon Wingo, whose brother Bob won the city 440 dash back in 1937, won the 220 dash in 22.8. He would be the school's final city champion.

Upper Peninsula: With the war over—and gasoline rationing a thing of the past—one might have thought the UP schools would return to a combined state championships to compete with Lower Peninsula schools. That wasn't to be the case. Over the years there have been attempts by some of the UP coaches to orchestrate a return, but they have been shot down by UP administrators who felt track and cross country weren't worth the expense—even though they participate fully in sports such as football and basketball. The Upper Peninsula Finals would continue on as a separate meet, even though it only represents little more than 3% of the state's population, according to the 2010 Census.

In the 1946 edition, Ironwood nosed out Escanaba by half of a point to win the UP finals held in Houghton. The winners got a huge break during the running of the day's final event. Needing a relay win to take first-place honors, but trailing by 20 yards, Ironwood got lucky when Menominee's anchor leg dropped the baton.

Munising moved into the winner's circle for the first time in Class C, while Chassell continued to dominate in Class D. Rob Mitchell of Negaunee became the first UP shot putter to crack the 50-foot barrier. Mitchell, who tossed 51-3¾ at the districts, had to settle for a best effort of 50-3 at the championship meet, more than two feet farther than any mark posted at the Lower Peninsula finals.

The Upper Peninsula was jolted earlier in the week when Professor D.P. Sherman, long time meet manager and Athletic Director at Michigan Tech, unexpectedly passed away just days before the UP finals. A three-minute ceremony preceded the finals and taps were played in honor of Sherman. For years he was not only the meet manager but doubled as the meet's starter.

1947

A record crowd of 5,000 fans descended upon the Michigan State campus for the 1947 championships. Four meet records were broken and two others tied as Saginaw High School swept to its third consecutive Class A title. Marvin Cichowski led the Trojans with a meet record 22.6 in the 200-yard low hurdles, defending his title.

Saginaw's dominance was such that the Trojans won six first places using nine individuals. Their winners included Warren Keys (22-3½ broad jump),

K.D. McKinnon (52-5¾ shot put), Jim Johnson (high jump 5-11¾), Bill Conley (440 dash 52.2), and the winning medley relay team of Jim Bond, Glenn Webb, Ray Garrett and Bob Parsons (3:49.2).

The medley relay was added for high school tracksters beginning with the 1947 season. The relay was composed of four individual competitors, with runners No.'s 1 and 4 running a 440, and the middle 2 and 3 runners sprinting 220 yards. This relay was the forerunner in Michigan to the 4x4.

Flint Central again finished in second but did boast of Class A's only double winner in sprinter Art Ingram. He nosed out defending 220 champ Bill Hervey of Saginaw Arthur Hill in both sprints. Arthur Hill placed third in the team totals behind Flint Central, earning the Saginaw Valley conference another 1-2-3 sweep.

After missing the open championship by less than a point 36 years earlier, Alma swept to the Class B crown, nipping Hastings by less than two points. Bob Shults tied the record in the 120-yard high hurdles at 15.4, providing the team champs with their only individual gold medal.

Running a leg on the state championship 880-yard relay team for Ecorse High was Jim Bibbs, who would go on to become the head track coach for many years at Michigan State University, before retiring in 1995.

One oddity in Class B had to be in the sprints when Ray Branch and Robert Branch of Hastings exchanged wins in the sprints, Ray taking the 100 and brother Robert the 220. The last brother duo to accomplish this rare double were Clayton and Herbert Shenk from Chelsea back in 1904. Birmingham's Jack Phister posted one of the more impressive performances on the afternoon when his time of 50.9 in the 440 tied a mark set by Jim Wright of Berkley back in 1933.

Paw Paw returned to the forefront in Class C, winning three events. The only C record to fall went to Glen Rowe of Ypsilanti Lincoln with a 23.0 in the 200 lows, and Milan's John Koczman in the shot put. Koczman, who spent the winter getting training tips from Michigan star Charles Fonville, hung up a new shot record with a toss of 51-9½, short of his personal best of 55-2, a throw that put him at No. 8 nationally.

Although he failed to defend his pole vault title of the year before, Al Dorow of Imlay City took first-place honors in the 120-yard high hurdles. Dorow was the quarterback at MSC when the Spartans began their 28-game unbeaten streak, igniting their breakthrough into football prominence. Dorow would later display his superb quarterbacking skills in the NFL. Dorow led the AFC in touchdown passes while competing for the New York Titans in 1960.

Baroda added the Class D track title to its state basketball crown with Baldwin finishing in the runner-up slot. Aiding Baroda's efforts were the Arend

brothers, Ken and Earl. Eight years down the road the youngest of the Arend brothers (Don), would win the Class A 180-yard low hurdles while competing for neighboring Benton Harbor High School.

Hemlock hurdler Dan Haven set the only new meet record in Class D, hurdling the 120s in 16.0.

Detroit: Tommy Stewart of Denby put on a gritty performance at the city championships at Redford High. After suffering a badly cut left elbow that left him unable to bend his left arm while running, he won both dashes and anchored the co-champion 880-yard relay for his Denby team. Taking the baton 20 feet behind Sylvester Norman of Northwestern, Stewart caught the Colt runner on the turn and won by five feet.

Cooley used its talent in the hurdles to take team honors. Don Harrower led a Cardinal 1-2 finish in the 120-yard highs and the Cardinals fared even better in the lows, sweeping the first three places over the 120-yard distance. Individual scoring honors went to Gordon Cronk of Redford, who placed second in the 220, third in the 100 and first in the broad jump with a fine leap of 22-0. The Redford ace also ran a leg on the 880-yard relay team that finished in the same time as Denby from a previous heat.

Percy Smith showed amazing improvement in winning the shot competition. After never before heaving the shot more than 47 feet, he surprised the field when he busted the iron ball out near the 51-foot mark in taking honors in this event.

Upper Peninsula: Typical UP weather greeted athletes at the 1947 UP finals, held for the first time in Escanaba. In spite of the breezy and chilly conditions, six meet records fell by the wayside.

Menominee defeated defending champion Sault Ste. Marie while L'Anse moved into the winner's circle in Class C. Don Shannon powered Powers to the Class D crown with a perfect afternoon, winning the 100-yard dash, broad jump, long jump and running a leg on the winning 880-yard relay team.

Never to be forgotten by Rock-Mid Peninsula High School will be Lester Bazinet, winner of his section in the Class D 440-yard run. Bazinet passed away in 1997 and left the students at his alma mater $380,000 dollars. Each year the interest is given out in scholarships.

1948

Although Saginaw won again in Class A it was a performer from the northern town of Charlevoix who stole the show. Tom Johnson of Muskegon Heights and Don Schiesswohl of Arthur Hill battled one another in a heralded dual in the Class A shot put. Johnson eventually won with a new Class A record of 54-4¾, eclipsing Bill Watson's mark set thirteen years earlier. The future University of Michigan and Green Bay Packer football great would see his record stand at his high school for 47 years.

That wasn't the only epic throw that weekend: Charlevoix's Bob Carey boomed the twelve-pound ball 54-7 versus the field in Class C. He would go on to Michigan State where he would become the last of the three-sport stars, an All-American in football, starting center on the basketball squad, and a Big 10 and Drake Relays champion in the shot put. His best put of 53-11¾ with the 16lb shot would stand as an MSC (and now MSU) record well into the 1970s. Fittingly enough, the Charlevoix strong boy set this mark in his last home appearance in a Spartan uniform. In his final performance as a collegian, Carey placed 6th in the NCAA championships.

Before embarking on a great career in the NFL, where he was the No. 1 draft pick of the Los Angeles Rams, Carey would earn nine varsity letters at Michigan State, the last athlete to accomplish this feat for the Spartans. Bob Carey was enshrined in the Michigan Sports Hall of Fame shortly after he passed away in 1994.

Bob's twin brother Bill also fared well, despite not taking a first place. Bill finished second to his brother Bob in the shot, and placed in the broad jump and high hurdles for the Red Rayders.

Saginaw won its fourth-straight team title and third in a row under Herb Korf, who had coached two state championship teams in Elmhurst, Illinois, before coming to Michigan. To wrap it up, Saginaw had to nail the 880-yard relay to hold off its rivals from crosstown Arthur Hill. Among the relay members on the winning relay squad was Carey's future teammate at MSC, Jim Ellis. The future Spartan star in the defensive secondary also helped the winning Trojan cause by chipping in with a second place in the 440.

Dick Henson of Dearborn was the only double winner in Class A, equaling the 200-yard low hurdle record of 22.6 and winning the 100 in 10.2. The sprint races that meet were run into a brisk headwind resulting in slower than normal times. Henson's feat duplicated his father Lyle Henson's sprint double back in 1924.

Bob Hensman of Wyandotte Roosevelt knocked off a 21-year old Class A record while winning the 440. His 50.3 was a tenth better than the 50.4 initially set by John Lewis of Detroit Northeastern in 1927 and equaled by Saginaw's Charles Schmeling in 1937.

Ypsilanti took home Class B honors, with David Hill's double win leading the way. Eugene Seidel also chipped in for the victors with a first-place performance in the Class B mile. His 4:32.8 was easily the day's fastest mile in any class.

Alma's Harold "Dub" Martin took home a pair of first-place medals and nearly had a third. He won the 200-yard low hurdles in 23.1 and the broad jump with a near-record leap of 21-7¾. Martin was barely nosed out of first in the 100-yard dash by South Haven's Charles Roland, a decision that was questioned by many nearby observers.

Bob Parks captured the 440 for Howell High School. He would go on to have a legendary career as the head coach of Eastern Michigan for 30 years, earning coaching honors that would fill an entire page. The Parks family will also go down in state track history as the first father/daughter combination to win state individual titles. Park's daughter Sue would win the 880-yard run in 1974.

Bob Parks winning the 440 for Howell. This shot is as they are coming off the first turn. Note that they are not running in lanes.

Although the Carey brothers stole the headlines, East Grand Rapids returned once more to the winner's circle in Class C. Bloomfield Hills captured honors in Class D thanks, in large part, to Dick Miner. Winning the maximum of four state titles including a record 5-9½ leap in the high jump, Miner also added firsts in both hurdles and anchored the winning 880-yard relay. The day-long affair attracted nearly 1000 individuals from 197 schools.

Detroit: Accounts from the city meet hailed the action there as the most exciting since the first meet held back in 1921. Cooley won the team title for the eighth time in 11 years with 3 records smashed and one tied. This was the first title for new head track coach George Cairnes who had taken over the job from long-time coach Claude Snarey, who opted to work with the golfers instead. Cooley followed up its city title by winning the Wayne Relays for the sixth-straight year.

Detroit Northwestern's Fletcher Gilders set a state record of 12-7¾ in the pole vault. Note the lack of a pit; back then, jumpers landed in a small pile of sawdust.

Fletcher Gilders from Northwestern won the pole vault at a height of 12-7¾, higher than Forrest Naveaux's state best back in 1942 by a scant 1/4 inch. Stan McConnor, moving down from winning the 880-yard run in 1946, became the first prep in state history to break the 50 second barrier in the 440. The future Eastern Michigan University record holder crossed the finish line with a time of 49.8. Sam Gandy, of Miller, was also under the former mark, initially set by John Lewis of Northeastern in 1948.

Jim Mitchell of Northwestern ran the 220 in 22.1 to tie the 220-record, while Cooley's quartet of Don Englander, Jim Doddie, Larry Pickrell and Joe LaRue set a new mark of 1:31.3 in the 880-yard relay, still well shy of the state mark of 1:30.0 blazed by Northeastern 22 years earlier in East Lansing.

Miller's Arron Gordon could lay claim to the title as the state's fastest miler of 1948. He posted the Motor City's fastest winning time in eight years with a 4:31.7. In 1951 Gordon would team up with three Canadians for coach Don Canham's Wolverines, running a 880 split of 1:54.2 to help break the World Indoor Record for the distance medley.

Upper Peninsula: Ironwood overcame a strong performance by Menominee's Mike Shatusky to take first place honors at the UP finals. Shatusky, a four

sports star for the Menominee Maroons, scored 16 points, but it wasn't enough to offset the victorious Red Devils. Ironwood scored 43 to give veteran coach Jack Kramer his fourth UP title since becoming the Red Devil's track coach in 1930.

Ron Nettell led Houghton to the Class C UP championship. He won both short dashes and cleared 11-4 4/5 inches in the pole vault to establish a new record by 1/8 of an inch. (They were splitting hairs at the finals in Escanaba.) Shatusky's winning leap of 5-9½ missed equaling the UP finals record by a scant 10th of an inch.

Eben more than doubled the score over second-place Chassell to cop team honors in Class D.

1949

It was estimated that 7,000 prep tracksters, representing 350 high schools, attempted to qualify for the state championships in 1949. Coach Herb Korf's Saginaw Trojans made it a record-setting five titles in a row, a record for consecutive state championships in Class A. Scoring in nine of the thirteen events on the card, Saginaw High amassed 44 points, won four first places, and set a new record in the medley relay.

Shot putter Don Schiesswohl would be better known as a football player; he was a key player on MSU's undefeated national championship team of 1952.

To make it a complete Saginaw day once again, coach Gene Mason's Arthur Hill squad grabbed the runner-up spot with 25 1/5 points, topped by Don Schiesswohl's near record throw of 54-½, just four inches shy of Tom Johnson's mark posted a year earlier. The gentleman shot putter from Muskegon Heights had told Schwiesswohl to "go set the record" following their heralded dual of 1948. At regionals Schwiesswohl had put the shot a state record 56-4¾, a Michigan mark that would not be bettered for five years.

Gaylord Nelson, running the anchor leg for the Trojan medley relay quartet, made up a 10-yard deficit and won going away in a meet record 2:33.7. Warren Keyes made it three straight years that a Keyes had won the broad jump. The defending champion leaped 21-5½ on his final jump to overtake Grand Rapids Ottawa Hills' Ralph Lock. Keyes' brother Tim had taken the win in 1947.

Jim Ellis won the 440 in a time of 50.5, despite drawing the outside lane. It should be noted that up to this date the 440 was contested with the runners cutting to the inside lane after about 150 yards. Large fields often presented a myriad of problems, as runners fought for the inside position.

The premier performer had to be Ypsilanti High's David Hill, who won all three of his events in Class B with meet records. He long jumped 22-1¾, blazed the 120 high hurdles in 14.9, and trimmed the 200-low hurdle mark down to 22.7. Interestingly enough, Hill could only net a tie for third in the high jump, an event that he won in 1947 and 1948. The future Michigan gridder's efforts were good enough to almost single-handedly propel Ypsilanti to a second-place finish, trailing only Class B champion Birmingham.

The coach for Birmingham's championship squad was Kermit Ambrose, who became a fixture in track and field in the state of Michigan for many years. He was one of the founders of the Michigan Interscholastic Track Coaches Association. For many decades he was a starter at meets across the state. As a coach and official, he was honored with virtually every award possible during his long career, including the MHSAA's Forsythe Award and MITCA's Sweeney Award. After his death at age 101, MITCA's highest award for cross country coaching was named after him.

In Class C, Dundee's Jack Goodrich won the same three titles as Hill, leading his team to the state championship and nearly matched Hill's marks. The premier event of the day in Class C was the 120 highs. A Class C high hurdle mark that had stood since 1938 was bettered three times during the day. Goodrich ran a 15.5 in a preliminary and then Harlan Benjamin of Milan ripped off a 15.4 in a second preliminary. Goodrich came back in the finals to nip Benjamin by a stride in the new record time of 15.0.

Another three-time winner in 1940 was Vestaburg's Gaylord Snyder in Class D. Vestaburg finished third in the team battle behind Michigan School for the Deaf and Bloomfield Hills. Ironically, Snyder won the same three events as did Hill and Goodrich and set a new mark in the 200 low hurdles. Thirty years down the

road in 1979, Snyder's son Robert would duplicate his father's victory in the long jump.

It should be noted that the year 1949 saw a number of athletes who placed in this meet go on to become prominent in football. Future University of Michigan football star Lowell Perry placed 3rd in the Class B long jump at Ypsilanti. Leroy Bolden captured a sixth-place medal in the 100-yard dash. He would start in the famed "pony backfield" for Michigan State College's national championship team of 1952. Although tipping the scales at only 170 pounds, Bolden played two years in the National Football League for the Cleveland Browns.

Future Central Michigan football and track legend Jim Podoley placed a distant 6th in the pole vault while competing for Mt Morris. While he never won a first-place medal at the state meet as a prep, he would come into his own in his freshman year at CMU. He earned Most Valuable honors an unprecedented four years in a row in IIAC championships for coach Lyle Bennett's Chips. Later he would shine in the NFL for the Washington Redskins.

Chuck Fairbanks fell far short of his 1948 teammate Bob Carey in the Class C shot put, but did manage to take a third place. Following his college days at MSC, he became the head football coach for the Oklahoma Sooners and then the New England Patriots. Could there have ever been a better set of ends at any school than Class C Charlevoix had in the fall of 1947 with Bob Carey and Chuck Fairbanks?

Detroit: Northwestern won its first city championship since 1931. Walter Jenkins of Miller heaved the shot a meet record 53-5. Earlier in the week he had bettered Edwin Turashoff's 31-year record with a mark of 52-3½ inches. On May 4 in a dual on Belle Isle against Cass Tech, Jenkins had thrown 55-9.

Coach Jimmy Russell's Colts produced six individual winners. Little Billy Smith led the Northwestern assault in the hurdles, covering the 120 highs in 15.4 and the 120 lows in 13.5. Marvin Banks edged Detroit Central sophomore Cliff Hatcher in defending his 880 title, while Don Owens cleared a 6-0 to share honors in the high jump. The Colts also claimed first-place honors in the first-ever running of the medley relay, edging the pre-meet favorites from Detroit Cooley in 2:33.2.

After clearing 12-6 in the pole vault, Northwestern's Fletcher Gilders hoped for more. Indoors he had cleared a national prep record 13-3½. The city and state YMCA diving and tumbling champion would make an even bigger splash in the water. Following a two-year stint in the army, the three-time city diving champion took his talents to Ohio State University. The 5-8 Gilders twice won the NCAA diving title.

Upper Peninsula: Menominee turned the tables on Ironwood to place first in the UP Class B finals. Harold Larson and Jack Anderson won the only two individual titles for the Maroons but it was a member of the victorious 880-yard relay team who would bring national attention upon Menominee and the Upper Peninsula. Billy Wells took his football talents to Michigan State College where he not only led the Spartans to their first Rose Bowl appearance in 1954 but would be named the outstanding player of the game. The handsome Wells also garnered notoriety by dating screen star Debbie Reynolds before going on to a successful career in the NFL.

Jim Cox won three events as Munising breezed to the Class C crown but Chassell had to sweat out the final results of the high jump before being assured of a narrow victory over Hermansville. Bob Pelkie of Gwinn leaped 20-10¼ inches in the broad jump to set a record that would stand for more than 20 years.

1950

Flint Northern snapped Saginaw's five-year win streak, a consecutive mark that perhaps could have been extended. Saginaw's star sprinter had inexplicably failed to show for the regionals, thus was automatically disqualified from competing in the state finals. The Trojans fell five points shy from annexing an unprecedented sixth-straight, lacking points many Trojan followers felt could easily have been obtained with their ace sprinter in action.

Bay City Central's Milt Mead stole the spotlight by leaping a record 6-4 in the high jump, a mark second in state meet history only to Detroit Eastern's Bernard Lucas' meet record 6-4¾ clearance in 1934. Mead's dominance at this meet was such that second place was a full eight inches short of Mead's winning height. He also managed to capture the broad jump title on his final effort of the day. Dearborn Fordson's Bill Baxter repeated his sprint double in 1949, again taking both short dashes (10.3/22.6) to join Mead as Class A's only double winner.

Flint Northern's 880 and medley relay teams both won on the road to a championship. The win was the first in the history for the city of Flint in Class A and gave Coach Bill Cave the rare double win, both as a coach and an athlete. He had won the 440 while competing for Monroe High School in 1941. Among the relay runners for the victorious Vikings 880 relay were Leroy Bolden and Ellis Duckett. They both would go on to have brilliant careers at Michigan State and would play prominent roles in the Spartan's Rose Bowl victory over UCLA in 1954.

Niles scored only 23 points but that proved enough to edge defending champion Birmingham in a well-balanced Class B contest. Birmingham won three firsts but was unable to overcome Niles' superior depth. John Bachman, son of former MSC football coach Charley Bachman, won the Class B shot put with a throw of 50-4¾. The elder Bachman was a state champ in the same event in the state of Illinois.

Perennial power East Grand Rapids easily repeated as Class C champs with five first places. It was in Class C that two of the better performers in any of the classes would continue their long rivalry. Milan's Harlan Benjamin turned the tables on 1949 hurdles winner Jack Goodrich from nearby Dundee. Benjamin captured the 120-yard high hurdles and the 180 lows, nipping Goodrich in the process. Benjamin's record-setting times in the highs (14.8) and the lows (20.3) were the best marks made in the hurdles in all classes. Goodrich did not go without a title, however, as he won the high jump.

It should be noted that the low hurdles made their third shift in Michigan history in 1950, moving from the 200-yard distance down to 180 yards. This would also mark the final year when all classes would compete at the same site. From this point onward, MSC would no longer host all four classes, but instead would share the host role with the University of Michigan until 1958.

Ancel Rodgers won both short dashes to lead Benton Harbor St. Johns to its first Class D state championship. George Corcoran of Mt. Morris St. Mary, only a sophomore, repeated as the mile king in Class D.

Detroit: Al Williams of Detroit Northwestern posted the fastest mile time in Michigan schoolboy history in winning the Detroit City Championship. Williams clipped 3.3 seconds off the previous fastest mark, set a full decade earlier by Mt. Morris's Ralph Brakcrog, with a time of 4:24.9. Williams was the only champion from Detroit to post a mark superior to performances made by the out-state youths in East Lansing.

Miller High won seven of the thirteen events and tied in another while piling up 75 points. Dave Mann was the leading point winner for coach Leroy Dues' powerhouse. Mann, who made it all the way to AAA as a professional baseball player, had firsts in the 100 (10.1) and 220 (22.4), a second in the broad jump, and ran the anchor leg on the winning 880-yard relay team. Orlin Jones, who would one day be the historian for Detroit Pershing, took first-place honors in the 120-yard high hurdles (15.2).

Upper Peninsula: Ironwood squeaked out a narrow one-point win amidst controversy at the Class B UP finals in Houghton. Only three teams were entered in the medley relay in which Ironwood was awarded three points for a third-place finish. Escanaba, who placed but one point behind the winning Red Devils, protested the scoring ruling (5-4-3). Only district champions were allowed to enter UP finals in the relays. Escanaba officials believed the scoring should have been based on the rules stated in the MHSAA bulletin (5-3-1) when less than five teams are entered. The Eskimos protest was denied at an UP council meeting a few days later.

There could be no controversy as to who was the star of the meet. John Leppi of Ironwood dominated the hurdles. His 20.4 in the first year of the 180-yard low hurdles would stand for 20 years. His record in the high hurdles wouldn't be broken for 13 years.

Munising and Hermansville took the trophies for the wins in Class C and D. UP track fans were hopeful of seeing their first sub-10 clocking in the century by Hermansville's Victor Fochesato. He had run a 9.9 for the 100-yards at the district meet but unfavorable conditions in Houghton slowed him to a 10.5.

1951

For the first time in nine years the Class A team trophy moved out of the Saginaw Valley. Propelled by Bob Brown's magnificent running, Grand Rapids Ottawa Hills won the Class A team title in the wind, mud and rain.

Brown, who earlier in the day ran a wind-aided 9.8 in the 100-yard dash prelims, sped a 10.0 in the afternoon. He then ran the 220 in 21.8, a remarkable achievement considering the track had turned into a thick soup from the heavy rains. Ottawa Hills made the victory even more notable, as the only Class B school that elected to compete in Class A.

The monsoon conditions made it a virtual impossibility to establish any new records. For the first time the meet was divided among two sites. Michigan State College hosted the Class A & C divisions, with the University of Michigan welcoming the entrants in Classes B and D. Afternoon field events at both MSC and the U of M were moved indoors to Jenison and Yost fieldhouse. Mt. Pleasant's Kay Keffer was able to take advantage of the favorable indoor conditions to boost the Class B record a scant 1/4 of an inch in the Class B pole vault. Keffer would go on to win the welterweight division boxing championship at Fort Bragg, North Carolina, in April 1954.

Thomas Yinger of Monroe came close to a record in the slop outdoors in the 180-yard low hurdles. His mark of 19.6 was wind-aided by a 2.4mps breeze--the allowable limit was 2.0). Yinger completed his day by capturing the 120-high hurdles in 15.0.

Pontiac Central's Walt Beach placed in both dashes and anchored the Chieftain's winning 880-yard relay before embarking on a great career in football.Following a four-year tour of duty in the armed forces, he enjoyed a brilliant tenure at Central Michigan University and then had a brief stint in the NFL with the Cleveland Browns.

Cadillac eased to the Class B title, nearly doubling the score over runner-up Mt. Pleasant. Bert Zagers won the 220, placed second in the broad jump and ran a leg on the winning 880-yard relay team to lead the Vikings. He later starred on the gridiron at MSC and enjoyed a brief career in the NFL as a running back for the Washington Redskins. He was the leading punt returner in the NFL in 1957, returning 14 punts for 2 TD's and a league leading average return of 15.5 yards.

Clarence "Junior" Stielstra of Ludington, winner of the Class B broad jump, also became the Big 10 champion in this event in 1955 as a member of the University of Michigan track squad.

Ann Arbor University High put together three firsts and a pair of seconds to win the Class C title in East Lansing. Otisville joined Ann Arbor University as first-time team winner, capturing the Class D crown, as all the members of its nine-man squad were able to garner valuable points.

Detroit: The rains had dissipated by the time the Detroit City League conducted its championships, nearly two weeks after the state meet for the out-state schools. Cliff Hatcher of Central ran the fastest 440 in Michigan schoolboy history with a 48.8 clocking. The "slender" Hatcher, who had taken city meet honors a year earlier in the 880-yard run, became the first high schooler in state history to break the 49-second barrier for the quarter mile.

Joe Howard of Detroit Northwestern improved the 120-yard high hurdle mark down to 14.4, again the fastest high hurdle mark posted in Michigan high school annals. Veteran Detroit track sleuth John Gallimore would label Howard as the "smoothest hurdler" he had ever seen in state track prep history.

Mackenzie, in bringing home the team trophy, captured its first-ever team championship. It had appeared to be a long shot at best, following the preliminaries on Tuesday. Harry Barton, the Stags' ace sprinter, pulled a muscle after qualifying in the 100-yard dash heat. The injury forced him out of the 220, depriving Mackenzie of valuable points. He recovered sufficiently three days later to take a second in the 100 behind Detroit Central's Bolivar McGowan.

Upper Peninsula: Once again chilly weather and brisk winds on a rain-soaked track greeted competitors at the UP championships. Ironwood won the Class B crown for the fifth time. Ken Hofer of Stephenson took the 100-yard dash. Hofer would become a legend in UP circles as the head football coach at Menominee. He treated football fans to a Class B state championship as recently as 1998 while using the old-time single wing offense.

Hofer wasn't the only UP legend competing at the UP finals. Carl (Buck) Nystrom of Marquette, a future All-American at Michigan State, placed in the 440 and long jump. Nor was Hofer the only competitor to coach a UP team to a state title in football. Jerry Cvengros, who took third place in the shot put for Ironwood, would guide Escanaba to the Class A state football crown in 1981.

Bessemer and Eben emerged victorious in the Class C & D finals held on the Escanaba High School track. Erland Maki of Crystal Falls, who earlier in the week turned in a no-hit pitching performance in baseball, won the 120-yard high hurdles and shot put for the Trojans.

1952

Rains again made for sloppy conditions, eliminating any chance for records. Saginaw High returned to the winner's circle once again, scoring the second lowest winning point total in state history. Five other teams were within five points of Saginaw in the tension-packed meet. The Trojans won despite dropping the baton in the half mile relay.

The team championship helped sooth Saginaw's bitter loss earlier in the season at the Central Michigan College relays, the largest high school track meet in the country. Twice the Trojans relay teams were disqualified, and any one of them would have given coach Herb Korf's speedsters the title.

Alonzo Harris of Pontiac won both dashes (10.3/22.6) to become the only double winner in Class A. Carl Diener of Saginaw Arthur Hill and R.J. Johnson from Flint Northern repeated as shot put and long jump champions respectively. Terry Barr, wearing the colors of Grand Rapids Central, won the 440-yard dash on the rain-soaked track in 51.5. He would later become a star running back at Michigan before embarking on a well-known career with the Detroit Lions.

The star performer in 1952 had to be East Jackson's Ray Eggelston, who became one of only five male athletes in state history to win four individual events and, in so doing, led his team to a co-championship with Ann Arbor University. The busy Eggelston won the broad jump (21-7½), high jump (5-10), and both hurdles. Rules thru 1952 permitted athletes to compete in as many field events as so desired, but no more than three running events. Eggelston also participated in the 440, placing fifth in

his section, one point away from single-handedly winning the state team title.

"My coach told me we could win the meet if I placed in the quarter mile," he smiled as he collected his medals. "I placed fifth and a fourth would have won." Eggelston's first-place finish in the high jump included some high dramatics. He had missed twice at 5-9, before he was called to run in the finals of the 180-yard low hurdles. With one jump still remaining, he had to leave the high jump pit to go and win the 180-yard lows. After but a five-minute rest, Eggelston cleared the bar at 5-9 and then went another inch higher to secure first place over runner-up Carl Shelton of Milan.

Roseville won its only track championship ever by taking the Class B title. Bob Zimmerman was a double winner for the Panthers, winning the broad jump and the 220. Dave Goodell of Mt. Pleasant posted the day's best mark. The son of Mt. Pleasant head coach Fred Goodell, he won the shot put with a heave of 53-4. A rain slick throwing ring perhaps prevented the Oiler's strongman from setting a new record. A week earlier he had reached 55-9 in winning the regional.

Whitehall High School finished one point behind the two co-winners, placing third in a competition that saw 42 Class C schools score in the meet. Osie Rostic, who would go on to gridiron fame at little Augustana College, won the 100, finished 2nd in the 220 and anchored the winning 880-yard relay. He failed to place in his specialty, the broad jump, where he held the West Michigan conference record until broken in 1999.

Brethren Norman-Dickson began its monopoly that would last for another seven years, easily taking the Class D crown by a resounding margin. Leading the way for Brethren was double winner Richard Beane. Before graduating in 1956, Beane would win five individual titles and run on four winning relay units. This combined total of nine first-place finishes equaled the accomplishments of Caro's Clare McDurman and Dearborn Heights Robichaud's Tyrone Wheatley.

Class D did produce one meet record, set in a morning preliminary before the rains came. Suttons Bay's Don Buerle established the new mark for the 100 with a time of 10.2. After the rains, Buerle's winning time during the afternoon's finals was nearly a second slower than his morning record dash.

Maurice Ruddy, the Class C/D cross country champion, won the mile run in Class D to win the only state title in history for little Maple Grove High School.

Detroit: Despite an ankle injury incurred while qualifying in the pole vault earlier in the week, Willie Wright managed to lead Miller High to the Detroit title with a trio of victories. He won the 120-yard highs, 120 low hurdles and the pole vault for the victors.

It was not until Wright had soared to 11-8 on his final attempt to win the vault before Miller had wrapped up the team title. If not for a disqualification in the 880-relay by Northern, which trailed Miller in the final standings by two points, the Eskimos would have won the championship.

Southwestern's medley relay unit of Lester Sherman, Basil Szabo, Dick Conz, and Milton Lewis set the only record on the windswept Sawyer Field oval with a 2:32.4 clocking. John McKenzie, of Detroit Mackenzie, posted the fastest half mile clocking in 13 years, defending his title with a time of 1:59.0.

The high jump in 1952 may have helped inspire current day rules for tiebreaking. Seven athletes who cleared 5-8 were all named as co-champions.

Upper Peninsula: A large contingent from Sault Ste. Marie High School easily won the Class B finals in Houghton. All 17 entrants who made the trip to the Copper Country placed for coach Ernie Kran's Blue Devils.

Undoubtedly very few people in attendance would ever envision that an incomparable dynasty would begin on this day. In the first year of its track program, Pickford won the UP Class D title—and would not relinquish it for 26 years. Its first championship trophy might have been the toughest to win over the years as the Panthers took the medley relay, the day's final event, to eke out a two-point win over runner-up Eben.

1953

Warm weather and only a slight breeze greeted the entrants for the 1953 edition, again divided between Ann Arbor and East Lansing. Flint Northern gave coach Bill Cave, back after a two-year stint in the armed forces, his second championship trophy with a convincing showing in Ann Arbor. The team collected 37 points to easily hold off second-place Pontiac (24).

With ideal conditions for the first time in three years, spectators reveled in an onslaught of records. Perhaps the most impressive mark was the hurdle time of Leon Burton in the 180-yard lows. His 19.1 was only bettered by the legendary Rex Cawley several years later, before the 330-yard hurdles replaced the event in 1977.

East Detroit's Ron Kramer pushed Burton to the finish line. Kramer would become one of the University of Michigan's all-time greats, as well as a premier tight end for Vince Lombardi's great teams in Green Bay. Burton, meanwhile, would star on the gridiron for Arizona State and the old New York Titans of the American Football League.

Alonzo Harris of Pontiac equaled George Hester's 30-year old meet record with a 21.7 clocking in the 220-yard dash. He added the broad jump title and in the process, defeated the two-time champion of the event, R.J. Johnson. Flint Northern's Johnson did get a pair of first-place medals for the championship Vikings, running on both of the relay teams, including the record-setting medley foursome. The other Class A record for the day went to Gerald Zitny of Dearborn Fordson. He raced the mile in 4:28.8, surpassing Rex Woolsey's record set 13 years earlier.

A freshman scored the most points of any individual in leading St. Louis to the Class C team title. John Palmer scored 17 3/8 of the 30 points amassed by St. Louis. He set a meet record in winning the 180-yard low hurdles in 20.0 and also won the broad jump and placed second in the 120-yard highs. As a senior, he would complete his four-year sweep in the 180-yard low hurdles, becoming the first athlete in Michigan history to win outright one event four consecutive years, a feat rarely matched since. Palmer won the first of his four LH championships in Class C, the other three years won while competing against Class B competition.

Palmer learned the tricks of his trade from his coach, himself a former state champ. Sherman Olmsted of St. Louis won the 120-yard high hurdles while a prep track star at Saginaw High School in 1936. In 1952 he also piloted the Sharks to the Class C basketball championship. The popular Olmsted, a track letter winner for Michigan's legendary teams in the late 1930s, passed away in early 1997.

Al Bigelow of Stanton took down a 31-year-old record in Class C when he won the 220 in 22.3.

In Class B, Battle Creek Lakeview totaled only 20 points, but that was enough as the Spartans won their only track state championship. Earl Glenn of Belleville set a meet record when he tossed the shot 54-8½, topping Bob Carey's all-class mark set in 1948 by less than an inch. Carl Shelton of Milan was a double winner in B, tying for first in the pole vault at 11-4, and had the best leap of any class in the high jump at 6-½.

Brethren walked away from the field once again in Class D by placing in all but one of the thirteen events, running up an impressive total of 67½ points. Its nearest rival was Detroit University School, which made its best team showing since the early part of the 20th century. DUS, with 27½ points, trailed Brethren by a whopping 40. Richard Beane set records in both hurdles for the victors and joined teammates Bert Burns, Darrell Leckrone and Bob Phillips in setting a third record in the 880-yard relay.

Oddly enough, Beane did not win the high hurdles. Though he set a record during the qualifying round, he placed second in the finals to Joe Thering of Beal City. Thering's winning time of 15.9 was one tenth slower than Beane's record of 15.8. Jerry Mitchell of Eau Claire won three events in Class D, including a record 22.9 in the 220-yard dash.

Detroit: No individual records were set, but both relay records toppled at the city championships, with Miller easily repeating as city champs. Perhaps a pair of Miller broad jumpers, Godfrey Little and Rex McLeod posted the best marks for the day sailing over 22-8 in a 1-2 finish. The broad jumpers, thanks in part to a generous rules interpretation by meet manager George Mead, set a number of personal bests. All jumps were measured from each competitor's take off point, as opposed from the traditional marking from the far edge of the board. Despite this generous (and incorrect) interpretation, Clifford Robinson's record, set back in 1924, still stood.

John Thomas, winner of the 100 and 220, teamed up with Little, McLeod and John Massingille to win the 880-yard relay. The Miller quartet posted the second fastest time in state history with its city record time of 1:30.6.

Detroit Northern's medley, comprised of Dave Benson, Dan McCuin, Dennis Gibson and Lee Daniels, surpassed any out-state marks with its clocking of 2:29.9.

Upper Peninsula: In as balanced a contest ever contested in the UP finals, Marquette took home honors in Class B by tallying but 23½ points, one more than the defending champs from Sault Ste. Marie. Houghton scored in twelve of the thirteen events to top honors in Class C. Bessemer's Bob Harris was the only triple winner of the entire meet, capturing wins in the high and low hurdle events as well as the broad jump.

Pickford again flexed its muscles and rolled to the Class D championships. Although near perfect weather greeted athletes in 1953, only four new records were set in the UP, all in Class D.

1954

Two perennial powerhouses matched up again in the Class A finals. Saginaw won its seventh title in ten years with a 35 to 32 victory over defending champion Flint Northern. Stocky Bob Maturen opened and closed the meet with clutch performances to lead the Trojans. During the morning broad jump event, he leaped 21-11½ on his next-to-last effort to secure first place. In the final event, with his team trailing Flint Northern by two points, Maturen pole vaulted 12-0 to tie for first and give Saginaw the points it needed.

Muskegon's Joel Boyden—a 6-4, 230lb giant—set a Class A record by hurling the shot a state record 57-0. Al Dixon from Kalamazoo came a tenth of a second away from becoming the first out-state trackster to break the 50 second barrier, but did manage to establish a new record. A Flint Northern foursome gave

the long standing 880-yard relay record a scare by clocking a 1:30.2. Paul Wiegerink of Grand Rapids Ottawa Hills took both hurdles, joining Maturen as a double winner in 'A'.

Sprinter John Langhorn of Saginaw had the envious honor of playing a major role for three state championship teams--at two different schools. Langhorn ran for Saginaw High in his sophomore year, transferred to Flint Northern for his junior campaign and moved back again to Saginaw for his senior season. All three teams were state champions. Earlier in the month the Trojans won their first CMU Relays team title since 1949.

Inkster began a three-year reign in Class B, with a talented Ludington team in close pursuit. The Vikings of Inkster won three firsts, and also placed second three times for their 39-point total. The Viking 880-yard relay put on the most flawless performance of the day. The champions picked up nearly ten yards on every exchange of the baton and finished 40 yards ahead of their nearest rival. The foursome, made up of Herman Frederick, Arthur Frederick, Charles Calloway and Otis Lee, were timed in 1:31.4, shaving 1.1 seconds off a 16-year old mark set by East Lansing. A 2-3-4 finish in the 100-yard dash, won by Glen Burgett of Sparta, contributed to the first state title ever won in any sport in Inkster's 13-year history.

The state title more than made up for a disappointing ending at the CMU Relays earlier in the month. A disqualification in the meet's closing event, the mile relay, took eight points away from Inkster, paving the way for Mt Pleasant's Oilers to win the championship trophy.

Ludington's Lee Snyder soared 12-4¼ to up the pole vault record in 'B.' John Palmer had little trouble moving up from Class C, as he lowered the B meet record in the 180-yard low hurdles. Palmer skimmed the sticks in 20.2 to become the first athlete to ever hold a record for one event in two different classes.

Although he placed only second in his section of the 880-yard run, Hart's Ed Vandenheuvel would make a name for himself in the sport. Vandenheuvel would go on to shatter all distance records at CMU, capping his career with a second-place finish at the NCAA cross country championships in 1958. In that race he finished more than 100 yards ahead of a certain Billy Mills from Kansas, who would six years later win Olympic gold at 10,000 in a race immortalized by the movie, "Running Brave."

Lansing Everett, winner of the Class C meet, set the only record for its class when Dick Content vaulted 11-10¾. One of the leading point scorers in Class C was Dave Whitsell of Shelby. The versatile Whitsell won the broad jump, and placed second in the 180-yard low hurdles and shot for the Tigers. Whitsell would then go on to a brilliant career in the NFL for three teams. He intercepted 46 passes during his pro career, with perhaps the biggest being an interception against the Detroit Lions in 1963. He picked off a pass thrown by the Lion's Earl Morrall, who prepped at neighboring Muskegon, and raced for a touchdown to clinch the NFC title for the World Champion Bears.

Most athletes are encouraged to heed the advice of their coach, but, in the case of 100-yard dash champ Dale Boyer from Scottville, it would have been wise not too have done so. Boyer's track coach at Scottville, Harold Hope, was a crop duster during the summer months. Hope encouraged his star athlete to try crop dusting. Boyer did did so, but lost his life when he crashed his plane while crop dusting. Ironically, coach Hope also suffered the same fate a few months later, when his plane went down with mechanical problems.

Brethren again dominated Class D, and the winning Bobcats contributed two new records for first year coach Doyle Eckhardt. Their dominance was so complete, winning eight out of the thirteen events. Brethren's Dick Spoor traveled the mile in 4:39.1, shearing 4.4 seconds from a 16-year old mark. Richard Beane shaved one tenth of a second off his high hurdles mark, set a year earlier in the prelims, making amends for his 1953 loss. Beane's winning time was 15.7 and he beat 1953 champ Joe Thering. Beane moved into select company with four wins: both hurdle events, the high jump, and a leg on Brethren's 880-yard relay team.

Detroit: Pershing won its first-ever title in the city championships. Coach Carl Holmes' Doughboys took only one first during the afternoon, but had enough depth to hold off second-place Miller. The two-time champion defenders, Miller hoped for a third-straight but received a jolt earlier in the week when the Trojan's top seeded medley relay team was disqualified. Miller's Marvin Pettway, who set a record for the 220-yard straightaway, turned in a blazing 21.7 furlong, but was not deemed by meet officials as a record. The officials cited the fact that Northern's Leonard Alkon ran the former mark of 22.1 in 1940 around one turn.

Eastern's Fred Hopgood's winning leap of 22-7 was the state's best mark in 1954 for the broad jump. Bob Williams of Pershing, likewise, posted the state's best time in his event, clocking a 1:58.7 for the 880. Willie Adkins of Northeastern carried off individual honors with 17½ points, earning all the points scored by the Falcons.

Upper Peninsula: Rare perfect weather greeted the 325 athletes representing the 35 schools gathered at the UP finals in Houghton, yet nary a record was broken. Much of the blame could be attributed to the poor weather leading up to the finals. Ironwood, for

example, competed in only the qualifying regional meet before entering the UP finals.

Class B's Sault Ste. Marie joined defending champs Houghton and Pickford in the winner's circle. James Contratto of Bessemer enjoyed a perfect day in Class C. Leading the speedboys to a second-place finish behind Houghton, Contratto won the long jump and low hurdles and ran a leg on each of Bessemer's winning relay teams.

1955

The 1955 championships would feature many of the best performances in state history. Fans would see the first championship appearance of one of Michigan's greatest track athletes of all-time, Hayes Jones of Pontiac. Jones scored enough points by himself (18 2/5) that he would have won the Class A championship as an individual entry. Second-place Flint Northern, as a team, combined to score 17 points.

Coach Walter Schoekle's Chieftain's for the next two years could have arguably been the best team ever assembled. A total of twelve Pontiac athletes would score in the 1955 meet with Jones leading the way. The 1964 Olympic gold medalist broke the 120-yard high hurdle record of Jackson's Horace Smith, dating back to 1942, with a time of 14.5. Jones took the long jump with a leap of 22-5, finished just behind future MSU football star Don Arend from Benton Harbor in the 180-low hurdles and shared third place in the high jump. Pontiac's domination could have been even more complete, but its top seeded 880-yard relay team had a couple of poor passes, eliminating any chance for a top finish.

Not to be outdone by Jones was Pete Dant of Alpena.He equaled the 100-yard dash record, initially set back in the 1920s by George Hester and Eddie Tolan, with a 9.8 and clocked speedy but wind-aided 21.4. Photos of Dant's finish put his lead over his closest rival at perhaps 10 yards. The would-have-been meet record was aided by a 2.2mps wind (legal limit 2.0). Records were taken very seriously at the state competitions with the wind gauge being monitored by two professors employed in the physics department at Michigan State.

William Campbell from Dearborn Fordson was another shining light in the 1955 meet, setting one record and aiding in another. Campbell cracked the 50-second barrier with a time of 49.7 and helped his mates set a new mark in the medley relay with his 220-leg. Teaming with Campbell were Dale Robinson, Bill Friend and Phillip Davis as they stunned the crowd with their 2:28.1, over a second and half faster than Flint Northern's 2:29.7 set in 1953. As a meet record it

In 1955, Pontiac jumpers Hudson Ray and Alex Barge both cleared this 6-3½ bar at the state finals. Ray stood 6-4, Barge 5-4.

CMU Hall of Famer had won his two qualifying heats before clocking a 46.5 in the finals. This earned Myers a place at the Olympic trials in Palo Alto, California, two weeks later, but he was far off form and placed a disappointing seventh in his heat.

Henry McNary came half a point shy of winning the Class C crown with his 17, which was the total for his Cassopolis team. McNary won both dashes and finished second in the long jump. Reed City took the crown with Don Miller leading the way with a pair of victories in the hurdles. The slim difference in the team title came when Roger Landrum of the victorious Coyotes shared an eight-way tie for third in the pole-vault. Brethren won its fourth-straight championship and, for the second consecutive year, Brethren, Spring Arbor and Freesoil finished 1-2-3 in Class D. Norman Burns accounted for one of the two records claimed, erasing the 21 year-record in the shot by Milt Glassner of Diamondale with a heave of 49-3¾. Gordon Fitzgerald bettered a mark set by his 1954 Spring Arbor teammate Dave Heimberger in winning the 880-yard run in 2:05.2.

Detroit: A year earlier, a mark in the prelims did not count as a record. But when Miller's Jerry Green ran 21.8 in the 220 qualifying this year, it was recognized. Good thing, as Green pulled a muscle in anchoring the Miller relay in the prelims and in the finals could only manage about half of the 100-yard dash before stopping. In addition to Green's 220 mark, Ermin Crownley pushed the shot put out to 53-10½ and the Miller 880-yard relay foursome improved that time down to 1:30.5. One of the members on the record-setting relay team for Miller was Woody Thomas. Thomas would go on to win five state team titles as a head coach, four of those coming as head mentor at Detroit Central.

Detroit Northern lowered its own record in the medley down to 2:28.8, run by the foursome of Clarence Willis, Joe Collins, Roosevelt Wilson and Dave Benson.

It should be pointed out that City League athletes did have an advantage over out-state tracksters. Starting in 1955, meet records could be set in either the finals or the qualifying meets, which were typically run several days earlier, giving athletes a forgiving break from Mother Nature.

Upper Peninsula: Weather was not a problem for a change at the UP finals. Stephenson won its first Class B title at the Escanaba meet. Munising's Gary DeLisle, with a time of 4:35.2, broke Eugene Danielson's 14-year record in the mile run to highlight the individual performances.

Houghton, which earlier in the spring won the Class C state championship in basketball (the only sport in which the Upper and Lower Peninsula matched

still stands, as the event was replaced with the 4x4 in 1961. As a state record It lasted until 1969.

The Smith brothers (Willie and Namon) joined forces with Frank Santovich and Charles Gatza to take the 880-yard relay in 1:32.9. Namon Smith, a Bay County Area Sports Hall of Famer, also took home a first-place medal with a win in the 100-yard dash.

Inkster edged Grand Rapids Central for the Class B crown in a meet that featured two edits to the record book. John Palmer once again lowered the Class B mark for the 180-yard low hurdles with a time of 20.1, while Larry Masteller from Adrian erased Berkley's James Wright's 1933 mark with his 50.6 time in the 440.

Dave Myers of Mt. Pleasant, winner of the 220 in 22.5, would go on to have a sensational collegiate career at nearby Central Michigan University. He wrapped up his Chippewa days by placing fourth in the 440-yard dash at the 1960 NCAA championships. The talents) easily repeated in Class C. Pickford won seven events to once again capture the championship trophy in Class D.

1956

Fan interest in track & field may have been at its peak in the middle 1950s. Crowds in excess of 2,000 or more were common for dual meets staged at Houseman Field in Grand Rapids. With athletes such as Hayes Jones and Pete Dant performing, one could understand the enthusiastic support for the sport. The city of Kalamazoo further glamorized the track & field by inviting the state champions from all classes to compete in the Celery City in the inaugural Champion of Champions meet. Sponsored by the Kalamazoo Junior Chamber of Commerce to raise money for the Olympic team, the initial meet on Memorial Day weekend attracted a crowd of 2,500, the most ever to witness a track and field event in Kalamazoo history.

Pontiac improved on its great showing in 1955 by scoring 61 points. Using the present-day format for points, this total may have been the most scored in state history. The Chieftains of 1956 could certainly boast having Michigan's all-time best prep team. Pontiac also became the first team from the state of Michigan to win the team title at the prestigious Mansfield Relays.

Hayes Jones again was phenomenal, setting two meet records, winning three individual events and running a leg on the winning 880-yard relay team for the Chieftains. Although Jones would go on to be best known as an Olympic gold medalist hurdler, it might have been in the long jump in 1956 where Jones made the biggest splash. Hayes not only bettered Ted Tyrocki's long standing record of 22-11¾ set 20 years earlier but he surpassed it on all four of his jumps, with 23-8 7/8 being his best.

Jones lowered his own meet record in the high hurdles with a new mark of 14.4, and added a win in the 180-yard low hurdles in 19.4, three-tenths off the meet record. Pete Dant was nearly as spectacular as Jones. Although Jones' record counted in the 120-yard high hurdles, Dant's mark of 9.7 in winning the 100-yard dash was wind-aided (2.2mps), less than half a mph over the allowable.

Jones wasn't the only Chieftain who would make a mark in sports. Jim Shorter, who ran a leg on Pontiac's winning 880 relay team, made a name for himself in the NFL. The former star at the University of Detroit, would intercept 15 passes during a seven-year pro career.

For the second consecutive year, Alpena's Dant surpassed the oldest record on the books, this time

with a 21.2 burst in the 220-yard dash, only to find out that an excessive wind helped him run that fast. In his two years of competition Dant produced the fastest times in state history for both dashes in all conditions but only his 9.8 in 1955 would get record recognition.

Bob Lake of Kalamazoo Central was the other record setter in Class A, just nipping the previous best in the 880-yard run with a time of 1:58.9. He would move up to the mile as a member of the Michigan State team, setting a Big 10 record in 1959 with a time of 4:08.6. Another case for a tie-breaker rule to be invoked incurred in the pole vault as seven competitors tied for first at 11-6.

A three-way tie also developed in the Class B pole vault. No such tie would occur at the Champ of Champs meet in Kalamazoo, however. Dowagiac's Bill Deering took honors there by clearing 12-5. Deering would pass along his skills to his sons, who would both win state titles for Dowagiac High School. The youngest of the Deering vaulters, Matt, winning the state title 40 years after his father's second state crown. Bill Jr. (15-6) became the second Deering to notch a state title by winning in 1989. As a pro, he vaulted 18-10¼ and thrice ranked in the top 10 in the U.S. in the prestigious annual rankings of *Track & Field News*.

Dean Look won the Class C pole vault in a meet record 12-6. He eventually played both pro football (New York Titans) and baseball (Chicago White Sox). A longtime NFL official, he worked three Super Bowls. In the 1981 NFC playoffs, when the 49ers' Joe Montana passed to Dwight Clark for "The Catch," it was Look who called it a touchdown.

John Palmer, finishing his brilliant career at St. Louis High, scored 17 points for individual honors. Palmer not only won the low hurdles for four years, but all four of his wins were in meet records. The other Class B record was set by Utica in the medley with a time of 2:31.9. Inkster took the team honors in Class B after trailing St. Louis by five points going into the final event. The Vikings won the 880-relay in a meet record 1:31.0 to top the team tally.

Coach Sherman Olmsted's St Louis ace displayed his amazing versatility by walking off with the trophy awarded to the outstanding performer in the first annual Champion of Champions meet in Kalamazoo. Palmer dusted his competition to win the low hurdles (19.7), tied for first in the shot put (52-½), and placed in two other events to easily walk off with the prestigious trophy. It should be noted, however, that Hayes Jones and Pete Dant did not compete, both stars having previous commitments.

Finally, after a few years where no Class C team was able to romp to a convincing championship, Lansing Everett piled up 45 points to easily take home the trophy. Everett's all-time best athlete, until a guy by the name of Ervin "Magic" Johnson came along, paced the victory. Dean Look topped all classes in setting a Class C record in the pole vault at 12-6. He also placed second in the 100, fourth in the 180 lows and ran a leg on the winning 880-yard relay team. Later on he not only played in the NFL, but also played one year of Major League Baseball in 1961.

Reed City's Don Miller took both hurdles in Class C. Eleven days later that he demonstrated that he was probably the state's second best hurdler behind the incomparable Jones in winning the 120 highs in the Champion of Champions meet.

Covert shocked Brethren and won in Class D. What was so unique about the upset was that this was Covert's first year in track & field. Just as Inkster in Class B, Covert overtook Brethren by winning the day's final event, the 880-yard relay. Ken Beane was a double winner for Brethren in the sprints, and his win in the 100 was a repeat from his freshman year.

Atis Grinsberg from Class D Schoolcraft was the most inspirational athlete of the day. Hampered by a broken right arm in a cast, Grinsberg set a Class D record in the broad jump with a leap of 21-1¾, placed second in the 100-yard dash and third in the 220. The other record set in Class D went to Baldwin's Robert Booker, clocked in 51.7 in winning the 440-yard dash.

Detroit: Controversy surrounded the city championships once again. Denby held a three-point lead going into the final event, needing only a sixth-place finish in the 880-yard relay. On the last lap, however, Bob Herrington tried to hand off to Lee Gould and the baton dropped. Gould recovered the stick, but remained motionless until Denby coaches frantically shouted at him to finish the race. He came in last, but the point for sixth meant the difference between victory and a tie as runner-up Pershing finished fourth. Meet officials ruled in Denby's favor following a heated 15-minute discussion about the legality of the exchange.

Bob Manning of Detroit Western was the meet's only double winner. Manning's 21.7 in the 220 tied the meet record, the only event that produced a new meet mark. Jerry Bocci aided Denby's march to the championship by winning the mile run in 4:27.1, easily the state's best effort in 1956.

Paul Jones matched his brother Orlin's high hurdle championship performance in 1951. The younger Jones, clocked in 15.1, would join Hayes Jones of Pontiac at EMU following the 1956 season, giving the Hurons perhaps the best 1-2 hurdles duo in the country.

Upper Peninsula: 1956 could very well have been the year when the chant of "UP Power" became popular. Stephenson, Crystal Falls, and Chassell swept the three lower classes at the state basketball finals in East Lansing.

"Marvelous Mel" Peterson of Stephenson, perhaps the finest basketball player to ever come out of the UP, jumped 5-10 5/8 to set a meet record in the high jump. Kingsford's Willie Erickson exceeded the broad jump mark set by George Shomin of Escanaba in 1941 with a leap of 21-1¾.

Bob Perry was the individual star in Class C. The Iron River sophomore smashed the records in the hurdles, winning the 120-yard highs in 15.7 and the 180-yard lows in 20.7, both times well under the previous all-time UP meet records.

Ishpeming's Tim Zhulkie registered the best efforts in Class B. Although Zhulkie had to buck a chilling north wind that swept down the track, he was still able to post meet records for the 100 (10.2) and 220 (22.6) yard dashes.

Sault Ste. Marie, Houghton and Pickford won the team titles. Houghton escaped with the Class C trophy when Iron River's Gary Baumier misjudged the finish line in the 220-yard dash. Leading with but 10 yards to go Baumier slowed up and eventually placed second. Iron River lost the championship by just one point.

Hayes Jones: The Secret Was Hard Work

To select one athlete as the most outstanding Michigan high school track athlete in history would be difficult.

However, if one were to pick Hayes Jones, it would be equally difficult to argue that choice. When your author asked veteran track followers over the years to name their all-time favorite, the name of the Pontiac speedster always popped up.

Jones first appeared on the Pontiac sports scene as a 50-yard dash winner in the Junior Olympics, but it wasn't until midway through his junior year in 1955 would track fans begin to see his greatness on the cinders. His family had moved to Pontiac from Starkville, Mississippi, where he said he learned to hurdle: "I'd have to jump over the fence in back of our house every day on my way to school."

Jones, shortly after he enrolled at Eastern Michigan University, downplayed his early days as a Pontiac Chieftain. "I was really happy when I made the varsity as a junior. I finished last so often, it was a wonder Coach [Wally] Schloerke didn't kick me off the varsity." Jones, obviously never in danger of being cut from the squad, suddenly blossomed into Michigan's supreme high school track and field athlete.

Jones wasn't a a star when he started at Pontiac.

Until his junior year at Pontiac Central, Jones trailed many of his talented classmates. And talented track athletes were in abundance in Pontiac in the mid-1950s.

A classmate and admirer of Jones from this era, John Osler, recently reflected on him. "His secret was hard work," recalled Osler. "Pontiac Recreation Director Charlie Irish would unlock the gate to the track and Hayes would set up the hurdles and work out hours on end all summer long." That work and perseveres quickly paid off.

Irish worked with Jones tirelessly during those summer workouts at Wisner Stadium. Jones would knock the timbers down and Irish would set them back upright. "I had so much respect for Mr. Irish and we became friends, and when he retired from recreation and moved to Phoenix, I would go and visit him," said Jones.

At the 1955 state finals in East Lansing, Jones tallied 18 2/5 points, a total that would have been good enough by itself to win the state Class A title. But Jones was far from a one-man team for the Chieftains. Pontiac amassed the highest total in state history for schools in Class A-B-C with 51 and 9/10 points, far ahead of runner-up Flint Northern, which totaled 17. This total would have been even more impressive if the top seeded 880-yard relay team had a successful baton pass. As it was, the powerful Chieftains had more point scorers (12) than runner-up Northern had entries (10).

Jones ran a meet record 120-yard hurdles in 14.5 seconds, was a close second in the 180 lows; leaped 22-5 to win the broad jump, and shared third in the high jump. His second-place finish to Benton Harbor's Don Arends, a future football star at Michigan State, would be the last time Jones would taste defeat in a prep hurdles event.

Pontiac's record points total would last only until the next year.

The 1956 track squad could lay claim as the top team of all-time, and one would find few dissenters. With Jones paving the way by sweeping both hurdle events, the Chieftains became the first Michigan high school to ever win the Mansfield Relays in Ohio. At the state championships Coach Shoerkey's powerhouse racked up 61 points, far ahead of Flint Northern, again second with 26.

Under today's formula (10-8-6-5-4-3-2-1) Pontiac would have scored more than 100 points. Throw in events not run by high school athletes in 1956 (3200-meter run, 4 x 800 relay, 4 x 100 relay and discus) and there is little question that Pontiac would have scored even more.

Jones understandably was the undisputed ringleader of this powerhouse. Hayes won the 120-yard high hurdles in 14.4, eclipsing his record mark of 14.5 set a year earlier. In the prelims Jones was clocked in a wind-aided 14.2. The 17-year old added the broad jump title and easily topped all opposition (19.4) in the 180 lows.

After a disappointing non-place winning effort in the 880-yard relay in 1955, Schloerke added Jones to the quartet in 1956. Joined by Archie Brooks, Jim Shorter and Charles Pann, Jones helped the team grab top honors, and ended up winning three first-place medals in addition.

Jones felt that his most impressive achievement during the Class A championships on the University of Michigan's Ferry Field track came in the broad jump. He not only shattered a record that had withstood the test of time for 20 years, but he bettered the former mark on all four of his allotted trials.

Ted Tyrocki of Lansing Eastern held the former record at 22-11¾. Jones's best leap was 23-8 7/8 inches, while his 3 other trials were measured at 23-7, 23-½ and 23-¾ inches. None of his long jump rivals would even surpass 21-feet. Even though Jones would markedly improve his broad jump during his college years, he found his niche as a legendary hurdler.

It was an easy decision for Pontiac Coach Schloerke to drop Jones as a high jumper and move him to the 880-yard relay. Even though Jones had leaped 6-2, he was no better than the third best high jumper on his own team. Hudson Ray and Alex Barge tied for first-place honors at the state meet in 1955 by clearing 6-3½. They repeated their 1-2 performance in 1956.

The Chieftains of '56 were so dominant that they were shut out in only 3 events (100, shot and pole vault). Bill Douglas won his section of the 880 and also took 6th place in the broad jump.

Indoors, Jones was unbeatable for 60-straight races over six years.

The rest of the Jones saga is well documented. He didn't travel across country to attend college, but moved just a few miles down the road to Ypsilanti where he steadily improved. In 1957, he won four events and set four meet records in an hour at the old Interstate Intercollegiate Athletic Conference championships, dashing 9.4 in the 100, hitting 14.5 in the highs, 22.9 in the 220 lows and long jumping 24-5/8. At AAU Nationals, he placed 4th in the 220 lows, 5th in the highs, and earned a trip to Europe where he won several majors. He competed in 58 events during the season—everything from the 100 to the high jump (6-4¾) and won 49 times. In his flagship event, he ended up ranked No. 7 in the world by *Track & Field News*—all as a freshman.

As a sophomore, Jones won AAU hurdle crowns indoors and out—and this time ranked No. 1 in the world at year's end. About the same time, he ended up with a hairline fracture in his ankle from a game of pick-up basketball. He almost quit the sport then, but a talk with college dean Charles Brown set him on course: "He told me how easy it was to quit, that keeping on going is hard, that the best game's to fight when hope is out of sight."

In 1959, he won the NCAA title in a meet record 13.6, finished second in the AAU and captured gold in the Pan-Am Games, ranking No. 2 globally behind World Record setter Martin Lauer of Germany.

As a senior at Eastern Michigan, Jones bypassed the NCAA meet but won the AAU title. His best time, 13.5, came in making the Olympic team behind Lee Calhoun and Willie May. The three repeated that order at the Rome Olympics in a U.S. sweep of the medals ahead of Lauer.

Jones had tasted glory. It wasn't enough. "I knew I couldn't quit until I had won the gold. It was something I had to do."

He dedicated the next four years to being atop that Olympic podium. It wasn't easy. He took a job teaching at Denby High in Detroit. With no coach he hopped the fence at Mumford High School to train himself. He was hired as Denby's track coach, but Avery Brundage, the Detroit-born president of the International Olympic Committee found out and sent a letter to the AAU. He warned that if Jones took the job, he would be banned from the 1964 Olympics for violating his amateurism.

Along the way Jones became the greatest indoor hurdler in world history, setting multiple World Indoor Records and winning 60 races in a row, a legendary streak that stretched for six years. Outdoors, he focused solely on the highs, and won four of the next five AAU National titles. He went into the 1964 Olympic Trials as the strong favorite, but was upset by Willie Davenport.

Teammate Blaine Lindgren, though, knew to never count Jones out. Before the Trials, Jones had told reporters, "I'm tired of running. I'm 25, in pitiful shape and I'm ready to retire."

Lindgren explained, "That's Hayes for you. He knows how to beat you off the track as well as on it. He's a master at psychological warfare. What I mean is that he'll come up to you before a race and casually say, 'I feel great today' or he might tell you something about being in bad shape. The nextthing you know, you're really wondering.

"It took me a while to figure him out. I used to really be nervous and tense around him because he has so much experience and has been around so long. But now I just try to accept it because everyone knows he'll be the favorite any place or any time."

At the Tokyo Olympics, Jones battled back to the top. He said going in, "I'm retiring after the Olympics and right now that gold medal is the most important thing in my life. It is my last chance to prove that I'm the best in the world. I was ranked the best in Rome in 1960, but I wasn't ready to be a champion then. I walked into the stadium and saw 100,000 people and lost my composure. Then I lost everything I had worked for. I cannot forget that experience."

In the Tokyo's Olympic Stadium, Jones was cool and focused. In the final, he blistered a 13.67 to edge Lindgren for the gold. Though he never set a World Record outdoors—save for one as the leadoff against the Russians in a 4 x 100 in 1961—he ascended to the sports' highest honor.

Jones triumphed on the sport's biggest stage.

This author was fortunate to see Jones perform at Eastern Michigan while I was a student at Central Michigan University. Unlike some of today's pampered athletes whose thoughts are "Me first," team second, Jones would participate in just about any event to give his EMU team a better chance for victory. Hayes Jones never forgot his roots, his friends, coaches and teammates he treasured from his youth in Pontiac. And where can one find those precious bronze and gold medals he earned in the Olympics? They are prominently displayed at the Pontiac City Hall, with a proclamation and a photo of the 1964 Olympic games finish of the 100 hurdles finals.

1957

With a new coach and without graduated superstar Hayes Jones, Pontiac still managed to win its third-straight championship in Class A. First-year head coach Dean Wilson's Chieftains copped the title, thanks to a 1-2-3 in the high jump. Hudson Ray, a 6-5 basketball star who liked to jump in his bare feet, won the event at 6-1, far below his record-setting leap of 6-5 5/8 at the CMU Indoor Invitational.

Flint Northern again finished a disappointing second, despite winning two out of the three sections in the 440-yard dash. It should be noted that from a period from 1931 through 1961, sections for both the 880 and 440 were run at the state meet. However, unlike today, the winner of each was called a state champion. And the top four places from each race scored points. Four places were honored and points awarded 5-3-2-1 for the place winners. So for 30 years, the MHSAA crowned two or three state champs in the 440 and 880 at every meet. Only after 1961 did officials see the wisdom of having only one winner based on time.

A cold and dreary day and a rain-soaked track dashed hopes of any records. Namon Smith, Bay City Central's miniature speed merchant, was the meet's top individual performer with 11 2/3 points. He nipped Jerry Fitzpatrick from Muskegon Catholic in the 100-yard dash. Fitzpatrick, captain of the 1961 Notre Dame Track Team, took first-place honors in the broad jump. In 1981 Fitzpatrick would see his daughter Cathy Fitzpatrick win the girls Class A 100-yard dash while competing for Muskegon Mona Shores.

The '50s produced a bevy of NFL stars from Michigan and many of were promising track athletes. Gary Ballman, three sport-standout from East Detroit, placed in both hurdle events. Following a great career at MSU, Ballman scored 252 points over an eleven-year career with four different teams in the NFL.

Placing second in his section of the 880-yard run for the second-straight year was John Bork from

Monroe. It is truly safe to say that Bork had not yet reached his potential. He blossomed into one of the state's all-time best middle distance runners while competing for Western Michigan University. Bork capped his brilliant career as a Bronco thinclad by winning the NCAA championship in 1961 (1:48.3), ten yards ahead of his closest pursuer.

St. Joseph ended the three-year hold by Inkster on the B crown. The two teams battled evenly all afternoon, and were tied at 27 after the final running event of the day. St. Joseph's points in the high jump meant the difference. Jason Harness tied for first in the high jump and in his four events amassed 16½ points to top all point winners. Field conditions in Ann Arbor were certainly no better than in East Lansing.

Willie Prewitt, who earlier in the month had leaped a state record 24-3¾ to break a Jesse Owens meet standard at the Mansfield Relays, could only manage a winning 20-5¾ on the soft runway. Runner-up Inkster had perhaps the best effort of the day from 440-yard dash champion Bill Wyatt. The winner of the Mansfield 440, he romped home an easy winner in 51.7.

Ballman's future football teammate at MSU, Carl Charon, helped lead Boyne City to the Class C title. Boyne City's 27 points easily outdistanced Mt. Clemens St. Mary (18) and Paw Paw (14). Following his MSU career, Charon had a productive two-year stint in the NFL as a defensive back with Buffalo, scoring three TD's and intercepting seven passes.

Future CMU track star Bob Waters repeated with the fastest time in Class C in the 440. He ran two seconds faster than times posted in the other two sections of the 440.

Sophomore Don Voorheis from Frankenmuth began his three-year domination in the sprints in Class C, taking first in the 220 and placing second in the 100 behind Portland's Steve Willard. Harold Arft, Armada's only state champion, successfully defended his 880-yard run title. Armada, the home town of NBC sportscaster Dick Enberg, also beamed with pride when Arft won the 880-yard run against all comers at the Champion of Champions meet in Kalamazoo.

Covert repeated as Class D champion thanks to a courageous effort by Quincy Johnson, who had been stricken with polio during the fall and missed about six weeks of school. He recovered to win the long jump and 220, and anchored Covert's winning 880-yard relay, leading all scorers with 18½ points. Hurdles winner Orville Emerson of runner-up Dansville joined Johnson as the day's only other double winner.

Detroit: Pershing scored fifteen points in the 880-yard run to hold off Detroit Cody for the title. Only one record was set and the meet produced one unusual finish. Miler Al Randall of Northwestern was ten yards in front with the finish line less than twenty yards away. He didn't win, however. His left foot struck the curbing of the track and he sprawled to the ground. The field had passed the disconsolate Randall before he was able to get to his feet, with Denby's Tom Bleakley winning.

Pershing's sprinting foursome of Ron Benson, Ron Bass, Ron Hale and Don Hale ran the second-fastest time in state history in the 880-yard relay. The meet record 1:30.2 fell just two-tenths of a second shy of Northeastern's feat set 30 years earlier in East Lansing.

The meet marked an end of an era for Detroit Miller High School and legendary head coach Leroy Dues. The following fall Miller High would become a junior high school, leaving behind a treasure chest of memories. Miller High's head basketball coach Will Robinson would depart to take over the roundball coaching reigns at Pershing. Following a great career with the Doughboys, where he produced one of Michigan's greatest teams in 1967, Robinson would become the first black to become a Division I head basketball coach when he took over the coaching duties at Illinois State.

Winning the PSL broad jump championship at 21-11¼ was Danny Watkins from Detroit Central. He would later attend nearby Wayne State where he set a long jump record of 24-9½ that lasted for years.

Upper Peninsula: The eastern half of the UP swept honors at the 1957 finals at Engineer Field in Houghton. Sault Ste. Marie won its fourth crown in six years while Pickford kept rolling along in Class D.

In Class C Munising returned to the winner's circle for the first time since 1950. Individually, Ishpeming's Bob Wills and Iron River's Bob Perry were the standouts. Wills won the 100-yard dash and unseated defending champion Perry in the 180-yard lows. Perry turned the table on Wills by winning the broad jump over the Ishpeming star. Perry earlier had successfully defended his title in the 120-yard high hurdles.

Munising's Francis Bray ran about 800 of the 880-yards without his shoe, but still triumphed to help the Mustangs claim their team title. After leading Chassell to the state basketball championship in March, Don Mattson took a pair of firsts in the long jump and shot put in Class D.

The UP finals would see Rod Paavala of Hancock top all vaulters with a best effort of 11-2. Paavala would win a gold medal at the 1960 Olympic Games-- not in track and field, but as a member of the victorious USA hockey team.

1958

Pontiac Central and Flint Northern, for the fourth consecutive year, finished 1-2 at the state Class A championships in Ann Arbor. Pontiac edged Flint Northern and Flint Central in the 880 relay thanks, in part, to a spectacular anchor leg by Bob Manning.

Manning, who had won the 100 and 220 in the 1956 and 1957 Detroit City meet while a student at Detroit Western, became a welcome addition for coach Dean Wilson's title winners. In addition to his leg on the victorious 880-yard relay, Manning duplicated his Detroit City League feat in capturing both dash races at the state level.

Veteran *Flint Journal* sports writer Doug Mintline called the 1958 track meet the most spectacular in state history. Pontiac avenged two earlier setbacks to Flint Northern to again capture the A title, but not before perennial runner-up Flint Northern ran into a stroke of misfortune in the meet's final event. Broad jump champion Reg Gillard was running in first place when he stepped on the cement curb just before the straightaway. Gillard was thrown off stride, and by the time he recovered, he had dropped into last place before heading into the first exchange zone. Northern's margin of defeat was by only a stride or two. A win for Northern would have given coach Norb Badar's crew the trophy.

One of Michigan's all-time prep track greats made his championship debut in the 1958 meet. Rex Cawley won two first-place medals in the hurdles. He cruised to an easy victory in the 180-yard lows in a meet record 19.0, the No. 4 time posted by a high school runner in the United States that year. His win in the 120-yard high hurdles was not as easy, however. Cawley and East Detroit's Gary Ballman were both clocked in 14.5 seconds, and it took the judges a full five minutes to determine that Cawley had edged the future MSU and NFL speedster.

Bill Alcorn shattered a sixteen-year old record, held by Forrest Naveaux of Monroe in the pole vault with a mark of 12-11¾. The Birmingham star was hard pressed for the victory by Muskegon's Dick Cahill, whose second-place 12-9½ also surpassed Naveaux's 1942 record of 12-7½. Grosse Point junior Rem Purdy cut more than three seconds off the all-time state mile record with a time of 4:21.8, making him the No. 6 prep miler nationally that year.

East Grand Rapids' second-place finish in the 880-yard relay propelled Reed Waterman's club to another Class B state title. The meet was highlighted by a spectacular performance by Willie Prewitt of Willow Run. Prewitt set a meet record with a leap of 23-2¾ in winning the broad jump for the third consecutive year.

His wind-aided 21.6 captured the 220. He capped his career by anchoring the Flyers to the 880-yard relay title. He had also been the heavy favorite in the 100, but false-started in the morning preliminaries. Sadly, though Prewitt earned MVP honors in his first year at Ferris State, he never competed beyond that.

Larry Horgan of Big Rapids inched the pole vault meet record up a notch with his winning 12-5¼ in Class B. Sam Hughes became the first state champ in North Muskegon history when he cleared 6-1 to capture the high jump. In 1989 Hughes was indeed a proud father as he watched his son Mark co-captain the University of Michigan to the NCAA basketball championship.

Don Voorheis stole the show in Class C, blazing his way to a pair of dash championships. The Frankenmuth speedster had the day's fastest times in the 100 and 220. He clipped .2 off the longtime 100 dash mark shared by Paw Paw's Alan Smith and Boyne City's Ham White, running away from the field in 9.8. He again brought the large crowd in Mt. Pleasant to its feet with a spectacular 21.0 in the 220—albeit one with a huge 4.5mps (10mph) tailwind that helped him along considerably.

Frankenmuth's Don Voorhies and his coach.

Boyne City edged Grosse Ile's one-man crew of Charles Peltz to bring the trophy back in Class C. Peltz won three individual titles by capturing both hurdles and the broad jump to account for 18 of Grosse Ile's 21-point total. His 19.6 clocking for the 180-yard low hurdles was a meet record. The champs got a 6-1½ leap from future Big 10 champion Steve Williams in the high jump. Bob Waters of Montrose, for the third-straight season, posted the fastest time in any of the three sections run in the 440-yard dash.

Class D tracksters capped a day meant for records with a memorable effort of their own. Brethren concluded its magical run in the '50s by taking its fifth title in seven years. Reports from the meet in Mt.

Pleasant mentioned five records tumbling from the record books. Ken Beane could have possibly been omitted as another record setter with his mark of 21.5 in the 220-yard dash. Since Voorheis's 220 mark, shortly following Beane's run, was documented as wind aided, the author speculates that Beane's burst was likewise helped by excessive winds. Beane did tie the mark in winning the 100-yard dash for the fourth-straight year with a time of 10.2.

Brethren won both relays in record-setting fashion: the medley in 2:35.1 and the 880-yard relay in 1:34.5. Included among the winning relay team members for Brethren were Lionel and Larry Connelly, first cousins of the most famous Brethren grad of all. Although not a member of the Norsemen track team, 1949 Brethren graduate James Earl Jones ("This is CNN!") would go on to become a legend in the film industry.

Many of the state champions displayed their talents at the 3rd annual Champion of Champions meet in Kalamazoo. All four of the state sprint stars toed the starting line in an eagerly awaited battle to determine Michigan's fastest sprinter. Bob Manning, the Class A champion, won the 100 and 220-yard dashes with Jim Drake of Lake Orion (Class B) and Ken Beane of Brethren (Class D) placing 2nd and 3rd respectively in each event. Many called state Class C record holder Don Voorheis as the pre-meet favorite, but it just wasn't his day. He finished far back in the pack in each race, but would make amends in Kazoo country two years later, winning the state AAU title as an MSU freshman.

Rex Cawley was dubbed the most outstanding performer with his twin victories in the hurdles, an honor he would duplicate the following year. Cawley was the only athlete ever to capture the MVP more than once. Sophomore Mac Hunter from Muskegon Heights leaped 23-3 to take honors in the long jump. Hunter, plagued with nagging injuries throughout his prep career, owned the Greater Muskegon long jump record for many decades with that leap.

Detroit: It took 30 years, but Redford easily captured its first-ever title. Earlier, coach Bruce Wawa's Thinclads edged Class A state champion Pontiac Central by one half point in taking the U of D relays, perhaps rightfully proclaiming bragging rights for the entire state. Redford's balance, plus firsts by miler Louis Molnar and shot putter Len Cranston, paced the winners to victory.

Cass Tech senior Claude Miller bilstered the 100 in 9.8 and covered 220 in 21.7. A strong wind aided the sprinters, and despite objections from head referee Leighton Boyd, meet directors awarded Miller records in both.

After sharing first place his first two years, Denby's Jerry DeHanau won the pole vault championship outright at 11-8. DeHanau had surprised Class A record holder Bill Alcorn at the University of Detroit Relays, defeating the Birmingham ace with a vault of 12-5½.

Upper Peninsula: Perhaps the greatest array of talent ever assembled in the UP graced the finals in Marquette. Bob Wills of Ishpeming and Bob Perry of Iron River capped their high school careers by each winning three firsts.

Rain and very cool temperatures undoubtedly hindered what surely could have been an all-out assault on the record book. One meet record that did fall came in the Class B shot put. Burly Dave Manders, future MSU and Dallas Cowboy star, shattered a twelve-year old record in the shot put, hurling the iron ball 52-7¾ inches. Manders would go on to play a full decade in the NFL.

Nothing changed in 1958 as far as team champions were concerned. Sault Ste. Marie, Munising and Pickford all successfully defended their titles.

The Decade of Brethren

Any track fan that followed the sport back in the 1950's would most likely recall the incredible mastery of the Norsemen from Norman Dickson Brethren. They would also undoubtedly be curious as to why their domination in track and field would not carry over into later years. Brethren was the scourge of track and field during this long-ago decade, punishing Class D (and higher) foes by procuring five state championships and a runner-up placing over a seven-year span. Except for a brief return to glory in 1963, where Brethren would place second in the team battle, this tiny school, nestled in the woods of Manistee County, would never again make such a splash.

Located miles from any major highway, Brethren is truly just a dot on the map. The high school drew from a sparsely populated district that covered more than 200 square miles. Some students would come from as much as 45 miles away, quite a round trip to practice a sport, let alone procure an education.

The track program at the school began with the 1949-50 school year and quickly the Norsemen made an immediate impact. With Fred Beane placing 2nd in three events, Brethren placed a very respectable fourth at the state Class D championships, a harbinger of better things to come. The name of Beane would prove to be a nightmare to rival schools, and a name that would bring more medals to a single family than

*Fred Beane's leadoff on the winning 4x2 in
1951 marked the first of 19 victories by
various members of the Beane family.*

perhaps any other household in prep history. The
Beane brothers would win an unprecedented 18 first-
place medals, far more than any other brother
combination in state annals. In addition, first cousins
of the Beane brothers would pad the Beane total over
the years by winning four more titles.

Although townsfolk talk in reverence of their track
dynasty of the '50s, it was a non-athlete who would
put this tiny little hamlet on the world map. One year
before the track team was founded, a man who aspired
to be an actor on the stage, would ultimately become a
household name throughout the world. The famous
actor James Earl Jones never had the opportunity to
participate in track, but his first cousins would aid in
winning many state laurels.

Brethren's dynasty took place without the aid of a
track. Although this was not unusual for many small
schools throughout the state, there wasn't even a track
to practice on in the entire county. The '50s and '60s
would find the Manistee County meet conducted in
either Traverse City or Ludington.

This didn't deter from the enthusiasm or diminish
the skills and speed developed by the small group of
prepsters. The track team ran its practice sessions on a
sand track; Brethren coaches believed the resistance
training may have helped. After enduring many
workouts on the soft under footing all spring, the
Norsemen would get a psychological lift when they hit
the manicured cinder layouts of the time.

Head Coach Bob Dunnavan, and later Doyle
Eckhart, would draw their talent from a pool that
seldom boasted of an enrollment of much more than 50
boys. Interest was so high in 1951 that 26 out of the 42
boys enrolled in school were members of the track
team. This same unbelievable percentage of
participants would remain a constant throughout the
decade.

Norman-Dickson Brethren would not hesitate to take
on all comers. The Norsemen rolled to the Class D title
at the Central Michigan Relays—at the time the
Nation's biggest track prep meet—in 1951, 1952, 1953,
1954, 1955, 1957 and 1958, with seconds in 1956 and
1959.

The CMU Relays would annually attract more than
2,000 athletes, and Brethren would challenge the Class
D powerhouse from the Upper Peninsula, Pickford.
Coach Webb Morrison's Panthers from the Eastern UP
had put together a quality program. From 1951 thru
1976 Pickford would win 27 straight UP state Class D
championships. In the '50s, only Brethren could boast
supremacy over coach Morrison's powerhouse.

In 1951 at the state championships Dunnavan's
thinclads nearly grabbed their first team title in but
their second year in track, placing one point behind
runner-up Benton Harbor St. John, and only seven
behind first-place Otisville. The foursome of Fred
Beane, Richard Beane, Burt Burns and Bob Phillips, all
African-Americans, won their school's initial first-
place prize, teaming up for the 880-yard relay.

At the 1951 CMU Relays, Brethren used its superior
strength in the sprint relays to place well ahead of
Otisville and Benton Harbor St. John. This small group
of families would be joined in later years by siblings
from the Thomas and Connolly households. Beginning
with the 1952 season, the names of Beane, Burns,
Phillips, Connolly and Thomas would signify
supremacy in track and field in Northern Michigan
circles.

Early into the 1952 season it was plain to see that
coach Dunnavan and his loyal assistant Doyle
Eckhardt had formed a powerhouse. At the Manistee
County meet, held on a makeshift track on the
Onekama Fair Grounds, Brethren won every event but
the shot put. The team also defended its championship
at the CMU Relays. With the big block letters N-D
stenciled across the fronts of their uniform tops, the
speedsters from Norman Dickson Brethren more than
doubled the score of their closest pursuers at the 1952
state meet.

Don Stroup took the graduated Fred Beane's spot on the 880-yard relay and greatly aided the state championship effort, winning a title in the high jump. Richard Beane won the first of his five individual titles in the 120-yard high hurdles on the muddy MSU cinders.

Brethren was even more dominant in 1953. The Norsemen, with their total of 67½ points, the highest total in state history. Scored on a 6-5-4-3-2-1 scale, the team won its second-straight team trophy by 40 points. Earlier, at the CMU Relays, the Norsemen were even more impressive, racking up an amazing 76 points, with first-place finishes in five relays.

At the state Class D championships Brethren, led by two record-breaking performances by hurdler Richard Beane, scored in all but two events (880-yard run and broad jump). Oddly enough, Beane set a record in the high hurdles during the morning preliminaries, but was nipped at the tape in the finals by Beal City's Joe Therring. Beane's record-breaking time of 20.8 over the 180-yard lows, however, did net him a first-place.

Doyle Eckhardt took over the reigns from a busy Bob Dunnavan in 1954. Dunnavan was busy enough being both teacher and superintendent. Eckhardt also was busy. The 1950 CMU grad served as the school principal, taught a full workload of classes and coached baseball, basketball and baseball. As a coach he earned $125—for the entire school year!

Eckhardt pointed out how difficult it had become to locate meets within their area. "We would go to every track meet we could up here," said Eckhardt, "but we had trouble getting meets with the bigger schools. We ran a dual meet in the early years with Cadillac. We won the meet and they didn't ask us back. We ran a triangular with Ludington and Manistee. We won and they didn't ask us back. So we had a little trouble finding track meets."

In early May, before three thousand rabid track fans at a jammed Alumni Field in Mt. Pleasant, the Norsemen easily breezed to their fourth-straight Central Michigan Relays title, scoring 30 points more then their closest competitor.

Fortunately for Brethren fans, an invite wasn't necessary for the state championships. Eckhardt's tracksters again easily copped their third-straight Class D state crown. Led once again by Richard Beane's four first-place finishes, Brethren captured eight out of 13 events, placed second in three more, and for good measure gobbled up a couple of third-place medals.

Robert Phillips took both short sprints, Richard Spoor successfully defended the mile, and Daryl Leckrone won the pole vault. Walter Thomas teamed up with Phillips, Beane and Leckrone to take the 880-yard relay. Beane had earlier equaled his own record (15.7) in winning the 120-yard high hurdles, just missed his own mark in the 180 lows (21.0) and took his third individual win in the high jump.

A couple more Beane's arrived on the scene in 1955. Richard's young brother Ken won the 100-yard dash as a freshman. By the time he would graduate, he had won the century four straight years, the second prep athlete in Michigan history to accomplish this. Charles Beane, a first cousin to Ken Beane, provided depth in the sprints and relays.

At the 1955 state championships in Ann Arbor, fans were again rewarded with an amazing display of first-place power. Ken Beane, Walter Thomas and Norman Burns were multiple winners for coach Eckhardt's speedsters. Burns led the way with three first-places. Burns, with a winning toss of 49-3¾ inches in the shot put, erased a 21-year-old record from the books. After winning the 440-yard dash, Burns teamed up with the two Beanes and Walter Thomas to easily capture the 880-yard relay.

The Norsemen went 1-2 in the 220, without using 100 champ Ken Beane. Walter Thomas led teammate Charles Beane to the tape to give the winners 11 big points en route to their fourth-straight state championship.

In 1956 upstart Covert—in its first year of track—dashed Brethren's bid for a fifth-straight title in East Lansing. Cousins Ken and Charles Beane lacked sufficient help to pull off the state title, settling for runner-up honors, three and a half points behind Covert. Ken Beane won the 100 and 220-yard dashes with cousin Charles placing in the same events. The Norsemen finally lost at the CMU relays, with UP power Pickford turning the trick.

In 1957 Brethren was topped as state champions, despite winning the CMU relays.

The Norsemen bounced back the next year to cap their amazing run in a blaze of glory. The thinclads took an early lead at the CMU Relays and were never threatened in Class D. Coach Eckhardt's Norsemen captured seven out of 16 first places, adding one second and a fourth for a whopping 64 points, more than 40 points ahead of the UP champs from Pickford.

Undaunted by the prospect of facing stiff competition at the Petoskey Relays, Eckhardt's plucky band of speedsters made the long trek north a triumphant success. In the C-D division Brethren once again challenged Pickford as well as the defending 1957 state champs from nearby Boyne City. The Ramblers from Boyne City had earlier won the Class C title at the CMU Relays, and would go on to win their second-straight Class C state title later in the month.

As daylight disappeared, a sudden chill set in. Eckhardt had to do some real prodding to get his now frozen speedsters to prepare them for the relay. "I told them that if they wanted that first-place trophy and some more medals, then they were going to have to win the relay," recalled Eckhardt. The meet ended on a fitting note for Brethren supporters; sprinter Kenny Beane held off Carl Charon on the final leg of the 880 relay to win in 1:35.9. That time was nearly four seconds faster than the winning time posted by Traverse City in the A-B division. "I can still remember Kenny Beane beating Carl Charon on the anchor leg to win that meet."

The Norsemen dazzled the spectators gathered by winning the C-D division with 47½ points to Boyne City's 42. Brethren's domination ended in with a record-breaking effort at the state championships in Mt. Pleasant. Ken Beane capped his career by winning the century for the fourth-straight year (10.2), and taking three more first-place medals. Beane blazed the 220 in an unofficial 21.5, a time that may have been too generous, and anchored one of the Norsemen two record-setting relay teams.

The Brethren medley foursome of Lionel Connolly, Frank Thomas, Lawrence Connolly and Charles Beane shattered the meet record by almost five seconds. Their time of 2:35.5 was only 0.2 away from the Class C state meet record.

Ken Beane anchored the 880-relay foursome to yet another Class D best (1.34.5.) So deep were the speedsters with the big N-D on their jersey tops that Carl Smith, winner of the open 440, was not called upon to run in either relay.

Brethren would remain competitive over the next decade, but only with a second-place finish in 1963 would the Norsemen throw a scare into their opponents. The last member of the "Fab Five" families to procure a first-place medal would be Roger Connolly in 1968. Over the next 30 years only hurdler Greg Kapus in the early '90s would bring a first-place medal back to the quiet community.

Although most of their siblings have long ago left the Brethren area to seek a better economic environment, the parents, those that are still alive, elected to stay and retire among the peaceful environs. Doyle Eckhardt, who first arrived in Brethren nearly fifty years ago, never left. When prodded on how much influence he played in the success of the era, he replied: "Aaaagh! I always figured if you had the talent than you only had to give them a little direction."

The state track scene has seen several parochial schools from major metropolitan cities dominate action at the state meets. But to see a group of athletes, predominately representing by only five families from such a sparsely populated area, may be a story never to be witnessed again by Michigan prep fans. But during the 1950's Brethren High School was the Hickory of "Hoosiers" fame in the Wolverine state.

1959

Could this have been the year with the most top-end talent ever? Headlining them all was a pair who would stand at the top of the Olympic victory stand in 1964. Rex Cawley put on an exhibition in East Lansing that would stand as perhaps the most memorable in state history. In Detroit, Henry Carr dazzled the fans.

Although many performed admirably, the 1959 state meet belonged to Cawley. Longtime track fans that witnessed his accomplishments have often mentioned this as the most memorable state meet performance of all-time. A thumbnail sketch of his day:

1. Tied Hayes Jones mark of 14.4 in the 120-yard high hurdles.

2. Won the 180-yard low hurdles in 19.2, only two-tenths of a second off the record he established in 1958.

3. In his final attempt in the broad jump he cleared 22-8¼ inches to win the event.

4. Trailing by twelve yards (some observers swear it was farther) against top notch sprinters on the final leg of the 4 x 220, Cawley nipped Flint Northern's Maurice Pea and Saginaw Arthur Hill's Jim Bublitz at the tape.

All this despite rain in the morning and raw temperatures in the afternoon that left the Michigan State track surface soggy and slow. One can only speculate what kind of times the 1959 boy wonder would have produced under better conditions. A week before, Cawley set a national record for the highs at 13.9.

Overshadowed by Cawley was the first-place finish by Flint Central, garnering its first title ever. Once again cross-town rival Flint Northern played the role of the bridesmaid, finishing second for the sixth-straight season. The only record-breaking performance in Class A came in the pole vault by Birmingham's Bill Alcorn, who would go down in Michigan history as one of the best pole vaulters in the pre-fiberglass era.

Among the six competitors who shared first place in the high jump was Jackson's Alonzo Littlejohn. The modest 6-1 height he cleared would hardly portend his accomplishments as a collegian for Western Michigan University. The two-time Mid-American champion tied for eighth at the 1961 NCAA championships. He proved that was no fluke the next year, tieing for second at 6-9.

A pair of lightning-fast dash men, Naosha Poe and Otis Harrison, vaulted Willow Run to its first Class B title. The duo accounted for 21 points, the same total that runner-up Cranbrook posted. Just as in Class A, the only new Class B mark came in the vault with Wendell Johnson of Birmingham Troy erasing Larry Hogan's old mark with a 12-8. Art Welch matched John Palmer's 1956 record-breaking low hurdle clocking of 20.0 in the 180s.

The Class B individual star was Flint Bendle's Paul Krause, who cleared 6-0 to win the high jump, vaulted 12-4 for second place, and jumped 20-7¼ for fourth. Krause, unlike Cawley and Carr, would make his niche in a different sport—playing football for the New York Giants. In his 15 years in the NFL, Krause set a record with 81 pass interceptions, a stat that helped put him into the NFL Hall of Fame in 1998.

One might think that Krause, the first Michigan prep athlete to make the NFL shrine in Canton, Ohio, would be the highest ranked draft pick to come out of the 1959 state Class B meet. Not so. That honor would belong to shot put champion Dave Behrman from Dowagiac, the first choice by Buffalo of the AFL, but also an opening round pick of the Chicago Bears in the rival NFL. Krause was only a second-round pick of the Washington Redskins.

Charles Peltz led Grosse Ile to the Class C state title with a two-point margin over Flint Dye. He repeated as hurdles champion but again it was Frankenmuth's Don Voorheis who stole the spotlight. Sticky mud, churned up by a heavy early morning rain, prevented Voorheis from lowering his 100-yard dash meet standard, but his 21.6 time in the 220 was a meet record.

Schoolcraft captured only one first place but had enough depth to hold off Covert for the Class D crown.

Detroit: Down the road at Detroit Pershing, site of the Motor City championships, Henry Carr flashed a preview of his talents by shattering both dash records. Unfortunately, out-state fans would never get to see Carr perform his brilliance outside the Motor City during his high school years. One can only speculate how much of an impact Carr's exploits made in

hastening the Detroit Public School League's entrance back to state competition following his graduation in 1961.

Carr, a sophomore at Southwestern, sped the 100-yard dash in 9.7 and the 220 in a quick 21.0 in qualifying races that longtime track writer Hal Schram called aided by an 8-10mph wind. That same day in qualifying, Felton Rogers of Eastern, future gridiron great at the University of Iowa, leaped 6-6 to set a new mark in the high jump.

Two days later at the finals, Carr nursed a sore hamstring and carefully stepped to wins in 10.1 and 21.8. Jerry Burrell of Northern erased Cliff Robinson's 35-year record in the broad jump by sailing 23-¾. Terry Moore, 16-year old Redford sophomore, lowered the mile record down to 4:23.6.

Upper Peninsula: Weather also dampened individual efforts at the UP finals held on the Northern Michigan College track in Marquette. Dick Koski of Wakefield was the day's individual star, winning four events in leading Wakefield to the Class C title. He overcame the elements to snare a record in the long jump with a leap of 21-3. His other wins in the high jump, shot put and 100 also were the UP's best marks in any class.

Marquette won the Class B championship and Pickford, of course, repeated in Class D, sweeping both sections of the 440 and 880-yard runs.

Cawley's Road To Gold

Back in the late 1990's, while attending a high school coaching convention in Lansing, I had the opportunity to sit down and interview 3 coaching legends, Norb Badar, Marty Crane and Bryan Westfield.

One question I asked was: "What was your most memorable moment at the state finals?"

I was blown away when they each came up with the same answer: Warren "Rex" Cawley and his blistering anchor leg in the 880-yard relay in 1959.

Not that their answer should have surprised me, as over time I've been given the same answer by others who were at those same 1959 Class A/B finals at MSU.

How I would have liked to have been there at the finals in 1959, but this 'plodding' trackster didn't qualify from the regional meet. If only Jeff Hollobaugh had written his book: How To Race The Mile, some 50 years earlier, than perhaps I may have made it to East Lansing with some of my teammates.

Those who were at the state A/B finals at MSU that day will not soon forget Cawley's epic dash in the

Rex Cawley went on to USC where he won the 1963 NCAA title at the 440 hurdles. The next year he captured the Olympic gold medal after breaking the World Record in the 400 hurdles at the Trials.

day's final event. Although the distance that Cawley trailed his competitors seems to lengthen with age, many swear that the Farmington speedster was some 20 yards behind the lead runners when he grasped the baton on his anchor leg.

After getting the baton from teammate Roy Jordan, Cawley took off like a streak of lightening. He passed runners as if they were mailboxes planted in the ground as a "Oohs" and "Aahs" rang up from the 5,000 spectators. Finally Cawley reeled in Flint Northern's Maurice Pea, nipping him at the finish line by inches. Earlier, Pea had placed 2nd in the 220-yard dash. Cawley's reported split for his anchor leg? A stunning 20.3.

No less than an authority than MSU football coaching legend Duffy Daugherty said, "I've never seen anybody run as fast as that kid.".

Cawley's come-from-behind victory capped a perfect day. Despite running on a cinder track that was soggy and slow from steady morning rains, he won the broad jump with a leap of 22-8¼, equaled the state record in the 120-yard high hurdles held by Hayes Jones, and just missed his own 180-yard low hurdle record with a time of 19.2.

My first, and only chance, to watch Cawley compete in person was at the CMU Relays in early May of 1959. For many years, the CMU Relays was billed as the largest track & field carnival in the country, attracting hundreds of teams from the state of Michigan to compete at Old College Field in Mt. Pleasant.

I was there as a member of my North Muskegon High School track team. The level of competition at CMU was so high that my Norsemen track team that would soon win the West Michigan Conference championship, scored nary a point at the Chip Relays.

My attention was quickly diverted to a heat of the 120-yard high hurdles, where I watched this slender athlete with a perfectly trimmed crew cut glide effortlessly over the hurdles as if they were not even there. Shortly after this heat, the PA announcer pronounced Cawley's time in this morning preliminary as 13.8 seconds and a new USA high school record!

Shortly thereafter he blazed over the 180-yard low hurdles in yet another high school record of 18.4 seconds. Those marks, however, would last only until Cawley moved into the blocks for the afternoon finals.

Cawley, who had earlier placed first in the high jump, then was timed in 13.7 to again lower his mark for the high hurdles. All eyes were on the Farmington speedster for the start of the finals of the 180-yard low hurdles. Cawley, again went under the USA high school record with a spectacular time of 18.3 seconds, well below the listed USA record of 18.5.

Four races and four national records! Or were they? Before long the announcer corrected himself, and reported that all of Cawley's performances that day had been wind-aided. The Free Press later reported that winds during his races were measured from 6-8 mph (the legal limit is 4.47mph, or 2.0mps).

Although I was a neophyte track aficionado, as well as a plodding runner, I did not notice any anemometer present.

Cawley's high school career would officially end with the state finals at MSU but that would just be a tune-up for the big meets ahead of him later that summer. Just a few days after his one-man show at MSU, Cawley participated in the Champion of Champions Meet in Kalamazoo.

The conditions were no better on the first of June as heavy rains again made for a soggy track. Cawley again won the highs in 14.4, the lows in 19.3 and was clocked at 21.4 for his split on the winning 880-relay team. He was an easy choice as the outstanding performer of the year, an award he had also won the previous year.

One has to wonder what Rex could have accomplished during his senior season at Farmington if only he could have had decent weather. The elements would certainly change as Cawley embarked on a very busy summer season.

Competing against the nations' finest track performers of all ages at the AAU Nationals in Boulder, Colorado, Cawley placed in all three hurdle events, the only man to ever do so.

In the 400-meter hurdles, the soon-to-be USC frosh continually missed his steps and was forced to chop his stride. In spite of his mistakes in the first time he had ever run the event, he was clocked in an eye-popping 51.3 and moved into the event finals.

The next day Cawley competed in the 200-meter low hurdles, where his semifinal race was one of the greatest ever. The more-experienced Hayes Jones won in 22.9, followed by Cawley. His 23.0 would be a World Junior Record for this race run around a curve. Rex drew the sharp-curved inside lane for the final in the heat that included the first two place winners at the recent NCAA championships, Jones and Kansas track star Charley Tidwell.

Running in the rain, Tidwell passed Jones on the curve to take a yard-and-a-half lead heading into the stretch. Jones, who had earlier defeated Tidwell at the NCAA finals, nearly caught Tidwell but the Kansas senior nipped the former Pontiac Central star at the finish line in a new World Record of 22.6.

"Running like some kind of a demon," as reported in *Track & Field News*, Cawley placed third, just 4 yards behind the winner.

Then came the highs, run over the college/international height of 42-inches. Cawley placed an amazing 5th in a race that featured the likes of Lee Calhoun and Hayes Jones.

After a grueling day on the track, a dog-tired Cawley entered the blocks for his fourth race of the day, the 400-meter finals. Understandably exhausted, he still managed to lug across the finish line in 6th.

His spectacular showing at the AAU Nationals earned him a trip on the European tour later in the summer, the only high school athlete selected.

Just a year after his heroics at the 1959 state championships, Cawley made it into the 400 hurdle finals at the 1960 Olympic Trials, where he placed a respectable 7th.

It only took one year at USC before Rex became the face of the Trojan program. Competing in sunny southern California, Cawley stole the show at the Mt. San Antonio Relays in late April of 1961.

He anchored the USC mile relay team to a collegiate record with a blistering 45.4. He also won the 400 hurdles in 50.6. A third meet record was achieved when he ran a leg on the 880-yard relay team.

In May of 1961, he broke the 50-second barrier for the first time over the 400 hurdles (49.9) but later suffered a cramp while running a blistering leg of the 880-relay.

Cawley would battle some nagging injuries over the next two years but all was well during the all-important Olympic year of 1964. Running in front of a huge crowd at the Olympic Trials held at the LA Coliseum, Cawley blew away the field with his World Record 49.1.

Then came the Tokyo Olympics, and Cawley was less than 100 percent healthy for the biggest race of his career. A leg injury troubled him for the first two rounds. Even in the finals the former Farmington star had trouble perfecting his steps through the first seven hurdles before straightening things out over the final three. He made it to the finish line ahead of John Cooper of Great Britain, winning the gold in 49.6.

"The tension of competing in the Olympics is indescribable," remarked Cawley shortly after winning the gold medal at the 1964 Olympiad. "Two hours before the race you do everything but climb walls. The pressure bears heavily on your mind and saps your strength. I was so nervous I couldn't stay still.

"Then once the gun goes off, the dam breaks and the tension eases. I didn't see anything but the tape."

Cawley would be one of three former Michigan prep stars to stand on the top step of the podium and receive a gold medal in Tokyo. Pontiac's Hayes Jones and Detroit's Henry Carr would all receive gold medals (Carr earned a second gold while running on the winning 4x400 relay).

1960

Pontiac Central literally threw itself to the 1960 Class A state championship. The best trio of high school putters in state history helped the Chieftains claim a fifth title in six years. Bill Pritchett, future Detroit Lion star Jerry Rush and Charlie Brown scored fourteen of Pontiac's 44 points.

Pritchett and Rush each eclipsed Muskegon's Joel Boyden's 57-0 record set in 1955, with Pritchett's 59-5¾ leading the way. Despite less than ideal conditions, another record was broken and three other existing marks were near casualties. Future University of Michigan record holder Al Ammerman of Dearborn leaped 6-4½ to erase Milt Mead's mark set a decade earlier.

The winds died down long enough for Flint Northern's Maurice Pea to sprint the 100-yard dash in 9.8 seconds, matching the mark held by three other sprinters of the past. Pea nearly set a new record in the 220 with his time of 21.3, but the winds were clocked at 2.7mps, just over the allowable 2.0.

Flint Northern, again, was second with 41 points, a total that would have won six out of the past ten meets. Steve Jacobson almost singlehandedly led Birmingham to a third-place finish. He fell about an inch shy of the broad jump mark of Hayes Jones at 23-7½. Ironically, he fouled on his first three trials before unleashing the second-best jump in meet history on his fourth and final attempt.

One could assume that if a team would win six first places at a state championship meet, then it would breeze to the team title. Not the case, however, for the Class B meet held at Houseman Field in Grand Rapids. Ecorse won six events, but needed its win in the 880-yard relay to hold off a very tough Cranbrook squad, taking the state championship with 48 3/11 points to Cranbrook's 46 6/11. Ecorse won the 880-yard relay over a Cranbrook foursome that included Barney Crouse and Larry DeWitt, 1-2 place winners in the 220-yard dash. DeWitt could very well have also captured the 100-yard title earlier in the afternoon, but eased up 20 yards short of the tape, believing he had crossed the line the winner. DeWitt wound up third, trailing winner Craig LaGrone of Detroit Lutheran West and his teammate Crouse.

In Class B, defending champ Bob Sherman set a meet record in the 120-yard highs with a 14.5 during the morning prelims and was later matched by Charles Gray of Ecorse. Gray won the final at 14.5, sharing the record with Sherman. The two would later play football together at the University of Iowa. Although not matching the incomparable career of Krause, Sherman also matriculated to the pro ranks, playing two years as a defensive back for the Pittsburgh Steelers.

A few days following his section win in the 880-yard run, Sparta's Rush Ring stunned track followers by pulling off a huge upset at the Champion of Champions classic in Kalamazoo. After winning at state in 2:03.3 on a rain-soaked track, Ring elected to move up to the mile in Kalamazoo. He set a new meet record (4:26.6) in defeating Jan Bowen of Alma and undefeated Class C titleholder Dick Pickering from East Jackson.

Jim Born of Dowagiac suffered an unfortunate accident on the turn of the 220-yard dash. As he was streaking around the curve, the judge on the curve inadvertently stepped onto the track and bumped Born. After breaking stride and losing several yards, he finished sixth.

Ecorse's Jerry Holmes was pushed to his record in the high jump by 6-10 All-State basketball star Bill Chmielewski of Detroit Holy Redeemer. Holmes leaped 6-2½ to better Bill Dale's meet record of 6-2 set back in 1942.

Haslett won the Class C title by scoring 19 points, second-lowest championship point total recorded in state history. Despite a driving rain, Dick Pickering of East Jackson set a meet record with his 4:33.4 mile. The rain forced the pole vault indoors for most of the competition. Rich Schlegelmilch of Burton Bentley vaulted 12-2 for the win, but then officials moved him back outdoors for his attempts at 12-7, even though the rain was coming down. He couldn't make the bar.

Placing sixth in the Class C high jump was perhaps Bangor's greatest all-around athlete, Pete Gent. Best remembered in Bangor for leading his basketball team to its only state championship back, Gent followed up his prep career by starring in basketball at Michigan State. Despite not having played any collegiate football, Gent played five years as an end for the Dallas Cowboys. Following his NFL career Gent made an even bigger name for himself as the author of the top selling novel Dallas North Forty.

Henry Carr's city meet was magnificent: 9.5 state record, 20.6 state record, 23-1½, and anchor on a state record relay.

By winning a section in the 440, Dick Smith became Montague's first champion. But Smith's performance didn't make him more popular than classmate Nancy Ann Fleming who was crowned Miss America the following fall in Atlantic City.

Covert and Schoolcraft again again took the top two spots in Class D, but Covert came out on top this time. Unionville pole-vaulter Ken Gangler smashed the oldest standing Class D record with a 11-6½, topping the mark of Anthony Mazey of Middleton in 1936. Gangler, however, did not compete in corduroy trousers and canvas-backed shoes as Mazey wore nearly a quarter of a century earlier.

Detroit: As good a meet as the Class A athletes put on in Ann Arbor, it may have paled in comparison to the Detroit city championships. Henry Carr, who had transferred to Northwestern, again was the individual hero by setting three records. During qualifying trials Carr was clocked in a state record 9.5 in the 100-yard dash. Unlike previous years, meet officials made certain that any records set by Carr would be official. Veteran head timer Ken Mateson had five timers and a wind gauge assigned to the meet.

The winds were clocked at an allowable 1.7mps when Carr blazed the 220 in a state record 20.6. This followed another meet record in the broad jump, with the 6-3 junior sailing 23-1½. His blazing anchor leg of the 880-yard relay helped the Colts to smash the record, easily posting the fastest time recorded in Michigan schoolboy history at 1:28.2. Not since Jesse

Owens' magic moment at Ann Arbor's Ferry Field had track fans been treated to such an impressive demonstration of talent. Four events, four wins and four records!

Carr's performances were not the only thrills experienced by the 4,500 fans that jammed the Redford track, the largest turnout in Motor City history. Frank Carissimi of Denby, with his winning time of 4:17.7, powered his way through splits of 64.3, 2:09.7 and 3:13.0 to record the fastest mile in Michigan prep history, breaking his own mark from six days earlier by a mere 0.3. Fred Hatcher of Northwestern heaved the shot 58-8 to set yet another meet standard.

Upper Peninsula: A fine 66°day paved the way for an onslaught on the UP record books. The pole vault mark fell in all three classes. Greg Miheve, Wakefield all sports standout, became the first UP prepster to clear 12 feet in the pole vault in nearly 25 years. Earl Stolberg of Iron Mountain had sailed over the bar at 12-3 in 1935.

Manistique edged Marquette by two points to take home the championship team trophy in Class B. Football sensation Ron Rubick, who would go on to star at Michigan State University as a running back, won the 100-yard dash for the victors. Bill Rademacher of Menominee, who would go on to become the head football coach at Northern Michigan, took the high hurdles in Class B.

Wakefield repeated as Class C winners while Pickford romped to another easy win in Class D.

Coach Webb Morrison's Panthers scored more points than the next three teams combined.

Denby's Frank Carissimi broke the state record with his 4:17.7 mile to win the Detroit title.

A couple years later, as a sophomore star at Wayne State, he made Sports Illustrated's "Faces In The Crowd" for maintaining a 14-race unbeaten streak in cross country despite taking a wrong turn and running an extra half-mile.

(Tom Venaleck photo)

1961

Wedding bells chimed for the bridesmaid as Flint Northern wiped out years of frustration. Coach Norb Badar's Vikings defeated crosstown rival Flint Southwestern for the Class A title by nearly ten points, after finishing second for an unprecedented seven straight years.

Many changes and milestones would come and go in 1961. The medley relay was replaced by the more conventional mile relay (4 x 440y) and sections were run for the last time in the 440-yard dash and the 880-yard run. The mile run was run in sections for this year only, and as in the 440 and 880, the winner of each section was called a state champion.

Bradell Pritchett of Pontiac surpassed the 60-foot barrier in the shot, his 60-4¾ breaking the state's all-time record—he had thrown a record 60-1½ earlier in the season. No one else in Michigan had ever topped 60-feet. A week later he threw another record, 61-3¼, at the Champion of Champions meet, and he ended his season with his biggest throw, 61-8¾, to win the Oakland County title.

Flint Central's John Shaw set the other new mark in Class A in winning the 880 in 1:57.2. Ottawa Hills, by taking the first mile relay, likewise became meet record holdes in the winning time of 3:26.1. Future Big 10 100-yard champ Dorie Reid of Ferndale copped both sprint titles in Class A.

Joe Falls of Pontiac Waterford had a big day in the hurdles, winning the highs (14.6) and taking second in the 180-yard lows behind Al Franklin of Flint Southwestern. Earlier in the spring, Falls and teammate Dennis Tripp placed one-two in the highs at the prestigious CMU Relays. This twosome undoubtedly gave press box wags some interesting leads for stories during the track season, coining such natural phrases such as "Waterford Falls and Tripps to victory."

Record breakers in Class B didn't have to take a back seat to anybody with a pair of individuals posting impressive performances. Paul Holmberg of Cass City ran a 440 meet record of 48.8. Holmberg's section-winning time far overshadowed all other section winners, including Flint Kearsley's Marty Crane. Nobody can challenge Crane's penchant for winning state championships, however. As legendary head mentor for perennial power Flint Beecher, Crane coached Beecher to ten state championships, more than any other boys coach in state history. Holmberg also became a noted coach. Twice his Livonia Stevenson girls were state runners-up in cross country.

Clio's Gordon Morey upset heavily favored Jan Bowen in the mile and in the process broke Ralph Brakcrog's meet record from 1940. Morey's 4:25.6 exceeded by twelve seconds his previous best clocking. Bowen went on to a great collegiate career, winning the Big 10 mile in 1963 for MSU.

Jim Vogler led Detroit Lutheran West to the Class B title with wins in both hurdles, including a record-breaking 19.6 clocking in the 180-yard lows prelims. He ran a faster 19.1 in the finals with a healthy wind (more than twice the allowable) at his back.

Saginaw Michigan Lutheran Seminary defeated East Jackson for the Class C crown. Alan Behnke and Dennis Gorsline paced the winners. Behnke and Gorsline teamed up with Dick Tesauro and Don Koeppen to edge East Jackson in the day's final event, helping secure the team championship. Oddly enough, a competitor who failed to win his event tied Class C's only record. Frankenmuth's Walt Reinbold won his preliminary heat of the 120-yard high hurdles at a record-equaling 14.8, but lost in the finals to double hurdle winner Dave McLaughlin of Chelsea.

Michigan School for the Deaf captured five firsts in winning the Class D championship. Interestingly enough, of the four records set in the meet, nary a one came from the victors. Gary Tesman of Centreville upped the pole vault mark to 11-10½. Randy Johncox of Schoolcraft easily surpassed the previous best in the shot put with a heave of 53-1½, and Neil Browne of Lawton became the new record holder in the mile with a winning time of 4:36.3. Dave Beracy from Ashley captured first place in the 180-yard low hurdles, the only state track champion in Ashley history.

The most impressive performance came from Centreville's Charles Washington. Washington became the first performer in Class D in 26 years to top competitors in all classes, leaping 6-2¾ in the high jump. Not since Anthony Mazy of Middleton had the day's best mark in the pole vault in 1936, had a Class D performer led the entire field.

Washington and Browne certainly demonstrated that they could compete in any class. At the prestigious Champion of Champions meet the following week in Kalamazoo, the two Class D stars won their specialties. Washington's winning leap of 6-2½ established a new meet mark while Browne, thrilling his followers who trekked over from nearby Lawton, defeated the Class A and B state champs in the mile run with his 4:28.9.

Detroit: Out-state fans, unfortunately, would not see Henry Carr appear outside the Motor City. He was far from his peak at the metro championships, suffering from a slightly pulled hamstring muscle. Northwestern still had far too much depth for the rest of the field and came home easy victors for the second-straight year.

Henry Carr limped through his final city meet, but all was not lost. In 1964 he won two Olympic gold medals.

Carr limped home in 10.1 in the 100-yard dash and defended his long jump crown with a jump of 22-9¼ in his only attempt. Earlier in the season he had crushed the state record in the 440 with his 47.8 and also tied his 220 record of 20.6.

Carr would go on to a storied career in the sport. At Arizona State, he set three World Records and won the 1963 NCAA 220. The same year he tied for the win at the AAU Championships. At the Tokyo Olympics the following year, he won the 200 in 20.36 and returned to anchor the U.S. 4 x 400 to a World Record victory. After his retirement from track, he played in the NFL for the New York Giants.

Second in the city long jump was Redford's Dennis Holland. Holland would ultimately lay claim to the longest jump in Michigan history with his 26-2½ leap in 1965. The three-time Mid-American champion at Western Michigan University would place third in the NCAA championships that same season.

Teammate Robert Harris edged Carr and Northwestern's Charles Shelton for first in the 220. Redford's Terry Moore set the only individual meet record, nipping by inches rival George Harris in a scintillating duel. Moore's winning time of 1:55.0 surpassed the record set earlier in qualifying by Harris at 1:56.2. Dick Sharkey of Redford romped home a victor in the mile in an impressive time of 4:20.2. Sharkey led Tony Mifsud and Louis Scott at the finish line, giving the fans a short preview of what they might expect when this speedy Motor City trio competed at the state meet the following year.

Dick Sharkey captured the mile at the 1961 city meet. At Michigan State, he was a two-time Big 10 champ in the two-mile.

Athletes who excelled in a sport other than track made their presence known during the city championships. Future U of M cage standout Oliver Darden captured the high jump championship. Percy Mun of Eastern won the shot put over a few well-known luminaries. Mun finished ahead of a pair of teammates who would go on to professional careers. Bill Yearby starred on the gridiron at the U of M, before joining the New York Jets of the AFC, while Detroit

high school basketball legend Reggie Harding would have a brief stint with the Detroit Pistons in the NBA.

To further demonstrate the incredible talent that year, fifth-place winner Harold Lucas from Southwestern would be a future first round NFL draft choice of the St. Louis Cardinals. Lucas helped power Michigan State University to national prominence in the 1965-66 seasons.

Ironically, it is doubtful that if any of the above noted runners-up in the shot put ever received more TV time than Mun. Anybody who has ever followed Big 10 football on TV could hardly have missed his imposing figure. The former Eastern standout was a well-known football referee for years. He could always be readily spotted as the umpire who courageously lined up opposite the center.

Upper Peninsula: Big winds negated an all-out assault on the record book in the UP finals. Newberry placed in ten of fifteen events to win the Class B crown. Wakefield was an easy winner in Class C while Pickford received one of its closest scares ever in winning its tenth-straight Class D championship. The Panthers edged neighborhood rival DeTour by only six points to keep its incredible victory string rolling.

The Return of Detroit

When the Detroit schools left the MHSAA in 1930, it didn't have quite the impact in the newspapers as one might expect. The rationale for the departure, according to the Detroit Free Press: "Newspaper files of that day indicate the school board at the time felt Detroit's schools had sufficient competition among themselves. Also, an emphasis was being placed on intramural sports at the schools."

In reality, the effects of the decision were huge. Generations of young athletes had been robbed of the chance to compete in the state championships, and many Detroiters had given up hope that their young athletes would ever be allowed back.

The winds of change started blowing in the summer of 1960, when the Citizens Advisory Committee on Health, Physical Education and Physical Fitness submitted a report, a year in the making, with 62 recommendations for the Detroit schools to enhance opportunities for students. Recommendation No. 24 urged that the PSL return to state competition in basketball, cross country, swimming, track, golf and tennis.

Additional public pressure fell upon the school board after Detroit Catholic Central won the state's

Class A basketball title that winter. A month earlier, the team suffered its only loss, defeated 53-56 for the city title by unbeaten Detroit Eastern, which was barred from going to the state tourney. Many Detroit fans said that the Catholic Central trophy was tarnished.

"Nonsense," a Kalamazoo-area athletic director told Detroit Free Press sports writer Hal Schram. "Maybe you can peddle that propaganda in Detroit but not around the state. If those schools want to be classified as state champions, let them earn it on the tournament road along with Catholic Central and the rest of us."

The superintendent of the Detroit schools, Samuel Brownell, was obligated to produce a response to Recommendation No. 24 by April 11, 1961. Brownell, who had become superintendent in 1956, had been heavily criticized by many, including Schram, for keeping Detroit out of the state championships. The highest paid public official in Michigan with his $30,000 salary, Brownell would have seemed to be in strong position with the board, which had signed him to another 5-year contract in February.

The editorial by Hal Schram, the Detroit Free Press *prep sports writer, that helped nudge Detroit schools in the right direction.*

But when the superintendent came back with a recommendation that Detroit should not return to statewide competition, he faced serious opposition. The board voted him down and came up with three alternatives: "1. Return to state competition for a two-year trial period. 2. Return to state competition for a two-year trial period in certain sports. 3. Not to return to state competition for the present because of a possible over-emphasis on competitive sports." The presence of option 3 indicates that Superintendent Brownell had at least some support on the board.

A public hearing was held on April 25. The board passed alternative 2 on a 4-3 vote. Despite the

opposition of the three women on the board and Superintendent Brownell, Detroit schools would be returning to state competition.

The MHSAA welcomed the news. "We're very pleased that the Detroit Board of Education plans to return to state competition. It's a good thing for outstate boys to compete with Detroit boys," said director Charles Forsythe.

While he noted this would end any debate about the legitimacy of the MHSAA's state champions over the previous three decades, he quickly added, "This is not to say that previous state champions were not true champions."

At the time of the return, there were five Detroit high schools with bigger enrollments than the largest outstate school. Leading the way was Cass Tech, with 3,829 students.

In cross country in the fall of 1961, the Detroit schools made their presence felt. In the Class A state meet in Ypsilanti, Dick Sharkey of Detroit Redford took the win ahead of Tony Mifsud of Detroit Cody. Redford captured the team title, with Northwestern (sixth) and Cody (ninth) also cracking the top 10.

Detroit was back. /JH/

1962

With Saginaw Valley teams having dominated the Class A meet in previous years, winning 16 of the last 17 editions, the return of the Detroit schools promised an epic matchup between the two leagues. Lansing State Journal writer Bob Hoerner called Flint Northern the favorite, but added, "the Detroit public schools… are darkhorses and could easily upset any pre-meet dope charts."

Instead, a pair of relative newcomers upset the applecart. Even though Detroit schools won four events and Flint Northern captured three, it was Grosse Pointe and Muskegon Heights that forged the second tie in the 64-year history of the Class A meet at rain-drenched Ferry Field in Ann Arbor.

The crowd of 7,000, that included this track buff, went away wet, but not disappointed. The highlight had to be the mile. Lou Scott of Detroit Eastern and Redford's Dick Sharkey, squared off for the third time of the season with Sharkey having won thir previous eight encounters. Sharkey, the 1961 state cross country champion, set the pace until the 135-pound Scott turned on a blazing kick in the third lap. Scott set a new state record of 4:17.4 on the sloppy track, setting the stage for yet another duel to be contested at the Detroit City championships the following week. There Sharkey and Scott battled stride for stride down the homestretch, with Scott again the winner as both shattered the state record, 4:13.2 – 4:13.4.

Behind Scott and Sharkey at the state finals was a notable athlete who never won a state crown. In his first season of running track as a senior, Birmingham Seaholm's Jack Bacheler, a 6-5 basketball player, finished 3rd in 4:28. His coach, Kermit Ambrose, was one of the sport's greatest legends, and must have greatly inspired Bacheler, who went on to compete in two Olympic Games. In the 1972 Olympic marathon, he placed 9th.

The finish of one of the greatest miles ever in Michigan history: Lou Scott beating Dick Sharkey as both break the state record.

At the start of the last race on the program in Class A, Grosse Pointe was tied with Flint Northern for the lead, followed by Muskegon Heights with 25. The Tigers third-place finish in the mile relay gave the Muskegon area its first state trophy since Bob Zuppke's Muskegon squad won the title in 1910. Grosse Pointe finished the relay in fourth, earning the suburban Detroiters the necessary points to tie Muskegon Heights at 30.

Gerry Cerulla of Wyandotte Roosevelt was the meet's lone double winner, capturing both hurdles (14.5/19.9). Larry Page of Monroe made up a huge deficit from a tiring Sam McMurray of Muskegon Heights to tie the 440-yard meet record at 49.7.

Detroit Eastern led the Motor City contingent by placing fourth in the team standings. Bill Yearby, first

round draft pick of the New York Jets in 1966, joined Scott in the winners' circle by copping the shot-put title. Other Detroit winners included Thurston's 4x4 (3:28.1) and Theodosis McBurrows of Mumford, whose 1:57.9 in the 880 tied Grosse Pointe's George Thomas at the line.

In Class B, four records were bettered and one tied, as Dowagiac won the title for 24-year-old first year coach Paul Watt. Mose Easley gave the Chieftains their only first-place finish with a victory in the 220, 30 years after his father won the same event for Dowagiac back in 1932.

Distance runners dominated the record-breaking in the B action on the MSU track. Charlotte's Mike Martens, with a 1:56.1, bettered the 880-yard record of Quentin Brelsford of Birmingham from 1938. Martens, the Champion of Champions winner in Kalamazoo, placed second in the 880 at the 1964 Big 10 championships for Michigan State.

Howell's Eric Zemper improved the B mile mark down to 4:22.3. Gary Rugg of Battle Creek Pennfield improved the shot record to 55-8½, while 1961 champ David McLaughlin of Chelsea clocked 14.8 in winning his preliminary heat of the 120-yard high hurdles.

McLaughlin had to settle for second place, however, as the finals of the 120 hurdles were won by Willie Betts of River Rouge in a slightly slower winning time of 14.9. Has there even been a state athlete who had a better freshmen year than Betts? He not only won the 180-yard low hurdles, but in March also led the Panthers to the state Class B basketball championship.

In Class C, Lansing Boys Training School was initially announced as the winner of the meet held in Mt. Pleasant. Lansing St. Mary coach Paul Pozenga questioned the outcome and politely asked for a recheck of the point totals. A spot check showed two recording errors that would give additional points to St. Mary's and a narrow 3½-point win over the Training School. The winners set one of two meet records, taking the 880-yard relay in 1:33.5, eclipsing the standard held by Paw Paw since 1935.

Centreville moved up a notch to Class C, but it made little difference for its standout high jumper Charles Washington. He again posted the best mark in any class for the day with a new Class C high jump mark of 6-3¾. In doing so he matched the feat of John Palmer of St. Louis—setting records back-to-back in two different classes.

Michigan School for the Deaf led a record-setting contingent of Class D schools to the title, outlasting Covert 41 to 37. Six records were set in one of the best meets ever held in Class D. MSD went 1-2-3 in the broad jump to help its cause. Don Smith successfully defended the broad jump with a record 21-5, with twin brother Ron placing second. This was the first time in state track history that a set of twins went 1-2 in the same event.

Coach Earl Robert's Tartars won two relays, including a record effort in the mile relay, to aid their winning cause. The individual star of the Class D state meet was David Woods of little Wolverine High. Woods won three first places, including meet records in the 120 high hurdles (15.5) and the 180-yard lows (20.5). Sandwiched between he won the shot put with a 49-11½. Teammate Fred Joles took the 880-yard run for Wolverine to give the northern school a perfect 4 for 4 in first places. Fred became the third member of the Joles family to win a state championship.

Defending his high jump state title was Mike Bowers of Litchfield. Talk about an improvement! Bowers, who failed to clear 6 feet in 1961, became a Big 10 champion at MSU, and would become the first athlete from the state of Michigan to clear seven feet in the high jump.

Ypsilanti's Chet Beasley sprinted the 220-yard dash in 22.4 while Hildred Lewis of Memphis lowered the D mile record down to 4:35.4.

The point scoring was altered somewhat for the 1962 championships with the addition of another place winner. Seven medals were awarded in each event, with team totals scored 7-6-5-4-3-2-1.

Upper Peninsula: Powerful Pickford made it 11 straight with another awesome display of power. Gary Leach paced the Panthers with victories in the 100 and 220, both times the fastest recorded in any class in the UP. Such was mighty Pickford's depth that Elwin Leach and Roger Hall each ran their sections of the 440 quicker than any performers in Class B or C.

Newberry pulled off a similar feat while winning its second-straight Class A-B championship. Jim Maki broke the half mile record with a 2:03.9, though it would only stand until the following heat when his teammate Gary Brueger crossed the tape in 2:03.6.

Ideal weather in Marquette led to a pounding of the record books. Fifteen records fell in all classes. The meet was not without controversy. Rudyard initially was declared the winner in Class C after Bob Koski of Wakefield and Phil Hinchcliff of Rudyard tied for third in the pole vault. Officials broke the tie to give Koski the sole claim to third, noting he had fewer misses at the previous height. A protest came from the Wakefield coach, and MHSAA director Charles Forsythe backed it up based on the rules at the time. That moved Wakefield into a first-place tie with Rudyard in the team race, the first team tie at the UP finals.

1963

Fans called the 1963 Class A finals one of the best ever. Records fell at a pace never before seen in state annals. Nine out of 13 records were toppled, and another mark tied, in a meet run under perfect conditions in East Lansing. Norb Badar's Flint Northern crew roared back to the top with crosstown rival Flint Central second.

Only marks held by legends Hayes Jones (broad jump) and Rex Cawley (180 lows), along with Bradell Pritchett's shot mark, were able to withstand the onslaught.

Two of the records set were near the top of the national high school list that year. Robichaud's Walt Wilson smashed the 880-yard run mark by nearly four full seconds with a 1:53.3, the No. 2 clocking in the nation, while Detroit Eastern's Lou Scott took down the state record in the mile at 4:13.2, ranking No. 3. A month later, Scott would run against Canadian phenomenon Steve Ball at the International Freedom Festival in Windsor, hammering the state record down to 4:11.3 as Ball cruised to a 4:06.4.

A pair of venerable records fell by the wayside. George Hester's 21.7 meet standard, set in 1923, finally fell as Niles' William Raynor sped the furlong in 21.4. The other ancient standard to be broken was the 880-yard relay, set by Detroit Northeastern back in 1927. Kalamazoo Central's foursome of Wayne Fisher, Walt Worthy, Mike Thompson and Norm Gottlieb blistered a 1:29.5, matching that time a week later in winning the Champion of Champions race.

Ernie Long of Flint Central skimmed the 120 highs in 14.2, breaking the record shared by Jones and Cawley. Al Washington of Flint Northern became the fourth performer in State Class A history to win the high jump three consecutive years, setting a record with his leap of 6-5. Earlier in the season he straddled a state record of 6-7¼. George Wesson of Detroit Southeastern flew to a meet record 49.0 in the 440-yard dash.

The pole vault had now moved into the fiberglass era. Only a stubborn Tim Dobb from Muskegon would insist on using the old-fashioned steel pole. Despite vaulting a personal best, Dobb fell well out the running for a place, an event won by Flint Central's Bill Lee at a meet record 13-6. Almost as newsworthy was the decision in 1963 to determine place winners based on attempts and misses. No longer would the vertical events necessarily end in a tie when the leading competitors all had the same height. The practice often led to a log jam of competitors at the top, such as the seven-way stand-off for first in the pole vault in 1956.

Although not a record breaker, shot put champion Jack Harvey of Birmingham Seaholm would certainly make a formidable contribution to the sport. Harvey went on to become a two-time Big 10 champion and record breaker in the shot put at the University of Michigan. A short time later, Harvey became the head track coach of the Wolverines.

Despite perfect conditions across the state, records at the other state championships, held at other venues, did not take the whipping seen in East Lansing. Only one meet record fell in Class B, and that mark came in a relatively new event, the mile relay. River Rouge dominated the competition, much like it dominated during the basketball season, as the Panthers doubled their winning score over runner-up East Grand Rapids, 52 to 26.

Willie Betts paced the Rouge romp by winning both hurdles, running a leg on the victorious 880 relay and placing third in the high jump. His 14.8 tied the existing meet record in the 120-yard high hurdles. Larry Rugg of Battle Creek Pennfield won the shot, keeping a title in the Rugg family for the third-straight year. Brother Gary won in 1962 (and in Class C the year before).

Lansing Boy's Training School tallied just 18 1/6 points, but it was enough to win the Class C title at Mt. Pleasant over second-place Vandercook Lake. Two records were eclipsed. In the 880, Allen Huffman of Homer won in 2:00.9, bettering the 25-year-old standard of Vincent Butler of Howard City. Lansing St. Mary's Tom Dalton whittled the mile mark down to 4:31.0, surpassing the time set by East Jackson's Richard Pickering in 1960.

Record-breaking was more prevalent at the Class D meet at the same site, with five new marks. Although Michigan School for the Deaf grabbed the state title with a 43-36 margin over Brethren, the Tartars failed to join the record-breaking parade. John Fry of Unionville improved the 120-yard high hurdle record by 0.2 with a 15.3. Darwin Hoag of Morrice tied the 100 at 10.2 after covering 220 in 22.3 in the morning preliminaries.

Centreville's Charles Washington returned for his senior year as the current high jump meet record holder in Classes D & C. Yet he wasn't even able to win the event, let alone better his previous meet record. Litchfield's Mike Bowers upset him at 6-2. A week later at the Champions meet, they tied for first place with a meet record 6-5.

Phil Huber of St Joseph Lake Michigan Catholic won the D 880 at 2:02.7. The curtain came down on the end of an era for the Beane delegation. Brethren's Fred Beane's win in the broad jump was the 22nd time that a Beane had contributed to a state title, a family performance that far surpassed all others in state track history.

Upper Peninsula: Victory in the meet's final event, the 880-yard relay, gave Kingsford its first A-B Upper Peninsula title. Ontonagon's Polar Bears likewise won their first-ever title, while it was business as usual for Pickford. The great weather that graced the Lower Peninsula meet greeted the UP athletes as well on the Northern Michigan University track in Marquette.

Records fell in six events in A-B. Dan Purple, Gwinn, became the second UP high jumper in history to better 6-0, setting a new standard of 6-1¾. Newberry's John Hendrickson ran 53.1 to break the UP's oldest existing record in winning the 440; the old mark was set in the UP's first official final in 1940.

Rene Harger of Munising shattered the existing standard in the 880 with his 2:01.6. Wakefield's Jim Hodge sailed over the twelve-foot barrier to set a new high in the pole vault while Ontonagon's Larry Makima won the Class C shot put in a record 51-9¼. Pickford won nearly half of all events to continue its dominance in Class D.

1964

For the first time since 1939, a Flint athlete failed to win a first place at the state championships. Perennial power Flint Northern, which had placed no worse than third for the past decade, failed to get a single point for the first time since 1939. Battle Creek Central moved into the winner's circle, edging runner-up Flint Central by two points.

Bearcat sprinter Arnie Williams captured both short sprints, including a record-matching performance with a 9.8 clocking in the 100. During the 220-yard dash, the winds were gusting from 8-12mph, blowing him to a 21.3. Lansing Everett's Henry Patino was the leading point winner, taking both hurdles and running a leg on the winning 880-yard relay. Patino had big wind assistance in sailing over the low hurdles in 18.8 seconds.

Two days after winning in Class A, the Everett 4 x 220 captured the Lansing City meet with a state record 1:28.2.

The most impressive performance for the day belonged to Ann Arbor's Ken Dyer, who left all other jumpers in his wake, never having a miss through his record-breaking 6-7¾ leap. He took his skills to Arizona State, where he excelled in football. A fourth-round draft pick of San Diego, Dyer had a three-year stint in the NFL, primarily as a defensive back.

Wayne Lambert of Saginaw Arthur Hill upped the pole vault mark, just shy of the fourteen-foot barrier, the only other record to fall under the windy conditions. With so many competitors now using the new fiberglass pole, and meeting easier standards, the pole vault competition ended nearly two hours after the final running event.

Aided by a 3.6mps wind—nearly double the legal limit—Dennis Lamiman of Roseville flew 24-3 to win the long jump.

Ron Kutchinski made the move up from Class B to win the 880 in 1:55.3, the only year that East Grand Rapids would appear as a Class A team. Four years later as a Big 10 champion for Michigan, he would compete in the Mexico City Olympics.

Many looked forward to the big mile match-up between Bob Richards of Bloomfield Hills, state leader at 4:16.2, and Art Link of Detroit Redford, who had run 4:16.8. But Link tore a muscle in his foot during the race, and Richards sailed home the winner in 4:17.3.

Willow Run took only two events, but placed well in 10 to nip defending champion River Rouge by three points in Class B. Erratic winds led to some bizarre records in the 1964 meet in East Lansing. Topping the list were developments in the 120-yard high hurdles.

In the morning prelims LaMar Miller of Willow Run briefly put himself in the record books with a time of 14.7. Nelson Graham from Mt. Morris, just minutes later, won the third heat in an even faster time of 14.5 to take the meet record away from Miller. Neither would take home the first-place medal, however. Whitehall's Don Witt won the finals at an even faster 14.3, but by then the winds were gusting too much for a legitimate record (the gauge read 2.5).

Multiple meet standards tumbled in one of the most impressive 'B' competitions of all-time. Ernest Ver Hage of Hudsonville Unity, upped the pole vault mark, while Robert Johnson of Vassar established another new standard in the shot with a 57-7. Ver Hage and Johnson would follow up by defeating their Class A counterparts the following week at the Champion of Champions meet in Kalamazoo.

Although Willie Betts could not defend his two-year title as the Class B hurdle king, the future Bradley University basketball star did contribute to a pair of records. Injured while competing in the CMU Relays, the River Rouge star healed well enough to run a leg on each of the Panthers' relays. Rouge lowered the

mile relay mark down to 3:26.3 and improved the 880 relay standard to 1:30.3. Both topped the times set in Class A.

Rich Tompkins took home a first-place medal by winning the 440 for Hart. Later in life he would coach Fremont to many state championships in cross country before retiring in 1997. Boice Bowman's 9.9 in the 100-yard dash gave him a share of the meet record with 1945 legend Bob Swain of East Grand Rapids.

It was a banner year for the Cereal City, as Battle Creek St. Phillip brought the Class C championship trophy back to Mid-Michigan. The Fighting Tigers won three events, including a record-breaking jaunt in the 880-yard relay, to win their first-ever team title for coach Don Pape.

Four other meet marks tumbled in Class C, with the oldest erased in the shot put. Cheboygan Catholic's Louie Fournier broke Bob Carey's 16-year-old record with a put of 55-1. Distance marks fell as well, with Jim Giachino of Kalamazoo University lowering the mile record by nearly a second. In front of the hometown folks at the Champions meet the following week, he posted a 4:20.1, earning him the MVP trophy. Dale Sage of Reese avenged his only defeat when he bested Montrose's Gary Baird in the 880, with a new record time of 2:00.9. Baird had earlier bested Sage in the regional with a 1:57.6.

Roland Carter of Carson City-Crystal set a new mark in the pole vault with a clearance at 12-9. Carter, who also won the 120-high hurdle's title, would make an even bigger name for himself as a collegian. A two-time Big 10 champion for MSU, he was unparalleled at barrier-breaking. He was the first athlete from the state of Michigan to clear 16-feet (1967), 17-feet (1972) and 18-feet (1976). Along the way he made the finals in the Olympic Trials in '72 and '76.

Dwight Lee, the Class C champ in the long jump (22-5¼), made the leap from Class C New Haven High to starting halfback at Michigan State. Lee also made it into the NFL, playing 13 games during the 1968 season for San Francisco and Atlanta.

Covert rode home on the coattails of Mark Patterson to easily win the Class D crown. Patterson just failed in his bid to join the ranks of four-time winners, when his 880-yard relay team placed second to defending state champion Michigan School for the Deaf. Patterson won three individual firsts, with wins in the pole vault, high jump and 120-yard high hurdles. Jerry Ruell of runner-up Lake City had his winning 20.1 time in the 180-yard low hurdles disallowed as a new record when, he too, had a following wind over the allowable limit.

Upper Peninsula: Great weather continued at the UP State finals held once again in Marquette. Ten new UP track records fell by the wayside.

Marquette (A-B), Wakefield (C) and Pickford (D) won the team championships. Highlighting the meet records was Dan Purple's 6-3¾ leap in the high jump, a record that would stand for the Gwinn star well into the 1970s. Rene Harger of Munising came very close to being the first UP runner to crack the two-minute barrier in the half-mile when he cut his own record down to 2:00.5.

Roger Huyck and stocky Roger Hewer led Pickford's mastery in Class D. Huyck recorded the quickest 440-yard dash in any class in UP history (52.8) while double hurdles champion Hewer lowered the 120-yard high hurdles mark to 15.6.

Misfortune prevented Tom Teeple of Perkins from entering the record book. He crossed the line first in the mile in 4:41.3, then was disqualified for inadvertently cutting off another runner.

1965

Kalamazoo Central supplanted archrival Battle Creek to win its first state Class A Championship since 1942. The Giants displayed great strength in the field events to defeat Flint Central 45-34, the third consecutive runner-up finish for Central coach Carl Krieger.

Fred Carver paved the way for the victorious Giants by winning the long jump (the term "broad jump" gradually fell out of use over the course of the decade) and was second in the high jump at 6-5½. Stan Allen of Detroit Eastern, using the new tie-breaking rules, took home the first-place medal with the same 6-5½. Central's Ron Thompson supplied additional field event points with a triumph in the shot (57-9¾), helping the Giants ward off Flint Central's superior speed. Central's Len Hatchett took both hurdle events to become the meet's only double winner in East Lansing.

Arnie Williams became another of the growing list of sprinters who had won the 100-yard dash at the state meet in 9.8 seconds. The only meet record set was by Detroit Southeastern's mile relay unit, which was clocked in 3:22.6. Coach Nick Cheolas' Jungaleers upset a great Roseville foursome at the tape by using blind hand-offs. The gamble paid off as the favored Roseville quartet had a squad that included 880 champion Pat Wilson and Bill Wehrwein. A future Big 10 champion in the 440, Wehrwein would team up with Wilson at MSU to win the 1968 and 1969 Big 10 titles in the mile relay.

The meet firmly established the return to power of the Detroit Public School League. Following a few down years, Detroit Northwestern had its best showing since its dominance back in the 1920s. The Colts'

third-place finish led five other Motor City squads who placed among the top 15 teams.

One of the best races saw Detroit Cass Tech's Brian Moore edge Tom Kearney of Bloomfield Hills in 4:13.4, just shy of Lou Scott's meet record. Placing fifth in the mile was Jack Magellsen of Flint Ainsworth. Although Magellsen would go on to set the school 880-yard record for Western Michigan University, he would be renowned in another sport. As the head girls volleyball coach at Portage Northern, he led the Huskies to nine state Class A championships.

River Rouge was dominant the entire afternoon in capturing Class B at Ann Arbor's Ferry Field. The Panthers secured 61 points, more than double the total of the closest pursuer. Medals and points were now given to the first eight place winners, a system still in use. Although the winning Panthers took both relays and added another pair of first-place finishes, the Rouge failed to add to the record-breaking.

The most impressive meet record set in 1965 belonged to 1968 Olympian Ron Kutchinski of East Grand Rapids. After winning the Class A title a year earlier, Kutchinski dropped down to B to win an event he first captured as a sophomore in 1963, running the two laps in a dazzling 1:53.8.

Jim Miller of Sturgis upped the high jump Class B standard to 6-5, and Bob Johnson of Vassar bettered his own record in the shot, improving to 58-5½. Johnson surpassed the 60-foot barrier in winning the Champion of Champions meet in Kalamazoo the following weekend.

Future Notre Dame and Chicago Bear wide receiver Jim Seymour from Royal Oak Shrine won the Class B 180-yard low hurdles.

Steve Bishop of Vicksburg defeated defending champion Dean Rosenberg of North Muskegon in the mile in 4:22.8 to post one of the meet's biggest upsets. Rosenberg was initially scheduled to run in the first and slowest seeded heat in the mile run. His coach, Wes Bunks, pleaded with meet officials to allow Rosenberg into the second heat, stating that Rosenberg's winning time in the regional was run in gale-force winds in Ludington. Meet officials agreed and inserted Rosenberg in the second heat, though not in advantageous starting position. A converted 440-runner, Bishop also nosed out Rosenberg at Champion of Champions in a meet record 4:18.7.

In Class C, Fowlerville came from behind in the final event to earn a tie with defending champion Battle Creek St. Phillip. Fowlerville coach Bob Mabre was not around to see it happen. He figured early in the meet that his team was not faring too well, and left to go on a canoe trip.

Three meet records fell in C. Jim Giachino of Kalamazoo University improved his mile mark to

4:23.7. Dale Sage of Reese improved his own 880 mark to 1:58.9, becoming the first C half miler to crack two-minutes. Imlay City's mile relay team set a standard of 3:31.7 win in the mile relay.

Perennial Class D power Covert won its second consecutive state championship on the CMU track. Coach Ron Clark's squad collected 38 points in winning its fifth Class D crown overall.

Despite the growing use of the fiberglass pole, Ed Papes of Freesoil became the only new record holder in the pole vault as he cleared the bar at an even twelve feet. Martin High School's Jim Pegg set a new Class D mark in the 880 with a winning time of 2:01.2. Grosse Pointe University Liggett's foursome of Craig Jennings, Mark Weiss, Roy Pingel and Burt Taylor set a mile relay record. Pingel, son of former MSU All-American football star and Michigan Hall of Famer Johnny Pingel, added a first place in the long jump.

Joe Chagnon from Kinde North Huron became his school's only champion with his win in the long jump.

Upper Peninsula: The second-ever tie in UP state history came in the Class C division in Houghton. The Gwinn Model Towners climbed to the top of the ladder for the first time in history while sharing the crown with L'Anse.

Pickford tallied the most points in UP history by again overwhelming the competition in Class D. The Panthers won eight events and only meet records in the hurdles by Channing's Paul Feak kept Pickford from adding another pair of firsts. Feak broke both hurdle marks in dethroning defending champion Roger Hewer of the Panthers.

An ailing Dick Berlinski shrugged off a painful knee injury to win both short sprints, and ran a leg on the winning 880-yard relay team to lead Kingsford. If a healthy Berlinski had been able to compete in the long jump, where he owned the record, it is likely the Flivvers would have been able to pass the victorious Soo team. Berlinski had won the long jump three years in a row.

Webster Morrison:
A Perfect Record

Any conversation regarding top coaches in the state of Michigan would not be complete without acknowledging Webster Morrison.

In 25 years as the head coach of Pickford High, from 1952 through 1976, Morrison never came home from the Upper Peninsula State Track Finals with anything less than the first-place trophy: 25 years and 25 state championships!

Would Morrison's Pickford teams have won 25 straight if they competed at the LP championships? Highly unlikely, but he would have won more than his fair share.

One needs to look no further than the success Pickford experienced at the nation's largest prep relays, the CMU Relays, held annually in late April in Mt. Pleasant. During the first 10 years Pickford entered these famed relays, beginning in 1956, the Panthers came away first 7 of the 10 years.

Morrison would send a team to these relays for 21 straight years, winning 10 titles in all, along with five 2nd place finishes and a more than respectable 3rd three times. Only in two of those 19 years did the Panthers not finish in the top three.

Morrison's 1965 squad was so dominant that this powerhouse set a relays record by scoring a whopping 94 points. To put this total in perspective, the winning team in Class C came out on top with 38 tallies.

How this dynasty began would make for a story by itself. Morrison wore many hats soon after becoming a coach at Pickford in 1945. It was a fairly common practice in the 1940s, and the early 1950s, for one man to coach multiple sports at his high school. Morrison did the same as he was the football, basketball and baseball coach at Pickford. Yet the school didn't sponsor a track team, until fate would step in, thanks to a typical rainy day in the Upper Peninsula in 1952.

Morrison's Pickford baseball squad was scheduled to play against Newberry, only to have Mother Nature intervene and postpone the contest. A restless coach and team, hungry to participate in anything, decided to enter a track meet in Sault Ste. Marie, with the original intention of just giving the baseball players a good workout.

Having never partaken in even one practice, nor having a track to practice on, Morrison entered his baseball team in the track gala. Pickford competed so well against the bigger schools that they decided to enter the Class D regional. The school got the OK from MHSAA commissioner Charles Forsyth to compete and the rest is history.

After qualifying about 10 athletes for the state finals, only the third meet of the season for the neophyte squad, Morrison and his team made the long journey across the Upper Peninsula to Houghton, where they would compete in their basketball uniforms.

Pickford's 1952 baseball/track team.

The meet was run in the rain and mud on the Michigan Tech track. Pickford's first championship might have been the toughest. Trailing the defending champs from Eben going into the final event, the Pickford 880 yard-relay team sloshed through the mud to win the race and also the meet—by a slim two points. Rarely would Pickford be challenged again until Morrison's final year.

Buoyed by the success with this early adventure, Pickford made track & field an official sport for 1953. The old basketball attire was abandoned. For many years thereafter, Pickford would wear those easy to recognize stylish uniforms with the big P for Pickford stenciled in white against a blue backdrop.

After breezing through UP foes over the next three years, Morrison was looking for some stiffer competition for his Panthers. In 1956 Pickford became the first team from the UP to compete in the CMU Relays.

Morrison crammed 7 of his best athletes from his 28-member squad into his station wagon for the 210-mile jaunt to Mt. Pleasant. This was before one could simply cross the straits of Mackinaw over the Mighty Mac Bridge. Prior to the opening of the bridge, it was necessary to cross the chilly straits in a ferry.

Working the meet as the PA announcer was a CMU student who would be later recognized as one of America's greatest announcers, Dick Enberg. Seven Pickford trackmen, all seniors, snapped Brethren's 5-meet winning streak at the nation's largest high school relays, outscoring the LP perennial power by 11 points. Morrison later lamented: "I wish we could have brought the entire squad because I feel we left a half-dozen boys at home who could help us. A lack of finances permitted us to bring only seven boys here."

Following the all-day affair on the Mt. Pleasant track, the Panthers headed back to their UP home where they arrived around 2:30am on Saturday. After little—if any—sleep, the 7 Pickford track members joined the rest of the team to participate in Sault Invitational on Saturday afternoon. Under brutal conditions, with biting winds and temperatures in the low 30s, Pickford was still able finish second to Sault Ste. Marie, who would later win the Class B title, by a mere 7 points.

Pickford placed among the leaders at the Chip Relays in 1957 & 58, but had to take a back seat to Brethren, one of the top Class D teams in MHSAA history.

However, beginning in 1959, Pickford would show their true colors and would take the winning trophy in 6 of the next 7 years, competing against many of the Lower Peninsula's finest teams.

Webster would acknowledge many years later, long after his retirement, that his 1965 powerhouse was probably his most talented of his 25 teams, although his 1960 squad could be in that argument as well.

After dethroning their arch rivals from Brethren by 25 points in 1959, placing in 14 of the 15 events, the 1960 aggregation would rank up with any Class D team in state history. Competing against 42 other Class D teams, Pickford overwhelmed all its LP competitors with 81 2/3 points, nearly 50 ahead of 2nd place Unionville. The Panthers won 8 events and tied for 1st in another. Tom Harrison, Freshman pole vaulter tied for 1st at 11-4¾.

The commanding victory was tempered by a season-ending injury to senior long jumper Jim Smith. On numerous occasions Hal Schram, the revered dean of high school prep reporting in the pre-Mick McCabe era, often had written stories on Pickford's surreal excellence in track & field.

Here is what the legendary 'Swami' penned so eloquently in his Detroit Free Press story following the 1960 relays: "Of the 1,200 schoolboys who braved chilly winds and threatening skies here Friday in the 20th annual Central Michigan Relays, Pickford's Jim Smith was by far the unluckiest.

"Smith, who came 210 miles south to help his Upper Peninsula team in its quest for its second straight Class D title, won the broad jump all right. On his first jump Jim stretched out to 19 feet 6 ½ inches, a quarter-inch better than Norm Kohns of Newaygo.

But it was his final jump which proved his undoing. Smith landed sideways, so to speak, and fractured a bone in his right leg. The 5-foot-11 senior, president of his school's FFA chapter, was also scheduled to anchor two of his team's relays later in the day.

" ' That finishes me,' Smith said in disgust. "Dad will have to find someone to do the chores for a while. Freddie can't do it all.'

"Freddie is his 14-year-old brother, an eighth-grader. Freddie and Jim do most of the work on their dad's farm, six miles west of Pickford.

"Even though Pickford lost the services of Smith for the remainder of the season, the Panthers easily won their 9th straight UP Class D title by 35 points.

"Morrison never would shy away from competition. 'We always try to run against the toughest competition we can because the stronger the teams are that we meet, the stronger we become. We never worry about losing meets throughout the season but we always aim for the finals.'

Yet another one of Morrison's treks into the LP was to take part in the Petoskey Relays, where he would face some of the stiffest competitors from the Northern half of the LP. From 1961 through 1975, Pickford took part at Petoskey, where crowds of 2,000 fans were often in attendance. During that 15-year run, Pickford never failed to bring home the huge first place trophy awarded to the winning Class D team.

How in the world did he compile this incomparable record for a quarter of a century? He surely didn't have Olympians on any of his teams. I don't believe he had one single athlete compete in track at a D1 university school.

A humble Morrison would often give out a response that would deflect away from his own coaching brilliance. This is a typical quote from Morrison during a 1971 interview: "It's the community spirit more than anything else. Our kids really work hard because they have a great deal of pride and they want to keep it up. Practically all of the boys in the school are out for track. They take great pride in successfully competing against larger schools."

Parents and towns people are "real fans," according to Morrison, and follow the team everywhere it competes. "This really motivates the boys," Morrison said.

No doubt that the Morrison quotes rang true. However, I disagree with this Morrison quote from a 1971 story: "we don't do anything different than most people." Who but Morrison could possibly convince a preposterous high percentage of his male students to participate in track?

Morrison's 1965 team had 75 of the 85 male students in the school on the track team. This team so dominated its opponents that it outscored the closest pursuer at CMU by more than 60 points. The next year only 3 of the 66 boys attending Pickford did not go out for track.

The day after basketball season was over, the gym would be quickly set up with track equipment: pole vault, high jump, and hurdles. Relay exchanges and starts were practiced and practiced and the team, as well as the entire town's focus, would turn to track.

Each year Morrison would hand out a workbook prior to the start of track season that would be nearly 40 pages thick. And this was well before the era when one could simply just cut & paste and—presto, the work is done. He had one entire page for team rules. Each track event had meticulous daily work-out schedules that were applicable from the slowest to the fastest runner.

Morrison would give each one of his seniors a key leadership role, ensuring that all his workouts would go off as planned for each discipline.

"From the time a boy is in junior high school, a complete record of every race in which he competes is kept," Morrison revealed. "The improvement and performances of the poorest runners are given as much attention as the best and we enter every boy out for track in as many meets as possible," said Morrison.

In the early years Morrison would have to improvise his workouts as many of the Pickford students had to be bussed to school each day. "We practice all sports during the noon hour so every boy can take part as 75% of our students ride busses to and from school. This limits our practice time to one hour a day, but this is enough if is well organized," was Morrison's explanation.

I once asked one of his star athletes from the mid 60s, Roger Hewer, why he thought Pickford was so dominant in track. Hewer quickly replied: "The coach. We didn't have a lot of great speed but we were strong in the events where you needed a lot of good coaching. We were good in the relays because we always had good exchanges. We had good hurdlers, and pole vaulters, events where good coaching played such a big role."

Hewer, an 8-time UP state champion, was spot on with his remarks. Out of the amazing 138 events won by Pickford during the Morrison dynasty, Pickford's

880 and medley/mile relay teams won 33 of the possible 50 races. Hurdlers coached by Morrison were victorious 24 times during this span.

Web Morrison

Only in the high jump did any of Morrison's tracksters fail to produce fewer than 4 champions in an event. During this streak Pickford averaged 5 and one-half state champions each year!

Born in Spring Valley, Minnesota in 1921, Morrison moved with his family to Pickford at a very young age, where he would spend most of his 89 years. After graduating from Pickford High in 1939, he earned his degree from Northern Michigan University. Morrison served as a pilot in the United States Naval Air Corp in the Pacific Theatre. He returned home after the war, but unfortunately his brother Bernard did not, losing his life on a bombing mission over Germany in 1944.

Morrison ended his unparalleled coaching career in dramatic fashion. The Panthers were not picked to win the 1976 UP finals. They needed a clutch performance from three sophomores and a lone senior as the Panthers led Bessemer by only a single point heading into the final event.

Once again, all that practice, practice, practice paid off as the Panthers had perfect handoffs from the foursome of Senior Neil Peffers and sophomores John Baker, Brent Izzard and Chris Stevenson. The 35 points earned by the victors was their lowest total since the first state championship team of 1952 tallied 32.

After 25 years as the track coach, Morrison did not retire from coaching leaving the cupboard bare. Pickford would win titles in 1977 and 1978 to run its streak up to 27 consecutive, before Crystal Falls Forest Park snapped it in 1979.

Morrison has won numerous awards over the years: Michigan Coach of the Year in 1969 and 1975, Inducted into the Upper Peninsula Hall of Fame in 1973, named the Eastern Upper Peninsula Sportsman of the year in 1975 and in 1989 was the recipient of the MHSAA's most coveted honor, winning the Charles E. Forsyth award.

The town of Pickford went so far to honor their tiny community's No. 1 son with "Web Morrison Day" in 1971. He spent his retirement years in Pickford where he stayed active in numerous community projects, while attending numerous Pickford athletic events with his wife Kay.

Fifty years after the anniversary of Pickford's first team, the Web Morrison Relays were inaugurated in his honor. Fittingly, this meet annually takes place on the last Saturday of each April, the same weekend when many years earlier Pickford shined at the CMU Relays.

Morrison passed away on December 13, 2010, survived by his wife of 65 years Kay, one daughter, 5 sons, and numerous grandchildren.

[Editor's Note: Many thanks to Roger Morrison, a very proud son, for sending me much of Web Morrison's entire scrapbook for this feature.]

1966

The Saginaw Valley conference returned to power, completing a 1-2-3 sweep in Class A. Flint Southwestern, with 40 points, became the third Flint school to win a state A title, nosing out crosstown rival Flint Central and Pontiac Central. For Flint Central, which matched Pontiac with 24 points, it was a fourth-straight year in the runner-up spot.

Charles Robinson became the sixth Class A sprinter to match the 100-yard dash record with his 9.8 clocking. The Detroit Mackenzie sprinter then ran the 220 around the turn in 21.5, establishing a record run around one curve. For most of the previous state championships held up to this period in time, the 220-yard dash was run on the straightaway.

Another hurdling superstar emerged out of Pontiac in the person of Bill Tipton. With a time of 14.0, the Pontiac junior established a meet record in the 120-

yard high hurdles. Tipton defeated the defending champion and former record holder Len Hatchett of Flint Central.

At the CMU Relays, Ron Shortt of Farmington became the first Michigan prep to clear 14-0 in the pole vault. Here, he went a few better, with a state record 14-5.

The mile relay again became an easy victim for record seekers as Detroit Pershing lowered the best time for the four-lap event down to 3:21.6. Steve Bhue of North Farmington led a group of six who would run under the 50-second barrier in the 440. Placing fourth was Roseville's Bill Wehrwein. Wehrwein would rapidly hone his skills at MSU. The Big 10 quarter mile champion not only set the MSU varsity record in the 440 (45.7), but also became a world indoor record holder for the 600-yard run.

Bill Wehrwein became a Big 10 champion.

Cranbrook finished the 1966 year unbeaten after edging Ecorse by just over a point in the Class B meet in East Lansing. Ron Streng of Detroit Lutheran West covered the mile in 4:21.1. Mike Lantry of Oxford finished first in the shot, but would make his mark at Michigan with his foot rather than his arm. He became the regular place-kicker for the Michigan football team.

Dearborn Heights Riverside set yet another record for the mile relay with a clocking of 4:25.1. Fremont's Bill Bekkering duplicated his father's state pole vault championship for the Packers back in the 1930s with a record-clearing vault of 13-6. He wasn't the only state champion to emulate his father. The winner of the 220, John Schneider of Marshall, was the son of John Schneider Sr., a member of Marshall's 880-yard relay team of 1947.

Haslett won its second state championship of the 1960s by just nipping two-time Class C Champion Battle Creek St. Phillip. The Vikings took no firsts, compared to St. Phillip's three, but had superior depth. Haslett found the CMU track to its liking, as earlier in the season the Vikings took the prestigious CMU Relays.

Three records fell in Mt. Pleasant with Akron-Fairgrove's Gordon Aldrich breaking the long time 440 standard set by Boyne City's Elwood Hauser back in 1938. Aldrich, with his 49.5, was the first boy under 50.0 in the Class C meet, pushed by Jack Bansfield of Haslett. He would add his name to the list of state champions who also won as a coach when he directed Corunna to the Class B title in 1999.

Jim Vogt of Freeland took the Class C 880 in 1:58.0, shortly before John Hogan of North Branch lowered the 180-low hurdles mark to 19.5

In Class D, Jim Pegg of Martin moved up to the mile with success. Already the 880 record holder, he added the mile standard with his 4:30.0.

Covert returned to the winner's circle by capturing its third-straight team championship. The Bulldogs certainly enjoyed a wonderful run in the mid 60s as they also won a pair of basketball state championships. Ironically, as a member of the Class D Al-Van league, Covert had never won a league championship.

Bernard Woods, was a double winner for the champs, as was Ann Arbor University's Dave Shipman, winner of both short dashes. One embarrassing moment for meet officials had to come in the pole vault. It appears as the meet referee had failed to recognize the tie-breaking rule change (based on fewer misses) enacted in 1963, resulting in a four-way tie for first in the pole vault. One of those vaulters involved in the logjam was Freesoil's Steve Papes. In 1970 Papes would become an All-American while competing for the Central Michigan University baseball team.

Upper Peninsula: After surviving a scare at the regional, escaping with a half-point victory over runner-up DeTour, it appeared that this might be the year for Pickford's winning streak to come to an end. However, DeTour fell to third place at the UP finals and coach Webb Morrison's Panthers rolled to a 51 to 35½ win over runner-up Channing.

Sault Ste. Marie coasted to an easy victory in Class A-B, nearly doubling the score over second-place Escanaba. The Lock City cindermen set one record when Dennis Daugherty cleared 12-5¼, breaking the record of Kingsford's Rich McCarthy set a year earlier.

Escanaba's Jim Hansen earned the second record by heaving the shot put 53-8 inches. Stephenson captured its third UP track & field title by winning in Class C. Winning the high and low hurdles in Class C was Barry Pierson of St. Ignace. Pierson, as a star defensive back for the Michigan Wolverines, was the player of the game in 1969 as Michigan shocked top-ranked Ohio State in a nationally televised football game.

1967

For the third time in six years a team from the Six-A league captured the Class A state championship. Despite brisk head winds clocked at nearly 20 miles per hour, six meet records were set and another tied in a meet that gave the fans plenty of great action. Battle Creek Central captured the team title, but it was the individual competition that drew most of the attention from the standing room only crowd of 5,000.

Pontiac Central's Bill Tipton had been on fire all year. The star hurdler had opened his indoor season by defeating the reigning NCAA champion in a collegiate meet. Outdoors, he was just as quick, equaling the national record of 13.5 at the Saginaw Valley Championships and winning the Mansfield Relays with a wind-aided 13.3. On the MSU track for the state finals, he couldn't be touched. He broke his own meet record of 14.0 with a 13.9 in a preliminary heat and then matched that in the final. The best that he could do bucking those 22mph winds was 19.3 in the 180-yard lows. Later that summer he ran two more national records at the U.S. Jaycee meet, hitting 13.4 twice.

Flint Central's Herb Washington, with times of 10.1 and 22.4, won the highly touted duel of the sprinters. Washington, who would win the NCAA dash title while at MSU, unseated defending champion Charles Robinson of Detroit Mackenzie.

Battle Creek captured just one first place while winning the championship, but it was a record-setting performance in the 880 relay (1:28.8). Flint Central, although finishing in second place for the sixth-straight year, captured three individual firsts: Washington's double win in the short dashes and Freels Bacon win in the high jump with a new state record leap of 6-8. Flint Southwestern's Lavern Miller was the individual point leader with 21 points.

John Mock of Mt. Clemens would begin a four-year assault on the record in the 880-yard run, lowering the state record to 1:53.1. Detroit Southeastern's Lorenzo Montgomery got a meet record with his 48.9 win in the 440. Dave Leitner of Grand Haven joined the record onslaught with a clearance of 14-6½ in winning the pole vault.

1967 marked the restoration of an event that was last run at the state level near the turn of the century. Back in 1910 John Bishop of Hillsdale won the two-mile run in 10:18.4. After a lapse of time totaling 57

years, Ken House of Detroit Finney won the event and easily established a new meet record at 9:25.7. House's victory would be the only state track title ever won by Detroit Finney.

Ecorse easily captured the Class B title in Ann Arbor over runner-up Howell. John Schneider ran the 100-yard dash in 9.9 in the morning prelims, tying a meet record shared by three other sprinters. The Marshall speedster also became a double winner on the afternoon by defending his 220-yard dash title. Stan Hawthorne from Ecorse took the 120-yard high hurdles in 14.5.

Taking honors in the Class B shot put (57-½) for Ecorse was Dave Pureifoy. Following a fine football career at Eastern Michigan University, he had a successful stint in the National Football League. Ecorse's only NFL player, Pureifoy played eleven years as a standout defensive lineman, mostly while in the employ of the Green Bay Packers.

Ben Streng of Detroit Lutheran West bucked strong winds to lower his own mile record with an impressive time of 4:19.1. The champions from Ecorse won both relays, including a 3:25.1 in the mile relay.

Laingsburg's Dave Carroll put on a one-man show to account for 25 of his team's 30 points to help Laingsburg capture Class C. It was the first state title for Laingsburg in any sport. Carroll won both sprints for the second-straight year and also paced his 880-yard relay squad to a second-place finish.

Doug Smith broke a 32-year record in the long jump by sailing 22-6¾, leading Traverse City St. Francis to a second-place tie with Hartford. Doug Smith exceeded Alan Smith's 1935 leap by only 1/4 of an inch.

Wayne Wills of Ortonville Brandon clipped better than a second off the 880-yard record with a time of 1:56.9. The most impressive performance from the Class C meet came from Middleville's Gary Van Elst. The future MSU football star powered the 12-pound ball out 60-5¾, an all-class meet record.

Detroit St. Charles made the last year that it would be in operation a memorable one as it easily captured the Class D crown over runner-up Ann Arbor University High, 64½ to 47. St. Charles would merge in the fall of 1967 with three other schools to form Detroit East Catholic. Al Henderson led the victors with 23 points. Henderson took first in the 440-yard dash (51.6), and shattered the old record in the long jump by better than a foot, leaping 22-8¾. With winds at East Lansing and Ann Arbor reported at 13-22 mph the author suspects the wind gauge was nowhere to be seen at Alumni Field in Mt. Pleasant.

Dave Shipman brought home a trio of first-place medals for second-place Ann Arbor University High.

He won both short dashes and ran a leg on the winning 880-yard relay team.

Upper Peninsula: While a young quarterback by the name of Lloyd Carr, future football coach at the University of Michigan, was leading his Northern Michigan University football team to an inter-squad victory, the UP Finals were taking place at nearby Marquette High School. Pickford left no room for doubt in Class D by outscoring its closest competitor by 49 points while winning its 16th-straight team championship.

L'Anse came from behind with a victory in the last event to win the Class C title. Carl Funke won the 100 and 220-yard dashes in record time to pace the winners. Sophomore hurdler Rich Salani of Hancock tied both hurdle marks in Class C.

Ishpeming won its first UP track championship in any class by winning the A-B division. Al Eckhart of Calumet set a new standard in the century with a time of 10.1. Jim Boyle of Escanaba was a double winner, with his time of 15.3 in the high hurdles, setting a new UP record.

1968

Controversy surrounded the Class A championship of 1968, with the decision as to who won the title delayed nearly 30 minutes after the final event. Once it was determined that Flint Northern would be disqualified after apparently winning the 880-yard relay, the team victory went to coach Jack Finn's Battle Creek Central Bearcats.

Northern finished in fourth place with 28 points following the disqualification, but if officials had ruled otherwise, a first-place finish would have been worth ten points, and just enough to edge out Battle Creek, which won with 37½. For the sixth-straight season the Vikings of Flint Central played the role of the runner-up, despite the heroics of sprinter Herb Washington.

Washington became the first sprinter in Class A to defend the dash titles since Alpena's Pete Dant swept both sprints in 1955 & 1956. Washington joined Dant and six others in tying the 100 record, originally set by Buck Hester back in 1923. The Flint Central star battled strong headwinds (6.7 mps) to capture the 100-yard dash in 9.8. What was most impressive about it was Washington's margin of victory. A full half-second separated the titleholder and runner-up Eugene Brown from Battle Creek Central. During the indoor season, Washington had tied the World Record for the 50-yard dash. At the Mansfield Relays, he dashed to a state record of 9.4 and then won the 220 in 21.0. Both wind-legal, and both breaking meet records set by Jesse Owens.

In a dazzling career at Michigan State, Washington set several World Indoor Records and won the NCAA Indoor dash crown in 1970 and '72. In '72 he just missed making the finals of the Olympics Trials with his 10.1 in the 100m. His career took an odd turn when he was offered a pro baseball contract after college. He became the first and only player in history to make

Herb Washington was one of the sport's fastest starters ever. (photo courtesy of MSU)

the big leagues solely as a designated runner. In over two years with the Oakland A's, he appeared in 104 major League games and three World Series. The Flint speedster stole 30 bases during his career without ever having swung a bat.

Although Washington was undeniably the star of the '68 state finals, four records were broken and two others tied at Ferry Field in Ann Arbor. Mike Holt of Detroit Henry Ford, and Detroit Kettering's Roger Cleaver set records in their specialties by the narrowest of margins. Holt, in capturing the 440-yard dash, and Cleaver's victories in the 880-yard run, both dipped just a tenth under the previous meet records.

Ecorse sped the four laps of the relay in an all-time best 3:20.5, while Richard Gross of Grosse Pointe took honors in the two-mile in 9:19.3. Larry Bickner's 14-6½ victory gave the Waterford Township pole-vaulter a share of the meet record in that event.

Bay City John Glenn, in only its third year of existence, captured the Class B State Track Championship at Ralph Young field in East Lansing. Coach Bob Beumont's squad piled up 42 points to defeat Detroit East Catholic, which took runner-up honors in its first year. Glenn ruled the roost despite failing to place first in a single event. The Bobcats came up with a big second-place finish in the final event of the day, the mile relay, to overtake East Catholic.

Mike Whitefield, from Kalamazoo Hackett, took first place in both hurdles, including a record-setting 19.3 effort in the 180-yard lows. Northville's Ron Gloetzner just inched the pole vault record up to 13-6, while the two-mile record fell to Flint Bendle's Paul Baldwin at 9:40.4.

Les Warren's victory in the 220-yard dash was the first state title won by an athlete from Coloma. Another noteworthy win in Class B came from Grand Rapids Central's Clarence Ellis who leaped a respectable 23-1½ to win the long jump. He would go on to star at Notre Dame and play four years as a defensive back in the NFL.

A change in scenery didn't bother Detroit East Catholic's Al Henderson. After winning the state title in 1967 in the 440 while competing for Detroit St. Charles, Henderson made the switch to East Catholic after St. Charles closed its doors. The results stayed the same as Henderson defended his title in 50.1.

DeWitt High School also won a state championship without the benefit of a first-place finish. DeWitt became the second school in a row from the CMAC conference to win the Class C title, after Laingsburg copped the crown in 1967.

The big news in Class C was the effort of Middleville's Gary Van Elst in the shot. The three-time football All-Stater, and a member of the All-American prep team, got off a prodigious heave. His 63-7 put shattered his record of 60-5¾ set a year earlier, it would stand for 30 years as the best mark in meet history in all classes. Although happy with the record, Van Elst had hopes of equaling or surpassing his winning 64-10¾ heave from the regional.

If one could look down the road a dozen years, it would probably seem a little too far-fetched that the leading thrower in the world would come out of the Class C meet. Oddly enough, it wasn't Van Elst who would reign supreme as the world's best in 1980. That distinction fell to Ralf Reichenbach from Akron-Fairgrove, runner-up in the shot put in Class C, more than ten feet behind Van Elst.

A foreign exchange student from Germany, Reichenbach returned home and eventually became a 70-foot plus thrower with the heavier 16-pound ball. He was rated the No. 1 shot putter in the world in 1980, even though he missed out on competing in the 1980 Olympics due to the U.S.-led boycott. A shadow would eventually be cast over Reichenbach's heroics, however, as he later admitted using steroids. It is very likely that steroids contributed to an untimely end for the West German native. He passed away in February of 1998 at the age of 47.

Ralph Stepaniak, in winning the 440-yard dash, became the only champion in history from Alpena Catholic Central, which closed in 1972. Shortly after graduating from high school Stepaniak would team up with Grand Rapids Central's Clarence Ellis in the defensive secondary at Notre Dame.

The same could be said for Burr Oak's Dorrie Carpenter. His victory in the 100-yard dash remains the school's only state track win. Unionville scored in ten events and ran away with the Class D title. Mendon and Pentwater finished deadlocked in second place with 29 points. Aiding Pentwater's second-place showing was Bob Graham's record-tying 15.3 win in the 120-yard high hurdles. Chuck Holubik of Deerfield lowered the 440-yard dash record down to 51.2, while Nick Welburn set a new mark in the two-mile.

Class D's only double winner was Roger Connelly of Brethren with victories in the high jump and 220. Connelly was a first cousin of Brethren's most famous alum, movie star James Earl Jones.

Upper Peninsula: The Menominee Maroons received a ride on a fire engine on its return home after winning the UP Class A-B championship in Marquette. Jeff Stevenson of Munising established a new A-B record of 15.2 in the 120-yard high hurdles.

L'Anse successfully defended its Class C title. Mike Harsh from L'Anse upset current record holder and defending champion Dick Salani with a record-breaking time of 15.5 in the 120 highs.

A large delegation of parents, students and old grads traveled to Marquette to cheer Pickford to its 17th-straight Class D championship. For the first time in UP history all pole vault winners cleared the 12-foot barrier, taking full advantage of the fiberglass pole.

1969

For the first time in years, a soft and sluggish track awaited competitors vying for the Class A state championships in East Lansing. Hurdler John Morrison led Redford Union to the first state championship of any kind in its school history, a 29-24 triumph over defending champion Battle Creek.

Morrison won the 120 highs, finished just behind Charles Langston of Flint Central in the 180 lows and ran a leg on the 880-yard relay team that earned five valuable points. Bob Junk took second in the mile to give the Panthers all the points they needed in the well-balanced meet.

Kevin Reabe of Waterford Kettering turned in perhaps the best performance of the day, a meet record 1:52.7, just a tad slower than the 1:52.5 state record he set in winning his regional. Mike Holt clipped one half of a second off his meet mark in defending his 440-yard dash championship. The speedster from Detroit Henry Ford ran one lap around the slow track in a very respectable 48.3, nipping runner-up Mike Murphy from Midland.

Another major sprint star arrived on the scene. Marshall Dill of Detroit Northern won the 220-yard dash in 22.1. Only Ken James of Detroit Mackenzie prevented the Northern sophomore from sweeping both sprints over the next three years. James edged Dill in the 100-yard dash with a time of 10.0, and became the only double winner in Class A by running a leg on the winning 880-yard relay team.

An athlete more renowned for his basketball skills took home the first-place medal in the high jump. Pontiac Central's Campy Russell became the first state champion in track & field to also go on and play in the NBA. Richard Schott became the first state champion for newly formed Grosse Pointe North with his win in the two-mile run.

Southgate's victory in the mile relay became the only state title won for its school, but joy for this foursome would be short-lived. Floyd Wells, Charles Fielhauer, and Charles Doran were joined by Bill Franklin and cranked out a winning time of 3:21.7. Franklin joined Alan Smith, and a few other state champions from the past, in giving the supreme sacrifice for his country. Just a year after Franklin would wear the crown of a state champion, he would be killed in action in Vietnam while serving as a U.S. Marine.

Ecorse breezed to the Class B championship with three first-place finishes, leading runner-up Oscoda by nine points. Better conditions prevailed in Ann Arbor as four records tumbled during the day. Brad Miller of Sturgis improved on a record set by his brother Jim in 1965, winning the high jump at 6-5½. Dave Boyer of Fremont improved the pole vault record by better than seven inches with a clearance of 14-1¾.

Jerry Shinkel of Detroit St. Anthony became the only titleholder in his school's brief history in winning the two-mile run in 9:32.9. Bob Swain's 100-yard dash record, set back in 1945, fell to Oscoda's Frank Bennett in 9.8.

The Burgers of Reading became the most productive family act since the Beane's dominated Class D in the 1950s. Brother's Ken, Ralph, and Tom Burger were joined by Steve Noland to give Reading 44 points, beating the 38 tallied by runner-up Shepherd. The Blue Jays received an excellent performance from Bill White who captured both hurdle races for the second-straight year.

Detroit East Catholic dropped down to Class C to win the 880-yard relay in a record time of 1:33.4. The only other record to topple in Class C was in the high jump, where future Big 10 champion Dennis Adama of Newaygo straddled 6-5.

Grass Lake needed 55 points to hold off a strong Athens unit to take team honors in Class D. Grass Lake won four first-place medals to Athens' one in winning by five points. The only record to fall in Class D came when Tracy Elliott of Elk Rapids, the 1968 Class C champ, dropped down to D and lowered the two-mile standard to 9:44.1. Craig Letherbury won the pole vault to become the first state champ from Tekonsha.

Upper Peninsula: Near-freezing temperatures awaited participants at the UP finals in Marquette. Gladstone found the frigid weather to its liking as it captured its first UP track championship.

Surprisingly, seven records were set, although two were registered in the two-mile run, an event that was only in its third year of competition. Hancock and Ontonagon had to be content to share the championship in Class C. Greg Eckhart of Calumet, brother of 100 record holder Al Eckhart, set a new standard in the 440 with a 52.4.

Pickford had an uncharacteristic struggle in Class D, but survived a challenge from Rapid River to win its 18th-straight championship in Class D. Two-mile champion Maurice Evans of Republic, while attending Lake Superior State, would become the first distance runner in UP history to qualify for the NCAA Division II Championships.

1970

A "near-tragic" accident almost marred the 1970 Class A championships won by Benton Harbor. Tiger coach George McGinnis was among 24 coaches and spectators who had to be escorted to the hospital after a section of bleachers collapsed. McGinnis was treated, and returned, just in time to see his team take home its first state championship in nearly 30 years.

Headwinds hampered the sprinters' assault on records, but it didn't slow down 880-yard sensation Kevin Reabe. The Waterford Kettering ace not only bettered his record-setting performance of a year earlier but his winning time of 1:50.9 over 880-yards would stand the test of time for 45 years as the de facto meet record. He would run even faster a few weeks later in winning the Golden West Invitational in

California in a state record 1:50.6. Reabe's performance over the Ann Arbor cinders was one of two distance marks established during the afternoon.

Richard Schott repeated in the two-mile, marking three years in a row that a resident of Grosse Pointe won the longer distance race. Schott set a new record in the process with a new best time of 9:15.8. Mel Reeves won both hurdles, and became the eighth schoolboy from Pontiac to win the high hurdles crown over the past 15 years.

Mike Pierce of Grand Blanc copped the mile championship in 4:14.5, just edging a disappointed Doug Brown by a tenth of a second. Brown, from Harper Woods Notre Dame, never won a state track title in high school, but a week later he would become the first Michigan prep to break 9:00 in the two mile, running 8:57.7 at the Golden West Invitational in Sacaramento.

Brown would go on to a great post high school track career, the first of a string of great Michigan runners who fueled Stan Huntsman's powerhouse University of Tennessee program. Brown won two NCAA titles in the steeplechase and set two American Records in the event. He qualified for the Olympic team three times. As a coach, he guided his alma mater to the 1991 NCAA championship.

Detroit Northern's Marshall Dill won both dashes to join Pontiac Northern's Reeves as double winners. Dill ran into strong head winds, slowing the times, but the Motor City junior still had one year remaining to display his skills. A foursome scored all of Benton Harbor's points. Rodney Rhodes, Leroy Hunt, Frank Atkinson and Don Hopkins, teamed up in the 880-yard relay to give the victors their only first-place finish on the afternoon.

In Class B, Ecorse failed to capture a single individual title, but had more than enough depth to win its fourth state championship in the past 10 years, doubling its total over second-place Cranbrook. Three records fell in Class B, two on the field. Jim Goodfellow of Oxford set the only mark run on the cinders, running the two-mile race in 9:28.2. Jim Stevenson of Muskegon Catholic upped the pole vault best to 14-7, while Brad Miller not only won the high jump title for the second-straight year, but made it 3 for 3 on the record book for the Miller clan.

Miller's leap of 6-6¼ was overshadowed by the eye-popping performance of Dennis Adama of Newaygo in Class C. Adama leaped over the bar at 6-8½, the best high jump performance ever in the state of Michigan in any class. Adama went on to a great career at Indiana, where he not only won three Big 10 titles indoors and out but was runner-up at the '74 NCAA outdoor meet.

Defending champion Reading had to share the crown in Class C with Grass Lake, the Class D titleholder in 1969. Each team completed the day with identical scores of 37½ points. The only other record set in Class C was the 3:30.6 for Shelby's mile relay.

A dropped baton during the running of the 880-yard relay did not deny Covert its seventh state Class D title over the past 15 years. Ed Robinson was the individual star for the afternoon. The Michigan School for the Deaf junior equaled the 100-yard dash record in Class D at 10.2, won the 220-yard dash and anchored the winning 880-yard relay for the Tartars.

Dill later starred at Michigan State.

Upper Peninsula: Nothing would change in Class D in the Upper Peninsula. Pickford smashed its way to victory by an overwhelming margin as the Panthers' dynasty continued.

The Gwinn Modeltowners not only won five first places while winning the UP championship in A-B but also set a record in each winning event. Gwinn's half and mile relay teams notched meet records, times that would stand into the next millennium. Jeff Hatfield and Larry Froberg tied for first at a record 12-7¾ inches in the pole vault. Mike Hatfield crushed the former UP record in the 440 (51.1) while sophomore Fred Teddy became the first UP two-miler to crack the ten-minute barrier.

Rudyard breezed to its first-ever UP title in Class C. Tim Nault of Norway was the individual star with three firsts, including a meet record of 21-8½ in the long jump, a mark that lasted for decades.

1971

Detroit Northern became the first Detroit public school league squad in 31 years to win the Class A state championship, and the Jayhawks did it in convincing fashion. Marshall Dill led an assault on the record books that would make 1971 stand out as one of the best meets in prep history.

Dill had come into the meet as the sprinter to watch—earlier in the season he had tied Herb Washington's state record of 9.4.

In East Lansing, Northern tallied the most points scored in 15 years with its 54-point total, dominating action in the star-studded field. Dill not only had a hand in three meet records but also smashed two MSU field records. Dill began his day by setting a new record in the 100-yard dash, a mark that had stood for 48 years. Dill's 9.7 clocking in the morning prelims erased the 9.8 record shared by many, but initially set by Detroit Northern alumnus George Hester in 1923.

Dill returned moments later to blaze the 220 prelims in 21.2, notching record number two. In the afternoon finals Dill, with a 9.6, clipped yet another tenth off the 100-record, nearly a full half second ahead of the second-place finisher. Dill's anchor leg helped the team run 1:27.0, a state record. He saved his best for last, blazing the 220 in 20.6 to smash not only the state record, but also the MSU track record as well.

Dill made even bigger headlines over the summer. He won both sprints at the All-American HS Championships in 9.4 and 20.8. A week later, he won both races at Golden West, running 9.6 and 21.0 into headwinds. Then he took on the best adult sprinters in the world, placing fourth in the 200 at the AAU Nationals. A week later he broke national prep records in the 100m and 200—10.1 and 20.1—to win the Freedom Festival in Windsor. He placed third in the 200 (21.1) in the U.S. vs Africa meet. He captured the silver medal at the Pan-American Games Cali, Columbia, in a national prep record 20.39. And he wrapped it all up by tieing the national prep record at 100m with his 10.1 in Canada at the end of summer.

Not only was he named the top high school athlete in the nation by *Track & Field News*, he was ranked No. 4 in the world at 200m

Seven records were shattered and one other tied, much to the amazement of the large throng of spectators at Ralph Young Field. Stan Vinson of

Detroit Chadsey sped the 440 in 48.0 to set one mark, while Flint Kearsley's David Baker established the other with his two-mile time of 9:15.4.

Amazingly enough, only the pole vault record held up at the end of the day, as all other field event records fell by the wayside. John Ross of Detroit Mackenzie removed legendary Olympian Hayes Jones from the record books with a 23-11 in the long jump.

Ron Gatheright of Mt. Clemens smashed the shot-put record with a heave of 62-1. Dean Oosterhouse of East Lansing concluded the barrage on the record books by tying the standard in the high jump at 6-8.

The decade of the 70s certainly was the decade of the sprinters and Class B was no exception. Roy Young of Mt. Morris became the new record holder in Class B with his 9.7 win in the Class B 100-yard dash. Bob Swain of East Grand Rapids had initially set the mark, shared by many, in 1945. Swain's 220 record barely held up as Young's 21.9 was just a tenth of a second off the standard set by the East Grand Rapids star in 1945.

Holly picked up its first state team championship by scoring 38 points to easily dethrone Ecorse for the Class B title. The B meet was held at a high school facility for only the second time in state history with Michigan Center playing the host role. The Grand Rapids West Catholic foursome of Pat Sabel, Larry Kubiak, Greg Herda and Rick Jackson sprinted the 880-yard relay in 1:30.0 for a meet record.

Detroit Country Day easily won the team title in Class C with 46 points. Muskegon Western Michigan Christian had its best-ever finish in state competition, placing second with 39 points.

Jack McClellan led the Yellow Jackets to the C title with wins in both dashes and ran the opening leg on the winning 880-yard relay team. Carson City-Crystal's Mike Burns set a new record by running the mile in 4:22.7. Muskegon Christian's Gary Veurink lowered the 120-yard high hurdles record to 14.6, and became a double winner when he captured the 180-yard low hurdles. The other record to fall in Mt. Pleasant was the pole vault, where Mason Co. Central's George Reader cleared the bar at 13-1½.

Unionville won three firsts and three seconds and finished high up in many other events to coast to the Class D title with 75 points. Camden-Frontier grabbed second place behind Unionville with 46½ points. The meet was held at Ferris State's track in Big Rapids, where only one record was broken. Rod Sedar of Aranac Eastern became the new holder of the pole vault record at 13-1½.

Ed Robinson of Michigan School for the Deaf concluded his great career by winning the 100-yard dash for the third-straight year. Robinson's time of 10.2, equaled a record shared by many. Robinson became Class D's only multiple winner in 1971 with his repeat triumph in the 220 and ran the anchor leg on the victorious 880-yard relay team.

Upper Peninsula: Paul Kitti helped his father, coach Walt Kitti, to the first UP track championship for the Calumet Copper Kings. The young Kitti and teammate Clayton Antilla each won two events to lead the victors. Kitti became the first UP runner to break the two-minute barrier for the half-mile run as the UP runners took an all-out assault on the record book.

Joe Cherette of Marquette accounted for one of the 16 records broken by skimming the high hurdles in 15.0. All three two-mile winners bested the previous records with junior Fred Teddy of Class C champion L'Anse posting the day's fastest time of 9:30.4.

Gary Santi of Ishpeming upset defending champion Gary Patrick of Calumet in the day's most exciting event. Although Santi's winning time of 9:35.7 would fall short of Teddy's record set in the preceding race, it remained a meet record for years. Another barrier fell in the distance events when Larry Green of Stephenson became the first UP runner to break 4:30 in the mile run.

Yet another UP record was eclipsed when Bob Bruno of Class D Wakefield sailed over the bar in the pole vault at thirteen feet. It should also be noted that Pickford rolled to its 20th-straight championship in Class D.

1972

Track technology moved a step ahead in 1972 when the state Class A track meet was run for the first time on an all-weather surface. The venue for Class A moved to Flint's Guy Houston stadium, named after the longtime Flint coach and administrator. Houston also made a name for himself in track in the early 1900s, twice capturing the state title in the 440-yard dash.

Another event, the 440-yard relay, was added for the 1972 campaign, and it couldn't have come at a better time for Oak Park High School. The five-man track delegation was in second place going into the meet's final event, trailing Saginaw, with host Flint Northwestern and Lansing Sexton bunched close behind. All were in the final heat and all had a shot at the title.

Heading into the final leg Northwestern and Oak Park were side by side. Oak Park's Dave Caplon gave 100-yard dash runner-up Mike Rollins a perfect hand-off, and Oak Park wrapped up the relay and its first state title. Northwestern, in its haste to nail the hand-off, failed on the exchange and ended up a distant fifth after the disqualification. A victory would have given the Colts the state title.

Northwestern's bright spot came with its 1-2 finish in the high jump. The Colt's Doug Gibbs, who had won at Mansfield, Flint city and regionals asked his buddy to come out for the track team for the 1972 season. Reggie Ferguson agreed and nosed out his pal at the state finals with a new record-breaking leap of 6-9. Gibbs settled for second at 6-6.

Farmington's Nat Durham became the first prep in state history to vault the 15-foot barrier. Durham trailed Flint Northern's Barry Benton after both had cleared 14-7. Benton would have been declared the winner if Durham failed at the next height, but the Farmington ace made a clutch clearance on his third and final trial to win the event.

"I picked up my pole and slammed it to the ground," said Durham, "then started shaking everybody's hand. I was in another world. Not for long. The judge motioned me over. He told me my jump was illegal. Illegal?"

The official insisted that Durham's falling pole had broken the plane and the make was actually a miss. Durham argued, then was sent away by his coach, who filed a formal protest. Eventually, a games committee agreed that the rule was "hazy," and after 20 minutes of waiting Durham could celebrate again. In any case, his hold on the state record would be short-lived, as rival Benton would clear 15-¾ at the Greater Flint meet the following week.

Nick Ellis of Detroit Cooley whittled the two-mile meet record to 9:14.8, while Detroit Pershing became the first school in state history to run under the 3:20.0 barrier in winning the mile relay. Reggie Jones of Saginaw was the meet's only double winner, capturing both short dashes (9.8/21.6). The day's most exciting race had to be the mile run. Dave Wood barely missed the record with a time of 4:13.9 in edging Detroit Northern's Amos Brown as they clocked identical times.

Detroit Redford's Clarence Chapman, winner of the long jump at 22-11, would follow his collegiate career at Eastern Michigan University with a seven-year career in the NFL, primarily as a defensive back with the New Orleans Saints. Employed also as a kick returner, he topped his tenure with the Saints by returning a kick-off all the way back for a touchdown during the 1977 season.

Cranbrook rode the back of Charles Monk and—when misfortune struck runner-up Mt. Morris—won the Class B title. Monk became the first performer in state history to win the 440 and 880 in the same meet, and added his third first by running the anchor leg on the winning mile relay team.

Mt. Morris would have won the meet, if it hadn't been disqualified in the 880-yard relay after turning in the second-best time. The squad bobbled one of the exchanges and by the time the runner gained possession of the baton, he was out of the zone. Roy Young repeated as dash champion in Class B, although, due to a slight knee injury, the Panther ace did not match his record performance from a year earlier. Earlier in the season Young was clocked in a wind-aided 9.4 seconds while placing second in the Mansfield Relays.

Four records fell in Class B, three of the marks being set in the field events. The oldest mark to topple was in the long jump where Port Huron Central's Bob Johnson erased Willie Prewitt's name from the record books with a leap of 23-6½. Ed Tyler, mammoth 6-3/300-pounder from Oxford, improved the Class B shot best to 59-0, while Charles Durrant of Portland leaped 6-8 in the high jump.

In the two-mile run Reed City's Herb Lindsay recorded the lone record broken on the MSU cinders. The future MSU and world-class distance ace toured the eight laps in 9:22.9. Earlier in the season, at the Mansfield Relays, Lindsay and Ellis battled for first place in the two-mile run. Lindsay's 9:23.2 was just an eyelash behind the Class A champion from Cooley.

Herb Lindsay starred at Michigan State and later became the sport's top road racer.

It was not a good day for defending champions. There were six former titleholders in the meet, but only Young was able to repeat as a winner.

Detroit DePorres began its domination by winning the Class C title at CMU with 58 points, with Battle Creek St. Phillips making a good showing to take

second with 46½. John Bennett of Cassopolis matched Monk's feat by winning the 440-880 double. Mike Burns of Carson City-Crystal improved his own record by winning the mile in 4:18.8.

Gary Veurink of Muskegon Christian lost his high hurdles crown to Alan Baker of DePorres. Baker, in winning the highs, equaled Veurink's record of 14.6 set a year earlier. Veurink did manage to defend in the 180-yard low hurdles, setting a meet record 19.4. Decatur clocked 1:31.7 in the 880-yard relay.

Shelby High School concluded its best year in school history since 1910 with the mile relay team taking home the first-place medal. Shelby's wrestling and basketball teams each won state championships over the winter months. Anchoring Shelby's winning mile relay team was 6-9 Paul Griffin, who could go on to a great career in the NBA. Griffin, along with Pontiac Central's Campy Russell, are the only state champs in track to ever compete in pro basketball.

Unionville racked up the most points in state history with 83¼ to easily repeat as champs in Class D. The victors captured five firsts in a superb display of power to easily lead the field. Two records were set on the Caro High School track. Rod Sedar of Aranac Eastern won the pole vault to marginally improve his own record up to 13-2. Lloyd Wilds of runner-up Mendon High cracked the 2:00 barrier for the first time in Class D with a 1:59.8.

Upper Peninsula: Escanaba edged Ishpeming by two points to claim honors at the UP finals in Marquette. Jeff Boyer of Gladstone set records in the high hurdles (14.7) and John Noblet of Escanaba did the same in the pole vault (13-6¾).

Larry Rogers led Houghton to the Class C championship by winning four individual events, the second to accomplish this feat in UP history. Rogers' marks in the high hurdles (14.9) and 180-yard lows (20.4) were UP records.

The day's outstanding performance was Fred Teddy's two-mile run for L'Anse. Teddy lowered his own record with a time of 9:22.7. It's unfortunate that Teddy would not match up in Class with the Lower Peninsula champion—Herb Lindsay. Teddy's clocking, a mere two-tenths faster than Lindsay, still stands as the UP's all-time fastest two-mile run in any class.

Pickford made it 21 in a row in Class D. The Panthers' Steve Peffers accounted for the only record in Class D with a time of 15.0 in the high hurdles.

1973

Saginaw reveled once again in victory, winning its first Class A state championship since 1954 before 6,000 fans at MSU's Ralph Young Field. Reggie Jones led the Trojans, placing his name amongst the legendary sprinters in Michigan prep history. He equaled Detroit Northern's Marshall Dill's 100-yard dash record of 9.6 and then ran the second fastest 220 time in state meet history (21.1).

Jones teamed up with Saginaw teammate's Willie Dawkins, Larry Foster and future MSU basketball star Bob Chapman to win the 880-yard relay and provide veteran head coach Claude Marsh with the points to hold off second-place Pontiac Central. In winning the 100-yard dash, Jones avenged his only defeat of the season. Pontiac's Lucky Smith had beaten him at the Mansfield Relays earlier in the season, but the Saginaw speedster reversed the tables in East Lansing, despite a quick 9.7 time run by the second-place Smith.

The following year, as a collegiate freshman, Jones led Tennessee to the NCAA championship, stunning track fans nationwide by blitzing the 100 in a wind-aided 9.18 (4.3mps). He had earlier led the qualifying in 9.34—a meet record in the second year of automatic timing at nationals. He was ranked No. 4 in the world in the 100 (and No. 5 in the 200) by *Track & Field News*. He would make the finals of the Olympic Trials 100 in 1976, but not the team.

Detroit Osborne's Kelsey Johnson tied the long jump record of 23-11 to share honors with John Ross of Detroit Mackenzie. Johnson, Osborne's only state champion, added 15 inches to his previous personal best. Ken DeLor of Grosse Pointe North sprinted the 440-yard dash in 48.0, tying the mark set by Stan Vinson of Detroit Chadsey in 1971.

Action in the newer events saw Detroit Kettering grab a share of the 440-yard relay record with Oak Park, winning the short relay sprint around the oval in 42.9. The two mile saw a memorable duel between Farmington's Mike McGuire and Pat Davey of Birmingham Brother Rice. McGuire won the battle in a meet record 9:12.0, eclipsing the 9:14.8 run by Nick Ellis of Detroit Cooley in 1972. With McGuire and Davey only juniors, the two-mile run in 1974 promised to be some race!

Although he didn't set a record, Wayne Bouvier of Washington Eisenhower had one of the better performances of the day with his repeat win in the Class A shot put at 61-3. Mark Lawrence of Waterford Mott, in winning the 120-yard high hurdles, joined Bouvier as his school's only Class A state champion.

Relays played the major role in determining the Class B champion. Ecorse won the 880 and mile relay and finished second to Mt. Morris in the 440. Runner-up Dearborn Heights Robichaud initially appeared to win the 880-yard relay but was disqualified on a baton exchange.

Class B distance runners certainly didn't have to take a back seat, with Greg Meyer of Grand Rapids West Catholic dueling Hastings' Tom Duits in the mile run. Meyers broke the four-lap meet record by 4.2 seconds with a 4:14.9. Duits, although placing second, also bettered the old best with a 4:16.1 clocking. Meyer went on to become a Big 10 champ in the steeplechase and a sub four-minute miler, as well as a Boston Marathon winner.

Robert Johnson repeated as the long jump champ in 1973. The Port Huron senior fell short of his record from the previous year, but still uncorked a fine effort with his leap of 22-9.

Alan Baker paced Detroit DePorres to an easy victory in the Class C state meet in Mt. Pleasant. He won both hurdles and ran a leg on the winning mile relay team as the Eagles swept all three relays. His 14.6 equaled the 120-yard high hurdles mark. DePorres team total of 73 points was well ahead of runner-up St. Louis, which finished with 48.

Mike McGuire went on to become one of the most successful distance coaches in the NCAA, guiding the Wolverine women to 12 Big 10 cross country titles. Here he is with Pioneer & Michigan star Alice Hill. (Peter Draugalis photo)

Despite unseasonably cool weather in Mt Pleasant, three records were broken and another tied. The most impressive came in the pole vault as six of the top eight topped 13-0. Steve Wren of Haslett won at 14-1.

James Keller of Cassopolis ran the two-mile run in 9:48.4 and the DePorres team clocked 44.1 in the 440-yard relay. Andy Kovac of St. Louis won the mile in 4:27.9, while Herb Lindsay of Reed City struggled in third. A year earlier, Lindsay had set a Class B record in the two-mile run. Lindsay would have his day, however, becoming a two-time Big 10 champion in the mile at Michigan State University. He finished second twice to Illinois' Craig Virgin in the Big 10 5000.

Mendon, the Class D runner-up in 1972, cruised to the title in 1973 in Class D by racking up 74 points. Lloyd Wilds, who won the 440 and 880-yard runs, as well as running a leg on the winning record-setting mile relay team, led the Hornets. It was in the 880 where Wilds shown the brightest. His 1:56.8 would stand up until four divisions in 2000 replaced the Class system.

The Class D meet in Caro would go down as one of the best. Six records fell and another tied. Freshman Dwight Jones of Grosse Pointe University Liggett lowered the 100-yard dash mark a whopping 0.3 with a clocking of 9.9. Len Lilliard of Ann Arbor St. Thomas upped the high jump standard to 6-3, while Wilds' Mendon teammate, Brad Courtney, improved the mile best to 4:24.3.

Greg Sanderson made it a clean sweep on the record assaults for all distance races by capturing the two-mile run in 9:38.0. Bob Marshall of Almont equaled the 120-yard high hurdle best at 15.3.

Upper Peninsula: Escanaba rode the shoulders of big Wayne Schwalbach to victory in the Class A-B UP meet in Marquette. Schwalbach raced to victories in the 100 and 220-yard dash and, for good measure, won the shot put as well. Placing second, with its best showing ever at the UP State finals, was Iron Mountain.

Who at that meet could ever envision the impact on sports from two members of this Mountaineer team? Steve Mariucci and Tom Izzo would become household names, but certainly not in track & field. Mariucci coached in the NFL for many years and Tom Izzo has guided MSU's basketball team to great success, including an NCAA championship in 2000.

Mariucci won a section of the 440 and ran on a leg on the two winning relay teams, the 880 and mile. In their final moment in an Iron Mountain uniform, it was only fitting that Mariucci would pass the baton to his teammate and best friend Izzo in the mile relay.

Despite Mark Flood's record leap of 22-½ inch, a mark that still stood at the end of the millennium, Crystal Falls fell short in denying Pickford's Panthers their 22nd-straight UP state championship. Rudyard won seven events to easily earn the team trophy in Class C.

1974

Pontiac Central returned to the winner's circle for the sixth time at the Class A meet held at Flint's Guy Houston Stadium. Although failing to get an individual win, the Chiefs piled up 52 points in eight events to easily outdistance Ann Arbor Pioneer.

Four records fell in Class A, with the distance runners again posting the most impressive performances. Pat Davey and Mike McGuire again dueled in the two-mile run with Davey turning the tables in 1974, edging McGuire in a state record best of 9:00.4. Until Davey broke the two-mile record, he was best known as the son of former boxing great Chuck Davey, whose loss to Kid Gavilan prevented the senior Davey from becoming the lightweight champion of the world. McGuire's second-place 9:03.7 would have won every other two mile in meet history.

McGuire became an All-American at Michigan, won the '81 Free Press Marathon and went on to a stellar coaching career for the Wolverines, with 12 Big 10 XC titles and over 100 All-Americans.

Ed Grabowski, of West Bloomfield, won the first title in his school's history by taking the mile run in 4:15.7. He beat a stellar field that included future Big 10 champ Steve Elliott of Pontiac and the 1973 victor, Don Hubbard of Ann Arbor Huron.

Jim Stokes repeated in the pole vault, easily establishing a new state and meet record over rival Dave Lipinski of Warren Fitzgerald (2nd at 14-9). The two had swapped the state record earlier in the season, with Stokes vaulting 15-4 at the Mansfield Relays and Lipinski winning the CMU Relays two weeks later with a 15-6. Stokes, a future Big 10 record holder at the University of Michigan, sailed better than half a foot higher than the previous meet best, clearing 15-6½. The other records set in Class A came from Detroit Central in the mile relay (3:18.5) and Detroit Kettering in the 440-yard relay at 42.8.

Livonia Bentley surprised the perennial powers in the sprints by capturing the 880-yard relay in a quick 1:29.0, the only points scored by Bentley during the day. Future Michigan football star Harlan Huckleby of Detroit Cass Tech won the 220-yard dash in 21.9.

Distance runners again stole the show at the Class B finals in East Lansing, headed by Hastings' Tom Duits. Duits posted the quickest time in state final history for all classes with his time of 4:13.2. Although the all-class record would only survive for one year, Duits' time survived as Class B's all-time best for 39 years. At the regional, Duits had become the first Michigan prep under 4:10 with his 4:09.4.

Flint Power's Dwayne Strozier won both sprints and anchored the Chargers record-setting 440-yard relay team. The 16-year-old junior dashed the 220 dash in a wind-aided 21.2 (2.7). He also just missed the 100-yard dash mark by one tenth of a second with his clocking of 9.8.

Dearborn Heights Robichaud dominated the relays to propel the Bulldogs to a narrow victory over second-place Linden. Robichaud won the 4x4 and set a new record in Class B, by taking honors in the 880-relay with its time of 1:29.3. Jeff Swanson of Battle Creek Pennfield repeated as the high jump winner in Class B with a 6-8½. Grosse Ile's Jeff Sinclair in the two-mile clocked 9:17.2.

The Class C meet in Mt. Pleasant saw another onslaught on the record books with a sparkling display of talent. Detroit DePorres piled up 58 points to win its third-straight team championship. Jon Abrams led the winners, copping the sprint double, and running a leg on the record tying 440-yard relay team.

In the long jump Detroit Country Day's Dave Merritt leaped 22-6¾. DePorres and St. Louis both dipped under the record in the mile relay, but still failed to win. Detroit Catholic's foursome of Ronald Strong, Mike Walton, Jasper Young and Darroll Gatson shattered the former mark by five full seconds with its 3:25.0. Gatson would later resurrect a shaky Michigan State University program as its head track coach. He was named the Big 10 Indoor coach of the year in 1999 after MSU won the Big 10 Indoor Track Championship for the first time since 1972.

Steve Wren of Haslett improved his pole vault to 14-6¾, while New Haven's Don Sims lowered the 120-yard high hurdles best to 14.3.

Defending champion Mendon tallied 60 points to easily hold off North Muskegon for the Class D title. Len Lilliard of Ann Arbor St. Thomas finished second to Mike Schaller of Bridgman in the high jump, breaking Lilliard's 1973 record with a mark of 6-3¾. Interestingly enough, Lilliard showed his athletic ability by setting a record in the shot put with a record heave of 53-8. Sophomore Jim Herendeen of Grass Lake won the pole vault for the second-straight year, upping the record to 13-3.

North Muskegon's 880-relay team won with a time of 1:31.6. The same Norsemen foursome of Ray Swanson, Ron Steele, Jim Pancy and Don Stafford earlier had appeared to set another mark by running the 440-relay in 44.0, only to be disqualified for a lane violation.

Upper Peninsula: Wayne Schwalbach broke a pair of records and ran a leg on the winning 880-yard relay to lead Escanaba to its third-straight Class A-B UP championship. Schwalbach set an all-time UP best throw of 58-7 in the shot and took advantage of a strong tailwind to run 9.9 in the 100-yard dash.

Rudyard successfully defended its Class C crown at Marquette High School. Barry Green won three events for the champs, including a record-setting clocking of 20.3 in the 180-yard low hurdles.

Joe Baker led Pickford to its 23rd consecutive UP championship by winning four events, including a record time of 20 seconds in the 180-yard lows.

1975

The fastest mile ever run in state history highlighted action at the Class A championships at Flint Northwestern High. Steve Elliott of Pontiac sped the four laps in 4:08.2, shattering the previous meet best posted back in 1963 by Detroit Eastern's Lou Scott. He also sliced Tom Duits' state record by 1.2 seconds. While running for the University of Michigan, Elliott would set a Big 10 meet record in the 1500 meters at 3:42.6.

Midland's Jeff Randolph dropped down from the two-mile run to push Elliott to the record and also broke 4:10 with his 4:09.2.

Harlan Huckleby, Detroit Cass Tech, won the 100-yard and 220-yard dashes and ran anchor on the Technicians' 440-yard relay team that set a record of 42.1, joined by Michael White, Roosevelt Smith and Thomas Seabron. Huckleby later scored 13 touchdowns during a six-year career as a running back for Green Bay of the NFL. Seabron, a powerful 6-3,

Keith Young
(Bob Parks photo)

215-pounder, not only was a teammate of Huckleby at Michigan but played in the NFL for San Francisco and St. Louis.

They weren't the only state champs and Michigan football stars from the Motor City to blossom in football. Mike Harden, who ran the opening leg on Detroit Central's winning mile relay team (3:20.6), went on to have a brilliant career in the NFL. During his eleven years as a defensive back with Denver and the LA Raiders, Harden intercepted 36 passes and scored five TD's, including a 100-yard return of a picked aerial during the 1985 season.

Keith Young repeated as the 880-yard champion with a great 1:51.3. He would join Davey the following year at the University of Tennessee, keeping the flood of Michigan's elite runners flowing toward the Volunteer state. A week following the state finals Young finished second at the International Prep Invitational in a 1:50.3 that would last for 13 years as the state record.

In the team battle, Flint Southwestern edged host Flint Northwestern by one point, earning the city of Flint its first state championship in eight years. Flint area schools dominated the Class A team race by capturing four of the top seven places among the field of 129 schools. The two front-runners were all knotted up at 30 points each going into the final event of the day the 440-yard relay. Southwestern finished behind first-place Cass Tech, but ahead of third-place Northwestern, earning the deciding points.

Another outstanding performance was the 23-7½ leap in the long jump by defending champion Terry Thames of Flint Northwestern. Saginaw blazed to a 1:28.2 win in the 880-yard relay. Running one of the legs for the victorious Trojan team was a very late bloomer, Ricky Flowers. In 1979 Flowers would win both the 440 and 220-yard dashes at the Big 10 championships while competing for Michigan State.

Taylor Center's Arnette Chisolm picked up the first-place medal for his win in the 120-yard high hurdles (14.2). He later became a very valuable performer for the Michigan Wolverines.

While the distance runners dominated action at the Class A meet, a sprinter from Flint Powers was the individual star at the Class B meet in East Lansing. Dwayne Strozier set individual records in both the 100-yard and 220-yard dash and anchored the Chargers' meet record 440-yard relay quartet.

Strozier had the fastest recorded time in meet history with his 9.5 effort in the 100-yard dash. Four sprinters clocked 9.8 or faster in the short sprint with Strozier's time the fastest posted in any class in state annals. He then returned to the track a little later in the afternoon and wiped out East Grand Rapids's Bob Swain's record that had lasted since 1945. Strozier's

20.8 clocking still remains as the Class B best, and second to only Marshall Dill's time of 20.6 set on the same Spartan surface in 1971.

Mike Helms of Fenton set the other record in Class B, posting a 1:53.8 for the 880. Distance runners seemed to be at their best in the mid-1970s, with two-mile record setter Jack Sinclair of Grosse Ile repeating in a fine 9:18.2. John Monahan, in winning the mile in 4:18.4, became the only state track champion from Detroit Austin Catholic.

Ed Poindexter's double win in the hurdles led Inkster to the team championship with 39 1/3 points. Runner-up Wyoming Park picked up 10 of its 31 points with a 1:31.1 time for the 880-yard relay.

Unionville-Sebewaing rolled up 72 points to win the state Class C title, 26 points ahead of runner-up Charlevoix. In a rarity for the era of the 1970s, not a single record was set on the CMU track.

Just the opposite took place in the Class D affair held at Caro High School. Upstaging the record-breaking rampage at the 1973 meet were the performers of 1975. Seven records bit the dust on the afternoon, with two other marks equaled, in perhaps the strongest Class D field in state history.

After posting three easy wins at Class C, Detroit DePorres dropped to Class D, where the Eagles had their hands full with runner-up Detroit East Catholic and others en route to their narrow four-point victory. DePorres' only first place came in the 440-yard relay, but had enough depth to again take home the championship trophy.

Headlining the Class D record breakers was high jumper Mike Winsor of Fulton-Middleton. His winning leap of 6-9¼ not only established the meet record for Class D, but also was an all-class record. He would later go on to a second-place finish at the '76 NCAA championships for Central Michigan, leaping 7-5 and pushing winner Dwight Stones to a World Record. A year later Winsor would jump his lifetime best of 7-5¼ in Germany.

Mike Walton led East Catholic to its second-place finish with victories in the 440 and 880 and a leg on the mile relay team. His time of 49.1 set a new record for Class D. Jim Herendeen of Grass Lake improved his own record in the pole vault to 13-9½.

Allendale's Dale Buist won the two mile in 9:35.6, while Dave Sykes of Litchfield knocked three-tenths of a second off the previous best in the 120-yard high hurdles with his 14.9. Orlin Swimmer of Morenci, an earlier winner in the long jump, had a 20.0 in the 180 lows.

A disappointed Dwight Jones of Grosse Pointe University Liggett could only tie his own records for the short dashes. He had blazed the century in 9.5 in winning the regional, but at the finals simply equaled his 1974 performance with times of 9.9 in the 100 and 22.0 for the 220. The Liggett sprint sensation did catch the eye of former distance ace Lou Scott, former mile record holder and 1968 Olympian. Scott, a former distance star at Arizona State University, secured Jones a full-ride track scholarship to his alma mater.

Mark Dentler made it four straight years for a mile champion from Mendon. Record holder Brad Courtney had won the mile at the previous three state meets.

Upper Peninsula: Calumet ended Escanaba's three years reign as ruler of the Upper Peninsula Class A-B division. For the first time in several years no records were broken as a downpour in the early afternoon interrupted the UP finals for approximately one hour.

The drop down from A-B to Class C certainly benefited Ishpeming, as the Hematites scored 43 points, ten more than second-place Norway. Sophomore Mike Dellangelo began a three-year reign as one of the UP's all-time top track & field performers. Dellangelo was the meet's only double winner and ran a leg on the winning mile-relay team. Chuck Cloninger did set a new record in Class C by winning the 880-yard run in 2:01.9.

Joe Baker won three more individual titles to again lead Pickford to an easy victory in Class D, the 24th-straight championship for Coach Webb Morrison's Panthers.

That Magic Mile

Steve Elliott wasn't fooling anybody. He had tried basketball and football, but ran into problems on the bus. Pontiac Central High School, in the midst of a court-ordered bussing controversy in 1972, was a tough place to be (the previous year, 10 buses had been fire-bombed).

So Elliott joined golf, swimming, and then baseball. A disagreement with the baseball coach left the sophomore without a sport. He wasn't about to go out for track; he was no runner.

But Roger Shepler, the legendary track coach at Central, had Elliott on his radar. He knew that the gritty youngster had run a 4:40 mile in junior high. He cornered him in the crowded hallway, and said, "Hey, I expect you on the track team."

" Well, coach…" muttered Elliott.

"No buts," ordered Shepler.

"Well, it's a little late…" said Elliott. Shepler didn't seem to hear him. Three weeks later, Elliott won the mile at the regional meet in 4:30.

The next year, Elliott got even better, thriving on 30-35 miles per week of training. In his first season of cross country, he finished 18th in the Class A individual finals, clocking 15:35 for three miles. The following spring he took second in the state championship mile as a junior, clocking 4:16.2.

A hundred miles away, Jeff Randolph was also improving quickly. Third in the cross country team race in 15:08 as a junior, he also placed third in the Class A two-mile in 1974, clocking 9:17.0 behind stars Pat Davey (9:00.4) and Mike McGuire (9:03.7). As seniors, the rivalry between the two grew, but they didn't even get a chance to race at the state cross country finals. Back then, individuals who qualified for the finals without their team were forced to compete in a separate race. (Before chip timing, officials rightly claimed it was a pain in the butt to score a major team championship with a bunch of non-team runners scattered throughout the field.) So Randolph won the individual race in 14:47 with a healthy 11-second margin over Sam James of Highland Park. Elliott ran a 14:47 as well, but had to settle for second in the team race behind Flint Northern star Keith Young's 14:38.

The two seniors got to know each other on a long van ride to New York, where they went to compete as part of a Michigan all-star team. On the ride back, Elliott recalls, "Randolph was saying that he's dropping down to the mile." Young, the state's best half-miler, jumped into the conversation too. "He said he was moving up to the mile. I'm sitting back there going, 'Hmmm , are these guys disrespecting me a little bit?' "

So Elliott ran hard that winter. Randolph had the same idea, but explains, "my dad, he was pretty adamant. He said, 'You're a swimmer too, and you're letterman in swimming. You need to seriously consider what you doing here. You're leaving the swim team without a senior letter swimmer if you go and run all winter.' So he made me go out for swimming again and it was the best thing that could've happened to me. I didn't have leg stress of running in the winter and slipping on ice. And it was real good off-season cardiovascular training. I was fit."

At an indoor meet at Eastern Michigan, Elliott faced off against Young, and his 4:13.1 broke the state record by 3.5 seconds, beating Young's 4:15.8 handily. Young and his coach Norb Badar decided he would stick with the half mile for the rest of the year. In the meantime, Randolph and his coach, Gary Jozwiak, continued to prepare for the mile. He started moving down to shorter events, regularly racing relays. His training volume didn't increase, but it certainly got more intense. Jozwiak, a fan of Jim Ryun's training, incorporated that intense interval-based program with his own ideas.

Nowadays, 4:30 milers who run 70 miles a week debate endlessly on the Internet whether Grant Fisher was undertraining at 50 miles per week. Randolph, though, says he never did more than 10 miles a week during track season. Cross country, of course, was a different story. In the fall he might hit 20 miles a week. "I never did any long runs," he recalls.

What Randolph was developing was the ability to sustain speed. He could easily reel off a workout of repeat quarters all under 60. Jozwiak admits, "That was why we thought he had a shot at putting them together and breaking the four-minute mile. We thought he had a chance to do that. He could take punishment when it came to workouts…. His recovery was great when he was doing repeats. He probably wondered if he was going to survive at the time."

Elliott, meanwhile, felt stuck in the 4:15 range. He says, "Coach Shepler started talking to me about negative splits. I said, 'Coach, what are you talking about?' He said, 'Well, we concentrate so much on going out fast and holding onto the middle two quarters, then coming home. Why don't we go out easy?' At the Oakland County meet, I went out in 2:10, and when we looked back on it we almost laughed, because the confidence of the guys were running with me just swelled like crazy. And I came back with close to 2:00 for the second half. We got done and it was 4:12. I thought it was the easiest run of my life."

May 31, 1975, on a beautiful all-weather track at Northwestern High School in Flint, the combatants lined up for four laps of destiny. The day felt cooler than normal, overcast with temperatures in the mid-60s. The athletes fidgeted at the line, their mood somber. Some of them had found out that morning that their hero, Steve Prefontaine, had been killed in a car crash the previous day.

The gun fired, and Randolph took it out for the first lap. Elliott took over on the second lap. Memories are hazy about just how fast they hit the lap splits. The first took about 60 seconds, and a pack of runners tried to hang with them. The second lap took about 62 or 63 seconds. The runners trailing Elliott and Randolph felt the pain.

Jozwiak, standing on the far side of the track, started yelling to Randolph. "You've got to pick it up!"

If he wanted to break the four-minute mile, he was going too slow. Randolph launched into the third lap with everything he had, Elliott battling him for every step. The rest of the field fell off dramatically.

Says Bill Spencer, who finished sixth, "When they heard that split, my sense was they just took off."

Recalls Sam James, "Randolph and Elliott, they were gone. There is no way: we weren't even in their area code. We were just fighting each other." The crowd, knowing they were witnessing a historic race, roared for them to go faster.

On the final turn, Elliott mounted his attack. He accelerated and swept past Randolph with ease. "Steve had the ability to turn it on and kick," says Randolph. "That's exactly what beat me in that mile. Because I could cruise, but at that time I wasn't able to suddenly just kick in a sudden speed change and go from a 62 or 63-second lap down to a 58-second. I just wasn't able to do that. So I had to get out there and push the pace, which is what I tried to do from early in that race. There's a photograph showing us coming off the last turn. It is so obvious that he is kicking in the afterburners and I'm sitting there just cruising along. He passed me on that last turn and that's when I realized, 'I've got to get it going, because he's moving faster than me.' I could cruise, I just couldn't kick."

Elliott hit the finish in 4:08.2, Randolph following in 4:09.2. They had crushed the championship record of 4:13.2 set in 1963 by Lou Scott of Detroit Eastern (who ran the 5000m in the 1968 Olympics). Both runners also bettered the state record of 4:09.4 set by Tom Duits of Hastings the year before.

James sprinted in like a maniac: "I just kept passing people. I went from eighth to third in the last 200." Spencer wasn't as fortunate: "My coach said not to get boxed in. I was boxed in for half the race." For decades it ranked as the greatest prep mile in Michigan history. "It was a great race," quips James. "I wish I could have watched it."

1. Steve Elliott (Pontiac Central) 4:08.2
2. Jeff Randolph (Midland) 4:09.2
3. Sam James (Highland Park) 4:15.7
4. Eric Burt (Ann Arbor Pioneer) 4:16.2
5. Doug Sweazey (Garden City East) 4:16.6
6. Bill Spencer (Grosse Pointe South) 4:18.0
7. Dan Heikkinen (Adrian) 4:18.2
8. Tony Badalamenti (St Clair Shores) 4:18.7

Elliott and Randolph both broke the state record.
(William Gallagher photo)

Elliott and Randolph tangled again the next weekend at the Tri-State meet in Fort Wayne, Indiana (the forerunner of the current Midwest Meet of Champions). Elliott won, but was disqualified for cutting off another runner on the first lap. The next weekend, Elliott traveled to Knoxville for the AAU Junior Championships. He ran 1500m in the qualifying heats in 3:48.1, the equivalent of a 4:06.4 mile. The next day in the finals, he defied probability by running another 3:48.1.

On June 21, the two rivals met again in Mt. Prospect, Illinois, a Chicago suburb, for the prestigious International Prep Invitational. The mercury topped 90-degrees. According to witnesses, the race played out the same. Randolph forged the pace and Elliott burned him with his kick on the final stretch to win by 2.8 seconds. Elliott's 4:07.4 set a state record that would last 39 years, until Grant Fisher broke it with a 4:02.02 at the 2014 Dream Mile in New York.

Track & Field News named Steve Elliott the top high school miler in the nation in 1975. Randolph ended the season ranked No. 5 in the U.S. Not until January 2015 did Michigan fans see another race with two or more of our preps breaking 4:10.

Not all great high school runners continue their careers in college, but many in the epic mile race did. Elliott starred at the University of Michigan, and though he never broke the four-minute mile, he came close with a 3:42.6 in the 1500 (4:00.5 converted). Randolph went on to be a two-time cross country All-

American for Wisconsin. James earned All-America honors five times at Tennessee and competed in the 1980 Olympic Trials in the steeplechase. Several of the others also made their mark in the college ranks, but ironically, the only one who would ever break the four-minute barrier was seventh-placer Dan Heikkinen. An All-American steeplechaser for Michigan, he ran 3:59.05 in 1982.

All of the runners involved in the race at Northwestern High figured that day was just a step in the event's progression. They all express shock that it took nearly 40 years for other Michigan high schoolers to top their achievements. "I didn't see us as being any more unique or outside of the normal curve," says Randolph. "It was just sort of the perfect storm of several runners at that level and it made for great competition. I figured it within the next few years records would fall and other kids would just come along and move ahead."

Elliott, now a grandfather, agrees. "I was so surprised it took so long." /JH/

/Adapted from the September/October 2015 issue of Michigan Runner. *Used by permission*/

1976

In Class A, a three-way tie for first developed in the high jump, the first tie at the winning height in 14 years. Could it be that all three leaders in the high jump negotiated the record height of 6-9½, with the same number of misses and then elected to agree to a tie? No explanation was given in any of the reports as to why there would have been a three-way tie. The jump-off rule to settle ties for first place had been in effect beginning with the 1963 season.

Teammates Dennis Lewis and Victor Freeman of Ypsilanti, along with Gary Martin of East Lansing, all successfully cleared the bar at the new record height, each jumper credited with a share of the record.

Flint area schools again swept the first two places in Class A at Houseman Field in Grand Rapids, with coach Norbert Badar's Flint Northern squad returning to the winner's circle for the first time in thirteen years. Defending champion Flint Southwestern's second-place finish made it another 1-2 sweep for the Flint public schools. Southwestern's sprinters teamed up to capture both of the short relays, with future Penn State and NFL veteran Booker Moore running a leg on each state championship relay units.

The Flint thinclads dominated the competition, capturing six firsts and five second-place medals in an enormous display of power.

Sophomore sprinter Mike Miller captured the 220 in 21.6 to take home a first-place medal for the champs, while Richard MacInnes won the other first for Northern in the 880-yard run. Miller later attended Tennessee, and his 10.11/20.15 performances at the 1982 NCAA meet got him third place in both sprints and recognition for the fastest-ever sprints by a Michigan native—albeit in the friendly altitude of Provo, Utah. After college he played in the NFL for a couple of seasons with the New York Giants.

In addition to the above-mentioned three-way tie for the record in the high jump, Flint Southwestern tied the existing meet record in the 880-yard relay in the quick time of 1:27.0.

Despite running in 85-degree heat, impressive times were registered in the distances. Sam James of Highland Park ran the two-mile in 9:04.7. He also made it to Tennessee where he became one of the nation's leading performers in the steeplechase, placing fifth in the 1979 NCAA championships. Grosse Pointe's Bill Weidenbach, son of former Michigan athletic director Jack Weidenbach, bested all milers in Grand Rapids with a 4:16.3.

Brad Simpson of Flint Southwestern pulled the day's biggest surprise by running the fastest 440 of the day in the next-to-last heat. He was also a member of the Colts record-tieing 880 relay. The mile relay team from Detroit Cass Tech posted the other record set during the day with its time of 3:18.2. John Kretschmer of Bloomfield Hills Lahser successfully defended his 1975 pole vault title by clearing 15-0. Randy Smith of Jackson won the 100, and later captured the Big 10 dash for MSU.

At Class B in Battle Creek, Flint Beecher was poised on the winner's stand, prepared to accept the first-place trophy. Most of the spectators had departed the stadium with the impression that Beecher, indeed, was the champion. For a moment, instant confusion reigned down on the track when the announcement was made that the state champion was Dearborn Heights Robichaud.

Beecher coach Marty Crane, who had kept a close eye on the standings, asked for a recheck in the team scoring. After Robichaud had already headed home with the first-place trophy, the discrepancy was found. Eight points had been inadvertently credited to Robichaud in the two-mile run, rather than to the rightful runner from Dearborn Divine Child. Crane's title would be the first of many for one of the state's winningest coaches.

An old event returned in 1976 and it would be the swan song for another. Competition in the discus came

Grosse Pointe North's Bill Weidenbach, the 1976 mile champ. (Jim Bikar photo)

back after a hiatus of 45 years. Unlike the heavier two-kilo discus thrown back in 1931, the high school discus was now a lighter 1.6-kilo. Sam Angell of Holland West Ottawa set the day's best mark with a heave of 161-9.

The low hurdles run at the 180-yard distance would give way to today's 330y/300m distance. It would mark the fourth change in yardage for the lows since the inaugural meet in 1895.

In Class B, Brian Blank of Grand Rapids Northview took the 440 in 48.3. Burton Bentley's Gordon Jackson leaped 6-9¼. Mike Hetts from Royal Oak Shrine threw the shot 58-10½.

The leading point winner in B was Mike Ball of Wyoming Park. He captured the 100-yard dash in 9.9, the 180 lows in 19.4 and fell just short of winner Randy Rife of Linden at the tape in the 220. Anthony Akins tied the 120 high highs meet record with his winning time of 14.2.

Detroit Benedictine won the Class C title at Ithaca, unseating the defending champions from Unionville-

Sebewaing. The winning Ravens set two records en route to the title. James Alderidge won the 880-yard run in 1:56.1 and the 440-yard relay clocked 44.0

This effort was enough to help offset USA's 1-2 sweep in the 180-yard low hurdles, with Mike Mischung and Dennis Dunkel dominating. Larry Booker of Wyoming Lee sped the 440 in 48.9 with Riverview Gabriel Richard setting a meet record in the 880-yard relay at 1:30.8. Ed LaBair captured the Class C mile title, one of only two state champions in Mayville history. He eventually became a 7-time Div. II All-American at Saginaw Valley.

Detroit DePorres easily capture its fifth-straight title in Class D by piling up 73½ points. Homer High had its highest finish ever by taking second to DePorres. Brian Houghton had the most impressive performance in Class D with his 48.4 in the 440-yard dash. Houghton became a double individual champ when he dusted a strong field to win the 220 in 22.3.

Jeff Jackson of Mt Pleasant Sacred Heart set a record in the 100-yard dash preliminaries that had to raise many eyebrows. Jackson was timed in 9.7 in the 100 to get credit for a new record, but was only able to place fourth in the finals, with a much slower 10.2.

One of the better races at the Class D meet on the Lansing Waverly track was the 120-yard high hurdles. Mike Jones of Saugatuck upset defending champion Dave Sykes of Litchfield, bettering Sykes' former record in the process with a time of 14.7. DePorres smashed its previous record, set a year earlier, by a full second with a 1:30.5 in the 880-yard relay.

Upper Peninsula: Sault Ste. Marie returned to the winner's circle at the UP A-B finals, nipping defending champion Calumet 43 to 40. Larry Babbitt of the winning Blue Devils had the day's most impressive performance when he shattered the 880-yard run record with a clocking of 1:56.3. All three UP division winners broke two-minutes, the first time this happened in UP history. Chuck Cloninger helped Ishpeming Westwood to the Class C championship by improving his 880 mark to 1:58.5.

Westwood edged neighboring Ishpeming 45 to 40 to claim the Class C title. Mike Dellangelo posted the day's best mark in Class C in lowering the 330-record down to 50.2.

Pickford had to come from behind to earn its 25th-straight UP championship, all under the coaching of Webb Morrison. The winning total of 35 points was the fewest points scored since it tallied 32 points while winning its first championship back in 1952. Following the meet, an end to an era came when the legendary Morrison announced his retirement as coach and superintendent of schools at Pickford.

Detroit's Season That Wasn't

The Detroit Public Schools athletes had a difficult spring, with no money in the budget for track and other spring sports after two millage failures. Roy Allen, assistant director of health and physical education, in February pleaded for schools to find donors who could help cover the $150,000 cost of running the spring program on a bare-bones budget. "We have told our coaches that they can do whatever is possible to sell their programs to a donor," said Allen, whose own son Marcus, a promising hurdler, would not be affected because he attended Redford St. Mary.

In March, two famous alumni stepped forward at a press conference to urge donors forward. Probate judge Willis Ward and Michigan Secretary of State Richard Austin had placed 1-2 in the PSL hurdles in 1931, for Northwestern and Cass Tech respectively. Private donations had saved PSL football ($146,000) and basketball ($50,000) but at the time of the press conference, only $1,000 was promised to track. Said Ward, "We're not sure just how much support we have but you don't know what's on the other side of the nountain until you've climbed it."

The drive only netted $15,000. By mid-April, Detroit teams still hadn't scheduled a meet. At Central High, Woodie Thomas had 80 athletes training daily. Said one, "Coach Thomas keeps telling us to keep at our practice, that there's still hope. I'm a senior, this is my last year, I could use some scholarship help to get to college."

The savior never came. Detroit's athletes had to make do with several unofficial meets, but still were allowed by the MHSAA to participate in regionals. At Grosse Pointe, Cass Tech took third, Kettering fourth, Murray-Wright fifth. The Cass Tech girls won. The Redford boys won their regional.

No one expected much from them at the state finals. Yet unheralded junior Deon Hogan of Kettering, who spent the season "working on his own," blasted the state record in the 440 with a 47.1. He also ran a leg on Kettering's 880-yard relay team that ran a quick 1:27.7. Joining Hogan, John Anthony and Paul Butler on the relay squad was future University of Michigan football standout Stanley Edwards. He would advance to the NFL, where he enjoyed a six-year career, primarily with the Houston Oilers.

The Detroit Redford mile relay of Randy Woodsen, Melvin Matthews, Ahamed Lile and Monte Callender set a meet record of 3:16.4.

The Detroit athletes who persevered accomplished more than anyone expected. But the loss was felt. Said Hogan, "Not having a track season set us back. A lot of people lost interest."

1977

Flint Southwestern captured its second state Class A title in three years at Guy Houston Stadium with a five-point victory over Grand Rapids Ottawa Hills. Four records were broken and another equaled, despite a stiff breeze that raked the track from east to west.

Much was expected of Ypsilanti's Dennis Lewis. Indoors, coming right off the basketball season, he leaped a national prep record 7-2 at the AFL-CIO meet in Cobo Hall. A week later, he did it again. In Flint, he captured a second state title with his 6-10. Lewis went on to world-class jumping, setting a national junior college record of 7-8 in 1985. He was ranked in the U.S. top 10 three times by *Track & Field News*.

Gary Carter of St. Clair Shores Lakeview won a furious two-mile with rival Weidenbach of Grosse Pointe North. The winning time of 9:00.4 tied Pat Davey's 1974 meet record. A week later Weidenbach would get his revenge, winning the International Prep Invitational in a state record 8:53.0, which lasted in the record books until 2000 brought us Dathan Ritzenhein.

Larry Verburg of Sterling Heights Ford won the 880 in 1:52.2. John Harvey of Flint Southwestern won the 330-yard low hurdles in the event's first year in 37.8. Ottawa Hills won the 440-relay in 42.5. James Ross of Detroit Mackenzie, winner of the long jump at 23-0, became the Big 10 champion in his specialty while competing for Michigan in 1981.

Flint Beecher won the Class B title in Battle Creek by an eyelash over Wyoming Rogers. The team from Rogers had been in position to win until placing fourth in the mile relay in 3:24.4. A tenth faster and the squad would have tied Beecher's 40 points for the win.

Rogers' Mike Erickson and Mark Poelman paced the second-place Golden Hawks with a pair of victories. Erickson became the first state prep athlete to win the low hurdle-440 double, while Poelman won the mile and 880, the latter in a meet record 1:52.9. The B high jump went higher than Class A, as Derick Futrell of Saginaw Buena Vista scaled 6-11¼.

Marcus Allen led Redford St. Mary to its first Class C state title in Ithaca with a double win in the hurdles.

Normally, Dennis Lewis had much better form. The Ypsilanti star eventually became a 7-8 jumper. (Charles Zirkle photo)

Jim Smith of Royal Oak Shrine won the 220-440 double and ran a leg on the winning 880-yard relay to lead all individuals. Charlie Grigg, with his win in the discus, was Roger City's first boys state track champ.

The Class D meet at Lansing Waverly remarkably had four winners who posted the fastest times of the day in any class. Stanley Young of Detroit DePorres sped the 100 in 9.5 in the prelims to match Dwayne Strozier's meet record. He also captured the 220 in a blistering 21.5, fastest time in Class D history for the 220 run around a turn.

DePorres could perhaps claim its 1977 squad as the finest ever in Class D ranks. The Eagles scored 92 points, at the time the highest point total ever, aided by five first-place medals, four of the marks going down as Class D bests. The DePorres foursome of Young, Darrold Gohlston, Mark McClendon and Leonard Thornton took the 880 relay in 1:29.4.

McLendon and Thornton were joined by Michael Hinton and Michael Taylor in capturing the mile relay in 3:29.0. Cedric Coles captured the discus at 153-1.

Joining Hogan and Young as one of the stars of the day was David Sykes of Litchfield. The future University of Wisconsin ace easily had the best times of the day in any class with his wins in both hurdles. He sizzled over the lows in 36.9 and won the highs in 14.1. He captured his third championship with a 21-9½ long jump.

Rules in 1977 evidently prohibited a hurdle record to be set when a competitor knocks over a hurdle. Reports on the 1977 Class D meet had Sykes knocking down the first hurdle en route to his victory. Using today's standards, this would not be a disqualification for record-breaking purposes. If true, then Sykes should have been recognized as the state Class D record holder in the high hurdles. The following week at the Midwest Meet of Champions, he proved that his time of 14.1 was no fluke. The Litchfield star placed third, improving his time to 14.0. Following a meeting of track experts gathered in Lansing in March of 1998, Sykes was rightfully declared the Class D record holder.

Upper Peninsula: Mark Dellangelo closed out a brilliant prep career by winning three events to headline the UP finals. He ran the 220 in 22.2 and the 440 in 50.1 to set new marks and also took the long jump. The speedster nearly brought Ishpeming's 880-yard relay team a victory by closing a big gap before losing to Westwood by one tenth of a second. Dellangelo's heroics, however, weren't enough to keep Rudyard from winning the Class C championship. Dean Miksa of Norway powered over the high hurdles in 14.7 in C.

Marquette trailed Escanaba by less than a point heading into the day's final event. The Eskimos placed second behind only Menominee, while Marquette trailed in third place, giving Escanaba a 53½ to 52 victory. Leading the way for the victors was Jim DeFresne, whose clocking of 9.9 for the 100-yard dash equaled the all-time UP best for the century.

Coaching legend Webb Morrison had retired, but he was in the stands lending support as Pickford rolled to its 26th Class D championship in a row. Mark Freebury of Cedarville broke a record that dated back to 1942 in winning the Class D division of the 100. Mark Oberlin took the 880-yard run for the third-straight year as the Crystal Falls senior equaled his own record of 1:59.0.

Norb Badar: The Catalyst

For many years Norb Badar had to ruminate over why his Flint Northern squads could not escape its runner-up label. Seven years, from 1954 thru 1960 Badar watched as his Viking thinclads finished in second place at the state track finals. However, good things would come to those who have patience.

Badar was reared in Cleveland and attended Baldwin Wallace College before crossing the Michigan border to enroll at Michigan Normal (EMU). As an athlete, he was one of the nation's best, though his specialty wasn't on the Olympic program—he ran the 220-yard low hurdles in 23.2. At Baldwin-Wallace he was part of a devastating 1-2 punch in the hurdles with his teammate, Harrison Dillard, who later won Olympic gold in the 100 and the 110 hurdles.

He would kick off what would prove to be a most successful teaching and coaching career in 1951, before hanging up his whistle in 1983, a career spanning 33 years where Badar would guide Flint Northern to four state Class A championships, to complement his nine second-place finishes.

When asked if he had doubts that he would ever win a state championship, the humble Badar simply said "No." When pressed to elaborate, he replied: "I just felt it wasn't the most important thing."

Badar coached in an era when high school track was dominated by teams from the Saginaw Valley Conference. Beginning with Saginaw Arthur Hill's state title in 1944, a Valley team would win seventeen Class A championships in eighteen years. Only Grand Rapids Ottawa Hills in 1951 was able to cut into the Valley dominance.

Not only did the Valley bring back the first-place trophy, but also from 1952 thru 1961 Norb Badar and his coaching pals from the Saginaw Valley placed first and second for 10 consecutive years.

Badar fondly remembered his teams' competitive battles with Pontiac Central in the late 1950s and early 1960s. "Dean Wilson was Pontiac's coach in 1956—he was a hell of a coach. After Dean there was Roger Shepler, he was a great coach as well. We had some really great, but respectful, battles. They truly had a great all-around program."

During Badar's seven-year run of having to be content with lugging the runner-up trophy back to Flint, his arch rivals from Pontiac were state champions five times, including the Hayes Jones-led Chieftain track team from 1956 that could make a case as the state's all-time top team.

Coaching in an area that has always been rich in talent, Badar's track teams won an amazing 13 city championships. He was so respected by his peers and friends in track and field, that just one year after his retirement, the Greater Flint City Track and Field Invitational would be renamed the Norb Badar Classic in 1984.

Badar coached a number of top-flight athletes, but he loved to talk about Keith Young: "Certainly, one of my favorites was Keith Young. In addition to his exploits in track Young was also a two-time state champion in cross-country. Young was one of the fastest guys in school. He could have been one of our best sprinters. He was smart enough to realize that with proper training and with his basic speed he could dominate by moving up to the half-mile." And with Badar to guide Young, he did dominate, winning state titles twice in cross country in addition to his track exploits.

While giving his acceptance speech as an inductee into the Flint Area Sports Hall of Fame in 2010, Young was quick to heap praise on Coach Badar,

"There's no way possible it would have happened if it wasn't for Norb Badar," said Young. "I just can't tell you enough about him. He was the catalyst. He was just brilliant. I had no idea what I was doing, but for some reason, working with my teammates and with his coaching, I was blessed to win in my first year."

Young would continue to Tennessee where he

Keith Young conferring with coach Norb Badar.

achieved All-American status in the 1500 meters and was a part of a world record distance relay team in 1977.

Badar was ahead of his time. He was not only able to convince Young, but other sprinters as well, that they could be more successful by moving up to the quarter, half, or even the mile.

In 1958 when Badar's team lost the state meet due a bad break in the meet's final event, the 880-yard relay. Broad jump champion Reg Gillard was running in first place for Northern when he stepped on the cement curb just before the straightaway. Gillard was thrown off stride, and by the time he recovered, he had dropped back in last place before heading into the first exchange zone. Northern's margin of defeat was by about a stride.

A win for Northern would have given Northern the winning trophy. But Badar just said: "Those things happen sometimes. I think we make too much of why we're out there as coaches and why kids are out there." Badar's proudest feat: "I never had to cut a kid from the team. That's what I like best about the sport." After winning six state championships (four in track & field) and having 19 top 10 finishes in his 33 years at the state finals, along with 13 city championships, there can be little doubt of the giant role Badar played at Flint Northern. Until this once proud school sadly closed its doors in 2013, not only did Flint Northern fail to win another team state championship, the Vikings never again had even an individual state champion.

Although he retired in 1983, his love for track and field never waned, serving as an active member for MITCA (Michigan Interscholastic Track Coaches Association) by annually attending meetings and rarely missing an important track event. Up until the new millennium Badar kept active as a part-time coach at Flint Powers.

Badar was one the first to receive the annual Art Jevert award, given to an individual who has made a significant contribution to track and field and/or cross country in the state of Michigan. Though he received many other awards, Badar never sought personal recognition.

"I prided myself as a coach but I wanted to be a good teacher," he said. "Sports are voluntary, when kids are more concerned about the prize at the end; their priorities are mixed up. Rewards and recognition are bonuses. Prizes are frosting, but don't look for them. Keep things in perspective."

Norb Badar passed away at the age of 89 on January 2, 2014.

_____

1978

By taking first place in eight of the 14 events, Detroit area teams dominated the Class A state meet, held once again at Flint's Guy Houston Stadium. Detroit Cass Tech, by amassing 43 points, won its first state title since the heyday of Eddie Tolan back in the 1920s. A 1-2 placing in the 120-yard high hurdles highlighted the Technicians victory for head coach Robert Glenn.

Marcus Allen led teammate Curtis Cade across the finish line in the hurdles and smashed Bill Tipton's 22-year-old record in the process. Allen's time of 13.8 was one of four records to fall during the day. High jumper Paul Piwinski of Warren Cousino cleared the bar at 6-10½. Shelby Johnson of Taylor Center covered the 330-yard lows in 37.0 and Pat Kelly of Grand Rapids Union launched the discus 166-10.

Flint Southwestern took three first-place medals, but fell short by nine points of winning its third state title in four years. Brian Carpenter led the runner-up Colts, winning the long jump at 23-6¾, and running a leg on the winning 440 and 880-yard relays. Carpenter, following his collegiate career at the University of Michigan, played for three different teams during a four-year career in the NFL, intercepting four passes from his defensive backfield position.

Deon Hogan moved down from the 440 to capture the 100 and 220-yard dashes. The Detroit Kettering ace clocked 9.8 for the 100. Portage Northern's Eric Henricksen had a great day by taking the mile in 4:13.9 and the two-mile in an impressive 9:04.9.

A busy man during the field events was Michael Petsch of Redford Union. Petsch displayed his versatility by winning the shot put with a 61-1¼, taking third in the discus and still having enough bounce to place sixth in the long jump.

Although no records were set in the Class B state championships in Marysville, the meet certainly had its share of dramatics. The team title hinged on the outcome of the mile relay. Muskegon Heights had a two-point lead over Flint Beecher as the teams settled into the starting blocks. In an exciting race freshman Jon Fralick produced a sterling anchor for Coach Marty Crane's Buccaneers, edging Muskegon Heights and tieing the Tigers for the team title at 39 points.

The meet's best performance perhaps came in the 880-yard run when Holly High School's Jeff Lewis upended previous meet record holder Mark Poelman of Wyoming Rogers, 1:53.1-1:54.5. Poelman had to settle for fifth in the mile run but history would ultimately ordain the top-notch competition he faced. Winning the mile run in 4:21.5 was Brian Diemer of Grand Rapids South Christian, who would eventually become a 3-time Olympian, winning steeplechase bronze in 1984. Diemer finished ahead of runner-up Gerry Donakowski, who, in 1986-87, would become a two-time national champion in the 10,000-meter run.

Mike Shea of Detroit DeLaSalle and Ded DeWeerd of Hudsonville running in different heats, posted identical times of 50.3 in the 440 to share first place. Mason's Eric Young defeated Muskegon Reeth Puffer's Johnny Williams in the 330-yard low hurdles, 38.3-38.4. Williams, following a superb gridiron career at the University of Wisconsin, would later be the leading rusher for the Michigan Panthers, champions of the now defunct United States Football League.

Class C was nearly as tight as Class B with Detroit Benedictine nosing out Whitehall by a scant point to take the team title. Whitehall certainly had the meet's outstanding individual in Martin Schulist. The future MSU star not only won both long distance races but set meet records. His two-mile mark of 9:20.0 would survive as a record for 26 years. The runner-up Vikings took four first-place medals but were unable to overtake Benedictine's superior depth. Benedictine' only win came in the 880-yard relay. John Darya, with his win the 880-yard run, remains Burton-Atherton's only state track champ.

Distance runners also headlined the Class D meet held at Lansing Sexton. Akron-Fairgrove, led by Jerry Curtis, dethroned six-time champ Detroit DePorres. Curtis took the two mile in a meet record 9:28.0.

Curtis, with a 4:24.0 in the mile, set yet another meet record. Evans Lalas of Frankfort joined Curtis as the meet's only other double victor, winning the 220 and 440-yard dashes.

Upper Peninsula: A packed house with more than 3,000 fans saw the UP finals at Marquette High School. Gary Dravecky won both throws to lead Ironwood to its first title in 18 years. Kingsford's Kevin French not only was the leading scorer at the A-B meet but also accounted for the only record in his class by equaling the 330-yard low hurdles record at 39.8, a record that would stand until the hurdles were raised in 1988.

Although it never landed a first place at the finals, Ishpeming Westwood had enough depth to win the Class C team title over St. Ignace. Roy Lyberg of L'Anse was the only double winner, including a record-breaking 10.1 for the 100-yard dash. Pickford made it 27 state titles in a row in Class D. The Panthers piled up 79 points and set five new records. John Adrzejak led the winners with three first-place finishes and accounted for two of the new marks with wins in the pole vault and low hurdles.

1979

High jumpers headlined the action at the state Class A championships, held once again at Flint's Guy Houston stadium. Not one, but two jumpers, cleared the seven-foot barrier for the first time at the state championships. The competition was so tough Jon English of Brother Rice could only manage a third-place finish despite leaping 6-11.

John McIntosh of Sterling Heights Stevenso, and Dave Elliott of Ann Arbor Pioneer set the new meet record at 7-0, with McIntosh winning on misses. Flint Northern won its fifth Class A title on the hometown track, but most of the individual honors belonged to the Detroit Public School League and Detroit area athletes. Ten of the 15 first-place medals went to the Motor City.

In the 120 hurdles, Ann Arbor Pioneer's Jeff Herndon matched the 13.8 set the previous year by Cass Tech's Marcus Allen. Paul Babits of Redford Union, with a winning 14-7, became the second Babits in three years to capture a pole vault title. Brother Bob still retained the family's bragging rights with his 14-11 in 1977.

The best near-miss on a record was the 61-10 shot put by Phil Wells of Warren Mott, missing the meet mark of 62-1 by a scant three inches, despite competing on a sprained ankle injured while warming up. Ken Brown paced Flint Northern to the title with the day's best leap at 21-1¾. He also ran a leg on the winning mile relay team for coach Norb Badar's thinclads.

Dearborn Heights Robichaud won four, including a 220 and 440 dash double by Mark Woodson, to capture Class B. Robichaud finished with 48 to outdistance Ecorse (32) and Flint Beecher (31).

Brian Diemer won an impressive distance double in Class B. The Grand Rapids South Christian senior didn't disappoint his legion of hometown followers by winning the mile run in 4:14.9, after earlier romping home an easy winner in the two-mile with a 9:22.2.

Ed Brown of Otisville LakeVille stretched over the 330-yard low hurdles in 37.1 to give track enthusiasts a harbinger of things to come for the future Saginaw Valley 400 hurdler. Bob Krikke made 1979 the year of the high jumpers by leaping 6-11½. Brian Miller of Grand Rapids Christian vaulted 14-8.

In Class C, Matt Baldus of Grant flopped over the bar at 6-10, setting a record that would survive for twenty years. DeWitt edged Detroit Benedictine by a point and a half to win its first state track title. DeWitt managed the win without the aid of a first-place finish. Benedictine won a pair, including a 1:29.2 in the 880-yard relay.

Whitehall once again showed up in the distances, only with a new name. Guy Jacobson jumped out of the shadows of his 1978 teammate Martin Schulist to win the double, clocking 9:20.6 to post the second-fastest time in Class C meet history and coming back for a meet record 4:15.8 mile.

Class D also became the first boys state final run on a metric track, the new Grand Blanc oval. Detroit DePorres continued its dominance by romping to its seventh title in eight years. The Eagles piled up 87 points to take the first-place trophy over runner-up Ann Arbor Gabriel Richard by nearly 40 points.

The meet was especially sweet for DePorres head coach Robert Lynch. He saw his son Vernon help spark the Eagles to the title by capturing both hurdles. Mike Taylor became another double winner in the 200 and 400. Jerry Campbell of DePorres got an automatic meet record with his 10.9 win in the 100-meters.

Vestaburg's Robert Snyder won the same event that his father once captured. Gaylord Snyder took three first-place medals for Vestaburg back in 1949. Thirty years later, his son Bob would bring home a medal in the long jump with his winning 21-3¼, just slightly better than Dad jumped three decades earlier on the cinder runway at Michigan State College.

Upper Peninsula: Confusion, false starts and cold weather all put a damper on the UP Finals in Marquette. A mandate issued from the MHSSA office that all marks set on the metric track would automatically become meet records led to confusion for the record books that would carry over to the next millennium. To further complicate the problem, the state also insisted that all marks made in the field events were to be measured only in metrics.

It is mind boggling to believe that nearly twenty years passed before anybody realized that Gary Dravecky's measured mark of 16.62 meters was a meet record. None of the officials or members of the media on hand in Marquette had a conversion table. Converting to the imperial distance would put Dravecky's mark at 56-6½, a record that was not recognized for more than for 20 years.

The same misfortune came to pass for Keenan Failing of Escanaba. Nobody realized that Failing's metrically measured mark of 1.95 in the high jump would convert to 6-4¾, a half inch higher than the record.

Kevin French led Kingsford to the Class A-B team championship. French won both hurdle events, taking the lows hurdles shortly after winning the 400. Ishpeming Westwood successfully defended in Class C, placing in nine of the 11 running events.

Perhaps the biggest news to headline the UP final was the new champion crowned in Class D. After winning an unprecedented 27 straight UP titles, an achievement unmatched by any other Michigan high school in any sport, Pickford saw Crystal Falls Forest Park walk away with the team trophy. The Panthers fell all the way down to fourth place.

1980

Detroit Central won its first state championship in track & field since 1911 with a convincing performance at Grand Rapids' Houseman Field. Central piled up 57½ points, the most scored since Pontiac Central totaled 61 in winning the crown back in 1956.

Coach Woody Thomas's corps of splendid sprinters paved the way by winning all three relays. The foursome of David Beasley, Demetrius Hallums, Steve Jones and Jeff Hardy shattered the record for the 4x2 in a state record time of 1:26.9. The Trail Blazers won by a remarkable two full seconds over their nearest competitor.

Demetrius Hallums led the charge by running a leg on two winning relay quartets and placing first in the 220-yard dash. Only a second-place finish in the 100-yard dash, where Hallums finished second by a whisker to Don Anderson of Detroit Cody, prevented him from taking four first-place medals.

The most impressive performance of the entire day had to be Derek Harper's wind-aided long jump. He sailed an even 25 feet to easily surpass any previous performance in Michigan prep history, windy or legal. He later jumped 25-6¾ for the Wolverines and captured a Big 10 long jump title.

Two other marks that did go into the books came from Jerome Rivers of Detroit Northern and James Browne of Brother Rice. Rivers ran 36.8 in the 330-yard lows and Browne heaved the discus 176-1. Browne also won the shot crown with a toss of 58-½. He later became a standout football star at Boston College and had a brief career in the NFL with the Oakland Raiders.

Cody's Don Anderson captured a unique double by adding the 440-yard title to his win in the 100-yard dash. A rare tie resulted in the 440 when Anderson and Rob Grainger of Portage Central, running in different heats, posted an identical time of 48.9.

In Sturgis, Coach Marty Crane's Flint Beecher squad easily extended its domination with its fourth Class B title in five years, scoring 57 points. Runner-up Dexter scored 42 with the help of Andreas Laut. The foreign exchange student from Germany made his stay in the USA a memorable one by capturing three first-place medals.

Laut took the first Class B 100 dash run at the metric distance in 10.6. Laut's other victories came in the 200 (21.5) and the long jump (22-8¼). Mt

Pleasant's Ron Finch twirled the discus out 167-3 after earlier winning the shot title.

Beecher dominated the track, although the Bucs only captured a pair of wins. Paul Richmond covered 800-meters in 1:54.8, while the mile relay squad emerged the victors in 3:22.2. Running a leg on the winning foursome for Beecher was Lonnie Young. Following a great gridiron career at MSU, he would go on to have a long and successful career in the NFL, primarily with the St. Louis Cardinals.

Young wasn't the only member from Beecher to go on to stardom in the NFL. Placing fourth in the shot put in 1979 was Carl Banks. An All-American at MSU, he would become an All-Pro linebacker for many years with the World Champion New York Giants.

Kenny Lay took honors in the 400-meter run for Muskegon Heights. A few years down the road Lay would become the fire chief in his native city, the second 400/440 champ from the Heights to return home to become a chief. Sam McMurray, the 1962 440 state Class A champion, stayed home in Muskegon Heights where he became the municipality's chief of police.

At the Class C finals in Middleville, Ecorse nearly doubled the score over second-place Grand Rapids South Christian. Jamie Weathers had a part in three wins, taking the 220 and 440-yard dash, and running the anchor for the record-setting mile relay. Weathers joined teammates Milton Lewis, Michael Dunlap and Willie Thomas in running four laps in 3:24.6.

Paul Diaz of St. Louis ran the 880-yards in a new meet standard of 1:54.9. Diaz added the mile title by edging 1979 champion Guy Jacobson of Whitehall, 4:20.8-4:21.2. Jacobson did successfully defend his two-mile run title with a 9:28.8.

Mike Krauss of Clinton won the discus at 169-11, while Detroit Lutheran West blistered the 440-yard relay in 43.9. Tim Johnson of Grand Rapids South Christian joined Diaz as a double champion with victories in both hurdles.

In Class D, Perennial power Detroit DePorres scored the most points in state history by exploding for 110 points. The Eagles 80-point margin over second-place Covert remains the biggest point differential of all-time.

Detroit DePorres won nine out of the 16 events to dominate the action on the Grand Blanc metric surface. Larry Jordan had a perfect day for the champs with wins in both short sprints (including a meet record 10.5) and running legs on the winning 400 and 800-meter relay teams.

Scott Jakubik of Onekama became the final meet record setter with his winning 13-10 in the pole vault.

Upper Peninsula: Mike Photenhauer and Greg Ostrenga placed 1-2 in the 1600 and 3200 runs to lead

Menominee to the Class A-B title. Photenhauer's 4:27.6 in the 1600-meter run would stand for 17 years as the meet record. Runner-up Escanaba had a triple winner in sprinter John Tolfa. He swept the 100, 200 and 400 meters to lead the Eskimos. In a tight finish Tolfa edged Menominee's Chris Hofer in the 200. Hofer would later emulate his father as a successful head football coach, guiding Kingsford to the Class B state championship in 1993.

Rod Garwood of Gwinn won the 300-low hurdles in 38.5, the best UP time clocked for the eleven years the lows were contested.

Munising won five events, including a pair of firsts in the short sprints by Chuck Secreast to outdistance Iron Mountain in Class C.

Pickford, who lost its 27-year hold on the D title in 1979, returned to its customary place at the top. Scoring 42 points, Pickford topped second-place Norway, winner of the Class D football championship earlier in the fall. Coaching the second-place Knights was Vic Fochesato, who 30 years earlier became the first UP sprinter to run the 100-yard dash under 10 seconds while competing for Hermansville.

1981

The Trailblazers of Detroit Central lived up to their nickname in 1981. Coach Woody Thomas' speedsters marked themselves as one of Michigan's all-time best squads with a remarkable 61 points, nearly doubling the total over second-place Detroit Cody. Central's total matched that earned by the famous Pontiac Central squad of 1956. The Trailblazers did it without scoring a single point in the field events. The entire meet proved to be a feast for the Detroit Public League schools as the Motor City lads captured six of the 16 events.

Central posted an impressive win, even though it was unable to record what might have been Michigan's best-ever performance in the 880-yard relay. The Trailblazers placed an unprecedented 2-3-5 in the 220-dash. Hurdler Tom Wilcher joined the 220 trio of Demetrius Hallums, David Beasley and William White in the eagerly anticipated relay.

As the lead runners settled into their blocks for the start of the relay, track enthusiasts asked not if Central would set a new record, but by how much? Shortly after veteran starter Kermit Ambrose fired his .32 caliber starter pistol, another blast shortly followed, an obvious signal for a false start. But who false started? Unfortunately, for track buffs like this author who traveled many miles to Flint's Guy Houston stadium, the lead runner for Detroit Central was a little over-anxious and guilty of a false start. One now can only

speculate what Central's time might have been if allowed a second chance.

All of the above runners would go on to compete very successfully at the next level. Beasley and White became mainstays for Eastern Michigan. Hallums became a standout performer for the Spartans of Michigan State while Wilcher not only became one of the nation's leading hurdlers but also was a standout tailback on the Wolverine's football team. Steve Jones and Marc Jett teamed up with Wilcher and Hallums to capture the 440-yard relay by the surprisingly wide margin of a second and a half.

The depth in the speed department was such that the mile relay foursome of Beasley, Wilcher, White and Wilfred Hart also romped home first. Wilcher, who would later win back-to-back titles as the head coach of Detroit Cass Tech in 1994-95, won the 120-yard hurdles in 13.5.

Don Anderson, future Purdue football star, won both short dashes. His winning time in the 100-yard dash of 9.6 equaled the Class A meet record set in earlier years by Marshall Dill and Reggie Jones. It would last forever, with 1981 being the last Class A meet run on a yard track. Anderson, winner of the 100

Earl Jones became one of America's legendary 800 runners.

and 440-yard dashes in 1980, joined Detroit Kettering's Deon Hogan as the only Class A athletes to ever win titles in the 100, 220 and 440. The Cody star not only became the only track champion in Detroit Cody history, but also became the only former Comet ever to make the grade in the NFL.

Junior Earl Jones of Taylor Center began his middle-distance dominance for the next couple of years by winning the 880-yard run in 1:54.6. Four years later Jones would become the American Record holder in the 800-meter run with his victory at the 1984 Olympic Trials.

Field event competition was highlighted by Traverse City's Scott Krupilski's win in the pole vault. The Trojans of TC would dominate this event during the 1980s with six champions over the next seven years.

Jamie Weathers came up big again for Ecorse High as the 1980 Class C champions made the move up to Class B a successful one. The Red Raiders were easy victors in Sturgis by scoring 56 points to dethrone the defending champions of Flint Beecher, in second place with 32.

Weathers won the 400 in 48.8, placed second in the 200 and anchored the 800 and 1600-meter relay teams to victories. The Raider foursome of Weathers, Brian Pope, Rodney Nedd and Willie Thomas clocked 3:20.5 in the 4x4.

Cadillac's Mark Smith, a future Mid-American Conference steeplechase champion, lowered the 3200 meet record to 9:11.6. He also finished second to Tim Cannon of Cranbrook in an exciting 1600 with Cannon the victor in 4:13.5.

Smith's Cadillac teammate, Jim Bowman, leaped beyond the 23-foot barrier in the long jump. He also placed in both dashes to help Cadillac take third in the team race, just a point behind runner-up Beecher. Bowman's third in the 100 meters was one place ahead of future CMU teammate Curtis Adams. Both Adams and Bowman would go on to great careers on the gridiron. Adams became the leading ground gainer in Chippewa history before embarking on a brief career in the NFL. Bowman followed up his collegiate career with a five-year stint in the NFL as a defensive back with the New England Patriots.

Ricky Swilley of Saginaw Buena Vista had a big day for the Knights. He took both shorts dashes and anchored the 400 relay team to a meet record. The Buena Vista quartet of Reggie Choice, Steve Crawford, Silas Houston and Swilley edged Muskegon Catholic by a tenth of a second. Jim McGrath, Southgate Schafer's only state champion, clocked 37.2 in the 300-meter low hurdles.

Detroit Lutheran West won its first title in 20 years with 44 points at the Class C finals held in Clare. The meet was the first metric finals ever held in Class C and produced a couple of suspicious records. Both the boys and the girls 100-meter races produced a raft of suspiciously fast times. The author suspects there is a distinct probability that each 100-meter race may have been run at a shorter distance or runners were given a boost by excessive winds.

The Challenge of Record-Keeping

The demand for more sites, with the addition of girls track in 1973 coupled with the move away from having colleges host the finals, made the measurement of records more difficult during this era. It was a rarity for a wind gauge at many of the state finals over the next 30 years. To further complicate the issue some state meets had final times posted to the one hundredth of a second, even though fully automatic timing was not in use at any of the sites until 1984, and not at all the sites until 2003. The rule book clearly states that when hand timing is used, times must be rounded up to the next highest tenth of a second, a practice often not enforced at some state meets.

Lutheran West captured both short sprint relays, got a first from Louis Cox in the high jump at 6-9 and Reginald Harris in the 110-meter high hurdles at 14.3. Nelson Hanson won Lincoln-Alcona's first state title by putting the shot 56-1¾.

Detroit DePorres made it nine titles in ten years with another resounding win at the Class D finals held in Caro. The Eagles totaled 92 points with Battle Creek St. Phillip taking home the second-place trophy with 50 points. Greg Henderson had a hand in four first-place finishes for the champs.

Henderson won both hurdles, including a meet record of 37.3 in the 300-meter lows and a leg on two of the three winning relay teams for the Eagles. Brian Burger had an impressive day for Reading with wins in the 200 meters (22.9) and the 400 meters (49.8).

A pair of marks were set in the field events. Dave Koenigsknecht of Fowler began his dominance in the long jump with a leap of 22-9¼. John Chandler of Mesick hurled the discus 158-1 to establish a new meet standard.

Upper Peninsula: The Menominee Maroons gave a nice going away present to coach Fran Mellinger, a second-straight Class A-B championship at the UP finals in Marquette. Retiring after 21 years as the coach of the Maroons, Mellinger saw his ace sprinters Chris Hofer and Craig Leitzke place 1-2 in the 100 and 200 to lead the victors.

Iron Mountain won its first UP track championship by outscoring Ironwood 57 to 39 in Class C. Led by double winner Tom Flaminio, the Mountaineers took five events and led from start to finish.

Cedarville capped a year to remember by winning the Class D crown for coach Tom Wilson. Back in 1970, Wilson had won the Class D 880 while competing for rival Pickford. Earlier in the fall the Trojan football team posted a perfect season while winning the state Class D football championship at the Pontiac Silverdome.

1982

Detroit Central won six first places and scored an all-time state best total of 78 points to easily win its third-straight Class A championship. Thomas Wilcher won the 110-meter highs and 300-meter lows and anchored one of three winning Central relay teams. David Beasley won the 400 and coach Woody Thomas' flyers swept the relays.

Central's 4 x 100 winning time of 41.7—the first now that the Class A meet was metric—would stand as a meet record for next 27 years. Wilcher's winning time of 13.6 was second only to his own 13.5 established a year earlier of 13.5 (the metric 110m is only 11 inches farther than 120 yards). Earlier, Wilcher pulled off a rare feat at the PSL championships, winning the high hurdles four consecutive years. Right on Wilcher's heels was his future teammate at the University of Michigan, Derrick Stinson of Muskegon, in 13.7.

Wilcher again set a record in the 300-meter lows with a time of 36.3. Wilcher and Stinson than took their talents to the International Prep Invitational in Naperville, Illinois, taking on the best high schoolers in the country. Just as in the State meet, Wilcher and Stinson finished an impressive 1-2 over the 36-inch intermediate hurdles, Wilcher setting a state record of 37.0 despite stumbling off the final hurdle.

They were not the only Michiganders to finish first and second at the famed IPI. What was highly unusual was that the one-two finish in the pole vault came from competitors from the same school --Traverse City Central. Scott Krupilski, after setting a new Class A record at Flint's Houston stadium with a vault of 15-8, teamed up with fellow Trojan Jim Hensel to place first and second in Naperville, the only time that has ever been accomplished in the long history of the meet. In between, Hensel soared over a state record 16-½ at the Traverse City Record-Eagle Honor Roll meet.

The versatile Krupilski, who consistently vaulted over eighteen feet following a great career at Fresno State, turned to the decathlon in the summer, scoring 6710 with college implements at the TAC/USA Junior Championships in Bloomington, and 6895 with prep implements to win the Junior Olympics six weeks later. Both marks were state records.

Running just fast enough to win, Earl Jones capped a great high school career with a middle-distance double. The future Eastern Michigan star breezed to an easy win in the 1600-meters in 4:18.1 and an equally comfortable victory in the 800 meters in 1:52.7. He gave a real hint of his talent at the Midwest Meet of Champions, winning the 1600 in 4:07.20—a state record—and anchoring the 4x4 with a sub-46 leg.

It still was difficult to comprehend that this brilliant performer, just two short years later, would set an American Record in winning the Olympic Trials in 1:43.74. A few weeks later Jones would win a bronze medal in the 800 at the 1984 Olympics in Los Angeles.

Terry McDaniel crushed a strong field to win the 100 and 200-meter dashes in very quick times of 10.5 and 21.3. McDaniels would find his niche, however, in another sport. Following a great career as an All-American defensive back at the University of Tennessee, he became an All-Pro defensive back for the Oakland Raiders.

There is little doubt that the combined boys/girls meet at historic Guy Houston Stadium would rank among the finest ever. Muskegon's Johnny Mitchell hurled the discus 179-10 to establish one of two field event records. Gary Price won the shot put at 58-7. Scott Reed from Lansing Everett made his first year out for track a hit by flopping over the high jump bar at 6-9. Reed placed second in the long jump by leaping 23-2, five inches behind the winning effort of 23-7 by Vincent Cox of Kalamazoo Loy Norrix.

Flint Ainsworth needed a single automobile to transport its three-man team to Grand Rapids for the State Class B championships. The trio of Tom Kaisson, Tim Fellows and Jim Featherstone tallied 45 points to win over Oak Park's 33.

Featherstone set a new B record in winning the 330-yard lows in 37.0. The Flint junior finished third behind Paul Niemi's record-setting 14.1 in the 120-yard highs. Tim Fellows won the shot and discus for Ainsworth. Fellows' 175-0 set a meet record for the discus while Kaisson finished a mere 1/4 inch behind Fellows in the shot. Ken Mitchell paced runner-up Oak Park with a dazzling 400 in 48.0.

In Class C, Detroit Lutheran West with 110½ points became the second team in 1982 to set a record for the highest total for a state final. Lutheran West became only the second team in state history to surpass the century mark in total points (Detroit DePorres in Class D the other with 100½).

The Leopards won eight events, including a sweep in the relays to dominate Class C. Joe Corbett was the only multiple winner, taking the 110 hurdles (14.5) and 100 dash (11.0) just five minutes apart. Competition was fierce in the 100. Corbett led Anthony Mahone of Detroit DePorres and Rob Bramer of Olivet to the tape.

Earlier in the season Mahone topped all Motor City sprinters by taking the 100 at the PSL-Detroit Catholic League championship meet.

Ethan Sheard of Lutheran West set a long jump record at 22-9¾. Coach Mike Unger's standout 800-meter relay team clocked 1:29.1. The Leopards relay units dominated, winning the 4 x 400 in 3:21.2 and the 4 x 100 in 42.8.

Lutheran West didn't hog all the limelight, however. Ron Simpson of Redford St. Mary ran the 1600 meters in 4:13.5, a record that lasted 18 years. The future MSU star came back minutes later to win the 800-meter run in 1:53.7, a mark that stood up for 23 years. Mike Krauss threw the discus 176-11. He later won the Big 10 title in 1987 for Michigan.

Detroit East Catholic won the only close team title chase with a narrow 64-62 win in Class D over Battle Creek St. Phillip. Long jumper Dave Koenigsknecht of Fowler surpassed the 23-foot barrier on three of his attempts to easily set the meet record. His best would be measured at 23-5¾. John Chandler hit 173-10 in the discus, a record that would not be broken for 21 years.

Upper Peninsula: Escanaba offset the individual strength of Kingsford and Marquette to win the Class A-B battle held once again in Marquette. Ironwood excelled in the relays to notch an easier than expected win over Iron Mountain in Class C. The Rangers set records in all three relays.

Iron Mountain's pair of All-State football players, Nick Johnson and Rob Landsee, placed 1-2 in the discus. Both played Div. I while Landsee enjoyed a brief stint in the NFL with the Philadelphia Eagles. John Furno of Iron Mountain raced the fastest 1600 in UP history with a clocking of 4:24.4. Wakefield unseated Cedarville as the champs in Class D.

1983

Lansing Everett became the first Capital City school to win a Class A title since Lansing High School won the inaugural event back in 1898. Everett's relatively easy Class A victory at Jackson's Withington Stadium evolved around the finesse of hurdler Steve Smith and the leaping ability of Scott Reed.

Smith claimed both hurdle titles, hitting 14.3 in the 110-meter highs and 36.3 in the 300 lows. Reed, who won the high jump and placed second in the long jump the previous year, reversed his placings. He captured the long jump with a 23-10¾ leap. In the high jump, he would go 6-10 but lose on the tie breaker formula to Tom Hughes of Dearborn Edsel Ford. Two years later he would be the Big 10 long jump champion.

Muskegon's Johnny Mitchell shattered his own discus meet record by a whopping 14 feet with his 193-3. The top-rated high schooler in the nation in 1983, he would later win the Olympic Festival at Minneapolis, Minnesota, against the nation's best throwers.

Gary Price of Monroe blasted the shot out to 63-½, adding more than a foot to Ron Gatheright's meet record from 1971. Perennial power Flint Northern grabbed the runner-up trophy, aided by wins in the 800 and 1600-meter relays—the long relay clocked 3:16.5, one of the best performances in meet history.

Anthony Mahone, who placed second in the 100 and first in the 200 meters in 1982 while competing for Detroit DePorres, made the transition to Class A with considerable aplomb by capturing both short sprint titles. The Detroit Denby junior edged defending champion Terry McDaniel and Flint Central's Derrick Leonard in the 100. He came back to win the 200 in 21.4. Placing sixth in the 200 was Flint Northwestern's Andre Rison, who played football for MSU and became an All-Pro wide receiver in the NFL.

Another Flint native who placed in the 1983 state championships and who would go on to a great career in the NFL was Mark Ingram, Rison's teammate at Northwestern. In the state finals, Ingram placed 7th behind Smith in the 110-meter highs and had a fourth-place finish in the long jump. At MSU he preceded Rison and highlighted his NFL career by leading the 1991 New York Giant receivers with five catches at Super Bowl XXV. And, oh yes, it was Mark Ingram Jr. who won the Heisman Trophy in 2009.

Flint Beecher posted the most lopsided victory in Class B history by scoring a best-ever total of 91 points to take honors in Class B at Caro. Coach Marty Crane's crew would undoubtedly have crashed the 100-point barrier had the 4 x 800 relay arrived a year earlier.

The Bucs 800-meter trio of Robert Fisher, Jamonty Washington and Howard Young placed 1-2-8. One could only speculate as to how fast the Bucs could have run 4x8 that year. For what it's worth, Crane opined, "We probably would have run in the 7:30s." Beecher's sprint duo of Jeff Sharpe and Blain Houston went 1-2 in the 100. Little wonder than that this dynamic team would win the 800-meter relay at 1:30.1. Fischer and Washington teamed with Andre Hall and John Garner to win the 4x4 in 3:20.0.

Beecher captured seven first-place medals with the Flint area grabbing an additional two more titles. Troy Eggelston of Powers High notched a win in the 400 meters, while Tim Fellows of Flint Ainsworth took the discus at 170-0. Fellows' win in the discus had to help make up for some of the disappointment he experienced by placing second in the shot put to Saginaw Eisenhower's Dan Foor. Fellows had easily topped his own meet record with a 60-1¼. Foor, however, upstaged him with an even longer 60-3.

Ypsilanti Lincoln's foursome of Wesley Jones, Rodney Turrentine, Mark Lewis and Ghassan Ramaden zipped the 400 relay in 42.6. In one of the more exciting races of the day, defending champion Jeff Costello of Grand Rapids Catholic edged Center Line's Phil Schoensee by a tenth in the 3200. Costello's winning time was 9:17.4 and prevented a Center Line sweep in the distance events. Schoensee's teammate, Don Johns, had earlier captured the mile in 4:15.1.

In Class C, defending champion Detroit Lutheran West won five events, but failed to repeat as team champs. The Leopards scored 61 points but trailed metro Detroit rival DePorres at 64¼.

Lutheran West's Joe Corbett pulled off a feat that was rarely matched in state annals. The busy Corbett, in succession, won the 110-meter high hurdles, the 100-meter dash and ran a leg on the winning 800-meter relay time. The only rest he would receive would be a short respite during the girls finals in the 100 hurdles and the 100 dash.

Corbett's 13.9 time for the high hurdles was wind aided, but remains four tenths of a second faster than any other time posted under all conditions at the Class C finals. His 10.7 time in the 100 meters set a meet record.

Eric Frederick of Lutheran West accounted for a new record of 36.5 in the 300-meter low hurdles, shattering his own mark established a year earlier. The most impressive performance for the victorious DePorres squad came in the 1600-meter relay. The quarter of Daren Warner, James Fuller, Cloyd Tiller and Darryl Carter set a time of 3:20.1, beating the excellent 3:21.3 by Lutheran West.

It's certain that few Class C athletes had a better collegiate career than Benzie Central's Paul Santer. He took the 800 in 1:56.2. Just three years later, he placed 2nd for Northwestern at the 1986 Big 10 championships with a 1:48.95. Unfortunately, life was too short for the likable Benzie Central star. He developed an inoperable brain tumor and passed away in December of 1996.

Detroit East Catholic repeated as champion in Class D with 80 points, while Akron-Fairgrove took second-place honors with 60. Robert Willhight, who figured in four first places for coach Chris Hurley's Chargers, led East Catholic. He won both dashes and anchored the 400 and 800-meter relay teams to the winner's platform.

Two middle distance stars shared the spotlight with East Catholic. Robert Moore set a 4:15.1 meet record in the 1600. The Allendale senior, who ran 40 to 60 miles a week the previous year in the hills of Brazil where his father was a missionary, also romped home a winner in the 3200 (9:32.1).

Trailing Moore in second place, with a very respectable time of 4:21.5, was the meet's hard luck performer, Carl Mayhand of Mason County Eastern. After the mile he won the 400 meters in 49.5. Then he thought he won won the 800 as well, only to get disqualified for committing an infraction during the race. Ironically, that's the event in which he would later win a national junior college title.

Dave Koenigsknecht stamped himself as Class D's all-time premier long jumper. He again leaped beyond the 23-foot barrier for his third-straight title to headline action in the field events. Dan Stanley from Marcellus became a double champion with victories in both hurdle events. His time of 14.3 in the 110 highs was labeled a new record, but is shy of David Sykes' disputed effort of 14.1 clocked back in 1977.

Upper Peninsula: Marquette won every field event in the UP Class A-B championships yet trailed Kingsford by one point when the final scores were tallied. Iron Mountain was the only easy winner in Marquette, yet its winning margin over second-place Ishpeming Westwood was less than 10 points.

John Furno had the day's outstanding performance when the Iron Mountain distance ace ran the 1600 meters in a record 4:21.9. For years Lower Peninsula track fans were led to believe that Furno's time was a blistering 4:12.9, due to a typo sent over the wires covering the UP finals. Encouraging Furno on to the record was an Iron Mountain native son who was serving as a finish line judge, Northern Michigan University assistant basketball coach Tom Izzo.

UP fans were deprived of seeing a match-up between Furno and John Currie of St. Ignace. Currie, running in the next heat, recorded a Class D record of 4:28.6 to win his division. In spite of Currie's record, his St. Ignace team lost to Wakefield by one point.

Marty Crane: Beecher's Problem Solver

Without question one of the most successful coaches over the years in Michigan's Lower Peninsula was Flint Beecher's Marty Crane, who won 10 state Class B championships during his long coaching tenure. Crane was not only an innovative mentor, but he was able to devise methods to keep his teams interested in track, and track alone, during the spring of each year.

It had become apparent during the latter part of the 20th century that track had taken a back seat in appeal to other sports. It became clear to Crane that basketball was cutting into participation in track and field.

The crafty Crane took a different route than others to combat this threat. Early in his coaching career he probed the mind of Eastern Michigan University coach Bob Parks, who told Crane the key to success in track and field at the high school level is to get your best athletes out for the sport.

"I was having problems for a few years with AAU basketball," said Crane. "So, I decided there had to be a solution to this. I decided to take matters into my own hands. I went into our gymnasium at the start of track and took the basketball rims down and put them in my garage. I figured they couldn't play basketball without rims," chuckled Crane.

"The next day the principal calls me in and says, 'Marty, we have a problem; the rims are missing. Do you know where they're at?' I said, 'Yeah and I'll tell you what, they'll be back up the day after the state meet.'"

From that day forward track & field became a booming sport at Flint Beecher and the Buccaneers became the dominant Class B power from the late 1970s thru the 1980s. Beecher was so dominant under Crane's tutelage that his teams won ten Class B championships and placed second in two others from 1976 through the 1993 season.

In 1984 the two-mile relay was added as a new event for Michigan High School track. "At the 1983

Marty Crane

state finals we were running 1-2-3 (in the 880-yard) with 120 meters to go. Our runner in third (Howard

Young) got bumped at the top of the curve, lost his composure for a little bit, and ended up eighth," recalled Crane. Robert Fisher and teammate Jamonty Washington crossed the finish line inches apart with a time under 1:55.

Crane chided his fellow coaches that the ghost of Beecher was going to come back to haunt them for waiting another year to add in the two-mile relay. No one felt sorry for Crane in 1983, however. Beecher piled up 91 points, the most earned by a Class A or B team in state history. A cinch ten points in the two-mile relay, if available in 1983, would have pushed the Buccaneers winning total over the century mark.

Unlike many of his coaching colleagues, Crane had little trouble convincing players from the football team to participate in track. No track mentor ever coached more athletes who would make it all the way into the NFL. Four of his former track stars signed NFL contracts totaling more than a million dollars.

Perhaps the most renowned of the track/football guys was NFL All Star linebacker Carl Banks. "It took me quite a while to convince Carl to come out," reflected Crane. "Carl's number one love was, surprisingly, basketball."

Lonnie Young, Courtney Hawkins and Thad McFadden were also among other former Beecher track stars that found their future in the NFL. In addition, Tyrone Jones ventured north to offer his talents to the Canadian Football League with the Winnipeg Blue Bombers. He was a smashing success as he was not only honored as the Most Valuable Player of the 1994 Grey Cup but also was selected as the defensive player of the year in the CFL in 1985.

Crane also had success of his own as a high school runner, winning his section of the 440-yard dash in 1961 while attending nearby Flint Kearsley. "In those days, we ran out of a chute with a whole bunch of runners. I got off to a slow start at the state finals, all of a sudden I realized I was in about twentieth place," recalled Crane with some degree of exaggeration. "As I got to the final curve I headed for the far wall and ran as fast as I could. I had no idea if I won."

When asked about early role models growing up in Flint back in the 1950s, Crane mentioned his dad and longtime Flint Northern coach Norb Badar. "My dad was a baseball nut and always steered me to get into baseball. When I was in about the seventh grade, Harry Burnett, who would eventually be my high school track coach, convinced me that I should become a runner.

"Track and field was so competitive while growing up in Flint," said Crane. "We had some fierce competition and tremendous turnouts for AAU meets during the summer."

His first championship as a coach nearly didn't come to pass due to a scoring glitch. With two events remaining in the 1976 finals, Crane shouted to his team: "They (Dearborn Heights Robichaud) can't beat us as we've clinched the championship."

"They began announcing the place finishers in reverse order at Battle Creek Harper Creek and when the PA announcer said we were second and Robichaud first the Robichaud team members were elated," said Crane. "They grabbed the trophy and ran around the track while our kids were all down in the dumps."

Crane said he immediately went up to the press box and asked the scorer: "Please tell me: where did they score? Perhaps I made a mistake somewhere. I had a hard time getting my point across. I wanted them to tell me in what events they had scored. Finally, I got my point across and they began inspecting the score sheet. When they scrolled down the sheet and said Robichaud earned eight points in the two-mile run my pulse quickened. I said 'No! That was Dearborn Heights Riverside! Robichaud didn't even have an entrant in the two-mile."

The official said: "Oh no! I'll have to take eight points away from Robichaud." Quickly the announcement was made and apologies given for the understandable error. The scorer asked the Robichaud bus driver to stop his bus as the Dearborn Heights team had already begun to head for home with the trophy in their possession.

"A member of my team was running alongside their bus yelling for the bus driver to stop," recalled Crane. "The bus driver didn't stop because he thought our runner was just mad so they just kept pulling away. Finally, the word got out to the State Police. They caught up to and stopped their bus, handed them the runner-up trophy and brought the first-place trophy to us while we were eating at Win Schulers," said the bemused Crane.

When asked to point out some of his most memorable athletes, Crane first brought up Anthony Akins. "He was probably the most talented kid that I coached. There wasn't anything he couldn't do. I've seen Anthony lead off the two-mile relay at an indoor MITCA state championship meet and then come back and win the high hurdles in the very next race."

Crane didn't just measure the success of an athlete on the time or distance earned during a track meet. "One of my favorites was Hubert Anthony. Hubert, who never won a state championship, certainly wasn't my most talented athlete but he had an unbelievable work ethic. I would literally have to take the discus out of his hands to send him home," said Crane.

While reviewing Beecher's success during his tenure, it would appear Crane's teams would always peak at the right time. "This wasn't always true," said Crane. "I remember one year when the meet was held in Kalamazoo. We stayed overnight and it rained like cats and dogs. Our kids were up until 2 or 4 in the morning. My assistant pulled up to our hotel late in the evening and when he looked up he saw Lonnie Young walking on the ledge, going from room to room of the Holiday Inn.

"When I looked at the kids when we got on the bus the next morning, I knew we were in trouble. We ended up runner-up in the meet but we should have won the state championship going away."

These types of down seasons were few and far between during the Crane era at Beecher High. What makes his 10 state titles even more amazing is that Beecher did not have its own track to practice or host its own track meets.

"We ran on the dirt road in front of the school. I told the kids that training is training. If you believe in yourself, train hard and work hard, you'll be successful.

"I was also fortunate to have such a valuable assistant in Randy Coleman," Crane quickly added. Many honors have been bestowed on Crane since his retirement from coaching in 2003 after 34 years. He has joined his mentor and former good friend, the late Norb Badar, into the Flint Area Sports Hall of Fame, the Michigan High School Coaches Association Hall of Fame and in 2014 entered the National High School Coaches Association Hall of Fame.

In accepting his latest honor, Crane acknowledged that he still is active in his beloved sport. "I'm what you call a track nut. I still officiate to this day and I'm still involved in a lot of things. Anything track and field-related, it seems like I'm there. I love the sport and I want to give back."

1984

Motor City teams dominated action at the Class A state championships held at Withington Stadium in Jackson. Detroit Central won its fourth title in five years, as the Detroit Public Schools had four teams finish in the top six. The 3200-meter relay became the final event added to the present-day list of boy's events and, fittingly, Detroit Central won that event.

That was the only win of the day for coach Woody Thomas' Trailblazers. Runner-up Detroit Cooley also took one first-place medal with Ted Harris winning the high jump at 6-10. Anthony Mahone repeated as the sprint king for the second-straight year, tieing Terry McDaniel's record at 10.5 for the 100 meters, and blazing the 200 in 21.0.

Omar Davidson scampered around the Jackson oval in 46.6. Mike Sargeant of Flint Powers won an impressive double in the throws at 61-8 and 174-11. Michael Parker of Jackson established a new mark for the 300-low hurdles, becoming the only hurdler in Michigan history to crack the 36 second barrier at the state meet with his 35.9. The Jackson ace also ran the anchor on the Vikings' winning 800-meter relay.

The most exciting race of the day came in the 1600. Jeff Wilson of Flint Kearsley lunged at the tape to nip Jeffrey Neal of Detroit Murray-Wright. Both were clocked in 4:13.1. The Trojans of Saginaw finished a respectable third, spearheaded by a couple of relay victories.

Saginaw nipped Grand Rapids Ottawa Hills at the tape to win the 400-meter relay in 42.6 and captured the 1600-meter relay in 3:17.1. Darnell Davis and Ernest Menzie each ran a leg on the winning relay teams for the Trojans.

Traverse City sent its fourth-straight pole vaulter to the winner's circle when Greg Nienhouse captured the pole vault crown at 14-5. Coach John Lober's vaulters would produce six champions over a seven-year span.

Detroit Benedictine won its third state championship—but its first in Class B—with an easy victory in Caro. Coach Ted Mac's Ravens had too much depth for the one-man gang from Ypsilanti Lincoln. Mark Lewis won both short sprints and ran a leg on Lincoln's winning 800-meter relay to take meet individual honors. He was denied a possible fourth medal when he placed third in the long jump.

Eaton Rapids hurdler Michael Miller won both hurdle races, and twice set a meet record in the 110 highs. He was clocked in 13.9 on his first race, but was forced to rerun it when judges ruled that an obstruction from another runner had cost several athletes a chance at the title. After a sufficient rest break, the Greyhounds' star hurdler kept his composure and once

again proved he was the best, winning in another 13.9. He still had enough energy left later in the program to win the 300-meter lows in 38 seconds flat.

Rusty Korhonen of Forest Hills Central overcame a painful tendon irritation to win the 1600 in 4:15.8. After crossing the finish, he had to be helped from the track. Holland Christian's Gary Allen shocked his competitors in the pole vault. Hampered by a sprained ankle at regionals, he had barely qualified for the state finals with a sub-par 11-10. At the finals, he had recovered enough to soar over 14-5 for the win.

Detroit DePorres added additional hardware to its bulging trophy case by winning its 11th state championship in 13 years. The Eagles' amazing streak was led by the sprinting duo of Claude Tiller and Keith Harris. Tiller ran 48.5 in the 400. Harris played a major role in the team win, capturing the 200 in 22.3 and running a leg on two winning relay teams. The 4x1 clocked 43.3 and Harris joined Tiller, Anthony Johnson, and Ralph Bland to win the 4x4 in 3:24.2.

Bronson's Jesse McGuire was the only double champion on the Clare track with victories in the 1600 (4:20.4) and 3200 (9:26.8). One of the more impressive performances had to be the long jump of New Haven's Brian Corbit. His meet record of 23-9 was more than two and a half feet over his nearest competitor, the largest margin in state long jump history.

Detroit East Catholic had an easy time capturing its third-straight Class D crown in Traverse City. The Chargers totaled a whopping 87 points as Robert Willhight visited the winner's stand four more times. Willhight repeated his accomplishment of 1983 by taking both sprints and running legs on two winning sprint relays.

Upper Peninsula: Marquette's Brody Reese made up a huge deficit in the 4x4 and nipped Menominee's anchor man at the tape by 0.03 to lift his team to a thrilling half-point victory over the Maroons. The 72½ to 72 victory was Marquette's first UP A-B championship in twenty years. The victors overcame a perfect day by Menominee's Mark Noon, who won all three short dashes and ran a leg on the winning 800-meter relay.

No tight race developed at the Class C UP finals in Marquette as Ishpeming Westwood won the crown by nearly 20 points. Westwood's 400-meter relay team won by one and a half seconds in 44.4. St. Ignace moved up to Class C, with star miler John Currie challenging the meet record with his 4:24.6 in the 1600. Felch North Dickinson scored 19 points in the relays to help post a narrow 44-42 edge over Bessemer in Class D.

1985

Lansing Everett returned to the winner's circle with a decisive victory at the Class A state finals. The team was so dominating that when one of its favorites, Ken Thompson, false started in the finals of the 110-meter high hurdles, it proved insignificant. Roget Ware of Lansing Sexton, who had placed fourth the year before while competing for Lansing Everett, won the race.

If not for the transfer of Ware from Everett to Lansing Sexton, the Vikings would have been an even stronger favorite. Everett nearly doubled the points over runner-up Detroit Cooley in front of the 7,000 spectators at Flint's Guy Houston Stadium. Everett won the 800-meter relay in 1:26.77, one of the fastest times in state history.

The same Everett foursome of Andy Bunnell, Rod Whittington, Chuck Phillips and Thompson blazed the 400-meter relay in 41.77, a state record that would last for 25 years. Phillips captured the 200 meters in 22.04 to supply the winners with more valuable points.

Future Michigan football star Allan Jefferson of Warren DeLaSalle placed a close second to Phillips in the 200, but won the 100. Andre Rison of Flint Northwestern—another with a future in football— placed 4th in the 100 and took third in the 200 meters behind Phillips and Jefferson.

Impressive field event winners in included Joe Applewhite of Grand Rapids Central with a 23-2 in the long jump, and Jackson's James Smith with a 6-10 high jump. Swartz Creek's Keith Lancaster interrupted Traverse City's four-year reign in the pole vault with his winning 14-4. His teammate Eric Koskinen won the two-mile in 9:16.0. He had won the event as a sophomore in 1983. Oddly enough, Lancaster and Koskinen would be the only state track champions in Swartz Creek for the next 29 years.

Torin Dorn of Southfield, winner of the 400 (48.04), took his talents in football to the University of North Carolina. He excelled on the gridiron as a defensive back in the NFL with the St Louis Rams.

Flint Beecher won its sixth state championship since 1976 with a come-from-behind victory at Jackson Northwest. Tied with Detroit Benedictine going into the 1600 relay, the Bucs got the points they needed when freshman Courtney Hawkins crossed in second place. The winners only had one individual champion, but coach Marty Crane's squad piled up points with three second-place finishes and a fourth.

Darryl Warner of Willow Run won both short sprints (11.02/22.16). Winning the 400 in 49.62 was Bill Sall of Hudsonville Unity Christian. Perhaps better known as a basketball star at Calvin College, Sall later became the head basketball coach at Ferris State.

A well-balanced field gathered on the Clare track for the Class C championships. Ecorse put together 43 points to defeat two members of the West Michigan "C" conference, Mason County Central and Muskegon Oakridge. One record fell during the meet, with DeWitt outlasting its neighborhood rivals of Bath High School in the 3200-meter relay. The DeWitt foursome of Dane DeWitt, Mike Simon, Mike Price and Kent Gartside became the first Class C team to break the eight minute barrier with its 7:58.2.

Runner-up Mason County Central of Scottville featured the meet's individual star in Jeff Barnett. He held off future MSU ace Dennis Topolinski of Orchard Lake St. Mary in the 1600, and won the 800 in 1:56.3. Brian Corbit of New Haven defended his long jump title at 22-8 ½.

Fowler destroyed a quality field to easily capture the Class D title at Hillsdale College. Detroit East Catholic won four events, as opposed to only a pair for the winners from Fowler. However, the Eagles of Mid-Michigan demonstrated superior depth. Fowler was especially impressive in the relays with two firsts and two seconds.

East Catholic received a perfect effort from Sean Jones to take the second-place trophy back to the Motor City. Jones won the 100, 200, 400 meters and ran the anchor leg for the Charger's victorious 800-meter relay. Allendale fell just short of copping runner-up honors with an impressive showing from distance ace Dave Wooday. He ran a leg on the Falcons' victorious 1600-meter relay and had the narrowest of wins in the 800 and 1600—with the runners-up in both events getting the same time Wooday did.

Upper Peninsula: Cold and rain threw a blanket around the competitors, and the record books, at the UP Finals in Marquette. The host school defended its A-B crown with a narrow win over Escanaba. Negaunee used its superior depth to pull out a 40-32 win over Houghton in Class C. Gino Marchetti of Iron Mountain easily topped all hurdlers to earn individual honors.

Crystal Falls had the easiest win of all in Class D. The Trojans piled up 64 points to earn a 22-point edge over its closest pursuers. Tom Ball of Pickford accounted for the only meet record set with his heave of 154-11 in the discus.

1986

The Class A championship trophy remained in the Capitol City for another year, as Lansing Sexton supplanted crosstown rival Everett as the state champion. Sexton gave head coach Paul Pozega his first state title since his Lansing St. Mary's squad won the Class C crown back in 1962.

It wasn't an easy win, however, as the Big Reds had to turn on the jets in the meet's final event to earn the come-from-behind victory. Sexton trailed front-running Kalamazoo Loy Norrix heading into the 1600-meter relay, but came through with a second-place to clinch. Roget Ware repeated as the high hurdles champ (13.8) and placed third in the 300 lows to pace the winners. Ware also ran legs on the victorious 400-meter relay and the 4x4.

One meet record toppled when Traverse City's Bim Scala removed the Trojan's Scott Krupilski from the record books with a vault of 15-9. Scala nosed out runner-up Mark Smith of Lansing Waverly in a spirited battle that saw Smith clear 15-5 before bowing out of the competition. Scala's effort to become the first Michigan vaulter to clear 16 feet at the state meet fell awry when his pole snapped while attempting 16-1.

Junior Keith Wheeler of Troy, with wins in the 400 meters (47.64) and the 300-meter low hurdles (36.73), became Class A's only individual double champion. Other impressive marks at Guy Houston Stadium were turned in by high jumper Melvin Kelly of defending champion Lansing Everett (6-10) and sprinter Allen Jefferson of Detroit DeLaSalle in the 100 meters (10.55). Jefferson's century time remained the meet record for 31 years.

Todd Williams, with a 9:11.63 victory in the 3200-meter run, gave the large crowd present at Houston Stadium a glimpse of his future abilities in the distance races. The Monroe junior would go to Tennessee and then the pro ranks, where he would be ranked the top U.S. runner at 10,000m for four years and become a two-time Olympian.

Flint Beecher won the boys and the girls Class B titles in Jackson, becoming the third school in history to win both titles in the same year. In successfully defending, coach Marty Crane's squad totaled 75 points to finish well ahead of Detroit Benedictine. The Buccaneers won four events and scored in six others en route to their seventh title since 1976.

Corunna's John Bruce vaulted 15-7, smashing the previous meet record by nearly a foot. The individual point leader was Charles Wilson of Benedictine, with wins in both short dashes and legs on the victorious 400 and 800 relays. Wilson teamed up with Charles Winston, Shon Summerville and Cedric Green on both, with the 4x2 setting a meet record at 1:28.21.

Paul Cochran of Midland Bullock Creek captured wins in both weight events.

In Class C, Mason County Central's Jeff Barnett virtually put on a one-man show to propel the track squad from Scottville to its first state title. In the blazing sun on the Bangor track, the tireless Barnett logged

four miles, putting on a feat similar to Clare McDurmon's leading Caro to the crown in 1932.

Barnett repeated as champion in the 800 (1:54.60), 1600 (4:18.16) and added the 3200 (9:40.13). All this, after he anchored the winning 4x8 in the morning (8:04.61). He took his talents to Michigan where he placed second in the steeplechase at the 1992 Big 10 championships.

Mason County received its other crucial points with a fourth and a seventh in the vault, edging out perennial power Detroit DePorres, 46 to 44.

Leading DePorres was sprinter Rodney Culver, one of the finest all-around athletes in DePorres history. Following a brilliant career with the Eagles, he moved to tradition-rich Notre Dame. Elected by his peers to captain the Fighting Irish in his senior year, he was the first African-American selected in Notre Dame history. Culver's NFL career, and life was cut tragically short. He was among more than 100 passengers who perished in an airplane crash in May of 1996 in the Florida Everglades.

Sophomore Aron Gowell of Shelby swept to the shot-discus double, on his way to becoming the only thrower in Michigan history to sweep both for three straight years. Terrance Williams of Ecorse, with his winning leap of 23-0, had the best mark in all classes in the long jump.

Brad Darr of Hudson grabbed the pole vault title at a height of 14-2. Later at Michigan, he would win the '92 Big 10 title and reach a PR 18-½ in one of his three NCAA All-American performances.

John Hood hurdled 37.62 to repeat as the 300 low hurdles champ. He was the only state champion in Pontiac Catholic's history.

Detroit East Catholic moved back into the winner's circle after a year's absence with a 75-45 win over defending champion Fowler. Willy Scott led the Chargers, winning both hurdles and running a leg on one of the three relays won by the victors. Jeffrey Morris from Detroit Servite was the meet's other double winner on the Hillsdale College track, with victories in the 200 (22.72) and the 400 (49.06).

Upper Peninsula: Todd LaCosse took all three short sprints to lead the Eskimos to the A-B championship. Because the UP back in 1979 threw all the former records set in yards into the trash can, LaCosse was credited with a new mark in the 200 with a time of 22.7. The time was obviously short of the 22.5 clocking run by former Escanaba sprinter Jim DeFresne in 1977. LaCosse, to his credit, however, would come back the following year to set a new record that would satisfy all track fans.

Kingsford was given credit for a new record in the 4x1, even though its 45.3 was a full second short of the 44.3 clocking it clocked in 1976 over the longer 440-

yard distance. Gwinn's Tim Gipson leaped 21-7, more than a foot and a half farther than his closest competitor.

Houghton won five events while winning Class C. Ishpeming Westwood ran 8:13.8 for the 3200-meter relay. Tough luck befell Iron Mountain's Gino Marchetti. After winning the 110-meter high hurdles for the second-straight year, he was apparently headed for a new record over the 300-meter low sticks. He tripped and fell while leading and watched in frustration as Jody Paradis of Munising crossed the finish line in 39.5. Future CMU quarterback Jeff Bender set a meet record in the discus (149-2) for Newberry.

Rudyard used its strength on the field to score a 47-45 1/5 win over Crystal Falls Forest Park in Class D. Mike Thiry of Carney-Nedeau was the star of the UP finals for any class. He posted meet records that still stand today in the 100 and 200-meter dashes, becoming the first UP dash man to break eleven in the 100 with his 10.9.

1987

With a plethora of talented letterman returning from its 1986 state championship team, Lansing Sexton was a big favorite to repeat in 1987. Coach Paul Pozega's thinclads responded to the pressure by racking up 64 points, 13½ points more than Kalamazoo Loy Norrix.

Nearly 5,000 spectators packed Alma's Bahlke Stadium to watch Sexton win its second-straight and the third for the capital city in the past four years. Roget Ware led the Big Reds, taking his third-straight 110-meter high hurdles title, and running a leg on three relay teams, two of which won.

If not for a fourth-place finish in his freshman season, Ware could have become the first Class A performer in the modern era to win four straight. He took his hurdling skills to Ohio State the following year where he took the Big 10 title.

Loy Norrix got a double win from weight specialist Kyle Wray in placing second in the team battle. Wray's best put of 60-1½, held off crosstown rival Jonathon Frazier of Kalamazoo Central. Wray's winning throw of 184-2 won the discus by a whopping 16 feet.

Corey Pryor of Jackson contributed to one of the two meet records set on the Alma surface with his hand-timed clocking of 10.4 for the 100. Placing third and fourth were his future MSU football teammates, Tico Duckett of Loy Norrix and Allan Haller of Lansing Sexton. Pryor topped the same twosome in the 200 in a quick 21.37.

Keith Wheeler of Troy convincingly defended in the 400 and 300lows. He won the 400 by better than a

Jackson's Corey Pryor winning the A 100. After a career at Michigan State, he would later become the Jackson coach. (MHSAA photo)

second with a clocking of 47.3. The Texas-bound senior, after placing second behind Ware in the high hurdles, romped to an easy win in the final year for the 300-meter low hurdles at 36.23.

Todd Williams repeated as the 3200 champ in 9:00.3. Earlier in the day he had run a leg on Monroe's fourth-place 3200-meter relay and just missed winning the 1600-meter crown by a tenth of a second. As a senior at Tennessee in 1991, he placed second in the 10,000, and third in the 5000 meters, helping coach Doug Brown's Volunteers win the NCAA Championship.

Cliff Dwelle of Lake Orion had nipped Williams in that 1600 at 4:12.9, a mark that was reported as a new meet record, but well short of the imperial record set by Pontiac Central's Steve Elliott in 1975. Elliott's mark over the longer mile distance would convert to a 4:06.8 for 1600.

Farmington's 7:48.5 captured the 4x8. Marcel Richardson of Lansing Everett leaped 23-4¾. Orlando Scott took the high jump at 6-9.

Flint Beecher placed in ten of the 17 events to easily repeat as state champion in Class B, with victories in the 4x2 and 4x8 and got an individual first in the shot from John Thornton (59-8½), less than five inches off the meet record. The 4x8 foursome of Stacy Watson, Michael Ford, Rhamon Cleveland and Aaron McFadden sped around the track in a meet record 7:52.3.

Dearborn's Andrew Tomasic tied the 300-meter low hurdles record of 37.1 initially set by Otisville LakeVille's Ed Brown back in 1979. With this being the final year for 30-inch setting, Tomasic and Brown would share the record forever.

Future Michigan and NFL wide receiver Derrick Alexander of Detroit Benedictine was able to win the 200 in his sophomore season, just nipping Scott Blackburn of Grand Rapids Catholic by 0.01.

Earlier in the competition Robert Harris of Willow Run, with his 10.61 win over Beecher's Courtney Hawkins in the 100-meter dash, defeated another future NFL receiver.

Tom Broene of Hudsonville Unity Christian matched the day's best high jump by clearing 6-9, while Bay City Handy's Joe Garrett had an impressive victory in the 400-meter dash (48.81).

Detroit Lutheran West won all three sprint relays to race to the Class C title in Bangor. Lutheran West got all its winning 50 points on four firsts, a third in the high jump and a fourth in the 400-meter dash. Greg Harris provided the only individual win for the Leopards in the 110-meter high hurdles.

Individual honors for the meet went to Rory Stace of Galesburg-Augusta. Stace who copped the high jump title at 6-7, became the third Class C jumper in meet history to hit the 23-foot barrier and won the 100 meters. His 10.81 kept Darryl Stallworth of Ecorse from also winning three championships. Stallworth went on to capture both the 200 (22.25) and 400 (49.43).

Aron Gowell of Shelby repeated in his junior year as king of the throws. Adam Norman of Kalkaska clocked a 9:24.21 in the 3200. Jay Pitcher of Ithaca took the vault at 14-5.

In Class D, Willy Scott of Detroit East Catholic had another big day, leading the Chargers to their second-straight crown. He defended both of his hurdle victories and long jumped a winning 22-10½. Jeff Morris of Detroit Servite blistered a 48.99 win in the 400.

Upper Peninsula: In Marquette, Todd LaCosse proved without a doubt that he was the top UP sprinter of the twentieth century. He set records in each of his wins: 10.9 for the 100, 22.2 in the 200 and 50.2 for the 400. Only the 400 mark would not stand into the next century for the Escanaba star. LaCosse also anchored Escanaba's 4x2 to victory to complete a perfect day. On a cold and rainy afternoon, he was the only athlete to set a meet record.

Gary Gregg's win in the 1600 managed to remove the oldest Escanaba school record. His 4:30.3 broke the mark of Eddie Holderman that dated all the way back to 1936. (Holderman would win a Big 10 title in the two mile for Purdue in 1940.)

Although Iron Mountain won the team battle in Class C, it was Munising's Jody Paradis who

Escanaba's Todd LaCosse (MHSAA photo)

dominated the individual competition. He won both hurdles and the 400 to singlehandedly lead Munising to third-place. Two records did fall in the field events, both from athletes from Newberry. Brandon Hauglie set a new standard at 6-5 in the high jump while Jeff Bender improved his own Class C best in the discus (150-6).

In Class D Jon Gollakner from team champion Crystal Falls Forest Park took the hurdles in 15.0.

1988

Two new leaders appeared at the top of the board in 1988. Southfield captured its first team title in school history by scoring 58 points at Eastern Michigan's Rynearson Stadium. Although having participated in most of the past 94 state track championships, Jackson High School enjoyed its most successful year as a team with a second-place finish behind Southfield.

Southfield got a stellar performance from sprinter Jeff Reynolds. Reynolds won the 200-meter dash (21.63), ran legs on two winning relays (4x1 and 4x2) and also ran a leg on the Southfield 1600-meter relay that was beaten by Detroit Cooley, 3:17.81-3:18.90.

With the increase in the 300-hurdle height from 30-inches to 36, the state meet program made its last major change. Steve Hearndon became the automatic meet record holder with a winning 38.20.

The day's most exciting race came in the 800-meter run. Rick Gledhill of Clinton Township Chippewa Valley, edged Tim Pitcher of Monroe in 1:50.63 to 1:50.74. While not superior to Kevin Reabe's 1:50.9 from 1970, they were the Nos. 2-3 performances in meet history. Two weeks later Rick Gledhill won the International Prep Invitational in 1:49.33, becoming the first in state history to dip under 1:50 for 800.

Marcel Richardson leaped 23-11½ to better the oldest meet record. On his first jump of the competition, he broke Hayes Jones' record set 32 years earlier. Richardson was far from satisfied. Three days earlier, the Lansing Everett star had jumped 25-3¼ at the Lansing Honor Roll Meet. It was the longest leap in state history, but officials took no wind

Marcel Richarson

information, even though the wind was gusting over 20mph. Following his initial meet record during the state finals, Richardson had to run on the 400 and 800-meter relays, efforts that took the life out of his legs.

Two weeks later, Richardson would get credit for a state record with his 25-2½ second-place finish at the International Prep Invitational (0.1 wind).

The Monroe 3200-meter relay of Derek Bork, Matt Schroeder, Chris Brown and Pitcher shattered the state record by better than six seconds with its 7:41.29. It would hold up for 16 years before being eclipsed by Saline in 2004 by a mere 0.02.

Toby Van Pelt, nephew of MSU All-American and NFL great Brad Van Pelt, took the pole vault at 15-3. Ron Williams from Chippewa Valley had a discus heave measured at 183-4.

Flint Beecher used its strength in the relays to post its ninth state Class B title. Coach Marty Crane's Bucs

compiled an impressive 77 points on the Sturgis track. Leading the way was the 3200-meter relay quartet of Corey Massey, Kenneth Ellis, Aron McFadden and Stacy Watson. Beecher's 7:48.7 easily shattered the meet record and would last for ten years.

For Watson and McFadden, it marked the third-straight year on a winning 4x8. Watson also won the 800 (1:55.79) and anchored the meet record 4x4 as well. Joining Watson and McFadden on the 1600 relay were Tony Triggs and Courtney Hawkins. The Bucs time of 3:19.69 would not be broken until 2004.

Beecher took the 4x1 (43.31) and only team runner-up Detroit East Catholic, with 4x2 win, prevented a complete Beecher relay sweep. Zekiel Miller led the Chargers by running a leg on the victorious relay team and taking first in the 400 meters (49.08).

Omaka Smith of Bay City Handy became a double winner in the 100 (10.81) and 200 (21.71). Richard Palmer of Mt. Clemens had one of Class B's all-time best efforts in the long jump with his leap of 23-1½. South Haven's Joe Sappanos went 6-9 in the high jump. He had spent the majority of the season on the South Haven tennis team, winning the state title in only his third meet.

Detroit Lutheran West won its fourth Class C title in the 1980s with 67 points, 17 more than runner-up Saginaw Nouvel. However, a burly shot putter and discus thrower from Shelby highlighted the action on the Alma track. Aron Gowell won the shot put (62-11) and discus (179-3) for the third-straight year, the only athlete in state history to accomplish the throws triple.

Two weeks earlier the Florida-bound Gowell had unleashed the twelve-pound ball 65-3 in winning the regional; it was the No. 2 throw in the nation.

Rick Lubbers of Grandville Calvin Christian cleared 14-7 in the vault, only 1/4 inch better than the previous mark posted by Steve Wren of Haslett 14 years earlier. Sprinter Tony Jackson of Saginaw Nouvel joined Gowell as a double winner by winning the dashes (11.0/21.9). Greg Harris had the only first-place showing for Lutheran West team by winning the 110-meter high hurdles in 14.5.

Jason Whitley of Charlevoix set an automatic record in the first year of the 300-meter intermediate hurdles. Even so, his time of 39.0 however, would last until the 1996 state finals. Another great mark in class C came from Williamston's Sean Conklin in the 400 meters (49.1).

In Class D, Fowler, although not winning an individual championship, placed in 13 of 17 events to win the crown in Traverse City. Mendon, while taking home the runner-up trophy, likewise failed to win an individual title.

Scott Goodman of Portland St. Patrick cleared 14-2 in the pole vault. Lawton's 3200-meter relay foursome of Keith Oxley, Tim VanWyk, Tony Lanphear and John Widner accounted for another Class D best with a 8:09.34. Juron Johnson of Baldwin, with two wins in the dashes, was the day's only double winner.

Upper Peninsula: In action under sunny skies and temperatures hovering in the 80s, Gwinn won its first title in 18 years. Depth paid off for second-year coach Dick Mettlach as the Model Towners placed in every event. Thrower Brandon Bruce won two of the three titles garnered. Corey Potvin of Escanaba clocked a meet record 14.6 in the highs.

The day's individual star would prove to be Darrin Laabs from Ironwood. He took three firsts and one second in leading Ironwood to the Class C title. He won the high hurdles in 15.0, posted the day's fastest time (40.3) in winning the 300 hurdles (40.3) and set a meet record of 6-6 in the high jump. Only a second-place finish in the long jump prevented Laabs from having a perfect day.

Against a well-balanced field in Class D, Crystal Falls edged Wakefield 44 to 40. John Payment matched Laabs' Class C record by clearing 6-6 in the high jump.

1989

Three of the most successful track stars in Michigan history competed at the state finals in 1989, but none would win a first place.

In Class A, held again at Rynearson Stadium in Ypsilanti, Darnell Hall, from Detroit Pershing, placed second behind Steve Sandles of East Detroit in the 400-meter dash. Later in life he would win an Olympic gold medal in the 4x4 relay.

Sophomore Brian Hyde of East Kentwood tripped and fell off the track while battling for the lead going into the final turn of the 1600-meter run. He finished out of the money, but later at William & Mary would set an American Collegiate Record in the 1500.

How many in the crowd at Class B in Jackson could ever imagine that the runner from Cadillac, who placed a distant seventh in the 800-meter run, would become the greatest miler in Michigan history? Paul McMullen, would bounce back the following year and become a state champion. It was during his collegiate career at Eastern Michigan University where he would become the nation's leading 1500/miler. He ran in the '96 Olympics and was a two-time World Championships finalist. Paul's brother Phil would prove to be another late bloomer. While competing for Western Michigan, Phil would place 5th at the NCAA championships in the decathlon.

Soggy conditions greeted the athletes at most sites throughout the state on June 3, the first time since 1969 where rain would be a factor. The modern all-weather tracks, however, were obviously better suited to handle inclement weather than the cinder tracks of the pre-1972 era.

Southfield survived two hours of delays, first by a tornado watch and then by a thunderstorm, before sprinting to its second-straight Class A team title, overcoming Monroe's supremacy in the distances. With wins in the 400 and 800-meter relays and a second to Monroe in the 4x8, Southfield closed the meet on a high note with a third in the 1600 relay.

The Monroe quartet of Derek Bork, Sean Sweat, Matt Schroeder and Tim Pitcher repeated as state champs with a 7:48.25 clocking. Pitcher won the 1600 meters, with Bork third, and a tired Pitcher battled to a second in the 800 behind Chippewa Valley's Aaron Grzymkowski.

Toby Van Pelt was not only able to repeat as pole vault champion but the Owosso senior with his 15-10 clearance in the pole vault, set the only meet record of the day. Van Pelt was one of four vaulters from the Big Nine conference to place in the top five.

Brian Grosso of Walled Lake Western became the first runner in state history to crack the nine-minute barrier in the 3200 at the state finals, though previous 2-mile records were intrinsically superior. Grosso traversed eight laps of the EMU track in 8:59.20.

In addition to winning the 400 (47.22), East Detroit's Steve Sandles became the only double individual winner by defeating defender Jeff Reynolds of Southfield in the 200. He also supplied valuable points for the champion Blue Jays by taking second in the 100 behind Terrance Smith of Bay City Central.

Smith, in winning the 100, accomplished a rare feat for his family. His father, Namon Smith, won the state 100 title for Bay City Central back in 1955, making the Smiths the second father/son duo ever to win the state Class A 100 dash (Lyle and Dick Hensen were the first). The younger Smith also erased the existing Bay City long jump record during the 1989 campaign, breaking his father's mark set 34 years earlier.

Bob Czachorski of Grandville nearly pulled off a double in the hurdles. In 37.76 he edged Catrin Cooper of Saginaw in the 300s and he placed second behind Benton Harbor's Larry Harden in the highs.

In Class B, Flint Beecher watched its bid for a fifth-straight go down the drain when its crack 1600-meter relay was disqualified after winning the regional. One of the members of the Bucs relay team was wearing a watch during his leg of the race, a violation of state rules at the time. With Beecher's relay team in the stands, Grand Rapids Northview made up a 39-38 deficit to Beecher by not only placing in the meet's final event, but winning the event outright.

Northview also won the 400 and 800-meter relays to rack up 30 of its meet-winning 48 points. Andy Korytkowski and Mickey Wallace each ran a leg on all three winning relay units. The win was especially sweet for Korytkowski's father, Al Korytkowski. Before taking over the head coaching reigns for Northview six years earlier, the Wildcats had gone ten straight years without winning even a dual meet.

The individual highlights of the meet belonged to Dearborn Heights Robichaud sophomore Tyrone Wheatley. He broke a 17-year old record in the long jump by leaping 23-10¾. He then took down another meet record by matching Andreus Laut's 10.5 for the 100 from 1980. Placing second to Wheatley in the long jump was future Michigan teammate Derrick Alexander of Detroit Benedictine.

Three future first round draft picks of the NFL competed in the field events. In addition to top draft picks Wheatley and Alexander, sixth-place shot put place finisher Rob Frederickson of St. Joseph would also be selected in the first round after completing a great football career at MSU.

Although Cadillac's Paul McMullen would grab more fame later, Randy Helling of Stevensville-Lakeshore would set the Class B standard in the 800-meter run with a time of 1:52.1.

Oxford senior Mike Goodfellow was the other athlete to win two individual events. Goodfellow won the 1600, and then outsprinted Jeff Kelke down the stretch to capture the 3200 in 9:31.3. Kelke became the second Class B casualty to be disqualified on a rule technicality for wearing a necklace. Goodfellow did fall short of setting the Oxford high school record, set back in 1970 by Goodfellow's uncle Jim Goodfellow, winner of the 1970 state championship.

Bill Deering of Dowagiac, with his clearance at 15-6, missed the meet record in the pole vault by only an inch. His father, Bill Deering Sr., won the vault for Dowagiac back in 1955 and 1956.

In Class C in Alma, Saginaw Nouvel piled up 71 points to win its first team title. Tony Jackson was the leading point producer, winning both short sprints and running a leg on the championship 4x2 squad. Jackson fell just short of a perfect day when the Panthers 4x1 placed second to Fulton-Middleton.

A pair of Northern Michigan tracksters were double winners. Charlevoix's Jason Whitley took the honors in the hurdles, while Jared Glover of Kingsley copped both long distance runs.

In Class D in Hillsdale, perennial power Detroit Lutheran West held off Fowler to take the crown. After winning the state championship for the previous two years in Class C, Lutheran West found a tougher opponent in Class D. The victors edged Fowler by only 6½ points, with Albert Rhoades winning the 100 high hurdles (14.8) and the long jump for Lutheran West.

Tom Becker led runner-up Fowler with wins in the 1600 (4:27.8) and 3200 (9:54.8). Juron Johnson of Baldwin again swept both short sprints for the second-straight year.

Upper Peninsula: John Payment of Brimley set shock waves throughout the entire state when he won the high jump at a state record 7-1 in Marquette. Payment is the only UP athlete to have a best-ever mark in any event for the entire state. Payment, whose previous best was 6-8¾, drew a huge crowd when the field announcer informed the audience that the bar was at 6-11. After it took Payment three tries to clear 6-11, he then cleared 7-0. Payment then cleared a record 7-1 on his first attempt, earning him a standing ovation from the frenzied crowd.

Randy Fountain of Pickford had the day's longest discus throw at 157-3.

Gwinn and Kingsford had to settle for a tie in Class A-B, a meet that would be the last state UP final for retiring Escanaba coach Jim Hirn. He had won seven state titles during his tenure with the Eskimos. Iron Mountain outlasted Ishpeming Westwood in Class C while Pickford returned to the winner's circle for the first time in nine years in Class D. Dave Bush had a perfect day for the victorious Panthers, winning both short sprints and running a leg on two winning relays.

1990

Following 20 years of near perfect conditions, athletes at the state finals had to battle downpours and tornado watches, infrequently interspersed with occasional sunshine. Pontiac Northern won its first state championship with 48½ points. For the third time in five years, Kalamazoo Loy Norrix had to settle for the runner-up trophy.

Northern's Damon Grady was the leading point winner on the Midland track. He took the 100 (10.69), placed second in the 200, third in the long jump and clinched the title for the Huskies by anchoring the 1600-meter relay to victory (3:17.73).

In spite of the inclement weather, good individual performances prevailed in Class A, with Darnell Hall the top draw. The Detroit Pershing senior easily won the 400 in 47.56, before embarking on a career that would propel him to world-class status. In 1992 he won an Olympic gold medal for helping the U.S. team through the heats in Barcelona. In 1995, he captured World Indoor gold and later that summer ran a PR of 44.34.

Kelvin Jackson of Loy Norrix blistered the 110 highs in 13.78. He also placed fifth in the 300 hurdles, won by Howard Triplett of Lansing Sexton in 37.80.

Shannon Norris of Lansing Eastern threatened to become the fourth high jumper in state history to clear seven feet in the high jump. In his first year out for track, Norris had to settle for 6-11, just an inch off the meet record in Class A.

Two other athletes emerged from the pack as double winners. Marcelo Ortiz of Dearborn Fordson took honors in the 800 and 1600-meter runs. Ortiz outlasted Brian Hyde of East Kentwood at the tape in 4:14.04-4:14.46. Ortiz had an easier time in the 800 meters, posting a 1:52.73 winner.

Jackson's Ali Shakoor took honors in the long jump and the 200, running 21.80 in a final that saw future MSU starting tailback Duane Goulbourne place seventh. Aaron Hayden, who made it into the NFL as a running back for the San Diego Chargers, ran a leg on Detroit Mumford's winning 800-meter relay team.

It's an oft-repeated myth that Tyrone Wheatley won a state team title all by himself. He scored 40 essential points for Robichaud, but the team needed more to beat runner-up Three Rivers, 49 to 46. (MHSAA photo)

In Class B, Tyrone Wheatley became the first Michigan athlete in 38 years to win four individual titles to highlight track action in all classes. The Robichaud Junior joined Caro's Clare McDurmon (1932), Detroit Central's Roy Ellis (1899), Grand Rapids Central's Joe

Horner (1907) and East Jackson's Ray Eggelston (1952) in this most select ring of honor.

Robichaud needed all of Wheatley's points, and then some, to win the state title over runner-up Three Rivers, 49 to 46. The all-time career rushing leader at the University of Michigan battled strong headwinds in winning the 110-meter highs (14.85) and the 100-meter dash (10.8h). Wheatley further added the 200-title (21.9h), and capped his momentous day by barely missing his long jump record with a 23-10.

Although Wheatley gobbled up most of the headlines, another champion who would have an even greater track career was Paul McMullen of Cadillac, who won the 1600 in 4:19.9. He would take his talents to Eastern Michigan University where under the coaching of Bob Parks he developed into an Olympian and two-time World Champs finalist.

Only a talent like Wheatley would prevent Sam Brown of Three Rivers from winning four first-place finishes of his own. Brown spearheaded Three Rivers' quest for the title by placing second to Wheatley in both short sprints and anchoring the winning 400 and 800-meter relays.

The lone record at Jackson Northwest came in the 300-meter intermediates, where Darnell Kellogg of Redford-Thurston won in 38.1. Winning the high jump at 6-7 was another who would go on to a great collegiate career. Jon Royce of Chelsea would dominate this event in the Big 10 while competing at Michigan.

Tom Johnson of Marysville came less than a foot from setting a meet record in the shot put at 59-4¾. He also annexed the discus by whirling the platter 167-6.

In Class C at Wyoming Park, a pair of strangers to state championship competition battled for the title. Fulton-Middleton won its first state final track trophy by nipping Edwardsburg 41-39. It was the first trophy for the runner-up since placing second in 1950.

In Class D, Reading captured its first championship in twenty years, tallying an impressive 80 points to edge Detroit Lutheran West. Todd Richards dominated on the Hillsdale track by winning three individual titles and running on the victorious 400-meter relay. He leaped 6-7 in the high jump, won the long jump by a foot at 22-½ and capped his perfect day by setting the meet record for the 300- hurdles (39.46) that would survive for more than a decade.

Upper Peninsula: Kingsford won the title against a very balanced A-B field. Only 10 points separated the Flivvers from fifth-place. Sprinter Desi Schultz from Gladstone was the only double winner. Negaunee won the 1600-meter relay in 3:30.4, a meet record though inferior to Gwinn's 3:30.4 for yards in 1970.

Jerry Cleary of Ontonagon won all three dashes and ran the anchor on the Gladiators' winning 4x2, but it wasn't enough to win the team Class C finals. Ishpeming Westwood outscored Cleary's runner-up Ontonagon team by eight points to take home the first-place trophy. Chris Lett, the UP cross-country champ in the fall, won a pair of races over the longer distances. His teammate Chris Salani won the discus before becoming the regular punter for Michigan State's Football team in the fall.

Pickford looked like the dynasty of old as the Panthers completely dominated in Class D, more than doubling the winning total over second-place Lake Linden Hubbell.

1991

Detroit Cooley saved its best for last in winning its first-ever team title at Grand Rapids' Houseman Field. Cooley's near record-setting effort in the 1600-meter relay was just enough to hold off runner-up Lansing Sexton, 48 to 42. The fleet foursome, comprised of Robert Adams, David Norman, Raphael Johnson and Marco West, covered the metric mile in 3:16.05, just shy of Detroit Redford's yards converted time of 3:15.3 back in 1977. West had an especially big day for coach Gene Ballard's champs. In addition to his anchor leg on the relay team noted above, he won the 400 (48.15) and placed second behind Ypsilanti's Kerch Patterson in the 200 meters.

Runner-up Sexton pushed Cooley in the 4 x 400 relay, as the Big Red's second place clocking of 3:17.04 was one of the best ever. Sexton's Howard Triplett, a member of that quartet, set the only meet record in the sweltering heat running the 300 hurdles in 37.59. Pontiac Northern's Jamell Humprey pushed Triplett to the record, finishing an eyelash behind the record setter in 37.60.

Sexton nearly had another state champion when shot putter Matt Beard placed less than two inches behind the winning heave of Flint Carman-Ainsworth's John Runyan. Beard and Runyan would again meet each other in competition, not on the track, but on the football gridiron. Beard became an academic All-American as a center for the Michigan State Spartans while Runyon played for Michigan before becoming an NFL All-Star (and later a congressman).

Neither Beard nor Runyon would be drafted into the NFL as high as the fourth place shot putter in Grand Rapids. Pete Chrplewicz of Sterling Heights Stevenson, after completing his career as a tight end for Notre Dame, would be the fifth player selected by the Detroit Lions in the 1997 draft.

A couple of records were threatened in the field events. Pontiac Central's Stephane Mayo, with his winning clearance at 6-11, missed the meet record in the high jump by only an inch. Grandville's Brett Organek won the discus crown by better than sixteen feet with a toss of 185-0.

The best distance effort on the hot afternoon belonged to East Kentwood's Brian Hyde, who won the 1600 in 4:12.74, the fastest metric mile in ten years.

Only a slight hamstring pull perhaps kept Dearborn Heights Robichaud from repeating as team champs in Class B. Robichaud tallied 31 points, nine behind eventual champion Oxford. Tyrone Wheatley was again a heavy favorite to win four individual first-place medals at the state meet, and was right on track to do so before the nagging injury occurred. While winning the 100 meters in 10.67, easily the day's fastest time in any class, the future Michigan grid star eased up halfway through the race after suffering a cramp in his right hamstring.

With Wheatley out of the 200, the door was left open for Oxford. Paving the way was versatile Eric Welch, who sprinted to victory in the 400 (48.4), and anchored two relay championships for the Wildcats: the 4x2 (1.29.99) and the 4x8 (8:01.38).

Until he went down early in the meet, Wheatley had made his presence felt. He needed but one jump to take his third-straight long jump title (23-0), and then captured his third meet record while winning the 110-meter high hurdles. Wheatley's 13.7 time was caught only on hand stop watches, as the FAT unit failed to catch him in the final picture. Meet referee Blake Hageman explained: "Wheatley was so far out in front it caused the timing device to malfunction. All the runners were in the picture but him."

Wheatley's total of nine individual titles is matched in Michigan prep history by only Caro's Clare McDurmon in the early 1930s. Wheatley will also be remembered in Mansfield, Ohio. In the 66 years running of the what had been for many years the Midwest's most prestigious meet, he was the only athlete to win the 100-meter dash three consecutive years.

In spite of the sweltering conditions, Jeff Christian, the only state track champion from Beaverton, had the day's best time in capturing the 3200-meter run (9:18.8). Another impressive mark was a 15-2 winning vault by Bob Bailey, of Remus Chippewa Hills, while successfully defending his title.

In Class C, Sherman Ross, by scoring 30 of his team's 50 points, led Cassopolis to its first team title. Ross won both short sprints, placed second in the 400 to Galesburg Augusta's Rick Tyson and ran a leg on the Ranger's second-place 1600-meter relay team. Such was Cassopolis's depth in the sprints, that the state 100 champion was not needed by the Rangers to win the 400-meter relay. Thomas McNary, Robert

Tyrone Wheatley was hit by injury as a senior.

Crawford, Robert Saxton and Mike Andrew teamed up to win the relay in 43.9.

The best individual match-up took place in the high jump, where Tracy Grudenich of Bellevue and Mike Pfeil of Fulton-Middleton waged a fierce battle. Each jumper matched the previous state Class C best by clearing 6-10. Although Grudenich took home the first-place medal based on fewer misses, each jumper would be credited with a share of the meet record.

The closest battle for a team title came in Class D. Todd Richards led Reading High to a successful defense of its crown with a 69-68 squeaker over Detroit Lutheran West. Richards, hampered somewhat from a knee injury from basketball season, defended two of his three titles. He did not even enter the 300 hurdles, where he held the meet record.

Coach Bob Lutz held Richards out of the 300-meter hurdles to run him in the 400 meters, an event that put less strain on his star's ailing knee. After placing second in the open 400 behind Manton's Don Johnson, Reading entered the final event needing to finish only one place behind Lutheran West to repeat as team champs. Richards came through under the intense pressure, anchoring the Rangers to a second-place finish in the 1600-meter relay, a step behind Lutheran West but a point ahead in the final tally.

Mendon's Bryan Happel pulled off a feat that was very uncommon in Class D. He had the day's best pole vault mark for any class in winning at 15-2½, a meet record.

Upper Peninsula: Near perfect weather awaited the athletes in Marquette. Kingsford's 400-meter relay team came the closest to a meet record. Although given credit for breaking a record with its 44.6, it was clearly inferior to the Flivver's 440 relay time of 44.3 back in 1976.

Menominee edged Ishpeming Westwood 46 to 43 to take home the team trophy in Class A-B, while

Ironwood had a much easier time in Class C, scoring 71 points to 47 and a half for runner-up Stephenson. Chris Lett was the individual star. The distance ace from Houghton posted the fastest times in all three classes with his wins in the 800, 1600 and 3200-meter run. Pickford was on another streak as it made it three in a row in Class D.

1992

Although trailing Traverse City by nine and a half points entering the afternoon's final event, defending Class A champion Detroit Cooley still loomed as the team to beat. All Cooley had to do to repeat was win the 1600-meter relay. With most of their relay members returning from a near record-setting quartet of 1991, the Cardinals were heavy favorites to win and, with the ten points awarded for first place, would nip Traverse City by a half point.

But fate was kind to veteran head coach John Lober and his Traverse City squad. Without a relay team qualified for the day's closing event, Trojan followers looked on helplessly as Cooley's crack foursome sprinted to a commanding lead after two laps. Suddenly, a Cooley runner dropped the baton on the third lap. The mishap moved Cooley back to last in its heat and preserved T.C.'s title.

If any team or coach deserved to win a state title in 1992, it was Lober and his Black and Gold Trojans. Traverse City won seven invitationals during the season, including the Huron and Spartan relays. Lober brought a contingent of 11 athletes to Grand Rapids, and ten scored. Although Traverse City did not win a single event, it did manage to score points in all four field events.

It would be the only state title Traverse City has won under its longtime coach, who remained very active with the team for another few decades.

Flint Kearsley, with its second-place total of 35, posted its best-ever finish, just two and a half points shy of Traverse City's total of 37½.

The rainy afternoon put a damper on athletes' quest for records. Times were especially slow in the running events throughout the Grand Rapids area. Only Trinity Townsend of Muskegon Heights was credited with posting a meet record on the track. Even so, his 48.14 seconds in the 400 meters was intrinsically inferior to Ken Mitchell's 48.0 record set over the longer 440-yard distance a decade earlier.

Townsend would later find the 800 distance more to his liking. At Michigan, he placed fourth in the 1996 NCAA, the only American to make the finals. The same year he would compete at the Olympic Trials.

Perhaps the day's best performance belonged to Grandville's Brett Organek. On his last toss of the day, he sailed the discus 196-5 to better Johnny Mitchell's record set back in 1983. Jon Runyan of Flint Carman-Ainsworth placed second to Organek in the discus, but did manage to set a Cavalier school record with his toss of 178-1. He also managed to successfully defend his state championship in the shot put (59-5).

Randy Kinder of East Lansing was the leading point producer at Houseman Field. The starring tailback for East Lansing's state championship football team, he nearly pulled off a sprint triple crown. The future tailback at Notre Dame won the 400 meters (48.88) and nipped defending co-champion Brad Fields of East Kentwood by 0.01 in the 200 (21.87). Earlier Fields, a future Michigan State speedster, had edged Kinder in the 100 meters (11.02) by the same 0.01 margin.

Khary Burnley of Cass Tech won the 110-high hurdles with a time of 14.25. Burnley gave much of the credit for his success to his father. In 1961, the last year that Detroit athletes did not compete at the state level, Mike Burnley won the Detroit City high hurdles championships while competing for Detroit Mumford.

Class B saw the return to power of Flint Beecher. Not only did head coach Marty Crane's Bucs win their tenth boy's state title, but the lady Bucs likewise captured the Class B crown at Wyoming Park High School. This marked the third time Beecher would win both team championships in the same year.

Team depth and unprecedented power in the relays propelled Beecher to both crowns. For the first time one school would sweep all four relays. Beecher would see 13 of its 16 boys break into the scoring column. Highlighting the romp was a convincing victory in the 1600-meter relay. McKinley Tipton, Jimmy Lacy, Garth Spight and Marcus Tipton battled raindrops as well as the opposition to win in 3:21.07, more than seven seconds ahead of second-place.

Andy Schoech from Bloomfield Hills Andover was the only individual double winner. He posted the day's fastest time in all classes in capturing the 100 (10.81) and the 200 (21.78), helping Andover to a second-place team finish.

In Class C, Detroit DePorres placed in only three events, but it was enough to win its 12th state team track championship. Adrian Edwards and Allen Heywood went 1-2 in the 100 meters, with Heywood winning the 200. DePorres also utilized the speed of Edwards and Heywood to win the 800-meter relay. Although the Eagles were shut out in all other events, their total of 41 points was enough to hold off runner-up Edwardsburg's final total of 37.

Athens won its first Boy's State Class D track championship with a hard fought 53-50 win over rival Litchfield. Earlier in the season, first year coach Larry

Brown's Indians had lost an invitational and a regional crown to Litchfield. The most impressive individual achievement at the Class D meet at Forest Hills Northern, was in the pole vault. Webberville's Brandon McCarty, son of harness racing driver Larry McCarty, won with with his 14-4¾ clearance.

Upper Peninsula: A week earlier, running in windchills that dipped to as low as 18 degrees in Marquette, Escanaba survived the cold to win the Class A-B title with 68 points, eight more than second-place Sault Ste. Marie.

Even though snow could occasionally be seen falling on the Marquette oval, Wade Hodge of Menominee became the first vaulter in UP history to clear fourteen feet. Nate Chylek and Charlie Bush each won a pair of events for the Eskimos. Chylek's 10.9 in the 100 might have tied the meet record but it was aided by winds gusting up to 25 miles per hour.

Houghton was the winner in a well-balanced Class C final. In Class D, it was business as usual for Pickford as the team raced to its fourth-straight, 15 points better than second-place Rock-Mid Peninsula. The Pickford team had some extra incentive to win the title after Coach Sam Lightfoot announced to his team on the bus ride over that he was retiring.

1993

Flint Carman-Ainsworth won the first team championship for a Flint school in 14 years at Grand Rapid's Houseman Field. Eleven years earlier, on the same Houseman field oval, head coach Kenn Domerese won a title in Class B, when the school was called Flint Ainsworth. Unlike 1982, when the Cavaliers won the hardware with just three athletes, team depth paid off in 1993.

The 4x1 squad won in a school record 42.6 and sophomore Mike Spaulding crossed the finish line first in the 300 hurdles (38.88). The most surprising first place came from junior Chuck Thrash in the high jump. Thrash, who barely reached the state meet in a tie for the third and final qualifying spot at regionals, shocked the field with a winning leap of 6-8. A runner-up finish in the high hurdles by Spaulding, and a fourth in the 800-meter relay gave the Cavaliers 44½ points, 3½ more than second-place Detroit Mumford.

Don Bryant of Farmington Hills Harrison edged Spaulding in the high hurdles. Although John Herrington's Hawks have won many a state championship in football, Bryant would be the first track titlist from Harrison.

The most impressive individual performance in Class A belonged to Midland Dow's Steven Hill. He set a meet record by clearing 16-½, erasing the 15-10 standard of Owosso's Toby Van Pelt. Hill switched to a bigger pole just three weeks before the state finals. "I wanted to set a record today, nothing less. After getting to 15-7, I didn't want to go for 15-11 to beat the record. I wanted 16-0. You get about six good jumps in a meet and I was running out."

Al Barnett from Belleville fell less than an inch shy of cracking the 60-foot mark in the shot put.

Helping Detroit Mumford bring home the runner-up trophy was Derrick Mason, who finished second in the long jump, placed in the 400, and ran legs on the 400 and 1600-meter relay teams that placed 2nd and 3rd respectively. He would go on to a sensational collegiate career in football at MSU, ending his Spartan career as the all-time leading kick returner in Big 10 history. He was drafted in the fourth round in the 1997 NFL draft by the Tennessee Oilers, in a career that would see Mason become a perennial NFL All-Star.

Mason's future MSU teammate as a wide receiver for the Spartans, Octavis Long, took fourth in the 100-meter dash. Winning the 100 meters was junior Micah Morris of Bay City Central, in his first year out for track.

The leading point producer in Class A was Flint Southwestern's Steve Ruffin. He won the 400 (47.94), the 200- (21.8) and anchored Southwestern's 4x4 to yet another first (3:20.23). The day truly belonged to Flint with nine winners. Janario Brown of Kearsley edged yet another Flint thinclad, Bill Thompson of Northwestern, to take the 800 (1:55.46), while teammate Gary Kinney won the 3200 in 9:31.12. Kinney had won as a sophomore in 1991 and taken second in 1992.

Class B performers didn't suffer any letdown on the Wyoming Park track. A pair of records fell by the wayside, and another equaled, as Class B competitors bettered their Class A compatriots in nearly half of the events. Chris Polk paced Detroit UD Jesuit to its first team title. He figured in the scoring of a perfect 40 points by winning the 200 and 400 meters, as well as running legs on state championship relay squads.

The Jesuit foursome of William Brooks, Jim Krol, Edzra Gibson and Polk bettered the meet record with a 1:28.23 clocking for the 4x2. Kareem Dillard replaced Krol and the U-D 1600-meter relay team romped to victory (3:20.36) by nearly six seconds. U-D Jesuit held off perennial power Flint Beecher, which came six points away from winning its 11th team state title.

Grand Rapids Catholic's David Gerrity, who would captain Notre Dame's track team in his senior year of college, joined Hill in clearing 16 feet at the state meet, just 1/4 inch behind Hill's measured vault of 16-½. Jim Gardiner, arguably the best pole vault coach in state prep history, saw his Cougar vaulters finish 1-2.

Garrity's teammate Mike Long vaulted 14-2 to claim second-place.

Northview's Ed Barnes, who earlier in the afternoon won the 100, showed his versatility by winning the longer hurdle race in 38.1, a time that equaled the meet record.

Vicksburg's Aaron Oakes easily defended his title with the day's best long jump of 23-2. Tim Strok of Riverview had the day's best time for the 110-meter high hurdles at a speedy 14.19.

Mark Goodfellow, with his win in the 1600, became the third Goodfellow from Oxford to win a state championship in a distance race. In 1970, Mark's uncle Jim took honors in the two-mile run, while brother Mike won both distance races in 1989.

In Class C, Eau Claire won its title by scoring 40 points at Byron Center. Napoleon and New Haven shared second with 36 points. The meet marked the debut of John Mack onto the state track scene. The New Haven frosh grabbed the win at 400 meters and ran on the winning 800-meter relay for New Haven.

In Class D, Akron-Fairgrove won the title for veteran head coach Jerry Lasceski. Coaching the Vikings in his 29th year, Lasceski had earlier led Akron-Fairgrove to a state title in 1978. Litchfield certainly made it interesting on the Forest Hills Northern track, finishing just two points behind the victors.

Jeff Beuche of Ann Arbor Gabriel Richard took the 800-meter run in 1:57.0, second only to Lee Wilds of Mendon in Class D history. Wilds ran 1:56.7 over the longer 880-yard distance back in 1973. Marty McGinn of Grass Lake raced to the 2nd fastest time in state history for the 3200-meter run in 9:29.5, but short of Jerry Curtis' mark of 9:28.4 run over the longer two-mile distance in 1978.

Upper Peninsula: In a big improvement from the previous year, sunny weather greeted the athletes for the 1993 finals in Marquette. Surprisingly, no records in A-B competition fell, as Escanaba successfully defended its team championship.

St. Ignace won its first team title by the narrowest of margins over Munising, escaping with the trophy by a slender half point margin in Class C. Rich Blowers from Manistique took part in three wins, including a record 40.0 over the 300 hurdles. Jeremiah Konell of Stephenson cleared 13-3 in the pole vault.

Although Felch North Dickinson took home the team trophy in Class D, Ryan Fountain of Pickford was clearly the individual star. Fountain set a meet record with his 55-1 in the shot and an all-class UP best with his 163-1 heave in the discus.

1994

Detroit Cass Tech returned to the winner's circle for the first time since 1978 by taking the Class A team title at Midland High School. An impressive array of depth in the sprint events propelled coach Tom Wilcher's Technicians to the easy victory. Although it was Tech's first title in 16 years, the path to the top was a familiar one for Wilcher. The former Michigan football and track standout was a member of three winning teams in the early 1980s for Detroit Central.

Said Wilcher, "The guys did what they were supposed to do and got what they were supposed to get—the state title."

Cass Tech blazed to history in the 800-meter relay. The foursome of Fred Wilkerson, Clarence Williams, Jabari Johnson and Darryl Rankins not only shattered the existing state record but also came only a tenth of a second from matching the national prep record. Hand-held watches timed the Green & White burners in 1:24.8, which would have tied the national record. The automatic timing mechanism had the race at 1:24.94, which officials rounded up to 1:25.0 because of a malfunction.

Johnson, Williams and Rankin placed second, fifth, and sixth respectively in the 200, while Wilkerson placed second in the 100. Winner Micah Morris of Bay City Central defended his title with a quick hand-held time of 10.4. Morris was nearly as impressive in the 200 as he led the field across the finish line in the 200 meters at 21.4.

Cass Tech's Dwayne Fuqua, son of former Pittsburgh Steelers' star Frenchy Fuqua, then teamed up with Wilkerson, Johnson and Clarence Williams to win the 1600-meter relay in 3:17.1.

Credited with a third record by officials was Brandon Guinn of Jackson, whose 37.5 for the 300 hurdles was inferior to the standard 37.59 by Howard Triplett of Lansing Sexton that had been automatically timed.

If Cass Tech's strength was in the sprints, then runner-up Ann Arbor Pioneer dominated in the distances. The Class A cross country team champion actually had more first places than Cass Tech. Pioneer's Todd Snyder won the 3200 in 9:17.1. Don McLaughlin, who ran a leg on the winning 3200-meter relay team earlier, placed third behind Snyder and Steve Schell of Dearborn Fordson.

Pioneer's other first place came from Elgin Bates' fine leap of 6-11 in the high jump. He edged Holt's Jeff Williams, who cleared a fine 6-10.

Michael Barker of Clio, the discus winner, nearly had a second victory in the shot put. Leading going into the final round, he was nosed out of first place by Detroit Cooley's Lionel Boston. Jim Rief of Flint Central successfully defended his 1600-meter run crown, but was unable to set a personal best after giving his all in the 3200-meter relay. His 1:53.0 split moved Central up to fifth place for the event.

Pontiac Northern's Gaven Herring turned in another impressive performance with a 47.0.

In Class B at Saginaw, a new champion emerged. Comstock won its first title by a narrow two-point margin over Ypsilanti Lincoln. Although the Colts won only the 800-meter relay, Randy Hunt was a major contributor during the day. In addition to his anchor on the winning relay (1:29.32), he placed second in the 200 and 400.

The lone record to fall came from Chelsea's David Beeman, who easily won the discus title by nearly 14 feet with his 175-3. Placing third behind Beeman was Muskegon Orchard View's Josh Keur, a future four-year starter at tight end on MSU's football team.

Chelsea took its third first-place medal earlier in the day when it won the 3200-meter relay in 7:58.68. Running a leg was Dan Wehrwein, son of Bill Wehrwein, a former Big 10 champion in the 440-yard dash. The elder Wehrwein has been a huge help over the years in assisting on this book project.

A double winner in Saginaw was Joe O'Connor of West Branch Ogemaw Heights. O'Connor became the first state champion from West Branch in 81 years. Ironically, he swept the same two events won by Earl Sheldon in 1912 and 1913. The Class B cross country champ in the fall, O'Connor won the 1600 (4:16.02) and the 800 (1:55.51).

Ted Adams, likewise, captured a pair of races in leading Ypsilanti Lincoln to its runner-up finish. Adams won both short dashes for the Railsplitters, and ran a leg on each of the third-place 400 and 800-meter relay teams. Lincoln won its third title by capturing the 1600-meter relay.

Aaron Oakes took honors in the long jump for the third consecutive year. The Vicksburg leaper sailed 23-1¼. Jackson Northwest's Lee Busby, with a 15-½, had the day's best effort in the pole vault.

In Class C, New Haven began a three-year run by at Bay City Western's oval. Coach Frank Reed brought only four boys, but that was enough to nip Breckenridge by two and a half points. For Breckenridge, it was the best finish yet. Casey Ward won the pole vault at 14-9. Breckenridge also nipped New Haven in the 800-meter relay by a tenth of a second in 1:30.2.

It was John Mack who led the victors to their first state title. He repeated as the 400-meter champ in 48.89, won the 200 in 22.5, and anchored the 1600-meter relay team to a third-in-a-row. Only the narrow loss in the 800-relay to Breckenridge, deprived Mack of winning four first-place medals in three consecutive years, a feat never accomplished in state prep history.

Tim Henge of New Lothrop and Cory Dunn of Jonesville had excellent marks in the field events. Henge's leap of 6-9 in the high jump was the first state title won in New Lothrop's history. Dunn's best long jump of 22-8½ was nearly two feet farther than his nearest competitor.

In Class D, Pittsford moved into the winner's circle for the first time. Coach Bruce Caswell's Wildcats would begin a reign of four straight state titles by amassing 66 points. Only shot putter Jeremy Sanford would win an individual first-place.

Upper Peninsula: Menominee captured the A-B title, thanks in large part to triple winner Steve Molnar, who won the 100 and 200 as well as the 300 hurdles. Future running star Rob Martin became the first runner in UP history to run under 50 seconds for 400 meters. He also won the 800 and anchored a pair of relay teams to victory.

Ishpeming Westwood sophomore David Paananen had the UP's second-best mark ever in the shot put with a 56-2½. Ron Roell and Matt Hoskins completed a magical year at Kingsford High School. After playing on the Class B state championship Flivver football team in the fall, they each won a state title in track.

Munising romped to the Class C crown by the widest margin ever in tallying 73 points on the Marquette track. Dave DeLisle led the Mustangs with the fastest times in the UP in the distance events. He won the 800 (2:00.0), 1600 (4:27.0), and 3200 (9:56.2), all after anchoring the winning 3200-meter relay. Coach Fran DesArmo's boys placed in 16 of 17 events on a day where no records were set.

Ontonagon won its first Class D championship in 24 years, outscoring second-place Powers-North Central 47 to 38. John Richard of Felch North Dickinson accounted for the only meet record with a 40.6 clocking over the 300-meter hurdles.

1995

It was deja vu at the running of the state finals held once again in the thumb area of Michigan. Detroit Cass Tech's girls and boys teams brought the team championship trophies back to the Motor City. Mother Nature was none too kind to the athletes, however. Rain and strong winds made for sub-par performances in virtually all events.

Only in the pole vault would a meet record be set. Phil Grzemkowski of Reese inched the Class C record up to 14-11. Even with the record, Grzemkowski fell short of equaling his personal best of 15-2 set earlier in the week.

Again, it was Cass Tech's strength in the relays that carried the Technicians to their fourth state title. Coach Tom Wilcher's speedsters won the 400, 800 and 1600-meter relays. The team was so deep that not a single runner was called upon to run a leg on all three relays. The Green and White tallied 47 points, 14 more than runner-up Detroit Chadsey. For Chadsey, it was its best showing ever. Tony Vann-Spann's win in the 400 (48.05) highlighted Chadsey's good day.

Vann-Spann also placed second in the 200 behind Jamal Allen of Southfield Lathrup. Allen also claimed the 100 to become Class A's only double winner on the afternoon.

Battling strong winds, Todd Snyder of Ann Arbor Pioneer turned the day's best individual performance. Snyder made it a perfect season for the distance awards. After successfully defending his cross country crown in the fall, he won the 3200 in 9:09.9. Just as he did in cross country, he defeated runner-up Steve Shell of Dearborn Fordson by about 15 yards.

Otis Floyd of Southfield impressed in the 300 hurdles with a solid 37.78. The best on the field came in the pole vault where East Lansing's Adam Gilroy cleared 15-1.

In Class B, Comstock romped to its second-straight title at Midland Dow. Comstock's margin of victory was the second biggest in Class B history, trailing only Flint Beecher's total set in 1983. Comstock garnered nary a point, of its 70, in a field event. Coach Tim Cashen's powerhouse produced six wins.

Leading the way for the victors was sprinter Randy Hunt, who slammed his way to a perfect afternoon by winning the 100, 200, and 400 and anchoring the winning 4x1. Although Hunt was the big star, Comstock was far from a one-man team. Shawn Bowden won the 110 highs for the Colts, while T.J. Fields, Quentin Hunter, J.B. Thomas and Terrance Bowden teamed up to take the 800-meter relay.

One event that took a licking was the high jump. The rain made for a slick surface and high winds, made the jumping treacherous. Fremont's Demetry McDonald had the best jump of the day in all classes when he cleared 6-6. Not since the early 1970s, when the Fosbury Flop technique became the dominant style, had the year's best jumpers failed to clear anything higher than 6-6 at the state finals. The winning height of 5-10 in the Class D high jump was the lowest winning clearance in 34 years.

In Class C, New Haven cruised to its second-straight title, matching Comstock's total of 70 points from the Class B meet. Once again it was John Mack paving the way for the Rockets. He matched Hunt's perfect slam of four wins by repeating as the 200 and 400-meter champ and running legs on the winning 800 and 1600-meter relays for Coach Frank Reed's thinclads.

Mack broke 49 seconds in winning his third-straight 400 title and posted the day's fastest time in any class with his 21.97 in the 200. He led teammate Bill Chenault across the finish line in the 200 to give the Rockets a 1-2 sweep for the furlong. If not for placing behind Mack in the 200, Chenault would also have brought back four first-place medals to New Haven. Earlier Chenault won the 100 meters (10.91) and joined Mack and teammates Glen Clark and Cliff Akers on the winning 800 and 1600-meter relay teams.

Having the best day in any class in the field events was Quincy's Jerry Stempien, who won the shot put by more than six feet with a toss of 57-8¼ and the discus by more than 16 feet over his closest competitor.

Dominating the distance events was Justin Curry from Carson City-Crystal. Curry, who led the Eagles to the team cross country title in the fall, won the 1600 (4:23.02) and the 3200 (9:38.5). The win in the 3200 was his third-straight, a feat no other Class C runner had matched.

In Class D, Pittsford could lay claim to being the team of the '90s. The Wildcats won their second-straight by scoring 57 points, but this would prove to be just a warm up for the next two years. Baldwin sophomore Juson Johnson sprinted the century in 10.86, the day's fastest time.

The busiest runner of the day may have been Central Lake's Ryan Shay. The sophomore distance ace repeated as the 3200 champ, and breezed home first in the 800 and 1600-meter runs.

Upper Peninsula: It was deja vu for the Menominee Maroons as they once again edged Marquette for the A-B title. Steve Molnar paced the winners by winning the sprint double and anchoring the winning 800-meter relay. Two all-time UP best performances were set on the Marquette oval.

Robin Martin nearly had the best time on either peninsula with his meet record of 1:55.9 over 800 meters. In addition, he led the Marquette 3200-meter relay team to an all-time UP best. While running at the University of Pennsylvania Martin would hold five school records, including the outdoor 800 meters (1:47.10) as well as the indoors (1:48.89).

David Paananen from Ishpeming Westwood notched his name into the record books with a heave of 169-4 in the discus, second only to Stempien's effort below the Big Mac bridge.

Although they didn't win the day's final race, a come-from-behind effort by anchor man Ty Nesberg picked up a second place for Munising to clinch the Class C UP championship.

A packed house at Marquette witnessed a pair of records fall in C, both on the field. Rob Katona of

Negaunee, as did Paananen, found the conditions favorable in the discus when he hurled the platter 156-1. Jeremy Richard from Ironwood cleared at 13-6 to set in the pole vault.

Powers-North Central won its first state title since the consolidation of Powers-Spaulding and Hermansville in Class D. The Jets won five events in outscoring second-place Ontonagon by twenty-five points.

1996

One who has chronologically followed this year-by-year history would certainly note that most of our lead paragraphs cover the Class A portion of the state meet. In 1996, however, John Mack and his New Haven Rockets get top billing. Coach Frank Reed ended his 33-year coaching career at New Haven on top, with his tracksters capturing their third-straight Class C state title.

New Haven sprinter Mack sprinted his way onto the all-time leader board in state titles won. No other trackster in Michigan's noble track history can come close to matching Mack's total of 13 gold medals. And Mack came oh-so close to having a perfect score.

Out of the 16 events entered (the maximum permitted under high school rules) Mack had two seconds and an ignominious 8th, medaling in all 16 events. Mack became one of only a handful of state prep athletes to win an event four-straight years when he romped home victorious in the 400 in a meet record 48.22.

Mack took the state title in the 200 meters three straight years, "He probably would have won it all four years if I hadn't have entered him in the long jump-- where he placed eighth--in his freshman year," lamented Coach Reed. A runner-up finish in the 4x4 in his freshman year, followed by a narrow loss to Breckenridge the following year in the 4 x 200, were the only defeats Mack would see in his brilliant career.

It had been 61 years since a state athlete put together back-to-back four first-place finishes, and Mack became only the third performer in state history to pull off this rare feat. (Eugene Beatty of Detroit Northeastern in 1927-28, and Alan Smith of Paw Paw back in 1934-35 being the other two). In addition to his 200 and 400 wins, Mack anchored the Rockets' championship 4 x 200 and 4 x 400 relays to victory, contributing to 40 of the 41 New Haven points.

Mack's talents extended beyond the dusty cinders of New Haven's antiquated track. His ability in the classroom led to an impressive Ivy League academic scholarship at Princeton University. He didn't disappoint his legion of followers back home, winning the Ivy League 400-meter championship in his freshman year and being named the MVP for the Tigers.

"John was the kind of kid you loved to have on your team," said coach Frank Reed. "He was a leader, he did everything, the whole works. If equipment needed to be put up, he'd put it up, and was the last one off the track field. He carried the water bucket and all. At track meets I didn't have to do anything. He would take charge of the kids, lead them all in warm ups, just a great leader."

Like New Haven, Detroit Cass Tech pulled of the hat trick by winning its third-consecutive state Class A championship. The Technicians totaled 62 points on the new Rockford oval, 18 more than runner-up Pontiac Northern.

It is perhaps only fitting that the athlete with the longest name in state history to win a state track title would also have one of the longest jumps. Okoineme

John Mack went on to star at Princeton.

Giwa-Agbomeirel, of Midland leaped 24-6 in wind-aided conditions on one of the oddest of runways, one that spanned the crest of the infield, so that the beginning of the runway was uphill, but the bulk of the run to the board was clearly downhill. Giwa-Agbomeirel's leap is second in meet history to Derek Harper's wind-aided 25-foot leap posted sixteen years earlier. Curiously, the 24-6 was given meet record status, but years later the MHSAA acknowledged the mark as wind-aided on its website.

Giwa-Agbomeirel would share the spotlight with Dearborn Fordson's Abdul Alzindani, who repeated \in the 1600 and followed up with a win effort in the 3200. His senior year Alzindani also won the Footlocker national XC title and outdoor nationals in the two mile.

Perhaps the most exciting race came in the 3200-meter relay. Ben Ufer anchored Ann Arbor Pioneer to

the narrowest of victories over runner-up Grand Blanc. Ufer was the grandson of the late Bob Ufer, one-time World Indoor Record holder and three-time indoor Big 10 champion for the U of M. But, of course, most people fondly remember Ufer has the long-time football radio voice of the "Meeechigan" Wolverines.

Flint Central's Stan Brown shot out of nowhere to win the shot. In eighth place going into his final trial, Brown catapulted past seven competitors in unleashing his winning 57-½.

Runner-up Pontiac Northern received a great effort from Godfrey Herring. After winning the 400 in 47.67, Herring anchored Northern's 4x4 relay team to victory (3:20.6). Crosstown rival Gerald Rasool of Pontiac Central also had a big day. Rasool, after placing second in the long jump at 23-11, took honors in the 100 (10.92).

In Class B, lanky Jeff DeLong led Whitehall to its first-ever title in Lowell. The consummate team player for the victorious Vikings, DeLong pulled Whitehall's 3200-meter relay up to fourth-place, then ran second in the 1600 and 800. Saving his best for last, the seemingly inexhaustible Viking star anchored Whitehall's 1600-meter relay team to victory, clinching the state title.

Tough luck honors went to Brent Lesniak of Dowagiac. He missed out on a first-place medal in the long jump by placing a half inch behind Harrison's Shane Kelly's 22-9½ leap. His second-place finish in the 100 was even closer. John Matthews of Wyoming Godwin Heights edged him at the tape by 0.01. Lesniak did get a first-place medal, however, running a leg on Dowagiac's 4 x 100-meter relay. A dropped baton in the 4 x 200 may have cost Dowagiac the championship.

In addition to Mack's heroics at the Class C state meet in Comstock Park, two other performances stood out. Pete Moe of Constantine ran 38.97 for the 300 hurdles. Ryan Harris of Buchanan sped 10.72 in winning the century.

Mr. Basketball finalist, Mike Burde of Newaygo, won the discus competition at 166-0.

With the lone exception being Whitehall, it was three-peat for team championships in 1996. Pittsford brought home the Class D title for the third-straight year with a commanding performance. Pittsford's winning total of 96 points was nearly 60 points more that runner-up Webberville, and third-highest point total in Class D history.

Individual standouts at the Class D finals held at Forest Hill Northern's Track complex were Juson Johnson of Baldwin and Ryan Shay of Central Lake. Johnson took the 100 for the third-straight year while Shay dusted the field to once again win the 3200.

Bruce Hungerford, who earlier in the season quarterbacked Fowler to the Class D football title, won the shot with a heave of 52-½. Hungerford would later become a junior college All-American in basketball while competing for Muskegon Community College.

Upper Peninsula: For the first time in more than 30 years the finals were not held in Marquette. Escanaba found the change to Kingsford more to its liking by walking off with the Class A-B championship.

David Paananen of Westwood won his third-straight shot title and made it two in a row in the discus to top all performers. Munising, although not nearly as dominant as in 1995, won top team honors in Class C, outpointing second-place Ironwood 41 to 36. After being a bridesmaid five-times in the past, Rapid River won its first Class D crown with a convincing 15-point margin over runner-up Powers-North Central.

1997

The city of Pontiac could proclaim itself as the King of Track in 1997. Pontiac Northern and Pontiac Central placed 1-2 in the Class A team competition, far outdistancing all other schools. Godfrey Herring led Northern's charge to a second title by winning two individual events and running a leg on the winning 4 x 400. Less than a hundredth-of-a-second kept Herring from a bigger sweep. The EMU-bound runner took second in the 100, the same time (10.81) as winner Lamar Courtney of Muskegon Mona Shores.

Undaunted with his narrow setback in the 100, Herring blazed the fastest 400 (46.95) and 200 (21.24) meters at the state meet in 13 years. "This is great," said Herring of the team finish. "If we can't win, we hope Central wins. But to win the state meet, it feels unbelievable."

A young sophomore from Kalamazoo Loy Norrix startled the crowd by unleashing a prodigious heave of 63-7 on his final throw to set a new Class A record.

T.J. Duckett, a 6-3/250 package of speed and power, also ran a leg on Loy Norrix's winning 4x1. His toss in the shot put came only an inch from equaling the oldest state all-class record on the books--a 63-8 by Gary Van Elst of Class C Middleville in 1968. Duckett's clutch last put pushed Joe Keller of Lansing Eastern back to second. Keller's mark of 61-6 was in itself a prodigious heave.

In the discus, leader Nate Golin of Grandville saw Chad Peters of Mount Pleasant sail the platter out to 177-9 on the final throw to take first-place honors.

Paul Terek, Livonia Franklin's first state track champion, broke the meet record and tied the state record in the pole vault by clearing the bar at 16-6. Jeff

Kus equaled the Class A mark in the high jump by scaling the bar at 7-0.

Jalilu Mayo performed yeoman-like chores for second-place Pontiac Central. He topped the field in the 110-meter highs (13.91), ran a leg on the winning 4 x 200 team and placed second in the 300 hurdles. Arthur Bouyer, following in the footsteps of his sister Nikki—winner of five state Class A titles in the hurdles, took honors in 300 IH with a winning 37.74.

Anthony Spires of Detroit Mumford, won the distance double, taking the 1600 (4:16.99) and 3200 (9:23.13).

In Class B at Lowell, misfortune again plagued Dowagiac. It would prove to be a bittersweet afternoon for Dowagiac star Brent Lesniak. The All-State football star won the long jump (22-6½) and garnered another first place medal by running lead-off on 4 x 200. Earlier he placed a close second in the 100 meters, 0.01 seconds behind Edward Johnson of River Rouge.

Dowagiac was a heavy favorite to take first in the 4 x 100. An over-anxious Lesniak was disqualified for false starting. The points lost by the Chieftains opened the door for nearby St. Joseph. The Bears needed a second-place in the meet's final event to give veteran coach Ron Waldvogel his first state Class B track title in his 31 years as the Bear's head mentor. Micah Zuhl, who earlier had taken first in the 400, ran a superb anchor to put St. Joseph second behind Ypsilanti Lincoln in the 4 x 400. The eight points scored by St. Joseph would be one point more than the hard luck Chieftains of Dowagiac.

Charles DeWildt of Grand Rapids Catholic Central had the most impressive performance on the field, with a vault of 15-8. He later defeated Class A champion Paul Terek at the Midwest Meet of Champions. In 2000 DeWildt would become a Big 10 Champion in his specialty while competing for Michigan. DeWildt's victory was won, however, with a heavy heart. His high school coach Jim Gardiner, pole vault mentor for many past state champions, had passed away just a day earlier.

In Class B, Nick Brockway of Richland Gull Lake ran the fastest 3200-meter run in 16 years (9:14.7) to record the top individual performance. Only a junior, he defeated 1600 champion Russ Gerbers by nearly 18 seconds. Gerbers, from Wyoming Park, would win the Midwest Meet in the 3200-meter run the follow week.

In Class C, Detroit DePorres ended New Haven's three-year reign by taking the title at Comstock Park. Failing to win a single event, the Eagles still had enough depth to capture their 13th state track championship. Jason Carver of Parchment was the day's only double winner in Class C with his wins in both short sprints.

In Class D, Ryan Shay capped a phenomenal career for Central Lake by winning the 1600 (4:17.13) and the 3200 (9:25.68). In all, he ended up with seven state track titles (plus four-straight in cross country). He went on to become Notre Dame's first-ever NCAA champion, winning the 10,000 in 2001. As one of America's top distance runners, he captured three USA titles. He tragically died at age 28 while competing in the 2007 Olympic Trials in the marathon victim of a cardiac arrhythmia.

Baldwin's Juson Johnson also put up some impressive numbers in Class D. He won the 100 for the fourth-straight year, and, but for the narrowest of margins in his freshman year, would have copped the 200 meters four straight years as well. The victories in the two sprints also gave Johnson seven straight titles, and he further padded his list of first-place medals by anchoring back-to-back 4x1 teams in 1995 and 1996.

Johnson's winning time of 10.77 not only was more than a half second faster than the runner-up but also was the fastest time posted in any class. Johnson nicely wrapped up his prep career by winning the prestigious Midwest Meet of Champions in a wind-aided (2.9) 10.58 seconds.

Pittsford dominated the scoring as no team has ever done in state prep annals, romping to its fourth-straight title by amassing 116 points, the highest total in history. Nick Grabowski took part in four winning events for the victors, winning the long jump and 400, as well as running a leg on a pair of victorious relay squads.

Upper Peninsula: Menominee took team honors at the A-B finals on a rainy day in Kingsford. It was Pete Remien of Ishpeming Westwood who was clearly the top performer during this dreary day. A rested Remien set an UP record in A-B by winning the 1600-meter run in 4:24.3. After a short rest, he placed second in the 400 before winning the 800 and 3200.

Calumet returned to the winner's circle for the first time in 20 years in Class C. Stephenson, which placed just behind the first-place Copper Kings, produced two of the three records set or equaled in Class C. Bradley Ruleau took the 100 in 11.1 while teammate Derek Sandahl won the 100-meter high hurdles in 15.0. Matt Chambers of Houghton equaled the record in the 300-meter hurdles with a 40.0.

It was again a big day for Rapid River fans, as the Rockets boys and girls teams repeated as UP Class D champs. Rapid River won three out of the four relays.

1998

East Lansing High School won its first Class A state title and its first overall in 57 years in the most dramatic

of fashion. Confronted with the prospect of having to win the day's last event to take home the trophy, Coach Jeff Smith's thinclads rose to the occasion and captured their must-win race by more than three seconds.

The ten points earned in the 4x4 was just enough to hold off Rockford, 39½ to 39. The Capitol City area ruled as Lansing Eastern and Lansing Sexton also placed in the top six.

All-State football star Shakla Dhladha took the only individual first-place for the Trojans with his 14.31 in the 110 highs. For the first time in memory there was a wind gauge present at the D1 finals, supplied by Jeff Hollobaugh, one of your authors,

No records were set at the Class A affair held on Bay City Western's track, but White Lake Lakeland's 3200-meter relay tie of 7:46.31 was second only to Monroe's state record effort set back in 1988. In second, Portage Central impressed with a 7:47.61. Lakeland's Nick Gow ran a leg of the relay and still had enough energy to repeat in the 800 (1:53.75) against a stellar field. "I knew I had to work my hardest," said Gow. "To win it again, it's an excellent feeling."

Junior Jason Hartmann of Rockford, along with sophomore Charles Rogers of Saginaw, won a pair of individual titles. Hartmann cruised to victories in the 1600 (4:12.80) and 3200 (9:24.54). Rogers edged defending champ Lemar Courtney of Muskegon Mona Shores in the century (10.70), then breezed to an easier win in the 200. His wind-aided 21.67 was more than a half second faster than second-place. Courtney recovered from his loss to Rogers by sprinting to victory in the 400 (48.82).

Junior T.J. Duckett repeated as shot champion, though his heave of 62-6½ was short of his near-record throw from 1997.

In Class B, Corunna capped a great year in cruising to the Class B state title in Saginaw. The Cavaliers, who took the state Class B cross country championship in the fall, won by 25 points over runner-up St. Joseph. Their only first-place finish came in the 800-meter relay (1:29.16), but coach Chris Curtis's squad displayed great depth by placing in ten of the 17 events.

Runner-up St. Joseph put together a meet record in the 3200-meter relay with Ben Watson, Lars Petske, Mike Mandarino and Matt Hutchinson blazing in 7:48.36. The other mark to fall was the 300 hurdles with Coopersville's John Bennink posting a 38.0.

Brian Manor of Standish Sterling moved into the record books by posting a time of 47.9 over 400 meters. Although Ken Mitchell's 440-yard clocking of 48.0 ran in 1982 is intrinsically superior to Manor's 47.9, both times would be listed in the record book.

Just as in Class A, the double winners came in identical events. Edwin Johnson of River Rouge blazed to victories in the 100 and 200 meters while Richland Gull Lake's Nick Brockway took the 1600 and 3200. Johnson and Brockway added to their laurels the following weekend at the Midwest Meet of Champions. Johnson captured both sprints on the Ohio Wesleyan oval while Brockway crushed all Midwest rivals in his specialty, breaking the tape first in the 3200 in 9:13.40.

The most dramatic win occurred in the shot. Joe Denay of Bay City Glenn waited until his final toss to eke out a win over Frankenmuth's Pat Walderzak by only a half-inch.

Andy Lixey of Tawas won the "slow" section of the 800 in 1:54.0, a full two seconds faster than the winning time produced in the top-seeded heat.

In Class C, New Haven's Travis Kelly came less that an inch away from singlehandedly winning the team title. Kelly, who won the 100, 200 and 400 meters, placed third in the long jump, a mere half-inch behind the second-place finisher. If Kelly had managed second, that would have placed New Haven one point ahead of the state championship team from Detroit DePorres.

Taking second behind Kelly in the 200 was Manchester's Nick Davis. Ignored by many of the major in-state schools, Davis took his football talents to the University of Wisconsin. Just months after running for Manchester High's track squad, he produced a dramatic 84-yard punt return for a touchdown against Penn State, putting Wisconsin into the Rose Bowl.

Aron Gebauer of Bad Axe produced the only meet record with a 15-4 in the pole vault. Kris Brown of Ann Arbor Greenhills rallied from a career-threatening accident in the fall to win the 800-meter run (1:56.91).

In Class D Grass Lake ran eight seconds faster than the existing 3200-meter relay record, yet failed to win the event. New Buffalo's foursome of Pat Butler, John Calo, Mark Lucas and Kyle Lindley nipped Grass Lake at the tape to take the meet record to 8:01.17.

Upper Peninsula: The quality at the finals in Marquette was in Class C. Pete Remien, running under less than ideal conditions, established a meet record in the 1600 in 4:18.7. The Ishpeming Westwood star and CMU prospect would place second behind Dave Cook of Portage Northern at the Midwest Meet of Champions, the highest placing ever for an UP athlete.

Greg Londo of Gwinn sped once around the Marquette oval during a heavy rain in 49.7 to set the first of his two records. He than lowered the 200-meter mark down to 22.5. In spite of the heroics of Remien and Londo, it was Calumet that would take home the team trophy. Dan Mattson of Calumet hurled the discus 159-0 for another meet mark.

Negaunee, led by a distance sweep from Caden Rouhomaki, held off Menominee to win team honors in Class A-B. St. Ignace won Class D honors over a school that was curious to say the least. Mohawk Keweenaw Academy, a for-profit reform school for youthful offenders, placed second in Class D. Due to confidentiality laws, runners from Keweenaw could only be listed by their first names. Aaron Litzner of the Saints set the only meet record, clocking 9:49.9 for the 3200-meter run.

1999

Detroit Mumford made amends for a disappointing third-place finish at the 1998 finals, overwhelming all foes at the finals in Midland. Mumford tallied 30 points in the hurdle events in cruising to an undefeated season. Johnnie Birdsong was the catalyst behind Mumford's triumph. He won the 110 highs in 14.21 and the 300 hurdles in 37.98. He also ran on Mumford's winning 1600-meter relay team that cruised to a victory by nearly five full seconds (3:17.80) over second-place Pontiac Central.

Gary Stanford, winner of the long jump, placed second behind his teammate Birdsong in the high hurdles. Mumford put three hurdlers in the top five over the 39-inch barriers. Brandon Jiles contributed yet another first for the victors by taking the 800-meter run in 1:53.10. He would later star for EMU and become a great coach in his own right, both at Mumford and Oak Park.

After winning seven state championships as the coach of Detroit DePorres, Mumford's Robert Lynch would become the first coach in state history to win state track titles at two different schools.

Kalamazoo Loy Norrix's T.J. Duckett, the National High School Player of the Year in football, exemplified his talent by nailing down honors as the nation's best with the twelve-pound iron ball.

Although short of his nation-leading toss of 67-0 at the conference championships, Duckett managed to erase the oldest record from the books. His heave of 64-½ bettered his own meet record and topped the all-class record set by Middleville's Gary Van Elst that stood for 31 years. Runner-up Brian Ottney from Troy would have to settle for second with a solid 60-9½. In the fall he joined Duckett on MSU's football team.

Said Duckett, "I wanted to come here and set a mark that would stand for a few years. I don't know if it will or not. The young guys are throwing longer than ever."

The day's major surprises came in the distance races. Junior John Hughes of Traverse City Central upset defending champion Jason Hartman of Rockford in the 1600, 4:10.45-4:11.19.

Hartman's young teammate, Dathan Ritzenhein, was warming up for bigger and better things in this race. His third-place 4:14.45 was the fastest ever recorded by a sophomore at the state meet. He then shocked the large gathering in Midland by outkicking Hartman for the first time ever to win the 3200. Ritzenhein was clocked in 9:16.16, and then amazed track followers by winning the two-mile run in 9:01.79 at the Footlocker Outdoor Championships in North Carolina.

One more major surprise awaited the faithful in Midland in the 100-meter dash. Junior Stuart Schweigert defeated cross-town rival Charles Rogers of Saginaw in a wind-aided 10.60.

In Class B, Corunna needed a little bit of luck to repeat. Romulus, winner of the 800-meter relay earlier, was apparently headed for victory in the 400-meter relay. A bad pass on the final exchange resulted in a dropped baton, opening the door for Corunna. Needing a top finish heading into the meet's final event, the 1600-meter relay, the Cavaliers responded with a win to again bring home the first-place trophy, three points ahead of Romulus.

Brad Teeple vaulted a meet record of 16-1 to defeat a talented field. Steve Manz of Ogemaw Heights moved all the way up to number one with the day's best toss of 176-0 as friendly winds helped the top three over 168-0.

In Class C, Buchanan won its first-ever title in Saginaw. Buchanan duplicated Corunna's feat by winning the 1600-meter relay to take home the trophy. Robert King of Bath sailed over the bar at 6-10¼ to set a meet record.

Although overlooked by the media attending the state finals, Adam Lyon's clocking of 14.31 established a new best for the 100-meter high hurdles. Defending hurdles champion Ken Klinger of Muskegon Oakridge, in placing second to the Mesick hurdler in 14.39 also surpassed the previous meet best. Brandon Hooks of DePorres won the 100 in a dazzling 10.74.

Otis Jordan's sprinting paced Harbor Woods Bishop Gallagher to the Class D state championship at Frankenmuth. Jordan copped the 100 and 200-meter dashes and ran legs on the winning 800 and second-place 400-meter relays. History was set at the Class D event as Michelle Batten, the first female ever to guide a men's team to a state track championship, coached Bishop Gallagher.

Upper Peninsula: Winds, rain and unusually warm temperatures hampered efforts at Marquette High School. Shawn Anderson of Manistique set the only meet record with his heave of 164-8 in the discus.

Escanaba, Calumet and Felch North Dickinson won their classes in the team competition.

2000

A major change in classifications took place beginning with the 2000 campaign in the Lower Peninsula, as teams were now placed in divisions with approximately equal numbers of schools in each, instead of classes based on enrollment figures.

The first state final of the new millennium would also prove to be the first state championship won by the boys from Portage Northern. Northern used the power of its big threesome of sprinter Kelly Baraka, hurdler Jim Campbell and thrower Joey Sarantos.

Although it was Northern's day to shine in the team competition, the year 2000 would be remembered by many for Dathan Ritzenhein's continued emergence as the nation's top distance runner. In cross country, he not only won the state finals but also the Footlocker nationals. Leading up to the state finals in track, he won the Roosevelt Memorial 3200 in Dayton in a national 11th grade record 8:41.10. He clocked a state record 4:05.9 in the 1600 at the OK Red Championships.

The diminutive Ritzenhein (5-7/110) didn't disappoint the home folks as he easily captured the 1600 and 3200 at the Division 1 finals. First came a 1:56 split in a losing 4x8 effort, as Saline put together a 7:47.81 to top the Rams' 7:50.59. A few hours later, Ritzenhein ran the 1600 in 4:08.08, a new meet record, though still inferior to Steve Elliott's 4:08.2 for the mile a quarter century earlier. Then he captured the 3200 in 9:00.63.

As usual, Ritzenhein was gracious afterwards. "These guys are all really good. It's great to run in a state that has so many good kids."

Two weeks later in Raleigh at the Footlocker Outdoor Championships, Ritzenhein astonished the large crowd by romping home an easy two-mile winner in 8:48.06, demolishing a national field.

Kelly Baraka, Portage Northern junior, didn't repeat as 200-meter champion, but did nip a pair of heralded sprinters to win the century in 10.56—getting the maximum allowable wind aid (2.0). Saginaw's Charles Rogers, dubbed by many as the No. 1 high school football player in the country, took second ahead of another highly recruited gridder, defending champ Stu Schweigert of Saginaw Heritage. Schweigert would have a productive 5-year career in the NFL after starring in college at Purdue.

Joey Sarantos picked up 18 points with a second-place finish in the discus and a first in the shot. He bettered his own best in the shot by more than a foot with a 61-11 on his final attempt. Northern coach Bill Fries had to know everything was going their way when hurdler Bill Campbell also added 18 points in the hurdles. After placing second in the 110-meter highs, Campbell surprised the 300 field with his 38.09 win. He was seeded only 16th after regionals.

Kalamazoo Central's all-junior 4x1quartet took home first-place. One of the foursome was football star Greg Jennings, who set Western Michigan University records as a wide receiver, and would become a star for the Green Bay Packers in the NFL.

Erik Mirandette won the pole vault at 14-0. Five years later he would end up in the newspapers again after a harrowing experience in Egypt in 2005. Working there for two years as a missionary, he was traveling on a motorcycle delivering medicine to AIDS victims when a suicide bomber attacked. Mirandette was badly wounded; his younger brother Alex and 15 others were killed.

At the D2 championships in Grandville, Romulus squeezed out a one-point victory over Detroit Renaissance. The battle came down to the final race of the day when the Romulus foursome of Jarvis Jordan, Caleb Beasly, Henry Staple and Ashley Terry needed to win the 4x4 after earlier taking the 4x8. They came through with the victory, and Renaissance was right on its heels in second.

In Division 3, Kevin Sule of Hemlock posted a winning 4:12.62 in the 1600, superior to Ron Simpson's former best in Class C. He also captured the 800-meter run as well as anchoring the victorious 4 x 800. Nate Hinkle's 6-8 made him the first champion ever from Grayling.

Clare trailed Albion into the final event, the 4 x 400 relay. The Pioneer foursome, led by Kyle Kolbe, clinched the title and picked up 10 points. Kolbe earlier won the 400-meter dash, placed second in the 200 and ran on a leg on Clare's runner-up 4 x 200, accounting for 36 of Clare's total of 47 points.

Tom Maczik of Reese was a double winner in the weight events, but came up short of matching his previous best marks of 61-11 ¾ in the shot put and 186-7 in the discus.

Kevin Singleton of Centreville scored 30 points in winning three events at the Division 3 meet held at Grand Rapids Forest Hills Northern, but it wasn't enough to catch Maple City Glen Lake. The former Class D field was enlarged to include a number of schools that had previously competed in Class C.

Upper Peninsula: Interest and quality of competition was lacking at the UP championships held in Kingsford. Although the meet was held in near-perfect conditions, the competitors could not touch previous records from the 1900s. Escanaba, Iron Mountain and Rapid River took the team titles as the Yoopers stayed with the traditional class format for another year.

Shawn Anderson of Manistique was perhaps the UP's boys track star of the year. During the regular season he became the first athlete from above the Mighty Mac to heave the iron ball over sixty feet in the shot put. Anderson also became the all-time UP leader in the discus with a best mark of 177-10 but fell far short of his early season efforts at the finals.

2001

Rockford's Dathan Ritzenhein, in his final meet on his home track, crushed the meet record in the 3200 with an astonishing 8:43.32 over the 8 laps. Reportedly he had been chasing the national record—8:36.3 for the full two miles. Blustery winds throughout the race made his feat even more amazing.

"It's disappointing," he told reporters. I thought I could have it today. There were so many people here, and every time I went around I felt better. I fell off the last three laps."

Ritzenhein's career after high school is the stuff of legend: three Olympic teams, an American Record 12:56.27 at 5000 and a solid place among the greatest U.S. runners of all-time.

Saginaw Heritage, helped by the running of 400-meter champion Soji Jibowu, took home team honors with 46 points, five points better than Detroit Cass Tech. Joey Sorantos had another big day in the throws for Portage Northern. He scored all his team's points and set an all-class meet record with his mighty 197-11 in the discus. He also successfully defended his shot crown with a mark of 61-7½".

In Division 2, after dominating the state playoff football scene for many years, Farmington Hills Harrison edged a pack of competitors to win its first track & field championship at Grand Rapids Forest Hills Northern High School.

In the process the Hawks set a meet record in the 4 x 100 relay. The foursome comprised of future MSU football standout Agim Shabaj, Charles Pickett, Chris Roberson and Marcus Woods sped one lap in 42.66. In the day's final event, Shabaj came back to anchor Harrison's 4x4 to victory to clinch its team title as runner-up Stevensville-Lakeshore watched first-place hopes go up in smoke.

However, Lakeshore could look forward to a rosy future with the arrival of a discus thrower who would lord over the event for the next three years. Sophomore Joe Hover set a meet record by more than four feet with his 180-7.

Although overshadowed by Ritzenhein's sterling performances in D1, Tim Ross of Caledonia had a day for himself in Division 2. In displacing defending champ Kurtis Marlow of Richland Gull Lake, Ross blistered a meet record 9:10.58. Earlier Ross dusted the field in the 1600 in 4:13.47.

The other record to fall was to Alma's Bryan Jackson in the 300-meter hurdles; his 37.84 would not fall for another 15 years.

In Division 3, a new track power emerged to begin the 21st century. Under the reins of coach Paul Nillson, Williamston High School began its dominance with a convincing state championship performance at Comstock Park. Williamston used its exceptional depth in the distances. Pat Maynard won the 3200 and anchored Williamston to first in the 4x8.

Brad Gebauer of Bad Axe set a new mark when he successfully cleared the bar at 15-9. As a senior at Michigan State, Gebauer would capture first at both the indoor and outdoor Big 10 championships. Burly Tim Shaw won his school's only track individual championship when he captured the 100. A star running back in football at Livonia Clarenceville, Shaw would take his skills to Penn State where he became a starting linebacker for Joe Paterno's Nittany Lions.

It would have been hard to believe at the time that the Division 4 state meet at Lowell High School would feature an athlete who would become a more recognizable name to sports fans around the world than Dathan Ritzenhein, yet, it's true. Braylon Edwards of Harper Woods Bishop Gallagher would have a football career at Michigan that would see him develop into the premier wide receiver in college football. He would sign for millions when he inked his contract as the 3rd player taken in the 2005 draft when taken by the Cleveland Browns.

Edwards showed an amazing display of athleticism in placing second in the high jump at 6-8, second in the 100 at 11.23 and then winning the 200-meters in 22.61. Nick Ogle set the only D4/Class D record when he cruised over the 300 hurdles in 39.30. Lutheran Westland claimed the D4 team title with but one individual champion in shot put winner Nate Meckes.

Upper Peninsula: Matt Wise of Calumet was clearly the individual star at the finals held in Kingsford. Wise would hang four first-place medals across his torso, including a record 40.5 clocking in the 300 hurdles. He also took first in the high hurdles and 200- as well as running a leg on Calumet's winning 800-meter relay. Sault Ste. Marie won the team honors on the first UP state championships that were run in divisions.

Newberry easily grabbed team honors in Division 2 while Rapid River would lay claim as the UP's first state champ in Division 3. Other than Wise's record equaling performance in Division 1, no other performances would top any former records set under the previous Class system.

2002

Kenneth Ferguson ruled the day at the Division 1 track finals in Rockford. The Mumford senior took home four first-place medals to help Robert Lynch's squad score 40 of 63 points, needing every one of them to nip rival Detroit Cass Tech by one point.

Ferguson put on a show that would compare favorably to such legends of the past as Bill Watson, Hayes Jones and Rex Cawley. Ferguson began his record-setting day by skimming over the hurdles in 13.65. Earlier in the season Ferguson ran an even faster 13.61 at the Roosevelt Memorial Relays in Dayton.

In the 4x2, Ferguson ran a blistering anchor to bring the baton home first in 1:27.32. Then in an absolutely stunning performance, he crushed the state record with a 35.90 in the 300 hurdles, nearly three full seconds ahead of the field. He capped his day by anchoring the 1600-meter relay team to a meet record of 3:14.28, far surpassing the previous best set 25 years earlier by Detroit Redford.

The future South Carolina standout followed the regular high school season by capturing the silver medal at the World Junior (U20) Championships in Kingston, Jamaica. He also won gold as the lead-off on the U.S. 4 x 400. Along the way he crushed 400 in 46.59, the No. 2 Michigan prep time ever.

Pierre Vinson kept Cass Tech in the chase for the team championship with wins in the short sprints as well as anchoring the winning 4x1. Only Ferguson's brilliant anchor leg in the 800 meter-relay kept Vinson from claiming four first-place medals and leading Cass Tech to the team title.

Tim Moore from Novi was the distance star, capturing first in the 1600 (4:14.00) and 3200 (9:21.9) after winning state and national titles in cross country the previous fall. Said his coach, Robert Smith, "There was a lot of pressure on him to prove he's the best distance runner in the state.

Farmington Hills Harrison successfully defended its Division 2 title against a well-balanced field at Grand Rapids Houseman Field. Agim Shabaj played a big role in the Hawks' win with a first-place in the 200 and the opening leg of Harrison's winning 1600-meter relay. Earlier, in the fall of 2001, Shabaj teamed up with Hawk quarterback Drew Stanton to win the state D3 football championship with a win over Fruitport. Fruitport's big football star was Markus Langlois, who would win the 2002 pole vault crown at Houseman

Field. Langlois also went to MSU where he became the Big 10 indoor champion in the pole vault in 2007.

Brian Sherwood of Fowlerville cleared 6-11 in winning the high jump. Junior Joe Hover of Stevensville-Lakeshore repeated as discus champion with an impressive 180-6, just a preview of what he would accomplish the following year.

Future Michigan defensive back Morgan Trent placed second in the long jump, behind the 23-0 of winner Michael Bailey of Lansing Waverly. Taking fifth in the shot, won by Chelsea's Joe Tripodi, was Saginaw's Lamar Woodley, who would be a four-year regular and a future All-American for the Wolverines before embarking on a long career in the NFL.

Tim Ross of Caledonia repeated his twin distance wins, with the day's fastest time in all classes with his clocking of 9:16.13 for the 3200.

In Division 3, Yale captured its first state championship since 1928 by the narrowest of margins at Comstock Park. Yale took the state title without the benefit of one first-place finish. Runner-up Battle Creek Pennfield had a double winner in distance performer Aaron Nasers, winner of the 800 and 1600-meter runs.

Kyle Dengler accounted for all 20 of Essexville Garber's points by sweeping the short sprints, including the 200 in 21.86. The only record to fall in D3 came in the 300 hurdles where Dan Fugate of Dundee won in 38.78. Future CMU football star Dan Bazuin from McBain placed second in the shot put behind winner Joe Brooks of Kingsley. What a year it was for McBain! In March, the Northern Michigan school won the state Class C basketball title with Bazuin scoring 15 points and pulling down 11 rebounds.

Highlighting the Division 4 state championships at Forest Hills Northern High School in Grand Rapids was an all-out assault on a record that had survived for nearly 30 years. The record time of 1:56.8, set in 1973 by Mendon's Lloyd Wilds, was not only broken, but beaten by three runners. Vershawn Miller of Detroit Benedictine (1:54.97) led Daniel Orozco of Lawton and Liam Boylan-Pett from Bath under Wilds' former mark.

Benedictine captured the D4 title in a meet that wasn't completed until 9:30 in the evening. Ben Petitpren won a marathon pole vaulting contest that got off to a very late start for the guys. The male vaulters had to wait around for eight and a half hours until a champion was crowned in the girls vault.

Upper Peninsula: Matt Wise won four events at the finals held once again in Kingsford. His gallant effort nearly propelled little Calumet to the UP D1 championship, but his team fell three points shy of victorious Marquette, a school with nearly three times the enrollment of the Copper Country lads.

Marquette received the benefit of the doubt of a 'generous' no call false start as the 1600-meter relay got underway. Marquette won the race and passed Calumet in the team standings to take the trophy. Marquette's Jamieson Cihak churned a 4:22.1 for the 1600 meters before winning the 3200.

Plenty of controversy surrounded the UP championships, but none perhaps more so than in the Division 2 finals. The Upper Peninsula had been reluctant to use fully-automatic timing (FAT) over the years but the many complaints with placings at this meet might have finally convinced the UP to join the rest of the state on a crucial meet management issue.

Norway and Stephenson were declared co-champs at the D2 finals with each team credited with 76 points. Many of the track fans in attendance felt the results would have been different if FAT had been used. Some good came out of the strife: this would be the last year the UP relied on hand times and spotters.

The outstanding performance came from Steve Schmidt of Stevenson, clocked in 10.8 in winning the century, the fastest time ever recorded in any class/division in UP history.

UP legend Brock Bower and his Bark River-Harris thinclads were able to bring home five first-place medals, the same as team winning Rapid River at the D4 finals, but fell well short of Rapid River's imposing total of 117. Bower won three events, including a 6-6 in the high jump, and ran a leg on the winning 400-meter relay as Bark River settled for a second-place tie in the team battle with Rock Mid Peninsula.

2003

Swirling and gusty winds put a damper on individual performances as once again the state prep finals returned to the Grand Rapids area. The only records set came in the Division 3 meet where this author suspects those gusty winds might have been at the runner's backs.

There was, however, no controversy with the record set in the discus event in Division 2. Joe Hover of Stevensville-Lakeshore spun the circular platter out to the 195-6 in mark, a D2 meet record. Earlier in the season Hover became the first Michigan high school track performer to surpass the 200-foot barrier, launching three state records in a row—201-2, 202-1 and 204-0—in a dual meet.

The loss to graduation of super star Kenneth Ferguson didn't prevent Detroit Mumford from again winning the Division 1 title at Grand Rapids' Houseman Field. Mumford needed 44 points to bring the winning trophy back to the Motor City. Instrumental in Mumford's win were its two victories in the 1600 and 3200-meter relays.

Perhaps the best performance came in the sprint relays. Pontiac Northern's 4 x 100 whisked around the windy oval in 41.92. Northern's 4 x 200 wasn't too shabby either: 1:27.04.

For this author, the most astonishing performance on the afternoon at the D1 finals was the performance of Rockford's Joe Staley. Standing 6-5 and tipping the scales at 230 pounds, Staley was a member on the runner-up 400-meter relay and the 800-meter relay that finished fourth. In addition, He was clocked at 21.9 when he placed sixth in the 200. Before he finished his four-year career at CMU as one of the nation's top football players, he had filled his once lean frame out to 300 pounds without a noticeable loss of speed. Following his college career, he became a perennial All-Pro lineman in the NFL for the San Francisco 49rs.

Winning the 200 meters ahead of Staley was Jeremy Orr of Detroit Henry Ford. In 2006 Orr would place fourth at the Big 10 championships in the 100 and 200 meters.

Although Hover notched the only record at the Division 2 finals held in Caledonia, John Childress produced a very notable mark in the 110 hurdles. The Flint Powers senior skimmed over the highs in a wind-aided 13.96. Childress, a future captain of the Michigan State Spartans track team, would later take fourth place at the 2006 Big 10 championships.

Farmington Hills Harrison repeated as team champs, nine points ahead of Stevensville-Lakeshore. Hover's teammate Jim Pancoast was the meet's only double winner, taking the 800 and 1600.

In Division 3, after a one-year absence, Williamston nearly doubled the total over runner-up Muskegon Oakridge to return to the winner's circle. The Hornets foursome of B.J. Pankow, Erik Schultink, Fil Marlatt and David Bills broke an 18-year-old record with a 7:57.98.

A perfect case in point that one doesn't have to possess monstrous size to become a state champion shot-putter would be that of John Plumstead of Benzie Central. At a modest 5-11 and 180 pounds, Plumstead, a future linebacker for the Army football team, had the day's best performance in any division with a mark of 57-11 ½.

A pair of Detroit parochial schools dueled for the Division 4 state title at Forest Hills Northern with Benedictine outpointing runner-up DePorres. The individual standout in D4 was Bath junior distance standout Liam Boylan-Pett. He broke his brother Will Boylan-Pett's meet record with a 4:19.47 in the 1600. He later captured the 800 in 1:55.38.

Just when fans thought Central Lake had finally run out of Shays, another child of Central Lake head coach Joe Shay won another state distance title. Junior Stephan Shay became the fourth of the Shay brothers to win a first-place medal when he won the 3200.

Upper Peninsula: Marquette produced the first UP foursome to run the 1600-meter relay under 3:30 seconds at the finals in Kingsford. The foursome stopped the FAT timer at 3:29.18 to help seal a team title. Chris Peterson of Marquette also set a new standard with a 40.21 in winning the 300 hurdles.

Everyone Knows It's Windy

Two "records" set on this windy afternoon in Comstock Park came in races where wind gauges are always necessary to validate records. However, meet officials, who did not have wind gauges (which can be bought for under $20), declared two marks as meet records: the 14.30 in the high hurdles by Derrick Cook of Oakridge and the 21.77 in the 200 by Andy Montague of Olivet. In addition, Kim Thompson of Detroit Country Day was credited for a time of 10.76 in the 100.

With winds hitting 23mph that day, all were likely wind-aided, since it would be unimaginable for any of those athletes to run that fast into a headwind.

The authors wish to make perfectly clear that this is not a slam on the athletes. Wind-aided races are a regular fact of life in our sport and all world-class sprinters/hurdler/jumpers have experienced them. When high school officials pretend that wind is absent when a wind gauge is absent, that does young athletes and the accurate reporting of the sport a disservice.

There are three losers when officials ignore wind assistance to give an athlete a record: the legitimate recordholder who loses their mark unfairly; the future athlete who has to chase a mark that is suspicious; and the "beneficiary" of the officials' generosity. Often the athlete is never able to run that fast again in legitimate circumstances and spends years chasing a suspicious mark.

That is why, in cases where meet officials have made shaky calls with regard to wind, the authors feel the right thing to do is correct the historical record. /JH/

Ishpeming won in Division 2 and Rapid River in Division 3. Brock Bower cleared 6-6, the second highest clearance in either Peninsula, to conclude a stellar career at Bark River-Harris. A basketball star as well, Bower brought the Breslin crowd to its feet with a rim-rattling dunk at the Class D basketball finals, though Bark River-Harris lost to heavily favored Detroit Rogers.

2004

Detroit Mumford won the boys and girls Division 1 state finals hosted, after a year's absence, at Ted Lewis Stadium in Rockford. The win was historically significant for head coach Robert Lynch of the Mustangs. After leading Detroit DePorres to seven state titles, Lynch would win his fourth at Mumford, for 11 overall, one more Lower Peninsula crown than won by Marty Crane of Flint Beecher.

Mumford needed only 44 points to earn top honors. Marcus Thigpen took first in the 100-meter dash and then followed that with the leadoff leg for the victorious 800-meter relay. Thigpen explained, "There's the pressure to keep this thing going. The seniors last year put it in our hands to handle this. It's a good kind of pressure. You don't want to be the ones to end it."

The Mustangs would place five points ahead of runner-up Flint Carman-Ainsworth to claim a third-consecutive title.

Saline's 3200-relay of Dustin Voss, Neil Atzinger, Carter Bishop and Alex Muhs posted a clocking of 7:41.27. Saline's time was even quicker than a Michigan all-star team would post the following week at the Midwest Meet of Champions in Ohio. Two weeks later the four would run even faster, 7:40.68, to win the national title in Raleigh, North Carolina.

Voss and Atzinger would place a solid second and third in a very quick 1600 won by junior Justin Switzer of Waterford Kettering in 4:09.11. Atzinger would then place second in the 800 later in the afternoon to Abraham Mach of East Lansing, whose 1:52.01 was the quickest state meet mark for the 800 since 1988.

In Division 2, an exciting conclusion to what had been a very nondescript meet took place at Caledonia. Flint Kearsley and Lansing Sexton, running 1-2 in the team competition, battled to the wire in the fastest 1600 meter-relay in D2/Class B history. The Kearsley foursome of Kyle Bergquist, Peter O'Brien, Tony Parcels and Dan Goodman were clocked in 3:19.11, just ahead of Sexton's 3:19.81.

Junior Dan Roberts of Vicksburg sailed around the track in 4:13.83 in winning the 1600. Roberts would later add the 3200 crown to his list of wins. Placing fifth in the 3200 was Riley Klingel of Fremont. Klingel won

the Division 2 cross country title in the fall of 2002. As a senior in 2004 he placed second behind Roberts at. Just before the 2005 outdoor season would begin in April, the state track scene was saddened with news that Klingel had been killed in an automobile accident on his way to school.

Winning the 3200-meter relay was a foursome from Cedar Springs. This would be the first state title for the Red Hawks since Walter Cole won the state shot championship exactly 100 years earlier. Also of note was the eighth-place performer in the D2 shot put. Kevin Grady of East Grand Rapids, who would end his brilliant high school career as the state's all-time leading rusher, taking his football talents to Michigan.

The highlight of Division 3 at Comstock Park came from Josh Perrin of Hillsdale breaking a 26-year-old meet record with his 9:12.14 in the 3200.

Zach Burrington of Muskegon Oakridge broke Brad Gebauer's record by ¼ inch when he sailed over the bar at 15-9¼. Burrington had earlier cleared 16-4 to win the West Michigan Conference Championships, and again cleared 16 feet in winning the Midwest Meet of Champions.

Detroit Country nearly doubled its winning total over second-place Frankenmuth to take team honors. Demea Carter had a big day for the victorious Yellow Jackets. In winning the long jump by a foot and a half, his 23-7 missed the meet record by a mere two inches. He also captured the 300-meter intermediate hurdles and placed second in the 100-meter dash.

In Division 4, Detroit St. Martin de Porres had just enough power in the sprints to overcome the distance strength of Bath and scratch out another state. Bath clearly had the top performer in Liam Boylan-Pett. After breezing to the 1600-meter title in 4:24.10, he set a meet record in the 800 with a 1:54.06. The following week at the Midwest Meet of Champion in Delaware, Ohio the future Columbia University star crushed the best of the Midwest with a 4:10.95.

The youngest of the incredible Shay brothers from Central Lake capped his career by setting a meet record in the 3200 meter-run. Stephen Shay, a future MSU distance ace, lowered the new record down to 9:22.07.

Andrew Kemp of Maple City Glen Lake had the best throw of the day in any division with his 170-1 in the discus.

Upper Peninsula: Jason Hofer of Menominee set a UP record for the 300 hurdles at 40.01 while Nick Zweifel of Norway did the same with a clocking of 49.34 in the 400.

Gladstone easily took team honors in Division 1; Norway breezed to a convincing title in D2 while Pickford and Rapid River continued their rivalry in D4, Pickford nipping its rival by just two points.

2005

Junior Ahmad Rashad would lead Flint Carman-Ainsworth to the Division 1 state championship, held once again at Rockford High School. Rashad blazed to victories in the 100 and 200, ran a leg on the second-place 400-meter relay and capped the day by running a 47-second anchor on Carman-Ainsworth's victorious 1600 meter-relay. The biggest challenge for Rashad, however, was accomplishing all of this just ten days his mother died from pancreatic cancer—and two days after her funeral.

"I gave it everything I had," he said. "It was a tough week, but I had to get through it."

Rashad just missed setting a meet record in the 100 by a scant 0.01 with his winning 10.56. That summer he would set a state record 10.52 (0.1 wind) at the AAU Junior Olympics in New Orleans, along with a speedy 21.02 (-0.1) that put him No. 2 all-time in state history behind only the legendary Marshall Dill of 1971.

Carman-Ainsworth ended the three-year reign of Detroit Mumford, which ended up ten points behind. The Mustangs added a couple of first-place medals to their vast collection. Mumford took honors in the 800-meter relay and Blake Figgins took the 800-meter run.

Justin Switzer of Waterford Kettering performed a feat unmatched in Michigan schoolboy history. In winning the 1600 meter-run for the second-straight year, Switzer, with a winning time of 4:09.35, became the first distance competitor to break the 4:10 barrier in consecutive years.

A quartet of future football stars would make their presence known at the D1 meet. Otis Wiley, future starting defensive back at Michigan State, ran the lead-off for Carman-Ainsworth's winning 1600-meter relay and placed second behind Matt Comer of Portage Northern in the 300 hurdles.

Winning the discus was sophomore Vince Helmuth of Saline. He would have bragging rights at the start of the 2007 football season with the Michigan Wolverines as he defeated second-place Terrance Taylor of Muskegon. Taylor was a starting defensive lineman for Michigan's 2006 team that played Southern California in the Rose Bowl. A teammate of Taylor's on Muskegon's 2004 Division 2 state championship football team, sophomore Ronald Johnson, placed eighth in the 400-meter dash in his only season of track. After leading Muskegon to its second undefeated season in three years, and another D2 state football title, Johnson would not follow Taylor to U-M, but instead would enroll at Southern California.

Lansing Sexton, which won back-to-back Class A championships in the late 1980s, would drop down a notch in class and win the Division 2 state title in Caledonia.

It's too bad that Switzer and Daniel Roberts from Vickburg could not have been paired up in the same 1600-meter race. Roberts set a new meet record with a time that was almost identical to Switzer's mark (4:09.45). Nobody was complaining that Roberts wasn't tested in his race, however, as Lex Williams of Dexter pushed him with a 4:09.98.

Williams did have his moment later in the afternoon when he lowered the meet record in the 3200 to 9:07.88. Following Landon Peacock of Cedar Springs in second place was another pair of Dexter runners, Dan Jackson and Tony Nalli in third and fourth. Dexter, not surprisingly, won the cross country championship the previous fall.

Clinton Inderbitzin of Allegan, with a clocking of 1:53.73, ran the fastest 800 in 16 years in D2/Class B. Impressive marks were also turned in by Sexton's Jon Allen in the long jump (23-4¼) and Chris Faison of Bloomfield Hills in the high jump (6-10).

In Division 3, Frankenmuth got big time efforts from Andrew Dodson and Mike Golden to win over Detroit Country Day. Dodson became the first D3/Class C athlete to clear 7-0 in the high jump. After winning the 200, and going into the meet's final event some 6.5 points behind, Frankenmuth's Golden grabbed the baton for the final leg of the 1600-meter relay and led the Eagles to the win and their first team title ever.

Okwara Uzoh from Berrien Springs set a new mark of 38.69 for the 300 hurdles while Unionville-Sebewaing would eliminate Williamston from the record board by winning the 3200-meter relay in 7:55.57.

It was a bittersweet state championship for the Detroit DePorres team at the Division 4 finals at Houseman Field in Grand Rapids. The 16th state track championship won by the school would mark the end of an era as it would close its doors at the end of the school year.

It was fitting that the only record in D4 was set by DePorres. The 4x1 relay of David Grimes, Taurian Washington, Cortez Smith and Anthony Bowman, with a time of 43.32, broke a 29-year-old record formerly held by DePorres.

Upper Peninsula: Gladstone went on a rampage in by racking up an all-time high of 150 points in winning D1. The school figured in one of only three records set during the day. The 400-meter relay foursome of Cevin Cosby, Seth Humpula, Charlie Stafford and Matt Petr broke the old mark that had lasted 29 years with a 43.93.

In the 65 years that the UP has officially held its own championships, the three fastest times ever recorded in the 800-meter relay were run on this day on the Kingsford High School Track. Second-place finisher Menominee and Gladstone in third all broke the former record held of Sault Ste. Marie of 1:32.04. The new mark would belong to the foursome from West Iron Country, comprised of Matt Konoske, James Wolf, Matt Westphal and Dustin Johnson with a final mark of 1:31.00.

The final mark to fall came in the 400 when Justin Wiles of Escanaba posted the quickest time in UP history with a 48.91.

Newberry edged Norway to take home the top trophy in Division 2 while Powers-North Central won its third UP title in Division 3.

2006

A great senior year loomed for Carman-Ainsworth's sprint sensation, Ahmad Rashad. He won the Nike Indoor Nationals in Maryland with a state record 6.73 over 60 meters. Outdoors, a knee injury hampered him, and he managed only one race, a 10.4 over 100 meters. He had to miss his final state meet. He went on to become an All-American at USC, with six Pac-10 sprint titles to his name and PRs of 10.10 and 20.56.

The state finals, held once again in the Grand Rapids area, would go down as perhaps the most bizarre in state history. Long delays due to inclement weather, disqualifications, no-show teams, state champs forgoing their senior year to leave early to play spring football, and competitors leaving early so they can get to the dance on time—all contributed to old time track buffs shaking their heads in disbelief.

Division 1 finals were contested for the first time on East Kentwood's new facility. Nobody was more surprised than Saline when at the end of the day the Hornets found their team total at the top of the leader board. Scoring just 39½ points, the Hornets won their first-ever title.

Leading the way, and scoring more than half of Saline's points, was double champion Vince Helmuth. Winning by the prodigious margin of some twenty feet, he not only defended his discus at 180-1, but had a resounding victory in the shot. His best effort with the 12-pound ball was 59-5, more than six feet farther than the second-place finisher.

"I want to come back and go for records next year," he said. That didn't happen, however. Helmuth completed his high school studies early and enrolled at Michigan, bypassing his senior year in track. His spring days would be spent on the gridiron where he participated in spring football drills for the Wolverines.

Plenty of top marks were recorded. Nicholas McCampbell from Detroit Cass Tech covered the 300 hurdles in a dazzling 37.43. Dimitri Banks of Detroit Murray-Wright sped 200 in 21.40 seconds. Logan Lynch from Temperance Bedford cleared the bar at 16-0 in winning the pole vault.

If anybody had mixed feelings about winning the state championship, it would aptly apply to Ypsilanti head coach Torin Moore. His team managed to share the Division 2 title with the host school, Grand Rapids Forest Hills Northern, each scoring 40 points.

It was a roller coaster ride all afternoon and evening for Coach Moore. A controversial first-place effort in the day's final event, the 1600-meter relay, was just one of the emotional trials and tribulations for Moore and his Braves. Many observers felt his anchor runner cut off, as well as impeded the progress of the second-place team from Adrian. Anything less than ten points would have given the state title to Forest Hills Northern. Officials did not call a DQ.

Ypsilanti missed out on a couple of golden opportunities to pick up that missing one point to win its first outright state track title since 1948. In the final, fastest seeded heat of the 400-meter relay, it looked like Ypsilanti would, at a minimum, have placed in the top eight, but the anchor never got the baton from the third runner.

Another lost opportunity cropped up in the high jump. After clearing the bar at 6-5, long jump champion Woody Payne readied for the next height. But before he would make any attempts at 6-6, rains came and the jumpers had to sit out a four-hour delay. Not wanting to miss the start of that evening's prom back in Ypsilanti, Payne passed on his final attempts and bolted back to Ypsi, leaving his team one point shy of outright victory.

Clint Allen from Muskegon Orchard View blazed a 10.44 for the 100-meter dash, faster than any other time ever recorded in any state final. Officials, however, did not make arrangements for a wind gauge, thus igniting a lively debate (including among the authors) about whether the mark should be accorded state record status. Proponents felt that Allen's past times made the mark credible (he had run 10.3 hand with no wind gauge at regionals). Opponents noted the fact the times from every athlete in the race would have been massive PRs, plus that winds in the area were gusting up to 5.4mps at the time (2.0mps is the maximum allowable wind for records).

While the MHSAA continues to list the 10.44 as a record, it was considered wind-aided by the high school editors at Track & Field News, as well as by Michtrack.org. In the end, an important rule of recordkeeping won out: about records, there must be no doubt. In this century, it is essential that sprint records be confirmed by an inexpensive wind gauge.

Allen went on to a successful career at Eastern Michigan, winning four MAC crowns in the 60 and three in the 100. He recorded a lifetime best of 10.39 (1.8 wind) at the Drake Relays as a sophomore. He also ran 10.21 at the SeaRay Relays, pushed by a massive 7.7 wind.

Landon Peacock from Cedar Springs, a transfer from Morley-Stanwood, came close to breaking the nine-minute barrier in the 3200 meters. Peacock's 9:01.66 came just moments before the four-hour delay due to thunder and lightning,

Josh Hembrough of Forest Hills Northern was the big star for the co-champs. He challenged Tyrone Wheatley's all-time Class B mark of 13.7 (hand) from 1990 with a 13.82. In the 4x2, Orchard Lake St. Mary blitzed a 1:28.38 for a near-record.

Jay Bilsborrow from Coldwater won the 800 and 1600. Earlier in the season Bilsborrow broke the Coldwater school record set in the 3200-meter run in 1968, a mark set by his father Jim Bilsborrow.

In Division 3 at Comstock Park, Williamston showed great balance and heavy firepower in the distance events. The foursome of David Ash, Tyler Sharp, Dan Nix and Chris Pankow, with a time of 7:49.83, not only shattered the previous 4x8 mark but the notched the fastest time of the day in any division.

Country Day's 800-meter relay of Chris Rucker, Erik Williams, Jonas Gray and Martin Corniffe broke the 24-year old mark set back in 1982 by Detroit Lutheran West with a time of 1:27.95.

In Division 4, Aaron Hunt led Potterville to its first-ever state track championship by winning the 800 and 1600 and clinched the title by running the anchor on the winning 1600-meter relay. Unfortunately for Potterville, few fans were present at the conclusion of the meet. Due to numerous rain delays throughout the day, it would be after 10:00pm before Hunt would cross the finish line.

A fourth first-place medal just eluded Hunt earlier in the day as he couldn't run down Jared Fischer from Unionville-Sebewaing in the 3200-meter relay. Brennan Pitcher, Matt Niziolek and Matt Eisengruber joined Fisher on the USA foursome that would set a meet record with an 8:01.17.

A sad note a week after the meet put a damper on the celebrations. McBain's Darin Bazuin, brother of CMU football great Dan Bazuin, took his own life only a week after winning the discus state title.

Upper Peninsula: Stormy weather was not a problem at the finals, held as usual at Kingsford. Despite sunny skies and ideal conditions not one record was set during the meet. Gladstone repeated as D1 champs, while Newberry and Rock-Mid Peninsula took the honors in Division 2 and 3.

2007

While Ann Arbor Pioneer can lay claim to the most team titles in MHSAA history on the girls side, the boys finally captured their first with a convincing showing at the D1 championships. It had to be a fun-filled bus ride back home to Ann Arbor as both the girls and boys team were state champions.

Coach Don Sleeman's Pioneers won three of the four relay events to earn 63 points, 30 more than runner-up East Kentwood, a young team on the cusp of becoming a track powerhouse.

With his victory in the 200, Pioneer sprinter James Smith was the lone individual winner and also participated on two of the winning relay teams.

Once again, records were hard to come by on the East Kentwood oval, with only a pair set in Division 1. Logan Lynch of Temperance Bedford cleared 16-1 in the pole vault, still 5 inches shy of the Class A record held by Paul Terek in 1997. Kyle Wilson from East Detroit sped around the track in 47.96, the fastest time in the 400 in a decade.

Future Michigan and NFL defensive lineman, Michael Martin from Detroit Catholic Central surpassed the 60-foot barrier for an impressive win in the shot. Earlier in the year he had won the heavyweight state title in wrestling.

In Division 2 in Zeeland, one had to look no further than results from the 3200 meter-run to recognize the talents of the distance corps from Dexter. By scoring 30 points in just this one event, the powerful Dreadnaughts needed but six more points to win their first track & field championship in Dexter history.

In more than a century of state championships, Dexter was the only school ever to have five place winners in a single event. Led by Dan Jackson's first-place finish in 9:07.38, Jackson was followed by Bobby Aprill and Jason Bishop, with Ben Stevenson coming in fifth and Ryan Neely in seventh.

Dexter scored in only three events, with Jackson adding the 1600, and it took a meet record by Fenton in the 3200 relay (7:52.31) to deny Dexter yet another distance triumph.

While Jackson and his mates clearly headlined the distances, Forest Hills Northern hurdling ace Josh Hembrough was the dominant force in the hurdles. he skimmed the 110 High Hurdles in a 13.70 to surpass the hand-held time of 13.7 of Tyrone Wheatley. Hembrough, who would win a gold medal in the deaf Olympics, nearly added a second record with his victory in the 300 hurdles (37.99). He capped his prep career by anchoring Forest Hills Northern to a victory in the 1600-meter relay.

Later, Hembrough would win a Big 10 hurdle crown for Purdue.

Another notable mark was the 4 x 100 of 42.53 of Detroit Renaissance, while Joe Wesley from Marine City cleared 16-0 in the pole vault.

In Division 3, Williamston was denied its fourth title in a short seven-year span when it lost by the narrowest of margins in the team D3 competition to Detroit Country Day.

Led by the sprinting efforts of future MSU football star Chris Rucker, Country Day was able to hold off Williamston by less than a point to take home the first-place trophy. Rucker sprinted to victories in the 100 and 400 and then ran a leg on the winning 800 and 1600-meter relays.

Maverick Darling of Ovid-Elsie was the winner of the 1600 in 4:15.07. "At 300," he said, "I just kicked it with what I had left. My body was pretty numb with 100 left and I just kept going."

Garnering the only individual victory for Williamston was a D3 record-setting performance of 1:53.86 in the 800-meter run by David Ash.

Aided by the double victory in the weight events by George Flanner, Ottawa Lake Whiteford captured its first state championship by winning the D4 title at Comstock Park. Flanner followed up his victory in the discus with a record effort of 58-5¼ in the shot.

Upper Peninsula: At the finals in Kingsford, Gladstone repeated for the fourth-straight time in D1. Mike Coyne set the only D1 record with a successful clearance of 13-7 in the pole vault.

Alex Winkler was the leading performer in leading Stephenson to its first UP State championship since 1966. Winkler won all four events entered for the victors by winning both hurdle events, as well as the day's best efforts in the long jump and 200 meters.

Rock Mid-Peninsula again captured the D3 crown with a narrow 81-74 win over Felch North Dickinson.

2008

The Division 1 team title was not decided until the day's final events as Flint Carman-Ainsworth nipped East Kentwood by a single point to capture its third crown. It was only fitting that these two track powers would place 1-2 in the 1600-meter relay, capping an exciting day on the Rockford oval.

Needing at least a second-place finish in the meet finale, Carman-Ainsworth kept the victorious East Kentwood squad well within its sight as it crossed the finish line less than a second behind the Falcons.

One should not feel too sorry for East Kentwood however, as it was about to embark the following

season on a streak that would see the team atop the podium for five of the next six state finals.

Windy conditions hindered the competitors at the D1 finals, held once again in the Grand Rapids area. Detroit Catholic Central's Michael Martin had the day's most impressive performance in the field events when he unleashed a 63-9 in the shot, second in meet history only to T.J. Duckett's 64-½ effort a decade earlier.

The repeat win in the shot made up for Martin failing to place in the platter: "It probably helped that I fouled in the discus. It's good to finish out strong with another state championship."

Leading the charge for the victors was hurdler Roscoe Payne. He won both hurdles and ran a leg on a pair of relay teams that paved the way for the Cavaliers' team title.

Although contested very early in the competition, the D1 team title could very well have been decided in the 800-meter relay. With Payne running the third leg of the relay, the Cavaliers edged East Kentwood to pick up 10 valuable points, 2 more than the runner-up Falcon foursome.

Despite the wind, Detroit Mumford captured the 3200 relay by a comfortable 5-second margin. Mumford's winning 7:44.79 was second only to its school record set in 2002.

Monroe senior Justin Heck had a memorable afternoon as he garnered a pair of wins in the 1600 (4:15.33) and 3200 (9:20.32). High jump champion Mitchell White from Livonia Stevenson was one of two who would have brief flings in the NFL Placing sixth in the high jump was Grand Haven's John Potter. He would join Martin and White as 2008 track place winners who would perform in the NFL, Martin as a defensive lineman, White a defensive back and Potter as a kicker.

At the D2 finals Williamston, a team that normally scores big in the distances, garner 20 valuable points in the field events to notch its fourth state championship of the first decade of the 21st century.

The winds that bedeviled Division 1 seemed milder in Zeeland, as Tommy Brinn of Otsego and Bobby Aprill of Dexter still managed to post outstanding times. Brinn broke a 19-year old record in the 800-meter run with his 1:51.76. Aprill churned out wins in the 1600 (4:12.98) and 3200 (9:16.41).

Donnie Stiffler was a double winner for Williamston by taking first-place honors in the shot and discus as the Hornets tallied 57 points, a comfortable 15 points better than nearby East Lansing.

Speed was of the essence on the lightning quick oval as Detroit Renaissance clocked a meet record 42.30 in the 4x1. A speedy East Lansing foursome, finished second in 42.5, also under the old best.

Sparta sophomore sprinter Brandon Vandriel defended his title with a wind-aided 10.52 in the 100.

Winning the long jump was future MSU football star Bennie Fowler. Competing for Detroit Country Day, Fowler won the long jump with a leap of 22-5¼. Later he was star of MSU's 2013 Big 10 Champions and winning Rose Bowl team, who made it into the NFL as an undrafted free agent, winning a Super Bowl ring with the Denver Broncos.

In Division 3 Albion nipped Allendale by a single point to earn its first track title. Again, as in Division 1, a relay race would prove to be the difference in determining the state champion.

Albion sped around the Comstock Park oval in a quick 43.28 for the 4x1, with Allendale close behind in second.

Although Albion took home the big team trophy, Allendale could boast of the day's outstanding individual in junior Zack Hill, who topped the 60-foot mark in the shot and set a discus meet record of 175-7.

Junior Hershey Jackson won the 100 for Allendale but the bigger story is what happened to Jackson in the 200-meter dash. An obviously injured Jackson lined up for the 200, probably hoping he could eke out a few points. Allendale didn't have a 4x4, while Albion had a chance to win the event. A big finish in the 200 would have sealed the win for Allendale. It wasn't going to happen; Jackson limped home in eighth in a pedestrian 38.95. In hindsight, a sixth would have given his team the win, a seventh would have been a tie.

In Division 4, with Jay Spitzley leading the way, Pewamo-Westphalia coasted to the title at Forest Hills Eastern. Spitzley won the high hurdles, ran a leg on a pair of winning relay teams, and earned a couple of points with a seventh in the long jump.

Upper Peninsula: Gladstone in D1, Ironwood in D2 and Felch North Dickinson in D3 easily ran off with their titles in Kingsford. Although no records were set, except for marks that were clearly inferior to former records made in the pre-division era, one statistical oddity came to pass.

Ironwood's Alan Peterson won the D2 1600 in 4:34.59, the same exact time clocked the previous year by Scott Bond of Munising.

2009

With one of the authors working the mic at the Division 1 finals at East Kentwood—and the other up in the booth doing a play-by-play for the webcast—the fans in attendance as well as those at home witnessed the start of a dynasty by the home team.

Utilizing an amazing number of talented sprinters, East Kentwood more than doubled the total of its

closest pursuer, Portage Northern, in winning the first of three straight track championships.

Teammates Jon Henry and Tyrone Green placed 1-2 in the 100, surprising many who had seen Green consistently beating Henry all season. "If you added up all the dual meets, he'd be state champion," said Henry.

Green told Mick McCabe of the *Detroit Free Press*, "I lost to a teammate. It's all about good sportsmanship between us."

The Falcons would then win the three remaining relays. Deonte' Hurst chipped in 10 more with his win in the 300 hurdles and coach Dave Emeott's speedsters never looked back.

A bizarre occurrence took place soon after the conclusion of one of East Kentwood's winning relays. The Falcons streaked to victory in the 4 x 100 race with an apparent record time of 41.47 seconds, but were denied the record due to a mismarked stagger line—on their home track.

1600 winner Michael Atchoo. (Pete Draugalis photo)

Andrew Evans of Portage Northern successfully defended his title in the discus. His winning 182-10, as impressive as it was, gave no clue as to his future potential. He became an SEC champion for Kentucky and placed third in the 2013 NCAA. He threw 218-6 with the heavier college/international platter and made the 2016 Olympic team.

Midland's Andrew Maxwell, a much-maligned starting quarterback for Michigan State before giving way to Conner Cook, showed his athletic ability by high jumping 6-7, second only to Holly junior Jonathon Beeler's winning 6-8.

Before heading west to continue his running career at Stanford, Troy's Michael Atchoo established a D1 record for the 1600 with his 4:07.71. As a Cardinal, Atchoo set a school record with a 3:57.14 indoor mile.

Also credited with a MHSAA record at the time—improperly—was Flushing long jumper Jeff Kline, who leaped 24-1. A video of the jump on YouTube confirmed that the leap in fact had a huge amount of wind assistance. In fact, pole vault officials on the adjacent runway had to hold the bar in place until the vaulters started each leap, because they were finding it nearly impossible to keep the bar up in the high winds.

Sophomore Nick Kaiser of Temperance Bedford surprised the field by winning the 800-meter run in 1:52.13. Reed Kamyszek outdistanced all foes with his win in the 3200. The Kenowa Hills junior would take his talents to Syracuse where he would place fifth at the 2013 ACC outdoor championships in the much longer 10,000-meter run.

In Division 2 at Zeeland, Hamilton captured its first track championship, piling up an impressive total of 61 to far outdistance Williamston in D2 action. The Hawkeyes won the 800 and 1600 relays and placed a close second behind Williamston in the 4x1. Hamilton picked up a whopping 18 points when Troy Sneller and Dakota Sale went 1-2 in the 300 Hurdles.

Tommy Brinn repeated as the state champion in the 800, but his time was well short of his record-breaking time of 1:51.76 established the previous year.

Brinn was attempting to win a couple of races that were paired closely together yet nearly accomplished his goal. He ran fast enough in the 400-meter dash to go under the meet record with a 48.08. However, that wasn't fast enough as Stephen Murphy, a first-year runner from Madison Heights Lamphere, beat Brinn to the tape. Murphy, who gave up baseball in his senior season, crossed the finish a stride ahead in 47.94.

In Division 3 at Comstock Park, Albion repeated as team champion, but runner-up Allendale had the day's top performer. Zack Hill set the meet record in D3/Class C annals with a 63-9½, toppling a mark set 41 years earlier by Middleville's Gary Van Elst. Only

T.J. Duckett's 64-foot effort in 1998 was superior to Hill's mark. Hill also established a new standard for the discus with his 181-0 toss.

In Division 4, Potterville coasted to its second title with a convincing win over conference rival Pewamo-Westphalia at Forest Hills Eastern.

Kurt Schneider of Auburn Hills Oakland Christian cleared 6-10½ for a meet record and the top high jump of the day in any division.

Upper Peninsula: Gladstone edged Marquette in the D1 portion, Ironwood held off Munising and St. Ignace to take honors in D2 and Crystal Falls Forest Park nipped rival Felch North Dickinson, 75 to 72½, to win in D3. The D1 title was the sixth in a row for coach Gary Whitmer's Braves.

Performances were not up to previous UP standards as Mother Nature hindered nearly all the marks at the Kingsford facility. Only one meet record fell in all 3 divisions, Terry Martin set a D2 standard in the discus with a 160-5.

2010

Leaving its home track for the short trip to neighboring Rockford did not hinder East Kentwood's attempt to winning a second-straight D1 championship. After romping to a convincing 45-point margin of victory in 2009, the Falcons outdid themselves in 2010.

Scoring in 12 of the 17 events, coach Dave Emeott's Falcons piled up an all-time best 92 points in crushing their nearest competitor by 48 points, the largest margin of victory in MHSAA D1/Class A history. East Kentwood once again dominated the speed events, with Jon Henry winning the 100 and 200 double and keying both short relays.

Headlining the EK rout was the record-setting 4 x 100 relay time of 41.46. The foursome of Dallas Wade, Deonte' Hearst, Kody Dantuma and Henry teamed up once again a week later, selected to represent Team Michigan at the Midwest Meet of Champions. In Fort Wayne they went even faster, blasting a 41.17 state record.

Normally not noted for its distance runners, East Kentwood garnered 10 valuable points when Isaac Cox raced to victory in 1:51.78, the fastest time recorded in the D1 era.

Omar Kaddurah from Grand Blanc posted a new 1600 record with a time of 4:07.67—a mark so fast one would think it would last for decades on the school record board.

Kaddurah was disappointed in his time, though, as after opening up at 58 for the first lap, his race plan fell apart and he found himself in third place. "It ended up being a race instead of the way I wanted it to be," he said. "At the state meet, the runners in there are all animals. You have to be an animal to get there… There's a whole bunch of people there and you have to know they're there and anything can happen."

Kaddurah summoned a 59-second last lap to leave his rivals behind.

Grand Blanc's Omar Kaddurah won the 1600.
(Pete Draugalis photo)

John Beeler from Holly came an inch shy of clearing seven feet with his winning clearance of 6-11. He was successful a week later when he cleared the 7-foot barrier while winning the Midwest Meet of Champions.

East Kentwood's Deonte' Hearst was denied a second-straight win in the 300 hurdles, as Northville's Ali Arastu won the event in 37.50. Arastu would later captain Michigan's team and place fourth in the 2013 NCAA 400H at 49.37.

High hurdle champion Drake Johnson would give his mother plenty of reasons to cheer when he later became a star running back right across the street from Ann Arbor Pioneer High at Michigan's famous Big House. When Johnson ended his career in the Wolverine's final game against eventual NCAA champion Ohio State in November of 2014, his mother was on the sidelines as coach of the cheerleading squad.

Yet another impressive performance came from Detroit Catholic Central in the 1600-meter relay. The Shamrocks capped the meet with one of the fastest times in state history (3:16.11).

While East Kentwood scored an impressive 92 points to win D1, neighboring Byron Center was very content with its modest 30-point total in Division 2, just one point more than Zeeland West. The Bulldogs scored in just three events, but that was all that was necessary to win their first state title.

Junior Derek Sievers contributed more than half of the winner's points with a win in the discus and a third-place showing the shot. He and his Byron Center teammate Jeff Sattler, winner of the 1600, would later become teammates at Michigan.

Field events highlighted the action once again in Zeeland. Junior Aaron Daugherty from Big Rapids repeated as the long jump champ with a fine leap of 23-1 ½, while Dartis Willis of Detroit Country Day, also a junior, cleared 6-10 to claim high jump honors.

Fowlerville's Max Babits would become the third member of the Babits family to win a state title in the pole vault when he cleared 16-½. A generation earlier his father Bob and uncle Paul were state pole vault champions while competing for Redford Union High School.

Ross Parsons, the 100 and 200-meter champion from DeWitt, would later become a place winner in the Big 10 dash for Michigan State.

In Division 3, Vassar won its first title while Concord did the same in D4. For Vassar, it was the highest placing since it placed second in 1921, the first year the state had more than one classification in determining state champions.

Vassar's 400-meter relay team of Madison Harper, Troy Hecht, Justin Locklear and Keif Vickers sweetened the pot by racing to a meet record of 43.25, while anchorman Vickers had earlier won the long jump as well as run on Vassar's second-place 800-meter relay.

Steve Machin of Whitmore Lake just missed a meet record by 0.01 in the 110 highs when his winning time of 14.31. Mason County Central's 3200-meter relay time was the No. 2 time ever recorded in a D3 final.

The most exciting race had to be the 300 hurdles. Chris Teitsma of Allendale led Michael Parker of Michigan Center and Maurice Jones of Jackson Lumen Christi to the finish line with a new record time of 37.30. All three went under the old 37.98 meet standard.

The D4 battle not decided until the day's final race, Concord edged Pewamo-Westphalia 52-49 at Jenison. Needing at least a top three finish in the 1600-meter relay, Concord placed second behind Detroit Loyola to give the Yellowjackets six points, enough to pass Pewamo-Westphalia in team totals.

Kyle Stacks, Ian Miller and Spencer Nousain won individual titles in the 1600, 400, and 3200-meter runs in leading Concord to victory.

Prior to this, Concord High had only produced only one state champion in its history.

The star of the meet, honored by MITCA as the state's top track and field performer of 2010, was Pewamo-Westphalia's Corey Noeker. He won four individual state titles in the high and low hurdles, as well as the 100 and 200-meter dashes.

Upper Peninsula: Better weather conditions worked to the advantage of the athletes at the finals in Kingsford. The host Flivvers set records in the 400 and 800-meter relays in D1, while Ironwood's Alan Peterson ran some fast times with his first-place finishes in the D2 distance events.

Gladstone's Kent King won the shot put for the fourth-straight year, a standard never before achieved in the event in MHSAA history.

Marquette ended Gladstone's 6-year reign in D1, while St. Ignace in D2 and Crystal Falls Forest Park in D3 repeated as champions in their divisions.

2011

Once again East Kentwood dominated all foes at the D1 state finals in Rockford by winning another decisive victory, outscoring all opponents by more than 40 points for the third-straight year.

And talk about a one-year improvement! One needn't look any further than what East Kentwood's Ricco Hall accomplished on the track in 2011. After his family moved to East Kentwood during the off-season, Hall was tested in the fall as only the fourth or fifth fastest runner on a talented and deep East Kentwood team. With nearly 8,000 spectators in attendance for the D1 finals, he set a new Division 1 dash record of 10.55, equaling the 25-year-old Class A record set 25 years earlier by Allan Jefferson.

Stunning EK coach Dave Emeott and perhaps himself, Hall then chopped more than a second off his previous personal best time while winning the 400 meters in 47.00, the fastest in the D1 era. "I was really focused on trying to get a good time," he said. "I started kicking around the 200 and it brought me all the way in."

Hall earlier was part of the winning 800-meter relay team that won the event by a staggering margin of more than 2 full seconds. The EK foursome of Hall, Chris James, Houston Glass and James Stovall took only 1:26.34 to circle the track twice.

Before departing East Kentwood to become a future All-American in track and field for the Nebraska Cornhuskers, Hall capped his perfect day by anchoring

Ricco Hall's first time under 48 took him all the way to 47.00. (Pete Draugalis photo)

East Kentwood's 1600-meter relay to a 3:19.95.

A number of performers returned to the track to defend the state titles they earned as juniors. Feerooz Yacoobi from Dearborn, a future football captain at Pennsylvania, won again in the shot put.

Drake Johnson repeated in the high hurdles. The Ann Arbor Pioneer star just missed setting a meet record in the event with his clocking of 13.73, second only to Kenneth Ferguson's record of 13.65 from 2002.

Distance runners had to battle sweltering heat throughout the afternoon, putting a damper on any record hopes in the longer races. Omar Kaddurah of Grand Blanc defended his 1600 title with a great of 4:12.41, still well short of his previous year.

A pair of former champions as sophomores bounced back to win their specialties as seniors. Nick Kaiser of Temperance Bedford won the 800 in 1:52.91 while Javonte Lipsey of Portage Northern did the same in the Intermediate hurdles (38.83).

In Division 2, performances in the field events highlighted the action at historic Houseman Field, the site of the state finals as far back as 1936.

Defending champion Byron Center tallied 36, six more than it scored in winning the 2010 crown, yet finished far back in fifth place, a full 20 points behind champion East Lansing.

One record was set and a few near misses took place in the field events area. Anthony Zettel from Ogemaw Heights set a new mark in the shot put with a heave of 61-8, before departing for Penn State where he would become an All-Big 10 performer on the Nittany Lions football team.

Derek Sievers placed third behind Zettel in the shot, but the Byron Center senior successfully defended in the discus with a 186-8.

Detroit Country Day's Dartis Willis came with big expectations. Indoors he had soared over the highest height in state history with his 7-2¼. Here he captured a repeat win at 6-11.

Winning the long jump for the third consecutive year was Aaron Daugherty of Big Rapids. After placing second behind Willis in the high jump, Daugherty still had enough energy left to leap 23-7½, second in D2/Class B history only to Tyrone Wheatley.

Auburn Hills Avondale, with 400 champion Trevon Salter running the anchor leg, set the only D2 record on the track when it was clocked in 1:28.11 in the 800-meter relay. Avondale added a win in the 4x1.

Aiding East Lansing's team hopes were wins in the two relays on the program, the 1600 and 3200.

In Division 3, Frankenmuth had to wait until the day's final event to win the team championship, when anchorman Luke Bade crossed the finish line inches ahead of Lansing Catholic to capture the 1600-meter relay. Bade played a huge role for the victors. In addition to his anchor in the last event, he earlier anchored the Eagles to victory in the 3200-relay and took first in the 800-meter run (1:54.32).

David Scouten of Brooklyn Columbia Central defied the odds to equal Zack Hill's discus meet record from 2009 with a toss of 181-0. Scouten also had captured the shot title with an impressive 59-6.

Only one outright record was set at the meet held once again at Comstock Park. Isaac Austin cleared 16 feet in the pole vault. He needed to set a record to secure first place as Brian Michell of Reed City had matched him at 15-9.

Placing second to Frankenmuth in the team competition was Union City. Chris Maye, with wins in the long jump, 100 and 200 scored 30 of Union City's 38 points.

In Division 4, The battle for the team championship came down to the day's final event, the 1600-meter relay. Big Rapids Crossroads topped Albion by a couple of meters to earn 10 valuable points and tie Albion for first place with 48 points. Trailing by two points at the end of the day was Muskegon Catholic, which had placed sixth in the relay.

Upper Peninsula: Marquette destroyed the competition with a dominant showing in the distance events. Mickey Sanders just edged teammate Austin Wissler by less than a tenth of a second to win the mile in 4:26.28 as Marquette finished 1-2-3. The victors did even better by taking the first four places in the 800 with Wissler winning in 1:58.35.

Sanders virtually ran alone while winning the 3200 by 25 seconds over his closest pursuer.

Marquette also showed some speed in the dashes, led by sprinter Garrett Pentecost, who captured both short sprints, including a meet record time of 10.95 in the 100-meter dash.

St. Ignace once again took honors in D2 while Cedarville nosed out neighboring Pickford to win it all in D3. Just one year after Gladstone's Kent King won an event for four consecutive years, St. Ignace high jumper Austin St. Louis matched that feat by doing the same in the high jump.

2012

While records fell right-and-left for the girls in the finals, such was not the case for the boys. In fact, the Grosse Pointe South's girls 3200-meter relay team ran a faster time then the boys did in the UP.

While most of the top performers during the girls meet were centered on the track, just the opposite was true for the boys.

In Division 1 at East Kentwood, Lake Orion won its first state title in totaling 50 points. It was not until the day's final event before Lake Orion capped its historical day with a win in the 1600-meter relay, the only first place earned by the champions.

D1 discus champ Matt Costello of Bay City Western made his biggest splash in another sport as Michigan's Mr. Basketball of 2012. He would later play a prominent role for Michigan State's basketball team, including a trip to the coveted Final Four in 2015. He had nearly earned yet another first-place medal in the shot put, but fell a couple inches shy of Swartz Creek's Kevin Weiler.

Highlighting a relatively quiet afternoon was Drake Johnson of Ann Arbor Pioneer, winning the 110-meter high hurdles for the third consecutive year, a feat matched in Class A/D1 annals only by Lansing Sexton's Roget Ware from 1985 through 1987. Johnson clocked his 14.24—more than a half-second slower than the year before—into a massive 4.3 headwind. "It's pretty hard to run fast into that kind of wind," he said.

Steven Bastien from Saline sailed 23-5 inches to take honors in the long jump. He would go on to become a Big 10 decathlon champ for Michigan.

Grand Blanc, a school better known for producing some of the fastest distance runners in MHSAA history, took home the runner-up trophy thanks in most part to its sprinters. The Bobcats won both the 400 and

800-meter relays and tallied all but 10 of their points in the short sprints and relays.

One could easily see why Milford won the cross-country championship in the fall, as it finished 1-2-6 in the 1600 and got a win from Brandon Wallace in the 800 (1:54.12) after earlier taking the 4x8 in 7:43.42.

Hurdle star Drake Johnson of Pioneer
(Pete Draugalis photo)

The first to cross the finish line at that same cross-country championship, Garret Zuk of White Lake Lakeland, did the same in the 3200-meter run with a fine time of 9:04.35.

The Division 2 meet at historic Houseman Field in downtown Grand Rapids saw some terrific performances. The Lansing Sexton foursome of Kendell Jackson, Adrian Sanchez, David Washington and Anthony Goodman set a meet record for the 800 relay with a 1:27.99.

Auburn Hills Avondale became a first year-champ by out-scoring Lansing Sexton 47-40. James Salisbury from Marine City cleared 16-1 to equal the meet record first set by Brad Teeple.

Riley Norman of Cadillac provided another notable mark with his winning toss of 61-2½ in the shot put, the No. 2 distance in Class B/D2 history.

The short sprints produced some quick times that surely had to raise some eyebrows. The 200 was so speedy that the first three place winners all broke the previous meet record of 21.70. Kassius Kelly of Livonia Clarenceville was clocked at 21.36, followed by Gary Jones of Allegan (21.61) and sophomore Ted Parcher from Linden (21.64).

Yet another fast time was turned in by Auburn Hills Avondale's Kyle Redwine, whose 10.53 was one of the fastest times in state history.

The only track double winner on the afternoon came from junior Connor Mora from Cedar Springs, winner of the 1600 and 3200-meter runs.

In Division 3, Lansing Catholic grabbed its first track state title with a dominant showing at Comstock Park. The victors took home five first-place medals, including winning three of the four relays. Running a leg on all three relays was Zach Zingsheim, who added his fourth medal to his collection by taking first in the 800-meter run (1:55.97).

Chris Maye, from runner-up Union City, nearly had a perfect day. Maye won both the 100 and 200 dashes and ran on the winning 400-meter relay. Only a second finish in the long jump to Lakeview's Dillon Wood kept Maye from a four-win sweep.

In Division 4, Albion moved down after winning D3 the previous year. Lawson Bright-Mitchell played a most valuable role for the coach Mike Jurasek's squad by anchoring three winning relays. However, he had to share his title in the 400 meters with Austin Sandusky from Morenci, as the two could not be separated on the photo, a dead-heat at 50.917 seconds.

Jacob Patrick, a junior from the tiny village of Litchfield, had the day's best throw in the discus—in all classes—with his 190-0 to establish a new meet record.

David Dantuma from Big Rapids Crossroads Academy won the boys D4 1600-meter run in 4:25.92, again—the same winning time from the previous year that winner Kyle Tait ran—and the two were from the same school!

Upper Peninsula: Performances were sub-par compared to past with one notable exception. While many of the competitors struggled at the finals in Kingsford, such was not the case for junior Kenner Broullire from Manistique. Broullire set the only record that was superior to anything from the pre-division era, with a 39.74 in the 300 hurdles.

Marquette and St. Ignace won for the third consecutive year in Divisions 1 & 2 while Pickford, after winning the Class D championship for 27 straight years, 25 under the leadership of the legendary Web Morrison, won but its second state title over the past 20 years in D3.

2013

The abnormally brutal weather during the winter carried over well into the track season for our Michigan athletes. The entire season was beset with poor conditions that continued into the first of June, the date of the state track championships held for the 13th-straight year in the Grand Rapids area.

While the gusty breezes prevalent for much of the day hampered the running events, the windy conditions were indeed very favorable for all the discus competitors. All four winners in the discus event in the

LP finals at East Kentwood unleashed throws that landed well beyond the 180-foot mark, unprecedented in prep history in the Wolverine State.

But what Walled Lake Central's Cullen Prena accomplished in Division 1 was startling. Prena had four throws that surpassed the 200-foot mark, with his best effort measured at 210-1, more than 12 feet farther than the previous record. Preva's throw, a monstrous 34 feet farther than the second-place finisher, would be a vast improvement by nearly 40 feet from his best effort from 2012, when he placed second to MSU basketball standout Matt Costello.

"I put my mind on the 210 ever since last season when I threw 188. To finally reach that goal was just an amazing feeling," said Prena.

Prena also captured the D1 shot title. The Oregon recruit had the day's best mark at 60-11.

While the D1 finals would say good bye to some of the greatest girl distance runners in MHSAA prep history, the boys events would get a preview of greatness to come from some talented underclassmen.

The first of the young superstars of the future to toe the starting line was sophomore Grant Fisher of Grand Blanc. Fisher and senior T.J. Carey from Lake Orion

The closest 1600 finish ever? T.J. Carey beat sophomore Grant Fisher by 0.006. It would be the last time Fisher lost in state finals competition. (Peter Draugalis)

would battle in one of the tightest finishes in history for the 1600. With the crowd on its feet in support of both runners, Carey just edged Fisher at the finish line by a tiny 0.006.

Placing a very respectable seventh with a time under 4:20 was another budding prodigy, freshman Anthony Berry from Traverse City. Windy conditions kept Carey's time to 4:15.76 seconds, the second slowest winning clocking in a dozen years.

Winning the D1 state title for the fourth time in five years was East Kentwood. However, this time it took only 43 points, nearly 30 less than the Falcons' other wins.

East Kentwood once again relied on its perennially strong relay teams to bring yet another trophy to its bulging trophy case, winning the 800 and 400-relays and placing a solid third in the 1600-meters. The well-balanced meet that produced only a pair of double champions, as more than ten teams scored 20 points or more, with Grand Blanc leading the second tier with 32 tallies.

Andrew Middleton held off another talented underclassman with his win in the 800-meter run. The Holt senior defeated Grand Rapids Kenowa Hills sophomore Donavan Brazier by a full second with his winning time of 1:53.36.

In Division 2, although Chelsea High School had been participating in the state finals for well over 100 years with its first individual state champion dating all the way back to 1904, the school earned its first team title by outscoring Grand Rapids Ottawa Hills 64-56.

The victorious Bulldogs delivered from all angles, utilizing the speed of double winner Berkley Edwards in the sprints, pole vault champion Michael Hovater in the field events, and the middle-distance talents from their victorious 3200-meter relay team to account for the bulk of their winning points.

Edwards came close to the meet record in the 200 meters at 21.37, albeit wind-aided (3.2), while his 10.58 in the 100 was boosted by a big 5.4mps wind.

Quincy Boyd had the day's next best mark in the discus at 189-2.

Cedar Springs' Connor Mora turned in the day's fastest time in the 1600-meters on this sunny, but windy afternoon. The future Michigan steeplechaser turned in a 4:10.38, more than five-seconds faster than turned in by the D1 runners and a whopping 10 seconds ahead of second.

Riley Norman repeated as the shot put champ but his winning throw of 59-10 was short of his 60-foot plus throw in 2012. Long Jumper Dontel Highsmith from Dowagiac busted a great leap of 23-5¼.

In Division 3, Wyoming Kelloggsville joined Chelsea as another first-time state championship team with a commanding victory at Comstock Park. Leading the way for Kelloggsville was TJ Burnett who ran the second fastest time in meet history with a 48.59, while also anchoring the 800 and 1600-meter relays to wins.

Matching Burnett's three wins was a distance performer from Mason Co. Central with the almost identical last name—Chase Barnett. His family has produced a number of state champs including Jeff Barnett, winner of four first-place medals in 1986.

Barnett nipped Nick Raymond from Erie-Mason by an eyelash in the 1600 (4:15.97) and also had a narrow win in the 800 over Jake Hall of Frankenmuth. Earlier in the morning he anchored his Spartans to the to a blazing 7:57.04 in the 4x8.

Evan Hartman from Niles Brandywine easily eclipsed the meet record in the discus with his 187-1.

In Division 4 at Hudsonville, Saugatuck deprived Albion of a repeat win. It would prove to be the first for Saugatuck and perhaps the last for Albion, scheduled to close the following fall.

Although short of his record set in 2012, Jacob Patrick from Litchfield had a mark of 187-2, second only to his 190-0 effort in D4 annals. Earlier in the season he had thrown 201-1 at the Hillsdale County Championships to join an elite club.

Luke Meyer from Addison cleared 6-8 in the high jump.

Upper Peninsula: After watching Marquette take home the last three D1 championships, Gladstone, winners from 2004-09, returned to the top of the awards stand, while Marquette lagged behind in fourth.

Highlighting the day's action was Jared Vuksan from Gladstone with a heave of 55-11¼ in the shot, second only to Escanaba's Wayne Schwalbach's best mark of 58-7 set back in 1974.

Gladstone, after winning four of the five field events, took a commanding lead into the running finals and tallied 112, with Menominee next in line with 80.

After a drought of 53 years, the Emeralds of Manistique High won their first championship since the heyday of former MSU running back Ron Rubic in 1960. Manistique had to wait out an interminably long rain delay to finally clinch. Holding a narrow lead over Ishpeming heading into the final event, the Emeralds defeated Ishpeming, thanks to a speedy anchor leg from Ryan Ramey.

Earlier Ramey had won the 200 and 400 before capping his day with his come-from-behind win in the 1600 relay. Manistique's Kannar Broulire, who improved his own best for the 300 hurdles to 39.35, produced the only meet record of the day.

After a five-year absence, Felch North Dickinson returned to the winner's circle with a convincing win in Kingsford. Junior Tim Hruska led the way for the champs with victories in both hurdles as well as the 100. Senior All-State basketball player Brett Branstrom (6-5) from Rock Mid Peninsula also was a three-event winner in the field events.

2014

Much better weather was in store for the state track finals in 2014 with a number of top-flight performances taking place throughout the Grand Rapids area. East Kentwood continued its dominance in the state's highest division with a fifth state championship in six years; the best run in Division1/Class A history since Saginaw High won five straight titles and six in a seven-year run from 1945-52.

The day's top performance came from Grand Rapids Kenowa Hills junior Donavan Brazier, who produced a 1:50.24 in the 800 meter-run. He took down one of the oldest records on the books when he surpassed the 880-yard mark of Kevin Reabe from Waterford Mott of 1:50.9 set 44 years earlier.

Perhaps most impressive was that Brazier ran his two laps with negative splits, clocking 55.5 for the first lap and speeding up to 54.7 on the second.

"I came in more confident this year," Brazier said. "I just felt good the whole way."

Brazier's was the only Class A/D1 record, but others who challenged the list. Noah Gary of Dexter had the No. 2 vault in meet history with his 16-2, second only to Paul Terek's 16-6 from 1997.

Dexter vaulter Noah Gary

Brandon Piwinski from Warren DeLaSalle was another junior who excelled out-dueling Cody Stemple from White Lake Lakeland in the high jump. Piwinski cleared 6-10 at the state finals after setting a school record 7-½ in the Macomb County to top the best his father, Paul, set for Warren Cousino in 1978. However, Dad still had one bragging right as he had gone a half-inch higher to win his state title 36 years earlier.

Kevin Weiler of Swartz Creek had his best effort in the shot land at 60-4½ after earlier winning the discus with a 176-5, making him one of three double winners at the Rockford complex.

Oak Park took home the runner-up team trophy with speedster Maurice Allen playing a leading role. He won the 400-meters in 48.19, the 200-meter dash in a quick 21.36 into a slight headwind and ran legs on a pair of place-winning relay squads.

Grand Blanc junior Grant Fisher breezed to victories in the 1600 and 3200. He blasted his final lap in 58.3 to win the 1600 in 4:10.82. The first five finishers in the metric mile were underclassmen, with the youngest being second-place finisher Anthony Berry, a sophomore from Traverse City Central.

The Footlocker national cross country champion the previous fall was content to let Royal Oak's Ben Hill set the pace in the 8-lapper before shifting into a devastating kick in the last 200, winning in 9:07.11 to 9:09.34.

The real fireworks would come in the post-season for Fisher. Two weeks after the state finals he competed in the Dream Mile at the New York Diamond League meet, where in victory he demolished the state record for the mile with his 4:02.02. A week later at the Brooks PR meet, he used another brutal kick to win by nearly four seconds in 8:51.28 for two miles. He also placed second in the 1500 at the USA Junior Championships, qualifying to run in the World Juniors later that summer in Eugene.

The very deep East Kentwood team captured a pair of firsts en route to its commanding victory, Antoine Lloyd winning the 100-hurdles in 13.95, and the 800-meter relay winning for the fifth time in the last six seasons.

In Division 2, competing throughout the entire season without a home track didn't deter Zeeland West from winning its first title, capping a dream season for a school that was still in only its tenth year as a four-year school.

The Dux had only one individual winner in Jason Tran in the 300 hurdles, but the rest of the team chipped in with a number of top three finishes.

Anthony Fitzgerald from Melvindale was clearly the meet's top individual performer, with a pair of top notch wins, high jumping 6-9 to win by three full inches, and winning the long jump by a full foot with a fine 23-1 to become one of two double winners that day.

Joshuwa Holloman contributed a pair of wins in the two short dashes (10.75/22.21) to lead Auburn Hills Avondale to a second-place team finish.

The event that came closest to a record occurred in the 4 x 100. Orchard Lake St. Mary posted a 42.53, the No. 4 time in meet history. For the third year in a row a runner from Cedar Springs won the 1600 when Austin Sargent outlasted 800-meter champion John Sattler from Byron Center.

In Division 3, Sanford-Meridian showed it is quality and not quantity that determines a team champion. First-time winners, the Mustangs hadn't won their conference or regional, but came away with the big one at Comstock Park. Fortunately for coach Dave Pettyplace, one of his athletes made a good call.

A regular on the school's baseball team had to make a tough decision as the Sanford-Meridian baseball team was competing in the district tournament. It appeared that senior John Wenzlick made the right choice, as he was a member of three winning Sanford-Meridian relay teams and one of those teams set a meet record.

What is extraordinary about this 1600-meter relay team is that the other three members of the foursome were first-year performers. Dan Johnson broke his wrist shortly before the baseball season and settled for a position on the track team. Seniors Kevin Scheibert and Jacob Ham had played travel basketball during the spring of their junior year, but gave up basketball to run track. And run they did! Needing to finish in the top five in the day's final event, the Sanford-Meridian foursome won in 3:21.44 and then celebrated shortly thereafter with the first-place team trophy.

Mason County Central, led by 1600-meter winner Chase Barnett, finished second with 39 points, six behind Sanford-Meridian.

Jaylen Ghoston from Madison Heights Madison busted an 18-year-old mark with his 48.17 in the 400.

In Division 4, Concord received a major boost to its already solid program after Albion closed its school doors following the previous school year. The Yellow Jackets added a number of former Albion athletes to their program, but none would have a bigger impact than senior sprinter Lawson Bright-Mitchell.

Bright-Mitchell won two individual events and anchored the 800 and 1600-meter relay squads to impressive victories. Concord easily had more than enough points (78) to dethrone defending champion Saugatuck.

Three of those victories resulted in new meet records for coach Mike Jurasek's squad. Bright-Mitchell, who won the 100-meter dash as a freshman at Albion, set a new record for the Class D/D4 century with a time of 10.70. The Yellow Jacket senior later erased a record that went all the way back to 1958 when he blazed the 200-meter dash in 21.62, superior to a hand time of 21.5 for Brethren's Ken Beane, likely run on a straightaway.

Concord's winning 1600-meter relay team concluded its day with a new D4 record of 3:24.19, a time second only to the Class D record of 3:22.9 set in 1981 by another school that has since closed its doors, Detroit DePorres.

Upper Peninsula: Kingsford won its first state title since 1990, and the first it could celebrate on its own track with a commanding win on the Flivver track.

Stealing much of the thunder away from the title, however, was a sophomore distance ace from Sault Ste Marie. Parker Scott ran the fastest time in UP history in the 1600 (4:18.09) and then followed that with a win in the 800 in 1:58.29, defending the titles he won in 2013 as a freshman.

Unfortunately for Blue Devil fans, Scott would not be running in future UP track meets as his family would move to Texas before the start of the next school year.

After winning back-to-back Division 7 football championships at Ford Field in Detroit, the Ishpeming Hematites added further laurels with a decisive win in D2 track.

In Division 3 Andy Cooper won four individual events to lead Munising to its first title in 18 years, winning the high jump, both hurdles and the 200 dash.

2015

There have been some amazing performances set at the MHSAA finals over the years, and now one can add 2015 to the list.

Typically, these performances came from a single individual who would virtually steal the show. One can go back more than a century to Joe Horner in 1907. The exploits of future Olympic gold medalists such as Ralph Craig, Eddie Tolan, Hayes Jones and Rex Cawley also dazzled, as did Bill Watson's magnificent performance in 1935 state meet. Of more recent vintage, state track fans were thrilled with the brilliance of distance runner Dathan Ritzenhein and hurdler Kenneth Ferguson.

However, the 2015 state finals showcased a pair of superstars wowing the fans that packed Rockford's track facility, and one could make a case for a distance relay team that would make track gurus across the nation stand up and take notice.

Almost lost in the shuffle was Saline winning the team title, depriving runner-up East Kentwood from its sixth crown in seven years.

With the field events still in progress, the first running event saw the Saline 3200-meter relay of Logan Wetzel, Josiah Humphrey, Austin Welch and Kevin Hall run a blistering meet record of 7:38.97.

The signature event for this classic state final would be the 1600-meter run. All eyes were on Grant Fisher, the defending champion widely regarded as the nation's top prep miler. Only a few knew that he would be attempting to break the fabled four-minute barrier. He had served notice of his fitness quietly a few weeks earlier, running a state record 3:42.89 in a 1500m race at Stanford—worth 4:00.73 for a full mile.

The timing crew had set up a second finish line 9.34m past the first, just in case anybody would be curious in the final time for a full mile.

Grant Fisher had a monstrous lead at the end of his historic four laps—even though the next three runners also broke 4:10. (Pete Draugalis photo)

Starting in the outside lanes, Fisher ran alone from the gun. He hit 400 in 59.8. As his lead grew to astounding levels, the athletes warming up on the infield swarmed to the side of the track. All knew something special was happening. Fisher passed

800m in 1:59.9. The skies seemed to grow darker, as through the race the winds started to pick up.

Fisher lost a little momentum on the third lap, his slowest at 62.6. He passed 1200m in 3:02.5. On the final 200, he sprinted hard, hoping to make history. With a last lap of 57.6, he zipped past the official finish line in a state record 4:00.28, continuing on for the full mile in 4:01.67, another state record. The timers had even gotten an FAT split on his 1500 (3:46.10—No. 2 in state history).

Following this epic performance, it was clear that many on-site reporters believed they had their lead story.

But wait… still to run his race was a tall and long-limbed senior from a school that was little known for producing track superstars. Visions of Cuban Olympic champion Alberto Juantorena came to mind while watching Donavan Brazier blaze effortlessly around the oval.

Brazier covered his first lap in 54.95 and in his trademark style sped up to a 54.03 to destroy the meet record with his 1:48.98.

It came as no surprise to the track aficionados on hand that maybe the Kenowa Hills dynamo would pull off something very special. After all, as a junior he was the New Balance 800-meter national champion and two weeks earlier, on the chilly shores of Lake Michigan in Grand Haven, won the regional qualifier by more than 10 seconds with a nation-leading time (and state record) of 1:48.07.

Both Fisher and Brazier were busy following the state finals by taking their act across the country from coast to coast. Less than a week after his great show in Rockford, Fisher took part in a mile race in St. Louis against professional runners. He finished third and made history, becoming the first Michigan prep and the seventh nationally to break 4:00 with his 3:59.38.

A few days later Fisher defended his adidas Dream Mile title in New York, beating a top national field with a 4:01.73 in the tactical contest.

Both Brazier and Fisher would next compete in Seattle at the Brooks PR meet. Undefeated against all prep rivals, Fisher suffered his first loss in a blazing fast two-mile run by Virginia junior Drew Hunter. Even in defeat he was never faster. He passed through 3200 in 8:40.7 en route to an 8:43.57 for two miles, both marks breaking Dathan Ritzenhein state records.

The Texas A&M-bound Brazier crushing the field in the 800-meter run with a state record 1:47.55 to become the No. 4 runner in U.S. history.

Although he didn't come away from Rockford with an individual first-place medal, Saline's Logan Wetzel would have been a meet MVP in many previous state finals. Wetzel picked up a pair of first-place medals for his role on the record-setting 3200 relay as well as Saline's victory in the 1600 relay, but had to be content to place second behind the pair of all-time greats in the 1600 and 800 runs.

The Villanova bound senior still managed to post 4:08.04 in the four-lapper and 1:52.74 in the two-lapper. In NYC at the Dream Mile, he finished fifth in 4:04.60 to become the No. 2 Michigan miler in history.

The weather got progressively worse throughout the day in the Grand Rapids area. By the time Fisher took to the track for the 3200, the winds were gusting hard. He still ran a meet record 8:53.41.

In Division 2, Orchard Lake St. Mary added the track championship to its trophy case with 52 points, 7.5 ahead host Zeeland East. The victorious Eagles won a pair of sprint relays and received a first-place finish from 300 hurdler Richard Bowen to highlight their victory.

Zeeland East's 3200-meter relay team, composed of Scott Binder, Scott Cramer, Matt Cramer and John Groendyke set a D2 meet record of 7:50.70.

Division 3 was a tight race for the team championship between a couple of new faces at the top of the leader board, Jackson Lumen Christi and Hillsdale, neither having placed in the top two before.

In Comstock Park, Jaylin Golson from Madison Heights Madison battled the winds win a second title in the 400. His 49.46 was more than a second slower than his meet record the year before.

The talent was so spread out that only Clinton High was able to win more than one of the 17 events, with victories from its 400-meter relay and Tyler Underwood in the 200.

Division 4's leading storyline in Hudsonville was the extremely tight battle for the team championship, with only seven points separating the first seven teams. The final totals showed Saugatuck and defending champion Concord tied for first with 40 points and Muskegon West Michigan Christian just a point back in third.

The battle was decided on the very last race. Saugatuck's Blake Dunn, winner of the 300 hurdles, dueled WMC's Elijah VanderVelde, a third place winner in the 400, down the stretch. Dunn outleaned VanderVelde at the finish line by less than a tenth of a second, the difference between an outright championship for the Muskegon parochials and a third-place finish for Saugatuck.

Aaron Watson from Union City was the point leader with victories in the 100 and 200; he also ran a leg on the first-place 4x1 and the fourth-place 4x4.

Blake Washington from Southfield Christian put together a meet record of 49.34 in the 400. Casey Williams of Saginaw Michigan Lutheran Seminary had the best long jump of the day with his 22-9¼.

Upper Peninsula: Records were hard to find in Kingsford. The top performances came in the division with the smallest school enrollments. Andy Cooper from Munising won the high jump at 6-2 and then set D3 records in both hurdles (14.96/40.13).

Don't look for Crystal Falls pole vaulter Billy Ragio to expect a great bargain on a piece of property in the future from realtor John Andrzejak. Ragio broke Andrzejak's record of 13-3 from 37 years earlier by Andrzejak while competing for Pickford, and later equaled in 2006 by Rock Mid Peninsula's Jimmi Cretens. Ragio topped it by a mere half-inch.

Munising more than doubled the score over second-place Rapid River to take team honors in D3, while Marquette and Ishpeming won in D1 and D2.

2016

Although it was common up until recent years for athletes to partake in more than one sport, such has not been the case in recent years. One of the biggest challenges coaches of the new millennium face is convincing many of their better athletes, especially those than took part in football, to join the track team in the spring.

After winning his first state championship over 40 years ago while coaching now-closed Detroit DePorres to a Class D title, veteran coach Robert Lynch had a quick answer for Oak Park's success in 2016: "The biggest thing we've got going for us is we got some football players to come out."

Lynch's Oak Park team had just one first-place winner, junior Cameron Cooper in the 800, but had just enough depth to defeat Rockford by nine points to earn Lynch his first championship at Oak Park, but No. 12 overall in his extraordinary coaching career.

Headlining action in the field events was Oxford strong-man Connor Bandel. He won both throws by more than a combined 33 feet! The Florida commit easily won in the discus with a mighty 198-11. Then he threw the shot 67-5¾, breaking an old meet record (T.J. Duckett's 17-year-old standard) and a young state record (the 67-2½ he had thrown to win the Oakland County meet eight days earlier).

Although his leap was wind-aided, Jackson High's Anthony Owens became the fifth athlete in meet history to jump beyond 24-feet in winning the long jump at 24-1¼. Although Terius Wheatley had to settle for second, he would now have the bragging rights in his own family. The Ann Arbor Pioneer junior's second-place leap, measured at 23-10¾ (aided by a 3.2 wind) was a miniscule ¼" longer than his legendary father, Tyrone Wheatley, recorded in 1989.

The leading point winner, and clearly the leading sprinter at the MHSAA state finals in 2016, was East

No one scored more points at D1 in 2016 than East Kentwood's Khance Meyers.
(Pete Draugalis photo)

Kentwood junior sprinter Khance Meyers. The Falcon speedster won took home of the first of his 3 first-place medals with a victory in the 100 (10.73).

That proved to be a warm-up for Meyers as in the very next event, he ran the opening leg of East Kentwood's 4 x 200-relay team to a new D1 record 1:26.27.

He may have saved his best performance for last as he blazed to victory in the 200-meters with a new D1 record of 21.24. That time also equaled the Class A FAT best of 21.24 recorded by Godfrey Herring of Pontiac Northern from the Class A finals in 1997.

In Division 2, just down the road in Zeeland, Orchard Lake St. Mary won a tight battle with Mason to repeat as champions. St. Mary's was shut out in the field events as Mason jumped out to an early lead, scoring 30 of its 44 points on three wins on the field. Justin Scavarda copped both weight events while his teammate Jarrett VanHavel won the pole vault.

OLSM quickly made its move early into the running event finals with back-to-back wins in the 100-meter dash and the 800-meter relay.

Kahlee Hamler, who won the 100, and Richard Bowens teamed up with Shemond Dabney, who placed in both hurdles, and Ky'Ren Cunningham to break the meet record with their 1:27.71. Bowens would later break a 15-year-old record with his 37.46 in the 300 hurdles.

Noah Jacobs from Corunna ran a fabulous solo 3200 meters to win in 8:55.57, 30 seconds ahead of his closest pursuer. Jacobs time was a D2 record and was third in state meet history only to legends Dathan Ritzenhein and Grant Fisher.

Alex Klemm of Macomb Lutheran North joined the high jump elite by clearing a meet record 7-0.

In Division 3, Sanford-Meridian returned to the winner's circle after a one-year absence, in a well-balanced D3 meet held at Comstock Park.

The winners tallied 36 of their points on victories in the 400 and 800 relays and a pair of seconds in the 100 and 200 by Christian Petre. Sanford-Meridian mirrored D2 champ Orchard Lake St. Mary by winning a state title without a single point in the field events.

The Mustang foursome of Christian Petre, Miles LeViere, Monte Petre and Andre Smith set a new meet record of 43.14 in the 400-relay.

In his first year out for the sport, Wyoming Lee sophomore Thomas Robinson took honors in both short dash races, running 11.09 and 22.20. Carl Meyers from Grand Rapids West Catholic joined Robinson as a double winner with victories in the shot and discus. His 62-9¾" in the shot was the top performance on the field.

In Division 4, Saugatuck made sure it would not have to share this trophy as it more than doubled the score, 66-32, over Evart.

Although only a junior in 2016, Saugatuck four-sport star Blake Dunn had a difficult decision to make. The state track finals fell on the same day as the district baseball finals. Confident that his baseball mates would win the district (and they did), Dunn opted, with the blessing of his baseball coach, to run in the track finals.

He produced a pair of meet records in the hurdles. Running into a headwind, Dunn was clocked in 14.33, just nipping the 32-year-old mark in Class D of Willy Scott. In the 300 hurdles, Dunn won by nearly two full seconds in 38.31. His exemplary high school career came to an end at the beginning of the following track season when he tore his ACL while long jumping.

Upper Peninsula: In leading Marquette to the D1 title, Lance Rambo had the top performance during the championships in Kingsford with a sub 2-minute clocking (1:59.23) in the 800-meter run.

No records fell during the day-long competition north of the Big Mac. Ishpeming was an easy winner in D2 while the only suspense came in D3. Rapid River placed second to Powers-North Central in the day's final event, the 1600-meter relay, to win over North Central by a narrow 4 points.

2017

The decade saw the geographical center for excellence in Michigan schoolboy track shift to Western Michigan as the Falcons of East Kentwood, and their head coach Dave Emeott, have been a dominant force at the state's most populous division.

East Kentwood won its sixth Division 1 title as Emeott has now equaled former Saginaw mentor Herb Korf for winning the most state wins in Class A/ D1 history. Korf captured his titles from 1946-1954.

In 2017 the Falcons showed their comfort running on their home track in East Kentwood, scoring in 9 of the 17 events.

Where competitors from the Saginaw Valley once dominated the track & field scene from the 1940s into the 1970s, the OK conference is doing the same more than a half century later. Placing second was conference rival Rockford, tallying an impressive 62, second only to the victor's haul of 78.5.

For the second time in three years, Michigan produced the nation's fastest 800 runner. Oak Park's Cameron Cooper didn't save his energy for an all-out assault on the 2-lap record, but took part in four grueling events in a valiant effort to help his Oak Park team defend its state championship. He began the day by running a blazing anchor 800 in 1:48.66 to give Oak Park the 4 x 800 win in 7:44.85.

He nearly snared another victory in the 1600-meter run in one of the afternoon's most exciting finishes. Rockford junior Cole Johnson, who did not run a leg on Rockford's 3200-relay team, set the pace for almost the entire race. Tucked in just behind, Cooper looked poised for the sprint win when he passed Johnson with about 100 meters remaining.

The Rockford star somehow found yet another gear and regained the lead in the final strides, crossing the finish in 4:08.60 with Cooper inches away in 4:08.96. The two would return to the track about an hour later to resume their rivalry in the 800. Cooper has just enough gas left in the tank to outlast an understandably tired Johnson in 1:51.22.

Cooper was not done yet. Although the LSU commit said, "I couldn't feel my legs," he held off East Kentwood's Khance Meyers to lead his foursome to victory in the 4 x 400 relay (3:17.58).

Three weeks after the state finals, Cooper traveled to Sacramento, California, where he won the 800 at the USATF Junior Nationals with a time of 1:47.59, making him the No. 5 prep in U.S. history.

Oak Park's Cameron Cooper managed three wins and a close second in a great day at D1.
(Pete Draugalis photo)

Although Cooper was the top performer, there were other outstanding performances on a near-perfect day. The East Kentwood sprinter that Cooper gamely held off in the 1600-relay, Khance Meyers, capped a sensational career.

The senior speedster again won the 100 and 200, with his winning 10.53 in the 100—into a slight headwind—establishing a D1 record. His mark of 21.27, also into a headwind, impressed. Meyers took the baton on the final leg of the 800 relay and stopped the clock at 1:26.07, a Division 1 record, second only to the hand-held time of Detroit Cass Tech of 1:25.0 set 23 years earlier.

Ironically, the record was set despite East Kentwood competing in the second of three heats. The Falcons were not one of the top eight teams based on their second-place finish in the regional behind Reeths-Puffer. But what a difference it makes when you add the state 100 and 200-dash champ to your lineup. Reeths-Puffer would place fifth in the state finals, but

its time would be fast enough to break a Greater Muskegon record that stood for 55 years.

Predominantly noted for producing outstanding distance runners, Rockford showed there is speed in Ram Country as well. The 4 x 100 squad of Melvin Mosely, Noah Stallworth, Josh Patterson and Nicholas Isley circled the oval in a meet record 41.20, missing the state record by a mere 0.03. A surprisingly quick Traverse City West team followed in 41.94.

Mason Phillips of Salem and East Kentwood's Andre Welch had a fierce battle in the long jump. On his first attempt in the competition, Welch leaped 24-1¾, a meager quarter-inch farther than the meet record. On his fourth attempt, Phillips surpassed Welch's short-lived record with a 24-2¾. Surprisingly, Phillips, a senior, was in his first year of track, having joined midway through the season. He went on to become a D2 All-American for Northwood University.

The only sophomore to even compete in the shot came away with the first-place medal. East Kentwood's Logan Brown tossed the ball 60-1½.

East Lansing hurdler Kentre Patterson had a most memorable afternoon. After leading all qualifiers in the morning preliminaries with a time of 13.74, Patterson won the afternoon's first final running event in a slightly slower 13.84. He would win his second hurdling event the hard way. Running in the second of three heats, Patterson was timed in 38.23 in winning the 'slower' seeded heat, but 0.04 faster than Allen Stritzinger from Warren DeLaSalle posted in the final heat.

In Division 2, another local favorite won, as Zeeland East tallied 71 points to beat Coldwater by 29. Lake Fenton's 3200-relay squad of Elijah Bordeau, Remington Clements, Thomas Mueller and Isaac Golson came close to a meet record in near-perfect conditions, clocking 7:50.92, just 0.22 shy of the mark.

Lake Odessa hurdler Noah Caudy and Corunna distance ace Noah Jacobs each ran off with a pair of first-place medals. Caudy became the first three-time winner in the high hurdles. Improving his time each year, Caudy won the highs at 14.05 and came back in the 300s with an even more impressive 37.85.

Although falling well short of his 3200 record from the 2016 state finals, Corunna's distance standout Noah Jacobs nevertheless had to be pleased with his showing. After winning the Division 2 XC title in the fall, Jacobs was diagnosed with an injury to his left tibia shortly before the start of the 2017 track season. The Wisconsin commit had to shelve his training for five weeks, putting him at less than 100% healthy for the state finals.

He won the 1600 earlier in the program with a 4:14.03, then captured his third-straight 3200 with a come-from-behind narrow victory over Coldwater's Shuaib Aljabaly, 9:11.63-9:11.84.

The winning Dux piled up 18 points in the shot event, thanks to 1-2 from Jonathan Berghorst and Branden Knoll. This same duo placed 2-3 in the discus, behind the winning toss of 180-1 from Coldwater's Connor Covert.

While Coldwater's best placing in the shot put was a third-place effort from Sam DeMeester, the Cardinals qualified an unimaginable total of seven participants in this single event, with four of the athletes earning a place. Although it is highly unlikely that such an award exists, surely the weight coach at Coldwater High would run away with that honor.

In Division 3 at Comstock Park, three of the new records occurring in the distance events. Chesaning edged Hillsdale 47-42 to claim its first title while the individual top honors went to Bridgman senior Brian Patrick. After a commanding win in the 1600 in 4:11.05, erasing a 17-year-old record, Patrick returned to the track a short time later and lowered the 800 mark to 1:53.81.

St. Louis senior Evan Goodell, although the top seed in the 1600, did not challenge Patrick in what surely would have been an interesting battle in the metric mile. Instead, he posted a winning 9:08.04 in the 3200 to lower a 13-year-old record by more than 4 seconds.

Thomas Robinson of Wyoming Lee set the final record in D3 with a time of 21.76 set, not in the finals, but in the morning prelims of the 200-meter dash. With a legal wind of 1.0, Robinson set a new record by the slimmest of margins, 0.01 seconds faster than the 21.77 by Andy Montague of Olivet in 2003. The Wyoming Lee junior also repeated in the 100 with his 10.85 win.

Another noteworthy doubler was Dan Stone of Frankenmuth. He won the discus by more than 12 feet (171-0), and also produced a winning 60-9¾ in the shot.

Connor Maloney made a bid at a record in the 400, as the Lansing Catholic senior's winning time of 48.63 was less than a half second shy of the record.

In Division 4 at Houseman Field in Grand Rapids, Whittemore-Prescott won its first title with 36 points, It was the lowest point total in a half century at the D4/Class D finals.

The winners earned the championship despite not winning a single event, nor was a single record set during the meet. Only one mark was even challenged. Mike Courterier from Johannesbrug-Lewiston, who won the pole vault by nearly two feet, had a winning 14-9, just 4 inches off the meet record.

Upper Peninsula: With temperatures hovering at an unseasonably balmy 80 degrees in Kingsford, Marquette easily won its third-straight D1 title, outscoring Iron Mountain by nearly 50 points.

In D2, Newberry won its first championship in 11 years as John Paramaski won 3 field events and also ran a leg on Newberry's 400-meter relay (45.03).

Matthew Revord of Munising upped the D3 pole vault record up to 13-6. Running virtually alone, Grady Kerst of Ishpeming won the 800 (2:00.65) by more than ten full seconds.

Rapid River, again, squeezed out a four-point victory to repeat in D3. The squad clinched the meet in meet record fashion, winning the 1600-relay (3:34.52) with runner-up Bessemer placing second in the meet's final event.

Earlier the day Bessemer Speedboys 4 x 800 relay team accounted for another record with an 8:29.88.

2018

When Donnie James produced a triple sprint win (10.82 - 21.28 - 47.49) at the Oakland County Championships for Oak Park, he was asked if he was going to try the same thing at the D1 state meet. "Heck no," he responded. "I'm going faster there!"

James didn't disappoint, though he had to recover from an early surprise. In the 100 final, he lined up against Jalen Ware of Muskegon Reeths-Puffer, who led the heats at 10.76. And though James produced a PR 10.70, he was just as shocked as anybody when Erik LaBonte of Traverse City West streaked by at the finish to win in 10.66.

*Donnie James (right) and Matthew Moorer were just
0.05 apart at the finish of the D1 200.
(Peter Draugalis photo)*

After leading off an eighth-place effort in the 4x2, James captured the 400 in 47.14, leading both Marcus Montgomery of Saginaw Heritage (47.65) and Matthew Moorer of Ypsilanti Lincoln (47.79). Then came the 200, and James ran 21.20 into a headwind for a new meet record.

For all those heroics, it would not be the day for Oak Park to unseat defending powerhouse East Kentwood. Not even close. The Falcons put together a 61-point effort to top Ann Arbor Pioneer (39) and Saline and Grand Blanc both at 37.

Perhaps the most stirring performance came from East Kentwood senior Trevor Stephenson, who won the best pole vault battle in state history, pressed hard the entire way by Saline's Eric Harris. Both made it over 16-0 without a miss. At a meet record 16-3½, Harris cleared, Stephenson passed. At a meet record 16-6½, they both cleared on their second attempts. At an outdoor state record 16-9½, Harris missed his second try, Stephenson made it. That gave Harris no choice but to pass to 17-½.

No one had ever seen a competition like it in Michigan. Two preps attempting the 17-foot barrier! Harris missed his one try and Stephenson all three, but they both ended the day as champions.

East Kentwood won with depth, having only two other winners. Logan Brown won his second straight shot with a toss of 57-1¾. Job Mayhue took the highs in 13.99, though a hamstring twinge kept him from the 300 hurdles final, an event he had the No. 1 seed in with his 37.15 performance at regionals.

It was a day of ones-upsmanship between the top two distance runners, Nick Foster of Pioneer and Cole Johnson of Rockford. At the cross country finals the previous fall, Foster caught a fading Johnson right before the line.

In the 4x8, Foster produced a magnificent come-from-behind anchor of 1:51.9 to give Pioneer a 7:45.64 win over perennial powerhouse Saline, while a far-back Rockford did not run Johnson. In the 1600, Johnson led for the better part of three laps before Saline's Anthony DeKraker and Foster passed him. But Johnson exploded on the final stretch, passing both on the inside to win with a 57.7 final lap. He topped Foster 4:08.47-4:08.64, with DeKraker at 4:10.35.

Then Johnson lined up for the 800 and outkicked Foster's teammate Netunji Paige, 1:53.11-1:53.41. In the 3200 it was all Foster. He needed a solid kick to win in 9:07.93 as three others broke 9:10. Johnson, not quite done, anchored his Rockford team to seventh in

the 4x4. Earlier in the season he had sped a 49.46 for 400—he didn't want to lose on the kick again.

In Division 2 at Zeeland, Coldwater captured the title with 60 points, no small thanks to its throwing crew, which went 1-2-3 in the shot, led by sophomore Dylan Targgart's 61-2. He also won the discus at 170-10. His brother Cole grabbed third in the shot and seventh in the discus.

With 36 points in the throws, Coldwater needed more to beat Zeeland East. Shuaib Aljabaly took the 1600 in 4:16.56 and finished third in the 3200 as Otsego's Alex Comerford dominated in 9:07.25. In between, Coldwater hurdler Adam Bailey was runner-up in the 300s behind Corbin DeJonge of Zeeland East (38.14).

Also notable was Thomas Robinson's sprint double. The Wyoming Lee senior won a windy 100 in 10.85 and came back with a 21.62 in the furlong. He ended his career with six state titles, after doubling the two previous years in D3.

Division 3 at Comstock Park saw Clare win by a mere two points over Berrien Springs. The Pioneers only had one winner, Noah Nivison in the discus at 156-7, but kept scoring when it counted.

Jackson Blanchard of Houghton Lake won a fine 14.23/37.79 hurdle double. Saugatuck junior Corey Gorgas owned the distances with his 1600 (4:15.74) and 3200 (9:17.32) victories. Logan Wells turned a nice double in consecutive races, anchoring Hart's 4x1 to a 43.83 win, and coming back minutes later to take the 400 in 48.89.

In Division 4 at Hudsonville, Kalamazoo Hackett won by 15 points over Sand Creek. Junior Heath Baldwin of Hackett captured the highs at 14.83w and the long jump at 22-2½w.

Sand Creek was propelled by the brilliant sprinting of junior Alec Muck, with wins at 10.98 and 22.02w. He also anchored the Aggies' third-place 4x1.

Upper Peninsula: Marquette scored a massive 110 points to beat Houghton in D1 in the clash at Kingsford. Clayton Sayen of Houghton made it a clean sweep of the dashes and then some, taking the 100 (11.47), 200 (23.19), 400 (51.25) and 800 (1:59.31), finishing his prep career with eight titles.

Ishpeming scored 100 on the nose to win D2—amazingly only winning one event, Hart Holmgren taking the long jump. However, it took depth, and six runner-up finishes certainly helped.

Bessemer pulverized D3 with 151 points, winning 10 events. It was the second-highest total in boys state history, after Ishpeming's 164 in D2 in 2015.

GIRLS HISTORY

It took many decades for girls track & field to reach equity with the boys, but it certainly wasn't for lack of interested athletes. In 1923 for instance, the first year of an indoor championship for Detroit girls, an astounding 500 girls entered! Sadly, girls athletics always took a backseat—usually to the boys—and were mostly forgotten in the difficult years of the Great Depression and World War II.

Here's a look at some of the steps along the way:

1913: While track & field for men and boys was booming across the nation, for females the sport barely existed. New York's all-female Vassar College hosted a field day for its student body beginning in 1895 and that was the extent of collegiate women's track. In Michigan, junior high school and elementary girls could sometimes compete in short sprints and a standing broad jump at a field day, and that was the extent of things. However, in 1913 one milestone was reached in the Great Lakes State.

On May 21, the women of Olivet College staged the first all-women's meet in state history. Organized by Marion Keese, the women's physical director of the college, the meet was quietly started at 3:30 a.m. because the men of the college had promised to mock the women. No starting pistol was used—to keep the noise level down and the men sleeping in their dorms. Adrian College won, three points ahead of the hosts. An athlete or two from Albion also competed. Vera Shrigley of West Branch was Adrian's big point-getter, with a win in the 100, second in the broad jump, and an anchor leg on the winning relay. Olivet's biggest star was Peggy Gordon of Traverse City, who was second in the 100 and also threw the shot 22-feet and the javelin 45-feet. A 220 was also contested, but no other events or results are known.

1922: This may have marked the first-ever meet in Michigan between girls from different high schools. On June 2, Bad Axe hosted the Huron County Championships and girls events were included. Sebewaing won, "taking practically every event."

1923: A milestone took place as the Detroit public schools offered the first city championship meets for girls, indoor and outdoors. We do know that 500 girls were entered in the indoor affair, which was organized by Lottie McDermott, supervisor of women's activities at the Detroit Department of Recreation. Outdoors, M. Peters of Northeastern won the 50-yard dash in 6 3/5 seconds, the mark lasting at least until 1928 as a meet record. Other events that were part of the championship slate: 75-yards, 60-yard hurdles, high jump, broad jump, baseball throw and 330-yard relay.

1924: Northern High won the Detroit crown, led by 50 dash winner Edith Clark in 6 4/5. St. Johns hosted a June high school meet for girls. In July, a Midwest women's meet was held on Detroit's Belle Isle, attracting clubs from as far away as Cleveland and Chicago. However, the runner-up team was Detroit Eastern's one-girl squad, Florence Wolf, who dominated the throws, winnng the shot (29-3), discus (74-6), baseball throw (200-3) and taking thirds in the javelin and basketball throw.

The Detroit Southwestern team at the first Detroit City championships for girls.

Said **C.**E. Brewer, Detroit's commissioner of recreation (Lottie McDermott's boss): "The old-fashioned idea that girls should not participate in the so-called 'violent' sports is becoming obsolete… Detroit has few known girl athletes because they have never had a chance to show what they can do. But there is certainly fine material here."

1926: New track programs for girls got started in Battle Creek, Benton Harbor and Croswell.

1928: On May 21, Niles hosted the first annual girls meet for athletes in Berrien and Cass counties. Niles won easily over Buchanan, Dowagiac and Three Oaks. Mildred Kalus of Three Oaks was written up as the star, though no events/times are available.

In Detroit on June 7, Northwestern won the city title. Virginia Anderson of Highland Park set a high jump record of 4-9, and Southeastern's Pauline Webster crushed the meet record in the 60-yard hurdles with her 8.4 (hurdle height unknown).

1934: On May 25, Battle Creek Lakeview won the Calhoun County championships over Athens, 29½-29. Homer placed third. The meet was held in conjunction with the boys competition. At the Sanilac County championships, an innovative format saw trophies go to the boys and girls team winners and a third trophy went to the best combined score. The headlines in the local paper gave all the glory to Deckerville's combined squad, beating Sandusky by one point. Sandusky didn't have any girl entrants.

The Great Depression and World War II nearly wiped out girls track from the state of Michigan. Never considered an essential activity, girls track virtually disappeared by the mid-1930s. After the war, small events emerged in scattered locations, usually intermural field day activities and meets aimed at elementary and junior high school girls. It wasn't until the 1960s that girls participation started becoming noticeable again.

1960s: Girls track started coming back, with the establishment of teams at various schools. At the same time, many of the very best talents found coaching and support in a growing club network. Among the prime movers in creating programs were Detroit TC (and later Michigan State) coach Jim Bibbs, Olympic hurdle champ Hayes Jones, Motor City Track Club's Richard Ford and Bettyre Robinson, Eastern Michigan coach Bob Parks, Red Simmons and Dick Beyst of the Wolverine Parkettes. All the same, the notion that girls track for high schools did not start until the MHSAA gave it the green light is not accurate. By the late 60s, dozens of schools sponsored girls track teams and participated in dual meets and invitationals. There were even some conferences, such as the Southern Thumb Association, that sponsored championship meets. In the Upper Peninsula, a girls state meet was organized a year before the MHSAA sanction.

1971: The MHSAA saw the writing on the wall. At the association's annual meeting in December, director Allen Bush said, "I anticipate there will be a fairly wide program for girls next year run on state-level competition… We're concerned with expanding programs for girls… We will advise [schools] to make preparations in their budgets for girls' sports in the coming years, planning for hiring of coaches, for one thing."

1972: In February, the Michigan Senate passed a bill allowing girls to compete on boys' teams in non-contact sports. While it languished waiting for approval from the House of Representatives, the MHSAA restated its opposition to mixed teams and instead pushed for more districts to add girls-only teams.

Critics took aim at the MHSAA's rules governing girls, which were couched in one-sided terms. Girls, for instance, were limited to "five practice or play periods per week including games or contests. Practice periods shall not exceed one and one-half hours in length per day." Bob Parks, who battled with the Ypsilanti district to add opportunities for girls, told the *Detroit Free Press* that rules like that made it difficult for girls to achieve excellence. Boys faced no such practice limitations.

At the same time, the Lansing district took the MHSAA to court over a case that started in tennis, arguing that girls should be allowed to participate on boys teams. Two Ann Arbor tennis players requested a court injunction, a legal move that was joined by Ypsilanti's Parks family.

Federal District Court Judge Damon Keith opened the door for girls with the April 26 injunction. As a result, the MHSAA ruled that girls could compete in any non-contact sports alongside boys. One of the early rules did not last long—that girls teams needed to have a female coach or faculty member supervising. Another gave girls more hoops to jump through while getting their required physical examinations.

Also in 1972, Detroit's Public School League brought back its girls championship after more than 40 years, and the Catholic League inaugurated its own championship. And on the college scene that spring Central Michigan University started the first collegiate program in the state under head coach Carole Howard.

The Early Stars of Girls Track

This is certainly not a complete listing, by any means, but we feel it is important to note who some of the high school pioneers were in girls track & field in Michigan.

Pam Bagian competing in the World Cross Country Championships senior race while still in high school.

Javelin thrower Louise Gerrish (Frank Hurley photo)

Pam Bagian (Wolverine Parkettes/Lincoln Park 1970): As a senior she ran 2:14.5 for 880-yards and 4:45.0 for 1500 to win a double at the Michigan AAU indoor meet in Ypsilanti. A few weeks earlier she ran 5:04.8 for the mile in New York at the AAU nationals.

Karen Buford (Motor City TC/Detroit Southeastern 1973): As a 9th-grader, she ran 6.8 for 60 yards at the Michigan AAU Indoor. In 1971, she ran a state record 6.5 for 50m.

Carolyn Coleman (Detroit TC/Ecorse 1970): Ran 6.7 for 60 yards in 1968, as well as 24.7 at the National Junior AAU 220.

Alfreda Daniels (Detroit Cass Tech 1973): Ran 6.5 for 60 yards, a long-standing state record, in 1972. Ran 11.6 for 100 meters at the Olympic Trials in '72.

Karen Dennis (Detroit TC/Detroit Chadsey 1967): Ran 24.8 at the Michigan AAU Indoor as a senior, and 24.4 at Michigan AAU outdoors. Fourth in National AAU Indoor 65. Later became the Ohio State head coach.

Louise Gerrish (Michigammes/Livonia Franklin 1966): As a high school sophomore, Gerrish placed third at the AAU Girls Nationals in the javelin, throwing a state record 144-8. The next year she won that meet at 141-10. She also placed third at AAU Indoor Nationals in the basketball throw (98-6). As a senior she placed third in the AAU Women's Nationals (160-10). State record of 163-10 in Cleveland 66.

Francie Kraker (Michigammes/Ann Arbor 1965): Won the girls 880 at the 1964 AAU Championships in California with a 2:17.4 performance, a time that was called a national high school record. In 1965, she clocked 2:12.6 and she later finished 5th in the AAU Senior Nationals. Competed in the 1968 Olympics in the 800, and four years later made it to the semifinals of the 1500 in the Munich Olympics, where she hit a PR of 4:12.76.

Debby Lansky (Wolverine Parkettes/Taylor Center 1971): In 1970 she won the AAU Junior Olympics in a meet record 9.9 for the 80-yard hurdles; she also anchored the record-setting 4x1 that year. Her 7.8 for the 60-yard hurdles stood for decades as the state record. As a senior in 1971, she clocked a state record 13.9. She ran in the 1976 Olympics.

Sue McLalin (Wolverine Parkettes/Redford Union 1972): Troubled with a serious case of scoliosis, McLalin sometimes competed in a back brace. At age 13 she set a state record for 13-year-olds with a 34-4 in the shot put. She was best as a long jumper, however. In 1971 she captured the AAU state title with a 17-5. As a senior she leaped 19-4½ to win the AAU Junior (Under 20) Nationals in Missouri after earlier placing 6th at the AAU Senior Nationals. As a frosh at Eastern Michigan, she placed 4th with an 18-9½ at the U.S.-Soviet Union indoor dual meet in Richmond, Virginia.

Lynn Olson (Lincoln Park 1972): Olson started dabbling in the racewalk as a frosh. She worked with noted walker Jeanne Bocci on technique. As a sophomore, she competed unofficially in the National AAU 10K, clocking 1:06:35. As a junior, she won the 1971 AAU Senior title in the exhibition mile walk in

7:53.8, an American Record in the new event. Her senior year she clocked 7:43.8 for the mile, just 8 seconds behind her coach's American Record. She also hit 7:06.0 for 1500m. As a frosh at Ferris State, she became the first woman to compete in the men's NAIA Nationals when she qualified for the 2-mile racewalk by winning the mile walk the first time it was held at the AAU National Indoor. She competed against 15 men.

Theresa Rulison (East Lansing/Wolverine Parkettes 1973): For one sparkling frosh season, Rulison emerged as a top half-miler. In the final event of an indoor pentathlon at Eastern Michigan, she ran 2:15.7 for 880y. At the state Junior Olympic qualifier outdoors, she qualified for both the 440 and the 880 (2:17.0). Deciding to focus on the half, she traveled to Knoxville for the 1970 AAU Junior Olympics, which she won in 2:12.4. The authors haven't found anything on her track career after that point. She later played basketball for Lansing Community College.

Florence Wolf (Detroit Eastern 1926?): Perhaps the first star of girls track in the state, Wolf could throw things. In 1923 she whipped a baseball 199-0 to win the event at the first Detroit city meet for girls. In 1924 she won three events against grown women in a meet on Belle Isle, and later won the baseball throw at a big meet at the state fairgrounds. In 1926, the summer of what probably was her senior year, she placed fourth in the AAU Nationals in the discus.

Francie Kraker was the best prep half-miler in the nation in 1964. She went on to make two Olympic teams and coached at the University of Michigan.

1972

A year before the MHSAA would approve a state meet for girls, coaches in the Upper Peninsula jumped the gun and held one of their own at Marquette High School on June 3. Coach Barb Krill's home team was ready, scoring in every event and piling up 67 points to defeat Iron Mountain by 21 in the 11-team field.

The individual star of the meet was Denise Redding of Gwinn, who won the long jump, the 50-yard dash and the 440 to put her team into third place.

1973

Long overdue, this year the MHSAA finally put together a girls state meet. While 6,000 fans filled Michigan State's Ralph Young Field for the Boys Class A State Championship, much smaller numbers would see history in the making down the road at East Lansing High School. There were 366 entrants, representing 119 schools, who would be the first-ever girls state meet competitors.

Competition at the state level in 1973 was an all-class affair with the first team title going to Lincoln Park. Skepticism certainly must have greeted the 366 enthusiasts, as media coverage was limited to a few short paragraphs in most newspapers, with summaries a scarcity.

The first state champions: Lincoln Park (photo courtesy of MHSAA)

Although the quantity was low at the onset, fans saw solid quality on display. This despite the fact that most of the participants at East Lansing were in their first season ever.

Detroit Cass Tech sent only one athlete to compete. Anita Lee set the example for future Technicians by winning the high jump (5-4) and the long jump (17-2¾).

Lincoln Park took two events en route to capturing the team trophy. Lynn Lovat earned first in the mile (5:23.6) and anchored the winning medley relay. Walled Lake Western kept the team championship in doubt the entire day before falling short of Lincoln Park by only 2½ points.

Clarkston High had the meet's outstanding athlete. Sue Latter won the 440-yard dash in 57.1 and the 880-yard run in a 2:17.7. In 1977, Latter went on to win the USA nationals in 2:03.8. In 1986, racing in Europe, she ran 2:00.31 for 800 and 4:23.93 for the mile.

Upper Peninsula: Defending champion Marquette made it official with another team win. Obviously, the success earned by the Pickford boys team carried down to the girls. Joanne Slater of Pickford became the meet's only double winner by capturing the 100 and 220-yard dashes.

1974

The 1974 girls state finals doubled to two divisions with interest increasing from girls throughout the state. Competitors were divided, with athletes of Class A and B schools meeting at Grand Rapids Houseman Field, while the smaller schools competed at Alma High School.

Anita Lee brought her Detroit Cass Tech teammates to Grand Rapids in 1974 and led the Technicians to the first of many team titles. Lee captured the long jump and the 80-yard low hurdles and was second in the high jump, scoring 23 of her team's 40 points. Walled Lake Western trailed again with 26½ points.

Despite this being only the second year for state championships, impressive marks were made at Houseman Field. Ypsilanti senior Sue Parks covered the half-mile in a sizzling 2:14.4; two years earlier she had clocked 2:07.9 for 800 at an AAU meet in Los Angeles.

Incidentally, the Parks family will be forever known as the first father/daughter state champs in Michigan prep history. Sue's father Bob, who became the longtime head track coach at Eastern Michigan University, won the Class B 440-yard dash in 1948 while competing for Howell High School. Sue followed her father into the coaching ranks, and is the current womens coach at Eastern Michigan University. The Parks combo undoubtedly pulled off the first father/daughter double in Division I track history when they led their respective schools to Mid-American Conference Championships in 1998.

Josephine Hobbs of Detroit Central was a double winner by taking the 100 and 220-yard dashes. Finishing second to Hobbs in both sprints was the 1973 champion in the 440 and 880-yard runs, Sue Latter of Clarkston.

One of the most exciting races of the day was the mile. Ninth grader Mary Ann Opalweski of Saginaw

MacArthur nipped Ann Forshee from Ann Arbor Huron at the wire in a fine 5:11.0. With this just the second year for the girls at the state level, records were a common occurrence. Only 1973 marks made in the long jump and 440-yard dash were safe from the record breakers.

The smaller schools met at Alma High School with Montrose easily capturing the C/D crown with 62 points. Schools from Mid-Michigan dominated the meet with Williamston, Bath, Haslett, and Fowlerville trailing Montrose.

The individual star of the C/D meet was Sue Bouck of Haslett, who matched the Class A-B best in the high jump and had the afternoon's best effort in the long jump with a leap of 17-10½. She placed second in the 80-yard hurdles, while posting the same time as first-place Linda Arnold of Grass Lake. Brenda Pryc paced Montrose to the team championship with a win in the 440-yard dash. She held off the busy Bouck with a time of 59.4.

Media coverage for the girls improved marginally in the second year of track but still lacked the respect given for the traditional boys state final meets. Participation in girls track proved popular enough that beginning with the 1975 season, state championships for the females would be held in all four classes.

Upper Peninsula: Gwinn High School hosted the third running of the UP girls finals. Although there were no notable individual achievements, the battle for the Class A-B team title was competitive. Escanaba edged L'Anse to win in Class C while Crystal Falls won in Class D. Interest in girls track took an upswing in the UP as 42 schools fielded teams, 14 more than competed in 1973.

1975

Interest in girls track continued to grow in 1975 with four sites playing host to the state championships. Livonia Franklin hosted the Class A meet, with Detroit Cass Tech repeating as state champs. Walled Lake Western earned second-place for the third-consecutive season.

Josephine Hobbs repeated as the dash champ in Class A, but headwinds and a slow track led to slower times than the preceding year. Anita Lee again paced the Technicians with victories in the high jump (5-6) and long jump (17-8).

Kim Hatchett of Pontiac Central posted a good time for the era by skimming over the 30-inch 110-yard low hurdles in 14.7. Runner-up Walled Lake Western nearly broke the four-minute barrier in the mile relay with its 4:00.1. Sophomore Kathy Wilson of Bloomfield

Hills Andover began her three-year domination of the mile by winning in 5:10.5.

At the Class B meet in Grand Rapids, Mary Ann Opalewski of Saginaw MacArthur sped the four laps in 5:04.5. The 4-10 sophomore stole the show as the 2,000 fans in attendance came to their feet in a standing ovation when she crossed the finish line. Muskegon Catholic and Ionia shared team honors, each scoring 35.

Ionia's Pam Moore won the only first place for either of the co-champs when she took the 220-yard dash in 25.5. Holt's Jane Pearce capped her three-year dominance in the shot put by tossing the shot 43-7. This mark for the eight-pound shot would stand until the weight of the shot was changed in 1980 to four kilos (8 lb, 13 oz).

Beth Brunn of Utica cleared 5-7 to establish the best all-class mark for the high jump. Rochelle Collins was also a standout performer at Houseman Field with wins in the 440 (58.0) and the 880-yard run (2:16.9). The freshman middle distance ace would dominate these two events for the next four years by racking up seven state titles.

In Kalamazoo at Class C, Bath captured the title by edging defending titleholder Montrose, 55 to 50. Mary Hull led the Bees with her 5:20.5 victory in the mile and ran a leg on the winning mile relay. Debbie Hughes of Fowlerville was a double champion in the 220 (25.0) and the long jump (17-2¼).

Linda Merrifield won her second-straight 100-yard dash title for Williamston and anchored the winning 440-yard relay quartet.

In Class D, Sue Behnke ran to victories in the 100 and 220-yard dashes, and was also a member of the winning 440-yard relay team, leading Battle Creek St. Philip to the championship. St. Philip's total of 67½ points easily outdistanced second-place Centreville, who had 42½.

Freshman Linda Arnold had a good day for Grass Lake with her 17-0 first-place in the long jump and a leg on the winning 880-yard relay. Concord's Debra Ramsed ran the quarter mile in the good time of 58.5.

Upper Peninsula: About 1,000 athletes converged on Marquette's Athletic Field for the combined running of the Boys and Girls UP championships. Escanaba and Marquette again finished 1-2 in the girls division. Records fell in 10 of the 13 events.

L'Anse won 5 of the 13 events to coast to an easy victory in Class C where records were shattered in 12 of the 13 events. Crystal Falls repeated in Class D.

1976

Detroit Cass Tech successfully defended its title by the narrowest of margins over a tightly-bunched field. Only five points separated the champions from the fifth-place finisher. Runner-up Detroit Pershing, at 34 points, trailed Cass Tech by only one point.

Performances vastly improved in the fourth state championship for the girls, with records falling in most events in all classes. Detroit Central's Josephine Hobbs defended her dash titles by winning the 100 and 220 for the third-straight year.

Ella Willis led Detroit Pershing to a second-place finish with a victory in the 880-yard run in a speedy 2:14.9. She would best be remembered for running a distance more than 56 times longer than her half-mile state title. Ellis, for many years, dominated women's long distance running in the state and won the prestigious Detroit Free Press Marathon three times. She won her first marathon, the 1975 Motor City Marathon on Belle Isle, while still in high school, clocking 3:13:51.

Kathy Wilson of Bloomfield Hills Lahser, cut her own record for the mile down to 5:06.4, thanks in part to the encouragement of her hometown fans, as the Class A state meet was held on her home track. Other impressive performances set at the A meet included a 11:16.9 by future Wisconsin distance ace Sally Zook of Traverse City in the two-mile, and a quick 56.1 time in the 440 by Ruth Hubbard of Walled Lake Western.

Sharon Upshaw of Mt. Clemens led the field events competitors with a good throw of 45-½ in the shot put, while Cynthia Tett from Grand Rapids Ottawa Hills sailed past the 18-foot mark in the long jump.

In Class B, perhaps as fine a field ever assembled graced the facilities at Comstock Park. Holt beat Muskegon Catholic Central with Johanna Matthyssen leading the way. The Holt senior ran the 440 in 56.1, a record that would remain in the record books for 34 years. Matthyssen also anchored two record-setting relays for the Rams. The 880-yard relay set a new standard at 1:45.0, and the mile relay likewise entered the record books in 4:03.0

Rochelle Collins of Immaculata lowered her own 880 record to 2:14.3, the best time posted in any class. Mary Ann Opalewski moved up from the mile to add the two-mile record to her list of honors, posting another all-class state best of 11:00.0 in the two-mile run. With her victory in the 110-yard hurdles, Janet Cook would be the only state track champion from Novi high for 35 years.

The field event sensation of the day, and one of the best in girls state history, was Beth Brunn of Utica. Brunn had the day's best long jump effort for all classes with her leap of 18-5¾. The Utica junior then had enough bounce left to set a new high jump record at 5-9, pushed by some of the best competitors ever.

Julie Hyde of Caro and Terri Johnson of Muskegon Catholic each jumped 5-8, a height that would have won the vast majority of all state titles in the event.

In Class C, sprinter Linda Merrifield led Williamston by winning both short sprints and anchoring the Hornets 440 relay team to a record. Only a second place in the long jump prevented Merrifield from sweeping a rare four firsts. Valerie Horne of runner-up Montrose prevented the Merrifield sweep by leaping 17-1¾ to win the long jump, less than 2 inches better than the Williamston star.

In Class D, Pam Brown won a pair of events to lead Morenci to the crown over Battle Creek St. Philip. Brown won the high jump at 5-7 and captured the 440 for the winners. Janet Hale of Maple City Glen Lake won the sprint double for the Lakers. Class D's most impressive performer had to be Abbie Currier of Lake City. Currier had the day's best throw in the discus in any class at 121-6 and almost hit the 40-foot barrier in the shot put. Earlier in the season Currier led Lake City to an undefeated season in basketball. She received a full-ride basketball scholarship to the University of Michigan where she became the U of M's all-time leading scorer by the time she graduated.

Upper Peninsula: Escanaba chalked up 91 points, the most ever earned by any team in UP history, to easily win its third-straight championship. The Eskimos won ten of the fourteen events with Nancy Gage and Jean White doubling. Marion Winnen led Ishpeming Westwood to the girls Class C championship. Winnen set a new record in the 880-yard run and placed second in the 100 and 220-yard dashes behind Newberry's Lori Bouchard.

Pickford's Lady Panthers won the girls UP title as well, with only 25 years to go to match the boy's consecutive winning streak.

1977

A golden era for girls track may well have gotten under way with the start of the 1977 season. For the next few years girls track would have a run that would propel Michigan high school tracksters up among the best in the country. Many records set would survive for decades.

Flint Central won the Class A title at Bloomfield Hills with 33 points, three more than Walled Lake Western. Only three events in Class A would not see a record fall. The next two years would see Delisa Walton of Detroit Mackenzie shatter two of those marks.

The future NCAA champion began her sophomore season in 1977 by winning the first of her three titles in the 440. Her winning 57.0 would prove to be, for

Walton, a very modest clocking. Miriam Boyd of Port Huron began a three-year winning streak in the girls two-mile run with a record 10:54.7. Kathy Wilson, of Bloomfield Hills Lahser, impressively concluded her three-year dominance in the mile run. Wilson, with a new record time of 4:59.8, became the first Michigan prep girl to break five minutes in the mile run at the state finals. (Lincoln Park's Lynn Lovatt was the first to break 5:00 in any meet, with her 4:56.0 at the 1971 Junior Nationals.)

The champs from Flint Central entered the record-breaking fray by winning the 880-yard relay in 1:41.9. Renee Turner equaled the 110-yard low hurdle best with a 14.5. Walled Lake Western lowered its record in the mile relay to 3:57.5.

One of the great stories to emerge out of the 1977 title chase had to be that of Molly Brennan of Waterford Mott. Although she would tie the meet record in the 220 at 24.5, it would be off the track and in the classroom where Brennan would make prep history. Following a great track and academic career at Michigan State, Brennan became the first state champion from Michigan to become a Rhodes Scholar.

Three field event records took a tumble. Cynthia Tett of Grand Rapids Ottawa Hills became the first to break the 19-foot barrier in the long jump with her record leap of 19-½ inch. Cathy Ballard of Mt Clemens L'Anse Creuse improved the high jump record to 5-8 and Lansing Waverly's Sheila Warren became the new record holder in the discus with a heave of 123-6.

Athlen Bowles of Detroit Henry Ford matched the 100-yard record at 11.0 while the last record to fall in 1977 came in the 440-relay, won by Mt Clemens in 48.2.

In Class B, Muskegon Catholic won in Comstock by eleven points over co-runners up Hastings and Fenton. Terri Johnson and Sue Bordeaux led Muskegon Catholic's charge, each hauling home three first-place medals. Bordeaux won the 100-yard dash for the Crusaders, and then teamed up with Johnson and two other teammates to win the 440 and 880 relays in meet records.

Johnson, who would later be an SEC champion for Alabama, tied the high jump record with the day's best leap of 5-9. She edged two-time champion Beth Brunn of Utica, who had to settle for a two-way tie for 3rd behind Johnson and second-place finisher Jodi Anderson of Saginaw Eisenhower. The Utica standout finished her career on a high note, however, by repeating in the long jump with a great 18-4¾, second only to her meet record posted a year earlier.

Anderson's teammate, Kelly Spatz, captured the mile, preventing cross-town rival Mary Ann Opalewski from winning the title four consecutive years. Spatz, who was soundly defeated by Opalewski at the regional, covered the distance in 5:08.4. Opalewski also finished second in the two-mile, but held on to her record.

Rochelle Collins continued her dominance in the middle-distances with another double victory. Collins bettered her previous best in the 880-yard run with a time of 2:12.5 and repeated as the 440-dash champ in a quick 56.8.

In Class C at St. Louis, North Muskegon emerged victorious with an 8-point edge over Detroit Lutheran West. The battle was highlighted by a tight scramble in the long jump. Judy Dalecki of Memphis and Debbie Dashke of East Jordan each had bests of 18-3½, but Dalecki had the better second jump. Four jumpers were able to better the 18-foot mark during the intense long jump competition.

Rogers City's Becky Klann ran a record-breaking 57.9 to win the 440. Sheri Anderson of Shelby won the discus at a record-breaking 121-1, while her West Michigan Conference rival, Annette Bohach of North Muskegon, began her three-year run as Michigan's best in the shot put. The 440-relay from Detroit Lutheran West claimed the final record at St. Louis.

Keela Yount, the defending mile champion, also took home honors in the 880-yard run. The DeWitt distance ace later became the head women's track coach at Central Michigan University.

In Class D, Brenda Johnson won both short sprints and anchored the winning 880 relay for team champion Grass Lake. Four records were set as Renee Naert of Akron-Fairgrove threw the shot 42-3½ inches, Donna Whitehead of Leelanau School won the long jump at 17-1¾ and Mt. Pleasant Sacred Heart took the mile relay in 4:10.7.

The meet's most impressive performance belonged to Lake City's Abbie Currier, who had the day's best throw in all classes by winning the discus at 130-9, a mark that would not be topped for 25 years.

Upper Peninsula: Marquette was able to finally dethrone Escanaba at the A-B track finals on its home oval. Coach Barb Crill was awarded the first-place trophy as a going away present in her last year. Marquette's mile relay team posted a mark of 4:07.9, a time that wasn't challenged in the decades following.

Becky Drake of Kingsford was the individual star, setting three records, including an 18-3 in the long jump. One other record was set when Stephenson's 880-relay team buzzed around the track in 1:48.4.

Janet Pratt won the 100 and 220-yard dashes to lead Rudyard to the girls Class C title. Connie Miettenen and Wanda Darling led Republic-Michigamme to its first-ever track title in Class D.

1978

Could there have ever have been a better array of talent than was assembled in Brighton for the 1978 girls state championships? Perhaps the following year would top this field, but only because many of the talented performers of 1978 on the track were juniors.

Headlining the action in Class A were a pair of speedsters from the Motor City who will long be remembered amongst the all-time best. Delisa Walton shattered the state record for the 880 with her 2:07.7. It would be the fastest two-lapper by a Michigan prep for the next 29 years. She followed up her smashing half-mile performance with an equally dazzling 440.

The Mackenzie junior dashed the one lap in 54.5, a mark that would last as a record for 33 years.

Of her improvement from the previous year, Walton said, "I wasn't strong last year. Then I developed my strength and my speed came automatically with it."

Walton had plenty of help from her teammates as Detroit Mackenzie easily took team honors with 41 points. Carman Rivers assisted the cause by taking the 220-yard dash and placing second in the 100. Walton joined Stag relay members Mira Jones, Melaine Tillman and Kimberly Watts to set yet another record with their 3:55.5 clocking in the mile relay.

Kim Turner of Detroit Mumford made her state debut a successful one by dethroning defending champion Renee Turner in the 110 hurdles with a 13.9.

Miriam Boyd of Port Huron set another record that was not surpassed for 18 years with her 10:36.8 in the 8-lapper. Boyd still had enough left to hop back on the track and polish off her competition in the mile with a 5:04.4.

Delisa Walton winning the national collegiate title In the 800 as a Tennessee frosh in 1980. (photo courtesy of Tennessee athletics)

Elaine Jones of Detroit Chadsey led three other runners across the finish line in the 100-yard dash under the previous record time of 11.0. However, winds were too strong for Jones' time of 10.8 to be accepted as a new record.

The lone mark to fall in the field events went to Josephine Mask of Lansing Sexton. The winner of the shot put hurled the discus a record 130-3. In winning the shot put, she had defeated cross-town rival Evelyn Johnson of Lansing Everett. Johnson' third-place medal in track was one more than her big brother ever won on the cinders—he turned out to be a decent basketball player, though—Earvin "Magic " Johnson.

In Class B at Otsego, UTEP-bound Rochelle Collins concluded her career at Detroit Immaculata in brilliant fashion. She not only won the 880 for the fourth consecutive year, but led her team to the team Class B championship. Immaculata just nipped Holt, 33 to 32.

Collins set a new meet record each time she won the state title. Her 2:11.1 in 1978 held up for decades as the Class B/D2 best. She nearly set another mark with her win in the 440. Her 56.3 trailed Johanna Matthyssen's 1976 record run by one-tenth of a

second. Oddly enough, it was that race where Collins, who placed second to Matthyssen, incurred her only loss at the state finals.

Lori Bennett, of Livonia Ladywood, flirted with the five-minute barrier in the mile run with a 5:00.3. Kim Willis of Southgate-Aquinas became the other new record holder, skimming over the 110-yard hurdles in 14.2

The Class C meet held in Haslett featured a pair of defending state champs. Muskegon Catholic, the 1977 Class B title holder, dropped down in enrollment and was paired off against cross-town rival North Muskegon, the defending State C champion.

Sue Bordeaux led the Muskegon Catholic Crusaders to victory, winning the 100 and 220-yard dashes and running a leg on the 880-yard relay that set a meet record of 1:44.8. That relay proved to be the turning point of the meet. Muskegon Catholic and North Muskegon were each battling for the lead as the relay teams blasted off following the gun. The Crusaders just edged North Muskegon at the tape with both teams easily under the previous record. However, he Norsemen received a crushing blow to their chances for a team title when were subsequently disqualified for cutting off a trailing team.

The two rival teams battled again later in the 440-yard relay, with a similar outcome. MCC and North Muskegon were each clocked in 49.9, with Catholic winning the lean at the tape. The Crusaders set this record with their speedster Bordeaux watching the action from the sideline. Rules at the time limited competitors to participate in only three running events. The Norse did have their shining moments with a pair of records set by Junior Annette Bohach in the weight events.

Bohach hurled the discus a new meet best of 127-0 and established a state record in the shot put. Her heave of 46-6 not only established a Class C best for the 8-pound ball, but was also the best toss thrown all-time in any class.

Beth Veldhoff of Blissfield won a unique double. She set a new meet record in the 880-yard run at 2:18.9 and took honors in the long jump for the Royals. Other records came in the 110-yard low hurdles and both distance runs. Jill Anderson made the home folks happy, as the Haslett native ran over the barriers in 14.7. Beth Lynn of Edwardsburg won the mile in 5:17.9, while Nora Green of Shepherd covered twice the distance in 11:16.1. Trailing both record setters was Melanie Weaver of Mason County Central.

In Class D in Lansing, winning a pair of firsts in the weight events was future Olympian Penny Neer of North Adams. With six records tumbling, one could easily assume that Neer would be one of the record setters. Not the case, however. Neer, who in 1985 would hurl the discus 201-4, had not as yet mastered the art of spinning while in high school. Her standing throw of 126-1 was good enough for the Class D title, adding to her earlier shot title.

The most eye-catching win belonged to Northport high jumper Kaye Leighton. The sophomore had the day's best leap in the high jump in any class at 5-8¾. Brenda Johnson won both sprints, including a record-breaking 11.3 in the 100-yard dash, to lead Grass Lake to the team title.

Johnson also anchored the 880-yard relay team to victory in a record time of 1:46.2, another mark that lasted for more than 30 years. Cindy Arnold also played a major role in the Warriors' victory by winning the 110-yard low hurdles in 15.0.

Another double winner was Mason County Eastern's Maria Shoup. The freshman took the 440 in 58.7 and then traveled the 880 in a record-breaking 2:20.1. Shoup would have a brilliant prep career for the Cardinals, winning 10 first-place medals, a number that would not be exceeded in girls track for thirty-years.

Upper Peninsula: Marquette won six events and broke four records, but still placed second behind Escanaba at the Class A-B finals in Marquette. Beth King's winning time in the 800-meter run of 2:22.0 would stand until 1999. Marquette's winning 1:46.6 in the 880 relay would last even longer.

Although falling short of her record jump, Becky Drake's 18-0 was easily the best performance of the day. Negaunee easily captured team honors in Class C. Connie Erickson won the throwing events to lead the Lady Minerettes. Engadine would win its only girls championship in Class D. Vicky Thomas of Engadine and Wendy Darling of runner-up Republic-Michigamme each took home three first-place medals to lead individual action.

1979

Action again sizzled on the tracks. However, temperatures that hovered near the 90-degree mark on the all-weather surfaces precluded the setting of any distance records for the girls. Many runners had to be treated for heat-related ailments.

In Class A at Brighton the competition was keen in the hurdles with Detroit Mumford's Kim Turner crushing East Lansing's Judi Brown in a meet record, 13.6 to 14.2. Turner also joined teammates Angela Sibby, Darlene Johnson and Lisa Madison to set a new record for the 880-yard relay at 1:41.4. Amazingly, both Turner and Brown would both later win Olympic medals. Brown, an NCAA champion for Michigan State would take the silver in the 400 hurdles at the '84

Olympics, and four years later Turner would capture the bronze in the 100 hurdles.

Kim Turner won two state titles. She would become an Olympic bronze medalist.

Port Huron's Miriam Boyd won the mile in 4:57.4, while Lisa Larsen of Battle Creek placed a distant fifth in 5:07.2. Larsen would prove to be the hard luck Olympian hopeful not once, not twice, but three times. In the 1984, 1988 and 1992 Olympic Trials, Larsen, a Boston Marathon winner, finished fourth.

Yet another 'late bloomer' that placed 4th in the mile run was Rochester's Jill Washburn. After taking her distance talents to Michigan State, she would move up in distance and set a Big 10 record in the 10,000.

It was a banner year for Flint Northern. The Lady Vikings added the track championship to their earlier state title earned in basketball. The Vikings carried a narrow lead over Detroit Mumford and Detroit Mackenzie entering the mile relay and responded to the challenge with a meet record time of 3:51.6.

The McGee twins, Pam and Paula, along with Levy String and Tonya Lowe, made up the record foursome. Pam McGee, who also won the shot, would later matriculate to Southern California, where she and Paula would lead the Lady Trojans to national prominence in women's basketball. In June of 2017 Pam's son Javale McGee played a key reserve role in leading the Golden State Warriors to the NBA title.

Delisa Walton continued her heroics on the Brighton track. The Detroit Mackenzie speedster repeated her double win earned the previous year by blazing to victories in the 440 and 880-yard runs. Walton ran the second fastest 880 time in the pre-2000 era with her 2:11.5. Pushing Walton to the tape was Sue Frederick of Ann Arbor Huron, running 2:11.9 in second.

Said Walton, "I strided the first lap and with 220 left I felt her on my heels. I started to pick it up then, but when I made the last curve I saw her right behind me. I thought it would be easier this year, but it wasn't."

Frederick would become a record-setter at Michigan and would win the Big 10 1500 in 1983. After her marriage, Sue Frederick Foster would return to her alma mater and take over the reigns as the women's cross country coach in Ann Arbor.

Lorri Thornton zoomed out to a distance of 19-7 to win the long jump. Elaine Jones of Detroit Chadsey won both sprints to join Boyd, Walton and Turner as double winners. The meet did produce one real oddity that occasionally occurs in track & field. Six cleared 5-5½ in the girls high jump with no ties. Rhonda Filius of Mona Shores won; the places were decided on misses.

In Class B at Houseman Field in Grand Rapids, Michelle Priefer figured in four first-place finishes for state champion St. Joseph. She won both hurdle events and ran a leg on record-breaking 440 and 880-yard relay teams. The Lady Bear's time of 49.1 for the 440-yard relay would survive until the start of the next millennium.

The two-mile run proved troubling, both to the girls and the meet officials. Concerned for the safety of the runners after three girls had passed out because of high temperatures, officials lost track of the lap count. Cheryl Scheffer of South Lyon and Lisa Last of Alma each had to run an extra lap. The official 11:12.9 was Scheffer's split at eight laps.

At Class C in Cassopolis, six records were broken and another tied. North Muskegon won the trophy 45-38 over Shepherd and joined fellow West Michigan Conference foe Mason County Central in setting three records that lasted for many years.

Annette Bohach hurled the eight-pound ball 48-6 to set an all-time best for all classes. This would prove to be the last year for the eight-pound shot implement. Bohach left little doubt that she could throw the 4kg college ball as well. At the Junior National meet two weeks later that she won with a 47-9.

Melanie Weaver of Mason County put herself in the record book with her double in the distances. A valedictorian and future Michigan star, Weaver won the mile in 5:01.0 and posted the day's fastest time for all classes in the two-mile. Her 10:52.2 lasted 34 years in Class C/D3, while her mile time would survive for 23 years.

The following Saturday at the Detroit Free Press Invitational, Weaver dueled with three-time Class A champ Miriam Boyd of Port Huron. Only a stride separated these two for the first six laps with Boyd setting the pace, with a confident and relaxed Weaver comfortably settled in second. Inexplicably, Boyd dropped out of the race, leaving Weaver alone in first where she finished in a career best of 10:42.5.

Other records bettered in the Class C meet were set by the Portland mile relay team at 4:07.0 and by sprinter Rochelle Bostic of Royal Oak Shrine, who sprinted 11.3 and 25.2.

At Class D in Grand Blanc, no records were set, but a major milestone was reached. For the first time in state history, a meet was held in meters. This would ultimately result in all meets being contested at the metric distances beginning with the 1982 season.

Indian River Inland Lakes won its only state championship in track with a 64-52 victory over Mason County Eastern. MCE's Maria Shoup, however, stole the show by winning four individual events. The future Western Michigan University sensation won the hurdles, the 880-yard run and the long jump to highlight the day.

This marked the first year where the girls were able to run in two hurdle events with the addition of the 220/200 low hurdles. Shoup matched the day's best time for the 200-meter lows with her 29.0, even though she only had a slight break after winning the 880-yard run. She took on all comers at the Free Press meet a week later, easily crossing in first before finding out she had been disqualified for running out of her lane.

Maria Shoup dominated the hurdles in high school. At Western Michigan, she won five MAC titles.

Upper Peninsula: The girls from Kingsford joined the Flivver boys as team champions. A new rule raised havoc for many of the runners at the meet in Marquette. Rigidly enforcing a new no-false start rule, eight runners were disqualified. Even the officials were in disagreement over the strict interpretation. Working his 20th year as an UP starter, head starter Gildo Canale overruled a false start issued by his assistant starter, provoking a sharp disagreement.

Although a pair of records was overlooked at the boys UP finals, an alert citizen from Negaunee eventually found a metric conversion book. Although not recognized as a meet record at the time, the 5-3¼ in the high jump by Linnea Laurilla from Negaunee was recognized a year later.

One of the UP all-time great track athletes completed her career in style. With her win in the long jump, Becky Drake of the victorious Flivvers became the first UP athlete to win one event four years in a row. Drake's victories in the 100 and 400 give her nine UP individual championships and she barely missed out on her tenth. Given but only a few minutes to rest after her win in the 400 meters, a tired Drake had to settle for second in the high jump. The UP Hall of Famer would take her all-around athletic skills to the golf course where she won the Upper Peninsula Ladies Golf Association championship four times. The Kingsford squad eventually boasted a pair of UP Hall of Famers. Hurdles champion Chris St. Louis was inducted into the UP Hall of Fame in 2002.

Negaunee's Lady Minerettes returned to the winner's circle in Class C, taking eight out of the 15 events and placing second in four others. Norway qualified only seven girls for the Class D finals, but coach Bob Giannunzio's runners recorded an easy victory by scoring 48 points. Norway's sprinters were so strong that they swept the first three places in the 100-meter dash and won all three relays. Linda Grodeski of the winning Lady Knights became the first UP girl to break 60 seconds in the 400-meter run.

1980

Flint Northern decimated the field at the Class A state finals on Grand Rapid's Houseman Field track, defeating Pontiac Central by 43 points. Tonya Lowe paced the talented Vikings to their second-straight title with wins in both hurdles and legs on two winning relay teams. Lowe would go on to earn honors while competing for Kentucky as the SEC athlete of the year in 1984. Northern swept the hurdle events and captured its sixth title of the day when Levy String passed the tape first in the 880-yard run in 2:14.8.

Lowe clocked a wind-aided 13.6 in the hurdles and also set a 220-yard low hurdle meet record with a 28.0. Northern's depth was so impressive that teammate Judy Tucker finished second to Lowe in a quick 14.1.

Tonya Lowe starred at Kentucky after her Flint Northern days. She made the semis of the 100 hurdles at the 1984 Olympic Trials.

Joining Lowe as the meet's outstanding individual was Kori Gifford of Bloomfield Hills Andover. She sped the 100-yard dash in 10.9 for one title, long jumped 18-11 for another, and ran a record-breaking 24.5 to capture her third of the day. Gifford nearly became the only performer in girls Class A history to win four individual titles in a single year by placing a respectable third in the 440. Gifford alone totaled 36 points, good enough to propel Andover to a third-place finish in the team competition.

Michelle Pfeiffer became the only state track champion in Davidson's school history with a 136-7 in the discus. Delores Bennett of Pontiac Central, second in the discus, led a 1-2 Pontiac sweep in the shot put with a record 44-8¼.

Mary Brunn edged defending champion Rhonda Filius on fewer misses at 5-7, joining her sister Beth as a state high jump champion for Utica. Jenny Weil of East Lansing romped home a winner in the two-mile run in an impressive 10:59.9.

At Class B in Sturgis, Grand Rapids South Christian prevented a sweep for Flint Beecher. Christian rode the back of distance ace Joan DeMaat to turn back the challenge of Beecher and win by a slim two points.

Girls performances had begun to level off after the great quality turned out by Michigan schools in the late 1970s. Although good performances were posted in Sturgis, only one record was set and another mark equaled.

Joan DeMaat, with a winning 4:57.9, cracked the five-minute barrier in the mile run. The ace of the Grand Rapids Christian team came back later to take the 800 in 2:17.9. The other Eagle first place couldn't have come at a more opportune time. Trailing going into the day's final event, the Christian foursome came through in clutch fashion to win the 4x4 and the team title by a scant two points.

Flint Beecher was able to match the meet record in the 800-meter relay with a 1:43.8. The Lady Bucs notched their other victory of the day by breezing home victorious in the 400-meter relay in 49.1.

Pallastean Harris of Montrose and Monica Williams of Port Huron joined DeMaat as double winners. Harris captured both short dashes while Williams dominated in the hurdles. Laurie Rogers of Saline matched her winning 5-7 from 1980 in defending her high jump championship.

The Class C meet in Cassopolis would be the last championship meet where the girls had to compete separately. The boys C teams were at Middleville. The next year they would both compete at Clare. North Muskegon won its third title in four years. Coach Karel Bailey's Norsewomen got just one first-place medal. Cindy Guy won the 100-yard dash, but the team placed in eight other events in defeating Detroit Lutheran West by ten points.

The highlight of the day came in the high jump. Ellie Hayden of Capac set an all-class record by winning at 5-11½. Beth Veldhoff of Blissfield, the 1978 long jump champ, set a new standard with a leap of 18-4¾.

Detroit Lutheran West matched Muskegon Catholic's 1978 best of 49.9 in the 440-yard relay. In the 220 hurdles, Karice Loveberry of Quincy lowered the meet record to 29.4.

In Class D, a tight battle was waged for the trophy with Ann Arbor Greenhills posting a narrow 42-41 win over Athens. Maria Shoup of Mason County Eastern won both hurdle races to give the future MVP of the Mid-American conference a total of eight state titles over three years. It took a record-setting jump from Sue Steeby of Michigan Lutheran Seminary at 18-3 to prevent Shoup from capturing yet another crown.

Andrea Kincannon lowered the best in the 200 meters to 25.6. Shoup's time of 14.8 in the 100-meter hurdles also was a meet record.

Upper Peninsula: Julie Drake succeeded older sister Becky as the individual star at Marquette. Only a second-place in the 400-meter dash prevented the Kingsford star from sweeping four events. Despite's Drake's heroics, Escanaba cruised to the Class A-B title, eight points ahead of runner-up Kingsford. Brenda Teague of Gwinn sailed 5-5 in the high jump for perhaps the day's single best performance.

The Merrick sisters led the Negaunee Lady Minerettes to their third-straight Class C championship. Jill Merrick captured the 1600-meter run for the fourth-straight year while twin sister Jan won the 200-meter

dash and long jump. The Merricks teamed up to collectively win 12 first-place medals during their prep career.

Followers of Norway High School will not soon forget the 1979-80 school year. The Lady Knights joined the boys football team as state champs for the entire state in winning the girls Class D basketball championship. Norway's track squad dominated the relays and short sprints to again repeat as UP girls champs. One of the stars of the state championship basketball squad put her name into the UP track record book: Joan Casanova set the 400 standard of 59.2.

1981

Flint Northern made it three in a row by again dominating action at Flint's Guy Houston Stadium. The Viking girls romped home first with 67 points, 32 more than Detroit Chadsey. Judy Tucker capped a near-perfect high school career by taking the 220-yard low hurdles in 28.7 and leaping 5-9 to set a meet mark in the high jump.

Tucker and teammate Leteia Hughley finished up with the super enviable record of never having participated in a losing track meet or a losing basketball game. Tucker won her hurdle race, even though she was relegated to run in a slower heat based on her regional performance. She teamed up with Hughley, Joanna Childress and Terri Barber to capture the 400-meter relay. Hughley took an individual title by leaping 18-8 in the long jump.

Cathy Fitzpatrick of Muskegon Mona Shores defeated a stellar field in the 100-yard dash in a meet record 10.8. Fitzpatrick, whose father Jerry was the 1956 Class A long jump champion, defeated future Big 10 champion Vivian McKenzie of Detroit Mumford. Elaine Jones, McKenzie's future teammate at Iowa, defeated both of them in the 220 in 24.6. Jones capped her day by blasting away the field in the 440-yard dash to win in 55.9.

The third record to fall during the day went to the mile relay foursome from Ann Arbor Pioneer, who sped the four laps in 3:51.3. Future Big 10 champion Kelly Graham covered the 110-yard low hurdles in 13.7 to just miss the meet record. Her 28.9 over the 220-yard timbers fell two tenths of a second short of the time posted by Tucker in the previous section.

In Class B in Sturgis, Flint Beecher earned the crown with 50 points, 14 more than Livonia-Ladywood. The Lady Bucs established the only records set.

Vivian McKenzie later starred for Iowa
(photo courtesy of Iowa Athletics)

Sharon Granberry's winning toss of 138-11 in the discus set a meet record, while the 800-meter relay of Leslie Arder, Geraldine Collier, Diane Wiley, and Sandy Harris set another mark at 1:42.7.

Joann Lanciaux of Fremont posted the day's fastest time in the mile with her 5:01.6. Martha Hans of Tecumseh was the meet's only double winner with victories in both hurdles. Karla Link of Fruitport won the high jump by an inch at 5-6 over Miss Basketball, Sue Tucker of Okemos.

At Class C in Clare, St. Louis won its first state title. Detroit Lutheran West's effort to capture both the boys and girls titles fell just short, but the Leopards did bring home the runner-up trophy. Janell Best led St. Louis to the title by winning the 400 (58.0) and 800 (2:19.7).

Whitehall matched Muskegon Catholic's record-setting 1978 effort in the 800m relay. The Viking foursome of Yvette Hunter, Michelle Cox, Tracey Brandel and Pam Sheesley posted a time of 1:44.3.

The only record to topple came when Mendy Matuzak of Lincoln-Alcona heaved the shot 40-2. She became the second champion from Lincoln-Alcona to win the shot on the same day as classmate Nelson Hanson won the same event in the boy's meet.

In Class D, Maria Shoup concluded her brilliant career at Mason County Eastern with a pair of titles. Shoup breezed over the 220 hurdles in a record 28.9 seconds to complement her earlier record set in the

long jump. The future Olympic Trials qualifier in the 400 hurdles leaped 18-5 in the long jump to establish a meet mark that would stand for 17 years.

Upper Peninsula: Escanaba won its sixth A-B championship in nine years by piling up 72 points in Marquette. However, it was Brenda Teague from Gwinn who easily had the day's most impressive performance. Teague leaped 5-8¼ to set an all-time UP best in the high jump. Teague's jump was the third best mark ever attained in Class B on either peninsula, at that point the highest ranking in any event by a UP female athlete.

Gusty winds that were clocked in excess of 25 miles per hour negated any record-setting performances in the running events. Kingsford found the drop down from Class A-B to its liking as it won the Class C title.

Cedarville and Norway each netted 45 points to share the Class D crown. Sherri Lee was a workhorse for Cedarville as she netted first-place medals in the 800, 1600 and 3200-meter runs. Freshman Gwen Wilkie won the first of four 200-meter dash titles she would garner during her career at DeTour.

1982

Vivian McKenzie led Detroit Chadsey to its first state championship as the meet was held once again at Flint's Houston Stadium. McKenzie won both dashes and anchored two winning relay teams, the 800-meter and 1600 meter. Chadsey's winning time of 1:40.0 set a new standard for the 800-meter relay, one of three records McKenzie would help set. The winners dethroned three-time defending champion Flint Northern as the Vikings had to settle for the runner-up trophy.

In the 100 meters McKenzie nipped Jackie Jones of Detroit Cooley and defending champion Cathy Fitzpatrick of Muskegon Mona Shores by a tenth of a second in 11.7.

McKenzie came back later in the afternoon to win the 200 in 24.2 to tie the mark set in the morning preliminaries by Fitzpatrick. Future Big 10 champion Joyce Wilson of Warren Tower High School defeated a hobbling Fitzpatrick in the 400 meters.

Fitzpatrick, who was the Greater Muskegon record holder in all sprint events, suffered a quadriceps pull a few days before the state finals, but was still able to score 22 points against some of the best sprint competition in Michigan history.

Another standout was Kelly Graham of Westland Glenn. She won both hurdles, clocking fast times of 13.7 in the 100 meters and 29.4 in the 200 hurdles.

Kayla Skelly of Midland became a double winner by capturing both distance events. The future MAC champion at Western Michigan won the 1600 in a quick 4:59.0, and came back later in the afternoon to post a near record time in the 3200 (10:46.3).

Adding to the quality of the competition was 800-meter champion Kathi Harris of Walled Lake Central. Harris, who would be an NCAA place winner while performing for Louisiana State University, defeated a strong field in her specialty in 2:15.3. Fourteen years later Harris just missed making the 1996 Olympic team in becoming the second woman from Michigan to break the two-minute barrier. At 32 years of age Harris finished fourth at the Olympic Trials in the spectacular time of 1:59.28, less than a yard away from making the team. In 1997, Harris (under her married name of Rounds) stunned track followers by winning the national title, earning the former Walled Lake athlete a place at the World Championships in Athens.

Chris Boehmer of Lapeer West soared 19-6¼ on her opening jump to put away the field in the long jump competition, the second-best ever at the Class A meet.

The Class B meet at Houseman Field saw one of only four team ties ever. Mt. Clemens L'Anse Creuse and Oak Park battled to a 32-all tie at the Class B finals at Houseman Field in Grand Rapids. One milestone would pass with the running of this meet. It would be the last state final contested in yards.

The individual honor at the meet went to Martha Hans of Tecumseh. The lanky redhead broke the existing meet records in the 110 hurdles as well as the 220 lows. Hans, with a 14.4, cut 0.2 off the best in the 110s and lowered the 220 hurdles record to 28.8.

Missy Thompson of Ludington ran the fastest mile/1600 of the day by covering the four laps in 4:57.4 to set a new meet record. The other mark to fall came in the shot put with Lisa Wesley of Detroit Northern tossing the 4kg ball 41-0.

In Class C, Detroit Lutheran West became the first school to win both boys and girls state track titles in the same year. The Lutheran West girls won four firsts, piling up 45 points to 27 for runner-up Cassopolis. Donna Smith of Lutheran West played a part in all four wins by taking both short sprints and running a leg on the 400 and 800-meter relays.

Two records fell by the wayside, held for the first time at Bangor High School. Bullock Creek's Marge Albaugh pushed the shot out to 41-10¾, with Manchester's Kari Agin easily setting a new mark for the girls 200-meter low hurdles. Agin posted a time of 28.7 in the final year the event would be run.

Sophomore Deb Hartline garnered second-place Cassopolis' only first-place medal by winning the high jump in the day's best mark of 5-8. Ann Hammond

became the only track state champion in Ida High School history with her win in the 400 meters.

At Class D in Caro, Becky Klein led Fowler to its first title. Klein ran a leg on the second-place 800-meter relay team and took second in the 200 behind Andrea Kincannon of Grosse Pointe Liggett. Klein's specialty was the 400, where she twice had the opportunity to display her talents. She edged Kincannon in the 400 meters in 57.6, with both runners eclipsing the former record. Klein's time would hold up as the Class D best for 20 years. The Fowler star then capped her day by anchoring Fowler's winning 1600-meter relay.

Covert bettered its record in the 4x1. The foursome of Betty Wright, Janice Lewis, Lisa Lewis and Meriel Toliver blazed around the oval in 50.5. Bradley Nixon of Ann Arbor Greenhills was a double winner in Class D with wins in both hurdles.

Upper Peninsula: Jean Tolfa matched her brother's triple-winning effort from 1980 in leading Escanaba to the girls Class A-B championship. She notched firsts in the 100, 200, long jump and anchored Escanaba's winning 800-meter relay.

Jenny Baldwin won the 100, 200 and 400 for Houghton but Negaunee had too much depth in winning its fourth Class C crown in five years. Cedarville didn't have to share the crown in Class D in 1982, but it certainly had to share the limelight with Gwen Wilkie of DeTour. The sophomore sensation won three firsts, all events won in the fastest time in any class at the UP meet.

1983

Flint Northern returned to the winner's circle for the fourth time in five years, edging Benton Harbor 59 to 52 in Class A action in Jackson. Hard luck befell Benton Harbor in the 800-meter relay, misfortune that may have cost the Lady Tigers a state title. Coach Ed Watson's top-seeded foursome was leading heading into the final leg, but failed to complete the final pass. Flint Northern took advantage of Harbor's miscue to post the 10 points that had appeared headed for the despondent Benton Harbor crew.

Flint Northern's 1600-meter relay composed of Terri Barner, Monica Taylor, and twin sisters Marlene and Carlene Isabelle posted an all-time best in their specialty by winning in 3:49.5. Carlene Isabelle accounted for the champions' other first place with a win in the 800-meter run in 2:15.6.

The girls low hurdles were changed in 1983 to the present day 300 meters with Carolyn Ferguson posting an automatic record with her win. The Benton Harbor star posted a great 43.0, just nipping Karen Brown of Detroit Central who was credited with the same time.

The best performance in the field belonged to Karen Sapp of Temperance Bedford, who launched a winning 45-3.

For the first time since 1977 the Class A meet failed to produce a double individual champion. Angie Prince

Class A's first 300 hurdle champion:
Carolyn Ferguson of Benton Harbor in 43.0.

of Detroit Pershing came close, as she finished second behind Benton Harbor's Jeanan Langston in the 100. Prince was the 200-meter champion in 24.9. Sapp, likewise, nearly doubled her victory total, but her toss of 131-7 in the discus was second best to Jeanette Long of Kalamazoo Central. Long, who placed fourth in the shot put, won the discus at 134-1.

At Class B in Caro, Kathy Kost led Mt. Clemens L'Anse Creuse to the title by winning three events. L'Anse Cruse finished with 42 points in a tight battle with St. Joseph, who trailed with 39. Kost ran the 100 in 12.2, leaped 18-4¼, and covered 400 in 56.5.

Kim Adent paced three runners under the five-minute barrier in an exciting 1600-meters. The St. Joseph ace nipped Dexter's Kelly McKillen at the tape with a 4:56.5, just shy of the mile mark set a year earlier by Missy Thompson of Ludington. Thompson would finish fourth in 5:00.5, slightly behind third-place finisher Kelly Champaign. The Livonia Ladywood runner scored an easy win over McKillen and Adent in the 3200, winning in 11:00.1.

South Lake's Laurie Vultaggio, with her second-straight title, had the day's best time for all classes in the 800. Vultaggio's 2:13.8 won by more than five seconds. Sharon Granberry made it three in a row with her victory in the discus. The Flint Beecher star capped her final season for the Bucs by also nailing down her first state title in the shot put.

In Class C at Bangor, Carson City-Crystal failed to win a first place, but Coach Ted Galbraith's squad piled up enough points to win the title. The Eagles tallied 39 points to hold off late charging Burton-Bentley who totaled 35. Donna Donakowski of Dearborn Heights Riverside, the only entry from her school, was the individual standout with a clean sweep in the distance races.

Donakowski won the 1600 in 5:00.3, nearly eleven seconds superior to second-place Penny Pennington of Carson City-Crystal. The Dearborn senior moved to the top of the record books with her 2:16.3 win in the 800. Donna, the sister of All-American distance aces Bill and Gerard Donakowski, made the famed racing family additionally proud with her 3200 victory over defending champion Carrie Lautner of Cass City.

DeWitt held off Burton-Bentley by a slim 0.2 to set a new record for the 4 x 400. Donna Wright of Parchment added another record in the discus with her 135-7.

In Class D at Traverse City, Fowler gave the Lansing area three state champions in 1983 with a repeat title. In the tightest team race of the afternoon coach Kim Spalsbury's Eagles squeezed past Ann Arbor Greenhills, 58½ to 58.

For the third-straight year Fowler captured the meet's final event, the 1600-meter relay, and then looked over its shoulder to see if Greenhills would finish in the top three. Greenhills had to settle for fourth in the relay, when a third-place finish would have met the title. The victory for Fowler culminated a perfect performance by senior sprinter Becky Klein. She defended her championship in the 400 in a quick 57.8, won the 200 (25.6), and anchored the 800-meter relay to victory in 1:46.8.

The champs saved their best for last with a clutch win in the 1600-meter relay. With Klein as the anchor, Jan Schmidtt, Kelly Hafner and Lana Hafner gave the star her fourth first-place medal of the day. The winning time of 4:02.1 set a meet record.

Kathy Doane set a meet mark in the 100-meter low hurdles at 14.6. This would be the last year that the girls 100-meter hurdles would be contested at the 30-inch setting. Beginning with the 1984 season another new set of marks would be added to the books with the raising of the 100-meter hurdles to the collegiate and international setting of 33 inches.

Larissa Szporluk established herself in Traverse City as one of Class D's finest. The Greenhills star won the 800 and 1600 with records that remained untouched in Class D up until the new millennium. She toured the two-lapper in 2:18.9 to barely nip Gina Van Laar of Allendale by a tenth of a second. They had battled earlier in the 1600, with Szporluk defeating the 1982 defending champion in 5:05.2.

Upper Peninsula: The spectators on hand at Marquette were treated to some tight finishes in the team races. Escanaba outdueled Marquette 60 to 57 to bring home the trophy in Class A-B. Hancock edged Negaunee 38-36 in Class C while Lake Linden Hubbell nosed out DeTour by three points in Class D.

Lynn Schollie led Hancock to its title by winning three individual events, including a record of 46.2 in the 300-meter hurdles. The star of stars once again for the girls was DeTour's Gwen Wilkie. She outdid her three first-place finishes a year earlier by streaking to four wins in 1993.

1984

Benton Harbor left little room for doubt that it was the top Class A squad in 1984 in Jackson. Coach Eddie Watson's speedsters nearly doubled their winning margin over second place Dearborn Edsel Ford by tallying 64 points. The Harborites made up for their disappointing showing in the 800-meter relay the previous year by smashing the state record. The foursome of Marita Rimpson, Linda McMillion, Sandra Rice and Carolyn Ferguson romped home winners in a meet record that would last for 10 years: 1:39.2.

Chauna Burton replaced Ferguson on the 400-meter relay team, as the Tigers again set a meet record of 47.9. Benton Harbor made five trips to the winners' stand, with Carolyn Ferguson paving the way with two individual firsts. Ferguson broke her own record set in 1983 with a 300-meter hurdles victory in 42.4. The Lady Tiger also garnered another first-place medal with a win in the 100 hurdles.

Angie Prince of Detroit Pershing and Latonja Curry of Grand Rapids Ottawa Hills hooked up in a tight race in the 200-meter dash. Prince edged Curry by a tenth in a quick 24.3. Curry had earlier earned her second-straight win in the long jump, spanning a windy 19-3¼.

A number of outstanding performances were in evidence on the Jackson track, complementing the record-breaking performances mentioned above. Ann Arbor Pioneer missed the 1600-meter relay mark by only two-tenths of a second with its 3:49.7.

Making a profound impact was a senior foreign exchange student from Melbourne, Australia: Michelle Bews of Birmingham Seaholm. The Class A state cross-country champ in the fall, she broke the five-minute barrier with her triumph in the 1600 (4:59.6), and then came back to take the 3200 (10:49.2).

Cammie Maki's win in the discus was the only state champion produced by Warren Lincoln High School.

The additions of the 3200-meter relay in 1984, and the raising of the 100-meter hurdles to 33 inches, were the last changes made to date in the format for girls track. The win for Benton Harbor in 1984 would prove to be the last Class A state championship won by a high school other than Ann Arbor Pioneer or Detroit Cass Tech, for many years.

In Class B it was quality, not quantity, which took home the team trophies in Caro. The Muskegon Heights foursome of Doris Hardiman, Janet Evans, Shenitha Walker and Sherry Kelly compiled 40 points to take the team title. The Hudsonville-Unity Christian duo of Tammy Oostendorp and Sue Bulkema tallied 35 points to help bring home the runner-up trophy.

To help further illustrate the individual domination of the meet on the Caro track, we can look at the two schools that tied for third place. Paulette Bryant of Southgate Aquinas and Tere Stouffer of Royal Oak Shrine each won three events to total all 30 of their school's points.

Bryant was certainly the individual star of the day. The Aquinas star won three events, setting meet records that were not eclipsed until Class B became Division 2. She began her assault on the record books with a time of 14.5 in the 100-meter hurdles. After a brief respite, she blasted off in the very next event to run a Class B meet record of 11.7 for the 100-meter dash. She capped her record-breaking assault with her 44.0 over the 300 lows. Stouffer, the Class B cross-country champion in the fall, took all three-distance races for her 30 points.

Muskegon Heights won the 800-meter relay in 1:43.5, beating its closest competitors by better than three full seconds. The Lady Tiger foursome returned to the track moments later to take the 400-meter relay in 49.9. Shenitha Walker had the lone individual championship for the winning Heights crew with her victory in the long jump.

In Class D in Clare, Kristi Jackson had a perfect afternoon in leading Detroit Country Day to its first title. Jackson took part in four first places, winning the 100-meter hurdles and 200-meter dash and anchoring the winning 800 and 400 relay teams. Country Day added five more points to give the victors a seven-point edge over second-place Burton Bentley.

The leading individual performance for the day came from Donna Wright of Parchment, who hurled the discus 150-7, setting a new Class C and all-class mark. Wright's throw was not topped in any class until the 1997 season. Yvonne Laderach of Erie-Mason, with a 42-0, made the day complete by setting a new meet record in the shot put.

The runners-up from Burton Bentley set two relay records to aid their cause. Although the Lady Bulldogs got an automatic record with their win in the 3200-meter relay in 9:42.9, the foursome of Laurie Diehl, Jennifer Erickson, Beth Cummings and Amanda Aldrich then sped around the track in 4:03.4 to set the record in the 4x4.

Jolene Crooks of Benzie Central, who earlier in the school year won the Class C cross country crown, was a double winner in the 800 (2:17.4) and 1600 (5:09.1).

At Class D in Traverse City, Potterville won its first title by romping home with 71 points. Cool weather and intermittent drops of rain may have had an adverse effect on the performances. The only record to fall came in the 300 hurdles, won by Sherri Jones of West Shore Christian Academy in Muskegon. The future Ferris State star clocked 44.85.

It was in the 300-meter hurdles where the victors from Potterville showed their overall team strength. Trailing Jones and second-place Lisa Nixon of Ann Arbor Greenhills in third, fourth, and fifth place, was the Potterville trio of Eleanor Marks, Shellie Nemeth and Heather Smalley. Cheryl Simpson joined the hurdling trio to win the 800-meter relay for the Vikings, while Marks took first in the 100-meter hurdles.

Upper Peninsula: Escanaba peaked at the right time in breezing to its fifth-straight Class A-B championship in Marquette. Every runner ran their best time of the season for head coach Gary Seehafer's Eskimos.

Ishpeming Westwood made it a clean sweep in Class C, joining the boys as UP team champions. Traci Babcock's 5:08.2 mile was clearly the day's best individual achievement. Babcock, of Iron Mountain, led her sister Wendy, who trailed in second place and Westwood's Jesse Green to the tape under 5:20, all well under any clocking posted in any other class at the UP finals.

DeTour's Gwen Wilkie again won four firsts to lead DeTour to a runner-up trophy behind nearby Pickford. Wilkie's four wins gave her a total of 12, the highest number of first-place finishes in UP history. Wilkie ran the 100-meter hurdles in a meet best 15.2.

1985

Ann Arbor Pioneer and Detroit Cass Tech initiated a rivalry unprecedented in state track history. One could hardly imagine the dominance that these two rivals would have over all other schools. For better than a decade only Ann Arbor Pioneer or Cass Tech would bring home a state championship trophy, and in most years, the school not bringing home the big trophy would settle for runner-up honors.

The 1985 state finals were important for another reason. The Lower Peninsula meets were the first that used fully-automatic timing—finally giving the timing at the meet the accuracy that a top-class competition deserves.

Pioneer began a six-year run with a narrow 56-50 win over Cass Tech, with Dearborn Edsel Ford a close third with 46 points. Perhaps overshadowing the team title chase, however, was distance sensation Laura Matson of Bloomfield Hills Andover.

Matson, who won the individual cross country crown in the fall, came in with big expectations, having won the Oakland County title 1600 in a state record 4:39.4. At the state finals she shattered the meet record by 10 full seconds with a 4:45.2, a mark that would stand for 26 years. The Andover star separated herself from the field by over 100 meters, with Edsel Ford runners taking three of the next four places. Matson, likewise, had little difficulty in winning the 800 meters with a 2:12.02, a time that trailed only Delisa Walton and Sue Frederick in meet history.

Denys Adams of Okemos, by winning the 3200-meter run (10:50.0), denied Edsel Ford a 1-2-3 sweep in this event. In the previous fall, the threesome of Mary Peruski, Kris Salt, and Elizabeth Lehenbauer placed 1-2-3 in the team portion of the Class A cross country championships, won easily by Edsel Ford.

Although the hurdle height for the 100-meter timbers had been raised to the present-day height of 33 inches for only a year, Nikki Williams of Ann Arbor Huron skimmed over them in 14.29, a record that would not be broken for a dozen years. Edsel Ford set another record in the 3200-meter relay, besting its mark set a year earlier with a time of 9:33.94.

Marita Rimpson joined Matson as the meet's only double champion with wins in both short sprints. Rimpson defended her own 100-meter title in 12.02 and won the 200 meters in 24.9.

The other record to fall came from the Cass Tech 400-meter relay foursome of Stacey Randolph, Angela Jones, Cynthia Merritt and Dana McKeithen. The Technicians flew around the oval in 47.81 to set a record that remained standing at the end of the century.

In Class B at Jackson Northwest, Hemlock edged Flint Beecher by one point to prevent a Beecher sweep of the Class B crowns. Hemlock placed 1-2 in the discus and 1-4 in the shot put to pile up valuable points. Beth Bourdo finished second in the discus and fourth in the shot put, both events won by Bourdo's teammate Sue Breternitz.

Julie Watson became the third member of the Huskies to score, and the distance ace did it in record-breaking fashion. She established a new mark in the 1600-meter run at 4:55.7 and placed second in the 3200 to Jackson Northwest's Erin Gillespie to clinch the first-ever state title for Hemlock. Gillespie's time of 10:53.33 was good enough to set a new Class B record.

The winners would need the 11-point margin going into the day's final running event. Flint Beecher won the 1600-meter relay in 3:59.2 to finish first, leaving the Lady Bucs just one point shy of Hemlock.

At Class C in Clare, Shirley Evans of champion Detroit Country Day began an amazing four-year run. The Motor City freshman sprinter would win the 100-200 meter double all four years while performing for the Yellow Jackets, a feat that stands unmatched in Lower Peninsula prep state annals. The future MSU sprinter also won the 400 meters in 58.4 and ran the anchor leg on the winning 800-meter relay, helping the champions score 40 of their 46 points.

A terrific rivalry came to an end as hometown favorite Jeani Stuppia made her last appearance on her home track a memorable one by defeating two-time champion Yvonne Laderach of Erie Mason in the shot put. Stuppia's 42-5 bettered Laderach's record of 42-0 set a year earlier. Laderach didn't go home shut out, however, as she beat Stuppia in the discus with a throw of 129-9.

Another rivalry grew among the distance runners. Over the next three years, Hart's Cathy Ackley and Jeanne Spitler of nearby Montague would win eight of the next nine championships in the distance events. Ackley won the 800 (2:18.0) and 1600-meter runs (5:15.4) in 1985, with Spitler crossing the line first in the 3200-meter run (11:24.55).

At Hillsdale College in Class D, Athens edged Akron-Fairgrove 65 to 61 to win a meet that saw nary a record broken on. Balance was the keyword of this meet as not one competitor would hop onto the awards stand more than once. Jenny Gradowski, the 3200-meter winner from Suttons Bay, was one who could boast of a double of sorts. She was the cross country champion in the fall.

Upper Peninsula: The finals in Marquette were clearly headlined by a pair of Class C distance stars. Jessie Green of Ishpeming Westwood defeated former record holder Traci Babcock in the 1600. Running in the rain and the cold Green led the Babcock sisters to the finish line in 5:05.3, three seconds quicker than Traci Babcock and ten seconds ahead of Wendy Babcock.

Traci Babcock did recover to record a meet best for the 3200-meter run (11.06.1).

Green led her Ishpeming Westwood teammate Kelly Jandron to a 1-2 in the 800, helping Westwood to the Class C championship. Escanaba once again cruised to the girls A-B title while Pickford was much the best in Class D.

1986

Ann Arbor Pioneer again romped to its second-straight Class A title by compiling an envious total of 85 points. Pioneer and runner-up Detroit Cass Tech so dominated the meet that, collectively, the two powerhouses won 8 out of the 16 events.

The Pioneers and the Technicians gobbled up all the hardware in the four relays with neither school boasting a double individual champion. Laura Matson, although unable to match her fabulous record time of 1995 in the blistering sun, still rolled to an easy 4:57.87 win in the 1600. In the 800, the Bloomfield Hills Andover star was pressed to the tape by Ann Lampkin of Detroit Redford, defending her 800-meter championship with a time of 2:12.5, one-tenth faster than Lampkin.

Pioneer claimed the only record set of the day at Guy Houston Stadium. The foursome of Seana Arnold, Kellie Henderson, Karin Surratt and Danielle Harpell lowered the 3200-relay best to 9:25.44. Ann Arbor Huron's Sonya Payne, NCAA place winner while competing for the University of Michigan, defended her 1985 title with a put of 44-10½.

Kristen Salt of Dearborn Edsel Ford posted an impressive performance in the sweltering heat with her 10:52.20 in the 3200-meter run.

A rarity occurred in the 100-meter dash when the automatic timer couldn't determine the winner. The photo showed that freshman Patrice Verdun of Flint Central and Michelle Bishop of Grand Haven finished in a dead heat at 12.05, the only tie in girls state history. Bishop narrowly averted another dead heat in the 200 meters. That photo showed Bishop crossing the line just 0.01 ahead of Terry Ford of Farmington Mercy.

At Class B in Jackson, Flint Beecher's girls made it a most enjoyable journey home with a first-place trophy on the bus. Coach Tyrone Armstrong's Lady Bucs bounced back from their one-point loss in 1985 to post a 42-29 win over Grand Rapids Christian.

Beecher's three championships came in the 400, 800 relay and 1600 relay with Pretoria Wilson taking a part in all three wins. Wilson kept the 400-crown in her family, succeeding sister Twynette as the champion with a 57.82 clocking. Twynette teamed up with her sister Pretoria on the winning relay teams.

Sue Breternitz of Hemlock came up with repeat wins in the shot and discus. Her mark of 41-11¼ in the shot put was far enough to set a new meet standard, one of two records to fall.

Grand Rapids Christian got a record-setting performance from its 3200-meter relay team on its way to capturing the second-place trophy. Taking a pair of firsts was Alana Davis of Jackson Lumen Christi with wins in both hurdles.

In Class C at Bangor, Detroit Country Day ran away from the field with 71 points to easily take the girls title. Country Day was first in four events and placed high in four others. Shirley Evans, who went on to become the 1992 Big 10 200 champ, repeated in both shorts sprints to aid the Yellow Jackets's cause.

The long jumpers enjoyed ideal conditions on the Bangor runway. Just as in the boy's long jump, the day's best effort in all classes came from the Class C ranks for the girls, as Chris Wilson of Ann Arbor Gabriel Richard leaped a record 18-7. Montague's Jeanne Spitler, with her wins in the 1600 and 3200, joined Evans as the meet's only other double winner.

At Class D in Hillsdale, Cheryl Boddy took all three sprints to lead Athens to the Class D crown. Boddy won the 100 (12.66), 200 (26.47) 400 (58.28).

Runner-up Akron-Fairgrove earned its only win from Alisa Swan, who threw 119-1 in the discus. Fowler's 3200-meter relay team was able to lower the meet record to 9:54.04, the only such mark of the day.

Upper Peninsula: Escanaba nearly doubled the total over its nearest competitor at the Class A-B finals in Marquette. The win was the seventh-straight for the Lady Eskimos, a team composed mainly of underclassmen.

Stephenson won two of the four relays and placed second in the other two to win team honor in Class C. Kathy Amos edged Colleen Colegrove from St. Ignace to set a meet record in the 100 meters at 12.7. Colegrove would turn the table on Amos and win the 200 in 26.2. The St. Ignace star also lowered her record for the 400 meters to 59.4 seconds.

Pickford outdid Escanaba and nearly tripled the score over its closest rival in Class D. Coach John Benin's Lady Panthers tallied 92 points on their journey to a third-straight championship, the most points tallied in UP girls history. When coach Fred Stage of second-place Rapid River was asked the reason for Pickford's success he replied: "The boys teams that won for 27 years in a row went off and they all had daughters, and here they are."

1987

In front of 4,900 fans at Alma's Bahlke Stadium, Pioneer of Ann Arbor breezed to its third-straight Class A title. Coach Bryan Westfield's powerhouse bettered its impressive 1996 total by compiling 90 points, with Detroit Cass Tech again the runner-up. The city of Ann Arbor claimed the only two records with Huron eclipsing Pioneer's mark set a year earlier in the 3200-meter relay. The foursome of Laura Simmering, Mara Matuszak, Amy Bennett and Tracy Boudreau edged their cross-town rivals by one and a half seconds in posting their new mark of 9:20.4.

Lisa Waite of the champion Pioneers topped the 140-foot barrier with her record heave of 140-3 in the discus. Waite's margin of victory over Ann Baker of Flint Carman-Ainsworth was nearly 15 feet.

The most impressive performance came from Kristen Salt of Dearborn Edsel Ford, who ran the second-best 1600 in meet history (4:53.6), pulling runner-up Seana Arnold of Ann Arbor Pioneer under the five-minute barrier as well. Salt defended her 3200-meter title with a meet record clocking of 10:49.7, which would not be broken for a full decade.

Darchelle Ross became the other individual dual champion with victories in both hurdles. The sophomore star from Detroit Cass Tech picked up her third first-place medal of the afternoon by running a leg on the victorious 1600-meter relay team.

Cheryl Pruitt of Detroit Henry Ford, running on a sore leg, breezed to the 400-meter title with a time of 55.6 that was announced as a state metric record but was well shy of the imperial mark of 54.2 posted 9 years earlier by Delisa Walton. "I know I wanted to win, but I didn't think my leg would allow me," she said. "I thank the Lord I was able to do it."

Patrice Verdun had a big day on the Alma surface. The defending co-champion in the 100 meters made sure there was no tie in 1987, winning the short dash outright in 11.98 and running a leg on Flint Central's winning 400-meter relay unit. Defending 200 champ Michelle Bishop of Grand Haven had to settle for a second behind Yvette Smiley of Cass Tech (24.89).

In Class B at Sturgis, victory was again doubly sweet for Flint Beecher as the Lady Bucs joined the boys in repeating. Beecher scored 58 points to easily secure first place over Grand Rapids Christian. Beecher won five events and placed in five others to secure the crown.

Coach Tyrone Armstrong's senior-dominated crew capped a great career in grand style by running Class B's fastest 1600-meter relay time in history. The Beecher foursome of Twynette Wilson, Pretoria Wilson, Michelle Westbrook and Ayuna Hairston won by more than seven full seconds, with a 3:55.64. The time, however, was intrinsically inferior to the standing 4 x 440y best of 3:56.5 by Holt High School back in 1978—and thus fueled many arguments among fans about what the proper record should be.

Twynette Wilson of Beecher hauled off the maximum four first-place medals by winning the 800-

meter run (2:14.65) and running legs on the Bucs' winning 400, 800, and 1600-meter relay teams.

Linden's Amy Warner had the day's best performance in all classes with her winning leap of 5-8 in the high jump. She overcame an obvious handicap, wearing a cast to protect an injured elbow.

The drama in Class C held at Bangor was for the runner-up trophy as Detroit Country Day racked up the most points in meet history in claiming its fourth-straight championship. Coach George Prosperi's squad tallied a whopping 85 points, 51 points more than second-place Hart.

The Yellow Jackets were so dominant that they became the first team in state history to sweep all four relays. Detroit DePorres did claim a share of one relay, running the same time as Country Day, but out of a different heat in the 400-meter relay. Peggy Evans duplicated her performance from her freshman year by taking part in four first-place titles. Evans again swept both short dashes for the third consecutive year and ran legs on the winning 800 and 1600-meter relay teams.

Despite its dominance, Country Day was not able to set any meet records. The only mark to fall came in the long jump where Kim Pearson of Muskegon Oakridge had the best jump outside Class A in state history with an 18-11½.

Pearson's fellow league competitors, Jeanne Spitler and Kathy Ackley, concluded their rivalry in spectacular fashion. Spitler won the 1600 (5:09.05) and the 3200-meter runs (11:17.45) with her West Michigan Conference rival placing second in each race. Somehow Ackley had enough energy to win the 800 meters in 2:18.4. During their high school careers, Ackley and Spitler would each win five state Class C distance titles.

In Traverse City at Class D, Akron-Fairgrove took the momentum early to win. It started with a narrow win in the 3200-meter relay. The foursome of Michelle Brown, Theresa Bischoff, Yvonne Siler and Robin Aldrich set the new Class D record in 9:52.30 with Fowler second at 9:52.33.

Carrie Ager of Central Lake tied the meet record 12.40 in the 100-meter dash in the only other event that seriously faced a record challenge.

Upper Peninsula: Gwinn made its best showing ever at the Class A-B finals in Marquette. The Model Towners placed second to perennial power Escanaba to bring home their only girls track trophy ever. Dindy North of Gwinn accounted for the only A-B record set during the cold and rainy day with a throw of 38-¾ in the shot put.

Laurie Bero became the second UP girl (Gwen Wilkie of DeTour the other) to win four individual titles

in one year in leading Escanaba to its eighth-straight team championship.

Ishpeming Westwood narrowly defeated Stephenson to win the Class C championship. Freshman Tracy Holappa from Ishpeming was a double winner in Class C, winning the 100 and 200-meter dashes, events she would own over the next four years. Pickford again romped to its fourth-straight Class D crown. Inclement weather contributed to zero records set during the competition.

1988

Ann Arbor Pioneer racked up 90 points to claim its fourth consecutive title on the nearby Eastern Michigan University track. The Lady Pioneers showed strength in both the sprints and the longer distances to put 22 points ahead of perennial power Detroit Cass Tech.

Leading the way for the victors was double winner Crystal Braddock, who sprinted 100 meters in a wind-aided 11.70, which was given meet record credit alongside Vivian McKenzie's 11.7 hand time from 1982. The Pioneer speedster also blazed the 200 with a 24.45.

"I'm very surprised by this," said Braddock. I didn't know I was going to win until the very end. I've been working on leaning because I thought this would be close."

Seana Arnold nearly matched her teammate's double, winning the 3200 meters (11:01.34) and placed second behind crosstown rival Laura Simmering of Ann Arbor Huron in the 1600-meter run.

Earlier in the day Simmering had placed second to teammate Tracy Boudreau in an exciting 800. Boudreau, the daughter of Bob Boudreau, 1967 state Class D mile champion from Flint St. Matthews, posted a quick one with her 2:12.22. The dynamic duo of Simmering and Boudreau had led the River Rats to a second-place finish in 3200-meter relay, behind the West Bloomfield foursome of Amira Danforth, Tracy Abbott, Maureen Reed and Stacy Abbot, who flashed around the oval in a meet record time of 9:17.46.

Cass Tech won the 800-meter relay (1:42.86) and Trinette Johnson earned the other win for the Lady Technicians by becoming the fifth long jumper to reach the 19-foot barrier in meet history. Darchelle Ross, the 1987 champion, placed second in both hurdle events in 1988 to add valuable points for the victors.

Latonya White of Flint Northern, with her victories in the weight events, became the first Flint area girl to win two events since 1981. She heaved the shot out to 42-7½, and came back to hurl the discus 136-4.

At Class B in Sturgis, a pair of distance records took a tumble. Detroit DePorres supplanted two-time champion Flint Beecher to win its first girls track title. A pair of Grand Rapids schools, however, figured in the only record-breaking of the day.

Team runner-up Wyoming Park edged Marshall by less than a second with its meet record 9:33.02 in the 3200-meter relay.

Heather Slay of East Grand Rapids had the best mark with her 3200-meter run of 10:49.59, a standard that would last for 13 years. Slay earlier had dusted the field to win the 1600 in 5:00.77.

Heather Slay of East Grand Rapids (MHSAA photo)

Cari Byrd won Oxford's first girls state track title with a convincing run over 800 (2:13.93). Pretoria Wilson of Flint Beecher capped her career with her third consecutive 400-meter title.

The champions from DePorres won a pair of sprint relays, and got a double victory in the hurdles from Tara Allen.

In the Class C meet in Alma, Shirley Evans ended one of the finest prep careers in state history by leading Country Day to its fifth-consecutive state championship. Evans never tasted defeat at the state finals in the 100 and 200. The Yellow Jacket sprinter made it a grand slam by winning the 100 (12.5) and the 200 (25.7) for the fourth-straight year, a feat unmatched in state history.

Shirley Evans of Detroit Country Day (MHSAA photo)

Evans also ran legs on five winning relays during her career at Country Day to make it 14 first-place medals in all, a record in itself. Evans teamed up with her sister Peggy, Ngina Burgette and Hameera Newman to take the 1600-meter relay in a time of 4:03.35.

Placing third in the 200 meters to Evans was Kelly Ley of Muskegon Catholic, the daughter of Rick Ley, former head coach in the National Hockey League for Hartford and later Vancouver.

New Haven took the second-place trophy with 45 points, 20 less than Country Day. Kristal Mack of New Haven sped around the track in 57.9 to set a meet record in the 400. Eight years later, Kristal's younger brother, John Mack, would set the Class C boys record in the 400, making the Mack duo the only brother-sister record holders in state history.

Sara Neely set a record that would survive for a dozen years with a toss of 44-0 in the shot put, the best mark of the day in any class.

In Class D at Traverse City, Akron-Fairgrove won the closest race for the team title, edging Fowler 54 to 51. The meet boasted four double champions with

Jennifer Foster of Akron-Fairgrove winning the 800 and 1600, Carrie Ager of Central Lake both short sprints, Laura Selby of Tekonsha the hurdles, and Angela Frick of Walkerville the 400 and the long jump. Frick had led her little West Michigan rural school to the Class D basketball title earlier in the school year.

Ager's wins in the 100 (12.4) and the 200 (25.6) matched the records for the two sprints to provide the only run on any records in Class D.

Upper Peninsula: Laurie Bero and Tammy Cook each won three events to pace Escanaba to its ninth-straight Class A-B title. Bero barely missed out on equaling her four-win performance from 1987 when she placed second behind Lynn Kleiman of Kingsford in the 100-meter hurdles. Cook set one record and equaled another on the Marquette High School track. In only her third race ever over the distance, she won the 400 meters, setting a meet record in her division. In addition to winning the 100 meters, the Escanaba speedster also tied the existing UP A-B record in the 200 with a clocking of 26.2.

Dindy North from Gwinn improved her own record in the shot put. She also had the second-best discus throw in meet history with a heave of 121-0, second only to Shelly Chapman's record set back in 1977.

Calumet survived a perfect day by Stephenson's Traci Jeschke to walk away with the Class C team trophy. She won two solo first-place medals and ran a leg on a pair of winning relays for the runner-up Eagles. Vicki Butchko from Manistique accounted for the only record set in Class C with her throw of 122-0 in the discus.

Pickford won its fifth-straight D championship in a meet that was dominated by two girls. Julie Wallis ran a total of four miles in sweeping the distances for the victors. Her time of 5:25.3 was the only record set in Class D. Julie Elsing led Rock to a second-place finish as she won four individual events.

1989

Crystal Braddock again sprinted to a pair of dash championships to spearhead Ann Arbor Pioneer's fifth-straight Class A title at Eastern Michigan University. Braddock ran the 100 in a clocking of 11.84 to set a new meet record.

This despite a very rainy day, with the precipitation so fierce that the one-hour break between the morning and afternoon sessions was stretched to two hours. "It hasn't rained like this since 1955," said longtime official Jon Gallimore.

Braddock also raced to the 200 title (24.90) and ran a leg on the victorious 1600-meter relay to help Ann Arbor score 70½ points. Detroit Cass Tech piled up 58

Crystal Braddock (center) winning the 100 over Trinette Johnson (left) and Patrice Verdun. (MHSAA photo)

points to again finish second for the fifth-straight season. Trinette Johnson topped the meet record with her leap of 19-8 to pace all individual efforts.

"It makes me feel good, but I would have liked to have jumped better," said Johnson. "I guess today wasn't the day for me to jump 21-feet."

Johnson finally hit that 21-footer five years later as a senior at Florida State. Her daughter also became a jumper of note. Texas prep Jasmine Moore reached best of 20-11¾ in her junior year. As a senior, she reached a triple jump best of 44-2½ to become the No. 4 prep jumper in U.S. history.

Darchelle Ross, after winning the event as a sophomore, reclaimed her title in her senior year by winning the 100-meter hurdles for the Lady Technicians. LaTonya White of Flint Northern, in capturing the shot put and discus, repeated her double from the previous season. White improved on her shot-put mark from 1988 with a put of 44-3 and hurled the discus from the slippery ring 123-1.

The final event during the marathon long meet was not completed until after 7:00pm. Perhaps saving the best for last was Gwen Wentland of Grand Blanc. She won the first title in state track history for the Grand Blanc girls at 5-7, a modest height as it would turn out for her. By the time she had retired from a professional jumping career, she had cleared a best of 6-5, competed in the World Championships, and been ranked among top 10 Americans by *Track & Field News* an astounding 15 years.

One of the better marks on the rain-soaked track came from Clarkston's 3200-meter relay team, with its 9:22.6.

At Class B in Wyoming Park, Detroit DePorres made it two in a row after a hard-fought battle with Wyoming Park.

Sprinter Danielle Pierce paced DePorres, winning both short sprints and taking a leg on the winning 800-meter relay. Wyoming Park received a big effort from Tamie Gipe to help the Vikings take the runner-up trophy. Wyoming Park picked up eight more points when its 3200-meter relay team pushed Lansing Catholic to the day's only meet record during the rain-interrupted meet.

Heather Slay, in repeating as 1600 and 3200 champion, perhaps turned in the most impressive performance of the day. The future NCAA place winner broke the five-minute barrier (4:59.1) and the eleven-minute barrier in the 3200 (10:56.3), the best times for all classes during the finals.

The leading point winner was Grand Rapids West Catholic's Jennifer Merritt, who won both hurdles and the high jump to claim 30 of the 34 points tallied by the Falcons.

At Class C at Alma College, a new star emerged on the scene. Onsted sophomore Naheed Irani began her reign, contributing to four firsts: the 300 hurdles, 200-meter dash and legs on the winning 400 and 800-meter relays. Onsted's 44 points topped the 35 of Redford St. Mary. Irani clocked an FAT meet record of 45.23 in the 300 hurdles.

Sharing the spotlight with Irani on the rain-soaked track was Stacey Kilburn of White Pigeon who swept the distances. Killburn copped the mile (5:02.49), the 800 (2:17:48), and still had enough energy to win the 3200-meter run by 15 seconds (11:22.37).

Connie Claus of Rogers City had a big day in the throws, repeating as the discus champion with a 137-9 and adding the shot at 40-6½. Cathy Fromwiller of Marlette also picked up a pair of wins by capturing the 100-meter dash and the long jump (18-1½).

Hillsdale hosted Class D, and the Fowler girls won a two-team duel for the championship over Detroit Lutheran West. The Lady Leopards finished in second place despite scoring 75 points, a total in previous years that would have been good enough to win *every* state title. Sherine Rowell and Marcy Sillman did most of the damage for the victorious Eagles. They placed 1-2 in the 300 hurdles with Rowell winning the 100 hurdles. Sillman nearly picked off two more first-place medals with her second in the 100 meters and her leg on the runner-up 1600-meter relay.

Jackie Clark of Camden-Frontier was a double winner in one of the most unusual combos since Beth Veldhoff of Blissfield won the long jump and 800 back in 1978. Clark set the only meet record in Class D with her 12.3 clocking in the 100 meters and later doubled back to win the much longer 800 in 2:19.5.

Tiia Sammallahati, a foreign exchange student from Finland, made her one year stay at Genesee High School a memorable one by winning the 3200 in 11:42.4.

Upper Peninsula: Marquette also received some unexpected help from a foreign exchange student in ending Escanaba's nine-year reign at the A-B finals. Hayley Murphy from South Africa capped an undefeated season by winning the 800 and 1600 meters and running on the winning 3200-meter relay.

Cheryl Jacobson of Escanaba contributed one of two records set during the finals. She set a meet best 39-5½ in the shot. The other record came in the Class C 100-meter dash when Tracy Holappa of Ishpeming tied the record of 12.7. Newberry took home its first girls track trophy when it nipped Iron River West Iron County in Class C.

Iron Mountain overcame the three distance wins earned by Pickford's Julie Wallis in snapping the Lady Panthers' five-year streak in Class D. She concluded her outstanding career undefeated four years running in the 800 and 1600-meter runs.

1990

Flashes of bright sunshine highlighted the Class A athletes on the Midland High School oval, but frequent downpours precluded any wholesale runs on the record book. For the first time since 1984, spectators at the girls Class A state finals would fail to see an Ann Arbor Pioneer-Detroit Cass Tech 1-2 finish. The Lady Pioneers did annex their sixth-straight title, but the Lady Technicians of Cass Tech had to settle for third, behind runner-up Ypsilanti. Bridget Mann's distance double helped steer coach Bryan Westfield's Lady Pioneers to an eight-point margin over neighboring Ypsi.

The Pioneer team was a young one. Said Westfield, "Even though they are sophomores and freshmen, they've run in some tough competition. But still, when you're 14 years old, you can make some dumb mistakes."

Mann's 1600 and 3200 triumphs, along with a winning performance from the 4 x 100, keyed the team effort. Nicole Wilson placed Ypsi's second place by taking the 100-200 double and winning her third first-place medal of the afternoon by running a leg on the Braves victorious 4 x 200. Wilson's bid to win a rare four first-place medals fell less than a tenth of a second short, as Ypsi's 4 x 100 quartet trailed victorious Ann Arbor Pioneer by an eyelash at the finish line.

Grand Blanc's Gwen Wentland, with her repeat victory in the high jump, had the day's best individual performance. The future world-class jumper cleared the bar at a meet record 5-10, six inches higher than any other jumper. She then attempted 6-0, a height which would beat Ellie Hayden's all-time state record of 5-11¼ that she had tied the previous summer. She missed three times, but later in the summer she would clear that bar to win the Canada-USA Games.

Wentland hadn't entered the fray at the state finals until until the bar reached 5-4, two hours after the first jumpers. The first female state champion in Grand Blanc's history further demonstrated her natural ability by placing third in the long jump.

Flint Northern's Marjona Howard, by sweeping the hurdles, joined Mann as a double winner. Howard edged long jump champion Katrina Jones of Lansing Eastern to win the high hurdles. She then had a much easier win in the 300-meter low hurdles. Her winning 43.46 was nearly a full two seconds faster than Jones.

The closest race of the day took place in the 400 meters. Detroit Henry Ford's Ijnanya Alhamisi outleaned Southfield's Janeen Jones in the 400. Both were clocked in 55.8.

In Jackson, Class B fans saw another familiar team return to the winner's circle. Detroit DePorres won its third-straight for head coach Pat Geraghty. Nicole Embry paced the Eagles by taking the 100 and running on a pair of winning sprint relays. She edged Collette Savage of Bay City John Glenn, 12.01 to 12.02. It was the fastest FAT 100 in meet history.

Even more impressive were the Eagles' winning times in the short relays. DePorres' 48.95 mark in the 4 x 100 was only a half second off the meet record. Its 1:42.72 for the 4 x 200 was also more than respectable.

The two distance races provided a pair of thrilling finishes for the large crowd. Frankenmuth's Jennifer Barber (5:11.7) nipped DePorres' Angel White and Wyoming Park's Kim Blouw in a blanket finish in the 1600. Barber then battled rival Laura Bell of Otisville LakeVille in the 3200. It was the third match-up in two weeks for the two distance aces, with each having claimed an earlier victory. Bell, with a 11:11.2, edged Barber by just three-tenths of a second, as both runners ran no more than a stride apart throughout the race.

Vonda Meder led runner-up Corunna to its best-ever finish in state annals by taking the 800 in 2:16.3, less than an hour after tying for second in the 400-meter dash. The tireless Meder also ran a leg on the Cavalier runner-up 4 x 800—trailing first-place Grand Rapids South Christian by only a second at the tape—and anchored the 4 x 400 to a third-place.

At Wyoming Park, the Class C headlines were dominated by Naheed Irani's four individual wins. That 40 points would have been good enough alone to propel Onsted to the team championship. Irani took first in the 200, 800 and 100-meter high hurdles, but glistened the brightest in the 300-meter lows. Despite

running on a wet surface, she churned a speedy 44.49 meet record for the low timbers, a record that would remain unbroken for two decades. Her teammate, Abbie Schaffer, pitched in with 10 more points in the high jump.

New Haven's Elizabeth Clark posted the most impressive mark in the field events with her 18-4½ in the long jump, a mark in Class C not surpassed that decade.

Valentine Stumpf of Roscommon won the 1600 in 5:14.6 to become the first state champion in her school's history.

Hillsdale College hosted Class D. Fowler displayed an impressive display of team depth in repeating as team champs. Coach Kim Spalsbury's Eagles failed to win one first-place medal, but combined plenty of second and third-place finishes to hold off second-place Detroit Lutheran West.

What was highly unusual was that Maple City Glen Lake's impressive showing of first-place power didn't bring a higher team finish. The Lady Lakers won four first-places, yet were unable to take home either of the team trophies. Junior Marnie Peplinski's wins in the low hurdles and long jump, as well as Teresa Proost's second-straight 400 title, would earn Glen Lake no better than third in the team picture. The Lady Lakers ended the afternoon with a first-place in the 4 x 400, serving notice that this young track squad would be hard to beat the following season.

Upper Peninsula: Marquette coach Dale Phillips had developed a distance program that would be the envy of all Upper Peninsula teams in the 1990s. The squad romped to an easy victory in Class A/B on its home oval. Carla Johnson led two other Marquette teammates to a 1-2-3 finish in the 3200.

Thanks to the running of Christie Nutkins, Newberry repeated as champs in Class C. Nutkins swept all three distance races and anchored her team to a win in the 3200-relay. Tracy Holoppa of Ishpeming matched Julie Wallis's unusual achievement from the year before, finishing undefeated in her specialty. Holoppa won the 100 and 200 four straight years in Class C.

Kara Scherer of Cedarville-DeTour, winner of all three short sprints in Class D, would begin a four-year undefeated streak of her own in the 200. Sherer's 26.3 in the 200 meters was the only record to fall in Class D. Pickford made it two for two as the Lady Panthers joined the boys as UP champs.

1991

Ann Arbor Pioneer cakewalked to its seventh-straight Class A state championship at Grand Rapids' Houseman Field. Bryan Westfield's Pioneers dominated unlike any other team in Michigan prep history, piling up 95 points, the most ever scored by any girls team in any class. The Lady Pioneers won seven of the 16 events, including a sweep of all the sprint relays.

Sophomore Bridget Mann repeated her distance double from 1990, sweeping the 1600 (5:12.0) and 3200 (11:43.5). Heather Brown then won both short sprints for the victors by capturing the 100 (11.9) and 200 (24.99). In addition, she also ran legs on two winning relay units, the 4 x 200 (1:42.7), and the 4 x 100. The foursome of Brown, Hayley Wilkins, Seena Walters and Vania Nelson blazed the 4 x 100 in a meet record 48.2. Nelson added points for the champs by placing second to her teammate Brown in the 100 meters and earning a third-place in the 200.

Said Brown of teammate Nelson, "It helps to have her by my side. It's a great competition for us. We've been chasing each other all year."

The relay record was the only new mark set on the sizzling surface. Hot and muggy conditions on the Houseman Field oval took a toll on the athletes, in particular the distance runners. No one came close to a meet record. Volunteers stood by with cold towels in each lane at the finish line, providing welcome relief for the competitors.

Three girls won the first state titles in track for their respective schools. Karen Eshman of Grosse Pointe South won the 100 hurdles (14.7). Holland West Ottawa's Alicia Bernier won the first of her four state titles in the 300 hurdles (44.68). Romeo's Jessica Ballenger took the shot crown with a heave of 41-8¾.

In perhaps the most thrilling finish of the afternoon, Arelia Berry from Flint Northwestern outlasted defending champion Ijnanya Alhamisi of Detroit Henry Ford to win the 400 in 56.05. Greenville's Sara Miner's time of 2:17.84 in winning the 800-meter run was noteworthy under the steamy conditions.

Ruth Thawngmung of Battle Creek Lakeview overcame a shaky start to capture the discus. She was forced to forfeit her first throw when she accidentally carried two disks into the ring. Shaken up from the ruling, she then fouled on her second throw. Needing a good mark to earn three more throws, she hurled a standing 126-6, which not only gave her three more tries but was far enough to win the event.

In the Class B meet at Wyoming Park, a well-balanced attack gave Otisville LakeVille its first state championship. Future MSU distance ace Laura Bell won the 1600 in the day's all-class best time of 5:04.17, narrowly defeating Chelsea's Lisa Monti and Petoskey's Kelly Smith. Monti, with a first-place winning time of 11:06.36, turned the table on Bell in the 3200, easily the day's fastest time for the event. Bell's

teammate Karri Kuzma added a second individual title for the Falcons, taking the shot put at 41-1½.

Smith had a hand in setting the only meet record during the blistering afternoon, running the anchor leg on Petoskey's 4 x 800-meter relay team. The future NCAA star at Colorado teamed with Wendy Johnechek, Diohariah Stevens and Katy Hollbacher to win the relay in 9:26.06, 11 seconds faster than any other team posted.

Defending champion Detroit DePorres finished second, well behind Lakeville, despite a trio of first-place medals garnered by sprinter Atemia McClure, who aced both the 100 (12.33) and 200 (25.33) and ran on the victorious 4 x 100-meter relay.

Flint Beecher's Chantella Byrd had a big afternoon for the Lady Bucs. Reed edged Melvindale's Laquanda George at the tape to win the 400, 57.11 to 57.14 and anchored Beecher's winning 800 and 1600-meter relay teams.

Although Smith would be unsuccessful in her quest to win the same event four-straight years, freshman Carla Ploeg, of Middleville, would begin her four-year string in the long jump. Ploeg won with a leap of 17-10. Rita Harden of Dearborn Heights Robichaud joined boy's classmate Tyrone Wheatley as a multiple champ. She took both hurdles, running 15.4 and 45.2.

In Class C at Byron Center, only a change in classification denied Onsted and its all-around track star Naheed Irani from winning a third-straight championship. Frankenmuth, which finished third in Class B in 1990, welcomed the move down to Class C as it ousted Onsted 64 to 52. Irani was certainly the individual star of the day. In winning three events, she now totaled 9 titles, behind only Mason County Eastern's Maria Shoup's 10 championships in girls prep history.

Frankenmuth's depth, which led to relay wins in the 1600 and 3200 meters, was too much for Irani's individual talent to overcome.

St. Louis' Linda Godefroidt posted excellent marks. She won the 1600 in a noteworthy 5:05.2 and pushed Southfield Christian's Joy Wright to a 2:17.3 mark while finishing second in the 800.

Grant's Kelly Oberlin leaped 5-8 in the high jump, and Theresa Hall of Byron threw 129-4 in the discus, the top marks posted for those events in any class.

Forest Hills Northern hosted the Class D finals. Maple City Glen Lake's talented foursome of Marnie Peplinski, Theresa Proost, Jennifer Plowman and Sue Hobbins was all that was needed for the Lakers to win their first title. Peplinski was the big scorer as she won the long jump, both hurdles and ran on the winning 4 x 400-meter relay team.

Marnie Peplinski scored 8 individual titles during her Glen Lake career—and ran on 4 winning relays. (MHSAA photo)

Upper Peninsula: Although the boys were unable to take advantage of the unusually warm weather at the finals in Marquette, the girls were able to amend the record book. Marquette's' girls, by totaling 102 points, became the first team in the UP to ever top the 100-point mark. They again used their distance power to win, sweeping the first three places in the 800 and 1600 and taking three of the top four in the 3200.

Carla Johnson of Marquette set a new standard in the 3200 with a time of 11:36.6. Lisa Corbiere from Sault Ste. Marie broke both hurdles' records in Class A-B. Newberry held on to win a third-straight Class C championship. Pickford again swept Class D.

Clearly the star of stars was sophomore sprinter Kara Scherer from Cedarville/DeTour. She established herself in this meet as one of the premier sprinters ever for schools above the Big Mac Bridge. Scherer set a record in the 200 (26.0) and won the 400 meters by nearly 30 yards, finishing four and half seconds in front of the second-place competitor. To round out her day Scherer sprinted the 100 meters in 12.6 to equal the Class D record.

1992

In Grand Rapids, Detroit Cass Tech won its first girls State Class A championship since 1976. Ann Arbor Pioneer failed to win the coveted trophy for the first time since 1984. Heavy rains, spills, and controversy may have taken some of the luster off Cass Tech's 62 to 51 victory over Pioneer.

Rains that slicked the Houseman Field complex not only prevented a run on the record book, but held down performances throughout the day. One exception would be Katja Pettinen of Lansing Eastern. The Finnish exchange student took advantage of winds unfavorable for runners to set a meet mark in the discus (144-9).

Cass Tech nailed down its team title in the day's final event, the 1600-meter relay. The quartet of Obiama Alhamisi, Cheryl Omar, Erica Shepherd and Lamika Harper tallied 10 points with a 4:00.44 clocking for the metric mile. Earlier in the day this foursome scored another 10 by nailing down the 3200-meter relay. Shepherd took home her third first-place medal when she won the 800 meters in 2:14.41, nearly four seconds faster than second-place.

Ann Arbor's Vania Nelson certainly did all she could to help her Lady Pioneers mount a successful defense of their team title. She won the 100 and 200 and anchored the 4 x 100 and 4 x 200 to state titles.

Coach Bryan Westfield's tracksters did well, but may have lost the meet in the distance events. The Lady Pioneers were looking for valuable points from distance ace Bridget Mann, winner of the 1600 and 3200-meter runs for the past two years. Misfortune befell Mann, however, less than halfway through the opening lap of the 1600-meter run.

Meet officials let an unusually large pack of 26 runners toe the line for the start of the 1600. Boxed in midway through the first lap, a runner stepped on the two-time defending champ, causing Mann to fall and injure herself. "It figures it would have to happen at the state meet," she said in a disgruntled, yet still humorous tone. "Why couldn't it have happened in some dippy meet?"

Although she failed to defend her state title in the 300-meter low hurdles, Holland West Ottawa's Alicia Bernier certainly had a big day. Bernier placed behind only Lansing Sexton's Deanna Bouyer in the 300 lows. Earlier in the day she had won the high jump and the 100-meter hurdles to personally account for 28 points.

A strict interpretation of a fuzzy rule put a tarnish on the Mona Shores 3200-meter relay unit. The foursome of Shannon Swinburne, Kristen Crouch, Mary Amy Hornik and Tami Schiller had assumed they were to receive medals after their runner-up finish behind Cass Tech. A piece of metal, less than a 1/4 inch, that held rubber bands together, was deemed grounds for disqualification. Designed to hold one's hair in place while the girls raced around the track, these rubber bands were ruled a "safety hazard" according to the rules of the time. Needless to say, Sailor supporters back in Muskegon did not greet this ruling with open arms.

For the third time in school history, Flint Beecher swept to the boys and girls state title in Class B. Just as their boy counterparts fared, the Lady Bucs used depth and power in the relays to hold off Petoskey 54 to 46. Of the four relays contested, coach Joe Wilkerson's Lady Bucs only failed to win the 4x8.

Petoskey's second-place was the highest ever for the Northmen. The school could boast of putting two of the best distance runners from one school on the track in girls state history. Sophomore Kelly Smith led teammate Katy Hollbacher around the oval in a 1-2 finish for the 1600 meters. What was especially significant was that both of the Petoskey distance aces broke the five-minute barrier, a rare occurrence in the 20th century. Smith won in 4:56.84, just ahead of Hollbacher's 4:58.94, each time far superior to any other marks posted in any other class during the day's final competition.

Hollbacher also had the day's best time in the 3200-meter run (10:55.38). Despite the dreary conditions, Smith made it a distance sweep for the Northmen by easily capturing the 800 at 2:15.54. Smith, from her sophomore year onward, would never taste defeat in the 800 or 1600 runs.

At Class C, Tracy Kangas and Janet Boldrey led Vermontville-Maple Valley to its first-ever team title. Kangas scored 20 points for the champs with her firsts in the shot put and discus. Boldrey ran a 2:18.3 in the 800 and a leg on the winning 3200 (9:43.7) and 1600-meter relays.

In Class D, Maple City Glen Lake's team could very well have stamped its squad as one of the best ever. Not only did the Lakers amass a record total with 86 points, but coach Bill Brendal's speedsters helped rewrite the record book.

The Lakers set two records and barely missed another. Marnie Peplinski and Theresa Proost finished their careers for the Lakers in spectacular fashion. For the second-straight year Peplinski had a "perfect" day, taking home four first-place medals. In all, Peplinski capped her career with 12 first-place medals. The future Central Michigan track star won the long jump for the third-straight year (17-5), and established new meet standards for the hurdles, 15.06 and 44.82. She teamed with Proost, Jennifer Plowman and Erin Atwood to nearly set another mark. Only in Class A was any team able to run faster than the Lakers' time of 4:03.90, a mark that is second only to Fowler's record of 4:02.1 set back in 1982.

Proost, by winning the 400-meter run, became one of six girls in state history to win the same event four-consecutive years. By winning the 100 and 200, Proost boosted her total collection of first-place medals to 10.

Upper Peninsula: Escanaba won the only Class A-B championship not won by Marquette during the 1990s with its performance on the shores of Lake Superior. The bone-chilling weather producing wind chills that hovered below the twenty-degree mark, which obviously agreed with the aptly named Eskimos.

Tiffany Hodge made her debut in 1992, and for the next four years would stamp herself as one of the leading UP hurdlers of all-time. She won the first two of ten first-places she would earn during her career for Menominee. She posted a wind-aided time of 15.2 second in winning the 100 hurdles.

Krista Beaver from Gladstone posted a blazing but windy 12.4 in the 100 meters.

Munising in Class C and Cedarville in Class D also took home team championship trophies. Kelly Peterson from Munising won the 400 and 800 for Munising and anchored the winning 1600-meter relay.

Three girls won nine out of the eleven individual events offered in Class D. Dana Feak of second-place Felch North Dickinson won all three distance events and ran a leg on the winning 3200-meter relay team. Brook Hine of Bessemer and Kara Scherer from the winning Cedarville team also won three events. Scherer was possibly denied a fourth win when Cedarville's 800-meter relay team was disqualified for a false start.

1993

Detroit Cass Tech repeated as Class A champs at the state finals held in Grand Rapids. What was surprising was Salem's second-place finish, one point better than perennial track power Ann Arbor Pioneer.

Nikki Bouyer of Lansing Sexton skimmed the 300-meter lows in 43.35, the best individual performance of the day.

Leading Cass Tech's convincing 29-point victory was Erica Shepherd, who played a role in three first-places for the Lady Technicians. Shepherd successfully defended her 800-meter title in 2:15.61, and ran legs on each of the winning 800 (1:41.55) and 1600-meter relays (3:54.34).

Sexton's Bouyer joined Detroit Northern's Chandra Burns and distance ace Christi Goodison as an individual double winner. Bouyer added the 100-meter high hurdles (14.6) to her low hurdle crown. Burns took the 100 meters (12.2) and the 200-meters (24.88), saying later, "I just convinced myself I wouldn't be beat."

Sexton's Nikki Bouyer produced the day's best performance. (MHSAA photo)

Sterling Heights Stevenson's Christi Goodison won the 1600 (5:01.2) and the 3200 (11:10.09).

Leading Salem to its best-ever finish was Latonya Wheeler, who capped her senior year by defending her 400-meter title (58.01); she had gone undefeated in her specialty over the previous two years. Brighton won its first state track title, with a 3200-meter relay composed entirely of underclassmen.

Across town Wyoming Park High School hosted the Class B finals, and track fans saw Petoskey's Kelly Smith set the only record in any class when she won the 1600-meter run in 4:55.49.

Reporters also credited Smith with establishing a meet standard for the 800 when she crossed the finish line first in 2:13.4. Somehow, over the years, track officials had seemingly omitted marks made over the longer imperial distance of 880 yards. In reality, Smith's time was slower than four 880 runners' marks made prior to 1983. Nevertheless, Smith was easily the standout athlete.

What was special about Smith's achievements was that she was less than 100 per cent physically. Nursing a bothersome sore foot, the Petoskey junior hadn't run for a few days leading up to the state meet. Her coaches advised her to drop out of the competition if pain developed during her races.

Although Petoskey's Smith was the meet standout, the leading scorer at the Class B state finals was Inkster's Charnell Lynn. She figured in all 40 of her team's points, enough to give Inkster its first-ever girls state track title. She won the 100, 200, and 400 and ran the anchor on the winning 400-meter relay.

Betsy Haverkamp of Grand Rapids South Christian turned in the day's fastest 3200-meter run. The future NCAA Division III place winner for nearby Calvin College won her event in the fine time of 10:52.7.

Placing in both hurdle events was Haverkamp's teammate from South Christian, Val Sterk. However, it would be in volleyball where Sterk would truly excel.

After leading MSU to the final four in 1996, Sterk would be named to the first team All-American squad, an honor she would duplicate the following year.

Jennifer Story, in winning both hurdle events, would become the first state track champion from Stanton-Central Montcalm. Liz Mast, of Caledonia, with her winning 137-0 in the discus, turned in the best field event performance.

In Class C at Byron Center, Shepherd won its first-ever title by racking up 45 points. The Lady Blue Jays had their lone first-place finish in the day's final event. The foursome of Amy McCaul, Andrea Campbell, Jamie White and Jodi Gelina won the 1600-meter relay in 4:05.46.

The leading point producer was Renee Pardon of Comstock Park, who won both short dashes and anchored the victorious 400-meter relay to account for 30 points, all the Panthers needed to carry home runner-up honors.

Freshman Carrie Gould, representing Burton-Bendle High School, easily won the 3200-meter run in 11:22.0.

In Class D, Litchfield won its first title. Pam Blonde led the victors by winning the discus with a 125-11. Blonde also ran a leg on Litchfield's winning 1600-meter relay team.

Upper Peninsula: The Class A-B team battle came down to the last race in Marquette. Needing a first-place finish in the 1600 relay, Michelle Olds made up a 10-yard deficit on Menominee's final runner to win at the tape in a thrilling finish.

Crista Beaver, with a time of 26.3, set a meet record in the 200 meters in A-B. Sophomore Tiffany Hodge from Menominee had a perfect day for the runner-up Maroons. Hodge took home four first-place medals, including a record-setting time of 15.4 for the 100-meter hurdles and a 47.1 over the 300-meter timbers.

Stephenson, aided by three first-place performances from Kelly Klein, won the Class C final. Rebecca Palmer of the victors accounted for the lone record in her class with a mark of 124-8 in the discus, the longest throw in UP history in any class until 2005.

Cedarville again rode the shoulders of Kara Scherer to repeat as winners in Class D. After being upset in the 100 and 400 dashes, Scherer came back to post a win in the 200-meter dash and then clinched the team championship for Cedarville by anchoring the winning 1600-meter relay. Sara Hood of Baraga accounted for the only record in Class D with her toss of 118-2 in the discus.

1994

Coach Bertha Smiley's Lady Technicians from Detroit Cass Tech continued their dominance in the team Class A competition by easily racing to their third-straight victory. Cass Tech's 65 points were 23 more than its city league rivals from Martin Luther King Jr. High could muster. Five times the Lady Technicians were the first to cross the finish line, including a near sweep of the four relays.

Just as the Cass Tech boy's romped to the all-time best in the 800 relay, the Lady Technicians' 800-meter relay foursome of Chantelle Nagbe, Julia Ford, Emily Higgins and Felicia Baker became the second team to break the 1:40.0 barrier in the 4 x 200. Cass romped home to victory in a meet record of 1:38.4, more than four seconds ahead of runner-up Detroit King.

Emily Higgins and freshman Julia Ford also won individual titles for the victors, as well as taking part in two state championship relay units. Higgins flashed to the 100-meter title in a quick 11.8, while Ford raced around the oval in 55.1. "I was happy to set the record," said Ford. "But I have more to do."

Cass Tech was so deep in talent that only Ford was needed to run a leg on yet another state championship relay squad. She teamed up with Okioma Alhamisi, Nicole Callaway and Katie Chapman to win the 1600-meter relay in 3:56.5, more than four seconds faster than second-place Ann Arbor Pioneer. Tech's 48.5 clocking in the 400-meter relay was more than a second faster than runner-up Pioneer.

Sharing the individual spotlight in Midland was Nikki Bouyer of Lansing Sexton. She repeated her hurdles double from 1993, just missing a new mark for the 100-meter hurdles with her hand-timed 14.3. The Lansing speedster took her fifth individual state title, and third consecutive win in the 300-meter low hurdles. A tiring Bouyer capped her day with a third in the 200-meter dash, after earlier anchoring the Big Red 800-meter relay team to a third-place.

Stacy Thomas displayed her versatility by partaking in an unusual double. The Flint Southwestern ace defended her 1993 high jump championship at 5-7, and placed inches behind first-place Sarah Herbert from East Detroit in the 800-meter run. Susie VonBernuth likewise barely missed a double victory, placing second to Summer Beydoun of Dearborn Fordson in the discus after winning the shot put with a heave of 41-1½.

In Class B at Saginaw, an unusual team battle was waged where the main combatants never were on the track at the same time. If ever there was any proof needed as to what is most valuable to win a state championship, superior sprinters or superior distance people, it may have been answered when River Rouge won the title with 58 points, 10 more than second-place Caledonia.

Neither team tallied a single point in the field events, so it was a pure sprint vs. distance battle.

Just as in 1993, the star of stars was Petoskey senior Kelly Smith. The future NCAA distance ace for the Colorado Buffaloes easily captured her two specialties, producing a sensational 4:48.41 clocking in the 1600-meter run. A short time later she returned to the oval to destroy the field in the 800 meters. Running virtually alone from the opening gun, only the clock was Smith's foe on this bright afternoon. When she crossed the finish line in 2:12.19 seconds, she was more than 8 seconds ahead of her closest opponent, the widest margin of victory in state prep history. Smith would go on to be runner-up in the 1500 meters at the 1998 NCAA Championships.

As amazing as her 800 performance was, Smith's time did not set a meet record. She fell short of matching Detroit Immaculata's Rochelle Collins 2:11.7 clocking over the slightly longer distance of 880 yards back in 1978. No such comparisons were needed for Smith's 1600-meter effort. Smith surpassed her previous mark set a year earlier by more than seven seconds.

Kenyetta Grigsby led the Panthers to victory by winning the 100 and 300 hurdles and running on two winning relay teams (400 and 800). Simby Bonner won the other first-place for the victors in the 200-meter dash (25.32) and garnered the remaining Panther points by placing second to defending champion Charnell Lynn (12.23) in the 100 meters.

Caledonia followers couldn't have expected more from their team. After easily winning the Class B cross country crown in the fall, the Fighting Scots used their distance talents to compile all their points. The foursome of Shannon Houseman, Barb Warner, Sarah Parbel and Karyn Duba began the day by shattering the meet record in the 3200-meter relay. The Lady Scots' time of 9:22.75 was 9 seconds faster than the winning time posted in Class A and stood as the standard for nine years.

Future MSU distance ace Duba, although running in the shadows of the incomparable Kelly Smith, sparkled for the Fighting Scots. After breaking five minutes in the 1600-meter run, she led Caledonia to an unprecedented 1-2-7 finish in the 3200 meters.

Shahla Bolbolan of Fremont highlighted the field event performers. She not only won the shot (43-3¼) and discus (142-10), but also set a Class B record in each event. Carla Ploeg of Middleville Thornapple-Kellogg completed her four-year sweep in the long jump with a fine effort of 18-2¼.

In Class C at Bay City Western, Clare waited until the final event of the afternoon before winning its only first-place. By this time coach Judy Johnson's Lady Pioneers had already clinched their first-ever state team title. The win in the mile relay just made the day a little sweeter for the victors.

One of the best performances of the day came in the discus. Dasha Yeakey, of Union City, hurled the platter out 140-11.

Bay City Glenn hosted Class D, where only one meet record fell. Cynthia White of Covert with a time of 12.10, won the 100-meter dash by nearly one full second. Maple City Glen Lake easily won the team title by racking up 67½ points. Only the Lady Lakers stood in the way of a Pittsford boys-girls sweep, as the Wildcats placed second to Glen Lake in the team race.

Upper Peninsula: Marquette garnered its fifth championship in five years with a convincing performance at the finals. Coach Dale Phillips' squad tallied points in 15 of 16 events, while winning ten, as it scored 84 points, 36 more than runner-up Menominee.

Sarah Heikkila had a perfect day, winning all three dashes and anchoring the winning 4x2. Heikkila's 26.3 in the 200 meters also equaled the A-B record. The top individual performance was Tiffany Hodge's effort in the 300 hurdles. The Menominee junior set the all-class UP record with her clocking of 45.3.

Ironwood strolled to a 21-point win in Class C on the Marquette track in a meet that produced no new records. Kelly Klein from Stephenson was the only triple winner in C.

The tightest finish in UP history headlined the action in Class D. Lake Linden-Hubbell and Felch North Dickinson shared first place with 38 points, just two points ahead of third-place Cedarville. Dana Feak, daughter of head coach Paul Feak, a former state champion back in the middle 1960s, was the individual star by sweeping all three distance events for the co-champs from North Dickinson.

Tawna Urmon certainly drew the plaudits from the fans that favor the smaller schools. Urmon, by winning the Class D long jump, became the first athlete from tiny Mackinac Island High School to win a UP championship.

1995

It was again an all-Cass Tech party at the Class A meet in Saginaw. The girls joined their boy counterparts at the top of the standings, winning a second-straight and their fourth title won in the past four years. Only Ann Arbor Pioneer was able to put up a challenge, placing 16 points behind the Lady Technicians' winning total of 71.

It is doubtful if there has ever been a deeper group of sprinters than Cass Tech's speedsters of 1995. Coach Bertha Smiley could have fielded a relay team of four individual state champions. Emily Higgins (the 1994 100-meter champion), Kanisa Williams (1995 & 1997 100 meters), Chantelle Nagbe (1995 200 & 1996 100 meters) and Julia Ford (1994 400-meter champion). Oddly enough, this foursome never once ran a race together.

It is likely that only rain and strong winds prevented the Cass Tech squad from improving on its own relay records. The only two seniors on the entire Tech squad, LaKeisha Snoddy and Higgins, teamed up with Williams and Nagbe to cruise to the 4x1 title (48.38). Ford then joined Snoddy, Nagbe and Traci Ball to blast the field in the 800-meter relay (1:41.0). Coach Smiley then had the luxury of putting three new faces with Ford to claim yet another 1600-meter crown (3:57.45), Cass Tech's fourth win in a row.

Said Nagbe of winning in bad weather, "You can't think about the weather. You can't think about anything. My coach said if you start thinking about anything while running, it takes away from the energy in your legs. So I don't think when I'm running."

Action in the field events highlighted the rest of the day. Suzie VonBernuth, with a winning put of 42-5, defended her shot championship, but it was in the discus where the Owosso senior made the most noise. VonBernuth sailed the platter out 146-0, more than 21 feet farther than the second-place finisher, and far enough to set a Class A record.

Jenny Engelhardt of Battle Creek Lakeview won the high jump at 5-8, one inch better than two-time defending champion Stacey Thomas of Flint Southwestern. The win for Engelhardt deprived Thomas of the chance to be the only Class A performer in girls history to win the same event four successive years. Thomas would, however, return to win the event in her senior campaign.

Sarah Hebert of East Detroit held off Cass Tech's Katie Chapman and Thomas once again to repeat as the 800 champ in 2:15.85. The year would mark the debut of a couple of the state of Michigan's all-time stars, Ayesha George and Sharon Van Tuyl. George, of Ann Arbor Pioneer, would begin a three-year reign in the 100 hurdles, while Van Tuyl, of Portage Northern, leaped onto the scene by winning the 1600-meter run. Van Tuyl tried to annex the distance double, but placed second to Alison Klemmer of Troy-Athens in the 3200-meter run. Klemmer would become a college All-American at Notre Dame in the 10,000-meter run.

In Class B at Midland Dow, the Lady Scots from Caledonia would only need 41 markers to win their first state track championship, seven less than their runner-up tally a year before. During the fall Caledonia used its depth in the distances to win a second state cross-country title. Coach Dave Hodgkinson's nationally ranked runners scored a record low of 21 points, with 6 runners placing in the top 8.

Only Carrie Gould of Flint Powers would prevent Caledonia from posting a near-perfect cross-country score. Gould, who had to sit out the 1994 track season after transferring from Burton Bendle, took the 1600 (5:05.2) and the 3200 (11:05.27).

The 3200-meter relay quartet of Shannon Houseman, Keri Bloem, Sarah Parbel and Barb Warner won by 17 seconds over second-place Pennfield. Each one of that foursome would score valuable points for head track coach Joe Zomerlei's squad throughout the day. Although Caledonia walked off with the big trophy, many other individuals shone brightly.

In addition to Carrie Gould, Kenyetta Grigsby of River Rouge was a double winner, successfully defending her hurdle wins from 1994. The big winner was Charnell Lynn of Willow Run. The transfer from Inkster won all three sprints to account for all thirty of Willow Run's points.

Placing second to Lynn in the 200 and 400 was Angie Stanifer, who anchored Tecumseh's winning 800-meter relay team. She took her talents to the University of Georgia and became a college All-American by placing sixth at the 1998 NCAAs in the 800-meter run (2:04.64).

The field events were highlighted by a pair of throwers who would dominate their disciplines over the next three seasons. Alana Robinson, of Grosse Ile, threw 139-11 in the discus, second only to the Class B meet record. Makiba Batten, of Detroit Renaissance, would begin a three-year reign in the shot with a heave of 41-1½.

Inclement weather in 1995 wasn't just limited to the state finals. Many regional sites also suffered from adverse conditions, leading to some runners having to run their races in the "slower" heats. Such was the case for Ann Lemire of Frankenmuth. Running in the first heat due to a slow regional time, Lemire battled the clock, only to see her time fall a tenth of a second behind first-place Erin White of Battle Creek Pennfield, running in the top-seeded heat.

At Class C, Liz Mulvaney and Heidi Goodenough helped lead Hemlock to the title. Mulvaney tallied 20 of Hemlock's 63 points with a double win in the weight events. She had the day's best effort in all classes with her winning throw of 42-6¼ in the shot put. For good measure, she also topped all other Class C discus throwers, hurling the platter 127-8. Goodenough took first-place honors by winning the 400 meters (58.33) and then clinching the meet for the Huskies by anchoring the 4x4 (4:10.38) to a first place.

Jessica Champine did her level best to bring a second-straight title back to Clare. She won both short sprints (12.30 and 25.54) and anchored Clare's 800-meter relay team to a third first-place finish.

Perhaps the best race in the meet came in the 1600-meter run. After having lost to rival Bethany Brewster of Saginaw Valley Lutheran four straight times during the regular season, Unionville-Sebewaing's Christie Achenbach nipped Brewster at the finish line to win the 1600 title, posting the fastest time of the day for any class (5:05.06). Later in the day Brewster did get a state title, finishing ahead of Achenbach in the 3200. Suttons Bay's Traci Knudsen in the 800 turned in an impressive 2:16.87.

In Class D, Maple City Glen Lake won its fourth championship in five years by outscoring runner-up Grass Lake 60 to 52. Central Lake's Zabrina Brock's winning 40-1¼ in the shot was the day's best mark. Brooke Formsma capped a memorable year by winning the long jump and 200. During the winter months, Formsma earned All-State honors while leading Battle Creek St. Phillip to its fourth-straight Class D volleyball championship.

Upper Peninsula: Although only one record was equaled at the finals, there were a number of impressive performances in A-B. Marquette once again waltzed to the team championship by piling up points in every event. Sarah Heikkila and Sault Ste. Marie's Maryea Pike staged a tight dual for sprinting supremacy. Pike edged the defending champion in the 100 and 200 meters with Heikkila prevailing in the 400 meters, equaling a meet record at 59.2 seconds.

Menominee's Tiffany Hodge completed her impressive career with wins in both hurdles and the long jump.

Ironwood blitzed the field in Class C, more than doubling the score over second-place Munising. Oddly enough, an Ironwood girl set neither of the two records broken in Class C. St. Ignace took the 400-meter relay at 51.8 while Gael Butkovich of Houghton cleared 5-5 in the high jump.

Coach Kathy Paul of Rock Mid Peninsula only had four girls entered at the Class D finals. However, quality ruled over quantity as the foursome of Crystal Aper, Faye Peterson, Jill Gobert and Andrea Beauchamp upset the field with a narrow one-point edge over Rapid River. Peterson and Gobert each won a pair of firsts, but the Lady Wolverines had to nervously watch the day's final event to see if they would be passed by Rapid River. A valiant anchor leg by Rapid River's Stacey Boyer in the 1600-meter relay fell just short and Mid Pen had its first victory.

1996

Detroit Cass Tech scored as much as it ever had in Rockford, but it would be only good enough to take runner-up honors. On top again after four years in second, Ann Arbor Pioneer exploded to the title by scoring 93 points, second only to its own winning total in 1991.

It was strictly a two-team race for team laurels, as third-place Troy scored 40 points less than the front runners. This did not preclude some impressive performances delivered by out-state competitors.

One of the state of Michigan's top female athletes concluded her brilliant career on a high note. Flint Southwestern's Stacey Thomas nipped Jenny Engelhardt of Battle Creek Lakeview to win the high jump crown. Thomas, who suffered her only loss to Engelhardt in 1995, won the event on fewer misses. Thomas cleared 5-8 on her first try while Engelhardt, who would win the Midwest Meet of Champions at 5-9, cleared on her second trial.

Although one of the leading points producers at the state track finals, Thomas would really make her mark in basketball. She averaged 25 points, grabbed 14 rebounds, 7 assists and 12 steals per outing. In addition to excelling on the hardwood and in the classroom, Thomas also somehow found time to win consistently on the Knights' cross-country team. Although not selected as Miss Basketball in the state of Michigan, she would, as early as her freshman year, help transform the Michigan women's basketball team from an also-ran into a Big 10 power.

The only meet record to fall came in the 3200-meter run. Sharon Van Tuyl, with a 10:25.76, shattered the former 18-year old record set by Miriam Boyd of Port Huron. "Everyone was telling me to run faster," she said. "So I did." Van Tuyl, who had raced to her second-straight Class A cross county championship in the fall, also added the 1600-meter title to her list of laurels.

Evlista Clemons claimed the first girls track title for tradition-laden Detroit Northwestern with her 2:13.28 clocking in the 800-meter run. She also won her specialty at the Midwest Meet of Champions the following weekend in Indianapolis.

Ann Arbor Pioneer, although scoring 93 points, would take first-place honors in only three events. The Lady Pioneers swept the 100-meter high hurdles in unprecedented fashion, Ayesha George leading teammates Robyn Woolfolk and Kendall Willis to the tape, the first 1-2-3 finish by one school in state history. Pioneer and Cass Tech would each win two relays.

Chantelle Nagbe of Cass Tech, who won the 200 a year earlier, captured the 100 in 12.74. Nagbe concluded her track career with a most impressive accomplishment: running a leg on a state championship 800-meter relay team for four consecutive years.

In Class B at Lowell, Tamika Craig of Dearborn Heights Robichaud could have walked off with the team title all by herself. She won three individual events and ran a leg on Robichaud's victorious 1600-meter relay. Flint Powers, with 28 points, was far back of Robichaud's winning total of 58. Craig won all three sprints and teamed up with Stephanie Gray, Juanita McGrew and Andrea McGrew to win the relay in 3:57.81.

Carrie Gould led Flint Powers to its second-place finish. With her win in the 1600-meter run (5:03.9), that made it eight straight state championship event wins. However, her quest for a ninth-straight ran into a roadblock when Caledonia's Shannon Houseman beat her in the 3200 in 11:04.2 to 11:10.1. Houseman had earlier teamed up with Keri Bloom, Jenny Sprague and Brooke Wierenga to win the 3200-meter relay for the third-straight year. The Lady Scots winning time of 9:25.4 was second in Class B only to their own record set in 1994, a record that stuck around for another 9 years.

Makiba Batten of Detroit Renaissance, by uncorking a toss of 147-7 in the discus, established the only meet record set at the meet. Batten also took the shot put. Erin White of Battle Creek Pennfield, with a fine time of 2:13.79, easily captured the 800-meter title.

Kenyetta Griggs returned to the winner's circle for the third-straight year in the 100-meter hurdles. The River Rouge star took her talents to the Midwest Meet of Champions the following weekend where she won the 100-meter hurdles and the long jump (18-6½).

Griggs placed second behind Kari Karhoff of Durand in the 300-meter low hurdles. Karhoff, who won the 400 meters in 1994 as a freshman, clocked an impressive 44.7. She took her talents to Central Michigan University, where she won Mid-American Conference titles at 400 and the 400 hurdles.

At Comstock Park in Class C, Clare High School, the 1994 Class C champions, moved back into the winner's circle by defeating defender Hemlock 58 to 43. Jessica Champine figured in 38 points for the champs by winning the 100 and 200-meter dashes, and running legs on the winning 4x1 and runner-up 4x2 relays. Lutheran Westland's win in the 4 x 200 kept Champine from having a perfect day.

Clare was certainly more than a one-woman team, as its 3200-meter relay team claimed a state title. The foursome of Michelle Schepperley, Meghan McNeilly, Beth Wolfe and Hylie Schepperley just missed the meet record with a clocking of 9:42.58.

Liz Mulvaney kept Hemlock in the hunt with wins in the weight events. Her heave of 43-3¾ inches was the day's best effort in any class in the shot put.

Highlighting the distance events in Class C was the performance of Saginaw Valley Lutheran's Bethany Brewster. Her clocking of 11:07.69 was second only to the 10:48.8 posted by Mason County Central's Melanie Weaver back in 1979. She had earlier won the 1600 in 5:08.99.

Class D was held at Forest Hills Northern. Nicole Miehlke of Manistee Catholic, with a 2:18.32 in the 800, would set the only meet standard.

No team has ever improved more in one season than Homer High School. Shut out at the 1995 state meet, the Lady Tigers used the one-two punch of Courtney Huffman and Liz Powers to amass 77 points to easily capture the Class D girls title. Huffman and Powers were individual double winners, and only a second-place finish in the 800-meter relay, behind Bellaire, denied the Homer aces a perfect afternoon.

Upper Peninsula: The girls state finals upstaged the boys at Kingsford High School. Although the boys were unable to come close to posting any records, the girls put five new marks on the books. Marquette continued its dominance in Class A-B by rolling up 88 points. Maryea Pike of Sault Ste. Marie was clearly the star of stars in A-B. She won all three dashes before anchoring the Soo 1600-relay team to victory in the second fastest time in nearly 20 years (4:10.3).

Ironwood won its third consecutive Class C title, but received a strong challenge from St. Ignace. Although placing second in the team competition St. Ignace contributed to all three records in Class C. Ann Pemble of the Saints equaled the 100-meter best in C at 12.7, while Richelle Robinson defeated future MSU cross country star Ann Somerville from Ironwood in the 400 meters in a record-breaking time of 59.2. The Saints also posted the UP's second fastest 1600-relay time in any class with a clocking of 4:09.9.

Rapid River's girls made it a clean sweep for the Rockets in Class D, edging Pickford 35 to 33. Cedarville's 3200-relay team lowered the record in Class D down to 10:15.2 while Pickford's Jill Rairigh became the discus leader in Class D. Tawna Ulmon won a pair of firsts for tiny Mackinac Island High. Ulmon had earlier become the first athlete from Mackinac Island to win a medal when she placed fifth in the long jump as an eighth grader.

1997

Nearly 8,000 fans in Rockford looked on as Ann Arbor Pioneer won its ninth state title in 14 years. Perennial power Detroit Cass Tech again settled for runner-up honors, 33 points behind. The Pioneers wasted no time in making their presence felt at Ted Carlson Memorial Stadium.

In sweeping the 100-meter highs for the second straight year, the Lady Pioneer trio of Ayesha George, Kendal Willis and Robyn Woolfolk all were reported to be under the meet record. With no wind gauge present, officials using questionable judgment called the 13.89 a meet record. "It felt great to get the record," George said. "It was a quick final and we had the wind at our back."

George ran the leadoff leg for the winning 400-meter relay, and placed third in the high jump in contributing valuable points for the victors. She also took first places honors in the hurdles the following week at the Midwest Meet of Champions.

Runner-up Cass Tech actually won more events (3) than Ann Arbor, but failed to match the Lady Pioneer's incredible depth. The Lady Technicians, in the very next event following Pioneer's sweep of the hurdles, nearly pulled off a sweep of their own. Kanisa Williams became the third Cass Tech speedster in four years to sprint to the 100-meter finish first. It was her second 100-meter title (she won as a sophomore in 1995). Teammate Tiarra Jones finished second.

Williams, who would win the 100 and 200 meters at the Midwest Meet, teamed up with Tracy Ball, Julia Ford and Meshia Maton to win the 800-meter relay for the Technicians. It was an unprecedented fifth-straight year that Cass Tech would win this event. Even more domineering were the school's 1600-meter squads. The green & white of Cass Tech would win this event for a sixth-straight season. Julia Ford, the daughter of Richard Ford, one of the founders of the legendary Motor City Track Club, ran a leg on four straight championship units.

Portage Northern's Sharon Van Tuyl returned to the spotlight once again in the distances. The starting goalie on Northern's boys hockey team once again copped an impressive distance double. After winning the 1600-meter run for the third consecutive year (4:57.82), Van Tuyl romped to an impressive win in the 3200 (10:31.16). She finished her prep career with seven titles.

Van Tuyl added further laurels to her impressive running resume by winning the two-mile run at the national high school meet in North Carolina in a personal best time of 10:25.59. Van Tuyl would go on to have an even better career at Boston College as a hockey goalie.

Erin White also won an event for a third consecutive year, but it would be her first title in Class A. White, who won the state Class B title in 1995 and 1996 while running for Battle Creek Pennfield, made the transfer to Class A with the same results. After winning the 800 meters (2:13.32) for Battle Creek Central, White would defeat all comers the following week at the Midwest Meet of Champions.

Michelle Davis of Lansing Sexton took first place in the 200 (24.71) and 400 meters (55.62) to become a double winner. Melissa Brosseau of Alpena, with a 44-9¾ toss in the shot, highlighted the field competition.

At Class B in Lowell, Detroit Renaissance won its first state championship in any sport. Although Makeba Batten was the big point producer, coach Rick Miotke's squad had to sweat out the meet's final event before walking off with the trophy. After qualifying in the regional with a time fast enough only to run in the third slowest of four 1600-meter relay heats, the foursome of Adriane Mayes, Julia Stevenson, Rashida Bradley and Julia Redd sped around the track in a school record 4:00.0. After nervously watching both the clock and competitors cross the finish line in the next two heats, the Lady Phoenix finished with four more points than runner-up Corunna.

Competition in the field events took the spotlight. Records in the discus took a beating with Alana Robinson of Grosse Ile hurling the platter 155-6. Batten, placed a more than respectable second in the discus with a mark of 147-0.

Lindsay Mulder erased from the record books one of the oldest marks with her win in the long jump. The Grandville Calvin Christian ace leaped 18-6 to better Beth Brunn's mark of 18-5¾ set 21 years earlier. Proving that her mark of 18-6 was no fluke, Mulder improved to 18-7 a week later in winning the long jump at the Midwest Meet.

Katie Clifford of Grand Rapids West Catholic had little difficulty in winning the 1600 (4:58.6) and 3200 (10:58.0).

It was business as usual for Caledonia in the girls 3200-meter relay. After winning their fourth-straight cross country title in the fall, the Lady Scots also won their fourth-consecutive 4 x 800. Shannon Houseman, who took her talents to Arizona State and later Michigan State, ran on each of the four 3200-meter relay squads.

In Class C at Comstock Park, Kingsley won its first state championship in girls track by scoring 38 points. The Lady Stags clinched the meet by taking their only win in the meet's final event. The relay of Alaina Olds, Amber Hays, Kate Rieger and Erin Ockut won the 4 x 400 to finish three points ahead of Napoleon.

Bethany Brewster was once again the top performer. The Saginaw Valley Lutheran distance ace, who had a time second only to Van Tuyl at the cross country finals in the fall, easily took her specialties on the track, with winning times of 5:00.55 for the 1600 and 11:09.23 in the 3200.

Joining Brewster as double winners were Jane Ludtke of White Cloud and Alanna Mestelle of White Pigeon. Mestelle took honors in the short sprints while Ludtke walked off with the first-place medals in the weight events.

Monyka Paul of St. Louis, winner of the high jump at 5-5, would improve that mark by three inches in winning her event at the Midwest Meet of Champions.

Just as in Classes B and C, a first-time champion was crowned in Class D at Forest Hills. And holding true to form, it took the 1600-meter relay to determine a champion. Mendon used the five points earned with its fourth-place finish in the day's final event to clinch the trophy.

Mendon's only first-place effort was a record in the 3200-relay. The 4 x 800 team of Kasey Culp, Christina Stephenson, Lena Rice and Michelle Klein were clocked in 9:44.6. Culp added valuable points by placing second in the 1600 and 3200. Winning those events was Betsey Speer from Whitmore Lake, who had placed second behind Culp at the state cross country finals by less than a stride.

Upper Peninsula: Marquette, whose strength has usually been found in the distance events, used a 1-2-3 sweep in the shot put to win its fifth-straight A-B championship.

The A-B meet was certainly upstaged by the Class C. Three records fell in Class C as Ironwood made it four team titles in a row. Three girls stole the show: Ann Somerville of Ironwood and Holly Brown and Richelle Robinson of second-place St. Ignace.

Somerville figured in a pair of records for the Red Devils but it was her anchor in the 1600-meter relay that was most impressive. Leading St. Ignace by two points entering the final event, Somerville dueled with Robinson of the Saints. Robinson, who had earlier won the 200 and 400, took the early lead on the final lap. Somerville held her form and defeated Robinson by two and a half seconds at the finish line. Earlier, the future MSU cross-country whiz had won the 1600 and 800, the latter in an all-UP class record of 2:21.3. Holly Brown won three events for St. Ignace, including a record of 17-5½ in the long jump.

Rapid River held off second-place Lake Linden-Hubbell to successfully defend the Class D championship. Sara Boyer and Lisa Froberg paced the Rockets with a pair of wins. Boyer clinched the championship with her anchor on the winning 4x4.

1998

It was business as usual for Ann Arbor Pioneer as the Lady Pioneers won a third-consecutive Class A championship in surprisingly easy fashion. Coach

Bryan Westfield's deep squad, with 82 points, nearly doubled the score on Detroit Cass Tech.

Sharon Van Tuyl again won the 1600 and 3200-meter runs. Only as a freshman, when she placed second in the 3200, did the Portage Northern distance ace fail to win. Coupled with her three state cross country victories, the Boston College-bound star won 10 state titles in track and cross country.

Class A power Cass Tech's Traci Ball was the individual standout at Bay City Western. Ball equaled the meet record in the 200 with a clocking of 24.38. She won the 400 in a near-record 54.81. Earlier, the Technician's foursome of Crystal Lee, Tiarra Jones, Ball & Me'shia Moton raced to a convincing win in 1:39.33.

Seemingly always peaking at the right time, the Lady Pioneers were led by hurdler Robyn Woolfolk, who defeated arch rival Tanisha Williams of Ypsilanti in the 100-meter hurdles in a quick 14.03. In addition, Woolfolk placed 2nd in the 300 hurdles behind Leshanta Blanton and ran on a leg on the winning 400-meter relay team that broke a six-year old school record with a 47.87.

Ypsilanti's Williams earned the hard luck award for the day. In addition to her narrow loss to Woolfolk in the hurdles, she equaled the day's best mark in the long jump with a 18-1½. Williams, however, had to settle for second place when Charnita Allen of Portage Central, who also had the same mark as Williams, took home the first-place medal with a better second jump. Later, Williams and her mates could only watch the 400 relay because they had dropped the baton at regionals. At the Washtenaw County Meet of Champions, Ypsi had defeated the eventual state champions.

In Class B at Saginaw, Detroit Renaissance easily repeated by racking up 66 points. The meet was highlighted by the girls weight events where Alana Robinson of team runner-up Grosse Ile and Renaissance's Makiba Batten concluded their four-year rivalry.

Robinson bested her rival, but needed to be at her best to do so. First she broke the meet record in the shot at 44-7, then added the discus crown as well. Robinson hurled the one-kilo platter 154-0, behind only her own meet record. Batten's second-place effort in the shot also exceeded the old meet record.

The victorious Phoenix team had a plethora of sprinters to compliment Batten, winning the 800-meter relay in 1:42.25, a meet record, and the 1600 relay in a quick 3:57.77. Only Albion's first in the 400 relay (49.2) denied Renaissance a relay sweep.

A new event was added for the girls in 1999. Stephanie Teeple from Sturgis, with a clearance of 10-4¼, would have the day's best performance in the pole vault.

In Class C, Kingsley held off Northern Michigan rival Benzie Central 55 to 46 to take home the girls title,

Bethany Brewster from Saginaw Valley Lutheran was clearly the class of the individual competitors. Not only did she win a distance triple, but she took her show on the road two weeks later and won the National Scholastic mile with a 4:50.43.

In between she won the distance double at the Midwest Meet of Champions. After winning the 1600 run in 4:56.86, she volunteered to enter the 3200 because Team Michigan lacked a third runner. This set up a dream match for the first time between Brewster and Class A record holder Van Tuyl.

Although Brewster had expended considerable energy in winning the 1600 run on the Ohio Wesleyan oval, the University of Wisconsin bound senior defeated Van Tuyl by 17 seconds. She wasted no time proving that she could run with the nation's elite as a Badger, winning 11 Big 10 crowns and making All-America six times.

Ironically, despite Brewster's accomplishments, she fell short of setting any meet records in Class C, a testament to the abilities of Mason County Central's Melanie Weaver some 19 years earlier.

Fowler continued its dominance in Class D by piling up 85 points. Brittany Hedgepeth of St. Joseph Lake Michigan Catholic was the individual star, with the day's best mark in all classes in the long jump, leaping 18-7½ to better Maria Shoup's 17-year old record. Hedgepeth, who also won the 100, set the other record in Class D with her 25.5 in the 200.

Mendon's 3200-meter relay foursome of Kasey Culp, Christyina Stephenson, Elyssa Vernon and Michelle Klein bettered its own record from 1997 with a time of 9:39.97.

Desha Feldpausch was the catalyst for the winning Fowler squad. She won both hurdles, anchored the winning 1600-meter relay team and barely missed out on a fourth first-place medal when her team's 800-meter relay team was nipped at the wire by Carsonville-Port Sanilac.

Upper Peninsula: Rain again played havoc at the finals in Marquette. There can be little doubt, however, that no two teams ever dominated an UP final in any class as did Marquette and Escanaba. The two teams combined to win every first-place medal but one. The only "outsider" to win a title was Allison Koskey from Negaunee when she took honors in the girls 300-meter hurdles. Marquette outscored rival Escanaba 102 to 84 to claim another team trophy. Krista O'Dell was the only triple winner in A-B, winning all three distance events. O'Dell's winning time in the 1600 was a A-B record.

Ironwood continued its roll in Class C, scoring 10 points more than second-place Ishpeming Westwood. Ann Somerville capped her great career for Ironwood by repeating her four victories from 1997.

Rapid River, which came a basket short from winning the girls Class D basketball finals in December, also had to settle for second place in the Class D track finals. St. Ignace, second for two years in a row behind Ironwood in Class C, found the drop to Class D more to its liking. Jane Rautiola, the only individual UP track champion from Painsdale-Jeffers, set the only record in Class D with her 11:53.0 in the 3200.

1999

If ever a dynasty was spawned during the 20th century in girls track & field, certainly Ann Arbor Pioneer would be at the top of the list. Only Pickford's boys could perhaps boast of a run as complete as the girls of Pioneer High School, but Pickford's domination came against a much smaller group of competitors.

Coach Brian Westfield's Lady Pioneers won their fourth-straight Class A championship and their tenth since 1985.

Tanisha (Nee Nee) Williams was clearly the star at the finals in Midland. Her 14.27 clocking over the 100-meter hurdles was the closest threat to a new record. She also posted a top mark in the long jump with a leap of 18-10¾.

If Pioneer can be classified as a dynasty in team competition, then surely the same could be said for the Lady Technicians of Detroit Cass Tech in the 800-meter relay. The 1:40.41 for Cass was the seventh-straight in this event, easily the most dominance by a single school in any event in the 105 years of Michigan track & field. Tiarra Jones, winner of the 100, and 200 champion Katrice Walton were joined by Eboni Jenkins and Meshia Moton on the winning relay.

Rockford scored 58 of its 60 points with its deep distance corps of six runners in their best-ever showing. It is doubtful if any school in the country could match Rockford's boy and girl runners that year. Two weeks after the state meet the boys and girls distance medley relay teams took first place against the best the nation had to offer at the National Scholastic in North Carolina.

Optimum running conditions were not available in Midland. Rockford's winning 3200-meter relay time of 9:22.34 paled in comparison to its effort at the national meet. There the Lady Rams placed 3rd in 9:07.88,

cutting nearly 10 seconds off West Bloomfield's state record of 9:17.46 set in 1988.

Southfield's speedsters romped to an impressive win in the 1600-meter relay. Carly Knazze and Melody Williams, who placed 1-3 respectively in the open 400, led the Blue Jays to a quick 3:51.51 clocking, more than a second faster than second-place Pioneer. Earlier, Williams and Tiarra Jones were caught in the same 12.01 for the 100, but the photo showed Jones the winner.

At Class B, Detroit Renaissance rolled to its third-straight championship, led by its sprinters. The Lady Phoenix won the 400 and 800-meter relays and placed 2-3-4 in the 200 meters. The day's best individual performance came from Becky Breisch of Edwardsburg in the discus; after taking first in the shot (42-8½), she threw the discus 151-5.

In Class C at Saginaw, a considerable amount of grumbling came from athletes, coaches, and spectators. The crowd was poorly informed of performances throughout the day. Many fans waited in anticipation for the girls 300-meter hurdles, where defending champion Amber Bright of Benzie Central had posted the state's fastest time in any class. She had already won the 100 hurdles in 14.91. However, Bright never got a chance to run her specialty. Officials scratched her when she did not report in time.

Despite her disappointment, Bright came back to anchor the winning 1600-meter relay (4:04.52). "I knew I had to score extra points to make up for what we lost," Bright said. "I couldn't let the team down."

The Lady Huskies managed to win the team trophy by 11 over Mason County Central.

A trio of records tumbled. Mason County Central's foursome of Crystal Fluter, Jenny Irwin, Kristie Lehrbass and Leanna Wolf, with a time of 9:30.56, shattered the former record by eight seconds.

Julia Redd surpassed a record that stood for 20 years with a 56.05 in the 400. Tiffany Simons of Detroit Dominican established the other Class C mark with her time of 24.94 in the 200 meters.

North Muskegon, which hadn't won a state track championship since winning three out of four years beginning in 1977, edged a well-balanced field to take honors in Class D. Lindsey Kowalski of Manistee Catholic rebounded from a narrow loss in the 100 to defeat defending champion Brittany Hedgepeth of St. Joseph Lake Michigan Catholic. Her winning time of 25.68 was just off Hedgepeth's meet record.

Upper Peninsula: It's too bad that Marquette's distance corps didn't match talents with Rockford. Hopefully, the new millennium will see athletes from the Upper Peninsula compete in all sports against their peers from the Lower Peninsula. The winds were severe on the shores of Lake Superior; sustained winds of 20mph with occasional gusts up to 60mph made records nearly impossible.

The Marquette foursome of Erica Helmilla, Angela Abernathy, Emily and Katie Anderson broke the UP record in 9:41.3. Katie Anderson accounted for the other record by winning the 800-meter run in 2:21.1.

Ironwood edged St. Ignace 49 to 46 to win a sixth-straight Class C championship. Bessemer won five events but could only place third in the team standings in Class D. Jacklyn Bebeau won the 100 and 200 meters and ran a leg on a pair of winning relay teams for the speedgirls.

2000

Running in front of the hometown fans, Rockford won its first girls track title. The Lady Rams used their incredible depth in the distance events to dethrone perennial power Ann Arbor Pioneer. Not only could Rockford boast of having the most talented array of distance runners in the state, there could be little doubt that it was tops in the entire country.

"The meet came down to the sprints, the hurdles and the distances, said Rockford head coach Randy VanderVeen. "We knew Ann Arbor Pioneer's and Cass Tech's strengths were the sprints and hurdles, and ours were the distances."

It didn't take long for the 8,000 fans in attendance to appreciate Rockford's greatness. The 4 x 800 relay of Renae Sobie, Aimee Keenan, Nora Colligan and Linsey Blaisdell smashed the meet record with a clocking of 9:13.87. Two weeks later at the Foot Locker Outdoor National Championships, Kalin Toedebusch replaced Sobie and Rockford became the first Michigan High School foursome to break the nine-minute barrier with a time of 8:57.52, at the time the No. 5 performance in U.S. prep history.

So dominant were the Rams at nationals that the combined Rockford teams had more first-place winners than any other state. Combined, Rockford won six titles, one more than the entire states of California, Florida and New York.

The Lower Peninsula Finals this year were the first to be held with divisional classifications, instead of the old class system. The crucial difference was that the divisions were balanced, with the top 25% of schools by size in Division 1, the next 25% in Division 2, etc. For the most part, not a lot changed on the track in the three largest divisions. The smallest division included bigger schools than in the past and saw deeper competition in the ensuing years.

The MHSAA started a whole new slate of meet records for the divisional era. In this book, we note many of the "new" records but often refer "Class B/Div.

2" records, for instance, in order to give proper acknowledgement to the legitimate records of the previous century.

At the finals in Rockford, the Lady Rams placed four girls in the top nine of the 1600 to accumulate 29 of their 87 1/3 points. Junior Linsey Blaisdell won in 4:50.95, while teammates Kalin Toedebusch (4:56.66) and Emily Blakeslee (4:56.57) ran 3-4.

This same Ram threesome swept the first three places in the 3200. Blakeslee took first in 10:55.71 just inches ahead of Toedebusch and Blaisdell who were credited with a tie for second.

Southfield, although finishing well behind Rockford in fourth, had a pair of double winners in sprinter Melanie Williams and Lindsay Bond. Williams sprinted to victories in the 200 (24.62) and the 400 (56.70) and placed a close second behind Tiarra Jones of Detroit Cass Tech in the 100. Bond, with her win in the 100 hurdles (14.24), prevented Ann Arbor from placing 1-2-3. Bond nipped Pioneer's Tiffany Hall to win the 300 hurdles crown.

In Division 2, Detroit Renaissance continued its dominance at the state finals by winning its fourth-straight team title. The 84 points earned by head coach Rick Miotke's champs would be the second highest total earned in D2/Class B history, trailing only the 87 scored by the girls from Flint Beecher in 1992. Renaissance amassed 84 points without scoring once in the field events.

It was a different story in the sprints. The 800-meter relay of LaTosha Jollet (100 champ), Erin Anderson (2nd in the 100 and 3rd in the 200), Jennifer Lawson (200 champ) and Julia Stevenson (4th in the 200 and 400) was so talented that its clocking of 1:39.92 was the fastest time ever posted in state Class B/D2 annals. So deep were the Lady Phoenix sprint corps that Fallon Jenkins and Brandis O'Neal joined Anderson and Jollet for the 400-meter relay to set another standard (48.69) that was unchallenged for 13 years.

Sara Jane Baker, a sophomore from Mattawan, was yet another D2 standout. After clearing 5-7 in the high jump, she led a stellar field in the 400-meter dash to the finish line with a time of 56.16 seconds.

Jamie Kryzminski of Corunna, a future distance standout at Michigan State, set a meet record in the 3200-meter run (10:45.23) after winning the 1600 in 4:54.07. Battle Creek Lakeview, anchored by 800-meter champion Jennifer Price, blistered a 3:56.07 to defeat Renaissance in the 1600 relay.

In Division 3 at Comstock Park, Yale had just enough firepower to edge Benzie by a single point. Amber Berrien led her team to victory with wins in the 200 and 400. The meet would see the emergence of a girl destined to become one of the best throwers in state history. Becky Breisch from Edwardsburg began her dominance in the shot put and discus with a pair of records that would last until she returned the next year. Her marks of 46-4¼ and 156-11 were not only D3/Class C meet records, but were also superior to any former marks set in any other class or division.

Two other former Class C marks fell in D3. Lansing Catholic Central defeated second-place Mason County Central in the 3200-meter relay, in the process lowering Mason County's 1999 record to 9:30.24. Tracy Ignatuk took the 800 record to 2:16.03.

At Division 4 at Forest Hills Northern, Saginaw Michigan Lutheran Seminary gave its coach the perfect going-away present. A team victory came on the last day of coaching for Daryl Weber. The victors won four events to finish 18 points ahead of Detroit DePorres.

Two records went down. Sarah Adelaine of Harbor Springs had a best 41-9 in the shot. Jenny Kulchar had a big day for Burton Atherton. After clearing the bar at 5-7, the best girls mark in the high jump in 22 years, Kulchar set a meet record in the 800-meter run in 2:17.87.

Upper Peninsula: The championships were held under ideal conditions and the top stars from across the Big Mac Bridge disappointed no one on hand in Kingsford. It was double your money in A-B with the O'Dell and Anderson twins stealing the show. Only in the 3200-meter relay did the highest class fail to break a record in events contested at 400 meters and longer.

Krista O'Dell came just a fraction from becoming the first UP girl to crack the five-minute barrier in the 1600 (5:00.1), just ahead of Katie and Emily Anderson from Marquette. Krista's twin sister, Kari, placed fifth after earlier running a leg on the victorious 3200-meter relay team with Krista and Linsey Olson and Erin Gannon.

O'Dell, who would place second at the Midwest Meet of Champions in the 1600, waged a thrilling dual with sophomore Natalie Cahill from Sault Ste. Marie in the 800. Running nearly stride for stride the entire race O'Dell passed Cahill on the stretch drive as both runners shattered the previous record by nearly five seconds. The Anderson twins capped the record-breaking onslaught by running 1-2 in the 3200-meter run, with Katie leading her twin sister Emily across the line in 10:59.6 as Marquette took the team title in A-B. Earlier Erica Helmila of Marquette set a new UP standard of 59.0 in the 400.

Westwood held off St. Ignace to take honors in Class C while Pickford nipped rival Rapid River by only three points to bring another state championship trophy back to an already crowded trophy case in Pickford. St. Ignace came close to breaking a record dating back to 1978 when it won the Class C 800-meter relay in

1:48.7, less than a half second slower than the mark set by Stephenson.

2001

In the tightest team battle since 1976, Ann Arbor Pioneer fought off Rockford to win the Division 1 title. Dramatically, the championship was decided on the day's last event. The Lady Pioneers outlegged Rockford in the 1600-meter relay to capture the team title, 81-80. It was a battle between Pioneers sprinters and hurdlers vs. Rockford's deep corps of long distance aces.

Taking advantage of coach Bryan Westfield's expert hurdle coaching paved the way for another state title. Westfield, a standout 400-meter hurdler in his day, passed his expertise off to his students. Although not winning the 300-meter hurdles, Venice Jones, Candice Davis and Aja Hunter placed 2-3-4 behind winner Lindsay Bond from Southfield to pile on much needed points. Earlier, Davis had nipped Bond in taking honors in the 100-meter hurdles.

The Rams confirmed their distance depth during the day by taking the 3200-meter relay, pulling off the rare feat of placing four in the 1600-meter run. Linsey Blaisdell successfully defended her championship; also placing were Nikki Bohnsack and Kalin and Kelsey Toedebusch.

Only Katie Boyles from Rochester Adams kept the Rams from sweeping the 3200, clocking a meet standard 10:42.06. Boyles had won four straight cross country crowns but this was her first on the track. "Track and I just haven't gotten along. It just hadn't worked out for me in the past. But I felt real good today."

In Division 2 at Forest Hills Northern, Detroit Renaissance powered to its fifth-straight team title. Battle Creek Lakeview made the team battle interesting by trailing the champs by only 3½ points. Junior sprinter LaTosha Jollet sped to a pair of victories in the short sprints and also ran the anchor leg for the Lady Phoenix 800-meter relay team. Renaissance won the event by an amazing margin of nearly five seconds.

The individual star was Mattawan junior Sara Jane Baker. The future standout heptathlete at Nebraska equaled a 25-year old record in clearing 5-9 in the high jump to equal a record initially set by Utica's Beth Brunn in 1976 and matched by Terri Johnson of Muskegon Catholic in 1977. Then in the 400, Baker posted the day's fastest time in all divisions with her repeat win in 56.66.

A duo from West Branch Ogemaw Heights shared the spotlight with Baker at the D2 finals. Jessica Kraft joined the sub five-minute club with a 4:57.65 in the 1600. She then placed second in the 3200 behind teammate Abigail Nelkie, who won in 10:47.44.

The focus in Division 3 at Comstock Park was on the throws. While Dathan Ritzenhein could arguably be called the state's number one distance performer of all-time, perhaps Becky Breisch of Edwardsburg could stake a similar claim in the throws. Breisch established records in all classes/divisions with her achievements. She whirled the discus 158-3 and muscled the shot out to 46-9¾.

Those distances would pale in comparison to what she would accomplish for the University of Nebraska. She would become an eight-time All American for the Lady Huskers, winning NCAA titles in the shot (2003) and the discus (2004). She just missed making the Olympic team when she placed fourth in the discus at the Olympic Trials. She bounced back to win the USA title in 2005 with a monster heave of 206-5.

Cass City would win its first state championship in the well-balanced Division 3 meet. Although over shadowed by Breisch, sophomore sprinter Julie Johnson of Laingsburg had a monster day. She scored all 30 of her team's points by winning all three sprints (12.45, 25.47, 57.04), helping her team to runner-up honors.

Another rising star was Wyoming Kelloggsville frosh Nicole Bush, who would dominate the distance races over her career. She won the 1600 (5:01.27) and 3200 (11:10.62).

Tracy Egnatuk of Albion not only defended her title in the 800 but established a meet record at 2:14.66. Track may not have been the Albion High School valedictorian's best sport. She was selected Class B/C/D high school swimmer of the year before joining the swim team at the University of Michigan. As a Wolverine trackster, she placed second in her freshman year in the 800 meters at the Big 10.

In Division 4 at Lowell, Reading had little trouble in breezing to the championship. Jeanie Lawton of Bishop Gallagher defended her title in the discus with a meet record 137-6.

Upper Peninsula: Sarah Duesing led Sault Ste. Marie to the title as the UP made the change from classes to division competition a year after the Lower Peninsula (albeit with three divisions). Highlighting Duessing's performance was her meet standard 5-8 in the high jump, second only to Sara Jane Baker's 5-9 effort at the Lower Peninsula finals. Only a record performance by Sarah Ducheny in the 100-meter hurdles deprived Duesing from winning four individual titles. Ducheny nipped Duesing at the tape in the 100-hurdles with a UP D1/Class A-B best of 15.4 seconds, just inches ahead of Duesing.

Taking home four first-place medals at the UP finals on the Kingsford High School track was Gladstone sprinter Tiffany Petr, who captured the 100, 200 and 400 as well as anchoring the winning 4 x 200.

Ironwood won a tightly contested battle in D2 by compiling a six-point advantage over St. Ignace. Westwood's Amber Smith was the top individual point winner in D2 by sweeping the distance events (800,1600 and 3200) as well as anchoring the winning 3200-meter relay.

Pickford picked up its tenth Division 3 title for head coach John Benin by outpointing rival Rapid River 64-59. Ashley Bishop fell four inches short of becoming the first girl from the UP to hit the 40-0 in the shot put.

2002

Ann Arbor Pioneer surpassed all expectations at the Division 1 finals in Rockford. Pioneer racked up a record total of 97 points and pulled off a feat that had only occurred one other time in girls track history. The Lady Pioneers swept all four relays, a feat that had only previously been accomplished in 1987 in Class C by Detroit Country Day. By winning the 800-meter relay, Ann Arbor ended the dominance of Detroit Cass Tech in this event after nine straight years.

Once again Pioneer dominated the hurdle events with Candice Davis winning the 100 hurdles and teammate Andrea Mosher following in second place. Mosher came back later in the afternoon to win the 300 hurdles in 43.19, making her the No. 6 hurdler in state history. Davis' time of 13.69 in the 100 hurdles set a new state record.

Said Davis, "I was going so fast I wasn't going over the hurdles on the correct leg. It felt like I couldn't get my leg up."

Of Pioneer's sweep in the relays, the 3200-meter foursome of Rachel Eyler, Jennifer Kraus, Alexandra Cassar and Clarissa Codrington came the closest in setting a new meet record. Their 9:14.03 missed by only two-tenths of a second. Laura Fortson and Keisha Townsend were members of three of the four winning relay units.

Once again Rockford compiled the second highest point total (76 points) for a second-place team in state D1/Class A history. Rockford's powerful distance corps again produced a mass of points, despite a controversy that led to the loss of their distance coach, Brad Prins. The Lady Rams also became a powerhouse in the girls pole vault. Bethany Hecksel and Janine Roslonic placed 1-2 while Stacy Orosz managed a tie for seventh.

Detroit Cass Tech continued its stranglehold on the short sprints with Katrice Walton of the Lady

Technicians sweeping the short dashes. She made it nine in a row for a Cass Tech runner in the 100 meters and then came back to recapture the 200-meter crown that she first won as a freshman back in 1999.

The Division 2 finals at Grand Rapids Houseman Field boasted a talented field that produced some of the best marks in Class B annals. It was business as usual for Detroit Renaissance as the Lady Phoenix captured their sixth-straight state title. LaTosha Jolett of the winners set the pace for the day's record onslaught by lowering her own best in the 200-meter dash down to 24.55 seconds.

A pair of young frosh took a bead on the hurdles races where both records fell. Meghan Stachota of Chesaning, with a 14.39, became her school's first state track champ. Another talented frosh making her state debut was Ypsilanti's Tiffany Ofili. After placing second to Stachota in the 100 hurdles, Ofili bounced back to set a new record with a clocking of 44.04 for the 300-meter lows.

Annie Diener of Pinconning bettered the long jump best by a scant ¼ with a 18-6¼. Diener needed that extra quarter of an inch to not only set a record, but to take first place, as Rhianna Stalter of Lake Odessa-Lakewood also matched the former record of 18-6. Sara Jane Baker of Mattawan just missed matching her own mark in the high jump when she cleared 5-8.

Although not setting any records, it was clear that Cadillac's Katie Erdman would become something special down the road. While the winds were very favorable for the sprinters, hurdlers, and long jumpers, they worked against the distance performers. Erdman won the 1600-meter run by an overwhelming 14 seconds (4:57.81) and the 800 meters by four seconds (2:13.51). After enrolling at Michigan the following fall, she would be the Big 10 freshman of the year in track with a personal best of 2:04.21 in the 800.

In Division 3, the girls from Yale matched the boys' feat and won the title. Courtney Kersten led the way for the victors by winning the 300-meter hurdles and clinched the meet when she crossed the finish line in first place with her anchor on the 1600-meter relay.

Sprinter Julie Johnson of Laingsburg would equal her three victories from 2001. Her 200m winning time of 24.82 would set a record that lasted until 2014. Vassar's Mary Raney's mark of 44-2 in the shot put was the best effort in any division.

Sophomore Nicole Bush from Wyoming Kelloggsville likewise had the day's best mark in the 3200-meter run on a day when the winds were not kind for distance runners. However, what was most noteworthy for Bush was her second in the 1600 behind Krishawnah Parker of Detroit Crockett. It would be the only race Bush would not win in her four-year career.

In Division 4, Maple City Glen Lake returned to the winner's circle after a seven-year drought. The Lady Lakers took the team trophy back to the shores of Leelanau County, despite not picking up a single first-place medal. Sprinter Stacy Dellar, who repeated as the winner of the 100 and 200, paced runner-up Lincoln-Alcona.

Jaenaie Lawton of Harper Woods Bishop Gallagher also returned to the winner's circle in the discus and shot put. She twirled the discus out to 135-11, second only to her record throw from 2001. Dessaray Cranford from Detroit Benedictine broke a 20-year old meet standard by zipping around the oval in 57.65.

Amanda Weber completed a tremendous year at Portland St. Patrick. After leading her team to the state Class D basketball title back in December, Weber capped her season by winning the D4 long jump title.

The girl who would make the biggest splash on the basketball courts was high jump runner-up Liz Shimek of Maple City Glen Lake. She placed second on misses at 5-5 to winner Porsha Ellis of Southfield Christian and parlayed her Miss Basketball crown into a brilliant NCAA career at Michigan State. The pride of little Empire, Michigan, would not only lead the Spartans to the national championship game in 2005, but would end her collegiate career as the top scorer and rebounder in MSU history.

Upper Peninsula: Ashley Bishop of Pickford and sophomore distance ace Amber Smith from Ishpeming Westwood were the top performers at the finals held in Kingsford. Bishop not only set a UP record of 42-½" in the shot put, but that performance was superior to any mark set in D4 or Class D in the Lower Peninsula. Her performance helped Pickford to its third-straight title with Rapid River likewise placing second for the third consecutive year.

Sophomore Amber Smith led Westwood to the Division 2 championship by again dominating the distance events. Smith's winning time of 5:04.1 set a UP record.

Gladstone racked up a massive total of 125 points to easily take team honors in a Division 1 meet that would see no division records fall.

2003

Rockford captured its second Division 1 title at Houseman Field in Grand Rapids, as perennial power Ann Arbor Pioneer had to settle for second. Unlike the state champs from 2000 that relied on their outstanding distance corps to bring home the bacon, coach Randy Vanderveen's Lady Rams had become a complete team by 2003. Sprinters and field events personnel all chipped in help Rockford rack up an impressive total of 77½ points.

The Lady Rams still prevailed with their distance power, led by Nikki Bohnsack. Fully recovered from a hip injury that sidelined her during the cross-country season, Bohnsack captured the 1600 and 3200 at Houseman Field and also anchored the 3200-meter relay to another victory. Fittingly, Rockford capped the day's events by edging runner-up Pioneer in the 1600-meter relay.

Said Bohnsack, "The whole team contributes. It's a great feeling. Everyone pulls for each other."

Pioneer did have its day in the sun, however. Hurdling wizard Candice Davis lowered her own record from the previous year to 13.66 seconds in winning the 100 hurdles. Astin Steward of Okemos set a discus standard at 154-9. Just missing a new mark was Flint Carman-Ainsworth's Kamitra Carroll, whose best effort in the shot was 45-6¼, less than an inch shy.

Ariss Seals, by winning the 100-meter dash, would be the seventh sprinter from Detroit Cass Tech to win the century over a ten-year span, an accomplishment no other school in either gender could claim.

At Division 2 in Caledonia, another long streak continued when Detroit Renaissance climbed the victory stand for the seventh-straight year. Individual honors went to Stephanie Allers of Coopersville. She began her day's work by hurdling a wind-aided 14.29 to beat a first-rate field to the finish, including defending champ and previous record holder Megan Strachota of Chesaning.

The future 5-time NAIA All-American at nearby Cornerstone University barely had time to catch her breath when she settled into the blocks for the very next event, the 100-meter dash. She settled for third behind double sprint champion Alisha Cole from Cadillac and Ypsilanti star Tiffany Ofili. Allers then outlasted a pair of Renaissance runners to emerge victorious in the 400-meter dash (57.43). She concluded her 8-race day (including prelims and semi-finals) by leading Coopersville to a second-place finish behind Renaissance in the 1600-meter relay. The eight points earned in this event propelled the Lady Broncos into second place, their best ever placing.

One other record of note was set in D2. The Renaissance foursome of Amber Hay, Alexandrea Cunningham, Elisha Logan and Kelly Sampson were timed in 9:19.83 for the 3200-meter relay. Watching proudly from the stands when Kelly Sampson crossed the finish line was her 94-year old grandfather Robert Sampson. That came 76 years after Robert Sampson won the state Class A high jump championship while competing for Detroit Cass Tech.

Courtney Kersten of Yale, winner of the 300-meter hurdles in Division 3 in 2002, made the step up in division without a hitch and won the event in 44.35.

At Division 3 in Comstock Park, one of the most impressive performers had her career come to a glorious finish. For the third-straight year Julie Johnson of Laingsburg would win all three sprints, but in 2003 she had a little help from her mates. Ironically, her most memorable race was not only her last race for Laingsburg High, but it was a race she didn't even win! Trailing Monroe Saint Mary Catholic Central by two points heading into the 1600-meter relay, Johnson received the baton trailing many teams. With a blazing anchor leg Johnson moved past many runners (including Monroe Saint Mary) to move into third place and give Laingsburg a share of the title with the ladies from Monroe.

Johnson would leave a lasting legacy behind her following the 2003 season. In addition to winning the 100, 200, and 400-meter dashes for three straight years, her time of 24.82 for the 200 meters remained at the top of the leader board for 11 years.

A trio of other competitors notched a pair of wins. Headlining was Nicole Bush of Wyoming Kelloggsville, who erased a long-standing record for the 1600 that was set by Melanie Weaver of Mason County back in 1979. Bush became the first D3/Class C performer in meet history to break the five-minute barrier.

Mary Raney from Vassar claimed a double win in the throws with victories in the shot put (42-½) and discus (134-0). Katie Pickette from Hopkins sped to a pair of first-place finishes in the hurdles, topped by a wind-aided 14.50.

In Division 4 action at Forest Hills Northern, Detroit Benedictine impressed. The girls, behind a sweep in the sprints from Dessaray Cranford, duplicated the boy's championship effort by outpointing runner-up Pewamo-Westphalia 53 to 44. Jessica Miela from Fife Lake-Forest Area had the only meet record when she vaulted 10-6.

Upper Peninsula: Escanaba won its first state championship in 11 years by nipping rival Marquette 94 to 90 in Kingsford. Sophomore speedster Stephanie Ostrenga, winner of the 200 and 400-meter dash, led the Esykmos.

There could be little question as to what performer in any division was the most impressive at the UP finals. Amber Smith of Ishpeming Westwood cruised to her third-straight sweep in the distance events, setting a 1600-meter record in the process. She won the 1600 by 30 seconds with a 5:01.53, recorded a second record by winning the 800 in 2:18.12 and just missed a third mark by about a second by winning the 3200 in 11:07.78.

The Patriots needed all of Smith's points, as Westwood would win a narrow victory over Iron Mountain in D2, 93 To 91.

Rapid River roared to an easy Division 3 crown by more than doubling the margin over runner-up Rock Mid Peninsula. Stephanie Boyer paced the way for the victors by winning three events. The lone D3 record to fall came in the 100 meters when Becky Baron of Rock Mid Peninsula sped the century in 12.50 seconds.

2004

Although the boys failed to create too many waves, the girls 2004 Lower Peninsula State Finals had more records broken than at a disco demolition night in old Comiskey Park. Nearly half the records fell in Division 4 while four more new marks were created in Division 3. A new wave of talented distance performers arrived on the scene to make these state finals one of the best in state history.

Detroit Mumford took home a pile of hardware back to the Motor City in Division 1. The Lady Mustangs joined the boys in taking first-place honors in Rockford. Headlining the Lady Mustangs achievements were the 400 and 800-meter relays. The 400-relay of Porsche Ries, Shayla Mahan, Dana Hill and Stephanie Porter blazed one lap in a meet record 47.78 seconds. Ries would become the first girl not from Detroit Cass Tech, to win the 100 in a full decade.

It's not often that Ann Arbor Pioneer sets a school record and does not win. However, in the 800-meter relay, the Lady Pioneers placed behind Mumford's 1:39.12, the second-fastest time in meet history.

So talented was Mumford's Ries, Chanell Wright, Jessica Jones and Jasmine Webb that only Ries ran a leg on the relay that broke the 4x1 record.

Pioneer would not be left out of the records, however. The 1600-meter relay of Melissa Phillips, Osameude Iyoha, Kiara Moore and Lauren Fortson clocked 3:46.43. Earlier Iyoha blasted a 42.85 in the 300 hurdles.

Rockford swept the first two places in the pole vault with winner Stacy Orosz improving the meet record to 11-6.

Geena Gall of Grand Blanc ran the second fastest time in meet history for the two-lapper with a 2:10.45. "I'm a lot stronger this year than last year," she said. Lisa Senakiewich from Davison had a sparkling time of 4:51.64 in the 1600 meters, winning by over six seconds against a strong field.

In Division 2 at Caledonia, Ypsilanti got a prodigious effort from Tiffany Ofili as Ypsi ended Detroit Renaissance's seven-year reign. Ofili swept both hurdles and placed second in the 100 to lead the Braves to an 8-point margin over Renaissance.

Bekah Smeltzer from Monroe Jefferson emerged as a distance star. The freshman, after warming up with a winning performance in the 1600, crushed the field in the 3200 with a record-setting 10:40.66.

Christine Krellwitz of Big Rapids joined three other high jumpers of the past in sharing the high jump record when she cleared the bar at 5-9. Angela Maxey certainly took advantage of the familiar surroundings at her hometown track as the Caledonia vaulter had the day's highest clearance in her event with an 11-8.

At the Division 3 finals at Comstock Park, three records fell and another was just missed by a whisker as Goodrich won its first state title. The middle distance runners set the tone for the day when they thumped the field by 24 seconds in the 3200-meter relay. The foursome of Samantha Minkler, Kayla O'Mara, Kaitlin O'Mara and Janee Jones, with a clocking of 9:24.33, smashed the previous mark held by Lansing Catholic by six seconds. Jones later just missed matching the D3 record for the 800 meters by 0.23 of a second with her 2:14.89.

The 1600 was so competitive that the first three place winners finished under the meet record set a year earlier by Nicole Bush. This time, the Wyoming Kelloggsville runner led Janee Jones of Goodrich and Sarah Squires of Unionville-Sebewaing all under the mark with her 4:53.35. Bush came back to win the 3200 in 10:57.16, second only to Mason County Central's Melanie Weaver 1979 meet record.

In the 400, junior Jaime Watson from nearby Allendale ran the one lap in 55.95, a remarkable four seconds ahead of her closest pursuer.

Houseman Field in Grand Rapids hosted Division 4. Perhaps overshadowing Detroit Benedictine's victory was the outstanding talent assembled there. An astonishing total of six meet records fell by the wayside in a meet that could be labeled the "best-ever" in D4/Division 4 history.

Talk about a building rivalry! How about the battles that would be fought in the distance events over the next few years between Marissa Treece of Maple City Glen Lake and Alexa Glencer of Ann Arbor Greenhills? Treece would win round one by setting records in the 1600 (5:00.56) and 3200-meter runs (11:11.91). These would last only a year.

Erin Dillon from Reading also set a pair of meet marks. The sophomore sprinted the 400 in 57.63 and came back with a 25.63 in the 200. She was a huge factor in Reading's second-place finish behind Benedictine, anchoring the second-place 800-meter relay and concluding her day with an anchor on the Rangers' 1600-meter relay.

Laurel Bennett of Mt. Pleasant Sacred Heart clocked 2:16.04 in the 800. Jessica Miela's pole-vault of 10-10½ won the Fife Lake Forest Area student the event for the third-straight year.

Upper Peninsula: Unlike their counterparts from the Lower Peninsula, the UP girls only set one meet record. Stephanie Ostrenga of Escanaba owned that distinction with her 57.56 in the D1 400.

The 2004 finals marked the final race as a high school prep for Ishpeming Westwood's Amber Smith. The senior class valedictorian had won 16 UP state championships during her remarkable four-year career, including all four UP Division 2 cross country crowns. She would follow in the footsteps of former distance legends Dathan Ritzenhein and Kelly Smith and attend Colorado, where she ran only a few races in four years because of persistent injuries.

Iron Mountain took honors in D2 while Rapid River had nearly 100 points over its closest pursuer in the D3 UP finals.

2005

Sophomore speedster Shayla Mahan of Detroit Mumford, Geena Gall from Grand Blanc and Jenny Morgan from Clarkston dazzled the fans in D1. Mahan would lead Mumford to its second-straight championship, with perennial power Ann Arbor Pioneer a distant second.

"We didn't take anything for granted," said Mumford coach Marc Parker. "We have so much respect for the Pioneer program and the quality of the team, we knew it would be difficult."

After leading the Mustangs to a 1-2 in the 100 with her meet record 11.95, Mahan helped key a pair of meet record relays. She ran the opening leg of the record shattering 800-meter relay that was clocked in a blistering time of 1:37.72. Also on the relay were Stephanie Porter, 100 runner-up Chanell Wright and 200/400 champion Jessica Jones on anchor.

Dana Hill joined Mahan, Wright and Porter on the 4 x 100 to run 47.15 seconds, crushing the old state record by a third of a second.

Clarkston's 3200-meter relay of Lyndsay Smith, Liz Mengyan, Lisa Sickman and Morgan decimated the meet record set by Rockford with a 9:09.45. Later in the afternoon Morgan would clock 4:48.07 to win one of the deepest 1600 races in state annals. The race was so competitive that second-place Geena Gall and Morgan's teammate Liz Mengyan would run the fourth and sixth-fastest times in meet history. The next week Mengyan would win the event at the Midwest Meet.

Morgan still had enough energy left to win the 3200

Jenny Morgan (left) racing younger sister Stephanie. (Pat Davey photo)

meters in 10:45.46. Gall came back to dominate the 800 with her 2:09.60. "I was a little disappointed after what happened in the mile," she said. A few weeks later she would set a state record 2:05.05 in winning the national title.

In Caledonia at Division 2, Detroit Renaissance returned to the winner's circle for the eighth time in nine years. However, it was Tiffany Ofili of runner-up Ypsilanti who stole the show.

The Michigan-bound Ofili set records in three events to headline the day. She leaped 18-9¼ in the long jump, took the 100 hurdles in 14.19, and then capped her day with a 42.82 in the 300 hurdles. After winning her 100-hurdle race Ofili went to the blocks for the 100. Alisha Cole prevented her from having a perfect day by winning, 12.34-12.50. Cole, a Cadillac senior, added the 200-meter dash to her first-place medal collection with a winning hand time of 24.6.

Renaissance nearly swept all four relays en route to its title, as only a second to Lansing Waverly in the 4 x 100 prevented a Lady Phoenix sweep. Renaissance, with a 3:56.45 posted the fourth-fastest time in meet history.

In Division 3 at Comstock Park, Goodrich had a memorable day as the Lady Martians totaled 93 points, the highest total in Class C/Division 3 history. Goodrich was so deep in the distance events that the Lady Martians didn't even need ace distance star Janee Jones to take top honors in the 3200-meter relay. She stayed rested to win the 1600 in a quick 4:58.19 and then claimed first in the 800 in 2:16.8. She was a member of the 1600 relay that placed second behind a meet record 4:01.89 by Albion.

The same Albion quartet of Alpha Clark, Joranda Chapman, Juandretta Oliver and Mika Clark had earlier teamed up to claim another record in the 800-meter relay with a 1:44.24.

Perhaps the best race was the girls 100-meter hurdles. After winning the Division 2 state title back in 2002 as a freshman, Chesaning's Meghan Strachota dropped down a division to capture the hurdles in her senior year with a meet record 14.36. Close on Meghan's heels were Michelle Elliott of Goodrich and Alexandria Lemonious from Detroit Communication Media Arts.

A milestone was set in the Division 3 pole vault when Katie Shaw of Lakeview, became the first Michigan schoolgirl to clear 12-feet in the pole vault at the state championships.

A very tight battle for the D4 championships took place at Houseman Field in Grand Rapids. First-time champion Saginaw Valley Lutheran nosed out Rochester Hills Lutheran Northwest and Ubly by two points.

The top individual performers at the D4 meet oddly enough did not come from any of the top three teams.

Distance stars Marissa Treece (Maple City Glen Lake) and Alexa Glencer (Ann Arbor Greenhills) put on a show. The meet record in the 1600 dropped to 4:56.15, with Treece edging out her Ann Arbor rival by one second. She later set a meet record at 3200 with her 11:07.84.

Another distance ace that would exceed her own previous mark was Mt. Pleasant Sacred Heart's Laurel Bennett. With a 2:13.95 Bennett was pushed to the new mark by runner-up Glencer, whose second-place time also was under the meet record.

Upper Peninsula: Escanaba's Stephanie Ostrenga won four individual titles on the Kingsford track in leading her team to the Division 1 championship. She began her day by winning the 100 in a meet record 12.58. Then she ran the fastest time in UP history (57.85) in the 400, adding another record to her list of honors.

Ostrenga later battled to a first-place finish in the 800-meter run and capped her day by becoming the first runner in history to win all races from 100 through 800 meters. She not only made the 200 meters her fourth championship of the day, but her 25.75 was the fastest in UP history.

The D2 and D3 meets were void of any record-setting performances for the second-straight year. Ishpeming-Republic Michigamme won its first state track title since 1977 in D2, while Rapid River scored its third-straight in D3.

2006

A familiar face received the winning trophy at East Kentwood as Ann Arbor Pioneer head coach Bryan

Westfield claimed his 14th state title as the head mentor at Pioneer.

Although Pioneer totaled an outstanding 80 points, the Lady Pioneers could muster only two wins, the 400-meter relay and Chidimma Uche's win in the 300 low hurdles.

Junior sprinter Shayla Mahan certainly could now lay claim to being Michigan's top female speedster. Mahan crushed the sprints, setting an all-time state record of 11.54 in the 100—with the wind at the maximum allowable 2.0 meters per second

Then disaster struck in the 4 x 100 when Mumford's lead-off false-started. Mahon was furious, and took out her frustrations on the 200, where she destroyed the state record with her 23.74 (0.9 wind). "I was relaxed on the curve, but at the line I got a little tight," she told *Free Press* writer Mick McCabe. "I'm hurting now and I never hurt after the 200. I think this means I can run even faster."

She could. Later in the summer she improved her state records to 11.53 and 23.49.

Erin Humphrey's win in the 400-meter dash completed the sprint records sweep. The Ypsilanti Lincoln senior posted a new all-class/division record with a time of 54.33, arguably superior to the 1978 hand clocking of 54.5 seconds run by Delisa Walton over the slightly longer 440-distance.

The other record came in the pole vault. Junior Amy Morrison from Fenton added more than two-feet to her regional qualifier of 10-0, winning at 12-1.

The Morgan sisters, Jenny and Stephanie, played a major role in Clarkston sharing second place with Detroit Mumford. The sisters each ran a leg on Clarkston's winning 3200-meter relay team that clocked 9:13.42. Senior Jenny then led her sophomore sister Stephanie across the 1600 finish, 4:56.48 to 4:56.86. Stephanie regrouped and captured the 800 in 2:14.54. Jenny then made it a perfect distance sweep for the duo by winning the 3200 in 10:38.51.

In Division 2 at Forest Hills Northern, Detroit Renaissance won its ninth title in ten years. Conspicuous with their absence was the previous year's runners-up from Ypsilanti. Not happy with the team's behavior the night before, the no-nonsense coach for the Braves loaded the girls up in the van and headed back to Ypsilanti without any of the qualifiers even making an appearance.

Sophomore Ramzee Fondren from Renaissance clocked 2:11.08 in the 800, faster than the 2:11.7 set over 880 yards by Rochelle Collins of Detroit Immaculata back in 1978. Once the conversions were factored in, it was close to a tie.

Although Fondren would be credited with the day's only record, there were numerous outstanding performances. Many of the spectators thought they might have been seeing double in two consecutive races. After Katherine McCarthy from Grand Rapids Kenowa Hills won the 400 in the fourth-fastest time in meet history (56.38), her twin Stephanie won the very next race, the 300-meter hurdles in 43.95 seconds, the third-fastest time in meet annals.

The comeback athlete of the meet had to be distance star Bekah Smeltzer from Monroe Jefferson. After winning the 1600 and 3200 as a freshman, Smeltzer would slip back to a pair of third-place finishes in 2005. However, in her junior season of 2006, she bounced back and nailed down both titles. Her 10:42.86 for the 3200 meters was just shy of her own meet record set back in 2004.

At Division 3 in Comstock Park, Kent City won its first-ever championship, nosing out two-time champion Goodrich. The Eagles trailed the defenders by four points going into the final race. A fifth-place effort delivered enough points to take the trophy.

Keyria Calloway from Detroit Crockett had a near-miss in the 200-meter dash. Her time of 24.85 just missed the 24.82 meet record by Julie Johnson of Laingsburg. Albion's 1600-meter relay time of 4:02.89 was second only to its record set the previous year.

Lauren Beresh of Morley Stanwood, in winning the shot for the third consecutive year, muscled the iron ball out to 44-4¼ inches, the best effort of the day in any division.

For the first time, the Division 4 finals were held at Forest Hills Eastern. Ubly would win its first state championship.

Alexa Glencer of Ann Arbor Greenhills finally made it to the top of the podium. After placing second to a pair of record holders over the past three years she exacted her revenge in her last opportunity.

Glencer nipped two-time winner Marissa Treece from Maple City Glen Lake at the finish line by less than a stride in 4:55.57. It was the third consecutive year these two finished under the meet record.

They would go head-to-head in the 3200 with the same results. Glencer won by the same slim margin and set a meet record of 10:56.48. As if this wasn't enough, she had also won the 800 in 2:15.90. In the process, she beat the two-time defending champ and meet record holder Laurel Bennett from Mt. Pleasant Sacred Heart.

Although just missing her own meet records in the 200 and 400, Erin Dillon of Reading would make it three straight years of wins.

Upper Peninsula: Calumet edged Marquette by just three points, with Escanaba a close third at the Division 1 finals in Kingsford. The Marquette 4 x 200 foursome of Alyssa Espamer, Jessica Trotochaud, Brettnee Balbierz and Catherine Angeli posted a winning time of 1:46.34, faster than a Marquette

foursome ran in 1978. However, the 1978 clocking of 1:46.6 was run over 880 yards, 4.67 meters further than 800 meters—the old mark was clearly superior. Fortunately, this same 2006 foursome from Marquette made sure there would be no doubters as to who has the 1600-meter relay record, as they concluded the day's festivities by erasing the former UP best with a 4:04.92.

For the third-straight track season, the girls competing in the Division 2 and Division 3 meets were unable to set any meet records. Ishpeming outlasted runner-up Norway to win a tight battle in D2 while Pickford returned to the winner's stand in D4.

2007

Drama was lacking as to who would walk away with the team championships at the 2007 finals, held once again in the Grand Rapids area. All of the team titles were decided by margins greater than 20 points.

In Division 1 at East Kentwood, Ann Arbor Pioneer once again dominated to win its 15th team title, becoming the first team in Lower Peninsula history—in any class—to surpass the 100-point barrier.

With incredible depth, the Lady Pioneers placed in 10 of the 12 running events en route to a record-crashing total of 104 points. As usual, hurdle mastery played a role. Ra'Jae Marable placed first in the 100 hurdles with teammates Chidimma Uche and Paige Madison finishing fourth and fifth. Uche claimed top honors in the longer 300 hurdles with Madison taking second and Amanda Maher eighth.

High jump ace Ariel Roberts added one field event title for the victors with her 5-7 win in the high jump while coach Bryan Westfield's squad took additional first-place honors in the 400 and 1600-meter relays.

Only one meet record was set. East Kentwood's Abby Shanahan took full advantage of her home runway when she cleared 12-2 in the pole vault. She eclipsed the record set a year earlier by Fenton's Amy Morrison, who would be competing in D2.

Detroit Mumford's Shayla Mahan was the meet's only double winner as she once again swept the 100 and 200. This time around she wouldn't get records because she had big headwinds to deal with. Her 100 of 11.76 was into a stiff 2.5 breeze, and her 200 of 24.11 was into a 1.5 (after a 23.89 semi).

Mahan, before she heard the wind reading, was upset. "I'm running against the clock, not the people. I would have been fine with a 23.8, but a 24.1 seems like I was jogging."

Later in the summer she showed what she really had under the hood, winning the Midwest 100 in a state record 11.37 and finishing 2nd at the USATF

Shayla Mahan, by the time she graduated, had claimed four state records: 100—11.37, 200—23.49, 4x1—47.15, 4x2—1:37.72, plus two indoor records: 60—7.26, 200—23.90. (Jeff Hollobaugh photo)

Junior championships at 11.38.

A pair of future Mid-America conference champs claimed victories during the afternoon activities. Taylor Kennedy's Victoria Chatman won the 400 in 55.51 while Lauren Quaintance won the first state championship in Walled Lake Northern's history by taking the 800 in 2:14.97.

In Division 2, Detroit Renaissance concluded its incredible run of state titles by breezing to its third in a row, and tenth in 11 years under head coach Rick Miotke. Renaissance was victorious in 4 events, with middle distance ace Ramzee Fondren playing a leading role in three. Fondren narrowly missed her own record time of 2:11.08 set in 2006 by a slim tenth of a second. In winning her third-straight 800 Fondren easily posted the fastest time of the day in all divisions.

Fondren earlier had won the 1600-meter run in a tight race to the wire with Meggan Freeland of Parma Western, posting a winning time of 4:59.85 to just edge out Freeland at 4:59.90. The future Tennessee Vol capped her Renaissance career in style by anchoring Renaissance's winning 1600-meter relay.

Byron Center's Mary Angell was the headline athlete of the entire meet by posting all-division records in two events. She twirled the discus out to 159-5 to better the previous record set in 2001 by Becky Breisch, and then again exceeded Breisch's all-class record in the shot put with a heave of 48-9¾.

Comstock Park hosted Division 3. Led by Amelia Bannister, Albion cruised to an easy victory. Bannister won two events and ran a leg on the winning 800-meter relay, all in meet records. Impressively enough, Albion, coached by Mike Jurasek, won five events during the day, setting new meet records in each.

Bannister set a new mark of 55.94 in the 400 and then just minutes later notched another record by winning the 800 in 2:14.03. She also ran a leg on the record-setting 800-meter relay team.

Earlier in the program, Juandretta Oliver long jumped 18-1, a full foot better than the runner-up. Albion's winning time of 49.74 in the 400-meter relay established a meet record.

Amy Myler from Ann Arbor Gabriel Richard led her team in taking home the runner-up trophy in D3. After crossing the finish line first in the 100-meter hurdles, she copped the 300 low hurdles crown with a meet record 44.82. She concluded her busy afternoon by running a leg on AAGR's meet record 1600-meter relay team, the first in meet history to break 4:00 (3:59.06).

In Division 4, although Ubly had little trouble in taking the team honors, the day's individual star was Maple City Glen Lake's distance ace Marissa Treece.

After being defeated in the 1600 and 3200 the year before, Treece destroyed the meet record in the four-lapper with the day's fastest 1600 time in any division, 4:51.73.

Treece still had enough gas left in the tank to win both the 800 and 3200 to account for all of her team's 30 points. The future Notre Dame track star missed setting the 800-record by a scant 0.01.

The winners from Ubly were led by sprinter Jade Kaufman, with her two victories in the 200 and 400-meter dash, a third in the 100 and an anchor on Ubly's meet record 4:04.48 in the 4 x 400.

Future Michigan State All-Big 10 volleyball star Allyson Karaba from North Muskegon showed her jumping ability by winning the high jump at 5-6.

Upper Peninsula: While all the Lower Peninsula state finals were runaway victories for the winners, action could not have been tighter at the UP meet.

Escanaba and Marquette dominated action in the D1 portion, with the two sharing the title with 101 points. The only record set in D1 was Gladstone's 400-meter relay team clocking of 51.22.

Ishpeming's runner-up finish in the 1600-meter-relay gave the Hematites enough points to surpass St. Ignace in D2.

Pickford edged Rapid River for the D3 title while freshman Erin Holmberg from Cook's Big Bay de Noc was the day's leading point producer. Holmberg won all 4 distance events to account for 40 of her teams 53 points. Holmberg established D3 records in the 1600 (5:22,79) and the 3200 (11:59.89), the first individual titles earned by a female track performer from Cook's Big Bay de Noc.

2008

A bevy of talented athletes took part in the state finals, with a few destined for future greatness in this first-rate sport. And would 2008 see the possible end of a track dynasty in girls track?

Ann Arbor Pioneer would capture its 16th state title held at the spacious Rockford facility, the last championship earned under the incomparable coaching career of Bryan Westfield. He would be honored as the National High School Coach of the year for an unprecedented fourth time.

Thanks to a brilliant all-around performance by Ariel Roberts, the Pioneers would rack up 59 points, four more than runner-up Jackson High. The daughter of former MSU and Denver Bronco running back Aaron Roberts contributed nearly half of the Pioneer points with wins in the high jump and low hurdles, and a second in the long jump.

The future all-ACC performer at North Carolina, with her clearance of 5-9, had the best mark in the high jump since Gwen Wentland cleared 5-10 back in 1990.

Ariel Roberts won two straight high jump titles.
(Pete Draugalis photo)

While brisk winds in Rockford made fast times difficult in the running events, such was not the case on the field.

Tia Brooks of East Kentwood smashed the meet record in the shot put with a best of 48-½. Just four years after graduating from high school, she would win at both the NCAA indoor and outdoor while competing for Oklahoma University. A member of the 2012 Olympic team, Brooks ended her pro career with a best of 64-8¾, an astounding 16-foot improvement over her mark in high school.

West Bloomfield's Leslie Aririguzo, who had won the high hurdles as a soph, came back as a senior to do it again, her 13.84 second only to the meet record of Candice Davis. "Last year was disappointing," she said of her third-place finish. "I thought it was going to come easy because I had won it the year before. It was a bad day."

Looking on with much interest at the D1 finals was the 1973 440 and 880-yard winner in the first state meet for girls, Sue Latter Addison. A national champion in the 880-yard run in 1977, mom would see her daughter Rebecca Addison capture a pair of state titles 35 years later.

The Grand Haven senior produced a winning 800 time of 2:13.79 that outdid mom's 880 clocking of 2:17.7 from 1973.

At Division 2 in Zeeland, after placing second for the previous two years, Forest Hills Northern finally won. Northern had just one individual champion in sprinter Marieme Mhaye, but had enough depth in other events to hold off Ypsilanti 54-40.

Windy conditions affected the competition all day. Katie Guikema from Grand Rapids South Christian won the long jump for the third-straight year, exceeding the 18-foot barrier on all three of her victories.

In Division 3, Ann Arbor Gabriel Richard copped the title as runner-up Leroy Pine River, with 42 points, had its best showing ever.

Albion's Amelia Bannister won two distinctly different events. For the second time in girls track history, an individual won the 100 and 800 meters in a single showing in the state finals. Bannister first captured the 100 in 12.21, then showed her endurance skills with a third-straight win in the 800.

Winning the high jump with a leap of 5-6 was Flint Hamady's Jasmine Thomas, who would parlay her leaping ability into becoming a future basketball star at Michigan State. She would earn player of the year honors for the MSU women's cagers following the 2012-13 season.

In Division 4 at Forest Hills Eastern, Potterville won its first state championship in 24 years with 49 points. The victors picked up 28 of their points in the relays with wins in the 4x2 and 4x4 and taking second behind a record-setting Pewamo-Westphalia foursome in the 4x1.

Upper Peninsula: Frigid conditions chilled the speed in Kingsford. Winter coats were the preference of attire for the thousands of spectators who braved the Artic-like temperatures.

Marquette tallied a whopping 124 points to easily capture yet another D1 crown. The leading individual scorer in D1 was the host school's Jaime Roberts. The versatile Flivver soph won both hurdles as well as the pole vault to lead Kingsford to second behind Marquette.

St. Ignace with 89 points won the D2 title over Ishpeming Westwood by 10 points. Munising sophomore Abbey Kelto matched Roberts' 3 victories in D1 by winning all three distance events in D2.

In Division 3, Brimley won its first team championship in school history by a narrow 4 points over Powers-North Central. Erin Holmberg of Cooks Big Bay De Noc was yet another triple winner in D3. However, a third-place in the 800 denied her the chance to match her 4 wins from 2007.

Bryan Westfield: Pioneer's Legendary Mentor

There has not been a team, boys or girls, that has dominated track & field as the Lady Pioneers of Ann Arbor. Folks up in the UP could boast of the 27-year run by the Pickford boys in Class D, but Pioneer had to battle many more schools in its class to earn a state championship.

Beginning with the 1985 season, and including 2008, Ann Arbor Pioneer won 16 state titles and placed second in six other years. Only in 1993 and 1994 did it fail to bring home a trophy yet still placed a very respectable third. In all, Pioneer placed in the top 3 in the toughest division in girls track for 23 consecutive years!

The underlying reason for Pioneer's success: Bryan Westfield. There was no secret, he insisted: "I don't think we do anything differently. We do get in the weight room and run down the hallways at Pioneer in the off-season. We don't work on specific events, just general conditioning so that by late February the kids our in generally pretty good cardiovascular shape."

It wasn't just the kids at Pioneer that benefited from the early training program. Other athletes from neighboring schools sought Westfield's advice and often times would train alongside Westfield's athletes during the off-season. He usually had around 90 girls on his team, a number that had to be the envy of any track coach during this era.

That number does not include the middle school kids from Ann Arbor as well as the athletes from nearby Dexter, Ann Arbor Huron, Ypsilanti, Saline and others who would be there in the off-season.

Not that track was the only sport going at Pioneer, or even the No. 1. "Swimming is another big sport at Pioneer," he said in 1998. "And their philosophy for conditioning is very similar to ours as well as their summer program."

Westfield at the 2007 finals, wearing a shirt adorned with one of his favorite sayings: "PUSH: Pray Until Something Happens." (Jeff Hollobaugh photo)

Westfield was instrumental in setting up a summer track program and many of his Pioneer athletes would take part in a number of summer meets. "Not all the girls would take part in summer competition," said Westfield, "but enough of them would participate that it would give them valuable exposure to travel as well as bringing the kids closer together."

He grew up in Detroit where he attended Holy Cross Lutheran School in his childhood days. He was first exposed to track and field while in junior high school when he would enter summer meets held on the old cinder track located on Belle Isle.

His family moved to Ann Arbor in the late 1950s where he enrolled at Ann Arbor High, the only public high school in town then.

"I ran high school track for coach Tim Ryan. He was a strong-willed, dynamic type of person. Although I developed a strong interest in track I didn't have a great deal of success."

Westfield was lucky enough to take part in a race that many track buffs (including Westfield and Hall of Fame coaches Norb Badar and Marty Crane) believed was the most memorable event ever contested in MHSAA prep history.

"I ran the anchor leg for Ann Arbor High in the 880-yard relay when Warren 'Rex' Cawley blew the field away. I was running with my mouth open the whole way in awe. That was one of the greatest days in track and field that I can remember," he said.

Cawley, of course, would go on to be an Olympic gold medalist in the 400-meter hurdles in 1964.

Following his graduation from Ann Arbor High, Westfield ventured east to Cornell to further his education and also run track. "I was blessed at Cornell to not only run for head coach Lou Montgomery, but in my sophomore year Olympic legend Glenn Davis became our assistant coach."

It was Davis who developed Westfield into a 400-meter hurdler where he qualified for the Olympic Trials in 1964. "That was a great experience and that really stimulated me to get involved further in this great sport. I came back to Ann Arbor and ran track for a few years for the Ann Arbor Track Club."

It was during this exciting era when Westfield developed his first taste for coaching. Before high school track for girls began in the early 1970s, Westfield began work in 1966 with veteran coach Red Simmons coaching a girls AAU team called the "Michigamees."

Although Westfield was teaching at Pioneer at this time, he didn't get a chance to a coach a high school team until 1978, when track and cross country were finally made available for the Lady Pioneers.

He credits the summer AAU program for jump-starting the girls high school teams to early success. Westfield was also quick to laud the work of his assistant coaches throughout the years. Many of those assistant coaches have gone on to success of their own, including Sue Parks, the head track coach at Eastern Michigan.

Most coaches would be more than satisfied to have one of their track athletes advance to compete at the college level. However, during 1998 alone, Westfield had a mind-boggling 16 former Pioneers participating in college track. During his coaching career he would see 200 Pioneers achieve All-State honors while 59 would be tabbed All-Americans.

Westfield's dynasty earned seven of its state titles in a streak from 1985 through 1991, a feat never matched by any boys or girls team in state history. In 2007 Pioneer became the first—and only—Lower Peninsula girls team to surpass the 100-point barrier.

Over the years Westfield would attempt to keep in touch with all of his athletes, and not just the stars.

One athlete that Westfield was very proud of was one who made her niche off the track---Diane Laurin. Growing up in Haiti, Laurin and her parents escaped political unrest and made it to Ann Arbor.

"Diane was a great student and a decent athlete," recalled Westfield. She walked on the Michigan team while concentrating on her studies. She is now Dr. Diane Laurin, working as a gynecologist in Maryland.

Every year Westfield would beam with pride when he would look in the stands at the state meets, where many former members of his Pioneer teams would be rooting on the current group of thinclads.

Although first diagnosed with esophageal cancer in 2014, Westfield would continue coaching his beloved Pioneer team through the 2015 season. Sadly, he passed away at age 72 just weeks after coaching in his final state meet.

More than 200 attendees attended a candlelight vigil just 12 hours after his death. However, there was a little laughter amongst the tears that were shed on this occasion. Summing up Westfield's character perfectly was one of Westfield's star runners, former state hurdles champion Candice Davis Price, who became a world-class athlete: "The tears are going to be hard tonight, because if he saw us all crying, he would make us run laps."

Four times Westfield was honored as the National Coach of the year, as well as an unheard of 17 times picked as the Michigan Track/Cross Country Coach of the Year. In addition to his 16 state track titles Westfield guided his Pioneer cross-country squads to three state championships and six runner-up finishes. He would be honored in the MITCA Hall of Fame in 2006 and the MHSAA Coaches Hall of Fame in 2014.

The candlelight vigil was held at the site where Westfield spent much of his life, now called the Westfield-Sleeman Track.

Former Westfield runner Seana Arnold Larson spoke for many on this solemn occasion. "He really helped guide everyone down the right path," the onetime 3200 state champ said. "To hear the people speak… it was the same story over and over about how he made them better, how he got them through a difficult time and how they were blessed to have him in their lives."

She added: "You would think that with his many state championships and all-state athletes, he'd always expected you to win. But if you had a bad day, he was the first person to say 'Get over it' and 'Let's move on.'"

Westfield truly cared for his athletes as well as his students. "If one of his students or athletes missed practice or class he was on the phone or at your door wondering why you were not at practice that day," said his daughter, Crystal Westfield, who assisted on Pioneer's track teams in his final years, and tragically also passed away from cancer later that year.

On July 23, 2015, just days after his passing, *USA Today* named Bryan Westfield America's Best 2014-15 coach.

Christienne Linton went on to star at Ohio State (Pete Draugalis photo)

2009

At the East Kentwood track, Romulus rode the talents of Christienne Linton to earn the first girls track title in its history.

A future All-American performer for the Buckeyes of Ohio State, Linton nearly singlehandedly won the team title by contributing to all 38 points earned by the Eagles. Romulus needed every one of Linton's points, as only two points separated the first three place winners in the D1 competition.

Linton won the long jump and the 300 hurdles, placed second in the 100 hurdles, and helped clinch the exciting team title by running a leg on the victorious 1600-meter relay team.

"It wasn't all about me," Linton told Mick McCabe of the *Free Press*. "I prayed. Before the relay I told the girls to keep doing what we've been doing all year."

There were many notable performances during this well-balanced meet. Rockford's Sarah Birkmeier became the first vaulter in state history to clear the 13-foot barrier when she won her specialty for the second-straight year.

Ariel Roberts had an exceptional day for Ann Arbor Pioneer as coach Bryan Westfield's powerhouse was attempting to win its 17th state championship. However, the future North Carolina all-around performer didn't get a win this time around. She was denied her third consecutive high jump win when West Bloomfield's Emelle McConney edged her with a personal best of 5-8.

Roberts also finished second in the 300 hurdles behind Linton's 42.86.

Denying Linton an opportunity to win a historic four first-place medals was Southfield's Bridget Owens, winner of the 100 hurdles. The future school record holder at Clemson at 12.71 seconds, Owens edged Linton, 14.13 to 14.19.

Megan Goethals led a talented group of distance runners in the 1600, where seven broke 5:00; the Rochester junior won in 4:51.20. Behind her was Courtney Calka of Livonia Stevenson and defending champion Rebecca Addison of Grand Haven. Addison would return to the track to defend her 800 title, with a future member of MSU's NCAA 2014 cross-country championship team, Sara Kroll, in 2nd place.

Showing little fatigue from her outstanding showing in the 1600, Goethels capped her day by taking charge of the 3200 with a meet record 10:37.50.

Yet to become another future Big 10 track star was the 400 champion. Flint Southwestern Academy's Dynasty McGee went on to become a third-place finisher at the 2014 Big 10 Championship while competing for Penn State.

Making her first appearance at the MHSAA finals was freshman sprinter Kyra Jefferson from Detroit Cass Tech. The daughter of '84 Olympic bronze medalist Thomas Jefferson, she won the 200 in 25.12.

Another well-balanced meet took place in Zeeland at the Division 2 finals. East Lansing took the team title with 36 points, the lowest winning point total in D2/Class B in 26 years.

One double winner at the D2 meet caught the eye of MSU coach Walt Drenth. Croswell-Lexington's Leah O'Connor won the 800 (2:15.41) and 1600 (5:03.38). With yet another year to go in her prep career, O'Connor would eventually blossom into one of the nation's great distance stars.

In Division 3, Frankenmuth breezed to the title with solid running from its relay teams. After winning the shorter 400 and 800-meter relays, the victors put an exclamation point to their title by crushing the field by more than 8 seconds in winning the 1600 relay. Leading the Eagles was future CMU star sprinter Kelsey Ritter.

Ritter crossed the finish line first in the 200 meters, was second in the 400 and ran a leg on two of the relays. She was edged in the 400 meters by Albion's Amelia Bannister, who had earlier repeated as the 100-meter champion and ran a leg on Albion's winning 400-relay squad. Oddly enough, after winning the 800-meter run for three straight years, Bannister did not attempt to make it four in a row in the two-lap event.

Rachel Hoffman was the meet's only performer to win three individual events. She took honors in the long jump and both hurdles, the first state champion from Shelby in 32 years. Allendale frosh Ali Wiersma, with her victory in the 3200-meter run, would begin her dominance in this event.

In Division 4, the Central Michigan Conference ruled. With 51 points, Potterville would lead fellow conference members Fowler and Pewamo-Westphalia to a 1-2-3 finish.

Highlighting Potterville's day was its meet record in the 800-relay. The foursome of Jenna Whipple, Kaila Cook, Jill Witaker and Kelsey Letson cruised to a 1:45.38. Pewamo-Westphalia would begin its supremacy in the 400-meter relay, an event it would win in 7 of the next 8 years.

Three athletes who competed during the day in three difference divisions would team up shortly down the road in basketball. D4 shot put champion Jasmine Hines from Central Lake, D3 high jump winner Jasmine Thomas from Flint Hamady and D2 place winner Annalisle Pickrel from Grand Rapids Catholic Central would eventually be teammates on Michigan State's basketball team.

Upper Peninsula: At the finals in Kingsford, Marquette edged Calumet 92-82 to once again take the honors in D1. Gladstone's Lindsey Lusardi, with wins in the 1600 and 3200, was the only D1 performer to win more than one event. Munising took the first-place trophy by an even ten points over runner-up Ishpeming Westwood in D2. Abbey Kelto led the winning Munising squad to victory by winning the same distance events as Lusardi.

Brimley had a much easier time in repeating as the UP D3 champs by piling up 84 points. Brimley's Jessica Graham had the most notable performance in all divisions by winning the high jump in less than ideal conditions at 5-4.

2010

Once again, a glittering array of talent graced the tracks in the Grand Rapids area. In Division 1, Rochester's Megan Goethals repeated as a double winner in the distances, as well as running a leg for her victorious 3200-relay team. Rochester, however, got some much-needed help in the sprints, with Ashley Keyes winning the 100-meter dash and running a leg on the winning 400-relay to lead Rochester to its first state title.

Goethal's winning time of 10:22.75 eclipsed the previous D1 and all-class record set in 1996 by Sharon Van Tuyl. Rochester's 3200-relay foursome also set a new meet record by a scant 0.02 of a second. Said the winner, "Just to get it done today and know that I could do it was a really good feeling."

Lurking in the shadows after a fourth-place finish was a very young Grosse Pointe South team that featured twin sisters who would star on the track over the next 4 years. Freshman Hannah Meier broke the D1 record in the 800-meter run. Her time of 2:08.83 was the fastest time in meet history in 32 years, second only to Delisa Walton's Class A mark 2:07.7 over the longer 880 yards in 1978.

Haley Meier would place behind Goethals' 4:47.37 in the 1600, just ahead of Traverse City's Julia Otwell, the third-place finisher. Otwell helped bring MSU the 2014 NCAA cross country championship.

In addition to Goethal's pair of wins, three other returning champs defended their titles in D1, including Alysha Johnson of Walled Lake Western in the shot and Southfield's Bridgette Owens in the 100-meter hurdles. Rockford's Sarah Birkmeier won the pole vault for the third-straight year.

In Division 2 at Zeeland West, Kristen Hixson of Remus Chippewa Hills set a meet record of 12-4. At Grand Valley she added more than two feet, clearing 14-4½ to win the NCAA D2 title in 2014.

Detroit Country Day's Kendall Baisden broke a 400-meter record that had stood for 34 years when she was

Two weeks after the state finals, Megan Goethals became the first Michigan girl to break 10:00 for 3200m. (Pete Draugalis photo)

Dearborn Divine Child won only one event but captured the team title with 61 points.

In Division 3 at Comstock Park, Frankenmuth swamped the opposition with a monstrous 50-point margin, the biggest ever in D3/Class C. Paving the way for the Frankenmuth onslaught were Kelsie Ritter and Emily Wee.

Ritter, after settling for second in the 100-dash, later won the 200 and 400 and ran a leg on the winning 4 x 400.

Wee set the only meet record of the day with her hurdle win in 44.82. She also ran on a pair of winning relay teams for the Eagles. Wee placed 3rd in the 100 hurdles behind a promising young freshman from Reed City, Sami Michell, and defending champion Rachel Hoffman.

In Division 4 at Jenison, a pair of Central Michigan Conference rivals would vie for the trophy with Pewamo-Westphalia edging out its rivals from Fowler 65-61.

An unusual number of records were broken. Angie Hengesbach lowered the 100 standard to 12.40 and also anchored the Pewamo-Westphalia 4 x 100 to a 50.41. The Pirates just missed setting another record in the 4 x 200 relay, but had to settle for the third-fastest time in meet history.

Kinde North Huron's Megan Heffner, after earlier winning the high jump, set a meet record with her winning time of 44.98 in the 300-meter hurdles. Future MSU basketball star Jasmine Hines accounted for the other record with her 42-7 effort in the shot put.

Upper Peninsula: Negaunee, although accounting for only two wins, took its first title since 1981 when it edged defending champion Marquette 95-92 in Kingsford.

The individual star of the entire meet was Kingsford's Jaime Roberts. In addition to her wins in the 100 hurdles and the long jump, she posted one of the best efforts on either peninsula with her clearance at 12-feet in the vault, more than three feet better than her best vault at the finals a year before.

With a runner-up finish in the 300 hurdles, Roberts pushed Selena Meser of Sault Ste. Marie to a new UP meet record time of 45.40.

It was strictly no contest in D2 as St. Ignace, scoring in every event, tallied 131 points to run away with the trophy. Junior Dani Gagne of Norway won the 100-meter dash in 12.83 to set the lone meet record. Cooks-Big Bay De Noc won its first girls UP title by scoring six more points than runner-up Ontonagon.

clocked in 54.91 seconds, destroying the yard mark of 56.1 by Holt's Johanna Matthyssen in 1976. Later that summer she set a state record of 52.59 to win the USATF Junior title.

Baisden earlier captured the 100 in 12.13 and would have been favored to win the 200, but had to leave the meet early to attend her grandfather's funeral.

Running on her home track, Rachel Schulist, coached by her father Martin Schulist, a double state champ in the mile and two mile while running for Whitehall in 1978, won the 3200-meter race in 10:59.40. Over the next few years at Michigan State she would blossom into one of the nation's best.

After winning the 1600 in a time that did not even break the five-minute barrier, who could possibly have envisioned O'Connor's accomplishments in the next few years? From a D2 1600 title for Croswell-Lexington High School in 5:01.99 to winning the NCAA indoor mile championship in a blazing 4:27.18. O'Connor was named the Big 10 indoor and outdoor women's Track Athlete of the Year for the 2014-15 school year,

2011

Featured in as part of ESPN "Outside the Lines," the story of Latipha Cross perhaps overshadowed all the outstanding accomplishments at the 2011 track and field finals. The Southfield junior overcame many traumatic obstacles on her difficult journey during her prep career, including child abuse, homelessness and two bouts fighting cancer.

And yet she was able to break one of the oldest records on the books, winning the D1 400 in 54.29, eclipsing Delisa Walton's 1978 mark.

Southfield's 400 winner, Latipha Cross
(Pete Draugalis photo)

Cross was one of many athletes who took advantage of the near perfect conditions for the state finals held at four different West Michigan sites.

The Meier twins led Grosse Pointe South to its first title, holding off Detroit Cass Tech and Ann Arbor Pioneer to bring home the win by virtue of its 54-50 win over the pair of past champions, deadlocked in second place.

After the twins each ran a leg on the Blue Devil 3200-meter relay team that placed 2nd to Ann Arbor Huron, Hannah Meier raced to victory in the 1600-meter run with a time of 4:42.60, breaking Laura

Matson's 26-year-old mark of 4:45.20. Finishing just a few strides behind her sister, with a 4:45.80, Haley also nearly beat Matson's record. All eight medalists finished under five, the first occurrence in MHSAA history.

Hannah Meier then sped around the track twice to set a D1 record in the 800 with a clocking of 2:07.37. Pushing Hannah to the 800 record and placing second was Rochester's Brook Handler, who would take her talents to the Michigan where as a team captain in 2015, she placed seventh in the NCAA 1500 in Eugene, Oregon.

Cass Tech sprint star Kyra Jefferson took home three first places on the Rockford oval with victories in the 100 and 200-meter dashes, and a leg on the winning 4 x 400 relay team. The future Florida Gator posted the No. 2 time in MHSAA meet history with her 23.87.

The closing relay packed considerable drama as Grosse Pointe South needed at least a seventh-place finish in the afternoon's final event to win the meet. The Blue Devils fared better than needed, placing 4th.

Turning in other notable performances in D1 were Nyki Caldwell from Dexter and Grand Blanc's Gabriella Anzalone. Caldwell won the high jump at 5-8 and a few years later at Wake Forest would be the ACC champion in the event. Anzalone won the 3200-meter run in 10:23.07, the sixth fastest time in meet history; she would go on to become All-Big 10 for Wisconsin.

Tory Schiller from Grand Ledge, voted by MITCA coaches as Miss Track for 2011, joined Jefferson and Hannah Meier as a double winner in the long jump and 300 hurdles.

In Division 2, Detroit Country Day's Kendall Baisden and Brittany Mann combined for five wins, earning all the points needed for Country Day to win the team championship.

Baisden left the track at the end of the day just 0.01 second shy of owning all three D2 sprint records. After setting a D2 record in the 100 meters at 11.92, and defending her title in the 400 (55.12), missing the record she already held. "I didn't mean to run that fast," she admitted. "It has been a long day. A lot of races. It's hot."

Then she took the 200 dash in 24.56, just shy of the 24.55 meet standard set by LaTosha Jollet in 2002.

Baisden's teammate, Brittany Mann, followed her 141-10 victory in the discus with a very modest winning shot heave of 41-0.

Brittany London from Middleville-Thornapple Kellogg won a tight battle with Stevensville-Lakeshore's Lauren Chorney. London cleared 12-1 while Chorney, later a Big 10 champion for MSU, would settle for second place at 11-10. Rachele Schulist from Zeeland West won the 1600 in 5:00.59.

Division 3 saw the tightest team battle, Benzie Central nipping perennial power Frankenmuth by one point. The big three individual stars were Benzie's Michaela Carnegie, Reed City's Sami Michell and Frankenmuth sprinter Angie Ritter.

After Theresa Warsecke, Bryce Cutler, and Taylor Nye provided Carnegie with a comfortable lead in the 4 x 800, Carnegie powered home on the anchor leg to cross the finish line in a meet record 9:22.71, 19 seconds ahead of the runner-up team.

Carnegie, in one of the closest finishes of the day, nipped defending champion Ali Wiersma from Allendale 4:57.59-4:57.79 to win the 1600. The Benzie Central ace still had enough energy to successfully defend the 800 in 2:16.96.

Reed City sophomore Sami Michell had a terrific day by winning three events, two of those setting D3 records. Her winning 14.07 in the 100 hurdles was the day's fastest in any division while her 300H meet record of 43.83 was just a fraction slower than Schiller's winning time in D1.

Ritter, who had earlier won the 400-meter dash, deprived Michell of a fourth win when she edged her by inches in winning the 200-meter dash, 26.25-26.30.

In Division 4 at Jenison, Pewamo-Westphalia piled up 81½ points, but that was not enough to defeat Fowler's 89. PW's points were the most ever earned by a team that did not come away as a team champion. No records were set at the D4 finals in Jenison, but Pewamo's 4 x 100 relay team came close, missing out of improving on its own record set in 2010 by less than a tenth of a second.

Upper Peninsula: At the finals in Kingsford, Marquette recaptured the title after placing behind Negaunee in 2009. Sault Ste. Marie and star runner Selena Meser challenged by winning four events.

First Meser won the 100 hurdles. Then she amazingly won back-to-back races, the 400 and the 300 hurdles. After getting a short break during the running of the 800, she recovered to win the 200.

St. Ignace, which scored a whopping 131 points to win D2 a year earlier, one-upped itself with a tally of 132. However, it was an athlete from third-place Norway who set the only record during the meet. Dani Gagni of Norway won three events and clocked 12.54 in the 100, the fastest UP time in the new century.

Brimley captured the D3 crown in the UP as Tabitha Graham bettered her sister's 2-year-old record in the high jump with a 5-5. Lauren Spranger got another best with her 58.70 in the one-lapper, a time that was superior to the LP Division 4 winner.

2012

Division 1 at East Kentwood once again saw the incomparable distance aces from Grosse Pointe South lead their team to a second title.

The foursome of Kelsie Schwartz, Ersula Farrow, and the Meier twins, Haley and Hannah, shattered the former 4 x 800-meter relay record by a mind-boggling 17 seconds with a state record of 8:48.29 in the first running event final. Though not a national prep record as noted by most in the sport, it was a National Federation record (the federation keeps its own list of national marks using criteria that are considered statistically shaky by many).

"We knew it was possible," said Haley Meier.

Ann Arbor Huron's Cindy Ofili then participated in the next three running event finals with a performance unequaled in state track history. She won the afternoon's first final, the 100 hurdles in 13.78, before quickly returning to the starting line of the 100 meters, which she won in 11.97.

Next came the 800-meter relay and the busy Ofili anchored the River Rats to victory there as well. Three consecutive events, and three victories, a first-time achievement in state history.

Ofili returned to the track 4 events later to win the 300 hurdles, becoming the first Class A/D1 girl to win three individual first-place medals.

Kyra Jefferson (Jeff Hollobaugh photo)

Ofili would excel in nearby Ann Arbor to such an extent that she would win multiple Big 10 titles. She captured the NCAA indoor hurdle crown in 2016. A dual citizen, she represented Great Britain internationally, finishing 4th in the 2016 Olympics.

Once again, the Meier twins paced the Blue Devils to the state championship with 77½ points, ahead of Ofili and Ann Arbor Huron's total of 64.

After recovering from a record-breaking effort in the 4 x 800, the same foursome nearly swept the 1600-meter run. Hannah and Haley again placed 1-2 for the metric mile event and were followed in third by freshman Ersula Farrow. The fourth member of the relay unit, Kelsie Schwartz, placed a more than respectable sixth.

Three of them nearly pulled off a sweep of the 800. Hannah Meier won in 2:08.57. Jamie Morrissey of Rochester Adams placed second while Haley Meier and Farrow followed in third and fourth place.

The runner-up Huron squad, in addition to Ofili's heroics, received valuable points from sprinter Maya Long, a future teammate of Ofili down the road at Michigan. Long beat Latipha Cross, the defending champ and meet record holder in the 400 meters, in a quick 54.80.

Kyra Jefferson of Cass Tech sped 23.83 in the 200 to defeat Long. It was the No. 2 time in meet history. Five years later she would win the NCAA title for Florida in a collegiate record 22.09.

As this outstanding meet was nearing a close, junior Erin Finn from West Bloomfield smashed the 3200-meter mark with an all-class record of 10:17.86, winning by an outlandish 23 plus seconds over her closest competitor.

Although events run on the track dominated the action at East Kentwood, there were some notable field event performances.

Cierra Pryor of Jackson flew past 19-feet in the long jump. Southfield Lathrup's Keianna Ingram cleared 5-9 in the high jump, and Katie Rancourt made her hometown fans happy with a victory in the pole vault at 12-6.

In Division 2 at Houseman Field, a furious battle between Detroit Country Day and Dearborn Divine Child settled nothing as both teams finished with 60 points. To say the state title was decided by the slimmest of margins would be an understatement. Dearborn Divine Child was trailing by 10 points and needed a win in the 1600 relay to force a tie with Country Day.

Veteran Divine Child coach Tony Mifsud's foursome edged East Grand Rapids and the rest of the field in the closing relay to snatch a share of the title with its archrivals. However, Mifsud, a star distance runner a half century ago in Detroit's PSL, could have only lamented on the many 'what ifs' that took place during the course of the meet.

Mifsud's Falcons finished second in the 800-meter relay to Country Day by less than two-tenths of a second. They placed third in the 400-meter relay, just 0.06 behind second-place Forest Hills Eastern. Paige Patterson, with a fourth in the 400 meters, was just a tenth of a second from procuring two more points.

However, nothing could have been closer than the final three places in the 300 hurdles, a race that saw places 6-7-8 in a near dead heat. Officials had to take a long look at the FAT photo to sort it out. The final photo showed Caro's Gabrielle Collins in 7th with a time of 46.844 with Divine Child's Mallory Myler in eighth at 46.845. An outright state championship was decided by the width of a credit card.

Country Day scored all 60 of its points in just 6 events, with victories in all. Thrower Brittany Mann scored the lone double for the Yellow Jackets. The future University of Oregon star won the discus competition by an astonishing 33 feet with her 156-8, and climbed the top rung of the awards stand with her second-straight title in the shot put (41-11).

Sydney Cureton sped to a new meet record in the 100 meters with her 11.90, just 0.02 faster than teammate Kendall Baisden a year earlier. Baisden, who also joined Cureton on the winning Yellow Jacket 400 and 800-meter relay teams, managed to break her own best with a time of 54.58 for the 400-meter run. Later in the summer she would run 52.60 for 3rd in the USATF Junior Championships.

The biggest mystery for this author is why weren't the two record-breaking Country Day sprinters entered in the 200? Surely the Yellow Jackets would not have had to share the trophy with Divine Child if one, or both, of these record breakers had entered the starting blocks for this race. With a PR (and state record) of 23.42 from her freshman year, Baisden would have been a formidable contender.

DeWitt senior Tori Desira not only defended her championship in the 300 hurdles, but in winning the 100-meter hurdles, pulled off a very rare feat, capturing the title she had last won as a frosh.

Sara Barron from Pontiac Notre Dame Prep successfully defended her title in the 800 and then defeated a star-studded field in the 1600 meters with a sparkling 4:51.67. Barron would break the school mile record the following year as a freshman at Vanderbilt.

Placing 2nd behind Barron was Ali Wiersma from Allendale. After recovering from the 1600, Wiersma would return to the track later in the afternoon to set a meet record in the 3200 with a time of 10:41.67.

Placing seventh in this same race was McKenzie Diemer, daughter of three-time Olympian and bronze medalist in the steeplechase in the 1984 Olympics, Brian Diemer.

In Division 3 at Comstock Park, Frankenmuth won its third state championship in four years. Stealing the show was Reed City junior Sami Michell, who became the second girl in history to win four individual state titles, and the first since Maria Shoup accomplished it 33 years earlier.

Michell flashed over the hurdles in a scintillating 42.23, a new state record. Earlier, she had bettered her own previous record in the 100-meter hurdles with a time of 13.84, and leaped 18-6½ inches to win the long jump, an amazing two feet longer than her closest competitor. Michell still had enough gas left in her tank to pick up her fourth win of the day in her final event, the 200.

Yet another of one of those anomalies that often appear in track and field took place in the 1600-meter run. Theresa Warsecke from Benzie Central won this event in 4:57.59, ironically the same exact time run the previous year by her Benzie Central teammate Michaela Carnegie.

Placing second was freshmen Annie Fuller from Manistee. It would prove to be the only time Fuller would taste defeat at an MHSAA final meet. Fuller did come back later in the program to win the 800 in a meet record 2:13.03.

In Division 4, Fowler repeated as champs in with 54 points, four more than Traverse City St. Francis. Past contender Pewamo-Westphalia had been bumped to D3.

Upper Peninsula: Marquette nosed out Negaunee 106-99 to take honors at the D1 meet held, as always, in Kingsford. Chelsea Jacques from Calumet lowered the Class A/B D1 record in the 100-meter dash to 12.55 to highlight the action in D1.

St. Ignace continued its dominance in D2 by amassing 142 points to again secure a state title. Rudyard's Hunter Perry set a record in the discus in UP Division 2, but less than a previous UP Class C heave of 124-8 by Rebecca Palmer from Stephenson in 1993.

Brimley outlasted Eben Junction Superior Central to take home the winning trophy in D3.

2013

Track and field fans bid adieu to a number of graduating superstars in 2013, but on the bright side a group of promising underclassmen ensured that girls track and field in the state of Michigan would remain at a high level.

Before departing to participate at the next level, with Grosse Pointe South's Meier twins enrolling at Duke, and Erin Finn taking the shorter route to join the University of Michigan, this outstanding trio saved its best for last with some eye-opening performances at the D1 finals, held once again at East Kentwood.

After warming up earlier in the program by winning another 3200-meter relay (9:01.98), Hannah and Haley Meier brought the large crowd to its feet with a record-smashing performance in the 1600-meter run. Running to a new meet record time of 4:39.23, Hannah would quickly turn and watch her twin sister Hannah cross the finish line in 4:42.43, the second fastest time ever. The results were not entirely unexpected. The week before the two had competed at the adidas GP meet in New York City over the full mile distance. Hannah ran a state record 4:40.48, passing by 1600 in a record 4:38.9. Haley clocked 4:42.11 for the mile.

Erin Finn followed close behind the Meier twins in a quick 4:45.37 with Grosse Pointe South soph Ersula Farrow placing fourth. And for the second time in the past three years, the first eight placers were well under the five-minute barrier.

Four events later Hannah Meier won the 800 meters in 2:06.35, breaking the meet record of 2:07.37 she set two years earlier as well as running a time all could agree was superior to the 1978 mark of 2:07.7 over 880 yards by Delisa Walton. Meier was pushed to the record by Farrow, whose 2:07.91 would have won almost any other year.

What was especially impressive from the above record performances was that the athletes were performing in less than ideal conditions. Although sunny skies prevailed throughout the day in the Grand Rapids area, brisk winds were evident that put a damper for the sprinters running into a strong headwind.

It was only appropriate that Hannah Meier would lead her Grosse Pointe South teammates to victory in the final event of the meet by anchoring the 1600-meter relay. The ten points earned by South gave the Blue Devils a total of 76 points and its third-straight D1 state championship.

Said Haley, "I couldn't think of a better way to finish our high school career, winning our third state title. Our team is just all about running for each other. We don't care about the trophies or any of that. We just run for each other and run the best we can."

After starting their collegiate careers at Duke, both twins ended up winning Big 10 titles in the mile for Michigan.

West Bloomfield's Finn, after expending considerable energy in the 1600, still had enough energy to shatter her own record in the 3200-meter run. Although she fell short of her goal to break the 10-minute barrier, Finn, virtually running solo, posted a spectacular 10:08.22

Hannah Meier
(Pete Draugalis photo)

West Bloomfield's Erin Finn
(Pete Draugalis photo)

. Yet another senior closing out her prep career was Cierra Pryor, the daughter of 1987 dash champ Corey Pryor, who for the second-straight year surpassed 19-feet (19-½) to repeat as the long jump champion. Placing behind seniors Pryor and Farmington's Aaron Howell in the long jump was one of two freshmen who would be a part of the new guard in the sport, East Kentwood's Sekayi Bracey.

Bracey became the new sprint queen with wins in the 100 (12.18) and 200 (24.82). Bracey would begin a rivalry with another incoming frosh, when she nipped Oak Park's Anna Jefferson in the 200. Jefferson had earlier had captured first place in the 400 with an impressive 55.44.

In Division 2, a senior dominated Divine Child squad, surely disappointed that it had to share the title with Detroit Country Day the year before, assured its followers there would be no drama by romping to an easy team win.

A relatively new school, running on its own track, pleased its fans by taking home the runner-up trophy, and providing the only record-setting performance of the day. The Grand Rapids Forest Hills Eastern 400-meter relay of Sam Reno, Camron Nelson, Jaclyn Goble and Alli Gutschow sped around the track in a meet record 48.40.

Senior Kendall Baisden of Detroit Country Day capped her sensational prep career with impressive wins in the 200 and 400. Only running into a strong head wind perhaps deprived Baisden from setting a new mark in the 200-meters, as her time of 24.65 was only a tenth of a second away from the current record.

Baisden accomplished the rare feat of winning the same event for four consecutive years with her convincing 400 victory. Traversing the one lap in the day's fastest time of 54.99, Baisden won the event by more than two seconds over her closest competitor. And, her competitor had to be the clock as Baisden, after winning her regional under adverse weather conditions, had been seeded in a slower heat.

That summer, Baisden romped to a state record of 52.03 to take second at the USATF Juniors. That put her on Team USA for the Pan-American Juniors in Colombia where she won silver in the 400 and gold on the relay. At the University of Texas, she piled on the honors, winning the World Juniors, the Pan-Am Games, and finishing 2nd in the NCAA.

Baisden was one of three to bag a pair of victories in D2. Junior Megan O'Neal from Remus Chippewa Hills had a very busy day. After running a leg on a non-placing 3200-meter relay, O'Neal posted the fourth fastest time in D2 history with her time of 4:52.21 in the 1600. Then she won the 800 in 2:14.88, before running out of gas and understandably finishing near the back of the pack in the 3200.

Senior Janina Pollatz of Grand Rapids Christian won both the long jump (18-7) and pole vault (11-8) before going to a great career at Eastern Michigan.

In Division 3 at Comstock Park, Pewamo-Westphalia showed it could handle being in a bigger division, scoring 54 points, 14 more than the one-person track team from Reed City.

Once again Sami Michell was the individual star by winning four individual events for the second consecutive year. She would end her career with a total of 12 individual first-place medals, the most by any athlete, boy or girl, in MHSAA annals.

A pair of up-and-coming sophomores contributed to the only records set. Annie Fuller from Manistee, after winning the 1600-meters in 4:56.11, the third-fastest time in meet history, came back to break her own record in the 800 with a 2:11.77, more than 3 seconds ahead of the runner-up.

Amber Way from Charlevoix broke one of the oldest meet standards in the books with her win in the 3200. Her 10:48.48 for the 3200-meter run topped the record set by Mason County Central's Melanie Weaver in 1979.

Kendall Baisden won the 400 four straight years.
(Jeff Hollobaugh photo)

At Division 4 in Jenison, another one of those brilliant freshmen appeared, this time with a powerful pedigree. Coming from a family renowned for its success on the football field, young Holly Bullough showed she had some outstanding skills as well.

With wins in the 800 and 1600, as well as placing 2nd in the 3200 run and anchoring the runner-up 3200-meter team, Bullough led Traverse City St. Francis to its first title, outscoring Reading 66-52.

The Gladiators overcame the loss of a possible 10 points in the 800-meter relay when, while leading, one of its runners tore her Achilles tendon.

It was Reading that had the lone record-holder. Michelle Davis ran on two winning relay teams and won the hurdles in 44.92.

Although short of the meet record, Miranda Johnson from Ottawa Lake Whiteford became the fourth girl in ClassD/D4 to surpass 18-feet in the long jump.

Upper Peninsula: The other budding freshman star in Michigan was running away from all her opponents far to the north at the finals in Kingsford.

While easily winning the three distances, as well as anchoring Marquette's 3200-meter relay team, Lindsey Rudden was credited with establishing three meet records in the D1 classification for the Upper Peninsula. However, all three of her records fell short of those set in previous years under the class system, something that Rudden would change in the ensuing years.

With Rudden added to Marquette's roster, Marquette more than doubled its score over runner-up Negaunee 145-62.

West Iron County took honors in D2. St. Ignace, which had been powerful in D2, moved down in enrollment to compete in D3 and, as one would expect, dominated in the lower class with 64 more points than its nearest foe.

2014

The quality in girls track and field in the state of Michigan, despite the loss to graduation of such notable stars as the Meier twins and Erin Finn, certainly did not take a step backwards as Michigan continued to churn out talent that ranked with the nation's best.

A couple of young sprinters resumed their rivalry, while the Detroit Metro area would continue to develop talent in the distance events that would attract college recruiters in droves.

Since the change was made at the turn of the new millennium from classes to divisions, girls track and field in Division 1 had been dominated by the likes of Ann Arbor Pioneer, Detroit Mumford, Rockford, and for the last three years, Grosse Pointe South. However, a new power in girls track would emerge in Oak Park beginning with the 2014 season.

One key reason was the coach, Brandon Jiles, himself the 1999 state champ at 800. Jiles had starred at Eastern Michigan and later devoted himself to coaching with mentor Robert Lynch. The two made Mumford legendary and when they moved to Oak Park, success followed.

With 92 points, Oak Park nearly doubled the total over its closest pursuers from Northville, without a senior in the lineup. The winners did most of their damage with a near-perfect performance in the relays, sweeping all but the 4 x 800.

Headlining the day's exciting action were the performances of a pair of standout sophomore sprinters, Oak Park's Anna Jefferson and East Kentwood's Sekayi Bracey.

Each would end the day with three first-place medals and one second. In the 200, the only individual race that the two speedsters were paired against one

Robert Lynch (left) and Brandon Jiles brought success with them to Oak Park. (Marvin Goodwin photo)

another, Bracey had a solid lead on the homestretch when Jefferson started making up ground fast.

"I could feel her," said Bracey. "I tried to stay relaxed and run my race."

Bracey nipped Jefferson in the 200 by inches. Bracey was clocked in 23.98, while Jefferson was close behind in 24.03, among the fastest times in meet history.

Earlier in the day Bracey won the long jump (18-7¼) and the 100 in 11.88. Jefferson, who was a member of the winning 400 and 800-meter relay squads for Oak Park, won only one individual race, but it was a dandy. She demolished the 400 in 53.50, a meet record by a huge margin.

So deep was the Oak Park powerhouse that the Knights were able to win the 4 x 400 with Jefferson

watching from the sidelines. Jefferson had earlier joined Carlita Taylor, Brianna Holloway and Tamea McKelvy to win the 4 x 200 in the second-fastest time in Michigan history at 1:38.15.

While Jefferson was dealt her only defeat by Bracey in the 200, she did get some solace by running the anchor on Oak Park's winning 400-relay that edged Bracey and her East Kentwood teammates by a stride. Oak Park was clocked in 47.35, with the Falcons less than a stride behind in 47.79.

The Birmingham Seaholm 4 x 800 of Rachel Dedanio, Brook Callahan, Patty Giradot and Audrey Belf got the running events off to a great start by breaking nine minutes in the 3200-meter with a 8:59.08, a time second only to the national record set by Grosse Pointe South's outstanding 2012 race.

After a long rest Belf would return to the track late in the afternoon to win the 3200-meter run in 10:17.08, a time second only to the record posted just a year earlier by Erin Finn.

This race was of such top quality that all eight-place winners were clocked under 10:45. To put this in a perspective, the eight-place winner (Cayla Eckenroth from Northville) would have won all but 4 of the 3200 state finals during the Class A era.

Eckenroth's Northville teammate Rachel Coleman placed second to Belf in 10:24.58. Coleman ran that fast time despite the fact she had won the 1600 earlier in the afternoon in 4:45.75. Coleman's four-lap time would rank only behind such legendary distances stars as Laura Matson, Erin Finn and the Meier twins.

Not all the notable performances in Division 1 were limited to the track. Junior Mackenzie Shell of Port Huron Northern sailed over the vault bar at 12-7. And Jailah Mason from Sterling Heights Stevenson cleared the high jump bar at 5-9¼, less than an inch away from the long-standing mark of 5-10 set 24 years earlier by Gwen Wentland.

Jaevyn Wortham from Macomb L'Anse Creuse, with a toss of 140-5, became the first discus thrower to win the event three times in Class A/D1 history.

After following Hannah Meier at Grosse Pointe South during her first two years on the South track team, Ersula Farrow won the 800-meters in 2:07.63, a time only behind Meier and the legendary Delisa Walton. Farrow came by her talent honestly. Her father, Erskine Farrow, won the Class A mile for Detroit Northern in 1980.

In Division 2 at Houseman Field in Grand Rapids, Remus Chippewa Hills had to be pleasantly surprised to tally 34 points, not win one event, yet at the end of the day be crowned the state champions. It would prove to be the lowest winning point total in 32 years. Chippewa Hills had to be a little nervous heading into the day's final events. Needing to place in the top eight in case Lansing Waverly would win the 1600-meter relay---and Waverly did win--the Warriors finished in the money at sixth to win the first state track title in school's history.

The days' top performance was turned in by Karrigan Smith of St. Johns. She won the event in 4:51.53, second only to Kelly Smith's 4:48.41 clocking 20 years earlier. Pushing Karrigan Smith to the record was the defending champion in this event, Megan O'Neil from Remus Chippewa Hills. O'Neil would also contribute 8 more valuable points for the state champs with a second-place finish behind Spring Lake's Carlyn Arteaga in the 800-meter run.

In Division 3 at Comstock Park, Frankenmuth won its fourth state title in six years with a dominating performance. The winners tallied 96 points, the highest total in Class C/D3 history, aided by a marvelous day from Angie Ritter.

After winning a pair of individual state titles as a frosh, but none during her sophomore and junior seasons, Ritter made a huge comeback as a senior. She won the 100 in a meet record 11.94, then took the 200 in another record, 24.72. Perhaps just as satisfying, that 200 took the school record away from her sister, Kelsey, who herself had won five individual D3 titles.

Ritter also anchored Frankenmuth to a record-shattering win in the 4 x 200 with a time of 1:41.17, more than two seconds ahead of a fast Pewamo-Westphalia team.

A couple of other records took a tumble, thanks to a pair of distance runners from Northern Michigan. Manistee's Annie Fuller for the third-straight year, improved on the 800 mark, this time with a 2:11.40. This came after she had earlier won the 1600 in 4:55.64, the third-fastest in Class C/D3 history.

Another junior from even farther north, Charlevoix's Amber Way, also improved on her own meet record with a swift 10:35.33 in the 3200, 26 seconds ahead of the next finisher.

The 2013 state champion, Pewamo-Westphalia, took home the runner-up trophy by finishing in style, winning the 4 x 400 in 4:01.16, one of the fastest times in meet history.

At Division 4 in Hudsonville, Reading improved from its second-place finish from the previous year to win the title with an impressive 81 points, 25 more than Traverse City St. Francis.

Leading the charge for Reading was senior Michelle Davis. She would walk away from this meet as the meet record-holder in three events, the 100 hurdles, the 400 and the 300 hurdles. However, Davis would not win one of the events for which she holds the record—for a very good reason.

Davis won the 100 hurdles in a meet record 15.05 and returned to the track to break a school and meet record for the 400 held by a Reading runner, Erin Dillon, with a 57.33. Already the record holder in the very next event, the 300-hurdles, Davis had little time to recover and ran well short of her best set the year before, holding on for 2nd behind Savannah Feldpausch from Fowler.

Miranda Johnson from Ottawa Lake Whiteford established a new mark for the 200-meter dash (25.15) and came just an inch short of the existing long jump record of 18-7 ½ owned by Brittany Hedgepath from 1998.

Upper Peninsula: Fans in attendance at the finals were treated to the first sub-5:00 four lapper in UP history when Marquette soph Lindsey Rudden defended her title with a 4:55.28. Unlike the onslaught of records during the LP finals, Rudden's mark would prove to be the only record earned during the finals held, as always, in Kingsford.

Marquette, with 145 points, cruised to the D1 championship, St. Ignace with 116 points, moved up from D3 to hold off West Iron Co. in D2, while Brimley won in D4 for the fifth time in seven years.

The ironman (or ironwoman) award, if they had one for the UP finals, would undoubtedly have gone to Marquette's Amber Huebner. The freshman took part in four grueling running events, the 400, 800, 1600 and 3200 meters, winning the unusual combination of the 400 and 3200, while placing second to Rudden in the 800 and 1600.

2015

Girls track and field in the state of Michigan has grown by leaps and bounds since the first state finals were held back in 1973. A huge reason for this growth can be attributed to Ann Arbor Pioneer coach Bryan Westfield.

The Lady Pioneers placed a very respectable fourth in what would prove to be their coach's last track finals.

Although the rain that persisted throughout the day put a slight damper on many of the events, there were still some outstanding performances at the state finals.

To absolutely nobody's surprise Oak Park easily defended its D1 state championship in Rockford. The biggest surprise was seeing former Grosse Pointe South star Ersula Farrow wearing the uniform of Oak Park. After being a bridesmaid to South's Hannah Meier for two years, Farrow won the 800-meters for the second-straight year with a time of 2:08.43, a time that gave her three of the six fastest times in meet history.

Ersula Farrow was a major force in the 800.
(Pete Draugalis photo)

Earlier in the meet Cuneo had posted the meet's biggest upset when she defeated the meet record holder in the 400-meter dash, Anna Jefferson, 55.32 to 56.10. "To actually prove to myself that I could do it," Cuneo said, "it was one of the best days I've ever had."

Bracey came a tenth of a second away from winning four first-place medals for her day's work. In the tightest race of the day, she finished inches short of catching Jefferson in the 400-meter relay.

Audrey Belf from Birmingham Seaholm ran nearly 10 seconds slower than her winning time from 2014, yet her 10:26.58 was still one of the fastest state finals times ever in the metric two-mile. Her Seaholm teammate, Rachel DaDamio, shone in winning the 1600 in 4:46.05.

Audrey Belf being interviewed by one of the authors.
(Pete Draugalis photo)

After winning three of the four relays in 2014, Oak Park found the missing link for success with the addition of Farrow to its 4 x 800 team. Farrow joined Jayla Fleming, Lashae Bowen and Dorriann Coleman to easily win in the second fastest time in history, 8:54.29.

While Oak Park had little trouble in winning all four relays it was only appropriate that making a gallant run in the day's final event was Ann Arbor Pioneer's relay.

Only Oak Park prevented Pioneer from winning the final race that Bryan Westfield would ever coach at a state final.

Although no records were set at the D1 finals, history was indeed recorded with the performance of East Kentwood's junior speedster Sekayi Bracey. By defending her three titles from the 2014 finals—the long jump, 100 and 200, Bracey carted off the most individual medals in the combined Class A/Division 1 era – 8 titles, with her senior season still lying ahead.

Bracey won another epic battle against some outstanding opponents in the 200-meters. She again edged Oak Park's Anna Jefferson with Rockford's Sammy Cuneo in close pursuit.

The D1 girls shot put was very competitive with Emily Meier from Canton hurling the 4kg iron ball 46-2, the second-best heave in D1 annals.

Meier placed 2nd in the discus behind Andrea Sietsema from Grand Rapids Forest Hills Central, who won at 145-5.

At Division 2 in Zeeland, no superpower teams appeared, so it took only 36 points for St. Johns to win the school's first girls state championship in any sport. So balanced was the team scoring that a total of 66 high school teams scored points on the brand new Zeeland track.

Contributing to all but four of St. John's 36 points was senior distance ace Karrigan Smith. The MSU commit captured the 1600, placed 3rd in the 800-meter run and ran a leg on a pair of second-place relay units, the 3200 and 1600-meter relays.

Miaisha Blair from Flint Southwestern leaped 18-9¼ to tie the meet record of Ypsilanti's Tiffany Ofili from a decade earlier.

Winning the first state title earned in Cedar Springs girls track history was Kenzie Weiler, who won the 3200 in 10:41.98.

Flint Powers junior Nikole Sargent won the shot at 45-4¾ for a No. 2 performance in meet history. It should be noted that Zeeland East placed three girls in this event, all throwing farther than 40 feet, no small feat indeed! Their coach, Ralph Neal, had won the Class A shot in 1995 for Monroe.

At Division 3 in Comstock Park, five points is all that separated the top three teams. With 62 points, Pewamo-Westphalia won its third title in six years with perennial contender Frankenmuth in second with 59½ and upstart Manistee close behind at 57.

Running without a track to even practice on, Manistee captured 4 first-place medals and added a second in the 1600-meter relay to give the top teams a real run for their money.

Annie Fuller went on to star for Michigan State.
(Peter Draugalis photo)

Manistee's Annie Fuller capped her brilliant career by winning the 1600 for the third time. In her 800 specialty, Fuller not only won a fourth-straight year but set a meet record each time. This feat was accomplished only one other time in boys or girls

history and, oddly enough, it took place in the same event. Rochelle Collins did it 40 years earlier for Detroit Immaculata.

U-M bound Kayla Keane placed 3rd behind Fuller and Holly Bullough of Traverse City St. Francis in the 1600 before returning to the track later in the afternoon to pull off the meet's biggest upset. After missing the past two-track seasons with injuries, Keane, the valedictorian at East Jordan, upset the heavily favored meet record holder in the 3200 meters, Amber Way from nearby Charlevoix.

Keane's winning 10:47.76 was second only to Way's mark of 10:35.33 from the previous year. With Keane headed to Ann Arbor to compete for the Wolverines and Way bound for East Lansing and MSU, they would soon meet again on the cross-country trails.

In Division 4, it was a reunion of sorts as the head coach of the newly crowned state champs from Harbor Springs, Emily Kloss, was a teammate at Fowler High School with Jill Feldpausch, the coach at Fowler. Harbor Springs edged Fowler 57-53½ points, keyed by a 1-2 finish in the 400 by Salix Sampson and Charlotte Cullip.

Upper Peninsula: Marquette surely made a statement that it could have competed at any level with its brilliant showing at the finals in Kingsford.

Junior Lindsey Rudden began her record-shattering day by running the anchor on Marquette's 3200-meter relay that smashed the meet record by more than 16 seconds. She then ran virtually alone for much of the 1600-meters, winning with a 4:56.31. Later, she crushed the 800 field by nearly 10 seconds with a meet record 2:13.94, and then perhaps saved the best for last.

Marquette's 1600-meter relay team comprised of Holly Blowers, Shayla and Amber Huebner joined Rudden to run the relay in 4:00.15, a time only bettered by Oak Park's winning foursome at the D1 finals in the Lower Peninsula.

Needless to say, Marquette romped to the team title while Ishpeming took the team trophy in D2 and Newberry in D3. Other than the records set by Rudden and her mates in the relay, the only other meet standard came in the pole vault with Sarah Audette of Lake Linden-Hubbell clearing the bar just a quarter inch over the former record of 10-0.

2016

Once again, the quality of girls competition was top notch, as records continued to tumble on a perfect day in early June. Topping the performers was a senior speedster from Northville who had improved rapidly since her freshman year on the track. After taking a back seat during her first three years to East Kentwood's Sekayi Bracey and Oak Park's Anna Jefferson, it was Chloe Abbott's turn to shine.

Abbott's day began innocently enough when she anchored Northville's 800-meter relay team to a more than respectable fourth-place finish, a race that would prove to be the fastest in meet history.

Two events later Abbott would launch from the starting blocks in the 400. Among the talented runners in the fastest seeded heat was two-time champion Anna Jefferson. Abbott blazed to the fastest 400 time in meet history with a 53.10, while Jefferson had to settle for 3rd. Sandwiched between Abbott and Jefferson was East Lansing's Taylor Manson, whose time of 53.56 would be the fifth fastest time in state meet annals.

Northville's Chloe Abbott triumphed in the 400 over Anna Jefferson (left) and Taylor Manson (right). All three would become NCAA standouts: Abbott for Purdue & Kentucky, Manson for Florida, and Jefferson for Virginia (Peter Draugalis photo)

"If you think about it for a long time," said Abbott, "you think, 'Oh wow, I did so well in the 400.' You get comfortable with it. I wanted to forget that I did that and focus on my next event, the 200."

Abbott would now be faced with another daunting task in the 200 meters, as one of her competitors in the finals would be future Purdue teammate Sekayi Bracey, shooting for her fourth-straight win. She had earlier in the day made it four straight in the 100. Abbott again emerged victorious, with a blistering 24.03.

She capped her momentous afternoon by anchoring Northville to a come-from-behind narrow win over Oak Park in the meet's final race, the 1600-meter relay. The finish was so close that Northville and Oak Park were credited with the same time, 3:50.58, with Ann Arbor Pioneer also just inches away at the finish line.

Bracey and Jefferson would have their day in the sun, however. Bracey earlier won her third-straight long jump with a 18-1 and then became the third in D1 history to win the same event four consecutive years by dashing to victory in the 100-meter dash.

Jefferson was instrumental in Oak Park obliterating a pair of relay records with wins in the 800 and 400-meter relays. She was joined by Janae Barksdale, Brianna Holloway and Tamea McKelvy on each of the record-setting teams. Oak Park's winning 1:36.66 shattered the state record by more than a full second. In the 4 x 100, the victors produced a jaw-dropping state record of 46.28, with Pioneer also under the old best at 47.12.

Holloway, not only a part of Oak Park's relays, also won the 300 hurdles in 42.71. Dorianne Coleman chipped in with 10 of Oak Park's 81½ points by winning the 800 (2:10.20).

It was a happy ride home for all the Oak Park participants following the day-long festivities. The girls not only won a third-straight team title, but made it a perfect day for the Detroit Suburbanites as the boys team also won.

Greenville's Landon Kemp may have been the most versatile of all the talented athletes at the Hudsonville Athletic Complex. Kemp raised the pole vault meet record to 13-4, placed 2nd in the long jump, and finished an impressive 5th in the 100-meter hurdles.

Competing in its first state finals without legendary coach Bryan Westfield, Ann Arbor Pioneer had a splendid runner-up showing with 64 points. Britten Bowen, in winning the 100-meter hurdles, became the 11th Pioneer hurdler to win the event.

A very young Pioneer 4 x 800 relay of Anne Forsyth, Sydney Dawes, Jacalyn Overdier and Alice Hill, all underclassmen, produced a sparkling 8:56.52.

In Division 2 at Zeeland, the team from Lansing Waverly won the title. Tra'chele Roberts led Waverly by assisting on 30 of its 42 points with a win in the 100 and anchor legs on the winning 400 and 800-meter relays.

Although placing 2 points behind Waverly with 40 points, Flint Powers' Nikole Sargeant had a pair of the day's better performances with her wins in the weight events. Matching her father Mike's dual win in the shot put and discus for Flint Powers in 1984, Nikole captured the discus with a heave of 147-9 and the shot put with a toss of 47-5½, the leading marks for both events in all classes at the state track finals.

A pair of budding stars may have burst onto the scene. Grand Rapids Catholic freshman Jakarri Alven ripped a 55.66 in the 400 the fastest time in meet history for someone not named Kendall Baisden.

Holland Christian sophomore Kayla Windemuller won the 1600 and 3200, with her victory in the 3200 coming in a bizarre race that displayed the best in sportsmanship. Windemuller overcame not just one fall to the track, but twice.

Christina Sawyer of Tecumseh, after seeing Windemuller take a spill late in the race, paused for a moment to allow her fellow runner to catch up. This display of sportsmanship may have cost Sawyer the race, but certainly captured the hearts of the crowd, as she placed just behind Windemuller at the finish line. Despite her two spills, Windemuller won in a time just under 11 minutes (10:59.52).

The pole vaulting LeRoux sisters of Spring Lake continued to dominate the event. After Allie took top honors in the vault in 2014, sister Gabriella won in 2015 and again in 2016, all at the same winning height of 11-8.

At Division 3 in Comstock Park, the Ithaca girls track team, coached by Gene Lebron, moved into the spotlight by winning its first title. Despite taking only one event, Ithaca had just enough firepower to outlast Adrian Madison.

Who would take home the coveted team trophy would not be decided until the day's final event, the 1600-meter relay. Ithaca, needing at least a 6th-place finish to clinch the title if Adrian Madison would win the relay—and it did—left itself a little breathing room by placing 4th.

Traverse City St. Francis distance ace Holly Bullough capped her great high school career by nearly being a part of four winning events, all while running with a painful stress fracture in her foot. She began her day's work by first anchoring the Gladiator 3200-meter relay team to a convincing victory, more than six seconds ahead of the second-place foursome from Ithaca.

Bullough, who had set a division record at the cross country state finals in the fall, inserted her name atop the meet record board by running 1600-meters in 4:52.63, breaking a 12-year old mark. She then romped to her third victory in the 800 meters, winning by nearly six second over her closest competitor in 2:12.22.

Showing the toughness that characterized the well-known Bullough/Morse football family over the years, Bullough completed her high school career by helping her 1600-relay team place second in the day's closing event.

The other meet record to fall at the D2 finals came in the pole vault, where Kasey Staley of Clare scaled at 12-4. Hailey Stockford of Sanford-Meridian repeated as champ in the 100 and 200-meter dashes.

Freshman Adelyn Ackley, in winning the 3200-meter run in 10:49.87, was one of three Hart runners in this event who placed in the top six.

Houseman Field in Grand Rapids hosted Division 4, where perennial power Fowler added yet another piece of hardware to its trophy case with a third state championship in six years. Winning three of the four relays, Fowler finished a dozen points ahead of second-place Concord.

Two meet records also were established in D4. Caylin Bonser of Harbor Springs twirled the discus out to 141-6 while Mendon's Mary Leighton lowered the 100-meter hurdle mark to 14.93.

Upper Peninsula: How does one score the most points in state history and yet not win one of the field events? That was part of the story at the finals held during a drizzly day in Kingsford. Marquette amassed 169 points, more than 100 more than runner-up Escanaba to easily win its sixth-straight D1 title.

Lindsey Rudden can begin writing her acceptance speech into the UP Hall of Fame based on her incomparable prep career. She played a part in winning 15 (out of a possible 16) state titles during her four years. She won the 800 and 1600 in each of her four seasons on the track, added the 3200 in her freshman year, and then ran legs on five Marquette winning relay teams.

Rudden and her Marquette classmates were so dominant that they had four runners place in the top five in the 1600-meter run.

It was the Marquette and Ishpeming show in Kingsford as the boys and girls team from each school won the championship in their respective divisions. The race to the D2 crown was much closer in D2 as Norway also topped the century mark in total points with 104, trailing victorious Ishpeming's 127.

Emily McDonald of Gwinn provided the day's lone D2 record with a 16-10 leap in the long jump.

The girls from Ontonagon won the first UP state finals contested in classes way back in 1974, but had to wait 42 more years before winning a second. Ontonagon tallied 72 points to edge out Newberry for honors at the D3 meet.

Ontonagon's Lori Wardynski recorded one of the two records set in D4 with a time of 47.27 in the 300 hurdles. The other new mark was notched by Natalie Beaulieu of Newberry in the 3200 (11:46.04).

2017

Ann Arbor Pioneer returned to the victory stand to claim a 17th state championship in yet another star-splashed state finals. Numerous records once again fell, many posted by underclassmen who will continue to insure Michigan's star quality far into the future.

After playing second fiddle for the past decade to Grosse Pointe South and then Oak Park, Pioneer used relay strength to win its first state championship under the coaching of Nancy Boudreau.

Junior Britten Bowen continued Pioneer's excellence in the 100 hurdles by posting the 12th hurdle victory for the event in school history.

It didn't take long for the huge crowd on hand at the East Kentwood complex to get a sampling of the D1 talent that would be showcased during the afternoon.

Less than 14 seconds after the gun was fired for the start of the afternoon finals, the day's first running event record would fall. Ann Arbor Pioneer's Britten Bowen and White Lake Lakeland's Grace Stark quickly burst out in front and they appeared to be dead even for much of the race. However, Bowen pulled away over the last hurdle after Stark had slightly lost her form while straining to run faster.

Just moments after the completion of this race, the guru of Michigan high school track, who also usually doubles as the announcer for D1, Jeff Hollobaugh, quickly informed the large crowd that they had just witnessed the fastest 1-2 finish in state history. Both Bowen, with a time of 13.40 and Stark (13.62), had eclipsed the record of yet another Pioneer hurdle ace from the past, Candice Davis.

Said Bowen, "I just needed to run my race. She [Stark] was going to do what she needed to do. It was going to be a race, so that's what we did. We gave them a race."

Although it was the first running event of the afternoon, it was not the first title Pioneer earned that day. Earlier in the morning the Pioneer foursome of Anne Forsyth, Elizabeth Kos, Sydney Dawes and Jacalyn Overdier captured first in the 4 x 800. To illustrate how strong the distances are in Michigan, Pioneer's winning 9:06.13 would not make the all-time top ten listing in meet history. Yet a few weeks later the team would deliver a 8:54.45 runner-up finish at the New Balance Outdoor Nationals in North Carolina.

The third winner for the victors was turned in by junior Anne Forsyth with a blistering 4:43.84. She would pick up 8 more valuable points by placing 2nd in the 3200-meter run behind Maggie Farrell of Battle Creek Lakeview. Farrell was clocked in 10:19.99, the fourth-fastest time ever posted at a state final.

Oak Park scored more than half of its 65 points by sweeping the 400, 800 and 1600-meter relays and grabbing 6th in the 3200-relay. Oak Park's 46.89 clocking in the 400 was second in history only to its own record set the previous year. The win in the 4 x 200 took only 1:38.38. Then the foursome of Carlita Taylor, Makayla Gates, Miyah Brooks and Janae Barksdale cruised 3:49.73 in the 4 x 400, the No. 3 time in meet history.

Tamea McKelvy was the leading point producer for the runner-ups. She won the 200-meter dash (24.14 into a stiff headwind), placed third in the 100 and ran legs on the victorious 400 and 800-meter relays.

Tamea McKelvy edged Anavia Battle in the 200 by 0.13. Both would later star in the college ranks, McKelvy at Texas, Battle at Ohio State. (Pete Draugalis photo)

East Kentwood's girls team scored a more than respectable 57 points in placing a close third in its attempt to match the boys victory. Corrine Jemison was the sole winner for the host school with the day's best heave in the discus of 151-0, the second best effort in meet history.

Greenville's outstanding all-around performer, Landon Kemp, was yet another star of stars. She won the pole vault at 13-3, just an inch shy of her meet record, placed 2nd in the long jump with the sixth best jump in meet history (19-3) and capped her day with a 5th in the record-setting 100-meter hurdle race.

Kemp showed her toughness in repeating as pole vault champ by clearing 13-3 on her third attempt at that height. The South Dakota State commit needed to clear as she had been second place on misses to Jessica Mercier of Waterford Kettering. Sophia Franklin of Okemos also cleared 13-0 in third.

Placing ahead of Kemp in the long jump was Angelica Floyd of Clinton Township Chippewa Valley. Her winning 19-3¾, the longest jump recorded in 18 years, is a D1 record, and put her at No. 4 in meet annals behind three girls from the Class A era.

Wyandotte Roosevelt's Kyanna Evans' winning time of 42.64 in the 300 hurdles stands as one of the best performances ever.

East Lansing's Taylor Manson breezed a 53.21 to just miss the 400 record of 53.10 set a year earlier by Chloe Abbott. A couple weeks later at New Balance Nationals she would go even faster, 53.18, for second.

In Division 2, Zeeland East came agonizingly close to matching the boys' victory on their home track. East placed 2nd to defending champion Lansing Waverly by one slim point (47-46) with the state title decided by 0.002 of a second.

Hurdler Mariel Bruxvoort of Grand Rapids South Christian barely held off a charging Suenomi Norinh at the finish, with both runners at 14.82. After a review of the FAT photo, Bruxvoort was declared the winner with a time of 14.811, with Norinh second at 14.813. The two-point differential between first and second place would give Waverly the championship trophy.

The importance of that finish was overshadowed at the time because much of the attention at the conclusion of the race was diverted to Michaiah Thomas from Detroit Country Day. She was well in the lead before disaster struck for the Yellow Jacket senior. She lost her balance after clipping the ninth hurdle and fell. Later she would place second to Bruxvoort in the 300 hurdles.

To further compound its woes, Zeeland East placed 7th in the 4 x 100 relay, just one-tenth of a second from a sixth-place finish that would have earned a tie for the title.

Norinh had earlier made it to the top of the victory stand with the day's best effort in any class by winning the high jump at 5-8. The junior came just an inch from equaling the state's oldest existing record in any event, the 5-9 first set 41 years earlier by Beth Brunn of Utica.

Waverly won the 400 and 800 relays and received 14 valuable points from Malin Smith with 2nd and 3rd placings in the discus and shot put. The meet was clinched by Waverly when freshman Priscilla Trainor earned 6 points with her 3rd in the 200. Winning that race in a wind-aided 24.26 was Carleton Airport's Zoe Eby, who had earlier won the 100.

The Holland Christian relay quartet of Madylin VanderZwaag, Michelle Kuipers, Elizabeth Bruxvoort and Kayla Windemuller, all underclassmen, smashed the former best by more than 10 seconds in winning the 4 x 800 in 9:09.41.

Windemuller would then defend each of her distance titles with victories in the 1600 (4:52.60) and 3200 runs (10:49.90). Placing second in each of those events was Christina Sawyer from Tecumseh.

Gabriella LeRioux of Spring Lake, in winning the pole vault for the third-straight year, set a new D2 mark of 12-6.

In Division 3 at Comstock Park, Adrian Madison ran off with the state title in a meet that was highlighted by a number of outstanding performances from the distance competitors.

Topping the distance stars was Lansing Catholic junior Olivia Theis, who smashed both the 1600 and 3200 meet records.

First Theis lowered the 1600 meet record to 4:50.10. Sophomore Adelyn Ackley of Hart and Olivia's sister, freshman Jaden Theis, placed 2nd and 3rd as the first five broke the 5-minute barrier.

In the 3200, Olivia Theis was pushed both by Ackley and Jaden. All three ran under the former mark, led by the elder Theis in 10:30.49.

Showing that she could run with any runner from any division, or any state, Olivia Theis would place second later in June at the National Championships with a much-improved time of 10:14.34 for the full two miles.

With 800 winner Amber Gall, a sophomore, running the anchor, Shepherd won the fastest 3200-relay in D3 history. The Blue Jay foursome of Rachel Mathers, Katelyn Hutchinson, Kylie Hutchinson and Gall set a new mark of 9:18.06. Runner-up Hart, who would have three runners place in the top eight in the 3200, also ran faster than the previous record. Not far behind in third was Lansing Catholic's all-underclass lineup that included the Theis sisters.

Adrian Madison, in winning its first state championship, was led by Megan Rosales, who won the 400 and the 300 hurdles shortly afterwards. She bookended her day with legs on winning 4 x 200 and 4 x 400 relays. Running the anchor on a team with Chelsea Short, Delaney Stersic and Sierra Hernandez, Rosales helped set a new D3 mark in the 1600-relay at 3:57.80.

At Division 4 at Housemen Field, Southfield Christian became another first-time team winner, led by junior Chika Amene who won all three short dashes and ran a leg on the winning 1600-meter relay.

Only a pair of meet records were set in D4. Mendon's Mary Leighton clocked 14.89 in the 100 hurdles. In the shot put, Erica Lechner of Harbor Springs threw 44-1 ½.

Upper Peninsula: Only two records fell during the finals at Kingsford. Emmy Kinney of West Iron County won the D2 400 in 59.18. Laura Guftafson of St. Ignace upped the D3 mark to 5-4 in the high jump.

It was business as usual for Marquette as it won its seventh-straight D1 title while St. Ignace edged Munising by 8 points to carry off the D2 trophy. Lake Linden-Hubbell returned to the winners' circle for the first time since 1983 by winning it all in D3.

2018

The headlines from the Division 1 meet at East Kentwood centered on White Lake Lakeland's Grace Stark. The junior hurdler, runner-up the year before, had been serving notice all season that she would be the event's biggest force.

A year before, she had finished second to Pioneer's Britten Bowen, who opted as a senior not to run for her school. That had no effect on the outcome this time around. After a 13.68 heat, Stark destroyed the final with a stunning 13.16 state record performance, run with a perfect 1.7 tailwind.

Behind her, Oak Park sophomore Aasia Laurencin, only a 15.08 hurdler the year before, came through with a 13.54 to become the state's No. 3 hurdler ever.

Grace Stark's 13.16 slashed 0.24 off the state record in the hurdles. (Peter Draugalis photo)

Minutes later, Stark lined up for the 100 final. She would not be denied, overcoming fast-starting Ava Qe'Neisha Young of East Kentwood to win, 11.74-11.87.

"That was a lot faster than I thought it would be," said Stark of her historic hurdles. "I'm used to running both events back-to-back, so I just wanted to keep that mentality.

Stark came back minutes later to win the 100. (Peter Draugalis photo)

Two weeks later, Stark would win the hurdles at New Balance Nationals in 13.24, and place 3rd in the 100 in a best of 11.47.

Oak Park clawed its way back from disaster to make it into the D1 winner's circle, topping Rockford, 66-59½.

Coach Brandon Jiles knew the Knights didn't have a lot of wiggle room. Dorriann Coleman successfully returned from injury to lead off the 4 x 800 in 2:13.57—helping the team to a 9:08.75 victory over Rockford (9:10.46) and Pioneer (9:12.63).

Laurencin's hurdle breakthrough also helped, but disaster hit in the 4 x 200 when Jada Roundtree, leading on the anchor, pulled up injured. "These girls are really tough… They're going to do whatever they need to do to get the job done," said Jiles.

And they did. Miyah Brooks came through with a 400 win in 55.12. Laurencin returned to win the 200 in 24.64. In the 4 x 400, an event Oak Park had won three of the previous four years, the foursome of Makayla Gates, Jayla Jones, Mariyah Archibald and Dorriann Coleman came up the winners in 3:51.01.

A huge state record—completely unexpected—came in the shot. East Kentwood senior Corinne Jemison came in with a best of 46-10½. After four rounds, she led at 46-1½, then she stunned spectators—and her throws coach Norm Zylstra—by lofting the ball 49-11¾, a state record by 5¾ inches and nearly two feet farther than the school record owned by Olympian Tia Brooks.

Jemison topped the 45-6½ of Lansing Waverly's Malin Smith, who earlier had thrown a meet record of 163-9 in the discus.

The distances served up plenty of excitement, as usual. Rockford's Ericka VanderLende, the D1 cross country champ, topped defending champion Anne Forsyth in the 1600, 4:45.17 to 4:48.28.

In the 800, senior Katie Osika of Waterford Mott went from the gun, churning out a 2:08.88 to top Hudsonville's Melanie Helder (2:09.28) and Oak Park's Coleman (2:10.22). It was Osika's last chance to join her sisters at the top of the podium. Ten years earlier, Shannon Osika had won the 3200, and a year later Shannon and Alyssa had teamed up on the 4x8 winners.

VanderLende's quest for a distance double ran into renewed opposition from Forsyth, who finished with an amazing 5:00.4 second half to take the 3200 in a meet record 10:08.07, well ahead of VanderLende's 10:12.26.

Just four days later, VanderLende made history, becoming the first Michigan prep to break 10:00 for the full two-mile, running 9:59.92 at the Brooks PR Invitational. She passed the 3200 mark in 9:56.5, a state record.

The Division 2 team battle at Zeeland came down to a pair of local rivals. Host Zeeland East nipped Holland Christian by a mere two points in a meet that was a record-smashing success.

Accounting for more than half of her team's points, Suenomi Norinh captured three state titles and fell just two-tenths of a second from a perfect afternoon with her runner-up finish in the 300 hurdles.

Winner in the 100-meter hurdles (14.63), and the long jump (18-1¼), Norinh won the high jump for the third consecutive year with the highest clearance in any division at 5-8.

The distance races were headlined by Kayla Windemuller of Holland Christian and Olivia Theis of Lansing Catholic, whose school had moved up a division.

Windemuller began her taxing day in the early hours by teaming up with Michelle Kuipers, Elizabeth Bruxvoort and Madylin VanderZwaag to win the 4 x 800 in 9:10.01, less than a second slower than they had run the previous year.

Then she blazed to a D2 record early in the afternoon in the 1600 with a 4:49.55, second only to the Class B mark of Petoskey's Kelly Smith back in 1994. Although the Holland Christian standout was able to top Olivia Theis in the 1600, Theis perhaps used her runner-up placing as a warm-up for the 3200 meters.

Theis took the longer win in 10:37.08, and could boast of holding the 3200 record in both D2 and D3. Placing second was Olivia's younger sister, Jaden.

Windemuller capped her day with a third to give her team 6 valuable points, just minutes after earning Holland Christian an additional 5 points with a 4th in the 800. That race was won by yet another Maroon runner, sophomore Michelle Kuipers, who had stunned by cutting six seconds off her best to win in 2:13.47.

Another record was established when Brianna Bredeweg of Allendale won the vault at 12-7, the highest height in state history for a sophomore.

In Division 3 at Comstock Park, St. Charles and Hart were deadlocked after all results were tabulated with 46 points. Both teams could reflect as to what could have been if not for placings determined by increments in the most minuscule of margins.

St. Charles dominated the sprints and short relays, and Hart the distance events. However, St. Charles can look back at a pair of field events that reaped big dividends for the co-champs.

Mikayle Williams placed second in the long jump, just a quarter of an inch longer than third place finisher Ella Suliman of Grass Lake. Williams also took a valuable 2 points in the pole vault, earning one more point than another vaulter who cleared the same 10-foot height in the pole vault, with Williams earning the championship saving point on fewer misses at the last height.

Hart likewise had a close call in the 800 where just 0.04 stood between Hart and a runner-up trophy.

In a valiant attempt to lead her team to a state championship, Hart's Adelyn Ackley likewise put the team ahead of individual glory by attempting to secure as many points as possible.

Earlier in the day she had joined Alayna Ackley, Brenna Aerts and McKenzie Stitt and anchored them to victory in the 4 x 800.

The D3 cross-country champion in the fall, she placed second in the 1600 behind Hanover-Horton's Judy Rector, whose 4:52.59 was No. 3 mark in meet history. Earning one valuable point with an 8th place finish was Adelyn's young sister, freshman Savannah.

Adelyn, one of four Ackleys who competed during the meet, later procured three much-needed points by placing 6th in the 800.

Rector, coming off her win in the 1600, nosed out 2017 D3 state champion Amber Gall of Shephard by 0.01 to take the 800.

The indefatigable Ackley, whose aunt Cathy Ackley was a five-time state champion for Hart back in the 1980s, somehow saved up enough energy to win the 3200-meter run (10:45.54) just minutes later.

Hart earned a whopping 20 points in the long run to move from the middle of the pack to earn a share of the trophy. Adelyn's older sister Alayna, recovering from a stress fracture, placed third for the Pirates, while younger sister Savannah netted 4 points with her fifth-place. Ninth grader Lynae Ackley, a cousin of the three sisters, placed a respectable 13th.

The individual star for the co-champs from St. Charles was senior sprinter Najiyah Holden. Holden earned first place honors in the 200, took 3rd in the 100 and anchored both the 4 x 100 and 4 x 200 relays to victory.

In Division 4 at Hudsonville, Fowler tallied an impressive 87 points to breeze to its ninth state championship. The mid-Michigan powerhouse has also carted off 8 runner-up trophies since championships for the girls first took place back in 1973.

Fowler won seven titles on the day and swept all four relays as well as taking three places in the 100 hurdles.

Southfield Christian's Chika Amene, winner of all three sprints a year before, nearly pulled off another three-peat. Only a narrow loss in the 400 to Beal City frosh Angela Kotecki kept the senior from the trifecta. Both were clocked in 57.33.

An inspired Samantha Saenz from Concord, after winning the 1600 the previous two years, again repeated in 2018 and also added the 800 and 3200 titles.

She told reporters that the day of her first state win in 2016 she learned that her sister had died. "Every time I cross the finish line it's so meaningful for me because my sister couldn't walk or talk. Just the fact I get to have that gift, it's a good feeling."

Upper Peninsula: The distance duo of sophomore Emily Paupore and senior Clara Johnson led Negaunee to its first title in eight years, snapping Marquette's quest to win its eighth straight.

The pair finished 1-2 in the 800, 1600 and 3200 meter runs while Paupore's winning time of 11:25.52 in the latter established a meet record. One other mark fell in D1 when Emily McLean of Sault Ste. Marie tossed the shot 38-1¼.

After being pushed to the limits to win D2 a year earlier, St. Ignace took all the drama out by scoring in all events to accumulate 160 points, 70 more than Iron Mountain.

High jumper Linnee Gustafson of St. Ignace joined the short list of state champs who won an individual title four-consecutive years.

Lake Linden-Hubbell successfully defended its crown in D3 as breezy conditions limited top performances in most of the events. Madeleine Peramaki set the only record in D3 with a 2:23.05 in the 800.

STATE CHAMPIONS

What follows is the result of 30 years of painstaking and passionate research by Jim Moyes; it is the most complete listing ever compiled of every high school state track & field champion in Michigan history. While current official MHSAA usage is to use the term "Lower Peninsula Finals" or its UP counterpart, for athletes and coaches it's the "state" meet, and it dates its existence to long before the MHSAA came into existence in 1924.

Which Meet? These are the meets that are included in this compilation:

1895-1897 – "Field Days" as they were called then, organized by the Michigan Inter-School Athletic Association, a group made up of students and faculty members. The group later took the name "Michigan High School Athletic Association" but had no connection to the current organization of that name.

1898-1907 – The Michigan Interscholastic, sponsored by the University of Michigan. Participation widened, but eventually Michigan started allowing out-of-state teams to participate.

1908-1911 – The M.A.C. Interscholastic, sponsored by Michigan Agricultural College (later MSU), restricted membership to Michigan schools, and had the sanction of the Michigan Schoolmasters Club, the forerunner of the Michigan Association of Secondary School Principals. It was conducted from 1909-on under the eligibility rules of the the Michigan Interscholastic Athletic Association, the forerunner of the MHSAA. The University of Michigan event remained an important meet during this time (and until 1924) but the authors do not consider it a state championship.

1912 – Organized solely by the Michigan Schoolmasters Club.

1913-1924 – The M.A.C. Interscholastic.

1925 – present – The Michigan High School Athletic Association.

Meet Records: The records listed below—as well as the record progressions marked by an asterisk (*) next to the performances—do not always match what meet officials and the MHSAA called meet records at the time. Rather, these are our determination of the meet records using proper statistical guidelines (considering wind readings, etc.). Records were reset when the transition was made from classes to divisions in 2000-2001. In the sprint events, notable hand-times are listed in some cases where historically interesting; we no longer consider them to be meet records.

Wind measurement: The rules on what is or isn't a legal wind have been with us for nearly 100 years. Even back in the 1890s, officials in our sport would disallow records if they felt the aiding wind was excessive. Unfortunately, for much of the history of the state finals, wind readings weren't consistently taken. Only in the last several years have we seen consistent officiating in this area in the LP Finals. To date we have not seen wind readings reported from the UP.

A "w" is included with performances in the 100, 200, 100/110H and LJ that were aided by excessive wind. An actual wind reading is given in meters-per-second where known. Legal wind, by the way, is 2.0mps (4.47mph) or less. Where no reading is noted and there is a "w", that indicates that either the original reading has been lost or that officials at the meet or trusted observers deemed the wind excessive.

In actuality, there were far, *far* more wind-aided performances in the course of the meet history than are noted here. However, we can only work with the information we have. That means that some of the marks noted as records might not be legitimate, but we'll never know. We can be sure that marks with a wind-reading are 100% reliable and the standard for future records.

Timing: All times in tenths of a second are hand-timed. All listed to the hundredth of a second are automatic times. In the crucial events (100, 200, 400, 100/110H, 300H & 4x1), once automatic timing became standard at the state finals, hand-times are not considered for records.

In some of the early UP meets that produced results in hundredths of a second, there were reports from coaches that automatic timing was not actually in use. We cannot be sure that the times in question have been recorded correctly.

The inaccuracy of hand-timing cannot be overstated. The commonly used 0.24 average conversion comes from a study of trained professional timers at the 1972 Munich Olympic Games. Consider that mythical for our purposes. The margin of error tends to be much bigger at high school meets, where timers have typically been volunteers with no actual training. The several years that I compared automatic times with official back-up hand-times at the Division I Finals (back when hand times were taken), the average error was 0.45 seconds.

Track configuration: The 1895-6 meets were held on a half-mile horse track. In 1912 the meet was held on a banked bicycle track, lap size unknown. Starting in 1914 at East Lansing, the 220-yard dash and hurdles were run on the straightaway. Prior to that the event had been run on the curve. When MSU reconfigured the track in 1970-71, the 220 was once again run on a curve.

Corrections & Additions Please! In some cases, we are missing the names of relay personnel. There are also probably spelling errors galore in the tens of thousands of names that have been typed up from blurry microfilms of decades-old newspapers. If you can offer us any help, please email jeffhollobaugh@gmail.com. /JH/

BOYS 100 METERS

Records

D1	10.53 (-0.2)	Khance Meyers	East Kentwood	2017
D2	10.53	Kyle Redwine	Auburn Hills Avondale	2012
D3	10.82	Chris Rucker	Detroit Country Day	2007
D4	10.70 (0.7)	Lawson Bright-Mitchell	Concord	2014
UPD1	10.95	Garrett Pentecost	Marquette	2011
UPD2	11.25	Brett Spigarelli	Iron Mountain	2003
(hand 10.8		*Steve Schmidt*	*Stephenson*	*2002)*
UPD3	11.23	Phillip Hood	Engadine	2010

Records by Class (pre-2000 for LP, pre-2001 for UP)

A	10.55	Allan Jefferson	Detroit DeLaSalle	1986
B	10.61	Robert Harris	Ypsilanti Willow Run	1987
C	10.72	Ryan Harris	Buchanan	1996
D	10.77	Juson Johnson	Baldwin	1997
(hand 10.5		*Larry Jordan*	*Detroit DePorres*	*1980)*
UPA	10.9	Todd LaCosse	Escanaba	1987
UPC	11.1	Bradley Ruleau	Stephenson	1997
UPD	10.9	Mike Thiry	Carney-Nadeau	1986

100 - Class A/Division 1 Champions

(y=100 yards)

Year		Name	School	Time
1895	all	Clarence Christopher	Lansing	10.4y
1896	all	W.W. Kittleman	Detroit Central	11.4y
1897	all	W.W. Kittleman	Detroit Central	10.8y
1898	all	Roy Ellis	Detroit Central	11.0y
1899	all	Roy Ellis	Detroit Central	11.6y
1900	all	Lyman Bennett	Michigan Military Academy	10.4y*
1901	all	Ralph Keeler	Detroit Central	10.6y
1902	all	Ralph Keeler	Detroit University School	10.2y*
1903	all	Ralph Keeler	Detroit University School	nt
1904	all	Clayton Schenk	Chelsea	nt
1905	all	George Widman	Detroit Central	10.2y*
1906	all	George Widman	Detroit Central	nt
1907	all	George Widman	Detroit Central	10.2y*
1908	all	Harvey Cornwell	Ann Arbor	10.2y*
1909	all	Win Spiegel	Detroit University School	10.2y*
1910	all	Thomas Tuomy	Detroit University School	10.2y*
1911	all	Joseph Comstock	Alpena	10.2y*
1912	all	Carman Smith	Bay City Eastern	10.2y*
1913	all	Alfred Gamble	Coldwater	10.2y*
1914	all	Herbert Henry	Detroit Eastern	10.0y*
1915	all	Herbert Henry	Detroit Eastern	10.6y
1916	all	Russell Cowan	Pontiac	10.2y
1917	all	Russell Cowan	Pontiac	10.8y
1918		No Meet – World War I		
1919	all	George Walker	Gobleville	10.4y
1920	all	Carl Blauman	Detroit Northwestern	10.4y
1921	A	George Hester	Detroit Northern	10.2y
1922	A	George Hester	Detroit Northern	10.2y
1923	A	George Hester	Detroit Northern	9.8y*
1924	A	Lyle Henson	Lansing Central	10.2y
1925	A	Eddie Tolan	Detroit Cass Tech	10.1y
1926	A	Eddie Tolan	Detroit Cass Tech	9.9y
1927	A	Eddie Tolan	Detroit Cass Tech	9.8y*
1928	A	Lester Nelson	Grand Rapids South	10.4y
1929	A	Leroy Oliver	Detroit Cass Tech	10.2y
1930	A	William Bryant	Detroit Cass Tech	10.4y
1931	A	Roy Kaiser	Grosse Pointe	10.6y
1932	A	Harsant Tantsi	Ann Arbor	10.4y
1933	A	Bob Kolbe	Saginaw Eastern	10.0y
1934	A	Bill Strehl	Grand Rapids Ottawa Hills	10.1y
1935	A	Wilbur Greer	Flint Central	10.1y
1936	A	Ira Hughes	Monroe	9.9y
1937	A	James McGhee	Pontiac	10.1y
1938	A	George Doran	Grand Rapids South	10.1y
1939	A	Bert Copeland	Benton Harbor	10.0y
1940	A	Bert Copeland	Benton Harbor	10.0y
1941	A	Bert Copeland	Benton Harbor	10.0y
1942	A	Bob Rogers	Kalamazoo Central	10.5y
1943		No Meet – World War II		
1944	A	Dean Ousterhaut	Saginaw Arthur Hill	10.5y
1945	A	Owen Jackson	Flint Central	10.0y
1946	A	John Fleming	Lansing Eastern	10.4y
1947	A	Art Ingram	Flint Central	10.1y

Year	Class	Name	School	Time
1948	A	Dick Henson	Dearborn	10.2y
1949	A	William Baxter	Dearborn Fordson	10.2y
1950	A	William Baxter	Dearborn Fordson	10.3y
1951	A	Bob Brown	Grand Rapids Ottawa Hills	10.0y
1952	A	Alonzo Harris	Pontiac	10.3y
1953	A	John Johnson	Kalamazoo Central	9.9y
1954	A	Marvin Pierce	Saginaw	10.0y
1955	A	Pete Dant	Alpena	9.8y*
1956	A	Pete Dant	Alpena	9.7yw
1957	A	Namon Smith	Bay City Central	10.3y
1958	A	Bob Manning	Pontiac Central	10.1y
1959	A	Don Watkins	Flint Central	10.2y
1960	A	Maurice Pea	Flint Northern	9.8y*
1961	A	Dorie Reid	Ferndale	9.9y
1962	A	Joe Parham	Muskegon Heights	10.0y
1963	A	Wilbur Johnson	Flint Northern	9.8y*
1964	A	Arnie Williams	Battle Creek Central	9.8y*
1965	A	Arnie Williams	Battle Creek Central	9.8y*
1966	A	Charles Robinson	Detroit Mackenzie	9.8y*
1967	A	Herb Washington	Flint Central	10.1y
1968	A	Herb Washington	Flint Central	9.8y* (-6.7)
1969	A	Ken James	Detroit Mackenzie	10.0y
1970	A	Marshall Dill	Detroit Northern	10.0y
1971	A	Marshall Dill	Detroit Northern	9.6y*
1972	A	Reggie Jones	Saginaw	9.8y
1973	A	Reggie Jones	Saginaw	9.6y*
1974	A	Chris Richards	Detroit Pershing	9.8y
1975	A	Harlan Huckleby	Detroit Cass Tech	9.8y
1976	A	Randall Smith	Jackson	9.8y
1977	A	Jerry Malone	Pontiac Northern	9.8y
1978	A	Deon Hogan	Detroit Kettering	9.8y
1979	A	Anthony Battle	Flint Southwestern	10.0y
1980	A	Don Anderson	Detroit Cody	9.7y
1981	A	Don Anderson	Detroit Cody	9.6y*
1982	A	Terry McDaniel	Saginaw	10.5*
1983	A	Anthony Mahone	Detroit Denby	10.7
1984	A	Anthony Mahone	Detroit Denby	10.5*
1985	A	Allan Jefferson	Warren DeLaSalle	10.78*
1986	A	Allan Jefferson	Detroit DeLaSalle	10.55*
1987	A	Corey Pryor	Jackson	10.4
1988	A	Martin Hill	Detroit Cass Tech	10.5
1989	A	Terrance Smith	Bay City Central	10.93
1990	A	Damon Grady	Pontiac Northern	10.69
1991	A	Kerch. Patterson	Ypsilanti	10.83
1992	A	Brad Fields	East Kentwood	11.02
1993	A	Micah Morris	Bay City Central	10.85
1994	A	Micah Morris	Bay City Central	10.4
1995	A	Jamal Allen	Southfield Lathrup	11.2
1996	A	Gerald Rasool	Pontiac Central	10.92
1997	A	Lemar Courtney	Muskegon Mona Shores	10.81
1998	A	Charles Rogers	Saginaw	10.70 (1.8)
1999	A	Stuart Schweigert	Saginaw Heritage	10.60w (2.2)
2000	D1	Kelly Baraka	Portage Northern	10.56* (2.0)
2001	D1	Kyle Brown	West Bloomfield	10.86
2002	D1	Pierre Vinson	Detroit Cass Tech	10.70
2003	D1	Rynar Hamilton	Jackson	10.83 (-1.2)
2004	D1	Marcus Thigpen	Detroit Mumford	10.82
2005	D1	Ahmad Rashad	Flint Carman-Ainsworth	10.56*
2006	D1	Dimitri Banks	Detroit Murray-Wright	10.75 (1.1)
2007	D1	James Jackson	Grand Ledge	10.94 (-1.4)
2008	D1	Darryl White	Romulus	10.76 (1.6)
2009	D1	Jon Henry	East Kentwood	10.89 (-2.8)
2010	D1	Jon Henry	East Kentwood	10.81 (-3.7)
2011	D1	Ricco Hall	East Kentwood	10.55* (1.4)
2012	D1	Austin Sanders	Ypsilanti	10.92
2013	D1	Joshuwa Holloman	Auburn Hills Avondale	11.11
2014	D1	Eli Minor	Oak Park	10.88
2015	D1	Jaron Flournoy	Westland John Glenn	10.56 (1.0)
2016	D1	Khance Meyers	East Kentwood	10.73 (0.3)
2017	D1	Khance Meyers	East Kentwood	10.53* (-0.2)
2018	D1	Erik LaBonte	Traverse City West	10.66 (0.2)

100 - Class B/Division 2 Champions

(y=100 yards)

Year	Class	Name	School	Time
1921	B	Kent Pritchard	Allegan	10.4y*
1922	B	Harley Sternaman	Owosso	10.4y*
1923	B	John Burridge	St Johns	10.3y*
1924	B	John Burridge	St Johns	10.2y*
1925	B	Clare Warner	St Johns	10.5y
1926	B	Paul Ruth	St Johns	10.4y
1927	B	Moulton Davis	St Joseph	10.3wy
1928	B	Moulton Davis	St Joseph	10.3y
1929	B	Fred Schatte	Monroe	10.4y
1930	B	Fred Schatte	Monroe	10.5y
1931	B	Virgil Davenport	Alma	10.7y
1932	B	Moses Easley	Dowagiac	10.5y
1933	B	William Guckleberg	Birmingham	10.3y
1934	B	Arthur Frontczak	Dowagiac	10.2y*
1935	B	Vinton Davis	St Joseph	10.3y
1936	B	Red Conley	Allegan	10.0y*
1937	B	Ron Mead	East Lansing	10.2y
1938	B	Ron Mead	East Lansing	10.2y
1939	B	Ron Mead	East Lansing	9.8yw
1940	B	Walter Derby	Fremont	10.3y
1941	B	Bo Miller	East Lansing	10.4y
1942	B	Jack Steelman	Birmingham	10.8y
1943		No Meet – World War II		
1944	B	Bob Swain	East Grand Rapids	10.3y
1945	B	Bob Swain	East Grand Rapids	9.9y*
1946	B	Ulysses Rogers	Ecorse	10.7y
1947	B	Ray Branch	Hastings	10.4y
1948	B	Charles Roland	South Haven	10.5y
1949	B	Elmore McKinney	Ecorse	10.4y
1950	B	Joe Ross	Birmingham	10.4y
1951	B	Henry Whitsett	Ecorse	10.5y
1952	B	Henry Whitsett	Ecorse	10.8y
1953	B	Glen Burgett	Sparta	10.1y
1954	B	Glen Burgett	Sparta	10.0y
1955	B	Art Frederick	Inkster	10.4y
1956	B	Charles Keyers	Inkster	10.5y
1957	B	Terry Montei	St Joseph	10.6y
1958	B	Jim Drake	Lake Orion	10.1y
1959	B	Naosha Poe	Willow Run	10.2y
1960	B	Craig LaGrone	Detroit Lutheran West	10.2y
1961	B	Craig LaGrone	Detroit Lutheran West	9.9y*
1962	B	Tom Reid	Stevensville-Lakeshore	10.1y
1963	B	Tom Reid	Stevensville-Lakeshore	10.1y
1964	B	Boice Bowman	River Rouge	9.9y*
1965	B	Clarence Sabbath	River Rouge	10.5y
1966	B	Ed Randle	Cranbrook	10.2y
1967	B	John Schneider	Marshall	10.1y
1968	B	Al Miller	Niles Brandywine	10.1y
1969	B	Frank Bennett	Oscoda	9.8y*
1970	B	Larry Schultze	Elkton-Pigeon-Bayport	10.2y
1971	B	Roy Young	Mount Morris	9.7y*
1972	B	Roy Young	Mount Morris	10.0y
1973	B	Terry Fields	Comstock	10.0y
1974	B	Dwayne Strozier	Flint Powers	9.8y
1975	B	Dwayne Strozier	Flint Powers	9.5y*
1976	B	Mike Ball	Wyoming Park	9.9y
1977	B	Wilbert Rowland	Port Huron Central	10.1y
1978	B	Paul Sugas	Plainwell	10.0y
1979	B	Scott Bayer	Parma Western	9.9y
1980	B	Andreas Laut	Dexter	10.5*
1981	B	Ricky Swilley	Saginaw Buena Vista	11.2
1982	B	Kevin Robinson	Dearborn Hts Robichaud	9.9y
1983	B	Jeff Sharp	Flint Beecher	10.6
1984	B	Mark Lewis	Ypsilanti Lincoln	10.6
1985	B	Darryl Warner	Willow Run	11.02*
1986	B	Charles Wilson	Detroit Benedictine	10.9
1987	B	Robert Harris	Willow Run	10.61*
1988	B	O'Maka Smith	Bay City Handy	10.81
1989	B	Tyrone Wheatley	Dearborn Hts Robichaud	10.5
1990	B	Tyrone Wheatley	Dearborn Hts Robichaud	10.8
1991	B	Tyrone Wheatley	Dearborn Hts Robichaud	10.67
1992	B	Andy Schoelch	Bloomfield Hills Andover	10.81
1993	B	Ed Barnes	Grand Rapids Northview	10.93
1994	B	Ted Adams	Ypsilanti Lincoln	10.97
1995	B	Randy Hunt	Comstock	11.36
1996	B	John Matthews	Wyoming Godwin Heights	11.21
1997	B	Edward Johnson	River Rouge	10.84
1998	B	Edward Johnson	River Rouge	10.92
1999	B	Antwan Henderson	Stevensville-Lakeshore	11.05
2000	D2	Sean Heard	Ypsilanti	10.73*
2001	D2	Daymond Hammler	Orchard Lake St Mary	10.85
2002	D2	Tim Scott	Fowlerville	10.80
2003	D2	Brian Brighton	Allen Park	10.82
2004	D2	Corey Pennywell	Dearborn Hts Crestwood	11.07
2005	D2	Clint Allen	Muskegon Orchard View	10.79
2006	D2	Clint Allen	Muskegon Orchard View	10.44w
2007	D2	Brandon Vandriel	Sparta	10.88
2008	D2	Brandon Vandriel	Sparta	10.52w
2009	D2	Brandon Vandriel	Sparta	10.98
2010	D2	Ross Parsons	DeWitt	10.80
2011	D2	John Hill	Detroit Country Day	10.79

Year	Name	School	Time
2012 D2	Kyle Redwine	Auburn Hills Avondale	10.53*
2013 D2	Berkley Edwards	Chelsea	10.58w (5.4)
2014 D2	Joshuwa Holloman	Auburn Hills Avondale	10.75
2015 D2	Joshuwa Holloman	Auburn Hills Avondale	10.71
2016 D2	Kahlee Hamler	Orchard Lake St Mary	10.99 (-0.9)
2017 D2	John Adams	Ferndale	10.94 (1.0)
2018 D2	Thomas Robinson	Wyoming Lee	10.85w (2.6)

100 - Class C/Division 3 Champions

(y=100 yards)

Year	Name	School	Time
1921 C	Joe Biers	Imlay City	10.4y*
1922 C	Harold Wright	Millington	10.4y*
1923 C	Donald Camp	Plainwell	10.5y
1924 C	Chuck Parker	Clinton	10.3y*
1925 C	Harold Gilbert	Croswell	10.4y
1926 C	Milton Jacobi	Marine City	10.3y*
1927 C	Ted Fuzz Oosting	Fremont	10.5y
1928 C	Don Craig	Romeo	10.6y
1929 C	Mark Stephenson	Constantine	10.4y
1930 C	Harry Samrick	East Grand Rapids	10.2y*
1931 C	Ham White	Boyne City	10.7y
1932 C	Ham White	Boyne City	10.5y
1933 C	Ham White	Boyne City	10.0y*
1934 C	Alan Smith	Paw Paw	10.2y
1935 C	Alan Smith	Paw Paw	10.0y*
1936 C	Burdet Warson	Homer	10.2y
1937 C	Arthur Mitchell	Northville	10.4y
1938 C	Arthur Mitchell	Northville	10.4y
1939 C	Tom Cherry	St Clair Shores South Lake	10.2y
1940 C	Frank Lee	East Grand Rapids	10.4y
1941 C	Dan Adcock	Holt	10.5y
1942 C	Richard Holland	Comstock Park	10.6y
1943	No Meet – World War II		
1944 C	Marvin Grostic	Fowlerville	10.5y
1945 C	Joe Banks	St Clair Shores Lakeshore	10.3y
1946 C	Art Marschner	Detroit University School	10.7y
1947 C	Victor Tate	Paw Paw	10.4y
1948 C	Ron Willett	St Clair Shores South Lake	11.1y
1949 C	Peter Coll	Detroit St Ambrose	10.9y
1950 C	John Vanderzee	Grosse Ile	10.7y
1951 C	Jerry Wolf	Ann Arbor University High	10.4y
1952 C	Osie Rostic	Whitehall	10.5y
1953 C	Dick Ewing	Okemos	10.1y
1954 C	Dale Boyer	Scottville	10.2y
1955 C	Henry McNary	Cassopolis	10.2y
1956 C	Tom Belmore	Ypsilanti Lincoln	10.3y
1957 C	Steve Willard	Portland	10.6y
1958 C	Don Voorheis	Frankenmuth	9.8y*
1959 C	Don Voorheis	Frankenmuth	10.2y
1960 C	Bill Lynch	Nashville	10.5y
1961 C	Dennis Gorsline	Michigan Lutheran Seminary	10.3y
1962 C	Dave Loomis	East Jackson	10.3y
1963 C	Cy Vallier	Merrill	10.3y
1964 C	Steven Strauch	Detroit St Theresa	9.9y
1965 C	Greg Braun	Fowlerville	10.4y
1966 C	Dave Carroll	Laingsburg	10.0y
1967 C	Dave Carroll	Laingsburg	10.4y
1968 C	Jim Holmes	Lansing Boys Vocational	10.1y
1969 C	Mike Valentine	East Jackson	10.0y
1970 C	Claude Bagsby	Detroit DePorres	10.5y
1971 C	Jack McClellan	Detroit Country Day	10.2y
1972 C	Dan Abrams	Detroit DePorres	10.1y
1973 C	Dave Ratajack	Detroit Country Day	10.3y
1974 C	Jan Abrams	Detroit DePorres	10.4y
1975 C	Mark Lehman	Whittemore-Prescott	10.2y
1976 C	Bob VanderBoon	GR Forest Hills Northern	10.2y
1977 C	Dan Morris	Harper Woods Lutheran E	9.9y
1978 C	Randy Lauterburg	Whitehall	10.2y
1979 C	John Moore	Eau Claire	10.2y
1980 C	Kipp Owen	Goodrich	9.9y
1981 C	Rob Bramer	Olivet	10.6w
1982 C	Joe Corbett	Detroit Lutheran West	11.0*
1983 C	Joe Corbett	Detroit Lutheran West	10.7*
1984 C	Scott Simon	St Charles	11.1
1985 C	Wiley Boulding	Kalamazoo Hackett	11.06*
1986 C	Rodney Culver	Detroit DePorres	10.81*
1987 C	Rory Stace	Galesburg-Augusta	10.81*
1988 C	Tony Jackson	Saginaw Nouvel	11.0
1989 C	Tony Jackson	Saginaw Nouvel	10.92
1990 C	Chad VanConet	Fulton-Middleton	11.42
1991 C	Sherman Ross	Cassopolis	11.0
1992 C	Adrian Edwards	Detroit DePorres	11.1
1993 C	Jeremy Davis	Manchester	11.57
1994 C	Thomas Dixon	Bangor	11.33
1995 C	Billy Chenault	New Haven	10.90
1996 C	Ryan Harris	Buchanan	10.72*
1997 C	Jason Carver	Parchment	10.77
1998 C	Travis Kelly	New Haven	11.27
1999 C	Brandon Hooks	Detroit DePorres	10.74
2000 D3	Vic Ornelas	Beaverton	11.04*
2001 D3	Tim Shaw	Livonia Clarenceville	11.03*
2002 D3	Kyle Dengler	Essexville Garber	11.02*
2003 D3	Kim Thompson	Detroit Country Day	10.76w
2004 D3	Jonathon Evans	Muskegon Oakridge	11.00*
2005 D3	Jonathon Evans	Muskegon Oakridge	10.91*
2006 D3	Chris Rucker	Detroit Country Day	10.82*
2007 D3	Chris Rucker	Detroit Country Day	10.82*
2008 D3	Hersey Jackson	Allendale	10.89
2009 D3	Dan Rau	Sanford-Meridian	10.83 (1.2)
2010 D3	Brent Vanenk	Grandville Calvin Christian	11.15
2011 D3	Chris Maye	Union City	10.83
2012 D3	Chris Maye	Union City	10.87
2013 D3	Alize Champion	Southfield Bradford Acad	11.03
2014 D3	Aaron Watson	Union City	10.90 (0.0)
2015 D3	Christian Petre	Sanford-Meridian	11.13 (0.0)
2016 D3	Thomas Robinson	Wyoming Lee	11.09 (-0.8)
2017 D3	Thomas Robinson	Wyoming Lee	10.84 (0.0)
2018 D3	Caleb Schutte	Grandville Calvin Christian	11.10 (1.6)

100 - Class D/Division 4 Champions

(y=100 yards)

Year	Name	School	Time
1927 D	Irwin Kemp	Trenton	10.6y*
1928 D	Leroy Lewis	Centreville	11.1y
1929 D	Fred Miles	Okemos	10.9y
1930 D	Fred Miles	Okemos	10.8y
1931 D	Gregory Mosher	Centreville	11.2y
1932 D	Rex Wolf	Prattville	11.1y
1933 D	Jim Sprague	South Lyon	10.4y*
1934 D	Clifton Frazier	Centreville	10.9y
1935 D	William Weise	Bear Lake	10.4y*
1936 D	Tom Cherry	St. Clair Shores South Lake	10.4y*
1937 D	Tom Cherry	St. Clair Shores South Lake	10.7y
1938 D	Dick LaBrasseur	Nahma	10.6y
1939 D	Gordon Craig	Bloomfield Hills	10.3y*
1940 D	Harold Flynn	Copemish	10.7y
1941 D	Bill La Gro	White Pigeon	10.6y
1942 D	Larry Pratt	Colon	10.8y
1943	No Meet – World War II		
1944 D	Henry Rolike	Lansing Boys Vocational	10.8y
1945 D	Arlon Dennison	Michigan School for Deaf	10.3y*
1946 D	Arlon Dennison	Michigan School for Deaf	10.6y
1947 D	Stephan Nykos	Grosse Ile	10.9y
1948 D	Bob Hocker	Benton Harbor St. John	10.8y
1949 D	Ancel Rodgers	Benton Harbor St. John	10.7y
1950 D	Ancel Rodgers	Benton Harbor St. John	10.8y
1951 D	Ancel Rodgers	Benton Harbor St. John	10.4y
1952 D	Don Beurle	Suttons Bay	10.2y*
1953 D	Jerry Mitchell	Eau Claire	10.6y
1954 D	Robert Phillips	Brethren	10.4y
1955 D	Ken Beane	Brethren	10.8y
1956 D	Ken Beane	Brethren	10.6y
1957 D	Ken Beane	Brethren	10.7y
1958 D	Ken Beane	Brethren	10.2y*
1959 D	Frank Thomas	Brethren	10.8y
1960 D	Roosevelt Davis	Covert	10.3y
1961 D	Chet Beasley	Ypsilanti St. John	10.5y
1962 D	Chet Beasley	Ypsilanti St. John	10.6y
1963 D	Darwin Hoag	Morrice	10.2y*
1964 D	Cliff Harris	Lake City	10.3y
1965 D	Cliff Harris	Lake City	10.4y
1966 D	Dave Shipman	Ann Arbor University High	10.3y
1967 D	Dave Shipman	Ann Arbor University High	10.4y
1968 D	Dorrie Carpenter	Burr Oak	10.3y
1969 D	Ed Robinson	Michigan School for Deaf	10.0y*
1970 D	Ed Robinson	Michigan School for Deaf	10.2y
1971 D	Ed Robinson	Michigan School for Deaf	10.2y
1972 D	Chester Harding	Covert	10.3y
1973 D	Dwight Jones	Grosse Pointe Univ Liggett	9.9y*
1974 D	Dwight Jones	Grosse Pointe Univ Liggett	10.0y
1975 D	Dwight Jones	Grosse Pointe Univ Liggett	9.9y*

1976 D	Stanley Young	Detroit DePorres	9.9y*		1998 D	Eric Colver	Webberville	10.95
1977 D	Stanley Young	Detroit DePorres (9.5* heat) 9.7y			1999 D	Otis Jordan	Harper Woods Gallagher	10.97
1978 D	Rod Strong	Mendon	10.1y		2000 D4	Trav. Montgomery	St. Joseph Lk MI Catholic	11.05*
1979 D	Jerry Campbell	Detroit DePorres	10.9*		2001 D4	Darry Anglin	Redford Borgess	10.94*
1980 D	Larry Jordan	Detroit DePorres	10.5*		2002 D4	Jason Smith	Redford Borgess	11.11
1981 D	Fred King	Covert	11.1		2003 D4	Carl Grimes	Detroit DePorres	10.99
1982 D	Brian Burger	Reading	11.2		2004 D4	Willie Knight	Decatur	11.29
1983 D	Robert Willhight	Detroit East Catholic	11.0		2005 D4	William Fulton	Inkster	10.77*
1984 D	Robert Willhight	Detroit East Catholic	10.81*		2006 D4	Matt Eichler	Litchfield	10.98
1985 D	Sean Jones	Detroit East Catholic	11.14		2007 D4	John Fahnenstiel	North Muskegon	11.26
1986 D	Leroy Williams	Baldwin	11.2		2008 D4	Josh Depree	Ottawa Lake Whiteford	11.10
1987 D	Dave Goodwin	Redford St Mary	10.96		2009 D4	Ethan Murray	Bellaire	11.15 (-2.7)
1988 D	Juron Johnson	Baldwin	11.11		2010 D4	Cory Noeker	Pewamo-Westphalia	11.16
1989 D	Juron Johnson	Baldwin	10.8		2011 D4	Lawson Bright-Mitchell	Albion	10.83
1990 D	Kouty Mawenh	Pentwater	11.16		2012 D4	Alex Lodes	Climax-Scotts	11.14
1991 D	Damon Butler	Detroit Lutheran West	11.66		2013 D4	Alexander Lodes	Climax-Scotts	11.32
1992 D	Carlor Perez	Athens	11.32		2014 D4	Lawson Bright-Mitchell	Concord	10.70* (0.7)
1993 D	Steve Richardson	Akron-Fairgrove	11.1		2015 D4	Aaron Watson	Union City	10.96 (0.0)
1994 D	Juson Johnson	Baldwin	11.16		2016 D4	Billy Wojnowski	Big Rapids Crossroads	11.15
1995 D	Juson Johnson	Baldwin	10.86		2017 D4	Alec Muck	Sand Creek	10.98 (1.5)
1996 D	Juson Johnson	Baldwin	11.08		2018 D4	Alec Muck	Sand Creek	10.98 (1.8)
1997 D	Juson Johnson	Baldwin	10.77*					

100 – UP Class AB/Division 1 Champions

(y=100 yards)

1940 UPB	Oliver Shampine	Munising	10.8y*		1980 UPAB	John Tolfa	Escanaba	11.4*
1941 UPB	Jim Pierce	Sault Ste. Marie	10.8y*		1981 UPAB	Craig Leitzke	Menominee	11.8
1942 UPB	Jim Pierce	Sault Ste. Marie	10.8y*		1982 UPAB	Guy Zablocki	Kingsford	11.5
1943	No Meet – World War II				1983 UPAB	Patrick Duffy	Kingsford	11.3*
1944 UPB	Bob Curley	Manistique	10.6y*		1984 UPAB	Mark Noon	Menominee	11.1*
1945 UPB	Bob Curley	Manistique	10.7y		1985 UPAB	Emmett Blake	Marquette	11.6
1946 UPB	Walter Olson	Ironwood	10.4y*		1986 UPAB	Todd LaCosse	Escanaba	11.1*
1947 UPB	Crawford	Sault Ste. Marie	10.9y		1987 UPAB	Todd LaCosse	Escanaba	10.9*
1948 UPB	Alfred Borsum	Newberry	10.8y		1988 UPAB	Corey Potvin	Escanaba	11.1
1949 UPB	Alfred Borsum	Newberry	10.9y		1989 UPAB	Desi Schultz	Gladstone	11.3
1950 UPB	Robert McDonald	Newberry	10.5y		1990 UPAB	Desi Schultz	Gladstone	11.2
1951 UPB	Ken Hofer	Stephenson	11.0y		1991 UPAB	Nate Chylek	Escanaba	11.1
1952 UPB	Joe Deldin	Kingsford	10.7y		1992 UPAB	Nate Chylek	Escanaba	10.9w
1953 UPB	Eddie Vergara	Iron River	10.7y		1993 UPAB	Geoff Grawn	Marquette	11.5
1954 UPB	Bob Visuri	Stephenson	10.8y		1994 UPAB	Steve Molnar	Menominee	11.2
1955 UPB	Eddie Vergara	Iron River	10.4y*		1995 UPAB	Steve Molnar	Menominee	11.5
1956 UPB	Tim Zhulkie	Ishpeming	10.2y*		1996 UPAB	Josh Jupe	Escanaba	11.6
1957 UPB	Bob Wills	Ishpeming	10.4y		1997 UPAB	Andy Kohrt	Menominee	11.5
1958 UPB	Bob Wills	Ishpeming	10.4y		1998 UPAB	Josh Tarbox	Menominee	12.0
1959 UPB	Richard Courier	Escanaba	11.0y		1999 UPAB	Benton Grady	Escanaba	12.3
1960 UPB	Ron Rubick	Manistique	10.7y		2000 UPAB	Ben Andrews	Escanaba	11.3
1961 UPB	Dave Perry	Munising	10.5y		2001 UPD1	Ben Andrews	Escanaba	11.3*
1962 UPAB	Bob Brown	Negaunee	10.6y		2002 UPD1	Matt Wise	Calumet	11.1*
1963 UPAB	Jim Cummings	Rudyard	10.4y		2003 UPD1	Andrew Shaver	Menominee	11.25*
1964 UPAB	Dick Berlinski	Kingsford	10.8y		2004 UPD1	Matt Kanoske	West Iron County	11.43
1965 UPAB	Dick Berlinski	Kingsford	10.7y		2005 UPD1	Justin Wiles	Escanaba	11.36
1966 UPAB	Neal DeRochey	Sault Ste. Marie	10.5y		2006 UPD1	Justin Wiles	Escanaba	11.27
1967 UPAB	Alfred Eckhart	Calumet	10.1y*		2007 UPD1	Ethan Shaver	Menominee	11.63
1968 UPAB	Bruce Jacobson	Ishpeming	10.5y		2008 UPD1	Jordan Michell	Marquette	11.41
1969 UPAB	Paul Symons	Negaunee	10.2y		2009 UPD1	Garde Kangas	Manistique	11.17*
1970 UPAB	Bob Leanes	Marquette	10.1y*		2010 UPD1	Dylan Tengesdahl	Kingsford	11.33
1971 UPAB	Clayton Antilla	Calumet	10.3y		2011 UPD1	Garrett Pentecost	Marquette	10.95*
1972 UPAB	Tony Nardi	Ishpeming	10.2y		2012 UPD1	Paul Frantti	Calumet	11.11
1973 UPAB	Wayne Schwalbach	Escanaba	10.4y		2013 UPD1	Cole Tengesdahl	Kingsford	11.26
1974 UPAB	Wayne Schwalbach	Escanaba	9.9y*		2014 UPD1	Kevin O'Keefe	Negaunee	11.38
1975 UPAB	Matt Paupore	Kingsford	10.4y		2015 UPD1	Trevor Roberts	Kingsford	11.39
1976 UPAB	Lance Wiertella	Sault Ste. Marie	10.3y		2016 UPD1	Patrick Burmeister	Marquette	11.40
1977 UPAB	Jim DeFresne	Escanaba	9.9y*		2017 UPD1	Trevor Roberts	Kingsford	11.25
1978 UPAB	Bob Nesbitt	Marquette	10.2y		2018 UPD1	Clayton Sayen	Houghton	11.47
1979 UPAB	John Tolfa	Escanaba	11.4*					

100 – UP Class C/Division 2 Champions

(y=100 yards)

1940 UPC	Mike O'Donnell	Escanaba St. Joseph	10.8y*		1955 UPC	Paul Monette	Houghton	10.9y
1941 UPC	Robert Lawson	Stephenson	10.8y*		1956 UPC	Gary Baumier	Iron River	10.7y*
1942 UPC	Robert Lawson	Stephenson	10.8y*		1957 UPC	Keith Pangborn	Munising	11.0y
1943	No Meet – World War II				1958 UPC	Dave Carpenedo	Bessemer	11.3y
1944 UPC	Francis Cappaert	Stephenson	10.9y		1959 UPC	Dick Koski	Wakefield	10.8y
1945 UPC	William Eilola	Hancock	11.0y		1960 UPC	Nick Predovik	Gwinn	10.9y
1946 UPC	Robert Broda	Munising	10.7y*		1961 UPC	Lawrence DeLucca	Sault Ste. Marie Loretto	10.4y*
1947 UPC	Ron Nettell	Houghton	11.3y		1962 UPC	Roger Relich	Bessemer	10.4y*
1948 UPC	Ron Nettell	Houghton	11.0y		1963 UPC	Al Perrault	Lake Linden	10.7y
1949 UPC	Jim Cox	Munising	11.0y		1964 UPC	Bill Fenlon	St. Ignace	10.7y
1950 UPC	Bill Mayo	L'Anse	10.7y*		1965 UPC	Ray Sibley	Wakefield	10.7y
1951 UPC	Robert Thompson	Baraga	11.3y		1966 UPC	Ray Sibley	Wakefield	10.5y
1952 UPC	Frank Stimac	Munising	11.1y		1967 UPC	Karl Funke	L'Anse	10.2y*
1953 UPC	Ed LaFleur	Lake Linden	11.5y		1968 UPC	Karl Funke	L'Anse	10.6y
1954 UPC	Fred Trevarthen	Bessemer	11.3y		1969 UPC	Jerry Mathias	Rudyard	10.5y
					1970 UPC	Tim Nault	Norway	10.3y

Year	Class	Name	School	Time
1971	UPC	Bob Teddy	L'Anse	10.4y
1972	UPC	Larry Rogers	Houghton	10.4y
1973	UPC	Gordy Peterson	Hancock	10.5y
1974	UPC	Harry Johnson	Houghton	10.1y*
1975	UPC	James Normand	Newberry	10.5y
1976	UPC	Roy Lyberg	L'Anse	10.2y
1977	UPC	Roy Lyberg	L'Anse	10.1y*
1978	UPC	Roy Lyberg	L'Anse	10.1y*
1979	UPC	Randy Poirer	Ishpeming Westwood	11.2*
1980	UPC	Chuck Secreast	Munising	11.4
1981	UPC	Mark Konopacke	Kingsford	12.0
1982	UPC	Bill Hauswirth	Houghton	11.6
1983	UPC	Troy Farley	Manistique	11.5
1984	UPC	Brian Cahill	St. Ignace	11.3
1985	UPC	John Demarest	Negaunee	11.3
1986	UPC	Dan Antilla	Calumet	11.5
1987	UPC	Chester Blom	Stephenson	11.3
1988	UPC	Jerry Cleary	Ontonagon	11.3
1989	UPC	Jerry Cleary	Ontonagon	11.2*
1990	UPC	Jerry Cleary	Ontonagon	11.2*
1991	UPC	Terry Johnson	Newberry	11.4
1992	UPC	Swan Lindeblad	Munising	11.2*
1993	UPC	David Brown	St. Ignace	11.2*
1994	UPC	Swan Lindeblad	Munising	11.4
1995	UPC	John LaValley	Norway	11.9
1996	UPC	Jim LaBlonde	Ironwood	11.3
1997	UPC	Bradley Ruleau	Stephenson	11.1*
1998	UPC	Greg Londo	Gwinn	11.4
1999	UPC	Shane Trotter	Iron River West Iron County	11.7
2000	UPC	Matt Mainville	Iron Mountain	11.3
2001	UPD2	Brett Spigarelli	Iron Mountain	11.7*
2002	UPD2	Steve Schmidt	Stephenson	10.8*
2003	UPD2	Brett Spigarelli	Iron Mountain	11.25*
2004	UPD2	Nick Laydon	Iron Mountain	11.77
2005	UPD2	Mike Houghton	Newberry	11.71
2006	UPD2	Paul Davis	St. Ignace	11.27
2007	UPD2	Derrick Frailing	West Iron County	11.64
2008	UPD2	Mike Carriere	Ishpeming	11.46
2009	UPD2	Ed Laplaunt	Newberry	11.43
2010	UPD2	Roman Alberti	Stephenson	11.47
2011	UPD2	Lance Pinter	Newberry	11.65
2012	UPD2	Parker Simmons	St. Ignace	11.45
2013	UPD2	Kennar Broulire	Manistique	11.37
2014	UPD2	Tony Floyd	Manistique	11.64
2015	UPD2	Nate Meyer	Ishpeming	11.64
2016	UPD2	Alex Dewald	Hancock	11.68
2017	UPD2	Montell Glover	Stephenson	11.41
2018	UPD2	Montell Glover	Stephenson	11.36

100 – UP Class D/Division 3 Champions

(y=100 yards)

Year	Class	Name	School	Time
1940	UPD	Obed Thraser	Alpha	10.8y*
1941	UPD	Morley Roberts	Rapid River	10.8y*
1942	UPD	Reno Fochesato	Hermansville	10.2y*
1943		No Meet – World War II		
1944	UPD	Bill MacEchern	Hermansville	11.1y
1945	UPD	Carr	Ewen	11.2y
1946	UPD	William Mosher	Marquette Pierce	11.2y
1947	UPD	Don Shannon	Powers	11.4y
1948	UPD	Bill Frigard	Eben	11.2y
1949	UPD	Vic Fochesato	Hermansville	11.1y
1950	UPD	Vic Fochesato	Hermansville	10.5y
1951	UPD	Anthony Stankiewicz	Alpha	11.4y
1952	UPD	Ronald Larson	Gwinn	11.4y
1953	UPD	Eldred Leach	Pickford	10.7y
1954	UPD	Eldred Leach	Pickford	10.8y
1955	UPD	Jaynce Leach	Pickford	10.9y
1956	UPD	Jaynce Leach	Pickford	10.5y
1957	UPD	Ken Harwood	Rapid River	11.2y
1958	UPD	Dick Olds	Marquette Pierce	11.2y
1959	UPD	Bill Kibble	Pickford	10.9y
1960	UPD	Bill Kibble	Pickford	10.6y
1961	UPD	Verne Lamoreaux	Cedarville	10.4y
1962	UPD	Gary Leach	Pickford	10.3y
1963	UPD	Gary Leach	Pickford	10.4y
1964	UPD	Jim Bishop	Cedarville	11.1y
1965	UPD	Bruce Reamer	Pickford	11.0y
1966	UPD	Dale Coullard	Pickford	11.1y
1967	UPD	Don Nye	Dollar Bay	10.4y
1968	UPD	Don Nye	Dollar Bay	10.6y
1969	UPD	Bob Leanes	Marquette Baraga	10.3y
1970	UPD	Bob Mileski	Powers	10.7y
1971	UPD	Gus Fillman	Engadine	10.8y
1972	UPD	Jeak Feak	Felch North Dickinson	10.5y
1973	UPD	Fred Kivisto	Ironwood Catholic	10.6y
1974	UPD	Joe Baker	Pickford	10.3y
1975	UPD	Mike Trevarthen	Bessemer	10.5y
1976	UPD	Mike Trevarthen	Bessemer	10.4y
1977	UPD	Mark Freebury	Cedarville	10.1y*
1978	UPD	Brent Izzard	Pickford	10.4y
1979	UPD	Mark Allison	Pickford	11.3*
1980	UPD	Mark Allison	Pickford	11.3*
1981	UPD	Patrick Hebert	Baraga	11.8
1982	UPD	Lewis Sawicky	Baraga	11.6
1983	UPD	Mike Thiry	Carney-Nedeau	11.6
1984	UPD	Mike Thiry	Carney-Nedeau	11.4
1985	UPD	Dale Hongisto	Wakefield	11.7
1986	UPD	Mike Thiry	Carney-Nedeau	10.9*
1987	UPD	Esley Gustafson	Iron Mountain N Dickinson	11.3
1988	UPD	Jeff Sappanen	Baraga	11.5
1989	UPD	Dave Bush	Pickford	11.2
1990	UPD	Randy Wood	Wakefield	11.2
1991	UPD	Mike Ojala	Ewen-Trout Creek	11.2
1992	UPD	Marty Laurila	Painesdale-Jeffers	11.3
1993	UPD	Tim Goard	Ontonagon	11.6
1994	UPD	Steve Mattson	Ontonagon	11.5
1995	UPD	Chris Gorzinski	Powers-North Central	11.8
1996	UPD	Bill Carlson	Pickford	12.0
1997	UPD	Mike Razmus	White Pine	11.6
1998	UPD	Mike Razmus	White Pine	11.8
1999	UPD	Al D.	Mohawk Keweenaw	11.9
2000	UPD	Chasey Zablocki	Lake Linden-Hubbell	11.8
2001	UPD3	Travis Bellefeuille	Bark River-Harris	11.2*
2002	UPD3	Travis Bellefeuille	Bark River-Harris	11.4
2003	UPD3	Andrew Mettler	Bessemer	11.46*
2004	UPD3	Josh LaTendresse	Chassell	11.75
2005	UPD3	Andrew Mettler	Bessemer	11.51
2006	UPD3	Craig Bilski	Powers-North Central	11.64
2007	UPD3	Grayson Hood	Engadine	11.87
2008	UPD3	Josh Siler	Crystal Falls Forest Park	11.72
2009	UPD3	Mike Schmaus	Ontonagon	11.30*
2010	UPD3	Phillip Hood	Engadine	11.23*
2011	UPD3	Tyler Arnold	Powers-North Central	11.62
2012	UPD3	Dylan Kirkley	Ontonagon	11.45
2013	UPD3	Tim Hruska	Iron Mountain N Dickinson	11.53
2014	UPD3	Tim Hruska	Iron Mountain N Dickinson	11.83
2015	UPD3	James Cryderman	St. Ignace	11.62
2016	UPD3	Greg Seppanen	Eben Junction Superior Cent	11.40
2017	UPD3	Brendan Middleton	Lake Linden-Hubbell	11.83
2018	UPD3	Brayden Tomes	Bessemer	11.92

BOYS 200 METERS

Records

D1	21.20 (-0.7)	Donnie James	Oak Park	2018
D2	21.36	Kassius Kelly	Livonia Clarenceville	2012
D3	21.76 (1.0)	Thomas Robinson	Wyoming Lee	2017
D4	21.62 (0.6)	Lawson Bright-Mitchell	Concord	2014

UPD1	22.46	Justin Wiles	Escanaba	2005
UPD2	22.70	Paul Davis	St. Ignace	2006
UPD3	22.73	Mike Schmaus	Ontonagon	2010

Records by Class (pre-2000 for LP, pre-2001 for UP)

A	21.37	Corey Pryor	Jackson	1987
(hand: 20.6y)		*Marshall Dill*	*Detroit Northern*	*1971)*
B	21.71	O'Maka Smith	Bay City Handy	1988
(hand: 20.8y)		*Dwayne Strozier*	*Flint Powers*	*1975)*
C	21.81	John Mack	New Haven	1996
D	21.75	Robert Wilhite	Detroit East Catholic	1984
UPAB	22.2	Todd LaCosse	Escanaba	1987
UPC	22.2y	Michael Dellangelo	Ishpeming	1977
UPD	22.3	Mike Thiry	Carney-Nadeau	1986

200 - Class A/Division 1 Champions

(y=220 yards)

1895 all	Clarence Christopher	Lansing	25.0y*
1896 all	Charles Widman	Detroit Central	25.6y
1897 all	W.W. Kittleman	Detroit Central	24.0y*
1898 all	Roy Ellis	Detroit Central	23.6y*
1899 all	Roy Ellis	Detroit Central	23.0y*
1900 all	Lyman Bennett	Michigan Military Academy	22.8y*
1901 all	Ralph Keeler	Detroit Central	24.0y
1902 all (tie)	Edward Trankla	Michigan Military Academy	23.6y
1902 all (tie)	Ralph Keeler	Detroit University School	23.6y
1903 all	Ralph Keeler (2)	Detroit University School	23.0y
1904 all	Herbert Schenk (3)	Chelsea	nt
1905 all	George Widman	Detroit Central	23.8y
1906 all	George Widman	Detroit Central	22.4y*
1907 all	George Widman (4)	Detroit Central	nt
1908 all	Art Widman	Detroit Central	23.3y
1909 all	Art Widman	Detroit Central	23.4y
1910 all	Thomas Tuomy	Detroit University School	23.2y
1911 all	Paul Kress	Alma	24.6y
1912 all	William Howard	Croswell	24.0y
1913 all	Alfred Gamble	Coldwater	23.8y

(220y straightaway)

1914 all	Clarence Kretzschmar	Detroit Eastern	23.8y
1915 all	Herbert Henry	Detroit Eastern	23.8y
1916 all	Leonard Merchant	St Joseph	22.6y
1917 all	William Brown	Detroit Central	23.8y
1918	No Meet – World War I		
1919 all	George Walker	Gobleville	23.2y
1920 all	Carl Blauman	Detroit Northwestern	23.4y
1921 A	George Hester	Detroit Northern	22.6y
1922 A	George Hester	Detroit Northern	22.1y*
1923 A	George Hester	Detroit Northern	21.7y*
1924 A	Lyle Henson	Lansing Central	22.1y
1925 A	Eddie Tolan	Detroit Cass Tech	22.4y
1926 A	Eddie Tolan	Detroit Cass Tech	22.2y
1927 A	Eddie Tolan	Detroit Cass Tech	21.9y
1928 A	Lester Nelson	Grand Rapids South	22.8y
1929 A	Leroy Oliver	Detroit Cass Tech	22.7y
1930 A	William Bryant	Detroit Cass Tech	23.5y
1931 A	Bernard Roberts	Monroe	23.7y
1932 A	David Baird	Saginaw Eastern	22.5y
1933 A	Louis Voorheis	Grand Rapids Catholic	22.2y
1934 A	Bill Strehl	Grand Rapids Ottawa Hills	23.2y
1935 A	Wilbur Greer	Flint Central	22.5y
1936 A	Pete Dykhouse	Grand Rapids Davis Tech	22.7cy
1937 A	James McGhee	Pontiac	22.1y
1938 A	George Doran	Grand Rapids South	21.9y
1939 A	Warren McCarger	Owosso	21.9y
1940 A	Bert Copeland	Benton Harbor	21.9y
1941 A	Earl Copeland	Benton Harbor	22.8y
1942 A	Bob Rogers	Kalamazoo Central	23.2y
1943	No Meet – World War II		
1944 A	Bud Elve	Grand Rapids Davis Tech	22.6y
1945 A	Owen Jackson	Flint Central	22.3y
1946 A	Bill Hervey	Saginaw	24.0y
1947 A	Art Ingram	Flint Central	22.2y
1948 A	Terry Nulf	Kalamazoo Central	23.0y
1949 A	William Baxter	Dearborn Fordson	22.6y
1950 A	William Baxter	Dearborn Fordson	22.6y
1951 A	Bob Brown	Grand Rapids Ottawa Hills	21.8y
1952 A	Alonzo Harris	Pontiac	22.6y
1953 A	Alonzo Harris	Pontiac	21.7y*
1954 A	Art Johnson	Flint Northern	21.8y
1955 A	Pete Dant	Alpena	21.4yw (2.3)

1956 A	Pete Dant	Alpena	21.6yw
1957 A	Phil Beck	Jackson	22.7y
1958 A	Bob Manning	Pontiac	21.8y
1959 A	Ron Watkins	Flint Central	21.8y
1960 A	Maurice Pea	Flint Northern	21.3yw (2.7)
1961 A	Dorie Reed	Ferndale	22.1y
1962 A	Dalton Kimble	Flint Northern	22.1y
1963 A	William Raynor	Niles	21.4y*
1964 A	Arnie Williams	Battle Creek Central	21.3yw (3.6)
1965 A	Thelbert Jeffries	Detroit Northwestern	21.6y
1966 A	Charles Robinson	Detroit Mackenzie	21.5y
1967 A	Herb Washington	Flint Central	22.4y
1968 A	Herb Washington	Flint Central	22.0y
1969 A	Marshall Dill	Detroit Northern	22.1y
1970 A	Marshall Dill	Detroit Northern	21.9y
1971 A	Marshall Dill	Detroit Northern	20.6y*
1972 A	Reggie Jones	Saginaw	21.6y
1973 A	Reggie Jones	Saginaw	21.1y
1974 A	Harlan Huckleby	Detroit Cass Tech	21.9y
1975 A	Harlan Huckleby	Detroit Cass Tech	21.9y
1976 A	Mike Miller	Flint Northern	21.6y
1977 A	Mike Miller	Flint Northern	22.5y
1978 A	Deon Hogan	Detroit Kettering	21.8y
1979 A	Robert Constant	Grand Haven	22.4y
1980 A	DeMetrius Hallums	Detroit Central	21.4y
1981 A	Don Anderson	Detroit Cody	21.3y
1982 A	Terry McDaniel	Saginaw	21.3
1983 A	Anthony Mahone	Detroit Denby	21.4
1984 A	Anthony Mahone	Detroit Denby	21.0
1985 A	Chuck Phillips	Lansing Everett	22.04*
1986 A	Ivan Cottman	Redford Borgess	21.84*
1987 A	Corey Pryor	Jackson	21.37*
1988 A	Jeff Reynolds	Southfield	21.63
1989 A	Steve Sandles	East Detroit	22.08
1990 A	Ali Shakoor	Jackson	21.80
1991 A (tie)	Kerchival Patterson	Ypsilanti	21.98
1991 A (tie)	Brad Field	East Kentwood	21.98
1992 A	Randy Kinder	East Lansing	21.87
1993 A	Steve Ruffin	Flint Southwestern	21.80
1994 A	Micah Morris	Bay City Central	21.50
1995 A	Jamal Allen	Southfield Lathrup	22.60
1996 A	David Kea	Detroit Cass Tech	22.57
1997 A	Godfrey Herring	Pontiac Northern	21.24w
1998 A	Charles Rogers	Saginaw	21.67w (2.5)
1999 A	Kelly Baraka	Portage Northern	21.66w (3.6)
2000 D1	Charles Rogers	Saginaw	21.3*
2001 D1	Carl Tabb	Ann Arbor Huron	21.79*
2002 D1	Pierre Vinson	Detroit Cass Tech	21.90
2003 D1	Jeremy Orr	Detroit Henry Ford	21.3 (-3.5)
2004 D1	Jeremy Orr	Detroit Henry Ford	21.82
2006 D1	Dimitri Banks	Detroit Murray-Wright	21.40* (1.5)
2006 D1	Ahmad Rashad	Flint Carman-Ainsworth	21.51
2007 D1	James Smith	Ann Arbor Pioneer	21.80 (-2.6)
2008 D1	DeShawn Williams	Detroit Cody	21.90 (1.8)
2009 D1	Aaron Taylor	Rochester Adams	21.91 (-3.9)
2010 D1	John Henry	East Kentwood	21.76 (-2.8)
2011 D1	D'Ontae Hopson	Jackson	21.56 (1.5)
2012 D1	Austin Sanders	Ypsilanti	21.94 (1.5)
2013 D1	Brandon Wilks	Southfield Lathrup	21.93(-1.1)
2014 D1	Maurice Allen	Oak Park	21.36* (-0.2)
2015 D1	Jaron Flournoy	Westland John Glenn	21.25w (5.3)
2016 D1	Khance Meyers	East Kentwood	21.24* (1.4)
2017 D1	Khance Meyers	East Kentwood	21.27 (-1.6)
2018 D1	Donnie James	Oak Park	21.20* (-0.7)

200 - Class B/Division 2 Champions

(y=220 yards)

Year		Name	School	Time
1921	B	Earl Kelly	Cadillac	23.4y*
1922	B	Harley Sternaman	Owosso	23.2y*
1923	B	John Burridge	St Johns	22.8y*
1924	B	Nick Nixon	Wyandotte Roosevelt	22.8y*
1925	B	Clare Warner	St Johns	23.4y
1926	B	Raymond Bunge	St Johns	22.9y
1927	B	Moulton Davis	St Joseph	22.4y*
1928	B	Moulton Davis	St Joseph	22.5y
1929	B	Milton Porteous	Birmingham	23
1930	B	Fred Schatte	Monroe	22.7y
1931	B	Russell Chrisman	Kingsford	24.2y
1932	B	Moses Easley	Dowagiac	22.8y
1933	B	William Guckelberg	Birmingham	22.7y
1934	B	Arthur Frontczak	Dowagiac	23.0y
1935	B	Vinton Davis	St Joseph	22.8y
1936	B	Raymond Zoller	Niles	22.9y
1937	B	Ron Mead	East Lansing	22.5y
1938	B	Ron Mead	East Lansing	21.9y
1939	B	Ron Mead	East Lansing	21.9y
1940	B	Walter Derby	Fremont	22.7y
1941	B	Bo Miller	East Lansing	22.9y
1942	B	Jack Steelman	Birmingham	23.4y
1943		No Meet – World War II		
1944	B	Bob Swain	East Grand Rapids	22.3y*
1945	B	Bob Swain	East Grand Rapids	21.8y*
1946	B	Ulysses Rogers	Ecorse	23.6y
1947	B	Robert Branch	Hastings	22.5y
1948	B	Charles Roland	South Haven	23.7y
1949	B	Bob Folin	Birmingham	23.5y
1950	B	Joe Ross	Birmingham	23.7y
1951	B	Bert Zagers	Cadillac	22.8y
1952	B	Bob Zimmerman	Roseville	23.9y
1953	B	Sam Orlikowski	Warren	22.4y
1954	B	Herman Frederick	Inkster	22.1y
1955	B	Dave Myers	Mt Pleasant	22.5y
1956	B	Charles Keyser	Inkster	23.0y
1957	B	Charles Keyser	Inkster	23.2y
1958	B	Willie Prewitt	Willow Run	21.6yw (3.6)
1959	B	Otis Harrison	Willow Run	22.6y
1960	B	Barney Crouse	Cranbrook	23.2y
1961	B	Barney Crouse	Cranbrook	21.2y*
1962	B	Mose Easely	Dowagiac	22.6y
1963	B	Tom Reid	Stevensville-Lakeshore	22.7y
1964	B	Boice Bowman	River Rouge	21.9y
1965	B	Jim Wood	Mount Morris	23.0y
1966	B	John Schneider	Marshall	22.3y
1967	B	John Schneider	Marshall	22.1y
1968	B	Les Warren	Coloma	22.1y
1969	B	Bill White	Dowagiac	22.6y
1970	B	Tom Budzyn	Riverview Gabriel Richard	22.4y
1971	B	Roy Young	Mount Morris	21.9y
1972	B	Roy Young	Mount Morris	22.0y
1973	B	Andre Jacobs	Dearborn Heights Robichaud	22.2y
1974	B	Dwayne Strozier	Flint Powers	21.2yw (2.7)
1975	B	Dwayne Strozier	Flint Powers	20.8y*
1976	B	Randy Rife	Linden	21.6y
1977	B	Vern Chontos	Lake Fenton	22.2y
1978	B	Vern Chontos	Lake Fenton	22.4y
1979	B	Mark Woodson	Dearborn Heights Robichaud	22.1y
1980	B	Andreus Laut	Dexter	21.5
1981	B	Ricky Swilley	Saginaw Buena Vista	22.4
1982	B	Ricky Swilley	Saginaw Buena Vista	22.0y
1983	B	Henry Woodmore	Auburn Hills Avondale	22.5
1984	B	Mark Lewis	Ypsilanti Lincoln	21.9
1985	B	Darryl Warner	Willow Run	22.16*
1986	B	Charles Wilson	Detroit Benedictine	22.3
1987	B	Derrick Alexander	Detroit Benedictine	22.18
1988	B	O'Maka Smith	Bay City Handy	21.71*
1989	B	Derrick Alexander	Detroit Benedictine	22.0
1990	B	Tyrone Wheatley	Dearborn Heights Robichaud	21.90
1991	B	Andy Schoelch	Bloomfield Hills Andover	22.15
1992	B	Andy Schoelch	Bloomfield Hills Andover	21.78
1993	B	Chris Polk	Detroit UD Jesuit	22.03
1994	B	Ted Adams	Ypsilanti Lincoln	22.28
1995	B	Randy Hunt	Comstock	22.53
1996	B	Chad Kring	Edwardsburg	22.90
1997	B	Edward Johnson	River Rouge	21.8
1998	B	Edward Johnson	River Rouge	21.82
1999	B	David Moss	Dearborn Heights Robichaud	22.15
2000	D2	Elton Anderson	Detroit Renaissance	22.44*
2001	D2	Nelson DeFord	Haslett	22.29*
2002	D2	Agim Shabaj	Farmington Hills Harrison	21.95*
2003	D2	Zach Labrecque	Battle Creek Harper Creek	21.94*
2004	D2	Dmitri Banks	Detroit Chadsey	22.15
2005	D2	Clint Allen	Muskegon Orchard View	21.7
2006	D2	Markgone Russell	Adrian	21.88*
2007	D2	James Rogers	Madison Heights Lamphere	22.05
2008	D2	Tony Fountain	Whitehall	22.12
2009	D2	Ryan Brooks	Williamston	22.14
2010	D2	Ross Parsons	DeWitt	21.82*
2011	D2	Gary Jones	Allegan	22.09
2012	D2	Kassius Kelly	Livonia Clarenceville	21.36*
2013	D2	Berkley Edwards	Chelsea	21.37w (3.2)
2014	D2	Joshuwa Holloman	Auburn Hills Avondale	22.21
2015	D2	Jonathan Fife	Flint Southwestern	21.55
2016	D2	Johnathon Shell	Sturgis	22.01 (-1.1)
2017	D2	Josh Nelson	River Rouge	22.30w (2.4)
2018	D2	Thomas Robinson	Wyoming Lee	21.62 (1.5)

200 - Class C/Division 3 Champions

(y=220 yards)

Year		Name	School	Time
1921	C	Bohn Grim	Sturgis	23.4y*
1922	C	Albert Fey	Dearborn	22.6y*
1923	C	Vernon Rupp	Morenci	22.9y
1924	C	Chuck Parker	Clinton	23.1y
1925	C	Harold Gilbert	Croswell	23.2y
1926	C	Milton Jacobi	Marine City	23.1y
1927	C	Joe Salerno	Yale	23.0y
1928	C	Joe Salerno	Yale	23.6y
1929	C	William Fenner	Rochester	23.3y
1930	C	Jerry Griffith	Rochester	24.0y
1931	C	Frederick Dougan	Berrien Springs	24.3y
1932	C	Ham White	Boyne City	23.5y
1933	C	Ham White	Boyne City	22.6y*
1934	C	Alan Smith	Paw Paw	22.7y
1935	C	Alan Smith	Paw Paw	22.7y
1936	C	BurDetroitte Warson	Homer	23.2y
1937	C	Caesar Harper	Vassar	23.2y
1938	C	Jack McNitt	Mesick	23.0y
1939	C	Tom Cherry	St Clair Shores South Lake	22.6y*
1940	C	Frank Lee	East Grand Rapids	22.4y*
1941	C	Bill Squires	Milan	23.1y
1942	C	Richard Holland	Comstock Park	23.9y
1943		No Meet – World War II		
1944	C	Joe Banks	St Clair Shores Lake Shore	22.7y
1945	C	Joe Banks	St Clair Shores Lake Shore	22.7y
1946	C	Keith Gundrum	Ypsilanti Roosevelt	24.0y
1947	C	Gerald Vredevelt	Grandville	23.0y
1948	C	Dave Boland	East Grand Rapids	23.0y
1949	C	Hubert Mead	Dundee	23.4y
1950	C	Ken Finger	St Clair Shores Lake Shore	23.0y
1951	C	Jerry Wolf	Ann Arbor University High	23.3y
1952	C	Jerry Wolf	Ann Arbor University High	23.3y
1953	C	Dick Bigelow	Stanton	22.3y*
1954	C	Henry McNary	Cassopolis	22.4y
1955	C	Henry McNary	Cassopolis	22.5y
1956	C	Jim Shirey	Pittsford	22.2yw
1957	C	Don Voorheis	Frankenmuth	23.7y
1958	C	Don Voorheis	Frankenmuth	21.0yw (4.5)
1959	C	Don Voorheis	Frankenmuth	21.6y*
1960	C	Bill Lynch	Nashville	21.6y*
1961	C	Ted Sternad	Fennville	22.7y
1962	C	Dave Loomis	East Jackson	22.3y
1963	C	Cy Vallier	Merrill	22.3y
1964	C	Steven Strauch	Detroit St Theresa	21.6y*
1965	C	Dave Austin	Battle Creek St Phillip	23.1y
1966	C	Dave Carroll	Laingsburg	22.1y
1967	C	Dave Carroll	Laingsburg	23.2y
1968	C	Jim Holmes	Lansing Boys Vocational	22.2y
1969	C	Ralph Burger	Reading	nt
1970	C	Claude Bagsby	Detroit DePorres	22.3y
1971	C	Jack McClellan	Detroit Country Day	22.2y
1972	C	Jan Abrams	Detroit DePorres	21.9y
1973	C	Dave Ratajack	Detroit Country Day	22.3y
1974	C	Jan Abrams	Detroit DePorres	22.4y
1975	C	Mark Lehman	Whittemore-Prescott	22.2y
1976	C	Jeff Hunter	Detroit Benedictine	22.3y
1977	C	Jim Smith	Royal Oak Shrine	23.3y
1978	C	Raynor Washington	Detroit Benedictine	22.7y
1979	C	Creston Gray	Detroit Benedictine	22.6y

1980 C	Jamie Weathers	Ecorse	23.0y
1981 C	Geoffrey Craig	Detroit Country Day	22.4
1982 C	Anthony Mahone	Detroit DePorres	21.8
1983 C	Eric Frederick	Detroit Lutheran West	21.8
1984 C	Keith Harris	Detroit DePorres	22.3
1985 C	Wiley Boulding	Kalamazoo Hackett	22.61*
1986 C	Scott Simon	St. Charles	22.4
1987 C	Daryl Stallworth	Ecorse	22.25*
1988 C	Tony Jackson	Saginaw Nouvel	21.9
1989 C	Tony Jackson	Saginaw Nouvel	22.31
1990 C	Sherman Ross	Cassopolis	22.5
1991 C	Sherman Ross	Cassopolis	22.5
1992 C	Allen Heywood	Detroit DePorres	22.6
1993 C	Jason Ross	Napoleon	22.71
1994 C	John Mack	New Haven	22.5
1995 C	John Mack	New Haven	21.97*
1996 C	John Mack	New Haven	21.81*
1997 C	Jason Carver	Parchment	22.06
1998 C	Travis Kelly	New Haven	22.23
1999 C	Kyle Colbe	Clare	22.15

2000 D3	Vic Ornelas	Beaverton	22.05*
2001 D3	Andrew Montague	Olivet	22.51
2002 D3	Kyle Dengler	Essexville Garber	21.86*
2003 D3	Andy Montague	Olivet	21.77*
2004 D3	Phil Damaska	Detroit Country Day	22.1
2005 D3	Mike Golden	Frankenmuth	22.09
2006 D3	Kenji Shaltry	Saginaw Nouvel	22.37
2007 D3	Kenji Shaltry	Saginaw Nouvel	21.99
2008 D3	James Person	Montrose	22.37
2009 D3	Todd Atchison	Albion	21.86 (0.4)
2010 D3	Brent Vanenk	Grandville Calvin Christian	22.14
2011 D3	Chris Maye	Union City	21.95
2012 D3	Chris Maye	Union City	21.85
2013 D3	Tyler Hendricks	Saginaw Nouvel	22.82
2014 D3	Brock Thumm	Watervliet	22.27 (0.0)
2015 D3	Tyler Underwood	Clinton	22.36w (4.2)
2016 D3	Thomas Robinson	Wyoming Lee	22.2
2017 D3	Thomas Robinson	Wyoming Lee (21.76* heat)	22.04 (0.0)
2018 D3	Giovanni Weeks	Kent City	22.36 (-0.3)

200 - Class D/Division 4 Champions
(y=220 yards)

1927 D	Irwin Kemp	Trenton	26.2y*
1928 D	Michael Orlovich	Dearborn Fordson	24.4y*
1929 D	Fred Miles	Okemos	23.6y*
1930 D	Fred Miles	Okemos	23.5y*
1931 D	Gregory Mosher	Centreville	24.9y
1932 D	Tom Reynolds	South Lake	24.4y
1933 D	Bernard Meyer	Portage	23.2y*
1934 D	Clifton Frazier	Centreville	24.3y
1935 D	William Weise	Bear Lake	24.3y
1936 D	Earl Walters	Centreville	23.4y
1937 D	Tom Cherry	St Clair Shores South Lake	23.9y
1938 D	Dick LaBrasseur	Nahma	23.3y
1939 D	Harold Hansen	Fruitport	23.7y
1940 D	Edward Kersey	Blanchard	23.3y
1941 D	Wayne Van Patten	Litchfield	23.8y
1942 D	Bob Schepers	McBain	24.1y
1943	No Meet – World War II		
1944 D	Henry Rolike	Boys Vocational	23.6y
1945 D	Arlon Dennison	Michigan School for Deaf	23.0y*
1946 D	Arlon Dennison	Michigan School for Deaf	24.1y
1947 D	Don Gast	Baroda	24.1y
1948 D	Bob Hocker	Benton Harbor St John	23.5y
1949 D	Ancel Rodgers	Benton Harbor St John	23.9y
1950 D	Ancel Rodgers	Benton Harbor St John	23.8y
1951 D	Ancel Rodgers	Benton Harbor St John	23.2y
1952 D	Jerry Mitchell	Eau Claire	25.1y
1953 D	Jerry Mitchell	Eau Claire	22.9y*
1954 D	Robert Phillips	Brethren	23.1y
1955 D	Walt Thomas	Brethren	24.2y
1956 D	Ken Beane	Brethren	23.6y
1957 D	Quincy Johnson	Covert	23.3y
1958 D	Ken Beane	Brethren	21.5yw
1959 D	Al Kaiser	Grass Lake	23.6y
1960 D	Dick Warren	Morrice	22.2y*
1961 D	Chet Beasley	Ypsilanti St John	23.1y
1962 D	Chet Beasley	Ypsilanti St John	22.4y
1963 D	Darwin Hoag	Morrice	22.5y
1964 D	Joe Lessard	Bellaire	22.3y
1965 D	Richard Carling	Ecorse St Francis	23.3y
1966 D	Dave Shipman	Ann Arbor University High	22.3y
1967 D	Dave Shipman	Ann Arbor University High	22.5y
1968 D	Roger Connolly	Brethren	22.7y
1969 D	Gary Siecrist	Grass Lake	22.7y
1970 D	Ed Robinson	Michigan School for the Deaf	23.0y
1971 D	Ed Robinson	Michigan School for the Deaf	22.5y
1972 D	Dan Carter	Grosse Pointe Univ. Liggett	22.6y

1973 D	Mark Lehman	Whittemore-Prescott	22.4y
1974 D	Dwight Jones	Grosse Pointe Univ. Liggett	22.0y*
1975 D	Dwight Jones	Grosse Pointe Univ. Liggett	22.0y*
1976 D	Brian Houghton	Detroit DePorres	22.3y
1977 D	Stanley Young	Detroit DePorres	21.6y*
1978 D	Evans Lalas	Frankfort	23.0y
1979 D	Mike Taylor	Detroit DePorres	22.4
1980 D	Larry Jordan	Detroit DePorres	21.8
1981 D	Brian Burger	Reading	22.9
1982 D	Brian Burger	Reading	22.7
1983 D	Robert Willhight	Detroit East Catholic	22.5
1984 D	Robert Willhight	Detroit East Catholic	21.75*
1985 D	Sean Jones	Detroit East Catholic	22.91
1986 D	Jeffrey Morris	Detroit Servite	22.72
1987 D	Jeff Simons	Detroit East Catholic	22.34
1988 D	Juron Johnson	Baldwin	22.42
1989 D	Juron Johnson	Baldwin	22.8
1990 D	Brad Brown	Pittsford	23.26
1991 D	Don Johnson	Manton	23.18
1992 D	Steve Richardson	Akron-Fairgrove	23.23
1993 D	Steve Richardson	Akron-Fairgrove	22.9
1994 D	Oliver Galvez	Ann Arbor Richard	23.09
1995 D	Juson Johnson	Baldwin	22.65
1996 D	Juson Johnson	Baldwin	22.72
1997 D	Juson Johnson	Baldwin	21.90
1998 D	Eric Culver	Mancelona	22.4
1999 D	Otis Jordan	Harper Woods Gallagher	22.15
2000 D4	Kelvin Singleton	Centreville	22.71*
2001 D4	Braylon Edwards	Harper Woods Gallagher	22.61*
2002 D4	Adam Crawford	Harper Woods Lutheran East	22.73
2003 D4	Daniel McKinney	Detroit Benedictine	22.41*
2004 D4	Anthony Bowman	Detroit DePorres	22.56
2005 D4	Anthony Bowman	Detroit DePorres	22.18*
2006 D4	Jared Spaulding	Marion	22.3h
2007 D4	Jared Spaulding	Marion	22.52
2008 D4	David Patrick	Genesee	22.64
2009 D4	Jesse Schwartz	Centreville	23.24
2010 D4	Cory Noeker	Pewamo-Westphalia	22.60
2011 D4	Lawson Bright-Mitchell	Albion	22.19
2012 D4	Alex Lodes	Climax-Scotts	22.79
2013 D4	Lawson Bright-Mitchell	Albion	22.44
2014 D4	Lawson Bright-Mitchell	Concord	21.62* (0.6)
2015 D4	Aaron Watson	Union City	22.33 (-4.3)
2016 D4	Alec Muck	Sand Creek	22.50
2017 D4	Alec Muck	Sand Creek	22.14
2018 D4	Alec Muck	Sand Creek	22.02w (2.9)

200 – UP Class AB/Division 1 Champions
(y=220 yards)

1940 UPB	Oliver Shampine	Munising	24.4y*
1941 UPB	Robert Curtis	Hancock	24.0y*
1942 UPB	Jim Pierce	Sault Ste. Marie	23.9y*
1943	No Meet – World War II		
1944 UPB	Bob Curley	Manistique	23.3y*
1945 UPB	Bob Curley	Manistique	23.5y
1946 UPB	Walter Olson	Ironwood	23.4y
1947 UPB	Mike Doyle	Menominee	23.7y
1948 UPB	Alfred Borsom	Newberry	23.5y
1949 UPB	Alfred Borsom	Newberry	23.7y

1950 UPB	Robert McDonald	Newberry	23.0y*
1951 UPB	Jerome Tooler	Sault Ste. Marie	23.5y
1952 UPB	Joe Deldin	Kingsford	23.5y
1953 UPB	Howard Larson	Marquette	23.4y
1954 UPB	Kenneth Kuzmierz	Sault Ste. Marie	23.8y
1955 UPB	Kaye Vandenboom	Marquette	23.6y
1956 UPB	Timothy Zhulkie	Ishpeming	22.6y*
1957 UPB	Mike Farley	Manistique	23.4y
1958 UPB	Bob WIlls	Ishpeming	23.1y
1959 UPB	Richard Courier	Escanaba	24.6y
1960 UPB	Ron McDonough	Manistique	23.5y

1961 UPB	Bob Luxmore	Iron Mountain	22.7y
1962 UPAB	Dick Berlinski	Kingsford	23.8y
1963 UPAB	Jim Cummings	Rudyard	22.9y
1964 UPAB	Chris Kitti	Calumet	23.5y
1965 UPAB	Dick Berlinski	Kingsford	23.0y
1966 UPAB	Neal DeRochey	Sault Ste. Marie	23.4y
1967 UPAB	Alfred Eckhart	Calumet	22.7y
1968 UPAB	Bruce Jacobson	Ishpeming	23.2y
1969 UPAB	Rick Lorenson	Gladstone	23.1y
1970 UPAB	Bob Leanes	Marquette	22.8y
1971 UPAB	Clayton Antilla	Calumet	23.1y
1972 UPAB	Wayne Schwalbach	Escanaba	23.6y
1973 UPAB	Gordy Peterson	Hancock	23.3y
1974 UPAB	Jeff Currier	Ironwood	23.3y
1975 UPAB	Lance Wiertella	Sault Ste. Marie	23.2y
1976 UPAB	Mark Creten	Escanaba	23.1y
1977 UPAB	Jim Defresne	Escanaba	22.5y*
1978 UPAB	Jim Defresne	Escanaba	23.0y
1979 UPAB	John Tolfa	Escanaba	23.5
1980 UPAB	John Tolfa	Escanaba	23.3
1981 UPAB	Chris Hofer	Menominee	23.3
1982 UPAB	Jerry Rudden	Escanaba	23.3
1983 UPAB	Guy Zablocki	Kingsford	23.4
1984 UPAB	Mark Noon	Menominee	22.9
1985 UPAB	Emmett Blake	Marquette	23.9
1986 UPAB	Todd LaCosse	Escanaba	22.7
1987 UPAB	Todd LaCosse	Escanaba	22.2*
1988 UPAB	Corey Potvin	Escanaba	22.7
1989 UPAB	Matt North	Gwinn	23.3

1990 UPAB	Desi Schultz	Gladstone	22.9
1991 UPAB	Nate Chylek	Escanaba	23.0
1992 UPAB	Nate Chylek	Escanaba	23.4
1993 UPAB	Todd Taylor	Escanaba	23.3
1994 UPAB	Steve Molnar	Menominee	22.5
1995 UPAB	Steve Molnar	Menominee	22.8
1996 UPAB	Craig Jensen	Kingsford	23.7
1997 UPAB	Adam Pennell	Marquette	23.7
1998 UPAB	Josh Tarbox	Menominee	24.0
1999 UPAB	Josh Tarbox	Menominee	23.0
2000 UPAB	Ben Andrews	Escanaba	23.1
2001 UPD1	Matt Wise	Calumet	22.5*
2002 UPD1	Matt Wise	Calumet	22.6
2003 UPD1	Pete Tuccini	Marquette	22.93*
2004 UPD1	Justin Wiles	Escanaba	23.02
2005 UPD1	Justin Wiles	Escanaba	22.46*
2006 UPD1	Justin Wiles	Escanaba	22.72
2007 UPD1	Josh Droese	Kingsford	23.13
2008 UPD1	Josh Droese	Kingsford	23.26
2009 UPD1	Garde Kangas	Manistique	22.79
2010 UPD1	Dylan Tengesdahl	Kingsford	22.75
2011 UPD1	Garrett Pentecost	Marquette	23.13
2012 UPD1	Paul Frantti	Calumet	22.77
2013 UPD1	Shaun Sullivan	Menominee	23.17
2014 UPD1	Kevin O'Keefe	Negaunee	22.60
2015 UPD1	Connor Hetrick	Negaunee	23.24
2016 UPD1	Ryan Jones	Sault Ste. Marie	23.12
2017 UPD1	Clayton Sayen	Houghton	22.63
2018 UPD1	Clayton Sayen	Houghton	23.19

200 – UP Class C/Division 2 Champions

(y=220 yards)

1940 UPC	Robert Mottord	Stephenson	24.2y*
1941 UPC	Robert Lawson	Stephenson	24.8y
1942 UPC	Robert Lawson	Stephenson	24.5y
1943	No Meet – World War II		
1944 UPC	William Eilola	Hancock	24.1y*
1945 UPC	William Eilola	Hancock	23.8y*
1946 UPC	Edward Sowa	Munising	24.2y
1947 UPC	Ron Nettell	Houghton	24.6y
1947 UPC	Edward Sowa	Munising	24.2y
1949 UPC	James Cox	Munising	23.6y*
1950 UPC	Howard Leslie	Ontonagon	23.8y
1951 UPC	Roy Baril	Lake Linden	24.4y
1952 UPC	Frank Stimac	Munising	24.5y
1953 UPC	Norm Weisinger	Ontonagon	25.3y
1954 UPC	Paul Monette	Houghton	25.6y
1955 UPC	Ray Sironen	Ewen	24.5y
1956 UPC	Bruce Davis	St. Ignace	23.9y
1957 UPC	Bruce Davis	St. Ignace	24.2y
1958 UPC	Dave Carpenedo	Bessemer	25.2y
1959 UPC	Ken Schei	Lake Linden	25.5y
1960 UPC	Greg Miheve	Wakefield	23.8y
1961 UPC	Lawrence DeLucca	Sault Ste. Marie Loretto	23.3y*
1962 UPC	Roger Relich	Bessemer	23.4y
1963 UPC	Jim Hodge	Wakefield	23.4y
1964 UPC	Bill Fenlon	St. Ignace	23.6y
1965 UPC	Ray Sibley	Wakefield	23.1y*
1966 UPC	Ray Sibley	Wakefield	23.9y
1967 UPC	Karl Funke	L'Anse	22.8y*
1968 UPC	Karl Funke	L'Anse	22.8y*
1969 UPC	Richard Salani	Hancock	23.5y
1970 UPC	Tim Nault	Norway	22.4y*
1971 UPC	Bob Teddy	L'Anse	23.6y
1972 UPC	John Otto	Houghton	23.6y
1973 UPC	Wayne Schwalbach	Escanaba	23.0y
1974 UPC	Fred Bennett	Munising	23.9y
1975 UPC	Bruce Witting	Hancock	23.5y
1976 UPC	Michael Dellangelo	Ishpeming	22.9y
1977 UPC	Michael Dellangelo	Ishpeming	22.2y*
1978 UPC	Roy Lybert	L'Anse	22.8y

1979 UPC	Randy Proirer	Ishpeming Westwood	23.2
1980 UPC	Chuck Secreast	Munising	23.3
1981 UPC	Tom Flamino	Iron Mountain	23.3
1982 UPC	Bill Hauswirth	Houghton	23.5
1983 UPC	Troy Farley	Manistique	23.1
1984 UPC	Rudy Nyman	Ishpeming Westwood	23.1
1985 UPC	Joe Fochesato	Norway	23.5
1986 UPC	Jerry Destrampe	Houghton	23.0
1987 UPC	Shawn Zimmer	L'Anse	23.8
1988 UPC	Jerry Cleary	Ontonagon	22.9
1989 UPC	Cory Hoffman	Norway	23.2
1990 UPC	Jerry Cleary	Ontonagon	23.0
1991 UPC	Jason Maki	Ironwood	23.1
1992 UPC	Lewis Page	Iron Mountain	23.8
1993 UPC	Rich Blowers	Manistique	23.2
1994 UPC	Chris Suggitt	Rudyard	22.8
1995 UPC	Jim LaBlonde	Ironwood	23.4
1996 UPC	Jim LaBlonde	Ironwood	22.9
1997 UPC	Jim LaBlonde	Ironwood	22.9
1998 UPC	Greg Londo	Gwinn	22.5
1999 UPC	Shane Trotter	Iron River West Iron County	22.8
2000 UPC	Gavin Cornwell	Rudyard	23.2
2001 UPD2	Eric Rocker	Newberry	23.5*
2002 UPD2	Jeremy Nelson	Ishpeming	23.1*
2003 UPD2	Jeremy Nelson	Ishpeming	22.9*
2004 UPD2	Chris Mattas	Norway	23.93*
2005 UPD2	Jeremy Putman	Munising	23.35*
2006 UPD2	Paul Davis	St. Ignace	22.70*
2007 UPD2	Alex Winkler	Stephenson	23.74
2008 UPD2	Nick Pennell	Ishpeming Westwood	23.40
2009 UPD2	Evan Everson	St. Ignace	23.56
2010 UPD2	Evan Everson	St. Ignace	22.94
2011 UPD2	Jared Clark	Rudyard	23.70
2012 UPD2	Parker Simmons	St. Ignace	23.66
2013 UPD2	Ryan Ramey	Menominee	23.82
2014 UPD2	Ryan LaBerge	L'Anse	23.33
2015 UPD2	Nate Meyer	Ishpeming	23.36
2016 UPD2	Alex Dewald	Hancock	23.52
2017 UPD2	Montell Glover	Stephenson	23.65
2018 UPD2	Montell Glover	Stephenson	22.98

200 – UP Class D/Division 3 Champions

(y=220 yards)

1940 UPD	Obed Thraser	Alpha	24.2y*
1941 UPD	Morley Roberts	Rapid River	24.6y
1942 UPD	Reno Fochesto	Hermansville	24.0y*
1943	No Meet – World War II		
1944 UPD	Alver Polossari	Chassell	24.7y
1945 UPD	Richard Loeffler	Powers	25.0y
1946 UPD	Richard Loeffler	Powers	25.0y
1947 UPD	Bill Frigrad	Eben	25.0y
1947 UPD	Kenneth LeBoeuff	Powers	25.8y

1949 UPD	Vic Fochesato	Hermansville	24.5y
1950 UPD	Vic Fochesato	Hermansville	23.9y*
1951 UPD	Anthony Stankewicz	Alpha	25.1y
1952 UPD	Jim Quinnell	Pickford	25.0y
1953 UPD	Eldred Leach	Pickford	24.3y
1954 UPD	Eldred Leach	Pickford	24.6y
1955 UPD	Jaynce Leach	Pickford	23.8y*
1956 UPD	Jaynce Leach	Pickford	23.0y*
1957 UPD	Ken Harwood	Rapid River	24.2y
1958 UPD	Dick Olds	Marquette Pierce	25.0y

Year	Class	Name	School	Time		Year	Class	Name	School	Time
1959	UPD	Bill Kibble	Pickford	24.6y		1989	UPD	Dave Bush	Pickford	23.6
1960	UPD	Bill Kibble	Pickford	24.0y		1990	UPD	Jamie Wiles	Lake Linden-Hubbell	23.2
1961	UPD	Gary Leach	Pickford	23.2y		1991	UPD	Mike Ojala	Ewen-Trout Creek	23.2
1962	UPD	Gary Leach	Pickford	23.1y		1992	UPD	Dan Thompson	DeTour	23.6
1963	UPD	Gary Leach	Pickford	23.0y*		1993	UPD	Dan Thompson	DeTour	23.3
1964	UPD	Jim Bishop	Cedarville	24.1y		1994	UPD	Tim Goard	Ontonagon	23.2
1965	UPD	Bill Wonnacott	Pickford	22.4y*		1995	UPD	Jeff Ives	Bark River-Harris	23.6
1966	UPD	Charles Dillon	Republic	24.2y		1996	UPD	Andy Begalle	Bessemer	23.9
1967	UPD	Dale Coullard	Pickford	23.6y		1997	UPD	Mike Razmus	White Pine	23.9
1968	UPD	Jerry Soumis	Chassell	23.5y		1998	UPD	Robert Taylor	Brimley	23.5
1969	UPD	Bob Mileski	Powers	23.5y		1999	UPD	Al D.	Mohawk Keweenaw	23.7
1970	UPD	Bob Mileski	Powers	23.2y		2000	UPD	Nicholas Albright	Engadine	23.7
1971	UPD	Mark Cambray	Channing	23.7y		2001	UPD3	Dustin Esslin	Pickford	23.7*
1972	UPD	Mike Wise	Pickford	24.0y		2002	UPD3	Dan Larrabee	Rapid River	23.2*
1973	UPD	Fred Kivisto	Ironwood Catholic	23.5y		2003	UPD3	Andrew Mettler	Bessemer	23.25*
1974	UPD	Mark Gill	Crystal Falls Forest Park	23.7y		2004	UPD3	Mike Houghton	Engadine	23.73
1975	UPD	John Begalle	Bessemer	23.9y		2005	UPD3	Andrew Mettler	Bessemer	23.67
1976	UPD	John Burt	Bessemer	23.7y		2006	UPD3	Steve Davis	Powers-North Central	23.55
1977	UPD	Mark Freebury	Cedarville	23.0y		2007	UPD3	Cory Thiry	Carney-Nedeau	24.03
1978	UPD	Bruce Cruickshank	Cedarville	23.1y		2008	UPD3	Mike Schmaus	Ontonagon	24.05
1979	UPD	Andy Kucharczyk	DeTour	23.5		2009	UPD3	Mike Schmaus	Ontonagon	23.38
1980	UPD	Mark Allison	Pickford	23.1		2010	UPD3	Mike Schmaus	Ontonagon	22.73*
1981	UPD	Lewis Sawicki	Baraga	23.5		2011	UPD3	Jordan Lavigne	Pickford	23.68
1982	UPD	Lewis Sawicki	Baraga	23.6		2012	UPD3	Dylan Kirkley	Ontonagon	23.50
1983	UPD	Roy Carpenedo	Bessemer	23.4		2013	UPD3	Lucas Gauthier	Munising	23.17
1984	UPD	Roy Carpenedo	Bessemer	23.2		2014	UPD3	Andy Cooper	Munising	23.89
1985	UPD	Dale Hongisto	Wakefield	24.4		2015	UPD3	Andy Greenfield	Munising	22.80
1986	UPD	Mike Thiry	Carney-Nedeau	22.3*		2016	UPD3	Iver Stenberg	Bark River-Harris	23.23
1987	UPD	Scott Grooms	Bessemer	23.7		2017	UPD3	Brayden Tomes	Bessemer	23.34
1988	UPD	Randy Woody	Wakefield	23.7		2018	UPD3	Brayden Tomes	Bessemer	23.70

BOYS 400 METERS

Records

Class	Time	Name	School	Year
D1	47.00	Ricco Hall	East Kentwood	2011
D2	47.94	Stephen Murphy	Madison Heights Lamphere	2009
D3	48.17	Jaylen Gholston	Madison Heights Madison	2014
D4	49.34	Blake Washington	Southfield Christian	2015
UPD1	48.91	Justin Wiles	Escanaba	2005
UPD2	50.76	Michael Glover	Stephenson	2017
(hand:	49.4	Nick Zweifel	Norway	2004)
UPD3	50.66	Phillip Hood	Engadine	2010

Records by Class (pre-2000 for LP, pre-2001 for UP)

Class	Time	Name	School	Year
A	46.95	Godfrey Herring	Pontiac Northern	1997
(hand:	46.6	Omar Davidson	Mt Clemens	1984)
B	48.14	Trinity Townsend	Muskegon Heights	1992
C	48.22	John Mack	New Haven	1996
D	48.99	Jeffrey Morris	Detroit Servite	1987
(hand:	48.4y	Brian Houghton	Detroit DePorres	1976)
UPAB	49.9	Rob Martin	Marquette	1994
UPC	49.7	Greg Londo	Gwinn	1998
UPD	51.0y	Tim Freebury	Cedarville	1976

400 - Class A/Division 1 Champions

(y=440 yards)

Year	Class	Name	School	Time		Year	Class	Name	School	Time
1895	all	Clarence Christopher	Lansing	57.4y*		1911(2)	all	Raymond Smith	Muskegon	55.8y
		(another report has winning time at 53.6y)				1912	all	Fred Hawkins	Adrian	54.4y
1896	all	Hazen Pingree	Detroit Central	54.4y*		1913	all	Warner Van Acken	Coldwater	52.4y*
1897	all	Chandler Tompkins	Lansing	55.0y		1914	all	Scott Burke	Richmond	53.0y
1898	all	Francis Longyear	Lansing	56.8y		1915	all	Scott Burke	Richmond	52.8y
1899	all	Thurlow Coon	Ann Arbor	56.4y		1916	all	Guy Houston	Grand Rapids Central	52.4y*
1900	all	Ivor Roberts	Ann Arbor	56.2y		1917	all	Guy Houston	Grand Rapids Central	54.4y
1901	all	Ivor Roberts	Ann Arbor	55.6y		1918		No Meet – World War I		
1902	all	Fred Keeler	Detroit University School	53.4y*		1919	all	Adam Siemons	Grand Rapids South	54.4y
1903	all	Rollie Lewis (2)	Charlevoix	nt		1920	all	Bill Weekes	Battle Creek	53.0y
1904	all	Ralph Sparling	Detroit University School	55.0y		1921	A	Marsh. McCausland	Detroit Eastern	51.8y*
1905	all	Lewis Torrent (3)	Muskegon	nt		1922	A	Harold Davis	Detroit Northwestern	52.2y
1906	all	Bob Woodcock (3)	Detroit University School	nt		1923	A	Dayton Dailey	Detroit Cass Tech	51.6y*
1907	all	Bob Woodcock (4)	Detroit University School	nt		1924	A	Everett Pauschert	Detroit Northern	51.2y*
1908	all	George Wall	Saginaw	56.4y		1925	A	Herman Miethe	Escanaba	51.5y
1909	all	Kenneth Croutchie	Muskegon	54.8y		1926	A	Herb Craig	Flint	52.6y
1910(1)	all	Ivan Gore	Traverse City	54.6y		1927	A	John Lewis	Detroit Northeastern	50.4y*
1910(2)	all	Norman Bassett	Grand Rapids Central	54.0y		1928	A	Leon Dykas	Detroit Northeastern	51.8y
1911(1)	all	William Howard	Croswell	54.0y		1929	A	Merrill Hershey	Detroit Western	50.7y
						1930	A	Leon Dykas	Detroit Northeastern	50.9y

400 - Class A/Division 1 Champions

Year	Class	Name	School	Time
1931(1)	A	Douglas Emery	Grand Rapids Central	52.3y
1931(2)	A	Byron Bury	Benton Harbor	53.5y
1932(1)	A	Hal Baker	Flint Central	52.4y
1932(2)	A	Darwin Jones	Grand Rapids South	52.8y
1933(1)	A	Carl Lauterhahn	Grand Rapids South	50.9y
1933(2)	A	John Thomas	Flint Central	52.3y
1934(1)	A	Lee Wigg	Ann Arbor	51.4y
1934(2)	A	Clay Tellman	Muskegon	52.0y
1935(1)	A	Roy Fehr	Royal Oak	52.6y
1935(2)	A	Lee Barnett	Lansing Central	52.7y
1936(1)	A	Mac Valleau	Flint Central	53.0y
1936(2)	A	Richard Holtzman	Grosse Pointe	53.6y
1937(1)	A	Emil Kovarcik	Muskegon Heights	51.8y
1937(2)	A	Charles Schmeling	Saginaw	52.9y
1938(1)	A	Charles Schmeling	Saginaw	50.4y*
1938(2)	A	Louis Carpenter	Flint Northern	51.9y
1939(1)	A	Bob Sutton	Kalamazoo Central	51.4y
1939(2)	A	Russell Peek	Muskegon	52.0y
1940(1)	A	Fred Swanton	Mt Clemens	51.2y
1940(2)	A	Jack Doran	Grand Rapids South	51.8y
1941(1)	A	William Cave	Monroe	51.6y
1941(2)	A	Nathan Howison	Midland	51.8y
1942	A (tie)	Rob Howison	Midland	52.6y
1942	A (tie)	Jim Gibson	Pontiac	52.6y
1943		No Meet – World War II		
1944(1)	A	Jim Morrish	Ferndale	52.7y
1944(2)	A	Herb Speerstra	Saginaw	53.4y
1945(1)	A	Bill Griggs	Dearborn	51.7y
1945(2)	A	Augustine Deruy	Hazel Park	52.6y
1946(1)	A	Bill Griggs	Dearborn	52.7y
1946(2)	A	Bob Werner	Muskegon Heights	53.1y
1947(1)	A	Jack Rose	Grand Rapids Creston	51.4y
1947(2)	A	Bill Conley	Saginaw	52.2y
1948(1)	A	Bob Hensman	Wyandotte Roosevelt	50.3y
1948(2)	A	Oscar Ingram	Flint Central	51.6y
1949(1)	A	James Ellis	Saginaw	50.5y
1949(2)	A	Kenneth Jones	Grand Rapids Ottawa Hills	51.2y
1950(1)	A	Charles Beesley	Wyandotte Roosevelt	50.6y
1950(2)	A	Harry Miller	Jackson	52.2y
1951(1)	A	Horace Armstead	Ferndale	50.6y
1951(2)	A	Glenn Davis	Alpena	51.4y
1952(1)	A	Terry Barr	Grand Rapids Central	51.5y
1952(2)	A	Ralph Gray	Grosse Pointe	53.4y
1953(1)	A	Terry Barr	Grand Rapids Central	50.7y
1953(2)	A	Ulus Silk	Flint Central	51.1y
1954(1)	A	Al Dixon	Kalamazoo Central	50.0y
1954(2)	A	Don Zysk	Grand Haven	51.2y
1955(1)	A	William Campbell	Dearborn Fordson	49.7y*
1955(2)	A	Levi Simpson	Ypsilanti	50.5y
1956	(3)A	Jim Nelligan	Lansing Sexton	50.8y
1956(1)	A	Larry Poehlman	Niles	51.0y
1956(2)	A	John Sharp	Flint Northern	50.0y
1957	(3)A	Jim Nelligan	Lansing Sexton	52.3y
1957(1)	A	Dennis Wright	Flint Northern	51.2y
1957(2)	A	John Sharp	Flint Northern	51.7y
1958	(3)A	John Harley	Dearborn	50.8y
1958(1)	A	Dennis Wright	Flint Northern	49.9y
1958(2)	A	Phil Gaines	Flint Northern	50.6y
1959	(3)A	Dave Curtis	Lansing Sexton	52.3y
1959(1)	A	Dennis Wright	Flint Northern	50.8y
1959(2)	A	Jim Moers	Wayne	51.6y
1960	(3)A	Dempsey Taylor	Ann Arbor	51.7y
1960(1)	A	Steve Meyer	Berkley	51.4y
1960(2)	A	Bob Siera	Dearborn	52.0y
1961	(3)A	Larry Page	Monroe	51.6y
1961(1)	A	Huey Edwards	Flint Northern	50.2y
1961(2)	A	Sam McMurray	Muskegon Heights	50.3y
1962	A	Larry Page	Monroe	49.7y*
1963	A	George Wesson	Detroit Southeastern	49.0y*
1964	A	Rodney Ford	Royal Oak Kimball	51.2y
1965	A	Wally Chany	Temperance Bedford	50.2y
1966	A	Steve Bhue	North Farmington	49.3y
1967	A	Loren. Montgomery	Detroit Southeastern	48.9y*
1968	A	Mike Holt	Detroit Henry Ford	48.8y*
1969	A	Mike Holt	Detroit Henry Ford	48.3y*
1970	A	Tim Pinnix	Port Huron	49.8y
1971	A	Stan Vinson	Detroit Chadsey	48.0y*
1972	A	Charles Davis	Ferndale	48.6y
1973	A	Ken DeLor	Grosse Pointe North	48.0y*
1974	A	Howard Mitchell	Detroit Mumford	48.8y
1975	A	Greg Anderson	Detroit Southeastern	48.4y
1976	A	Brad Simpson	Flint Southwestern	48.6y
1977	A	Deon Hogan	Detroit Kettering	47.1y*
1978	A	Randall Woodson	Detroit Redford	47.8y
1979	A	James Woods	Detroit Redford	48.0y
1980	A (tie)	Rob Grainger	Portage Central	48.9y
1980	A (tie)	Donald Anderson	Detroit Cody	48.9y
1981	A	Marcus Sanders	Lansing Sexton	47.7y
1982	A	David Beasley	Detroit Central	47.4
1983	A	Rodney Benson	Detroit Cass Tech	47.5
1984	A	Omar Davidson	Mt Clemens	46.6*
1985	A	Torin Dorn	Southfield	48.04*
1986	A	Keith Wheeler	Troy	47.64*
1987	A	Keith Wheeler	Troy	47.3
1988	A	Derrick Harris	Detroit Cooley	48.78
1989	A	Steve Sandles	East Detroit	47.22*
1990	A	Darnell Hall	Detroit Pershing	47.56
1991	A	Marco West	Detroit Cooley	48.15
1992	A	Randy Kinder	East Lansing	48.88
1993	A	Steve Ruffin	Flint Southwestern	47.94
1994	A	Gaven Herring	Pontiac Northern	47.0
1995	A	Tony Vann-Spann	Detroit Chadsey	48.05
1996	A	Godfrey Herring	Pontiac Northern	47.67
1997	A	Godfrey Herring	Pontiac Northern	46.95*
1998	A	Lamar Courtney	Muskegon Mona Shores	48.82
1999	A	Charles Rogers	Saginaw	47.82
2000	D1	Derold Sligh	Saginaw Heritage	48.60*
2001	D1	Soji Jibowu	Saginaw Heritage	48.28*
2002	D1	Willie Spencer	Grand Rapids Union	48.25*
2003	D1	Justin Thomason	Port Huron	49.53
2004	D1	Terry Fambro	East Lansing	48.41
2005	D1	Andre Barnes	West Bloomfield	48.87
2006	D1	Cedric Everson	Detroit Mumford	48.74
2007	D1	Kyle Wilson	East Detroit	47.96
2008	D1	Varick Tucker	Belleville	48.71
2009	D1	Nathan Saliga	Romeo	48.84
2010	D1	Phillip Washington	West Bloomfield	48.42
2011	D1	Ricco Hall	East Kentwood	47.00*
2012	D1	Shane Barron	Flint Carman-Ainsworth	48.10
2013	D1	Gabe Hodge	Davison	48.57
2014	D1	Maurice Allen	Oak Park	48.13
2015	D1	Skyler Bowden	Saline	47.87
2016	D1	Montel Wood	Wayne Memorial	47.30
2017	D1	Matthew Moorer	Ypsilanti Lincoln	47.42
2018	D1	Donnie James	Oak Park	47.14

400 - Class B/Division 2 Champions

(y=440 yards)

Year	Class	Name	School	Time
1920	B	Lloyd Miller	Vassar	53.8y*
1921	B	Charles Bailey	Petoskey	55.0y
1922	B	Ollie Steiner	Niles	52.6y*
1923	B	Lewis Ealy	Allegan	52.7y
1924	B	Bob Rogers	Wyandotte Roosevelt	56.3y
1925	B	Louis Peters	Niles	54.3y
1926	B	Robert Hickey	Charlotte	54.3y
1927	B	Ben Sims	St Joseph	53.3y
1928	B	Robert Seekall	Three Rivers	53.5y
1929	B	Mac Crane	Ypsilanti	53.4y
1930	B	Bernard Roberts	Monroe	53.3y
1931(1)	B	George Jackson	Ypsilanti Central	54.4y
1931(2)	B	Harold McCracken	Cadillac	54.5y
1932(1)	B	George Jackson	Ypsilanti Central	52.7y
1932(2)	B	Bob Kemmerling	Three Rivers	54.4y
1933(1)	B	James Wright	Berkley	50.9y*
1933(2)	B	Orin Cain	Niles	52.8y
1934(1)	B	Leon Jones	Dearborn	52.3y
1934(2)	B	Robert Prenkert	Niles	53.6y
1935(1)	B	Bunny Fulkerson	Howell	51.5y
1935(2)	B	Ralph Gildenstein	East Detroit	52.7y
1936(1)	B	Lawton Williams	Hastings	52.7y
1936(2)	B	Jack McNutt	Kalamazoo State High	54.9y
1937(1)	B	Edward Klett	Dowagiac	53.9y
1937(2)	B	Phil Carey	Birmingham	54.2y
1938(1)	B	Bob Hamilton	Buchanan	52.1y
1938(2)	B	Arthur Dehn	Belding	52.2y
1939(1)	B	James Kerwin	Grand Rapids Lee	51.8y
1939(2)	B	Richard Daron	Ludington	53.0y
1940(1)	B	Phil Hanson	Alma	51.3y
1940(2)	B	Clare Chandler	Allegan	51.6y
1941(1)	B	Melvin Detroitwiler	Mt Pleasant	51.5y
1941(2)	B	Charles Betts	East Grand Rapids	54.0y
1942(1)	B	Harold Short	Melvindale	53.4y
1942(2)	B	Tom Kennedy	Niles	54.3y
1943		No Meet – World War II		
1944	B (tie)	Stanley Van Gilder	Niles	53.2y

Year	Class	Name	School	Time		Year	Class	Name	School	Time
1944	B (tie)	Neal Martin	Cadillac	53.2y		1971	B	Clarence Leslie	Muskegon Heights	49.6y
1945(1)	B	Burt Lankhorst	Fremont	52.1y		1972	B	Charles Monk	Cranbrook	49.6y
1945(2)	B	Gerald Connoly	Ypsilanti Roosevelt	53.1y		1973	B	Rick Harwick	Caro	49.9y
1946(1)	B	Jack Phister	Birmingham	53.0y		1974	B	David Furst	Niles Brandywine	49.0y
1946(2)	B	Lee Walker	Hillsdale	55.3y		1975	B	Brian Blank	Grand Rapids Northview	49.1y
1947(1)	B	Jack Phister	Birmingham	50.9y*		1976	B	Brian Blank	Grand Rapids Northview	48.3y*
1947(2)	B	Wardell Gilliam	River Rouge	51.4y		1977	B	Michael Erickson	Wyoming Rogers	48.5y
1948(1)	B	Mark Thompson	Niles	53.1y		1978	B (tie)	Mike Shea	Detroit DeLaSalle	50.3y
1948(2)	B	Bob Parks	Howell	54.1y		1978	B (tie)	Ded DeWeerd	Hudsonville	50.3y
1949(1)	B	Merle Rewalt	Allegan	53.5y		1979	B	Mark Woodson	Dearborn Heights Robichaud	49.7
1949(2)	B	Bob Dunn	South Haven	54.0y		1980	B	Kenneth Lay	Muskegon Heights	49.6
1950(1)	B	Louis Vargha	Plymouth	52.6y		1981	B	Jamie Weathers	Ecorse	48.8
1950(2)	B	Eric Heizer	Birmingham	53.2y		1982	B	Ken Mitchell	Oak Park	48.0y*
1951(1)	B	Tom Peyette	East Grand Rapids	53.2y		1983	B	Troy Eggelston	Flint Powers	49.1
1951(2)	B	Bob Brasington	Mt Pleasant	55.2y		1984	B	Derrick Walker	Detroit Benedictine	49.3
1952(1)	B	Ron Suess	Manistee	53.8y		1985	B	Bill Sall	Hudsonville Unity Christian	49.62*
1952(2)	B	Ned Sharples	Birmingham	54.5y		1986	B	Sam New	Auburn Hills Avondale	50.10
1953(1)	B	Bob Wagner	Roseville	51.7y		1987	B	Joe Garrett	Bay City Handy	48.81*
1953(2)	B	Junior Mailand	Alma	51.9y		1988	B	Zekiel Miller	Detroit East Catholic	49.08
1954(1)	B	Larry Masteller	Adrian	51.3y		1989	B	Latony Triggs	Flint Beecher	48.4
1954(2)	B	Don Harsh	Charlotte	53.4y		1990	B	Thomas Smith	Milan	49.14
1955(1)	B	Larry Masteller	Adrian	50.6y*		1991	B	Erik Welch	Oxford	48.4
1955(2)	B	Bill Wyatt	Inkster	51.0y		1992	B	Trinity Townsend	Muskegon Heights	48.14*
1956 (3)	B	Clyde Battle	Romulus	52.8y		1993	B	Chris Polk	Detroit UD Jesuit	49.17
1956(1)	B	Dick Barstow	St Louis	52.2y		1994	B	John Thompson	Big Rapids	49.37
1956(2)	B	Bill Wyatt	Inkster	52.8y		1995	B	Randy Hunt	Comstock	49.71
1957 (3)	B	Bruce Berndt	St Joseph	53.4y		1996	B	Eric Hansen	Big Rapids	49.7
1957(1)	B	Bill Wyatt	Inkster	51.7y		1997	B	Micah Zuhl	St Joseph	49.6
1957(2)	B	Dick Barstow	St Louis	52.6y		1998	B	Brad Manor	Standish Sterling	47.9
1958 (3)	B	Larry Sharon	Ecorse	52.0y		1999	B	Ashley Terry	Romulus	49.76
1958(1)	B	Tom Noteware	Cranbrook	51.7y		2000	D2	Elton Anderson	Detroit Renaissance	49.16*
1958(2)	B	Everette Griffin	River Rouge	51.8y		2001	D2	Nelson DeFord	Haslett	49.10*
1959 (3)	B	Mike Aderhold	Hastings	53.3y		2002	D2	Dayrl Jackson	Benton Harbor	49.31
1959(1)	B	Roger Williams	South Haven	51.0y		2003	D2	Hermon Tate	Farmington Hills Harrison	49.18
1959(2)	B	Larry Sharon	Ecorse	51.5y		2004	D2	Devon Jackson	Dowagiac	49.25
1960 (3)	B	Tom Dunton	Battle Creek Lakeview	53.8y		2005	D2	Michael Smoot	Trenton	48.36*
1960(1)	B	Harry Seymour	Ecorse	54.3y		2006	D2	Kyle Terpak	Riverview	49.09
1960(2)	B	Tod Williams	Cranbrook	54.0y		2007	D2	Jarrod Hamilton	Ferndale	49.11
1961 (3)	B	Glen Duddles	Grand Blanc	51.4y		2008	D2	Adrien Bouyer	Battle Creek Lakeview	48.81
1961(1)	B	Paul Holmberg	Cass City	48.8y*		2009	D2	Stephen Murphy	Madison Heights Lamphere	47.94*
1961(2)	B	Marty Crane	Flint Kearsley	51.1y		2010	D2	Dan Pung	Zeeland West	49.12
1962	B	Dick Gaston	South Haven	50.7y		2011	D2	Trevor Salter	Auburn Hills Avondale	48.70
1963	B	Mike Erwin	East Grand Rapids	50.7y		2012	D2	Nathan Chapman	Auburn Hills Avondale	48.71
1964	B	Rich Tompkins	Hart	51.0y		2013	D2	Marcel Wyckoff	Detroit East English	48.39
1965	B	Eric Peterson	River Rouge	50.2y		2014	D2	Colby Clark	Stevensville-Lakeshore	48.67
1966	B	Gary Gleton	Ecorse	51.0y		2015	D2	Steven Linton	St. Johns	49.04
1967	B	Al Henderson	Detroit St Charles	51.6y		2016	D2	Steven Linton	St. Johns	48.26
1968	B	Al Henderson	Detroit East Catholic	50.1y		2017	D2	Cameron Oleen	Fruitport	49.21
1969	B	Art Small	Ecorse	50.0y		2018	D2	Jacob Denison	Tecumseh	49.27
1970	B	Perry Richardson	Paw Paw	49.8y						

400 - Class C/Division 3 Champions

(y=440 yards)

Year	Class	Name	School	Time		Year	Class	Name	School	Time
1921	C	Cook	Wayne	55.2y*		1941(2)	C	Henry Tomei	St Clair Shores South Lake	52.9y
1922	C	Vern Canedy	Eaton Rapids	54.0y*		1942(1)	C	Ted Wisner	Grandville	53.5y
1923	C	Alan McLean	Plainwell	53.8y*		1942(2)	C	Bob Frentheway	Imlay City	55.3y
1924	C	Paul Sutton	Morenci	nt		1943		No Meet – World War II		
1925	C	Glen McCaslin	Wayland	54.7y		1944(1)	C	Morton Pritchard	Evart	nt
1926	C	Theral Dutch Kanitz	Milan	54.5y		1944(2)	C	Ted Wisner	Grandville	nt
1927	C	Donald Payne	Plainwell	53.2y*		1945(1)	C	Vernon MacKenzie	Fowlerville	53.8y
1928	C	Eugene Atkins	Vassar	53.5y		1945(2)	C	Earl Baldwin	Tecumseh	54.7y
1929	C	Ronald Weaver	Berrien Springs	52.4y*		1946(1)	C	Dick Cepela	Grand Rapids Wyoming Park	53.2y
1930	C	Donald Martin	Oxford	52.0y*		1946(2)	C	Gerald Connoly	Ypsilanti Roosevelt	54.3y
1931(1)	C	Clarence Daybird	Harbor Springs	54.6y		1947(1)	C	Keith Van Duzen	Belding	52.4y
1931(2)	C	James Shrader	Caro	55.6y		1947(2)	C	Dick Holmgren	Grand Rapids Lee	54.3y
1932(1)	C	Tyrus Carter	Kalamazoo St Augustine	53.9y		1948(1)	C	Karl Newman	East Grand Rapids	53.7y
1932(2)	C	James Wright	Berkley	54.0y		1948(2)	C	Dave Hickman	Ypsilanti Roosevelt	55.3y
1933(1)	C	Dee Weaver	Buchanan	51.3y*		1949(1)	C	Dave Hickman	Ypsilanti Roosevelt	51.7y
1933(2)	C	Tyrus Carter	Kalamazoo State High	52.4y		1949(2)	C	Karl Newman	East Grand Rapids	54.1y
1934(1)	C	Chuck Taylor	South Lyon	53.5y		1950(1)	C	Tom Peyette	East Grand Rapids	52.7y
1934(2)	C	Lee Stewart	Romeo	53.9y		1950(2)	C	Marvin Staplin	Ypsilanti Roosevelt	53.1y
1935(1)	C	Chuck Taylor	South Lyon	52.6y		1951(1)	C	Marvin Staplin	Ypsilanti Roosevelt	53.8y
1935(2)	C	Errol Graydon	Kalkaska	52.7y		1951(2)	C	Charles Baker	Shelby	54.9y
1936(1)	C	Garner Osborne	Milford	53.4y		1952(1)	C	John Oney	Ypsilanti Roosevelt	54.0y
1936(2)	C	Warren Ampey	Paw Paw	54.5y		1952(2)	C	Jim Madar	Holly	54.4y
1937(1)	C	Elwood Hauser	Boyne City	53.4y		1953(1)	C	Bill Cowan	Glen Arbor Leelanau School	51.7y
1937(2)	C	Lovell Lewis	Shelby	53.0y		1953(2)	C	Harry Paulson	White Cloud	52.5y
1938(1)	C	Elwood Hauser	Boyne City	50.8y*		1954(1)	C	Wayne Marine	Ann Arbor University	52.8y
1938(2)	C	Rudy Marcelletti	Paw Paw	53.0y		1954(2)	C	Gerald Inman	Galesburg	53.5y
1939(1)	C	Willis Glas	Ann Arbor University	52.0y		1955(1)	C	Robert Booker	Baldwin	51.4y
1939(2)	C	Dale Buerger	Flint Bendle	52.2y		1955(2)	C	Paul Frankhauser	Marion	52.7y
1940(1)	C	Stanley Porter	Morenci	52.1y		1956 (3)	C	Jim Kreider	Okemos	54.3y
1940(2)	C	Don Harris	Corunna	53.0y		1956(1)	C	Bob Waters	Montrose	53.0y
1941(1)	C	Fran. Miskokomon	Algonac	51.4y		1956(2)	C	But Bowens	Glen Arbor Leelanau School	53.5y
						1957 (3)	C	Bob Snow	Honor	53.8y

1957(1)	C	Bob Waters	Montrose	51.9y
1957(2)	C	Ed Bowen	Glen Arbor Leelanau School	53.7y
1958 (3)	C	Gerry Beard	Ann Arbor University	53.5y
1958(1)	C	Bob Waters	Montrose	52.4y
1958(2)	C	Gene Cross	Paw Paw	53.2y
1959 (3)	C	Larry Tarno	Burton Bentley	54.9y
1959(1)	C	Buck Miley	Flint Dye	54.1y
1959(2)	C	Dick Ekine	Leslie	54.2y
1960 (3)	C	Dick Smith	Montague	53.8y
1960(1)	C	Mike Elliott	Centreville	52.8y
1960(2)	C	Warren Kent	Haslett	53.0y
1961 (3)	C	Joe Everett	Saranac	52.7y
1961(1)	C	Bob Milles	Homer	51.6y
1961(2)	C	Harold Dunkel	Parma Western	52.6y
1962	C	Larry Davenport	Lansing St Mary	51.4y
1963	C	Ed Kennard	Glen Arbor Leelanau School	52.1y
1964	C	Jim Bauman	Battle Creek St Phillip	51.8y
1965	C	Dick Hilton	Glen Arbor Leelanau School	50.9y
1966	C	Gordon Aldrich	Akron-Fairgrove	49.5y*
1967	C	Len Moeller	Breckenridge	50.4y
1968	C	Ralph Stepaniak	Alpena Catholic	50.5y
1969	C	Chris Boogs	Detroit St Rita	50.2y
1970	C	Lon Bohannon	Shepherd	51.0y
1971	C	Tom Burger	Reading	50.7y
1972	C	John Bennett	Cassopolis	51.0y
1973	C	George Fuller	Detroit Servite	49.5y*
1974	C	Mike Walton	Detroit East Catholic	49.5y*
1975	C	Joe Green	Bath	49.6y
1976	C	Larry Booker	Wyoming Lee	48.9y*
1977	C	Jim Smith	Royal Oak Shrine	49.5y
1978	C	Russell Haines	Cassopolis	50.3y
1979	C	Gregg Lockwood	Freeland	50.8
1980	C	Jamie Weathers	Ecorse	50.4
1981	C	Bruce Davis	Dundee	49.8
1982	C	Phillip Morrow	Lakeview	49.9
1983	C	Mike White	Harper Woods Lutheran East	49.1

1984	C	Claude Tiller	Detroit DePorres	48.5*
1985	C	Fred Dalton	Ecorse	49.51*
1986	C	Tim Stersic	Kalamazoo Hackett	50.66
1987	C	Daryl Stallworth	Ecorse	49.43*
1988	C	Sean Conklin	Williamston	49.1
1989	C	Ron Beachy	Constantine	50.68
1990	C	Rick Tyson	Galesburg-Augusta	49.8
1991	C	Rick Tyson	Galesburg-Augusta	49.1
1992	C	Tim Thomas	Saginaw Nouvel	49.3
1993	C	John Mack	New Haven	49.67
1994	C	John Mack	New Haven	48.89*
1995	C	John Mack	New Haven	48.99
1996	C	John Mack	New Haven	48.22*
1997	C	Nick Anders	Centreville	48.88
1998	C	Travis Kelly	New Haven	48.96
1999	C	Calvin Treadwell	Buchanan	49.50
2000	D3	Kyle Kolbe	Clare	49.32*
2001	D3	Jeffrey Stoll	Tawas	49.43
2002	D3	Josh Rodgers	Clare	49.77
2003	D3	Jason Stewart	Suttons Bay	49.30*
2004	D3	Phil Damaska	Detroit Country Day	48.70*
2005	D3	Brandon Wright	Union City	48.94
2006	D3	Travis Tamez	Essexville Garber	49.50
2007	D3	Chris Rucker	Detroit Country Day	49.02
2008	D3	Tony Rasch	Perry	49.83
2009	D3	Jeff Burd	Vermontville Maple Valley	49.38
2010	D3	Michael Rossman	Madison Heights Foley	49.84
2011	D3	Cody Foreman	Whittemore-Prescott	48.97
2012	D3	Alex Thelen	Pewamo-Westphalia	50.29
2013	D3	T.J. Burnett	Wyoming Kelloggsville	48.59*
2014	D3	Jaylen Gholston	Madison Heights Madison	48.17*
2015	D3	Jaylen Gholston	Madison Heights Madison	49.46
2016	D3	Felix Biewald	Elkton-Pigeon-Bayport	49.36
2017	D3	Konnor Maloney	Lansing Catholic	48.63
2018	D3	Logan Wells	Hart	48.89

400 - Class D/Division 4 Champions

(y=440 yards)

1927	D	Frank Coleman	Okemos	55.8y*
1928	D	Frank Coleman	Okemos	56.6y
1929	D	Ralph James	Newaygo	56.2y
1930	D	Ivan Walcott	Comstock Park	56.2y
1931(1)	D	Ivan Walcott	Comstock Park	56.1y
1931(2)	D (tie)	Rex Glidden	Alba	57.5y
1931(2)	D (tie)	William Williams	Dimondale	57.5y
1932(1)	D	Charles Defer	South Lake	54.4y*
1932(2)	D	William Williams	Dimondale	55.9y
1933(1)	D	Earl Sattler	Dimondale	55.2y
1933(2)	D	Marshall Somerville	Richland	54.1y*
1934(1)	D	Earl Sattler	Dimondale	55.3y
1934(2)	D	Keith Baumgardner	Centreville	56.1y
1935(1)	D	George Gargett	St Clair Shores Lakeview	54.7y
1935(2)	D	Jim Whinsonant	Royal Oak Madison	55.1y
1936	D	Frank Figgles	Onekama	56.3y
1937(1)	D	Edward McDonald	Pentwater	54.5y
1937(2)	D	Thomas Miller	Onekama	55.2y
1938(1)	D	Don Sawyer	Bloomfield Hills	54.2y
1938(2)	D	Leo Latkin	Mt Morris St Mary	55.4y
1939(1)	D	William Griswold	Michigan School for Deaf	55.1y
1939(2)	D	Earl Cady	Potterville	57.0y
1940(1)	D	William Griswold	Michigan School for Deaf	52.2y*
1940(2)	D	Leon Brunnell	St Joseph Catholic	54.7y
1941	D	Jim Merriman	Bear Lake	54.6y
1942	D	Bob Mosher	Lansing Blind School	53.0y
1943		No Meet – World War II		
1944	D	Race Hice	Lansing Boys Vocational	55.4y
1945	D	Charles Whitetree	Michigan School for Deaf	53.2y
1946	D	Don DeFord	Stevensville	57.9y
1947	D	Rolland Burwell	Baldwin	55.9y
1948(1)	D	Morris Hughes	Michigan School for Deaf	55.3y
1948(2)	D	Frank Hamlin	Vestaburg	56.2y
1949(1)	D	Ber. Veneklassen	Three Oaks	53.4y
1949(2)	D	Sig Mollenkott	Galien	55.1y
1950	D	John Newman	Benton Harbor St John	54.3y
1951(1)	D	Lloyd Salacina	Newaygo	55.3y
1951(2)	D	Barry Schultz	Michigan School for Deaf	55.9y
1952(1)	D	Dean Rhodes	Fairview	56.2y
1952(2)	D	Don French	Edwardsburg	56.7y
1953(1)	D	Bert Burns	Brethren	53.4y
1953(2)	D	Don Bartz	Stevensville	53.9y
1954(1)	D	Robert Decker	Galien	54.4y
1954(2)	D	Richard Lotre	DeWitt	54.6y
1955(1)	D	Norman Burns	Brethren	53.4y

1955(2)	D	Lyford Young	Freesoil	54.0y
1956(1)	D	Robert Booker	Baldwin	51.7y*
1956(2)	D	Clayton Turner	Akron	54.1y
1957(1)	D	Larry Simmons	Hartland	55.6y
1957(2)	D	Jerome Crockett	Covert	56.0y
1958(1)	D	Mike Snyder	Woodland	54.1y
1958(2)	D	Carl Smith	Brethren	55.1y
1959(1)	D	Mike Snyder	Woodland	55.0y
1959(2)	D	Dale Sylvester	Fairgrove	56.2y
1960(1)	D	Paul Joles	Wolverine	52.8y
1960(2)	D	Mike Johnson	Mason County Eastern	53.3y
1961(1)	D	Mike Johnson	Mason County Eastern	52.1y
1961(2)	D	Wilbert Reed	Michigan School for Deaf	53.4y
1962	D	Abram Powell	Michigan School for Deaf	51.9y
1963	D	Abram Powell	Michigan School for Deaf	51.8y
1964	D	Abram Powell	Michigan School for Deaf	52.1y
1965	D	Jack Larson	St Joseph Catholic	51.3y*
1966	D	Bernard Woods	Covert	51.9y
1966	D	Bernard Woods	Covert	51.9y
1968	D	Chuck Holubik	Deerfield	51.2y*
1969	D	Craig Laingsburg	Ypsilanti Roosevelt	52.0y
1970	D	Art Smith	Covert	51.6y
1971	D	Terry Balzer	Unionville	51.8y
1972	D	Terry Balzer	Unionville	51.9y
1973	D	Lloyd Wilds	Mendon	51.5y
1974	D	George Butts	Flint Holy Rosary	51.0y*
1975	D	Mike Walton	Detroit East Catholic	49.1y*
1976	D	Brian Houghton	Detroit DePorres	48.4y*
1977	D	Dave Koppin	Detroit Country Day	49.9y
1978	D	Evans Lalas	Frankfort	50.5y
1979	D	Mike Taylor	Detroit DePorres	49.6
1980	D	Brian Burger	Reading	50.1
1981	D	Brian Burger	Reading	49.8
1982	D	Al Smith	Covert	49.0
1983	D	Carl Mayhand	Mason County Eastern	49.5
1984	D	Michael Gatson	Detroit East Catholic	49.51*
1985	D	Sean Jones	Detroit East Catholic	50.07
1986	D	Jeffrey Morris	Detroit Servite	49.06*
1987	D	Jeffrey Morris	Detroit Servite	48.99*
1988	D	Keith Seybert	Mt Pleasant Sacred Heart	50.01
1989	D	Matt Okma	Suttons Bay	50.8
1990	D	Don Johnson	Manton	50.46
1991	D	Don Johnson	Manton	49.62
1992	D	Terry Baker	Mendon	51.13
1993	D	Todd VanderKlay	Mendon	51.9
1994	D	Dieter Brown	Battle Creek St Phillip	50.24

Year	Class	Name	School	Time
1995	D	Dieter Brown	Battle Creek St Phillip	50.87
1996	D	Steve Bailey	Athens	50.71
1997	D	Nick Grabowski	Pittsford	50.72
1998	D	Derek Shoup	Mason County Eastern	49.4
1999	D	Kelvin Singleton	Centreville	49.06
2000	D4	Kelvin Singleton	Centreville	49.53*
2001	D4	Simon Smith	Mancelona	50.01
2002	D4	Kenneth Coleman	Baldwin	49.92
2003	D4	Eric Lunning	Fairview	51.02
2004	D4	Dave Messer	Blanchard-Montabella	49.79
2005	D4	Kyle Fortin	Fairview	49.43*
2006	D4	Kyle Fortin	Fairview	50.05
2007	D4	Aaron Hilborn	Kingston	50.1
2008	D4	Josh Depree	Ottawa Lake Whiteford	49.51
2009	D4	Ben Lawson	Mayville	51.06
2010	D4	Ian Miller	Concord	49.49
2011	D4	Ian Miller	Concord	49.89
2012	D4	Nolen Mitchell	Albion	52.92
2012	D4	Austin Sandusky	Morenci	52.92
2013	D4	Zack McGowen	White Cloud	50.60
2014	D4	Austin Sandusky	Morenci	50.48
2015	D4	Blake Washington	Southfield Christian	49.34*
2016	D4	Deion Gatson	Cassopolis	50.20
2017	D4	Patrick Harris	Hale	50.04
2018	D4	Patrick Harris	Hale	50.04

400 – UP Class AB/Division 1 Champions

(y=440 yards)

Year	Class	Name	School	Time
1940	UPB	Donald Kirkpatrick	Kingsford	53.5y*
1941(1)	UPB	Clar. Grabowski	Escanaba	54.5y
1941(2)	UPB	Stuart Oakes	Sault Ste. Marie	54.1y
1942(1)	UPB	Clar. Grabowski	Escanaba	53.9y
1942(2)	UPB	Aldo Andreoli	Iron Mountain	54.0y
1943		No Meet – World War II		
1944	UPB	R. Mazurek	Ironwood	54.5y
1945(1)	UPB	Jack Brosco	Sault Ste. Marie	55.2y
1945(2)	UPB	J. Manning	Escanaba	54.5y
1946(1)	UPB	Gerrish	Sault Ste. Marie	54.6y
1946(2)	UPB	Jim Ross	Escanaba	55.0y
1947(1)	UPB	Allen Schuster	Manistique	55.0y
1947(2)	UPB	Rod Halstead	Calumet	54.7y
1948(1)	UPB	Matt Nikkari	Newberry	55.1y
1948(2)	UPB	William Chubb	Marquette	55.1y
1949(1)	UPB	William Chubb	Marquette	53.9y
1949(2)	UPB	Jack Anderson	Menominee	55.0y
1950(1)	UPB	Hugo Schobert	Manistique	54.5y
1950(2)	UPB	Steve Petros	Marquette	54.6y
1951(1)	UPB	Keith Goddard	Kingsford	55.8y
1951(2)	UPB	Gil Mroz	Sault Ste. Marie	55.4y
1952(1)	UPB	Tom Taylor	Newberry	55.8y
1952(2)	UPB	Carl Senogles	Sault Ste. Marie	57.3y
1953(1)	UPB	Jim Laurin	Stephenson	55.9y
1953(2)	UPB	Harlan Yelland	Escanaba	57.2y
1954(1)	UPB	Allen Default	Menominee	55.2y
1954(2)	UPB	Frank Holmberg	Newberry	56.0y
1955(1)	UPB	Ken Dixner	Manistique	54.9y
1955(2)	UPB	Mike Kaifish	Calumet	56.1y
1956(1)	UPB	John Fletcher	Sault Ste. Marie	54.3y
1956(2)	UPB	Carl Dougivoto	Stephenson	54.3y
1957(1)	UPB	John Fletcher	Sault Ste. Marie	55.3y
1957(2)	UPB	Tom Westlake	Calumet	54.9y
1958(1)	UPB	Wendell Gilroy	Sault Ste. Marie	55.9y
1958(2)	UPB	Bill Cooper	Sault Ste. Marie	55.9y
1959(1)	UPB	Wendell Gilroy	Sault Ste. Marie	55.0y
1959(2)	UPB	Bill Axel	Marquette	55.1y
1960(1)	UPB	John Fisher	Escanaba	53.8y
1960(2)	UPB	Raoul Robar	Ishpeming	54.4y
1961(1)	UPB	Clayton Haupt	Newberry	54.5y
1961(2)	UPB	John Fisher	Escanaba	53.8y
1962	UPAB	Ben Yagodzinski	Escanaba Holy Name	54.6y
1963	UPAB	John Hendrickson	Negaunee	53.1y*
1964	UPAB	Ken Berg	Marquette	53.4y
1965	UPAB	Brian Stanway	Sault Ste. Marie	52.6y*
1966	UPAB	Jeff Gill	Kingsford	53.3y
1967	UPAB	Pat Verette	Iron Mountain	53.6y
1968	UPAB	Greg Eckhart	Calumet	53.3y
1969	UPAB	Greg Eckhart	Calumet	52.4y*
1970	UPAB	Michael Hatfield	Gwinn	51.1y*
1971	UPAB	Jimmy Lee	Rudyard	51.9y
1972	UPAB	Leon Hank	Sault Ste. Marie	51.8y
1973	UPAB	Jeff Currier	Ironwood	51.6y
1974	UPAB	Jeff Currier	Ironwood	52.2y
1975	UPAB	Tim Baroni	Calumet	51.7y
1976	UPAB	Steve Zablocki	Kingsford	51.2y
1977	UPAB	Terry Awrey	Kingsford	52.5y
1978	UPAB	Alan Smith	Gladstone	53.1y
1979	UPAB	Kevin French	Kingsford	51.8
1980	UPAB	John Tolfa	Escanaba	50.8*
1981	UPAB	John Tolfa	Escanaba	50.6*
1982	UPAB	Guy Zablocki	Kingsford	52.3
1983	UPAB	Guy Zablocki	Kingsford	52.0
1984	UPAB	Mark Noon	Menominee	51.4
1985	UPAB	Tim Casparson	Menominee	52.2
1986	UPAB	Todd LaCosse	Escanaba	51.0
1987	UPAB	Todd LaCosse	Escanaba	50.2*
1988	UPAB	Ron Pratt	Kingsford	51.6
1989	UPAB	Chris Richard	Kingsford	52.4
1990	UPAB	Keith Collins	Negaunee	50.6
1991	UPAB	Mono McDonald	Sault Ste. Marie	51.5
1992	UPAB	Mono McDonald	Sault Ste. Marie	52.2
1993	UPAB	Matt Searle	Gladstone	51.2
1994	UPAB	Rob Martin	Marquette	49.9*
1995	UPAB	Tom Thompson	Menominee	52.7
1996	UPAB	Dillon Carr	Ishpeming Westwood	52.2
1997	UPAB	Brian Savard	Sault Ste. Marie	53.1
1998	UPAB	Brian Savard	Sault Ste. Marie	52.2
1999	UPAB	Brian Branam	Escanaba	51.8
2000	UPAB	Brian Branam	Escanaba	51.0
2001	UPD1	Aaron Faulkner	Negaunee	51.3
2002	UPD1	Jay Wiles	Escanaba	51.2
2003	UPD1	Pete Tuccini	Marquette	50.75*
2004	UPD1	Justin Wiles	Escanaba	50.22*
2005	UPD1	Justin Wiles	Escanaba	48.91*
2006	UPD1	Justin Wiles	Escanaba	49.79
2007	UPD1	Josh Droese	Kingsford	50.56
2008	UPD1	Jacob Bennette	Sault Ste. Marie	51.53
2009	UPD1	Garde Kangas	Manistique	50.68
2010	UPD1	Erik Kliesner	Kingsford	51.26
2011	UPD1	Adrian DeLaRosa	Menominee	51.39
2012	UPD1	Kyle Lester	Sault Ste. Marie	51.27
2013	UPD1	Chris Sedenquist	Gladstone	51.39
2014	UPD1	Tyler Roberts	Kingsford	51.08
2015	UPD1	Andrew Banitt	Marquette	51.59
2016	UPD1	Clayton Sayen	Houghton	51.70
2017	UPD1	Clayton Sayen	Houghton	50.24
2018	UPD1	Clayton Sayen	Houghton	51.25

400 – UP Class C/Division 2 Champions

(y=440 yards)

Year	Class	Name	School	Time
1940	UPC	John Kemp	L'Anse	57.2y*
1941	UPC	John Lawrence	Stephenson	nt
1942	UPC	Arnold Engman	Baraga	55.1y*
1943		No Meet – World War II		
1944	UPC	Emil Platzke	Ewen	55.2y
1945	UPC	Richard Anderson	L'Anse	54.5y*
1946(1)	UPC	Kujula	Newberry	55.0y
1946(2)	UPC	Don Potter	Munising	56.4y
1947(1)	UPC	Burton Stern	Hancock	58.2y
1947(2)	UPC	Stanley Dudo	L'Anse	56.6y
1948(1)	UPC	Bob Hillier	Munising	56.0y
1948(2)	UPC	Lloyd DeMars	Munising	56.2y
1949(1)	UPC	Robert Hiller	Munising	54.4y*
1949(2)	UPC	Stanley Dudo	L'Anse	56.3y
1950(1)	UPC	Stanley Dudo	L'Anse	55.8y
1950(2)	UPC	Mannisto	Bessemer	55.4y
1951(1)	UPC	Glenn Gransell	L'Anse	58.2y
1951(2)	UPC	Roy Pingel	Bessemer	57.1y
1952	UPC	Glenn Gransell	L'Anse	56.5y
1953	UPC	Spencer Carlson	Houghton	57.4y
1954	UPC	Paul Smith	Houghton	57.2y
1955(1)	UPC	Don Borich	Bessemer	56.8y
1955(2)	UPC	Fred Haberlen	Ontonagon	57.4y
1956(1)	UPC	Bill Schinderle	Iron River	56.9y
1956(2)	UPC	Paul Repath	Houghton	57.0y
1957(1)	UPC	Don Borich	Bessemer	55.6y
1957(2)	UPC	Romilly Gilbert	Wakefield	58.0y
1958(1)	UPC	Roger Kangas	Houghton	57.8y
1958(2)	UPC	Romilly Gilbert	Wakefield	nt

Year	Class	Name	School	Time
1959	UPC	Garth McMaster	Sault Ste. Marie Loretto	56.3y
1960(1)	UPC	Dave Peterson	Stephenson	54.5y
1960(2)	UPC	Jim Ghiardi	Gwinn	54.5y
1961(1)	UPC	Dewey Maki	Wakefield	55.9y
1961(2)	UPC	Don Sawaski	Wakefield	54.3y*
1962	UPC	Don Sawaski	Wakefield	54.5y
1963	UPC	Coolidge Fraser	St. Ignace	55.1y
1964	UPC	Thomas Makinen	Bessemer	53.2y*
1965	UPC	Ladd Honkala	Bessemer	53.5y
1966	UPC	Bob Fredrickson	L'Anse	53.3y
1967	UPC	Russel Brittain	Crystal Falls	53.2y*
1968	UPC	Ken Kennedy	Houghton	54.7y
1969	UPC	Don Michaelson	L'Anse	54.0y
1970	UPC	Barry Hafeman	Stephenson	52.1y*
1971	UPC	Don Michaelson	L'Anse	52.6y
1972	UPC	John Otto	Houghton	51.7y*
1973	UPC	John Otto	Houghton	52.3y
1974	UPC	Dave Rogge	L'Anse	52.2y
1975	UPC	Michael Dellangelo	Ishpeming	51.8y
1976	UPC	Michael Dellangelo	Ishpeming	50.2y*
1977	UPC	Michael Dellangelo	Ishpeming	50.1y*
1978	UPC	Charles Otto	Houghton	51.4y
1979	UPC	Steve Flaminio	Iron Mountain	53.0
1980	UPC	Dan Pousakowski	Iron River West Iron County	51.7
1981	UPC	Tom Flamino	Iron Mountain	51.5
1982	UPC	Jim Estola	Ironwood	51.8
1983	UPC	Craig Allen	Iron Mountain	51.5
1984	UPC	Craig Allen	Iron Mountain	50.4
1985	UPC	Andy Luepnitz	St. Ignace	52.4
1986	UPC	Jody Paradis	Munising	51.8
1987	UPC	Jody Paradis	Munising	52.5
1988	UPC	Craig Podgornik	Iron Mountain	51.1
1989	UPC	Keith Collins	Negaunee	53.3
1990	UPC	Jerry Cleary	Ontonagon	51.5
1991	UPC	Keith Collins	Negaunee	50.9
1992	UPC	Lewis Page	Iron Mountain	52.5
1993	UPC	Jesse Janeau	Iron River West Iron County	51.9
1994	UPC	Chris Suggitt	Rudyard	50.9
1995	UPC	Jason Wender	Iron Mountain	52.6
1996	UPC	Brian Lorente	St. Ignace	51.7
1997	UPC	John Sturos	Calumet	52.0
1998	UPC	Greg Londo	Gwinn	49.7*
1999	UPC	Shane Trotter	Iron River West Iron County	52.3
2000	UPC	Jeremiah Beckman	Manistique	51.7
2001	UPD2	Eric Rocker	Newberry	51.5*
2002	UPD2	Nick Zweifel	Norway	53.4
2003	UPD2	Nick Zweifel	Norway	52.12*
2004	UPD2	Nick Zweifel	Norway	49.4*
2005	UPD2	J Pann	Newberry	51.15*
2006	UPD2	Paul Davis	St. Ignace	52.82
2007	UPD2	Brandon Lawrence	Manistique	52.01
2008	UPD2	Kyle Phillips	Stephenson	52.47
2009	UPD2	Jacob Herres	Stephenson	53.25
2010	UPD2	Evan Everson	St. Ignace	51.31
2011	UPD2	Austin St. Louis	St. Ignace	55.82
2012	UPD2	Nate Meyer	Ishpeming	53.43
2013	UPD2	Ryan Ramey	Menominee	51.12*
2014	UPD2	Ryan Ramey	Menominee	51.95
2015	UPD2	Nate Meyer	Ishpeming	54.33
2016	UPD2	David Lavake	St. Ignace	55.47
2017	UPD2	Michael Glover	Stephenson	50.76*
2018	UPD2	Montell Glover	Stephenson	51.30

400 – UP Class D/Division 3 Champions

(y=440 yards)

Year	Class	Name	School	Time
1940	UPD	Mills	Trenary	58.6y*
1941	UPD	John Narkooli	Rock	?
1942	UPD	Snorre Holle	Hermansville	55.9y*
1943		No Meet – World War II		
1944	UPD	Lester Treankler	Alpha	57.0y
1945	UPD	McCreanor	Eben	57.8y
1946(1)	UPD	Lester Treankler	Alpha	57.0y
1946(2)	UPD	Elmer Vesser	Powers	58.3y
1947(1)	UPD	John Dove	Chassell	55.6y*
1947(2)	UPD	Lester Bazinet	Rock	56.3y
1948(1)	UPD	Bob Urpila	Trout Creek	56.9y
1949(1)	UPD	Don Maki	Eben	56.5y
1949(2)	UPD	Charles Lombard	Hermansville	57.5y
1950(1)	UPD	Bob Kern	Eben	57.6y
1950(2)	UPD	Glenn Gregg	Gwinn	56.8y
1951(1)	UPD	Donald Goodrich	Bergland	58.9y
1951(2)	UPD	James Laurin	Carney	59.3y
1952(1)	UPD	Leroy Libby	Marquette Pierce	58.1y
1952(2)	UPD	James Laurin	Carney	57.2y
1953(1)	UPD	Jim Graham	Pickford	55.5y*
1953(2)	UPD	Lloyd LaCasse	Hermansville	57.3y
1954(1)	UPD	Ronell Leach	Pickford	57.0y
1954(2)	UPD	Don Groleau	Nahma	57.7y
1955(1)	UPD	Ken Harwood	Rapid River	55.0y*
1955(2)	UPD	Russell Barger	Chassell	57.9y
1956(1)	UPD	Roger Wahl	Pickford	57.0y
1956(2)	UPD	Ken Harwood	Rapid River	57.7y
1957(1)	UPD	Dick Plont	DeTour	57.1y
1957(2)	UPD	Corwin Williams	Pickford	57.7y
1958(1)	UPD	Paul MacDonald	Cedarville	58.3y
1958(2)	UPD	Kent Lang	Cooks	56.8y
1959(1)	UPD	Jim Ghiardi	Gwinn	55.3y
1959(2)	UPD	Bruce Taylor	Pickford	56.8y
1960(1)	UPD	Ron Pennington	Pickford	55.0y*
1960(2)	UPD	Jim Carlson	Rapid River	55.2y
1961(1)	UPD	Elwin Leach	Pickford	?
1961(2)	UPD	Tony Lee	DeTour	54.6y*
1962	UPD	Elwin Leach	Pickford	54.0y
1963	UPD	Bob Huyck	Pickford	53.7y*
1964	UPD	Bob Huyck	Pickford	52.8y*
1965	UPD	Bob Huyck	Pickford	52.7y*
1966	UPD	Mickey Adams	DeTour	53.8y
1967	UPD	Carl Smith	Channing	55.4y
1968	UPD	Tomothy Tischer	DeTour	54.2y
1969	UPD	Tomothy Tischer	DeTour	53.5y
1970	UPD	Michael Wise	Pickford	53.4y
1971	UPD	Michael Wise	Pickford	52.5y*
1972	UPD	Michael Wise	Pickford	53.4y
1973	UPD	Mark Johns	Wakefield	53.3y
1974	UPD	Mark Johns	Wakefield	53.1y
1975	UPD	Tim Freebury	Cedarville	53.3y
1976	UPD	Tim Freebury	Cedarville	51.0y*
1977	UPD	Ronald Carlson	DeTour	53.0y
1978	UPD	John Andrzejak	Pickford	53.0y
1979	UPD	Greg Croasdell	Rock-Mid Peninsula	52.6
1980	UPD	Greg Belleville	Engadine	51.5
1981	UPD	Paul Raboin	Norway	53.2
1982	UPD	Brent Madalinski	Bark River-Harris	51.6
1983	UPD	Dale Hongisto	Wakefield	53.1
1984	UPD	Dale Hongisto	Wakefield	52.1
1985	UPD	Mike Christian	Felch North Dickinson	53.3
1986	UPD	Richard Ledy	DeTour	52.7
1987	UPD	Scott Grooms	Bessemer	52.5
1988	UPD	Mike Miskovich	Wakefield	52.9
1989	UPD	Dave Blake	Rudyard	53.2
1990	UPD	Mike Ojala	Ewen-Trout Creek	52.1
1991	UPD	Mike Ojala	Ewen-Trout Creek	52.0
1992	UPD	Chris Jaruzel	Brimley	54.2
1993	UPD	Dan Thompson	DeTour	52.0
1994	UPD	Nathan Ferrier	Rock-Mid Peninsula	52.6
1995	UPD	Nathan Ferrier	Rock-Mid Peninsula	52.0
1996	UPD	Dave Larrabee	Rapid River	52.5
1997	UPD	Mike Hammill	Crystal Falls Forest Park	52.8
1998	UPD	Dennis Savard	St. Ignace	53.0
1999	UPD	Al D.	Mohawk Keweenaw	52.5
2000	UPD	Nick Albright	Engadine	53.5
2001	UPD3	Nick Albright	Engadine	53.0*
2002	UPD3	Anthony Wilson	Cedarville	53.2
2003	UPD3	Brad Hunter	Pickford	52.50*
2004	UPD3	Andrew Mettler	Bessemer	51.93*
2005	UPD3	Andrew Mettler	Bessemer	51.40*
2006	UPD3	Justin Wigand	Rock-Mid Peninsula	53.53
2007	UPD3	Harlan Chartrand	Brimley	51.94
2008	UPD3	Harlan Chartrand	Brimley	51.94
2009	UPD3	Phillip Hood	Engadine	51.48
2010	UPD3	Phillip Hood	Engadine	50.66*
2011	UPD3	Brett Bryant	Rapid River	52.75
2012	UPD3	Dylan Kirkley	Ontonagon	52.73
2013	UPD3	Cole Potvin	Cooks-Big Bay de Noc	51.62
2014	UPD3	Cole Potvin	Cooks-Big Bay de Noc	51.17
2015	UPD3	Bryce Holle	Powers-North Central	51.78
2016	UPD3	Lucas Sundling	Cooks-Big Bay de Noc	52.07
2017	UPD3	Lucas Sundling	Rapid River	52.41
2018	UPD3	Lucas Sundling	Rapid River	53.06

BOYS 800 METERS

Records

D1	1:48.98	Donavan Brazier	Grand Rapids Kenowa Hills	2015
D2	1:51.76	Tommy Brinn	Otsego	2008
D3	1:53.81	Brian Patrick	Bridgman	2017
D4	1:54.06	Liam Boylan-Pett	Bath	2004
UPD1	1:58.06	Alvin Moore	Gladstone	2005
UPD2	1:59.36	Scott Bond	Munising	2007
UPD3	2:01.08	Isaiah Aili	Bessemer	2018

Records by Class (pre-2000 for LP, pre-2001 for UP)

A	1:50.63	Rick Gledhill	Clinton Township Chippewa Valley	1988
B	1:52.1	Randy Helling	Stevensville-Lakeshore	1989
C	1:53.7	Ronald Simpson	Redford St Mary	1982
D	1:56.8y	Lloyd Wilds	Mendon	1973
UPAB	1:55.9	Rob Martin	Marquette	1995
UPC	1:58.4y	Charles Cloninger	Ishpeming Westwood	1976
UPD	1:59.0y	Mark Oberlin	Crystal Falls Forest Park	1976
	1:59.0y	Mark Oberlin	Crystal Falls Forest Park	1977

800 – Class A/Division 1 Champions

(y=880 yards)

Year	Class	Name	School	Time
1896	all	Guy Dayrell	Grand Rapids	2:14.0y*
1897	all	Frank Mera	Detroit Central	2:16.4y
1898	all	William Roberts	Detroit Central	2:21.2y
1899	all	Ralph Dubois	Ann Arbor	2:16.6y
1900	all	Abbott Widdicomb	Grand Rapids Central	2:10.6y*
1901	all	Edward Hayes	Detroit Central	2:13.0y
1902	all	Edward Hayes	Detroit Central	2:04.0y*
1903	all	Martin Daane	Grand Rapids	2:07.8y
1904	all	Jacob Williams	Detroit University School	nt
1905	all	Alexander Walker	Detroit University School	2:07.8y
1906	all	William Balhatchet	Michigan Military Academy	2:03.3y*
1907	all	Henry Sullivan	Grand Rapids Central	2:05.6y
1908	all	Henry Sullivan	Grand Rapids Central	2:03.8y
1909	all	Henry Sullivan	Grand Rapids Central	2:06.2y
1910	all	Leland Wesley	Adrian	2:07.8y
1911	all	Frederick Lumley	Detroit Central	2:10.8y
1912	all	Earl Sheldon	West Branch	2:04.0y
1913	all	Earl Sheldon	West Branch	2:04.5y
1914	all	Fletcher Gallagher	Bay City Eastern	2:06.8y
1915	all	William Welsch	Allegan	2:06.4y
1916	all	Dave Forbes	Grand Rapids Central	2:04.0y
1917	all	Harold Jones	Grand Rapids Central	2:11.0y
1918		No Meet – World War I		
1919	all	Bill Weekes	Battle Creek	2:05.0y
1920	all	Bill Weekes	Battle Creek	2:04.8y
1921	A	Joyce Wanamaker	Highland Park	2:04.4y
1922	A	Ray Hart	Saginaw Arthur Hill	2:07.4y
1923	A	Ray Hart	Saginaw Arthur Hill	2:03.1y
1924	A	Don Seeger	Detroit Northwestern	2:02.9y*
1925	A	Milton Kendrick	Mt Clemens	2:01.5y*
1926	A	Ralph Munson	Kalamazoo Central	2:04.0y
1927	A	William Smith	Detroit Cass Tech	2:04.8y
1928	A	Rha Arnold	Detroit Western	1:59.9y*
1929	A	Howard Braden	Flint Northern	2:01.5y
1930	A	Raymond Roe (1)	Detroit Northwestern	2:00.4y
1930	A	Karl Kahler (2)	Detroit Redford	2:02.6y
1931	A	Clayton Penny	Grand Rapids Union	2:04.5y
1932	A	Howard Davison	Grand Rapids Ottawa Hills	2:03.1y
1933	A	Forrest Spencer	Lansing Eastern	2:03.9y
1934	A	Sam Leppert	Saginaw	2:02.6y
1935	A	Harold Davidson	Grand Rapids Ottawa Hills	2:03.3y
1936	A	Bill Sikes	Lansing Eastern	2:03.5y
1937	A	Harry Leonard	Grand Rapids Davis Tech	2:05.4y
1938 (1)	A	Bud Russell	Saginaw	2:01.5y
1938 (2)	A	Rene Hall	Saginaw	2:03.0y
1939 (1)	A	Ed Robins	Grosse Pointe	2:02.6y
1939 (2)	A	Norm Kruse	Grand Rapids Creston	2:05.0y
1940 (1)	A	Harold Carpenter	Royal Oak	1:59.0y*
1940 (2)	A	Robert Earl Betts	Lansing Eastern	2:04.2y
1941 (1)	A	John Bultema	Muskegon	2:02.8y
1941 (2)	A	Gilbert McMickens	Kalamazoo Central	2:04.3y
1942 (1)	A	Gordon McMickens	Kalamazoo Central	2:02.4y
1942 (2)	A	Frank Olszewski	Grand Rapids Union	2:02.9y
1943		No Meet – World War II		
1944 (1)	A	Donald Knapp	Battle Creek Central	2:03.6y
1944 (2)	A	Charles Hackley	Kalamazoo Central	2:05.4y
1945 (1)	A	Wilbert Beattie	Grand Rapids South	2:01.3y
1945 (2)	A	Don Makielski	Ann Arbor	2:02.7y
1946 (1)	A	Ed Draugellis	Grand Rapids Catholic	2:03.3y
1946 (2)	A	Jim Kepford	Muskegon	2:05.3y
1947 (1)	A	Jim Kepford	Muskegon	2:00.6y
1947 (2)	A	Leon Malone	Flint Central	2:04.0y
1948 (1)	A	Jim Kepford	Muskegon	2:02.0y
1948 (2)	A	Bob Parsons	Saginaw	2:02.2y
1949 (1)	A	Joe Host	Grand Rapids Catholic	2:01.0y
1949 (2)	A	Don Douglas	Ann Arbor	2:03.1y
1950 (1)	A	Joe Host	Grand Rapids Catholic	2:00.6y
1950 (2)	A	Barr Braman	Royal Oak	2:01.8y
1951 (1)	A	George Jayne	Ann Arbor	2:00.3y
1951 (2)	A	Joe Host	Grand Rapids Catholic	2:02.8y
1952 (1)	A	Bob Pildner	Saginaw	2:04.2y
1952 (2)	A	Robert Schaller	Grosse Pointe	2:04.6y
1953 (1)	A	Ernie Bennetts	Hazel Park	1:59.5y
1953 (2)	A	Dale Vandenberg	Grand Rapids Catholic	2:01.6y
1954 (1)	A	Dale Vandenberg	Grand Rapids Catholic	1:59.5y
1954 (2)	A	Milt Theros	Ann Arbor	2:01.7y
1955 (1)	A	Bill Douglas	Pontiac	2:00.0y
1955 (2)	A	Bob Lake	Kalamazoo Central	2:00.9y
1956 (1)	A	Bob Lake	Kalamazoo Central	1:58.9y*
1956 (2)	A	Bill Douglas	Pontiac	1:59.7y
1956 (3)	A	Harold Stancie	Battle Creek	2:01.6y
1957 (1)	A	Bob Duke	Dearborn Fordson	2:04.0y
1957 (2)	A	Larry Beamer	Pontiac	2:04.0y
1957 (3)	A	Wylie Rogers	Flint Central	2:05.0y
1958 (1)	A	Wylie Rogers	Flint Central	1:59.7y
1958 (2)	A	Harvey Martin	Flint Northern	2:00.1y
1958 (3)	A	Roger Coates	Pontiac Central	2:01.0y
1959 (1)	A	Geo. Freidriechsen	Flint Central	2:00.0y
1959 (2)	A	Jim Reily	Birmingham	2:00.7y
1959 (3)	A	Gary Crenshaw	Flint Central	2:02.2y
1960 (1)	A	Bob Fulcher	Hazel Park	1:59.4y
1960 (2)	A	Ted Kelly	Dearborn	2:02.1y
1960 (3)	A	Fran McDougal	Saginaw Arthur Hill	2:03.3y
1961 (1)	A	John Shaw	Flint Central	1:57.2y*
1961 (2)	A	Chester Harris	Flint Southwestern	2:00.3y
1961 (3)	A	Paul Kinney	Royal Oak Dondero	2:00.7y
1962	A (tie)	George Thomas	Grosse Pointe	1:57.9y
1962	A (tie)	Theo. McBurrows	Detroit Mumford	1:57.9y
1963	A	Walt Wilson	Dearborn Heights Robichaud	1:53.3y*
1964	A	Ron Kutchinski	East Grand Rapids	1:55.3y
1965	A	Pat Wilson	Roseville	1:54.2y
1966	A	Tony Kneft	Detroit Catholic Central	1:55.9y
1967	A	John Mock	Mt Clemens	1:53.1y*
1968	A	Roger Cleaver	Detroit Kettering	1:53.0y*
1969	A	Kevin Reabe	Waterford Kettering	1:52.7y*
1970	A	Kevin Reabe	Waterford Kettering	1:50.9y*
1971	A	Bob Mills	Ann Arbor Huron	1:54.5y

1972	A	Dave Fortney	Ypsilanti	1:52.8y
1973	A	Steve Brown	Grand Rapids Ottawa Hills	1:55.5y
1974	A	Keith Young	Flint Northern	1:53.7y
1975	A	Keith Young	Flint Northern	1:51.3y
1976	A	Richard MacInnes	Flint Northern	1:55.3y
1977	A	Larry Verburg	Sterling Heights Ford	1:52.2y
1978	A	Mark Pruente	Pontiac Central	1:53.7y
1979	A	Tim Kenney	Detroit Mumford	1:52.4y
1980	A	David Johnson	Flint Northwestern	1:52.3y
1981	A	Earl Jones	Taylor Center	1:54.6y
1982	A	Earl Jones	Taylor Center	1:52.7
1983	A	John McCleary	Birmingham Brother Rice	1:52.1
1984	A	Tim Monahan	Grosse Pointe North	1:55.3
1985	A	Derrick Coleman	Detroit Denby	1:53.60
1986	A	Scott Colvin	Grand Blanc	1:53.80
1987	A	Kevin Williams	Davison	1:53.1
1988	A	Rick Gledhill	Clinton Twp Chippewa Valley	1:50.63*
1989	A	Aaron Grzymkowski	Clinton Twp Chippewa Valley	1:54.09
1990	A	Marcelo Ortiz	Dearborn Fordson	1:52.73
1991	A	Todd Snyder	Brighton	1:53.1
1992	A	David Norman	Detroit Cooley	1:54.16
1993	A	Janairo Brown	Flint Kearsley	1:55.46
1994	A	Brandon Dutton	Brighton	1:55.7
1995	A	Rob Stowe	Greenville	1:54.64

1996	A	Dan Snyder	St. Johns	1:55.64
1997	A	Nick Gow	White Lake Lakeland	1:54.80
1998	A	Nick Gow	White Lake Lakeland	1:53.79
1999	A	Brandon Jiles	Detroit Mumford	1:53.10
2000	D1	Tom Greenless	Milford	1:52.59*
2001	D1	Eric Caruthers	Muskegon Mona Shores	1:53.92
2002	D1	Courtland Keteyian	Lake Orion	1:53.10
2003	D1	Christopher Haag	Warren DeLasalle	1:52.94
2004	D1	Abraham Mach	East Lansing	1:52.01*
2005	D1	Blake Figgins	Detroit Mumford	1:52.98
2006	D1	Brad Anderson	Rochester Adams	1:54.21
2007	D1	Isaiah Ward	Detroit Mumford	1:54.03
2008	D1	Joe Reynolds	Rochester Adams	1:53.92
2009	D1	Nick Kaiser	Temperance Bedford	1:52.13
2010	D1	Isaac Cox	East Kentwood	1:51.78*
2011	D1	Nick Kaiser	Temperance Bedford	1:52.91
2012	D1	Brandon Wallace	Milford	1:54.12
2013	D1	Andrew Middleton	Holt	1:53.36
2014	D1	Donavan Brazier	Grand Rapids Kenowa Hills	1:50.24*
2015	D1	Donavan Brazier	Grand Rapids Kenowa Hills	1:48.98*
2016	D1	Cameron Cooper	Oak Park	1:51.68
2017	D1	Cameron Cooper	Oak Park	1:51.22
2018	D1	Cole Johnson	Rockford	1:53.11

800 – Class B/Division 2 Champions

(y=880 yards)

1921	B	Don Henry	Petoskey	2:09.4y*
1922	B	Harold Stevens	Plymouth	2:08.4y*
1923	B	Phillip Knuth	St Joseph	2:06.4y*
1924	B	Claud Cramer	St Johns	2:06.5y
1925	B	Robert Burns	Niles	2:05.4y*
1926	B	Claud Cramer	St Johns	2:04.0y*
1927	B	Ralph Bazley	Ferndale	2:07.0y
1928	B	Earl Sonnenberg	Wyandotte Roosevelt	2:05.0y
1929	B	Earl Sonnenberg	Wyandotte Roosevelt	2:03.5y*
1930	B	Tim Quinn	Ludington	1:58.8y*
1931	B	Tim Quinn	Ludington	1:59.5y
1932	B	Otto Hecksel	Grand Haven	2:06y
1933	B	Clayton Brelsford	Birmingham	2:01.7y
1934	B	Harold Dean	Alma	2:04.0y
1935	B	Richard Dickerson	Dearborn	2:03.8y
1936	B	Quentin Brelsford	Birmingham	2:06.1y
1937	B	Quentin Brelsford	Birmingham	2:03.0y
1938 (1)	B	Quentin Brelsford	Birmingham	1:57.6y*
1938 (2)	B	Carl Rausch	Cadillac	2:02.3y
1939 (1)	B	John Purdue	Albion	2:04.5y
1939 (2)	B	Albert Borton	Hastings	2:06.0y
1940 (1)	B	Melvin Detroitwiler	Mt Pleasant	2:03.4y
1940 (2)	B	Robert Price	Belding	2:04.7y
1941	B	Albert Bailey	South Haven	2:02.0y
1942 (1)	B	Robert Price	Belding	2:05.7y
1942 (2)	B	Lewis Jeffries	Niles	2:07.0y
1943		No Meet – World War II		
1944 (1)	B	Don Arnold	Niles	2:05.0y
1944 (2)	B	Joe Pray	Charlotte	2:05.7y
1945 (1)	B	Herb Kebschull	St Joseph	2:04.0y
1945 (2)	B	Don Thaden	East Lansing	2:04.5y
1946 (1)	B	Herb Kebschull	St Joseph	2:04.8y
1946 (2)	B	Carl Lemcool	Traverse City	2:06.3y
1947 (1)	B	Chuck Franks	Fenton	2:04.4y
1947 (2)	B	Dale Boyd	Fremont	2:04.6y
1948 (1)	B	Dale Boyd	Fremont	2:03.3y
1948 (2)	B	Chuck Franks	Fenton	2:05.4y
1949 (1)	B	Morris Tubbergen	Fremont	2:05.0y
1949 (2)	B	Eugene Sowles	Coldwater	2:05.2y
1950 (1)	B	Dick Horie	Livonia Bentley	2:01.9y
1950 (2)	B	Tom Tyler	Niles	2:04.8y
1951 (1)	B	Dick Horie	Livonia Bentley	2:03.3y
1951 (2)	B	Paul Hook	Adrian	2:04.8y
1952 (1)	B	Lavel Rogers	Inkster Roosevelt	2:07.6y
1952 (2)	B	Ray Vandersteen	Grand Ledge	2:08.7y
1953 (1)	B	Dick Teugh	Kalamazoo State High	2:02.6y
1953 (2)	B	Fred Tshirhart	Milan	2:03.3y
1954 (1)	B	Roy Butler	Inkster	2:02.7y
1954 (2)	B	Jim Pauget	Troy	2:02.8y
1955 (1)	B	Don Pounds	Walled Lake	2:03.9y
1955 (2)	B	Paul Maloney	Detroit Servite	2:05.1y
1956 (1)	B	Larry Taylor	Fenton	2:04.2y
1956 (2)	B	Bob Kenippe	Ludington	2:05.6y
1956 (3)	B	Ernest Hudson	River Rouge	2:07.6y
1957 (1)	B	Ernest Hudson	River Rouge	2:04.0y
1957 (2)	B	Fred Lavery	Cranbrook	2:05.0y
1957 (3)	B	Dennis Fitzgerald	Portage	2:07.1y

1958 (1)	B	Bill Baldwin	Flint Kearsley	1:59.3y
1958 (2)	B	Paul Underhill	South Lyon	2:01.2y
1958 (3)	B	Don Cottingham	Three Rivers	2:05.1y
1959 (1)	B	Mart. Hammerstein	Temperance	1:59.3y
1959 (2)	B	Paul Underhill	South Lyon	2:01.6y
1959 (3)	B	Bill Baldwin	Flint Kearsley	2:04.0y
1960 (1)	B	Ron Horning	Sturgis	2:03.3y
1960 (2)	B	Rush Ring	Sparta	2:03.3y
1960 (3)	B	Ray Wood	Belding	2:02.1y
1961 (1)	B	Mike Martin	Charlotte	1:59.6y
1961 (2)	B	Dick McDonald	Temperance	2:01.0y
1961 (3)	B	Ray Wood	Belding	2:01.2y
1962	B	Mike Martin	Charlotte	1:56.1y*
1963	B	Ron Kutchinski	East Grand Rapids	1:56.7y
1964	B	Jim Burger	Milan	2:01.4y
1965	B	Ron Kutchinski	East Grand Rapids	1:53.8y*
1966	B	Rich Stevens	Dearborn Heights Riverside	1:54.8y
1967	B	Larry Reese	Holly	1:58.2y
1968	B	Steve Freese	Three Rivers	1:55.8y
1969	B	Ron Cool	Grand Rapids Northview	1:57.5y
1970	B	Dan Smith	Muskegon Heights	1:55.3y
1971	B	Dan Keswick	Fenton	1:55.6y
1972	B	Charles Monk	Cranbrook	1:53.8y*
1973	B	David Karns	Fenton	1:55.9y
1974	B	David Furst	Niles Brandywine	1:53.9y
1975	B	Mike Helms	Fenton	1:53.6y*
1976	B	Lewis Yeo	Grand Rapids West Catholic	1:55.2y
1977	B	Mark Poelman	Wyoming Rogers	1:52.9y*
1978	B	Jeff Lewis	Holly	1:53.1y
1979	B	Terry Ross	Dearborn Heights Robichaud	1:56.3y
1980	B	Paul Richmond	Flint Beecher	1:54.8
1981	B	Bob Boynton	East Grand Rapids	1:54.9
1982	B	Rich Horston	Oak Park	1:54.3y
1983	B	Robert Fischer	Flint Beecher	1:54.4
1984	B	John Goble	Petoskey	1:54.9
1985	B	John Brazier	Grand Rapids Catholic	1:54.86
1986	B	Mike Hanninen	Chesaning	1:56.5
1987	B	Jeff Boks	Bay City Handy	1:56.21
1988	B	Stacy Watson	Flint Beecher	1:55.79
1989	B	Randy Helling	Stevensville-Lakeshore	1:52.1*
1990	B	Todd Koning	Hudsonville Unity Christian	1:54.0
1991	B	Andy Sorenson	Tawas	1:55.47
1992	B	Brian Recor	Marine City	1:56.67
1993	B	Dan Rader	Fremont	1:56.0
1994	B	Joe O'Connor	West Branch Ogemaw Hts	1:55.51
1995	B	Joel Sellentine	Ortonville Brandon	1:56.23
1996	B	Adrian Ashby	Stockbridge	1:56.3
1997	B	Mike Bucholtz	Ludington	1:56.3
1998	B	Andy Lixey	Tawas	1:54.00
1999	B	Phillip Stead	Dearborn Divine Child	1:54.88
2000	D2	Justin Blakely	Big Rapids	1:54.80*
2001	D2	Jay Brown	Muskegon Orchard View	1:54.26*
2002	D2	Jim Pancoast	Stevensville-Lakeshore	1:54.66
2003	D2	Jim Pancoast	Stevensville-Lakeshore	1:53.74*
2004	D2	Kent Debruin	Vicksburg	1:54.39
2005	D2	Clinton Inderbitzin	Allegan	1:53.73*
2006	D2	Jay Bilsborrow	Coldwater	1:53.63*
2007	D2	Peek Delorean	Detroit Crockett	1:54.61

Year	Class	Name	School	Time
2008	D2	Tommy Brinn	Otsego	1:51.76*
2009	D2	Tommy Brinn	Otsego	1:55.49
2010	D2	Trevor Brinn	Otsego	1:55.00
2011	D2	Nick Wharry	Ionia	1:56.39
2012	D2	Conner Mora	Cedar Springs	1:56.41
2013	D2	Luke Johnson	Ludington	1:53.53
2014	D2	John Sattler	Byron Center	1:53.34
2015	D2	Sam Plaska	Zeeland East	1:55.11
2016	D2	Daniel Steele	Sturgis	1:54.92
2017	D2	Jonathan Groendyk	Zeeland East	1:53.40
2018	D2	Josiah Morse	Essexville Garber	1:55.63

800 – Class C/Division 3 Champions

(y=880 yards)

Year	Class	Name	School	Time
1921	C	Harold Stevens	Plymouth	2:17.0y*
1922	C	Arthur Miller	Otsego	2:11.6y*
1923	C	Kenneth Higgins	Cass City	2:13.2y
1924	C	Orland Barton	Plainwell	2:15.6y
1925	C	Leo Halloran	Wayland	2:10.9y*
1926	C	Edward Tanney	Bangor	2:08.6y*
1927	C	Edward Tanney	Bangor	2:09.8y
1928	C	Oliver Cejka	Kingsford	2:08.3y*
1929	C	George Robinson	Battle Creek Lakeview	2:06.5y*
1930	C	John Caplis	Wayne	2:04.4y*
1931	C	William Chase	St Clair	2:07y
1932	C	Arbutus Shaw	Algonac	2:10.4y
1933	C	Richard Brockway	Paw Paw	2:07.5y
1934	C	Dudley Straubel	Frankfort	2:06.3y
1935	C	John Woodbury	Yale	2:05.7y
1936	C	Bob Ellis	Lowell	2:07.5y
1937	C	Keith Cruikshank	Flint Bendle	2:03.0y*
1938 (1)	C	Vincent Butler	Howard City	2:01.6y*
1938 (2)	C	Steve Hustafa	Paw Paw	2:06.4y
1939 (1)	C	Max Whitetree	Flint Hoover	2:07.1y
1939 (2)	C	Robert Archer	Croswell	2:07.9y
1940 (1)	C	Max Whitetree	Flint Hoover	2:02.1y
1940 (2)	C	John Stoutjesdyke	East Grand Rapids	2:04.1y
1941 (1)	C	Dick Meldrum	Ypsilanti Roosevelt	2:05.3y
1941 (2)	C	Donald Kahler	Imlay City	2:05.3y
1942 (1)	C	Dick Meldrum	Ypsilanti Roosevelt	2:07.3y
1942 (2)	C	Vernon Ward	Mesick	2:09.1y
1943		No Meet – World War II		
1944 (1)	C	Tom Dickinson	Cranbrook	2:05.9y
1944 (2)	C	Charles Herrington	Bad Axe	2:09.6y
1945 (1)	C	Art Snyder	Grandville	2:04.0y
1945 (2)	C	Stan Johnson	Grand Rapids Lee	2:08.0y
1946 (1)	C	Don Krahnnenberg	East Grand Rapids	2:05.4y
1946 (2)	C	Corliss Keehn	Evart	2:07.9y
1947 (1)	C	William Joliffe	Charlevoix	2:04.8y
1947 (2)	C	Howard Camfield	Grand Rapids Wyoming Park	2:08.3y
1948 (1)	C	Arlue Moore	St Clair Shores Lake Shore	2:06.3y
1948 (2)	C	Wesley Baxendale	St Clair Shores South Lake	2:08.7y
1949 (1)	C	David McLaughlin	East Grand Rapids	2:06.3y
1949 (2)	C	Wesley Baxendall	St Clair Shores South Lake	2:07.1y
1950 (1)	C	William Ross	Paw Paw	2:03.5y
1950 (2)	C	David McLaughlin	East Grand Rapids	2:06.0y
1951 (1)	C	Don Ross	Mattawan	2:08.2y
1951 (2)	C	Bill Ross	Paw Paw	2:09.7y
1952 (1)	C	Jim Allen	Whitehall	2:07.5y
1952 (2)	C	Don Ross	Mattawan	2:08.5y
1953 (1)	C	Jim Allen	Whitehall	2:04.0y
1953 (2)	C	Ken Maxwell	Marlette	2:04.6y
1954 (1)	C	Ken Maxwell	Marlette	2:01.7y
1954 (2)	C	Ed Goodrich	South Lyon	2:03.5y
1955 (1)	C	Ronald Post	Comstock Park	2:04.0y
1955 (2)	C	James Wildey	Comstock Park	2:06.3y
1956 (1)	C	Bill Gries	Reed City	2:03.3y
1956 (2)	C	Dick Cordes	Comstock Park	2:03.4y
1956 (3)	C	Harold Arft	Armada	2:05.3y
1957 (1)	C	Ron Hopkins	Lansing Everett	2:03.0y
1957 (2)	C	Harold Arft	Armada	2:03.1y
1957 (3)	C	Dick Cordes	Comstock Park	2:05.7y
1958 (1)	C	Dick Cordes	Comstock Park	2:02.5y
1958 (2)	C	Gary Gray	Ypsilanti Roosevelt	2:03.0y
1958 (3)	C	Fred Wenz	Paw Paw	2:05.5y
1959 (1)	C	Gerry Gray	Ypsilanti Roosevelt	2:05.4y
1959 (2)	C	Dick Fraser	Glen Arbor Leelanau School	2:06.2y
1959 (2)	C	Gary Gripman	Quincy	2:06.2y
1960 (1)	C	Larry Hamilton	East Jackson	2:02.8y
1960 (2)	C	Dick Frazier	Glen Arbor Leelanau School	2:02.8y
1960 (3)	C	Wayne Gripman	Quincy	2:04.0y
1961 (1)	C	Steve Cole	Bellevue	2:02.4y
1961 (2)	C	Larry Hamilton	East Jackson	2:03.5y
1961 (3)	C	Joe Zimmer	Richland	2:03.8y
1962	C	Richard Seppelt	Homer	2:02.4y
1963	C	Alan Huffman	Homer	2:00.9y*
1964	C	Dale Sage	Reese	2:00.4y*
1965	C	Dale Sage	Reese	1:58.9y*
1966	C	Jim Vogt	Freeland	1:58.0y*
1967	C	Wayne Wills	Ortonville Brandon	1:56.9y*
1968	C	Charles Brink	Akron-Fairgrove	2:01.2y
1969	C	Al Martin	Saginaw SS Peter & Paul	1:58.5y
1970	C	Dale Bauman	Battle Creek St Phillip	1:57.6y
1971	C	Dave Garcia	Saginaw SS Peter & Paul	1:58.0y
1972	C	John Bennett	Cassopolis	1:56.3y*
1973	C	Mike Wilcox	Byron	1:57.1y
1974	C	Andy Kovac	St Louis	1:58.6y
1975	C	James Aldridge	Detroit Benedictine	1:58.4y
1976	C	James Aldridge	Detroit Benedictine	1:56.1y*
1977	C	Jim Gerhardt	Saginaw SS Peter & Paul	1:58.2y
1978	C	John Darya	Burton Atherton	1:57.2y
1979	C	Paul Diaz	St. Louis	1:56.3y
1980	C	Paul Diaz	St Louis	1:54.9y*
1981	C	Mike Danielson	Muskegon Oakridge	1:55.7
1982	C	Ronald Simpson	Redford St. Mary	1:53.7*
1983	C	Paul Santer	Benzie Central	1:56.2
1984	C	Bob Jones	Saginaw SS Peter & Paul	1:57.9
1985	C	Jeff Barnett	Mason County Central	1:56.30
1986	C	Jeff Barnett	Mason County Central	1:54.60
1987	C	Neal Newman	Detroit Country Day	1:55.91
1988	C	Marc Zweedyk	Grandville Calvin Christian	1:56.0
1989	C	Marc Zweedyk	Grandville Calvin Christian	1:57.41
1990	C	Mike Barnes	Grosse Pointe Liggett	1:57.11
1991	C	John Miller	Leslie	1:58.7
1992	C	Don Watkins	Berrien Springs	1:58.5
1993	C	Chad Rich	Sandusky	1:58.01
1994	C	Chad Rich	Sandusky	1:57.65
1995	C	John Bachholzky	Almont	1:58.17
1996	C	Steve Morales	Kent City	1:55.17
1997	C	Nick Bacholzky	Almont	1:55.32
1998	C	Kris Brown	Ann Arbor Greenhills	1:56.91
1999	C	Kevin Sule	Hemlock	1:57.19
2000	D3	Kevin Sule	Hemlock	1:54.44*
2001	D3	Aaron Nasers	Battle Creek Pennfield	1:55.35
2002	D3	Aaron Nasers	Battle Creek Pennfield	1:54.51
2003	D3	Fil Marlatt	Williamston	1:54.85
2004	D3	Jacob Dubois	East Jackson	1:55.12
2005	D3	Daniel Clark	Jackson Lumen Christi	1:54.22*
2006	D3	David Ash	Williamston	1:57.09
2007	D3	David Ash	Williamston	1:53.86*
2008	D3	Jaramey Bierlein	Saginaw Swan Valley	1:57.0
2009	D3	Nick Radionoff	Benzie Central	1:55.86
2010	D3	Ben Wynsma	Suttons Bay	1:55.64
2011	D3	Luke Bade	Frankenmuth	1:54.32
2012	D3	Zach Zingsheim	Lansing Catholic	1:55.97
2013	D3	Chase Barnett	Mason County Central	1:57.41
2014	D3	Zach Hardway	Hillsdale	1:54.37
2015	D3	Patrick Ludlow	Jackson Lumen Christi	1:55.30
2016	D3	Anthony Evilsizor	Constantine	1:54.68
2017	D3	Brian Patrick	Bridgman	1:53.81*
2018	D3	Devin Gibbs	Leslie	1:55.88

800 – Class D/Division 4 Champions

(y=880 yards)

Year	Class	Name	School	Time
1927	D	Arthur Ford	Trenton	2:13.4y*
1928	D	Lawrence Pedo	Vulcan	2:08.1y*
1929	D	Eldred Townsend	Maple Rapids	2:11.0y
1930	D	Morrell Mason	South Lake	2:11.8y
1931	D	Gerald Engle	Ann Arbor St Thomas	2:11.7y
1932	D	Gerald Engle	Ann Arbor St Thomas	2:10.3y
1933	D	John Devine	Ann Arbor St Thomas	2:10.8y
1934	D	John Martin	Bear Lake	2:13y
1935	D	Wallace Smith	Royal Oak Madison	2:12.6y
1936	D	Gerald Stockel	Dimondale	2:22.1y
1937	D	Ellsworth Matthews	Bear Lake	2:12.8y
1938	D	Ellsworth Matthews	Bear Lake	2:09.3y
1939	D	George Wilson	Michigan School for Deaf	2:12.4y
1940	D (tie)	Richard Klett	Michigan School for Deaf	2:07.6y*
1940	D (tie)	John Burgess	Albion Starr Commonwealth	2:07.6y*
1941	D	Dick Klett	Michigan School for Deaf	nt
1942	D	John Chapman	Mt Morris St Mary	2:12.6y

Year	Class	Name	School	Time
1943		No Meet – World War II		
1944	D	winner unknown		
1945	D	Ralph Unruh	Baroda	2:08.3y
1946 (1)	D	Ralph Unruh	Baroda	2:11.0y
1946 (2)	D	Fred Minor	Michigan School for the Deaf	2:12.3y
1947	D	Bill Golden	St Joseph Lake Mich Catholic	2:08.2y
1948	D	Robert Arend	Baroda	2:11.8y
1949	D	Robert Arend	Baroda	2:09.7y
1950	D	Merlin Gay	Central Lake	2:09.7y
1951 (1)	D	Don Reed	Michigan School for Deaf	2:10.5y
1951 (2)	D	Don Wiegandt	Dearborn Edison	2:11.0y
1952	D	George Sheerer	Litchfield	2:11.0y
1953	D	Cliff Proctor	Kent City	2:08.8y
1954	D	Dave Heimberger	Spring Arbor	2:06.5y*
1955	D	Gordon Fitzgerald	Spring Arbor	2:05.2y*
1956 (1)	D	Gerald Jones	Newaygo	2:08.8y
1956 (2)	D	John Kondziela	Petoskey St Francis	2:08.8y
1957 (1)	D	John Phelps	Dansville	2:10.2y
1957 (2)	D	Bob Lyons	Beal City	2:11.8y
1958 (1)	D	Don Rasmussen	Stanton	2:03.7y*
1958 (2)	D	Bob Lyons	Beal City	2:06.4y
1959 (1)	D	Richard Tonkin	Fairgrove	2:07.3y
1959 (2)	D	Jim Rodebaugh	Schoolcraft	2:11.5y
1960 (1)	D	Bob Scripter	Michigan School for Deaf	2:07.9y
1960 (2)	D	Richard Quast	Marion	2:08.4y
1961 (1)	D	Gerald Blakely	Michigan School for Deaf	2:06.0y
1961 (2)	D	Al Feldpausch	Fowler	2:07.0y
1962	D	Fred Joles	Wolverine	2:04.0y
1963	D	Phil Huber	St Joseph Catholic	2:02.7y*
1964	D	Tom Taylor	Schoolcraft	2:05.2y
1965	D	Jim Pegg	Martin	2:01.2y*
1966	D	Mike Bill	Litchfield	2:02.2y
1967	D	Brian McDonald	Flint St Matthew	2:04.7y
1968	D	Bob Berg	Lake City	2:02.1y
1969	D	Dave Spencer	Lawrence	2:02.4y
1970	D	Pat Shanahan	Flint Holy Rosary	2:01.0y*
1971	D	Van Middlesworth	Climax-Scotts	2:02.6y
1972	D	Lloyd Wilds	Mendon	1:59.8y*
1973	D	Lloyd Wilds	Mendon	1:56.8y*
1974	D	Wayne Wilds	Mendon	1:58.5y
1975	D	Mike Walton	Detroit East Catholic	1:58.0y
1976	D	John Wright	Ann Arbor St Thomas	1:58.1y
1977	D	Steve Courtney	Mendon	1:59.6y
1978	D	Jim Pohl	Mt Pleasant Sacred Heart	1:58.0y
1979	D	Jim Pohl	Mt Pleasant Sacred Heart	1:57.9
1980	D	Ray Robinson	Detroit DePorres	1:57.9
1981	D	Ray Robinson	Detroit DePorres	1:58.4
1982	D	Don Wolbrink	Allendale	1:57.2
1983	D	Brad Reynolds	Maple City Glen Lake	1:58.2
1984	D	Tim Seward	Detroit East Catholic	2:01.3
1985	D	Dave Woday	Allendale	2:00.2
1986	D	Tony Hill	Concord	1:58.31
1987	D	Darrin Ainkley	Pittsford	1:57.90
1988	D	Robert Smith	Warren Bethesda Christian	2:00.59
1989	D	Rob Puroll	Bellaire	1:58.6
1990	D	David Shaw	Litchfield	2:01.06
1991	D	Tom Becker	Fowler	1:58.24
1992	D	David Shaw	Litchfield	1:58.64
1993	D	Jeff Beuche	Ann Arbor Gabriel Richard	1:57.0
1994	D	Ryan Fink	Onekema	2:00.29
1995	D	Ryan Shay	Central Lake	2:00.88
1996	D	Kris Brown	Ann Arbor Greenhills	1:59.85
1997	D	Mark Caswell	Pittsford	1:59.52
1998	D	Ryan Morris	Centreville	1:58.7
1999	D	John Calo	New Buffalo	1:58.17
2000	D4	Garnett Kohler	Brown City	1:56.19*
2001	D4	Kris Kane	Grass Lake	1:57.60
2002	D4	Vershawn Miller	Detroit Benedictine	1:54.97*
2003	D4	Liam Boylan-Pett	Bath	1:55.38
2004	D4	Liam Boylan-Pett	Bath	1:54.06*
2005	D4	Aaron Hunt	Potterville	1:56.64
2006	D4	Aaron Hunt	Potterville	1:55.2
2007	D4	Glen Barker	North Muskegon	1:57.19
2008	D4	Jon Hatfield	Pittsford	1:59.49
2009	D4	Collin Ward	Potterville	1:58.26
2010	D4	Warren Witchell	Dansville	1:57.05
2011	D4	Kyle Tait	Big Rapids Crossroads	1:57.61
2012	D4	David Dantuma	Big Rapids Crossroads	1:59.91
2013	D4	Max Hodges	Evart	1:58.40
2014	D4	Bryce DeGrammont	Mio	1:58.09
2015	D4	Luke Anderson	Harbor Beach	1:57.31
2016	D4	Daniel Mikovits	Concord	1:58.50
2017	D4	Daniel Mikovits	Concord	1:59.00
2018	D4	Stephen Barker	Deckerville	1:56.82

800 – UP Class AB/Division 1 Champions

(y=880 yards)

Year	Class	Name	School	Time
1940	UPB	Everett Mayo	Ironwood	2:10.8y*
1941	UPB	Albert Robbins	Iron Mountain	2:07.4y*
1942	UPB	Fred Babich	Ironwood	2:10.3y
1943		No Meet – World War II		
1944	UPB	John Groos	Escanaba	2:09.2y
1945	UPB	John Holt	Sault Ste Marie	2:04.7y*
1946	UPB	Toivo Savonen	Ironwood	2:09.5y
1947	UPB	Don Bichler	Escanaba	2:09.7y
1948	UPB	Jim Foley	Menominee	2:09.2y
1949	UPB	Jack Veeser	Iron River	2:09.8y
1950	UPB	Bill Rushford	Marquette	2:10.0y
1951	UPB	Dave Zerbel	Escanaba	2:09.2y
1953	UPB	Don Embs	Sault Ste. Marie	2:06.6y
1954	UPB	Melvin Werth	Ironwood	2:07.5y
1955	UPB	James Stafford	Sault Ste. Marie	2:06.5y
1956	UPB	James Stafford	Sault Ste Marie	2:04.6y*
1952 (1)	UPB	Don Embs	Sault Ste. Marie	2:09.0y
1957 (1)	UPB	Jim Brunelle	Escanaba	2:12.9y
1957 (2)	UPB	Kenneth Pelto	Calumet	2:12.3y
1958 (1)	UPB	Jim Collins	Negaunee	2:13.2y
1958 (2)	UPB	Bob King	Manistique	2:14.0y
1959 (1)	UPB	Fred Matson	Munising	2:09.0y
1959 (2)	UPB	Larry Wall	Menominee	2:11.6y
1960 (1)	UPB	Robert Beach	Hancock	2:09.9y
1960 (2)	UPB	Wayne Olson	Manistique	2:06.2y
1961 (1)	UPB	Gary Kruger	Newberry	2:05.1y
1961 (2)	UPB	Jim Maki	Newberry	2:05.9y
1962	UPAB	Gary Kruger	Newberry	2:03.6y*
1963	UPAB	Rene Harger	Munising	2:01.1y*
1964	UPAB	Rene Harger	Munising	2:00.5y*
1965	UPAB	Carl Narkooli	Gwinn	2:05.2y
1966	UPAB	John Ketola	Gwinn	2:03.2y
1967	UPAB	Bill Parkkonen	Ishpeming	2:05.2y
1968	UPAB	Doug Schupp	Iron Mountain	2:04.0y
1969	UPAB	Cliff Young	Gladstone	2:05.0y
1970	UPAB	Doug Schupp	Iron Mountain	2:00.6y
1971	UPAB	Paul Kitti	Calumet	1:59.2y*
1972	UPAB	Leon Hank	Sault Ste. Marie	2:00.1y
1973 (1)	UPAB	Ken Callow	Menominee	2:00.5y
1973 (2)	UPAB	Fred Breitsman	Escanaba	2:04.3y
1974 (1)	UPAB	Ken Callow	Menominee	2:01.6y
1974 (2)	UPAB	Larry Babbitt	Sault Ste. Marie	2:00.1y
1975	UPAB	Larry Babbitt	Sault Ste. Marie	2:00.6y
1976	UPAB	Larry Babbitt	Sault Ste Marie	1:56.3y*
1977	UPAB	Scott Melchoir	Menominee	2:02.2y
1978	UPAB	Chuck Gendron	Gwinn	2:02.7y
1979	UPAB	Chuck Gendron	Gwinn	2:00.9
1980	UPAB	Chuck Gendron	Gwinn	1:58.6
1981	UPAB	Tom Bruce	Sault Ste Marie	2:02.6
1982	UPAB	John Kingston	Marquette	1:59.5
1983	UPAB	Tracy Lokken	Gwinn	2:02.1
1984	UPAB	Mike Nowack	Menominee	2:03.2
1985	UPAB	Fran Champeau	Menominee	2:03.7
1986	UPAB	Tim Casperson	Menominee	2:01.4
1987	UPAB	Eric Werner	Marquette	2:02.0
1988	UPAB	Chris Richard	Kingsford	1:58.9
1989	UPAB	Chris Richard	Kingsford	2:01.2
1990	UPAB	Kelly Keefe	Marquette	2:00.8
1991	UPAB	Kelly Keefe	Marquette	2:00.6
1992	UPAB	Tony Perion	Escanaba	2:07.6
1993	UPAB	Sawn Seaberg	Menominee	2:03.5
1994	UPAB	Rob Martin	Marquette	2:02.3
1995	UPAB	Rob Martin	Marquette	1:55.9*
1996	UPAB	Ryan Horgan	Escanaba	2:01.39
1997	UPAB	Peter Remien	Ishpeming Westwood	2:01.91
1998	UPAB	Caden Rouhomaki	Negaunee	2:00.77
1999	UPAB	Scott Stesney	Menominee	2:02.63
2000	UPAB	Clifford Lindsey	Sault Ste. Marie	2:01.7
2001	UPD1	Clifton Lindsey	Sault Ste. Marie	2:02.1*
2002	UPD1	Griffin Savings	West Iron County	2:00.0*
2003	UPD1	David Echelbarger	Negaunee	2:01.96
2004	UPD1	Stuard Kramer	Marquette	2:02.72
2005	UPD1	Alvin Moore	Gladstone	1:58.06*
2006	UPD1	Dillon Johnston	Marquette	2:03.45
2007	UPD1	Dillon Johnston	Marquette	2:00.16
2008	UPD1	Josh Ostrenga	Escanaba	2:02.90
2009	UPD1	Austin Wissler	Marquette	2:01.95
2010	UPD1	Austin Wissler	Marquette	2:02.30
2011	UPD1	Austin Wissler	Marquette	1:58.35

2012	UPD1	Andrew Bennitt	Marquette	2:03.10
2013	UPD1	Parker Scott	Sault Ste. Marie	2:00.90
2014	UPD1	Parker Scott	Sault Ste. Marie	1:58.59
2015	UPD1	Andrew Banitt	Marquette	2:00.82
2016	UPD1	Lance Rambo	Marquette	1:59.23
2017	UPD1	Ryan Sanderson	Sault Ste. Marie	2:01.35
2018	UPD1	Clayton Sayen	Houghton	1:59.31

800 – UP Class C/Division 2 Champions

(y=880 yards)

1940	UPC	Elton Carlson	Newberry	2:13.2y*
1941	UPC	Herbert Nordeen	Gwinn	2:14.9y
1942	UPC	Michael Serafin	Newberry	2:08.2y*
1943		No Meet – World War II		
1944	UPC	Emil Platske	Ewen	2:14.3y
1945	UPC	Louis Lee	L'Anse	2:12.8y
1946	UPC	Francis Bedell	L'Anse	2:13.3y
1947	UPC	William Swartz	L'Anse	2:12.6y
1948	UPC	Alex Gembolis	Wakefield	2:12.8y
1949	UPC	Bob Morrison	Munising	2:11.1y
1950	UPC	Bob Morrison	Munising	2:10.0y
1951	UPC	Charles Franti	Ewen	2:13.9y
1952	UPC	Nurkkalla	L'Anse	2:12.3y
1953	UPC	James Strong	Ontonagon	2:12.4y
1954	UPC	Humphrey	Ewen	2:15.0y
1955	UPC	Ric Fenske	Houghton	2:14.3y
1956	UPC	Gerald Lambert	St. Ignace	2:12.0y
1957	UPC	Gerald Lambert	St. Ignace	2:12.1y
1958 (1)	UPC	Walsh	Munising	2:14.7y
1958 (2)	UPC	Clark Westman	L'Anse	nt
1959	UPC	Ralph Leiveska	Ontonagon	2:14.4y
1960	UPC	Bill Crouch	St. Ignace	2:09.7y
1961 (1)	UPC	Mike Leanes	Marquette Baraga	2:13.9y
1961 (2)	UPC	Bob Crouch	St. Ignace	2:09.0y
1962	UPC	Mike Leanes	Marquette Baraga	2:08.1y*
1963	UPC	Fred Hagen	Houghton	2:08.1y*
1964	UPC	Prentice Brown	St. Ignace	2:08.1y*
1965	UPC	David Hegg	Ontonagon	2:03.1y*
1966	UPC	Mark Dougovito	Stephenson	2:07.4y
1967	UPC	John Dedo	Stambaugh	2:05.5y
1968	UPC	Dan Floyd	Ontonagon	2:06.4y
1969	UPC	Craig Struble	L'Anse	2:06.1y
1970	UPC	Mitchell Irwin	Rudyard	2:04.4y
1971	UPC	Joseph Brown	L'Anse	2:02.7y*
1972	UPC	Dave Forslund	Bessemer	2:04.8y
1973 (1)	UPC	Malcom Irwin	Rudyard	2:02.7y*
1973 (2)	UPC	Randy DeWitt	Rudyard	2:03.8y
1974	UPC	Ken English	Rudyard	2:03.8y
1975	UPC	Charles Cloninger	Ishpeming Westwood	2:01.9y*
1976	UPC	Charles Cloninger	Ishpeming Westwood	1:58.4y*
1977	UPC	John Davis	Rudyard	2:03.1y
1978	UPC	Jim McNamee	St. Ignace	2:02.5y
1979	UPC	Paul Orchard	Iron River West Iron County	2:02.8
1980	UPC	Darrell Laver	St. Ignace	2:00.9
1981	UPC	Darrell Laver	St. Ignace	2:00.3
1982	UPC	Tim Somerville	Ironwood	2:01.1
1983	UPC	Craig Allen	Iron Mountain	1:59.0
1984	UPC	Craig Allen	Iron Mountain	1:59.3
1985	UPC	Ron Meyer	Iron River West Iron Country	2:02.2
1986	UPC	Mark Balko	Munising	2:01.2
1987	UPC	Don Reynolds	Negaunee	2:01.8
1988	UPC	Shane Jacques	Calumet	1:59.3
1989	UPC	John Novara	Iron Mountain	2:01.5
1990	UPC	Dan Schnell	Stephenson	2:03.0
1991	UPC	Chris Lett	Houghton	1:59.6
1992	UPC	Matt Peters	Hancock	2:05.8
1993	UPC	David DeLisle	Munising	2:00.8
1994	UPC	David DeLisle	Munising	1:59.6
1995	UPC	Tom Miller	Houghton	2:01.2
1996	UPC	Kevin Knierim	Newberry	1:59.6
1997	UPC	Greg Londo	Gwinn	2:02.2
1998	UPC	Peter Remien	Ishpeming Westwood	1:59.7
1999	UPC	Dave Campbell	Calumet	2:01.0
2000	UPC	Pat Kerwin	Munising	2:02.6
2001	UPD2	Matt Mcnamara	Newberry	2:03.9*
2002	UPD2	Jake Rankinen	Ishpeming Westwood	2:03.8*
2003	UPD2	Nick Adams	St. Ignace	2:02.00*
2004	UPD2	Andrew Schultz	Newberry	2:02.22
2005	UPD2	Dan Skog	Norway	2:02.92
2006	UPD2	Brandon Lawrence	Manistique	2:03.97
2007	UPD2	Scott Bond	Munising	1:59.36*
2008	UPD2	Dominic Beckman	Ironwood	2:02.78
2009	UPD2	Dominic Beckman	Ironwood	2:03.29
2010	UPD2	Alan Peterson	Ironwood	2:00.32
2011	UPD2	David Hebert	West Iron County	2:03.27
2012	UPD2	Jano Newlin	Stephenson	2:10.21
2013	UPD2	Grant Holmstrom	Hancock	2:07.45
2014	UPD2	Jared Joki	Ironwood	2:06.58
2015	UPD2	Tommy Potter	Ishpeming	2:11.64
2016	UPD2	Tanney Huotari	Iron Mountain	2:08.37
2017	UPD2	Grady Kerst	Ishpeming	2:00.65
2018	UPD2	Michael Kulas	Iron Mountain	2:09.14

800 – UP Class D/Division 3 Champions

(y=880 yards)

1940	UPD	Richard Feak	Channing	2:17.0y*
1941	UPD	Frederick Blowers	Nahma	2:11.7y*
1942	UPD	Lloyd Rose	Marquette Pierce	2:14.5y
1943		No Meet – World War II		
1944	UPD	Kenneth Maga	Hermansville	2:16.3y
1945	UPD	Emil Platske	Ewen	2:14.5y
1946	UPD	Walter Soumis	Chassell	2:15.6y
1947	UPD	William Larson	Powers	2:15.7y
1948	UPD	Walter Soumis	Chassell	2:15.2y
1949	UPD	Mike Phalen	Nahma	2:16.6y
1950	UPD	Emil Ayotte	Hermansville	2:13.0y
1951	UPD	Karlo Vartti	Eben	2:13.2y
1952 (1)	UPD	Karlo Vartti	Eben	2:12.3y
1953	UPD	Dean Rye	Pickford	2:10.5y*
1954	UPD	Dean Rye	Pickford	2:10.6y
1955	UPD	Steve Johnson	Rapid River	2:10.2y*
1956	UPD	William Wallis	Pickford	2:07.7y*
1957 (1)	UPD	Don McConkey	Pickford	2:20.1y
1957 (2)	UPD	Darrel Ledy	DeTour	2:19.9y
1958 (1)	UPD	Ted O'Brien	Pickford	2:18.5y
1958 (2)	UPD	Wes Wilibee	Rapid River	2:18.3y
1959 (1)	UPD	Gary Crawford	Pickford	2:12.8y
1959 (2)	UPD	Mike Groleau	Nahma	2:13.4y
1960 (1)	UPD	Dave Beacom	Pickford	2:09.1y
1960 (2)	UPD	Gerald Stevenson	DeTour	2:09.7y
1961 (1)	UPD	Don Pomeroy	Nahma	2:12.1y
1961 (2)	UPD	Jerry Stephenson	DeTour	2:10.9y
1962	UPD	Don Pomeroy	Nahma	2:06.0y*
1963	UPD	Ed Breclaw	Vulcan	2:03.6y*
1964	UPD	Dick Soczek	DeTour	2:06.0y
1965	UPD	Paul Adams	Pickford	2:03.0y*
1966	UPD	Jim Belinski	Pickford	2:07.7y
1967	UPD	Dave Lamb	Pickford	2:08.0y
1968	UPD	Bob Wonnacott	Pickford	2:10.7y
1969	UPD	Mark Cambray	Channing	2:09.9y
1970	UPD	Tom Wilson	Pickford	2:05.3y
1971	UPD	John Staff	Ewen-Trout Creek	2:01.7y*
1972	UPD	Louis Feak	Felch North Dickinson	2:04.1y
1973 (1)	UPD	Mark Johns	Wakefield	2:03.6y
1973 (2)	UPD	Pierre Soumis	Chassell	2:03.5y
1974 (1)	UPD	Mark Oberlin	Crystal Falls Forest Park	2:06.6y
1974 (2)	UPD	Martin Wilson	Pickford	2:03.9y
1975	UPD	Mark Oberlin	Crystal Falls Forest Park	2:02.7y
1976	UPD	Mark Oberlin	Crystal Falls Forest Park	1:59.0y*
1977	UPD	Mark Oberlin	Crystal Falls Forest Park	1:59.0y*
1978	UPD	Duane Stevenson	Pickford	2:04.0y
1979	UPD	Greg Belleville	Engadine	2:05.4
1980	UPD	Richard Postma	Rudyard	2:03.7
1981	UPD	Paul Raboin	Norway	2:04.9
1982	UPD	Lewis Sawicki	Baraga	2:03.4
1983	UPD	John Currie	St. Ignace	2:01.4
1984	UPD	Doug Buckler	Wakefield	2:05.5
1985	UPD	Joe Berthume	Engadine	2:05.2
1986	UPD	Garett Cornwell	Rudyard	2:04.5
1987	UPD	Daren Pershinski	Engadine	2:04.6
1988	UPD	Daren Pershinski	Engadine	2:02.2
1989	UPD	Chad Miskovich	Wakefield	2:06.9
1990	UPD	Gary Spolarich	White Pine	2:01.8
1991	UPD	Gary Spolarich	White Pine	2:01.5
1992	UPD	E. Buddy Londo	Wakefield	2:08.4
1993	UPD	Ryan Grondin	Powers-North Central	2:02.1
1994	UPD	Fran Broeders	Felch North Dickinson	2:05.2
1995	UPD	Jason Carter	Eben Junction Superior Cent	2:04.4
1996	UPD	Greg Londo	Wakefield	2:03.6
1997	UPD	Curtis Grondin	Powers-North Central	2:05.9

1998	UPD	Aaron Litzner	St. Ignace	2:04.0
1999	UPD	Dustin Pitrone	Bessemer	2:04.5
2000	UPD	Mike Holmgren	Rapid River	2:04.1
2001	UPD3	Ryan Holm	Wakefield	2:04.8*
2002	UPD3	Ryan Holm	Wakefield	2:03.9*
2003	UPD3	Brad Hunter	Pickford	2:03.59*
2004	UPD3	Luke Moilanen	Powers-North Central	2:04.02
2005	UPD3	Casey Trevarthen	Bessemer	2:04.74
2006	UPD3	Mike Turton	Eben Junction Superior Cent	2:07.96
2007	UPD3	Tyler Veraghen	Powers-North Central	2:04.83
2008	UPD3	Tyler Veraghen	Powers-North Central	2:03.97
2009	UPD3	Tyler Veraghen	Powers-North Central	2:03.41*
2010	UPD3	Tyler Kantiz	Cedarville	2:06.99
2011	UPD3	Gabe Belson	Felch North Dickinson	2:07.87
2012	UPD3	Tyler Keinitz	Eben Junction Superior Cent	2:06.56
2013	UPD3	Josh Hester	Cedarville	2:03.63
2014	UPD3	Dan Blair	Rapid River	2:05.71
2015	UPD3	Brett Hannah	Munising	2:01.45*
2016	UPD3	Brett Hannah	Munising	2:02.12
2017	UPD3	Isaiah Aili	Bessemer	2:07.35
2018	UPD3	Isaiah Aili	Bessemer	2:01.08*

BOYS 1600 METERS

Records

D1	4:00.28	Grant Fisher	Grand Blanc	2015
D2	4:09.45	Daniel Roberts	Vicksburg	2005
D3	4:11.50	Brian Patrick	Bridgman	2017
D4	4:16.94	Larry Julson	Potterville	2009
UPD1	4:18.09	Parker Scott	Sault Ste. Marie	2014
UPD2	4:27.21	Alan Peterson	Ironwood	2010
UPD3	4:33.24	Thomas Bohn	Cedarville	2018

Records by Class (pre-2000 for LP, pre-2001 for UP)

A	4:08.2y	Steve Elliot	Pontiac Central	1975
B	4:13.1y	Tom Duits	Hastings	1974
C	4:13.5	Ron Simpson	Redford St Mary	1982
D	4:15.1	Robert Moore	Allendale	1983
UPAB	4:24.3	Peter Remien	Ishpeming Westwood	1997
UPC	4:18.7	Peter Remien	Ishpeming Westwood	1998
UPD	4:28.6	John Currie	St. Ignace	1983

1600 - Class A/Division 1 Champions

(y=mile / 1609.34m)

1895 all	Fisher	Ann Arbor	5:30.0y*
1898 all	Perley Jones	Lansing	5:18.0y*
1899 all	Chester Barlow	Greenville	5:04.2y*
1900 all	Abbott Widdicomb	Grand Rapids	4:55.0y*
1901 all	Martin Daane	Grand Rapids	4:48.4y*
1902 all	Henry Nancrede	Ann Arbor	4:59.0y
1903 all	Martin Daane (2)	Grand Rapids	nt
1904 all	Charles Behrens (2)	Grand Rapids	nt
1905 all	Eddie Hanavan	Detroit Central	4:51.4y
1906 all	Eddie Hanavan	Detroit Central	4:43y*
1907 all	Eddie Hanavan (2)	Detroit University School	nt
1908 all	Mark Kennedy	Stockbridge	4:47.0y
1909 all	George Cowley	Muskegon	4:43.6y
1910 all	Leland Wesley	Adrian	4:45.4y
1911 all	Fred Cooper	Alma	4:48.0y
1912 all	Earl Sheldon	West Branch	4:41.8y*
1913 all	Earl Sheldon	West Branch	4:33.6y*
1914 all	Robert Meehan	Battle Creek	4:40.6y
1915 all	Harry Thompson	Detroit Eastern	4:38.8y
1916 all	Jake VanderVisse	Grand Rapids Central	4:42.4y
1917 all	Jake VanderVisse	Grand Rapids Central	4:44.8y
1918 all	No Meet (WW I)		
1919 all	Charles Cooper	Detroit Central	4:46.8y
1920 all	Jack Bowen	Grand Rapids Central	4:39.6y
1921 A	Leslie Brenton	Detroit Northwestern	4:44.0y
1922 A	Harold Sutton	Detroit Central	4:39.4y
1923 A	Theodore Hornberger	Ann Arbor	4:41.7y
1924 A	Don Kingsford	Grand Rapids South	4:46.0y
1925 A	Leroy Potter	Coldwater	4:33.0y*
1926 A	Don Kingsford	Grand Rapids South	4:35.8y
1927 A	Ray Swartz	Kalamazoo Central	4:41.5y
1928 A	Ray Swartz	Kalamazoo Central	4:32.2y*
1929 A	Otto Pongrace	Detroit Eastern	4:34.6y
1930 A	James Carr	Detroit Redford	4:42.0y
1931 A	Harold Homer	Muskegon	4:46.5y
1932 A	Lucille Kaiser	Lansing Eastern	4:36.2y
1933 A	Harold Sparks	Saginaw Arthur Hill	4:36.6y
1934 A	Lorimer Miles	Kalamazoo Central	4:31.3y*
1935 A	Pete Fager	Saginaw	4:32.6y
1936 A	Paul Herman	Jackson	4:45.6y
1937 A	Louis Gray	Lansing Eastern	4:37.9y
1938 A	Leroy Schwartzkopf	Saginaw	4:32.9y
1939 A	Rex Woolsey	Jackson	4:39.2y
1940 A	Rex Woolsey	Jackson	4:30.8y*
1941 A	Al Wehner	Monroe	4:35.3y
1942 A	Rutillo Enzastiga	Flint Central	4:37.2y
1944 A	Dick Dombos	Kalamazoo Central	4:37.5y
1945 A	Wilson Gay	Midland	4:37.5y
1946 A	Wilson Gay	Midland	4:36.5y
1947 A	Tom Goretzka	Battle Creek Central	4:37.7y
1948 A	Tom Goretzka	Battle Creek Central	4:39.3y
1949 A	Ray Palmer	Jackson	4:34.3y
1950 A	George Jayne	Ann Arbor	4:35.9y
1951 A	Jim Arnold	Battle Creek	4:41.3y
1952 A	Don Witbrodt	Bay City Central	4:38.3y
1953 A	Gerald Zitny	Dearborn Fordson	4:28.8y*
1954 A	Larry Favorite	Battle Creek Central	4:28.9y
1955 A	Sherry Shaffer	Holland	4:35.0y
1956 A	Steve Rhoades	Grand Rapids Ottawa Hills	4:33.6y
1957 A	Roger Coates	Pontiac	4:38.9y
1958 A	Rem Purdy	Grosse Pointe	4:21.8y*
1959 A	Jerry Bashaw	Lincoln Park	4:29.2y
1960 A	Mac Poll	Lansing Sexton	4:33.7y
1961 A	Mike Kaines	Waterford Township	4:30.8y
1961 A (1)	Mike Selts	Garden City	4:32.2y
1962 A	Lou Scott	Detroit Eastern	4:17.4y*
1963 A	Lou Scott	Detroit Eastern	4:13.2y*
1964 A	Bob Richards	Bloomfield Hills Andover	4:17.3y
1965 A	Brian Moore	Detroit Cass Tech	4:13.4y
1966 A	Jim Love	Flint Central	4:19.0y
1967 A	Ken Hartman	Southfield	4:18.2y
1968 A	Gary Harris	Kalamazoo Loy Norrix	4:19.0y
1969 A	Steve Denforth	Temperance Bedford	4:16.8y
1970 A	Mike Pierce	Grand Blanc	4:14.5y
1971 A	Steve Norris	St Joseph	4:16.3y
1972 A	Dave Wood	Grand Rapids Union	4:13.9y
1973 A	Don Hubbard	Ann Arbor Huron	4:16.9y
1974 A	Ed Grabowski	West Bloomfield	4:15.7y
1975 A	Steve Elliott	Pontiac Central	4:08.2y*
1976 A	Bill Weidenbach	Grosse Pointe North	4:16.3y
1977 A	Lou Cappo	Flushing	4:17.2y
1978 A	Eric Henrickson	Portage Northern	4:13.5y
1979 A	Charles Broski	Hazel Park	4:14.7y
1980 A	Erskine Farrow	Detroit Northern	4:16.7y
1981 A	Bill Stone	Holt	4:12.6y

Year	Name	School	Time
1982 A	Earl Jones	Taylor Center	4:18.1
1983 A	Joseph Mihalic	Warren Tower	4:17.4
1984 A	Jeff Wilson	Flint Kearsley	4:13.1
1985 A	Guy Pace	Ann Arbor Pioneer	4:18.0
1986 A	Mark Reinardy	East Kentwood	4:15.35
1987 A	Cliff Dwell	Lake Orion	4:12.9
1988 A	Chris Buursma	Grandville	4:13.37
1989 A	Tim Pitcher	Monroe	4:13.4
1991 A	Brian Hyde	East Kentwood	4:12.74
1992 A	Ryan Kennedy	Rochester	4:15.76
1993 A	Jim Reif	Flint Central	4:17.22
1994 A	Jim Reif	Flint Central	4:18.3
1995 A	Abdul Alzandani	Dearborn Fordson	4:17.2
1996 A	Abdul Alzandani	Dearborn Fordson	4:14.11
1997 A	Anthony Spires	Detroit Mumford	4:16.99
1998 A	Jason Hartmann	Rockford	4:12.8
1999 A	John Hughes	Traverse City Central	4:10.45
2000 D1	Dathan Ritzenhein	Rockford	4:08.08*
2001 D1	Jon Wojcik	Wyandotte Roosevelt	4:13.40
2002 D1	Tim Moore	Novi	4:14.00
2003 D1	Christopher Catton	Grand Blanc	4:17.91
2004 D1	Justin Switzer	Waterford Kettering	4:09.11
2005 D1	Justin Switzer	Waterford Kettering	4:09.35
2006 D1	Cole Sanseverino	Monroe	4:16.85
2007 D1	Cole Sanseverino	Monroe	4:13.90
2008 D1	Justin Heck	Monroe	4:15.33
2009 D1	Michael Atchoo	Troy	4:07.71*
2010 D1	Omar Kaddurah	Grand Blanc	4:07.67*
2011 D1	Omar Kaddurah	Grand Blanc	4:12.41
2012 D1	Brian Kettle	Milford	4:20.22
2013 D1	T. J. Carey	Lake Orion	4:15.76
2014 D1	Grant Fisher	Grand Blanc	4:10.82
2015 D1	Grant Fisher	Grand Blanc	4:00.28*
2016 D1	Anthony Giannobile	Ann Arbor Skyline	4:11.48
2017 D1	Cole Johnson	Rockford	4:08.60
2018 D1	Cole Johnson	Rockford	4:08.47

1600 - Class B/Division 2 Champions

(y=mile / 1609.34m)

Year	Name	School	Time
1921 B	Don Henry	Petoskey	4:52y*
1922 B	Gilbert Otto	Niles	4:52.4y
1923 B	Leroy Potter	Coldwater	4:46.0y*
1924 B	Leroy Potter	Coldwater	4:37.0y*
1925 B	Albert Hathaway	Petoskey	4:47.9y
1926 B	James O'Connor	Allegan	4:47.6y
1927 B	James O'Connor	Allegan	4:44.4y
1928 B (tie)	Carlton Hoyt	Dowagiac	4:49.4y
1928 B (tie)	Carl Putnam	Caro	4:49.4y
1929 B	Thomas Grimes	Niles	4:44.6y
1930 B	Welcome Steele	St Joseph	4:43.4y
1931 B	Charles Dennis	Ludington	4:36.5y*
1932 B	Charles Dennis	Ludington	4:38.3y
1933 B	J. Nelson Gardner	Hastings	4:34.6y*
1934 B	Ford Hess	South Haven	4:38.3y
1935 B	Bill Davison	Big Rapids	4:40.8y
1936 B	Ed Holderman	Escanaba	4:34.3y*
1937 B	Ralph Cooley	Howell	4:38.2y
1938 B	Casimer Rakowski	Manistee	4:37.8y
1939 B	Ralph Brakcrog	Mt Morris	4:43.1y
1940 B	Ralph Brakcrog	Mt Morris	4:28.2y*
1941 B	Russell Bradley	Charlotte	4:32.7y
1942 B	Bill Holloway	Mt Morris	4:37.8y
1944 B	Vernon Pearson	St Joseph	4:46.5y
1945 B	Russ Gabier	Cadillac	4:38.7y
1946 B	George Howe	Fenton	4:36.6y
1947 B	George Howe	Fenton	4:37.4y
1948 B	Eugene Seidl	Ypsilanti	4:32.8y
1949 B	Cliff Poehlman	Niles	4:41.0y
1950 B	Robert Hall	Lowell	4:34.3y
1951 B	Jack Boughton	Roseville	4:48.1y
1952 B	Bill Pyle	Alma	4:45.2y
1953 B	Bob Mannsfield	Farmington	4:29.5y
1954 B	Jerry Butts	Big Rapids	4:35.5y
1955 B	Gerald Dayharsh	Hart	4:35.2y
1956 B	Walter Schafer	Ludington	4:37.4y
1957 B	Robert Carigon	Lowell	4:37.3y
1958 B	Roger Humbarger	Wyoming Godwin Heights	4:39.3y
1959 B	Roger Humbarger	Wyoming Godwin Heights	4:33.3y
1960 B	John Ogden	Cranbrook	4:34.2y
1961 B (2)	Jeff Taylor	Otsego	4:31.9y
1961 B	Gordon Morey	Clio	4:25.6y*
1962 B	Eric Zemper	Howell	4:22.3y*
1963 B	Ken Coates	Wyoming Park	4:28.0y
1964 B	Dean Rosenberg	North Muskegon	4:27.9y
1965 B	Steve Bishop	Vicksburg	4:22.8y
1966 B	Ron Streng	Detroit Lutheran West	4:21.1y*
1967 B	Ron Streng	Detroit Lutheran West	4:19.1y*
1968 B	Ron Cool	Grand Rapids Northview	4:30.0y
1969 B	James Anglin	Richland Gull Lake	4:23.9y
1970 B	Bill Chenoweth	Charlotte	4:22.2y
1971 B	Dan Tamminga	Grand Rapids Christian	4:19.4y
1972 B	Kim Stafford	Parchment	4:25.5y
1973 B	Greg Meyer	Grand Rapids West Catholic	4:14.9y*
1974 B	Tom Duits	Hastings	4:13.1y*
1975 B	John Monahan	Detroit Austin	4:18.4y
1976 B	Mark Poelman	Wyoming Rogers	4:18.0y
1977 B	Mark Poelman	Wyoming Rogers	4:19.5y
1978 B	Brian Diemer	Grand Rapids South Christian	4:21.5y
1979 B	Brian Diemer	Grand Rapids South Christian	4:14.9y
1980 B	Tim Cannon	Cranbrook	4:17.0
1981 B	Tim Cannon	Cranbrook	4:13.5
1982 B	Simon Hatley	Wyoming Rogers	4:20.8y
1983 B	Don Johns	Center Line	4:15.1
1984 B	Jay Korhonen	GR Forest Hills Central	4:15.8
1985 B	Scott Ritter	Warren Fitzgerald	4:19.46
1986 B	Brad Kirk	Otsego	4:18.0
1987 B	Ian Smith	Plainwell	4:18.76
1988 B	Ron Froeschke	St. Joseph	4:18.64
1989 B	Michael Goodfellow	Oxford	4:22.1
1990 B	Paul McMullen	Cadillac	4:19.9
1991 B	Trevor Smith	Allegan	4:17.34
1992 B	Mike Smedley	Buchanan	4:17.33
1993 B	Mark Goodfellow	Oxford	4:17.03
1994 B	Joe O'Connor	West Branch Ogemaw Heights	4:16.02
1995 B	Troy Lively	Caro	4:19.82
1996 B	Kevin Rossiter	Monroe St. Mary Catholic	4:19.19
1997 B	Russ Gerbers	Wyoming Park	4:19.1
1998 B	Nick Brockway	Richland Gull Lake	4:16.17
1999 B	Kurtis Marlowe	Richland Gull Lake	4:19.64
2000 D2	Justin Blakely	Big Rapids	4:15.82*
2001 D2	Tim Ross	Caledonia	4:13.47*
2002 D2	Tim Ross	Caledonia	4:15.96
2003 D2	Jim Pancoast	Stevensville-Lakeshore	4:13.59
2004 D2	Daniel Roberts	Vicksburg	4:13.83
2005 D2	Daniel Roberts	Vicksburg	4:09.45*
2006 D2	Jay Bilsborrow	Coldwater	4:14.59
2007 D2	Dan Jackson	Dexter	4:15.84
2008 D2	Bobby Aprill	Dexter	4:12.98
2009 D2	Brandon Hoffman	Parma Western	4:18.08
2010 D2	Jeff Sattler	Byron Center	4:16.35
2011 D2	Jeff Sattler	Byron Center	4:18.18
2012 D2	Conner Mora	Cedar Springs	4:13.97
2013 D2	Conner Mora	Cedar Springs	4:10.38
2014 D2	Austin Sargent	Cedar Springs	4:15.85
2015 D2	Morgan Beadlescomb	Algonac	4:13.58
2016 D2	Morgan Beadlescomb	Algonac	4:13.18
2017 D2	Noah Jacobs	Corunna	4:14.03
2018 D2	Shuaib Aljabaly	Coldwater	4:16.56

1600 - Class C/Division 3 Champions

(y=mile / 1609.34m)

Year	Name	School	Time
1921 C	Stub Van Housen	Boyne City	4:54.8y*
1922 C	Donald Seeger	Cass City	4:44.8y*
1923 C	John Goodall	Cass City	4:57.8y
1924 C	Byron Boyd	Ithaca	4:57.6y
1925 C	Myron Smith	Woodland	4:54.9y
1926 C	Arthur Sheldon	Lawton	4:49.9y
1927 C	J. Perry Austin	Three Oaks	4:57.3y
1928 C	Howard Middleswood	Farmington	4:47.9y
1929 C	Clarence Arnold	Charlevoix	4:44.6y*
1930 C	Ralph Wheaton	Paw Paw	4:48.7y
1931 C	Bob Moreland	Kalamazoo St Augustine	4:52.4y
1932 C	Clarence Heacock	Almont	4:42.1y*
1933 C	Harry Clark	Wyoming Godwin Heights	4:45.6y
1934 C	Harry Clark	Wyoming Godwin Heights	4:45.4y
1935 C	George Miller	Grandville	4:42.5y
1937 C	Charles Pierce	Plainwell	4:42.3y
1938 C	Clarence Melvin	Fowlerville	4:40.2y*
1939 C	Stanley Gondek	Milan	4:45.1y
1940 C	Ralph Golding	Keego Harbor	4:39.9y*

Year	Name	School	Time
1941 C	Harold Flynn	Flint Hoover	4:37.6y
1942 C	Wardell Lyke	Mesick	4:38.5y
1944 C	John Klever	Grant	4:35.1y*
1944 D	Allan Stone	Whitehall	5:00.1y
1946 C	Allen Hosler	Milan	4:35.6y
1947 C	Mel Sharrar	St Louis	4:45.4y
1948 C	Mel Sharrar	St Louis	4:40.9y
1949 C	Phillip Kavanaugh	Kalamazoo St Augustine	4:41.0y
1950 C	Jerry Leland	Ypsilanti Roosevelt	4:36.3y
1951 C	Tom Hoffmeyer	Lansing Everett	4:45.0y
1952 C	Jerry Gonser	Saline	4:48.1y
1953 C	Ben Raver	Flint Dye	4:38.8y
1954 C	James MacField	Reed City	4:41.8y
1955 C	Jim Chemenko	Capac	4:36.9y
1956 C	Jim Chemenko	Capac	4:38.8y
1957 C	Ron Little	Almont	4:41.2y
1958 C	Tim Hutton	Grosse Pointe St Paul	4:43.7y
1959 C	Dick Pickering	East Jackson	4:42.0y
1960 C	Dick Pickering	East Jackson	4:33.4y*
1961 C (1)	Ron Ward	North Branch	4:44.1y
1961 C	LeRoy Smith	East Jordan	4:41.1y
1962 C	Thomas Dalton	Lansing St Mary	4:35.4y
1963 C	Thomas Dalton	Lansing St Mary	4:31.0y*
1964 C	Jim Giachino	Kalamazoo University	4:30.6y*
1965 C	Jim Giachino	Kalamazoo University	4:23.7y*
1966 C	Neil Elmer	Springport	4:35.0y
1967 C	Steve Joy	Benzie Central	4:30.3y
1968 C	Andy Jugan	Orchard Lake St Mary	4:30.5y
1969 C	Mike Hamilton	Manchester	4:29.0y
1970 C	Steve Oalma	Central Montcalm	4:28.1y
1971 C	Mike Burns	Carson City-Crystal	4:22.9y*
1972 C	Mike Burns	Carson City-Crystal	4:18.8y*
1973 C	Andy Kovak	St Louis	4:27.5y
1974 C	Steve Bunn	Hartford	4:25.9y
1975 C	Kevin Cain	Addison	4:26.3y
1976 C	Ed LaBair	Mayville	4:23.5y
1977 C	Brad Shaw	Addison	4:26.1y
1978 C	Martin Schulist	Whitehall	4:18.1y*
1979 C	Guy Jacobson	Whitehall	4:15.8y*
1980 C	Paul Diaz	St. Louis	4:20.8y
1981 C	Tim Broekema	Kalamazoo Christian	4:21.1
1982 C	Ron Simpson	Redford St Mary	4:13.5*
1983 C	Kirk Scharch	Unionville-Sebewaing	4:17.1
1984 C	Jesse McGuire	Bronson	4:20.4
1985 C	Jeff Barnett	Mason County Central	4:21.99
1986 C	Jeff Barnett	Mason County Central	4:18.16
1987 C	Greg Parker	Capac	4:19.04
1988 C	David Hahn	Three Oaks River Valley	4:21.9
1989 C	Jared Glover	Kingsley	4:22.15
1990 C	Steve Johnson	Breckenridge	4:23.02
1991 C	Mike Ball	Hudson	4:21.2
1992 C	Chris Heggelund	Laingsburg	4:18.3
1993 C	Matt Smith	Charlevoix	4:23.54
1994 C	Art Smith	Bangor	4:20.81
1995 C	Justin Curry	Carson City-Crystal	4:23.02
1996 C	Ryan Wenk	Shelby	4:22.52
1997 C	Matt Zissler	Hemlock	4:20.20
1998 C	Curtis King	Mason County Central	4:24.61
1999 C	Jacques Henning	Harbor Springs	4:18.44
2000 D3	Kevin Sule	Hemlock	4:12.62*
2001 D3	Aaron Nasers	Battle Creek Pennfield	4:17.40
2002 D3	Aaron Nasers	Battle Creek Pennfield	4:21.29
2003 D3	Jacob Dubois	East Jackson	4:19.02
2004 D3	Jacob Dubois	East Jackson	4:17.67
2005 D3	David Brent	Monroe St. Mary Catholic	4:14.93
2006 D3	Dan Nix	Williamston	4:22.00
2007 D3	Maverick Darling	Ovid-Elsie	4:15.07
2008 D3	Maverick Darling	Ovid-Elsie	4:16.97
2009 D3	Alex Wilson	Kent City	4:17.82
2010 D3	Alex Wilson	Kent City	4:15.77
2011 D3	Stu Crowell	Parchment	4:19.97
2012 D3	Joe Oehrli	Reed City	4:19.14
2013 D3	Chase Barnett	Mason County Central	4:15.97
2014 D3	Chase Barnett	Mason County Central	4:17.71
2015 D3	Keenan Rebera	Lansing Catholic	4:17.09
2016 D3	Abe Visser	Grandville Calvin Christian	4:16.62
2017 D3	Brian Patrick	Bridgman	4:11.50*
2018 D3	Corey Gorgas	Saugatuck	4:15.74

1600 - Class D/Division 4 Champions

(y=mile / 1609.34m)

Year	Name	School	Time
1927 D	Arthur Sheldon	Lawton	5:02.7y*
1928 D	Ralph Griffith	Sand Creek	4:52.9y*
1929 D	Frederick Walker	Crystal	5:06.7y
1930 D	Orla Currier	Okemos	5:00.0y
1931 D	Frederick Walker	Crystal	5:05.9y
1932 D	Howard Dengmore	Hanover	4:56.8y
1933 D	Arnold Borders	Napoleon	4:53.9y
1934 D	Harold Olson	Bergland	4:46.2y*
1935 D	Robert Roe	Clayton	4:56.6y
1936 D	Maynard Calhoun	Dimondale	5:05.1y
1937 D	John Eldridge	Bear Lake	5:00.6y
1938 D	John Eldridge	Bear Lake	4:43.5y*
1939 D	Calvin Kelsey	Albion Starr Commonwealth	4:55.3y
1940 D	Calvin Kelsey	Merritt	4:47.9y
1941 D	Edson Carey	Onekama	4:45.9y
1942 D	Paul Noe	Mt Morris St Mary	4:57.6y
1944 D	Allan Stone	Whitehall	5:00.1y
1945 D	Allan Stone	Whitehall	5:00.5y
1946 D	Ed LaPointe	Baldwin	5:04.0y
1947 D	Junior Dongoille	St Joseph Lake Mich Catholic	4:46.8y
1948 D	Ivan Davis	Merrill	4:44.9y
1949 D	George Corcoran	Mt Morris St Mary	4:46.0y
1950 D	George Corcoran	Mt Morris St Mary	4:52.3y
1951 D	Jim Chapman	Spring Arbor	4:55.2y
1952 D	Morris Ruddy	Maple Grove	4:59.4y
1953 D	Richard Spoor	Brethren	4:48.9y
1954 D	Richard Spoor	Brethren	4:39.1y*
1955 D	Les Grable	Dimondale	4:43.4y
1956 D	Les Grable	Dimondale	4:41.1y
1957 D	Vern Reed	Vermontville	4:48.1y
1958 D	Bill Steffel	Petoskey St Francis	4:39.9y
1959 D	Dave Jacobs	Beal City	4:46.5y
1960 D	Dave Jacobs	Beal City	4:42.9y
1961 D	Neil Browne	Lawton	4:36.3y*
1962 D	Hildred Lewis	Memphis	4:35.4y*
1963 D	Paul Pung	Portland St Patrick	4:37.5y
1964 D	George Danks	Brethren	4:49.2y
1965 D	George Danks	Brethren	4:40.8y
1966 D	Jim Pegg	Martin	4:30.0y*
1967 D	Bob Boudreau	Flint St Matthew	4:32.8y
1968 D	Tom Atwater	Lawton	4:34.1y
1969 D	Dennis Hicks	Ecorse St Francis	4:39.7y
1970 D	Roy Heminger	Litchfield	4:42.1y
1971 D	Roy Heminger	Litchfield	4:37.9y
1972 D	Brad Courtney	Mendon	4:31.5y
1973 D	Brad Courtney	Mendon	4:24.3y*
1974 D	Brad Courtney	Mendon	4:28.8y
1975 D	Mark Dentler	Mendon	4:30.2y
1976 D	Bill Lannen	Mt Pleasant Sacred Heart	4:24.5y
1977 D	Robert Duerksen	Mancelona	4:32.2y
1978 D	Jerry Curtis	Akron Fairgrove	4:24.0y*
1979 D	Roderick Brevard	Detroit East Catholic	4:19.1*
1980 D	Ray Robinson	Detroit DePorres	4:37.8
1981 D	Shaun Davies	Bellaire	4:29.4
1982 D	Ron Landry	Oakland Christian	4:26.0
1983 D	Robert Moore	Allendale	4:15.1*
1984 D	Dave Schuiteman	North Muskegon	4:24.57
1985 D	Dave Woday	Allendale	4:26.9
1986 D	Dave Dubin	Ann Arbor Greenhills	4:23.83
1987 D	Don Price	Fulton-Middleton	4:33.10
1988 D	Ken Matzem	Mason County Eastern	4:28.02
1989 D	Tom Becker	Fowler	4:27.8
1990 D	Tom Becker	Fowler	4:22.93
1991 D	Tom Becker	Fowler	4:21.43
1992 D	Bret Clements	Bath	4:28.05
1993 D	Casey Shay	Central Lake	4:21.9
1994 D	Eric Bierstetal	Fowler	4:23.1
1995 D	Ryan Shay	Central Lake	4:28.73
1996 D	Ryan Shay	Central Lake	4:22.00
1997 D	Ryan Shay	Central Lake	4:17.13
1998 D	Ron Hein	Galien	4:32.4
1999 D	Ron Hein	Galien	4:29.76
2000 D4	Will Boylan-Pett	Bath	4:23.16*
2001 D4	Will Boylan-Pett	Bath	4:21.12*
2002 D4	Will Boylan-Pett	Bath	4:21.66
2003 D4	Liam Boylan-Pett	Bath	4:19.47*
2004 D4	Liam Boylan-Pett	Bath	4:24.10
2005 D4	Aaron Hunt	Potterville	4:24.29
2006 D4	Aaron Hunt	Potterville	4:23.16
2007 D4	Alex Harris	Royal Oak Shrine	4:22.04
2008 D4	Tim Jagielski	Waldron	4:24.05
2009 D4	Larry Julson	Potterville	4:16.94*
2010 D4	Kyle Stacks	Concord	4:19.44
2011 D4	Kyle Tait	Big Rapids Crossroads	4:25.92
2012 D4	David Dantuma	Big Rapids Crossroads	4:25.92

2013 D4	Nick Vander Kooi	Fremont Providence Christian	4:25.89
2014 D4	Luke Anderson	Harbor Beach	4:17.49
2015 D4	Luke Anderson	Harbor Beach	4:17.77

2016 D4	Santana Scott	Evart	4:22.89
2017 D4	Jeremy Kloss	Harbor Springs	4:25.73
2018 D4	Alex Grifka	Ubly	4:27.90

1600 - UP Class AB/Division 1 Champions

(y=mile / 1609.34m)

1940 UPB	Joe Herbert	Menominee	4:55.3y*
1941 UPB	Eugene Danielson	Wakefield	4:40.8y*
1942 UPB	Clarence Vicklund	Iron Mountain	4:47.3y
1944 UPB	Roy Williams	Escanaba	4:46.1y
1945 UPB	Coy Tyrell	Manistique	4:46.1y
1946 UPB	Coy Tyrell	Manistique	4:43.3y
1947 UPB	Glen Porterfield	Menominee	4:40.9y
1948 UPB	Joe Supanich	Calumet	4:46.1y
1949 UPB	Joe Supanich	Calumet	4:45.5y
1950 UPB	Rod Mattson	Ironwood	4:44.7y
1951 UPB	Donald Quick	Manistique	4:45.4y
1952 UPB	Truman Van Luven	Sault Ste. Marie	4:47.2y
1953 UPB	Dick Casey	Escanaba	4:44.6y
1954 UPB	Gary DeLisle	Munising	4:41.7y
1955 UPB	Gary DeLisle	Munising	4:35.2y*
1956 UPB	Bob Kuntze	Stephenson	4:44.1y
1957 UPB	Tom Anderson	Negaunee	4:52.6y
1958 UPB	Tom Anderson	Negaunee	4:52.5y
1959 UPB	Bob Beauchamp	Iron River	4:46.0y
1960 UPB	Peter Ladoceur	Escanaba	4:52.1y
1961 UPB	Ken Johnson	Marquette	4:48.9y
1962 UPAB	Ken Johnson	Marquette	4:33.9y*
1963 UPAB	Bruce Swanson	Ishpeming	4:37.6y
1964 UPAB	Bruce Swanson	Ishpeming	4:39.5y
1965 UPAB	Rod LaFond	Newberry	4:42.1y
1966 UPAB	Al Schupp	Iron Mountain	4:38.6y
1967 UPAB	Gordon Leppanen	Ishpeming	4:40.3y
1968 UPAB	Dave Hasse	Menominee	4:36.3y
1969 UPAB	Paul Williams	Newberry	4:38.9y
1970 UPAB	Paul Williams	Newberry	4:36.9y
1971 UPAB	Ivan Plude	Menominee	4:30.5y*
1972 UPAB	Mark Patrick	Rudyard	4:33.9y
1973 UPAB	Gerrry Krause	Escanaba	4:33.0y
1974 UPAB	Kurt Behrendt	Ironwood	4:42.4y
1975 UPAB	Kevin Holmes	Escanaba	4:37.2y
1976 UPAB	Mike Wickens	Gwinn	4:32.2y
1977 UPAB	Mike Ostrenga	Menominee	4:30.9y
1978 UPAB	Don Rondeau	Kingsford	4:36.4y
1979 UPAB	Mike Photenhauer	Menominee	4:28.0*

1980 UPAB	Mike Photenhauer	Menominee	4:27.6*
1981 UPAB	Tom Bruce	Sault Ste Marie	4:38.8
1982 UPAB	John Kingston	Marquette	4:29.5
1983 UPAB	Jon Ottoson	Marquette	4:36.6
1984 UPAB	Tracy Lokken	Gwinn	4:29.9
1985 UPAB	Fran Champeau	Menominee	4:41.0
1986 UPAB	Dennis Murvich	Kingsford	4:35.9
1987 UPAB	Gary Cregg	Escanaba	4:30.3
1988 UPAB	Rhett Fisher	Escanaba	4:36.0
1989 UPAB	Jon Berry	Gwinn	4:37.8
1990 UPAB	Larry Lapachin	Ironwood	4:32.0
1991 UPAB	Jason Ladd	Menominee	4:35.9
1992 UPAB	Bob Knapp	Kingsford	4:44.9
1993 UPAB	Bob Knapp	Kingsford	4:36.7
1994 UPAB	Bob Knapp	Kingsford	4:36.8
1995 UPAB	Andy Ramos	Gwinn	4:36.7
1996 UPAB	Peter Remien	Ishpeming Westwood	4:35.0
1997 UPAB	Peter Remien	Ishpeming Westwood	4:24.3*
1998 UPAB	Caden Ruohomaki	Negaunee	4:34.6
1999 UPAB	Scott Stesney	Marquette	4:41.6
2000 UPAB	Clifton Lindsey	Sault Ste. Marie	4:27.0
2001 UPD1	Clifton Lindsey	Sault Ste. Marie	4:27.5*
2002 UPD1	Jamieson Cihak	Marquette	4:22.3*
2003 UPD1	Nick Richer	Negaunee	4:37.93
2004 UPD1	Stuart Kramer	Marquette	4:33.04
2005 UPD1	Chris Davis	Gladstone	4:37.94
2006 UPD1	Jared Johnston	Marquette	4:31.46
2007 UPD1	Jared Johnston	Marquette	4:29.05
2008 UPD1	Jake Isaaccson	Menominee	4:34.03
2009 UPD1	Mickey Sanders	Marquette	4:32.25
2010 UPD1	Mickey Sanders	Marquette	4:40.78
2011 UPD1	Mickey Sanders	Marquette	4:26.28
2012 UPD1	Andrew Stenberg	Escanaba	4:45.14
2013 UPD1	Parker Scott	Sault Ste. Marie	4:31.98
2014 UPD1	Parker Scott	Sault Ste. Marie	4:18.09*
2015 UPD1	Lance Rambo	Marquette	4:28.84
2016 UPD1	Lance Rambo	Marquette	4:25.26
2017 UPD1	Colton Yesney	Negaunee	4:24.81
2018 UPD1	Colton Yesney	Negaunee	4:23.49

1600 - UP Class C/Division 2 Champions

(y=mile / 1609.34m)

1940 UPC	Phillip Fyvie	Newberry	4:56.7y*
1941 UPC	R. LePage	Lake Linden	4:49.2y*
1942 UPC	Phillip Fyvie	Newberry	4:53.7y
1944 UPC	George Williams	Wakefield	4:55.9y
1945 UPC	George Williams	Wakefield	4:50.1y
1946 UPC	Erven Maki	Wakefield	5:05.0y
1947 UPC	Marshall King	Hancock	4:48.6y*
1948 UPC	George Karling	Wakefield	4:55.1y
1949 UPC	Bob Hitch	L'Anse	4:54.0y
1950 UPC	Robert Hitch	L'Anse	4:44.0y*
1951 UPC	Elmer Rantanen	Munising	4:54.9y
1952 UPC	Spenser Carlson	Houghton	5:04.2y
1953 UPC	Roger Ryynanen	Painesdale	4:52.4y
1954 UPC	Roger Ryynanen	Painesdale	4:49.1y
1955 UPC	Roger Ryynanen	Painesdale	4:44.2y
1956 UPC	Edward Hocking	Wakefield	nt
1957 UPC	Bernard Bugg	Munising	4:56.6y
1958 UPC	B. Briggs	Munising	4:56.0y
1959 UPC	John Hendrickson	Lake Linden	5:06y
1960 UPC	John Hendrickson	Lake Linden	4:52.6y
1961 UPC	Joe Stevens	L'Anse	4:57.6y
1962 UPC	Joe Stevens	L'Anse	4:45.7y
1963 UPC	Charles Ghidorzi	Crystal Falls	4:53.7y
1964 UPC	Dick Tretheway	Bessemer	4:47.8y
1965 UPC	Bob Jackson	Gwinn	4:48.6y
1966 UPC	Ken Kline	Stephenson	4:46.6y
1967 UPC	Lyle Ross	Rudyard	4:50.9y
1968 UPC	Stanley Johns	Wakefield	4:53.3y
1969 UPC	Bob Holmes	Crystal Falls	4:49.7y
1970 UPC	James Hagen	St. Ignace	4:39.5y*
1971 UPC	Larry Green	Stephenson	4:28.3y*
1972 UPC	Larry Green	Stephenson	4:36.0y
1973 UPC	Brad Benam	Munising	4:29.8y
1974 UPC	Brad Benam	Munising	4:32.4y

1975 UPC	Charles Williams	Newberry	4:37.8y
1976 UPC	Reg McGuire	Ontonagon	4:32.3y
1977 UPC	Pierre Ogea	Ishpeming	4:35.5y
1978 UPC	Bob Nettell	Hancock	4:36.5y
1979 UPC	Paul Orchard	Iron River West Iron Country	4:25.2*
1980 UPC	Darrell Laver	St. Ignace	4:28.9
1981 UPC	John Furno	Iron Mountain	4:32.9
1982 UPC	John Furno	Iron Mountain	4:24.4*
1983 UPC	John Furno	Iron Mountain	4:21.9*
1984 UPC	John Currie	St. Ignace	4:24.6
1985 UPC	Mark St. Amour	Iron Mountain	4:33.8
1986 UPC	Mark Balko	Munising	4:33.6
1987 UPC	Jeff Legeret	Iron Mountain	4:34.7
1988 UPC	Bob Schnell	Stephenson	4:29.0
1989 UPC	Chris Lett	Houghton	4:31.7
1990 UPC	Chris Lett	Houghton	4:31.6
1991 UPC	Chris Lett	Houghton	4:23.9
1992 UPC	David Schnell	Stephenson	4:47.0
1993 UPC	David DeLisle	Munising	4:33.5
1994 UPC	David DeLisle	Munising	4:27.0
1995 UPC	Tom Miller	Houghton	4:31.5
1996 UPC	Kevin Knierim	Newberry	4:25.1
1997 UPC	Aaron Litzner	St. Ignace	4:35.1
1998 UPC	Peter Remien	Ishpeming Westwood	4:18.7*
1999 UPC	Dave Campbell	Calumet	4:37.6
2000 UPC	Corey King	Hancock	4:33.4
2001 UPD2	Matt Mcnamara	Newberry	4:37.7*
2002 UPD2	Brent Malaski	Rudyard	4:35.6*
2003 UPD2	Jake Rankinen	Ishpeming Westwood	4:37.37
2004 UPD2	Andrew Schultz	Newberry	4:38.53
2005 UPD2	Andrew Schultz	Newberry	4:37.30
2006 UPD2	Scott Bond	Munising	4:46.57
2007 UPD2	Scott Bond	Munising	4:34.59*
2008 UPD2	Alan Peterson	Ironwood	4:34.59*
2009 UPD2	Dominic Beckman	Ironwood	4:34.33*

2010	UPD2	Alan Peterson	Ironwood	4:27.21*	2015	UPD2	Jared Joki	Ironwood	4:43.35
2011	UPD2	David Hebert	West Iron County	4:34.62	2016	UPD2	Nate Carey	Iron Mountain	4:45.04
2012	UPD2	Jono Newlin	Stephenson	4:53.12	2017	UPD2	Grady Kerst	Ishpeming	4:29.11
2013	UPD2	Dan Kulas	Iron Mountain	4:42.03	2018	UPD2	Nick Niemi	Ironwood	4:42.87
2014	UPD2	Jared Joki	Ironwood	4:45.18					

1600 - UP Class D/Division 3 Champions

(y=mile / 1609.34m)

1940	UPD	Ernest Leonardi	Alpha	4:46.8y*	1980	UPD	Doug Bernard	Cooks-Big Bay de Noc	4:29.3*
1941	UPD	Joe Clabots	Rock	4:48.6y	1981	UPD	John Ackley	Cedarville	4:41.0
1942	UPD	P. Crowe	Watersmeet	4:58.8y	1982	UPD	Daniel Giesen	Norway	4:34.7
1944	UPD	Frank Hoholik	Alpha	5:22.3y	1983	UPD	John Currie	St. Ignace	4:28.6*
1945	UPD	James Niemi	Ewen	5:08.7y	1984	UPD	Melvin Willis	Brimley	4:43.3
1946	UPD	Robert Ostrom	Rapid River	5:06.4y	1985	UPD	Charlie Cox	Crystal Falls Forest Park	4:41.3
1947	UPD	Elmer Wesman	Ewen	4:57.0y	1986	UPD	Charlie Cox	Crystal Falls Forest Park	4:39.5
1948	UPD	winner unknown			1987	UPD	Deren Pershinsky	Engadine	4:33.7
1949	UPD	Louis Nordeen	Gwinn	4:54.9y	1988	UPD	Deren Pershinsky	Engadine	4:30.2
1950	UPD	Don Johnson	Eben	5:11.0y	1989	UPD	Glen Avena	Crystal Falls Forest Park	4:38.6
1951	UPD	Don Johnson	Eben	5:04.5y	1990	UPD	Gary Spolarich	White Pine	4:32.5
1952	UPD	Patrick Culbert	Gwinn	4:52.3y	1991	UPD	Gary Spolarich	White Pine	4:32.7
1953	UPD	Ron Groleau	Nahma	4:55.4y	1992	UPD	Ryan Grondin	Powers-North Central	4:50.2
1954	UPD	Ron Groleau	Nahma	4:50.9y	1993	UPD	Ryan Grondin	Powers-North Central	4:38.5
1955	UPD	Carl Hanna	Pickford	4:47.5y	1994	UPD	Jason Maki	Eben Junction Superior Central	4:39.1
1956	UPD	Donald Stephenson	Pickford	4:45.0y*	1995	UPD	Curtis Grondin	Powers-North Central	4:39.5
1957	UPD	Steven Johnson	Rapid River	4:54.0y	1996	UPD	Curtis Grondin	Powers-North Central	4:44.1
1958	UPD	Mike Groleau	Nahma	4:58.9y	1997	UPD	Curtis Grondin	Powers-North Central	4:45.1
1959	UPD	Mike McCarthy	Pickford	4:51.0y	1998	UPD	Aaron Litzner	St. Ignace	4:29.5
1960	UPD	Dwight Harwood	Rapid River	4:47.4y	1999	UPD	Mike Holmgren	Rapid River	4:47.0
1961	UPD	John LaVallee	Garden	4:46.5y	2000	UPD	Mike Holmgren	Rapid River	4:38.9
1962	UPD	John LaVallee	Garden	4:41.3y*	2001	UPD3	Ryan Holm	Wakefield	4:36.3*
1963	UPD	Don Gattra	Vulcan	4:41.9y	2002	UPD3	Ryan Holm	Wakefield	4:35.2*
1964	UPD	Doug Ehle	Cedarville	4:42.4y	2003	UPD3	Brad Hunter	Pickford	4:36.18
1965	UPD	John Stano	Ironwood St. Ambrose	4:42.4y	2004	UPD3	Sam Kilpela	Painesdale-Jeffers	4:37.30
1966	UPD	Don Innerebner	Champion	4:47.8y	2005	UPD3	Tyler Crossman	Rapid River	4:42.63
1967	UPD	Mike Skytta	Champion	4:42.0y	2006	UPD3	Richard Gibson	Pickford	4:44.29
1968	UPD	Mike Skytta	Champion	4:44.2y	2007	UPD3	Tyler Crossman	Rapid River	4:41.53
1969	UPD	Stanley Johns	Wakefield	4:43.6y	2008	UPD3	Tyler Crossman	Rapid River	4:34.01*
1970	UPD	Bob Jacquart	Ironwood Catholic	4:38.4y*	2009	UPD3	Jonathan Kilpela	Painesdale-Jeffers	4:35.05
1971	UPD	Dennis Brunnnie	Wakefield	4:43.7y	2010	UPD3	Tony Silva	Crystal Falls Forest Park	4:44.12
1972	UPD	Mike Carr	Powers-North Central	4:40.3y	2011	UPD3	Jacob Mahoski	Munising	4:41.12
1973	UPD	Mike Carr	Powers-North Central	4:34.7y*	2012	UPD3	Andrew Kelto	Munising	4:51.14
1974	UPD	Jim Leach	Pickford	4:45.2y	2013	UPD3	Josh Hester	Cedarville	4:37.79
1975	UPD	Jim Leach	Pickford	4:39.5y	2014	UPD3	Brett Hannah	Munising	4:41.62
1976	UPD	Roger Behrens	DeTour	4:42.1y	2015	UPD3	Brett Hannah	Munising	4:38.09
1977	UPD	Mark Oberlin	Crystal Falls Forest Park	4:35.6y	2016	UPD3	Brett Hannah	Munising	4:37.76
1978	UPD	John Tibert	White Pine	4:35.4y	2017	UPD3	Isaiah Aili	Bessemer	4:39.82
1979	UPD	Adre Soumis	Chassell	4:33.9*	2018	UPD3	Thomas Bohn	Cedarville	4:33.24*

BOYS 3200 METERS

Records

D1	8:43.32	Dathan Ritzenhein	Rockford	2001
D2	8:55.57	Noah Jacobs	Corunna	2016
D3	9:08.04	Evan Goodell	St. Louis	2017
D4	9:22.07	Stephan Shay	Central Lake	2004
UPD1	9:50.43	Colton Yesney	Negaunee	2018
UPD2	9:47.28	Jake Rankinen	Ishpeming Westwood	2003
UPD3	10:10.1	Ryan Holm	Wakefield	2001

Records by Class (pre-2000 for LP, pre-2001 for UP)

A	8:59.20	Brian Grosso	Walled Lake Western	1989
B	9:11.6	Mark Smith	Cadillac	1981
C	9:20.0y	Martin Schulist	Whitehall	1978
D	9:25.68	Ryan Shay	Central Lake	1997
UPAB	9:35.7y	Gary Santi	Ishpeming	1971
UPC	9:22.7y	Fred Teddy	L'Anse	1972
UPD	9:49.9	Aaron Litzner	St. Ignace	1998

3200 - Class A/Division 1 Champions

(y=2 miles / 3218.68m)

1901	all	Chester Barlow	Greenville	10:52.0y*	1905	all	Will Ben-O'liel	Ann Arbor	10:36.0y
1902	all	Floyd Rowe	Battle Creek	nt	1906	all	Will Ben-O'liel	Ann Arbor	10:34.5y
1903	all	Floyd Rowe	Battle Creek	11:10.0y	1907	all	Will Ben-O'liel	Ann Arbor	11:32.7y
1904	all	Floyd Rowe	Battle Creek	10:29.0y*	1908	all (tie)	Bill Mann	Muskegon	
							10:29.0y*		

1908 all (tie) Charles Henderson	Ann Arbor		1991 A	Gary Kinnee	Flint Kearsley	9:33.70
10:29.0y*			1992 A	Chris Rudolph	Detroit Henry Ford	9:24.34
1909 all	Bill Mann	Muskegon	10:42.6y	1993 A	Gary Kinnee	Flint Kearsley	9:31.12
1910 all	John Bishop	Hillsdale	10:18.4y*	1994 A	Todd Snyder	Ann Arbor Pioneer	9:17.1
1967 A	Ken House	Detroit Finney	9:25.7y*	1995 A	Todd Snyder	Ann Arbor Pioneer	9:09.9
1968 A	Richard Gross	Grosse Pointe	9:19.3y*	1996 A	Abdul Alzindani	Dearborn Fordson	9:26.70
1969 A	Richard Schott	Grosse Pointe North	9:26.4y	1997 A	Anthony Spires	Detroit Mumford	9:23.13
1970 A	Richard Schott	Grosse Pointe North	9:15.8y*	1998 A	Jason Hartmann	Rockford	9:24.54
1971 A	David Baker	Flint Kearsley	9:15.4y*	1999 A	Dathan Ritzenhein	Rockford	9:16.16
1972 A	Nick Ellis	Detroit Cooley	9:14.8y*	2000 D1	Dathan Ritzenhein	Rockford	9:00.63*
1973 A	Mike McGuire	Farmington	9:12.0y*	2001 D1	Dathan Ritzenhein	Rockford	8:43.32*
1974 A	Pat Davey	Birmingham Brother Rice	9.00.4y*	2002 D1	Tim Moore	Novi	9:21.90
1975 A	Tom Calvert	Jackson	9:13.7y	2003 D1	Dustin Voss	Saline	9:08.58
1976 A	Sam James	Highland Park	9:04.7y	2004 D1	Neal Naughton	Walled Lake Western	9:08.81
1977 A	Gary Carter	St Clair Shores Lakeview	9:00.4y*	2005 D1	John Black	Birmingham Brother Rice	9:14.59
1978 A	Eric Hendricksen	Portage Northern	9:04.9y	2006 D1	Pete Loy	Warren DeLaSalle	9:27.45
1979 A	Brian Olsen	Jackson	9:14.5y	2007 D1	David Emery	Pinckney	9:22.1
1980 A	Doug Tolson	Wayne Memorial	9:13.8y	2008 D1	Justin Heck	Monroe	9:20.32
1981 A	Bill Brady	Mt Clemens	9:22.3y	2009 D1	Reed Kamyszek	Grand Rapids Kenowa Hills	9:16.66
1982 A	Jamie Elliott	Royal Oak Dondero	9:21.5	2010 D1	Reed Kamyszek	Grand Rapids Kenowa Hills	9:14.49
1983 A	Erik Koskinen	Swartz Creek	9:19.5	2011 D1	Evan Chiplock	Saginaw Heritage	9:20.90
1984 A	Tim Fraleigh	Ann Arbor Pioneer	9:25.9	2012 D1	Garret Zuk	White Lake Lakeland	9:04.35
1985 A	Eric Koskinen	Swartz Creek	9:16.00	2013 D1	Grant Fisher	Grand Blanc	9:04.33
1986 A	Todd Williams	Monroe	9:11.63	2014 D1	Grant Fisher	Grand Blanc	9:07.11
1987 A	Todd Williams	Monroe	9:01.40	2015 D1	Grant Fisher	Grand Blanc	8:53.41
1988 A	Brian Grosso	Walled Lake Western	9:15.29	2016 D1	Jacob Lee	Fenton	9:07.72
1989 A	Brian Grosso	Walled Lake Western	8:59.20*	2017 D1	Dominick Dimambro	Fenton	9:07.79
1990 A	Bill Stricklen	Sterling Heights Ford	9:13.54	2018 D1	Nick Foster	Ann Arbor Pioneer	9:07.93

3200 - Class B/Division 2 Champions

(y=2 miles / 3218.68m)

1967 B	Norm Cepela	Wyoming Rogers	9:48.2y*	1993 B	Bob Busquaert	St Clair Shores Lakeview	9:26.51
1968 B	Paul Baldwin	Flint Bendle	9:40.4y*	1994 B	Tom Chorny	Fruitport	9:30.80
1969 B	Jerry Shinkel	Detroit St Anthony	9:32.9y*	1995 B	Tom Chorny	Fruitport	9:25.99
1970 B	Jim Goodfellow	Oxford	9:28.2y*	1996 B	Nick Brockway	Richland Gull Lake	9:22.59
1971 B	Doug O'Berry	Oxford	9:35.7y	1997 B	Nick Brockway	Richland Gull Lake	9:14.7
1972 B	Herb Lindsay	Reed City	9:22.9y*	1998 B	Nick Brockway	Richland Gull Lake	9:21.77
1973 B	Devon Hind	Auburn Hills Avondale	9:24.9y	1999 B	Andrew Vyncke	Marysville	9:32.14
1974 B	Jack Sinclair	Grosse Ile	9:17.2y*	2000 D2	Kurtis Marlowe	Richland Gull Lake	9:16.72*
1975 B	Jack Sinclair	Grosse Ile	9:18.2y	2001 D2	Tim Ross	Caledonia	9:10.58*
1976 B	Kevin Marcy	Dearborn Divine Child	9:33.2y	2002 D2	Tim Ross	Caledonia	9:16.13
1977 B	Neil Miller	Harper Woods Gallagher	9:20.4y	2003 D2	Chris Burke	Dexter	9:26.42
1978 B	Tom Fountain	Mt Pleasant	9:25.1y	2004 D2	Daniel Roberts	Vicksburg	9:18.48
1979 B	Brian Diemer	Grand Rapids South Christian	9:22.2y	2005 D2	Lex Williams	Dexter	9:07.88*
1980 B	Mark Smith	Cadillac	9:24.0	2006 D2	Landon Peacock	Cedar Springs	9:01.66*
1981 B	Mark Smith	Cadillac	9:11.6*	2007 D2	Dan Jackson	Dexter	9:07.38
1982 B	Jeff Costello	Grand Rapids Catholic	9:26.0y	2008 D2	Bobby Aprill	Dexter	9:16.41
1983 B	Jeff Costello	Grand Rapids Catholic	9:17.4	2009 D2	Kyle Anderson	Milan	9:24.68
1984 B	Phillip Schoensee	Center Line	9:24.5	2010 D2	Mark Beams	Vicksburg	9:24.24
1985 B	Steve Cashman	Grand Rapids Catholic	9:28.12	2011 D2	August Pappas	Chelsea	9:31.98
1986 B	David Ritter	Warren Fitzgerald	9:28.2	2012 D2	Bryce Bradley	Chelsea	9:24.41
1987 B	Mark Osborne	Hillsdale	9:31.3	2013 D2	Tanner Hinkle	Mason	9:13.41
1988 B	Erik Dickerson	Gaylord	9:31.04	2014 D2	Nathan Mylenek	Pontiac Notre Dame Prep	9:37.96
1989 B	Michael Goodfellow	Oxford	9:31.3	2015 D2	Noah Jacobs	Corunna	9:27.49
1990 B	Arbria Shepherd	Stockbridge	9:30.4	2016 D2	Noah Jacobs	Corunna	8:55.57*
1991 B	Jeff Christian	Beaverton	9:18.80	2017 D2	Noah Jacobs	Corunna	9:11.63
1992 B	Jeff Christian	Beaverton	9:21.95	2018 D2	Alex Comerford	Otsego	9:07.25

3200 - Class C/Division 3 Champions

(y=2 miles / 3218.68m)

1967 C	Duane Temple	Fulton-Middleton	10:07.1y*	1990 C	Michael Ball	Hudson	9:41.38
1968 C	Tracy Elliot	Elk Rapids	9:56.0y*	1991 C	Kurt Long	Sandusky	9:41.7
1969 C	Mark Collier	Flint St Agnes	10:00.1y	1992 C	Mike Ball	Hudson	9:28.4
1970 C	Dave Hinz	East Jackson	9:40.1y*	1993 C	Justin Curry	Carson City-Crystal	9:33.2
1971 C	Herb Lindsay	Reed City	10:00.4y	1994 C	Justin Curry	Carson City-Crystal	9:33.81
1972 C	Tim Karas	Orchard Lake St Mary	9:54.7y	1995 C	Justin Curry	Carson City-Crystal	9:38.50
1973 C	James Keller	Cassopolis	9:48.4y	1996 C	Dan Hoekstra	Kalamazoo Christian	9:35.30
1974 C	Jeff Pullen	Leroy Pine River	9:37.8y*	1997 C	Dan Hoekstra	Kalamazoo Christian	9:31.88
1975 C	Rich Holmes	Leroy Pine River	9:42.7y	1998 C	Jon Schiemann	Saginaw Valley Lutheran	9:34.13
1976 C	Paul Drake	Reese	9:39.4y	1999 C	Jake Flynn	Benzie Central	9:33.15
1977 C	Martin Schulist	Whitehall	9:39.8y	2000 D3	Tristen Perlberg	Saginaw Valley Lutheran	9:18.89*
1978 C	Martin Schulist	Whitehall	9:20.0y*	2001 D3	Pat Maynard	Williamston	9:25.69
1979 C	Guy Jacobson	Whitehall	9:20.6y	2002 D3	Steve Czymbor	Hemlock	9:37.69
1980 C	Guy Jacobson	Whitehall	9:28.8y	2003 D3	Josh Perrin	Hillsdale	9:27.51
1981 C	Eric Stuber	Williamston	9:24.1	2004 D3	Josh Perrin	Hillsdale	9:12.14*
1982 C	Kirk Scharich	Unionville Sebewaing	9:34.5	2005 D3	Josh Hofbauer	Harbor Springs	9:34.55
1983 C	Kirk Scharich	Unionville Sebewaing	9:23.3	2006 D3	Maverick Darling	Ovid-Elsie	9:28.07
1984 C	Jesse McGuire	Bronson	9:26.8	2007 D3	Maverick Darling	Ovid-Elsie	9:14.27
1985 C	Jesse McGuire	Bronson	9:42.14	2008 D3	Maverick Darling	Ovid-Elsie	9:18.98
1986 C	Jeff Barnett	Mason County Central	9:40.13	2009 D3	Alex Wilson	Kent City	9:25.40
1987 C	Adam Norman	Kalkaska	9:24.21	2010 D3	David Madrigal	Durand	9:25.13
1988 C	Tim Topolinski	Orchard Lake St Mary	9:41.4	2011 D3	Caleb Rhynard	Shepherd	9:36.89
1989 C	Jared Glover	Kingsley	9:34.49	2012 D3	Bryce Stroede	Hanover-Horton	9:36.96
				2013 D3	Keenan Rebera	Lansing Catholic	9:32.46

Year		Name	School	Time
2014	D3	Keenan Rebera	Lansing Catholic	9:28.34
2015	D3	Abe Visser	Grandville Calvin Christian	9:24.49
2016	D3	Evan Goodell	St. Louis	9:21.00
2017	D3	Evan Goodell	St. Louis	9:08.04*
2018	D3	Corey Gorgas	Saugatuck	9:17.32

3200 - Class D/Division 4 Champions

(y=2 miles / 3218.68m)

Year		Name	School	Time
1967	D	Nick Welburn	Lawton	10:11.2y*
1968	D	Nick Welburn	Lawton	10:05.1y*
1969	D	Tracy Elliott	Elk Rapids	9:44.1y*
1970	D	Steve Rockey	Litchfield	9:46.7y
1971	D	Greg Sanderson	Lawton	10:17.9y
1972	D	Tim Baker	Mendon	9:53.7y
1973	D	Greg Sanderson	Lawton	9:38.0y*
1974	D	Mark Dentler	Mendon	10:04.2y
1975	D	Dale Buist	Allendale	9:35.6y*
1976	D	John Whitney	Littlefield	9:50.4y
1977	D	Jerry Curtis	Akron-Fairgrove	9:54.2y
1978	D	Jerry Curtis	Akron-Fairgrove	9:28.4y*
1979	D	Roderick Brevard	Detroit East Catholic	9:33.7
1980	D	Andy Moyad	Ann Arbor Greenhills	10:03.3
1981	D	Bill Duren	Ann Arbor Greenhills	9:47.3
1982	D	Tim Miller	Battle Creek St. Phillip	9:34.9
1983	D	Robert Moore	Allendale	9:32.1
1984	D	Dan Ebright	Suttons Bay	9:32.87
1985	D	Matt Holappa	Ann Arbor Greenhills	9:59.54
1986	D	Jeff Thomas	Mancelona	9:38.43
1987	D	Bob Brent	Hale	9:44.20
1988	D	Matt Joseph	Ann Arbor Greenhills	9:43.55
1989	D	Tom Becker	Fowler	9:54.8
1990	D	Jay Caruso	Whitmore Lake	9:49.3
1991	D	Mike Richardson	Central Lake	9:46.17
1992	D	Adam Dusseau	Ottawa Lake Whiteford	9:35.5
1993	D	Marty McGinn	Grass Lake	9:29.5
1994	D	Marty McGinn	Grass Lake	9:35.96
1995	D	Ryan Shay	Central Lake	9:47.98
1996	D	Ryan Shay	Central Lake	9:44.76
1997	D	Ryan Shay	Central Lake	9:25.68*
1998	D	Nathan Shay	Central Lake	9:56.3
1999	D	Ron Hein	Galien	10:08.86
2000	D4	Andy Duemling	Ubly	9:39.95*
2001	D4	Will Boylan-Pett	Bath	9:31.50*
2002	D4	Michael Putzke	New Buffalo	9:34.35
2003	D4	Stephan Shay	Central Lake	9:44.03
2004	D4	Stephan Shay	Central Lake	9:22.07*
2005	D4	Curtis Barclay	Hale	9:57.12
2006	D4	Victor Ramirez	Wyoming Lee	9:36.84
2007	D4	Alex Harris	Royal Oak Shrine	9:51.10
2008	D4	Kevin Oblinger	Mt Pleasant Sacred Heart	9:45.68
2009	D4	Christian Birky	Saugatuck	9:32.24
2010	D4	Spencer Nousain	Concord	9:39.09
2011	D4	Casey Voisin	Mt Pleasant Sacred Heart	9:39.86
2012	D4	Sean Kelly	Saugatuck	9:40.51
2013	D4	Sean Kelly	Saugatuck	9:35.99
2014	D4	Jesse Hersha	Concord	9:38.54
2015	D4	Jesse Hersha	Concord	9:39.87
2016	D4	Santana Scott	Evart	9:42.83
2017	D4	Jeremy Kloss	Harbor Springs	9:46.25
2018	D4	Nathan Stout	Wyoming Potter's House	9:44.08

3200 – UP Class AB/Division 1 Champions

(y=2 miles / 3218.68m)

Year		Name	School	Time
1967	UPAB	Gordon Pekuri	Menominee	10:20.0y*
1968	UPAB	Gordon Pekuri	Menominee	10:11.5y*
1969	UPAB	Gordon Pekuri	Menominee	10:06.0y*
1970	UPAB	Gary Patrick	Calumet	10:02.9y*
1971	UPAB	Gary Santi	Ishpeming	9:35.7y*
1972	UPAB	Gary Patrick	Calumet	9:36.0y
1973	UPAB	Glen Santi	Ishpeming	9:58.1y
1974	UPAB	Dave Baker	Ironwood	10:17.5y
1975	UPAB	Ron McKerchie	Sault Ste. Marie	10:09.8y
1976	UPAB	Kurt Malmgren	Marquette	9:52.4y
1977	UPAB	Kurt Malmgren	Marquette	9:39.4y
1978	UPAB	Mike Photenhauer	Menominee	9:47.9y
1979	UPAB	Dean Borg	Gwinn	9:45.2
1980	UPAB	Mike Photenhauer	Menominee	9:50.7
1981	UPAB	Jim Harris	Escanaba	10:07.5
1982	UPAB	Jon Ottoson	Marquette	10:14.3
1983	UPAB	Jon Ottoson	Marquette	9:59.3
1984	UPAB	Tracy Lokken	Gwinn	10:00.8
1985	UPAB	Dan Beaudry	Escanaba	10:04.1
1986	UPAB	Dennis Murvich	Kingsford	10:03.4
1987	UPAB	Gary Gregg	Escanaba	9:49.6
1988	UPAB	Don Bovin	Gladstone	9:57.8
1989	UPAB	Don Bovin	Gladstone	10:12.6
1990	UPAB	Chad Waucansch	Sault Ste. Marie	10:06.1
1991	UPAB	Chad Waucausch	Sault Ste. Marie	9:49.3
1992	UPAB	Ryan Potila	Ishpeming Westwood	10:22.4
1993	UPAB	Ryan Potila	Ishpeming Westwood	9:57.1
1994	UPAB	Andy Ramos	Gwinn	10:06.0
1995	UPAB	Andy Ramos	Gwinn	9:52.9
1996	UPAB	Peter Remien	Ishpeming Westwood	10:17.87
1997	UPAB	Peter Remien	Ishpeming Westwood	9:59.45
1998	UPAB	Caden Ruohomaki	Negaunee	10:25.09
1999	UPAB	John Ganon	Escanaba	10:14.75
2000	UPAB	Jamison Cihak	Marquette	10:07.4*
2001	UPD1	Jamison Cihak	Marquette	10:00.0*
2002	UPD1	Jamison Cihak	Marquette	10:02.0
2003	UPD1	Beau Poquette	Kingsford	10:08.50
2004	UPD1	Alex Tiseo	Marquette	10:09.96
2005	UPD1	Jake Meeuwsen	Kingsford	10:19.80
2006	UPD1	Jake Meeuwsen	Kingsford	10:12.04
2007	UPD1	Jake Meeuwsen	Kingsford	10:06.75
2008	UPD1	Jake Isaaccson	Menominee	10:19.53
2009	UPD1	Mickey Sanders	Marquette	10:08.01
2010	UPD1	Mickey Sanders	Marquette	10:10.54
2011	UPD1	Mickey Sanders	Marquette	9:53.14*
2012	UPD1	Devin Berg	Calumet	10:19.36
2013	UPD1	Eric Cousineau	Escanaba	10:10.10
2014	UPD1	Jacob Colling	Houghton	10:07.67
2015	UPD1	Lance Rambo	Marquette	9:58.02
2016	UPD1	Joey Wolfe	Escanaba	9:59.78
2017	UPD1	Adam Bruce	Gladstone	10:20.53
2018	UPD1	Colton Yesney	Negaunee	9:50.43*

3200 – UP Class C/Division 2 Champions

(y=2 miles / 3218.68m)

Year		Name	School	Time
1967	UPC	Ron Stromgren	Stephenson	10:36.0y*
1968	UPC	William McNamee	St. Ignace	10:25.2y
1969	UPC	Keith Whitman	L'Anse	10:18.2y
1970	UPC	Fred Teddy	L'Anse	9:55.4y*
1971	UPC	Fred Teddy	L'Anse	9:30.4y*
1972	UPC	Fred Teddy	L'Anse	9:22.7y*
1973	UPC	Brian Weng	Stephenson	9:53.6y
1974	UPC	Brian Weng	Stephenson	9:57.1y
1975	UPC	Greg Harger	Munising	9:49.0y
1976	UPC	Greg Harger	Munising	9:45.0y
1977	UPC	Kevin King	Ishpeming	9:57.0y
1978	UPC	Jeff Mount	Hancock	10:02.2y
1979	UPC	Pierre Ogea	Ishpeming	9:57.0
1980	UPC	Tom Verme	Munising	10:03.2
1981	UPC	Martin Humphrey	Iron Mountain	9:49.7
1982	UPC	Martin Humphrey	Iron Mountain	9:46.9
1983	UPC	John Furno	Iron Mountain	9:34.0
1984	UPC	Larry Gray	Ishpeming Westwood	10:00.1
1985	UPC	Arnie Kinnunen	Calumet	10:01.6
1986	UPC	Pete Marcotte	Ishpeming Westwood	10.07.0
1987	UPC	Jeff Legeret	Iron Mountain	9:54.6
1988	UPC	Pete Marcotte	Ishpeming Westwood	9:46.7
1989	UPC	Chris Lett	Houghton	9:49.0
1990	UPC	Chris Lett	Houghton	10:00.9
1991	UPC	Chris Lett	Houghton	9:48.1
1992	UPC	Dave DeLisle	Munising	10:27.0
1993	UPC	Dave DeLisle	Munising	9:52.0
1994	UPC	Dave DeLisle	Munising	9:56.2
1995	UPC	Tom Miller	Houghton	9:55.1
1996	UPC	Dave Elwing	Munising	9:48.4
1997	UPC	Aaron Litzner	St. Ignace	9:56.9
1998	UPC	Peter Remien	Ishpeming Westwood	9:56.8
1999	UPC	Dave Campbell	Calumet	10:03.6
2000	UPC	Chris Marana	Ishpeming Westwood	10:16.7
2001	UPD2	Dave Harvey	Munising	10:03.2*
2002	UPD2	Brent Malaski	Rudyard	10:19.53
2003	UPD2	Jake Rankinen	Ishpeming Westwood	9:47.28*

Year	Class	Name	School	Time
2004 UPD2		Brandon Newlin	Stephenson	10.33.03
2005 UPD2		Mark Kinnunen	Munising	10:15.62
2006 UPD2		Mark Kinnunen	Munising	10:19.49
2007 UPD2		Alan Peterson	Ironwood	10:15.09
2008 UPD2		Alan Peterson	Ironwood	10:06.78
2009 UPD2		Jake Mahoski	Munising	10:20.40
2010 UPD2		Alan Peterson	Ironwood	9:50.90
2011 UPD2		Trevor Vetort	Stephenson	10:28.76
2012 UPD2		Conner Cappaert	Stephenson	10:42.55
2013 UPD2		Dan Kulas	Iron Mountain	10:15.40
2014 UPD2		Jared Joki	Ironwood	10:19.36
2015 UPD2		Jared Joki	Ironwood	10:19.36
2016 UPD2		Nate Carey	Iron Mountain	10:11.44
2017 UPD2		Nick Niemi	Ironwood	10:20.23
2018 UPD2		Nick Niemi	Ironwood	10:21.85

3200 – UP Class D/Division 3 Champions

(y=2 miles / 3218.68m)

Year	Class	Name	School	Time
1967 UPD		Lief Benson	Eben	10:31.5y*
1968 UPD		Floyd Lamoreaux	Cedarville	10:32.1y
1969 UPD		Maurice Evans	Republic	10:27.0y*
1970 UPD		Eric Rike	Pickford	10:33.8y
1971 UPD		Brian Aho	Painesdale	10:26.3y*
1972 UPD		James Skinner	Pickford	10:00.4y*
1973 UPD		Jim Skinner	Pickford	10:00.6y
1974 UPD		James Koivu	Wakefield	10:31.9y
1975 UPD		Mark Palosaari	Chassell	10:23.3y
1976 UPD		Mark Palosaari	Chassell	10:09.3y
1977 UPD		Gary Mishica	Lake Linden-Hubbell	10:19.2y
1978 UPD		Andrie Soumis	Chassell	10:13.4y
1979 UPD		Mark Horwitz	Norway	10:03.7
1980 UPD		Doug Bernard	Cooks-Big Bay de Noc	9:58.9*
1981 UPD		Keith Slack	Engadine	10:07.2
1982 UPD		Eugene Soumis	Chassell	10:22.2
1983 UPD		Melvin Willis	Brimley	10:34.6
1984 UPD		Melvin Willis	Brimley	10:05.1
1985 UPD		Carley Cox	Crystal Falls Forest Park	10:25.0
1986 UPD		Deren Pershinske	Engadine	10:14.8
1987 UPD		Deren Pershinske	Engadine	10:03.6
1988 UPD		Glenn Avena	Crystal Falls Forest Park	10:03.6
1989 UPD		Glenn Avena	Crystal Falls Forest Park	10:28.7
1990 UPD		Cal Ledy	Pickford	10:24.2
1991 UPD		Dan Malamao	Eben Junction Superior Central	10:23.6
1992 UPD		Ryan Grondin	Powers-North Central	10:39.9
1993 UPD		Ryan Grondin	Powers-North Central	10:29.5
1994 UPD		Jason Maki	Eben Junction Superior Central	10:32.4
1995 UPD		Norman Siren	Ontonagon	10:25.0
1996 UPD		Norman Siren	Ontonagon	10:36.2
1997 UPD		Norman Siren	Ontonagon	10:39.2
1998 UPD		Aaron Litzner	St. Ignace	9:49.9*
1999 UPD		Mike Holmgren	Rapid River	10:34.3
2000 UPD		Mike Holmgren	Rapid River	10:24.2
2001 UPD3		Ryan Holm	Wakefield	10:10.1*
2002 UPD3		Ryan Holm	Wakefield	10:22.78
2003 UPD3		Ryan Holm	Wakefield	10:16.84
2004 UPD3		Sam Kilpela	Painesdale-Jeffers	10:15.78
2005 UPD3		Tyler Crossman	Rapid River	10:20.28
2006 UPD3		Tyler Crossman	Rapid River	10:30.98
2007 UPD3		Tyler Crossman	Rapid River	10:19.56
2008 UPD3		Tyler Crossman	Rapid River	10:10.25
2009 UPD3		Jonathan Kipela	Painesdale-Jeffers	10:11.92
2010 UPD3		Tim Dunstan	Dollar Bay	10:16.20
2011 UPD3		Jacob Mahoski	Munising	10:43.20
2012 UPD3		Andrew Kelto	Munising	10:36.29
2013 UPD3		Brett Hannah	Munising	10:43.79
2014 UPD3		Brett Hannah	Munising	10:49.47
2015 UPD3		Brett Hannah	Munising	10:40.50
2016 UPD3		Brett Hannah	Munising	10:42.70
2017 UPD3		Austin Plotkin	Brimley	10:30.94
2018 UPD3		Uriah Aili	Bessemer	10:25.39

BOYS 110-METER HURDLES

Records

D1	13.65	Kenneth Ferguson	Detroit Mumford	2002
D2	13.70	Josh Hembrough	Grand Rapids Forest Hills Northern	2007
D3	14.23 (0.4)	Jackson Blanchard	Houghton Lake	2018
D4	14.35 (-1.4)	Cory Noeker	Pewamo-Westphalia	2009
UPD1	15.15	Chris Peterson	Marquette	2003
(hand	14.8	Matt Wise	Calumet	2001)
UPD2	15.34	Tony Cook	Munising	2003
UPD3	14.96	Andy Cooper	Munising	2015

Records by Class (pre-2000 for LP, pre-2001 for UP)

A	13.78	Kelvin Jackson	Kalamazoo Loy Norrix	1990
(hand	13.5y	Thomas Wilcher	Detroit Central	1981)
B	14.19	Tim Strok	Riverview	1993
(hand	13.7	Tyrone Wheatley	Dearborn Heights Robichaud	1991)
C	14.31	Adam Lyon	Mesick	1999
D	14.34	Willy Scott	Detroit East Catholic	1987
UPAB	14.6	Corey Potvin	Escanaba	1988
UPC	14.7y	Dean Miksa	Norway	1977
UPD	15.0y	Steven Peffers	Pickford	1972
	15.0	Jon Gollakner	Crystal Falls Forest Park	1987

110H – Class A/Division 1 Champions

(42-inch hurdles)
(y=120 yards / 109.73m)

Year	Name	School	Time
1895 all	Clarence Christopher	Lansing	16.0y
1897 all	Otis Cole	Lansing	18.0y
1898 all	Clarence Christopher	Lansing	19.0y*
1899 all	Walter Tucker	Ann Arbor	19.2y
1900 all	Bob Dawson	Pontiac	18.4y*
1901 all	Raymond Stewart	Ann Arbor	16.6y*
1902 all	Frank Nicol	Detroit Central	16.4y*
1903 all	Frank Nicol	Detroit University School	17.0y
1904 all	Earl Smith	Detroit Central	16.8y
1905 all	John N Patterson	Detroit University School	16.2y*
1906 all	Dana Torrey	Detroit University School	16.0y*
1907 all	Ralph Craig	Detroit Central	17.2y
1908 all	Allen Garrells	Detroit Central	15.0y LH
1909 all	Jimmie Craig	Detroit Central	16.4y
1910 all	Pinky Schaffer	Muskegon	16.4y
1911 all	Edward Krautheim	Muskegon	17.3y
1912 all	Cecil Corbin	Alpena	18.2y
1913 all	Sidney Wyatt	Detroit Eastern	17.0y
1914 all	Howard Armstrong	Muskegon	17.0y
1915 all	Raymond Beardsley	Muskegon	18.0y
1916 all	Rod McKenzie	Grand Rapids Central	16.4y
1917 all	Charles Gleason	Detroit Eastern	17.6y
1918	No Meet – World War I		
1919 all	Edward McCallum	Detroit Central	17.0y

Year	Name	School	Time
1920 all	Harold Price	Grand Rapids Central	17.0y
1921 A	George Snider	Detroit Northwestern	16.4y
1922 A	Deabert Toepfer	Detroit Eastern	16.6y
1923 A	Edward Spence	Detroit Western	16.5y
1924 A	Edward Spence	Detroit Western	16.0y*
1925 A	Bill Loving	Detroit Cass Tech	16.5y
1926 A	Bill Loving	Detroit Cass Tech	16.1y
1927 A	Eugene Beatty	Detroit Northeastern	16.1y
1928 A	Eugene Beatty	Detroit Northeastern	16.5y
1929 A	Jack Heston	Detroit Northwestern	16.2y
1930 A	Willis Ward	Detroit Northwestern	16.0y
1931 A	Boyd Pantlind	Grand Rapids Central	15.8y*
1932 A	Ed Kalawart	Grand Rapids Ottawa Hills	16.2y
1933 A	Walt Karcewski	Grand Rapids Davis Tech	15.9y
1934 A	Norbert Miknavich	Grand Rapids Union	16.5y

(39-inch hurdles)

Year	Name	School	Time
1935 A	Gayle Robinson	Muskegon	15.6y*
1936 A	Sherman Olmsted	Saginaw	15.3y*
1937 A	Willie Campbell	Monroe	15.3y*
1938 A	Floyd Bates	Flint Central	15.0y*
1939 A	Paul White	River Rouge	15.1y
1940 A	Hezikah Bibbs	Flint Northern	15.3y
1941 A	Horace Smith	Jackson	14.6y*
1942 A	Bill Hamilton	Flint Northern	15.3y
1943	No Meet – World War II		
1944 A	Garion Campbell	Monroe	15.2y
1945 A	Amien Carter	Saginaw	15.5y
1946 A	Jesse Thomas	Flint Central	15.4y
1947 A	Frank Allen	Flint Northern	15.3y
1948 A	Rollie Hanson	Saginaw Arthur Hill	15.4y
1949 A	Leonard Porterfield	Saginaw Arthur Hill	15.5y
1950 A	Ernest Jodoin	Wyandotte Roosevelt	15.4y
1951 A	Tom Yinger	Monroe	15.0y
1952 A	Duane Root	Wyandotte Roosevelt	15.6y
1953 A	Phil Smith	Dearborn	15.2y
1954 A	Paul Wiegerink	Grand Rapids Ottawa Hills	14.7y
1955 A	Hayes Jones	Pontiac	14.5y*
1956 A	Hayes Jones	Pontiac	14.4y*
1957 A	Jerry Meyer	Berkley	15.1y
1958 A	Rex Cawley	Farmington	14.5y
1959 A	Rex Cawley	Farmington	14.4y
1960 A	Leon Prentis	Pontiac Central	15.0y
1961 A	Joe Falls	Waterford Township	14.6y
1962 A	Gary Cerulla	Wyandotte Roosevelt	14.5y
1963 A	Ernie Long	Flint Central	14.2y*
1964 A	Henry Patino	Lansing Everett	14.3y
1965 A	Len Hatchett	Flint Central	14.4y
1966 A	Bill Tipton	Pontiac Central	14.0y*
1967 A	Bill Tipton	Pontiac Central	13.9y* (-5.8)
1968 A	Robert Johnson	Pontiac Central	14.6y

Year	Name	School	Time
1969 A	John Morrison	Detroit Redford Union	14.3y
1970 A	Melvin Reeves	Pontiac Northern	14.4y
1971 A	Steve Dart	East Lansing	14.8y
1972 A	Paul Zalynski	Allen Park	14.4y
1973 A	Mark Lawrence	Waterford Mott	14.2y
1974 A	Roger Brownlee	Mt Clemens	14.1y
1975 A	Arnette Chisolm	Taylor Center	14.2y
1976 A	Rob Cummings	Flint Carman	14.5y
1977 A	Brett Hanson	Wayne Memorial	14.2y
1978 A	Marcus Allen	Detroit Cass Tech	13.8y*
1979 A	Jeff Herndon	Ann Arbor Pioneer	13.8y*
1980 A	Mike Boyd	Lansing Hill	13.9yw
1981 A	Thomas Wilcher	Detroit Central	13.5y*
1982 A	Thomas Wilcher	Detroit Central	13.6
1983 A	Steve Smith	Lansing Everett	14.3
1984 A	Tony Norris	Lansing Sexton	14.1
1985 A	Roget Ware	Lansing Sexton	14.40*
1986 A	Roget Ware	Lansing Sexton	13.8
1987 A	Roget Ware	Lansing Sexton	13.87*
1988 A	Scott Larson	Ann Arbor Huron	14.55
1989 A	Larry Harden	Benton Harbor	14.09
1990 A	Kelvin Jackson	Kalamazoo Loy Norrix	13.78*
1991 A	Jamell Humphrey	Pontiac Northern	14.53
1992 A	Khary Burnley	Detroit Cass Tech	14.74
1993 A	Don Bryant	Farmington Hills Harrison	14.52
1994 A	William Brooks	Detroit UD Jesuit	14.20
1995 A	Gregg Richardson	Lansing Everett	14.3
1996 A	Jerome Rodgers	Pontiac Northern	14.43
1997 A	Jalilu Mayo	Pontiac Central	13.91
1998 A	Shakla Dhladhla	East Lansing	14.31w(3.0)
1999 A	Johnnie Birdsong	Detroit Mumford	14.21(-0.6)
2000 D1	Mike Smith	Flint Central	14.34* (1.0)
2001 D1	Mike Smith	Flint Central	14.28*
2002 D1	Kenneth Ferguson	Detroit Mumford	13.65*
2003 D1	Edmund Graham	Flint Central	14.17 (-1.1)
2004 D1	Rob Fiorillo	Holly	14.48
2005 D1	Daniel Kinney	Romulus	14.38
2006 D1	Nicholas McCampbell	Detroit Cass Tech	14.15w (2.7)
2007 D1	Shane Wells	Romulus	14.45
2008 D1	Roscoe Payne	Flint Carman-Ainsworth	13.99w (4.9)
2009 D1	Renaldo Powell	Wayne Memorial	14.13 (-2.7)
2010 D1	Drake Johnson	Ann Arbor Pioneer	14.17 (-3.0)
2011 D1	Drake Johnson	Ann Arbor Pioneer	13.73 (1.0)
2012 D1	Drake Johnson	Ann Arbor Pioneer	14.24 (-4.3)
2013 D1	Freddie Crittenden	Utica	14.36(-2.6)
2014 D1	Antoine Lloyd	East Kentwood	13.95 (0.2)
2015 D1	Robie Webster	Ypsilanti Lincoln	14.00 (0.9)
2016 D1	Kentre Patterson	East Lansing	14.03 (-1.3)
2017 D1	Kentre Patterson	East Lansing	13.84 (-1.9)
2018 D1	Job Mayhue	East Kentwood	13.99 (-0.7)

110H – Class B/Division 2 Champions

(42-inch hurdles)
(y=120 yards / 109.73m)

Year	Name	School	Time
1921 B	George Haggerty	Ypsilanti Central	17.4y*
1922 B	Lewis Darling	Niles	17.2y*
1923 B	Harold George	Petoskey	17.3y
1924 B	Harold George	Petoskey	17.4y
1925 B	Brett Shaunding	Allegan	17.2y*
1926 B	Moulton Davis	St Joseph	16.8y*
1927 B	Clare Huggett	St Johns	16.8y*
1928 B	Edwin Jackson	Dearborn	16.9y
1929 B	Ted Bath	Niles	16.2y*
1930 B	Kurt Warmbein	St Joseph	17.5y
1931 B	Isadore Schulman	South Haven	17.1y
1932 B	Kurt Warmbein	St Joseph	16.5y
1933 B	John McKee	Birmingham	16.3y
1934 B	Walter Sabbath	River Rouge	16.8y

(39-inch hurdles)

Year	Name	School	Time
1935 B	Harold Slim Howard	Alma	15.6y*
1936 B	Lawrence Hardke	St Joseph	15.4yw
1937 B	Lavern Zander	Ionia	15.7y
1938 B	Carl Henry	Belding	15.4y*
1939 B	William Arndt	Ionia	15.6y
1940 B	Ray Merideth	Melvindale	15.5y
1941 B	Leslie Murphy	Ionia	15.8y
1942 B	Bob Blakely	Milford	15.9y
1943	No Meet – World War II		
1944 B	Clyde Hoag	South Haven	16.3y
1945 B	Keith Gundrum	Ypsilanti Roosevelt	15.8y
1946 B	Doug White	Charlotte	15.9y
1947 B	Bob Shultz	Alma	15.4y*
1948 B	David Hill	Ypsilanti Central	16.2y
1949 B	David Hill	Ypsilanti Central	14.9y*

Year	Name	School	Time
1950 B	William Brendel	Grand Blanc	15.8y
1951 B	Jim Lincoln	Greenville	15.0y
1952 B	Fred Hanke	Marshall	16.1y
1953 B	Bill Cook	Greenville	15.4y
1954 B	Jack Boomer	Mt Pleasant	15.3y
1955 B	Ernest Malzahn	Utica	15.4y
1956 B	Ernest Malzahn	Utica	15.1y
1957 B	John Williams	Ecorse	15.3y
1958 B	Rollin Douma	East Grand Rapids	15.2y
1959 B	Bob Sherman	Durand	15.2y
1960 B	Charles Gray	Ecorse	14.5y*
	(Bob Sherman-Durand ran 14.5* in the heats)		
1961 B	Jim Vogler	Detroit Lutheran West	14.7y
1962 B	Willie Betts	River Rouge	14.9y
1963 B	Willie Betts	River Rouge	14.8y
1964 B	Don Witt	Whitehall	14.3yw (2.5)
	(Nelson Graham-Mt Morris ran 14.5* in the heats)		
1965 B	Walter Thomas	Ecorse	15.0y
1966 B	Melvin Allen	Romulus	15.0y
1967 B	Stan Hawthorne	Ecorse	14.5*y
1968 B	Mike Whitefield	Kalamazoo Hackett	14.6y
1969 B	Tim Drumbeller	Riverview	14.2y*
1970 B	Larry Walker	River Rouge	14.9y
1971 B	Paul Jorgenson	Greenville	14.7y
1972 B	Chris Langley	Oscoda	14.6y
1973 B	Eric Rush	Montrose	15.0y
1974 B	Ed Poindexter	Inkster	14.7y
1975 B	Ed Poindexter	Inkster	14.3y
1976 B	Athony Akins	Flint Beecher	14.2y*
1977 B	Clarence Guyton	Inkster Cherry Hill	14.5y
1978 B	Larry Wiley	Flint Beecher	14.2y*
1979 B	Darryl Goree	Dearborn Heights Robichaud	14.3y

Year	Name	School	Time
1980 B	Jeff Ernst	Coldwater	14.7
1981 B	Greg Blade	Ecorse	14.7
1982 B	Paul Niemi	Oxford	14.1y*
1983 B	Andre Hall	Flint Beecher	14.2
1984 B	Mike Miller	Eaton Rapids	13.9*
1985 B	Terry Strong	Flint Beecher	14.82*
1986 B	Terry Strong	Flint Beecher	14.3
1987 B	Mike White	Three Rivers	14.57*
1988 B	Steve Nederveld	Mason	15.10
1989 B	Steve Nederveld	Mason	14.60
1990 B	Tyrone Wheatley	Dearborn Heights Robichaud	14.85
1991 B	Tyrone Wheatley	Dearborn Heights Robichaud	13.7*
1992 B	Tim Lynch	Corunna	14.35*
1993 B	Tim Strok	Riverview	14.19*
1994 B	Rob Herrick	Corunna	14.25
1995 B	Shawn Bowden	Comstock	14.74
1996 B	Jason Fiengo	Richland Gull Lake	14.88
1997 B	Jason Fiengo	Richland Gull Lake	14.39
1998 B	Ryan Krug	St. Joseph	14.38
1999 B	Carleton McCauley	Romulus	14.83
2000 D2	William Agee	Detroit Southwestern	14.48*
2001 D2	Zack Tocco	Comstock	14.80
2002 D2	John Childress	Flint Powers	14.31*
2003 D2	John Childress	Flint Powers	13.96w
2004 D2	Rich Lacroix	Marine City	14.38
2005 D2	Tymel Dodd	Lansing Sexton	14.70
2006 D2	Josh Hembrough	GR Forest Hills Northern	13.82*
2007 D2	Josh Hembrough	GR Forest Hills Northern	13.70*
2008 D2	Evan Carpenter	Chelsea	14.71
2009 D2	Vanier Joseph	Redford Thurston	14.35
2010 D2	Chris Williams	Saginaw	14.24
2011 D2	Justin Balczak	Cedar Springs	14.19
2012 D2	Austin Loewen	Williamston	14.46
2013 D2	Austin Loewen	Williamston	14.44w (5.4)
2014 D2	Fred Boyd	Dearborn Divine Child	14.60
2015 D2	Noah Caudy	Lake Odessa Lakewood	14.70
2016 D2	Noah Caudy	Lake Odessa Lakewood	14.21 (-1.2)
2017 D2	Noah Caudy	Lake Odessa Lakewood	14.05 (0.5)
2018 D2	Anthony Hudson	Harper Woods	14.68w (2.2)

110H – Class C/Division 3 Champions

(42-inch hurdles)
(y=120 yards / 109.73m)

Year	Name	School	Time
1921 C	Paul Longhurst	Vassar	20.0y*
1922 C	Robert Soule	Plainwell	17.8y*
1923 C	Alan McClean	Plainwell	17.3y*
1924 C	Donald McLean	Allegan	17.5y
1925 C	Donald McLean	Plainwell	17.5y
1926 C	Gerald Miller	Otsego	17.2y*
1927 C	Theodore Nagelvoort	Oak Ridge	17.0y*
1928 C	Burnell Morland	Paw Paw	18.1y
1929 C	Johnny Tooker	Kalamazoo St Augustine	15.2yLH*
1930 C	Theo Thomas	Constantine	14.4yLH*
1931 C	Louie Morse	Buchanan	14.5yLH
1932 C	Clare McDurmon	Caro	16.9y*
1933 C	Clare McDurmon	Caro	16.1y*
1934 C	Kenneth Thompson	East Grand Rapids	17.2y

(39-inch hurdles)

Year	Name	School	Time
1935 C	Lawrence Schram	Algonac	16.2y
1936 C	Louis Oswalt	Paw Paw	16.2y
1937 C	Elmer Miller	Belding	16.0y*
1938 C	Dick Bergman	Charlevoix	15.6y*
1939 C	Don Turnispseed	Mancelona	15.6y*
1940 C	Lawrence Beckman	Shelby	15.6yw
1941 C	Don Harm	St Clair Shores South Lake	16.0y
1942 C	John Glosque	Imlay City	16.1y
1943	No Meet – World War II		
1944 C	Duane Formsma	Grand Rapids Wyoming Park	16.3y
1945 C	Wallace Johnson	Romulus	15.7y
1946 C	Keith Gundrum	Ypsilanti Roosevelt	15.8y
1947 C	Al Dorow	Imlay City	15.7y
1948 C	Richard Corbat	Oxford	15.8y
1949 C	Jack Goodrich	Dundee	15.0y*
1950 C	Harland Benjamin	Milan	14.8y*
1951 C	Richard Hicks	Portage	15.8y
1952 C	Ray Eggelston	East Jackson	15.8y
1953 C	Charles Harding	Berrien Springs	15.6y
1954 C	Tom Lick	Marlette	15.2y
1955 C	Don Miller	Reed City	15.3y
1956 C	Don Miller	Reed City	14.9y
1957 C	Ron Holowasko	Boyne City	15.6y
1958 C	Chuck Peltz	Grosse Ille	15.0y
1959 C	Chuck Peltz	Grosse Ille	15.4y
1960 C	Russ Husted	Burton Atherton	15.1y
1961 C	Dave McLaughlin	Chelsea	15.0y
1962 C	Roger Davidsom	Deckerville	16.7y
1963 C	Don Lowe	Vandercook Lake	15.2y
1964 C	Roland Carter	Carson City	15.4y
1965 C	Ralph Baker	Constantine	15.2y
1966 C	Ralph Skinner	Battle Creek St Phillip	15.3y
1967 C	Sam Kirkland	Clinton Boysville	15.6y
1968 C	Bill White	Shepherd	15.4y
1969 C	Bill White	Shepherd	14.5y*
1970 C	Cliff Dukes	White Cloud	14.9y
1971 C	Gary Veurink	Muskegon Christian	14.6y
1972 C	Alan Baker	Detroit DePorres	14.6y
1973 C	Alan Baker	Detroit DePorres	14.6y
1974 C	Donald Sims	New Haven	14.3y*
1975 C	Dan Gohs	Vassar	14.7y
1976 C	Mike Mission	Unionville-Sebewaing	14.7y
1977 C	Marcus Allen	Redford St Mary	14.5y
1978 C	Don York	Flint Hamady	15.0y
1979 C	Roger Barbour	Stockbridge	14.6y
1980 C	Tim Johnson	Grand Rapids South Christian	14.6y
1981 C	Reginald Harris	Detroit Lutheran West	14.3*
1982 C	Joe Corbett	Detroit Lutheran West	14.5
1983 C	Joe Corbett	Detroit Lutheran West	13.9w
1984 C	Greg Singer	Bangor	14.7
1985 C	Lorenzo Browner	Detroit Lutheran West	14.96*
1986 C	Tony Fleming	Detroit DePorres	14.84*
1987 C	Greg Harris	Detroit Lutheran West	14.57*
1988 C	Greg Harris	Detroit Lutheran West	14.5
1989 C	Jason Whitley	Charlevoix	14.99
1990 C	Steve Sampson	Petersburg-Summerfield	15.21
1991 C	Andrew Gitersonke	Blissfield	15.20
1992 C	Eric Russell	Parchment	14.60
1993 C	Jason Nordbeck	Benzie Central	15.23
1994 C	Jason Elder	Jonesville	15.55
1995 C	Ernest Bentz	Montague	14.71
1996 C	Saul Tilmann	Howard City Tri County	14.81
1997 C	Saul Tilmann	Howard City Tri County	14.41w
1998 C	Ken Klinger	Muskegon Oakridge	15.01
1999 C	Adam Lyon	Mesick	14.31*
2000 D3	Adam Lyon	Mesick	14.96*
2001 D3	Benard Gleton	Detroit Crockett	14.76*
2002 D3	Joe LeFevre	Macomb Lutheran North	14.47*
2003 D3	Derrick Cook	Muskegon Oakridge	14.30*
2004 D3	Tyler Bassage	Quincy	14.74
2005 D3	Joey Latz	Ovid-Elsie	14.94
2006 D3	Joey Latz	Ovid-Elsie	14.58
2007 D3	Keith Curtis	Berrien Springs	14.63
2008 D3	Keith Curtis	Berrien Springs	14.71
2009 D3	Michael Parker	Michigan Center	14.87 (-1.2)
2010 D3	Steven Machin	Whitmore Lake	14.31
2011 D3	Jake McFadden	Clare	14.36
2012 D3	Jake McFadden	Clare	14.71
2013 D3	Teo Redding	Warren Michigan Collegiate	14.65
2014 D3	Josh Harris	New Haven	14.96 (0.5)
2015 D3	Zach Stadnika	Macomb Lutheran North	14.67 (0.0)
2016 D3	Andrew Storm	Marlette	14.82 (-0.1)
2017 D3	Jackson Blanchard	Houghton Lake	14.81 (-1.5)
2018 D3	Jackson Blanchard	Houghton Lake	14.23* (0.4)

110H – Class D/Division 4 Champions

(42-inch hurdles)
(y=120 yards / 109.73m)

Year	Name	School	Time
1927 D	Clarence Swartz	Trenton	19.0y*
1928 D	Staughton Dalzell	Muir	19.8y

(30-inch hurdles)

Year	Name	School	Time
1929 D	Bernard Osthaus	Newaygo	15.9yLH*
1930 D	Bill Chase	South Lake	15.2yLH*
1931 D	Bill Chase	South Lake	14.8yLH*

(42-inch hurdles)

Year	Name	School	Time
1932 D	John Brown	Centreville	18.3y*
1933 D	Lester Walters	Centreville	17.1y*
1934 D	Lester Walters	Centreville	16.6y*

(39-inch hurdles)

Year	Name	School	Time
1935 D	Thomas Scott	Saranac	16.8y
1936 D	Russell McCurdy	Onekama	16.6y*
1937 D	Robert Hall	Bloomfield Hills	17.7y

Year	Name	School	Time
1938 D	Robert Hall	Bloomfield Hills	16.3y*
1939 D	Bernard Zeeb	Bath	18.5y
1940 D	Bill Miller	Byron	16.9y
1941 D	Orvin Shauver	Bath	16.9y
1942 D	Richard Keck	DeWitt	17.2y
1943	No Meet – World War II		
1944 D	Jack East	Glen Arbor Leelanau School	17.4y
1945 D	James Ostler	Glen Arbor Leelanau School	17.0y
1946 D	Dan Haven	Hemlock	17.7y
1947 D	Daniel Haven	Hemlock	16.0y*
1948 D	Dick Miner	Bloomfield Hills	17.2y
1949 D	Gaylord Snyder	Vestaburg	16.3y
1950 D	John Fortenberry	Dearborn Edison Institute	16.2y
1951 D	Norman Rushton	Central Lake	16.8y
1952 D	Richard Beane	Brethren	17.2y
1953 D	Joe Thering	Beal City	15.9y*
1954 D	Richard Beane	Brethren	15.7y*
1955 D	Roland Joles	Wolverine	16.4y
1956 D	Roland Joles	Wolverine	16.0y
1957 D	Orville Emerson	Dansville	16.4y
1958 D	Dick Paisley	Beal City	15.7y*
1959 D	Norm Kuhns	Newaygo	15.9y
1960 D	Wes Butcher	Spring Arbor	15.2y*
1961 D	Chet Dow	Goodrich	15.8y
1962 D	David Woods	Wolverine	15.5y
1963 D	John Fry	Unionville	15.3y
1964 D	Mark Patterson	Covert	15.4y
1965 D	Terry Barnes	Centreville	15.8y
1966 D	Carl Archambeau	Arenac-Eastern	15.6y
1967 D	Jeff Sinclair	Detroit St Charles	16.0y
1968 D	Bob Graham	Pentwater	15.3y
1969 D	Tom Rathburn	Athens	15.6y
1970 D	Mike Gordon	Mt Clemens St Mary	15.4y
1971 D	Dean Ehy	Camden-Frontier	15.5y
1972 D	Greg Ardis	Lake City	15.4y
1973 D	Bob Marshall	Almont	15.3y
1974 D	Robin Ray	Mendon	15.4y
1975 D	David Sykes	Litchfield	14.9y*
1976 D	Mike Jones	Saugatuck	14.7y*
1977 D	David Sykes	Litchfield	14.1y*
1978 D	Courtney Vance	Detroit Country Day	14.7y

Year	Name	School	Time
1979 D	Vernon Lynch	Detroit DePorres	14.9
1980 D	Vernon Lynch	Detroit DePorres	14.4
1981 D	Greg Henderson	Detroit DePorres	14.8
1982 D	Dwayne Grice	Detroit East Catholic	14.8
1983 D	Dan Stanley	Marcellus	14.3
1984 D	Bill Krumbach	Gaylord St Mary	15.27*
1985 D	Steve Waldron	Sand Creek	14.91*
1986 D	Willy Scott	Detroit East Catholic	14.50*
1987 D	Willy Scott	Detroit East Catholic	14.34*
1988 D	John Bull	Onekema	15.16
1989 D	Albert Rhodes	Detroit Lutheran West	14.80
1990 D	Sean Harper	Detroit Lutheran West	14.74
1991 D	Joel Robinette	Litchfield	14.86
1992 D	Greg Kapus	Brethren	15.06
1993 D	Fran Turner	Lake Mich. Catholic	14.3
1994 D	Greg Kapus	Brethren	14.98
1995 D	Matt Miller	Pittsford	15.04
1996 D	Matt Miller	Pittsford	15.24
1997 D	Zwannah Hage	Warren Bethesda Christian	14.86
1998 D	Emeka Nwosu	Detroit Loyola	15.32
1999 D	Brandon Hollenbeck	Frankfort	15.23
2000 D4	Matt Wiesen	Maple City Glen Lake	15.08*
2001 D4	Nick Ogle	Camden-Frontier	15.17
2002 D4	Alan Ball	Detroit DePorres	15.09
2003 D4	Alan Ball	Detroit DePorres	14.62*
2004 D4	Jon Thelen	Pewamo-Westphalia	15.10
2005 D4	Jon Thelen	Pewamo-Westphalia	14.88
2006 D4	Bryan Sevensma	Maple City Glen Lake	14.80
2007 D4	Adam Duerksen	Mancelona	15.21
2008 D4	Jay Spitzley	Pewamo-Westphalia	14.69w
2009 D4	Cory Noeker	Pewamo-Westphalia	14.35* (-1.4)
2010 D4	Cory Noeker	Pewamo-Westphalia	14.70
2011 D4	Austin Fedewa	Pewamo-Westphalia	15.02
2012 D4	Josh Jenkins	Reading	14.82
2013 D4	Andy Houser	Pittsford	15.34
2014 D4	David Dykstra	White Cloud	15.37 (0.9)
2015 D4	Austin Olson	Lutheran Westland	14.81 (0.5)
2016 D4	Blake Dunn	Saugatuck	14.33w (4.5)
2017 D4	Griffin Greider	Morenci	14.96 (-0.9)
2018 D4	Heath Baldwin	Kalamazoo Hackett	14.83w (2.2)

110H – UP Class AB/Division 1 Champions

(39-inch hurdles)
(y=120 yards / 109.73m)

Year	Name	School	Time
1940 UPB	George Shomin	Escanaba	16.8y*
1941 UPB	George Shomin	Escanaba	16.7y*
1942 UPB	George Shomin	Escanaba	16.1y*
1943	No Meet – World War II		
1944 UPB	Bob Crepeau	Escanaba	16.5y
1945 UPB	Bill Peterson	Escanaba	16.5y
1946 UPB	Jack Finn	Escanaba	16.5y
1947 UPB	Frank Furlong	Newberry	17.1y
1948 UPB	Keith Ewing	Sault Ste. Marie	16.5y
1949 UPB	Keith Ewing	Sault Ste. Marie	16.2y
1950 UPB	John Leppi	Ironwood	15.5y*
1951 UPB	John Leppi	Ironwood	15.7y
1952 UPB	Richard Lake	Manistique	16.4y
1953 UPB	Carmody	Munising	16.6y
1954 UPB	Dan Miron	Kingsford	16.1y
1955 UPB	David Wise	Sault Ste. Marie	16.0y
1956 UPB	Dick Robinson	Marquette	16.6y
1957 UPB	Robert Perry	Iron River	15.9y
1958 UPB	Robert Perry	Iron River	16.0y
1959 UPB	John Lasio	Calumet	16.9y
1960 UPB	Bill Rademacher	Menominee	16.3y
1961 UPB	Charles Johnson	Newberry	15.7y
1962 UPAB	Gene Pearson	Marquette	15.4y*
1963 UPAB	Mike Dissinger	Marquette	15.5y
1964 UPAB	Bob Pearson	Marquette	15.8y
1965 UPAB	Jim Boyle	Escanaba	16.5y
1966 UPAB	Jim Boyle	Escanaba	15.5y
1967 UPAB	Jim Boyle	Escanaba	15.3y*
1968 UPAB	Jeffrey Stevenson	Munising	15.4y
1969 UPAB	Allen Berg	Escanaba	15.1yw
1970 UPAB	Bob Schacht	Marquette	15.1y*
1971 UPAB	Joe Cherrette	Marquette	15.0y*
1972 UPAB	Jeff Boyer	Gladstone	14.7y*
1973 UPAB	Steve Merrick	Negaunee	15.6y
1974 UPAB	Paul Bohn	Escanaba	15.7y
1975 UPAB	Peter Riley	Calumet	15.8y
1976 UPAB	Paul Gwinn	Marquette	15.1y
1977 UPAB	Mark Bonenfant	Calumet	15.0y
1978 UPAB	Kevin French	Kingsford	15.5y

Year	Name	School	Time
1979 UPAB	Kevin French	Kingsford	15.2
1980 UPAB	Chris Brayak	Escanaba	15.4
1981 UPAB	Alan Verbrigghe	Gladstone	16.1
1982 UPAB	Jim Eastin	Escanaba	15.4
1983 UPAB	James Zigman	Kingsford	15.2
1984 UPAB	Steve Driscoll	Marquette	16.2
1985 UPAB	Randy Phare	Kingsford	15.9
1986 UPAB	Corey Potvin	Escanaba	15.7
1987 UPAB	Corey Potvin	Escanaba	15.1
1988 UPAB	Corey Potvin	Escanaba	14.6*
1989 UPAB	Scott Nevenhoven	Marquette	15.4
1990 UPAB	Scott Nevenhoven	Marquette	15.0
1991 UPAB	Scott Nevenhoven	Marquette	14.9
1992 UPAB	Gavin Pike	Sault Ste. Marie	14.8
1993 UPAB	Matt Hoskins	Kingsford	15.9
1994 UPAB	Matt Hoskins	Kingsford	15.3
1995 UPAB	Matt Hoskins	Kingsford	15.6
1996 UPAB	Brian Tourangeau	Escanaba	16.19*
1997 UPAB	Kowayne Burns	Marquette	16.15*
1998 UPAB	Chad LaCombe	Menominee	16.09*
1999 UPAB	Chad LaCombe	Menominee	16.36
2000 UPAB	Christopher Peterson	Marquette	16.60
2001 UPD1	Matt Wise	Calumet	14.8*
2002 UPD1	Matt Wise	Calumet	15.2
2003 UPD1	Chris Peterson	Marquette	15.15*
2004 UPD1	Jason Hofer	Menominee	15.55
2005 UPD1	Joseph Levandoski	Marquette	16.11
2006 UPD1	Geoff Smart	Kingsford	15.93
2007 UPD1	Dillon Menard	Negaunee	16.20
2008 UPD1	Dillon Menard	Negaunee	15.81
2009 UPD1	Dillon Menard	Negaunee	15.36
2010 UPD1	Wes Jacobson	Kingsford	15.30
2011 UPD1	Dan Bingel	Negaunee	16.10
2012 UPD1	Zach Taggart	Marquette	15.59
2013 UPD1	Brian Hines	Menominee	15.96
2014 UPD1	Jason Bell	Negaunee	15.95
2015 UPD1	Jason Bell	Negaunee	15.77
2016 UPD1	Joe Grasso	Negaunee	16.14
2017 UPD1	Aaron Bolo	Iron Mountain	15.79
2018 UPD1	Calvin Thibault	Gladstone	16.12

110H – UP Class C/Division 3 Champions

(39-inch hurdles)
(y=120 yards / 109.73m)

Year	Class	Name	School	Time
1940	UPC	Mike O'Donnell	Escanaba St. Joseph	17.3y*
1941	UPC	John Ludlow	Newberry	17.1y*
1942	UPC	Paul Nygren	Stephenson	16.3y*
1943		No Meet – World War II		
1944	UPC	Pat McKindles	L'Anse	17.2y
1945	UPC	Charles Atkocunis	Stephenson	17.3y
1946	UPC	Frank Furlong	Newberry	17.6y
1947	UPC	Ken Seaton	Hancock	17.3y
1948	UPC	Richard Nebel	Munising	17.3y
1949	UPC	Phil Creten	Gladstone	16.5y
1950	UPC	Richard Nebel	Munising	16.3y*
1951	UPC	Erland Maki	Crystal Falls	16.8y
1952	UPC	Gerald Salmela	Wakefield	17.7y
1953	UPC	Bob Harris	Bessemer	17.1y
1954	UPC	Raymond Reynolds	Houghton	19.3y
1955	UPC	Jim Olson	Wakefield	16.6y
1956	UPC	Robert Perry	Iron River	15.7y*
1957	UPC	Gary Robbins	Munising	17.3y
1958	UPC	Dick Miller	Munising	17.2y
1959	UPC	Greg Miheve	Wakefield	17.1y
1960	UPC	Greg Miheve	Wakefield	16.6y
1961	UPC	Tom Miheve	Wakefield	15.9y
1962	UPC	Pearce Olson	Lake Linden	15.9y
1963	UPC	Tom Camarich	Ontonagon	16.1y
1964	UPC	Terry Salmi	Wakefield	16.6y
1965	UPC	Jerry Lutri	Stephenson	16.8y
1966	UPC	Barry Pierson	St. Ignace	16.7y
1967	UPC	Richard Salani	Hancock	15.6y*
1968	UPC	Michael Harsh	L'Anse	15.5y*
1969	UPC	Jeffrey Stevenson	Munising	15.0yw
1970	UPC	Reggie Barefield	Rudyard	16.0y
1971	UPC	Al Meiner	Norway	15.7y
1972	UPC	Larry Rogers	Houghton	14.9y
1973	UPC	Barry Green	Rudyard	15.2y*
1974	UPC	Barry Green	Rudyard	15.3y
1975	UPC	Dean Miksa	Norway	15.7y
1976	UPC	Dean Miksa	Norway	15.0y*
1977	UPC	Dean Miksa	Norway	14.7y*
1978	UPC	Jim Watwood	Hancock	15.3y
1979	UPC	Paul Bucklin	Houghton	15.4
1980	UPC	Kevin Harmon	Munising	15.1
1981	UPC	Doug Tomoski	Iron River West Iron County	15.7
1982	UPC	Jim Passint	Ironwood	15.8
1983	UPC	Sean Ellsworth	Ironwood	15.9
1984	UPC	Kirk Harmon	Munising	15.6
1985	UPC	Gino Marchetti	Iron Mountain	15.1
1986	UPC	Gino Marchetti	Iron Mountain	15.1
1987	UPC	Jody Paradis	Munising	15.0
1988	UPC	Darin Laabs	Ironwood	15.0
1989	UPC	Mike Shephard	St. Ignace	15.1
1990	UPC	Darren Sorenson	St. Ignace	15.4
1991	UPC	Aaron Pinsky	Ironwood	15.3
1992	UPC	Mike Bond	Houghton	15.7
1993	UPC	Jereimish Konnell	Stephenson	15.6
1994	UPC	Criag Michelin	Munising	15.4
1995	UPC	Ty Nesberg	Munising	15.9
1996	UPC	Ty Nesberg	Munising	15.4
1997	UPC	Derek Sandahl	Stephenson	15.0
1998	UPC	Derek Sandahl	Stephenson	15.5
1999	UPC	Dave Silk	Negaunee	16.4
2000	UPC	Matt Wise	Calumet	15.5
2001	UPD2	Jim Clement	St. Ignace	15.7
2002	UPD2	Tony Cook	Munising	15.6
2003	UPD2	Tony Cook	Munising	15.34*
2004	UPD2	Lee Denman	Munising	16.11
2005	UPD2	Andrew Mendina	Norway	16.04
2006	UPD2	Jake Meneghini	Norway	17.01
2007	UPD2	Alex Winkler	Stephenson	15.93
2008	UPD2	Jake Meneghini	Norway	16.03
2009	UPD2	Jake Meneghini	Norway	16.00
2010	UPD2	Tanney Mayo	West Iron County	16.09
2011	UPD2	Trevor Cochrane	Bark River-Harris	16.77
2012	UPD2	James Sutton	Newberry	16.61
2013	UPD2	Vincente Carlson	Ishpeming Westwood	15.70
2014	UPD2	Jacob Jarvis	Hancock	15.65
2015	UPD2	Vincente Carlson	Ishpeming Westwood	15.35
2016	UPD2	Charlie Gerhard	Iron Mountain	17.36
2017	UPD2	Alex Johnson	Newberry	15.99
2018	UPD2	Inocencio Stankevich	Norway	16.00

110H – UP Class D/Division 3 Champions

(39-inch hurdles)
(y=120 yards / 109.73m)

Year	Class	Name	School	Time
1940	UPD	Tony Del Santo	Channing	17.0y*
1941	UPD	Turlio Marana	Hermansville	16.6y*
1942	UPD	Turlio Marana	Hermansville	16.5y*
1943		No Meet – World War II		
1944	UPD	D. Antilla	Channing	17.4y
1945	UPD	Stocky Salo	Eben	18.4y
1946	UPD	Kauppila	Eben	17.9y
1947	UPD	Stocky Salo	Eben	17.6y
1948	UPD	Leslie Niemi	Eben	18.4y
1949	UPD	Paul Tormala	Chassell	17.4y
1950	UPD	Paul Tormala	Chassell	17.0y
1951	UPD	Ralph Heitila	Chassell	17.2y
1952	UPD	George Tomasi	Hermansville	17.3y
1953	UPD	Kenneth Posio	Eben	17.1y
1954	UPD	John Anderson	Dollar Bay	17.8y
1955	UPD	Alden Tormala	Chassell	18.2y
1956	UPD	Alden Tormala	Chassell	17.1y
1957	UPD	Alden Tormala	Chassell	17.6y
1958	UPD	Ken Tormala	Chassell	16.8y
1959	UPD	Ken Tormala	Chassell	16.5y*
1960	UPD	Larry Laurich	Marquette Pierce	16.0y*
1961	UPD	Larry Laurich	Marquette Pierce	15.7y*
1962	UPD	Roger Hewer	Pickford	16.8y
1963	UPD	Steve Butula	Baraga	16.6y
1964	UPD	Roger Hewer	Pickford	15.8y
1965	UPD	Paul Feak	Channing	15.4y*
1966	UPD	Paul Feak	Channing	15.3y*
1967	UPD	Erik Rike	Pickford	16.2y
1968	UPD	Dale Morin	Rapid River	16.0y
1969	UPD	Martin Storey	Pickford	15.4y
1970	UPD	Martin Storey	Pickford	15.3y*
1971	UPD	Steven Peffers	Pickford	15.3y*
1972	UPD	Steven Peffers	Pickford	15.0y*
1973	UPD	Mark Flood	Crystal Falls Forest Park	15.7y
1974	UPD	Joe Baker	Pickford	15.5y
1975	UPD	Joe Baker	Pickford	15.6y
1976	UPD	Pete Burla	Bessemer	15.5y
1977	UPD	Dan Lato	Crystal Falls Forest Park	15.5y
1978	UPD	Robert Koski	Rock-Mid Peninsula	15.6y
1979	UPD	Robert Koski	Rock-Mid Peninsula	15.2
1980	UPD	Daniel Beckwith	Pickford	15.9
1981	UPD	John Sheski	Bark River-Harris	16.4
1982	UPD	Robert Ross	White Pine	16.5
1983	UPD	Darwin Hill	Cedarville	15.9
1984	UPD	Charlie Anderson	Rudyard	15.8
1985	UPD	Jon Gollakner	Crystal Falls Forest Park	15.7
1986	UPD	Jon Gollakner	Crystal Falls Forest Park	15.1
1987	UPD	Jon Gollakner	Crystal Falls Forest Park	15.0*
1988	UPD	Travis Schnicke	Crystal Falls Forest Park	15.8
1989	UPD	Kurt Sparkman	Rudyard	15.7
1990	UPD	Phil Croasdell	Rock-Mid Peninsula	16.0
1991	UPD	Jack Croci	Felch North Dickinson	16.4
1992	UPD	Rodney Trudell	Rock-Mid Peninsula	15.9
1993	UPD	Bob Hessel	Cedarville	15.8
1994	UPD	Chris Wining	Rapid River	15.3
1995	UPD	John Richard	Felch North Dickinson	15.7
1996	UPD	Tony Eskofski	Rapid River	16.1
1997	UPD	Richard Hanna	Pickford	16.3
1998	UPD	Don Rickley	St. Ignace	16.8
1999	UPD	Andy Livermore	Engadine	16.8
2000	UPD	Jeff Richardson	Felch North Dickinson	16.0
2001	UPD3	Jerry Reuther	Rapid River	15.9*
2002	UPD3	Brock Bower	Bark River-Harris	15.5*
2003	UPD3	Brock Bower	Bark River-Harris	15.59*
2004	UPD3	Glen Erickson	Rapid River	16.63
2005	UPD3	Jordan Gobert	Rock-Mid Peninsula	16.32
2006	UPD3	Joe Gorecki	Bark River-Harris	15.63
2007	UPD3	Grayson Hood	Engadine	15.21*
2008	UPD3	Peter Leeman	Felch North Dickinson	15.97
2009	UPD3	Jeff Zar	Rapid River	16.63
2010	UPD3	Jordan Baker	Cedarville	16.16
2011	UPD3	Jordan Baker	Cedarville	15.63
2012	UPD3	Trevor Cochrane	Bark River-Harris	15.90
2013	UPD3	Tim Hruska	Felch North Dickinson	16.17

2014 UPD3	Andy Cooper	Munising	16.11		2017 UPD3	Garrett O'Neil	Felch North Dickinson	16.34
2015 UPD3	Andy Cooper	Munising	14.96*		2018 UPD3	Jamie Jett	Bessemer	16.97
2016 UPD3	Garrett O'Neil	Felch North Dickinson	17.09					

BOYS 300-METER HURDLES

Records

D1	35.90	Kenneth Ferguson	Detroit Mumford	2002
D2	37.46	Richard Bowens	Orchard Lake St Mary	2016
D3	37.30	Chris Teitsma	Allendale	2010
D4	38.31	Blake Dunn	Saugatuck	2016
UPD1	39.74	Kenneth Broullire	Manistique	2012
UPD2	39.35	Kenneth Broullire	Manistique	2013
UPD3	40.13	Andy Cooper	Munising	2015

Records by Class (pre-2000 for LP, pre-2001 for UP)

A	37.59	Howard Triplett	Lansing Sexton	1991
B	38.53	Ryan Johnson	Dowagiac	1994
(hand	*38.0*	*John Bennink*	*Coopersville*	*1998)*
C	38.97	Pete Moe	Constantine	1988
D	39.46	Todd Richards	Reading	1990
UPAB	40.5	John Schneider	Sault Ste. Marie	1988
UPC	40.0	Richie Blowers	Manistique	1993
	40.0	Matt Chambers	Houghton	1997
UPD	40.6	John Richard	Felch North Dickinson	1994, 1995

300H – Class A/Division 1 Champions

(220-yard/ 201.17m low hurdles; 30 inches)

1896 all	Hazen Pingree	Detroit Central	29.0*
1897 all	Otis Cole	Lansing	28.2*
1898 all	Clarence Christopher	Lansing	28.4
1899 all	Bob Dawson	Pontiac	29.8
1900 all	Cyrus Peel	Detroit Western	27.2*
1901 all	John H. James (2)	Detroit University School	27.0*
1902 all	Frank Nicol	Detroit Central	26.4*
1903 all	Frank Nicol	Detroit University School	26.4*
1904 all	Earl Smith	Detroit Central	27.2
1905 all	Jose Malcomson	Detroit University School	25.8*
1906 all	Jose Malcomson	Detroit University School	25.6*
1907 all	Ralph Craig	Detroit Central	27.6
1908 all	Allen Garrels	Detroit Central	26.0
1909 all	Jimmie Craig	Detroit Central	27.8
1910 all	Jimmie Craig	Detroit Central	26.6
1911 all	Carman Smith	Bay City Eastern	26.6
1912 all	Carman Smith	Bay City Eastern	27.4
1913 all	Fred Williams	Detroit Eastern	28.4
1914 all	Fred Williams	Detroit Eastern	27.8
1915 all	Howard Handley	Alma	27.0
1916 all	Rod McKenzie	Grand Rapids Central	26.6
1917 all	Lloyd Kurtz	Kalamazoo Central	28.0
1918	No Meet – World War I		
1919 all	Edward McCallum	Detroit Central	27.8
1920 all	Harold Price	Grand Rapids Central	28.2
1921 A (tie)	George Snider	Detroit Northwestern	27.0
1921 A (tie)	Harold Belf	Highland Park	27.0
1922 A	Bill Meyers	Detroit Cass Tech	26.2
1923 A	Edward Spence	Detroit Western	26.3
1924 A	Edward Spence	Detroit Western	24.6*
1925 A	Bill Loving	Detroit Cass Tech	24.8
1926 A	Bill Loving	Detroit Cass Tech	25.6
1927 A	Eugene Beatty	Detroit Northeastern	25.3
1928 A	Eugene Beatty	Detroit Northeastern	25.9
1929 A	Charles Eknovich	Detroit Northeastern	25.0
1930 A	Willis Ward	Detroit Northwestern	26.1
1931 A	Frank Hoff	Lansing Eastern	26.4
1932 A	Harvey Woodstra	Grand Rapids Ottawa Hills	26.6
1933 A	Walt Karcewski	Grand Rapids Davis Tech	25.2
1934 A	Harold Huebner	Dearborn Fordson	26.3

(200-yard/ 182.88m low hurdles; 30 inches)

1935 A	Gayle Robinson	Muskegon	23.3*
1936 A	Perry Mason	Monroe	23.4
1937 A	Perry Mason	Monroe	22.9*
1938 A	Floyd Bates	Flint Central	22.4w
1939 A	Dale Kaulitz	Lansing Eastern	22.8*
1940 A	Russell Reader	Dearborn	22.9
1941 A	Russell Reader	Dearborn	23.3

1942 A	Horace Smith	Jackson	23.0
1943	No Meet – World War II		
1944 A	Garion Campbell	Monroe	22.8*
1945 A	Ben DeVette	Muskegon	23.1
1946 A	Marvin Chichowski	Saginaw	23.6
1947 A	Marvin Chichowski	Saginaw	22.6*
1948 A	Dick Henson	Dearborn	22.6*
1949 A	Sylvester Collins	Flint Northern	22.7

(180-yard/ 164.6m low hurdles; 30 inches)

1950 A	Clifford Walker	Kalamazoo Central	20.4*
1951 A	Tom Yinger	Monroe	19.6w
1952 A	Dale Griffin	Jackson	20.8
1953 A	Leon Burton	Flint Northern	19.1*
1954 A	Paul Wiegerink	Grand Rapids Ottawa Hills	19.5
1955 A	Don Arend	Benton Harbor	19.5
1956 A	Hayes Jones	Pontiac	19.4
1957 A	Dick Bezile	Traverse City	20.1
1958 A	Rex Cawley	Farmington	19.0*
1959 A	Rex Cawley	Farmington	19.2
1960 A	Joe Mason	Saginaw Arthur Hill	19.0w (3.6)
1961 A	Al Franklin	Flint Southwestern	19.7
1962 A	Gerry Cerulla	Wyandotte Roosevelt	19.9
1963 A	John Smith	Bay City Central	19.2
1964 A	Henry Patino	Lansing Everett	18.8w (3.6)
1965 A	Len Hatchett	Flint Central	19.3
1966 A	Bill Tipton	Pontiac Central	19.6
1967 A	Bill Tipton	Pontiac Central	19.3 (-8.9)
1968 A	Robert Johnson	Pontiac Central	20.2
1969 A	Charles Langston	Flint Central	19.3
1970 A	Melvin Reeves	Pontiac Northern	19.6
1971 A	Gary Block	Dearborn	19.5
1972 A	Paul Sherd	Rockford	19.6
1973 A	Tom Swies	Dearborn Fordson	19.8
1974 A	Stan Benefield	Highland Park	19.3
1975 A	Keith Edwards	Grand Rapids Creston	19.3
1976 A	Keith Edwards	Grand Rapids Creston	19.1

(300m low hurdles; y=330-yards [301.76m]; 30 inches)

1977 A	John Harvey	Flint Southwestern	37.8y*
1978 A	Shelby Johnson	Taylor Center	37.0y*
1979 A	Allen Jones	Midland	38.0
1980 A	Jerome Rivers	Detroit Northern	36.8y*
1981 A	Brian Vier	Grosse Pointe North	37.4y
1982 A	Thomas Wilcher	Detroit Central	36.3*
1983 A	Steve Smith	Lansing Everett	36.4
1984 A	Michael Parker	Jackson	35.9*
1985 A	Lannie Jackson	Ann Arbor Huron	37.23*
1986 A	Keith Wheeler	Troy	36.73*
1987 A	Keith Wheeler	Troy	36.23*

(300m Intermediate hurdles; 36 inches)

Year	Name	School	Time
1988 A	Steve Hearndon	Wayne Memorial	38.20*
1989 A	Bob Czachorski	Grandville	37.76*
1990 A	Howard Triplett	Lansing Sexton	37.80
1991 A	Howard Triplett	Lansing Sexton	37.59*
1992 A	Jeff Brust	Walled Lake	39.69
1993 A	Mike Spaulding	Flint Carman-Ainsworth	38.88
1994 A	Brandon Guinn	Jackson	37.5
1995 A	Otis Floyd	Southfield	37.78
1996 A	Nevara Smith	Detroit Cass Tech	38.58
1997 A	Arthur Bouyer	Lansing Sexton	37.74
1998 A	Joel Gaff	Traverse City Central	38.72
1999 A	Johnnie Birdsong	Detroit Mumford	37.98
2000 D1	Jim Campbell	Portage Northern	38.09*
2001 D1	Kenneth Ferguson	Detroit Mumford	38.32
2002 D1	Kenneth Ferguson	Detroit Mumford	35.90*
2003 D1	Mark Knight	Bay City Central	38.32
2004 D1	Matt Comer	Portage Northern	37.85
2005 D1	Matt Comer	Portage Northern	37.73
2006 D1	Nicholas McCampbell	Detroit Cass Tech	37.43
2007 D1	Kevin Lanier	White Lake Lakeland	38.38
2008 D1	Roscoe Payne	Flint Carman-Ainsworth	37.69
2009 D1	Deonte' Hurst	East Kentwood	38.01
2010 D1	Ali Arastu	Northville	37.50
2011 D1	Javonte Lipsey	Portage Northern	37.44
2013 D1	Ross Williams	Birmingham Groves	37.96
2013 D1	Javonte Lipsey	Portage Northern	38.83
2014 D1	Mike Carey	Birmingham Brother Rice	38.07
2015 D1	Robie Webster	Ypsilanti Lincoln	38.03
2016 D1	Tahawn Kimbrough	Fraser	38.25
2017 D1	Kentre Patterson	East Lansing	38.23
2018 D1	Keshaun Harris	Lansing Waverly	37.81

300H – Class B/Division 2 Champions

(220-yard/ 201.17m low hurdles; 30 inches)

Year	Name	School	Time
1921 B	George Haggerty	Ypsilanti Central	26.2*
1922 B	Jack Stem	Hastings	27.4
1923 B	Dowe Keene	Allegan	26.5
1924 B	Dowe Keene	Allegan	nt
1925 B	Lothaire Hall	Niles	26.8
1926 B	Carl Nordberg	St Joseph	26.6
1927 B	Clare Huggett	St Johns	27.6
1928 B	Jack Hyatt	Three Rivers	27.0
1929 B	Fred Shaw	Dearborn	25.8*
1930 B	William James	Hastings	27.8
1931 B	Isadore Schulman	South Haven	27.3
1932 B	Kurt Warmbein	St Joseph	26.2
1933 B	William Cramer	Dearborn	26.6
1934 B	Walter Sabbath	River Rouge	26.3

(200-yard/ 182.88m low hurdles; 30 inches)

Year	Name	School	Time
1935 B	Don Porteous	Birmingham	23.5*
1936 B	Lawrence Hardke	St Joseph	23.9
1937 B	Lavern Zander	Ionia	23.7
1938 B	Gail Cheney	Charlotte	22.8w
1939 B	Curt Alward	Traverse City	23.7
1940 B	Warren Hart	Mt Morris	23.0*
1941 B	Harold Roberts	Three Rivers	23.8
1942 B	Jack Wagner	Hastings	24.6
1943	No Meet – World War II		
1944 B	Fred Wolters	Ypsilanti Central	24.1
1945 B	Bill Bair	Ypsilanti Roosevelt	23.4
1946 B	Ralph Brown	Redford Union	24.5
1947 B	Ralph Brown	Redford Union	23.1
1948 B	Harold DubMartin	Alma	23.1
1949 B	Dave Hill	Ypsilanti Central	22.7*

(180-yard/ 164.6m low hurdles; 30 inches)

Year	Name	School	Time
1950 B	Junior Sielstra	Ludington	20.6*
1951 B	Junior Sielstra	Ludington	20.6*
1952 B	Jack Kerchkoff	Roseville	22.1
1953 B	Gene Fox	Battle Creek Lakeview	20.6*
1954 B	John Palmer	St Louis	20.2*
1955 B	John Palmer	St Louis	20.1*
1956 B	John Palmer	St Louis	20.0*
1957 B	Don Masengale	Ionia	20.2
1958 B	Rollin Douma	East Grand Rapids	19.3w (3.0)
1959 B	Art Welch	River Rouge	20.0*
1960 B	Charles Gray	Ecorse	20.3
1961 B	Jim Vogler	Detroit Lutheran West	19.1w (4.5)
1962 B	Willie Betts	River Rouge	20.0*
1963 B	Willie Betts	River Rouge	20.3
1964 B	Lamar Miller	Willow Run	18.9*
1965 B	Jim Seymour	Royal Oak Shrine	20.2
1966 B	Richard Elsasser	Dexter	19.9
1967 B	Wayne Hartwick	Erie-Mason	19.9
1968 B	Mike Whitefield	Kalamazoo Hackett	19.3
1969 B	Tim Drumbeiler	Riverview	20.1
1970 B	Terry Dooley	Harper Woods	20.2
1971 B	Dean Sommerfield	Saginaw Carrollton	20.0
1972 B	Charles Wend	Stevensville-Lakeshore	20.3
1973 B	Ed Poindexter	Inkster	19.9
1974 B	Ed Poindexter	Inkster	19.8
1975 B	Ed Poindexter	Inkster	19.5
1976 B	Mike Ball	Wyoming Park	19.4

(300m low hurdles; y=330-yards [301.76m]; 30 inches)

Year	Name	School	Time
1977 B	Mike Erickson	Wyoming Rogers	38.0y*
1978 B	Eric Young	Mason	38.3y
1979 B	Ed Brown	Otisville LakeVille	37.1*
1980 B	Greg Green	Wyoming Rogers	38.2
1981 B	Jim McGrath	Southgate Schaffer	37.2
1982 B	Jim Featherston	Flint Ainsworth	37.0y*
1983 B	Andre Hall	Flint Beecher	37.3
1984 B	Mike Miller	Eaton Rapids	38.0
1985 B	Travis Cardinal	Vicksburg	38.28*
1986 B	Steve Newsome	Eaton Rapids	38.10*
1987 B	Andrew Tomasic	Dearborn	37.1

(300m Intermediate hurdles; 36 inches)

Year	Name	School	Time
1988 B	Scott Howitz	Millington	38.3*
1989 B	Richard Palmer	Mt Clemens	38.3
1990 B	Darnell Kellogg	Redford Thurston	38.1*
1991 B	Blake Novak	Milan	38.5
1992 B	Todd Wiersman	Hudsonville	39.53*
1993 B	Ed Barnes	Grand Rapids Northview	38.1*
1994 B	Ryan Johnson	Dowagiac	38.53*
1995 B	Chad Pratt	Alma	39.91
1996 B	Dan Glander	Clawson	39.10
1997 B	Jaquan Wright	Ypsilanti Lincoln	38.75
1998 B	John Bennink	Coopersville	38.0*
1999 B	Jau Nichols	Whitehall	39.22
2000 D2	Jau Nichols	Whitehall	38.28*
2001 D2	Bryan Jackson	Alma	37.84*
2002 D2	Kyle Shaw	Three Rivers	38.43
2003 D2	Kevin Davis	Farmington Hills Harrison	38.64
2004 D2	Eric Christy	St. Clair	39.09
2005 D2	Tymel Dodd	Lansing Sexton	38.92
2006 D2	Cameron Murphy	Farmington Hills Harrison	38.98
2007 D2	Josh Hembrough	GR Forest Hills Northern	37.99
2008 D2	Trey Crongeyer	Cheboygan	39.65
2009 D2	Troy Sneller	Hamilton	38.83
2010 D2	Dalton Bates	North Branch	39.07
2011 D2	Mason Borders	Chelsea	38.14
2012 D2	David Washington	Lansing Sexton	38.18
2013 D2	Nick Robbins	GR Forest Hills Eastern	38.05
2014 D2	Jason Tran	Zeeland West	38.79
2015 D2	Richard Bowens	Orchard Lake St Mary	38.42
2016 D2	Richard Bowens	Orchard Lake St Mary	37.46*
2017 D2	Noah Caudy	Lake Odessa Lakewood	37.85
2018 D2	Corbin DeJonge	Zeeland East	38.14

300H – Class C/Division 3 Champions

(220-yard/ 201.17m low hurdles; 30 inches)

Year	Name	School	Time
1921 C	Cleo Everts	Vassar	28.8*
1922 C	Robert Soule	Plainwell	27.4*
1923 C	Donald Camp	Plainwell	27.9
1924 C	Lavere Sproul	Clinton	27.3*
1925 C	Donald McLean	Plainwell	27.3*
1926 C	Lincoln Rush	Otsego	28.0
1927 C	Fred Shaw	Dearborn	27.3*
1928 C	Osborn Slosser	Yale	28.2
1929 C	Event not held		
1930 C	Event not held		
1931 C	Event not held		
1932 C	Clare McDurmon	Caro	27.5
1933 C	Clare McDurmon	Caro	25.4*
1934 C	James Jennings	Paw Paw	26.8

(200-yard/ 182.88m low hurdles; 30 inches)

Year	Name	School	Time
1935 C	Louis Oswalt	Paw Paw	23.5*
1936 C	Garrett Stukkie	Lowell	25.0
1937 C	Bruce Smith	Mancelona	24.0
1938 C (tie)	Don Turnipseed	Mancelona	23.9
1938 C (tie)	Dick Bergman	Charlevoix	23.9
1939 C	Jim Sutton	Algonac	23.7

Year	Class	Name	School	Time
1940	C	Harold Dugan	Romulus	23.4*
1941	C	Bud Ward	Imlay City	23.8
1942	C	George Brown	Ann Arbor University	23.5
1943		No Meet – World War II		
1944	C	Bill Bair	Ypsilanti Roosevelt	24.1
1945	C	Wallace Johnson	Romulus	24.0
1946	C	Orin Schultz	Romulus	24.2
1947	C	Glen Rowe	Ypsilanti Lincoln	23.0*
1948	C	Glen Rowe	Ypsilanti Lincoln	23.4
1949	C	Jack Goodrich	Dundee	23.5

(180-yard/ 164.6m low hurdles; 30 inches)

Year	Class	Name	School	Time
1950	C	Harlan Benjamin	Milan	20.3*
1951	C	Ray Eggelston	East Jackson	20.9
1952	C	Ray Eggelston	East Jackson	21.2
1953	C	John Palmer	St Louis	20.0*
1954	C	Tom Lick	Marlette	20.5
1955	C	Don Miller	Reed City	20.6
1956	C	Don Miller	Reed City	20.5
1957	C	William Schlee	Hart	20.9
1958	C	Charles Peltz	Grosse Ile	19.6*
1959	C	Charles Peltz	Grosse Ile	20.6
1960	C	Dehn Solomon	Delton Kellogg	20.5
1961	C	Dave McLaughlin	Chelsea	19.8
1962	C	Roger Davidson	Deckerville	20.5
1963	C	Don Lowe	Vandercook Lake	20.1
1964	C	Dick Soderberg	Portland	20.1
1965	C	Ron Winkleman	Ida	20.2
1966	C	John Hogan	North Branch	19.5*
1967	C	Bob Williamston	Hartford	20.8
1968	C	Bill White	Shepherd	20.5
1969	C	Bill White	Shepherd	19.5*
1970	C	Ken Burger	Reading	19.9
1971	C	Gary Veurink	Muskegon Christian	19.9
1972	C	Gary Veurink	Muskegon Christian	19.4*
1973	C	Alan Baker	Detroit DePorres	19.9
1974	C	Harry Davis	Detroit Country Day	19.5
1975	C	Dave Merritt	Detroit Country Day	20.0
1976	C	Mike Mischung	Unionville-Sebewaing	20.2

(300m low hurdles; y=330-yards [301.76m]; 30 inches)

Year	Class	Name	School	Time
1977	C	Marcus Allen	Redford St Mary	38.3y*
1978	C	John Church	Ithaca	39.1y
1979	C	LaVaughn McNary	Cassopolis	38.2*
1980	C	Tim Johnson	Grand Rapids S. Christian	39.0y
1981	C	Mike Patterson	Dundee	38.4
1982	C	Erik Frederick	Detroit Lutheran West	37.9*
1983	C	Erik Frederick	Detroit Lutheran West	36.5*
1984	C	Tony Nickel	Michigan Center	37.8
1985	C	John Hood	Pontiac Catholic	37.8
1986	C	John Hood	Pontiac Catholic	37.62*
1987	C	Josh Whitley	Charlevoix	38.81

(300m Intermediate hurdles; 36 inches)

Year	Class	Name	School	Time
1988	C	Jason Whitley	Charlevoix	39.0*
1989	C	Jason Whitley	Charlevoix	39.21*
1990	C	Dwayne Johnson	Bangor	40.02
1991	C	Chad Mills	Ithaca	39.3
1992	C	Mark Risch	Blissfield	39.3
1993	C	Nathan Porter	Goodrich	39.3
1994	C	Carl Dosch	Newaygo	40.07
1995	C	Jason Morris	Centreville	40.13
1996	C	Pete Moe	Constantine	38.97*
1997	C	Elliot Turner	Cassopolis	39.75
1998	C	Adam Stuber	Mancelona	39.27
1999	C	Mike Seeger	Bath	39.80
2000	D3	Kevin Davis	Albion	39.65*
2001	D3	Kevin Davis	Albion	39.08*
2002	D3	Dan Fugate	Dundee	38.78*
2003	D3	Trent McCloskey	Mason County Central	39.18
2004	D3	Demea Carter	Detroit Country Day	39.09
2005	D3	Okwara Uzoh	Berrien Springs	38.68*
2006	D3	Kevin Bacon	Vassar	39.55
2007	D3	Kevin Bacon	Vassar	38.28*
2008	D3	Keith Curtis	Berrien Springs	39.33
2009	D3	Michael Parker	Michigan Center	37.98*
2010	D3	Chris Teitsma	Allendale	37.30*
2011	D3	Jake McFadden	Clare	39.15
2012	D3	Jake McFadden	Clare	38.88
2013	D3	Jesse Ring	Bangor	39.17
2014	D3	Andrew Duckett	Niles Brandywine	39.17
2015	D3	Andrew Duckett	Niles Brandywine	39.04
2016	D3	Andrew Storm	Marlette	39.14
2017	D3	Jackson Blanchard	Houghton Lake	38.50
2018	D3	Jackson Blanchard	Houghton Lake	37.79

300H – Class D/Division 4 Champions

(220-yard/ 201.17m low hurdles; 30 inches)

Year	Class	Name	School	Time
1927	D	Lloyd Brown	Centreville	27.4*
1928	D	Staughton Dalzell	Muir	29.6
1929	D	Event not held		
1930	D	Event not held		
1931	D	Event not held		
1932	D	Lester Walters	Centreville	27.7
1933	D	Lester Walters	Centreville	26.4*
1934	D	Lester Walters	Centreville	26.5

(200-yard/ 182.88m low hurdles; 30 inches)

Year	Class	Name	School	Time
1935	D	Frank Kohler	St Clair Shores Lakeview	25.0*
1936	D	Vaughn Smoyer	Napoleon	25.3
1937	D	Earl McDonald	Ellsworth	25.7
1938	D	Gordon Craig	Bloomfield Hills	23.8*
1939	D	Gordon Craig	Bloomfield Hills	23.9
1940	D	Bernard Zeeb	Bath	24.4
1941	D	Bernard Zeeb	Bath	24.5
1942	D	George Wilson	Benton Harbor St John	26.1
1943		No Meet – World War II		
1944	D	Paul Odette	Glen Arbor Leelanau School	24.9
1945	D	James Ostler	Glen Arbor Leelanau School	nt
1946	D	Dick Miner	Bloomfield Hills	25.7
1947	D	Dick Miner	Bloomfield Hills	24.5
1948	D	Dick Miner	Bloomfield Hills	24.8
1949	D	Gaylord Snyder	Vestaburg	23.6*

(180-yard/ 164.6m low hurdles; 30 inches)

Year	Class	Name	School	Time
1950	D	John Fortenberry	Dearborn Edison Institute	21.5*
1951	D	Norton Averill	Otisville	22.4
1952	D	Gerald Peterson	New Troy	23.3
1953	D	Richard Beane	Brethren	20.8*
1954	D	Richard Beane	Brethren	21.0
1955	D	Roland Joles	Wolverine	21.8
1956	D	Roland Joles	Wolverine	22.0
1957	D	Orville Emerson	Dansville	21.9
1958	D	Wes Butcher	Spring Arbor	20.6*
1959	D	Norman Kuhns	Newaygo	21.3
1960	D	Brown Jordan	Michigan School for Deaf	20.1
1961	D	Dave Beracy	Ashley	20.7
1962	D	David Woods	Wolverine	20.5*
1963	D	John Fry	Unionville	20.4*
1964	D	Jerry Ruell	Lake City	20.1*
1965	D	Terry Barnes	Centreville	20.7
1966	D	Clarence Baber	Covert	20.2
1967	D	Allen Childs	Unionville	20.7
1968	D	Mike Taverniti	Potterville	20.6
1969	D	John White	Grass Lake	20.3
1970	D	Mike Gordon	Mt Clemens St Mary	20.4
1971	D	Art Morris	Covert	20.8
1972	D	Mike Gaeth	Unionville	20.2
1973	D	Kevin Clark	Lake City	20.6
1974	D	Kevin Clark	Lake City	20.5
1975	D	Orlin Swimmer	Morenci	20.0*
1976	D	David Sykes	Litchfield	20.2

(300m low hurdles; y=330-yards [301.76m]; 30 inches)

Year	Class	Name	School	Time
1977	D	David Sykes	Litchfield	36.9y*
1978	D	Mike Shenemen	Bellaire	39.1y
1979	D	Vernon Lynch	Detroit DePorres	38.8
1980	D	Greg Henderson	Detroit DePorres	38.7
1981	D	Greg Henderson	Detroit DePorres	37.3
1982	D	Jeff Clark	Camden-Frontier	38.7
1983	D	Dan Stanley	Marcellus	38.4
1984	D	Dave Sella	Allendale	38.95*
1985	D	Dave Sella	Allendale	38.3
1986	D	Willy Scott	Detroit East Catholic	39.31
1987	D	Willy Scott	Detroit East Catholic	39.37

(300m Intermediate hurdles; 36 inches)

Year	Class	Name	School	Time
1988	D	Pat Wilson	Decatur	39.89*
1989	D	Sean Harper	Detroit Lutheran West	40.5
1990	D	Todd Richards	Reading	39.46*
1991	D	Joel Robinette	Litchfield	39.50
1992	D	Todd Mrozinski	Onekema	40.81
1993	D	Jake Baxter	Pittsford	40.50
1994	D	Greg Kapus	Brethren	39.84
1995	D	Jason Hoolsema	Peck	40.95
1996	D	Matt Miller	Pittsford	40.23
1997	D	John Westbrook	North Muskegon	40.61
1998	D	Drake Wilkins	Harper Woods Gallagher	40.2
1999	D	Drake Wilkins	Harper Woods Gallagher	40.57
2000	D4	Marcello Johnson	Burton Bentley	39.85*
2001	D4	Nick Ogle	Camden-Frontier	39.30*
2002	D4	Rob Greer	Lutheran Westland	39.20*
2003	D4	Ryan McDowell	Morenci	40.11

Year	Class	Name	School	Time
2004 D4		Steve Labusa	Manton	40.29
2005 D4		Keagan Puse	Ottawa Lake Whiteford	39.78
2006 D4		Bryan Sevensma	Maple City Glen Lake	38.77*
2007 D4		Adam Duerksen	Mancelona	39.39
2008 D4		Adam Duerksen	Mancelona	40.30
2009 D4		Cory Noeker	Pewamo-Westphalia	38.88
2010 D4		Cory Noeker	Pewamo-Westphalia	38.95
2011 D4		Jesse Schwartz	Centreville	40.15
2012 D4		Josh Jenkins	Reading	40.16
2013 D4		Clayton Meldrum	Kalamazoo Christian	40.66
2014 D4		Blake Dunn	Saugatuck	40.22
2015 D4		Blake Dunn	Saugatuck	39.31
2016 D4		Blake Dunn	Saugatuck	38.31*
2017 D4		Derek Flory	Marcellus	39.89
2018 D4		Derek Flory	Marcellus	39.49

300H – UP Class AB/Division 1 Champions

(220-yard/ 201.17m low hurdles; 30 inches)

Year	Class	Name	School	Time
1940 UPB		Harry Ingersol	Calumet	25.9*
1941 UPB		Fred Rydholm	Marquette	25.7*
1942 UPB		George Shomin	Escanaba	24.9*
1943		No Meet – World War II		
1944 UPB		Bob Crepeau	Escanaba	24.9*
1945 UPB		Marshall Treado	Ironwood	25.0
1946 UPB		Jack Peterson	Escanaba	24.8*
1947 UPB		Jack Peterson	Escanaba	24.6*
1948 UPB		Keith Ewing	Sault Ste. Marie	24.6*
1949 UPB		Keith Ewing	Sault Ste. Marie	23.8*

(180-yard/ 164.6m low hurdles; 30 inches)

Year	Class	Name	School	Time
1950 UPB		John Leppi	Ironwood	20.4*
1951 UPB		John Leppi	Ironwood	21.4
1952 UPB		Richard Lake	Manistique	22.0
1953 UPB		Eddie Vergara	Iron River	21.7
1954 UPB		Dan Miron	Kingsford	21.6
1955 UPB		Eddie Vergara	Iron River	21.5
1956 UPB		Bob Wills	Ishpeming	21.1
1957 UPB		Bob Wills	Ishpeming	20.8
1958 UPB		Robert Perry	Iron River	21.2
1959 UPB		Dan Pearce	Marquette	22.1
1960 UPB		Robert Brown	Newberry	21.2
1961 UPB		Don Anderson	Newberry	20.7
1962 UPB		Robert Brown	Newberry	21.0
1963 UPAB		Bob Pearson	Marquette	21.9
1964 UPAB		Bob Pearson	Marquette	21.7
1965 UPAB		Brad Shouldice	Sault Ste. Marie	21.7
1966 UPAB		Brad Shouldice	Sault Ste. Marie	21.4
1967 UPAB		Bill Zhulkie	Ishpeming	20.6
1968 UPAB		Bob Narotzky	Ishpeming	21.4
1969 UPAB		Joe Lasnoski	Escanaba Holy Name	21.2
1970 UPAB		Robert Schact	Marquette	20.2*
1971 UPAB		Rich Sherwood	West Iron	20.6
1972 UPAB		Jeff Boyer	Gladstone	20.5
1973 UPAB		Steve Merrick	Negaunee	20.7
1974 UPAB		Mike Cvengros	Escanaba	20.3
1975 UPAB		Ross Coltman	Calumet	20.3
1976 UPAB		Ross Coltman	Calumet	20.1*

(300m low hurdles; y=330-yards [301.76m]; 30 inches)

Year	Class	Name	School	Time
1977 UPAB		Bryan Viau	Escanaba	39.8y*
1978 UPAB		Kevin French	Kingsford	39.8y*
1979 UPAB		Kevin French	Kingsford	40.0
1980 UPAB		Rod Garwood	Gwinn	38.9*
1981 UPAB		Bill Forrester	Sault Ste Marie	40.3
1982 UPAB		Jim Eastin	Escanaba	40.7
1983 UPAB		Jim Eastin	Escanaba	40.1
1984 UPAB		Willie Lake	Menominee	40.1
1985 UPAB		Hank Gretzinger	Gwinn	41.5
1986 UPAB		Phil Zagrodnik	Menominee	40.0
1987 UPAB		Jim LaFave	Marquette	41.7

(300m Intermediate hurdles; 36 inches)

Year	Class	Name	School	Time
1988 UPAB		John Schneider	Sault Ste. Marie	40.5*
1989 UPAB		Aaron Pinski	Ironwood	42.9
1990 UPAB		Jeff Povolo	Kingsford	40.6
1991 UPAB		Matt Gibson	Kingsford	40.6
1992 UPAB		Gavin Pike	Sault Ste. Marie	40.7
1993 UPAB		Steve Molnar	Menominee	41.2
1994 UPAB		Steve Molnar	Menominee	40.7
1995 UPAB		Nick Kelley	Menominee	42.4
1996 UPAB		Josh Edwards	Kingsford	41.5
1997 UPAB		Brian Tourangeau	Escanaba	42.0
1998 UPAB		Dave Siik	Negaunee	41.5
1999 UPAB		Chad LaCombe	Menominee	41.5
2000 UPAB		Steve Davis	Gladstone	43.2
2001 UPD1		Matt Wise	Calumet	40.5*
2002 UPD1		Matt Wise	Calumet	40.5*
2003 UPD1		Chris Peterson	Marquette	40.21*
2004 UPD1		Jason Hofer	Menominee	40.01*
2005 UPD1		James Cappeart	Gladstone	41.23
2006 UPD1		James Cappeart	Gladstone	41.27
2007 UPD1		Casey Danhoff	Gladstone	42.86
2008 UPD1		Billy Morrow	Gladstone	41.96
2009 UPD1		Billy Morrow	Gladstone	41.30
2010 UPD1		Wes Jacobson	Kingsford	40.81
2011 UPD1		Kenneth Broullire	Manistique	41.72
2012 UPD1		Kenneth Broullire	Manistique	39.74*
2013 UPD1		Bryan Hines	Menominee	41.59
2014 UPD1		Jason Bell	Negaunee	41.72
2015 UPD1		Jason Bell	Negaunee	41.31
2016 UPD1		Bradley Zeaborg	Marquette	42.32
2017 UPD1		Charlie Gerhard	Iron Mountain	41.34
2018 UPD1		Calvin Thibault	Gladstone	40.04

300H – UP Class C/Division 2 Champions

(220-yard/ 201.17m low hurdles; 30 inches)

Year	Class	Name	School	Time
1940 UPC		Kakkala	Gwinn	25.7*
1941 UPC		John Ludlow	Newberry	nt
1942 UPC		John Ludlow	Newberry	24.9*
1943		No Meet – World War II		
1944 UPC		Pat McKindles	L'Anse	24.9*
1945 UPC		Charles Atkocunis	Stephenson	25.5
1946 UPC		Frank Furlong	Newberry	25.2
1947 UPC		Jim Tourville	Houghton	25.9
1948 UPC		Jim Tourville	Houghton	25.9
1949 UPC		Dick Nebel	Munising	24.9*

(180-yard/ 164.6m low hurdles; 30 inches)

Year	Class	Name	School	Time
1950 UPC		Dick Nebel	Munising	21.4*
1951 UPC		James Pratt	Houghton	22.9
1952 UPC		Gerald Salmela	Wakefield	23.0
1953 UPC		Bob Harris	Bessemer	22.9
1954 UPC		James Contratto	Bessemer	22.1
1955 UPC		Ralph Hurley	Houghton	22.8
1956 UPC		Robert Perry	Iron River	20.7*
1957 UPC		John Sanreget	Houghton	22.8
1958 UPC		Dick Miller	Munising	23.0
1959 UPC		Tom Miheve	Wakefield	22.6
1960 UPC		Bob Koski	Wakefield	22.2
1961 UPC		Tom Miheve	Wakefield	21.3
1962 UPC		Cal Shirey	Gwinn	21.9
1963 UPC		Ernie Brumbaugh	Norway	21.3
1964 UPC		Gary Bordeau	Lake Linden	22.0
1965 UPC		Jack Bennett	Gwinn	22.1
1966 UPC		Barry Pierson	St. Ignace	21.9
1967 UPC		Richard Salani	Hancock	20.7*
1968 UPC		Richard Salani	Hancock	21.0
1969 UPC		Bill Tarbox	Hancock	20.9
1970 UPC		James Bonetti	Norway	21.5
1971 UPC		Larry Rogers	Houghton	20.8
1972 UPC		Larry Rogers	Houghton	20.4*
1973 UPC		Barry Green	Rudyard	20.6
1974 UPC		Barry Green	Rudyard	20.3*
1975 UPC		Mike Kelly	Houghton	20.8
1976 UPC		Tom Robinson	Iron River West Iron County	20.3*

(300m low hurdles; y=330-yards [301.76m]; 30 inches)

Year	Class	Name	School	Time
1977 UPC		Brien Ricci	Hancock	39.9y*
1978 UPC		Scott Dobson	Ishpeming	41.0y
1979 UPC		Dale Warren	Iron Mountain	40.9
1980 UPC		Dale Warren	Iron Mountain	39.5*
1981 UPC		Scott LaCombe	Munising	41.0
1982 UPC		William Popp	Iron Mountain	40.4
1983 UPC		Scott Rasner	Stephenson	40.2
1984 UPC		Kirk Harmon	Munising	39.9
1985 UPC		Gino Marchetti	Iron Mountain	39.6
1986 UPC		Jody Paradis	Munising	39.5*
1987 UPC		Jody Paradis	Munising	41.1

(300m Intermediate hurdles; 36 inches)

Year	Class	Name	School	Time
1988 UPC		Darin Laabs	Ironwood	40.3
1989 UPC		Mike Shephard	St. Ignace	41.7
1990 UPC		Darren Sorenson	St. Ignace	41.2
1991 UPC		Kevin Coleman	Ironwood	41.9
1992 UPC		Richie Blowers	Manistique	42.3
1993 UPC		Richie Blowers	Manistique	40.0

Year	Class	Name	School	Mark
1994	UPC	Dan Dinnocenzio	Ironwood	40.2
1995	UPC	Francis Kmiecik	Ironwood	42.0
1996	UPC	Matt Chambers	Houghton	40.4
1997	UPC	Matt Chambers	Houghton	40.0
1998	UPC	Scott Carhpun	Stephenson	41.9
1999	UPC	Dave Siik	Negaunee	41.5
2000	UPC	Nick Baumgartner	West Iron County	40.4
2001	UPD2	Jim Clement	St. Ignace	41.9*
2002	UPD2	Justin Allen	Norway	42.4
2003	UPD2	Justin Allen	Norway	42.03*
2004	UPD2	Lee Denman	Munising	40.98*
2005	UPD2	Andrew Mendina	Norway	42.35
2006	UPD2	Alex Winkler	Stephenson	42.01
2007	UPD2	Alex Winkler	Stephenson	41.97
2008	UPD2	Jake Dellanelo	Ishpeming Westwood	43.40
2009	UPD2	JaKe Meneghini	Norway	41.90
2010	UPD2	Cubby Litzner	St. Ignace	41.08
2011	UPD2	Caleb Litzner	St. Ignace	41.49
2012	UPD2	Josh Carlson	Ironwood	44.21
2013	UPD2	Kenneth Broullire	Manistique	39.35*
2014	UPD2	Jacob Jarvis	Hancock	40.36
2015	UPD2	Vincente Carlson	Ishpeming Westwood	42.59
2016	UPD2	Riley Jarocki	Ironwood	44.72
2017	UPD2	Inocenio Stankevich	Norway	42.46
2018	UPD2	Charlie Gerhard	Iron Mountain	41.10

300H – UP Class D/Division 3 Champions

(220-yard/ 201.17m low hurdles; 30 inches)

Year	Class	Name	School	Mark
1940	UPD	Tony Del Santo	Channing	26.7*
1941	UPD	Turlio Marana	Hermansville	24.4*
1942	UPD	Wayne Burge	Alpha	25.0
1943		No Meet – World War II		
1944	UPD	Bill MacEchern	Hermansville	25.0
1945	UPD	Waino Salo	Eben	25.4
1946	UPD	Waino Salo	Eben	24.9
1947	UPD	Waino Salo	Eben	25.2
1948	UPD	Dean Lind	Rapid River	27.0
1949	UPD	Don Hurst	Marquette Pierce	26.5

(180-yard/ 164.6m low hurdles; 30 inches)

Year	Class	Name	School	Mark
1950	UPD	Harold Kallio	Eben	22.4*
1951	UPD	William Kallio	Eben	22.6
1952	UPD	Allen Dighera	Negaunee St. Paul	23.3
1953	UPD	John Nordeen	Gwinn	23.0
1954	UPD	John Nordeen	Gwinn	22.6
1955	UPD	David Fountain	Pickford	22.8
1956	UPD	David Fountain	Pickford	21.8*
1957	UPD	Jim Lockhart	Pickford	23.3
1958	UPD	Alden Tormala	Chassell	23.1
1959	UPD	Ken Tormala	Chassell	22.9
1960	UPD	Jack Ruthledge	Pickford	21.9
1961	UPD	Larry Laurich	Marquette Pierce	21.2*
1962	UPD	Gene Fuller	Rapid River	22.0
1963	UPD	Roger Hewer	Pickford	22.3
1964	UPD	Roger Hewer	Pickford	22.6
1965	UPD	Paul Feak	Channing	21.1*
1966	UPD	Melvin Leach	Pickford	21.2
1967	UPD	Erik Rike	Pickford	21.7
1968	UPD	Don Nye	Dollar Bay	21.8
1969	UPD	Martin Storey	Pickford	21.1*
1970	UPD	Martin Storey	Pickford	20.4*
1971	UPD	Ron Beacom	Pickford	20.8
1972	UPD	Steve Peffers	Pickford	20.6
1973	UPD	Mark Flood	Crystal Falls Forest Park	20.7
1974	UPD	Joe Baker	Pickford	20.0*
1975	UPD	Joe Baker	Pickford	20.8
1976	UPD	Neil Peffers	Pickford	21.0

(300m low hurdles; y=330-yards [301.76m]; 30 inches)

Year	Class	Name	School	Mark
1977	UPD	John Andrzejak	Pickford	40.4y*
1978	UPD	John Andrzejak	Pickford	39.7y*
1979	UPD	Greg Croasdell	Rock-Mid Peninsula	40.7
1980	UPD	Daniel Beckwith	Pickford	40.9
1981	UPD	John Sheski	Bark River-Harris	41.0
1982	UPD	Jack Laimakka	Wakefield	41.6
1983	UPD	Joe Chapman	DeTour	40.7
1984	UPD	Jim Matrella	Bessemer	40.2
1985	UPD	Mark Nelson	DeTour	40.9
1986	UPD	Marc Nelson	DeTour	39.9
1987	UPD	Sean Norton	Lake Linden-Hubbell	42.5

(300m Intermediate hurdles; 36 inches)

Year	Class	Name	School	Mark
1988	UPD	Kurt Sparkman	Rudyard	42.3*
1989	UPD	Pete Avena	Crystal Falls Forest Park	42.7
1990	UPD	Pete Avena	Crystal Falls Forest Park	42.2*
1991	UPD	Jake Tyner	Eben Junction Superior Central	42.9
1992	UPD	Rodney Trudell	Rock-Mid Peninsula	43.8
1993	UPD	John Richard	Felch North Dickinson	42.6
1994	UPD	John Richard	Felch North Dickinson	40.6*
1995	UPD	John Richard	Felch North Dickinson	40.6*
1996	UPD	Brian Bouty	Powers-North Central	42.3
1997	UPD	Brian Bouty	Powers-North Central	42.6
1998	UPD	Kurt Miller	DeTour	42.4
1999	UPD	Matt Barron	Rock-Mid Peninsula	41.9
2000	UPD	Janssen Baij	Felch North Dickinson	41.8
2001	UPD3	Jordan Wilcoxen	Engadine	43.0*
2002	UPD3	Joe Nyberg	Pickford	42.3*
2003	UPD3	David Sanderson	Cedarville	42.40*
2004	UPD3	David Sanderson	Cedarville	41.91*
2005	UPD3	Grayson Hood	Engadine	42.36
2006	UPD3	Grayson Hood	Engadine	42.56
2007	UPD3	Grayson Hood	Engadine	40.63*
2008	UPD3	Peter Leeman	Felch North Dickinson	42.37
2009	UPD3	Mike Schmaus	Ontonagon	41.45
2010	UPD3	Mike Schmaus	Ontonagon	40.42*
2011	UPD3	Jordan Baker	Cedarville	41.12
2012	UPD3	Trevor Cochrane	Bark River-Harris	41.28
2013	UPD3	Tim Hruska	Felch North Dickinson	41.89
2014	UPD3	Andy Cooper	Munising	40.77
2015	UPD3	Andy Cooper	Munising	40.13*
2016	UPD3	Garrett O'Neil	Felch North Dickinson	42.75
2017	UPD3	Garrett O'Neil	Felch North Dickinson	41.97
2018	UPD3	Brayden Tomes	Bessemer	41.94

BOYS HIGH JUMP

Records

Class	Mark	Name	School	Year
D1	6-11	Jonathon Beeler	Holly	2010
	6-11	Owen Hughes	Okemos	2011
D2	7-0	Alex Klemm	Macomb Lutheran North	2016
D3	7-0	Andrew Dodson	Frankenmuth	2005
D4	6-10½	Kurt Schneider	Auburn Hills Oakland Christian	2009
UPD1	6-5	Jake Richmond	Kingsford	2004
UPD2	6-4	James Sutton	Newberry	2013
UPD3	6-6	Brock Bower	Bark River-Harris	2002, 2003

Records by Class (pre-2000 for LP, pre-2001 for UP)

Class	Mark	Name	School	Year
A	7-0	John McIntosh	Sterling Hts Stevenson	1979
	7-0	Dave Elliott	Ann Arbor Pioneer	1979
	7-0	Jeff Kus	Grand Ledge	1997
B	6-11½	Bob Krikke	G R Christian	1979
C	6-10¼	Robert King	Bath	1999

D	6-9¼	Mike Winsor	Fulton-Middleton	1989
UPAB	6-8	Bret Nerat	Menominee	1990
UPC	6-6	Darin Laabs	Ironwood	1988
UPD	7-1	John Payment	Brimley	1989

HJ – Class A/Division 1 Champion

Year	Name	School	Mark
1895 all	Clarence Christopher	Lansing	4-10*
	(another report has mark at 5-0)		
1896 all	John Prentis	Detroit Central	5-2*
1897 all	Neil Snow	Detroit Central	5-8*
1898 all	Clarence Christopher	Lansing	4-11
1899 all	Roy Ellis	Detroit Central	5-3*
1900 all	George Haller	Detroit School for Boys	5-2
1901 all	Jimmy Keena	Detroit University School	5-4½
1902 all	Jimmy Keena	Detroit University School	5-5*
1903 all	George Lawton	Detroit Central	5-7*
1904 all	John Neil Patterson	Detroit University School	5-7½
1905 all	John Neil Patterson	Detroit University School	5-9*
1906 all	John Neil Patterson	Detroit University School	6-1¼*
1907 all (tie)	Roger Hawkins	Detroit Central	5-7
1907 all (tie)	Clifton Dick	Muskegon	5-7
1908 all	Tom Stalker	Detroit Central	5-7¾
1909 all	Frank Higgins	Manistee	5-2
1910 all	Warren Sargeant	Shelby	5-6¼
1911 all	Austin Chambers	Detroit Central	5-3¾
1912 all	Phillip Kelleher	Battle Creek	5-6
1913 all	Howard Armstrong	Muskegon	5-7
1914 all (tie)	Mosher Luther	Grand Rapids Central	5-8
1914 all (tie)	Howard Armstrong	Muskegon	5-8
1915 all	Vic Crawford	Detroit Cass Tech	5-7¼
1916 all	Paul Walker	Dowagiac	5-7½
1917 all	Conant Hatch	St Joseph	5-6
1918	No Meet – World War I		
1919 all	Paul Sweet	Battle Creek	5-8
1920 all	Leroy Niesch	Detroit Eastern	5-10
1921 A	Bob Herrman	Lansing Central	5-7
1922 A	John Huntington	Detroit Eastern	5-9¾
1923 A	John Huntington	Detroit Eastern	5-9¼
1924 A	Charles Ruggles	Detroit Northern	5-9
1925 A	Max Holbrook	Coldwater	5-10
1925 A (tie)	Edward Gaines	Detroit Cass Tech	5-10
1925 A (tie)	William Loving	Detroit Cass Tech	5-10
1926 A	Nelson Schrier	Kalamazoo Central	5-9½
1927 A	Thad Dennis	Detroit Northwestern	6-¼
1928 A	Robert Sampson	Detroit Cass Tech	6-¾
1929 A	Willis Ward	Detroit Northwestern	6-1¾*
1930 A	Arnold Deneau	Detroit Mackenzie	5-10½
1931 A	William Burrell	Kalamazoo Central	5-10
1932 A	Jack Powell	Kalamazoo Central	5-8¾
1933 A	Jack Powell	Kalamazoo Central	5-10¼
1934 A (tie)	William Watson	Saginaw	5-11
1934 A (tie)	Ray McDonald	Grand Rapids South	5-11
1935 A	William Watson	Saginaw	6-1¼
1936 A	James Keegstra	Grand Rapids Central	5-11¾
1937 A	Gordon Miller	Grand Rapids Creston	5-8½
1938 A	Floyd Bates	Flint Central	6-2 7/8*
1939 A	Otis Wade	River Rouge	6-¼
1940 A (tie)	George Rich	Battle Creek	5-9
1940 A (tie)	Ed Murphy	Pontiac	5-9
1941 A	Cliff Fielder	Flint Northern	5-10
1942 A	Olin Evans	River Rouge	5-11
1943	No Meet – World War II		
1944 A (tie)	Dick Rifenburg	Saginaw Arthur Hill	5-8½
1944 A (tie)	George Osborn	Saginaw Arthur Hill	5-8½
1944 A (tie)	Pete Van Henennamm	Grand Rapids Central	5-8½
1944 A (tie)	Jack Hampton	Battle Creek Central	5-8½
1945 A (tie)	Bob Bradley	Battle Creek Central	5-10½
1945 A (tie)	Ted Judson	Ann Arbor	5-10½
1946 A	Bob Bradley	Battle Creek	6-1
1947 A	Jim Johnson	Saginaw	5-11¾
1948 A (tie)	Milt Mead	Bay City Central	5-9¾
1948 A (tie)	Dick Tunney	Saginaw Arthur Hill	5-9¾
1948 A (tie)	Bill Ware	Battle Creek Central	5-9¾
1949 A	Milt Mead	Bay City Central	6-2
1950 A	Milt Mead	Bay City Central	6-4*
1951 A	Elmer Hawkins	Flint Northern	5-11
1952 A	Howard Neely	Ypsilanti	6-0
1953 A	Williard Neely	Ypsilanti Central	5-11¼
1954 A (tie)	Williard Neely	Ypsilanti	6-¼
1954 A (tie)	Dick McKinney	Ferndale	6-¼
1955 A (tie)	Hudson Ray	Pontiac	6-3½
1955 A (tie)	Alex Barge	Pontiac	6-3½
1956 A	Hudson Ray	Pontiac	6-3¾
1957 A	Hudson Ray	Pontiac Central	6-1
1958 A	Gene Lawson	Highland Park	6-3½
1959 A (tie)	Alonzo Littlejohn	Jackson	6-1
1959 A (tie)	John Baldy	Monroe	6-1
1959 A (tie)	Jesse Campbell	Ann Arbor	6-1
1959 A (tie)	Rolf Langerfelt	Grosse Pointe	6-1
1959 A (tie)	Al Ammerman	Dearborn	6-1
1959 A (tie)	Troy Palmer	Ferndale	6-1
1960 A	Al Ammerman	Dearborn	6-4½*
1961 A (tie)	Al Washington	Flint Northern	6-2
1961 A (tie)	Jim Worthy	Kalamazoo Central	6-2
1962 A	Al Washington	Flint Northern	6-2½
1963 A	Al Washington	Flint Northern	6-5*
1964 A	Ken Dyer	Ann Arbor	6-7¾ *
1965 A	Stan Allen	Detroit Eastern	6-5¼
1966 A	Donald Lavalais	Pontiac Central	6-6
1967 A	Freels Bacon	Flint Central	6-8*
1968 A	Russ Carson	Flint Central	6-6
1969 A	Campy Russell	Pontiac Central	6-4
1970 A	Dave Lekovich	Bloomfield Hills Lahser	6-6
1971 A	Dean Oosterhouse	East Lansing	6-8*
1972 A	Reggie Ferguson	Flint Northwestern	6-9*
1973 A	Tom Siebert	Kalamazoo Central	6-6
1974 A	Darrell Williams	Grand Rapids Ottawa Hills	6-8
1975 A	Mike Braman	Midland	6-7
1976 A (tie)	Dennis Lewis	Ypsilanti	6-9½*
1976 A (tie)	Gary Martin	East Lansing	6-9½*
1976 A (tie)	Victor Freeman	Ypsilanti	6-9½*
1977 A	Dennis Lewis	Ypsilanti	6-10*
1978 A	Paul Piwinski	Warren Cousino	6-10½*
1979 A	John McIntosh	Sterling Hts Stevenson	7-0*
	(Dave Elliott/Ann Arbor Pioneer also jumped 7-0*)		
1980 A	Walt Reynolds	East Lansing	6-7
1981 A	Mark Smith	Lansing Sexton	6-9
1982 A	Scott Reed	Lansing Everett	6-9
1983 A	Tom Hughes	Dearborn Edsel Ford	6-10
1984 A	Ted Harris	Detroit Cooley	6-10
1985 A	James Smith	Jackson	6-10
1986 A	Melvin Kelly	Lansing Everett	6-10
1987 A	Orlando Scott	Lansing Sexton	6-9
1988 A	Joe Beaman	Jackson	6-10
1989 A	Dan Reddan	Rochester	6-9
1990 A	Shannon Norris	Lansing Eastern	6-11
1991 A	Stephane Mayo	Pontiac Central	6-11
1992 A	Mario Patterson	Adrian	6-10
1993 A	Chuck Thrash	Flint Carman-Ainsworth	6-8
1994 A	Elgin Bates	Ann Arbor Pioneer	6-11
1995 A	Elvin Jones	Ferndale	6-4
1996 A	Elvin Jones	Ferndale	6-6
1997 A	Jeff Kus	Grand Ledge	7-0*
1998 A	William Nash	Milford	6-9
1999 A	Nate Blevins	GR Forest Hills Central	6-6
2000 D1	Michael Weishuhn	Pinckney	6-8*
2001 D1	Michael Weishuhn	Pinckney	6-8*
2002 D1	Adam Kring	Port Huron Northern	6-7
2003 D1	Ashard Moore	Ann Arbor Huron	6-6
2004 D1	Eltaro Hooper	Ypsilanti Lincoln	6-10¼*
2005 D1	Ryan Libiran	Okemos	6-9
2006 D1	Keonte Johnson	Pontiac Northern	6-7
2007 D1	Eric Thornton	Canton	6-7
2008 D1	Michael White	Livonia Stevenson	6-6
2009 D1	Jonathon Beeler	Holly	6-8
2010 D1	Jonathon Beeler	Holly	6-11*
2011 D1	Owen Hughes	Okemos	6-11*
2012 D1	Rre Goynes	Redford Union	6-6
2013 D1	Robert Atwater	Lincoln Park	6-10
2014 D1	Brandon Piwinski	Warren DeLaSalle	6-10
2015 D1	Brandon Piwinski	Warren DeLaSalle	6-7
2016 D1	Kalebb Perry	Mt Pleasant	6-7
2017 D1	Conner Bush	Plymouth	6-6
2018 D1	Cassidy Henshaw	Traverse City Central	6-9

HJ – Class B/Division 2 Champion

1921 B	Kent Pritchard	Allegan	5-9*		1966 B	Eric Jackson	Clintondale	6-2
1922 B	Kent Pritchard	Allegan	5-5¾		1967 B	Larry Tyler	Detroit Cathedral	6-3
1923 B	Max Holbrook	Coldwater	5-7½		1968 B	Ron DeVries	Erie-Mason	6-3
1924 B	Max Holbrook	Coldwater	5-7¼		1969 B	Brad Miller	Sturgis	6-5½*
1925 B	Ernest Zavits	St Johns	5-8		1970 B	Brad Miller	Sturgis	6-6¼*
1926 B	Charles Crabill	Niles	5-4		1971 B	Jesse Meyers	Midland Bullock Creek	6-3
1927 B	George Williams	Birmingham	5-8¼		1972 B	Charles Durrant	Portland	6-8*
1928 B	Ray March	Petoskey	5-6¾		1973 B	Jeff Swanson	Battle Creek Pennfield	6-4
1929 B (tie)	James Crawford	Niles	5-6¾		1974 B	Jeff Swanson	Battle Creek Pennfield	6-8½*
1929 B (tie)	Norm Borton	Alma	5-6¾		1975 B	Ralph Smith	Holly	6-4
1930 B	Edward Murphy	Escanaba	5-8¼		1976 B	Gordon Jackson	Burton Bentley	6-9¼*
1931 B	Harold Powers	Mt Pleasant	5-9*		1977 B	Derrick Futrell	Saginaw Buena Vista	6-11¼*
1932 B	Kurt Warmbein	St. Joseph	5-10 5/8*		1978 B	Bob Krikke	Grand Rapids Christian	6-7½
1933 B (tie)	Rex Overbeck	Birmingham	5-10 1/8		1979 B	Bob Krikke	Grand Rapids Christian	6-11½*
1933 B (tie)	Victor Wellwood	Redford Union	5-10 1/8		1980 B	Mike Velis	Grosse Ile	6-7
1934 B	Allen Cisco	Dowagiac	5-7		1981 B	Charles Jones	Flint Beecher	6-5
1935 B	William F. Williams	Albion	5-9¼		1982 B	Don Durant	Warren Fitzgerald	6-8
1936 B	Norman Goodwin	Allegan	5-10¼		1983 B	Dan Durant	Warren Fitzgerald	6-9
1937 B	Frank McCarthy	Birmingham	5-8		1984 B	Eddie Wilcox	Oak Park	6-9
1938 B (tie)	Earl Stevens	Buchanan	5-9¾		1985 B	Tom Badour	Essexville Garber	6-8
1938 B (tie)	William Schelb	Allegan	5-9¾		1986 B	Tom Badour	Essexville Garber	6-8
1939 B	Arthur Darr	Dowagiac	5-5½		1987 B	Tom Broene	Hudsonville Unity Christian	6-9
1940 B	Ed Geisler	Dowagiac	5-9¼		1988 B	Jon Sappanos	South Haven	6-9
1941 B	Bill Dale	Wayne	5-10¼		1989 B	Scott Eagle	Fowlerville	6-8
1942 B	Bill Dale	Wayne	6-2*		1990 B	Jon Royce	Chelsea	6-7
1943	No Meet – World War II				1991 B	John Tiburt	Grandville Calvin Christian	6-7
1944 B (tie)	Tom Doland	Hastings	6-¾		1992 B	Brian Howard	Stockbridge	6-7
1944 B (tie)	Harold Townsend	Hastings	6-¾		1993 B	Taron Burgess	Flint Beecher	6-8
1945 B	Tom Doland	Hastings	5-7½		1994 B	Demetry McDonald	Fremont	6-7
1946 B	Howard McCants	River Rouge	5-7½		1995 B	Demetry McDonald	Fremont	6-6
1947 B (tie)	Thomas Knoll	Niles	5-11		1996 B	Steve Paulsen	Fremont	6-8
1947 B (tie)	David Hill	Ypsilanti Central	5-1		1997 B	Steve Paulsen	Fremont	6-9
1948 B	David Hill	Ypsilanti Central	5-11		1998 B	Steve Paulsen	Fremont	6-8
1949 B	David Heinzman	Plymouth	6-0		1999 B	Andy Hawley	Jackson Lumen Christi	6-9
1950 B	Rex Corless	Coldwater	6-0		2000 D2	Nate Hinkle	Grayling	6-8*
1951 B	Dick Booth	Cadillac	5-11½		2001 D2	Josh Brown	Kalkaska	6-9*
1952 B	Mark Booth	Cadillac	5-10		2002 D2	Brian Sherwood	Fowlerville	6-11*
1953 B	Carl Shelton	Milan	6-½		2003 D2	Andrew Denker	Warren Fitzgerald	6-7
1954 B (tie)	Lee Snyder	Ludington	5-9½		2004 D2	Christopher Faison	Bloomfield Hills Lahser	6-9
1954 B (tie)	Jim Foley	Romulus	5-9½		2005 D2	Chris Faison	Bloomfield Hills Lahser	6-10
1955 B	Jim Foley	Romulus	6-0		2006 D2	Brad Birkholtz	Hamilton	6-6
1956 B	Walter Ector	River Rouge	6-1¼		2007 D2	Kurt Poehlman	Niles	6-10
1957 B (tie)	Jason Harness	St Joseph	5-9		2008 D2	Gerry Hammons	St. Clair Shores South Lake	6-6
1957 B (tie)	Joe Locey	Kalamazoo St Augustine	5-9		2009 D2	Brad James	Haslett	6-9
1958 B	Sam Hughes	North Muskegon	6-1		2010 D2	Dartis Willis	Detroit Country Day	6-10
1959 B	Paul Krause	Flint Bendle	6-0		2011 D2	Dartis Willis	Detroit Country Day	6-11*
1960 B	Jerry Holmes	Ecorse	6-2½*		2012 D2	Louis Lamberti	Petoskey	6-8
1961 B	Al Portratz	Airport	6-1½		2013 D2	Louis Lamberti	Petoskey	6-7
1962 B (tie)	Tom Zuppke	Stevensville-Lakeshore	6-1		2014 D2	Anthony Fitzgerald	Melvindale	6-9
1962 B (tie)	Al Portratz	Airport	6-1		2015 D2	Nathan Whitting	Freeland	6-6
1963 B	David Shepard	Stockbridge	6-1½		2016 D2	Alex Klemm	Macomb Lutheran North	7-0*
1964 B	John Northern	Dowagiac	6-1¾		2017 D2	Luke Clarelli	Harper Woods	6-6
1965 B	Jim Miller	Sturgis	6-5*		2018 D2	Jaden Zaitshik	Lake Fenton	6-7

HJ – Class C/Division 3 Champion

1921 C	Bud Pio	Union City	5-6*		1941 C (tie)	Francis Coen	St. Clair Shores Lakeview	5-8
1922 C	Lyle Bennett	Rockford	5-6¾*		1941 C (tie)	Seth Smith	Frankfort	5-8
1923 C	Alton Vance	Nashville	5-4		1942 C	Fred Johnson	Grandville	5-7
1924 C	George Anderson	Breckenridge	5-4		1943	No Meet – World War II		
1924 C (tie)	Graham	Farmington	5-4		1944 C (tie)	Duane Formsma	Grand Rapids Wyoming Park	5-4¾
1925 C	Harold Gilbert	Croswell	5-5¾		1944 C (tie)	Laurence De Cou	Marine City	5-4¾
1926 C (tie)	Laguar Farnsworth	Wayland	5-5		1945 C	Donald Meyers	Algonac	5-8¾
1926 C (tie)	Charles Price	East Tawas	5-5		1946 C (tie)	Tom Coates	Ann Arbor University High	5-5¾
1926 C (tie)	Fred Voegeli	Bangor	5-5		1946 C (tie)	Dick Grubbs	Grand Rapids Wyoming Park	5-5¾
1927 C	Minnow Fish Walters	Fremont	5-6¼		1946 C (tie)	Al Jones	Morenci	5-5¾
1928 C	Theodore Bass	Cassopolis	5-7¼*		1947 C (tie)	Carl Carrington	Paw Paw	5-10¾
1929 C (tie)	James Thompson	Paw Paw	5-6¾		1947 C (tie)	Robert Eggelston	East Jackson	5-10¾
1929 C (tie)	Gerald Kempher	Belding	5-6¾		1948 C	Alex Andrulis	Hart	5-10¼
1930 C	Fred Allen	Wayne	5-7¾*		1949 C	Alex Andrulis	Hart	5-11
1931 C	Clare McDurman	Caro	5-11¼*		1950 C (tie)	William Carrington	Paw Paw	5-10
1932 C	Clare McDurman	Caro	5-5½		1950 C (tie)	Jack Goodrich	Dundee	5-10
1933 C (tie)	Hubert Hoot Lockhart	Frankfort	5-7½		1950 C (tie)	Fred Smith	Battle Creek St Phillip	5-10
1933 C (tie)	Thomas Scott	Saranac	5-7½		1951 C	Gary Cullen	Ypsilanti Lincoln	5-10¼
1933 C (tie)	Clare McDurman	Caro	5-7½		1952 C	Ray Eggelston	East Jackson	5-10
1934 C	Oliver Tilli	Ravenna	5-7¼		1953 C (tie)	Frank Kristal	St. Louis	5-10½
1935 C	Roy Breen	Grand Rapids Lee	6-0 3/8*		1953 C (tie)	Chester Warsco	Berrien Springs	5-10½
1936 C	Bill Stauffer	Lowell	5-9¼		1954 C	Al Warman	Clarkston	6-0
1937 C	Bill Stauffer	Lowell	5-8¾		1955 C (tie)	Jim Vollmer	Wyandotte Smith	5-10¾
1938 C	Dick Bergman	Charlevoix	5-10		1955 C (tie)	Don Wilson	Grosse Ile	5-10¾
1939 C	William Hollenbeck	Frankfort	5-9¾		1956 C	Casey Clark	Berrien Springs	6-¾*
1940 C	George Brown	Ann Arbor University	5-7½		1957 C	Mike Schmalbach	Mt Pleasant Sacred Heart	5-8¾
1941 C (tie)	Verl Harris	St. Clair Shores South Lake	5-8		1958 C	Steve Williams	Boyne City	6-1½*
1941 C (tie)	Tom Paton	Okemos	5-8		1959 C (tie)	Jim Roe	East Jackson	5-11
1941 C (tie)	Blaine Cooper	Marine City	5-8		1959 C (tie)	Jim Miller	Elsie	5-11

Year	Name	School	Mark
1960 C (tie)	Privet Ilmar	Middleville	5-9¼
1960 C (tie)	Jim Miller	Elsie	5-9¼
1961 C (tie)	Calvin Scott	Ypsilanti Roosevelt	5-10
1961 C (tie)	Dwight Hinds	New Boston	5-10
1962 C	Charles Washington	Centreville	6-3¾*
1963 C	Mike Rabbers	Richland	6-¼
1964 C	Gary Knickerbocker	Manchester	6-1½
1965 C	Harvey Loiselle	Flint Holy Redeemer	6-3
1966 C	Ralph Schmaltz	Bridgman	6-1¼
1967 C	Mike Christopher	Farmington Our Lady-Sorrows	5-11
1968 C	Bob Kimble	Comstock	6-2
1969 C	Dennis Adama	Newaygo	6-5*
1970 C	Dennis Adama	Newaygo	6-8½*
1971 C	Chris Villadsen	Scottville Mason County Central	6-2
1972 C	Mark Stoimenoff	Battle Creek St Phillip	6-7¼
1973 C	Mike Winsor	Fulton-Middleton	6-4½
1974 C	Tom Duncan	Detroit DePorres	6-7
1975 C	Ed Vanderberg	Kalkaska	6-5
1976 C	Mike Bishop	Saginaw SS Peter & Paul	6-6
1977 C	Gregg Tarrant	Bath	6-6
1978 C	Gregg Tarrant	Bath	6-7
1979 C	Matt Baldus	Grant	6-10*
1980 C	Richard Johnson	Bangor	6-6
1981 C	Louis Cox	Detroit Lutheran West	6-9
1982 C	Louis Cox	Detroit Lutheran West	6-8
1983 C	Kevin Johnson	Cassopolis	6-6
1984 C	Mike Wilson	Caledonia	6-8
1985 C	Mike Schmid	St Joseph Lake Mich Catholic	6-8
1986 C	Mike Schmidt	St Joseph Lake Mich Catholic	6-8
1987 C	Rory Stace	Galesburg-Augusta	6-7
1988 C	Gregg Bott	St. Louis	6-5
1989 C	Bruce Daniels	Jonesville	6-4
1990 C	Mike Pfeil	Fulton-Middleton	6-7
1991 C	Tracy Grudenich	Bellevue	6-10*
1992 C	Paul Caarballo	Royal Oak Shrine	6-8
1993 C	Gerry Burns	Harbor Springs	6-7
1994 C	Tom Henge	New Lothrop	6-9
1995 C	Steve Palmer	Centreville	6-5
1996 C	Josh Ode	Freeland	6-4
1997 C	David Gregwer	Scottville Mason County C	6-6
1998 C	Jon Deephouse	Muskegon West Mich Christian	6-5
1999 C	Robert King	Bath	6-10¼*
2000 D3	Andy Hawley	Jackson Lumen Christi	6-7*
2001 D3	Mario Guerrero	Saginaw Swan Valley	6-5
2002 D3	Ryan Dixion	Saginaw Swan Valley	6-4
2003 D3	Blain Smith	Laingsburg	6-4
2004 D3	Andrew Dodson	Frankenmuth	6-9*
2005 D3	Andrew Dodson	Frankenmuth	7-0*
2006 D3	Erving Warren	Coloma	6-8¼
2007 D3	Kevin Bacon	Vassar	6-7
2008 D3	Jarod Sawyer	Manchester	6-6
2009 D3	Ryan Aaron	Madison Heights Madison	6-8
2010 D3	Darnell McKinney	Saginaw Buena Vista	6-4
2011 D3	Brendan Banker	Ida	6-3
2012 D3	Travis McCuaig	Morley-Stanwood	6-8
2013 D3	Travis McCuaig	Morley-Stanwood	6-9
2014 D3	Quincy Collings	Hopkins	6-9
2015 D3	Nate McKeown	Hesperia	6-7
2016 D3	Joe Conley	Saranac	6-6
2017 D3	Spencer Eves	Hillsdale	6-7
2018 D3	Sam Spaulding	Berrien Springs	6-7

HJ – Class D/Division 4 Champion

Year	Name	School	Mark
1927 D	Elton Daniels	Okemos	5-3¼*
1928 D	Norman Smith	Newaygo	5-2¾
1929 D (tie)	Norman Smith	Newaygo	5-5¾*
1929 D (tie)	Homer Patterson	Wyoming Godwin Heights	5-5¾*
1930 D	Bill Chase	South Lake	5-7*
1931 D	Bill Chase	South Lake	5-5½
1932 D (tie)	Victor Hawley	Napoleon	5-3¾
1932 D (tie)	William Weise	Bear Lake	5-3¾
1933 D	William Weise	Bear Lake	5-8½*
1934 D	William Weise	Bear Lake	5-9¼*
1935 D	William Weise	Bear Lake	5-9¼*
1936 D (tie)	Leo Kelly	Onekama	5-4
1936 D (tie)	Jack Nelson	Onekama	5-4
1937 D	David Mitchell	Montgomery	5-6¼
1938 D	Jack Bengnot	Elberta	5-8
1939 D	Robert Craig	Morrice	5-6
1940 D (tie)	George Floyd	Bloomfield Hills	5-5½
1940 D (tie)	Richard Klett	Michigan School for Deaf	5-5½
1941 D	Jim Lopker	St Joseph Catholic	5-7½
1942 D (tie)	Richard Keck	DeWitt	5-3½
1942 D (tie)	Ernest Ware	Bear Lake	5-3½
1943	No Meet – World War II		
1944 D (tie)	Bob Jackson	Glen Arbor Leelanau School	5-1 7/8
1944 D (tie)	Art Arntz	Benton Harbor St John	5-1 7/8
1945 D (tie)	Robert Brown	Bloomfield Hills	5-2½
1945 D (tie)	Don Bartz	Stevensville	5-2½
1945 D (tie)	Harry Lintner	Galien	5-2½
1945 D (tie)	Leonard Pickering	Bloomfield Hills	5-2½
1945 D (tie)	Bob Murphy	Benton Harbor St John	5-2½
1946 D	Don Plonta	Bayport	5-7
1947 D	Bill Reese	Galien	5-7
1948 D	Dick Miner	Bloomfield Hills	5-9½*
1949 D	Monroe Dial	Michigan School for Deaf	5-10 1/8*
1950 D (tie)	Richard Ewald	Michigan School for Deaf	5-7
1950 D (tie)	Fred Parker	Wyandotte Smith	5-7
1950 D (tie)	Eugene Hairs	Benton Harbor St John	5-7
1951 D	Eugene Haire	Benton Harbor St John	5-7½
1952 D	Don Stroup	Brethren	5-5
1953 D	Hans Becherer	Detroit University School	5-9
1954 D	Richard Beane	Brethren	5-7¾
1955 D	Rod DeYoung	Ellsworth	5-8¾
1956 D (tie)	Charles Sanders	Crystal	5-7¾
1956 D (tie)	Howard Blanks	Covert	5-7¾
1957 D	Ron Kamaloski	Onekema	5-8
1958 D	Ron Kamaloski	Onekema	5-10¾*
1959 D (tie)	Jack Rynn	Baldwin	5-7
1959 D (tie)	John Englert	Dryden	5-7
1959 D (tie)	Sidney Woods	Covert	5-7
1959 D (tie)	Phillip Hild	Benton Harbor St John	5-7
1960 D	Richard Wesler	Gobles	5-9
1961 D	Charles Washington	Centreville	6-2¾*
1962 D (tie)	Warren Clark	Bellaire	5-10¾
1962 D (tie)	Mike Bowers	Litchfield	5-10¾
1963 D	Mike Bowers	Litchfield	6-2
1964 D	Mark Patterson	Covert	5-11
1965 D	Loren VanBevern	Unionville	6-0
1966 D	Phil Trockelman	Bellaire	6-1¼
1967 D	Jim VanWagoner	Ovid	6-1
1968 D	Roger Connolly	Brethren	5-11
1969 D	Denny Reed	Whitmore Lake	5-11
1970 D	Byron Blasdell	Bellaire	5-11¼
1971 D	John Burla	Michigan School for Deaf	5-11
1972 D	John Gast	Bridgman	6-1
1973 D	Len Lilliard	Ann Arbor St Thomas	6-3*
1974 D	Mike Schaller	Bridgman	6-3¾*
1975 D	Mike Winsor	Fulton-Middleton	6-9¼*
1976 D	Gary Sykes	Litchfield	6-5¾
1977 D	Dave Downey	Battle Creek St Phillip	6-5
1978 D	Gary Sykes	Litchfield	6-4½
1979 D	Doug Koenigsknecht	Fowler	6-4¼
1980 D	Doug Koenigsknecht	Fowler	6-4½
1981 D	Charles Walker	Covert	6-4½
1982 D	Kurt Partlo	Akron-Fairgrove	6-6
1983 D	Kurt Partlo	Akron-FairGrove	6-7¼
1984 D	Kerry Zaremba	Morrice	6-7¾
1985 D	Ryan Pschigoda	Bridgman	6-7
1986 D	Don Dekilder	Gobles	6-8
1987 D	Jeff Crosby	Martin	6-4
1988 D	Jim McHugh	Pentwater	6-6
1989 D	Jim McHugh	Pentwater	6-5
1990 D	Todd Richards	Reading	6-7
1991 D	Todd Richards	Reading	6-6
1992 D	Chester Harding	Covert	6-4
1993 D	Chris Bills	Litchfield	6-4
1994 D	Chris Bills	Litchfield	6-7
1995 D	Kevin Alspaugh	Wyoming Lee	5-10
1996 D	Kevin Alspaugh	Wyoming Lee	6-3
1997 D	Joshua Ortman	Fulton-Middleton	6-4
1998 D	Morgan Bailey	Covert	6-1
1999 D	Kip Hartman	Mt Pleasant Sacred Heart	6-4
2000 D4	Jeff Johnson	Onekama	6-2*
2001 D4	Joe Baysdell	Brown City	6-9*
2002 D4	Andrew Hayton	Sand Creek	6-6
2003 D4	Justin Traxler	Adrian Madison	6-3
2004 D4	Brandon Bullard	Galien	6-6
2005 D4	Chris Bullard	New Buffalo	6-8
2006 D4	Greg Kinney	Fife Lake Forest Area	6-2
2007 D4	Travis Leflore	Royal Oak Shrine	6-5
2008 D4	Keaton Wolfe	Martin	6-5
2009 D4	Kurt Schneider	Auburn Hills Oakland Christian	6-10½*
2010 D4	Stephen Sykes	Litchfield	6-6
2011 D4	Stephen Sykes	Litchfield	6-8

2012 D4	Todd Brassow	Saginaw Mich Luth Seminary	6-5
2013 D4	Luke Meyer	Addison	6-8
2014 D4	Hunter Weeks	Homer	6-7
2015 D4	Jarid Walton	Coleman	6-5

2016 D4	Bryce Washington	Southfield Christian	6-5
2017 D4	Daniel Lanfear	Harbor Beach	6-6
2018 D4	Peter Kalthoff	Hillsdale Academy	6-5

HJ – UP Class AB/Division 1 Champion

1940 UPB	Don Kirkpatrick	Kingsford	5-7*
1941 UPB	Bob Stephens	Escanaba	5-9½*
1942 UPB (tie)	George Shomin	Escanaba	5-9¾*
1942 UPB (tie)	Ronald Rouse	Escanaba	5-9¾*
1942 UPB (tie)	Bob Stephens	Escanaba	5-9¾*
1943	No Meet – World War II		
1944 UPB	Bob Crepeau	Escanaba	5-7
1945 UPB	J. Rucinski	Iron River	5-8½
1946 UPB	Jack Finn	Escanaba	5-7
1947 UPB	Orval Deitz	Sault Ste Marie	5-7
1948 UPB	Mike Shatusky	Menominee	5-9½
1949 UPB	Bill Peterson	Ironwood	5-4½
1950 UPB	Jim Alrick	Sault Ste Marie	5-10 1/8*
1951 UPB (tie)	Ward VanLaanan	Iron Mountain	5-7
1951 UPB (tie)	Frank Young	Marquette	5-7
1952 UPB	Ward VanLaanan	Iron Mountain	5-6
1953 UPB	Bill Caley	Menominee	5-9
1954 UPB	James Borque	Sault Ste. Marie	5-7¾
1955 UPB	Bob Leroy	Stephenson	5-7
1956 UPB	Mel Peterson	Stephenson	5-10 5/8*
1957 UPB	Bill Cooper	Sault Ste. Marie	5-9 3/8
1958 UPB	Bob Perry	Iron River	5-8
1959 UPB	Warren Luoma	Ishpeming	5-9¼
1960 UPB	Joh Prato	Munising	5-10
1961 UPB (tie)	Con Yagodzinski	Escanaba Holy Name	5-9¼
1961 UPAB (tie)	Lee Carr	Kingsford	5-9¼
1962 UPAB (tie)	Con Yagodzinski	Escanaba Holy Name	5-9
1962 UPAB (tie)	Lee Carr	Kingsford	5-9
1963 UPAB	Dan Purple	Gwinn	6-1¼*
1964 UPAB	Dan Purple	Gwinn	6-3¾*
1965 UPAB	Harry Frank	Rudyard	5-10
1966 UPAB	Paul Miller	Escanaba	6-¼
1967 UPAB	Paul Miller	Escanaba	5-9
1968 UPAB	Ron Foster	Rudyard	5-10
1969 UPAB	Cliff Stiles	Gwinn	6-0
1970 UPAB	John Beauparant	Menominee	5-11
1971 UPAB	Rich Berry	Marquette	6-2
1972 UPAB	Dan Hollingsworth	Sault Ste. Marie	6-1
1973 UPAB	John Hirn	Escanaba	6-2
1974 UPAB	Dale Wickman	Kingsford	6-1
1975 UPAB	Lance Collins	Escanaba	6-2¼
1976 UPAB	Gary Taivalkoski	Calumet	6-0

1977 UPAB	Gary Taivalkoski	Calumet	6-4½*
1978 UPAB	John Whitney	Marquette	6-2
1979 UPAB	Keenen Failing	Escanaba	6-4¾*
1980 UPAB	Al LaFountain	Marquette	6-6*
1981 UPAB	Al LaFountain	Marquette	6-4
1982 UPAB	Jim Zigman	Kingsford	5-10
1983 UPAB	Guy Nuechterlein	Marquette	6-2
1984 UPAB	Troy Carlson	Gladstone	5-11
1985 UPAB	Greg Buzzo	Marquette	6-2
1986 UPAB	Troy Carlson	Gladstone	6-2
1987 UPAB	Dan Viitala	Gwinn	6-4
1988 UPAB	Keith Gering	Kingsford	6-1
1989 UPAB	Bret Nerat	Menominee	6-5
1990 UPAB	Bret Nerat	Menominee	6-8*
1991 UPAB	Bret Nerat	Menominee	6-3
1992 UPAB	Jeff LaValley	Marquette	6-6
1993 UPAB	Bob Ball	Marquette	6-0
1994 UPAB	Mark Kavanaugh	Sault Ste. Marie	6-3
1995 UPAB	Matt Hoskins	Kingsford	6-2
1996 UPAB	Jim Malone	Kingsford	6-4
1997 UPAB	Kevin Vogel	Escanaba	6-0
1998 UPAB	Kyle Bell	Negaunee	6-0
1999 UPAB	Drew Buyarski	Menominee	6-1
2000 UPAB	Drew Buyarski	Menominee	6-0
2001 UPD1	Joe Shoup	Escanaba	6-3*
2002 UPD1	Tim Thomas	Gwinn	6-0
2003 UPD1	Jason Hofer	Menominee	6-0
2004 UPD1	Jake Richmond	Kingsford	6-5*
2005 UPD1	Travis Baril	Sault Ste. Marie	6-3
2006 UPD1	Travis Baril	Sault Ste. Marie	6-4½
2007 UPD1	Adam Gilbertson	Sault Ste. Marie	6-0
2008 UPD1	Adam Gilbertson	Sault Ste. Marie	6-0
2009 UPD1	Max Vandewiele	Escanaba	6-2
2010 UPD1	Kris Benaglio	Negaunee	6-3
2011 UPD1	James Bosk	Gladstone	6-0
2012 UPD1	Luke Zambon	Iron Mountain	5-10
2013 UPD1	Justin Pederson	Gladstone	6-3
2014 UPD1	Zane Radloff	Negaunee	6-0
2015 UPD1	Brandon Kowalkowski	Kingsford	6-0
2016 UPD1	Taylor Althouse	Marquette	5-10
2017 UPD1	Jedidiah Weber	Marquette	6-2
2018 UPD1	Raphael Millado	Marquette	6-2

HJ – UP Class C/Division 2 Champion

1940 UPC	Bill Mikulich	Eben	5-8*
1941 UPC	Tom St. Germaine	Baraga	5-8*
1942 UPC (tie)	Zakeimeir	Newberry	5-4¾
1942 UPC (tie)	Ed Edwards	L'Anse	5-4¾
1943	No Meet – World War II		
1944 UPC	Marco Sertich	Wakefield	5-6
1945 UPC (tie)	William Glasson	Baraga	5-0 1/3
1945 UPC (tie)	Eugene Valko	Ironwood St. Ambrose	5-0 1/3
1945 UPC (tie)	William Osterman	Baraga	5-0 1/3
1945 UPC (tie)	Tom Emblad	L'Anse	5-0 1/3
1946 UPC	William Glasson	Baraga	5-11*
1947 UPC (tie)	Paul Thurston	Gwinn	5-6
1947 UPC (tie)	Tom Emblad	L'Anse	5-6
1948 UPC	results unknown		
1949 UPC	George Brunette	L'Anse	5-6¼
1950 UPC	Jim Wojciehowski	Wakefield	5-8
1951 UPC	Dominic Certano	Bessemer	5-3
1952 UPC	John Sporich	Wakefield	5-4
1953 UPC	Kriss Novak	Wakefield	5-8
1954 UPC	Juan Mentink	Houghton	5-3
1955 UPC	David LaJeunesse	Houghton	5-7
1956 UPC	Einar Anderson	Houghton	5-8
1957 UPC	Richard Koski	Wakefield	5-4
1958 UPC	Richard Koski	Wakefield	5-11¾*
1959 UPC	Richard Koski	Wakefield	5-9¼
1960 UPC	John Haarala	Houghton	5-4
1961 UPC (tie)	Joe Haywood	Rudyard	5-8
1961 UPC (tie)	Clark Suchovsky	Stephenson	5-8
1961 UPC (tie)	Allen Stump	St. Ignace	5-8
1962 UPC	Dan Purple	Gwinn	5-10
1963 UPC	Byron Johnson	Bessemer	5-10½
1964 UPC	Don Stipech	Houghton	5-8
1965 UPC	Phil Paananen	Houghton	5-9

1966 UPC	Bill McGee	Marquette Baraga	5-10¼
1967 UPC	Chuck Tandlund	Ontonagon	5-9
1968 UPC	Richard Salani	Hancock	5-9¾
1969 UPC	Richard Salani	Hancock	5-8
1970 UPC	Wickstrom	Stephenson	5-11
1971 UPC	Brian Adams	Norway	5-10
1972 UPC	Mike Burley	Bessemer	5-11
1973 UPC	Dave Hutchenson	Ontonagon	6-1*
1974 UPC	Dave Hutchenson	Ontonagon	6-0
1975 UPC	Mark Campbell	Norway	6-1*
1976 UPC	Duane Manier	Ishpeming Westwood	6-2*
1977 UPC	Mark Sarder	West Iron	6-0
1978 UPC	Edwin Pope	St. Ignace	6-3¼*
1979 UPC	Jeff Miles	Ontonagon	5-9¾
1980 UPC	Chris Patritto	Ironwood	6-0
1981 UPC	Mark Konopacke	Kingsford	6-1
1982 UPC	Tom Nufer	Houghton	6-0
1983 UPC	Kory Spiroff	Ishpeming	6-2
1984 UPC	Kory Spiroff	Ishpeming	6-2
1985 UPC	Bill Laitala	Negaunee	6-1
1986 UPC	Scott Monette	Houghton	6-4*
1987 UPC	Brandon Hauglie	Newberry	6-5*
1988 UPC	Darin Laabs	Ironwood	6-6*
1989 UPC	Dennis Johnson	Stephenson	6-3
1990 UPC	Phil Bal	Ishpeming	6-4
1991 UPC	Phil Bal	Ishpeming	6-3
1992 UPC	Kris Brown	St. Ignace	6-2
1993 UPC	Wil Gehrett	Newberry	6-2
1994 UPC	Bob DeVillez	Newberry	6-0
1995 UPC	Bob DeVillez	Newberry	6-3
1996 UPC	Mark Jasper	Stephenson	6-4
1997 UPC	Josh Cone	Calumet	6-1
1998 UPC	Josh Cone	Calumet	6-2

1999 UPC	John Hokenson	Manistique	5-10
2000 UPC	Jim Clement	St. Ignace	6-0
2001 UPD2	Rick St Amour	Munising	6-3*
2002 UPD2	Rick St Amour	Munising	6-2
2003 UPD2	Nicholas Buckland	Iron Mountain	5-10
2004 UPD2	Nick Zweifel	Norway	6-0
2005 UPD2	Dustin Brancheau	Ishpeming-Rep Michagammee	6-0
2006 UPD2	Dustin Brancheau	Ishpeming-Rep Michagammee	5-10
2007 UPD2	Bryan Gottschalk	Ironwood	5-10
2008 UPD2	Austin St. Louis	St. Ignace	6-1
2009 UPD2	Austin St. Louis	St. Ignace	6-2
2010 UPD2	Austin St. Louis	St. Ignace	5-9
2011 UPD2	Austin St. Louis	St. Ignace	5-9
2012 UPD2	James Sutton	Newberry	6-3½*
2013 UPD2	James Sutton	Newberry	6-4*
2014 UPD2	Leroy Ward-Harbaum	Newberry	5-8
2015 UPD2	Luke Redlon	Gwinn	5-10
2016 UPD2	Aaron Bolo	Iron Mountain	5-8
2017 UPD2	Jason Osborn	Rudyard	5-11
2018 UPD2	Charlie Gerhard	Iron Mountain	6-3

HJ – UP Class D/Division 3 Champion

1940 UPD	Aaro Sutela	Rock	5-9¼*
1941 UPD	Bill Mikulich	Eben	5-4¾
1942 UPD	Wil Tuominen	Marquette Pierce	5-7
1943	No Meet – World War II		
1944 UPD	D. Antilla	Channing	5-0
1945 UPD (tie)	Tom Osborn	Chassell	5-4
1945 UPD (tie)	Albert Leppanen	Marquette Pierce	5-4
1946 UPD	Haapala	Chassell	5-9
1947 UPD	Tom Osborn	Chassell	5-5
1948 UPD	Dick Whitens	Hermansville	5-4½
1949 UPD	Ray McKay	Ironwood St. Ambrose	5-6½
1950 UPD	Paul Tormala	Chassell	5-6
1951 UPD	Ralph Heitala	Chassell	5-5
1952 UPD	George Tomasi	Hermansville	5-6
1953 UPD	Morris Nance	Trenary	5-6¾
1954 UPD	Willis Norgard	Dollar Bay	5-7
1955 UPD (tie)	Ray McConkey	Pickford	5-4
1955 UPD (tie)	Wayne Christoff	Rapid River	5-4
1955 UPD (tie)	Bernard Newhouse	Nahma	5-4
1956 UPD	Wayne Christoff	Rapid River	5-9
1957 UPD (tie)	Ken Harwood	Rapid River	5-6
1957 UPD (tie)	Darrel Ledy	DeTour	5-6
1958 UPD	Robert Kiamerus	DeTour	5-8
1959 UPD	Gary Soumis	Chassell	5-6
1960 UPD	Robert Kiamerus	DeTour	nh
1961 UPD	John LaVallee	Garden	5-9¾*
1962 UPD	John LaVallee	Garden	5-11½*
1963 UPD	Tom Olson	Channing	5-8
1964 UPD	Dave Klamerus	DeTour	5-9
1965 UPD	Dan Dutcher	Cedarville	5-10
1966 UPD	Dave Klamerus	DeTour	5-9
1967 UPD	Felix Sacheck	Bark River	5-5
1968 UPD	Louis Binoniemi	Dollar Bay	5-6½
1969 UPD	Dale Morin	Rapid River	5-6
1970 UPD	Ted Balley	DeTour	5-8
1971 UPD	Michael Applekamp	Bergland	6-3*
1972 UPD	Mike Carlisle	Ewen-Trout Creek	5-10
1973 UPD	Jerry Leskela	Ewen-Trout Creek	6-0
1974 UPD	Mike Carlisle	Ewen-Trout Creek	5-10
1975 UPD	Ricky Woods	Felch North Dickinson	6-2½
1976 UPD	Don Stefanski	DeTour	6-2
1977 UPD	Dave Dupart	Powers-North Central	6-3½*
1978 UPD	Doug Galer	Pickford	6-3¾*
1979 UPD	John Casanova	Crystal Falls Forest Park	6-1½
1980 UPD	Dorn Siegler	Felch North Dickinson	6-4*
1981 UPD	Christopher Smith	Pickford	6-2
1982 UPD	Dan Densmore	Cedarville	6-0
1983 UPD	Paul Truckey	Wakefield	6-3
1984 UPD	Steve Kezerle	Crystal Falls Forest Park	6-2
1985 UPD	Steve Kezerle	Crystal Falls Forest Park	6-1
1986 UPD	Pat Belinsky	Bessemer	5-11
1987 UPD	John Payment	Brimley	6-6*
1988 UPD	John Payment	Brimley	6-0
1989 UPD	John Payment	Brimley	7-1*
1990 UPD	Kevin Sutton	Brimley	6-6
1991 UPD	Kevin Sutton	Brimley	6-3
1992 UPD	Charles Tomblinson	Rock-Mid Peninsula	6-0
1993 UPD	Andy Gramlich	Carney-Nedeau	6-5
1994 UPD	Andy Gramlich	Carney-Nedeau	6-3
1995 UPD	Tom Granquist	Powers-North Central	5-11
1996 UPD	Josh Haske	Cedarville	6-1
1997 UPD	Damien Waara	Baraga	5-10
1998 UPD	Sean Duffin	Carney-Nedeau	5-10
1999 UPD	Sean Duffin	Carney-Nedeau	6-2
2000 UPD	Sean Duffin	Carney-Nedeau	6-4
2001 UPD3	Brock Bower	Bark River-Harris	6-4*
2002 UPD3	Brock Bower	Bark River-Harris	6-6*
2003 UPD3	Brock Bower	Bark River-Harris	6-6*
2004 UPD3	Mark Roell	Felch North Dickinson	6-0
2005 UPD3	Ryan Duman	Cedarville	6-2
2006 UPD3	Mark Roell	Felch North Dickinson	6-3
2007 UPD3	Mark Roell	Felch North Dickinson	6-2
2008 UPD3	Peter Leeman	Felch North Dickinson	6-1
2009 UPD3	Paul Roell	Felch North Dickinson	5-11
2010 UPD3	Mike Schmaus	Ontonagon	6-0
2011 UPD3	Brett Gervais	Lake Linden-Hubbell	5-9
2012 UPD3	Martin Payment	Cedarville	5-11
2013 UPD3	Brett Branstrom	Rock-Mid Peninsula	6-1
2014 UPD3	Andy Cooper	Munising	6-0
2015 UPD3	Andy Cooper	Munising	6-2
2016 UPD3	Morgan Cox	Powers-North Central	5-8
2017 UPD3	Nicholas Edington	Pickford	6-2
2018 UPD3	Terry Brower	Rock Mid Peninsula	6-1

BOYS POLE VAULT

Records

D1	16-9.5	Trevor Stephenson	East Kentwood	2018
D2	16-1	Jamie Salisbury	Marine City	2012
D3	16-0	Isaac Austin	Kent City	2011
D4	15-1	Curtis Bell	Coleman	2014
UPD1	13-7	Mike Coyne	Gladstone	2007
UPD2	13-6	Matthew Revord	Munising	2017
UPD3	13-3½	Bill Ragio	Crystal Falls Forest Park	2015

Records by Class (pre-2000 for LP, pre-2001 for UP)

A	16-6	Paul Terek	Livonia Franklin	1997
B	16-1	Brad Teeple	Sturgis	1999
C	15-4	Aaron Gebauer	Bad Axe	1998
D	15-2½	Bryan Happel	Mendon	1991
UPAB	14-0	Wade Hodge	Menominee	1992
UPC	13-4	Jeremy Richards	Ironwood	1995
UPD	13-3	John Andrzejak	Pickford	1978

PV – Class A/Division 1 Champions

Year	Name	School	Mark
1895 all	Clarence Christopher	Lansing	8-3*
	(another report has mark at 8-10)		
1896 all	Clarence Christopher	Lansing	9-1*
1897 all	Clarence Christopher	Lansing	9-1*
1898 all (tie)	Clarence Christopher	Lansing	9-0
1898 all (tie)	Charles Lesher	Lansing	9-0
1899 all	Charles Seiffer	Adrian	9-0
1900 all	Jimmy Keena	Detroit University School	9-7*
1901 all	H. A. Osborn	Detroit Central	9-8*
1902 all	George Read	Ann Arbor	10-0*
1903 all	Victor Dyer	Michigan Military Academy	10-6*
1904 all	Edward Raper	Battle Creek	10-9*
1905 all (tie)	Ward Richards	Ann Arbor	10-0
1905 all (tie)	Stuart Marker	Detroit Central	10-0
1906 all	Joe Horner	Grand Rapids Central	10-9*
1907 all	Joe Horner	Grand Rapids Central	11-1½*
1908 all	George Shaw	Muskegon	10-11
1909 all	George Shaw	Muskegon	11-2*
1910 all	Claude Cross	Muskegon	10-9
1911 all	Clarence Loveland	Grand Rapids Central	10-½
1912 all	Forrest Bailey	Morenci	11-2½*
1913 all	Elmer Reich	Detroit Eastern	10-9
1914 all	Elmer Reich	Detroit Eastern	10-6
1915 all (tie)	Roy Workman	Plainwell	10-5
1915 all (tie)	Miles Casteel	St. Johns	10-5
1916 all	Arthur Cross	Muskegon	10-9
1917 all (tie)	Harold Bailey	Breckenridge	10-8
1917 all (tie)	Marion Slaughter	Detroit Central	10-8
1918	No Meet – World War I		
1919 all	Rudel Miller	Kalamazoo Central	10-5
1920 all (tie)	Burwell Jones	Detroit Central	10-9
1920 all (tie)	Don Gainder	Kalamazoo Central	10-9
1921 A	Don Gainder	Kalamazoo Central	10-9
1922 A (tie)	Albert Thorp	Highland Park	11-1
1922 A (tie)	Dan Nielsen	Muskegon	11-1
1923 A	Percy Prout	Detroit Central	11-9*
1924 A	Bill Hathaway	Kalamazoo Central	10-8½
1925 A (tie)	Bill Hathaway	Kalamazoo Central	11-6
1925 A (tie)	Ray Newman	Pontiac	11-6
1926 A	Ray Newman	Pontiac	11-9*
1927 A	Baxter Hathaway	Kalamazoo Central	11-10*
1928 A	Robert Balmer	Lansing Central	10-7
1929 A	Morgan Wilson	Muskegon	11-10¼*
1930 A	Eddie Lasky	Hamtramck	11-6
1931 A	Harold Stein	Monroe	11-6
1932 A	Harold Stein	Monroe	12-¾*
1933 A	Harold Stein	Monroe	12-2¼*
1934 A (tie)	Herbert McMillan	Flint Northern	11-9
1934 A (tie)	Harold Stein	Monroe	11-9
1935 A (tie)	Joe Kahnowski	Grand Rapids Catholic	11-6½
1935 A (tie)	Millard Huitman	Grand Rapids Central	11-6½
1936 A (tie)	Paul Ingell	Muskegon	11-2¼
1936 A (tie)	Bob Quance	Pontiac	11-2¼
1936 A (tie)	Art Gutz	River Rouge	11-2¼
1937 A	Al Engel	Saginaw	10-9
1938 A	Ted Wonch	Lansing Eastern	12-0
1939 A	Jim Jenkins	Monroe	12-4¼*
1940 A (tie)	Samuel Calvert	Hazel Park	12-0
1940 A (tie)	Jim Naveaux	Monroe	12-0
1941 A	Forrest Naveaux	Monroe	12-0
1942 A	Forrest Naveaux	Monroe	12-7½*
1943	No Meet Held – World War II		
1944 A	Jack Hampton	Battle Creek	11-9
1945 A	Bill Dennison	Pontiac	11-4½
1946 A	Arnold Smith	Alpena	11-1½
1947 A	Bob Nagle	Lansing Eastern	11-10
1948 A (tie)	Ray Marshall	Monroe	11-8
1948 A (tie)	Phil Daubert	Saginaw Arthur Hill	11-8
1949 A (tie)	Gerald Embry	Battle Creek Central	11-6
1949 A (tie)	Jim Bonney	Jackson	11-6
1949 A (tie)	Tom Reynolds	Pontiac	11-6
1950 A	Roger Maugh	Ann Arbor	12-1
1951 A	Bob Dust	Saginaw Arthur Hill	11-10
1952 A	Stuart Galka	Grand Rapids Catholic	12-0
1953 A (tie)	George Best	Battle Creek	11-11
1953 A (tie)	Jim Henkle	Jackson	11-11
1953 A (tie)	Pete Sabo	Grand Rapids Ottawa Hills	11-11
1954 A (tie)	Roger Shepler	Lansing Eastern	12-4
1954 A (tie)	Bob Maturen	Saginaw	12-4
1954 A (tie)	Tom Lampel	Saginaw Arthur Hill	12-4
1955 A	Richard Donnell	Battle Creek	12-4
1956 A (tie)	Ron McCrumb	Birmingham	11-6
1956 A (tie)	Bill McFarlane	Birmingham	11-6
1956 A (tie)	Jim Collins	Flint Northern	11-6
1956 A (tie)	Dick Cahill	Muskegon	11-6
1956 A (tie)	Ron Filius	Muskegon	11-6
1956 A (tie)	Mike Worden	Redford Union	11-6
1956 A (tie)	Art Smith	Saginaw	11-6
1957 A	Bill McFarlan	Birmingham	12-1
1958 A	Bill Alcorn	Birmingham	12-11¾*
1959 A	Bill Alcorn	Birmingham	13-3*
1960 A	Joe Baldy	Monroe	12-9
1961 A (tie)	Roger Mason	Birmingham Seaholm	12-6
1961 A (tie)	William Schnarr	Lansing Everett	12-6
1961 A (tie)	Tony Gairno	Monroe	12-6
1961 A (tie)	Mickey Pickle	Muskegon	12-6
1962 A	Dick Wells	Grand Rapids Ottawa Hills	13-1¼
1963 A	Bill Lee	Flint Central	13-6*
1964 A	Wayne Lambert	Saginaw Arthur Hill	13-11¾*
1965 A	Robert Keyes	Jackson	13-8
1966 A	Ron Shortt	Farmington	14-5*
1967 A	Dave Leitner	Grand Haven	14-6½*
1968 A	Larry Bickner	Waterford Township	14-6½*
1969 A	Mark Whittaker	Flint Southwestern	13-9¼
1970 A	Jim Shelton	Grosse Pointe North	14-0
1971 A	Roger Blanchard	Detroit Redford Union	14-4
1972 A	Nat Durham	Farmington	15-0*
1973 A	Jim Stokes	Flint Kearsley	14-3
1974 A	Jim Stokes	Flint Kearsley	15-6½*
1975 A	John Kretsehmer	Bloomfield Hills Lahser	14-8
1976 A	John Kretschmer	Bloomfield Hills Lahser	15-0
1977 A	Bob Babits	Redford Union	14-11
1978 A	Jon Lunderberg	Holland	13-11
1979 A	Paul Babits	Redford Union	14-7
1980 A	Marc Rohman	East Lansing	14-1
1981 A	Scott Krupilski	Traverse City	14-10¼
1982 A	Scott Krupilski	Traverse City	15-8*
1983 A	Mark Blodgett	Traverse City	14-5
1984 A	Greg Nienhouse	Traverse City	14-5
1985 A	Keith Lancaster	Swartz Creek	14-4
1986 A	Bim Scala	Traverse City	15-9*
1987 A	Tom Guy	Traverse City	13-11
1988 A	Toby VanPelt	Owosso	15-3
1989 A	Toby VanPelt	Owosso	15-10*
1990 A	Greg Pattee	Flushing	14-11
1991 A	Ben Robbins	Grand Haven	14-7
1992 A	Ben Robbins	Grand Haven	14-10
1993 A	Steve Hill	Midland Dow	16-½*
1994 A	Courtney Wenzel	Midland	14-6
1995 A	Adam Gilroy	East Lansing	15-1
1996 A	Jay Schultz	Bay City Central	15-5
1997 A	Paul Terek	Livonia Franklin	16-6*
1998 A	Chip Owen	Holland West Ottawa	15-3
1999 A	Chip Owen	Holland West Ottawa	15-2
2000 D1	Erik Mirandette	East Kentwood	14-0*
2001 D1	Andy Marska	Port Huron Northern	14-6*
2002 D1	Bryan Lancaster	Ann Arbor Huron	14-9*
2003 D1	Scott Levering	GR Forest Hills Central	13-7
2004 D1	Benny Lopez	Grand Ledge	14-10*
2005 D1	Ryan Santa	Livonia Churchill	15-0*
2006 D1	Logan Lynch	Temperance Bedford	16-0*
2007 D1	Logan Lynch	Temperance Bedford	16-1*
2008 D1	Nick Goyette	Davison	14-3
2009 D1	Ryan Staley	Flushing	15-4
2010 D1	Nate Hop	Hudsonville	15-7
2011 D1	Andrew Herring	Dexter	15-7
2012 D1	Dan Emery	Battle Creek Lakeview	15-4
2013 D1	Dylan Kole	Grand Rapids Kenowa Hills	14-10
2014 D1	Noah Gary	Dexter	16-2*
2015 D1	Nick Burkhalter	South Lyon	15-6
2016 D1	Jonny De Haan	Rockford	15-0
2017 D1	Cole Snyder	Macomb Dakota	15-6
2018 D1	Trevor Stephenson	East Kentwood	16-9½*
(En route Eric Harris/Saline cleared 16-3½* & 16-6½*, Stephenson 16-6½*)			

PV – Class B/Division 2 Champions

Year	Name	School	Mark
1921 B	Leo Smith	Allegan	9-0*
1922 B	Leo Smith	Allegan	10-0*
1923 B	Harold George	Petoskey	10-6*
1924 B	Harold George	Petoskey	10-7*
1925 B	Ray Hiscock	Allegan	10-10¾*
1926 B	Carl Nordberg	St. Joseph	11-5*

1927 B	David Gafill	Birmingham	10-¾
1928 B	Ralph Briney	St. Joseph	11-3¼
1929 B	Allan Findley	Niles	11-0
1930 B	William Stoner	Monroe	11-5*
1931 B	Bob Erickson	St. Joseph	11-5½*
1932 B	Bob Erickson	St. Joseph	11-6*
1933 B (tie)	Gayle Oldt	River Rouge	11-6*
1933 B (tie)	Bob Erickson	St. Joseph	11-6*
1934 B	Gayle Oldt	River Rouge	11-11¼*
1935 B (tie)	Allen Cisco	Dowagiac	11-0
1935 B (tie)	Charles O'Dell	Three Rivers	11-0
1936 B (tie)	Jack Williams	Plymouth	10-11¾
1936 B (tie)	Lloyd Waterman	Three Rivers	10-11¾
1937 B	Jim Bekkering	Fremont	11-6
1938 B	Jim Bekkering	Fremont	11-6
1939 B (tie)	William Price	Belding	11-3
1939 B (tie)	Douglas Fuzz Prough	Plymouth	11-3
1940 B (tie)	William Price	Belding	11-6
1940 B (tie)	Douglas Fuzz Prough	Plymouth	11-6
1941 B	Roy Dygert	East Lansing	12-¼*
1942 B	Fred Zoellin	Birmingham	11-6¼
1943	No Meet Held – World War II		
1944 B	Bob Sullivan	Belleville	11-3
1945 B	Bob Sullivan	Belleville	11-5¼
1946 B	Bob Sullivan	Belleville	11-1¾
1947 B	Leon McGowen	Fremont	11-3
1948 B (tie)	Arthur Ott	Adrian	11-5¼
1948 B (tie)	Jim Wagenschutz	Plymouth	11-5¼
1949 B	Rollie McGinnis	Birmingham	11-7½
1950 B	Ken Moore	Flint Bendle	11-3
1951 B	Kay Keffer	Mt Pleasant	12-2½*
1952 B	Louis Postula	Marshall	11-6
1953 B (tie)	Carl Shelton	Milan	11-4
1953 B (tie)	Jim Roberts	Three Rivers	11-4
1954 B	Lee Snyder	Ludington	12-4¼*
1955 B	Bill Deering	Dowagiac	12-1
1956 B (tie)	Ed Freeman	Cass CIty	11-10
1956 B (tie)	Bill Deering	Dowagiac	11-10
1956 B (tie)	Norman Tree	St. Louis	11-10
1957 B	Frank Fink	Walled Lake	12-0
1958 B	Larry Horgan	Big Rapids	12-5¼*
1959 B	Wendall Johnson	Troy	12-8*
1960 B (tie)	Mike Wells	Durand	12-1
1960 B (tie)	Paul Krause	Flint Bendle	12-1
1961 B (tie)	Rick Schlegelmilch	Burton Bentley	12-4
1961 B (tie)	Mike Edwards	St. Clair Shores Lake Shore	12-4
1962 B	Richard Petty	Vassar	12-4
1963 B	Dan Greene	Tecumseh	12-6
1964 B	Ernest Ver Hage	Hudsonville Unity Christian	13-5¼*
1965 B	Mike May	Vassar	13-2
1966 B	Bill Bekkering	Fremont	13-6*
1967 B	Rick Good	Montrose	13-1
1968 B	Ron Gloetzner	Northville	13-7*
1969 B	Dave Boyer	Fremont	14-1¾*
1970 B	Jim Stevenson	Muskegon Catholic	14-7*
1971 B	David Henson	Holland West Ottawa	13-4
1972 B	Terry Hart	Corunna	13-8
1973 B	Matt Peterson	Essexville Garber	14-0
1974 B	Mark Langlois	Muskegon Catholic	14-3
1975 B	Karl Bontrager	Midland Bullock Creek	14-4
1976 B	Tom Splan	Petoskey	14-4
1977 B	Matt Heydlauff	Chelsea	13-11
1978 B	Jeffery Smith	Battle Creek Harper Creek	13-11
1979 B	Brian Miller	Bay City Glenn	14-8*
1980 B	Donald Biscupski	Tecumseh	14-2½
1981 B	John Bartos	Corunna	14-3½
1982 B	Ed Lumm	Holly	13-8
1983 B	Bob Hawkins	Haslett	14-4
1984 B	Gary Allen	Holland Christian	14-5
1985 B	Kraig Koeze	Wyoming Park	13-10
1986 B	John Bruce	Corunna	15-7*
1987 B	Mark Crosby	Sturgis	14-5
1988 B	Tim Szezepanski	Grand Rapids West Catholic	14-9
1989 B	Bill Deering	Dowagiac	15-6
1990 B	Bob Bailey	Remus Chippewa Hills	14-4
1991 B	Bob Bailey	Remus Chippewa Hills	15-2
1992 B	Jamie Mauer	Sparta	13-11
1993 B	David Gerrity	Grand Rapids Catholic	16-¼*
1994 B	Lee Busby	Jackson Northwest	15-½
1995 B	Dan Fuja	Corunna	14-10
1996 B	Matthew Deering	Dowagiac	15-0
1997 B	Charles Dewildt	Grand Rapids Catholic	15-8
1998 B	Geoff Fairbanks	Tecumseh	15-4
1999 B	Brad Teeple	Sturgis	16-1*
2000 D2	Nicholas Schaibly	Haslett	14-9*
2001 D2	Mark Langlois	Fruitport	15-0*
2002 D2	Mark Langlois	Fruitport	15-3*
2003 D2	Steve Davis	Allegan	14-6
2004 D2	Mike Fisher	Byron Center	14-6
2005 D2	Marcus Breidinger	Alma	14-9
2006 D2	Matt Fisher	Byron Center	14-7
2007 D2	Joe Wesley	Marine City	16-0*
2008 D2	Joe Wesley	Marine City	14-8
2009 D2	Austin DeWildt	Grand Rapids Catholic	15-2
2010 D2	Max Babits	Fowlerville	16-½*
2011 D2	Jamie Salisbury	Marine City	16-1*
2011 D2	Jamie Salisbury	Marine City	15-3
2013 D2	Michael Hovater	Chelsea	14-10
2014 D2	Mitchell Mueller	Algonac	15-9
2015 D2	Mitchell Mueller	Algonac	15-6
2016 D2	Jarrett VanHaval	Mason	15-3
2017 D2	Bont Remongton	Allendale	13-10
2018 D2	Alex Inosencio	Parma Western	15-8

PV – Class C/Division 3 Champions

1921 C	Earl New	Plainwell	10-1*
1922 C	Bud Pio	Union City	10-6*
1923 C	Donald Seed	Cass City	11-0*
1924 C (tie)	Harold Nixon	Almont	10-11
1924 C (tie)	Fred Allyn	Farmington	10-11
1925 C (tie)	Harold Nixon	Almont	10-6
1925 C (tie)	William Irwin	Newaygo	10-6
1926 C	Laguar Farnsworth	Wayland	11-¾*
1927 C	Fred Petoskey	St. Charles	10-6
1928 C	Russell Goosen	East Grand Rapids	11-3¼*
1929 C	Russell Goosen	East Grand Rapids	11-6*
1930 C	Gilson Pearsall	Algonac	10-8
1931 C (tie)	Gilson Pearsall	Algonac	11-0
1931 C (tie)	Richard Soule	Paw Paw	11-0
1932 C	Warren Pearsaul	East Lansing	11-¾
1933 C	Bruce McMahon	Lowell	11-3
1934 C	Henry Hoffman	Northville	11-5¾
1935 C (tie)	Henry Hoffman	Northville	11-6*
1935 C (tie)	Peter Hawryiciew	Ypsilanti Lincoln	11-6*
1936 C	Donald Wilber	East Grand Rapids	10-10
1937 C	Max Brink	Grant	10-4
1938 C	Arthur Cuthbertson	Algonac	11-3
1939 C	Donald Mortemore	Lambertville	10-11
1940 C	Jay De Cou	Marine City	11-6*
1941 C	Donald Mortemore	Lambertville	11-3
1942 C	Jay De Cou	Marine City	11-7½*
1943	No Meet Held – World War II		
1944 C (tie)	Don Lester	Algonac	10-2
1944 C (tie)	Al Snyder	Grandville	10-2
1945 C	Harold Phillips	Corunna	10-8
1946 C	Al Dorow	Imlay City	11-¼
1947 C	Eugene Burch	Romulus	11-1
1948 C	Paul Hemenger	Algonac	11-4
1949 C (tie)	John Kinnane	Lansing Everett	11-6½
1949 C (tie)	Jack Kelly	St. Clair Shores Lake Shore	11-6½
1950 C	Jack Kelly	St. Clair Shores South Lake	11-6
1951 C (tie)	Howard Young	Ann Arbor University High	10-8¾
1951 C (tie)	Claude Lewis	Dundee	10-8¾
1951 C (tie)	Robert Packard	Morenci	10-8¾
1952 C	Howard Young	Ann Arbor University High	11-6
1953 C	George Price	Lansing Everett	11-9*
1954 C	Dick Content	Lansing Everett	11-10¾*
1955 C	Richard Locke	Quincy	11-6
1956 C	Dean Look	Lansing Everett	12-6*
1957 C (tie)	Robert Shaw	Marlette	11-4½
1957 C (tie)	Chad Johnson	Paw Paw	11-4½
1958 C	Doug Newville	Boyne City	12-3¾
1959 C (tie)	Dick Hall	Burton Atherton	11-6
1959 C (tie)	Rick Schlegelmilch	Burton Bentley	11-6
1959 C (tie)	George Schull	Harrison	11-6
1960 C	Rick Schlegelmilch	Burton Bentley	12-2
1961 C	Bob Curtis	Muskegon Reeths-Puffer	11-9
1962 C	Gary Tesman	Centreville	12-1¾
1963 C	Larry McBride	Charlevoix	12-0
1964 C	Roland Carter	Carson City	12-9*
1965 C	Rick Ford	Morenci	12-7
1966 C	Mike Vance	Flint St. John	12-2
1967 C	Tom Warner	Middleville	12-3
1968 C	Jim Olds	Hartford	12-11½*
1969 C	Tom Clausen	Wyoming Lee	12-9

Year	Name	School	Mark
1970 C	Ian Livock	Gobles	12-11½*
1971 C	George Reader	Mason County Central	13-1½*
1972 C	Tom Glass	Farwell	12-10
1973 C	Steve Wren	Haslett	14-1*
1974 C	Steve Wren	Haslett	14-6¾*
1975 C	Randy Baltzer	Unionville-Sebewaing	13-6
1976 C	Scott Walters	Paw Paw	14-½
1977 C	Kevin Ladiness	Erie Mason	13-4
1978 C	Dave Elbers	Reese	13-6
1979 C	Tony Mudd	Niles Brandywine	13-9
1980 C	Tony Mudd	Niles Brandywine	13-5
1981 C	Tim Weber	St. Louis	13-9¾
1982 C	Jim Purman	Reese	13-6
1983 C	Randy Darr	Hudson	14-0
1984 C	Tracy Weber	Reese	13-5
1985 C	Mike Armstrong	Muskegon Oakridge	14-0
1986 C	Brad Darr	Hudson	14-2
1987 C	Jay Pitcher	Ithaca	14-5
1988 C	Rick Lubbers	Grandville Calvin Christian	14-7*
1989 C	Joe Felske	Reese	13-7
1990 C	Scott Wazny	Goodrich	14-2
1991 C	David Swartz	Goodrich	14-1
1992 C	Chris Weber	Dundee	13-9
1993 C	Casey Ward	Breckenridge	14-6
1994 C	Casey Ward	Breckenridge	14-9*
1995 C	Phil Grzemkowski	Reese	14-11*
1996 C	Lynn Randle	Byron	14-1
1997 C	Al Keener	Bronson	14-3
1998 C	Aaron Gebauer	Bad Axe	15-4*
1999 C	Mike Bolster	Petersburg-Summerfield	13-6
2000 D3	Brad Gebauer	Bad Axe	14-6*
2001 D3	Brad Gebauer	Bad Axe	15-9*
2002 D3	Brad Gebauer	Bad Axe	15-0
2003 D3	Tom Stomant	Portland	14-6
2004 D3	Zach Burrington	Muskegon Oakridge	15-9¼*
2005 D3	Lance Bice	Addison	14-3
2006 D3	Loey Latz	Ovid-Elsie	14-6
2007 D3	Kyle Lund	Lakeview	14-9
2008 D3	Kyle Lund	Lakeview	13-9
2009 D3	Isaac Austin	Kent City	14-6
2010 D3	Jacob Elbers	Reese	15-0
2011 D3	Isaac Austin	Kent City	16-0*
2012 D3	Scott Watson	Stockbridge	14-6
2013 D3	Jeff Dempsey	Bath	14-7
2014 D3	Jacob Battani	Almont	13-9
2015 D3	Nate Fasbender	Reed City	14-0
2016 D3	Jacob Battani	Almont	15-6
2017 D3	Reese Nemeth	Hillsdale	15-0
2018 D3	Zach Flint	Manton	13-6

PV – Class D/Division 4 Champions

Year	Name	School	Mark
1927 D	Lee Hawkins	Woodland	10-¾*
1928 D	Oliver	Middleton	10-4*
1929 D	Norman Smith	Newaygo	10-2½
1930 D	Gerald Vigland	Elberta	10-11¾*
1931 D	Donald Schultz	Middleton	10-6
1932 D	Howard Elzinga	Ellsworth	11-0*
1933 D	Linel Jolis	Maple Rapids	9-9
1934 D	Ralph Borseth	Bergland	11-4½*
1935 D	Thomas Scott	Saranac	10-0
1936 D	Anthony Mazey	Middleton	11-5*
1937 D	Sylvester Buck Flarity	Onekema	11-1½
1938 D	Sylvester Buck Flarity	Onekema	10-5½
1939 D (tie)	James Moore	Bloomfield Hills	10-6
1939 D (tie)	Gerald Clark	Byron	10-6
1939 D (tie)	Mark Krieger	St. Joseph Lake Mich Catholic	10-6
1940 D	Warren Cooper	Ida	10-6
1941 D	Marlin Roberts	Galien	10-3
1942 D (tie)	Ernest Ware	Bear Lake	10-6
1942 D (tie)	Joe Toth	Mt Morris St. Mary	10-6
1943	No Meet Held – World War II		
1944 D	Art Winfield	Bloomfield Hills	unknown
1945 D (tie)	Bill Roka	Michigan School for Deaf	10-2
1945 D (tie)	Don Bartz	Stevensville	10-2
1946 D	Bill Reese	Galien	9-9
1947 D	Bill Reese	Galien	11-3
1948 D (tie)	Bill Reese	Galien	10-0
1948 D (tie)	Nole Noggle	Galien	10-0
1949 D (tie)	Woods Proctor	Bloomfield Hills	9-11
1949 D (tie)	Arien Heise	Woodland	9-11
1950 D	Robert Willingham	Otisville	10-9
1951 D	Jack Bond	New Buffalo	11-3
1952 D	Marvin Penny	Merrill	9-9
1953 D	Tom McCormick	Otisville	10-3
1954 D	Daryl Leckrone	Brethren	10-9
1955 D	William Elzinga	Ellsworth	10-8
1956 D (tie)	Tom Hoag	Crystal	11-3
1956 D (tie)	William Elzinga	Ellsworth	11-3
1957 D	Tom Hoag	Crystal	11-0
1958 D	Bob Doehrer	Galien	11-2
1959 D	John Jackinowicz	Petoskey St. Francis	10-8
1960 D	Ken Gangler	Unionville	11-6½*
1961 D	Gary Tesman	Centreville	11-10½*
1962 D	Charles Rochow	Bay City St. Mary	11-1
1963 D	Mark Patterson	Covert	11-4
1964 D	Mark Patterson	Covert	11-5
1965 D	Ed Papes	Freesoil	12-0*
1966 D (tie)	Bernard Woods	Covert	11-10
1966 D (tie)	Steve Papes	Freesoil	11-10
1966 D (tie)	Gary Adams	Litchfield	11-10
1966 D (tie)	Tom Bontekoe	Marion	11-10
1967 D	Doug Miller	Lake City	11-11¾
1968 D	Doug Miller	Lake City	11-11¼
1969 D	Craig Letherbury	Tekonsha	12-8*
1970 D	Don Winchester	Mt Morris St Mary	12-2
1971 D	Rod Seder	Aranac-Eastern	13-1½*
1972 D	Rod Seder	Aranac-Eastern	13-2*
1973 D	Jim Herendeen	Grass Lake	12-7
1974 D	Jim Herendeen	Grass Lake	13-3*
1975 D	Jim Herendeen	Grass Lake	13-9½*
1976 D	Jim Herendeen	Grass Lake	13-6
1977 D	Steve Hiner	Potterville	12-0
1978 D	John Roop	Kingsley	13-7
1979 D	Carl Martel	Flint Holy Rosary	13-5¾
1980 D	Scott Jakubik	Onekema	13-10*
1981 D	Jim Patnaude	Owendale-Gagetown	13-7
1982 D	Jim Patnaude	Owendale-Gagetown	13-7
1983 D	Joe Rioux	Kingsley	13-2
1984 D	John Dietrich	Gobles	13-4
1985 D	Kelly Jones	Pittsford	12-10
1986 D	Scott Hale	Webberville	13-3
1987 D	Carl Aldrich	Akron-Fairgrove	13-1
1988 D	Scott Goodman	Portland St. Patrick	14-2*
1989 D	Bryan Happel	Mendon	13-9
1990 D	Bryan Happel	Mendon	14-½
1991 D	Bryan Happel	Mendon	15-2½*
1992 D	Brandon McCarty	Webberville	14-4¾
1993 D	Jim McLaughlin	Kingston	13-1
1994 D	Craig Happel	Mendon	13-9
1995 D	Eric Diller	Fairview	11-11
1996 D	Terry Kuster	Camden-Frontier	12-1
1997 D	William Oakley	Webberville	12-9
1998 D	Rusty Gardner	Mendon	12-6
1999 D	Kurt Daugherty	Webberville	12-0
2000 D4	Kyle Ray	Mendon	12-10*
2001 D4	Ben Walker	Bellaire	12-7
2002 D4	Ben Petitpren	Brown City	13-9*
2003 D4	Tony Thomas	Onekema	13-7
2004 D4	Bryant Wilson	Hale	14-5*
2005 D4	Bryant Wilson	Hale	14-0
2006 D4	Breg Bruns	Litchfield	14-0
2007 D4	Aaron Chamberlain	Webberville	14-0
2008 D4	Matt Magda	Jonesville	14-0
2009 D4	Trent Morris	Reading	14-0
2010 D4	Tim Canfield	Unionville-Sebewaing	13-11
2011 D4	Tim Canfield	Unionville-Sebewaing	15-0*
2012 D4	Tyler Fogarty	Onekema	13-5
2013 D4	Gavin Towery	Homer	13-4
2014 D4	Curtis Bell	Coleman	15-1*
2015 D4	Jacob Kulhanek	Merrill	13-7
2016 D4	Jacob Kulhanek	Merrill	13-9
2017 D4	Mike Couterier	Johannesburg-Lewiston	14-9
2018 D4	Cole Hallett	Sand Creek	13-6

PV – UP Class AB/Division 1 Champions

Year	Name	School	Mark
1940 UPB	Tom Finch	Escanaba	10-0?
1941 UPB	Phil Anderson	Ironwood	11-3½*
1942 UPB	Walter Curik	Ironwood	11-5*
1943	No Meet Held – World War II		
1944 UPB	Wayne Crebo	Escanaba	10-6
1945 UPB	Clifford Weir	Escanaba	10-3

Year	Class	Athlete	School	Mark
1946 UPB		Clifford Weir	Escanaba	11-0
1947 UPB		Engle	Marquette	10-6
1948 UPB		Lawrence Sobolewski	Ironwood	11-4
1949 UPB (tie)		Lawrence Sobolewski	Ironwood	11-2
1949 UPB (tie)		Axel Anderson	Escanaba	11-2
1949 UPB (tie)		Leonard Staley	Sault Ste. Marie	11-2
1950 UPB		Axel Anderson	Escanaba	10-10
1951 UPB		John Prokos	Escanaba	11-7*
1952 UPB (tie)		Richard Parkkonen	Negaunee	10-4½
1952 UPB (tie)		Bob Melchoir	Stephenson	10-4½
1952 UPB (tie)		Henry Brown	Sault Ste. Marie	10-4½
1952 UPB (tie)		Tom Roberts	Ironwood	10-4½
1953 UPB (tie)		Bob Melchoir	Stephenson	10-9
1953 UPB (tie)		Ron England	Menominee	10-9
1954 UPB		Pat LaFave	Manistique	11-0
1955 UPB		Pete Feira	Iron Mountain	11-0
1956 UPB		Dale Manske	Escanaba	10-8
1957 UPB		Rod Paavola	Hancock	11-2
1958 UPB		Mike Stemac	Escanaba Holy Name	10-8
1959 UPB (tie)		Al Johnson	Iron Mountain	11-5
1959 UPB (tie)		Mike Stemac	Escanaba Holy Name	11-5
1960 UPB		Mike Stemac	Escanaba Holy Name	11-8½*
1961 UPB (tie)		Bob Heikkala	Calumet	10-8
1961 UPB (tie)		Brian Johnson	Ironwood	10-8
1962 UPAB		Ray Luke	Munising	11-3
1963 UPAB		Quentin Minkin	Ironwood	11-11½*
1964 UPAB		Jim Konrad	Kingsford	11-6
1965 UPAB		Rich McCarthy	Kingsford	12-0*
1966 UPAB		Dennis Daugherty	Sault Ste. Marie	12-5½*
1967 UPAB		Mitchell	Sault Ste. Marie	12-0
1968 UPAB		John Vardigan	Escanaba	12-2½
1969 UPAB		Dennis Bastian	Calumet	12-3
1970 UPAB		Terry Froberg	Gwinn	12-7¾*
1971 UPAB		John Noblet	Escanaba	12-10¾*
1972 UPAB		John Noblet	Escanaba	13-6¾*
1973 UPAB		Mike Stewart	Menominee	12-6
1974 UPAB		Kurt Kitti	Calumet	12-10
1975 UPAB		Mike Bruce	Marquette	12-0
1976 UPAB		Pat Lemire	Menominee	12-7½
1977 UPAB		Steve Row	Calumet	12-7
1978 UPAB		Rob Noblet	Sault Ste. Marie	12-9
1979 UPAB		Bruce Pepin	Escanaba	11-9¾
1980 UPAB		Mike Wilson	Menominee	12-0
1981 UPAB		Kevin Johnson	Menominee	12-6
1982 UPAB		Kevin Johnson	Menominee	12-7½
1983 UPAB		Greg Olson	Marquette	12-0
1984 UPAB		Darrell Reed	Kingsford	12-5
1985 UPAB		Ken Vanderlinden	Gladstone	12-6
1986 UPAB		Ken Vanderlinden	Gladstone	13-0
1987 UPAB		Brian Gonyou	Marquette	12-6
1988 UPAB		Tim Driscoll	Marquette	13-0
1989 UPAB		Chris Durkee	Gwinn	12-0
1990 UPAB		Scott Creten	Gladstone	13-0
1991 UPAB		Jeff Maynard	Ishpeming Westwood	13-3
1992 UPAB		Wade Hodge	Menominee	14-0*
1993 UPAB		Nick Jensen	Gladstone	12-0
1994 UPAB		Dennis VanAble	Ishpeming Westwood	12-6
1995 UPAB		Nick Jensen	Gladstone	13-6
1996 UPAB		Randy Laurilla	Ishpeming Westwood	13-0
1997 UPAB		Casey Young	Gladstone	12-0
1998 UPAB		Casey Young	Gladstone	12-6
1999 UPAB		Casey Young	Gladstone	13-6
2000 UPAB		Tony Bartol	Gladstone	13-0
2001 UPD1		Dan Maloney	Escanaba	12-6*
2002 UPD1		Eric Jarvi	Negaunee	12-6*
2003 UPD1		Luke Gustafson	Menominee	12-0
2004 UPD1		Jake Skewis	Negaunee	12-6*
2005 UPD1		Seth Hampula	Gladstone	13-3*
2006 UPD1		Brad Hooper	Negaunee	13-6*
2007 UPD1		Mike Coyne	Gladstone	13-7*
2008 UPD1		Mike Coyne	Gladstone	13-0
2009 UPD1		Joel Revord	Negaunee	13-0
2010 UPD1		Josh Syverson	Gladstone	13-6
2011 UPD1		Zach Sturdy	Gladstone	12-0
2012 UPD1		Zach Sturdy	Gladstone	12-6
2013 UPD1		Ausin Caya	Negaunee	12-0
2014 UPD1		Ryan Camo	Kingsford	13-0
2015 UPD1		Jake Budd	Houghton	11-0
2016 UPD1		Kyle McKenzie	Gladstone	11-6
2017 UPD1		Kameron Simpkin	Houghton	12-9
2018 UPD1		Dayton Miron	Escanaba	12-6

PV – UP Class C/Division 2 Champions

Year	Class	Athlete	School	Mark
1940 UPC		Leonard Hill	Eben	10-0*
1941 UPC		Leroy Baker	Escanaba St. Joseph	10-3*
1942 UPC (tie)		Onnie Koskamaki	L'Anse	10-2
1942 UPC (tie)		Green	Eben	10-2
1943		No Meet Held – World War II		
1944 UPC		Mike Polovitz	Wakefield	11-½*
1945 UPC		Tom Emblad	L'Anse	10-9
1946 UPC (tie)		Welters	Newberry	10-8
1946 UPC (tie)		Jack Raymond	Munising	10-8
1947 UPC		Tom Emblad	L'Anse	11-4½*
1948 UPC		Ronald Nettell	Houghton	11-4 5/8*
1949 UPC (tie)		Alex Gembolis	Wakefield	11-0
1949 UPC (tie)		Clarence Rivers	Negaunee	11-0
1950 UPC (tie)		Les Young	Gladstone	9-11
1950 UPC (tie)		Ralph Everson	L'Anse	9-11
1951 UPC		Ralph Everson	L'Anse	10-2
1952 UPC (tie)		Robert Mattson	Wakefield	9-11¼
1952 UPC (tie)		Carl Bricco	Painesdale	9-11¼
1953 UPC		Jerry Kastner	Houghton	10-9¾
1954 UPC		Einard Anderson	Houghton	10-9
1955 UPC (tie)		Harold Linn	Wakefield	11-1¼
1955 UPC (tie)		Joe Leshinski	Houghton	11-1¼
1956 UPC		Joe Leshinski	Houghton	11-4
1957 UPC (tie)		Sam Bagnieski	Painesdale	10-10
1957 UPC (tie)		Harold Benink	Baraga	10-10
1958 UPC		Greg Miheve	Wakefield	10-8
1959 UPC		Greg Miheve	Wakefield	11-6½*
1960 UPC		Greg Miheve	Wakefield	12-½*
1961 UPC (tie)		Larry Stelmaszek	L'Anse	11-0
1961 UPC (tie)		John Haarala	Houghton	11-0
1961 UPC (tie)		Jim Hodge	Wakefield	11-0
1962 UPC		Jim Hodge	Wakefield	11-9
1963 UPC		Jim Hodge	Wakefield	12-1½*
1964 UPC		Roger Koski	Wakefield	11-6
1965 UPC		Jim Smith	Wakefield	10-10
1966 UPC		David Aultman	Crystal Falls	11-6
1967 UPC		David Aultman	Crystal Falls	11-9
1968 UPC		David Aultman	L'Anse	12-4*
1969 UPC		Harold Wiberg	Stephenson	11-5
1970 UPC		Mitchell Irwin	Rudyard	12-10*
1971 UPC		Brian Adams	Norway	12-5
1972 UPC		Ed Lester	St. Ignace	11-6
1973 UPC		Mike Lord	Stephenson	12-0
1974 UPC		Mitch Lord	Stephenson	12-10*
1975 UPC		Frank Devine	Norway	11-11
1976 UPC		Brett Gauthier	Ishpeming	12-8¼
1977 UPC		Dennis Nault	Ishpeming Westwood	12-7
1978 UPC		Dan Drabek	Ontonagon	12-6
1979 UPC		Larry Rasmussen	Negaunee	12-5¼
1980 UPC		Daniel Harrington	Ishpeming Westwood	12-9½
1981 UPC		Tim Korcal	Newberry	12-3½
1982 UPC		Dean Johnson	Munising	12-3
1983 UPC		Dave Vaara	Ironwood	12-7
1984 UPC		Mark Quelette	Ishpeming	12-2
1985 UPC		Paul Johnson	Munising	12-7¼
1986 UPC		Bob Miklesch	Ironwood	12-6
1987 UPC		Pat Ark	Houghton	12-6
1988 UPC		Al Miner	Norway	12-10¾*
1989 UPC		Steve Carlson	Ishpeming Westwood	12-0
1990 UPC		Tony Mariuzza	Ishpeming Westwood	12-0
1991 UPC		Robert Riggs	Ironwood	12-6
1992 UPC		Curtis Brown	St. Ignace	12-0
1993 UPC		Jeremiah Konell	Stephenson	13-3*
1994 UPC		Jeremiah Konell	Stephenson	12-6
1995 UPC		Jeremy Richards	Ironwood	13-4*
1996 UPC		Jeremy Richards	Ironwood	12-6
1997 UPC		Jason Leach	Manistique	12-0
1998 UPC		Kevin Letson	Ironwood	12-0
1999 UPC		Joe Dolaski	Munising	12-9
2000 UPC		Troy Sayles	St. Ignace	12-0
2001 UPD2		Sam Winkler	Stephenson	12-6*
2002 UPD2		Aaron Gutchess	St. Ignace	11-6
2003 UPD2		Adam Brown	Newberry	12-0
2004 UPD2		Aaron Gutchess	St. Ignace	12-0
2005 UPD2		Aaron Gutchess	St. Ignace	12-0
2006 UPD2		Derrick Clark	St. Ignace	12-0
2007 UPD2		Kurt Davis	Munising	12-0
2008 UPD2		Troy Seaberg	Munising	11-6
2009 UPD2		Troy Seaberg	Munising	11-6
2010 UPD2		Lance Pinter	Newberry	12-0
2011 UPD2		Joe Samotucha	Stephenson	12-0
2012 UPD2		Richard Bentley	St. Ignace	11-6

2013 UPD2	Cole Stevens	Ironwood	12-0		2016 UPD2	Mitchell Peterson	St. Ignace	11-6
2014 UPD2	Noah Olgren	Ishpeming	12-0		2017 UPD2	Matthew Revord	Munising	13-6*
2015 UPD2	Isaac Aukee	Ironwood	11-6		2018 UPD2	Rico Braucher	Ironwood	11-6

PV – UP Class D/Division 3 Champions

1940 UPD	Aaro Sutela	Rock	10-2*		1977 UPD	Ronald Carlson	DeTour	13-2½*
1941 UPD	Aaro Sutela	Rock	10-3?		1978 UPD	John Andrzejak	Pickford	13-3*
1942 UPD	John Minerich	Hermansville	10-9¼*		1979 UPD	Gary Christensen	Pickford	12-6¼
1943	No Meet Held – World War II				1980 UPD	Gary Christensen	Pickford	12-6½
1944 UPD	John Minerich	Hermansville	11-0*		1981 UPD	John Edington	Pickford	12-10
1945 UPD	J. Paul Brisson	Eben	10-6¼		1982 UPD	Dean Hartwig	Rapid River	12-8
1946 UPD	F. Haapala	Chassell	10-9		1983 UPD	Bob Hardwick	Rapid RIver	12-6
1947 UPD (tie)	Stocky Salo	Eben	10-3		1984 UPD	Tom Healy	Hancock	11-6
1947 UPD (tie)	Lempi	Eben	10-3		1985 UPD	Tony Ragio	Crystal Falls Forest Park	12-0
1948 UPD (tie)	Dick Whitens	Hermansville	10-6		1986 UPD	Don Johnson	Pickford	12-3
1948 UPD (tie)	Eino Valeen	Rock	10-6		1987 UPD	Dann Craft	Crystal Falls Forest Park	12-0
1949 UPD	Paul Begovac	Trenary	11-5*		1988 UPD	Darren Wallis	Pickford	12-0
1950 UPD	Paul Tormala	Chassell	10-0		1989 UPD	Shawn Bortolini	Crystal Falls Forest Park	12-6
1951 UPD	William Killio	Eben	11-0		1990 UPD	Craig Lancour	Rapid River	13-0
1952 UPD (tie)	Donald Strjanen	Rock	9-9		1991 UPD	Corey Ness	Rapid River	12-0
1952 UPD (tie)	John Belanger	Hermansville	9-9		1992 UPD	Shon Cottle	Pickford	11-6
1953 UPD	John Belanger	Hermansville	10-2		1993 UPD	Corey Ness	Rapid River	12-6
1954 UPD (tie)	Gerald Mattson	Eben	10-3		1994 UPD	Chris Wolf	Rapid River	11-0
1954 UPD (tie)	Alan Morin	Chassell	10-3		1995 UPD	Jason Saari	Wakefield	12-6
1955 UPD	Frank Bailey	DeTour	10-6		1996 UPD	Chad Parrett	Rapid River	12-0
1956 UPD	Frank Bailey	DeTour	10-8		1997 UPD	Jim Linn	Wakefield	11-6
1957 UPD (tie)	Steve Johnson	Rapid River	10-6		1998 UPD	Jim Linn	Wakefield	11-0
1957 UPD (tie)	Wayne Harrison	Pickford	10-6		1999 UPD	Casey Britton	Powers-North Central	12-0
1957 UPD (tie)	Gerald Paavola	Doelle	10-6		2000 UPD	Mike Holmgren	Rapid RIver	11-6
1958 UPD	Wayne Harrison	Pickford	10-7		2001 UPD3	Paul Linn	Wakefield	11-6*
1959 UPD	Gary Soumis	Chassell	10-6		2002 UPD3	Cory Candro	Rapid River	11-0
1960 UPD	Arnold Putala	Baraga	11-5½*		2003 UPD3	Joe Pociopa	Eben Junction Superior Central	12-0*
1961 UPD	John Aimli	Baraga	11-0		2004 UPD3	Joe Chernach	Crystal Falls Forest Park	12-6*
1962 UPD	Mike Aalto	Rock	11-3		2005 UPD3	Justin Giezer	Rapid River	12-0
1963 UPD	Tom Harrison	Pickford	11-8*		2006 UPD3	Jimmi Cretens	Rock-Mid Peninsula	13-¾*
1964 UPD	John Bennin	Pickford	11-6		2007 UPD3	Jimmi Cretens	Rock-Mid Peninsula	13-3*
1965 UPD	Pete LeClair	Baraga	11-4		2008 UPD3	Pat Hampston	Bessemer	11-6
1966 UPD	Neil Harrison	Pickford	11-11½*		2009 UPD3	Derek Berglund	Rapid River	12-6
1967 UPD	Frank Stec	Pickford	11-3		2010 UPD3	Brett Gervais	Lake Linden-Hubbell	11-6
1968 UPD	Tomothy Tischer	DeTour	12-3¾*		2011 UPD3	Daniel Knapp	Felch North Dickinson	12-6
1969 UPD	Jerry Bawks	Pickford	12-5¼*		2012 UPD3	Robert Metter	Rapid River	12-6
1970 UPD	Jerry Bawks	Pickford	12-11½*		2013 UPD3	Robert Metter	Rapid River	12-0
1971 UPD	Robert Bruno	Wakefield	13-1*		2014 UPD3	Bill Ragio	Crystal Falls Forest Park	12-0
1972 UPD	Dana Hill	Pickford	12-7		2015 UPD3	Bill Ragio	Crystal Falls Forest Park	13-3½*
1973 UPD	Dana Hill	Pickford	12-6		2016 UPD3	Bill Ragio	Crystal Falls Forest Park	13-0
1974 UPD	Tim O'Connor	Pickford	12-8		2017 UPD3	Luke Gustafson	Rapid River	12-0
1975 UPD	Tim O'Connor	Pickford	12-6		2018 UPD3	Matthew Revord	Munising	13-0
1976 UPD	Joe Converse	Engadine	12-4					

BOYS LONG JUMP

Records

D1	24-2¾ (0.3)	Mason Phillips	Salem	2017
D2	23-7½	Aaron Daugherty	Big Rapids	2011
D3	23-7	Demea Carter	Detroit Country Day	2004
D4	22-11¾	Tyrell Hall	Marion	2014
UPD1	21-6½	Justin Wiles	Escanaba	2006
UPD2	20-11	Cody Kangas	Hancock	2003
UPD3	21-1	Brett Gervais	Lake Linden-Hubbell	2011

Records by Class (pre-2000 for LP, pre-2001 for UP)

A	23-11½	Marcel Richardson	Lansing Everett	1988
B	23-10¾	Tyrone Wheatley	Dearborn Heights Robichaud	1989
C	23-9	Brian Corbit	New Haven	1984
D	23-5¾	Dave Koenigsknecht	Fowler	1982
UPAB	22-5	Chuck Atwater	Manistique	1974
UPC	21-8½	Tim Nault	Norway	1970
UPD	22-½	Mark Flood	Crystal Falls Forest Park	1973

LJ – Class A/Division 1 Champion

1895 all	Clarence Christopher	Lansing	18-7½*		1901 all	H. A. Osborn	Detroit Central	19-11
1896 all	Clarence Christopher	Lansing	21-6½*		1902 all	Horace Edmands	Kalamazoo Central	20-4
1897 all	Otis Cole	Lansing	20-7		1903 all	Clarence McCarty (4)	Wayne	19-11¼
1898 all	Roy Ellis	Detroit Central	20-6		1904 all	Lewis Torrent	Muskegon	20-3¼
1899 all	Roy Ellis	Detroit Central	20-8		1905 all	Cullen Corliss (4)	Detroit University School	20-9
1900 all	Frank Thompson	Pontiac	19-7		1906 all	Ward Richards (4)	Ann Arbor	21-0

1907 all	Ord Page (3)	Grand Rapids Central	20-5
1908 all	Fred Pierson	Traverse City	19-9½
1909 all	Howard Schaffer	Muskegon	20-9
1910 all	Paul Kress	Alma	20-3¾
1911 all	William Howard	Croswell	21-½
1912 all	Carman Smith	Bay City Eastern	20-½
1913 all	R. Harry Leslie	Croswell	20-8
1914 all	Jerry Marks	Oscoda	20-3¾
1915 all	Vernon Parks	St Johns	21-3¼
1915 all	Glen Thompson	Rockford	21-½
1916 all	Lawrence Townsend	St Johns	20-6
1917 all (tie)	Harry Clark	Detroit Cass Tech	19-10
1917 all (tie)	Howard Shears	Otsego	19-10
1918	No Meet – World War I		
1919 all	Leroy Neish	Detroit Eastern	19-11½
1920 all	Thomas Shepherd	Kalamazoo Central	20-5½
1921 A	Paul Cook	Muskegon	20-8
1922 A	Bill Meyers	Detroit Cass Tech	20-9¼
1923 A	Phil Northrup	Detroit Northwestern	21-5½
1924 A	Raymond Smith	Battle Creek	22-6½*
1925 A	Clifford Robinson	Detroit Northwestern	22-10*
1926 A	Dick Chapman	Grand Rapids South	21-6½
1927 A	Eugene Beatty	Detroit Northeastern	21-8
1928 A	Eugene Beatty	Detroit Northeastern	21-3
1929 A	Thad Dennis	Detroit Northwestern	22-4
1930 A	William Friday	Detroit Cass Tech	21-7½
1931 A	Douglas Emery	Grand Rapids Central	21-11
1932 A	Ed Kalawart	Grand Rapids Central	22-2½
1933 A	Sanford Farrell	Grand Rapids Central	21-10½
1934 A	Chester Peevy	Grand Rapids South	20-10
1935 A	William Watson	Saginaw	22-4
1936 A	Ted Tyrocki	Lansing Central	22-11¾*
1937 A	Ted Tyrocki	Lansing Central	22-9
1938 A	Edward Dragg	Dearborn Fordson	22-1
1939 A	Hugh Davis	Lansing Central	21-7¼
1940 A	Bert Copeland	Benton Harbor	22-1
1941 A	Earl Copeland	Benton Harbor	22-2½
1942 A	Bob Whitfield	Kalamazoo Central	21-5
1943	No Meet – World War II		
1944 A	Archie England	Grand Rapids South	21-4½
1945 A	Jesse Thomas	Flint Central	21-11¼
1946 A	Jesse Thomas	Flint Central	21-4¾
1947 A	Tim Keyes	Saginaw	22-3½
1948 A	Warren Keyes	Saginaw	22-4½
1949 A	Warren Keyes	Saginaw	21-5¾
1950 A	Milt Mead	Bay City Central	21-5¼
1951 A	R.G. Johnson	Flint Northern	21-7½
1952 A	R.G. Johnson	Flint Northern	21-8¾
1953 A	Alonzo Harris	Pontiac	21-2
1954 A	Bob Maturen	Saginaw	21-11½
1955 A	Hayes Jones	Pontiac	22-5
1956 A	Hayes Jones	Pontiac	23-8¾*
1957 A	Jerry Fitzpatrick	Muskegon Catholic	21-8¾
1958 A	Reg Gillard	Flint Northern	22-2
1959 A	Rex Cawley	Farmington	22-8
1960 A	Steve Jacobson	Birmingham	23-7½
1961 A	Bob Barnett	Flint Central	21-10½
1962 A	Bob Barnett	Flint Central	21-10¾
1963 A	William Whittaker	Flint Southwestern	23-5¾
1964 A	Dennis Lamiman	Roseville	24-3w (3.6)
1965 A	Fred Carver	Kalamazoo Central	22-5¼
1966 A	Ira Russell	Detroit Cass Tech	23-3½
1967 A	Lavern Miller	Flint Southwestern	22-10½
1968 A	Lloyd Hoke	Highland Park	23-4½
1969 A	Roland Garcia	Pontiac Central	22-3¾
1970 A	Deima Williams	Flint Northwestern	23-1¾
1971 A	John Ross	Detroit Mackenzie	23-11*
1972 A	Clarence Chapman	Detroit Redford	22-11
1973 A	Kelsey Johnson	Detroit Osborn	23-11*
1974 A	Terry Thames	Flint Northwestern	23-1
1975 A	Terry Thames	Flint Northwestern	23-7½
1976 A	Stan Wilkins	Detroit Chadsey	22-9½
1977 A	James Ross	Kalamazoo Central	23-0
1978 A	Brian Carpenter	Flint Southwestern	23-6¾
1979 A	Ken Brown	Flint Northern	23-1¼
1980 A	Derek Harper	Pontiac Northern	25-0w
1981 A	Clayton Alexander	Flint Northwestern	23-4½
1982 A	Vincent Cox	Kalamazoo Loy Norrix	23-7
1983 A	Scott Reed	Lansing Everett	23-10¾
1984 A	Jerome Greer	Southfield	23-3¼
1985 A	Joseph Applewhite	Grand Rapids Central	23-2
1986 A	Thomas Pryor	Jackson	21-8½
1987 A	Marcel Richardson	Lansing Everett	23-4¾
1988 A	Marcel Richardson	Lansing Everett	23-11½*
1989 A	Aaron Bailey	Ann Arbor Pioneer	23-5½
1990 A	Ali Shakoor	Jackson	22-10½
1991 A	Izell Watkins	Romulus	23-8¾
1992 A	Mario Patterson	Adrian	22-10½
1993 A	Dion Woolfolk	Ann Arbor Pioneer	22-9
1994 A	Eric Peters	Grosse Pointe North	23-3
1995 A	Mark Windom	Grand Rapids Union	22-6
1996 A	Oki Giwaagbomeirel	Midland	24-6w
1997 A	Jon Hall	Pontiac Central	21-1
1998 A	Joe Alls	Sterling Heights Stevenson	22-6½
1999 A	Gary Stanford	Detroit Mumford	22-4¾
2000 D1	Steve Wolf	Sterling Heights Stevenson	22-1½*
2001 D1	Greg Jennings	Kalamazoo Central	21-9
2002 D1	Justin Hoskins	Grand Rapids Creston	23-¾*
2003 D1	Evan Walker	Belleville	23-1*
2004 D1	Justin Hoskins	Grand Rapids Creston	23-5*
2005 D1	Harrel Jonte	Taylor Truman	23-1¼
2006 D1	Michael Stafford	Harrison Twp L'Anse Creuse	23-1¼
2007 D1	Cordell Miller	Lansing Everett	23-3¾
2008 D1	Cordell Miller	Lansing Everett	23-1
2009 D1	Jeff Kline	Flushing	24-1w
2010 D1	Aaron Dewberry	Portage Northern	21-11½
2011 D1	Jordan Levigne	Pickford	20-8
2012 D1	Steven Bastien	Saline	23-5*
2013 D1	Ato Condelee	Holland West Ottawa	23-¾w (5.5)
2014 D1	Austin Edwards	Grand Ledge	22-11 (0.6)
2015 D1	Austin Edwards	Grand Ledge	22-4¾
2016 D1	Anthony Owens	Jackson	24-1¼w (2.5)
2017 D1	Mason Phillips	Salem	24-2¾* (0.3)
2018 D1	AJ Abbott	West Bloomfield	23-7¼w (4.9)

LJ – Class B/Division 2 Champion

1921 B	Kent Pritchard	Allegan	21-6*
1922 B	Kent Pritchard	Allegan	21-4
1923 B	Oscar Renshaw	Coldwater	20-4¼
1924 B	Harold George	Petoskey	21-3½
1925 B	Burrell Tripp	Allegan	21-¼
1926 B	Joseph Lysaght	Kalamazoo State High	21-¼
1927 B	Harry Holman	Kalamazoo State High	20-9¾
1928 B	Ray March	Petoskey	21-1¾
1929 B	Edwin Jackson	Dearborn	21-2¾
1930 B	Clare McDurman	Caro	19-7½
1931 B	Kurt Warmbein	St Joseph	20-2½
1932 B	John McKee	Birmingham	21-5¾
1933 B	George Humm	Allegan	21-4
1934 B	Richard Heller	River Rouge	21-1½
1935 B	Allen Cisco	Dowagiac	21-2½
1936 B	Harold Wagenschutz	Plymouth	21-7½*
1937 B	Jerome Kladzyk	Bad Axe	20-11¾
1938 B	William Schelb	Allegan	20-10
1939 B	James Cook	Kalamazoo State High	21-5¼
1940 B	Jim Barbour	East Lansing	20-6½
1941 B	Clay Cochrane	Niles	20-10
1942 B	Fred Bouwman	Fremont	21-6¼
1943	No Meet – World War II		
1944 B	Emil Carlstrom	Berkley	19-9½
1945 B	Jerry Kalke	St Joseph	21-8¾*
1946 B	Sam Mitchell	Adrian	19-9¼
1947 B	Tom Mitchell	Adrian	21-4¾
1948 B	Harold DubMartin	Alma	21-7¾
1949 B	Dave Hill	Ypsilanti	22-1¾*
1950 B	Newell Heath	Hastings	20-9¾
1951 B	Junior Sielstra	Ludington	21-5¾
1952 B	Bob Zimmerman	Roseville	20-4¾
1953 B	Jack McDonald	Adrian	20-7¾
1954 B	William Benham	Tecumseh	21-5½
1955 B	John Palmer	St Louis	21-5¼
1956 B	Willie Prewitt	Willow Run	22-¼
1957 B	Willie Prewitt	Willow Run	20-5¾
1958 B	Willie Prewitt	Willow Run	23-2¾*
1959 B	Herman Brooks	Willow Run	21-7¼
1960 B	Clarence Brown	Ecorse	21-6
1961 B	Milt Waters	Dowagiac	21-7¼
1962 B	Dean Scott	Otsego	21-1½
1963 B	Boice Bowman	River Rouge	22-4
1964 B	Lamar Miller	Willow Run	21-11¾
1965 B	Pat Howard	Albion	21-7¼
1966 B	Paul Schneider	Harper Woods Lutheran East	21-5
1967 B	Gordon Wood	Detroit Lutheran West	22-10½
1968 B	Clarence Ellis	Grand Rapids Central	23-1½
1969 B	John DeJonge	Grand Rapids Christian	22-5¾
1970 B	John Stuyvenberg	Northville	22-11

Year	Name	School	Mark		Year	Name	School	Mark
1971 B	John Stuyvenberg	Northville	22-2½		1995 B	Marion Collier	Mt Clemens Clintondale	21-9½
1972 B	Robert Johnson	Port Huron Central	23-6½*		1996 B	Shane Kelly	Harrison	22-9½
1973 B	Robert Johnson	Port Huron Central	22-9		1997 B	Brent Lesniak	Dowagiac	22-6½
1974 B	Alvin Charles	Muskegon Reeths-Puffer	22-11¾		1998 B	Brent Lesniak	Dowagiac	23-0
1975 B	Mike Moses	Holly	22 1¾		1999 B	Nic Farrell	Jackson Lumen Christi	22-10½
1976 B	Everett Charleston	Dearborn Heights Robichaud	22-3¾		2000 D2	Ray Graves	Romulus	22-7*
1977 B	Mark Young	Saginaw Buena Vista	22-10½		2001 D2	Michael Bailey	Lansing Waverly	22-½
1978 B	Jeff Rowe	Linden	22-2		2002 D2	Michael Bailey	Lansing Waverly	23-0*
1979 B	Gary Armstrong	East Grand Rapids	22-4		2003 D2	Steve Ellsworth	Auburn Hills Avondale	22-¾
1980 B	Andreas Laut	Dexter	22-8¼		2004 D2	Marcus Crawford	River Rouge	22-2
1981 B	Jim Bowman	Cadillac	23-½		2005 D2	Jon Allen	Lansing Sexton	23-4¼*
1982 B	Vince Davis	Willow Run	22-6		2006 D2	Woodell Payne	Ypsilanti	22-8¾
1983 B	Jamonty Washington	Flint Beecher	22-6¾		2007 D2	Zach Heerspink	Hamilton	21-9½
1984 B	Anthony Green	Willow Run	22-3		2008 D2	Bennie Fowler	Detroit Country Day	22-5¼
1985 B	Eric Tuss	Inkster Cherry Hill	22-5		2009 D2	Aaron Daugherty	Big Rapids	22-11¼
1986 B	Derrick Harris	Flint Beecher	22-5¼		2010 D2	Aaron Daugherty	Big Rapids	23-1½
1987 B	Gerald Nazarebno	Riverview Gabriel Richard	22-6¼		2011 D2	Aaron Daugherty	Big Rapids	23-7½*
1988 B	Richard Palmer	Mt Clemens	23-1½		2012 D2	Eric Wilson	Redford Thurston	22-7½
1989 B	Tyrone Wheatley	Dearborn Heights Robichaud	23-10¾*		2013 D2	Dontel Highsmith	Dowagiac	23-5¼
1990 B	Tyrone Wheatley	Dearborn Heights Robichaud	23-10		2014 D2	Anthony Fitzgerald	Melvindale	23-1
1991 B	Tyrone Wheatley	Dearborn Heights Robichaud	23-0		2015 D2	Anthony Fitzgerald	Melvindale	22-5
1992 B	Aaron Oakes	Vicksburg	22-4¼		2016 D2	Zach Stadnika	Macomb Lutheran North	22-4¾w
1993 B	Aaron Oakes	Vicksburg	23-2		2017 D2	Sy Barnett	Williamston	22-9¾w
1994 B	Aaron Oakes	Vicksburg	23-1¼		2018 D2	Tony Martin	Saginaw	22-7

LJ – Class C/Division 3 Champion

Year	Name	School	Mark		Year	Name	School	Mark
1921 C	Bud Pio	Union City	20-0*		1970 C	Bill Hack	Grass Lake	21-0
1922 C (tie)	Bud Pio	Union City	20-0*		1971 C	Al Spencer	Akron-Fairgrove	21-7¾
1922 C (tie)	Bernard Otto	Jackson	20-0*		1972 C	Scott Davis	Addison	21-6½
1923 C	Alton Vance	Nashville	20-0*		1973 C	Sam Onstott	St Louis	21-9¼
1924 C	Fred Allyn	Farmington	20-6½*		1974 C	Dave Merritt	Detroit Country Day	22-6¾*
1925 C	Russell Garrett	Augusta	20-1¾		1975 C	Dave Merritt	Detroit Country Day	22-5½
1926 C	Milton Jacobi	Marine City	21-1½*		1976 C	James Henry	New Haven	22-5¾
1927 C	Joe Salerno	Yale	20-5		1977 C	Ted Lepper	Bronson	21-7¼
1928 C	Joe Salerno	Yale	21-3¾*		1978 C	Brian Phillips	Howard City Tri County	21 1¾
1929 C	Charles Eggstaff	Kalamazoo State High	19-11¾		1979 C	John Harrington	Buchanan	21-6
1930 C	George Ward	Bridgman	20-10½		1980 C	Jeff Baumback	Fennville	21-1¼
1931 C	George Ward	Bridgman	21-1½		1981 C	Craig Weber	Harbor Beach	21-7¾
1932 C	Clare McDurman	Caro	20-9½		1982 C	Ethan Sheard	Detroit Lutheran West	22-9¾*
1933 C	Ham White	Boyne City	22-1*		1983 C	Tim Davis	Mt Clemens Lutheran North	22-8¾
1934 C	Alan Smith	Paw Paw	21-½		1984 C	Brian Corbit	New Haven	23-9*
1935 C	Alan Smith	Paw Paw	22-6½*		1985 C	Brian Corbit	New Haven	22-8½
1936 C	Donald Wilber	East Grand Rapids	22-3½		1986 C	Terrance Williams	Ecorse	23-0
1937 C	Starr Keesler	Okemos	21-1½		1987 C	Rory Stace	Galesburg-Augusta	23-0
1938 C	Arthur Cuthbertson	Algonac	21-4 ¾		1988 C	Joe Jefferson	Orchard Lake St Mary	22-5
1939 C	Robert Brandt	Paw Paw	21-2½		1989 C	Darius Fykes	Flint Hamady	22-6
1940 C	John Hellyer	Glen Arbor Leelanau School	20-9¾		1990 C	Paul Whitlock	Union City	21-1
1941 C	Don Harm	St Clair Shores South Lake	21-¼		1991 C	James Harrison	Williamston	21-10½
1942 C	Fred Johnson	Grandville	21-9¼		1992 C	Chuck Davis	Byron	21-9¼
1943	No Meet – World War II				1993 C	Jermaine Thomas	Eau Claire	22-½
1944 C	N. J. Hanks	Marysville	20-9¾		1994 C	Cory Dunn	Jonesville	22-8½
1945 C	Luther Butler	Romulus	20-5½		1995 C	Chris Mansfield	Morenci	21-6
1946 C	Bob Fancett	Rockford	20-5¾		1996 C	Jason Thompson	Southgate Aquinas	22-6
1947 C	Richard Donovan	Paw Paw	20-1		1997 C	Jason Thompson	Southgate Aquinas	22-2
1948 C	Bob Black	St Clair Shores Lake Shore	21-3½		1998 C	Jared Owens	Niles Brandywine	21-2¾
1949 C	Jack Goodrich	Dundee	21-7¼		1999 C	Jeff Bowen	Muskegon Oakridge	22-1½
1950 C	Fred Newman	East Grand Rapids	20-9¾		2000 D3	Jeff Bowen	Muskegon Oakridge	21-11½*
1951 C	Gary Cullen	Ypsilanti Lincoln	20-6¾		2001 D3	Jason Stewart	Suttons Bay	21-8
1952 C	Ray Eggelston	East Jackson	21-7½		2002 D3	Jason Stewart	Suttons Bay	22-5½*
1953 C	John Palmer	St Louis	20-3¾		2003 D3	Demea Carter	Detroit Country Day	22-6½*
1954 C	David Whitsell	Shelby	20-2		2004 D3	Demea Carter	Detroit Country Day	23-7*
1955 C	Fred Garsa	Deckerville	21-3¼		2005 D3	Kyle Holmes	Detroit Country Day	22-0
1956 C	Rog Quinn	Lansing Everett	21-1		2006 D3	Jon Reed	Stanton-Central Montcalm	21-3¼
1957 C	Carl Charon	Boyne City	20-9¾		2007 D3	Marck Berden	Saginaw Swan Valley	21-10
1958 C	Charles Peltz	Grosse Ile	21-3½		2008 D3	Paris Gooch	Flint Beecher	22-5
1959 C	Jim Roe	East Jackson	21-4¼		2009 D3	Ryan Hopson	Albion	22-10½
1960 C	William Hopkins	Breckenridge	21-7¼		2010 D3	Keif Vickers	Vassar	21-10¼
1961 C	Al Behnke	Michigan Lutheran Seminary	21-0		2011 D3	Chris Maye	Union City	22-8
1962 C	Steve Maynard	Lansing Boys Training School	21-4½		2012 D3	Dillon Wood	Lakeview	22-4½
1963 C	Michael Rabbers	Richland	21-4 ¾		2013 D3	Jake Cowsert	Watervliet	21-1½
1964 C	Dwight Lee	New Haven	22-5¼		2014 D3	Austin Hawkins	Hillsdale	22-3½w (2.7)
1965 C	Van French	Baldwin	21-1½		2015 D3	Austin Hawkins	Hillsdale	21-2
1966 C	Terry Robe	Jackson St Mary	21-11¼		2016 D3	John Mitrzyk	Standish-Sterling	21-5½ (0.0)
1967 C	Doug Smith	Traverse City St Francis	22-6¾*		2017 D3	Sam Forsyth	Chesaning	21-6½
1968 C	Mike Clark	New Haven	22-6¾*		2018 D3	Bryce Ruhl	Quincy	21-¾
1969 C	Delbert Gregory	Dundee	21-9					

LJ – Class D/Division 4 Champion

Year	Name	School	Mark		Year	Name	School	Mark
1927 D	William Sutherby	Trenton	18-1¼*		1932 D	Charles Young	McBain	20-1¾
1928 D	Charles Dildine	St Clair Shores Lake Shore	19-4½*		1933 D	Gordon Bera	Richland	20-0
1929 D	Raymond Scott	McBain	18-10½		1934 D	Lester Walters	Centreville	20-0
1930 D	Murrell Mason	South Lake	20-2*		1935 D	William Wiese	Bear Lake	20-11*
1931 D	Floyd Cummings	Ann Arbor St Thomas	18-7¼		1936 D	Milo Palen	Napoleon	19-0

1937 D	Woody Newman	Mt Morris St Mary	18-9¾
1938 D	Basil Edwards	Dimondale	20-7¼
1939 D	Gordon Craig	Bloomfield Hills	20-3¾
1940 D	Rene La Franier	Mt Morris St Mary	20-4
1941 D	Rene La Franier	Mt Morris St Mary	20-11¼*
1942 D	Melvin Helmbolt	McBain	20-7
1943	No Meet – World War II		
1944 D	George Wilson	Benton Harbor St John	19-7
1945 D	Bennie Osborne	Benton Harbor St John	20-2¾
1946 D	Don Plonta	Bayport	19-1¾
1947 D	Morris Hughes	Michigan School for Deaf	19-10½
1948 D	Forrest Bass	Bath	20-6
1949 D	Gaylord Snyder	Vestaburg	20-9
1950 D	Richard Molnar	Wyandotte Smith	20-7¾
1951 D	Richard Molnar	Wyandotte Smith	21-1¼*
1952 D	Bruce Garbutt	Detroit University School	19-1½
1953 D	Jerry Mitchell	Eau Claire	20-3¾
1954 D	Jerry Mitchell	Eau Claire	20-11½
1955 D	Henry White	Freesoil	20-11¼
1956 D	Atis Grinsberg	Schoolcraft	21-1¾*
1957 D	Quincy Johnson	Covert	19-2½
1958 D	Pat Finch	Fairview	20-5
1959 D	Dick Johnson	Grosse Pointe University	20-8½
1960 D	Paul Joles	Wolverine	21-¾
1961 D	Don Smith	Michigan School for Deaf	20-1
1962 D	Don Smith	Michigan School for Deaf	21-5*
1963 D	David Beane	Brethren	20-6½
1964 D	Abram Powell	Michigan School for Deaf	21-4
1965 D	Roy Pingel	Grosse Pointe University	20-8¼
1966 D	Joe Chagnon	Kinde North Huron	20-11
1967 D	Al Henderson	Detroit St Charles	22-8¾*
1968 D	Jerry Kerperian	Flint St Matthew	20-8½
1969 D	Bill Hack	Grass Lake	21-3¼
1970 D	Ken Papes	Freesoil	21-5
1971 D	Al Strieter	Unionville	20-11
1972 D	Alland Streiter	Unionville	21-10½
1973 D	Kevin Clark	Lake City	20-4½
1974 D	Jeff Jackson	Mt Pleasant Sacred Heart	22-¾
1975 D	Orlin Swimmer	Morenci	21-8
1976 D	Jeff Jackson	Mt Pleasant Sacred Heart	21-6
1977 D	David Sykes	Litchfield	21-9½
1978 D	Scott Heath	Freesoil	22-0
1979 D	Robert Snyder	Vestaburg	21-3¼
1980 D	Pat Hurst	Battle Creek St. Phillip	22-½
1981 D	Dave Koenigsknecht	Fowler	22-9¼*
1982 D	Dave Koenigsknecht	Fowler	23-5¾*
1983 D	Dave Koenigsknecht	Fowler	23-½
1984 D	Ryan Pschigoda	Bridgman	22-4¾
1985 D	Ryan Pschigoda	Bridgman	22-5¼
1986 D	Paul Hurst	Battle Creek St Phillip	22-2
1987 D	Willy Scott	Detroit East Catholic	22-10½
1988 D	Chauncey Turman	Litchfield	22-5
1989 D	Albert Rhodes	Detroit Lutheran West	21-9½
1990 D	Todd Richards	Reading	22-2½
1991 D	Todd Richards	Reading	21-7
1992 D	Peter Amstutz	Athens	21-4
1993 D	Dave Cardenas	Adrian Madison	21-3¼
1994 D	Mike Kennealy	Au Gres	21-5½
1995 D	Jerrid Blacker	Port Hope	20-11
1996 D	Nick Salazar	Pittsford	21-4
1997 D	Nick Grabowski	Pittsford	21-6
1998 D	Luke Allen	Centreville	21-1
1999 D	Kelvin Singleton	Centreville	20-6
2000 D4	Kelvin Singleton	Centreville	22-1*
2001 D4	Jesse Magda	Reading	20-8¾
2002 D4	Kenneth Coleman	Baldwin	21-2¾
2003 D4	Olajuwon Pinson	Eau Claire	21-9½
2004 D4	Matt Epkey	Fowler	21-5¾
2005 D4	Matt Epkey	Fowler	21-5¾
2006 D4	Aaron Trieber	Saginaw Valley Lutheran	21-3¾
2007 D4	Patrick Patterson	Eau Claire	21-10¾
2008 D4	David Shockley	Detroit Loyola	21-3
2009 D4	Erric Garner	Springport	21-2
2010 D4	Erric Garner	Springport	21-5½
2011 D4	Ricky Richardson	Homer	22-½
2012 D4	Adam Abbott	Detroit Cristo Rey	22-3½*
2013 D4	Demetrius Nelson	Genesee	21-7
2014 D4	Tyrell Hall	Marion	22-11¾*
2015 D4	Casey Williams	Saginaw Mich Luth Seminary	22-9¼
2016 D4	Delvon Hines	Melvindale ABT	20-9¼
2017 D4	Derek Flory	Marcellus	20-11
2018 D4	Heath Baldwin	Kalamazoo Hackett	22-2½w (3.5)

LJ – UP Class AB/Division 1 Champion

1940 UPB	Roland Kehler	Escanaba	19-7*
1941 UPB	George Shomin	Escanaba	21-0*
1942 UPB	Dick Keskey	Marquette	19-10
1943	No Meet – World War II		
1944 UPB	Joe Devine	Calumet	19-1½
1945 UPB	Jack Brosco	Sault Ste. Marie	19-5¼
1946 UPB	Walter Olsen	Ironwood	19-7 5/8
1947 UPB	Aikens	Sault Ste Marie	20-2
1948 UPB	Stanley Kasieta	Ironwood	20-9½
1949 UPB	Harold Larson	Menominee	19-10¼
1950 UPB	Forrest Barrow	Kingsford	19-11¾
1951 UPB	Jerome Tooler	Sault Ste. Marie	20-1
1952 UPB	Ward VanLaanan	Iron Mountain	21-1½*
1953 UPB	Ray Cummings	Manistique	19-7¼
1954 UPB	Marlin Buckmaster	Stephenson	19-7¼
1955 UPB	William Erickson	Kingsford	20-8¼
1956 UPB	William Erickson	Kingsford	21-¾
1957 UPB	Bob Perry	Iron River	19-4¾
1958 UPB	Bob Wills	Ishpeming	20-7½
1959 UPB	George Fornnarino	Sault Ste. Marie	20-3¾
1960 UPB	Gerald Schinderle	Iron Mountain	19-9¼
1961 UPB	Richard Dubord	Escanaba Holy Name	19-10¾
1962 UPAB	Dick Berlinski	Kingsford	20-6¾
1963 UPAB	Dick Berlinski	Kingsford	21-1½*
1964 UPAB	Dick Berlinski	Kingsford	20-10½
1965 UPAB	Bob Van Kirk	Sault Ste. Marie	20-10
1966 UPAB	Duane Contols	Marquette	20-6½
1967 UPAB	Jim Boyle	Escanaba	20-5½
1968 UPAB	Jeff Stevenson	Munising	19-8½
1969 UPAB	Jeff Stevenson	Munising	19-8½
1970 UPAB	Mike Hatfield	Gwinn	21-7*
1971 UPAB	Gary Mainville	Kingsford	21-10*
1972 UPAB	Chuck Atwater	Manistique	21-½
1973 UPAB	Travey Blake	Calumet	21-3
1974 UPAB	Chuck Atwater	Manistique	22-5*
1975 UPAB	James Massoglia	Calumet	19-11
1976 UPAB	Jerry Garceau	Gwinn	20-2½
1977 UPAB	Don Theverkauf	Menominee	21-4¾
1978 UPAB	Rick Callies	Menominee	20-10¾
1979 UPAB	Mike Berquist	Marquette	20-10¾
1980 UPAB	Chuck Voelker	Calumet	20-4½
1981 UPAB	Mike Ward	Sault Ste Marie	20-10
1982 UPAB	Pat Duffy	Kingsford	21-6¾
1983 UPAB	Emmet Blake	Marquette	20-1
1984 UPAB	Pat Duffy	Kingsford	21-0
1985 UPAB	Greg Haslow	Escanaba	19-4½
1986 UPAB	Tim Gipson	Gwinn	21-7
1987 UPAB	Cory Thomosgard	Gwinn	20-¾
1988 UPAB	Roman Gasowski	Marquette	20-9
1989 UPAB	Shannon Black	Marquette	21-2
1990 UPAB	Dave Bramscheiber	Menominee	19-8¼
1991 UPAB	Mono McDonald	Sault Ste. Marie	21-¼
1992 UPAB	Mono McDonald	Sault Ste. Marie	20-9¾
1993 UPAB	Bill Cody	Escanaba	20-2½
1994 UPAB	Nick Kelly	Menominee	19-8
1995 UPAB	Andy Manthey	Marquette	21-¾
1996 UPAB	Josh Jupe	Escanaba	20-7¼
1997 UPAB	Korey Sahr	Menominee	19-11½
1998 UPAB	Tadd Russell	Menominee	19-0
1999 UPAB	Casey Young	Gladstone	20-5
2000 UPAB	Drew Buyarksi	Menominee	20-2
2001 UPD1	Adam Konrad	Gladstone	20-1¾*
2002 UPD1	Mark McDodonough	Sault Ste. Marie	20-4*
2003 UPD1	Steve Short	Kingsford	20-5¼*
2004 UPD1	Marc McDonough	Sault Ste. Marie	21-6¼*
2005 UPD1	Brandon Erdman	Menominee	20-4½
2006 UPD1	Justin Wiles	Escanaba	21-6½*
2007 UPD1	Joby Sullivan	Iron Mountain	19-11½
2008 UPD1	Dillon Menard	Negaunee	20-5½
2009 UPD1	Matt Rastello	Calumet	20-6
2010 UPD1	Tanner Maccoux	Menominee	20-11
2011 UPD1	Justin Pederson	Gladstone	20-4¾
2012 UPD1	Salmi Cole	Houghton	20-2½
2013 UPD1	Justin Pederson	Gladstone	21-½
2014 UPD1	Justin Brilinski	Menominee	19-9½
2015 UPD1	Trevor Roberts	Kingsford	20-10½
2016 UPD1	Mike Jamar	Kingsford	20-1¼
2017 UPD1	Wyatt Goodwin	Marquette	20-2¾
2018 UPD1	Raphael Millado	Marquette	19-6

LJ – UP Class C/Division 2 Champion

1940 UPC	Mike O'Donnell	Escanaba St. Joseph	19-2½*
1941 UPC	Richard Moilanen	Baraga	19-4*
1942 UPC	G. Simon	Stephenson	19-11¾*
1943	No Meet – World War II		
1944 UPC	Rene Adams	Houghton	18-2½
1945 UPC	William Eilola	Hancock	19-1½
1946 UPC	Kujula	Newberry	18-7
1947 UPC	Edward Sowa	Munising	20-2*
1948 UPC	Gene Smith	Gladstone	20-7*
1949 UPC	Lloyd Seavoy	L'Anse	20-3½
1950 UPC	Robert Thompson	Baraga	18-1¾
1951 UPC	James Seavoy	L'Anse	19-5
1952 UPC	Dan Dobbek	Ontonagon	19-8
1953 UPC	Bob Harris	Bessemer	18-11½
1954 UPC	James Contratto	Bessemer	19-4½
1955 UPC	Phil Belisle	Lake Linden	18-10
1956 UPC	Einar Anderson	Houghton	19-9
1957 UPC	Bob Hurley	Houghton	18-6¾
1958 UPC	Dick Koski	Wakefield	19-8
1959 UPC	Richard Koski	Wakefield	21-3*
1960 UPC	Jim Ghiardi	Gwinn	20-1¾
1961 UPC	Clark Suchovsky	Stephenson	20-9½
1962 UPC	Clark Suchovsky	Stephenson	20-6½
1963 UPC	Fred Hagan	Houghton	19-5½
1964 UPC	Ray McDonald	L'Anse	20-1¾
1965 UPC	Ray Sibley	Wakefield	19-10½
1966 UPC	Ray Sibley	Wakefield	20-8½
1967 UPC	Jerry LaFeunesse	Houghton	20-1½
1968 UPC	Ken Anderson	Lake Linden	19-11½
1969 UPC	Mike Gill	Rudyard	20-8½
1970 UPC	Tim Nault	Norway	21-8½*
1971 UPC	Larry Rogers	Houghton	21-5
1972 UPC	Larry Rogers	Houghton	20-8
1973 UPC	Earl Dougovita	Stephenson	20-7
1974 UPC	Barry Green	Rudyard	20-10
1975 UPC	Mike Dellangelo	Ishpeming	20-3
1976 UPC	Mike Dellangelo	Ishpeming	21-5¼
1977 UPC	Mike Dellangelo	Ishpeming	20-10½
1978 UPC	Zigmond Derochowski	Ontonagon	20-6¾
1979 UPC	Frank Kleinke	Stephenson	20-6½
1980 UPC	Dale Warren	Iron Mountain	20-5
1981 UPC	Dean Johnson	Munising	19-10
1982 UPC	Dean Johnson	Munising	21-7½
1983 UPC	Mike Morton	Ishpeming	18-11
1984 UPC	Brian Cahill	St. Ignace	20-9
1985 UPC	Jerry Destrampe	Houghton	19-11¾
1986 UPC	Jerry Destrampe	Houghton	21-5
1987 UPC	Mike Rubatt	Ironwood	21-1
1988 UPC	Stan Sharik	Houghton	21-1
1989 UPC	Mark Gilles	Lake Linden-Hubbell	20-3
1990 UPC	Jeremy Watt	Iron Mountain	20-4
1991 UPC	Nathan Pollard	Stephenson	19-9½
1992 UPC	Jim Gilmer	Ontonagon	20-1
1993 UPC	Mike Nordstrom	L'Anse	20-0
1994 UPC	Swan Lindeblad	Munising	20-7
1995 UPC	Reid Mortier	Iron Mountain	20-½
1996 UPC	Derek Sandahl	Stephenson	20-6½
1997 UPC	Derek Sandahl	Stephenson	21-7¾
1998 UPC	Jesse Haile	Iron River West Iron Country	20-10
1999 UPC	Brent Schupp	Iron Mountain	21-4½w
2000 UPC	Gavin Cornwell	Rudyard	21-4½
2001 UPD2	Brad Zimmerman	Norway	19-11½*
2002 UPD2	Cody Kangas	Hancock	19-6½
2003 UPD2	Cody Kangas	Hancock	20-11*
2004 UPD2	Zane Johnson	St. Ignace	20-3
2005 UPD2	Dustin Brancheau	Ishpeming-R Michagammee	18-11
2006 UPD2	Dustin Brancheau	Ishpeming-R Michagammee	19-5
2007 UPD2	Alex Winkler	Stephenson	20-4
2008 UPD2	Cory Torni	Ironwood	19-8½
2009 UPD2	Jordan Thomas	Norway	20-7
2010 UPD2	Roman Alberti	Stephenson	19-11
2011 UPD2	Lance Pinter	Newberry	20-¼
2012 UPD2	Lance Pinter	Newberry	20-¼
2013 UPD2	Josh Whittington	Ishpeming	20-3
2014 UPD2	Ryan Rogers	West Iron County	19-7
2015 UPD2	Brandon Olson	West Iron County	19-3
2016 UPD2	Aaron Bolo	Iron Mountain	18-10
2017 UPD2	John Paramski	Newberry	18-10
2018 UPD2	Hart Holmgren	Ishpeming	19-5½

LJ – UP Class D/Division 4 Champion

1940 UPD	Aaro Sutela	Rock	19-0*
1941 UPD	Reno Fochesetto	Hermansville	20-1*
1942 UPD	Reno Fochesetto	Hermansville	20-5 5/8*
1943	No Meet – World War II		
1944 UPD	Bill MacEchern	Hermansville	18-6½
1945 UPD	Stanley Ivlo	Ewen	18-10
1946 UPD	Don Shannon	Powers	19-1
1947 UPD	Don Shannon	Powers	19-4¾
1948 UPD	Bill Frigard	Eben	20-6½*
1949 UPD	Robert Pelkie	Gwinn	20-10¼*
1950 UPD	Harold Kallio	Eben	18-2¼
1951 UPD	Raymond Saly	Gwinn	19-0
1952 UPD	Anthony Stankiewicz	Alpha	20-0
1953 UPD	Vic Dani	Hermansville	17-10½
1954 UPD	John Nordeen	Gwinn	19-1¼
1955 UPD	Bernard Newhouse	Nahma	19-3
1956 UPD	Frank Bailey	DeTour	19-7
1957 UPD	Don Mattson	Chassell	18-6¼
1958 UPD	Dan Ojala	Ewen	19-½
1959 UPD	Terry Sayen	Gwinn	20-½
1960 UPD	Verne Lamoreaux	Cedarville	19-8
1961 UPD	Anthony Lee	DeTour	20-10¼*
1962 UPD	Don Pomeroy	Nahma	19-6½
1963 UPD	Bill Rushford	Rapid River	19-5½
1964 UPD	Dave Hanna	Pickford	19-9
1965 UPD	Dave Hanna	Pickford	19-9¾
1966 UPD	Melvin Leach	Pickford	19-5½
1967 UPD	Dan Safford	Rapid River	19-7½
1968 UPD	Frank Teddeucci	Pickford	19-8
1969 UPD	Ken Anderson	Lake Linden	21-3*
1970 UPD	Mark Cambray	Channing	20-8
1971 UPD	Rocky Belongie	Ewen-Trout Creek	21-0
1972 UPD	Schwiderson	Brimley	21-2
1973 UPD	Mark Flood	Crystal Falls Forest Park	22-½*
1974 UPD	Joe Baker	Pickford	21-4½*
1975 UPD	Joe Baker	Pickford	20-8
1976 UPD	Clint Monett	Republic-Michigamme	20-0
1977 UPD	Dan Short	Lake Linden-Hibbell	20-9
1978 UPD	Chris Stevenson	Pickford	20-6¾
1979 UPD	Dwayne Hammersmith	Rock-Mid Peninsula	20-9¼
1980 UPD	Jeff Andrews	Brimley	20-5½
1981 UPD	Lewis Sawicky	Baraga	20-5
1982 UPD	David Nelson	Wakefield	20-8
1983 UPD	David Nelson	Wakefield	20-3½
1984 UPD	Joe Newton	Felch North Dickinson	19-9
1985 UPD	Kenneth Wiser	Brimley	19-3
1986 UPD	Rob Tervo	Rudyard	19-4
1987 UPD	Chuck Pelkey	Cedarville	20-11½
1988 UPD	Mike Gillies	Lake Linden-Hubbell	19-11¾
1989 UPD	James Lindholm	Felch North Dickinson	19-4
1990 UPD	Mark Gillis	Lake Linden-Hubbell	20-6½
1991 UPD	Kevin Sutton	Brimley	20-0
1992 UPD	Charles Kline	Lake Linden-Hubbell	20-¼
1993 UPD	Mike Decker	Republic-Michigamme	20-3
1994 UPD	Mike Simeoni	Crystal Falls Forest Park	20-1¼
1995 UPD	Mike Simeoni	Crystal Falls Forest Park	19-7¼
1996 UPD	Mike Simeoni	Crystal Falls Forest Park	20-¾
1997 UPD	Casey Blenkhorn	Pickford	19-½
1998 UPD	Lee M.	Mohawk Keweenaw	19-6
1999 UPD	Sean Duffin	Carney-Nedeau	20-¼
2000 UPD	Sean Duffin	Carney-Nedeau	20-5
2001 UPD3	Brock Bower	Bark River-Harris	19-7½*
2002 UPD3	Brock Bower	Bark River-Harris	20-2*
2003 UPD3	Ben Laurin	Carney-Nedeau	19-10
2004 UPD3	Daniel Thompson	Bark River-Harris	19-10¼
2005 UPD3	Craig Bilski	North Central	19-10¼
2006 UPD3	Craig Bilski	North Central	20-10*
2007 UPD3	Alex Kopsi	Watersmeet	20-5
2008 UPD3	Damien Smith	Iron Mountain N Dickinson	20-8
2009 UPD3	C.J. Paquin	Cedarville	19-9½
2010 UPD3	Brett Gervais	Lake Linden-Hubbell	20-6½
2011 UPD3	Brett Gervais	Lake Linden-Hubbell	21-1*
2012 UPD3	Kane Rasner	Stephenson	19-9
2013 UPD3	Alex Smith	Bessemer	20-5
2014 UPD3	Bill Ragio	Crystal Falls Forest Park	18-9½
2015 UPD3	Brian Harju	St. Ignace	18-11
2016 UPD3	Noah Berg	Felch North Dickinson	18-5
2017 UPD3	Garrett O'Neil	Felch North Dickinson	18-10

BOYS TRIPLE JUMP

Records

All	43-11	Chandler Tompkins	Lansing	1896

TJ – All Classes Champion

1895 all	Clarence Christopher	Lansing	42-1
1896 all	Chandler Tompkins	Lansing	43-11
1897 all	Clarence Christopher	Lansing	43-5½

(In 1895 there was also a standing hop, step and jump, which Christopher won with a 27-7.)

BOYS SHOT

Records

D1	67-5¾	Connor Bandel	Oxford	2016
D2	61-8	Anthony Zettel	West Branch Ogemaw Heights	2011
D3	63-9½	Zack Hill	Allendale	2009
D4	58-5¼	George Flanner	Ottawa Lake Whiteford	2007
UPD1	55-11¼	Jared Vuksan	Gladstone	2013
UPD2	51-11¾	Matt Payment	Newberry	2006
UPD3	52-7¼	Jason Miller	Ontonagon	2007

Records by Class (pre-2000 for LP, pre-2001 for UP)

A	64-½	T.J. Duckett	Kalamazoo Loy Norrix	1999
B	60-3	Dan Foor	Saginaw Eisenhower	1983
C	63-7	Gary Van Elst	Middleville	1968
D	58-6¾	Steve Buhr	Cheboygan Catholic	1984
UPAB	58-7	Wayne Schwalbach	Escanaba	1974
UPC	54-6½	Gary Dravecky	Ironwood	1979
UPD	55-1	Ryan Fountain	Pickford	1993

SP – Class A/Division 1 Champions

(16lb / 7.26k shot)

1895 all	Chandler Tompkins	Lansing	33-11*
1896 all	Chandler Tompkins	Lansing	32-9
1897 all	Chandler Tompkins	Lansing	34-7¼*
1898 all	Waldo Avery	Detroit Central	31-3
1899 all	James Forrest	Ann Arbor	34-10*

(12lb / 5.44k shot)

1900 all	Chauncey Brewer	Marshall	38-11*
1901 all	Raynor Brewer	Detroit University School	38-11*
1902 all	Leon Hewitt	Grand Rapids Central	38-2
1903 all	Leon Hewitt	Grand Rapids Central	41-7*
1904 all	Walter Cole (2)	Cedar Springs	40-7
1905 all	Kenneth Arthur	Detroit University School	44-9*
1906 all	Joe Horner	Grand Rapids Central	46-0*
1907 all	Joe Horner	Grand Rapids Central	50-4*
1908 all	Harry Sonnanstein	Michigan Military Academy	42-¼
1909 all	Arthur Kohler	Lansing Central	46-7
1910 all	Arthur Kohler	Lansing Central	51-6¾*
1911 all	Lee Chilson	Sparta	43-0
1912 all	J. D. Cross	Wayne	46-3
1913 all	Hugh Blacklock	Grand Rapids Central	44-5½
1914 all	Pat Smith	Bay City Eastern	44-0
1915 all	George Kimball	Muskegon	47-4½
1916 all	Clarence Fessenden	Newaygo	46-2
1917 all	Paul Bowersox	Otsego	41-8
1918	No Meet – World War I		
1919 all	Leon. Shunt Turnbull	Detroit Eastern	41-8
1920 all	Glenn Brooks	Chelsea	41-2
1921 A	John Stuart	Detroit Eastern	42-3
1922 A	Dick Doyle	Kalamazoo Central	47-3½
1923 A	Paul Smith	Saginaw	46-1
1924 A	Harry VanNortwick	Detroit Northwestern	44-9½
1925 A	Fred Barrett	Lansing Central	47-2
1926 A	Merrill Gowman	Detroit Eastern	44-11¾
1927 A	Henry Harper	Pontiac	45-5¼
1928 A	Edwin Turashoff	Detroit Cass Tech	48-1½
1929 A	Joseph Beer	Detroit Eastern	44-3
1930 A	Jack Fundis	Detroit Northwestern	43-2
1931 A	Henry Darling	Ann Arbor	47-2
1932 A	Henry Darling	Ann Arbor	47-2½
1933 A	Paul Hippo Allen	Pontiac	47-9
1934 A	William Watson	Saginaw	48-7¾
1935 A	William Watson	Saginaw	53-10½*
1936 A	George Angelson	Royal Oak	49-3½
1937 A	George Angelson	Royal Oak	51-4
1938 A	Lewis Smiley	Ferndale	46-¼
1939 A	Burgess Lawson	Grand Rapids Ottawa Hills	50-5¾
1940 A	Robert H Smith	Battle Creek	47-8¼
1941 A	Maurice Hofmeister	Benton Harbor	47-9¼
1942 A	Jim Hunt	Jackson	47-7¾
1943	No Meet – World War II		
1944 A	Dick Rifenburg	Saginaw Arthur Hill	46-11
1945 A	Bill Cordell	Owosso	46-9
1946 A	K D McKinnon	Saginaw	47-10¾
1947 A	K D McKinnon	Saginaw	52-5¾
1948 A	Tom Johnson	Muskegon Heights	54-4¾*
1949 A	Don Schieswohl	Saginaw Arthur Hill	54-0
1950 A	Henry Coddington	Jackson	50-10¾
1951 A	Carl Diener	Saginaw Arthur Hill	51-10½
1952 A	Carl Diener	Saginaw Arthur Hill	52-3¼
1953 A	Jim Miller	Lansing Eastern	51-1¾
1954 A	Joel Boyden	Muskegon	57-0*
1955 A	Tom Jozwiak	Detroit Catholic Central	53-½
1956 A	Thelvius Winieckie	Saginaw Arthur Hill	53-11¾
1957 A	Oscar Hahn	Midland	54-¼
1958 A	Jerry Barto	Grand Rapids Catholic	54-7
1959 A	Bob Hayes	Midland	55-3
1960 A	Bradell Pritchett	Pontiac Central	59-5¾*
1961 A	Bradell Pritchett	Pontiac Central	60-4¾*
1962 A	Bill Yearby	Detroit Eastern	54-9½

1963 A	Jack Harvey	Birmingham Seaholm	57-11½		1991 A	Jon Runyan	Flint Carman-Ainsworth	57-6
1964 A	Jim Foss	Garden City	56-¾		1992 A	Jon Runyan	Flint Carman-Ainsworth	59-5
1965 A	Ron Thompson	Kalamazoo Central	57-9¾		1993 A	Al Barnett	Belleville	59-11½
1966 A	Doug Yancy	Flint Southwestern	59-3¼		1994 A	Lionel Boston	Detroit Cooley	56-3½
1967 A	Guile Ceffalo	East Detroit	59-11½		1995 A	Ralph Neal	Monroe	56-3¾
1968 A	Stu Hanley	Lansing Sexton	56-11		1996 A	Stan Brown	Flint Central	57-½
1969 A	Steve Nelson	Battle Creek Central	59-6¾		1997 A	T.J. Duckett	Kalamazoo Loy Norrix	63-6*
1970 A	Ron Gatheright	Mt Clemens	58-8¾		1998 A	T.J. Duckett	Kalamazoo Loy Norrix	62-6½
1971 A	Ron Gatheright	Mt Clemens	62-1*		1999 A	T.J. Duckett	Kalamazoo Loy Norrix	64-½*
1972 A	Wayne Bouvier	Washington Eisenhower	58-6¾		2000 D1	Joey Sarantos	Portage Northern	61-11*
1973 A	Wayne Bouvier	Washington Eisenhower	61-3		2001 D1	Joey Sarantos	Portage Northern	61-7½
1974 A	Calvin Reed	Detroit Kettering	57-10		2002 D1	Tom Berishaj	Sterling Heights Stevenson	57-3
1975 A	Brad Selden	Clinton Twp Chippewa Valley	59-0		2003 D1	Hady Rahman	Livonia Stevenson	54-2
1976 A	Steve Wallace	Dearborn	57-6¾		2004 D1	Adam Amon	Davison	54-8
1977 A	Mike Petsch	Redford Union	56-9		2005 D1	Gerald Gersham	Southfield	57-6½
1978 A	Mike Petsch	Redford Union	61-1¼		2006 D1	Vince Helmuth	Saline	59-5
1979 A	Phillip Wells	Warren Mott	61-10		2007 D1	Michael Martin	Detroit Catholic Central	60-11½
1980 A	James Browne	Birmingham Brother Rice	58-½		2008 D1	Michael Martin	Detroit Catholic Central	63-9*
1981 A	Dan Kenwell	West Bloomfield	57-3		2009 D1	Ethan Dennis	Grandville	57-9¾
1982 A	Gary Price	Monroe	57-7		2010 D1	Feerooz Yacoobi	Dearborn	55-10¾
1983 A	Gary Price	Monroe	63-1½*		2011 D1	Feerooz Yacoobi	Dearborn	59-4
1984 A	Mike Sargeant	Flint Powers	61-8		2012 D1	Kevin Weiler	Swartz Creek	55-10½
1985 A	Chuck Bartz	Troy	55-1		2013 D1	Cullen Prena	Walled Lake Central	60-11
1986 A	Jonathon Frazier	Kalamazoo Central	57-6½		2014 D1	Kevin Weiler	Walled Lake Central	60-4½
1987 A	Kyle Wray	Kalamazoo Loy Norrix	60-1½		2015 D1	Connor Bandel	Oxford	59-7½
1988 A	Marc deManigold	Grosse Pointe North	58-10½		2016 D1	Connor Bandel	Oxford	67-5¾*
1989 A	Allen Jackson	Lansing Sexton	55-5		2017 D1	Logan Brown	East Kentwood	60-1½
1990 A	Scott Faculak	Flint Carman-Ainsworth	54-7¾		2018 D1	Logan Brown	East Kentwood	57-1¾

SP – Class B/Division 2 Champions

1921 B	Maurice Johnson	Coldwater	41-2*		1970 B	John Wallace	Cranbrook	54-11½
1922 B	Glenn Eastham	Caro	42-4*		1971 B	Jeff Middledorf	Harper Woods Lutheran East	56-3¾
1923 B	Earl VanNorden	Otsego	41-11		1972 B	Ed Tyler	Oxford	59-0*
1924 B	Hazen Herkimer	Monroe	43-9¾*		1973 B	Brad Seldon	Clinton Twp Chippewa Valley	54-7½
1925 B	John Lagoni	Niles	41-10¾		1974 B	Randy Foss	Mason	58-10
1926 B	Ivan Simpson	St. Johns	41-10½		1975 B	Tom Ferenc	Detroit DeLaSalle	56-0
1927 B	Elmer Metras	Dowagiac	42-11¾		1976 B	Mike Hetts	Royal Oak Shrine	58-10½
1928 B	Wayne Webb	Ypsilanti Central	42-4		1977 B	Lee Wolverton	Linden	55-1½
1929 B	Bernard McNutt	Allegan	44-10*		1978 B	Mark Roscczewski	Oxford	55-6¼
1930 B	Bernard McNutt	Allegan	46-8½*		1979 B	Jim Lamb	Linden	55-11½
1931 B	Les Heidamos	Three Rivers	45-9¾		1980 B	Ron Finch	Mt Pleasant	56-7¾
1932 B	Earl Garn	Cadillac	44-0		1981 B	Carl Kloosterman	Lowell	55-1¼
1933 B	Frank Koppitsch	Dearborn	44-8½		1982 B	Tim Fellows	Flint Ainsworth	56-8¼
1934 B	Frank Koppitsch	Dearborn	48-10½*		1983 B	Dan Foor	Saginaw Eisenhower	60-3*
1935 B	Dan Kinsey	Plymouth	47-4¾		1984 B	Eric Moore	University of Detroit High	56-1½
1936 B	Dan Kinsey	Plymouth	50-8¾*		1985 B	Ben Simon	Remus Chippewa Hills	54-7
1937 B	John Barklarz	Ecorse	42-3½		1986 B	Paul Cochran	Midland Bullock Creek	55-5¼
1938 B	Dan Sullivan	Wayne	46-6		1987 B	John Thornton	Flint Beecher	59-8½
1939 B	Dan Sullivan	Wayne	53-9½*		1988 B	Marty Malcolm	Standish-Sterling	55-4½
1940 B	Harold Oehmke	East Detroit	46-9¾		1989 B	John Knack	Gaylord	56-10
1941 B	Harold Oehmke	East Detroit	47-9¼		1990 B	Tom Johnson	Marysville	59-4¾
1942 B	Ed Vanderly	Traverse City	47-4		1991 B	Joe Lemieux	Grand Rapids West Catholic	56-1
1943	No Meet – World War II				1992 B	Christian Youngs	Hastings	54-10
1944 B	Dick Lee	Ypsilanti Central	45-5¾		1993 B	David Beeman	Chelsea	55-1
1945 B	George Smith	Wayne	46-0		1994 B	David Beeman	Chelsea	57-7½
1946 B	George Smith	Wayne	48 4¾		1995 B	Tim Moore	Onsted	54-4
1947 B	Dick Groves	Birmingham	46-5½		1996 B	Tim Moore	Onsted	57-4
1948 B	Gary Walters	Battle Creek Lakeview	47-9		1997 B	Jake Frysinger	Grosse Ile	57-2
1949 B	Dick Fisher	Trenton	49-8½		1998 B	Joe Denay	Bay City Western	56-1
1950 B	John Bachman	East Lansing	50-4¾		1999 B	Tim Hoogewind	Wyoming Park	55-5½
1951 B	Tom Wood	Grand Blanc	51-8¼		2000 D2	Aaron Targgart	Coldwater	53-4¼*
1952 B	Dave Goodell	Mt Pleasant	53-4		2001 D2	Joe Tripodi	Chelsea	55-11½*
1953 B	Earl Glenn	Belleville	54-8½*		2002 D2	Joe Tripodi	Chelsea	57-8¼*
1954 B	Dave Sikarskie	Petoskey	48-5¾		2003 D2	Matt Jennings	Cadillac	57-0
1955 B	Dave Sikarskie	Petoskey	51-3¾		2004 D2	Chris Wohlgamuth	Stevensville-Lakeshore	57-7½
1956 B	Dick McMacken	Howell	51-4		2005 D2	Jon Boles	Lansing Sexton	56-10
1957 B	Dick McMacken	Howell	52-1½		2006 D2	Mike Kuras	Lake Odessa-Lakewood	54-11¾
1958 B	Tom Brown	Kalamazoo University	52-8¼		2007 D2	Mike Kuras	Lake Odessa-Lakewood	56-2
1959 B	Dave Behrman	Dowagiac	53-6¾		2008 D2	Donny Stiffler	Williamston	58-8*
1960 B	Jack Patterson	Fenton	53-2		2009 D2	Alex Rose	West Branch Ogemaw Heights	58-7½
1961 B	Paul Rakow	Detroit Lutheran West	52-9		2010 D2	Anthony Zettel	West Branch Ogemaw Heights	58-3¾
1962 B	Gary Rugg	Battle Creek Pennfield	55-8½*		2011 D2	Anthony Zettel	West Branch Ogemaw Heights	61-8*
1963 B	Larry Rugg	Battle Creek Pennfield	54-1		2012 D2	Riley Norman	Cadillac	61-2½
1964 B	Robert Johnson	Vassar	57-5*		2013 D2	Riley Norman	Cadillac	59-10
1965 B	Robert Johnson	Vassar	58-5½*		2014 D2	Aaron Curtis	Coopersville	56-3¼
1966 B	Mike Lantry	Oxford	54-7¼		2015 D2	Logan Targgart	Coldwater	57-3¾
1967 B	Dave Pureifoy	Ecorse	57-½		2016 D2	Justin Scavarda	Mason	57-10½
1968 B	Bob Frye	Vassar	55-10¼		2017 D2	Jonathan Berghorst	Zeeland West	56-1½
1969 B	Joe Connell	Muskegon Catholic	54-8		2018 D2	Dylan Targgart	Coldwater	61-2

SP – Class C/Division 3 Champions

1921 C	Earl VanNorden	Otsego	40-2½*		1923 C	Lavere Sproul	Clinton	40-10
1922 C	Earl VanNorden	Otsego	41-11*		1924 C	Lavere Sproul	Clinton	40-1

Year	Athlete	School	Mark
1925 C	Frank Anderson	Newaygo	39-5
1926 C	Joe Savoldi	Three Oaks	40-9
1927 C	Russell Pell	Plainwell	41-6¾
1928 C	Burnel Morland	Paw Paw	43-5½*
1929 C	Elmer Layer	Lowell	43-8*
1930 C	Frank McCrory	Ontonagon	43-10½*
1931 C	Frank McCrory	Ontonagon	45-7*
1932 C	Charles Smith	Caro	45-2
1933 C	Paul Paynich	Paw Paw	46-2*
1934 C	Bill Vivian	East Grand Rapids	47-9½*
1935 C	Mike Mandjiak	Kalamazoo St. Augustine	49-¼*
1936 C	Les Bruckner	Milan	43-9½
1937 C	L. A. Snyder	Corunna	40-8½
1938 C	Richard Williams	East Grand Rapids	44-2½
1939 C	Marion Thompson	Ravenna	43-5
1940 C	Stan Bocek	Corunna	45-7¼
1941 C	Stan Bocek	Corunna	49-2*
1942 C	Stan Bocek	Corunna	48-6½
1943	No Meet – World War II		
1944 C	Deane Dingman	Fowlerville	41-11½
1945 C	Roy Dornbos	Comstock Park	46-5½
1946 C	Bill Ghesquiere	Detroit University School	46-6¾
1947 C	John Koczman	Milan	51-8*
1948 C	Bob Carey	Charlevoix	54-7½*
1949 C	Joe Hovanesian	Okemos	45-8
1950 C	Joe Williamson	Glen Arbor Leelanau School	50-9¾
1951 C	Eugene Pearce	Holt	48-2½
1952 C	Bill Fenton	St Louis	49-8¾
1953 C	Tom Bullen	Clarkston	48-4¼
1954 C	Bob Burchfield	Lansing Everett	48-3
1955 C	Ed Fritz	Houghton Lake	47-10¼
1956 C	Tom Chapman	Marine City	52-0
1957 C	Larry Wheaton	Burton Bentley	49-7
1958 C	Joe Waluk	Orchard Lake St Mary	52-8½
1959 C	Pat Emerick	Imlay City	51-3¾
1960 C	Mike Mocese	Lansing St Mary	51-1¼
1961 C	Gary Rugg	Battle Creek Pennfield	52-5½
1962 C	Mike Rocca	Battle Creek Springfield	47-11
1963 C	Tom Moon	Olivet	50-9½
1964 C	Louis Fournier	Cheboygan Catholic	55-1*
1965 C	Ron Gaetner	Saginaw St Peter & Paul	52-11¼
1966 C	Gary Van Elst	Middleville	56-10*
1967 C	Gary Van Elst	Middleville	60-5¾*
1968 C	Gary Van Elst	Middleville	63-7*
1969 C	Mike Austrauskas	Mason County Central	55-1¾
1970 C	George Bennett	Cassopolis	55-8¾
1971 C	Scott Belt	New Haven	53-3½
1972 C	Mike Moon	Clinton	52-4¼
1973 C	Gary Bradley	Perry	51-10½
1974 C	Harry Bradley	Perry	54-10¾
1975 C	Harry Bradley	Perry	56-6
1976 C	Neil Masse	Lake Fenton	54-5½
1977 C	Greg Johnson	New Haven	55-¾
1978 C	Mike Parsons	Constantine	51-9¾
1979 C	Gary Kinsey	Farwell	55-1 /4
1980 C	Jim Zambron	Sandusky	53-3¼
1981 C	Nelson Hanson	Lincoln Alcona	56-1¾
1982 C	Dan Holloway	Detroit DePorres	59-11½
1983 C	Dan Holloway	Detroit DePorres	56-9¼
1984 C	Doug Geno	Battle Creek Pennfield	54-10
1985 C	Scott Humes	St Joseph Lake Mich Catholic	56-5¾
1986 C	Aron Gowell	Shelby	55-8¼
1987 C	Aron Gowell	Shelby	57-0
1988 C	Aron Gowell	Shelby	62-11¼
1989 C	Eric Wheeler	Fennville	52-7¼
1990 C	Troy Gowell	Shelby	51-6¼
1991 C	Craig Engel	Michigan Lutheran Seminary	53-11¾
1992 C	Brian Wildfong	Mancelona	58-11¾
1993 C	Brian Wildfong	Mancelona	56-8¾
1994 C	Jerry Stempien	Quincy	53-7
1995 C	Jerry Stempien	Quincy	57-8¼
1996 C	Pat Walderzak	Frankenmuth	55-3¾
1997 C	Dale Cowper	Marlette	57-11
1998 C	Derek McLaughlin	Berrien Springs	58-8¾
1999 C	Derek McLaughlin	Berrien Springs	57-11½
2000 D3	Tom Maczik	Reese	58-3¾*
2001 D3	Phil Teeple	Durand	52-4¾
2002 D3	Joe Brooks	Kingsley	58-5¾*
2003 D3	John Plumstead	Benzie Central	57-11½
2004 D3	John Plumstead	Benzie Central	55-10
2005 D3	Jacob Smith	Hopkins	53-1¾
2006 D3	Donny Stiffler	Williamston	52-7½
2007 D3	Nate English	Hillsdale	59-8½*
2008 D3	Zack Hill	Allendale	60-7½*
2009 D3	Zack Hill	Allendale	63-9½*
2010 D3	David Scouten	Brooklyn Columbia Central	55-9
2011 D3	David Scouten	Brooklyn Columbia Central	59-6
2012 D3	Dan Liesman	Lansing Catholic	54-5
2013 D3	Clayton Walderzak	Standish-Sterling	55-2½
2014 D3	Jonathan Williams	Berrien Springs	56-0
2015 D3	Carl Myers	Grand Rapids West Catholic	54-6
2016 D3	Carl Myers	Grand Rapids West Catholic	62-9¾
2017 D3	Dan Stone	Frankenmuth	60-9¾
2018 D3	Jacob Ager	Boyne City	59-10

SP – Class D/Division 4 Champions

Year	Athlete	School	Mark
1927 D	Lee Hawkins	Woodland	40-3¼*
1928 D	Ralph Pendall	Middleton	42-3¾*
1929 D	Bernard Blair	Middleton	37-6
1930 D	Bernard Blair	Middleton	40-10
1931 D	James Desy	Mackinaw City	39-8¾
1932 D	James Desy	Mackinaw City	43-5¼*
1933 D	Albert Terwilliger	Howard City	40-¾
1934 D	Milt Glassner	Dimondale	47-5*
1935 D	Milt Glassner	Dimondale	45-1½
1936 D	Stanley McRae	Pellston	42-3
1937 D	Jack Van Orman	Ellsworth	39-6¾
1938 D	Jack Bengnot	Elberta	43-11¼
1939 D	Ivan Watkins	Osseo	43-4
1940 D	Duane McIlquham	Pentwater	39-8½
1941 D	Duane Lord	Clayton	41-6¾
1942 D	Jack Fitzpatrick	Mt Pleasant Sacred Heart	45-2½
1943	No Meet – World War II		
1944 D	Henry Rolike	Boys Vocational	41-3
1945 D	Arlon Dennison	Michigan School for Deaf	40-½
1946 D	Gordon Allison	Baldwin	41-7¾
1947 D	John Wittboldt	Grosse Ile	43-3¼
1948 D	Roland Moore	Michigan School for Deaf	43-2½
1949 D	Sig Mollenkott	Galien	43-4
1950 D	Norman Armstrong	Albion Starr Commonwealth	42-2¼
1951 D	Frank Casteluccio	New Buffalo	47-0
1952 D	John Boyce	Martin	45-4¾
1953 D	Lee Parker	Weidman	43-7¾
1954 D	Lee Parker	Weidman	46-6¼
1955 D	Norman Burns	Brethren	49-3¾*
1956 D	George Smith	Copemish	45-7½
1957 D	Murray Marsh	Dimondale	46-2
1958 D	Murray Marsh	Dimondale	50-4½*
1959 D	Marvin Burns	Brethren	46-1¾
1960 D	Randy Johncox	Schoolcraft	46-4¾
1961 D	Randy Johncox	Schoolcraft	53-1½*
1962 D	David Woods	Wolverine	49-11½
1963 D	Dave Takacs	Michigan School for Deaf	45-10½
1964 D	Dave Takacs	Michigan School for Deaf	49-2½
1965 D	Calvin Young	Freesoil	52-1
1966 D	Mario Evans	Covert	52-1
1967 D	Jim Byrne	Genesee	52-1¼
1968 D	Jim Byrne	Genesee	50-9½
1969 D	Ken Papes	Freesoil	51-10
1970 D	Fred Troop	Harbor Springs	49-10½
1971 D	Duane Reemer	Camden-Frontier	49 1½
1972 D	Tim Ruff	Bridgman	48-1
1973 D	Tim Ruff	Bridgman	52-11½
1974 D	Leonard Lilliard	Ann Arbor St Thomas	53-8*
1975 D	Richard Shaffer	Camden-Frontier	50-5¼
1976 D	Steve McDaniel	Potterville	55-11½*
1977 D	Bob Saylor	Potterville	53-6½
1978 D	Trent Grossman	Centreville	52-10
1979 D	Cole Dickson	Akron-Fairgrove	49-9¾
1980 D	John Robinson	Saginaw MI Lutheran Seminary	48-5¼
1981 D	John Chandler	Mesick	54-2
1982 D	John Chandler	Mesick	53-7
1983 D	Craig Peterson	Onekema	53-9½
1984 D	Steve Buhr	Cheboygan Catholic	58-6¾*
1985 D	Steve Buhr	Cheboygan Catholic	52-7
1986 D	Jeff Naert	Akron-Fairgrove	54-0
1987 D	Leonard Patrick	Litchfield	52-10½
1988 D	Matt Beach	Pittsford	50-6¼
1989 D	Matt Beach	Pittsford	47-6
1990 D	Raymond Moore	Covert	48-7¾
1991 D	Raymond Moore	Covert	52-3
1992 D	Greg Spranger	Traverse City St. Francis	49-2
1993 D	David Horn	Litchfield	51-6¾
1994 D	Jeremy Sanford	Pittsford	50-0
1995 D	Jeff Buckmaster	North Muskegon	49-9¼
1996 D	Bruce Hungerford	Fowler	52-½

1997 D	Jason Stalter	Mason County Eastern	52-½
1998 D	John Hansen	Frankfort	57-6¾
1999 D	Cobey Buckner	Camden-Frontier	55-¾
2000 D4	Jay Davidson	Frankfort	56-0*
2001 D4	Nate Meckes	Lutheran Westland	54-9
2002 D4	Dilyn Gerber	Camden-Frontier	52-2¼
2003 D4	Dilyn Gerber	Camden-Frontier	53-2
2004 D4	Evan bernard	Detroit Loyola	53-5¾
2005 D4	Derron McLauy	Adrian Madison	56-11½*
2006 D4	Brent McCarrick	Morrice	52-9½
2007 D4	George Flanner	Ottawa Lake Whiteford	58-5¼*

2008 D4	Chris Mullen	New Buffalo	51-2¼
2009 D4	Eric Labuhn	Ubly	50-10
2010 D4	Roger Stewart	White Pigeon	53-7½
2011 D4	Roger Stewart	White Pigeon	56-2¼
2012 D4	Tomas Smith	Au Gres-Sims	51-5¼
2013 D4	Bobby Drew	Saugatuck	52-7½
2014 D4	Tyler Crenshaw	Brown City	51-8
2015 D4	Cole Vanooster	Kalamazoo Christian	54-6
2016 D4	Jacob Lechner	Harbor Springs	53-4¼
2017 D4	Paxton Titus	Livington Christian	55-9½
2018 D4	Daniel Smith	Carson City-Crystal	52-9

SP – UP Class AB/Division 1 Champions

1941 UPB	Erwin Johnson	Ironwood	44-9*
1942 UPB	Erwin Johnson	Ironwood	46-¾*
1943	No Meet – World War II		
1944 UPB	B. Mottes	Iron Mountain	42-1¼
1945 UPB	Rob Mitchell	Negaunee	45-9½
1946 UPB	Rob Mitchell	Negaunee	50-3*
1947 UPB	Johnson	Newberry	42-10
1948 UPB	Walter Stano	Ironwood	42-4¾
1949 UPB	Ben Pederson	Marquette	45-0
1950 UPB	Harry Culver	Marquette	44-8½
1951 UPB	Thomas Englehard	Ishpeming	44-4½
1952 UPB	Harman Misuraco	Ironwood	43-10
1953 UPB	Pat Cvengros	Ironwood	45-11
1954 UPB	Carl Nolingberg	Iron River	44-9
1955 UPB	Ed Dennis	Kingsford	46-8½
1956 UPB	Barry Armstrong	Sault Ste. Marie	48-4
1957 UPB	Barry Armstrong	Sault Ste. Marie	48-11
1958 UPB	David Manders	Kingsford	52-7¾*
1959 UPB	Roger Johnson	Marquette	45-5½
1960 UPB	Roger Johnson	Marquette	48-10¾
1961 UPB	Jim Trottier	Escanaba Holy Name	49-3¾
1962 UPAB	Joe Hase	Munising	47-5½
1963 UPAB	Mike Dissinger	Marquette	48-1½
1964 UPAB	Bill Sarnowski	Escanaba	50-7½
1965 UPAB	Bill Sarnowski	Escanaba	52-6
1966 UPAB	James Hansen	Escanaba	53-8*
1967 UPAB	Roy DeWitt	Gladstone	48-6½
1968 UPAB	Dave Dragoo	Menominee	50-5¼
1969 UPAB	John Miklesh	Ironwood	49-9
1970 UPAB	Dan Young	Escanaba Holy Name	52-8
1971 UPAB	Gary Brawley	Escanaba	56-5*
1972 UPAB	Ron Bigardi	West Iron Co.	51-7
1973 UPAB	Wayne Schwalbach	Escanaba	52-6½
1974 UPAB	Wayne Schwalbach	Escanaba	58-7*
1975 UPAB	Steven Engman	Marquette	50-7¾
1976 UPAB	John Hart	Calumet	52-2
1977 UPAB	Jack Hart	Calumet	53-4¾
1978 UPAB	Gary Dravecky	Ironwood	53-0
1979 UPAB	Bill Theisen	Menominee	49-11

1980 UPAB	Paul Christopherson	Menominee	48-4
1981 UPAB	Jed Comyne	Menominee	49-6
1982 UPAB	Jed Comyne	Menominee	55-9¼
1983 UPAB	Craig Wolf	Marquette	49-9
1984 UPAB	Steve Gonyou	Marquette	46-7¾
1985 UPAB	Paul Sundquist	Escanaba	46-11¾
1986 UPAB	Russell Bruce	Gwinn	48-4
1987 UPAB	Tim Evans	Menominee	49-11½
1988 UPAB	Bruce Brandon	Gwinn	46-11
1989 UPAB	Mike Martilla	Ironwood	49-4¼
1990 UPAB	Mike Martilla	Ironwood	53-½
1991 UPAB	Brian Honkala	Ishpeming Westwood	49-4¾
1992 UPAB	Charlie Bush	Escanaba	50-4
1993 UPAB	Gary Glowacki	Sault Ste. Marie	51-9½
1994 UPAB	David Paananen	Ishpeming Westwood	56-2½
1995 UPAB	David Paananen	Ishpeming Westwood	55-0
1996 UPAB	David Paananen	Ishpeming Westwood	54-4¼
1997 UPAB	Bob Kaikkonen	Escanaba	51-1
1998 UPAB	Josh Mileski	Gladstone	51-5
1999 UPAB	Dan Jones	Gladstone	51-7
2000 UPAB	Travis Beuchamp	Gladstone	50-6
2001 UPD1	Brad Sutter	Gladstone	50-8*
2002 UPD1	Brad Sutter	Gladstone	51-1*
2003 UPD1	Curtis Bizeau	Escanaba	47-8
2004 UPD1	Adam Sutter	Gladstone	46-11¾
2005 UPD1	Josh Frantii	Calumet	48-¼
2006 UPD1	Saun Voris	Sault Ste. Marie	47-6¾
2007 UPD1	Kent King	Gladstone	47-3½
2008 UPD1	Kent King	Gladstone	50-2
2009 UPD1	Kent King	Gladstone	52-½*
2010 UPD1	Kent King	Gladstone	52-½*
2011 UPD1	Tony Bonacci	Sault Ste. Marie	50-3¼
2012 UPD1	Jared Vuksan	Gladstone	51-3¾
2013 UPD1	Jared Vuksan	Gladstone	55-11¼*
2014 UPD1	Cody Malanowski	Gladstone	49-1½
2015 UPD1	Payton Muljo	Maequette	43-6½
2016 UPD1	Payton Muljo	Maequette	44-½
2017 UPD1	Michael Pizziola	Negaunee	43-9
2018 UPD1	Cooper Twardzik	Calumet	42-2½

SP – UP Class C/Division 2 Champions

1940 UPC	Warren Millard	Ontonagon	41-6*
1941 UPC	Robert Lowell	Lake Linden	41-2
1942 UPC	John Ludlow	Newberry	43-2*
1943	No Meet – World War II		
1944 UPC	D. Peoples	Gladstone	40-3
1945 UPC	Charles Atkocunis	Stephenson	40-11½
1946 UPC	Bruce Emblad	L'Anse	44-7*
1947 UPC	Donald Uitto	Houghton	42-3¾
1948 UPC	Lloyd Seavoy	L'Anse	43-7
1949 UPC	Jim Cox	Munising	43-8
1950 UPC	David Honz	Bessemer	48-0*
1951 UPC	Erland Maki	Crystal Falls	45-7¾
1952 UPC	Roy Pingel	Bessemer	44-7½
1953 UPC	Ray Sironen	Ewen	42-2
1954 UPC	Ray Sironen	Ewen	46-7
1955 UPC	Eugene Velesano	Wakefield	45-3
1956 UPC	Tom Prout	Houghton	41-5
1957 UPC	Jim Corgiat	Bessemer	43-1½
1958 UPC	Jim Corgiat	Bessemer	46-7½
1959 UPC	Richard Koski	Wakefield	42-8¾
1960 UPC	Dave Marshall	St. Ignace	43-6
1961 UPC	Steve Yatchak	Wakefield	44-8¼
1962 UPC	Steve Yatchak	Wakefield	49-8½*
1963 UPC	Larry Makimaa	Ontonagon	51-3¼*
1964 UPC	Larry Makimaa	Ontonagon	51-6½*
1965 UPC	Jerry Lutri	Stephenson	48-7
1966 UPC	Don Bussiere	Ontonagon	47-11¼
1967 UPC	Don Bussiere	Ontonagon	49-0

1968 UPC	Mike Smolcich	Wakefield	50-5¾
1969 UPC	Ken Kioski	Ontonagon	49-7½
1970 UPC	Don Michaelson	L'Anse	46-10
1971 UPC	Ron Lutri	Stephenson	49-4
1972 UPC	Mike Bal	Norway	46-6½
1973 UPC	Kurt Hogue	Newberry	49-2¾
1974 UPC	Jim Antilla	Ontonagon	47-9½
1975 UPC	Keith Woick	Houghton	48-11¾
1976 UPC	Pete Cheverette	Negaunee	46-6
1977 UPC	Steve Tollefson	L'Anse	47-1
1978 UPC	Jim Schram	Iron River West Iron County	48-4¾
1979 UPC	Gary Dravecky	Ironwood	54-6½*
1980 UPC	Jeff Lewis	Ontonagon	47-6¼
1981 UPC	Pete Kafczynski	Ironwood	49-2½
1982 UPC	Pete Kafczynski	Ironwood	50-4½
1983 UPC	Mark Rostagno	Iron RIver West Iron County	47-11½
1984 UPC	Chuck Klingbeil	Houghton	50-11¾
1985 UPC	Mike Rostagno	Iron River West Iron County	54-2
1986 UPC	Gregory Montgomery	Negaunee	52-2
1987 UPC	Gregory Montgomery	Negaunee	51-¾
1988 UPC	Scott Burton	Ishpeming Westwood	52-10½
1989 UPC	Shawn Hood	Iron Mountain	48-8
1990 UPC	Brian Honkala	Iron River West Iron County	49-8¾
1991 UPC	Ed Livermore	Negaunee	45-5¾
1992 UPC	Shawn McMullin	Ironwood	45-4
1993 UPC	Dan Hudson	Rudyard	46-11½
1994 UPC	Dan Hudson	Rudyard	52-10
1995 UPC	Tom Lawlor	Rudyard	48-10

1996 UPC	Tom Lawlor	Rudyard	49-4½
1997 UPC	Anders Hill	Hancock	51-3½
1998 UPC	Dan Mattson	Calumet	53-6
1999 UPC	Shawn Anderson	Manistique	52-0
2000 UPC	Shawn Anderson	Manistique	54-2½
2001 UPD2	Jake Holcomb	Newberry	50-11*
2002 UPD2	Jim Bourdlais	Newberry	51-8¼*
2003 UPD2	Jeff Weissgerber	Stephenson	50-2¾
2004 UPD2	Cory Veitengruger	Manistique	46-11
2005 UPD2	Matt Payment	Newberry	49-3¾
2006 UPD2	Matt Payment	Newberry	51-11¾*
2007 UPD2	Cody Kilgore	Newberry	45-6

2008 UPD2	Nate Isola	Ishpeming Westwood	45-0
2009 UPD2	Garret Maki	Hancock	42-8½
2010 UPD2	Gerrit Mortensen	St. Ignace	49-1
2011 UPD2	Garrett Maki	Hancock	49-¼
2012 UPD2	Joey Ostman	St. Ignace	45-1½
2013 UPD2	Chasz Jonet	West Iron Co.	43-10¼
2014 UPD2	Gary Hawthorne	Hancock	51-½
2015 UPD2	Brandon Kempainen	L'Anse	42-7½
2016 UPD2	Bryant Schram	West Iron Co.	48-1¼
2017 UPD2	John Paramski	Newberry	48-7
2018 UPD2	Bryant Schram	West Iron County	48-1½

SP – UP Class D/Division 3 Champions

1940 UPD	Tony Del Santo	Channing	37-7*
1941 UPD	George LaBrasseur	Nahma	41-9*
1942 UPD	William Roberts	Grand Marais	45-1*
1943	No Meet – World War II		
1944 UPD	E. Johnson	Greenland	37-1¾
1945 UPD	M. Jalkanen	Chassell	41-7¼
1946 UPD	Lofback	Mass	40-8½
1947 UPD	Don Shannon	Powers	38-9½
1948 UPD	Glen Arnold	Powers	38-5¾
1949 UPD	Gerald Froberg	Gwinn	39-6
1950 UPD	Harold Kallio	Eben	40-10¾
1951 UPD	William Kallio	Eben	41-3
1952 UPD	Alden Garceau	Negaunee St. Paul	41-2
1953 UPD	Dick Shephard	Bark River	43-2
1954 UPD	Burt Peterson	Cooks	39-11¾
1955 UPD	Louis Pitko	DeTour	40-1
1956 UPD	Ken Kauthen	Cooks	43-9
1957 UPD	Don Mattson	Chassell	44-6
1958 UPD	Raymond Koski	Chatham-Eben	46-2¾*
1959 UPD	Ted Stevenson	Pickford	42-7
1960 UPD	Ted Stevenson	Pickford	45-7¼
1961 UPD	Dwayne Johnson	Rapid River	45-1
1962 UPD	Dwayne Johnson	Rapid River	46-6*
1963 UPD	Tom McKee	Pickford	45-11½
1964 UPD	Bill Carlson	Eben	44-2½
1965 UPD	Tom Tellefson	DeTour	48-8¾*
1966 UPD	Craig Lindeman	Channing	45-11¼
1967 UPD	Michael Rankinen	Perkins	47-10¾
1968 UPD	Michael Rankinen	Republic-Michigamme	50-4¼*
1969 UPD	Vic Cox	National Mine	44-7
1970 UPD	Tom Nye	Cedarville	46-2
1971 UPD	Gary King	Engadine	46-5
1972 UPD	Gary King	Engadine	45-10½
1973 UPD	Gary Cottle	Pickford	45-0
1974 UPD	Mike Hytinen	National Mine	47-3
1975 UPD	John Bley	White Pine	48-10½
1976 UPD	George Staisil	Painesdale-Jeffers	48-3
1977 UPD	Mickey Lauscher	Perkins	48-1
1978 UPD	Dan Lato	Crystal Falls Forest Park	45-3
1979 UPD	Melvin Dean	DeTour	47-8

1980 UPD	Mickey Lane	Wakefield	46-2¼
1981 UPD	Mickey Lane	Wakefield	52-8½*
1982 UPD	Mickey Lane	Wakefield	52-2½
1983 UPD	Tim LaJoie	Pickford	52-2
1984 UPD	Don Willa	Powers-North Central	47-9¾
1985 UPD	Tom Ball	Pickford	46-7½
1986 UPD	Jeff Davis	Rudyard	50-3
1987 UPD	Sean Norton	Lake Linden-Hubbell	46-3¼
1988 UPD	Jim Suggitt	Rudyard	48-11
1989 UPD	Randy Fountain	Pickford	50-2
1990 UPD	William Porter	Eben Junction Superior Central	46-10½
1991 UPD	Steve Lane	Wakefield	49-11
1992 UPD	Ryan Fountain	Pickford	47-10
1993 UPD	Ryan Fountain	Pickford	55-1*
1994 UPD	Bill Tyler	Rapid River	45-10½
1995 UPD	Jared Maki	Ontonagon	47-6
1996 UPD	Jarod Maki	Ontonagon	48-0
1997 UPD	Aaron Fezzey	Lake Linden-Hubbell	45-9
1998 UPD	Craig Paquin	Powers-North Central	45-8
1999 UPD	Jeff Richard	Felch North DIckinson	48-8½
2000 UPD	Jon Laessig	Wakefield	46-11
2001 UPD3	Eric Wilbee	Rapid River	47-3¾*
2002 UPD3	Jack Bricco	Rapid River	51-1*
2003 UPD3	Steve Bowen	Cooks-Big Bay de Noc	47-10½
2004 UPD3	Justin Gustafson	Rapid River	44-5
2005 UPD3	Josh Winkler	Brimley	46-2½
2006 UPD3	Jason Miller	Ontonagon	46-10½
2007 UPD3	Jason Miller	Ontonagon	52-7¼*
2008 UPD3	John Troyer	Engadine	47-1
2009 UPD3	Michael Cantin	Pickford	45-2
2010 UPD3	Garrett Maki	Hancock	47-5
2011 UPD3	Jacob Pikka	Wakefield	49-6
2012 UPD3	Jacob Pikka	Wakefield	47-5
2013 UPD3	Brett Branstrom	Rock Mid Peninsula	47-11½
2014 UPD3	Jacob Pearson	Rapid River	46-10
2015 UPD3	Ben Stasewich	Munising	44-2½
2016 UPD3	Brenden Gatien	Powers-North Central	46-11½
2017 UPD3	Jacob Witt	Ewen-Trout Creek	45-5½
2018 UPD3	Tyler Busch	Bessemer	46-6

BOYS DISCUS

Records

D1	210-1	Cullen Prena	Walled Lake Central	2013
D2	195-6	Joe Hover	Stevensville-Lakeshore	2003
D3	187-1	Evan Hartman	Niles Brandywine	2013
D4	190-0	Jacob Patrick	Litchfield	2012
UPD1	160-5	Terry Martin	Manistique	2009
UPD2	155-8	Terry Martin	Manistique	2008
UPD3	154-8	Brett Branstrom	Rock Mid Peninsula	2012

Records by Class (pre-2000 for LP, pre-2001 for UP)

A	196-5	Brett Organek	Grandville	1992
B	176-0	Steve Manz	West Branch Ogemaw Heights	1999
C	179-3	Aron Gowell	Shelby	1988
D	173-10	John Chandler	Mesick	1982
UPAB	169-4	David Paananen	Ishpeming Westwood	1995
UPC	164-8	Shawn Anderson	Manistique	1999
UPD	163-11	Ryan Fountain	Pickford	1993

DT – Class A/Division 1 Champions

(2kg / 4.41lb—college/international weight)

Year	Name	School	Mark
1902 all	John Garrels	Detroit Central	101-10*
1903 all	Thomas Rosenberger	Ann Arbor	98-11
1904 all	Clayton Schenk	Chelsea	93-9
1905 all	Kenneth Arthur	Detroit University School	100-10
1906 all	Ralph Strellinger	Orchard Lake	109-10*
1907 all	Joe Horner (3)	Grand Rapids Central	109-0
1908 all	Will Runner (2)	Shelby	101-0
1909 all	Clem Quinn	Saginaw	100-0
1910 all	Arthur Kohler	Lansing Central	119-8*
1911 all	Lawrence Hendricks	Muskegon	105-6
1912 all	J. D. Cross	Wayne	112-2
1913 all	Theodore Wedemeyer	Chelsea	104-11
1914 all	Pat Smith	Bay City Eastern	109-0
1915 all	George Kimball	Muskegon	114-1
1916 all	Lawrence Bishop	Lansing Central	nm
1917 all	Lester Beltz	Lansing Central	104-1
1918	No Meet – World War I		
1919 all	Herman DeRuiter	Grand Rapids South	102-4
1920 all	Glenn Hookey Brooks	Chelsea	101 3/5y
1921 A	John Mulder	Muskegon	112-0
1922 A	Dick Doyle	Kalamazoo Central	113-10
1923 A	James Oade	Lansing Central	114-6
1924 A	Bennie Oosterbaan	Muskegon	122-0*
1925 A	T. Rex Wilson	Ann Arbor	126-11*
1926 A	Merrill Gowman	Detroit Eastern	110-10
1927 A	Henry Harper	Pontiac	111-11
1928 A	Harold Tanis	Holland	110-4
1929 A	George Huber	Detroit Northwestern	127-0*
1930 A	Jack Fun	Detroit Northwestern	116-10
1931 A	Bob Sprau	Muskegon	114-0

(1.62kg / 3.58lb—high school weight)

Year	Name	School	Mark
1976 A	Skip Ballish	Royal Oak Dondero	157-9*
1977 A	Andy Gheen	Alpena	161-8*
1978 A	Pat Kelly	Grand Rapids Union	166-10*
1979 A	Mike Hammond	Livonia Bentley	159-1
1980 A	James Browne	Birmingham Brother Rice	176-1*
1981 A	Bob Pittaway	Salem	173-9

Year	Name	School	Mark
1982 A	Johnny Mitchell	Muskegon	179-10*
1983 A	Johnny Mitchell	Muskegon	193-3*
1984 A	Mike Sargeant	Flint Powers	174-11
1985 A	Matt Larcinese	Belleville	163-10
1986 A	Kyle Wray	Kalamazoo Loy Norrix	172-5
1987 A	Kyle Wray	Kalamazoo Loy Norrix	184-2
1988 A	Ron Williams	Clinton Twp Chippewa Valley	183-4
1989 A	Zaim Cunmulaj	North Farmington	163-11
1990 A	Thomas Jenkins	Taylor Truman	158-10
1991 A	Brett Organek	Grandville	185-0
1992 A	Brett Organek	Grandville	196-5*
1993 A	Andy Filisko	Ann Arbor Huron	167-11
1994 A	Michael Barker	Clio	163-1
1995 A	Anthony Luebbert	Lake Orion	151-7
1996 A	Shawn Eagle	Port Huron Northern	170-8
1997 A	Chad Peters	Mt Pleasant	177-9
1998 A	Joe Keller	Lansing Eastern	178-3
1999 A	Nick Brzenzinski	Detroit Catholic Central	167-10
2000 D1	Jack Gitler	Berkley	178-5*
2001 D1	Joey Sarantos	Portage Northern	197-11*
2002 D1	Paul Sarantos	Portage Northern	180-7
2003 D1	Okezie Aguwa	Okemos	173-11
2004 D1	Joe Prieur	Flint Carman-Ainsworth	161-4
2005 D1	Vincent Helmuth	Saline	184-4
2006 D1	Vincent Helmuth	Saline	180-1
2007 D1	Kevin Mays	Flint Carman-Ainsworth	170-7
2008 D1	Andrew Evans	Portage Northern	180-8
2009 D1	Andrew Evans	Portage Northern	182-10
2010 D1	Justin Gaumer	Holly	170-5
2011 D1	Connor Kostrzewa	Traverse City West	160-1
2012 D1	Matt Costello	Bay City Western	178-6
2013 D1	Cullen Prena	Walled Lake Central	210-11*
2014 D1	Kevin Weiler	Swartz Creek	176-5
2015 D1	Connor Bandel	Oxford	175-2
2016 D1	Connor Bandel	Oxford	198-11
2017 D1	Randy Prince	Port Huron Northern	173-0
2018 D1	Aidan Martini	Grand Blanc	167-2

DT – Class B/Division 2 Champions

(2kg / 4.41lb—college/international weight)

Year	Name	School	Mark
1921 B	Earl Kelly	Cadillac	96-0*
1922 B	Glenn Eastham	Caro	101-0*
1923 B	Harland Ranson	Coldwater	102-6*
1924 B	Hazen Herkimer	Monroe	119-6*
1925 B	Albert McCabe	Petoskey	108-4
1926 B	Henry Doc Dirsksey	Grand Haven	108-9
1927 B	Ken Barnhill	Charlotte	119-10*
1928 B	Carl Thiel	Dearborn	112-1
1929 B	Carl Thiel	Dearborn	121-1*
1930 B	Bernard McNutt	Allegan	125-3*
1931 B	Otto Hecksel	Grand Haven	117-10

(1.62kg / 3.58lb—high school weight)

Year	Name	School	Mark
1976 B	Sam Angell	Holland West Ottawa	161-9*
1977 B	John Hankerb	Jackson Lumen Christi	151-11
1978 B	Bill Beyersdorf	Hemlock	154-2
1979 B	David Prieskorn	Ypsilanti Lincoln	159-8
1980 B	Ron Finch	Mt Pleasant	167-3*
1981 B	Sheldon Singleton	Flint Beecher	160-7
1982 B	Tim Fellows	Flint Ainsworth	175-0*
1983 B	Tim Fellows	Flint Ainsworth	170-0
1984 B	Paul Boughton	Comstock	165-8
1985 B	Jim Bowen	Brooklyn	160-4
1986 B	Paul Cochran	Midland Bullock Creek	174-8
1987 B	Dan Bright	Sturgis	158-9
1988 B	John Thawnghmung	Battle Creek Lakeview	154-6
1989 B	Jim Vanderbeek	Hudsonville	167-5
1990 B	Tom Johnston	Marysville	167-6

Year	Name	School	Mark
1991 B	Greg Duggins	Hudsonville	163-6
1992 B	Scott Gavin	Otisville LakeVille	154-8
1993 B	Rollie Ferris	Delton Kellogg	168-7
1994 B	David Beeman	Chelsea	175-3*
1995 B	Pete Owen	Bloomfield Hills Andover	160-5
1996 B	Ben Howell	West Branch Ogemaw Hts	168-3
1997 B	Jake Frysinger	Grosse Ile	162-8
1998 B	Frank Garofalo	Mt Morris	169-6
1999 B	Steve Manz	West Branch Ogemaw Heights	176-0*
2000 D2	Mike Preston	Auburn Hills Avondale	169-5*
2001 D2	Joe Hover	Stevensville-Lakeshore	180-7*
2002 D2	Joe Hover	Stevensville-Lakeshore	180-6
2003 D2	Joe Hover	Stevensville-Lakeshore	195-6*
2004 D2	Andrew Hartline	Stevensville-Lakeshore	168-4
2005 D2	Adam Mayhew	Richland Gull Lake	173-10
2006 D2	Lonnie Pugh	Grosse Ile	179-4
2007 D2	Brad Wentzel	Allegan	170-0
2008 D2	Donny Stiffler	Williamston	180-2
2009 D2	Jack Dennis	Caro	180-2
2010 D2	Derek Seivers	Byron Center	177-6
2011 D2	Derek Seivers	Byron Center	186-8
2012 D2	T. J. Beelen	Zeeland East	189-8
2013 D2	Quincy Boyd	Zeeland East	189-2
2014 D2	Logan Targgart	Coldwater	168-7
2015 D2	Justin Scavarda	Mason	172-2
2016 D2	Justin Scavarda	Mason	182-6
2017 D2	Connor Covert	Coldwater	180-1
2018 D2	Dylan Targgart	Coldwater	170-10

DT – Class C/Division 3 Champions

(2kg / 4.41lb—college/international weight)

Year	Name	School	Mark
1921 C	Frank Mote	Greenville	98-8*
1922 C	Lyle Bennett	Rockford	101-7*
1923 C	Alan McLean	Plainwell	112-9*
1924 C	Lavere Sprowl	Clinton	108-6
1925 C	Harold Gilbert	Croswell	92-5
1926 C	Wayne Grange	Morenci	99-4
1927 C	Russell Pell	Plainwell	113-9*
1928 C (tie)	Art Rhody	Kingsford	102-0
1928 C (tie)	Johnny Siwick	Kalamazoo St Augustine	102-0
1929 C	Elmer Layer	Lowell	109-1
1930 C	Elmer Layer	Lowell	120-2*
1931 C	Frank McCory	Ontonagon	121-7*

(1.62kg / 3.58lb—high school weight)

Year	Name	School	Mark
1976 C	Brian Lamontagne	New Haven	140-4*
1977 C	Charlie Grigg	Rogers City	159-5*
1978 C	Roger Plont	Ravenna	158-11
1979 C	Bruce Pfeifle	Perry	150-3
1980 C	Mike Krauss	Clinton	169-11*
1981 C	Mike Krauss	Clinton	159-3
1982 C	Mike Krauss	Clinton	176-11*
1983 C	Darin Geyerbiehl	Bad Axe	161-2
1984 C	Dan Flores	Flint Hamady	152-6
1985 C	Darren Fether	Napoleon	175-11
1986 C	Aron Gowell	Shelby	171-1
1987 C	Aron Gowell	Shelby	165-11

1988 C	Aron Gowell	Shelby	179-3*
1989 C	Tom McGee	Elkton-Pigeon-Bayport	143-11
1990 C	Todd Winter	Unionville-Sebewaing	157-4
1991 C	Chris McEwan	Almont	152-0
1992 C	Brian Borgman	WIlliamston	148-8
1993 C	Jeff Schuberg	Morley-Stanwood	154-10
1994 C	Glenn Schneider	Pewamo-Westphalia	155-9
1995 C	Jerry Stempien	Quincy	172-3
1996 C	Mike Burde	Newaygo	166-0
1997 C	Nick Squires	Clare	168-4
1998 C	Matt Groh	Decatur	167-7
1999 C	Tom Maczik	Reese	172-4
2000 D3	Tom Maczik	Reese	174-4*
2001 D3	Ian Morrison	Riverview Gabriel RIchard	163-8
2002 D3	Dan Reppuhn	Birch Run	159-7
2003 D3	Peter Maxwell	Beaverton	161-2
2004 D3	Levon Mock	Bangor	162-2
2005 D3	Truman Smth	Morley-Stanwood	153-6
2006 D3	Spence Krauss	Clinton	155-4
2007 D3	Spencer Krauss	Clinton	166-5
2008 D3	Zack Hill	Allendale	175-7*
2009 D3	Zack Hill	Allendale	181-0*
2010 D3	David Scouten	Brooklyn Columbia Central	167-9
2011 D3	David Scouten	Brooklyn Columbia Central	181-0*
2012 D3	Evan Hartman	Niles Brandywine	167-2
2013 D3	Evan Hartman	Niles Brandywine	187-1*
2014 D3	Michael Schauer	Laingsburg	172-8
2015 D3	Joshua Coston	Carson City-Crystal	161-3
2016 D3	Carl Meyers	Grand Rapids West Catholic	172-1
2017 D3	Dan Stone	Frankenmuth	171-0
2018 D3	Noah Nivison	Clare	156-7

DT – Class D/Division 4 Champions

(2kg / 4.41lb—college/international weight)

1927 D	Lee Hawkins	Woodland	111-1*
1928 D	Frank Coleman	Okemos	94-5
1929 D	Ken Little	Wyoming Godwin Heights	104-4
1930 D	Bernard Blair	Middleton	110-6
1931 D	Donald Reed	Centreville	98-2

(1.62kg / 3.58lb—high school weight)

1976 D	Jim Oleniczak	Onekema	133-4*
1977 D	Cedric Coles	Detroit DePorres	153-1*
1978 D	Todd Triplett	Detroit DePorres	145-1
1979 D	Mark Comella	Gaylord St. Mary	142-1
1980 D	John Chandler	Mesick	150-11
1981 D	John Chandler	Mesick	158-1*
1982 D	John Chandler	Mesick	173-10*
1983 D	Joe Bertram	Fowler	148-0
1984 D	Joe Rachor	Kingsley	158-8
1985 D	Joe Bertram	Fowler	157-7
1986 D	Joe Mueller	Litchfield	157-2
1987 D	Joe Mueller	Litchfield	168-2
1988 D	Mike Shaver	North Muskegon	153-10
1989 D	Matt Beach	Pittsford	145-5
1990 D	Kevin Ford	Detroit Lutheran West	143-2
1991 D	Clay Morehead	Inland Lakes	142-5
1992 D	Bill Campbell	Marion	146-0
1993 D	Greg Spranger	Traverse City St Francis	154-6
1994 D	David Fry	Akron-Fairgrove	141-10
1995 D	Chris Heckel	Litchfield	138-2
1996 D	Neil Andries	Adrian Madison	144-2
1997 D	Justin Nye	Litchfield	156-8
1998 D	Kyle Brink	Akron-Fairgrove	148-4
1999 D	Kyle Brink	Akron-Fairgrove	151-0
2000 D4	Kyle Brink	Akron-Fairgrove	160-7*
2001 D4	David Johnson	Covert	165-0*
2002 D4	Greg Oliver	Webberville	154-1
2003 D4	Chas Eldridge	Fulton-Middleton	160-1
2004 D4	Andrew Kemp	Maple City Glen Lake	170-1*
2005 D4	Derron McLaury	Adrian Madison	158-7
2006 D4	Darin Bazuin	McBain	157-7
2007 D4	George Flanner	Ottawa Lake Whiteford	160-6
2008 D4	Jack Ramon	Beal City	158-4
2009 D4	Nathan DeKam	McBain Northern Mich Christian	163-2
2010 D4	Ben Denomme	Manton	155-1
2011 D4	David Patrick	Litchfield	164-9
2012 D4	Jacob Patrick	Litchfield	190-0*
2013 D4	Jacob Patrick	Litchfield	187-2
2014 D4	Tucker Scharf	Unionville-Sebewaing	148-6
2015 D4	Kyle Smith	Breckenridge	149-0
2016 D4	Paxton Titus	Livingston Christian	162-11
2017 D4	Paxton Titus	Livingston Christian	169-10
2018 D4	Cody Finney	Coleman	151-1

DT – UP Class AB/Division 1 Champions

(1.62kg / 3.58lb—high school weight)

1976 UPAB	Joe Little	Marquette	140-1*
1977 UPAB	Mike Hirm	Escanaba	158-2*
1978 UPAB	Gary Dravecky	Ironwood	142-5
1979 UPAB	Steve Koller	Sault Ste Marie	151-1
1980 UPAB	Dennis Svoboda	Menominee	129-4
1981 UPAB	Greg Eastman	Escanaba	142-7
1982 UPAB	Rick Frazer	Escanaba	135-5
1983 UPAB	Tim Mattson	Marquette	130-7
1984 UPAB	Tim Mattson	Marquette	141-4
1985 UPAB	Doug Liesenring	Gladstone	136-6
1986 UPAB	Todd Seppi	Kingsford	149-4
1987 UPAB	Mark Derusha	Escanaba	140-8
1988 UPAB	Brandon Bruce	Gwinn	143-0
1989 UPAB	Brandon Bruce	Gwinn	155-10
1990 UPAB	Brandon Bruce	Gwinn	145-11
1991 UPAB	Eric Sunilla	Menominee	151-11
1992 UPAB	Charlie Bush	Escanaba	144-2
1993 UPAB	David Dellangelo	Negaunee	150-2
1994 UPAB	Rob Roell	Kingsford	149-7
1995 UPAB	David Paananen	Ishpeming Westwood	169-4*
1996 UPAB	David Paananen	Ishpeming Westwood	147-9
1997 UPAB	Jeff Sarnowski	Sault Ste. Marie	143-7
1998 UPAB	Josh Mileski	Gladstone	135-5
1999 UPAB	Jerald Sawyer	Sault Ste. Marie	137-3
2000 UPAB	Kurt Wilson	Gladstone	146-7
2001 UPD1	Jereld Sawyer	Sault Ste. Marie	158-0*
2002 UPD1	Jereld Sawyer	Sault Ste. Marie	156-2
2003 UPD1	Pete Moyryla	Calumet	131-7
2004 UPD1	Josh Frantti	Calumet	136-3
2005 UPD1	Jacaob Britton	Gladstone	147-11
2006 UPD1	Brada Hooper	Negaunee	132-4
2007 UPD1	Cody Woods	Menominee	130-8
2008 UPD1	Mike Goetz	Sault Ste. Marie	139-9
2009 UPD1	Terry Martin	Manistique	160-5*
2010 UPD1	Kent King	Gladstone	128-5
2011 UPD1	Ian Wienke	Kingsford	138-9
2012 UPD1	Hilding Beaudoin	Kingsford	143-1
2013 UPD1	Jared Vuksan	Gladstone	153-2
2014 UPD1	Jonah Carlson	Kingsford	140-11
2015 UPD1	Brad Ohtonen	Houghton	129-1
2016 UPD1	Brad Ohtonen	Houghton	120-2
2017 UPD1	Jesse Helminen	Calumet	132-0
2018 UPD1	Cooper Twardzik	Calumet	135-7

DT – UP Class C/Division 2 Champions

(1.62kg / 3.58lb—high school weight)

1976 UPC	Pete LaFreniere	Negaunee	140-2*
1977 UPC	Greg Peake	Rudyard	139-11
1978 UPC	Dan Wyers	St. Ignace	145-9*
1979 UPC	Gary Dravecky	Ironwood	151-10*
1980 UPC	Frank Agin	Houghton	134-9
1981 UPC	Nick Johnson	Iron Mountain	138-11
1982 UPC	Nick Johnson	Iron Mountain	145-6
1983 UPC	Tom LeVeque	Munising	144-11
1984 UPC	Tom LeVeque	Munising	148-3
1985 UPC	Ron Stimac	Houghton	141-0
1986 UPC	Jeff Bender	Newberry	149-2
1987 UPC	Jeff Bender	Newberry	150-6
1988 UPC	Terry Alderson	Ishpeming Westwood	149-1
1989 UPC	Shawn Hood	Iron Mountain	151-0
1990 UPC	Chris Salani	Hancock	136-5
1991 UPC	Brandon Ducsay	Newberry	136-9
1992 UPC	Rich Simpson	Houghton	143-10
1993 UPC	Sean McLafferty	St. Ignace	138-2
1994 UPC	Dan Hudson	Rudyard	150-3
1995 UPC	Bob Katona	Negaunee	156-1*
1996 UPC	Tom Lawlor	Rudyard	139-1
1997 UPC	Dan Mattson	Calumet	153-0
1998 UPC	Dan Mattson	Calumet	159-0*
1999 UPC	Shawn Anderson	Manistique	164-8*
2000 UPC	Shawn Anderson	Manistique	160-3

Year	Class	Name	School	Mark
2001 UPD2	Andrew Downey	Newberry	154-1*
2002 UPD2	Jim Bourdlais	Newberry	138-7
2003 UPD2	Jason Julien	Hancock	139-8
2004 UPD2	Matt Payment	Newberry	137-1
2005 UPD2	Matt Payment	Newberry	142-3
2006 UPD2	Matt Payment	Newberry	146-9
2007 UPD2	Terry Martin	Manistique	150-0
2008 UPD2	Terry Martin	Manistique	155-8*
2009 UPD2	Brady Burby	Rudyard	126-5

Year	Class	Name	School	Mark
2010 UPD2	Grant Simmons	St. Ignace	117-2
2011 UPD2	Garrett Maki	Hancock	127-7
2012 UPD2	Ryan Marshall	St. Ignace	126-8
2013 UPD2	Gage Hawthorne	Hancock	125-4
2014 UPD2	Gage Hawthorne	Hancock	142-3
2015 UPD2	Levi Hoskins	L'Anse	139-9
2016 UPD2	Gage Hawthorne	Hancock	140-2
2017 UPD2	John Paramski	Newberry	119-5
2018 UPD2	Josh Boulden	Norway	131-3

DT – UP Class D/Division 3 Champions

(1.62kg / 3.58lb—high school weight)

Year	Class	Name	School	Mark
1976 UPD	Mickey Lauschor	Perkins	130-6*
1977 UPD	Mickey Lauschor	Perkins	147-2*
1978 UPD	James Noble	White Pine	144-5
1979 UPD	John Casanova	Crystal Falls Forest Park	134-1
1980 UPD	Jon Stage	Carney-Nedeau	136-5
1981 UPD	Ken Rohrer	Cedarville	127-9
1982 UPD	Mark Vivio	Norway	153-9*
1983 UPD	Tim Ball	Pickford	140-3
1984 UPD	Thomas Ball	Pickford	143-4
1985 UPD	Thomas Ball	Pickford	154-11*
1986 UPD	Jeff Davis	Rudyard	149-6
1987 UPD	Randy Fountain	Pickford	141-8
1988 UPD	Randy Fountain	Pickford	147-0
1989 UPD	Randy Fountain	Pickford	157-3*
1990 UPD	Larry Hatfield	Pickford	130-9
1991 UPD	Filip Martin	Crystal Falls Forest Park	134-1
1992 UPD	Ryan Fountain	Pickford	146-0
1993 UPD	Ryan Fountain	Pickford	163-1*
1994 UPD	Scott Holmes	Crystal Falls Forest Park	137-4
1995 UPD	Kevin Lee	DeTour	142-1
1996 UPD	Chris Sherwin	Rapid River	126-3

Year	Class	Name	School	Mark
1997 UPD	Chris Sherwin	Rapid River	140-9
1998 UPD	Josh O.	Mohawk Keweenaw	125-9
1999 UPD	Kyle Rairigh	Pickford	137-8
2000 UPD	Jack Bricco	Rapid River	132-0
2001 UPD3	Eric Wilbee	Rapid River	145-8*
2002 UPD3	Richard Poma	Rapid River	148-1*
2003 UPD3	Richard Poma	Rapid River	149-1*
2004 UPD3	Juston Gustafson	Rapid River	133-11
2005 UPD3	Ryan Martin	Crystal Falls Forest Park	141-7
2006 UPD3	Mark Harrison	Crystal Falls Forest Park	134-4
2007 UPD3	Garrett Nowack	Powers-North Central	139-6
2008 UPD3	Garrett Nowack	Powers-North Central	141-0
2009 UPD3	David Koskela	Lake Linden-Hubbell	132-8
2010 UPD3	Joseph Serotzke	Lake Linden-Hubbell	124-4
2011 UPD3	Brett Branstrom	Rock Mid Peninsula	143-3
2012 UPD3	Brett Branstrom	Rock Mid Peninsula	154-8*
2013 UPD3	Brett Branstrom	Rock Mid Peninsula	153-9
2014 UPD3	Jacob Pearson	Rapid River	130-10
2015 UPD3	Brandon Kau	Stephenson	135-9
2016 UPD3	Logan Hardwick	Rapid River	132-2
2017 UPD3	Logan Hardwick	Rapid River	138-10
2018 UPD3	Logan Hardwick	Rapid River	144-11

BOYS HAMMER

Record

A	168-0	George Kimball	Muskegon		1915

Champions

(7.26kg / 16lb – college/international weight)

Year	Class	Name	School	Mark
1895 all	Vernon Eddy	Jackson	57-5½*
1896 all	Leroy King	Detroit Central	78-3*
1897 all	Oron Bury	Ann Arbor	80-0*
1898 all	Fred Lehman	Adrian	87-5*
1899 all	Walter Riebling	Detroit Central	76-4

(5.44kg / 12lb – high school weight)

Year	Class	Name	School	Mark
1900 all	Walter Tucker	Ann Arbor	112-7*
1901 all	Charles Curtis (2)	Wayne	unknown
1902 all	Charles Curtis	Wayne	128-11*
1903 all	Tho. Rosenberger (3)	Ann Arbor	unknown
1904 all	Ray Durfee	Wayne	139-2*
1905 all	Kenneth Arthur	Detroit University School	127-10

Year	Class	Name	School	Mark
1906 all	Ralph Strellinger (2)	Michigan Military Academy	135-6
1907 all	Joe Horner (3)	Grand Rapids Central	unknown
1908 all	Arthur Kohler	Lansing Central	161-0*
1909 all	Arthur Kohler	Lansing Central	165-9*
1910 all	Arthur Kohler	Lansing Central	164-10
1911 all	Frank Quail	Croswell	125-7
1912 all	J. D. Cross	Wayne	141-8
1913 all	Hugh Blacklock	Grand Rapids Central	126-9
1914 all	George Kimball	Muskegon	146-6
1915 all	George Kimball	Muskegon	168-0*
1916 all	Harry Walters	Otsego	128-3
1917 all	Karl Schmidt	Saginaw	116-0
1919 all	Leonard S. Turnbull	Detroit Eastern	118-4

BOYS JAVELIN

Records

A	176-11	Milford Haveman	Kalamazoo Central		1931
B	163-10	Paul McKinley	Cadillac		1929
C	162-11	James Wood	Northville		1924
D	170-5	Cleo Beaumont	Okemos		1930

JT – Class A Champions

Year	Class	Name	School	Mark
1922 A	Lowell Palmer	Grand Rapids Central	155-3*
1923 A	Julius Chatman	Detroit Northwestern	158-9*
1924 A	Ray Cooley	Kalamazoo Central	161-8*
1925 A	John Widman	Detroit Northwestern	156-9
1926 A	Kalman Bator	Detroit Southwestern	155-7

Year	Class	Name	School	Mark
1927 A	Edwin Turashoff	Detroit Cass Tech	157-2
1928 A	Edwin Turashoff	Detroit Cass Tech	165-1*
1929 A	Jack Hernley	Lansing Eastern	171-8*
1930 A	Wally Weber	Mt Clemens	171-10*
1931 A	Milford Haveman	Kalamazoo Central	176-11*

JT – Class B Champions

1924 B	Gerald Miller	Otsego	140-4*		1928 B	Ray March	Petoskey	149-7
1925 B	Lothaire Hall	Niles	159-5*		1929 B	Paul McKinley	Cadillac	163-10*
1926 B	Virgil Pressler	Hillsdale	151-2		1930 B	Harry Hanson	Dearborn	147-10
1927 B	Tony Zitta	St Joseph	143-0		1931 B	Paul McKinley	Cadillac	153-3

JT – Class C Champions

1924 C	James Wood	Northville	162-11*		1928 C	Johnny Siwick	Kalamazoo St Augustine	154-0
1925 C	Hubert Warner	Wayland	119-8		1929 C	Murray Sherman	Hazel Park	151-6
1926 C	Gerald Miller	Otsego	153-8		1930 C	Max Adams	Otsego	161-1
1927 C	Lyle Bouch	Corunna	150-2		1931 C	Paul Paynich	Paw Paw	160-7

JT – Class D Champions

1927 D	Irwin Kemp	Trenton	132-5*
1928 D	Clifford Jones	Wyoming Godwin Heights	151-2*
1929 D	Cleo Beaumont	Okemos	160-4*
1930 D	Cleo Beaumont	Okemos	170-5*
1931 D	Raymond Greensburg	Centreville	156-6

OUTMODED EVENTS

Some of the above-listed events that are no longer contested, such as the triple jump, the javelin and hammer, are still mainstream events in the sport and thus are given full recognition. Others that did not make that cut are a reflection of the experimentation that characterized the sport's early years, when folks were basically introducing new events to see what would stick. Obviously, bicycles didn't. We have not included the wrestling events that were included in the early state meet (and the punting and dropkicking), since those became their own high school sport(s).

40-yard Dash

| 1897 all | Chandler Tompkins | Lansing | 5.0 |
| 1898 all | Jordan | Ann Arbor | 5.0 |

40-yard Hurdles

| 1897 all | Bach | Ann Arbor | nt |
| 1898 all | Clarence Christopher | Lansing | 5 3/5 |

880-yard Walk

1895 all	Vernon Eddy	Jackson	3:55
1896 all	Ramage	Lansing	4:14
1897 all	Standish	Detroit	3:40 2/5

One Mile Walk

1898 all	Standish	Detroit	9:13 1/5
1899 all	Perry	Ann Arbor	9:18
1900 all	Morgan	Saginaw	7:48 4/5

440-yard Bicycle Race

1896 all	Phelps	Ann Arbor	1:13
1897 all	Baldwin	Detroit	35 4/5
1898 all	McCarrick	Lansing	35 3/5
1900 all	Rappely (2)	West Saginaw	nt
1901 all	Prall	Pontiac	nt

880-yard Bicycle Race

1895 all	Stoffiet	Ann Arbor	1:14
1896 all	Ulp	Ann Arbor	1:13
1897 all	Dodds	Detroit	1:25 1/5

One Mile Bicycle Race

1895 all	Goodsley	Ann Arbor	3:08
1896 all	Ulp	Ann Arbor	2:33
1897 all	Dodds	Detroit	2:22 4/5
1898 all	McCarrick	Lansing	2:58
1900 all	Olin	Grand Rapids	2:37 3/5
1901 all	Butler	Ann Arbor	nt

One Mile Tandem Bicycle Race

| 1897 all | Banfield & Butler | Ann Arbor | 2:39 2/5 |

Two Mile Bicycle Race

| 1897 all | Dayrell | Grand Rapids | 5:41 |

Standing High Jump

1895 all	Chandler Tompkins	Lansing	4-5

Standing Hitch Kick

1895 all	Wright	Ann Arbor	17¼ over head

Running Hitch Kick

1895 all	Gibson	Grand Rapids	8-5
1897 all	Gibson	Grand Rapids	

Standing Broad Jump

1895 all	Chandler Tompkins	Lansing	9-9
1896 all	Chandler Tompkins	Lansing	10-3
1897 all	Cole	Lansing	9-11

Standing Hop-Step-Jump

1895 all	Clarence Christopher	Lansing	27-7

BOYS 4 x 100 RELAY

Records

D1	41.30	Rockford	Melvin Mosely, Noah Stallworth, Josh Patterson, Nicholas Isley	2017
D2	42.30	Detroit Renaissance	Steven Worthy, Randy Moore, Xavier Parnell, Quinn Parnell	2008
D3	43.14	Sanford-Meridian	Christian Petre, Miles LeViere, Monte Petre, Andre Smith	2016
D4	43.32	Detroit DePorres	David Grimes, Taurian Washington, Cortex Smith, Anthony Bowman	2005
UPD1	43.78	Kingsford	Cole Peterson, Dyland Tengesdahl, Paul DeYeart, Wes Jacobson	2010
UPD2	45.03	Newberry	John Paramski, Jeff Rahilly, Andre James, Brandon Christensen	2017
UPD3	44.76	Lake Linden-Hubbell	Kellen Klein, Aaron Hainault, Carter Crouch, Brendan Middleton	2017

Records by Class (pre-2000 for LP, pre-2001 for UP)

A	41.77	Lansing Everett	Andy Bunnell, Rod Whittington, Chuck Phillips, Ken Thompson	1985
B	42.76	Oak Park	Ketwain Meredith, Mark McCleskey, Abdur Karim, Ocie Hardy	1994
C	43.35	Buchanan	Ernest Johnson, Marvin Treadwell, Mark Weedon, Ryan Harris	1996
(hand 42.8		*Detroit Lutheran West*	*Joe Corbett, Kinzel Forrest, Ethan Sheard, Chris Howie*	*1982)*
D	43.78	Detroit East Catholic	Jamal Walker, Robert Willhight, DeAngelo Bates, Marlon Harris	1984
UPAB	44.3y	Kingsford	Brian Phillips, Matt Paupore, Mark Swanson, Todd Gayan	1976
UPC	44.4	Ishpeming Westwood	Rudy Nyman, Mark Quelette, Bryan Ross, Dan Perry	1984
UPD	45.0y	Pickford	Pete Lamb, John Baker, Brent Izzard, Chris Stevenson	1978

4 x 100 – Class A/Division 1 Champions

(y=4 x 110 yards)

1972	A	Oak Park	42.9y*	Tony Craighead, Henry Staton, Dave Caplon, Mike Rollins
1973	A	Detroit Kettering	42.9y*	Anthony Thompson, Eddie Woods, Eldon Parham, Charles Carroll
1974	A	Detroit Kettering	42.8y*	Joe Boyd, Eugene Singleton, Sallie Boone, Charles Carroll
1975	A	Detroit Cass Tech	42.1y*	Michael White, Thomas Sebron, Roosevelt Smith, Harlan Huckleby
1976	A	Flint Southwestern	42.6y	Rodney Feaster, Reggie Mitchell, James Brewer, Booker Moore
1977	A	Grand Rapids Ottawa Hills	42.5y	Greg Tolliver, Ken Chandler, Dale Williams, James Foster
1978	A	Flint Southwestern	42.5y	Brian Carpenter, Anthony Battle, Reggie Mitchell, Norman Graham
1979	A	Detroit Cass Tech	42.2y	Reggie Ashley, Fredell Cason, Duan Hanks, John Hollaway
1980	A	Detroit Central	42.5y	David Beasley, Steve Jones, George Brooks, Demetrius Hallums
1981	A	Detroit Central	42.1y*	Marc Jett, Steve Jones, Thomas Wilcher, Demetrius Hallums
1982	A	Detroit Central	41.7*	Michael Thomas, William White, Marc Jett, Thomas Wilcher
1983	A	Flint Central	42.3	Archie Smyers, Daryl Greer, Daryl Gilliam, Derrick Leonard
1984	A	Saginaw	42.6	Timmie Prince, Darnell Davis, Tracy Lawrence, Ernest Menzie
1985	A	Lansing Everett	41.77*	Andy Bunnell, Rod Whittington, Chuck Phillips, Ken Thompson
1986	A	Lansing Sexton	42.42	Maurice Brandon, James Cunningham, Allen Haller, Paris Milton
1987	A	Lansing Sexton	42.20	Roget Ware, Allan Haller, Paris Milton, Stanley Wheeler
1988	A	Southfield	42.51	Bobby Johnson, Jeff Reynolds, Ron Hairston, Jason Booker
1989	A	Southfield	42.90	Bobby Johnson, Chris Porter, Lawrence Reynolds, Marvin Reynolds
1990	A	Saginaw	42.73	Devin Hall, Eric Ferguson, Virgel Tellis, Lee Couch
1991	A	Detroit King	43.0	Marcus Culver, Alvin Wars, Otta Clinton, Edward Davis
1992	A	Lansing Sexton	43.59	Darvis Cunningham, Danny Martinez, Jamaro Randall, Ali Ansari
1993	A	Flint Carman-Ainsworth	42.60	Jerron Mosley, Earl Chatman, Chris Abeare, Cedric Mosley
1994	A	Highland Park	42.0	Alvilla Greene, Andre Crosby, Terrance Reed, Tony Brown
1995	A	Detroit Cass Tech	43.10	Antonio Rush, Steve Jenkins, Jonathon King, Clarence Williams
1996	A	Troy	41.9	Asheen Sarna, Tarron Adams, Drew Patrick, Chuck Conner
1997	A	Kalamazoo Loy Norrix	42.59	Justin Rumph, John Bradford, Todd Duckett, Little John Flowers
1998	A	Lansing Sexton	42.63	Shawn Foster, Ron Beard, Javis Lewis, Richard Carter
1999	A	Benton Harbor	42.22	Marcus Hall, Tommie Lewis, Steve Holloway, Quincy Roberts
2000	D1	Kalamazoo Central	42.65*	Darius Johnson, Jerome Harrison, Gregory Jennings, Charles Johnson
2001	D1	Detroit Cass Tech	42.86	Felix Fielder, Lorenzo Mallette, Robert Height, Pierre Vinson
2002	D1	Detroit Cass Tech	42.65*	Felix Fielder, Lorenzo Mallette, Robert Height, Pierre Vinson

2003	D1	Pontiac Northern	41.92*	Henry Jackson, Anthony Cato, Phil Davis, Duron Shannon
2004	D1	Pontiac Northern	42.11	Henry Jackson, Anthony Cato, Anthony Bullock, Devin Harney
2005	D1	Detroit Cass Tech	42.50	Jonathon Folse, Tyrone Rembert, Sundiata Hankins, Jonathan Klyce
2006	D1	Livonia Stevenson	42.79	Nana Adomako, Kevin Murawsla, Pat Clasgens, Brian Chandler
2007	D1	East Kentwood	42.20	Christian Jesse, Serak Haile, Zeke Crossley, Kevin Jackson
2008	D1	East Kentwood	42.25	Dallas Wade, Christina Jessie, Zeke Crossley, Kevin Jackson
2009	D1	East Kentwood	41.47#	Dallas Wade, Kody Dantuma, Eric Dudley, Jon Henry (#=stagger mismeasurement)
2010	D1	East Kentwood	41.46*	Dallas Wade, Kody Dantuma, Deonte' Hurst, Jon Henry
2011	D1	Rockford	42.38	Brian Fischer, Brandon Lubenow, Colin Remtema, Chris Essenberger
2012	D1	Grand Blanc	42.13	Jamil Banks, Jalen Cureton, Damonta' Madden, Alton Yarbrough
2013	D1	East Kentwood	42.41	Justin Harris, Onrekus Carter, Kewon Getter, Devin McKinney
2014	D1	Oak Park	41.47	Davon Frior, Ricardo Brown, Eli Minor, Keyshawn Dunwoody-Spears
2015	D1	East Kentwood	42.20	Shane Harris, Michael Catching, Tristen Frey, Kevin Smith
2016	D1	Detroit Cass Tech	42.26	Jaylen-Kelly Powell, Donovan Johnson, Savalas Morgan, Donovan Peoples-Jones
2017	D1	Rockford	41.20*	Melvin Mosely, Noah Stallworth, Josh Patterson, Nicholas Isley
2018	D1	Farmington Hills Harrison	42.39	Moet Andrews, Ben Williams, Rod Heard, Joe Stevens

4 x 100 – Class B/Division 2 Champions

(y=4 x 110 yards)

1972	B	Oxford	43.9y*	Art DeGroot, Brad Boylan, Jeff Chapman, Huston Kennedy
1973	B	Mt Morris	43.9y*	Ron Gamble, Shelton Pinnix, Tim Tucker, Don Gamble
1974	B	Flint Powers	43.7y*	Rob McCall, Steve Charland, Bruce Waggoner, Dwayne Strozier
1975	B	Flint Powers	43.4y*	Bob LeBrasseur, Tony Leoni, Mike Woodbeck, Dwayne Strozier
1976	B	Muskegon Heights	43.8y	Charles Kirks, Stanley Ezel, Willie Townsel, Brian Sydnor
1977	B	Muskegon Heights	43.7y	Frank Merriweather, Stanley Ezel, Willie Townsel, Charles Kirks
1978	B	Albion	44.5y	Ed Reese, Chris Thomas, Anthony Ridley, Jeff McCormick
1979	B	Ecorse	43.7y	Michael Dunlap, Chris London, Calvin Warren, Calvin Butler
1980	B	Saginaw Buena Vista	43.3*	Tim Houston, Kernef Jackson, Silas Houston, Ricky Swilley
1981	B	Saginaw Buena Vista	42.7*	Reggie Choyce, Steve Crawford, Silas Houston, Ricky Swilley
1982	B	Ypsilanti Willow Run	43.4y	Derrick Houston, Vince Davis, Doni Jones, Pat Warner
1983	B	Ypsilanti Lincoln	42.6*	Wesley Jones, Rodney Turrentine, Mark Lewis, Ghassan Ramadan
1984	B	Detroit Benedictine	43.6	Dwayne Walker, Keith Nichols. Cedric Green, Cory Teasley
1985	B	Detroit Benedictine	43.26*	Charles Winston, Charles Wilson, Shon Somerville, Cedric Green
1986	B	Detroit Benedictine	43.2	Charles Winston, Charles Wilson, Shon Somerville, Cedric Green
1987	B	Mt Clemens	43.5	Walter Randle, Jeff Fishback, Richard Palmer, Jodie Blanchett
1988	B	Flint Beecher	43.31	LeWane Harris, Herbert Ford, Steve Beaugard, Courtney Hawkins
1989	B	Grand Rapids Northview	43.3	Andy Korytkowski, Brent Dickerson, Jody Moore, Mickey Wallace
1990	B	Three Rivers	43.4	Mike Shea, Dennis Posey, Mark Thurman, Sam Brown
1991	B	Jackson Lumen Christi	43.58	Devin Grimes, Wes Mueller, Steve Fletcher, Joe Martines
1992	B	Flint Beecher	43.78	Chris Williams, Jimmy Lacy, Onleton Perry, Antwan Williams
1993	B	Highland Park	43.90	Alvilla Greene, Andre Crosby, Dedan Jackson, Anthony Brown
1994	B	Oak Park	42.76*	Ketwain Meredith, Mark McCleskey, Abdur Karim, Ocie Hardy
1995	B	Comstock	44.36	T.J. Fields, Quentin Hunt, Terrance Bowden, Randy Hunt
1996	B	Dowagiac	43.32	Brent Lesniak, Marco Wolverton, Alfred Williams, James Crump
1997	B	St Joseph	43.81	Mike Morphy, Chris Winkle, Chris Heydahl, Micah Zuhl
1998	B	Dowagiac	43.0	James Bates, Adam Bisnett, Brent Lesniak, Mike Bishop
1999	B	Williamston	43.5	Pat Garrett, Travis Smith, Adams Davis, Allan Dosenberry
2000	D2	Detroit Renaissance	43.28*	Jason Davis, Elton Anderson, Darryl Nunn, Kenneth Stanford
2001	D2	Farmington Hills Harrison	42.66*	Agim Shabaj, Charles Pickett, Chris Roberson, Marcus Woods
2002	D2	Lansing Waverly	42.98	Justin Boyd, Michael Bailey, Terry Tyson, Abram McCoy
2003	D2	Farmington Hills Harrison	42.94	Marcus Woods, Charles Pickett, Robert McCall, Charles Stewart
2004	D2	Fenton	43.05	Michael Peck, Shawn Debo, Matt Temple, Matt Maygar
2005	D2	Lansing Waverly	42.95	Dante Dunn, Jamell Matthias, Cameron Duncan, Byron Horn
2006	D2	Orchard Lake St Mary	42.86	Dionte Allen, Taurian Washington, Aaron Gant, Anthony Bowman
2007	D2	Detroit Renaissance	42.53*	Steven Worthy, Randy Moore, Xavier Parnell, Quinn Parnell
2008	D2	Detroit Renaissance	42.30*	Steven Worthy, Randy Moore, Xavier Parnell, Quinn Parnell
2009	D2	Williamston	42.75	Austin Palmer, Chad Rhiness, Cam Lounsbury, Ryan Brooks
2010	D2	Cadillac	42.66	Tyler Ellsworth, Tyler Hewtt, Jake Hurrell, Cody Zagers
2011	D2	Auburn Hills Avondale	42.75	Takemi Smith, Jeff Douglas, Xavier Burns, Trevon Salter
2012	D2	Auburn Hills Avondale	42.83	Henry Paul, Jeff Douglas, Myles Wright, Kyle Redwine
2013	D2	Parma Western	42.67	Payton Wheeler, Devin Cole, Brendon Maynard, Levert Franklin-Potter
2014	D2	Orchard Lake St Mary	42.53	Ross Moore, Tyson Smith, Kahlee Hamler, Ryan Johnson
2015	D2	Orchard Lake St Mary	42.56	Ross Moore, Justin Myrick, Kahlee Hamler, Ryan Johnson
2016	D2	Lansing Sexton	43.13	Devin Taylor, Dijimon Slaughter, Dariyon Gregory, Cody Blankenburg
2017	D2	Wyoming Godwin Heights	42.86	Christopher Lubbett, Tamar Williams, Kelvyn Valdez, Maurice Vincson
2018	D2	Zeeland East	43.06	Corbin DeJonge, Gabe Taylor, Alex Stockdale, Bryce Metzger

4 x 100 – Class C/Division 3 Champions

(y=4 x 110 yards)

1972	C	Decatur	44.6y*	Steve Jannsen, Scott Athey, Tom Creagan, Doug Athey
1973	C	Detroit DePorres	44.2y*	Charles Walls, Joseph Walker, William Brown, Jan Abrams
1974	C	Detroit DePorres	44.2y*	Jan Abrams, Rick O'Leary, Joe Walker, John Frazier
1975	C	Charlevoix	44.5y	Joe Kauffman, Kevin Martin, Joe Speer, Mark Streeter
1976	C	Detroit Benedictine	44.0y*	Lawrence Drake, John Manchell, Ronald Johnson, Jeff Hunter
1977	C	Redford St Mary	44.7y	Paul Price, Tyrone Hodges, Enrique Washington, Kurt Weidle
1978	C	Whitehall	44.4y	Mark VanBlargan, Kevin Babcock, Lawrence Coleman, Randy Lauterburg
1979	C	Detroit Lutheran West	43.9y*	Charles Grace, Tom Wickman, Wilfred Allen, Ed Baxter
1980	C	Detroit Lutheran West	43.9y*	Charles Grace, Ethan Sheard, Kinzel Forrest, Chris Howie
1981	C	Detroit Lutheran West	43.3*	Joe Corbett, Kinzel Forrest, Ethan Sheard, Chris Howie
1982	C	Detroit Lutheran West	42.8*	Joe Corbett, Kinzel Forrest, Ethan Sheard, Chris Howie
1983	C	Detroit DePorres	44.1	William Bonnet, Darryl Carter, Anthony Johnson, James Scott
1984	C	Detroit DePorres	43.3	Keith Harris, Anthony Fleming, Bryant Stallworth, Ralph Bland
1985	C	Detroit Country Day	43.81*	Byron Pitts, Steve Hann, Sam Hims, Brian Stephens

1986	C	St Charles	44.61	Mark Zielinski, Matt Rusz, John Spannagel, Scott Simon
1987	C	Detroit Lutheran West	44.45	Steve Drohan, Greg Harris, Oscar Ford, Albert Rhodes
1988	C	Eau Claire	43.0	Kevin Moore, Dennis Alexander, Doug Miller, Todd Anderson
1989	C	Fulton-Middleton	44.21	Tom Cecchini, Spencer Wright, Chad Van Conent, Bill Thompson
1990	C	Detroit Country Day	44.14	Emmanuel Dizon, Jason Wallace, Chris Castillo, David Williams
1991	C	Cassopolis	43.9	Thomas McNary, Robert Crawford, Robert Saxton, Mike Andrews
1992	C	Constantine	44.60	Nick Juday, Matt Grile, Justin Topolski, Brian Stears
1993	C	Napoleon	44.11	Matt Bischoff, Jay Patrick, Brent Perkins, Jason Ross
1994	C	Detroit Benedictine	44.23	Antoine Flowers, Jason Wyatt, Armand Williams, Marvin Savage
1995	C	Breckenridge	44.16	Joe Bushre, Chad Spiekerman, Greg Ryan, Torry Gagne
1996	C	Buchanan	43.35*	Ernest Johnson, Marvin Treadwell, Mark Weedon, Ryan Harris
1997	C	New Haven	43.71	Travis Kelly, Cliff Akers, Tedaro France, Richard Sparks
1998	C	Cassopolis	43.69	C.J. Ward, Charlie Reese, Ronald Austin, Zachary Stratton
1999	C	Albion	43.36	Dominic Reid, Tonae Hannah, Kevin Davis, Marcus Ashley
2000	D3	Albion	44.16*	Dominic Reid, Tonae Hannah, Daniel Clark, Kevin Davis
2001	D3	Albion	44.44	Daniel Clar, Kevin Davis, Andre Smith, Jermaine Moore
2002	D3	Detroit Country Day	43.72*	Phil Damaska, Job Gupta, Brandon Horn, Kim Thompson
2003	D3	Imlay City	43.42*	Franco Folino, Brian Beebe, Jonathan Fielder, Gregory Gogola
2004	D3	Detroit Country Day	43.42*	Chris Rucker, Earnie Jackson, Martin Corniffe, Jared Owens
2005	D3	Albion	43.50	Marquis Merritt, Rickey Whitfield, Mike Ridley, Toronzo Lymon
2006	D3	Detroit Country Day	43.37*	Chris Rucker, Erik Williams, E.J. Whitlow, Jonas Gray
2007	D3	Albion	43.51	Mike Ridley, Durant Crum, Todd Atchison, Corwin Anderson
2008	D3	Albion	43.28*	Todd Atchison, Mike Ridley, Patrick Dewalt, Durant Crum
2009	D3	Albion	43.82	Patrick Dewalt, Ryan Hopson, Dion Mitchell, Todd Atchison
2010	D3	Vassar	43.25*	Madison Harper, Troy Hecht, Justin Locklear, Keif Vickers
2011	D3	Saranac	43.58	Rehmert, Leland, Bryan Roth, Jacob Conley
2012	D3	Union City	43.64	Aaron Watson, Josh Holton, Chris Maye, Zach Smith
2013	D3	Ann Arbor Gabriel Richard	43.99	Ashton Hundley, Kwami Abobor-Hererra, Matt Mackey, Blaise Stearns
2014	D3	Sanford Meridian	43.45	Charles Ellithorpe, Kevin Scheibert, Jacob Wenzlick, Jacob Ham
2015	D3	Clinton	44.51	Zech Johnson, Tyler Underwood, Noah Poore, Mathew Sexton
2016	D3	Sanford Meridian	43.14*	Christian Petre, Miles LeViere, Monte Petre, Andre Smith
2017	D3	Grandville Calvin Christian	43.36	Jared Piersma, Caleb Schutter, Tyler Houskamp, Marcus Lubbers
2018	D3	Hart	43.83	Kegan Strait, Angel Aguilar, Orian Torres, Logan Wells

4 x 100 – Class D/Division 4 Champions

(y=4 x 110 yards)

1972	D	Onekama	45.2y*	Rich Barryhill, Steve Ward, Carl Milarch, Dennis Manke
1973	D	Lawrence	45.5y	Dana Rowe, Jim McCree, Phil Johnson, Larry Whiteman
1974	D	Grass Lake	44.6y*	Dale Wyman, Randy Siegrist, Rod Grieshaber, Roger Crouch
1975	D	Dansville	44.7y	Alan Gardner, Jeff Casak, Gene Douglas, Andy Wheelden
1976	D	Detroit DePorres	43.6y*	Gregory Johnson, Terrane Hines, Stanley Young, Deron Early
1977	D	Grosse Pointe Univ Liggett	44.3y	John Engel, Will Hummel, Jim Catchings, David McKinney
1978	D	Ann Arbor Gabriel Richard	43.8y	George Pitts, Mark Fox, Mark Cameron, George Kokales
1979	D	Flint Academy	44.7	Quintin Reese, Derrick Relerford, Therman Sisco, Preston Walker
1980	D	Detroit DePorres	44.3	Larry Jordan, Darryl Carter, Vernon Lynch, Jerry Campbell
1981	D	Detroit DePorres	44.6	Darren Warner, Darryl Carter, Clint Childs, Keith Harris
1982	D	Battle Creek St Phillip	44.8	Bill Bush, Dave Mangan, Keith Williams, Mike Disher
1983	D	Detroit East Catholic	43.6*	Keith Thompson, Michael Gatson, Robert Hall, Robert Willhight
1984	D	Detroit East Catholic	43.78*	Jamal Walker, Robert Willhight, DeAngelo Bates, Marlon Harris
1985	D	Fowler	44.46	Dean Koenigsknecht, Ken Armbrustmacher, Matt Braun, Bill Snyder
1986	D	Detroit East Catholic	44.12	Zekiel Miller, Allen Mayes, Reginald Golfin, Jamal Walker
1987	D	Deerfield	44.90	Todd Nighswander, Chad Crots, Troy Haas. Jim Lott
1988	D	Covert	44.61	Anthony Strong, Earl Cox, Kenny Johnson, James Smith
1989	D	Detroit Lutheran West	44.40	Kevin Ford, Terrance Goff, Damon Butler, Albert Rhodes
1990	D	Reading	44.64	David Burger, Todd Richards, Jason Rodesiler, Aaron Burger
1991	D	Athens	44.62	John Hardy, Jamey Wyman, Scott Casselman, Carlos Perez
1992	D	Detroit Lutheran West	45.60	Brian Sparks, Devlin Scarber, LaRon Ellerbee, Reggie Dawton
1993	D	Pittsford	45.4	Travis Miller, Adam Abfall, Jake Baxter, Travis Wollett
1994	D	Pittsford	45.24	Shawn Reed, Brandon Brown, Jake Baxter, Kevin Dickey
1995	D	Baldwin	45.36	Marion Carter, Donte Hill, Jason Mason, Juson Johnson
1996	D	Baldwin	44.33	Juson Johnson, Dwight Thompson, Jason Mason, Robert Helm
1997	D	Pittsford	44.57	Dustin Ewing, Andy Towne, Brock Wollett, Kevin Dickey
1998	D	St Joseph Lake Michigan Catholic	44.6	J.J. Megna, Paul Querbach, John Roche', Travontii Montgomery
1999	D	Covert	44.24	Clifford Chandler, Javell Clay, Brandon Flournoy, Laquan Gordon
2000	D4	St Joseph Lake Michigan Catholic	44.00*	Travontii Montgomer, Paul Querbach, John Roche, Greg Deja
2001	D4	Redford Borgess	43.69*	Jose Kiocannon, Jason Smith, Dejuan Kea, Darryl Anglin
2002	D4	Redford Borgess	44.55	Donald Ferrell, Dejuan Kea, Edward Burney, Jason Smith
2003	D4	Detroit DePorres	43.98	Daryl Graham, Alan Ball, Anthony Bowman, Carl Grimes
2004	D4	Detroit DePorres	43.70	David Grimes, Anthony Bowman, Carlos Simpson, Carl Grimes
2005	D4	Detroit DePorres	43.32*	David Grimes, Taurian Washington, Cortex Smith, Anthony Bowman
2006	D4	Climax-Scotts	45.08	Tyler Langs, Jordan Langs, Dallas Halasz, Scott Bogard
2007	D4	Genesee	44.10	James Patilla, DeWayne Jackson, Jeremy Benton, David Patrick
2008	D4	Pewamo-Westphalia	44.28	Dale Spitzley, Cory Noeker, Jason Fedewa, Jay Spitzley
2009	D4	Pewamo-Westphalia	43.86	Dale Spitzley, Austin Fedewa, Alex Thelen, Cory Noeker
2010	D4	Muskegon Catholic	44.00	Jamicha Cooper, Tyler DePung, Major Metcalf, Damon Armstrong
2011	D4	Muskegon Catholic	44.12	Michael Heybloom, Tyler DePung, Zach Campbell, Damon Armstrong
2012	D4	Albion	44.70	Gary Chambers, Eliyah Yasha, Carles Summerour, Nolen Mitchell
2013	D4	Climax-Scotts	44.41	Alexander Lodes, Kirk Gibson, Sam Eshuis, Zach Nabozny
2014	D4	Southfield Christian	44.22	Nicholas Mitchell, Mitchell Jones, Aldred Williams, Blake Washington
2015	D4	Union City	44.30	Jalen Boes, Spencer Connell, Thomas Anderson, Aaron Watson
2016	D4	Melvindale ABT	43.75	Shakim Fields, Delvon Hines, Jamar Sanders, Damon Testley
2017	D4	Fulton-Middleton	44.43	Ben Fisher, Jon Baker, Adam Duflo, Tristan Johnson
2018	D4	Breckenridge	44.00	Lukas Ebright, Caleb Hurt, Hunter Collins, Caden Foster

4 x 100 – UP Class AB/Division 1 Champions

(y=4 x 110 yards)

1972	UPAB	Rudyard	46.0y*	
1973	UPAB	Iron Mountain	45.3y*	Dennis Nepper, Tom Swanson, Randy Awrey, Mike Branz
1974	UPAB	Iron Mountain	45.3y*	
1975	UPAB	Ironwood	45.4y	
1976	UPAB	Kingsford	44.3y*	Brian Phillips, Matt Paupore, Mark Swanson, Todd Gayan
1977	UPAB	Menominee	45.3y	Rick Callies, Shawn Cumbie, Mike Boettcher, Mike Honeychurch
1978	UPAB	Calumet	46.0y	Mark Peterson, Russell Kiviniemi, Mark Bonenfant, Michael Mihelich
1979	UPAB	Kingsford	45.9	Mark Forgette, Michael Konopacke, Mark Konopacke, Tomothy Goyan
1980	UPAB	Menominee	45.3	Craig Lietzke, Marty Hynnek, Alex Barker, Chris Hofer
1981	UPAB	Menominee	45.6	Craig Lietzke, Marty Hynnek, Alex Barker, Chris Hofer
1982	UPAB	Menominee	45.7	John Spies, Tom Dessert, Tim Lietzke, Mark Noon
1983	UPAB	Menominee	45.7	John Spies, Tim Lietzke, Mark Noon, Kevin Johnson
1984	UPAB	Marquette	45.6	Steve Nelson, Brian Levandowski, Emmet Blake, Greg Olson
1985	UPAB	Marquette	46.3	Doug Heslip, Mark Lynaugh, Greg Place, Emmett Blake
1986	UPAB	Kingsford	45.3	Ron Pratt, Mark Edens, Mark Willis, Todd Seppi
1987	UPAB	Kingsford	45.4	Ron Pratt, Herman Hinz, Mark WIllis, Mark Edens
1988	UPAB	Marquette	45.2	Greg Geoffriion, Boris Martycz, Mike Grange, Jeff LaFave
1989	UPAB	Kingsford	45.7	Paul Guilliani, Matt Flaminio, Dale Powell, Doug Roberts
1990	UPAB	Kingsford	45.1	Paul Guillani, Matt Flaminio, Dale Powell, Sean O'Neil
1991	UPAB	Kingsford	44.6	Matt Gibson, Matt Flaminio. Tim Casari, Aric Casillas
1992	UPAB	Escanaba	45.5	Ryan Friedhoff, Todd Taylor, Steve Groos, Nathan Chylek
1993	UPAB	Kingsford	45.9	Scott Giullani, Mike Raketich, Andy LaBlanc, Ryan Milkey
1994	UPAB	Escanaba	45.8	Jamie Hirn, Kevin Kang, Ryan Freidhoff, Scott Victorson
1995	UPAB	Marquette	45.3	Chad Wilkinson, Matt Tuccini, Andy Manthey, DayDale Manthley
1996	UPAB	Escanaba	45.7	
1997	UPAB	Menominee	45.7	Eli Wolf, Nathan Twork, Korey Sahr, Andy Kohrt
1998	UPAB	Menominee	45.41*	Joe Hensley, Nathan Twork, Brian Kass, Josh Tarbox
1999	UPAB	Menominee	46.06	Scott Stesney, Kris Erickson, Shannon Mathison, Ethan Rayhorn
2000	UPAB	Escanaba	46.0	Eddie Dwyer, Jim Hansen, Robert Lee, Ben Andrews
2001	UPD1	Escanaba	45.0*	Nick Mullin, Jay Wiles, Ed Dwyer, Ben Andrews
2002	UPD1	Hancock	46.2	Ryan Ricci, Andy Sarazin, Andy Soli, Pete Jones
2003	UPD1	Menominee	45.34*	Nick Parrette, Justin Tuma, William Depas, Andrew Shaver
2004	UPD1	Gladstone	44.35*	Cevin Cosby, Charlie Stafford, Matt Petr, Matt Holm
2005	UPD1	Gladstone	43.93*	David Grimes, Taurian Washington, Cortex Smith, Anthony Bowman
2006	UPD1	Menominee	45.28	Ethan Shaver, Andy Ozcus, Richie Barbeau, Jordan Noha
2007	UPD1	Menominee	44.81	Matt LaCanne, Kurt Roubal, Blake Chouinard, Ethan Shaver
2008	UPD1	Menominee	45.07	Fabian Delarosa, Jake Pedersen, Anthony Wilson, Ethan Shave
2009	UPD1	Kingsford	45.45	Adam Mattord, Dylan Tengesdahl, Justin Heupel, Wes Jacobson
2010	UPD1	Kingsford	43.78*	Cole Peterson, Dylan Tengesdahl, Paul DeYeart, Wes Jacobson
2011	UPD1	Menominee	44.78	
2012	UPD1	Menominee	45.03	Chris Briar, Jared Theisen, Shaun Sullivan, Leonard Briggs
2013	UPD1	Menominee	44.70	Bryan Hines, Aaron Forsberg, Shaun Sullivan, Leonard Briggs
2014	UPD1	Menominee	45.09	Aeron Forsberg, Justin Brilinski, Nate Marcin, Devon Harris
2015	UPD1	Marquette	45.16	Patrick Burmeister, Scott Tripp, Michael Millado, Brett Place
2016	UPD1	Marquette	45.01	Brandon Kowalkowski, Jonathan Schmutzler, Brandan McGuire, Ben Moreau
2017	UPD1	Kingsford	45.25	Tommy List, Trevor Povolo, Brad Vanremort, Trevor Roberts
2018	UPD1	Escanaba	45.33	Scout Wunder, Logan Carroll, Ryan Randall, Tyler Cook

4 x 100 – UP Class C/Division 2 Champions

(y=4 x 110 yards)

1972	UPC	Houghton	46.5y*	
1973	UPC	Rudyard	46.0y*	
1974	UPC	Hancock	45.6y*	Bruce Witting, Paul Peterson, Steve Salani, Marty Tarbox
1975	UPC	Hancock	45.0y*	Bruce Witting, Rick Pardini, Paul Peterson, Marty Tarbox
1976	UPC	Hancock	45.0y*	Bruce Witting, Brian Ricci, Rick Pardini, Marty Tarbox
1977	UPC	Rudyard	45.4y	
1978	UPC	Ontonagon	46.0y	
1979	UPC	Hancock	46.2	Robert Carlson, Greg Nominelli, Tom Loshaw, Matt Huhta
1980	UPC	Munising	45.9	Dean Johnson, Byron Pond, Bruce Radloff, Chuck Secreast
1981	UPC	Ironwood	46.2	Jim Manchester, Mike Blodgett, Mark Mazzon, John Komaromy
1982	UPC	Ironwood	44.9*	Jim Manchester, Mike Blodgett, Mark Mazzon, John Komaromy
1983	UPC	Ishpeming Westwood	45.5	Rudy Nyman, Mark Quelette, Kevin Kangas, Dan Perry
1984	UPC	Ishpeming Westwood	44.4*	Rudy Nyman, Mark Quelette, Bryan Ross, Dan Perry
1985	UPC	Houghton	45.4	John Sanregret, Jerry Destrampe, Rick Jurkanis, Brady Schaefer
1986	UPC	Houghton	45.0	John Sanregret, Jerry Destrampe, Rick Jurkanis, Brady Schaefer
1987	UPC	Iron Mountain	46.4	Steve Johnson, Steve Cowling, Steve Chiamulera, Tom Marchetti
1988	UPC	Stephenson	45.3	Tim Hanson, David Ledkins, Randy Klein, Chester Blom
1989	UPC	Ishpeming Westwood	45.6	Jared Frisk, Bob Nelson, Todd Poirier, Doug Etelmaki
1990	UPC	Ishpeming Westwood	45.4	Brian Johnson, Bob Nelson, Todd Poirer, Jared Frisk,
1991	UPC	Negaunee	46.4	Kevin Downey, Erif Leaf, Jon Beckman, Brett Koski
1992	UPC	Norway	46.8	John Olson, Mike Zahn, Andy Smith, Matt Edger
1993	UPC	Manistique	45.5	Jason Lockwood, Richie Blowers, Andy LaVigne, Derek LaPointe
1994	UPC	Munising	45.4	Bill Comish, Bryan Behing, Parker Young, Swan Lendeblad
1995	UPC	Negaunee	45.8	Nathan Mager, Chris Ewald, Eric Keranen, John Laitale
1996	UPC	Ironwood	45.3	Jeremy Richards, John Nemetz, Graham Niemi, Jim LaBlonde
1997	UPC	Ironwood	45.6	Graham Niemi, Ian Powell, John Schlais, Jim LaBlonde
1998	UPC	Calumet	45.7	Matt Koljonen, Greg Perala, Eric Bastian, Brian Johnson
1999	UPC	Munising	45.8	Ben Perry, Blair Tweedale, Jordan Miron, Brandon Spaulding
2000	UPC	Iron Mountain	45.1	Matt Mainville, Adam Husing, Jeff Taff, Mark Lafreniere
2001	UPD2	Ishpeming	46.0*	Adam Jandron, Chad Kurian, Jeremy Nelson, Jordan Austin
2002	UPD2	Stephenson	45.9*	Nate Lesperance, Thad Boettcher, Mike Shampo, Stece Schmidt

2003	UPD2	Iron Mountain	46.50*	Nick Laydon, Alexander Lundy, Nicholas Buckland, Brett Spigarelli
2004	UPD2	Norway	45.53*	Josh Querio, Chris Mattas, Jim DeBartolo, Andrew Medina
2005	UPD2	Norway	45.42*	David Grimes, Taurian Washington, Cortex Smith, Anthony Bowman
2006	UPD2	Norway	45.95	Phil Milbrath, Kyle Zweifel, Jordan Marchetti, Chris Mattas
2007	UPD2	Stephenson	45.66	Robert Strobel, Coty Jones, Brent Parrett, David Strobel
2008	UPD2	St. Ignace	45.35*	Jesse Becker, Antony Lester, Derek Marshall, Kyle Smock
2009	UPD2	St. Ignace	45.11*	Anthony Lester, Robby Robinson, Evan Emerson, Caleb Litzner
2010	UPD2	Rudyard	45.66	Caleb Solo, Ben Gable, Jared Clark, Ben Coffee
2011	UPD2	St. Ignace	45.70	Caleb Litzner, Galloway Thurston, Wyatt Orm, Joe Ostman
2012	UPD2	St. Ignace	46.22	James Helma, James Cruderman, Gally Thurston, Parker Simmons
2013	UPD2	Ishpeming	45.16	Eric Kostreva, Tyrus Millimaki, Derek DeCaire, Hunter Wirtanen
2014	UPD2	Ishpeming Westwood	46.56	Fred Boburka, Skyler Dakota, Jordan Hebert, Ryan Hunt
2014	UPD2	St. Ignace	46.56	Brandon Oja, Joe Fullerton, Jimmy Swanson, James Cryderman
2015	UPD2	Ishpeming	46.27	Isaac Olson, Halen Carello, Nick Comment, Ozzy Corp
2016	UPD2	Ishpeming	47.48	Isaac Olson, Jaren Kipling, Ozzy Corp, Matt Makil
2017	UPD2	Newberry	45.03*	John Paramski, Jeff Rahilly, Andre James, Brandon Christensen
2018	UPD2	Newberry	45.35	Brandon Christensen, Jaylen James, Jeff Rahilly, Andre James

4 x 100 – UP Class D/Division 3 Champions

(y=4 x 110 yards)

1972	UPD	Wakefield	47.5y*	Dan Nurmi, Mark Daniels, Lauri Maki, Dave Inkala
1973	UPD	Pickford	46.8y*	Bob Storey, Audie Potter, Kevin LaVictor, Bill Ames
1974	UPD	Pickford	46.6y*	Neil Peffers, Kevin LaVictor, Audie Potter, Steve McConkey
1976	UPD	Pickford	45.6y*	Neil Peffers, John Baker, Brent Izzard, Chris Stevenson
1977	UPD	Pickford	46.1y	Pete Lamb, John Baker, Brent Izzard, Chris Stevenson
1978	UPD	Pickford	45.0y*	Pete Lamb, John Baker, Brent Izzard, Chris Stevenson
1979	UPD	Powers-North Central	46.3	Jeff Menard, Jeff Poquette, Mark Fochesato, Dale Miller
1980	UPD	Powers-North Central	46.1	Marc Fochesato, Brian Hilsabeck, Dale Miller, Jeff Poquette
1981	UPD	Baraga	45.9	Pat Herbert, Ed Moberg, Lewis Sawicky, Tom Michaels
1982	UPD	Cedarville	46.4	Kurt Hill, Doug Scalf, Rob Freebury, Todd Soderlund
1983	UPD	Felch North DIckinson	46.7	Joe Newton, Jim Johnson. Mike Mooney, Rick Opsahl
1984	UPD	Felch North DIckinson	46.3	Joe Newton, Jim Johnson, Esley Gustafson, Rick Opsahl
1985	UPD	Crystal Falls-Forest Park	47.2	Jon Gallakner, Jim Nocerini, Mike Palo, Mark Mielcarek
1986	UPD	Bessemer	46.5	Pat Bulinski, Scott Trudgeon, Mike Contratto, Scott Grooms
1987	UPD	Crystal Falls-Forest Park	47.4	TomTotsch, Chris Nocerini, John Lovato, John Gollakner
1988	UPD	Wakefield	47.2	Rick Hemming, Dave Rautiola, Dane Velesano, Randy Woody
1989	UPD	Pickford	46.9	Dave Bush, Jason Firack, Paul McConkey, Guy Blanchard
1990	UPD	Pickford	46.3	Dave Dodds, Matt Bawks, Guy Blanchard, Dave Bush
1991	UPD	Brimley	46.5	Kevin Sutton, Tom Hurst, Jon Bowerman, Chris Jaruzel
1992	UPD	Rapid River	48.7	Kris Heidbrier, Cory Ness, Chris Wolf, Todd Anderson
1993	UPD	Ontonagon	46.9	Steve Mattson, Tom Goard, Dave Block. Roy Fiszer
1994	UPD	Powers-North Central	46.4	Nick Charles, Chris Gorzinski, Tom Granquist, Ryan Veeser
1995	UPD	Powers-North Central	46.1	Nick Charles, Chris Gorzinski, Tom Granquist, Ryan Veeser
1996	UPD	Crystal Falls Forest Park	46.2	Shawn Zaupa, Mark Stoor, Dyrek Darmer, Mike Simeoni
1997	UPD	Rapid River	47.2	Chad Parrett, Nathan Wolf, Joe Smith, Josh Kniss
1998	UPD	Mohawk Keweenaw	46.4	
1999	UPD	Felch North Dickinson	47.7	Dan Larson, Jared Gerguson, Steve Anderson, Regan Budek
2000	UPD	Pickford	47.2	Nick Rye, Gordon Grover, Dustin Esslin, Tyler Lofdahl
2001	UPD3	Bark River-Harris	46.9*	Jamie Kleikamp, Brock Bower, Brendan Pirlot, Travis Bellefeuille
2002	UPD3	Bark River-Harris	46.1*	Brendon Pirlot, Westin Bellefuille Brock Bower, Travis Bellefeuille
2003	UPD3	North DIckinson	46.75*	Travis Steinbrecher, Kevin Roell, Ryan Carey, Cicholas Mattson
2004	UPD3	Brimley	47.29	Jeff Graham, Travis Lynn, Kyle Dillon, Albert Bertram
2005	UPD3	Baraga	46.47*	Dan Giddings, Joel Stark, Dave Dillon, Joe Patovisti
2006	UPD3	Bark River-Harris	46.46*	Josh Aiken, Josh Thompson, Joe Gorecki, Jason Knauf
2007	UPD3	Rock Mid Peninsula	45.67*	Todd Winkelbauer, Justin Wigand, Keith Reynolds, Jimmy Cretens
2008	UPD3	Crystal Falls Forest Park	46.73	Dustin Basirico, Fred Hubbard, Bob Reid, Josh Siler
2009	UPD3	Crystal Falls Forest Park	46.53	Dustin Basirico, Mick Velesano, Bob Reid, Josh Siler
2010	UPD3	Crystal Falls Forest Park	46.76	Levi Oleksy, Cole Noblet, Jacob Siler, Josh Siler
2011	UPD3	Crystal Falls Forest Park	46.36	Kurt Lavacque, Collin Gendron, Cole Noblet, Jacob Siler
2012	UPD3	Bark River-Harris	47.01	Jacob Kleiman, Hunter Messersmith, Dane Messersmith, Scott Jorasz
2013	UPD3	Bessemer	45.91	Art Rundell, Taylor Smith, Derek Gheller, Alex Smith
2014	UPD3	Lake Linden-Hubbell	46.96	Konrad Klein, Luke Monette, Tyler Roose, Trent Ambuehl
2015	UPD3	Munising	46.21	Alex Hill, Alec Blank, Garret Elore, Austin Kelto
2016	UPD3	Newberry	46.68	John Paramski, Andre James, Adam Hildebrandt, Jaylen James
2017	UPD3	Lake Linden-Hubbell	44.76*	Kellen Klein, Aaron Hainault, Carter Crouch, Brendan Middleton
2018	UPD3	Rudyard	46.25	Kenneth Bowers, Maxwell Trotter, Noah Garrison, Jesse Carter-Powell

BOYS 4 x 200 RELAY

Records

D1	1:26.07	East Kentwood	Stephen Bracey, Jacoby Welch, AJ Jeffries, Khance Meyers	2017
D2	1:27.71	Orchard Lake St Mary	Richard Bowens, Shermond Dabney, Kanlee Hamler, Ky'Ren Cunningham	2016
D3	1:27.95	Detroit Country Day	Chris Rucker, Erik Williams, Jonas Gray, Matin Corniffe	2006
D4	1:29.69	Redford Borgess	Jose Kiocannon, Jason Smith, KeJuan Kea, Darryl Anglin	2001
UPD1	1:30.73	Kingsford	Eric Kliesner, Dyland Tengesdahl, Paul DeYeart, Wes Jacobson	2010
UPD2	1:33.18	Norway	Chris Mattas, Lane Thaler, Jim DeBartolo, Nick Zweifel	2004
	1:33.18	St. Ignace	Anthony Lester, Robby Robinson, Evan Emerson, Caleb Litzner	2009
UPD3	1:35.18	Powers-North Central	Craig Bilski, Andy Fazer, Jared Triest, Steve Davis	2006

A	1:25.0	Detroit Cass Tech	Fred Wilkerson, Clarence Williams, Jabari Johnson, Daryl Rankins	1994
B	1:28.23	Detroit UD Jesuit	William Brooks, Jim Krol, Edzra Gibson, Chris Polk	1993
C	1:29.1	Detroit Lutheran West	Dwight Tyson, Kinzel Forrest, Erik Frederick, Chris Howie	1982
D	1:29.4y	Detroit DePorres	Leonard Thornton, Mark McClendon, Darold Gholston, Stanley Young	1977
UPAB	1:32.1y	Gwinn	Bob Octaluk, Jeff Hatfield, Ron Storti, Marty Klena	1970
UPC	1:32.7	Ironwood	John Kamaromy, Mike Blodgett, Mark Mazzon, Jim Manchester	1982
UPD	1:35.0y	Powers-North Central	Marc Fochesato, Brian Hilsabeck, Dale Miller, Jeff Poquette	1980

4 x 200 – Class A/Division 1 Champions

(unknown distance)

1895	all	Grand Rapids	nt	

(y=4 x 220 yards)

Year	Class	School	Time	Team
1905	all	Detroit University School	1:34.0y*	Jose Malcomson, Ernest Vaughn, Percy Dunphy, DeForest Candler
1906	all	Detroit University School	1:33.8y*	Bob Woodcock, Jose Malcomson, Lysle White, Ernest Vaughn
1907	all	Detroit Central	1:35.2y	Ralph Craig, Allen Garrels, Tom Stalker, George Widman
1908	all	Ann Arbor	1:39.2y	Elmer Lehnforf, Edgar Roper, Harry Mills, Harvey Cornwell
1909	all	Detroit Central	1:37.4y	Jim Craig, Russell Stoddard, E. Montgomery, Art Widman
1910	all	Detroit Central	1:38.4y	Herbert Rosenthal, Jim Craig, E. Gaunt, John Bruce
1911	all	Detroit Central	1:38.4y	Harold Holland, Austin Chambers, John Bruce, Frederick Lumley
1912	all	Ann Arbor	nt	Ralph Speck, John Edwards, Martin Galt, Harold Smith
1913	all	Lansing Central	1:38.0y	Bayard Harvey, Lester Roscoe, Arthur Prine, Robert Healey
1914	all	Lansing Central	1:37.4y	Bayard Harvey, Robert Ehingher, Arthur Prine, Robert Healey
1915	all	Detroit Eastern	1:38.4y	Herbert Henry, Clarence Kratschmayer, John Wojciechowske Fred Williams
1916	all	Grand Rapids Central	1:36.0y	Rod McKenzie, Jake VanderVisse, Wendell Bacon, Guy Houston
1917	all	Grand Rapids Central	1:41.0y	Ernest Beard, Frank Stekette, Myron Hopkins, Guy Houston
1918		No Meet – World War I		
1919	all	Grand Rapids South	1:33.0y*	Rollin Davis, Emmett Bolden, Herman DeRuiter, Adam Siemons
1920	all	Detroit Northwestern	1:36.6y	Carl Blauman, Harold Davis, F. Day, George Snider
1921	A	Detroit Northwestern	nt	Art McDonald, Carl Blauman, Harold Davis, French Easton
1922	A	Detroit Northern	1:33.3y	Leonard Caplan, Dunton Barlow, Miles Turpin, George Hester
1923	A	Detroit Northwestern	1:31.8y*	Stanley Kilpatrick, Lawson Parker, Lowell Blanchard, Victor Leschinsky
1924	A	Detroit Northwestern	1:33.1y	Wallin McMinn, E McMinn, John Widman, Jimmie Tait
1925	A	Detroit Northwestern	1:31.5y*	Charles Ross, Wallin McMinn, John Widman, Jimmie Tait
1926	A	Kalamazoo Central	1:31.7y	Edgar Fenker, Sidney Brooks, George Hanselman, Darrell Calkins
1927	A	Detroit Northeastern	1:30.0y*	Eugene Beatty, Love Snowden, Norman Schmidt, John Lewis
1928	A	Detroit Northeastern	1:33.5y	Love Snowden, Leon Dykas, Charles Eknovich, Eugene Beatty
1929	A	Detroit Northwestern	1:32.9y	Thad Dennis, Floyd Penic, George Seros, Billy Burgess
1930	A	Ann Arbor	1:34.8y	Lyle Wagoner, Karl Wenger, Harry Matthews, Pete Zahner
1931	A	Grand Rapids Central	1:34.6y	Bill Drueke, Bob Sproul, Boyd Pantlind, Douglas Emery
1932	A	Grand Rapids Ottawa Hills	1:32.1y	Harold Jefferson, Harvey Woodstra, Fred Stiles, Ed Kalawart
1933	A	Saginaw	1:33.8y	Burnell Tarleton, Earl Perry, Garvin Sanders, Bob Kolbe
1934	A	Grand Rapids Ottawa Hills	1:32.3y	Art Bullen, Hal Blackburn, Chuck Luce, Bill Strehl
1935	A	Grand Rapids Davis Tech	1:32.2y	Jerry Bullen, Preston Schoon, Pete Dykehouse, Alonzo Lewis
1936	A	Monroe	1:32.5y	Ira Hughes, Percy Zimmerman, Perry Mason, Willie Campbell
1937	A	Pontiac	1:33.4y	Don Nelson, Bill Stoddard, Sam Seay, Jim McGhee
1938	A	Grand Rapids South	1:32.3y	Otto Veenkamp, Jimmy Krestakos, Red Kremer, George Doran
1939	A	Saginaw	1:34.7y	Johnny De Groat, Pete Wagner, Harlen Floyd, Bob Lyttle
1940	A	Battle Creek	1:32.6y	Bill Brewer, Matt Woods, Teddy Wilson, Eugene Ketchum
1941	A	Benton Harbor	1:32.9y	Willie Moore, Maurice Akright, Ed Peppel, Bert Copeland
1942	A	Kalamazoo Central	1:33.0y	Bob Whitfield, Neil Clark, Dave Wenzel, Bob Rogers
1943		No Meet – World War II		
1944	A	Grand Rapids Catholic	1:34.6y	Frank Walijewski, Jerry Bockheim, Dan O'Hearn, Robert Vandenberg
1945	A	Saginaw	1:32.7y	Jim Blenkhorn, Darrell Byers, Marvin Chicowski, Jim Hickey
1946	A	Saginaw	1:34.4y	Jim Blenkhorn, Vern Revell, Darrell Byers, Marvin Chicowski
1947	A	Grand Rapids Creston	1:34.1y	Russell Newton, Robert Foley, Jack Rose, Al Rasikas
1948	A	Saginaw	1:32.9y	Ray Garrett, Bob St John, Jim Ellis, Bill Conley
1949	A	Saginaw	1:31.6y	Gaylord Nelson, Ray Garrett, Bill Conley, Jim Ellis
1950	A	Flint Northern	1:31.0y	Leroy Bolden, Ellis Duckett, Sylvester Collins, Walt McMullin
1951	A	Pontiac	1:34.8y	Ron Fowler, Buddy Harris, Alonzo Harris, Walter Beach
1952	A	Mt Clemens	1:34.2y	Joe Folson, John Samuels, Willie Thomas, Melvin Becks
1953	A	Flint Northern	1:31.0y	R.G. Johnson, Art Johnson, John Langhorne, Leon Burton
1954	A	Flint Northern	1:30.2y*	Ernie Landsdowne, Jim Logan, Dave Copeland, Art Johnson
1955	A	Bay City Central	1:32.8y	Willie Smith, Frank Santovich, Charles Gatza, Namon Smith
1956	A	Pontiac	1:31.9y	Hayes Jones, Archie Brooks, Jim Shorter, Charles Spann
1957	A	Kalamazoo Central	1:32.5y	Joel Johnson, Jerry MacComber, Larry Brownell, Dave Snyder
1958	A	Pontiac Central	1:30.4y	Don Sowell, Jim Hawkins, Jim Keller, Bob Manning
1959	A	Farmington	1:32.0y	Mike Agee, Tom Grimshaw, Roy Jordan, Rex Cawley
1960	A	Flint Northern	1:32.8y	James Hodo, Hugh Edwards, J.B. Elzy, Maurice Pea
1961	A	Flint Northern	1:30.3y	Dennis McGee, Huey Edwards, Ed Johnson, Dalton Kimble
1962	A	Flint Northern	1:31.1y	Ed Johnson, Willie Buck, Clifton Finklea, Dalton Kimble
1963	A	Kalamazoo Central	1:29.5y*	Wayne Fisher, Walt Worthy, Mike Thompson. Norm Gottlieb
1964	A	Lansing Everett	1:30.9y	Henry Patino, Rich Ryals, Les Koren, Tom Smith
1965	A	Detroit Northwestern	1:30.0y	Richard Campbell, John Hawkins, James Kimball, Thelbart Jeffries
1966	A	Flint Southwestern	1:30.3y	Daryl Smith, Al Renick, George McNair, Gary Bosh
1967	A	Battle Creek Central	1:28.8y*	Andrew Johnson, Larry Evans, Jesse Wright, Eugene Brown
1968	A	Battle Creek Central	1:29.1y	Andrew Johnson, Jesse Wright, Jerry Miller, Eugene Brown
1969	A	Detroit Mackenzie	1:29.5y	Carlos Woods, Ken James, John Ware, Darryl Arnold
1970	A	Benton Harbor	1:28.9y	Leroy Hunt, Frank Atkinson, Don Hopkins
1971	A	Detroit Northern	1:27.0y*	William Nance, Brad Rogers, Tyrone Kelly, Marshall Dill
1972	A	Detroit Mackenzie	1:28.2y	Andre Payne, Ron Duncan, Ed Glass, Gary Quick

1973	A	Saginaw	1:29.9y	Larry Foster, Bob Chapman, Willie Dawkins, Reggie Jones
1974	A	Livonia Bentley	1:29.0y	Bill Brown, Rich Hammil, Darrell Ditzhazy, Brian Murphy
1975	A	Saginaw	1:28.2y	Ricky Flowers, Reggie Carter, Dan Abraham, Henry McClung
1976	A	Flint Southwestern	1:27.0y*	James Feaster, Booker Moore, Brad Simpson, James Brewer
1977	A	Detroit Kettering	1.27.7y	Stanley Edwards, John Anthony, Paul Butler, Deon Hogan
1978	A	Flint Southwestern	1:28.4y	Anthony Battle, Norman Graham, Brian Carpenter, Reggie Mitchell
1979	A	Detroit Pershing	1:28.0y	John Hill, Ron Jackson, James Lanum, DeWayne Robinson
1980	A	Detroit Central	1:26.9y*	David Beasley, Steve Jones, Jeff Hardy, Demetrius Hallums
1981	A	Detroit Cooley	1:29.3y	James Johnson, Ricky Simpson, Ray Calloway, Alex Hall
1982	A	Detroit Central	1:27.1	Davis Beasley, Vincent Hall, Marc Jett, William White
1983	A	Flint Northern	1:27.9	Will Palmer, Quinton Estes, Chris Williams, Anthony Bowie
1984	A	Jackson	1:27.7	Kurt Russell, Fred Parker, James Smith, Michael Parker
1985	A	Lansing Everett	1:26.77*	Andy Bunnell, Rod Whittington, Chuck Phillips, Ken Thompson
1986	A	Detroit Cooley	1:28.10	Clearnes Harris, Rodney Thompson, Benjamin Purkett, Daryl Stallworth
1987	A	Lansing Sexton	1:27.92	Stanley Wheeler, Roget Ware, Allan Haller, Paris Milton
1988	A	Southfield	1:27.41	Bobby Johnson, Jeff Reynolds, Ron Hairston, Jason Booker
1989	A	Southfield	1:28.2	Bobby Johnson, Jeff Reynolds, Cassidy Wright, Marvin Reynolds
1990	A	Detroit Mumford	1:28.82	Cecil Flanigan, Aaron Hayden, Maurice Allen, Robert Ellington
1991	A	Saginaw	1:28.01	Mike Grant, Mike Brown, Kevin Bond, Nate Simington
1992	A	Battle Creek Central	1:29.13	Jeremy Miller, Ricky Weaver, Quincy Armstrong, Reggie Vick
1993	A	Detroit Cass Tech	1:28.60	Antonio Rush, Clarence Williams, Jabari Johnson, Kerry Walker
1994	A	Detroit Cass Tech	1:25.0*	Fred Wilkerson, Clarence Williams, Jabari Johnson, Daryl Rankins
1995	A	Detroit Cass Tech	1:28.78	Steve Jenkins, Nevara Smith, Darryl Rankins, Clarence Williams
1996	A	Pontiac Central	1:28.9	Jonathon Hall, Jalilu Mayo, Gerald Rasool, Roland Eaton
1997	A	Pontiac Central	1:28.52	Jonathon Hall, Gerald Rasool, Jalilu Mayo, Sherrod Maye
1998	A	Detroit Central	1:28.31	Andre Henry, Dangelo Smith, Harold Harris, Steve Cooper
1999	A	Pontiac Central	1:28.03	Tarrance Daugherty, Peter Durham, Kalandrus Powell, Antawain Ball
2000	D1	Saginaw	1:28.16*	Lawrence Easter, Roy Manning, Jeremiah McLaurin, Charles Rogers
2001	D1	Detroit Cass Tech	1:27.50*	Lorenzo Mallette, Pierre Vinson, Lance Gailliard, Johnie Drake
2002	D1	Detroit Mumford	1:27.32*	Kelvin Jackson, Lorenzo Williams, Thomas Rogers, Kenneth Ferguson
2003	D1	Pontiac Northern	1:27.04*	Henry Jackson, Anthony Cato, Darryn Moore, Phil Davis
2004	D1	Detroit Mumford	1:27.14	Marcus Thigpen, Keith Hewlett, Andrew Hollie, Cedric Everson
2005	D1	Detroit Mumford	1:27.66	Cedric Everson, Emanuel Killebrew, Vincent Brown, Tayan Jackson
2006	D1	Romulus	1:28.07	Darryl White, Mario Crawford, Donzell Carter, Shane Wells
2007	D1	Ann Arbor Pioneer	1.27.95	Paris Horgrow, Dennis Fortson, James Wade, James Smith
2008	D1	Flint Carman-Ainsworth	1:28.00	Tyjuan Jones, Sean Bradley, Roscoe Payne, Jahmar Rashad
2009	D1	East Kentwood	1:26.72*	Jon Henry, Tyrone Green, Dallas Wade, Christian Jessie
2011	D1	East Kentwood	1:26.34*	Ricco Hall, Chris James, Houston Glass, Jalen Stovall
2012	D1	Grand Blanc	1:28.21	Stefon White, Jalen Cureton, Damonta' Madden, Alton Yarbrough
2013	D1	East Kentwood	1:27.72	Houston Glass, Devin McKinney, Kewon Getter, Kevin Smith
2014	D1	East Kentwood	1:27.09	Ashley Bailey, Kevin Smith, Devin McKinney, Michael Catching
2015	D1	Monroe	1:27.42	Dathan Dickerson, Corey Gooodloe, Marlon Martin, Stephen Blunt
2016	D1	East Kentwood	1:26.27*	Khance Meyers, Ansel Jeffries, Shane Harris, Andre Welch
2017	D1	East Kentwood	1:26.07*	Stephen Bracey, Jacoby Welch, AJ Jeffries, Khance Meyers
2018	D1	Detroit King	1:26.74	Jaeveyon Morton, Dylan Brown, Dequan Finn, Jalen McGaughy

4 x 200 – Class B/Division 2 Champions

(y=4 x 220 yards)

1909	B	Traverse City	1:42.6y*	Harry Wait, Walter Hanson, Fred Pierson, Lester Simpson
1910	B	Shelby	1:39.6y*	Steve Lyttle, Erwin Anderson, Clifford Harrison, Vern Souter
1911	B	Alpena	1:41.0y	Clarence Desjardens, Cecil Corbin, Edward Harris, Joseph Comstock
1913	B	St. Louis	1:40.4y	Elmer Hanna, Robert Durkee, Thomas Brewer, Wright Harrison
1914	B	Coldwater	1:39.6y*	Frank Sullivan, Roscoe Stewart, Harold Corson, Alfred Gamble
1915	B	Alma	1:39.6y*	Howard Handley, James Howe, Harold Davis, Malcom Smith
1916	B	Paw Paw	1:39.2y*	Kirk Harrington, Grant McFarlind, Clark McFarlind, Art Nunn
1917	B	Alma	1:44.8y	James Howe, Howard Walker, Verne Hirschberger, Herbert Wheaton
1918		No Meet – World War I		
1919	B	Bangor	1:41.4y	Loren Fausnaugh, Jim Northrup, Merlin Hepenstein, Ralph Dibble
1920	B	Petoskey	1:43.6y	Don Bailey, Harold Riggles, Don Henry, Don Hamill
1921	B	Allegan	1:37.4y*	Gerald Ritchie, Paul Streeter, Dow Keene, Kent Pritchard
1922	B	Allegan	1:36.8y*	Gerald Ritchie, Wayne Edgerton, Dow Keene, Kent Pritchard
1923	B	Allegan	1:35.1y*	Donald Fleser, Dow Keene, Wayne Edgerton, Lewis Ely
1924	B	Wyandotte Roosevelt	1:33.5y*	Earl Reidel, Lloyd Seestadt, Bob Rogers, Nick Nixon
1925	B	Niles	1:36.5y	Loren Dittmar, Louis Peters, Lothaire Hall, Lawrence Kendrick
1926	B	Kalamazoo State High	1:42.2y	Andrew Kline, Harry Holman, William Dole, Robert Godfrey
1927	B	Allegan	1:38.3y	Henry Sisson, Bernard McNutt, Haskell Baker, Ted Lange
1928	B	Wyandotte Roosevelt	1:35.7y	Walter Dysert, Melvin Moore, Norman Horen, Charles McColl
1929	B	Monroe	1:34.7y	Fred Schatte, John Benedict, Bruce Clark, Ronald Sayle
1930	B	Monroe	1:32.9y*	Fred Schatte, Bruce Clark, John Benedict, Bernard Roberts
1931	B	River Rouge	1:36.5y	Merlin Navarre, Leonard Fraser, Clarence Sabbath, Harold Michaelis
1932	B	Allegan	1:34.9y	George Humm, Harold Bussey, Ken Plotts, Chuck Smith
1933	B (tie)	Birmingham	1:34.4y	William Guckleberg, Clark Matthews, Don Donaldson, John McKee
1933	B (tie)	Allegan	1:34.4y	Red Conley, George Humm, Harold Bussey, Chuck Smith
1934	B	Dowagiac	1:33.7y	Charles Mosher, Allen Cisco, Mark Van Riper, Arthur Frontczak
1935	B	Niles	1:34.3y	Melvin Rahn, Homer Keck, Bob Prenkert, Raymond Zoller
1936	B	Niles	1:35.4y	Willard Sarley, Gerald Day, Dewayne Masten, Raymond Zoller
1937	B	Birmingham	1:37.3y	Clark Collins, Frank O'Donnell, Phil Carey, Byron Colgrove
1938	B	East Lansing	1:32.5y*	Bob McCarthy, Dick Morris, John Miller, Ron Mead
1939	B	Kalamazoo State High	1:34.8y	James Thomas Torgenson, Karl Shuart Gerald Koopsen
1940	B	Fremont	1:34.7y	Fred Bowman, Howard Detroiters, Dave Jackson, Walter Derby
1941	B	Mt Pleasant	1:34.1y	Andrew Clark, John Burgess, Melvin Detroitwiler, Terry Carey
1942	B	Birmingham	1:34.7y	Stan Peterson, Bob Murray, Joe Armstrong, Jack Steelman
1943		No Meet – World War II		
1944	B	East Grand Rapids	nt	Jim Miller, Don Krannenberg, Bob Lee, Bob Swain

1945	B	East Grand Rapids	1:33.0y	Jim Miller, Don Krannenberg, Bob Lee, Bob Swain
1946	B	Ecorse	1:35.9y	Bill Yarborough, Andrew McKinney, Rufus Underwood, Ulysses Rogers
1947	B	Ecorse	1:35.5y	Bill Yarborough, Ben Cook, James Bibbs, Ulysses Rogers
1948	B	Ypsilanti Central	1:34.6y	Dave Hill, Russell Van Slyke, Lawrence Perry, Normal Walker
1949	B	Birmingham	1:33.7y	Joel Ross, Jere McMillin, Rollie McGinnis, Bob Folin
1950	B	Sturgis	1:34.6y	Carl Harker, Joe Linder, Jack Frahrup, Mke Krebeer
1951	B	Cadillac	1:35.5y	Duane Eley, Bert Zagers, Walt Ransome, Dale Stevens
1952	B	Roseville	1:37.4y	Bob Wagner, Calvin Ford, Jack Kirchkoff, Bob Zimmerman
1953	B	Inkster	1:33.1y	Otis Lee, Herman Frederick, Guy Rogers, Lavel Rogers,
1954	B	Inkster	1:31.4y*	Herman Frederick, Arthur Frederick, Charles Calloway, Otis Lee
1955	B	Inkster	1:32.6y	Charles Keyser, Bill Wyatt, Charles Calloway, Art Frederick
1956	B	Inkster	1:31.0y*	Charles Calloway, Charles Bond, Bill Wyatt, Charles Keyser
1957	B	Inkster	1:34.5y	Warren Jenkins, Ed Sluter, Bill Wyatt, Charles Keyser
1958	B	Willow Run	1:31.8y	Naosha Poe, Melvin Austin, Otis Harrison, Willie Prewitt
1959	B	Willow Run	1:33.2y	Noasha Poe, Melvin Austin, Cliff Beelers, Otis Harrison
1960	B	Ecorse	1:34.4y	Harry Seymour, Ben Stevenson, Sam Palmore, Charles Gray
1961	B	Cranbrook	1:31.6y	John Schafer, Bob Hicks, George Bisbee, Barney Crouse
1962	B	River Rouge	1:32.6y	Will Gohlston, Leo Welch, Ted Burnley, Vern Smith
1963	B	River Rouge	1:33.8y	John Sykes, Willie Betts, Boice Bowman, Theodore Burnley
1964	B	River Rouge	1:30.3y*	Clarence Sabbath, Willie Betts, John Sykes, Boice Bowman
1965	B	River Rouge	1:32.1y	Chester Wright, Will Wright, Eugene Wilson, Clarence Sabbath
1966	B	Cranbrook	1:31.0y	Ed Randle, Bruce Hunter, Warren Craig, Craig Tallberg
1967	B	Ecorse	1:31.7y	Charles Griffin, Eric George, Art Small, Dewayne Gardner
1968	B	Detroit East Catholic	1:31.3y	Al Henderson, Jeff Sinclair, James Carruthers, Al Jones
1969	B	Ecorse	1:31.7y	Ron Trotter, Darryl Stalworth, Ellis Felten, Oscar Suddarth
1970	B	Wyoming Park	1:31.4y	James Veenendall, James Courter, Daniel Rittenhouse, William Buchanan
1971	B	Grand Rapids West Catholic	1:30.0y*	Pat Sobel, Larry Kubiak, Greg Herda, Rick Jackson
1972	B	Ecorse	1:32.3y	Deforest Stallworth, Stanley Gardner, Dwayne Stallworth, Edward Perkins
1973	B	Ecorse	1:31.9y	Carlos Henderson, Stanley Gardner, Dwayne Stallworth, Deforest Stallworth
1974	B	Dearborn Heights Robichaud	1:29.3y*	Ron Woodson, Calvin Green, Johnny Allen, Wes Jones
1975	B	Wyoming Park	1:31.1y	Dave Fopma, Chuck Walker, Dan Molyneux, Mike Ball
1976	B	River Rouge	1:30.2y	Wesley Thomas, Tracy DeWitt. Kelvin McGhee, Frank Fields
1977	B	Flint Beecher	1:30.0y	Ken Miller, Henry Young, James Carr, Ken Banks
1978	B	Dearborn Heights Robichaud	1:30.6y	James Rhea, Mark Woodson, Bruce Swasey, Earl Kendall
1979	B	Ecorse	1:30.2y	Michael Dunlap, Chris London, Calvin Butler, Calvin Warren
1980	B	Oak Park	1:30.4	Darryl Jones, Paul Estelle, Mike Sturduvant, James Taylor
1980	B	Saginaw Buena Vista	1:30.4y	Tim Houston. Kernef Jackson, Ken Haynes, Ricky Swilley
1981	B	Ecorse	1:29.0*	Rodney Nedd, Brian Pope, Willie Thomas, Jamie Weathers
1982	B	University of Detroit Jesuit	1:30.1y	Marc Crenshaw, Sekou Molette, Hugh Barrington, Chris Aldridge
1983	B	Flint Beecher	1:30.1	Jeff Sharp, Andre Hall, Carl Ellison, Blain Houston
1984	B	Ypsilanti Lincoln	1:30.1	Zach Price, Mark Lewis, Ghassan Ramada, Randy Robertson
1985	B	Detroit Benedictine	1:29.42	Charles Winston, Charles Wilson, Shon Somerville, Cedric Green
1986	B	Detroit Benedictine	1:28.3*	Charles Winston, Charles Wilson. Shon Somerville, Cedric Green
1987	B	Flint Beecher	1:30.15	Lewane Harris, Courtney Hawkins, Lee Speights, Stacy Watson
1988	B	Detroit East Catholic	1:28.50	Zekiel Miller, Derald Penn, Reginald Golfin, Jeff Simmons
1989	B	Grand Rapids Northview	1:28.8	Andy Korytkowski, Mickey Wallce, Brent Dickerson, Shane Sieracki
1990	B	Three RIvers	1:29.6	Mike Shea, Dennis Posey, Mark Thurman, Sam Brown
1991	B	Oxford	1:29.99	Vidal Fragoso, Steve McCracken, Cliff Wells, Erik Welch
1992	B	Flint Beecher	1:29.71	Antwan Williams, Obleton Perry, Jimmy Lacy, Garth Spight
1993	B	Detroit UD Jesuit	1:28.23*	William Brooks, Jim Krol, Edzra Gibson, Chris Polk
1994	B	Comstock	1:29.32	J.B. Thomas, Aaron Gardner, Nathan Smeltzer, Randy Hunt
1995	B	Comstock	1:32.01	T.J. Fields, J.B. Thomas, Terrance Bowden, Quentin Hunt
1996	B	Wyoming Godwin Heights	1:30.3	Tim Matthews, William Hall, Marlon Crosby, Larry Copeland
1997	B	Dowagiac	1:29.72	Brent Lesniak, Jamie White, Jonas Crump, Marco Wolverton
1998	B	Corunna	1:29.16	Dustin Bower, Kasper Kazmer, Keagan Kazmer, Robbie Currie
1999	B	Romulus	1:30.97	Fred Russell, Ashley Terry, Derrik Radford, Mike Woods
2000	D2	Ypsilanti Lincoln	1:29.60*	Shaun Reed, Kenny Williams, Aaron Brewer, Stanley Roberson
2001	D2	Ypsilanti	1:30.01	De'Andre Nixon, Jason Bird, Mike Gleason, Sean Heard
2002	D2	Lansing Waverly	1:28.67*	Justin Boyd, Michael Bailey, Terry Tyson, Abram McCoy
2003	D2	Linden	1:30.37	Ryan Norman, Jordan Norman, Jeff Krause, Mett Keenan
2004	D2	Flint Kearsley	1:29.62	Kyle Bergquist, Chris Velez, Peter O'Brien, Tony Parcels
2005	D2	East Lansing	1:28.90	Matt Paris, Isaac Harper, Forest Raymond, Jean Pitts
2006	D2	Orchard Lake St Mary	1:28.38*	Diote Allen, Taurian Washington, Aaron Gant, Anthony Bowman
2007	D2	East Lansing	1:28.42	Will Slanger-Grant, Austin Lintemuth, Ali Philman, Isaac Harper
2008	D2	East Lansing	1:28.93	Will Slanger-Grant, Austin Lintemuth, Ali Philman, Isaac Harper
2009	D2	Hamilton	1:28.49	Austin Schild, Matt Tyink, David Ptacek, Zach Heerspink
2010	D2	Flint Southwestern	1:28.17*	Johnathon Clark, Michael Johnson, Kendric Roberts, Justin Clark
2011	D2	Auburn Hills Avondale	1:28.11*	Nathan Chapman, Takemi Smith, Jeff Douglas, Trevon Salter
2012	D2	Lansing Sexton	1:27.99*	Kendell Jackson, Adrian Sanchez, David Washington, Anthony Goodman
2013	D2	Grand Rapids Ottawa Hills	1:28.16	Shawn Kneeland, Sam Beal, Jacori Millbrooks, Tayland Avery
2014	D2	Orchard Lake St Mary	1:29.18	Ross Moore, Kahlee Hamler, Ryan Johnson, Tyler Conchran
2015	D2	Orchard Lake St Mary	1:28.67	Ross Moore, Kahlee Hamler, Kahlee Hamler, Ky'Ren Cunningham
2016	D2	Orchard Lake St Mary	1:27.71*	Richard Bowens, Shermond Dabney, Kanlee Hamler, Ky'Ren Cunningham
2017	D2	Wyoming Godwin Heights	1:29.38	Maurice Vinson, Christopher Libbett, Kelvyn Valdez, Tamar Williams
2018	D2	Zeeland East	1:29.67	Gabe Taylor, Alex Stockdale, Bryce Metzger, Corbin DeJonge

4 x 200 – Class C/Division 3 Champions

(y=4 x 220 yards)

1921	C	Plymouth	1:40.4y*	Floyd Miller, Lavern Williams, Ward Walker, Harold Stevens
1922	C	Dearborn	1:37.6y*	Albert Fey, William Sweitzer, Louis Pfeiffer, Forrest McGuigan
1923	C	Plainwell	1:35.7y*	Alan McLean, Donald McLean, Archie Sunnerville, Donald Camp
1924	C	Morenci	1:37.6y	Paul Sutton, Donald Schoonover, James Miller, Allan Morningstar
1925	C	Wayland	1:38.4y	Glen McCasland, Walter Robsen, Lloyd Broker, Leo Halloran
1926	C	Otsego	1:37.3y	L. Waters, Gerald Miller, Lincoln Rush, Melbourne Button

1927	C	Plainwell	1:36.1y	Ron Hutchinson, Robert Scott, Donald Payne, Russell Pell
1928	C	Yale	1:36.8y	Osborn Slosser, Francis Staley, Joe Salerno, Everett Williams
1929	C	Plainwell	1:37.0y	Herman Scott, John Crosby, Lyle Earl, John Dean
1930	C	Kalamazoo St. Augustine	1:36.8y	Lee Muth, Larry Maher, Henry Kennedy, Johnny Tooker
1931	C	Algonac	1:37.4y	Walter Thomas, Lawrence Avers, Charles Bell, Gilson Pearsall
1932	C	Kalamazoo State High	1:34.8y*	Forrest Tanner, Ty Carter, Paul Krielick, Lawrence Russell
1933	C	Lowell	1:36.2y	Ray Dinson, Greg Harris, Jim Green Joe Schwab
1934	C	Paw Paw	1:34.7y*	James Jennings, Dave Warner, Al Murvin, Alan Smith
1935	C	Paw Paw	1:34.0y*	Dave Warner, Louis Oswalt, Joseph Lula, Alan Smith
1936	C	Paw Paw	1:38.8y	Louis Lelli, Dave Warner, Warren Ampey, Louis Oswalt
1937	C	Grant	1:39.8y	Jack Holton, Max Saur, Leon Brink, Max Brink
1938	C	Algonac	1:34.1y	Edward Stevens, Arthur Cuthbertson, Graham Grant, James Clark
1939	C	Flint Bendle	1:36.3y	Vincent Balsamo, Bill Ferrier, Dan Middleton, Dale Buerger
1940	C	Comstock Park	1:37.2y	Albert DeVoogd, Glen Haney, Ed Steffens, Richard Holland
1941	C	St. Clair Shores South Lake	1:34.7y	Art Willet, Don Knight, Don Harm, Henry Tomei
1942	C	Ann Arbor University High	1:34.6y	Miguel Suarez, John Gault, Bob Jamison, George Brown
1943		No Meet – World War II		
1944	C	St. Clair Shores Lake Shore	1:36.6y	Howard Tanner, Joe Banks, George Starling, Richard Green
1945	C	St. Clair Shores Lake Shore	1:35.2y	Richard Green, John Williams, James Mahon, Joe Banks
1946	C	Ypsilanti Roosevelt	1:37.0y	Jerry Connolly, Clark Pester, Don Vest, Keith Gundrum
1947	C	Ypsilanti Roosevelt	1:38.1y	Jerry Connolly, Don Vest, Emil Bair, Clark Pester
1948	C	East Grand Rapids	1:34.2y	Karl Newman, Bill Durkee, Charles Webber, Alan Pardoe
1949	C	East Grand Rapids	1:35.4y	Karl Newman, Bill Durkee, Al Pardoe, Jim Chamberlain
1950	C	East Grand Rapids	1:34.1y	Fred Newman, Tom Payette, Alan Pardoe, Charles Webber
1951	C	Ann Arbor University High	1:37.9y	Wayne Marine, Dave Zahn, Bill Weiner, Bon Hobbs
1952	C	Whitehall	1:37.7y	Osie Rostic, Jerry Lewis, Clayton Anthony, John Mull
1953	C	Okemos	1:36.5y	Bob Davidson, Lyle Davis, Gerald Rouse, Dick Ewing
1954	C	Lansing Everett	1:34.3y	Ted Ohmer, Gary Munson, Gene Guile, Dean Look
1955	C	Roseville Eastern	1:35.0y	Frank Serazlo, Dan Hamilton, Ourillo Carrizalas, Pete Carrizalas
1956	C	Lansing Everett	1:34.7y	Jerry Squires, Rog Quinn, Dick Gilmore, Dean Look
1957	C	Mt Clemens St Mary	1:34.3y	Bill Nebel, Frank Presley, Barney Peltier, Jack Nebel
1958	C	Ypsilanti Roosevelt	1:35.4y	Bill McKenzie, Bob Kidd, Phil Clark, Bob Wilcox
1959	C	Nashville	1:37.0y	Dennis Lamie, Bill Lynch, Vic Mauer, Ray Rousch
1960	C	Haslett	1:36.2y	Jim Chambers, Don Bongard, Warren Kent, James Sherman
1961	C	Michigan Lutheran Seminary	1:34.4y	Dennis Gorsline, Dick Tesauro, Alan Behnke, Don Koeppen
1962	C	Lansing St Mary	1:33.5y*	Dick McCloy, Tom Radigan, Dan Bozzo, Bill Van Zwoll
1963	C	Capac	1:33.6y	Ken Adamski, Louie Berard, Jon Ceranski, John Staniloiu
1964	C	Battle Creek St Phillip	1:32.6y*	Dave Austin, Jim Bauman, Herb Tillman, Mike Poyer
1965	C	Farwell	1:33.0y	Duane Updyke, Rod Rumrill, Bill McLand, Dennis Dawson
1966	C	Battle Creek St Phillip	1:32.8y	Jack Schroeder, Ralph Skinner, Jerry Quartermain, John McVeigh
1967	C	Detroit Country Day	1:33.9y	Andy Ditzhazy, John Means, Randall Dowis, Casey McWilliams
1968	C	Detroit Country Day	1:33.9y	Andy Ditzhazy, John Means, Tom Shriner, Jeff Wilson
1969	C	Detroit East Catholic	1:33.4y	Ben Jolie, Herman Riley, Jim Carruthers, Al Jones
1970	C	Reading	1:34.1y	Ken Burger, Fred Mason, Bill Bridgeon, Tom Burger
1970	C	Shepherd	1:34.0y	Pat Farnam, Rick Lantz, Neal Brickner, Doug White
1971	C	Detroit Country Day	1:32.7y	Jack McClellen, Jim Miller, Dave Ratajack, Mike Page
1972	C	Decatur	1:31.7y*	Tim Creagan, Doug Athey, Scott Athey, Steve Jannsen
1973	C	Detroit DePorres	1:32.3y	Charles Walls, William Brown, Benson Triplett, Tony Tillman
1974	C	Detroit Servite	1:31.2y*	Dennie Hayden, Alvin Pelt, James Phillips, George Fuller
1975	C	Wyoming Lee	1:32.1y	Jeff Lark, Phil Cole, Scott Kidder, Larry Booker
1976	C	Riverview Gabriel Richard	1:30.8y*	Ken Naszrodi, John Putz, Mike Partipilla, Doug Kourin
1977	C	Royal Oak Shrine	1:32.4y	Jim Smith, Nate McDonald, Jim Baver, Darwin Gibson
1978	C	Detroit Benedictine	1:31.5y	William Crews, John Manchell, Ron Johnson, Ray Washington
1979	C	Detroit Benedictine	1:29.2y*	Joe Curtis, Garrett Alexander, Creston Gray, Ray Washington
1980	C	Detroit Benedictine	1:32.2	Donald Barnes, Thomas Manchell, Garrett Alexander, Joseph Curtis
1981	C	Detroit Lutheran West	1:30.5	Dwight Tyson, Kinzel Forrest, Eric Webster, Chris Howie
1982	C	Detroit Lutheran West	1:29.1*	Dwight Tyson, Kinzel Forrest, Erik Frederick, Chris Howie
1983	C	Detroit Lutheran West	1:29.2	Joe Corbett, Mark Garner, Brett Dawsey, Erik Frederick
1984	C	Flint Hamady	1:31.0	Robert Jackson, Sylvester Johnson, Ray Buckner, Lionel White
1985	C	Flint Academy	1:31.34	Tyrone Motley, Sebastian Robinson, Michael Lewis, Richard Russell
1986	C	Detroit DePorres	1:31.45	Marcus Norwood, Rodney Colver, Bryant Stalworth, Tony Fleming
1987	C	Detroit Lutheran West	1:30.47	Greg Harris, Ben Jones, Oscar Ford, Tom Robinson
1988	C	Eau Claire	1:29.8	Kevin Moore, Dennis Alexander, Doug Miller, Todd Anderson
1989	C	Saginaw Nouvel	1:31.24	Warren Strong, Dave Lopez, Sheldon Murphy, Tony Jackson
1990	C	Parchment	1:31.60	Steve Maentz, Phil Collison, Eric Russell, Pat Russell
1991	C	Eau Claire	1:32.5	Rodney Stevens, Mike Robinson, James Atterberry, Eric Campbell-Johnson
1992	C	Detroit DePorres	1:32.0	Haywood Allen, Ronald Bogus, Herbie Harris, Adrian Edwards
1993	C	New Haven	1:31.07	Billy Chenault, Fred Jamison, John Mack, Greg Bryant
1994	C	Breckenridge	1:30.2	Dave Gillis, Chad Colllins, Torry Gagne, Dan Gillis
1995	C	New Haven	1:30.83	Billy Chenault, Glen Clark, Cliff Akers, John Mack
1996	C	New Haven	1:30.56	Clifford Akers, Tedaro France, John Mack, Travis Kelly
1997	C	Centreville	1:30.48	Kelvin Singleton, John Coomer, Ryan Morris, Nick Anders
1998	C	Cassopolis	1:31.88	Ronald Austin, Zachary Stratton, Malachi Walker, Karlton O'Daniel
1999	C	Albion	1:30.17	Dominic Reed, Tonae Hannah, Kevin Davis, Darryl Nicholson
2000	D3	Berrien Springs	1:31.13*	David Snide, Kenny Fetke, Joe Cecil, San Cezil
2001	D3	Stockbridge	1:31.82	Gerald Gendernalik, Ray Partin, Eric Bradbury, Matt Kunzelm
2002	D3	Detroit Country Day	1:30.78*	Phil Damaska, Jon Gupta, Derrick Carter, Kim Thompson
2003	D3	Dearborn Heights Robichaud	1:30.94	Renaldo Major, Maurice Love, Devin Laird, Issac Hendricks
2004	D3	Detroit Country Day	1:29.04*	Chris Rucker, Earnie Jackson, Martin Corniffe, Phil Damaska
2005	D3	Detroit Country Day	1:29.78	Jonas Gray, Erik Williams, Martin Corniffe, Chris Rucker
2006	D3	Detroit Country Day	1:27.95*	Chris Rucker, Erik Williams, Jonas Gray, Matin Corniffe
2007	D3	Detroit Country Day	1:28.39	Chris Rucker, Erik Williams, Brian Tan, Jonas Gray
2008	D3	Albion	1:29.83	Todd Atchison, Mike Ridley, Patrick Dewalt, Durant Crum
2009	D3	Albion	1:30.39	Patrick Dewalt, Ryan Hopson, Darius Crum, Todd Atchison

2010	D3	Livonia Clarenceville	1:30.51	LeVonte Brooks, Moses Hobson, Leonard Hogan, Kassius Kelly
2011	D3	Lansing Catholic	1:29.89	LeVonte Brooks, Moses Hobson, Leonard Hogan, Kassius Kelly
2012	D3	Lansing Catholic	1:29.73	Conner Caporale, Zach Zingsheim, Matt Macksood, Cedric Lee
2013	D3	Wyoming Kelloggsville	1:31.10	Cameron Love, Maquis Thurman, T.J. Burnett, Reginald Roberts
2014	D3	Sanford Meridian	1:28.99	Charles Ellithorpe, Jacob Wenzlick, Jacob Ham, Kevin Scheibert
2015	D3	Marlette	1:30.78	Hunter McGinnis, Andrew Storm, Connor Thomas, Michael Morrison
2016	D3	Sanford Meridian	1:29.21	Christian Petre. Miles LaViere, Monte Petre, Andre Smith
2017	D3	Chesaning	1:29.55	Zach McFarlan, Brady Friaser, Brandon Keys, Sam Forsyth
2018	D3	Coloma	1:28.61	Caleb Ellis, Sincere Taylor, Josh Young, Derek Plitt

4 x 200 – Class D/Division 4 Champions

(y=4 x 220 yards)

1927	D	Trenton	1:39.7y*	Henry Lebeau, William Sutherby, Clarence Swartz, Irwin Kemp
1928	D	Okemos	1:39.5y*	Howard McClure, Ralph Guile, Fred Miles, Frank Coleman
1929	D	Centreville	1:40.0y	T Yearson, Gregory Mosher, Lee Barnes, D Breckenridge
1930	D	Centreville	1:39.7y	Leon Barnes, Carl Awe, Gregory Mosher, Rex Beckwith
1931	D	Centreville	1:39.9y	Lester Walters, Donald Tessman, Munson Perry, Gregory Mosher
1932	D	St. Clair Shores South Lake	1:38.4y*	Ed Kurtshals, George Farrell, Charles Defer, Tom Reynolds
1933	D	Portage	1:39.3y	John Kuiper, Bert Wilson, Olin Kinney, Bernard Meyer
1934	D	Centreville	nt	Earl Walters, Clifton Frazier, Munson Perry, Donald Tesman
1935	D	St. Clair Shores Lakeview	1:37.4y*	Alvin Wunderlich, Frank Kohler, Edward Stanley, Basil Williams
1936	D	Onekama	1:38.7y	Leo Kelly, Russell McCurdy, Thomas Miller, Frank Figgles
1937	D	Bloomfield Hills	1:40.2y	Richard Shepherd, Don Sawyer, Richard Flannery, Arthur Gibson
1938	D	Bloomfield Hills	1:37.9y	Richard Shepherd, Robert Hall, Sam Vettraino, Gordon Craig
1939	D	Bloomfield Hills	1:38.5y	Richard Shepherd, Leon Sawyer, Richard Flannery, Gordon Craig
1940	D	Michigan School for Deaf	1:37.2y*	Carl Mobley, Wayne Hiar, William Griswold, Tommy O'Connell
1941	D	White Pigeon	1:37.6y	George Catton, Jack Eckerle, Lloyd Black, Dale Gray
1942	D	White Pigeon	1:36.4y*	Lloyd Black, Robert Thulin, George Catton, Louis LaGro
1943		No Meet – World War II		
1944	D	Glen Arbor Leelanau School	nt	Paul Odette, Lee Funderburg, Jack East, Bob Jackson
1945	D	Michigan School for Deaf	1:39.4y	Tony Hudecek, Melvin Brow, Charles Whitetree, Arlon Dennison
1946	D	Michigan School for Deaf	1:40.9y	Tony Hudecek, Caesar Bladecki, Melvin Brow, Arlon Dennison
1947	D	Baroda	1:38.8y	Ken Arend, Art Shedler, Earl Arend, Donald Gast
1948	D	Bloomfield Hills	1:36.5y	Jack MacGregor, Richard Blake, Dick Miner, Richard Pohl
1949	D	Michigan School for Deaf	1:38.8y	Charles Allen, Gene Ramberg, Monroe Dials, Richard Ewald
1950	D	Michigan School for Deaf	1:36.9y	Don Boone, Ted Corrin, Charles Allen, Richard Ewald
1951	D	Brethren	1:39.5y	Fred Beane, Richard Beane, Burt Burns, Bob Phillips
1952	D	Brethren	1:42.3y	Richard Beane, Bert Burns, Don Stroup, Bob Phillips
1953	D	Brethren	1:36.4y*	Richard Beane, Burt Burns, Daryl Leckrone, Bob Phillips
1954	D (tie)	Brethren	1:37.1y	Richard Beane, Walter Thomas, Daryl Leckrone, Bob Phillips
1954	D (tie)	Spring Arbor	1:37.1y	John Sipes, Dean Latta, Bill Barkwell, Paul Lynch
1955	D	Brethren	1:37.2y	Walt Thomas, Charles Beane, Norman Burns, Ken Beane
1956	D	Covert	1:36.8y	Art Nelson, John Young, Howard Blanks, Quincy Johnson
1957	D	Covert	1:39.4y	Jerome Crockett, Sid Woods, Jack Henry, Quincy Johnson
1958	D	Brethren	1:34.5y*	Lawrence Connolly, Frank Thomas, Charles Beane, Ken Beane
1959	D	Parma Western	1:39.1y	Larry Peterson, Steve Clark, Harold Dunker, Neil Cornstubble
1960	D	Grass Lake	nt	Dick Beal, Rick Corey, Dave Daken, Al Kaiser
1961	D	Michigan School for Deaf	1:35.5y	Don Smith, Wilbert Reed, Caswell Hassell, Brown Jordan
1962	D	Michigan School for Deaf	1:35.0y	Gary Blumerick, Dom Zito, Don Smith, Caswell Hassell
1963	D	Michigan School for Deaf	1:35.0y	Bill Hoffmeyer, Anson Mitchell, Dom Zito, Abram Powell
1964	D	Michigan School for Deaf	1:35.4y	Abram Powell, Bill Hoffmeyer, Richard Townsend, Steve Kovacs
1965	D	Ann Arbor University High	1:34.3y*	Sam Sturgis, Steve Spellman, Ralph Leing, Bill Bierwaltes
1966	D	Kalamazoo University	1:33.1y*	Mike Griffith, Dean Panse, Tom Mull, Mike Walters
1967	D	Ann Arbor University High	1:32.9y*	George Ging, Van Johnson, Dave Shipman, Jeff Donahey
1968	D	Unionville	1:34.9y	Art Alegria, Terry Houthoofd, Jim Weber, Steve Settler
1969	D	Grass Lake	1:34.6y	John White, Kevin Reithmiller, Bill Hack, Gary Siecrist
1970	D	Michigan School for Deaf	1:35.9y	Ken Hack, Bruce Kline, Dan Kuehn, Ed Robinson
1971	D	Michigan School for Deaf	1:34.2y	Dan Kuehn, Bruce Kline, Craig Schlorff, Ed Robinson
1972	D	Unionville	1:32.9y*	Ray Gokey, Dave Bitzer, Terry Balzer, Mike Gaeth
1973	D	Carsonville	1:34.4y	Jack Lechnyr, Jim Lechnyr, John Lechnyr, Jim Winkley
1974	D	North Muskegon	1:31.6y*	Ray Swanson, Ron Steele, Jim Pancy, Don Stafford
1975	D	Detroit DePorres	1:31.5y*	Charles Henry, Brian Houghton, Anthony Fuller, Stanley Young
1976	D	Detroit DePorres	1:30.5y*	Terrance Hines, Deron Early, Leonard Thornton, Brian Houghton
1977	D	Detroit DePorres	1:29.4y*	Leonard Thornton, Mark McClendon, Darold Gholston, Stanley Young
1978	D	Detroit DePorres	1:31.1y	Leonard Thornton, Robert Farmer, Vernon Lynch, Mike Taylor
1979	D	Detroit Country Day	1:31.9	Geoffrey Craig, Mark Fentreff, Ed Guindbi, David Kromm
1980	D	Detroit DePorres	1:30.5	Jerry Campbell, Greg Henderson, Vernon Lynch, Larry Jordan
1981	D	Detroit DePorres	1:31.1	Lebron Campbell, Greg Henderson, Clint Childs, Darryl Carter
1982	D	Detroit East Catholic	1:31.7	Stacy Cook, Eric King, Kevin Carter, Dwayne Grice
1983	D	Detroit East Catholic	1:31.2	Keith Thompson, Sean Jones, Kevin Carter, Robert Willhight
1984	D	Detroit East Catholic	1:29.92	Sean Jones, Michael Gatson, Kevin Carter, Robert Willhight
1985	D	Detroit East Catholic	1:31.89	Willy Scott, Jamal Walker, Reginald Golfin, Sean Jones
1986	D	Detroit East Catholic	1:31.95	Allen Mayes, Jamal Walker, Reginald Golfin, Jeff Simmons
1987	D	Detroit East Catholic	1:31.93	Derald Penn, Alton Mayes, Reginald Goffin, Jeff Simmons
1988	D	Ann Arbor Gabriel Richard	1:32.73	Josh Herrala, John Akujobi, Pat Richard, Kevin Henry
1989	D	Baldwin	1:32.2	Everett Goodson, Juron Johnson, Lavelle Jennings, Michael Turner
1990	D	Detroit Lutheran West	1:31.25	Damon Butler, Patrick VanHorn, Kevin Ford, Sean Harper
1991	D	Detroit Lutheran West	1:32.18	Laron Ellerbee, Howard Hughey, Damon Butler, Patrick VanHorn
1992	D	Detroit Lutheran West	1:33.10	Barrett Glover, Deulin Scarber, LaRon Ellerbee, Reggie Dawton
1993	D	Reading	1:33.5	Tony Britton, Kurt Willmont, Matt Myers, James Stumpf
1994	D	Battle Creek St Phillip	1:33.26	Ben McVeigh, Mike Hughes, J.J. Eldridge, Dieter Brown
1995	D	Pittsford	1:34.34	Brandon Brown, Dustin Ewing, Brock Wollett, Nick Salazar
1996	D	Pittsford	1:32.25	Dustin Ewing, Brandon Brown, Brock Wollett, Nick Salazar
1997	D	Pittsford	1:31.09	Dustin Ewing, Nick Salazar, Nick Grabowski, Brock Wollett,

1998	D	Mason County Eastern	1:31.1	James McCarthy, Derek Shoup, David Stanulis, Bob Reams
1999	D	Harper Woods Gallagher	1:31.13	Otis Jordan, Darnell Hood, Drake Williams, Markus Curry
2000	D4	Redford Borgess	1:30.00*	Darryl Anglin, Jose Kineannon, Daryl Robinson, Jason Smith
2001	D4	Redford Borgess	1:29.69*	Jose Kiocannon, Jason Smith, KeJuan Kea, Darryl Anglin
2002	D4	Redford Borgess	1:29.98	Edward Bruney, DeJuan Kea, Donald Ferrell, Jason Smith
2003	D4	Detroit Benedictine	1:30.34	Tayan Jackson, Andre King, Tony Lawrence, Daniel McKinney
2004	D4	Detroit DePorres	1:31.30	David Grimes, Anthony Bowman, Carlos Simpson, Carl Grimes
2005	D4	Detroit DePorres	1:29.83	David Grimes, Taurian Washington, Cortez Smith, Anthony Bowman
2006	D4	Flint Hamady	1:32.56	Deon Reed, Brendon Scott, Jordan Luster, Joshua Trouser
2007	D4	Springport	1:32.04	Leonard Sheldon, Tyler Tarpley, Eric Sargent, Jesse Holmes
2008	D4	Pewamo-Westphalia	1:31.70	Dale Spritzley, Jason Fedewa, Cory Noeker, Jay Spitzley
2009	D4	Muskegon Catholic	1:31.94	Major Melcalf, D'onte Foster, Jared Johnson, Steve Mitchell
2010	D4	White Pigeon	1:31.17	Mitch Johnson, Corey Wynkoop, Ryan Shoesmith, Tanner Nichols
2011	D4	Muskegon Catholic	1:32.83	Michael Heybloom, Tyler DePung, Zach Campbell, Damon Armstrong
2012	D4	Albion	1:32.18	Gary Chambers, Eliyah Yasha, Carles Sommerour, Nolen Mitchell
2013	D4	Albion	1:32.85	Jamil Short, Terrance Byrd, Bryan Peoples, Lawson Bright-Mitchell
2014	D4	Concord	1:31.46	Brett Lehman, Lonelie Langston, Chevy Burk, Lawson Bright-Mitchell
2015	D4	Detroit Loyola	1:31.84	Treveon Vaughn, Hunter Harris, Nicholas Lee, Harvey Caddell
2016	D4	Muskegon Catholic	1:31.30	Ben Treutler, Walker Christofferson, Logan Helton, Christian Martinez
2017	D4	Muskegon Catholic	1:32.25	Ben Treutler, Dawson Stiegman, Cameron Martinez, Tommy Watts
2018	D4	Fulton-Middleton	1:31.15	Tristan Johnston, Jon Baker, Adam Duflo, Nate Alwood

4 x 200 – UP Class AB/Division 1 Champions

(y=4 x 220 yards)

1940	UPB	Ironwood	1:38.1y*	Leonard Carpenter, Joe Kuker, Bennie Vronch, Verhelst
1941	UPB	Escanaba	1:37.5y*	Stuart Peterson, Bob Dufresne, Clarence Grabowski, Bob Craig
1942	UPB	Escanaba	1:38.4y	Bob DuFresne, Bob Morin, Fred Chepekis, Clarence Grabowski
1943		No Meet – World War II		
1944	UPB	Ironwood	1:38.1y	
1945	UPB	Sault Ste. Marie	1:37.8y	
1946	UPB	Ironwood	1:38.6y	
1947	UPB	Menominee	1:37.2y*	Mike Doyle, Jack McCormick, Ken Monson, Mike Shatusky
1948	UPB	Ironwood	1:37.5y	Erwin Erickson, H. Levinstein, Fred Halemo, H. Shaughnesy
1949	UPB	Menominee	1:35.4y*	Jack Anderson, Billy Wells, Emil Pontow, Billy Pontow
1950	UPB	Newberry	1:36.6y	Swanson, Boggs, Tom Taylor, Robert McDonald
1951	UPB	Sault Ste. Marie	1:40.0y	
1952	UPB	Sault Ste. Marie	1:38.7y	Dale Ferguson, Jim Booth, Jerome Tooler, John Bonnaci
1953	UPB	Sault Ste. Marie	1:38.6y	Ken Kusmiera, Henry Brown, Terry Martin, John Bonnaci
1954	UPB	Sault Ste. Marie	1:38.3y	Ken Kusmiera, Joe Stabile, Jack Young, Bob Flemal
1955	UPB	Iron River	1:37.9y	Eddie Vergara, Don Lundin, Jerry Gallagher, Gary Baumler
1956	UPB	Sault Ste. Marie	nt	
1957	UPB	Sault Ste. Marie	1:39.1y	Bill Cooper, John Fletcher, Larry Bosley, Fred Thompson
1958	UPB	Stephenson	1:39.9y	
1959	UPB	Marquette	1:37.9y	
1960	UPB	Manistique	1:36.5y	Ron Rubick, Dpug Tyrrell, Ron McDonough, Rqay Roussin
1961	UPB	Newberry	1:36.9y	Bob Brown, Gary Krueger, Charles Johnson, Don Anderson
1962	UPAB	Newberry	1:35.2y*	Bob Brown, Charles Johnson, Gary Krueger, John McCutcheon
1963	UPAB	Kingsford	1:36.0y	
1964	UPAB	Escanaba	1:34.3y*	Peter Bertrand, Chuck Brooks, Denny Remo, Wally Schultz
1965	UPAB	Kingsford	1:33.5y*	Dick Berlinski, Paul Santoni, Rich Freeman, Dave Raymond
1966	UPAB	Calumet	1:34.9y	George Oikarinen, Alfred Eckhart, Mark Kitti, Dennis Bal
1967	UPAB	Calumet	1:34.3y	Peter Oikarinen, George Oikarinen, Alfred Eckhart, Dennis Bal
1968	UPAB	Ishpeming	1:34.5y	
1969	UPAB	Marquette	1:35.5y	Dave Myers, Mike Brissette, Joe LaPorte, Jerry Slattery
1970	UPAB	Gwinn	1:32.1y*	Bob Octaluk, Jeff Hatfield, Ron Storti, Marty Klena
1971	UPAB	Rudyard	1:32.7y	
1972	UPAB	Rudyard	1:33.9y	
1973	UPAB	Iron Mountain	1:33.2y	Mike Branz, Mike Galbreath, Steve Mariucci, Jared Cudnohofsky
1974	UPAB	Escanaba	1:32.7y	Mike Cvengros, Dan Young, Jon Walch, Wayne Schwalbach
1975	UPAB	Escanaba	1:34.0y	
1976	UPAB	Escanaba	1:32.5y	Jon Walch, Brian Viau, Mark Creten, Jim Dufresne
1977	UPAB	Marquette	1:33.6y	
1978	UPAB	Marquette	1:34.2y	Bob Taylor, Mike Berquist, Bob Nesbitt, Curt Johnson
1979	UPAB	Kingsford	1:34.9	Randy Gardepy, Michael Konopacke, Mark Konopacke, Peter Dalberto
1980	UPAB	Escanaba	1:33.6	Mike Liebel, Eric Larson, Chris Murray, Chris Brayok
1981	UPAB	Menominee	1:32.2	Craig Leitske, Alex Barker, Marty Hynnek, Chris Hofer
1982	UPAB	Kingsford	1:34.2	Guy Zablocki, Jamie Krieg, Dave Dault, Andy Bittinger
1983	UPAB	Kingsford	1:33.5	Dave Dault, Jim Engman, Darren Dayart, Patrick Duffy
1984	UPAB	Menominee	1:33.8	John Spies, Tom Dessert, Marv Fernstrun, Mark Noon
1985	UPAB	Escanaba	1:35.2	Bill Cook, Gerg Haslow, Wade Walker, Scott Johnson
1986	UPAB	Gladstone	1:34.3	Troy Carlson, Ken Vanderlinden, Tom Quinn, Jon Parker
1987	UPAB	Escanaba	1:33.3	Corey Potvin, Joe Grondine, Jim Jandron, Todd LaCosse
1988	UPAB	Marquette	1:33.6	Frank Holowitz, Mike Grange, Boris Martysz, Jeff LaFave
1989	UPAB	Gwinn	1:34.8	Scott Owens, Craig Hoffman, Brandon Bruce, Matt North
1990	UPAB	Kingsford	1:32.6	Paul Guillani, Mike Flaminio, Dale Powell, ATony Sparapani
1991	UPAB	Escanaba	1:33.2	Todd Taylor, Steve Gross, Nate Chylek, Joe McGuigan
1992	UPAB	Escanaba	1:34.5	Reid Friedhoff, Todd Taylor, Steve Gross, Nate Chylek
1993	UPAB	Escanaba	1:35.4	Joe McGuigan, Scott Victorson, Marty Kulak, Reid Friedhoff
1994	UPAB	Ishpeming Westwood	1:35.2	Aric Sundquist, Ben Waterman, Jason Arsenault, Dan Waterman
1995	UPAB	Menominee	1:34.5	Tom Thompson, Jason Home, T.J. Bushcher, Stve Molnar
1996	UPAB	Escanaba	1:34.5	Marc Prebish, Jose Jupe, Ryan Horgan, Kevin Dyfresne
1997	UPAB	Menominee	1:34.8	Eli Wolfe, Nathan Twork, Korey Sahr, Andy Kohrt
1998	UPAB	Escanaba	1:35.0	Ben Andrews, Robert Lee, Brian Branam, Benton Gady
1999	UPAB	Escanaba	1:36.2	Brian Branam, Jason Braun, Ben Andrews, Benton Gady

2000	UPAB	Escanaba	1:33.6	Brian Branam, Robert Lee, Ben Andrews, Bob Skerbeck
2001	UPD1	Calumet	1:32.7*	Matt Wise, Eric Bausano, Matt Heiminen, Chris Plower
2002	UPD1	Escanaba	1:33.2	Bryan Jacobs, Brandon Mcmillan. Brandon Eis, Jay Wiles
2003	UPD1	Marquette	1:32.71*	Shinsuke Tsuchiya, Leonard Angel, Jordan Divine, Pete Tuccini
2004	UPD1	Sault Ste. Marie	1:32.02*	Mark Bisdorf, Kyle Ward, Dion Josiah, Marc McDonough
2005	UPD1	West Iron County	1:31.00*	Matt Konoske, James Wolf, Matt Westphal, Dustin Johnson
2006	UPD1	Gladstone	1:34.30	James Cappeart, Josh Sargeant, Steve Therrian, Charlie Stafford
2007	UPD1	Menominee	1:33.03	Matt LaCanne, Kurt Roubal, Blake Chouinard, Ethan Shaver
2008	UPD1	Escanaba	1:32.94	Mitch Vaneffen, Max Vanderwiele, John Keepers, Paul Wakefield
2009	UPD1	Gladstone	1:34.37	Alex Harvala, Matt Cseter, Kevin Pardon, Charlie Pfotenhauer
2010	UPD1	Kingsford	1:30.73*	Eric Kliesner, Dyland Tengesdahl, Paul DeYeart, Wes Jacobson
2011	UPD1	Marquette	1:32.15	Matt Mills, Aaron Detmers, Theo Sanyal, Alex Gagnon
2012	UPD1	Menominee	1:32.33	Elijah Mojzych, Bobby Olson, Saun Sullivan, Leonard Briggs
2013	UPD1	Menominee	1:32.09	Chase LaCombe, Aaron Forsberg, Shaun Sullivan, Leonard Briggs
2014	UPD1	Kingsford	1:31.94	Jaxson Ferree, Quintin Pratt, Tyler Roberts, Cole Tengesdahl
2015	UPD1	Marquette	1:33.60	Patrick Burmeister, Scott Tripp, Michael Millado, Brett Place
2016	UPD1	Kingsford	1:34.10	Brandon Kowalkowski, Jonathan Schmutzler, Brandon McGuire, Ben Moreau
2017	UPD1	Iron Mountain	1:34.48	Jake Dumais, Jaden Vincenzi, Adrian Barraza, Jacon Tucker
2018	UPD1	Negaunee	1:34.06	Steven Gooseberry, Jacob Sikora, Robbie Williams, Drew Dushane

4 x 200 – UP Class C/Division 2 Champions

(y=4 x 220 yards)

1940	UPC	L'Anse	1:42.7y*	
1941	UPC	Stephenson	1:40.7y*	
1942	UPC	Stephenson	1:40.2y*	Robert Lawson, Joe Hanske, Ray Peterson, George Simon
1943		No Meet – World War II		
1944	UPC	Gladstone	1:40.6y	
1945	UPC	Hancock	1:40.1y*	
1946	UPC	Munising	1:39.6y*	Donald Potter, Ed Sowa, Ray Ranta, Bob Broda
1947	UPC	L'Anse	1:40.3y	
1948	UPC	L'Anse	1:42.6y	
1949	UPC	Munising	1:37.2y*	Jim Cox, Doug Miron, Dick Nebel, Robert Hillier
1950	UPC	L'Anse	1:39.6y	
1951	UPC	Bessemer	1:42.7y	Roy Pingel, Ed Fabiny, Robert McKie, William Contratto
1952	UPC	Bessemer	1:41.9y	James Contratto, William Contratto, Hal Hansen, Roy Pingel
1953	UPC	Ontonagon	1:42.6y	Norm Weiiisinger, Robert Mattson, Bob Keefer, Tim Routanen
1954	UPC	Bessemer	1:41.0y	Norman, Crockett, Richard Ceno, Fred Trevarthen, James Contratto
1955	UPC	Houghton	1:40.4y	
1956	UPC	Bessemer	1:39.8y	Phil Masse, Don Borich, Art DaPra, David Carpenedo
1957	UPC	St. Ignace	1:40.2y	
1958	UPC	Bessemer	1:42.6y	Jim Corgiat. George Baksic, Bob Slomkoski, Dave Carpenedo
31959	UPC	Lake Linden	1:40.7y	
1960	UPC	Gwinn	1:36.2y*	
1961	UPC	Wakefield	1:38.1y	Jim Hodge, Bob Erickson, Dewey Maki, Don Sawaski
1962	UPC	Bessemer	1:36.3y	Marshall Tillner, Don Erickson, John Bonovetz, Roger Relich
1963	UPC	Wakefield	1:37.3y	Mickey Ginolifi, Terry Salmi, John Howe, Jim Hodge
1964	UPC	Wakefield	1:37.2y	Ray Sibley, Joe Miskovich, Terry Salmi, Mickey Ginolfi
1965	UPC	L'Anse	1:35.8y*	
1966	UPC	L'Anse	1:38.3y	
1967	UPC	Wakefield	1:35.6y	John Francisco, Mike Porcarelli, Roger Norkoli, Ray Subey
1968	UPC	L'Anse	1:34.1y*	Karl Funke, Jim Grigsby, Bob Teddy, Don Michaelson
1969	UPC	Hancock	1:35.8y	Richard Salani, Bill Tarbox, Jeff Kangas, Bill Anderson
1970	UPC	Rudyard	1:33.2y*	Tony Matthias, Steve Lindsay, Fred Besteman, Richard Besteman
1971	UPC	L'Anse	1:35.3y	Ron Thompson, Doug Thomas, Jimmy Lee, Fred Besteman
1972	UPC	Houghton	1:34.9y	Eric Caulley, Mike Johnson, Gerald Johnson, Fred Besteman
1973	UPC	Houghton	1:35.9y	
1974	UPC	Houghton	1:36.6y	
1975	UPC	Ishpeming	1:34.9y	
1976	UPC	Ishpeming	1:34.3y	
1977	UPC	Ironwood	1:33.7y	
1978	UPC	Ishpeming	1:34.5y	
1979	UPC	Ishpeming	1:36.0	David Lakanen, Troy Ogea, Neil Paavalo, Randall Poirer
1981	UPC	Ironwood	1:34.6	Jim Manchester, Mike Blodgett, Mark Mazzon, John Kamaromy
1982	UPC	Ironwood	1:32.7*	John Kamaromy, Mike Blodgett, Mark Mazzon, Jim Manchester
1983	UPC	Iron Mountain	1:33.4	Jim Poupre, Craif Allen, Dan Bianco, Chris Menza
1984	UPC	Ishpeming Westwood	1:33.7	Rudy Nyman, Mark Quelette, Bryan Ross, Dan Perry
1985	UPC	Houghton	1:33.5	Rick Jurkanis, John Sanregret, Jerry Destrampe, Brady Schaefer
1986	UPC	Houghton	1:32.9	John Sanregret, Rick Jurkanis, Jerry Destrampe, Brady Schaefer
1987	UPC	Ironwood	1:36.1	Daren Laabs, Tom Asunto, Shris Carlson, Daren Kinnunen
1988	UPC	Stephenson	1:35.1	Kevin Bowers, David Ledkins, Randy Klein, Chester Blom
1989	UPC	Ishpeming Westwood	1:33.9	Jared Frisk, Bob Nelson, Todd Porier, Doug Etelmaki
1990	UPC	Ontonagon	1:34.2	Jim Gilmer, Pete Miilu, Tom Brookens, Jerry Cleary
1991	UPC	Negaunee	1:34.1	Kevin Downey, Brett Koski, Jon Beckman, Chris Nelson
1992	UPC	Houghton	1:38.8	Dorin Mentink, Scott Karna, Micah Stipech, Bill Schwandt
1993	UPC	St. Ignace	1:34.8	Joe Visnaw, Brad Ledy, Shawn McLafferty, David Brown
1994	UPC	St. Ignace	1:34.7	Ed Lester, Sean McLafferty, Brad Ledy, Leonard Thomas
1995	UPC	Ironwood	1:35.6	Jeremy Richards, John Nemetz, Tim Moon, Jim LaBlonde
1996	UPC	Iron Mountain	1:35.5	Terry Blagec, Kevn Anderson, Tony Torrearo, Ryan Smith
1997	UPC	Stephenson	1:34.5	Bradley Ruleau, Jason Wachel, Zach Truitt, Brian Collins
1998	UPC	Calumet	1:34.6	Matt Koljonen, Greg Perala, Eric Bastian, Brian Johnson
1999	UPC	St. Ignace	1:35.9	Steven MacDonald, Ed Tallman, Dennis Savard, Andy Stempki
2000	UPC	Iron Mountain	1:34.0	Matt Mainville, Adam Husing, Jeff Taff, Mark Lafreniere
2001	UPD2	Newberry	1:34.3*	Tony Bergman, Dan Hiltunen, Matt McNamara, Eric Rocker
2002	UPD2	Stephenson	1:34.8	Mike Ruleau, Mike Shampo, Steve Schmidt, John Palmer

2003	UPD2	Iron Mountain	1:34.03*	Matt Gerard, Alexander Lundy, Nicholas Buckland, Brett Spigarelli
2004	UPD2	Norway	1:33.18*	Chris Mattas, Lane Thaler, Jim DeBartolo, Nick Zweifel
2005	UPD2	Norway	1:33.95	Chris Mattas, Nick Zweifel, Jim DeBartolo, Lane Thaler
2006	UPD2	St. Ignace	1:34.06	Jesse Becker, Derrick Clark, Zach Pierson, Paul Davis
2007	UPD2	Norway	1:33.92	Phil Milbrath, Jordan Thomas, Jeremy Wilson, Jordan Marchetti
2008	UPD2	Ishpeming Westwood	1:34.03	John Yeager, Jake Dellangelo, T.J. Black, Nick Pennell
2009	UPD2	St. Ignace	1:33.18*	Anthony Lester, Robby Robinson, Evan Emerson, Caleb Litzner
2010	UPD2	Rudyard	1:34.74	Arik Hesselink, Drew Otten, Jared Clark, Ben Coffee
2011	UPD2	St. Ignace	1:37.23	Caleb Litzner, Galloway Thurston, Wyatt Orm, Joe Ostman
2012	UPD2	Newberry	1:37.66	Taylor Weeks, John Nolan, Kyle Archer, Pierce Legault
2013	UPD2	West Iron County	1:34.50	Tyler Stafford, Andrew Peterson, Nik Thoney, Ryan Rogers
2014	UPD2	Ishpeming	1:35.39	Tyrus Millimaki, Adams Prisk, Nate Meyer, Derek Decaire
2015	UPD2	West Iron County	1:36.40	Phil King, Brandon Olson, Nik Thoney, Rusty Johnson
2016	UPD2	Ishpeming	1:37.90	Isaac Olson, Evan Gravedoni, Jaren Kipling, Kazmine Langness
2017	UPD2	Ishpeming	1:35.69	Isac Olson, Hunter Smith, Cooper Harris, Matthew Trawick
2018	UPD2	Newberry	1:34.05	Andre James, Jeff Rahilly, Jaylen James, Brandon Christensen

4 x 200 – UP Class D/Division 3 Champions

(y=4 x 220 yards)

1940	UPD	Alpha	1:46.3y*	Elwood Davis, Joe Polivka, John Bosko, Obed Thrasher
1941	UPD	Hermansville	1:40.9y*	
1942	UPD	Channing	1:39.7y*	
1943		No Meet – World War II		
1944	UPD	Chassell	1:47.0y	
1945	UPD	Ewen	1:43.4y	
1946	UPD	Powers	1:43.5y	
1947	UPD	Powers	1:42.7y	
1948	UPD	Eben	1:43.4y	
1949	UPD	Eben	1:40.3y	
1950	UPD	Hermansville	1:41.4y	Maule, Christenson, Nelson, Vic Fochesato
1951	UPD	Trenary	nt	
1952	UPD	Pickford	1:43.3y	Eldred Leach, Royce Miller, Charlie Izzard, Jim Quinell
1953	UPD	Pickford	1:39.5y*	Eldred Leach, Jim Graham, Jim Quinnell, Roland McCready
1954	UPD	Pickford	1:39.5y*	Eldred Leach, Jim Graham, Jim Quinnell, Roland McCready
1955	UPD	Pickford	1:38.7y*	Jim Roe, David Taylor, Jaynce Leach, David Fountain
1956	UPD	Pickford	1:38.4y*	Roger Wahl, Dave Taylor, Dave Fountain, Jaynee Leach
1957	UPD	DeTour	1:41.5y	
1958	UPD	Rapid River	1:45.4y	Ray Pratt, Jim Carlson, Phil Deneau, Allen Shanaquet
1959	UPD	Pickford	1:38.4y*	Gary Crawford, Milford Galer, Kenneth Stevenson, Ronald Rapson
1960	UPD	Pickford	1:37.3y*	Bill Kibble, Noel Hanna, Donald Thompson, Ronald Pennington
1961	UPD	Pickford	1:37.4y	Elwin Leach, Gary Leach, Donald Thomspon, Noel Hanna
1962	UPD	Pickford	1:35.7y*	Elwin Leach, Roger Hill, Donald Cruickshank, Gary Leach
1963	UPD	Pickford	1:38.1y	Roger Hewer, Bob Huyck, Tom Harrison, Gary Leach
1964	UPD	Pickford	1:36.1y	Roger Reamer, Chuck Bennin, Roger Hewer, Bob Huyck
1965	UPD	Pickford	1:35.5y*	Roger Reamer, Chuck Bennin, Roger Hewer, Bob Huyck
1966	UPD	Channing	1:38.1y	
1967	UPD	Pickford	1:38.0y	Dale Coullard, Ron Harrison, Gary Bawks, Wayne Stevenson
1968	UPD	Pickford	1:38.9y	Ron Harrison, Nick Hill, Wayne Stevenson, Eric Rike
1969	UPD	Pickford	1:37.3y	John Williams, Wayne Stevenson, Marty Storey, Ken Batho
1970	UPD	Channing	1:36.5y	
1971	UPD	Channing	1:35.6y	
1972	UPD	Wakefield	1:36.5y	Mike Ravelli, Mark Daniels, Dave Inkala, Pete West
1973	UPD	Crystal Falls Forest Park	1:36.9y	
1974	UPD	Crystal Falls Forest Park	1:36.5y	
1975	UPD	Felch North DIckinson	1:35.9y	Steve Feak, Ricky Woods, Brian Lindeman, Tom Kramer
1976	UPD	Bessemer	1:35.8y	Mike Trevarthen, John Burt, Leonard Janssen, Greg Smith
1977	UPD	Bessemer	1:36.1y	
1978	UPD	Pickford	1:35.5y*	Pete Lamb, John Baker, Mark Allison, Ed LaPreze
1979	UPD	Rock-Mid Peninsula	1:36.1	Keith Anderson, Greg Croasdell, Robert Koski, Dwayne Hammersmith
1980	UPD	Powers-North Central	1:35.0*	Marc Fochesato, Brian Hilsabeck, Dale Miller, Jeff Poquette
1981	UPD	Cedarville	1:36.9	Todd Soderlund, Rob Freebury, Roger Bock, Rory Hooper
1982	UPD	Wakefield	1:35.4	Rick Doney, Dave Nelson, Dale Hongisto, Jim Buckler
1983	UPD	St. Ignace	1:35.7	Kevin Laver, Brad Erskin, Preston Allers, Dan St. Andrew
1984	UPD	Felch North DIckinson	1:35.4	Joe Newton, Jim Johnson, Michael Christian, Richard Opsahl
1985	UPD	Crystal Falls Forest Park	1:36.3	John Gollakner, Jim Nocerini, Mike Palo, Mark Mielcarek
1986	UPD	Bessemer	1:35.9	Pat Bulinski, Scott Trudgeon, Mike Contratto, Scott Grooms
1987	UPD	Bessemer	1:37.2	Scott Trudgeon, Brian Bonovetz, Garth Stengard, Scott Grooms
1988	UPD	Wakefield	1:37.5	Rick Hemming, Dave Rautiola, Dane Valesano, Mike Miskovich
1989	UPD	Pickford	1:36.6	Jason Firack, Dave Bush, Steven Kyle, Guy Blanchard
1990	UPD	Pickford	1:35.3	Dave Dodds, Matt Bawks, Guy Blanchard, Dave Bush
1991	UPD	Pickford	1:36.7	Tom Dumback, Dave Dodds, Shon Cottie, Matt Bawks
1992	UPD	DeTour	1:40.2	Craig Bosley, Ben Fountain, Melvin Bennette, Dan Thoompson
1993	UPD	Rapid River	1:36.7	Scott McLaughlin, Cory Ness, Chris Wolf, Ben Larrabee
1994	UPD	Ontonagon	1:35.2	Jeff Bobula, Steve Mattson, Mark Moore, Tim Goard
1995	UPD	Powers-North Central	1:36.2	Nick Charles, Chris Gorzinski, Tom Granquist, Tyan Vesser
1996	UPD	Powers-North Central	1:36.6	Nick Charles, Chad Holle, Barry Cory, Brian Bouty
1997	UPD	Powers-North Central	1:37.8	Nick Charles, Andrew McPherson, Jason Gorzinski, Brian Bouty
1998	UPD	St. Ignace	1:37.0	Steven MacDonald, Don Rickley, Andy Stempki, Dennis Savard
1999	UPD	Mohawk Keweenaw	1:38.1	Karim H., L.W.P., Richard B., Al D.
2000	UPD	Rock-Mid Peninsula	1:36.0	Luke Maulding, Ciry Williams, Jim Brayak, Steve Koski
2001	UPD3	Rock-Mid Peninsula	1:35.1*	Cory Williams, Jake Gobert, Luke Maulding, Steve Koski
2002	UPD3	Rapid River	1:35.2	Terry Eskofski, Jon Bovin, Jerry Reuther, Dan Larrabee
2003	UPD3	Felch North Dickinson	1:37.71	Travis Steinbrecher, Kevin Roell, Ryan Carey, Nicholas Mattson
2004	UPD3	Felch North Dickinson	1:37.71	Brandon Lindeman, Barrys Holsworth, Kevin Roell, Travis Steinbrecher,

2005	UPD3	North Central	1:35.99	Steve Davis, Craig Bilski, Jeremy Felton, Barlow Heider
2006	UPD3	Powers-North Central	1:35.18*	Craig Bilski, Andy Fazer, Jared Triest, Steve Davis
2007	UPD3	Felch North Dickinson	1:36.36	Damian Smith, Pete Leeman, Paul Roell, John Nurmi
2008	UPD3	Crystal Falls Forest Park	1:36.26	Fred Hubbard, Bob Reid, Josh Siler, Mick Valesano
2009	UPD3	Felch North Dickinson	1:39.97	Terry Mays, Dillon Steinbrecher, Mike Miller, Joe Hruska
2010	UPD3	Crystal Falls Forest Park	1:36.23	Levi Oleksy, Cole Noblet, Jacob Siler, Josh Siler
2011	UPD3	Crystal Falls Forest Park	1:37.52	Alex Takala, Collin Gendron, Cole Noblet, Jacob Siler
2012	UPD3	Pickford	1:36.69	Jacob Richard, Phillip Coullard, Jared Levigne, Jordan Levigne
2013	UPD3	Bessemer	1:36.68	Art Rundell, Derek Gheller, Jess Mazzon, Taylor Smith
2014	UPD3	Bark River-Harris	1:35.74	Jake Greenfield, Alex Mathias, Sam Martin, Hunter Messersmith
2015	UPD3	St. Ignace	1:38.10	Brandon Oja, Gage Kreski, David LaVake, James Cryderman
2016	UPD3	Powers-North Central	1:36.90	Dylan Gagne, Trenton Schaff, Tyler Bentley, Morgan Cox
2017	UPD3	Rapid River	1:35.41	Lucas Sundling, Cam Willemsen, Luke Gustafson, Austin Wickland
2018	UPD3	Bessemer	1:36.72	Tad Rowe, Andy Aspinwall, Jared Janczak, Jamie Jett

BOYS 4 x 400 RELAY

Records

D1	3:13.90	Detroit Mumford	Dekoven Lynch, Hoisea Jones, Jimmie Jones, Kenneth Ferguson	2002
D2	3:19.11	Flint Kearsley	Kyle Bergquist, Peter O'Brien, Tony Parcels, Dan Goodman	2004
D3	3:21.44	Sanford Meridian	Dan Johnson, Kevin Scheibert, Jacab Ham, Jacob Wenzlick	2014
D4	3:24.19	Concord	Lonelle Langston, Lawson Bright-Mitchell, Chase Hinkle, Zach Hudson	2014
UPD1	3:29.18	Marquette	Jeremy Sergey, Chris Peterson, Jordan Divine, Pete Tuccini	2003
UPD2	3:32.9	Newberry	Jim Miller, Matt Mcnamara, Eric Rocker, Dan Hiltunen	2001
UPD3	3:34.52	Rapid River	Conner Bryant, Luke Gustafson, Cam Willemsen, Austin Wickland	2017

Records by Class (pre-2000 for LP, pre-2001 for UP)

A	3:16.05	Detroit Cooley	Robert Adams, David Norman, Raphael Johnson, Marco West	1991
B	3:19.69	Flint Beecher	Tony Triggs, Courtney Hawkins, Aaron McFadden, Stacy Watson	1988
C	3:20.1	Detroit DePorres	Darren Warner, James Fuller, Claude Tiller, Darryl Carter	1983
D	3:22.9	Detroit DePorres	Lebron Campbell, Darren Warner, Garfield Lemonious, Greg Henderson	1981
UPAB	3:30.3	Negaunee	Brian Healey, Dan Atkins, Chris Nelson, Keith Collins	1990
UPAB	3:30.4y	Gwinn	Mike Newell, Cliff Stiles, Jeff Hatfield, Mike Hatfield	1970
UPC	3:31.4	Ironwood	Darryl Petrusha, Jim Kivisto, Jim Estola, Mike McPherson	1982
UPD	3:31.8	Cedarville	Jamie Leach, Glenn Wandrie, Paul Freebury, Roger Bock	1980

4 x 400 – Class A/Division 1 Champions

(Mile Relay)

| 1908 | all | Detroit Central | 3:49.2* | Russell Stoddard, Don James, Art Widman, Allen Garrels |

(Mile Medley Relay – 440y-220-220-880)

| 1947 | A | Saginaw | 3:49.2* | Jim Bond, Glenn Webb, Ray Garrett, Bob Parsons |

(3/4 Medley Relay – 440y-220-220-440)

1948	A	Benton Harbor	2:34.5*	Dick Silverthorn, Nello Burnett, Gary Reakes, Stan Weber
1949	A	Saginaw	2:33.7*	Dick Gnirs, Nathan Taylor, Dick Conley, Gaylord Nelson
1950	A	Flint Northern	2:32.4*	Ken Rankin, John Martin, Walt McMullen, Walt Skidmore
1951	A	Grand Rapids Catholic	2:35.8	Lawrence Yeo, Jack Doran, Lavern Wolf, Terrence Evarhart
1952	A	Dearborn Fordson	2:36.4	Don Bender, Bob Wayne, Hector Colinga, Jim Kruther
1953	A	Flint Northern	2:29.7*	Jerome Miller, Art Johnson, R.G. Johnson, Gary Crowell
1954	A	Lansing Eastern	2:29.9	Tom Jenkins, Bruce Kyburz, Al Koss, Don Higel
1955	A	Dearborn Fordson	2:28.1*	Dale Robinson, Bill Friend, William Campbell, Phillip Davis
1956	A	Flint Northern	2:30.9	Francis Price, Arden Relerford, John Dennis, Phil Gaines
1957	A	Lansing Sexton	2:35.6	Fred Johnson, Terry Boyes, Jim Nelligan, Bernie Patterson
1958	A	Flint Central	2:30.7	Bill Foster, Henry Young, Paul Morrison, Ken Baxter
1959	A	Flint Central	2:29.5	Bill Foster, Paul Morrison, Ron Watkins, Jim Huesel
1960	A	Muskegon Catholic	2:31.7	Mike Sigman, Tom Pasco, Tom Hornik, Jerome Winston

(4 x 400; y=4 x 440 yards)

1961	A	Grand Rapids Ottawa Hills	3:26.1y*	Dick Fenske, Alan Johnson, Dick Schulz, Bob Carpenter
1962	A	Detroit Thurston	3:28.1y	Jerry McCabe, Ron Voightritter, Don Voightritter, Richard Gordon
1963	A (tie)	Detroit Mackenzie	3:24.5y*	Dennis Lugar, Cottrell Poole, Duane Varner, Charles Poindexter
1963	A (tie)	Flint Northern	3:24.5y*	Rozeal Graves, Andy Johnson, Frank Gause, Cliff Finklea
1964	A	Detroit Southeastern	3:28.2y	John Saddler, Ralph Thomas, Aaron Thomas, Larry Stanfield
1965	A	Detroit Southeastern	3:22.6y*	John Saddler, Larry Stanfield, Obra Purneil, Ralph Thomas
1966	A	Detroit Pershing	3:21.6y*	John Kitchen, Dale Hardeman, Regenald Bradford, Andre Broadfax
1967	A	Birmingham Seaholm	3:22.0y	Jim Labello, Bob Baxter, Neal Marzela, Roger Holtz
1968	A	Ecorse	3:20.5y*	Marion Pittman, Clio Turner, Art Small, Dan Haig
1969	A	Southgate	3:21.7y	Floyd Wells, Charles Fielhauer, Bill Franklin, Bruce Doran
1970	A	Flint Northern	3:20.9y	Dan Forte, Mike Kelly, Broderick Crump, John Butler
1971	A	Detroit Northern	3:23.7y	Brad Rogers, Luray Cooper, Garfield Randle, Bill Nance
1972	A	Detroit Pershing	3:19.5y*	Tim Harris, Tommy Clark, Darrel Davis, Eugene Ellerbie
1973	A	Grosse Pointe North	3:22.5y	Fred Minturn, Ed Brannan, Tom Przeslawski, Ken DeLor
1974	A	Detroit Central	3:18.6y*	Jerome Stanton, Haven Robinson, Frank Manners, Arvie Jones
1975	A	Detroit Central	3:20.6y	Mike Harden, Dennis Manners, Walter Baker, Jerome Stanton
1976	A	Detroit Cass Tech	3:18.2y*	Darryl Tucker, James Davies, Calvin Williams, Benson Triplett
1977	A	Detroit Redford	3:16.4y*	Randall Woodson, Melvin Matthews, Ahamed Lile, Monte Callendor
1978	A	Detroit Redford	3:20.9y	Randall Woodson, Ahamed Lile, Kenneth Watkins, James Woods
1979	A	Flint Northern	3:18.7y	Patrick Blakely, Ken Brown, Herb McGowan, James Younger
1980	A	Detroit Central	3:18.6y	David Beasley, Andre Topp, James Elder, Thomas Wilcher

1981	A	Detroit Central	3:17.9y	David Beasley, Thomas Wilcher, Wilfred Hart, William White
1982	A	Detroit Central	3:16.1*	Vincent Hall, William White, Wilfred Hart, David Beasley
1983	A	Flint Northern	3:16.5	Roderick McClure, Kenford Wilson, Stanley Ruth, Anthony Bowie
1984	A	Saginaw	3:17.1	Nathaniel Chisolm, Darnell Davis, Darrell Jones, Ernest Menzie
1985	A	Detroit Mumford	3:18.21	Roy Holt, David Singleton, Kent Vinson, Neil Crosby
1986	A	Pontiac Northern	3:17.60	Jessie Hodge, Rico Walker, Reggie Wynns, Craig McFerrin
1987	A	Ann Arbor Huron	3:17.90	Franklin Gay, Earl Flanagan, Kevin Hudson, Jerry Douglas
1988	A	Detroit Cooley	3:17.81	John Washington, Willie Jones, Richard Gregory, Derrick Harris
1989	A	Detroit Cooley	3:19.6	Willie Jones, Derrick Harris. Hamanuel Williams, Marco West
1990	A	Pontiac Northern	3:17.73	Jamell Humphrey, Marcus Steed, Dionne Finney, Damon Gandy
1991	A	Detroit Cooley	3:16.05*	Robert Adams, David Norman, Raphael Johnson, Marco West
1992	A	Detroit Mumford	3:21.78	Darian Dew, Cecil Flanigan, Joe Stevens, Derrick Mason
1993	A	Flint Southwestern	3:20.23	Anthony Torns, Ivan Norman Scott Thomas, Steve Ruffin
1994	A	Detroit Cass Tech	3:17.1	Fred Wilkerson, Clarence Williams, Jabari Johnson, Dwayne Fuqua
1995	A	Detroit Cass Tech	3:19.04	Nevara Smith, David Downs, Jonathon King, Brian Jones
1996	A	Pontiac Northern	3:20.6	Kareem Manley, Jerome Rodgers, Jason Lopez, Godfrey Herring
1997	A	Pontiac Northern	3:19.03	Kareem Manley, Godfrey Herring, Jason Wingo, Jason Lopez,
1998	A	East Lansing	3:19.63	Grant Ogbu, Dana Thomas, Brent Burns, Brad Miller
1999	A	Detroit Mumford	3:17.80	James Connor, Juan Bowles, Johnnie Birdsong, Brandon Jiles
2000	D1	Saginaw Heritage	3:19.34*	Derold Sligh, Robert Ellerman, Soji Jibowu, Stuart Schweigert
2001	D1	Detroit Mumford	3:20.70	Kenneth Ferguson, Jimmie Jones, Hoisea Jones, Dokoven Lynch
2002	D1	Detroit Mumford	3:13.90*	Dokoven Lynch, Hoisea Jones, Jimmie Jones, Kenneth Ferguson
2003	D1	Detroit Mumford	3:20.42	Isaiah Marshall, Tyjuan Sims, Keith Hewlett, Jimmie Jones
2004	D1	West Bloomfield	3:19.32	Andre Barnes, Brett Scafuri, Brandon Thrasher, Matt Koenigsknecht
2005	D1	Flint Carman-Ainsworth	3:19.29	Otis Wiley, Tyjuan Jones, Rodney Harris, Ahmad Rashad
2006	D1	Detroit Mumford	3:21.41	Darien Lewis, Kendrick Price, Isiah Ward, Cedric Everson
2007	D1	Ann Arbor Pioneer	3:18.50	James Smith, Dennis Fortson, Kevin Hughbanks, James Wade
2008	D1	East Kentwood	3:20.56	Deonte' Hurst, Chad Weesies, Christian Jessie, Kevin Jackson
2009	D1	East Kentwood	3:21.14	Deonte' Hurst, Chad Weesies, Isaac Cox, Christian Jesse
2010	D1	Detroit Catholic Central	3:16.11	Billy Riga, Josh Gatt, Jake Spuller, Spencer Hall
2011	D1	East Kentwood	3:19.95	Chris James, Ernie Morton, Joe Riggins, Ricco Hall
2012	D1	Lake Orion	3:21.42	Corey Ester, Zach Arnold, David Diaz, Nick Balavich
2013	D1	Lake Orion	3:19.76	Spencer Holland, Pat Rooker, Jestin Tigue, Gabe Hodge
2014	D1	East Lansing	3:16.56	Lawrence Davis, Jared Howenstein, Marq Adams, Antonio Clarke
2015	D1	Saline	3:22.91	David Alberdi, Logan Wetzel, Josiah Davis, Skyler Bowden
2016	D1	Saline	3:19.37	Brian Blankenship David Alberdi, Harrison Koch, Austin Welch
2017	D1	Oak Park	3:17.58	Dewan Hawthorne, Bryce Pickett, Javonne Kirksey, Cameron Cooper
2018	D1	Grand Blanc	3:22.94	Austin Rippee, Quin Broussard, Carter Merrell, Jeronn Body

4 x 400 – Class B/Division 2 Champions

(Mile Medley Relay – 440y-220-220-880)

1947	B	Marshall	3:51.9*	William Ward, Robert Morris, John Schneider, William Behenke

(3/4 Medley Relay – 440y-220-220-440)

1948	B	River Rouge	2:38.2*	Wardell Gilliam, Stan Stefanick, Alfred Driscoll, Wallace Salisbury
1949	B	Birmingham	2:33.4*	Eric Heizer, Jere McMillin, Bob Folin, Sandy Gruber
1950	B	Ypsilanti Central	2:37.0	Harold Duede, John Hill, Douglas Smith, John Baker
1951	B	Birmingham	2:40.8	Art Fredericks, Jack Hooper, Jim Newman, Ned Sharples
1952	B	Niles	2:39.4	Charles Allen, Al Marazita, Gordon Rollert, Larry Cochran
1953	B	Adrian	2:33.0*	Lyn Dibble, Hal Anglin, Jack McDonald, Larry Masteller
1954	B	Battle Creek Lakeview	2:34.2	Dale Talliaferrio, Rodney Smith, Dan Danklefsen, Dave Chidester
1955	B	Grand Rapids Central	2:33.7	Ernie Brazil, John Faasen, Fred Johnson, Earl Mandeville
1956	B	Utica	2:31.9*	Art Barrett, Ray Vaderweghe, Steve Stonebreaker, Brian Castle
1957	B	South Haven	2:36.0	Gary Smith, Joe Cunningham, Larry Flora, Skip Williams
1958	B	River Rouge	2:33.5	Sam Young, Bob Miller, Art Welch, Warren Corless
1959	B	Eaton Rapids	2:30.5*	Jay Shirley, Ron Elston, Mike Richardson, Howard Hilliard
1960	B	Flint Kearsley	2:35.8	Marvin Owen, John Williams, Dale Kritzman, Martin Crane

(4 x 400; y=4 x 440 yards)

1961	B	East Grand Rapids	3:32.9y*	Craig Miller, Mike Kerwin, Bob Paup, Bruce Osterink
1962	B (tie)	Detroit St Joseph	3:32.9y*	Carl Wiatr, S Passalaqua, Sam Patton, Jerome Patton
1962	B (tie)	River Rouge	3:32.9y*	Ted Burnley, Bill Dunson, Vernon Smith, Dennis Jones
1963	B	East Grand Rapids	3:28.2y*	Bob Paup, Mike Kerwin, Ron Kutchinski, McKee Tiff
1964	B	River Rouge	3:28.2y*	Willie Betts, Ron Lane, John Sykes, Eric Peterson
1965	B	River Rouge	3:26.3y*	Allen Walker, George Miles, Ron Lane, Eric Peterson
1966	B	Dearborn Heights Riverside	3:25.1y*	Gary Abell, Art Hoffman, Paul Cooke, Rich Stevens
1967	B	Ecorse	3:26.0y	Leslie Ritz, Art Small, Cleo Turner, Dan Haig
1968	B	Grand Rapids Central	3:27.6y	Bob Grosema, Chris Marchand, Joe Day, Eddie Edwards
1969	B	Ecorse	3:25.1y*	Oscar Suddarth, Carl Jones, Bob Hernandez, Art Small
1970	B	Muskegon Heights	3:25.9y	James Jackson, Bobby Henderson, Clarence Leslie, Dan Smith
1971	B	Detroit Lutheran West	3:25.3y	Len Hoopem Martin Nash, Layne Gobrooge, Tim Kostelnik
1972	B	Cranbrook	3:21.3y*	Elbert Gates, Bill Brunstad, Jack Campbell, Charles Monk
1973	B	Ecorse	3:25.1y	Deforest Stallworth, Herman Lyons, Robert Miles, Greg Warfield
1974	B	Dearborn Heights Robichaud	3:24.3y	Larry Johnson, Calvin Green, Ron Woodson, John Wilson
1975	B	Flint Beecher	3:22.1y	Greg Knox, Mike Mosby, Ron Simpson, Tony Akins
1976	B	Flint Beecher	3:23.9y	Bernard Carpenter, Ricky Franklin, Ricky Curtis, Anthony Akins
1977	B	Dearborn Heights Robichaud	3:23.3y	David Metthews, Terry Ross, Mack Woodson, Oscar Randall
1978	B	Flint Beecher	3:23.1y	Henry Young, Jerome Hogan, Tim Roman, John Fralik
1979	B	Muskegon Heights	3:23.6y	Kenneth Lay, Sebastian Hughey, Cedric Scott, Kevin Mays
1980	B	Flint Beecher	3:22.2	Lonnie Young, Kenneth Hawthorne, Troy McKeown, Van Deloney
1981	B	Ecorse	3:20.5*	Jamie Weathers, Brian Pope, Rodney Nedd, Willie Thomas
1982	B	Detroit Northern	3:21.6y	Terrance Keys, Dennis Howard, Carlton McGinnis, Keith King
1983	B	Flint Beecher	3:20.0*	Andre Hall, John Garner, Robert Fischer, Jamonty Washington
1984	B	Dearborn Divine Child	3:25.6	Mark Kitlinski, Mike Gallagher, Brian Kulka, John Laney
1985	B	Inkster	3:21.09	Earl Truss, Charles McKay, Michael Henderson, David Laws
1986	B	Flint Beecher	3:22.4	Terry Strong, Michael Ford, Kenneth Campbell, Courtney Hawkins

1987	B	River Rouge	3:23.78	James Jackson, Donald Jones. Mike Jackson, Alex Gassaway
1988	B	Flint Beecher	3:19.69*	Tony Triggs, Courtney Hawkins, Aaron McFadden, Stacy Watson
1989	B	Grand Rapids Northview	3:24.0	Andy Korytkowski, Mickey Wallace, Mike Savickas, Shane Sieracki
1990	B	Oxford	3:25.5	Vidal Fragoso, Charles Kniffen, Dave Berney, Eric Welch
1991	B	Flint Beecher	3:24.02	Marcus Tipton, Jimmy Lacy, Michael Jones, Garth Spight
1992	B	Flint Beecher	3:21.07	McKinley Tipton, Jimmy Lacy, Garth Spight, Marcus Tipton
1993	B	Detroit UD Jesuit	3:20.36	Edzra Gibson, Kareem Dillard, William Brooks, Chris Polk
1994	B	Ypsilanti Lincoln	3:24.7	James Yeargin, Dan West, Brian Gentz, Eric Carlson
1995	B	Plainwell	3:27.3	Mike Plugis, Tim Fisher, Stewart Murphy, Ben Blake
1996	B	Whitehall	3:22.98	Josh Meeuwenberg, Carey Brown, Derek Sines, Jeff DeLong
1997	B	Ypsilanti Lincoln	3:24.5	Jaquan Wright, Josh Spencer, Micah Steiner, Jason Fullterton
1998	B	Dearborn Heights Robichaud	3:21.21	Raypheal Brown, David Moss, Levi Peoples, Leonte Lillard
1999	B	Corunna	3:24.28	Jared Aldrich, Jim Skodak, Adam Sanderson, Robbie Currie
2000	D2	Romulus	3:22.31*	Jarvis Jordan, Caleb Beasly, Henry Staple, Ashley Terry
2001	D2	Farmington Hills Harrison	3:23.61	Fermon Tate. Brian Coats, Terrill Mayberry, Agim Shabaj
2002	D2	Farmington Hills Harrison	3:21.03*	Agim Shabaj, Fermon Tate, Kevin Davis, Terrill Mayberry
2003	D2	Flint Kearsley	3:22.08	Dan Goodman, Tony Parcels, Dan Vioght, Pete O'Brien
2004	D2	Flint Kearsley	3:19.11*	Kyle Bergquist, Peter O'Brien, Tony Parcels, Dan Goodman
2005	D2	Lansing Sexton	3:21.06	Tymel Dodd, Brian Merrill, Brian Tucker, Jacob Wyatt
2006	D2	Ypsilanti Central	3:23.48	Andre Oyebamiji, Shae Malveaux, Clent Simmons, Lapell Powell
2007	D2	Grand Rapids Forest Hills Northern	3:22.14	Tom Borgeling, David Marmian, Steve Lucas, Josh Hembrough
2008	D2	Zeeland West	3:21.56	Mike Bareman, Andy Plaska, Derrick Kingshott, Bobby Bassett
2009	D2	Hamilton	3:22.40	Dakota Sale, Troy Sneller, David Ptacek, Michael Hoffman
2010	D2	Auburn Hills Avondale	3:23.19	Nathon Chapman, Don Gordon, Zach Miklja, Trevon Salter
2011	D2	East Lansing	3:21.40	Gavin Midlam, Lawrence Collins, Tim Kulang, Dan Tyler
2012	D2	Lansing Sexton	3:23.94	Herman Mason, Adrian Sanchez, Anthony Goodman, Kendell Jackson
2013	D2	Detroit East English	3:22.76	Anton Cutris, Desmond King, Juwan Green, Marcel Wyckoff
2014	D2	Lansing Waverly	3:24.05	Martin Bennett, Florian Schwarb, Qadir Muhammad, Dartanian Cook
2015	D2	Adrian	3:25.23	Thomas Apling, Gavin Stepansky, Jzavion McGowen, Austin Laskowsky
2016	D2	Zeeland East	3:21.26	Kaylin Barton, Dan Cramer, John Groendyk, Corbin DeJonge
2017	D2	Zeeland East	3:23.75	Dan Cramer, Jonathan Groendyk, Corbin DeJonge, Gabe Taylor
2018	D2	Lansing Catholic	3:23.27	Ryan Schroeder, James Fedewa, Jack Fedewa, Ryan Ruiter

4 x 400 – Class C/Division 3 Champions

(Mile Medley Relay – 440y-220-220-880)

1947	C	Grand Rapids Lee	3:58.8*	Jack Formsma, Elmer Kuipers, Richard Timmer, Glenn Marema

(3/4 Medley Relay – 440y-220-220-440)

1948	C	Grand Rapids Lee	2:38.1*	Jack Formsma, Glen Marema, Elmer Kuipers, Dick Holmgren
1949	C	East Grand Rapids	2:38.3	John Parrish, Bill Durkee, Allen Pardoe, Tom Payette
1950	C	East Grand Rapids	2:35.5*	John Parrish, Gordon Hope, Alan Pardee, Fred Newman
1951	C	Plainwell	2:40.7	John Haskins, Bill Thompson, John Robinson, Richard Madden
1952	C	Grand Rapids Lee	2:42.4	Gordon Lanninga, Dale Phelps, Don Hulst, Don Hughes
1953	C	St Louis	2:38.4	Duane Dietrich, Dick Ross, Frank Kristal Leo Coston
1954	C	Athens	2:37.3	Larry Cline, Bob Wynn, Bob Klein, Phil Cline
1955	C	Athens	2:37.4	Dick Gilchrist, John Burke, Robert Wyn, Melvin Harvey
1956	C	Lansing Everett	2:35.3*	Jerry Squires, Dallas Brink, Dick Gilmore, Bill Morehouse
1957	C	Flint Dye	2:39.6	Charles Taylor, Jerry Meyers, Don Evans, Nevitt Cromer
1958	C	Saginaw SS Peter & Paul	2:37.1	Bernie Call, Paul Halas, Bob Navarro, Dan Jacobi
1959	C	Nashville	2:37.5	Dennis Lamie, Bill Lynch, Vic Mauer, Ray Rousch
1960	C	Cassopolis	nt	Clarence Blakely, Ejnor King, Bill Robinson, Bill Lorrer

(4 x 400; y=4 x 440 yards)

1961	C	Battle Creek St Philip	3:33.9y*	Don Kajcienski, Herbert Harmon, Tom Walker, Frank Quartermain
1962	C	Battle Creek St Phillip	3:34.9y	Chet Kajcienski, Herb Harmon, Dennis Cripps, Jim Bauman
1963	C	Bellevue	3:34.0y	Larry Evans, Dave Stanley, Jack Hanley, Jim Smith
1964	C	Battle Creek St Phillip	3:35.1y	Jonathon Cowles, Jim Cvetnich, Anthony Jaskie, Herb Tillman
1965	C	Imlay City	3:31.7y*	John Schoenfeld, Spencer Tellar, Rick Vincent, John Reinbold
1966	C	Battle Creek St Phillip	3:31.4y*	Bill Human, Mike McVeigh, Jerry Quartermain, Jack Schroeder
1967	C	Akron-Fairgrove	3:32.7y	Mike Kruchkow, Gordon Aldrich, Alan Arnold, Charles Brink
1968	C	Akron-Fairgrove	3:31.8y	Mike Kruchkow, Al Spencer, Alan Arnold, Charles Brink
1969	C	Central Montcalm	3:33.5y	Bill Brundage, Steve Palma, Dennis Thomsen, Dennis Waldron
1970	C	Shelby	3:30.6y*	Dave Felt, Lloyd Gowell, Bruce Mitteer, Rick VanLaan
1971	C	Detroit DePorres	3:32.6y	Lawrence Scott, Alan Baker, James O'Leary, Lawrence Ellis
1972	C	Shelby	3:31.1y	Mike Riggle, Bob Gosselin, Paul Griffin, Rick VanLaan
1973	C	Detroit DePorres	3:31.1y	Alan Baker, Benson Triplett, Dana Dorsey, Anthony Tilden
1974	C	Detroit East Catholic	3:25.0y*	Ronald Strong, Mike Walton, Jasper Young, Darroll Gatson
1975	C	Unionville-Sebewaing	3:26.6y	Tim Androl, Rod Luther, Randy Baker, Mike Mischung
1976	C	Harper Woods Lutheran East	3:25.5y	Tom Geyer, Ken Batts, Steve Callies, Chris Englert
1977	C	Montrose	3:26.8y	Dale Bloss, Andy Bragg, Russ Lund, John Pryc
1978	C	Clare	3:27.3y	Dean Doherty, Charles Sharlow, Tim Gibson, Al Rodgers
1979	C	Detroit Benedictine	3:27.1y	Ron Goolsby, Derwin Caffe, Charles Webster, Ferman Tate
1980	C	Ecorse	3:24.6y*	Milton Lewis, Michael Dunlap, Willie Thomas, Jamie Weathers
1981	C	Muskegon Oakridge	3:25.9	Scott Denio, Mike Dietz, Bill Wright, Mike Danielson
1982	C	Detroit Lutheran West	3:21.2*	Clifton Camp, Erik Frederick, Mark Garner, Dwight Tyson
1983	C	Detroit DePorres	3:20.1*	Darren Warner, James Fuller, Claude Tiller, Darryl Carter
1984	C	Detroit DePorres	3:24.2	Anthony Johnson, Ralph Bland, Claude Tiller, Keith Harris
1985	C	Ecorse	3:25.10	Jamel Adams, Earl Greene, Fred Dalton, Arvin Bowman
1986	C	Flint Hamady	3:26.31	Lance Huddleston, Rick White, Tony Nelson, David Rawls
1987	C	Detroit Lutheran West	3:24.45	Marcus Tarver, Lionel Sims, Tom Robinson, Ben Jones
1988	C	Williamston	3:24.5	Aaron Keiser, Rob Saylor, Jon Somerville, Sean Conklin
1989	C	Saginaw Nouvel	3:28.98	Tom McCartney, Casey McGovern, Sheldon Murphy, Dave Lopez
1990	C	Leslie	3:27.7	Curt Jordan, John Miller, Ty Huttenlocker, Art Bischoff
1991	C	Leslie	3:26.5	Steve DeBruler, Todd Craddock, Ty Huttenlocker, John Miller
1992	C	Leslie	3:28.0	Ty Huttenlocker, John Miller, Lasse Nilsen, Matthew Johnson
1993	C	Scottville Mason County Central	3:28.28	Dave Hartman, Roger Bailey, Brad Patterson, Greg Patterson

1994	C	New Haven	3:25.55	Greg Bryant, Billy Chenault, Fred Jamison, John Mack
1995	C	New Haven	3:29.95	Travis Kelly, Billy Chenault, Emmanuel Yates, John Mack
1996	C	New Haven	3:24.41	Travis Kelly, Tedaro France, Richard Sparks, John Mack
1997	C	New Haven	3:26.75	Richard Sparks, Tedaro France, Clifton Akers, Travis Kelly
1998	C	Sanford Meridian	3:29.63	Jason Hall, Justin Wood, Mike Gray, Brian McDonald
1999	C	Buchanan	3:25.85	Brad Benninghoff, Jonathon Yasko, Calvin Treadwelll, Melvin Treadwell
2000	D3	Clare	3:25.41*	Aaron Warner, Joe Paisley, Kyle Kolbe, Josh Rodgers
2001	D3	Benzie Central	3:26.27	Jordan Dennis, Ian Hunsinger, Kai Johansson, Brad Giglio
2002	D3	Jackson Lumen Christi	3:25.58	Keegan Farrell, Scott Bull, Charles Henry, Scott Sinclair
2003	D3	Detroit Country Day	3:25.47	Kim Thompson, Martin Comiffe, Rohit Khanna, Dermea Carter
2004	D3	Hudson	3:24.65*	Scott Rupnow, Ben Bloom, Brad Wilson, Brandon Murphy
2005	D3	Frankenmuth	3:22.37*	Casey Bierlein, Kevin Horn, Kendall Judson, Mike Golden
2006	D3	Detroit Country Day	3:23.14	Brian Tan, Chris Jackson, Martin Corniffe, Chris Rucker
2007	D3	Detroit Country Day	3:26.57	Brian Tan, Chris Jackson, Jonas Gray, Chris Rucker
2008	D3	Vermontville Maple Valley	3:24.71	Ron Morehouse, Charles Wymer, Nick Thurlby, Jeff Burd
2009	D3	Vermontville Maple Valley	3:23.86	Ron Morehouse, Josh Hall, Nick Thurlby, Jeff Burd
2010	D3	Frankenmuth	3:23.50	Ben Carter, Daniel Zeddies, Charles Wenzel, Lucas Bade
2011	D3	Frankenmuth	3:22.70	Ben Carter, Veitengruber, Jeremy Borchard, Luke Bade
2012	D3	Lansing Catholic	3:24.63	Matt Macksood, Jimmy Hicks, Connor Caporale, Zach Zingsheim
2013	D3	Wyoming Kelloggsville	3:24.27	Dionte Williams, Jordan Shannon, Reginald Roberts, T.J. Burnett
2014	D3	Sanford Meridian	3:21.44*	Dan Johnson, Kevin Scheibert, Jacob Ham, Jacob Wenzlick
2015	D3	Adrian Madison	3:28.45	Christopher Kangas, Isiah Wyatt-Young, Connor Mellon, Colby Weitenhagen
2016	D3	Hillsdale	3:23.96	Aaron Smith, Sam Nash, Charles Hohlbrook, Devin VanDusen
2017	D3	Lansing Catholic	3:23.56	Ryan Schroeder, Noah Alvarado, Ryan Ruiter, Konnor Maloney
2018	D3	Berrien Springs	3:23.42	Payton White, Nate Nannfeldt, Noah Sheline, Evan Griffiths

4 x 400 – Class D/Division 4 Champions

(Mile Medley Relay – 440y-220-220-880)

1947	D	Flint Utley	4:03.7*	Bob Gunnels, Ray Lord, Carl Carlson, Dwight Dockery

(3/4 Medley Relay – 440y-220-220-440)

1948	D	Luther	2:47.2*	Harold Miller, Elwin Purchase, Elin Reed, Eddie Slatkowski
1949	D	Luther	2:42.3*	Harold Miller, Elin Reed, Elwin Purchase, Eddie Slatkowski
1950	D	Albion Starr Commonwealth	2:40.1*	Bill Pulsifer, Norm Armstrong, Al Lovely, Walt McNay
1951	D	Otisville	2:42.4	Bob Price, Boyd Haddix, Norton Averill, Rollie Hughes
1952	D	Spring Arbor	2:48.1	Charles Terman, Don Jones, Ward Sites, Paul Lynch
1953	D	Spring Arbor	2:40.7	Del Marter, Bill Barkwell, Chuck Terman, Paul Lynch
1954	D	Vermontville	2:43.2	Bill Ames, Mike Newman, Bill Gaedert, Bob Stewart
1955	D	Spring Arbor	2:41.3	Paul Andrews, Fred Whims, Wes Bailor, Lowell Dunkel
1956	D	Spring Arbor	nt	Dave Webb, Sam Manson, Bill Getsinger, Howard Snyder
1957	D	Dansville	2:44.0	Roger Lininger, Larry Soule, Jerry Wing, Kaye Douglas
1958	D	Brethren	2:35.5*	Lionel Connelly, Frank Thomas, Larry Connelly, Charles Beane
1959	D	Grass Lake	2:40.6	Dick Beal, Dick Corey, Al Kaiser, Dave Daken
1960	D	Grass Lake	2:38.9	John Lindamood, Dick Beal, Al Kaiser, Dave Daken

(4 x 400; y=4 x 440 yards)

1961	D	Michigan School for Deaf	3:37.4y*	Gerald Blakely, Abram Powell, Don Smith, Caswell Hassell
1962	D	Michigan School for Deaf	3:35.4y*	Gerald Vernon, Steve Kovacs, Ron Smith, Caswell Hassell
1963	D	Michigan School for Deaf	3:35.8y	Bill Angelback, Frank Fickies, Steve Kovacs, Abraham Powell
1964	D	Grosse Pointe University	3:39.5y	Warren Finke, Craig Jennings, Roy Pingel, Burt Taylor
1965	D	Grosse Pointe University	3:35.2y*	Craig Jennings, Mark Weiss, Roy Pingel, Burt Taylor
1966	D	Litchfield	3:36.1y	Gary Adams, Don Bill, Mike Bill, John Johnston
1967	D	Michigan School for Deaf	3:39.0y	Dick Townsend, Mike Miller, Roy Jones, Everette Williams
1968	D	Mendon	3:31.7y*	Harold Jones, Bob Jones, Dick Rabbers, Jim Bingeman
1969	D	Athens	3:34.4y	Stan Hargus, Carl Holt, Doug Keeton, John Royer
1970	D	Flint Holy Rosary	3:37.3y	Pat Shanahan, Carl Herstein, Dennis Darpal, Phil Lewis
1971	D	Unionville	3:33.5y	Joe Clearhart, Dave Hofmeister, Mike Gaeth, Terry Balzer
1972	D	Unionville	3:33.0y	Lauren Gainforth, Joe Claerhart, Terry Balzer, Mike Gaeth
1973	D	Mendon	3:29.8y*	Lloyd Wilds, Wayne Wilds, Brad Courtney, Randy Steinberger
1974	D	Flint Holy Rosary	3:31.0y	Mark Kelley, Jim Stevenson, Mark Ecker, George Butts
1975	D	Detroit East Catholic	3:31.5y	Ernest Wilson, Curtis Young, Michael Peoples, Michael Walton
1976	D	Homer	3:30.3y	Anthony Armstrong, Steve Snyder, Brian Mull, Charlie Prater
1977	D	Detroit DePorres	3:29.0y*	Mark McClendon, Leonard Thornton, Michael Hinton, Michael Taylor
1978	D	Litchfield	3:29.1y	Dave Smith, Brad Nelligan, Mike Ballard, Gary Sykes
1979	D	Detroit DePorres	3:25.6*	Greg Henderson, Vernon Lynch, Ray Robinson, Mike Taylor
1980	D	Detroit DePorres	3:27.9	Lee Hardy, Greg Henderson, Jerry Campbell, Ray Robinson
1981	D	Detroit DePorres	3:22.9*	Lebron Campbell, Darren Warner, Garfield Lemonious, Greg Henderson
1982	D	Detroit East Catholic	3:27.5	Stacy Cook, Eric King, Terrance Wallace, Kevin Carter
1983	D	Detroit East Catholic	3:26.1	Sean Jones, Sylvester Angel, Michael Gatson, Kevin Carter
1984	D	Allendale	3:30.10	Tim Kirk, Dave Woday, Scott Forgas, Dave Sella
1985	D	Allendale	3:28.00	Tim Kirk, Jose Medina, Dave Woday, Dave Sella
1986	D	Detroit East Catholic	3:28.51	Zekiel Miller, Willy Scott, Jeff Simmons, Martin Meekins
1987	D	Schoolcraft	3:30.25	Brad Johnson, Andy RIdge, Buzz Phelps, Bob Kaufman
1988	D	Lawton	3:29.03	Keith Oxley, Tim VanWyk, John Widner, Tony Lanphear
1989	D	Bellaire	3:28.0	Eric Nicholie, Robert Wilcox, Joel Reed, Rob Puroll
1990	D	Bellaire	3:27.79	Fabrice Lahoucine, Eric Nicholie, Joel Reed, Rob Puroll
1991	D	Detroit Lutheran West	3:27.57	Howard Hughey, LaRon Ellerbee, Richard Smith, Pat VanHorn
1992	D	Mendon	3:31.96	Mike Strayley, Todd Vanderkey, Randy Monroe, Terry Baker
1993	D	Battle Creek St Phillip	3:33.1	Kyle Maichele, Mike Hughes, Dieter Brown, William Maddix
1994	D	Au Gres	3:31.20	Otie McKinley, Ken McFarlane, Brian Kelly, Mike Kennealy
1995	D	Au Gres	3:31.12	Robert Sims, Robert Tremble, Ken McFarlane, Mike Kennealy
1996	D	Pittsford	3:29.08	Nick Grabowski, Matt Miller, Mark Caswell, Nick Salazar
1997	D	Pittsford	3:29.24	Mark Caswell, Nick Salazar, Rob Draper, Nick Grabowski
1998	D	Centreville	3:30.4	Kasey Sahli, Kelvin Singleton, Kori Sahli, Ryan Morris
1999	D	Grass Lake	3:27.27	Russell Rogan, Steve Sherwood, Ryan Mayer, Kris Kane
2000	D4	Pewamo-Westphalia	3:28.01*	Joe Klein, Justin Miller, Jeremy Weber, Josh Weber

2001	D4	Detroit Benedictine	3:28.24	Tony Lawrence, Marvin Reed, Vershawn Miller, Daniel McKinney
2002	D4	Detroit Benedictine	3:25.28*	Marvin Reed, Nick Lawrence, Marvin Reed, Vershawn Miller
2003	D4	Detroit Benedictine	3:27.25	Andre King, Tony Lawrence, Alvin Jackson, Daniel McKinney
2004	D4	Fowler	3:28.74	Ryan Halfman, Kyle Schmitt, Tyler Thelen, Matt Epkey
2005	D4	Fowler	3:27.70	Chase Weber, Blake Mueller, Tyler Thelen, Matt Epkey
2006	D4	Potterville	3:28.34	Jordan Houston, Tom Roush, Tim Slocum, Aaron Hunt
2007	D4	Pittsford	3:27.39	Kyle Schaedler, Jon Hatfield, Chris Smith, Mike Norton
2008	D4	Jonesville	3:28.45	Chad McOscar, Earl Stanhope, Chad Falk, Matt Magda
2009	D4	Potterville	3:29.50	Frankie Diaz, Caleb Jones, Larry Julson, Collin Ward
2010	D4	Detroit Loyola	3:25.86	Stefon Johnson, Jason Marzette, Travis Steinbeck-Riley, Najee A' ve
2011	D4	Big Rapids Crossroads	3:27.49	Jalen Carter, David Dantuma, Colby Conklin, Kyle Tait
2012	D4	Albion	3:29.94	Gary Chambers, Nolen Mitchell, Markeese Boyd, Zach Hudson
2013	D4	White Cloud	3:31.86	Taylor Rodriguez, Hunter Redman, David Dykstra, Hunter Redman
2014	D4	Concord	3:24.19*	Lonelle Langston, Lawson Bright-Mitchell, Chase Hinkle, Zach Hudson
2015	D4	Saugatuck	3:32.06	Aaron Rasmussen, Cole Hartman, Joe Brown, Blake Dunn
2016	D4	Centreville	3:28.28	Jared Zrank, Chase LeBarre, Ross Hunter, Nolan Troyer
2017	D4	Manton	3:27.37	Jacob Cergnul, Josh Cergnul, Treh Heisel, Jayden Perry
2018	D4	Concord	3:30.96	Zeavion Jones, TJ Kessman, Vincent Giuliano, Brayn Smith

4 x 400 – UP Class AB/Division 1 Champions

(Mile Medley Relay – 440y-220-220-880)
| 1947 | UPB | Menominee | 3:55.8* | |

(3/4 Medley Relay – 440y-220-220-440)
1948	UPB	Escanaba	2:44.6*	Dick Pryal, Don Carlson, John Beaumier, Gary Abrahamson
1949	UPB	Sault Ste. Marie	2:42.6*	
1950	UPB	Sault Ste. Marie	2:40.6*	Bonnaci, Fowler, Bob Mohrer, Gil Mroz
1951	UPB	Newberry	2:44.6	McIntyre, Monte Mohr, Jack Taylor, Thomas Taylor
1952	UPB	Ishpeming	2:45.0	Duane Doney, Len Altobello, Bob Sharland, Phillipi
1953	UPB	Sault Ste. Marie	2:45.4	Dave Sowasky, Henry Brown, Terry Martin, John Headley
1954	UPB	Ishpeming	2:41.5	
1955	UPB	Newberry	2:38.9*	Frank Holmberg, Joe Marceny, Gary Teska, Dave McLean
1956	UPB	Sault Ste. Marie	2:43.7	Tom Slater, Richard Leonard, Mike Reed, Billy Cooper
1957	UPB	Menominee	2:45.8	Dennis Boettcher, Tom Foley, Fritz Wolff, Jan Thoney
1958	UPB	Menominee	2:42.4	
1959	UPB	Stephenson	2:39.1	
1960	UPB	Marquette	2:38.3*	

(4 x 400; y=4 x 440 yards)
1961	UPB	Marquette	3:42.1y*	
1962	UPAB	Newberry	3:40.6y*	
1963	UPAB	Newberry	3:40.0y*	
1964	UPAB	Marquette	3:37.5y*	
1965	UPAB	Kingsford	3:37.8y	
1966	UPAB	Sault Ste. Marie	3:31.4y*	
1967	UPAB	Ishpeming	3:37.6y	
1968	UPAB	Gladstone	3:39.0y	
1969	UPAB	Ishpeming	3:37.7y	
1970	UPAB	Gwinn	3:30.4y*	Mike Newell, Cliff Stiles, Jeff Hatfield, Mike Hatfield
1971	UPAB	Menominee	3:32.7y	Ivan Plude, Leigh Pickl, Sid Homa, Pete Eisenseph
1972	UPAB	Marquette	3:33.9y	
1973	UPAB	Iron Mountain	3:31.8y	Steve Mariucci, Tom Izzo, Mark Noskey, Jared Cudnohofsky
1974	UPAB	Menominee	3:34.3y	Ken Callow, Dave Theyerkayf, Rod Branyan, Steve Sexsmith
1975	UPAB	Ironwood	3:34.1y	
1976	UPAB	Sault Ste. Marie	3:32.0y	
1977	UPAB	Menominee	3:34.9y	Joe Mackovitz, Micky Rynning, Mike Ostrenga, Scott Melchoir
1978	UPAB	Kingsford	3:36.1y	Kevin French, Tony Zablocki, Jeff Quas, David Unger
1979	UPAB	Gwinn	3:34.4	Rod Garwood, Chuck Gendron, Darryl Henry, Dusty Trail
1980	UPAB	Escanaba	3:31.8	Mike Liebel, Eric Larson, Chris Murray, Heff Wright
1981	UPAB	Menominee	3:32.9	Troy Clausen, Bruce Behrendt, Rich Olson, Marty Hynnek
1982	UPAB	Marquette	3:33.3	John Tish, Brody Reese, Mike Parejko, John Kingston
1983	UPAB	Marquette	3:34.9	Raul Desolza, Guy Neuchterlein, Brody Reese, Carl Erickson
1984	UPAB	Marquette	3:35.4	Bill Ralph, Mike Wichar, Brian Levandowski, Brody Reese
1985	UPAB	Menominee	3:38.0	Dave Boye, Phil Zagrodnik, Kevin Woods, Tim Casperson
1986	UPAB	Menominee	3:31.2	Marv Fernstrum, Kevin Woods, Phil Zagrodnik, Tim Casperson
1987	UPAB	Gwinn	3:33.1	David Leisch, Andrew Nordeen, Tony Jones, Folden Peterson
1988	UPAB	Marquette	3:32.5	Boris Martysz, Frank Holowitz, Tim Morrissette, Roman Gasowski
1989	UPAB	Kingsford	3:36.0	Jeff Povolo, Erick Klieman, Steve LaLonde, Chris Richard
1990	UPAB	Negaunee	3:30.3*	Brian Healey, Dan Atkins, Chris Nelson, Keith Collins
1991	UPAB	Gladstone	3:32.9	Matt Searle, Chris Hayes, Chad Maslowski, Brian Hampton
1992	UPAB	Sault Ste. Marie	3:38.8	Gavin Pike, Ron MArble, Phil McDonald, Brian Stillers
1993	UPAB	Menominee	3:31.4	Chip Burns, Briam Hemer, Shawn Seaberg, Tom Thompson
1994	UPAB	Marquette	3:31.4	Tim Lamirand, Todd Hartwig, Matt Tuccine, Robin Martin
1995	UPAB	Marquette	3:32.5	Tom Keefe, Todd Hartwig, Matt Tuccini, Robin Martin
1996	UPAB	Ishpeming Westwood	3:36.7	Jason Sundquist, Dean Schultz, Peter Remien, Dillon Car
1997	UPAB	Menominee	3:37.7	Shane Mundt, Joey Gasparick, Jamie Fehrenbach, Shawn Mckenny
1998	UPAB	Menominee	3:36.6	Shane Mundt, Eric Frusti, Chad LaCombe, Joe Gasparick
1999	UPAB	Marquette	3:34.3	Scott Stesney, Kris Erickson, Shannon Mathison, Ethan Rayhorn
2000	UPAB	Marquette	3:32.8	Justin Kleinschmidt, Shani Davis, Pete Tuccini, Fred Jaeckl
2001	UPD1	Sault Ste. Marie	3:33.1*	Daniel Brown, Josh Anderson, John Anderson, James Shannon
2002	UPD1	Marquette	3:32.0*	Jared Gogek, Evan Milton, Jordan Divine, Pete Tuccini
2003	UPD1	Marquette	3:29.18*	Jeremy Sergey, Chris Peterson, Jordan Divine, Pete Tuccini
2004	UPD1	Escanaba	3:30.11	Matt Harrison, Brandon Eis, Justin Wiles, Jay Wiles
2005	UPD1	Gladstone	3:33.50	James Cappeart, Mat Holm, Therrian, Charlie Stafford
2006	UPD1	Gladstone	3:32.24	James Cappeart, Charlie Stafford, Joe Mileski, Steve Therrian
2007	UPD1	Kingsford	3:32.84	Rich Paupore, Dan Sjoquist, Sean Williams, Josh Droese

2008	UPD1	Escanaba	3:32.22	Paul Wakefield, John Keepers, Josh Ostrenga, Mitch Vaneffen
2009	UPD1	Menominee	3:35.69	Adrian Delarosa, Anthony Wilson, James Graham, Jordan McMahon
2010	UPD1	Marquette	3:31.47	Forest Gilfoy, Aaron Detmers, Owen Jordan, Aaron Wissler
2011	UPD1	Marquette	3:30.21	Forest Gilfoy, Alex Gagnon, Aaron Detmers, Austin Wissler
2012	UPD1	Marquette	3:33.75	Alex Gagnon, Tyler Balko, Danny Brisson, Zach Taggart
2013	UPD1	Kingsford	3:37.04	Jaxson Ferree, Jacob Allen, Jack Glodowski, Tyler Roberts
2014	UPD1	Kingsford	3:31.18	Jaxson Ferree, Jake Allen, Jack Glodowski, Tyler Roberts
2015	UPD1	Marquette	3:33.35	Riley Lynch, Matthew Millado, Nathan Schlorke, Andrew Banitt
2016	UPD1	Marquette	3:35.34	Matthew Millado, Julien Malherbe, Jesse Elsenbroek, Garrett Rudden
2017	UPD1	Marquette	3:33.63	Julien Malherbe, Matthew Millad, Alex Duvall, Collin Shinner
2018	UPD1	Marquette	3:35.87	Julien Malherbe, Nathan Zika, Mathurin Gagnon, Garret Rudden

4 x 400 – UP Class C/Division 2 Champions

(Mile Medley Relay – 440y-220-220-880)
| 1947 | UPC | Houghton | 4:01.6* | |

(3/4 Medley Relay – 440y-220-220-440)
1948	UPC	Houghton	2:45.6*	
1949	UPC	Wakefield	2:43.7*	Duane Lane, Rudy Valesano, Joh Niemi, Paul Gottwald
1950	UPC	Houghton	2:46.4	
1951	UPC	Houghton	2:47.7	
1952	UPC	Bessemer	2:48.6	Jim Biessel, Hal Hansen, William Contratto, Roy Pingel
1953	UPC	Bessemer	2:43.4*	Jim Biessel, Norm Crockett, James Contratto, Richard Ceno
1954	UPC	Bessemer	2:44.2	Leonard Selin, Fred Trevarthen, James Contratto, Norman Crockett
1955	UPC	Bessemer	2:44.0	Phillip Masse, Richard Ceno, Fred Travarthen, Stanley Marshalek
1956	UPC	Bessemer	2:41.5*	Phil Masse, David Carpenedo, Art DaPra, Don Borich
1957	UPC	St. Ignace	2:45.9	
1958	UPC	Bessemer	2:46.1	Jim Corgiat Darryl Pricco, George Baksie, Bob Slomkoski
1959	UPC	Sault Ste. Marie Loretto	2:45.1	
1960	UPC	Stephenson	2:40.1*	

(4 x 400; y=4 x 440 yards)
1961	UPC	Stephenson	3:44.9y*	Clark Suchovsky, D. Grinsteiner, T. Phillips, J. Dougovito
1962	UPC	Bessemer	3:45.8y	Tom Makinen, Bob Carpenedo, Louis Marconeri, John Bonovetz
1963	UPC	Houghton	3:45.3y	
1964	UPC	Ontonagon	3:41.1y*	Howard Hegg, Jim Torvinen, David Hegg, Larry Makimaa
1965	UPC	L'Anse	3:38.8y*	
1966	UPC	Stephenson	3:41.1y	
1967	UPC	L'Anse	3:43.5y	
1968	UPC	Stephenson	3:39.8y	Dennis Freis, Byron Lord, Dennis Axeljun, Mark Dougovito
1969	UPC	Stephenson	3:42.7y	Darrell Freis, Bill Koldos, Dennis Alexejun, Barry Hafeman
1970	UPC	Ontonagon	3:35.4y*	Dan Milla, Jerry Stork, Mickey McGuire, Jim Younk
1971	UPC	Norway	3:36.9y	
1972	UPC	Bessemer	3:36.6y	Gary Strelcheck, Tim Marczak, Mike Hoffner, Dave Forslund
1973	UPC	Rudyard	3:38.3y	
1974	UPC	Negaunee	3:37.0y	
1975	UPC	Ishpeming	3:37.3y	
1976	UPC	Ishpeming Westwood	3:34.4y*	
1977	UPC	Rudyard	3:33.2y*	
1978	UPC	Manistique	3:33.8y	D.J. Brady, Bill Giles, Ben Culey, John Pistulka
1979	UPC	Ontonagon	3:38.2	Ross Longhini, Howie Seid, Dave Lange, Bob Westphall
1980	UPC	Iron Mountain	3:34.6	Tom Flaminio, Chet Shields, Robert Helberg, Steve Flaminio
1981	UPC	Ironwood	3:32.9*	Mark Kivisto, Jim Estola, Tom Berquist, Mike McPhearson
1982	UPC	Ironwood	3:31.4*	Darryl Petrusha, Jim Kivisto, Jim Estola, Mike McPherson
1983	UPC	Ishpeming Westwood	3:33.6	Dave Froberg, Gregg Milton, Rob Maki, Dan Perry
1984	UPC	Ishpeming Westwood	3:31.9	Bryan Ross, Darrell Mailanen, Rudy Nyman Dan Perry
1985	UPC	St. Ignace	3:36.5	Brad Erskine, Kit Huskey, Dennis St. Andrew, Andy Leupnetz
1986	UPC	Ishpeming Westwood	3:32.9	Al Harvala, Bill Moore, Darrel Moilanen, John Carter
1987	UPC	Iron Mountain	3:35.2	Jim Flaminio, John Novara, Jeff Webb, Bill Potter
1988	UPC	Iron Mountain	3:32.7	Kevin Veale, John Novara, Craig Podgornik, Bill Potter
1989	UPC	Negaunee	3:34.2	Jon Waara, Brian Healey, Chris Nelson, Keith Collins
1990	UPC	Rudyard	3:35.7	Erik Olson, Jon Broog, Jay FInk, Dave Blake
1991	UPC	Negaunee	3:33.4	Jon Beckman, Brian Bartle, Chris Nelson, Keith Collins
1992	UPC	Hancock	3:42.6	Jason VanHoui, Mark Peters, Petr Belej, Matt Peters
1993	UPC	Rudyard	3:35.7	Jeremy Hauswirth, Lenny Becker, Chris Suggitt, Eric Schemmel
1994	UPC	St. Ignace	3:33.1	Brad Ledy, Sean McLafferty, Leonard Thomas, Brian Lorente
1995	UPC	Iron Mountain	3:35.1	Kevin Anderson, Bob Feredy, Tony Formell, Jason Wenders
1996	UPC	St. Ignace	3:32.8	Joel Kelso, Mike Stempki, Charlie Pierson, Brian Lorente
1997	UPC	St. Ignace	3:31.7	Joel Kelso, Charlie Pierson, Lewis Stempki, Mike Stempki
1998	UPC	Munising	3:35.6	Brian Spaulding, Shawn Pyle, Paul Lukowski, Ben Perry
1999	UPC	Newberry	3:34.8	Troy Bergman, Vince Randazzo, Eric Rocker, Matt McNamara
2000	UPC	Manistique	3:34.1	George Wood, Cheyne Herro, Darren Smith, Jermiah Beckman
2001	UPD2	Newberry	3:32.9*	Jim Miller, Matt Mcnamara, Eric Rocker, Dan Hiltunen
2002	UPD2	Norway	3:36.8	Justin Allen, Chad Beauchamp, Tony Mendina, Nick Zweifel
2003	UPD2	Ishpeming	3:35.00	Sean Palo, Ryan Mirinac, Alex Beerling, Eric Palo
2004	UPD2	Norway	3:33.49	Jim DeBartolo, Lane Thaler, Dan Skog, Nick Zweifel
2005	UPD2	Manistique	3:33.57	Adam Jewett, Dustin Matchinski, Cody Kangas, Brandon Lawrence
2006	UPD2	Ishpeming	3:36.69	Ryan Lusardi, Cory McCullough, Jake Lehmaann, Dustin Brancheau
2007	UPD2	Manistique	3:36.86	Cody Kangas, Pat McDonald, Garde Kangas, Brandon Lawrence
2008	UPD2	Manistique	3:36.07	Joe Delisle, Cody Kangas, Garde Kangas, Brandon Lawrence
2009	UPD2	St. Ignace	3:37.92	Anthony Lester, Evan Everson, Robby Robinson, Kevin Guillard
2010	UPD2	Stephenson	3:39.92	Jake Herres, Brett Parrett, Roman Alberti. Nolan Lakasik
2011	UPD2	Rudyard	3:44.69	Jared Clark, David Jarvie, AJ Jones, Brandon Hughes
2012	UPD2	Ishpeming	3:39.04	Zach Kinnunen, Ryan Leonard, Adam Prisk, Nate Meyer
2013	UPD2	Manistique	3:42.38	Kennar Broulire, Robert Ayitte, Ryan Ramey, Bryson Lawrence
2014	UPD2	Ishpeming	3:39.01	Jaren Kipling, Ozzy Corp. Adam Prisk, Nate Meyer

2015	UPD2	Ishpeming	3:45.18	Mark Holmgren, Derek Mahoski, Daren Guichin, Nate Meyer
2016	UPD2	Ishpeming	3:48.79	Donald Denofre, Daren Guichin, Kazmine Longness, Derek Mahoski
2017	UPD2	Ironwood	3:43.47	Ellio Gudgeon, Ian Hughes, Karl Bissell, Nick Niemi
2018	UPD2	Iron Mountain	3:40.31	Jake Dumais, Charlie Gerhard, Jaden Vicenzi, Michael Kulas

4 x 400 – UP Class D/Division 3 Champions

(Mile Medley Relay – 440y-220-220-880)

| 1947 | UPD | Marquette Pierce | 4:16.3* | |

(3/4 Medley Relay – 440y-220-220-440)

1948	UPD	Eben	2.55.4*	
1949	UPD	Chassell	2:49.1*	
1950	UPD	Alpha	2:50.5	
1951	UPD	Marquette Pierce	2:52.1	
1952	UPD	Pickford	2:47.5*	Larry Crawford, Charles Izzard, Ronell Leach, Royce Miller
1953	UPD	Nahma	2:50.7	
1954	UPD	Pickford	2:49.0	Eldred Leach, Jim Graham, Jim Quinnell Roland McCready
1955	UPD	Pickford	2:47.9	Fred McCready, Bill Wallis, Phillip Stevenson, Gerald Wallis
1956	UPD	Pickford	2:49.7	Allen Lordson, Gerald Wallis, Carl Dosenbach, Jim Roe
1957	UPD	Pickford	2:47.3*	Allen Lordson, Terry Gough, Garald Wallis, Darrell Izzard
1958	UPD	Pickford	2:47.7	Ron Pennington, Bill Kibble, Don Thompson, Larry Hatfield
1959	UPD	Pickford	2:47.0*	David Beacom, Donald Thompson, Bruce Taylor, Andrew Stevenson
1960	UPD	Pickford	2:42.0*	Chester Crawford, Jack Rutledge, Wayne Zwolinski, Gary Leach

(4 x 400; y=4 x 440 yards)

1961	UPD	DeTour	3:45.0y*	
1962	UPD	Pickford	3:49.6y	Donald Cruickshank, Dick Beacom, Jim LaVictor, John Jeske
1963	UPD	DeTour	3:43.8y*	Ron Zwolinski, Gary Cloudman, Dick Soczek, Jim Stevenson
1964	UPD	Pickford	3:42.8y*	George Rye, David Wilson, Gene Thompson, Paul Adams
1965	UPD	DeTour	3:41.8y*	
1966	UPD	Pickford	3:35.5y*	Dick Fountain, Bud Jeske, Bill Bawks, Jim Belinski
1967	UPD	Pickford	3:47.0y	Dick Fountain, Bud Jeske, Kenneth Bartho, David Lamb
1968	UPD	Pickford	3:45.8y	Rick Wonnacott, Bob Wonnacott, Ken Batho, Bob Rapson
1969	UPD	Wakefield	3:44.1y	Bruce Rukkila, Stan Wasielewski, Dale Johns, Stanley Johns
1970	UPD	Pickford	3:38.9y	Rick Wonnacott, Mike Wise, Chuck Hill, Tom Wilson
1971	UPD	Pickford	3:42.3y	Bob Galer, John Walter, Steve Andrzejak, Don Wilson
1972	UPD	Wakefield	3:42.8y	Tim Makela, Jim Carey, Paul Kolesar, Mark Johns
1973	UPD	Pickford	3:35.3y*	Mark McDonald, Dana Hill, Steve Andrzejak, Bruce Bawks
1974	UPD	Pickford	3:42.3y	Mark McDonald, Dana Hill, Steve Andrzejak, Bruce Bawks
1975	UPD	Pickford	3:38.8y	Steve Fountain, Tim Leach, Kevin Hamilton, Mike Ordiwdy
1976	UPD	DeTour	3:37.4y	
1977	UPD	Pickford	3:35.6y	Bruce Wagner, Mike McCord, John Andrzejak, Bob Bosley
1978	UPD	White Pine	3:38.5y	
1979	UPD	Crystal Falls Forest Park	3:39.0	Kelly Boyle, Dan Kivimaki, David Reitmeyer, Tracy Smith
1980	UPD	Cedarville	3:31.8*	Jamie Leach, Glenn Wandrie, Paul Freebury, Roger Bock
1981	UPD	Bark River-Harris	3:37.3	John Sheski, Dan Glimn, Chuck Gorecki, Brent Madalinski
1982	UPD	Wakefield	3:34.3	Rick Doney, Jack Liimakka, Doug Buckler, Jim Buckler
1983	UPD	St. Ignace	3:35.5	Kevin Laver, Randy Marshall, Richard Frazier, John Currie
1984	UPD	Bessemer	3:34.8	Ken Coleberg, Jim Mattrella, Jeff Golembeski, Ron Carpenedo
1985	UPD	Rudyard	3:42.4	Barry Nayback, Terin Salo, Fred Seames, Ed Folkersma
1986	UPD	Rapid River	3:38.9	Paul Stage, Mark Lenards, Tom Fix, Tom Thibault
1987	UPD	Wakefield	3:41.0	Rich Hemming, Dane Valesano, Mike Miskovich, Brian Pedrin
1988	UPD	Wakefield	3:38.0	Rick Hemming, Dane Rautiola, Duane Valesano, Mike Miskovich
1989	UPD	Eben Junction Superior Central	3:39.3	Mike Johnson, Jake Tyner, Tom Cox, Walt Thompson
1990	UPD	Lake Linden-Hubbell	3:39.0	Chris Perreault, James Keranen, Alex Acevedo, James Wilis
1991	UPD	Pickford	3:35.0	Ben Leach, Matt Bawks, Cal Ledy, Todd Dumbeck
1992	UPD	Pickford	3:46.4	Jason Kronemeyer, Ben Leach, Dave Dodds, Cal Ledy
1993	UPD	Felch North DIckinson	3:40.0	Fran Broeders, Kurt Kramer, Chad Bruno, John Richard
1994	UPD	Felch North DIckinson	3:37.7	Fran Broeders, Dominic Cherubini, Jamie Steinbrecher, John Richard
1995	UPD	Chassell	3:41.6	Ben Bachman, Mike Beiring, Jou Soumis, Jesse Soumis
1996	UPD	Crystal Falls Forest Park	3:41.3	Shawn Zaupa, Josh Ketola, Mike Hammel, Mike Simeoni
1997	UPD	Rapid River	3:43.1	Zach Nutt, Todd Stage, Nathan Wolf, Andy Schoenenberger
1998	UPD	Rapid River	3:41.4	Adam Cole, Greg Erkkila, Eric Lundin, Greg Bruno
1999	UPD	Felch North DIckinson	3:39.4	Jared Ferguson, Janssen Baij, Brad Sundholm, Nick Carlson
2000	UPD	Rock-Mid Peninsula	3:40.5	Luke Maulding, Jim Brayak, Jake Gobert, Steve Koski
2001	UPD3	Rock-Mid Peninsula	3:39.4*	Luke Maulding, Chris Sicotte, Jake Gobert, Steve Koski
2002	UPD3	Pickford	3:41.2	Brad Hunter, Doug Wallis, Adam Wallis, Joe Nyberg
2003	UPD3	Rock-Mid Peninsula	3:46.34	Anthony West, Josh Moore, Terry Verbrigghe, Chris Sicotte
2004	UPD3	Bessemer	3:40.53	Brandon Kupitz, Dane Hautala, Andrew Mettler, Casey Trevarthen
2005	UPD3	Bessemer	3:41.08	Brandon Kupitz, Aaron Zaleski, Casey Trevarthen, Andrew Mettler
2006	UPD3	Rock Mid Peninsula	3:40.04	Cory Winklebauer, Todd Winklebauer, Trey Beauchamp, Justin Wigand
2007	UPD3	Rock-Mid Peninsula	3:37.51*	Todd Winkelbauer, Keith Reynolds, Matt Viau, Justin Wigand
2008	UPD3	Cedarville	3:43.50	Zach McFarlane, Jake Wellnitz, Clayton Meyers, Jason Duncan
2009	UPD3	Crystal Falls Forest Park	3:39.90	Mick Valesano, Tim Martin, Alex Takala, Tony Greco
2010	UPD3	Crystal Falls Forest Park	3:44.44	Alex Takala, Jake Divine, Derek Aberly, Tim Martin
2011	UPD3	Pickford	3:42.45	Isaac Leach, Austin Brunning, Paul Morrison, Alec Firack
2012	UPD3	Crystal Falls Forest Park	3:36.32*	Alex Takala, Mark Hallman, Jake Divine, Derek Aberly
2013	UPD3	Pickford	3:42.01	Jarred Levigne, Justin Portice, Alec Firack, Austin Bruning
2014	UPD3	Powers-North Central	3:41.73	Tristen Harper, Josh Granquist, Jason Whitens, Bryce Holle
2015	UPD3	Powers-North Central	3:43.41	Dylan Gagne, Tyler Bentley, Tristen Harper, Bryce Holle
2016	UPD3	Powers-North Central	3:38.04	Dylan Gagne, Tyler Bentley, Trenton Schaff, Bryce Holle
2017	UPD3	Rapid River	3:34.52*	Conner Bryant, Luke Gustafson, Cam Willemsen, Austin Wickland
2018	UPD3	Bessemer	3:37.74	Tim Rowe, Cade Mazzon, Isaiah Aili, Brayden Tomes

BOYS 4 x 800 RELAY

Records

D1	7:38.97	Saline	Logan Wetzel, Josiah Humphrey, Austin Welch, Kevin Hall	2015
D2	7:50.70	Zeeland East	Scott Binder, Dan Cramer, Matt Cramer, John Groendyke	2015
D3	7:49.83	Williamston	David Ash, Tyler Sharp, Dan Nix, Chris Pankow	2006
D4	8:01.17	Unionville-Sebewaing	Brennan Pitcher, Matt Niziolek, Matt Eisengruber, Jared Fischer	2006
UPD1	8:02.4	Marquette	Jamison Cihak, Evan Milton, Conrad Esslin, Joe Graci	2001
UPD2	8:21.18	Ironwood	Mike McPherson, Alan Peterson, John Jacisin, Dominic Beckman	2007
UPD3	8:29.88	Bessemer	Tim Rowe, Cade Mazzon, Isiah Aili, Braydan Tomes	2017

Records by Class (pre-2000 for LP, pre-2001 for UP)

A	7:41.29	Monroe	Derek Bork, Matt Schroeder, Chris Brown, Tim Pitcher	1988
B	7:48.36	St Joseph	Ben Watson, Lars Petske, Mike Mandarino, Matt Hutchinson	1998
C	7:58.2	DeWitt	Dana DeWitt, Mike Simon, Mike Price, Kent Garside	1985
D	8:01.2	New Buffalo	Pat Butler, John Calo, Mark Lucas, Kyle Lindley	1998
UPAB	8:11.7	Marquette	Patrick Brown, Tom Brown, Ty Shesky, Robin Martin	1995
UPC	8:13.8	Ishpeming Westwood	Peter Marcotte, Al Harvala, Bill Moore, John Carter	1986
UPD	8:26.4	Rudyard	Ed Folkersma, Terin Salo, Shawn Ostrander, Garet Cornwell,	1986

4 x 800 – Class A/Division 1 Champions

1984	A	Detroit Central	7:50.5*	Omar Johnson, Anderson Bowles, James Johnson, Orssie Bumpus
1985	A	Detroit Mumford	7:53.09	David Singleton, Kendrick Williams, Roy Holt, Kent Vinson
1986	A	Detroit Murray-Wright	7:50.02	Ervin Fielder, Derek Wilson, Earl Harris, Asika Snelling
1987	A	Farmington	7:48.5*	Chris Inch, Alen Stebbins, Ron Smedley, Brandon London
1988	A	Monroe	7:41.29*	Derek Bork, Matt Schroeder, Chris Brown, Tim Pitcher
1989	A	Monroe	7:48.25	Derek Bork, Sean Sweat, Matt Schroeder, Tim Pitcher
1990	A	Troy	7:57.40	Ramsey Wilson, Ed Andrews, Alex Ramso, Jeff Cox
1991	A	Pontiac Northern	7:53.36	Marcus Steed, Ernest Sledge, Gavin Herring, Dionne Finney
1992	A	Detroit Catholic Central	7:58.00	Aaron Sheposh, Brandon Dalziel, Eric McKeon, Steve Witer
1993	A	Detroit Mumford	7:53.95	Joe Stevens, Shelby Thomas, Keenan Tindle, Eric Williams
1994	A	Ann Arbor Pioneer	7:49.1	Don McLaughlin, Keith Braxton, Ben Ingram, Steffan Hacker
1995	A	Pontiac Northern	8:04.5	Delshawn White, Kareem Manley, Greg Meyers, Godfrey Herring
1996	A	Ann Arbor Pioneer	7:56.30	Keith Brayton, Mike Humes, Eric Richtmyer, Ben Ufer
1997	A	White Lake Lakeland	7:49.58	Lance Binoniemi, Ryan Jones, Nick Gow, Anthony Sager
1998	A	White Lake Lakeland	7:46.31	Anthony Sager, Rich Oltesvig, Nick Gow, B.J. McCool
1999	A	Milford	7:52.18	Brandon Lawson, Brad Rutkowski, Eric D'Andrea, Tom Greenles
2000	D1	Saline	7:47.81*	Sean Moore, Steve Sherer, Mike Kusner, Nick Battle
2001	D1	Grand Ledge	7:47.52*	Brendan Robinson, Aaron Fedewa, Andy Thorson, Bobby Sherman
2002	D1	Detroit Mumford	7:43.46*	Isiah Marshall, Daniel Rounds, Jimmie Jones, Hoisea Jones
2003	D1	Detroit Mumford	7:48.02	Isiah Marshall, Blake Figgins, Keith Hewitt, Jimmie Jones
2004	D1	Saline	7:41.27*	Dustin Voss, Neil Atzinger, Carter Bishop, Alex Muhs
2005	D1	Milford	7:45.30	Joel Vanderworp, Andrew McKeachie, Michael Anderson, Dana Pitcock
2006	D1	Detroit Mumford	7:52.76	Michael Barry, Cedric Everson, Isiah Ward, Kendick Price
2007	D1	Ann Arbor Pioneer	7:45.20	Chris Fortson, Mike Wiesbuch, Shane Kunselman, James Wade
2008	D1	Detroit Mumford	7:44.79	George Jackson, Isiah Ward, Shaka Dukes, Kris Washington
2009	D1	Detroit Catholic Central	7:47.57	Brandon Schneider, Austin Zebrowski, Alex Toloff, Spencer Hall
2010	D1	Temperance Bedford	7:43.8	Tommy Valade, Chad Machinski, Dan Thompson, Nick Kaiser
2011	D1	Pinckney	7:49.45	Eric Fagan, Cal Magier, Jake Magier, Zac Meston
2012	D1	Milford	7:43.42	Shawn Welch, Kyle Monagle, Paul Ausum, Brandon Wallace
2013	D1	Saline	7:47.49	Anthony Lamus, Andrew Kitto, Ryan Wilkie, Matt Elms
2014	D1	Saline	7:40.54*	Logan Wetzel, Ryan Wilkie, Ruan Gauche, John Davis
2015	D1	Saline	7:38.97*	Logan Wetzel, Josiah Humphrey, Austin Welch, Kevin Hall
2016	D1	Rockford	7:43.92	Grayson Harding, Isaac Harding, Cole Johnson, Matthew MacGregor
2017	D1	Oak Park	7:44.85	Dewan Hawthorne, Javonn Kirksey, Michael Campbell, Cameron Cooper
2018	D1	Ann Arbor Pioneer	7:45.64	Netunji Paige, Aldo Pando-Girard, John Florence, Nick Foster

4 x 800 – Class B/Division 2 Champions

1984	B	Inkster Cherry Hill	7:58.9*	Ed Mulrooney, Richard Smith, Quinn Lawrence, Larry Dison
1985	B	Jackson Lumen Christi	8:04.08	Steve Gibson, Robert Wood, Todd Ross, David Ziolkowski
1986	B	Flint Beecher	8:02.8	Michael Ford, Rhaman Cleveland, Stacy Watson, Aaron McFadden
1987	B	Flint Beecher	7:52.3*	Stacy Watson, Michael Ford, Rhamon Cleveland, Aaron McFadden
1988	B	Flint Beecher	7:48.65*	Corey Massey, Kenneth Ellis, Aaron McFadden, Stacy Watson
1989	B	Essexville Garber	7:53.8	Mike Zolnierek, Fred Scharffe, Paul Navarre, Mike Nesbitt
1990	B	Algonac	8:04.8	Nick White, Mike Tesmer, Mike DeVlaminck, Ryan Hammang
1991	B	Oxford	8:01.38	Mark Goodfellow, Kurt Stephenson, Vidal Fragoso, Erik Welch
1992	B	Flint Beecher	8:03.69	McKinley Tipton, Marcus Brown, Ronald Allen, Marcus Tipton
1993	B	Fremont	7:56.70	Walter Florence, Scott Waterstredt, Brent Luchies, Dan Rader
1994	B	Chelsea	7:58.68	Dan Wehrwein, Scott Hawley, Ryan Schultz, Cory Brown
1995	B	Ludington	8:07.53	Keith Vroman, James Carlson, Mike Bucholtz, Roger Tominski
1996	B	Ludington	8:03.74	Mike Bucholtz, David Nickleson, Jeremy Horstman, James Carlson
1997	B	St. Joseph	7:57.2	Shawn Gast, Matt Hutchinson, Ben Watson, Lars Petzke
1998	B	St. Joseph	7:48.36*	Ben Watson, Lars Petske, Mike Mandarino, Matt Hutchinson
1999	B	Corunna	7:59.08	Robbie Currie, Aaron Lindell, Jared Aldrich, Kris Krzyminsk
2000	D2	Romulus	8:00.03*	Jarvis Jordan, Ashley Terry, Henry Staple, Caleb Beasly
2001	D2	Petoskey	7:59.60*	Adam Rensel, Nick Touran, Donovon Irish, Travis Biziorek
2002	D2	Holland Christian	8:00.13	Tyler Zwagerman, Brain Kragt, Rick Vogelzang, Neal Karsten

2003	D2	Wyoming Park	7:57.59*	Mark Vandermeer, Conrad Coipel, Chris Witbrodt, Joel Kirach
2004	D2	Cedar Springs	7:58.86	Dan Cramer, Tom Thornton, Rodney Smith, Mike Bigney
2005	D2	Chelsea	7:55.42*	Dan Lewis, Al Stewart, Brendan Smith, Ian Girard
2006	D2	Chelsea	8:02.53	Al Stewart, Brendan Smith, Riley Feeney, Ian Girard
2007	D2	Fenton	7:52.31*	Alex Ralston, Joe Kryza, Jesse Anderson, Joe Dimambro
2008	D2	Zeeland West	8:00.78	Bobby Bassett, Derrick Kingshott, Dan Kung, Chris Schulist
2009	D2	Linden	8:02.41	Jake Hord, Kyle LeMieux, Dylan Ryan, Brendan Sage
2010	D2	Grand Rapids Forest Hills Eastern	7:56.40	Garrett Cullen, Chad Scott, Erik Bates, Spencer Ferris
2011	D2	East Lansing	8:00.15	Shane Glynn-Hebron, Daniel Richardson, Nick Pridnis, Robbie Glew
2012	D2	Zeeland West	7:55.62	Braden Werley, Sam Plaska, Jordan Lambert, Brad Mesbergen
2013	D2	Chelsea	7:55.84	Zack Rabbitt, Tony Vilmelye, David Trimas, Jacob Stubbs
2014	D2	Mason	7:56.72	Mason VanDyke, Ashton Griswold, Paul Piozak, Nathan Jones
2015	D2	Zeeland East	7:50.70*	Scott Binder, Dan Cramer, Matt Cramer, John Groendyke
2016	D2	Fruitport	7:54.39	Kody Brooks, Cameron Oleen, Seth Glover, Noah Hendricks
2017	D2	Lake Fenton	7:50.92	Elijah Bordeau, Remington Clements, Thomas Mueller, Isaac Gilson
2018	D2	Chelsea	7:56.48	Connor Gilbreath, Jensen Holm, Carson Rabbitt, Tom Oates

4 x 800 – Class C/Division 3 Champions

1984	C	Bath	8:03.0*	Dave Courser, Brad Pullman, Ray Rosenberry, Brad Abendroth
1985	C	DeWitt	7:58.2*	Dana DeWitt, Mike Simon, Mike Price, Kent Gartside
1986	C	Scottville Mason County Central	8:04.61	Chris Thurow, Tom Johnson, Dave Keefer, Jeff Barnett
1987	C	Leroy Pine River	8:10.11	Scott Detroittloff, Steve Detroittloff, Matt Lagrow, Rob Wing
1988	C	St. Joseph Lake Michigan Catholic	8:04.3	Brian Humes, Mark Feltner, Byron Delaney, Jack Loresti
1989	C	Constantine	7:59.43	Mike Russell, Eric Hagenbuch, Scott Outman, Joe McBride
1990	C	Edwardsburg	8:10.22	Brad Apel, Todd Gizzi, Shawn Neff, Pat Etherington
1991	C	Sandusky	8:04.7	Kurt Long, Dan Lawler, Ryan Rich, Britt Owen
1992	C	Charlevoix	8:06.8	Mike Sevenski, Matt Smith, Jason Frabis, Zach Pajtas
1993	C	Charlevoix	8:08.51	Jake Porath, Mike Bush, Matt Dickinson, Matt Smith
1994	C	Charlevoix	8:08.56	Matt Dickinson, Chris LeButt, Mike Bush, Brian Martinus
1995	C	Charlevoix	8:14.99	Brian Martinus, Chris LeButt, Matt Dickinson, Mike Bush
1996	C	Lutheran Westland	7:59.45	Jason Collins, Sam Patterson, Phil Kimmell, Brad Polkinghorn
1997	C	St. Louis	7:58.74	Tyler Allen, Ryan Lantzer, Andrew Luehm, Eric Salladay
1998	C	Kent City	8:10.57	John Ebers, Jason Burbachyn, John Miron, Steve Morales
1999	C	Hemlock	8:01.0	Brent Handley, Kevin Sule, Andy Goodenough, Rusty Flewillin
2000	D3	Hemlock	7:58.30*	Rusty Flewelling, Andy Goodenough, Troy Sanchez, Kevin Sule
2001	D3	Williamston	7:58.48	Mike Salisbiry, Fill Marlatt, Jason Stover, Pat Maynard
2002	D3	Williamston	8:05.33	B.J. Pankrow, David Bills, Erik Schultink, Fil Marelette
2003	D3	Williamston	7:57.98*	B.J. Pankrow, David Bills, Erik Schultink, Fil Marelette
2004	D3	Grand Rapids West Catholic	8:00.80	Erich Tanis, Chris Leikert, Ed DeVries, Sam Passenger
2005	D3	Unionville-Sebewaing	7:55.57*	Matt Eisengruber, Justin Rackam, Cam Wildner, Jared Fischer
2006	D3	Williamston	7:49.83*	Daicd Ash, Tyler Sharp, Dan Nix, Chris Pankow
2007	D3	Erie Mason	8:03.77	Josh Adams, Brandon Griffin, Alex Russeau, Jesiah Rodriguez
2008	D3	Grand Rapids West Catholic	8:01.89	Antonio Schafer, Colin Valliere, Ryan Scott, Mike Gravelyn
2009	D3	Allendale	8:00.12	Alex Shepherd, Chris Ruens, David Cheatham, Josh Moskalewski
2010	D3	Mason County Central	7:54.74	Jared Lauber, Jacob Hernandez, Dan Deller, Chris Conrad
2011	D3	Frankenmuth	8:02.49	Veitengruber, Jake Hall, Ben Sievert, Luke Bade
2012	D3	Lansing Catholic	8:01.27	Joe Marrah, Austin Winter, Jimmy Hicks, Zach Zingsheim
2013	D3	Mason County Central	7:57.04	Drew Griffin, Alex Meyers, Travess Smith, Chase Barnett
2014	D3	Jackson Lumen Christi	7:57.87	Karl Berkemeier, Patrick Soltis, Keaton Coffman, Patrick Ludlow
2015	D3	Hanover-Horton	8:00.20	Brennan Burk, Dakota Yeaster, Austin Shepherd, Lucas Crisanti
2016	D3	Bridgman	8:02.42	Elliott Hanke, Karl Hanke, Kole Hanke, Brian Njugunal
2017	D3	Charlevoix	8:03.13	Noah Carson, David Ritter, Alan Rittter, Luke Buday
2018	D3	Caro	8:05.71	Yami Albrecht, Caleb Cotton, Bryden Miller, Aaron Hulbert

4 x 800 – Class D/Division 4 Champions

1984	D	Ann Arbor Greenhills	8:10.87*	John Vorhess, Matt Hallop, Dave Dubin, Eban Rosenthal
1985	D	Fowler	8:16.33	Mike Pohl, Tom Armbrustmacher, Rick Klein, Steve Bierstetel
1986	D	Fowler	8:13.23	Steve Bierstetel, Tom Wirth, Rick Klein, Mike Pohl
1987	D	Fowler	8:13.8	Steve Bierstetel, Marty Fox, Paul Wirth, Mike Pohl
1988	D	Lawton	8:09.34*	Mark Key, Ian Fyvie, Tony Lanphear, John Widner
1989	D	Fowler	8:19.3	Lyle Feldpausch, Terry Schneider, Paul Wirth, Marty Fox
1990	D	Reading	8:10.49	Douglas Corcoran, Jason Rodesiler, Nick Wheeler, Darin Corcoran
1991	D	Schoolcraft	8:14.14	Scott Lockwood, Ken Mayes, Brian Lockwood, Geoff Coates
1992	D	Bath	8:12.25	Brent Clements, Duane McKenna, Mark Schlegel, Bob Hergert
1993	D	Camden-Frontier	8:15.6	Steve Stempen, Chris Shiffler, Ryan Rutz, Jake Snyder
1994	D	Grass Lake	8:14.49	Zach Hall, Trevor McGinn, Jason Embury, Martin McGinn
1995	D	Traverse City St. Francis	8:35.74	Pat Butler, Kyle Lindley, Adam Homolka, Grant Hill
1996	D	Grass Lake	8:16.9	Colin Dunham, Trevor McGinn, Russel Rogan, Zach Hall
1997	D	Grass Lake	8:11.7	Kevin Rogan, Colin Dunham, Ryan Mayer, Trevor McGinn
1998	D	New Buffalo	8:01.2*	Pat Butler, John Calo, Mark Lucas, Kyle Lindley
1999	D	Grass Lake	8:17.4	
2000	D4	McBain	8:06.65*	Derek Byrne, Kyle Eisenga, Greg Bonham, Brent Eisenga
2001	D4	Ubly	8:06.90	Keith Langoski, Eric Dekoski, Andy Duemling, Kyle Walsh
2002	D4	Detroit Benedictine	8:08.76	Andre King, Nick Lawrence, Marvin Reed, Vershawn Miller
2003	D4	Lawton	8:11.68	John Kuiper, Euan Escanilla, Andy Waite, Dan Orozoco
2004	D4	Vandercook Lake	8:13.36	Ray Lowe, Randall Wilcox, Adam Whitworth, Adam Sprangel
2005	D4	Potterville	8:09.49	Eric Clark, Corey Lucas, Jerris Dahlgren, Aaron Hunt
2006	D4	Unionville-Sebewaing	8:01.17*	Brennan Pitcher, Matt Niziolek, Matt Eisengruber, Jared Fischer
2007	D4	Potterville	8:12.60	Grant James, Larry Julson, Josh Lawrence, Collin Ward
2008	D4	Potterville	8:13.76	Larry Julson, Frankie Diaz, Kyle Lamb, Collin Ward
2009	D4	Hillsdale Academy	8:03.94	Ethan Smith, Joel Calvert, Ethan Gehrke, Tom Lundberg
2010	D4	Big Rapids Crossroads	8:02.43	Ethan Smith, Joel Calvert, Ethan Gehrke, Tom Lundberg
2011	D4	Big Rapids Crossroads	8:13.39	David Dantuma, Travis Blake, Jalen Carter, Colby Conklin

2012	D4	Albion	8:11.92	Bryan Peoples. Jamie Malcolm, Lonelle Langston, Zach Hudson
2013	D4	Saugatuck	8:11.11	Alex Auschutz, Sean Kelly, Joe Brown, Zach Kerr
2014	D4	Muskegon Western Michigan Christian	8:11.39	Elijah Vandervelde, Max Purvis, David Gilson, Braxton Snuffer
2015	D4	Muskegon Western Michigan Christian	8:07.82	David Gilson, Seth Vanderkooi, Jacob Ray, Braxton Snuffer
2016	D4	Hillsdale Academy	8:13.94	Greg Whalen, Sam Brady, Connor Oakley, Noah Heckenlively
2017	D4	Hillsdale Academy	8:06.95	Greg Whalen, Nick Rush, Connor Oakley, Noah Heckenlively
2018	D4	Hillsdale Academy	8:14.88	Nick Rush, John O'Connor, Connor Oakley, Ian Calvert

4 x 800 – UP Class AB/Division 1 Champions

1984	UPAB	Menominee	8:28.2*	Steve Koesling, Tim Casperson, Tim Mockus, Mike Nowack
1985	UPAB	Marquette	8:25.8*	John Lahti, Craig Rigby, Brian VendeBerg, Erick Werner
1986	UPAB	Escanaba	8:13.5*	Mike Malmstead, Glen Greg, Rhett Fisher, Dennis Miron
1987	UPAB	Escanaba	8:18.3	Roman Gasowski, Jeff Osowski, Pete Easton, Eirk Werner
1988	UPAB	Gwinn	8:18.6	Chris Peterson, John Berry, Greg Lahti, Eric Erickson
1989	UPAB	Marquette	8:27.5	Bryan Bjork, Scott Zorza, Jim Harbin, Jim Henning
1990	UPAB	Negaunee	8:14.8	Brian Spencer, Chris Cape, Brian Healey, Chris Nelson
1991	UPAB	Marquette	8:19.7	Ray Uimari, Jason Liberty, Jason Berglund, Kelly Keefe
1992	UPAB	Menominee	8:35.9	Matt Haight, Chris Davis, Wade Hodge, Jason Ladd
1993	UPAB	Escanaba	8:19.6	Jason Homa, Takuhide Negai, Tom Thompson, Shawn Seaberg
1994	UPAB	Marquette	8:19.6	Ty Shesky, Tom Brown, Robin Martin, Tom Lamirand
1995	UPAB	Marquette	8:11.7*	Patrick Brown, Tom Brown, Ty Shesky, Robin Martin
1996	UPAB	Escanaba	8:24.6	Matt Prey, Adam Weasler, Craig Miller, Ryan Horgan
1997	UPAB	Menominee	8:33.0	John Blake, Steve Campbell, Jamie Fehrenbach, David Ross
1998	UPAB	Negaunee	8:24.6	Jason Silk, Caden Ruohomaki, Jon Paul Katona, Rick Sanderson
1999	UPAB	Kingsford	8:29.2	Joe Roberts, Bill Losks, Mike McDonald, Curt Van Dussen
2000	UPAB	Marquette	8:14.9	Fred Jaecklein, Justin Kleinschmidt, Evan Mitton, Shani Davis
2001	UPD1	Marquette	8:02.4*	Jamison Cihak, Stuard Kramer, Alex Guakdoni, Joe Graci
2002	UPD1	Sault Ste. Marie	8:26.7	Anthony Abrmason, Craif Cooper, Daniel Brown, Eric Worley
2003	UPD1	Marquette	8:27.75	Andrew Gualdoni, Alex Tiseo, Jordan Divine, Stuart Kramer
2004	UPD1	Marquette	8:13.46	Alex Tiseo, Dillon Johnston, Ben Montgomery, Stuart Kramer
2005	UPD1	Gladstone	8:22.43	Kyle Kelly Chris Davis, Alvin Moore, Tom Seronko
2006	UPD1	Marquette	8:20.43	Dillon Johnston, Jared Johnston, Andt Kramer, Nik Klene
2007	UPD1	Escanaba	8:20.05	Allison Harvey, Heather Rusch, Derek Saari, Josh Ostrenga
2008	UPD1	Gladstone	8:21.20	Matt Cester, Joe Mileski, Ben Carson, Marcus Whitmer
2009	UPD1	Marquette	8:26.25	Forest Gilfoy, Sam West, Kelly McCommons, Austin Wissler
2010	UPD1	Marquette	8:28.02	Forest Gilfoy, Aaron Detmers, Kelly McCommons, Aaron Wissler
2011	UPD1	Marquette	8:22.36	Marty Gray, Forest Gilfoy, Chris Kyle, Austin Wissler
2012	UPD1	Manistique	8:25.57	John Rahm, Bryson Lawerence, Ryan Ramey, Robert Atyotte
2013	UPD1	Escanaba	8:24.69	Jordan Ogren, Eric Cousineau, Andrew Stenberg, Jake Walker
2014	UPD1	Marquette	8:21.07	Troy Sergey, Brady Aboussleman, Andrew Kilpela, Andrew Bannitt
2015	UPD1	Marquette	8:19.24	Michael Millado, Matthew Millado, Nathan Schlorke, Andrew Benitt
2016	UPD1	Houghton	8:15.38	Bruce Scott, Hunter Richards, Sean Hyslop, Quentin Stachowiak
2017	UPD1	Houghton	8:15.70	Seth Helman, Patrick Donnel, Nicholas Wilson, Clayton Sayen
2018	UPD1	Marquette	8:30.74	Julien Malherbe, Nathan Zika, Garret Zueger, Mathurin Gagnon

4 x 800 – UP Class C/Division 2 Champions

1984	UPC	Negaunee	8:20.1*	Steve Terres, Todd Reynolds, Dave Tilly, Terry Bartle
1985	UPC	Iron River West Iron County	8:18.2*	Scott Remer, Adam Cook, Dave Remer, Ron Meyer
1986	UPC	Ishpeming Westwood	8:13.8*	Peter Marcotte, Al Harvala, Bill Moore, John Carter
1987	UPC	Iron Mountain	8:20.2	Jim Flaminio, John Novara, Bill Potter, Jeff Webb
1988	UPC	Iron Mountain	8:16.2	John Bouche, Steve Smithson, John Novara, Bill Potter
1989	UPC	Ishpeming Westwood	8:33.2	Todd Anderson, Scott Larson, Rich Conrad, Mike Conrad
1990	UPC	Ishpeming Westwood	8:25.0	Tony Eppert, Chris Anderson, Mike Conrad, Rich Conrad
1991	UPC	Stephenson	8:20.0	Tim Nordin, Dave Schnell, Joe Houle, Dan Schnell
1992	UPC	Stephenson	8:54.6	Mike FInch, Jon Haight, Joe Nordin, Chad Pyle
1993	UPC	Houghton	8:23.7	David Evensen, Dan Munoz, Tom Miller, Corey Carlson
1994	UPC	Munising	8:20.1	George Schulz, Mike Peters, Dan Munoz, Dave DeLisle
1995	UPC	Houghton	8:21.9	Tony Dupont, Matt Bradley, Julian Pike, Tom Miller
1996	UPC	Munising	8:18.0	Brian Spaulding, Abe Austin, Shawn Pyle, Dan Munoz
1997	UPC	Negaunee	8:24.4	Caden Ruohomaki, Dave Siik, Chris Katona, Dana Ferguson
1998	UPC	Calumet	8:25.9	Casey Heikkinen, Jeremy Rowe, Ryan Kangas, Dave Campbell
1999	UPC	Newberry	8:19.5	Erick Rocker, Vince Randazzo, Chris Labadie, Matt McNamara
2000	UPC	Munising	8:23.3	Henry Loope, Matt Anderson, Chad Seeberg, Pat Kerwin
2001	UPD2	Ironwood	8:28.9*	Josh Hakamaa, Evan Marvin, Jesse Daniels, Drew Douglass
2002	UPD2	Ishpeming	8:34.1	S. Palo, Ryan Kruger, Alew Beerling, Erick Palo
2003	UPD2	Ishpeming	8:31.43	Sean Palo, Ryan Marinac, Alex Beerling, Eric Palo
2004	UPD2	Norway	8:30.53	Chris Mattas, Lane Thaler, Jim DeBartolo, Nick Zweifel
2005	UPD2	Republic-Michagamme	8:24.72*	Sean Palo, Kyle Schinella, Ryan Lusardi, Justin Dillon
2006	UPD2	Munising	8:38.57	Kurt Davis, Kyle Storm, Mark Kinnenen, Scott Bond
2007	UPD2	Ironwood	8:21.18*	Mike McPherson, Alan Peterson, John Jacisin, Dominic Beckman
2008	UPD2	Ironwood	8:27.42	Mike McPherson, Alan Peterson, John Jacisin, Dominic Beckman
2009	UPD2	Munising	8:37.02	Dan Carlson, Lucas Schener, Jake Mahoski, Rick Coltson
2010	UPD2	Rudyard	8:32.66	Brock Lewis, Tyler Rice, David Jarvie, David McDonoff
2011	UPD2	Ishpeming	8:52.97	
2012	UPD2	Stephenson	9:06.50	Brandon Kau, Ken Truitt, Conner Cappaert, Jono Newlin
2013	UPD2	Manistique	8:37.97	Bryson Lawrence, William Pomery, Robert Ayotte, Ryan Ramey
2014	UPD2	Ishpeming	8:58.02	Kyle Selmser, Mathias Rein, Daren Guichin, Tommy Potter
2015	UPD2	Ishpeming	9:03.59	Mark Holmgren, Tommy Potter, Daren Guichin, Nate Meyer
2016	UPD2	Iron Mountain	8:54.81	Tanner Huotari, Michael Kulas, Davin Steva, Nate Carey
2017	UPD2	Ishpeming	8:37.40	Kyle Pruett, Joffery Braun, Daren Guichin, Grady Kerst
2018	UPD2	Iron Mountain	8:44.88	Jake Dumais, Caleb Plumley, Jaden Vicenzi, Michael Kulas

4 x 800 – UP Class D/Division 3 Champions

1984	UPD	Crystal Falls Forest Park	8:49.9*	Joe Veeser, Ed Veeser, David Graff, Darwin Aberly
1985	UPD	Rudyard	8:31.0*	Ed Folkersma, Terin Salo, Garett Cornwell, Bill Sage
1986	UPD	Rudyard	8:26.4*	Ed Folkersma, Terin Salo, Shawn Ostrander, Garet Cornwell,
1987	UPD	Bessemer	8:41.8	Pete Conrad, Garth Stengard, Ed Hocking, Brian Bonovetz
1988	UPD	Eben Junction Superior Central	8:35.6	Mike Decet, Duane Colbus, Tom Cox, Blake Penberthy
1989	UPD	Crystal Falls Forest Park	8:40.5	Pete Avena, Eric Heimert, Lee Siler, Glen Avena
1990	UPD	Pickford	8:35.5	Travis Michalsky, Brent Cottle, Cal Ledy, Benji Leach
1991	UPD	Pickford	8:34.3	Travis Michalsky, Mike Taylor, Ben Leach, Cal Ledy
1992	UPD	Pickford	8:56.5	Jason Kronemeyer, Josh Rose, Ben Leach, Cal Ledy
1993	UPD	Pickford	8:41.6	Steve Stec, Bobby McConkey, Josh Rose, Cal Ledy
1994	UPD	Ontonagon	8:37.3	Ryan Kamppainen, Chris Roehm, Jason Fronti, Tom LeGault
1995	UPD	Brimley	8:34.1	Ken Graham, James Lawrence, Cory McCormick, Paul Graham
1996	UPD	Rapid River	8:48.3	Todd Stage, Jim Hilgendorf, Andy Schounenberger, Zach Nutt
1997	UPD	Rapid River	8:44.2	Todd Stage, Andy Schounenberger, Cole Adam, Eric Lundin
1998	UPD	DeTour	8:46.8	
1999	UPD	Rapid River	8:38.4	Garon Quinn, Greg Erkkila, Dustin Selin, Mike Holmgren
2000	UPD	Detour	8:32.0	Donald Newell, Matt Brunk, Nathan Lehman, Ribert Young
2001	UPD3	Wakefield	8:33.53*	Josh Lamaide, Mark Piotrowski, Paul Suomi, Ryan Holm
2002	UPD3	Pickford	8:34.3	Joe Nyberg, Mahlon Collins, Adam Wallis, Brad Hunter
2003	UPD3	Wakefield	8:42.06	Cory Niemela, Keith Mattila, Casey Mosher, Ryan Holm
2004	UPD3	Powers-North Central	8:30.10*	Justin Gorzinski, Stephen Moilanen, Luke Moilanen, Adam Christopherson
2005	UPD3	Pickford	8:36.68	Carl Morrison, Kurt Harrison, Richard Gibson, Chris Thompson
2006	UPD3	Rock-Mid Peninsula	8:43.40	Chris Tritt, Jason Norkozi, Carl Branstrom, Brad Verbrigghe
2007	UPD3	Powers-North Central	8:39.60	David Dugree, Josh Hood, Tyler Veraghen, Steve Davis
2008	UPD3	Crystal Falls Forest Park	8:44.37	Tony Silva, Ben Shuck, Tony Greco, Josh Aberly
2009	UPD3	Crystal Falls Forest Park	8:50.31	Tony Silva, Jake Divine, Tony Freco, Josh Aberly
2010	UPD3	Crystal Falls Forest Park	8:45.58	Tony Silva, Jake Divine, Derek Aberly, Mark Hallman
2011	UPD3	Crystal Falls Forest Park	8:39.32	Tony Silva, Derek Aberly, Mark Hallman, Jake Divine
2012	UPD3	Crystal Falls Forest Park	8:40.77	Mark Hallman, Jon Curtis, Derek Aberly, Jake Divine
2013	UPD3	Eben Junction Superior Central	8:43.06	Nick Maki, Greg Seppanen, Tucker Spranger, Tyler Kienitz
2014	UPD3	Bessemer	8:48.65	Tim Buerger, Lance Berwald, Paul Buerger, Zack Mazurek
2015	UPD3	Bessemer	8:46.45	Tim Rowe, Lance Berwald, Braydon Tomes, Jess Mazzon
2016	UPD3	Bessemer	8:38.27	Tim Rowe, Cade Mazzon, Isaiah Aili, Brayden Tomes
2017	UPD3	Bessemer	8:29.88*	Tim Rowe, Cade Mazzon, Isiah Aili, Braydan Tomes
2018	UPD3	Bessemer	8:31.15	Tim Rowe, Cade Mazzon, Tad Rowe, Uriah Aili

Saginaw's Reggie Jones dominated the Class A sprints in 1973.
A year later, he was NCAA champ and the No. 4 sprinter on earth.
(Track & Field News photo)

GIRLS CHAMPIONS

GIRLS 100 METERS

Records

D1	11.54 (2.0)	Shayla Mahan	Detroit Mumford	2006
D2	11.90	Sydney Cureton	Detroit Country Day	2012
D3	11.94 (0.7)	Angie Ritter	Frankenmuth	2014
D4	12.40	Abbey Hengesbach	Pewamo-Westphalia	2010
	12.40 (-0.6)	Jordan Goodman	Mason County Eastern	2015
UPD1	12.55	Chelsea Jacques	Calumet	2012
UPD2	12.54	Dani Gagne	Norway	2011
UPD3	12.50	Becky Baron	Rock-Mid Peninsula	2003

Records by Class (pre-2000 for LP, pre-2001 for UP)

A	11.84	Crystal Braddock	Ann Arbor Pioneer	1989
B	12.01	Nicole Embry	Detroit DePorres	1990
C	12.10	Shirley Evans	Detroit Country Day	1986
D	12.10	Cynthia White	Covert	1994
UPAB	12.6	Michelle Blake	Menominee	1984
UPC	12.9	Eryn Mercer	St. Ignace	2000
UPD	12.6	Darlene Allen	Norway	1979
	12.6	Kara Scherer	Cedarville	1991

100 – Class A/Division 1 Champions

(y=100 yards)

1973 All	Carol Stieve	South Haven	11.6y*		1996 A	Chantelle Nagbe	Detroit Cass Tech	12.74
1974 A/B	Josephine Hobbs	Detroit Central	11.0y*		1997 A	Kanisa Williams	Detroit Cass Tech	11.90
1975 A	Josephine Hobbs	Detroit Central	11.3y		1998 A	Tiarra Jones	Detroit Cass Tech	11.88 (2.0)
1976 A	Josephine Hobbs	Detroit Central	11.0y*		1999 A	Tiarra Jones	Detroit Cass Tech	12.01 (2.0)
1977 A	Athlen Bowles	Detroit Henry Ford	11.0y*		2000 D1	Tiarra Jones	Detroit Cass Tech	11.98* (0.7)
1978 A	Elaine Jones	Detroit Chadsey	10.8yw		2001 D1	Karla Marshall	Detroit Cass Tech	12.25
1979 A	Elaine Jones	Detroit Chadsey	11.1y		2002 D1	Katrice Walton	Detroit Cass Tech	12.07 (-)
1980 A	Kori Gifford	Bloomfield Hills Andover	10.9y*		2003 D1	Ariss Seals	Detroit Cass Tech	12.31 (-0.6)
1981 A	Cathy Fitzpatrick	Muskegon Mona Shores	10.8y*		2004 D1	Porsche Ries	Detroit Mumford	12.10
1982 A	Vivian McKenzie	Detroit Chadsey	11.7*		2005 D1	Shayla Mahan	Detroit Mumford	11.95*
1983 A	Jeanan Langston	Benton Harbor	11.9		2006 D1	Shayla Mahan	Detroit Mumford	11.54* (2.0)
1984 A	Marita Rimpson	Benton Harbor	11.8		2007 D1	Shayla Mahan	Detroit Mumford	11.76 (-2.5)
1985 A	Marita Rimpson	Benton Harbor	12.12*		2008 D1	Jordan Clark	Southfield Lathrop	12.09 (-1.5)
1986 A (tie)	Patrice Verdun	Flint Central	12.05*		2009 D1	Charlotte Cahill	North Farmington	12.10 (-2.9)
1986 A (tie)	Michelle Bishop	Grand Haven	12.05*		2010 D1	Ashley Keyes	Rochester	12.39 (-2.7)
1987 A	Patrice Verdun	Flint Central	11.98*		2011 D1	Kyra Jefferson	Detroit Cass Tech	11.72 (1.4)
1988 A	Crystal Braddock	Ann Arbor Pioneer	11.70w		2012 D1	Cindy Ofili	Ann Arbor Huron	11.97 (-4.0)
1989 A	Crystal Braddock	Ann Arbor Pioneer	11.84*		2013 D1	Sekayi Bracey	East Kentwood	12.18 (0.0)
1990 A	Nicole Wilson	Ypsilanti	11.98		2014 D1	Sekayi Bracey	East Kentwood	11.88 (0.5)
1991 A	Heather Brown	Ann Arbor Pioneer	11.9		2015 D1	Sekayi Bracey	East Kentwood	11.83 (0.8)
1992 A	Vania Nelson	Ann Arbor Pioneer	12.34		2016 D1	Sekayi Bracey	East Kentwood	12.08
1993 A	Chandra Burns	Detroit Northern	12.2		2017 D1	Anavia Battle	Wayne Memorial	11.95 (-1.5)
1994 A	Emily Higgins	Detroit Cass Tech	11.8		2018 D1	Grace Stark	White Lake Lakeland	11.74 (1.7)
1995 A	Kanisa Williams	Detroit Cass Tech	12.3					

100 – Class B/Division 2 Champions

(y=100 yards)

1975 B	Rhonda Edwards	Stevensville-Lakeshore	11.4y*		1991 B	Atemia McClure	Detroit DePorres	12.33
1976 B	Joyce Horne	Three Rivers	11.4y*		1992 B	Atemia McClure	Detroit DePorres	12.33
1977 B	Susan Bordeaux	Muskegon Catholic	11.4y*		1993 B	Carla Wallin	Grand Rapids Northview	12.95
1978 B	Catherine Sharp	Detroit Immaculata	11.3y*		1994 B	Charnell Lynn	Inkster	12.23
1979 B	Louise Chauvin	Mt Clemens L'Anse Creuse	11.3y*		1995 B	Charnell Lynn	Ypsilanti Willow Run	12.4
1980 B	Pallastean Harris	Montrose	11.9*		1996 B	Tamika Craig	Dearborn Hts Robichaud	12.63
1981 B	Sandy Harris	Flint Beecher	12.4		1997 B	Latonya Jones	Saginaw Buena Vista	12.33
1982 B	Kathy Kost	Mt Clemens L'Anse Creuse	11.3y*		1998 B	Latonya Jones	Saginaw Buena Vista	12.67
1983 B	Kathy Kost	Mt Clemens L'Anse Creuse	12.2		1999 B	Erin Anderson	Detroit Renaissance	12.72
1984 B	Paulette Bryant	Southgate Aquinas	11.7*		2000 D2	LaTosha Jollet	Detroit Renaissance	12.34*
1985 B	Danita Sims	Flint Beecher	12.43*		2001 D2	LaTosha Jollet	Detroit Renaissance	12.30*
1986 B	Tammy Bryans	Hastings	12.4		2002 D2	Patrice Beasley	Romulus	12.11*
1987 B	LaDonna Holmes	Muskegon Heights	12.42*		2003 D2	Alisha Cole	Cadillac	12.12w
1988 B	LaDonna Holmes	Muskegon Heights	12.21*		2004 D2	Angela Pierce	Clinton Township Clintondale	12.66
1989 B	Danielle Pierce	Detroit DePorres	12.3		2005 D2	Alisha Cole	Cadillac	12.34
1990 B	Nicole Embry	Detroit DePorres	12.01*		2006 D2	Erica Mann	Battle Creek Lakeview	11.99w

Year	Class	Name	School	Time
2007 D2		Erica Mann	Battle Creek Lakeview	12.29
2008 D2		Marieme Mbaye	GR Forest Hills Northern	12.45
2009 D2		Ashley Abraham	Detroit Renaissance	12.50
2010 D2		Kendall Baisden	Detroit Country Day	12.13
2011 D2		Kendall Baisden	Detroit Country Day	11.92*
2012 D2		Sydney Cureton	Detroit Country Day	11.90*
2013 D2		Josey Yesmunt	DeWitt	12.18
2014 D2		Josey Yesmunt	DeWitt	12.33
2015 D2		Camron Nelson	GR Forest Hills Eastern	12.44
2016 D2		Tra'chels Roberts	Lansing Waverly	12.55 (-2.1)
2017 D2		Zoe Eby	Carleton Airport	12.26 (0.0)
2018 D2		Payten Williams	Bridgeport	12.06w (2.2)

100 – Class C/Division 3 Champions

(y=100 yards)

Year	Name	School	Time
1974 C/D	Linda Merrifield	Williamston	11.4y*
1975 C	Linda Merrifield	Williamston	11.5y
1976 C	Linda Merrifield	Williamston	11.0y*
1977 C	Gina Erwin	Scottville Mason County C	11.9y
1978 C	Sue Bordeaux	Muskegon Catholic	11.6y
1979 C	Rochelle Bostic	Royal Oak Shrine	11.1y
1980 C	Cindy Guy	North Muskegon	11.4y
1981 C	Donna Smith	Detroit Lutheran West	11.9w
1982 C	Donna Smith	Detroit Lutheran West	12.7*
1983 C	Lisa Hardiman	GR Forest Hills Northern	12.2*
1984 C	Felica Diaz	Detroit DePorres	12.6
1985 C	Shirley Evans	Detroit Country Day	12.15*
1986 C	Shirley Evans	Detroit Country Day	12.10*
1987 C	Shirley Evans	Detroit Country Day	12.1
1988 C	Shirley Evans	Detroit Country Day	12.5
1989 C	Cathy Fromwiller	Marlette	12.61
1990 C	Cathy Fromwiller	Marlette	12.8
1991 C	Alvera Clark	New Haven	12.6
1992 C	Angie Sneider	Morenci	12.9
1993 C	Renee Pardon	Comstock Park	12.86
1994 C	Dorothea Game	Detroit Dominican	12.31
1995 C	Jessica Champine	Clare	12.30
1996 C	Jessica Champine	Clare	12.21
1997 C	Alana Mestelle	White Pigeon	12.27
1998 C	Alana Mestelle	White Pigeon	12.48 (-)
1999 C	Tifany Simon	Redford Borgess	12.41
2000 D3	Jennifer Delamater	Blanchard-Montabella	12.74*
2001 D3	Julie Johnson	Laingsburg	12.45*
2002 D3	Julie Johnson	Laingsburg	12.42*
2003 D3	Julie Johnson	Laingsburg	12.36*
2004 D3	Kayria Callaway	Detroit Crockett	12.53
2005 D3	Keyria Calloway	Detroit Crockett	12.34*
2006 D3	Keyria Calloway	Detroit Crockett	12.16*
2007 D3	Mary Ramsey	Parchment	12.43
2008 D3	Amelia Bannister	Albion	12.21*
2009 D3	Amelia Bannister	Albion	12.36 (1.2)
2010 D3	Kaisha Martrin	Dowagiac	12.24
2011 D3	Raven Blaser	Wyoming Godwin Heights	12.24
2012 D3	Kimberly Balls	Bridgeport	12.48
2013 D3	Brianna Denneen	Buchanan	12.22
2014 D3	Angie Ritter	Frankenmuth	11.94* (0.7)
2015 D3	Hailey Stockford	Sanford-Meridian	12.07 (0.5)
2016 D3	Hailey Stockford	Sanford-Meridian	12.27 (-1.0)
2017 D3	Shiyon Taylor	Parchment	12.41 (0.0)
2018 D3	Jenna Odykirk	Farwell	12.63 (-2.1)

100 – Class D/Division 4 Champions

(y=100 yards)

Year	Name	School	Time
1975 D	Sue Behnke	Battle Creek St Phillip	11.5y*
1976 D	Janet Hale	Maple City Glen Lake	11.4y*
1977 D	Brenda Johnson	Grass Lake	11.6y
1978 D	Brenda Johnson	Grass Lake	11.3y*
1979 D	Penny Zeneberg	Mt Pleasant Sacred Heart	12.4*
1980 D	Sue Steeby	Saginaw Michigan Lutheran	12.4*
1981 D	Andrea Kincannon	Grosse Pointe Univ. Liggett	12.6
1982 D	Andrea Kincannon	Grosse Pointe Univ. Liggett	12.5
1983 D	Jane Pincombe	Schoolcraft	12.4*
1984 D	Melanie Lovely	Concord	13.01*
1985 D	Kiffany Bailey	Fulton-Middleton	13.06
1986 D	Cheryl Boddy	Athens	12.66*
1987 D	Carrie Ager	Central Lake	12.4
1988 D	Carrie Ager	Central Lake	12.4
1989 D	Jackie Clark	Camden-Frontier	12.3*
1990 D	Bridgett Stewart	Redford St Mary	12.32*
1991 D	Yvonne Hall	Detroit Lutheran West	12.79
1992 D	Theresa Proost	Maple City Glen Lake	12.92
1993 D	Stacey McCallum	Fairview	12.7
1994 D	Cynthia White	Covert	12.10*
1995 D	Jill Hall	Ann Arbor Gabriel Richard	12.99
1996 D	Liz Powers	Homer	13.05
1997 D	Brittany Hedgepath	St Joseph Lake Mich Catholic	12.73
1998 D	Brittany Hedgepath	St. Joseph Lake Mich Catholic	12.4
1999 D	Brittany Hedgepath	St. Joseph Lake Mich Catholic	12.62
2000 D4	Jenna Gaines	Breckenridge	12.77*
2001 D4	Angela Sherman	Southfield Christian	13.12
2002 D4	Stacy Dollar	Lincoln-Alcona	12.60*
2003 D4	Dessaray Cranford	Detroit Benedictine	12.54*
2004 D4	Seonetta Berlin	Detroit Benedictine	12.61
2005 D4	Monique Lee	New Haven	12.42*
2006 D4	Jasmine Wright	Eau Claire	12.62
2007 D4	Tasha Balls	Saginaw Buena Vista	12.81
2008 D4	Kristy Bengel	Pewamo-Westphalia	12.89
2009 D4	McKenzie Decker	Centreville	12.70 (-1.7)
2010 D4	Abbey Hengesbach	Pewamo-Westphalia	12.40*
2011 D4	Lindsey Hufnagel	Fowler	12.60
2012 D4	Marissa Ingersoll	Fife Lake Forest Area	12.74
2013 D4	Ashey White	Detroit Edison Academy	12.79
2014 D4	Jordan Goodman	Mason County Eastern	12.55 (0.6)
2015 D4	Jordan Goodman	Mason County Eastern	12.40* (-0.6)
2016 D4	Lindsey Lehman	Concord	12.30w (3.7)
2017 D4	Chika Amene	Southfield Christian	12.71
2018 D4	Chika Amene	Southfield Christian	12.44 (1.7)

100 – UP Class AB/Division 1 Champions

(50-yards)

Year	Name	School	Time
1972 UP-All	Denise Redding	Gwinn	6.4*

(y=100 yards)

Year	Name	School	Time
1972 UP-All	Colleen Larret	Menominee	12.1y*
1973 UP-All	Joanne Slater	Pickford	12.1y*
1974 UPAB	Denise Porath	Escanaba	11.7y*
1975 UPAB	Pat Rector	Gwinn	11.7y*
1976 UPAB	Nancy Gage	Escanaba	11.8y
1977 UPAB	Becky Drake	Kingsford	11.3y*
1978 UPAB	Becky Drake	Kingsford	11.4y
1979 UPAB	Becky Drake	Kingsford	12.7*
1980 UPAB	Julie Drake	Kingsford	12.8
1981 UPAB	Jean Tolfa	Escanaba	13.4
1982 UPAB	Jean Tolfa	Escanaba	13.0
1983 UPAB	Michelle Blake	Menominee	12.9
1984 UPAB	Michelle Blake	Menominee	12.6*
1985 UPAB	Tammy Cook	Escanaba	13.2
1986 UPAB	Tammy Cook	Escanaba	12.8
1987 UPAB	Tammy Cook	Escanaba	12.8
1988 UPAB	Tammy Cook	Escanaba	12.9
1989 UPAB	Jennifer Ostland	Gladstone	13.0
1990 UPAB	Jennifer Ostlund	Gladstone	12.9
1991 UPAB	Tammy Albon	Sault Ste. Marie	12.7
1992 UPAB	Crista Beaver	Gladstone	12.4w
1993 UPAB	Betsy Bourdeau	Escanaba	12.7
1994 UPAB	Sarah Heikkila	Marquette	12.8
1995 UPAB	Maryea Pike	Sault Ste. Marie	13.4
1996 UPAB	Maryea Pike	Sault Ste. Marie	13.2
1997 UPAB	Laura Lacrosse	Escanaba	13.3
1998 UPAB	Laura Lacrosse	Escanaba	13.6
1999 UPAB	Maija Emblad	Marquette	13.2
2000 UPAB	Tiffany Petr	Gladstone	12.7
2001 UPD1	Tiffany Petr	Gladstone	13.0*
2002 UPD1	Tiffany Petr	Gladstone	12.8*
2003 UPD1	Ashley Taccolini	Menominee	12.68*
2004 UPD1	Joan LaPointe	Houghton	13.42
2005 UPD1	Stephanie Ostrenga	Escanaba	12.58*
2006 UPD1	Alyssa Espamer	Marquette	12.85
2007 UPD1	Brittnee Bialbierz	Marquette	13.01
2008 UPD1	Catherine Angeli	Marquette	12.90
2009 UPD1	Katy LaFayette	Marquette	12.96
2010 UPD1	Courtney Laferniere	Marquette	12.79
2011 UPD1	Michaela Newberry	Iron Mountain	12.79
2012 UPD1	Chelsea Jacques	Calumet	12.55*
2013 UPD1	Chelsea Jacques	Calumet	12.62
2014 UPD1	Chelsea Jacques	Calumet	12.73

| 2015 UPD1 | Chelsea Jacques | Calumet | 12.69 |
| 2016 UPD1 | Izzie Peterson | Marquette | 12.60 |

| 2017 UPD1 | Isabelle Peterson | Marquette | 12.85 |
| 2018 UPD1 | Olivia Allen | Kingsford | 13.09 |

100 – UP Class C/Division 2 Champions
(y=100 yards)

1974 UPC	Betty Kuusisto	L'Anse	12.2y*
1975 UPC	Betty Kuusisto	L'Anse	12.4y
1976 UPC	Lori Bouchard	Newberry	11.8y*
1977 UPC	Jan Merrick	Negaunee	11.7y*
1978 UPC	Cheryl Thomas	Iron River West Iron Coumty	11.8y
1979 UPC	Jan Merrick	Negaunee	12.7*
1980 UPC	Ann Sporalski	Hancock	13.0
1981 UPC	Robin Eick	Stephenson	14.0
1982 UPC	Jenny Baldwin	Houghton	12.8
1983 UPC	Lynn Scholie	Hancock	12.9
1984 UPC	Tina Antilla	Calumet	12.8
1985 UPC	Kathy Amos	Ontonagon	13.1
1986 UPC	Kathy Amos	Ontonagon	12.7*
1987 UPC	Tracy Holappa	Ishpeming	13.1
1988 UPC	Tracy Holappa	Ishpeming	12.9
1989 UPC	Tracy Holappa	Ishpeming	12.7*
1990 UPC	Tracy Holappa	Ishpeming	12.9
1991 UPC	Brenna Plante	Calumet	12.9
1992 UPC	Jeannie Hetrick	Newberry	12.9
1993 UPC	Angela Arthur	Ironwood	13.10
1994 UPC	Tamara Clark	Iron Mountain	13.0
1995 UPC	Angela Arthur	Ironwood	13.3

1996 UPC	Anna Pemble	St. Ignace	12.7*
1997 UPC	Holly Brown	St. Ignace	13.00*
1998 UPC	Emily Karry	Hancock	13.23
1999 UPC	Emili Karry	Hancock	13.23
2000 UPC	Eryn Mercer	St. Ignace	12.90*
2001 UPD2	Eryn Mercer	St. Ignace	12.9*
2002 UPD2	Tara Bjorne	Manistique	12.9*
2003 UPD2	Rachel Ronquist	Newberry	13.28*
2004 UPD2	Katelyn Argall	Ishpeming	13.47
2005 UPD2	Krystal Stevenson	Manistique	13.15*
2006 UPD2	Taylor Watters	Ishpeming Westwood	13.24
2007 UPD2	Jessica Wood	Ishpeming	13.49
2008 UPD2	Taylor Watters	Ishpeming Westwood	13.17
2009 UPD2	Jamie Dompier	Chassell	12.89*
2010 UPD2	Dani Gagne	Norway	12.83*
2011 UPD2	Dani Gagne	Norway	12.54*
2012 UPD2	Dani Gagne	Norway	12.62
2013 UPD2	Hailey LaFleur	Iron Mountain	13.49
2014 UPD2	Rachel Hetherington	St. Ignace	13.08
2015 UPD2	Emmy Kinner	West Iron County	13.19
2016 UPD2	Emmy Kinner	West Iron County	13.33
2017 UPD2	Michaela Peramaki	Munising	12.79
2018 UPD2	Taylor Talerico	Iron Mountain	13.45

100 – UP Class D/Division 3 Champions
(y=100 yards)

1974 UPD	Barbara Short	Lake Linden-Hubbell	11.9y*
1975 UPD	Joanne Slater	Pickford	12.0y
1976 UPD	Barbara Short	Lake Linden-Hubbell	11.8y*
1977 UPD	Wanda Darling	Republic-Michigamme	11.8y*
1978 UPD	Wanda Darling	Republic-Michigamme	12.0y
1979 UPD	Darlene Allen	Norway	12.6*
1980 UPD	Darlene Allen	Norway	12.7
1981 UPD	Darlene Allen	Norway	13.4
1982 UPD	Gwen Wilkie	DeTour	12.7
1983 UPD	Gwen Wilkie	DeTour	12.8
1984 UPD	Gwen Wilkie	DeTour	12.7
1985 UPD	Denise Beauchamp	Bark River-Harris	13.1
1986 UPD	Cindy Schwiderson	Pickford	13.2
1987 UPD	Diana Hongisto	Wakefield	13.3
1988 UPD	Janelle Maki	Crystal Falls Forest Park	13.4
1989 UPD	Chastity Pool	Felch North Dickinson	12.9
1990 UPD	Kara Scherer	Cedarville	12.7
1991 UPD	Kara Scherer	Cedarville	12.6*
1992 UPD	Kara Scherer	Cedarville	12.8
1993 UPD	Janeen Forslund	Bessemer	12.9
1994 UPD	Cristina Koski	Lake Linden-Hubbell	12.9
1995 UPD	Beth Ives	Bark River-Harris	13.6

1996 UPD	Dawn Aavolainen	Lake Linden-Hubbell	13.2
1997 UPD	Dawn Savolainen	Lake Linden-Hubbell	13.2
1998 UPD	Holly Brown	St. Ignace	13.3
1999 UPD	Jacklyn Bebeau	Bessemer	13.3
2000 UPD	Molly Bacon	Rapid River	13.2
2001 UPD3	Molly Bacon	Rapid River	13.0*
2002 UPD3	Becky Baron	Rock-Mid Peninsula	13.0*
2003 UPD3	Becky Baron	Rock-Mid Peninsula	12.50*
2004 UPD3	Breanne Marshall	Rapid River	13.70
2005 UPD3	Holly Seppala	Lake Linden-Hubbel	13.54
2006 UPD3	Lauren Marshall	Rapid River	13.20
2007 UPD3	Lauren Marshall	Rapid River	13.37
2008 UPD3	Maria Valesano	Crystal Falls Forest Park	13.17
2009 UPD3	Maria Valesano	Crystal Falls Forest Park	12.93
2010 UPD3	Olivia Soumis	Ontonagon	12.83
2011 UPD3	Alexis Mason	Brimley	12.95
2012 UPD3	Jamie Dompier	Chassell	12.70
2013 UPD3	Jamie Dompier	Chassell	12.83
2014 UPD3	Mary Grandahl	Crystal Falls Forest Park	13.34
2015 UPD3	Taylor Bryant	Newberry	13.60
2016 UPD3	Lori Wardynski	Ontonagon	13.40
2017 UPD3	Hailee Demers	Bark River-Harris	13.30
2018 UPD3	Masyn Alexa	North Dickinson	13.19

GIRLS 200 METERS

Records

D1	23.74 (0.9)	Shayla Mahan	Detroit Mumford	2006
D2	24.55	LaTosha Jollet	Detroit Renaissance	2002
D3	24.72 (0.0)	Angie Ritter	Frankenmuth	2014
D4	25.15 (1.0)	Miranda Johnson	Ottawa Lake Whiteford	2014
UPD1	25.65	Stephanie Ostrenga	Escanaba	2005
UPD2	26.42	Dani Gagne	Norway	2012
UPD3	26.36	Jamie Dompier	Chassell	2012

Records by Class (pre-2000 for LP, pre-2001 for UP)

A	24.38 (1.0)	Tracy Ball	Detroit Cass Tech	1998
B	25.00	Charnell Lynn	Inkster	1993
C	24.94	Tiffany Simon	Redford Borgess	1998
D	25.58	Carrie Ager	Central Lake	1988
UPAB	26.0	Lisa Wiedenhoefer	Marquette	1978
UPC	26.2	Colleen Colegrove	St. Ignace	1986
UPD	26.3	Kara Scherer	Cedarville	1993

200 – Class A/Division 1 Champions
(y=220 yards)

| 1973 All | Cheryl Sowles | Cadillac | 26.6y* |

Year	Athlete	School	Time
1974 A/B	Josephine Hobbs	Detroit Central	24.8y*
1975 A	Josephine Hobbs	Detroit Central	25.3y
1976 A	Josephine Hobbs	Detroit Central	24.5y*
1977 A	Molly Brennan	Waterford Mott	24.5y*
1978 A	Carman Rivers	Detroit Mackenzie	24.6y
1979 A	Elaine Jones	Detroit Chadsey	24.8y
1980 A	Kori Gifford	Bloomfield Hills Andover	24.5y*
1981 A	Elaine Jones	Detroit Chadsey	24.6y
1982 A	Vivien McKenzie	Detroit Chadsey	24.2w
1983 A	Angie Prince	Detroit Pershing	24.9
1984 A	Angie Prince	Detroit Pershing	24.3*
1985 A	Marita Rimpson	Benton Harbor	24.90*
1986 A	Michelle Bishop	Grand Haven	25.22
1987 A	Yvette Smiley	Detroit Central	24.89*
1988 A	Crystal Braddock	Ann Arbor Pioneer	24.45w
1989 A	Crystal Braddock	Ann Arbor Pioneer	24.90
1990 A	Nicole Wilson	Ypsilanti	24.82*
1991 A	Heather Brown	Ann Arbor Pioneer	24.99
1992 A	Vania Nelson	Ann Arbor Pioneer	25.85
1993 A	Chandra Burns	Detroit Northern	24.88
1994 A	Shree Jones	Detroit Cooley	25.4
1995 A	Chantelle Nagbe	Detroit Cass Tech	25.83
1996 A	Nicole Ball	Ypsilanti	26.39
1997 A	Michelle Davis	Lansing Sexton	24.71*
1998 A	Tracy Ball	Detroit Cass Tech	24.38* (1.0)
1999 A	Katrice Walton	Detroit Cass Tech	25.02 (-0.5)
2000 D1	Melanie Williams	Southfield	24.62* (-1.4)
2001 D1	Crystal Lee	Detroit Cass Tech	25.34
2002 D1	Katrice Walton	Detroit Cass Tech	24.95
2003 D1	Tenisha Griggs	Southfield Lathrup	24.2 (-3.3)
2004 D1	Tenisha Griggs	Southfield Lathrup	24.47*
2005 D1	Jessica Jones	Detroit Mumford	25.02
2006 D1	Shayla Mahan	Detroit Mumford	23.74* (0.9)
2007 D1	Shayla Mahan	Detroit Mumford	24.11 (-1.5)
2008 D1	Elise Glass	Dearborn Edsel Ford	24.94w (3.7)
2009 D1	Kyra Jefferson	Detroit Cass Tech	25.12 (-4.2)
2010 D1	Diisa Swint-Cook	Oak Park	24.78 (-2.8)
2011 D1	Kyra Jefferson	Detroit Cass Tech	23.87 (1.1)
2012 D1	Kyra Jefferson	Detroit Cass Tech	23.83w (3.3)
2013 D1	Sekayi Bracey	East Kentwood	24.82
2014 D1	Sekayi Bracey	East Kentwood	23.98 (0.5)
2015 D1	Sekayi Bracey	East Kentwood	24.62w (2.4)
2016 D1	Chloe Abbott	Northville	24.03
2017 D1	Tamea McKelvy	Oak Park	24.14 (-1.8)
2018 D1	Aasia Laurencin	Oak Park	24.64 (0.7)

200 – Class B/Division 2 Champions

(y=220 yards)

Year	Athlete	School	Time
1975 B	Pam Moore	Ionia	25.5y*
1976 B	Rhonda Edwards	Stevensville-Lakeshore	25.1y*
1977 B	Julie Boerman	Grand Rapids Christian	25.8y
1978 B	Julie Boerman	Grand Rapids Christian	25.5y
1979 B	Angela Collins	Inkster	25.6y
1980 B	Pallastean Harris	Montrose	24.7*
1981 B	Michelle Morris	Oak Park	25.3
1982 B	Micelle Morris	Oak Park	25.4y
1983 B	Karen Wallace	Battle Creek Lakeview	25.5
1984 B	Tammy Oostendorp	Hudsonville Unity Christian	25.1
1985 B	Anjer Delaine	Milan	26.17*
1986 B	Jill Bigelow	Greenville	25.90*
1987 B	Amy VanWormer	Cadillac	25.53*
1988 B	Amy VanWormer	Cadillac	25.28*
1989 B	Danielle Pierce	Detroit DePorres	25.0
1990 B	Colette Savage	Bay City John Glenn	25.7
1991 B	Atemia McClure	Detroit DePorres	25.33
1992 B	Atemia McClure	Detroit DePorres	25.82
1993 B	Charnell Lynn	Inkster	25.00*
1994 B	Simby Donner	River Rouge	25.32
1995 B	Charnell Lynn	Ypsilanti Willow Run	25.7
1996 B	Tamika Craig	Dearborn Heights Robichaud	25.65
1997 B	Tamika Craig	Dearborn Heights Robichaud	24.8
1998 B	Latonya Jones	Saginaw Buena Vista	25.44
1999 B	Moran Arnold	Chelsea	25.93
2000 D2	Jennifer Lawson	Detroit Renaissance	25.11*
2001 D2	LaTosha Jollet	Detroit Renaissance	25.04*
2002 D2	LaTosha Jollet	Detroit Renaissance	24.55*
2003 D2	Alisha Cole	Cadillac	24.77
2004 D2	Zanita Clipper	Ypsilanti	25.80
2005 D2	Aslish Cole	Cadillac	24.6
2006 D2	Erica Mann	Battle Creek Lakeview	25.22
2007 D2	Ashlee Abraham	Detroit Renaissance	25.01
2008 D2	Iris Campbell	Yale	25.52
2009 D2	Ashlee Abraham	Detroit Renaissance	25.66
2010 D2	Paige Patterson	Dearborn Divine Child	25.24
2011 D2	Kendall Baisden	Detroit Country Day	24.56
2012 D2	Paige Patterson	Dearborn Divine Child	24.91
2013 D2	Kendall Baisden	Detroit Country Day	24.65w (2.4)
2014 D2	Josie Yesmunt	DeWitt	25.00
2015 D2	Zoe Eby	Carleton Airport	25.54
2016 D2	Zoe Eby	Carleton Airport	25.17w (2.3)
2017 D2	Zoe Eby	Carleton Airport	24.26w (2.3)
2018 D2	Payten Williams	Bridgeport	24.73 (1.3)

200 – Class C/Division 3 Champions

(y=220 yards)

Year	Athlete	School	Time
1974 C/D	Debbie Hughes	Fowlerville	26.0y*
1975 C	Debbie Hughes	Fowlerville	25.5y*
1976 C	Linda Merrifield	Williamston	25.2y*
1977 C	Rose Hejl	Blissfield	26.1y
1978 C	Susan Bordeaux	Muskegon Catholic	25.8y
1979 C	Rochelle Bostic	Royal Oak Shrine	25.2y*
1980 C	Darlene Fortman	Detroit Lutheran West	25.5y
1981 C	Donna Smith	Detroit Lutheran West	25.2*
1982 C	Donna Smith	Detroit Lutheran West	25.3
1983 C	Lisa Hardiman	GR Forest Hills Northern	25.9
1984 C	Kristi Jackson	Detroit Country Day	25.6
1985 C	Shirley Evans	Detroit Country Day	25.7
1986 C	Shirley Evans	Detroit Country Day33333333	25.67*
1987 C	Shirley Evans	Detroit Country Day	25.42*
1988 C	Shirley Evans	Detroit Country Day	25.7
1989 C	Naheed Irani	Onsted	26.23
1990 C	Naheed Irani	Onsted	25.8
1991 C	Naheed Irani	Onsted	25.3
1992 C	Renee Pardon	Comstock Park	26.8
1993 C	Renee Pardon	Comstock Park	26.02
1994 C	Carie Burger	Reading	26.18
1995 C	Jessica Champine	Clare	25.54
1996 C	Jessica Champine	Clare	25.33*
1997 C	Alana Mestelle	White Pigeon	25.36
1998 C	Tiffany Simon	Redford Borgess	25.84 (-)
1999 C	Tiffany Simon	Redford Borgess	24.94*
2000 D3	Amber Berrien	Yale	25.32*
2001 D3	Julie Johnson	Laingsburg	25.47
2002 D3	Julie Johnson	Laingsburg	24.82*
2003 D3	Julie Johnson	Laingsburg	25.20
2004 D3	Allison Strouse	Lansing Catholic Central	25.89
2005 D3	Keyria Calloway	Detroit Crockett	25.65
2006 D3	Keyria Calloway	Detroit Crockett	24.85
2007 D3	Andrea Duffey	Williamston	26.13
2008 D3	Kelsey Ritter	Frankenmuth	25.55
2009 D3	Kelsey Ritter	Frankenmuth	25.32 (1.6)
2010 D3	Kelsey Ritter	Frankenmuth	25.29
2011 D3	Angie Ritter	Frankenmuth	26.25
2012 D3	Sami Michell	Reed City	25.28
2013 D3	Sami Michell	Reed City	24.98
2014 D3	Angie Ritter	Frankenmuth	24.72* (0.0)
2015 D3	Hailey Stockford	Sanford Meridian	25.11w (9.1)
2016 D3	Hailey Stockford	Sanford Meridian	25.29
2017 D3	Shiyon Taylor	Parchment	25.96 (0.0)
2018 D3	Najiyah Holden	St Charles	25.61 (-0.6)

200 – Class D/Division 4 Champions

(y=220 yards)

Year	Athlete	School	Time
1975 D	Sue Behnke	Battle Creek St Phillip	26.6y*
1976 D	Janet Hale	Maple City Glen Lake	26.0y*
1977 D	Brenda Johnson	Grass Lake	26.4y
1978 D	Brenda Johnson	Grass Lake	26.2y
1979 D	Robin Wellman	Inland Lakes	25.7*
1980 D	Andrea Kincannon	Grosse Pt University Liggett	25.6*
1981 D	Andrea Kincannon	Grosse Pt University Liggett	26.2
1982 D	Andrea Kincannon	Grosse Pt University Liggett	26.3
1983 D	Becky Klein	Fowler	25.6*
1984 D	Melanie Lovely	Concord	26.18*
1985 D	Jennifer Foster	Akron-Fairgrove	26.92
1986 D	Cheryl Boddy	Athens	26.47
1987 D	Becky Underwood	Warren Bethesda Christian	26.00*

1988 D	Carrie Ager	Central Lake	25.58*
1989 D	Yolanda Hansen	Baldwin	27.3
1990 D	Yolanda Hanson	Baldwin	26.18
1991 D	Tina Lademan	Johannesburg-Lewiston	26.59
1992 D	Theresa Proost	Maple City Glen Lake	26.72
1993 D	Stacey McCullum	Fairview	26.4
1994 D	Brooke Formsma	Battle Creek St Phillip	26.39
1995 D	Brooke Formsma	Battle Creek St Phillip	26.19
1996 D	Jennifer Bryant	Detroit East Catholic	27.30
1997 D	Brittany Hedgepath	St. Joseph Lake Mich Catholic	26.25
1998 D	Brittany Hedgepath	St. Joseph Lake Mich Catholic	25.5
1999 D	Lindsey Kowalski	Manistee Catholic	25.68
2000 D4	Marquita McGowen	Detroit Deporres	26.1*
2001 D4	Stacy Dellar	Lincoln-Alcona	26.52*
2002 D4	Stacy Dellar	Lincoln-Alcona	25.72*
2003 D4	Dessaray Cranford	Detroit Benedictine	25.98

2004 D4	Erin Dillon	Reading	25.63*
2005 D4	Erin Dillon	Reading	25.89
2006 D4	Erin Dillon	Reading	25.70
2007 D4	Jade Kaufman	Ubly	25.44*
2008 D4	Heather Lowery	Morrice	26.83
2009 D4	Lindsey Hufnagel	Fowler	26.14 (-1.9)
2010 D4	Lindsey Hufnagel	Fowler	26.57
2011 D4	Lindsey Hufnagel	Fowler	26.06
2012 D4	Lauren Buckel	Traverse City St. Francis	26.49
2013 D4	Miranda Johnson	Ottawa Lake Whiteford	25.94
2014 D4	Miranda Johnson	Ottawa Lake Whiteford	25.15* (1.0)
2015 D4	Lindsey Lehman	Concord	25.92 (-4.7)
2016 D4	Lindsey Lehman	Concord	25.70
2017 D4	Chika Amene	Southfield Christian	25.71
2018 D4	Chika Amene	Southfield Christian	25.53w (6.0)

200 – UP Class AB/Division 1 Champions

(y=220 yards)

1972 UP-All	Mary Frankini	Iron Mountain	28.0y*
1973 UP-All	Joanne Slater	Pickford	27.4y*
1974 UPAB	Denise Porath	Escanaba	28.5y
1975 UPAB	Pat Rector	Gwinn	26.5y*
1976 UPAB	Nancy Gage	Escanaba	27.0y
1977 UPAB	Julie Drake	Kingsford	26.8y
1978 UPAB	Lisa Wiedenhoefer	Marquette	26.0y*
1979 UPAB	Lisa Pancheri	Kingsford	27.1
1980 UPAB	Julie Drake	Kingsford	26.6
1981 UPAB	Michelle Blake	Menominee	27.3
1982 UPAB	Jean Tolfa	Escanaba	26.9
1983 UPAB	Michelle Blake	Menominee	26.7
1984 UPAB	Laura Gidley	Gwinn	26.5
1985 UPAB	Laura Gidley	Gwinn	28.0
1986 UPAB	Brenda Guiliana	Kingsford	27.0
1987 UPAB	Tammy Cook	Escanaba	27.3
1988 UPAB	Tammy Cook	Escanaba	26.5
1989 UPAB	Cheryl French	Gwinn	27.2
1990 UPAB	Jennifer Ostlund	Gladstone	27.2
1991 UPAB	Crista Beaver	Gladstone	27.1
1992 UPAB	Crista Beaver	Gladstone	27.4
1993 UPAB	Crista Beaver	Gladstone	26.3
1994 UPAB	Sarah Heikkila	Marquette	26.3

1995 UPAB	Maryea Pike	Sault Ste. Marie	26.6
1996 UPAB	Maryea Pike	Sault Ste. Marie	27.1
1997 UPAB	Laura Lacrosse	Escanaba	27.3
1998 UPAB	Jill Kimmes	Marquette	27.3
1999 UPAB	Tiffany Petr	Gladstone	27.4
2000 UPAB	Tiffany Petr	Gladstone	26.9
2001 UPD1	Tiffany Petr	Gladstone	26.87*
2002 UPD1	Jamie Lyberg	Gladstone	27.3
2003 UPD1	Stephanie Ostrenga	Escanaba	26.65*
2004 UPD1	Stephanie Ostrenga	Escanaba	26.43*
2005 UPD1	Stephanie Ostrenga	Escanaba	25.65*
2006 UPD1	Catherine Angeli	Marquette	26.09
2007 UPD1	Brittnee Balbierz	Marquette	26.46
2008 UPD1	Catherine Angeli	Marquette	26.46
2009 UPD1	Selena Meser	Sault Ste. Marie	27.09
2010 UPD1	Courtney Leferniere	Marquette	26.29
2011 UPD1	Salena Meser	Sault Ste. Marie	26.75
2012 UPD1	Chelsea Jacques	Calumet	26.69
2013 UPD1	Chelsea Jacques	Calumet	26.62
2014 UPD1	Chelsea Jacques	Calumet	26.5
2015 UPD1	Chelsea Jacques	Calumet	26.23
2016 UPD1	Izzie Peterson	Marquette	26.90
2017 UPD1	Olivia Allen	Kingsford	26.53
2018 UPD1	Olivia Allen	Kingsford	27.07

200 – UP Class C/Division 2 Champions

(y=220 yards)

1974 UPC	Pam Seldon	L'Anse	29.2y*
1975 UPC	Sue Soderberg	Ishpeming Westwood	28.2y*
1976 UPC	Lori Bouchard	Newberry	26.8y*
1977 UPC	Janet Pratt	Rudyard	26.6y*
1978 UPC	Cheryl Thomas	Iron River West Iron County	26.8y
1979 UPC	Jan Merrick	Negaunee	26.9
1980 UPC	Jan Merrick	Negaunee	26.7
1981 UPC	Joanna Carlson	Negaunee	27.5
1982 UPC	Jennie Baldwin	Houghton	26.9
1983 UPC	Lynne Scholie	Hancock	26.4*
1984 UPC	Colleen Colegrove	St. Ignace	27.1
1985 UPC	Colleen Colegrove	St. Ignace	27.2
1986 UPC	Colleen Colegrove	St. Ignace	26.2*
1987 UPC	Tracy Holappa	Ishpeming	27.3
1988 UPC	Tracy Holappa	Ishpeming	27.0
1989 UPC	Tracy Holappa	Ishpeming	27.2
1990 UPC	Tracy Holappa	Ishpeming	26.8
1991 UPC	Karrie Chaudler	L'Anse	26.8
1992 UPC	Angela Arthur	Ironwood	27.8
1993 UPC	Angela Arthur	Ironwood	27.1
1994 UPC	Angela Arthur	Ironwood	26.8
1995 UPC	Angela Arthur	Ironwood	26.8

1996 UPC	Richelle Robinson	St. Ignace	26.8
1997 UPC	Richelle Robinson	St. Ignace	26.7
1998 UPC	Emily Karry	Hancock	27.1
1999 UPC	Emily Karry	Hancock	26.9
2000 UPC	Eryn Mercer	St. Ignace	26.9
2001 UPD2	Eryn Mercer	St. Ignace	26.7*
2002 UPD2	Tara Bjorne	Manistique	27.6
2003 UPD2	Hillary Lucarelli	Ishpeming Westwood	28.06*
2004 UPD2	Vanessa Anderson	Hancock	27.72*
2005 UPD2	Krystal Stevenson	Manistique	27.34*
2006 UPD2	Krystal Stevenson	Manistique	27.00*
2007 UPD2	Kelsey Cryderman	St. Ignace	27.37
2008 UPD2	Taylor Watters	Ishpeming Westwood	28.15
2009 UPD2	Jamie Dompier	Chassell	26.47*
2010 UPD2	Dani Gagne	Norway	26.96
2011 UPD2	Dani Gagne	Norway	27.09
2012 UPD2	Dani Gagne	Norway	26.42*
2013 UPD2	Carli Johnson	West Iron Co.	28.30
2014 UPD2	Rachel Hetherington	St. Ignace	26.86
2015 UPD2	Emmy Kinner	West Iron Co.	27.16
2016 UPD2	Emmy Kinner	West Iron Co.	27.53
2017 UPD2	Emmy Kinner	West Iron Co.	27.25
2018 UPD2	Olivia Berutti	Iron Mountain	27.72

200 – UP Class D/Division 3 Champions

(y=220 yards)

1974 UPD	Barbara Short	Lake Linden-Hubbell	29.7y*
1975 UPD	Joanne Slater	Pickford	27.2y*
1976 UPD	Barbara Short	Lake Linden-Hubbell	26.9y*
1977 UPD	Vickie Thomas	Engadine	26.6y*
1978 UPD	Vickie Thomas	Engadine	27.0y
1979 UPD	Darla Koller	Norway	27.6
1980 UPD	Darla Koller	Norway	26.6*
1981 UPD	Gwen Wilkie	DeTour	26.9
1982 UPD	Gwen Wilkie	DeTour	26.6*
1983 UPD	Gwen Wilkie	DeTour	26.5*
1984 UPD	Gwen Wilkie	DeTour	26.7
1985 UPD	Lori Kempainen	White Pine	28.4

1986 UPD	Tricia Harris	Rapid River	27.6
1987 UPD	Diana Hongisto	Wakefield	28.0
1988 UPD	Maggie Clawson	Pickford	27.6
1989 UPD	Sue Harteau	Felch North Dickinson	27.8
1990 UPD	Kara Scherer	Cedarville	26.3*
1991 UPD	Kara Scherer	Cedarville	26.0*
1992 UPD	Kara Scherer	Cedarville	26.6
1993 UPD	Kara Scherer	Cedarville	26.3
1994 UPD	Cristina Koski	Lake Linden-Hubbell	26.9
1995 UPD	Stacey Boyer	Rapid River	27.5
1996 UPD	Tawna Urmon	Mackinac Island	26.9
1997 UPD	Dawn Savolainen	Lake Linden-Hubbell	27.6
1998 UPD	Richelle Robinson	St. Ignace	26.8

1999 UPD	Jacklyn Bebeau	Bessemer	26.8	
2000 UPD	Stephanie Boyer	Rapid River	27.3	
2001 UPD3	Stephanie Boyer	Rapid River	27.0*	
2002 UPD3	Stephanie Boyer	Rapid River	26.7*	
2003 UPD3	Stephanie Boyer	Rapid River	26.65*	
2004 UPD3	Becky Baron	Rock Mid Peninsula	26.66	
2005 UPD3	Caitlin Mortinsen	Pickford	27.80	
2006 UPD3	Angela Guisfredi	Lake Linden-Hubbell	27.37	
2007 UPD3	Lauren Marshall	Rapid River	27.55	
2008 UPD3	Brittany Engman	Dollar Bay	28.07	

2009 UPD3	Maria Valesano	Crystal Falls Forest Park	26.87
2010 UPD3	Maria Valesano	Crystal Falls Forest Park	26.69
2011 UPD3	Brittany Engman	Dollar Bay	27.36
2012 UPD3	Jamie Dompier	Chassell	26.36*
2013 UPD3	Jamie Dompier	Chassell	26.38
2014 UPD3	Autumn Arseneau	Engadine	27.43
2015 UPD3	Hannah Plemons	Wakefield	27.74
2016 UPD3	Camryn Crossdell	Rock Mid Peninsula	27.96
2017 UPD3	Laura Lyons	Lake Linden-Hubbell	27.53
2018 UPD3	Masyn Alexa	North Dickinson	27.18

GIRLS 400 METERS

Records

D1	53.10	Chloe Abbott	Northville	2016
D2	54.58	Kendall Baisden	Detroit Country Day	2012
D3	55.94	Amelia Bannister	Albion	2007
D4	57.33	Michelle Davis	Reading	2014
UPD1	57.85	Stephanie Ostrenga	Escanaba	2005
UPD2	59.18	Emmy Kinner	West Iron County	2017
UPD3	58.70	Lauren Spranger	Eben Junction Superior Central	2011

Records by Class (pre-2000 for LP, pre-2001 for UP)

A	54.81	Tracy Ball	Detroit Cass Tech	1998
	(hand 54.5y	Delisa Walton	Detroit Mackenzie	1978)
B	56.40	Januala Bennett	Niles	1999
	(hand 56.1y	Johanna Matthyssen	Holt	1976)
C	56.05	Julia Redd	Detroit Dominican	1999
D	58.28	Cheryl Boddy	Athens	1986
	(hand 57.6	Becky Klein	Fowler	1982)
UPAB	59.0	Erica Helmila	Marquette	2000)
UPC	59.2	Richelle Robinson	St. Ignace	1996)
UPD	58.8	Kara Scherer	Cedarville	1991)

400 – Class A/Division 1 Champions

(y=440 yards)

1973 All	Sue Latter	Clarkston	57.1y*
1974 A/B	Mahalia Ewell	Flint Northwestern	58.9y
1975 A	Gloria Fuller	Detroit Northern	57.8y
1976 A	Ruth Hubbard	Walled Lake Western	56.7y*
1977 A	Delisa Walton	Detroit Mackenzie	57.0y
1978 A	Delisa Walton	Detroit Mackenzie	54.5y*
1979 A	Delisa Walton	Detroit Mackenzie	55.5y
1980 A	Cherri Laycock	Clio	55.9y
1981 A	Elaine Jones	Detroit Chadsey	55.9y
1982 A	Joyce Wilson	Warren Tower	55.9
1983 A	Barb Stinson	Jackson	56.4
1984 A	Vera Pruitt	Detroit Chadsey	56.6
1985 A	Cheryl Pruitt	Detroit Henry Ford	57.59*
1986 A	Angela Jones	Detroit Cass Tech	56.90*
1987 A	Cheryl Pruitt	Detroit Henry Ford	56.60*
1988 A	Jimalatrice Thomas	Detroit Osborn	57.27
1989 A	Charlotte Williams	Detroit Pershing	57.90
1990 A	Ijnanya Alhamisi	Detroit Henry Ford	55.80
1991 A	Arelia Berry	Flint Northwestern	56.05
1992 A	Latonya Wheeler	Salem	59.10
1993 A	Latonya Wheeler	Salem	58.01
1994 A	Julia Ford	Detroit Cass Tech	55.1
1995 A	Angelina Edwards	Flint Central	57.36

1996 A	Rosia Williams	Detroit Pershing	55.97
1997 A	Michelle Davis	Lansing Sexton	55.62
1998 A	Tracy Ball	Detroit Cass Tech	54.81*
1999 A	Carly Knazze	Southfield	55.87
2000 D1	Melanie Williams	Southfield	56.70*
2001 D1	Amber Walker	Detroit Northwestern	56.98
2002 D1	Becky Horn	Battle Creek Central	55.51*
2003 D1	Becky Horn	Battle Creek Central	56.63
2004 D1	Jessica Jones	Detroit Mumford	54.98*
2005 D1	Jessica Jones	Detroit Mumford	55.23
2006 D1	Erin Humphrey	Ypsilanti Lincoln	54.33*
2007 D1	Victoria Chatman	Taylor Kennedy	55.51
2008 D1	Brittani Williams	Jackson	56.08
2009 D1	Dynasty McGee	Flint Southwestern Academy	56.03
2010 D1	Rachel Jerrils	Rockford	56.61
2011 D1	Latipha Cross	Southfield	54.29*
2012 D1	Maya Long	Ann Arbor Huron	54.80
2013 D1	Anna Jefferson	Oak Park	55.44
2014 D1	Anna Jefferson	Oak Park	53.50*
2015 D1	Sammy Cuneo	Rockford	55.32*
2016 D1	Chloe Abbott	Northville	53.10*
2017 D1	Taylor Manson	East Lansing	53.21
2018 D1	Miyah Brooks	Oak Park	55.12

400 – Class B/Division 2 Champions

(y=440 yards)

1975 B	Rochelle Collins	Detroit Immaculata	58.0y*
1976 B	Johanna Matthyssen	Holt	56.1y*
1977 B	Rochelle Collins	Detroit Immaculata	56.8y
1978 B	Rochelle Collins	Detroit Immaculata	56.2y
1979 B	Yvonne Matthyssen	Holt	58.5y
1980 B	Melanie Detters	Durand	56.9
1981 B	Kathy Kost	Mt Clemens L'Anse Creuse	57.2
1982 B	Karen Wade	Ypsilanti Lincoln	57.1y
1983 B	Kathy Kost	Mt Clemens L'Anse Creuse	56.5
1984 B	Tammy Oostendorp	Hudsonville Unity Christian	57.5
1985 B	Twynette Wilson	Flint Beecher	57.44*
1986 B	Pretoria WIlson	Flint Beecher	57.7
1987 B	Pretoria Wilson	Flint Beecher	57.00*

1988 B	Pretoria Wilson	Flint Beecher	57.75
1989 B	Heather Akers	Cadillac	58.6
1990 B	Sarah Colladay	Big Rapids	58.0
1991 B	Chantella Byrd	Flint Beecher	57.11
1992 B	Laquanda George	Melvindale	58.85
1993 B	Charnell Lynn	Inkster	59.07
1994 B	Kari Karhoff	Durand	56.70
1995 B	Charnell Lynn	Ypsilanti Willow Run	57.45
1996 B	Tamika Craig	Dearborn Hts Robichaud	56.67*
1997 B	Lindsay Mulder	Grandville Calvin Christian	57.22
1998 B	Januala Bennett	Niles	56.8
1999 B	Januala Bennett	Niles	56.40*
2000 D2	Sara Jane Baker	Mattawan	56.17*
2001 D2	Sara Jane Baker	Mattawan	56.66

2002 D2	Jessica Jones	Detroit Renaissance	56.99
2003 D2	Stephanie Allers	Coopersville	57.43
2004 D2	Ernanda Daskeviciute	Pontiac Notre Dame Prep	57.37
2005 D2	Katherine McCarthy	Grand Rapids Kenowa Hills	57.44
2006 D2	Katherine McCarthy	Grand Rapids Kenowa Hills	56.38
2007 D2	Lindsey McKnight	Sparta	57.09
2008 D2	Olivia Detroyer	Chelsea	56.49
2009 D2	Olivia Detroyer	Chelsea	57.64
2010 D2	Kendall Baisden	Detroit Country Day	54.91*

2011 D2	Kendall Baisden	Detroit Country Day	55.12
2012 D2	Kendall Baisden	Detroit Country Day	54.58*
2013 D2	Kendall Baisden	Detroit Country Day	54.99
2014 D2	Zoe Eby	Carleton Airport	56.35
2015 D2	Abby Porter	Grand Rapids South Christian	56.87
2016 D2	Jakarri Alven	Grand Rapids Catholic Central	55.66
2017 D2	Jakarri Alven	Grand Rapids Catholic Central	56.48
2018 D2	Emma Fountain	Ludington	57.49

400 – Class C/Division 3 Champions
(y=440 yards)

1974 C/D	Brenda Pryc	Montrose	59.4y*
1975 C	Lori Davis	Haslett	1:00.5y
1976 C	Becky Klann	Rogers City	59.4y*
1977 C	Becky Klann	Rogers City	57.9y*
1978 C	Linda Noud	Galesburg Augusta	59.3y
1979 C	Nancy Bardwell	Burton Bentley	57.6y*
1980 C	Janell Best	St. Louis	57.8y
1981 C	Janell Best	St Louis	58.0
1982 C	Ann Hammond	Ida	59.3
1983 C	Andrea Kincannon	Grosse Pt University Liggett	58.8
1984 C	Jeana Vandermuelen	Middleville-Thornapple	59.0
1985 C	Shirley Evans	Detroit Country Day	58.4
1986 C	Coleen Wruble	Harbor Beach	59.37*
1987 C	Becky Hicks	Tawas	58.31*
1988 C	Kristal Mack	New Haven	57.9
1989 C	Beth Lerner	Edwardsburg	58.60
1990 C	Lynn Beutler	Erie-Mason	57.87*
1991 C	Jamie WIlson	Whitehall	58.6
1992 C	Kary Tomaw	East Jackson	1:00.2
1993 C	Tracey Knudsen	Suttons Bay	58.46
1994 C	Jodi Gelina	Shepherd	58.03
1995 C	Heidi Goodenough	Hemlock	58.33

1996 C	Megan DuMonte	Hart	58.34
1997 C	Kelly Nuechterlein	Frankenmuth	58.28
1998 C	Amber Ranney	Fennville	58.19
1999 C	Julia Redd	Detroit Dominican	56.05*
2000 D3	Amber Berrien	Yale	57.41*
2001 D3	Julie Johnson	Laingsburg	57.04*
2002 D3	Julie Johnson	Laingsburg	57.18
2003 D3	Julie Johnson	Laingsburg	57.48
2004 D3	Jaime Watson	Allendale	55.95*
2005 D3	Jaime Watson	Allendale	55.98
2006 D3	Stephanie Byrne	Bad Axe	57.29
2007 D3	Amelia Bannister	Albion	55.94*
2008 D3	Kelsey Ritter	Frankenmuth	58.21
2009 D3	Amelia Bannister	Albion	56.84
2010 D3	Kelsey Ritter	Frankenmuth	56.27
2011 D3	Angie Ritter	Frankenmuth	57.26
2012 D3	Devyn Powell	Leroy Pine River	57.77
2013 D3	Ce'aira Richardson	Bridgeport	56.92
2014 D3	Ce'aira Richardson	Bridgeport	57.11
2015 D3	Megan Rosales	Adrian Madison	57.58
2016 D3	Hailey Nielsen	Jonesville	58.34
2017 D3	Megan Rosales	Adrian Madison	57.02
2018 D3	Renee Kutcha	Jackson Lumen Christi	58.75

400 – Class D/Division 4 Champions
(y=440 yards)

1975 D	Debra Ramsed	Concord	58.5y*
1976 D	Pam Brown	Morenci	59.9y
1977 D	Pam Brown	Morenci	58.7y
1978 D	Maria Shoup	Mason County Eastern	58.7y
1979 D	Barb Loudenslager	Colon	59.7
1980 D	Kelly Wellman	Inland Lakes	1:02.2
1981 D	Becky Klein	Fowler	58.6
1982 D	Becky Klein	Fowler	57.6*
1983 D	Becky Klein	Fowler	57.8
1984 D	Kelly Hafner	Fowler	1:00.18*
1985 D	Lisa Nixon	Ann Arbor Greenhills	58.93*
1986 D	Cheryl Boddy	Athens	58.28*
1987 D	Becky Underwood	Warren Bethesda Christian	58.83
1988 D	Angela Frick	Walkerville	59.5
1989 D	Theresa Proost	Maple City Glen Lake	59.5
1990 D	Theresa Proost	Maple City Glen Lake	59.71
1991 D	Theresa Proost	Maple City Glen Lake	59.79
1992 D	Theresa Proost	Maple City Glen Lake	59.01*
1993 D	Leslie Keeney	Litchfield	1:00.1
1994 D	Catherine McGaw	Grass Lake	1:00.64
1995 D	Patrice Cannon	Wyoming Lee	1:01.68
1996 D	Wendy Lautner	Onekema	59.99

1997 D	Wendy Lautner	Onekema	1:00.7
1998 D	Amber Berrien	Carsonville-Port Sanilac	59.9
1999 D	Sherita Green	Southgate Aquinas	1:00.26
2000 D4	Julia Redd	Detroit Dominican	58.01*
2001 D4	Amanda Lyon	Mesick	59.61
2002 D4	Dessaray Crawford	Detroit Benedictine	57.65*
2003 D4	Dessaray Crawford	Detroit Benedictine	58.39
2004 D4	Erin Dillon	Reading	57.63*
2005 D4	Erin Dillon	Reading	57.98
2006 D4	Erin Dillon	Reading	57.70
2007 D4	Jade Kaufman	Ubly	58.93
2008 D4	Tori Gillespie	Marion	1:00.46
2009 D4	Lindsey Hufnagel	Fowler	58.03
2010 D4	Lindsey Hufnagel	Fowler	58.91
2011 D4	Lindsey Hufnagel	Fowler	58.76
2012 D4	Lauren Buckel	Traverse City St. Francis	59.93
2013 D4	Lauren Buckel	Traverse City St. Francis	59.54
2014 D4	Michelle Davis	Reading	57.33*
2015 D4	Salix Sampson	Harbor Springs	58.99
2016 D4	Alexandra Hanson	Brown City	58.11
2017 D4	Chika Amene	Southfield Christian	58.83
2018 D4	Angela Kotecki	Beal City	57.53

400 – UP Class AB/Division 1 Champions
(y=440 yards)

1972 UP-All	Denise Redding	Gwinn	1:04.0y*
1973 UP-All	Rene Eberling	Norway	1:07.0y
1974 UPAB	Sue Flippen	Escanaba	1:02.7y*
1975 UPAB	Sharon Schultz	Escanaba	1:03.2y
1976 UPAB	Sharon Schultz	Escanaba	1:01.9y*
1977 UPAB	Katie Miller	Marquette	1:00.4y*
1978 UPAB	Beth King	Marquette	1:00.8y
1979 UPAB	Becky Drake	Kingsford	1:00.3*
1980 UPAB	Linda Ewald	Menominee	1:01.1
1981 UPAB	Lisa Phelan	Escanaba	1:00.6
1982 UPAB	Elizabeth Sarvello	Marquette	1:00.3*
1983 UPAB	Laura Gidley	Gwinn	1:00.5
1984 UPAB	Laura Gidley	Gwinn	1:00.8
1985 UPAB	Jean Ammel	Escanaba	1:02.5
1986 UPAB	Jean Ammel	Escanaba	1:00.8
1987 UPAB	Vina Poquette	Menominee	1:02.0
1988 UPAB	Tammy Cook	Escanaba	59.2*
1989 UPAB	Cheryl French	Gwinn	1:01.8
1990 UPAB	Anne Borowski	Ironwood	1:01.6
1991 UPAB	Jennie Drake	Kingsford	1:01.6

1992 UPAB	Jennie Drake	Kingsford	1:03.8
1993 UPAB	Lisa Larson	Marquette	1:01.8
1994 UPAB	Sarah Heikkila	Marquette	1:00.1
1995 UPAB	Sarah Heikkila	Marquette	59.2*
1996 UPAB	Maryea Pike	Sault Ste. Marie	1:00.2
1997 UPAB	Chrissy Barnes	Marquette	1:02.2
1998 UPAB	Erica Helmila	Marquette	1:02.3
1999 UPAB	Erica Helmila	Marquette	1:01.6
2000 UPAB	Erica Helmila	Marquette	59.0*
2001 UPD1	Tiffany Petr	Gladstone	1:02.2*
2002 UPD1	Jamie Lyberg	Gladstone	1:01.6*
2003 UPD1	Stephanie Ostrenga	Escanaba	1:00.75*
2004 UPD1	Stephanie Ostrenga	Escanaba	58.56*
2005 UPD1	Stephanie Ostrenga	Escanaba	57.85*
2006 UPD1	Catherine Angeli	Marquette	59.91
2007 UPD1	Catherine Angeli	Marquette	1:00.32
2008 UPD1	Catherine Angeli	Marquette	1:01.40
2009 UPD1	Kristin Nelson	Iron Mountain	1:01.22
2010 UPD1	Courtney Laferniere	Marquette	59.26
2011 UPD1	Selema Meser	Sault Ste. Marie	58.72
2012 UPD1	Shayla Huebner	Marquette	1:01.68

2013 UPD1	Shayla Huebner	Marquette	59.29
2014 UPD1	Amber Huebner	Marquette	1:00.44
2015 UPD1	Shayla Huebner	Marquette	58.71
2016 UPD1	Olivia Allen	Kingsford	1:01.22
2017 UPD1	Olivia Allen	Kingsford	59.53
2018 UPD1	Olivia Allen	Kingsford	59.51

400 – UP Class C/Division 2 Champions
(y=440 yards)

1974 UPC	Kathy Talus	Negaunee	1:05.3y*
1975 UPC	Marian Winnen	Ishpeming Westwood	1:01.7y*
1976 UPC	Pam Pierce	Iron Mountain	1:02.3y
1977 UPC	Janet Pratt	Rudyard	1:00.7y*
1978 UPC	Pamela Pierce	Iron Mountain	1:00.4y*
1979 UPC	Carrie Talus	Negaunee	1:02.3
1980 UPC	Jennie Baldwin	Houghton	1:01.0
1981 UPC	Debbie Hoots	Stephenson	1:01.9
1982 UPC	Jenny Baldwin	Houghton	1:00.4*
1983 UPC	Michell Tregembo	Ironwood	1:02.1
1984 UPC	Colleen Colegrove	St. Ignace	1:00.8
1985 UPC	Colleen Colegrove	St. Ignace	1:00.3*
1986 UPC	Colleen Colegrove	St. Ignace	59.4*
1987 UPC	Heidi Knutson	Ishpeming Westwood	1:00.5
1988 UPC	Traci Jeschke	Stephenson	1:00.7
1989 UPC	Chris Buhto	Iron River-West Iron County	1:02.3
1990 UPC	Anne Kolaszewski	Stephenson	1:02.8
1991 UPC	Anne Borowski	Ironwood	1:02.0
1992 UPC	Kelly Peterson	Munising	1:04.4
1993 UPC	Kelly Peterson	Munising	1:01.5
1994 UPC	Kelly Peterson	Munising	1:02.0
1995 UPC	Kathy Beasley	Hancock	1:01.2
1996 UPC	Richelle Robinson	St. Ignace	59.2*
1997 UPC	Richelle Robinson	St. Ignace	1:00.2
1998 UPC	Erin McCarthy	Norway	1:01.3
1999 UPC	Emili Karry	Hancock	59.7
2000 UPC	Ashley Veran	Hancock	1:01.3
2001 UPD2	Kristen Pedo	Iron Mountain	1:00.9*
2002 UPD2	Ashley Verran	Hancock	1:01.5
2003 UPD2	Kate Hagenbuch	Hancock	1:01.37*
2004 UPD2	Elena Renier	Norway	1:02.16
2005 UPD2	Chelsea Hanert	Newberry	1:00.89*
2006 UPD2	Kelsey Cryderman	St. Ignace	1:01.41
2007 UPD2	Kelsey Cryderman	St. Ignace	1:00.96
2008 UPD2	Hannah Hegbloom	Ishpeming Westwood	1:06.48
2009 UPD2	Kara Dale	Ishpeming	1:00.99
2010 UPD2	Kara Dale	Ishpeming	1:00.30*
2011 UPD2	Kara Dale	Ishpeming	1:00.75
2012 UPD2	Dani Gagne	Norway	1:00.65
2013 UPD2	Hailey LaFleur	Iron Mountain	1:03.02
2014 UPD2	Emmy Kinner	West Iron County	1:00.98
2015 UPD2	Emmy Kinner	West Iron County	1:02.18
2016 UPD2	Emmy Kinner	West Iron County	1:02.76
2017 UPD2	Emmy Kinner	West Iron County	59.18*
2018 UPD2	Emily Coveyou	St Ignace	1:04.11

400 – UP Class D/Division 3 Champions
(y=440 yards)

1974 UPD	Chris Dishaw	Crystal Falls Forest Park	1:05.6y*
1975 UPD	Chris Dishaw	Crystal Falls Forest Park	1:02.4y*
1976 UPD	Chris Dishaw	Crystal Falls Forest Park	1:02.9y
1977 UPD	Lydia St. Juliana	Powers-North Central	1:02.9y
1978 UPD	Jean Mettlach	Crystal Falls Forest Park	1:03.1y
1979 UPD	Linda Grodeski	Norway	59.6*
1980 UPD	Joan Casanova	Norway	59.2*
1981 UPD	Mary Freebury	Cedarville	1:01.5
1982 UPD	Joan Casanova	Norway	1:00.1
1983 UPD	Lori Kempainen	White Pine	1:01.6
1984 UPD	Lori Kempainen	White Pine	1:02.3
1985 UPD	Lori Kempainen	White Pine	1:03.4
1986 UPD	Jodi Hosang	Lake Linden-Hubbell	1:02.1
1987 UPD	Jeri Hosang	Lake Linden-Hubbell	1:03.0
1988 UPD	Julie Elsing	Rock-Mid Peninsula	1:02.1
1989 UPD	Gina Weatherly	Pickford	1:03.6
1990 UPD	Kara Scherer	Cedarville	1:01.1
1991 UPD	Kara Scherer	Cedarville	58.8*
1992 UPD	Kara Scherer	Cedarville	1:01.2
1993 UPD	Jennifer Menard	Bessemer	1:01.6
1994 UPD	Dana Feak	Felch North DIckinson	1:00.3
1995 UPD	Stacey Boyer	Rapid River	1:01.3
1996 UPD	Tawna Ulman	Mackinaw Island	1:02.5
1997 UPD	Sue Burns	Felch North Dickinson	1:03.7
1998 UPD	Richelle Robinson	St. Ignace	59.5
1999 UPD	Molly Bacon	Rapid River	1:02.2
2000 UPD	Molly Bacon	Rapid River	1:01.3
2001 UPD3	Molly Bacon	Rapid River	1:01.4*
2002 UPD3	Stephanie Boyer	Rapid River	1:02.1
2003 UPD3	Stephanie Boyer	Rapid River	1:02.15*
2004 UPD3	Caitlin Mortinsen	Pickford	1:02.71
2005 UPD3	Caitlin Mortinsen	Pickford	1:01.44*
2006 UPD3	Angela Guisfredi	Lake Linden-Hubbell	1:01.54
2007 UPD3	Erin Holmberg	Cooks-Big Bay de Noc	1:01.20*
2008 UPD3	Erin Holmberg	Cooks-Big Bay de Noc	1:02.70
2009 UPD3	Lauren Spranger	Eben Junction Superior Central	1:00.73*
2010 UPD3	Lauren Spranger	Eben Junction Superior Central	1:00.53*
2011 UPD3	Lauren Spranger	Eben Junction Superior Central	58.70*
2012 UPD3	Lauren Spranger	Eben Junction Superior Central	58.97
2013 UPD3	Jamie Dompier	Chassell	1:00.62
2014 UPD3	Mary Grandahl	Crystal Falls Forest Park	1:04.72
2015 UPD3	Paige Blake	Ontonagon	1:03.10
2016 UPD3	Paige Blake	Ontonagon	1:03.26
2017 UPD3	Sarah Bailey	DeTour	1:00.52
2018 UPD3	Fahren Kolpack	Ontonagon	1:01.35

GIRLS 800 METERS

Records
D1	2:06.35	Hannah Meier	Grosse Pointe South	2013
D2	2:11.08	Ramzee Fondren	Detroit Renaissance	2006
D3	2:09.61	Annie Fuller	Manistee	2015
D4	2:13.95	Laurel Bennett	Mt Pleasant Sacred Heart	2005
UPD1	2:13.94	Lindsay Rudden	Marquette	2015
UPD2	2:18.2	Amber Smith	Ishpeming Westwood	2003
UPD3	2:21.61	Amy Kerst	Munising	2011

Records by Class (pre-2000 for LP, pre-2001 for UP)
A	2:07.7y	Delisa Walton	Detroit Mackenzie	1978
B	2:11.7y	Rochelle Collins	Detroit Immaculata	1978
C	2:16.3	Donna Donakowski	Deaborn Hts Riverside	1983
D	2:18.32	Nicole Miehlke	Manistee Catholic	1996
UPAB	2:15.8	Krista O'Dell	Escanaba	2000
UPC	2:21.3	Ann Somerville	Ironwood	1997
UPD	2:24.0	Joan Casanova	Norway	1980

800 – Class A/Division 1 Champions
(y=880 yards)

1973 All	Sue Latter	Clarkston	2:17.7y*	

1974 A/B	Sue Parks	Ypsilanti	2:14.4y*
1975 A	Leslie Laviolette	Ann Arbor Huron	2:19.4y
1976 A	Ella Willis	Detroit Pershing	2:14.9y
1977 A	Vicki Simpson	Madison Hts Lamphere	2:16.5y
1978 A	Delisa Walton	Detroit Mackenzie	2:07.7y*
1979 A	Delisa Walton	Detroit Mackenzie	2:11.5y
1980 A	Levy String	Flint Northern	2:14.8y
1981 A	Cynthia Dixon	Detroit Chadsey	2:15.2y
1982 A	Kathi Harris	Walled Lake Central	2:15.3
1983 A	Carlene Isabelle	Flint Northern	2:15.6
1984 A	Stephanie Robertson	Midland	2:15.7
1985 A	Laura Matson	Bloomfield Hills Andover	2:12.02
1986 A	Laura Matson	Bloomfield Hills Andover	2:12.50
1987 A	Charlotte Williams	Detroit Pershing	2:15.0
1988 A	Tracy Boudreau	Ann Arbor Huron	2:12.22
1989 A	Amira Danforth	West Bloomfield	2:13.90
1990 A	Amira Danforth	West Bloomfield	2:15.96
1991 A	Sara Minier	Greenville	2:17.84
1992 A	Erica Shepherd	Detroit Cass Tech	2:15.41
1993 A	Erica Shepherd	Detroit Cass Tech	2:15.61
1994 A	Sarah Hebert	East Detroit	2:15.8
1995 A	Sarah Hebert	East Detroit	2:15.85
1996 A	Evista Clemon	Detroit Northwestern	2:13.28

1997 A	Erin White	Battle Creek Central	2:13.32
1998 A	Julie Stowers	Brighton	2:16.8
1999 A	Rachel Sturtz	Traverse City Central	2:14.74
2000 D1	Ashley Patten	Lake Orion	2:11.95*
2001 D1	Ashley Patten	Lake Orion	2:11.72*
2002 D1	Ashley Patten	Lake Orion	2:14.30
2003 D1	Lisa Senakiewich	Davison	2:13.18
2004 D1	Geena Gall	Grand Blanc	2:10.45*
2005 D1	Geena Gall	Grand Blanc	2:09.60*
2006 D1	Stephanie Morgan	Clarkston	2:14.54
2007 D1	Lauren Quaintance	Walled Lake Northern	2:14.20
2008 D1	Rebecca Addison	Grand Haven	2:13.75
2009 D1	Rebecca Addison	Grand Haven	2:12.50
2010 D1	Hannah Meier	Grosse Pointe South	2:08.83*
2011 D1	Hannah Meier	Grosse Pointe South	2:07.37*
2012 D1	Hannah Meier	Grosse Pointe South	2:08.57
2013 D1	Hannah Meier	Grosse Pointe South	2:06.35*
2014 D1	Ersula Farrow	Grosse Pointe South	2:07.63
2015 D1	Ersula Farrow	Oak Park	2:08.43
2016 D1	Dorriann Coleman	Oak Park	2:10.20
2017 D1	Mallory Barrett	Milford	2:11.06
2018 D1	Katie Osika	Waterford Mott	2:08.88

800 – Class B/Division 2 Champions
(y=880 yards)

1975 B	Rochelle Collins	Detroit Immaculata	2:16.9y*
1976 B	Rochelle Collins	Detroit Immaculata	2:14.3y*
1977 B	Rochelle Collins	Detroit Immaculata	2:12.5y*
1978 B	Rochelle Collins	Detroit Immaculata	2:11.7y*
1979 B	Laurie Call	Saginaw MacArthur	2:18.0y
1980 B	Joan DeMaat	Grand Rapids Christian	2:17.9
1981 B	Jennifer Rioux	Livonia Ladywood	2:14.2
1982 B	Lorie Vultaggio	South Lake	2:13.2y
1983 B	Lorie Vultaggio	South Lake	2:13.8
1984 B	Teresa Stouffer	Royal Oak Shrine	2:18.5
1985 B	Valerie Ambrose	Riverview Gabriel Richard	2:19.56
1986 B	Joan Arndt	Livonia Ladywood	2:15.5
1987 B	Twynette Wilson	Flint Beecher	2:14.65
1988 B	Cari Byrd	Oxford	2:13.93
1989 B	Vonda Meder	Corunna	2:18.6
1990 B	Vonda Meder	Corunna	2:16.3
1991 B	Kendra Akers	Milan	2:20.3
1992 B	Kelly Smith	Petoskey	2:15.54
1993 B	Kelly Smith	Petoskey	2:13.4
1994 B	Kelly Smith	Petoskey	2:12.19
1995 B	Erin White	Battle Creek Pennfield	2:19.38
1996 B	Erin White	Battle Creek Pennfield	2:13.79

1997 B	Dru Bishop	Fenton	2:18.3
1998 B	Dru Bishop	Fenton	2:14.99
1999 B	Katherine Kenagy	Stevensville-Lakeshore	2:16.67
2000 D2	Jennifer Price	Battle Creek Lakeview	2:13.93*
2001 D2	Jessica Kraft	West Branch Ogemaw Heights	2:13.69*
2002 D2	Katie Erdman	Cadillac	2:13.51*
2003 D2	Sarah Schmidt	New Boston Huron	2:16.64
2004 D2	Katherine McCarthy	Grand Rapids Kenowa Hills	2:15.35
2005 D2	Ramzee Fondren	Detroit Renaissance	2:15.79
2006 D2	Ramzee Fondren	Detroit Renaissance	2:11.08*
2007 D2	Ramzee Fondren	Detroit Renaissance	2:11.18
2008 D2	Christina Farrow	Detroit Renaissance	2:14.54
2009 D2	Leah O'Connor	Croswell-Lexington	2:15.41
2010 D2	Leah O'Connor	Croswell-Lexington	2:15.08
2011 D2	Sara Barron	Pontiac Notre Dame Prep	2:13.49
2012 D2	Sara Barron	Pontiac Notre Dame Prep	2:13.83
2013 D2	Megan O'Neal	Remus Chippewa Hills	2:14.88
2014 D2	Carlyn Arteaga	Spring Lake	2:16.09
2015 D2	Carlyn Arteaga	Spring Lake	2:14.93
2016 D2	Mya Veen	Plainwell	2:14.75
2017 D2	Lauren Biggs	Ludington	2:12.13
2018 D2	Michelle Kuipers	Holland Christian	2:13.49

800 – Class C/Division 3 Champions
(y=880 yards)

1974 C/D	Cindy Tarrant	Bath	2:23.0y*
1975 C	Diane Tomes	Ottawa Lake Whiteford	2:25.3y
1976 C	Mandy Johnson	Scottville Mason County C	2:22.5y*
1977 C	Keela Yount	DeWitt	2:23.2y
1978 C	Beth Veldhoff	Blissfield	2:18.9y*
1979 C	Anne Simon	Shepherd	2:18.0y*
1980 C	Anne Simon	Shepherd	2:18.9y
1981 C	Janel Best	St Louis	2:19.7
1982 C	Mary Lunneen	Berrien Springs	2:18.1
1983 C	Donna Donakowski	Dearborn Heights Riverside	2:16.3*
1984 C	Jolene Crooks	Benzie Central	2:17.4
1985 C	Cathy Ackley	Hart	2:18.00
1986 C	Jenny Erickson	Burton-Bentley	2:22.23
1987 C	Cathy Ackley	Hart	2:18.4
1988 C	Cathy Ackley	Hart	2:19.7
1989 C	Stacey Kilburn	White Pigeon	2:17.48
1990 C	Naheed Irani	Onsted	2:22.5
1991 C	Joy Wright	Southfield Christian	2:17.3
1992 C	Janet Boldrey	Vermontville-Maple Valley	2:18.3
1993 C	Jeni Brewer	Southgate Aquinas	2:19.6
1994 C	Michelle Kline	Napoleon	2:19.20
1995 C	Traci Knudsen	Suttons Bay	2:16.87

1996 C	Kathryn Murphy	Vermontville Maple Valley	2:16.73
1997 C	Amy Jordan	Tawas	2:17.41
1998 C	Bethany Brewster	Saginaw Valley Lutheran	2:18.24
1999 C	Caryn Waterson	Benzie Central	2:17.41
2000 D3	Tracy Egnatuk	Albion	2:16.03*
2001 D3	Tracy Egnatuk	Albion	2:14.66*
2002 D3	Sarah Stornant	Portland	2:18.90
2003 D3	Monique Hoyle	Delton Kellogg	2:21.13
2004 D3	Janee Jones	Goodrich	2:14.89
2005 D3	Janee Jones	Goodrich	2:16.18
2006 D3	Amelia Bannister	Albion	2:15.50
2007 D3	Amelia Bannister	Albion	2:14.03*
2008 D3	Amelia Bannister	Albion	2:16.42
2009 D3	Rachel Whitley	Leroy Pine River	2:16.09
2010 D3	Michaela Carnegie	Benzie Central	2:16.16
2011 D3	Michaela Carnegie	Benzie Central	2:16.96
2012 D3	Annie Fuller	Manistee	2:13.03*
2013 D3	Annie Fuller	Manistee	2:11.77*
2014 D3	Annie Fuller	Manistee	2:11.40*
2015 D3	Annie Fuller	Manistee	2:09.61*
2016 D3	Holly Bullough	Traverse City St. Francis	2:12.22
2017 D3	Amber Gall	Shepherd	2:14.81
2018 D3	Judy Rector	Hanover-Horton	2:13.44

800 – Class D/Division 4 Champions
(y=880 yards)

1975 D	Janet Chappell	Battle Creek St Phillip	2:28.4y*
1976 D	Betty Wilds	Mendon	2:25.8y*
1977 D	Karen Hall	Indian River Inland Lakes	2:20.3y*
1978 D	Maria Shoup	Mason County Eastern	2:20.1y*
1979 D	Maria Shoup	Mason County Eastern	2:21.9
1980 D	Robin Magee	Ann Arbor Greenhills	2:23.1

1981 D	Dawn Rich	Deckerville	2:23.1
1982 D	Roxanne Wiersma	Allendale	2:23.6
1983 D	Lorissa Szporluk	Ann Arbor Greenhills	2:18.9*
1984 D	Sue Gunn	Ann Arbor Greenhills	2:21.92
1985 D	Michelle Wait	Covert	2:24.69
1986 D	Andl Clark	Grass Lake	2:23.90
1987 D	Jacki Clark	Camden-Frontier	2:22.70

Year	Class	Name	School	Time
1988 D		Jennifer Foster	Akron-Fairgrove	2:20.78
1989 D		Jackie Clark	Camden-Frontier	2:19.5
1990 D		Dawn Noble	Lawton	2:23.53
1991 D		Amy Langschied	Deerfield	2:20.62
1992 D		Amy Langschied	Deerfield	2:23.59
1993 D		Liz Martin	Maple City Glen Lake	2:23.2
1994 D		Lyndsay Burchardt	Pittsford	2:18.39*
1995 D		Sarah Ward	Camden-Frontier	2:22.33
1996 D		Nicole Miehlke	Manistee Catholic	2:18.32*
1997 D		Jenny Drenth	Central Lake	2:19.72
1998 D		Jenny Drenth	Central Lake	2:21.0
1999 D		Michelle Rolf	Rochester Hills Lutheran NW	2:24.54
2000 D4		Jenny Kulchar	Burton Atherton	2:17.87*
2001 D4		Jenny Kulchar	Burton Atherton	2:18.92
2002 D4		Amanda Lyon	Mesick	2:20.26
2003 D4		Katie Lawrence	Potterville	2:19.63

Year	Class	Name	School	Time
2004 D4		Laurel Bennett	Mt Pleasant Sacred Heart	2:16.04*
2005 D4		Laurel Bennett	Mt Pleasant Sacred Heart	2:13.95*
2006 D4		Alexa Glencer	Ann Arbor Greenhills	2:15.90
2007 D4		Marissa Treece	Maple City Glen Lake	2:13.96
2008 D4		Emily Wickemeyer	Athens	2:22.02
2009 D4		Ana Capotosto	Saugatuck	2:20.60
2010 D4		Elainee Poling	Pittsford	2:21.33
2011 D4		Shelly Albaugh	Hillsdale Academy	2:19.21
2012 D4		Shelly Albaugh	Hillsdale Academy	2:17.09
2013 D4		Holly Bullough	Traverse City St. Francis	2:16.53
2014 D4		Holly Bullough	Traverse City St. Francis	2:15.52
2015 D4		Kaitlin Grigg	Maple City Glen Lake	2:22.29
2016 D4		Kensington Garvey	Blanchard Montabella	2:21.58
2017 D4		Haili Gusa	Ubly	2:18.92
2018 D4		Samantha Saenz	Concord	2:16.31

800 – UP Class A/Division 1 Champions

(y=880 yards)

Year	Class	Name	School	Time
1972 UP-All		Alice Ahearn	Iron Mountain	2:36.2y*
1973 UP-All		Ann Pulcurich	Marquette	2:38.8y
1974 UPAB		Jenne Taccolini	Marquette	2:34.6y*
1975 UPAB		Kim Groleau	Marquette	2:31.1y*
1976 UPAB		Kim Groleau	Marquette	2:27.9y*
1977 UPAB		Katie Miller	Marquette	2:22.2y*
1978 UPAB		Beth King	Marquette	2:22.0y*
1979 UPAB		Michelle Hall	Escanaba	2:32.5
1980 UPAB		Holly Corbiere	Sault Ste Marie	2:26.7
1981 UPAB		Sherri Ahola	Gladstone	2:29.4
1982 UPAB		Sherri Ahola	Gladstone	2:22.9
1983 UPAB		Kyrin Smith	Marquette	2:22.3
1984 UPAB		Maribeth Anderson	Sault Ste. Marie	2:29.3
1985 UPAB		JoAnn Aho	Gwinn	2:29.0
1986 UPAB		Liz Cibula	Escanaba	2:26.6
1987 UPAB		Sherrill VanBeynen	Marquette	2:30.6
1988 UPAB		Liz Cibula	Escanaba	2:27.5
1989 UPAB		Hayley Murphy	Marquette	2:25.1
1990 UPAB		Kim Trewhella	Negaunee	2:25.6
1991 UPAB		Bobie Rodriguez	Marquette	2:28.8
1992 UPAB		Jennie Drake	Escanaba	2:31.2
1993 UPAB		Sarah Lahti	Negaunee	2:30.3
1994 UPAB		Lasa Larson	Marquette	2:27.3

Year	Class	Name	School	Time
1995 UPAB		Michele Scherer	Marquette	2:27.3
1996 UPAB		Michele Scherer	Marquette	2:22.5
1997 UPAB		Sarah Caruso	Sault Ste. Marie	2:25.9
1998 UPAB		Krista O'Dell	Escanaba	2:22.9
1999 UPAB		Katie Anderson	Marquette	2:21.1*
2000 UPAB		Krista O'Dell	Escanaba	2:15.8*
2001 UPD1		Mandi Long	Menominee	2:21.3*
2002 UPD1		Ginger Polich	Ironwood	2:24.0
2003 UPD1		Jessica Kalafut	Menominee	2:28.31
2004 UPD1		Kate Abbott	Houghton	2:26.12
2005 UPD1		Stephanie Ostrenga	Escanaba	2:25.18
2006 UPD1		Jeanee Bennetts	Escanaba	2:26.72
2007 UPD1		Erica Beversluis	Escanaba	2:24.98
2008 UPD1		Kelly Lufkin	Houghton	2:25.22
2009 UPD1		Jessica Fluette	Marquette	2:28.22
2010 UPD1		Faith Gunderson	Menominee	2:25.04
2011 UPD1		Tara Kiilunen	Calumet	2:25.34
2012 UPD1		Jessica Fluette	Marquette	2:24.69
2013 UPD1		Lindsay Rudden	Marquette	2:16.46*
2014 UPD1		Lindsay Rudden	Marquette	2:21.39
2015 UPD1		Lindsay Rudden	Marquette	2:13.94*
2016 UPD1		Lindsay Rudden	Marquette	2:16.00
2017 UPD1		Clara Johnson	Negaunee	2:23.46
2018 UPD1		Emily Paupore	Negaunee	2:23.70

800 – UP Class C/Division 2 Champions

(y=880 yards)

Year	Class	Name	School	Time
1974 UPC		Geri Meyers	Ontonagon	2:43.1y*
1975 UPC		Marion Winnen	Ishpeming Westwood	2:30.8y*
1976 UPC		Marion Winnen	Ishpeming	2:27.5y*
1977 UPC		Janet Pratt	Rudyard	2:27.6y
1978 UPC		Carrie Talus	Negaunee	2:24.8y*
1979 UPC		Carrie Talus	Negaunee	2:26.3
1980 UPC		Marion Walker	St. Ignace	2:23.4*
1981 UPC		Beth Collins	Negaunee	2:29.0
1982 UPC		Beth Collins	Negaunee	2:23.3*
1983 UPC		Beth Collins	Negaunee	2:29.3
1984 UPC		Jesse Green	Ishpeming Westwood	2:33.8
1985 UPC		Jesse Green	Ishpeming Westwood	2:22.4*
1986 UPC		Brita Sturos	Calumet	2:30.5
1987 UPC		Julie Csmarich	Ontonagon	2:29.2
1988 UPC		Julie Csmarich	Ontonagon	2:25.2
1989 UPC		Tammy Anderson	Ishpeming	2:28.8
1990 UPC		Christie Nutkins	Newberry	2:30.6
1991 UPC		Tammy Anderson	Ishpeming	2:28.0
1992 UPC		Kelly Peterson	Munising	2:32.2
1993 UPC		Jill Pollack	Ironwood	2:26.1
1994 UPC		Jill Pollack	Ironwood	2:27.2
1995 UPC		Jill Pollack	Ironwood	2:24.6

Year	Class	Name	School	Time
1996 UPC		Ann Somerville	Ironwood	2:23.2
1997 UPC		Ann Somerville	Ironwood	2:21.3
1998 UPC		Ann Somerville	Ironwood	2:22.8
1999 UPC		Chelsea Finco	Ironwood	2:27.8
2000 UPC		Jessica Koski	Ishpeming Westwood	2:27.4
2001 UPD2		Amber Smith	Ishpeming Westwood	2:22.3
2002 UPD2		Amber Smith	Ishpeming Westwood	2:20.2*
2003 UPD2		Amber Smith	Ishpeming Westwood	2:18.2*
2004 UPD2		Amber Smith	Ishpeming Westwood	2:18.59
2005 UPD2		Christina Mishica	Hancock	2:26.77
2006 UPD2		Christina Mishica	Hancock	2:28.21
2007 UPD2		Christina Mishica	Hancock	2:28.47
2008 UPD2		Abbey Kelto	Munising	2:33.50
2009 UPD2		Amy Kerst	Munising	2:29.18
2010 UPD2		Amy Kerst	Munising	2:24.74
2011 UPD2		Jaclyn Waara	West Iron County	2:28.99
2012 UPD2		Hannah Palmeter	Ironwood	2:25.05
2013 UPD2		Holly Blowers	Manistique	2:29.56
2014 UPD2		Holly Blowers	Manistique	2:29.56
2015 UPD2		Khora Swanson	Ishpeming	2:28.53
2016 UPD2		Khora Swanson	Ishpeming	2:34.15
2017 UPD2		Libby Becker	St. Ignace	2:27.19
2018 UPD2		Elizabeth Becker	St Ignace	2:24.50

800 – UP Class D/Division 3 Champions

(y=880 yards)

Year	Class	Name	School	Time
1974 UPD		Vicky Pearson	Rapid River	2:32.8y*
1975 UPD		Vicky Pearson	Rapid River	2:39.4y
1976 UPD		Mary Richowski	Baraga	2:32.7y*
1977 UPD		Laurie Engman	Dollar Bay	2:31.4y*
1978 UPD		Mary Radecki	Rudyard	2:29.3y*
1979 UPD		Mary Radecki	Rudyard	2:29.2*
1980 UPD		Joan Casanova	Norway	2:24.0*
1981 UPD		Sherri Lee	Cedarville	2:29.4
1982 UPD		Sue Smith	Cedarville	2:26.3
1983 UPD		Marion Walker	St. Ignace	2:30.0
1984 UPD		Gail Keranen	Lake Linden-Hubbell	2:33.7
1985 UPD		Joni Muffler	Rapid River	2:29.4

Year	Class	Name	School	Time
1986 UPD		Joni Muffler	Rapid River	2:30.0
1987 UPD		Julie Wallis	Pickford	2:27.9
1988 UPD		Julie Wallis	Pickford	2:30.2
1989 UPD		Julie Wallis	Pickford	2:34.4
1990 UPD		Jill Wallis	Pickford	2:30.5
1991 UPD		Stacey Majurin	White Pine	2:30.2
1992 UPD		Dana Feak	Felch North Dickinson	2:35.2
1993 UPD		Dana Feak	Felch North Dickinson	2:31.8
1994 UPD		Dana Feak	Felch North Dickinson	2:30.3
1995 UPD		Amber Veldman	Ontonagon	2:26.3
1996 UPD		Kim Curtis	Pickford	2:28.4
1997 UPD		Kim Curtis	Pickford	2:30.5
1998 UPD		Randi Johnson	St. Ignace	2:29.5

1999 UPD	Beth Koski	Baraga	2:26.8	
2000 UPD	Rachel Morrison	Pickford	2:28.2	
2001 UPD3	Rachel Morrison	Pickford	2:32.0*	
2002 UPD3	Danniel Holmgren	Rapid River	2:29.8*	
2003 UPD3	Rosanna Chapman	Pickford	2:30.40	
2004 UPD3	Dani Holmgren	Rapid River	2:27.77*	
2005 UPD3	Dani Holmgren	Rapid River	2:29.80	
2006 UPD3	Katey Kingsbury	Brimley	2:29.49	
2007 UPD3	Erin Holmberg	Cooks-Big Bay de Noc	2:23.72*	
2008 UPD3	Katie Granquist	Powers-North Central	2:27.92	
2009 UPD3	Lauren Spranger	Eben Junction Superior Central	2:27.28	
2010 UPD3	Lauren Spranger	Eben Junction Superior Central	2:23.82	
2011 UPD3	Amy Kerst	Munising	2:21.61*	
2012 UPD3	Lauren Spranger	Eben Junction Superior Central	2:24.17	
2013 UPD3	Sarah Cullip	St. Ignace	2:29.38	
2014 UPD3	Carlie Angie	Lake Linden-Hubbell	2:35.25	
2015 UPD3	Natalie Beaulieu	Newberry	2:26.63	
2016 UPD3	Heidi Hagen	Pickford	2:28.05	
2017 UPD3	Mariah Wilmer	Lake Linden-Hubbell	2:27.08	
2018 UPD3	Madeleine Peramaki	Munising	2:23.05	

GIRLS 1600 METERS

Records

D1	4:39.23	Hannah Meier	Grosse Pointe South	2013
D2	4:49.55	Kayla Windemuller	Holland Christian	2018
D3	4:50.10	Olivia Theis	Lansing Catholic	2017
D4	4:51.73	Marissa Treece	Maple City Glen Lake	2007
UPD1	4:55.28	Lindsey Rudden	Marquette	2014
UPD2	5:01.53	Amber Smith	Ishpeming Westwood	2003
UPD3	5:17.20	Amy Kerst	Munising	2011

Records by Class (pre-2000 for LP, pre-2001 for UP)

A	4:45.20	Laura Matson	Bloomfield Hills Andover	1985
B	4:48.41	Kelly Smith	Petoskey	1994
C	5:00.3	Donna Donakowski	Dearborn Heights Riverside	1983
D	5:05.2	Lisa Szporluk	Ann Arbor Greenhills	1983
UPAB	5:00.1	Krista O'Dell	Escanaba	2000
UPC	5:05.3	Jesse Green	Ishpeming Westwood	1985
UPD	5:25.3	Julie Wallis	Pickford	1988

1600 – Class A/Division 1 Champions

(y=mile / 1609.34m)

1973 All	Lynn Lovat	Lincoln Park	5:23.6y*	
1974 A/B	Mary Ann Opalewski	Saginaw MacArthur	5:11.0y*	
1975 A	Kathy Wilson	Bloomfield Hills Lahser	5:10.5y*	
1976 A	Kathy Wilson	Bloomfield Hills Lahser	5:06.4y*	
1977 A	Kathy Wilson	Bloomfield Hills Lahser	4:59.8y*	
1978 A	Marian Boyd	Port Huron	5:04.4y	
1979 A	Mariam Boyd	Port Huron	4:57.4y*	
1980 A	Tina Jordan	Detroit Mumford	5:00.5y	
1981 A	Catherine Schmidt	Grosse Pointe North	5:04.1y	
1982 A	Kayla Skelly	Midland	4:59.0	
1983 A	Angie Mogielski	Redford Union	4:59.5	
1984 A	Michelle Bews	Birmingham Seaholm	4:59.6	
1985 A	Laura Matson	Bloomfield Hills Andover	4:45.20*	
1986 A	Laura Matson	Bloomfield Hills Andover	4:57.87	
1987 A	Kristen Salt	Dearborn Edsel Ford	4:53.60	
1988 A	Laura Simmering	Ann Arbor Huron	4:56.00	
1989 A	Nichole Chinavare	Clarkston	5:12.2	
1990 A	Bridget Mann	Ann Arbor Pioneer	5:04.79	
1991 A	Bridget Mann	Ann Arbor Pioneer	5:12.0	
1992 A	Christi Goodison	Sterling Hts Stevenson	5:01.95	
1993 A	Christi Goodison	Sterling Hts Stevenson	5:01.02	
1994 A	Michelle Slater	Rochester Adams	5:03.1	
1995 A	Sharon Van Tuyl	Portage Northern	5:09.7	
1996 A	Sharon Van Tuyl	Portage Northern	4:54.00	
1997 A	Sharon Van Tuyl	Portage Northern	4:57.82	
1998 A	Sharon Van Tuyl	Portage Northern	4:56.9	
1999 A	Teresa Bongiovanni	Romeo	5:00.48	
2000 D1	Linsey Blaisdell	Rockford	4:50.95*	
2001 D1	Linsey Blaisdell	Rockford	4:58.43	
2002 D1	Nicki Bohnsack	Rockford	5:02.63	
2003 D1	Nicki Bohnsack	Rockford	4:55.06	
2004 D1	Lisa Senakiewicz	Davison	4:51.64	
2005 D1	Jenny Morgan	Clarkston	4:48.07*	
2006 D1	Jenny Morgan	Clarkston	4:56.48	
2007 D1	Katie Haines	Rockford	5:00.32	
2008 D1	Rebecca Addison	Grand Haven	4:50.80	
2009 D1	Megan Goethals	Rochester	4:51.20	
2010 D1	Megan Goethals	Rochester	4:47.37*	
2011 D1	Hannah Meier	Grosse Pointe South	4:42.60*	
2012 D1	Hannah Meier	Grosse Pointe South	4:43.05	
2013 D1	Hannah Meier	Grosse Pointe South	4:39.23*	
2014 D1	Rachel Coleman	Northville	4:45.76	
2015 D1	Rachel DaDamio	Birmingham Seaholm	4:46.06	
2016 D1	Rachel Bonner	Port Huron	4:49.29	
2017 D1	Anne Forsyth	Ann Arbor Pioneer	4:43.84	
2018 D1	Ericka VanderLende	Rockford	4:45.17	

1600 – Class B/Division 2 Champions

(y=mile / 1609.34m)

1975 B	Mary Ann Opalewski	Saginaw MacArthur	5:04.5y*	
1976 B	Sue Jarvis	Livonia Ladywood	5:17.0y	
1977 B	Kelly Spatz	Saginaw Eisenhower	5:08.4y	
1978 B	Lori Bennett	Livonia Ladywood	5:00.3y*	
1979 B	Ann Rouman	Big Rapids	5:05.2y	
1980 B	Joan DeMaat	Grand Rapids Christian	4:57.9*	
1981 B	Jo Ann Lanciaux	Fremont	5:01.6	
1982 B	Missy Thompson	Ludington	4:57.4y*	
1983 B	Kim Adent	St. Joseph	4:56.5*	
1984 B	Teresa Stouffer	Royal Oak Shrine	5:03.3	
1985 B	Julie Watson	Hemlock	4:55.77*	
1986 B	Sharon Kinsler	Saginaw MacArthur	5:13.7	
1987 B	Heather Slay	East Grand Rapids	5:12.20	
1988 B	Heather Slay	East Grand Rapids	5:00.77	
1989 B	Heather Slay	East Grand Rapids	4:59.1	
1990 B	Jennifer Barber	Frankenmuth	5:11.7	
1991 B	Laura Bell	Otisville LakeVille	5:04.17	
1992 B	Kelly Smith	Petoskey	4:56.84	
1993 B	Kelly Smith	Petoskey	4:55.49*	
1994 B	Kelly Smith	Petoskey	4:48.41*	
1995 B	Carrie Gould	Flint Powers	5:05.2	
1996 B	Carrie Gould	Flint Powers	5:03.9	
1997 B	Katie Clifford	Grand Rapids West Catholic	4:58.8	
1998 B	Jamie Krzyminski	Corunna	5:05.4	
1999 B	Jamie Krzyminski	Corunna	5:02.80	
2000 D2	Jamie Krzyminski	Corunna	4:54.07*	
2001 D2	Jessica Kraft	West Branch Ogemaw Heights	4:57.65	
2002 D2	Katie Erdman	Cadillac	4:57.81	
2003 D2	Jackie Gaydos	Allen Park	4:55.63	
2004 D2	Bekah Smeltzer	Monroe Jefferson	4:59.46	
2005 D2	Jessica Armstron	Wayland	5:02.68	
2006 D2	Bekah Smeltzer	Monroe Jefferson	4:57.10	
2007 D2	Ramzee Fondren	Detroit Renaissance	4:59.85	

2008 D2	Meggan Freeland	Parma Western	4:59.36
2009 D2	Leah O'Connor	Croswell-Lexington	5:03.38
2010 D2	Leah O'Connor	Croswell-Lexington	5:01.99
2011 D2	Rachel Schulist	Zeeland West	5:00.59
2012 D2	Sara Barron	Pontiac Notre Dame Prep	4:51.67*
2013 D2	Megan O'Neal	Remus Chippewal Hills	4:52.21
2014 D2	Karrigan Smith	St. Johns	4:51.53*
2015 D2	Karrigan Smith	St. Johns	4:59.08
2016 D2	Kayla Windemuller	Holland Christian	4:58.90
2017 D2	Kayla Windemuller	Holland Christian	4:52.60
2018 D2	Kayla Windemuller	Holland Christian	4:49.55*

1600 – Class C/Division 3 Champions

(y=mile / 1609.34m)

1974 C/D	Cathy Newman	Williamston	5:24.0y*
1975 C	Mary Hull	Bath	5:20.5y*
1976 C	Keela Yount	DeWitt	5:22.3y
1977 C	Keela Yount	DeWitt	5:22.2y
1978 C	Beth Lynn	Edwardsburg	5:17.9y*
1979 C	Melanie Weaver	Mason County Central	5:01.0y*
1980 C	Anne SImon	Shepherd	5:15.1y
1981 C	Carrie Lautner	Cass City	5:08.5
1982 C	Carrie Lautner	Cass City	5:09.8
1983 C	Donna Donakowski	Dearborn Heights Riverside	5:00.3*
1984 C	Jolene Crooks	Benzie Central	5:09.1
1985 C	Cathy Ackley	Hart	5:15.4
1986 C	Jeanne Spitler	Montague	5:10.65
1987 C	Jeanne Spitler	Montague	5:09.05
1988 C	Cathy Ackley	Hart	5:06.6
1989 C	Stacey Kilburn	White Pigeon	5:02.49
1990 C	Valentine Stumpf	Roscommon	5:14.59
1991 C	Lorenda Godefroidt	St. Louis	5:05.2
1992 C	Lorenda Godefroidt	St Louis	5:07.4
1993 C	Lorenda Godefroidt	St. Louis	5:08.59
1994 C	Traci Knudsen	Suttons Bay	5:06.7
1995 C	Christie Achenbach	Unionville-Sebewaing	5:05.06
1996 C	Bethany Brewster	Saginaw Valley Lutheran	5:08.88
1997 C	Bethany Brewster	Saginaw Valley Lutheran	5:00.55
1998 C	Bethany Brewster	Saginaw Valley Lutheran	5:07.11
1999 C	Jenny Irwin	Mason County Central	5:09.51
2000 D3	Rachel Kirvan	Lansing Catholic	5:05.63*
2001 D3	Nicole Bush	Wyoming Kelloggsville	5:01.27*
2002 D3	Krishawna Parker	Detroit Crockett	5:00.26*
2003 D3	Nicole Bush	Wyoming Kelloggsville	4:58.48*
2004 D3	Nicole Bush	Wyoming Kelloggsville	4:53.35*
2005 D3	Janee Jones	Goodrich	4:58.19
2006 D3	Alissa Ott	Detroit Country Day	5:14.20
2007 D3	Hilary Snyder	Jackson Lumen Christi	5:07.49
2008 D3	Karie McDonald	Frankenmuth	5:12.24
2009 D3	Cara Cremeans	Jackson Lumen Christi	5:05.88
2010 D3	Ali Wiersma	Allendale	4:59.86
2011 D3	Michaela Carnegie	Benzie Central	4:57.59
2012 D3	Theresa Warsecke	Benzie Central	4:57.59
2013 D3	Annie Fuller	Manistee	4:56.11
2014 D3	Annie Fuller	Manistee	4:55.64
2015 D3	Annie Fuller	Manistee	4:57.40
2016 D3	Holly Bullough	Traverse City St. Francis	4:52.63*
2017 D3	Olivia Theis	Lansing Catholic	4:50.10*
2018 D3	Judy Rector	Hanover-Horton	4:52.59

1600 – Class D/Division 4 Champions

(y=mile / 1609.34m)

1975 D	Joyce Bahr	Onekema	5:29.7y*
1976 D	Joan Alderink	Southfield Christian	5:16.4y*
1977 D	Virginia Schmitz	Walkerville	5:33.4y
1978 D	Mary Peterson	Suttons Bay	5:32.0y
1979 D	Julie Lantis	Grass Lake	5:20.6
1980 D	Robin Magee	Ann Arbor Greenhills	5:24.5
1981 D	Robin Magee	Ann Arbor Greenhills	5:06.3*
1982 D	Gina VanLaar	Allendale	5:09.9
1983 D	Larissa Szporluk	Ann Arbor Greenhills	5:05.2*
1984 D	Gina VanLaar	Allendale	5:14.57
1985 D	Theresa Padilla	Camden-Frontier	5:18.23
1986 D	Cindy Schneider	Fowler	5:21.47
1987 D	Theresa Padillaa	Camden-Frontier	5:24.5
1988 D	Jennifer Foster	Akron-Fairgrove	5:16.55
1989 D	Mary Lantinga	Battle Creek St Phillip	5:17.4
1990 D	Mary Lantinga	Battle Creek St Phillip	5:20.20
1991 D	Farrah Petiprin	Akron-Fairgrove	5:26.22
1992 D	Amy Langschied	Deerfield	5:16.16
1993 D	Liz Martin	Maple City Glen Lake	5:19.5
1994 D	Liz Martin	Maple City Glen Lake	5:18.25
1995 D	Sarah Carter	St. Joseph Lake Mich Catholic	5:16.82
1996 D	Brook Creed	Walkerville	5:24.15
1997 D	Betsy Speer	Whitmore Lake	5:13.55
1998 D	Brooke Creed	Walkerville	5:08.5
1999 D	Jennifer Kamps	North Muskegon	5:21.74
2000 D4	Katie Forsyth	Bath	5:14.52*
2001 D4	Katie Forsyth	Bath	5:13.47*
2002 D4	Lauren Fairbanks	Rogers City	5:09.94*
2003 D4	Laura Rolf	Rochester Hills Lutheran NW	5:05.62*
2004 D4	Marissa Treece	Maple City Glen Lake	5:00.56*
2005 D4	Marissa Treece	Maple City Glen Lake	4:56.15*
2006 D4	Alexa Glencer	Ann Arbor Greenhills	4:55.57*
2007 D4	Marissa Treece	Maple City Glen Lake	4:51.73*
2008 D4	Bridget Bennett	Mt Pleasant Sacred Heart	5:08.18
2009 D4	Nikki Wurster	Homer	5:08.16
2010 D4	Bridget Bennett	Mt Pleasant Sacred Heart	5:06.09
2011 D4	Kirsten Olling	Breckenridge	5:07.68
2012 D4	Nicole Zeinstra	Holland Black River	4:59.91
2013 D4	Holly Bullough	Traverse City St. Francis	5:07.37
2014 D4	Holly Bullough	Traverse City St. Francis	5:01.34
2015 D4	Tessa Fornari	Waterford Our Lady	5:08.39
2016 D4	Samantha Saenz	Concord	5:10.99
2017 D4	Samantha Saenz	Concord	5:10.64
2018 D4	Samantha Saenz	Concord	5:00.46

1600 – UP Class AB/Division 1 Champions

(y=mile / 1609.34m)

1972 UP-All	Theresa Plotske	Ewen-Trout Creek	6:13.1y*
1973 UP-All	Barb LaComb	Marquette	6:08.3y*
1974 UPAB	Martha Fitzgerald	Ironwood	5:54.7y*
1975 UPAB	Denise Pintello	Gwinn	5:35.3y*
1976 UPAB	Sue Rogers	Escanaba	5:28.9y*
1977 UPAB	Cynie Cory	Marquette	5:26.0y*
1978 UPAB	Lisa Bernard	Escanaba	5:42.6y
1979 UPAB	Kim Peterson	Gwinn	5:35.6
1980 UPAB	Kim Peterson	Gwinn	5:25.0*
1981 UPAB	Kim Peterson	Gwinn	5:30.9
1982 UPAB	Kara Braak	Marquette	5:24.1*
1983 UPAB	Kyrin Smith	Marquette	5:24.9
1984 UPAB	Kris Koski	Gwinn	5:32.8
1985 UPAB	Karen Anderson	Sault Ste. Marie	5:29.7
1986 UPAB	Liz Cibula	Escanaba	5:27.4
1987 UPAB	Lisa Werner	Marquette	5:26.6
1988 UPAB	Lisa Werner	Marquette	5:23.7*
1989 UPAB	Hayley Murphy	Marquette	5:31.4
1990 UPAB	Bobie Rodriguez	Marquette	5:33.6
1991 UPAB	Bobie Rodriguez	Marquette	5:25.9
1992 UPAB	Sara Cowen	Escanaba	5:38.6
1993 UPAB	Julie Jacobetti	Negaunee	5:39.4
1994 UPAB	Julie Jacobetti	Negaunee	5:32.4
1995 UPAB	Tarra Hodge	Menominee	5:29.7
1996 UPAB	Terri Campbell	Ishpeming Westwood	5:24.1
1997 UPAB	Krista O'Dell	Escanaba	5:26.7
1998 UPAB	Krista O'Dell	Escanaba	5:19.5
1999 UPAB	Katie Anderson	Marquette	5:21.7
2000 UPAB	Krista O'Dell	Escanaba	5:00.1*
2001 UPD1	Mandi Long	Menominee	5:20.9*
2002 UPD1	Natalie Cahill	Sault Ste. Marie	5:25.9
2003 UPD1	Karen Koljonen	Calumet	5:29.84
2004 UPD1	Kylee St. Arnauld	Marquette	5:24.33
2005 UPD1	Kelly McClure	Iron Mountain	5:19.73*
2006 UPD1	Jeanee Bennetts	Escanaba	5:27.13
2007 UPD1	Jeanee Bennette	Escanaba	5:35.28
2008 UPD1	Kelly Lufkin	Houghton	5:23.94
2009 UPD1	Lindsey Lusardi	Gladstone	5:23.51
2010 UPD1	Tara Kiilunen	Calumet	5:28.39
2011 UPD1	Lindsey Lusardi	Gladstone	5:23.17
2012 UPD1	Stacey Mathieu	Menominee	5:31.76
2013 UPD1	Lindsey Rudden	Marquette	5:05.50*
2014 UPD1	Lindsey Rudden	Marquette	4:55.28*
2015 UPD1	Lindsey Rudden	Marquette	4:56.31
2016 UPD1	Lindsey Rudden	Marquette	5:03.31
2017 UPD1	Clara Johnson	Negaunee	5:27.73
2018 UPD1	Emily Paupore	Negaunee	5:15.23

1600 – UP Class C/Division 2 Champions

(y=mile / 1609.34m)

1974 UPC	Mellisa Papworth	Hancock	5:59.3y*	
1975 UPC	Kathy Siegel	Houghton	5:49.9y*	
1976 UPC	Kathleen Siegel	Houghton	5:43.4y*	
1977 UPC	Jill Merrick	Negaunee	5:44.2y	
1978 UPC	Jill Merrick	Negaunee	5:33.0y	
1979 UPC	Jill Merrick	Negaunee	5:32.8*	
1980 UPC	Jill Merrick	Negaunee	5:26.7*	
1981 UPC	Carrie LeDuc	Kingsford	5:33.7	
1982 UPC	Lori Hill	Munising	5:30.8	
1983 UPC	Traci Babcock	Iron Mountain	5:15.3*	
1984 UPC	Traci Babcock	Iron Mountain	5:08.2*	
1985 UPC	Jesse Green	Ishpeming Westwood	5:05.3*	
1986 UPC	Wendy Babcock	Iron Mountain	5:25.9	
1987 UPC	Brita Sturos	Calumet	5:30.4	
1988 UPC	Brita Sturos	Calumet	5:29.2	
1989 UPC	Christie Nutkins	Newberry	5:35.1	
1990 UPC	Christie Nutkins	Newberry	5:32.9	
1991 UPC	Erin Koller	Stephenson	5:26.1	
1992 UPC	Angel Kusz	Ironwood	5:41.4	
1993 UPC	Jill Pollack	Ironwood	5:31.4	
1994 UPC	Myra Peterson	Calumet	5:32.9	
1995 UPC	Elizabeth Pietila	Hancock	5:22.4	
1996 UPC	Elizabeth Pietila	Hancock	5:24.3	
1997 UPC	Ann Somerville	Ironwood	5:13.5	
1998 UPC	Ann Somerville	Ironwood	5:16.7	
1999 UPC	Randi Johnson	St. Ignace	5:35.4	
2000 UPC	Lisa Weber	Manistique	5:28.3	
2001 UPD2	Amber Smith	Ishpeming Westwood	5:12.1*	
2002 UPD2	Amber Smith	Ishpeming Westwood	5:04.1*	
2003 UPD2	Amber Smith	Ishpeming Westwood	5:01.53*	
2004 UPD2	Amber Smith	Ishpeming Westwood	5:09.90	
2005 UPD2	Christina Mishica	Hancock	5:30.86	
2006 UPD2	Christina Mishica	Hancock	5:35.37	
2007 UPD2	Christina Mishica	Hancock	5:21.03	
2008 UPD2	Abbey Kelto	Munising	5:43.27	
2009 UPD2	Abbey Kelto	Munising	5:37.15	
2010 UPD2	Abbey Kelto	Munising	5:32.99	
2011 UPD2	Jaclyn Waara	West Iron County	5:34.61	
2012 UPD2	Sarah Cullip	St. Ignace	5:34.78	
2013 UPD2	Natalie Beaulieu	Newberry	5:34.37	
2014 UPD2	Holly Blowers	Manistique	5:26.30	
2015 UPD2	Katie Etelamaki	Ishpeming Westwood	5:32.91	
2016 UPD2	Khora Swanson	Ishpeming	6:02.99	
2017 UPD2	Madeleine Peramaki	Munising	5:38.69	
2018 UPD2	Elizabeth Becker	St Ignace	5:23.52	

1600 – UP Class C/Division 3 Champions

(y=mile / 1609.34m)

1974 UPD	Cindy Froberg	Rapid River	6:24.3y*	
1975 UPD	Bonnie Bates	Crystal Falls Forest Park	5:59.7y*	
1976 UPD	Cathy Spencer	Pickford	5:42.0y*	
1977 UPD	Ardis Hancock	Engadine	5:52.0y	
1978 UPD	Leah Johns	Wakefield	5:41.6y*	
1979 UPD	Mary Radecki	Rudyard	5:35.7*	
1980 UPD	Mary Radecki	Rudyard	5:28.6*	
1981 UPD	Sherri Lee	Cedarville	5:36.6	
1982 UPD	Cheryl Bird	Rapid River	5:34.7	
1983 UPD	Tracy Tessmer	Pickford	5:34.4	
1984 UPD	Tracy Tessmer	Pickford	5:40.3	
1985 UPD	Kristin Kroll	White Pine	5:30.6	
1986 UPD	Julie Wallis	Pickford	5:29.9	
1987 UPD	Julie Wallis	Pickford	5:29.3	
1988 UPD	Julie Wallis	Pickford	5:25.3*	
1989 UPD	Julie Wallis	Pickford	5:29.8	
1990 UPD	Jil Wallis	Pickford	5:47.9	
1991 UPD	Dana Feak	Felch North Dickinson	5:41.5	
1992 UPD	Dana Feak	Felch North Dickinson	5:52.0	
1993 UPD	Dana Feak	Felch North Dickinson	5:33.1	
1994 UPD	Dana Feak	Felch North Dickinson	5:32.0	
1995 UPD	Faye Peterson	Rock-Mid Peninsula	5:37.1	
1996 UPD	Jill Clement	Cedarville	5:38.7	
1997 UPD	Kim Curtis	Pickford	5:37.8	
1998 UPD	Randi Johnson	St. Ignace	5:25.4	
1999 UPD	Beth Koski	Baraga	5:44.2	
2000 UPD	Amanda Erkkila	Rapid River	5:48.4	
2001 UPD3	Meridith Cochran	Cedarville	5:47.71*	
2002 UPD3	Danniel Holmgren	Rapid River	5:36.4*	
2003 UPD3	Danniel Holmgren	Rapid River	5:44.15	
2004 UPD3	Danniel Holmgren	Rapid River	5:38.54	
2005 UPD3	Dani Holmgren	Rapid River	5:32.20*	
2006 UPD3	Jasmine Ledy	Pickford	5:33.38	
2007 UPD3	Erin Holmberg	Cooks-Big Bay de Noc	5:22.79*	
2008 UPD3	Erin Holmberg	Cooks-Big Bay de Noc	5:21.06*	
2009 UPD3	Erin Holmberg	Cooks-Big Bay de Noc	5:33.02	
2010 UPD3	Erin Holmberg	Cooks-Big Bay de Noc	5:23.22	
2011 UPD3	Amy Kerst	Munising	5:17.20*	
2012 UPD3	Brittany Richard	Cooks-Big Bay de Noc	5:51.65	
2013 UPD3	Sarah Cullip	St. Ignace	5:36.43	
2014 UPD3	Emma Bohn	Cedarville	5:52.16	
2015 UPD3	Natalie Beaulieu	Newberry	5:23.45	
2016 UPD3	Natalie Beaulieu	Newberry	5:24.54	
2017 UPD3	Cami Daavattila	Dollar Bay	5:41.78	
2018 UPD3	Madeleine Peramaki	Munising	5:27.66	

GIRLS 3200 METERS

Records

D1	10:08.07	Anne Forsyth	Ann Arbor Pioneer	2018
D2	10:37.08	Olivia Theis	Lansing Catholic	2018
D3	10:30.49	Olvia Theis	Lansing Catholic	2017
D4	10:56.48	Alexa Glencer	Ann Arbor Greenhills	2006
UPD1	11:25.52	Emily Paupore	Negaunee	2018
UPD2	11:07.78	Amber Smith	Ishpeming Westwood	2003
UPD3	11:46.04	Natalie Beaulieu	Newberry	2016

Records by Class (pre-2000 for LP, pre-2001 for UP)

A	10:25.76	Sharon Van Tuyl	Portage Northern	1996
B	10:49.59	Heather Slay	East Grand Rapids	1988
C	10:50.2y	Melanie Weaver	Mason County Central	1979
D	11:14.56	Larissa Szporluk	Ann Arbor Greenhills	1984
UPAB	10:59.6	Emily Anderson	Marquette	2000
UPC	11:06.1	Traci Babcock	Iron Mountain	1985
UPD	11:53.0	Jane Rautiola	Painesdale-Jeffers	1998

3200 – Class A/Division 1 Champions

(y=2 mile / 3218.68m)

1975 A	Carla Amble	Ann Arbor Huron	11:28.9y*		1977 A	Miriam Boyd	Port Huron	10:54.7y*
1976 A	Sally Zook	Traverse City	11:16.9y*		1978 A	Miriam Boyd	Port Huron	10:36.8y*
					1979 A	Miriam Boyd	Port Huron	10:54.7y

Year	Class	Name	School	Time
1980	A	Jenny Weil	East Lansing	10:59.8y
1981	A	Leslie Olin	Flushing	11:16.0y
1982	A	Kayla Skelly	Midland	10:46.3
1983	A	Kelly Schumate	Clio	10:56.6
1984	A	Michelle Bews	Birmingham Seaholm	10:49.2
1985	A	Denys Adams	Okemos	10.50.0
1986	A	Kristen Salt	Dearborn Edsel Ford	10:52.20
1987	A	Kristen Salt	Dearborn Edsel Ford	10:49.7
1988	A	Seana Arnold	Ann Arbor Pioneer	11:01.34
1989	A	Karen Perry	Kalamazoo Loy Norrix	11:03.20
1990	A	Bridget Mann	Ann Arbor Pioneer	11:08.3
1991	A	Bridget Mann	Ann Arbor Pioneer	11:43.5
1992	A	Christi Goodison	Sterling Hts Stevenson	10:58.25
1993	A	Christi Goodison	Sterling Hts Stevenson	11:10.09
1994	A	Eileen Fleck	East Lansing	10:55.3
1995	A	Alison Klemmer	Troy Athens	10:56.88
1996	A	Sharon Van Tuyl	Portage Northern	10:25.76*
1997	A	Sharon Van Tuyl	Portage Northern	10:31.16
1998	A	Sharon Van Tuyl	Portage Northern	10:51.03
1999	A	Marne Smiley	Sterling Heights Stevenson	11:07.62
2000	D1	Emily Blakeslee	Rockford	10:55.71*
2001	D1	Katie Boyles	Rochester Adams	10:42.06*
2002	D1	Nicki Bohnsack	Rockford	11:10.70
2003	D1	Nicki Bohnsack	Rockford	10:57.35
2004	D1	Annie Otwell	Traverse City Central	10:49.90
2005	D1	Jenny Morgan	Clarkston	10:45.56
2006	D1	Jenny Morgan	Clarkston	10:38.51*
2007	D1	Tiffany Abrahamian	Rochester	10:50.92
2008	D1	Shannon Osika	Waterford Mott	10:42.08
2009	D1	Megan Goethals	Rochester	10:37.50*
2010	D1	Megan Goethals	Rochester	10:22.75*
2011	D1	Gabrielle Anzalone	Grand Blanc	10:23.07
2012	D1	Erin Finn	West Bloomfield	10:17.86*
2013	D1	Erin Finn	West Bloomfield	10:08.23*
2014	D1	Audrey Belf	Birmingham Seaholm	10:17.08
2015	D1	Audrey Belf	Birmingham Seaholm	10:26.58
2016	D1	Maddy Trevisan	Farmington	10:35.85
2017	D1	Maggie Farrell	Battle Creek Lakeview	10:19.99
2018	D1	Anne Forsyth	Ann Arbor Pioneer	10:08.07*

3200 – Class B/Division 2 Champions

(y=2 mile / 3218.68m)

Year	Class	Name	School	Time
1975	B	Paula Leavesley	Carleton Airport	12:09.8y*
1976	B	Mary Ann Opalewski	Sag MacArthur	11:00.0y*
1977	B	Cheryl Scheffer	South Lyon	11:04.5y
1978	B	Cheryl Scheffer	South Lyon	11:05.5y
1979	B	Cheryl Scheffer	South Lyon	11:12.9y
1980	B	Lisa Last	Alma	11:01.5
1981	B	Kelly McKillen	Dexter	11:15.8
1982	B	Kelly McKillen	Dexter	11:18.7y
1983	B	Kelly Champagne	Livonia Ladywood	11:00.1
1984	B	Teresa Stouffer	Royal Oak Shrine	11:14.2
1985	B	Erin Gillespie	Jackson Northwest	10:53.33*
1986	B	Denys Adams	Okemos	11:22.7
1987	B	Jenny Ledrick	GR Forest Hills Central	11:31.7
1988	B	Heather Slay	East Grand Rapids	10:49.59*
1989	B	Heather Slay	East Grand Rapids	10:56.3
1990	B	Laura Bell	Otisville LakeVille	11:11.2
1991	B	Lisa Monti	Chelsea	11:06.36
1992	B	Katy Hollbacher	Petoskey	10:55.38
1993	B	Betsy Haverkamp	Grand Rapids South Christian	10:52.7
1994	B	Karyn Duba	Caledonia	11:00.06
1995	B	Carrie Gould	Flint Powers	11:05.27
1996	B	Shannon Houseman	Caledonia	11.04.2
1997	B	Katie Clifford	Grand Rapids West Catholic	10:58.0
1998	B	Anne McGrath	Grand Rapids Catholic Central	11:11.37
1999	B	Jamie Krzyminski	Corunna	11:20.99
2000	D2	Jamie Krzyminski	Corunna	10:45.23*
2001	D2	Abigail Nelkie	West Branch Ogemaw Heights	10:47.44
2002	D2	Jill LeBlanc	Richland Gull Lake	11:35.43
2003	D2	Caitlin Clifford	Bloomfield Hills Lasher	10:53.81
2004	D2	Bekah Smeltzer	Monroe Jefferson	10:40.66*
2005	D2	Jessica Armstrong	Wayland	11:08.62
2006	D2	Bekah Smeltzer	Monroe Jefferson	10:42.86
2007	D2	Molly Waterhouse	Vicksburg	10:49.82
2008	D2	Brooke Eilers	Holland Christian	10:59.65
2009	D2	Jordan Tomecek	Milan	11:07.43
2010	D2	Rachele Schulist	Zeeland West	10:59.40
2011	D2	Breanne Lasner	Freeland	11:06.55
2012	D2	Ali Wiersma	Allendale	10:40.22*
2013	D2	Meg Darmofal	Mason	10:49.49
2014	D2	Kaela Theut	East Grand Rapids	11:01.30
2015	D2	Kenzie Weiler	Cedar Springs	10:41.98
2016	D2	Kayla Windemuller	Holland Christian	10:59.52
2017	D2	Kayla Windemuller	Holland Christian	10:49.90
2018	D2	Olivia Theis	Lansing Catholic	10:37.08*

3200 – Class C/Division 3 Champions

(y=2 mile / 3218.68m)

Year	Class	Name	School	Time
1975	C	Cynthia Sprague	Lansing Catholic	11:46.5y*
1976	C	Kirsten Hansen	Napoleon	11:27.9y*
1977	C	Kathleen Seibel	Decatur	11:50.5y
1978	C	Nora Green	Shepherd	11:16.1y*
1979	C	Melanie Weaver	Mason County Central	10:52.2y*
1980	C	Connie Kidder	Burton Bendle	11:47.2y
1981	C	Cindy Reed	Napoleon	11:23.3
1982	C	Carrie Lautner	Cass City	11:19.66
1983	C	Donna Donakowski	Dearborn Heights Riverside	11:17.2
1984	C	Casey O'Neil	Blissfield	11:34.6
1985	C	Jeanne Spitler	Montague	11:24.55
1986	C	Jeanne Spitler	Montague	11:26.75
1987	C	Jeanne Spitler	Montague	11:17.45
1988	C	Becky Duda	Goodrich	11:27.7
1989	C	Stacey Kilburn	White Pigeon	11:22.37
1990	C	Jenifer Vite	Buchanan	11:41.81
1991	C	Megan Smedley	Buchanan	11:30.00
1992	C	Jennifer Miller	Grosse Pointe University Liggett	11:22.7
1993	C	Carrie Gould	Burton Bendle	11:22.0
1994	C	Christie Achenbach	Unionville-Sebewaing	11:32.23
1995	C	Bethany Brewster	Saginaw Valley Lutheran	11:17.74
1996	C	Bethany Brewster	Saginaw Valley Lutheran	11:07.69
1997	C	Bethany Brewster	Saginaw Valley Lutheran	11:09.33
1998	C	Bethany Brewster	Saginaw Valley Lutheran	11:12.93
1999	C	Naomi Wendland	Saginaw Mi Lutheran Seminary	11:08.22
2000	D3	Jessica Campbell	Hillsdale	11:16.45*
2001	D3	Nicole Bush	Wyoming Kelloggsville	11:10.62*
2002	D3	Nicole Bush	Wyoming Kelloggsville	11:10.07*
2003	D3	Nicole Bush	Wyoming Kelloggsville	10:57.18*
2004	D3	Nicole Bush	Wyoming Kelloggsville	10:57.16*
2005	D3	Erin Batt	Hillsdale	11:24.80
2006	D3	Adrienne Pastula	Hillsdale	11:09.99
2007	D3	Adrienne Pastula	Hillsdale	11:07.70
2008	D3	Devyn Ramsey	Benzie Central	11:12.65
2009	D3	Ali Wiersma	Allendale	11:04.55
2010	D3	Ali Wiersma	Allendale	10:57.56
2011	D3	Ali Wiersma	Allendale	11:04.29
2012	D3	Lindsey Burdette	Hanover-Horton	11:01.29
2013	D3	Amber Way	Charlevoix	10:48.48*
2014	D3	Amber Way	Charlevoix	10:35.33*
2015	D3	Kayla Keane	East Jordan	10:47.76
2016	D3	Adelyn Ackley	Hart	10:49.87
2017	D3	Olvia Theis	Lansing Catholic	10:30.49*
2018	D3	Adelyn Ackley	Hart	10:45.54

3200 – Class D/Division 4 Champions

(y=2 mile / 3218.68m)

Year	Class	Name	School	Time
1975	D	Vicky Havens	Litchfield	12:31.0y*
1976	D	Molly Bitz	Ottawa Lake Whiteford	12:20.9y*
1977	D	Sharon Zoyhoski	Maple City Glen Lake	12:21.5y
1978	D	Laura Vroon	Southfield Christian	11:40.0y*
1979	D	Robin Magee	Ann Arbor Greenhills	11:28.8*
1980	D	Lisa Einheuser	Pontiac Catholic	12:19.4
1981	D	Robin Magee	Ann Arbor Greenhills	11:31.3
1982	D	Jodi Watters	Mt Pleasant Sacred Heart	11:34.9
1983	D	Jenny Franssen	Concord	11:40.7
1984	D	Larissa Szporluk	Ann Arbor Greenhills	11:14.56*
1985	D	Jenny Gradowski	Suttons Bay	11:31.85
1986	D	Jenny Payne	Traverse City Pathfinder	11:22.82
1987	D	Theresa Padilla	Camden-Frontier	11:56.57
1988	D	Theresa Padilla	Camden-Frontier	11:50.57
1989	D	Tia Sammallahti	Genesee	11:42.4
1990	D	Mary Lantinga	BC St Phillip	11:48.77
1991	D	Holly Minsel	Ottawa Lake Whitford	12:19.56
1992	D	Cherokee Hoaglund	Marion	11:52.5
1993	D	Stephanie Klein	Mendon	12:03.9

1994 D	Ellen Schultz	Maple City Glen Lake	11:31.69
1995 D	Brook Creed	Walkerville	11:50.76
1996 D	Brook Creed	Walkerville	12:05.97
1997 D	Betsy Speer	Whitmore Lake	11:29.21
1998 D	Brook Creed	Walkerville	11:14.7
1999 D	Candi Mason	Potterville	12:13.67
2000 D	Camille Doan	Concord	11:31.99*
2001 D4	Katie Kelly	Kinde-North Huron	11:33.78
2002 D4	Katie Kelly	Kinde-North Huron	11:30.61*
2003 D4	Caitlin Kelly	Kinde-North Huron	11:17.01*
2004 D4	Marissa Treece	Maple City Glen Lake	11:11.91*
2005 D4	Marissa Treece	Maple City Glen Lake	11:07.84*
2006 D4	Alexa Glencer	Ann Arbor Greenhills	10:56.48*

2007 D4	Marissa Treece	Maple City Glen Lake	10:57.57
2008 D4	Nikki Wurster	Homer	11:32.74
2009 D4	Nikki Wurster	Homer	11:28.61
2010 D4	Bridget Bennett	Mt Pleasant Sacred Heart	11:21.31
2011 D4	Kirsten Olling	Breckenridge	11:34.35
2012 D4	Kirsten Olling	Breckenridge	11:00.67
2013 D4	Kirsten Olling	Breckenridge	11:03.75
2014 D4	Kirsten Olling	Breckenridge	11:17.24
2015 D4	Tessa Fornari	Waterford Our Lady	11:33.70
2016 D4	Ava Strenge	Battle Creek St. Phillip	10:59.56
2017 D4	Ava Strenge	Battle Creek St. Phillip	11:17.75
2018 D4	Samantha Saenz	Concord	11:15.51

3200 – UP Class AB/Division 1 Champions

(y=2 mile / 3218.68m)

1975 UPAB	Vicky Davidson	Escanaba	13:13.8y*
1976 UPAB	Cindy Courenne	Escanaba	12:35.4y*
1977 UPAB	Deb Fredenburg	Escanaba	12:17.5y*
1978 UPAB	Kim Peterson	Gwinn	12:08.8y*
1979 UPAB	Penny Martin	Marquette	12:14.2
1980 UPAB	Kim Peterson	Gwinn	11:53.9*
1981 UPAB	Denise Gentile	Menominee	12:20.1
1982 UPAB	Kara Braak	Marquette	11:55.9
1983 UPAB	Kara Braak	Marquette	12:07.4
1984 UPAB	Lorraine Boucher	Escanaba	12:03.5
1985 UPAB	Lorraine Boucher	Escanaba	11:57.9
1986 UPAB	Lorraine Boucher	Escanaba	11:57.5
1987 UPAB	Kelly Abramson	Marquette	12:06.2
1988 UPAB	Sarah Hynnek	Menominee	11:59.3
1989 UPAB	Sarah Hynnek	Menominee	11:59.3
1990 UPAB	Carla Johnson	Marquette	11:53.7*
1991 UPAB	Carla Johnson	Marquette	11:36.6*
1992 UPAB	Julie Jacobetti	Negaunee	12:13.8
1993 UPAB	Julie Jacobetti	Negaunee	12:14.8
1994 UPAB	Lucy Lea	Marquette	11:57.6
1995 UPAB	Lucy Lea	Marquette	12:03.4
1996 UPAB	Angela Sandretto	Ishpeming Westwood	11:48.0

1997 UPAB	Angela Sandretto	Ishpeming Westwood	11:41.6
1998 UPAB	Krista O'Dell	Escanaba	11:50.7
1999 UPAB	Emily Anderson	Marquette	11:46.1
2000 UPAB	Emily Anderson	Marquette	10:59.6*
2001 UPD1	Natalie Cahill	Sault Ste. Marie	11:38.2*
2002 UPD1	Natalie Cahill	Sault Ste. Marie	12:01.3
2003 UPD1	Karen Koljonen	Calumet	11:57.59
2004 UPD1	Kylee St. Arnauld	Marquette	11:57.56
2005 UPD1	Kelly McClure	Iron Mountain	12:02.55
2006 UPD1	Andrea Millimaki	Marquette	12:01.09
2007 UPD1	Kelly Lufkin	Houghton	12.22.32
2008 UPD1	Lindsay Lusardi	Gladstone	11:59.40
2009 UPD1	Lindsay Lusardi	Gladstone	11:42.41
2010 UPD1	Lindsay Kiilunen	Calumet	11:52.98
2011 UPD1	Tara Kiilunen	Calumet	12:05.46
2012 UPD1	Tara Kiilunen	Calumet	11:50.70
2013 UPD1	Lindsay Rudden	Marquette	11:26.38*
2014 UPD1	Amber Huebner	Marquette	11:48.80
2015 UPD1	Amber Huebner	Marquette	11:42.71
2016 UPD1	Clara Johnson	Negaunee	11:54.09
2017 UPD1	Clara Johnson	Negaunee	12:02.08
2018 UPD1	Emily Paupore	Negaunee	11:25.52*

3200 – UP Class C/Division 2 Champions

(y=2 mile / 3218.68m)

1975 UPC	Paula Anderson	Ishpeming	12:53.9y*
1976 UPC	Sherry Wright	Hancock	12:06.3y*
1977 UPC	Melissa Papworth	Houghton	12:33.3y
1978 UPC	Sherri Wright	Hancock	12:01.0y*
1979 UPC	Pat Arseneault	Ishpeming	12:02.8
1980 UPC	Barb LaLonde	St. Ignace	12:20.0
1981 UPC	Ann Cevigney	Ishpeming	12:05.2
1982 UPC	Lorie Mileski	Negaunee	12:16.0
1983 UPC	Traci Babcock	Iron Mountain	11:41.2*
1984 UPC	Traci Babcock	Iron Mountain	11:13.8*
1985 UPC	Traci Babcock	Iron Mountain	11:06.1*
1986 UPC	Wendy Babcock	Iron Mountain	11:20.4
1987 UPC	Joanna McLane	Manistique	12:23.4
1988 UPC	Christie Nutkins	Newberry	12:28.4
1989 UPC	Christie Nutkins	Newberry	12:28.4
1990 UPC	Christie Nutkins	Newberry	12:00.8
1991 UPC	Christie Nutkins	Newberry	12:13.9
1992 UPC	Gala Derwin	Munising	12:31.0
1993 UPC	Myra Peterson	Calumet	12:08.0
1994 UPC	Myra Peterson	Calumet	12:24.7
1995 UPC	Julie Jacobetti	Negaunee	12:23.5
1996 UPC	Elizabeth Pietila	Hancock	11:40.9

1997 UPC	Elizabeth Pietila	Hancock	11:37.8
1998 UPC	Elizabeth Pietila	Hancock	11:36.4
1999 UPC	Trisha Nylund	Crystal Falls Forest Park	12:21.7
2000 UPC	Hanna Vissering	Ishpeming Westwood	11:46.0
2001 UPD2	Amber Smith	Ishpeming Westwood	11:34.2*
2002 UPD2	Amber Smith	Ishpeming Westwood	11:49.9
2003 UPD2	Amber Smith	Ishpeming Westwood	11:07.78*
2004 UPD2	Amber Smith	Ishpeming Westwood	11:18.87
2005 UPD2	Christina Mishica	Hancock	12:23.05
2006 UPD2	Christina Mishica	Hancock	12:27.41
2007 UPD2	Abbey Kelto	Munising	12:21.61
2008 UPD2	Abbey Kelto	Munising	12.14.37
2009 UPD2	Abbey Kelto	Munising	12:11.70
2010 UPD2	Abbey Kelto	Munising	12:21.74
2011 UPD2	Sarah Cullip	St. Ignace	12:43.63
2012 UPD2	Sarah Cullip	St. Ignace	12:16.17
2013 UPD2	Natalie Beaulieu	Newberry	12:12.55
2014 UPD2	Natalie Beaulieu	Newberry	12:21.37
2015 UPD2	Katie Etelamaki	Ishpeming Westwood	12:02.45
2016 UPD2	Khora Swanson	Ishpeming	13:21.21
2017 UPD2	Madelaine Peramaki	Munising	12:58.11
2018 UPD2	Elizabeth Becker	St Ignace	11:56.41

3200 – UP Class D/Division 3 Champions

(y=2 mile / 3218.68m)

1975 UPD	Laurie Engman	Dollar Bay	12:38.4y*
1976 UPD	Judy Voegtline	Republic-Michigamme	12:58.5y
1977 UPD	Maruene Verbrigghe	Eben	13:04.8y
1978 UPD	Tammy Klima	Crystal Falls Forest Park	13:14.2y
1979 UPD	Leah Johns	Wakefield	12:13.0*
1980 UPD	Mary Radecki	Rudyard	12:29.1
1981 UPD	Sherri Lee	Cedarville	12:17.4
1982 UPD	Lynn Sokolowski	White Pine	12:27.4
1983 UPD	Tracy Tessmer	Pickford	12:33.1
1984 UPD	Tracy Tessmer	Pickford	12:18.3
1985 UPD	Stephanie Todd	Chassell	12:16.7
1986 UPD	Tracy Tessmer	Pickford	12:22.9
1987 UPD	Patty Thurber	Bark River-Harris	12:21.0
1988 UPD	Julie Wallis	Pickford	12:16.7
1989 UPD	Julie Wallis	Pickford	12:42.4
1990 UPD	Jean Charlebois	Eben Junction Superior Central	12:47.0

1991 UPD	Jean Charlevois	Eben Junction Superior Central	12:35.9
1992 UPD	Dana Feak	Felch North Dickinson	13:08.2
1993 UPD	Debbie Hermes	Cooks-Big Bay de Noc	12:41.2
1994 UPD	Dana Feak	Felch North Dickinson	12:14.9
1995 UPD	Faye Peterson	Rock-Mid Peninsula	12:27.6
1996 UPD	Jill Clement	Cedarville	12:23.3
1997 UPD	Jane Rautiola	Painesdale-Jeffers	12:15.4
1998 UPD	Jane Rautiola	Painesdale-Jeffers	11:53.0*
1999 UPD	Beth Koski	Baraga	12:16.8
2000 UPD	Jenny Moreau	Carney-Nedeau	12:51.5
2001 UPD3	Courtney Brown	Pickford	13:06.2*
2002 UPD3	Danniel Holmgren	Rapid River	13:03.5*
2003 UPD3	Dani Holmgren	Rapid River	12:32.68*
2004 UPD3	Dani Holmgren	Rapid River	12:00.18*
2005 UPD3	Dani Holmgren	Rapid River	12:08.30
2006 UPD3	Jasmine Ledy	Pickford	12:24.23
2007 UPD3	Erin Holmberg	Cooks-Big Bay de Noc	11:59.89*

2008 UPD3	Erin Holmberg	Cooks-Big Bay de Noc	12:14.50
2009 UPD3	Erica Johnson	Felch North Dickinson	12:15.21
2010 UPD3	Erin Holmberg	Cooks-Big Bay de Noc	12:41.71
2011 UPD3	Erica Johnson	Felch North Dickinson	11:51.06*
2012 UPD3	Emily Chartrand	Brimley	12:29.29
2013 UPD3	Sarah Cullip	St. Ignace	12:30.12

2014 UPD3	Lily Wieringa	Bessemer	13:14.61
2015 UPD3	Emma Bohn	Cedarville	11:49.16*
2016 UPD3	Natalie Beaulieu	Newberry	11:46.04*
2017 UPD3	Lela Rautiola	Chassell	12:47.38
2018 UPD3	Madeleine Peramaki	Munising	12:26.31

GIRLS 100m HURDLES

Records

D1	13.16 (1.7)	Grace Stark	White Lake Lakeland	2018
D2	14.19	Tiffany Ofili	Ypsilanti	2005
D3	13.84	Sami Michell	Reed City	2012
D4	14.89 (-1.1)	Mary Leighton	Mendon	2017
UPD1	15.68	Jamie Roberts	Kingsford	2010
UPD2	16.05	Natalie Bertucci	Republic-Michigamme	2005
UPD3	15.97	Holly Seppala	Lake Linden-Hubbel	2006

Records by Class (pre-2000 for LP, pre-2001 for UP)

A	14.22	Ayesha George	Ann Arbor Pioneer	1997
B	14.60	Kenyetta Grigsby	River Rouge	1996
(hand 14.2y		*Kim Willis*	*Southgate Aquinas*	*1977)*
C	14.82	Dawn Schottenloher	Bronson	1986
D	15.06	Marnie Peplinski	Maple City Glen Lake	1992
UPAB	15.3	Tiffany Hodge	Menominee	1987
UPC	16.0	Bobbi Jo Bergman	Ishpeming	1987
UPD	15.2	Gwen Wilkie	DeTour	1984

100H – Class A/Division 1 Champions

(80y hurdles, 30")

1973 All	Sharon Solack	Livonia Stevenson	11.1*
1974 A/B	Anita Lee	Detroit Cass Tech	10.7*

(100m hurdles, 30"; y=110 yards)

1975 A	Kimberly Hatchett	Pontiac Central	14.7y*
1976 A	Kimberly Hatchett	Pontiac Central	14.5y*
1977 A	Renee Turner	Flint Central	14.5y
1978 A	Kim Turner	Detroit Mumford	13.9y*
1979 A	Kim Turner	Detroit Mumford	13.6y*
1980 A	Tonya Lowe	Flint Northern	13.6yw
1981 A	Kelly Graham	Westland Glenn	13.7y
1982 A	Kelly Graham	Westland Glenn	13.7
1983 A	Marie Palinkas	Roseville	14.1

(100m hurdles, 33")

1984 A	Carolyn Ferguson	Benton Harbor	14.5*
1985 A	Nikki Williams	Ann Arbor Huron	14.29*
1986 A	Sabrina Jordan	Ann Arbor Pioneer	14.46
1987 A	Darchelle Ross	Detroit Cass Tech	14.45
1988 A	Karen Spiers	Rochester Adams	14.49
1989 A	Darchelle Ross	Detroit Cass Tech	14.32
1990 A	Marjona Howard	Flint Northern	14.43
1991 A	Karen Ehresman	Grosse Pointe South	14.7
1992 A	Alicia Bernier	Holland West Ottawa	15.02
1993 A	Nikki Bouyer	Lansing Sexton	14.60
1994 A	Nikki Bouyer	Lansing Sexton	14.3

1995 A	Ayesha George	Ann Arbor Pioneer	14.9
1996 A	Ayesha George	Ann Arbor Pioneer	14.89
1997 A	Ayesha George	Ann Arbor Pioneer	13.89w
		(George 14.22* semifinal)	
1998 A	Robyn Woolfolk	Ann Arbor Pioneer	14.03w (2.1)
1999 A	Tanisha Williams	Ypsilanti	14.27* (1.2)
2000 D1	Lindsay Bond	Southfield	14.24* (-0.5)
2001 D1	Candice Davis	Ann Arbor Pioneer	14.15*
2002 D1	Candice Davis	Ann Arbor Pioneer	13.69* (-)
2003 D1	Candice Davis	Ann Arbor Pioneer	13.66* (-1.2)
2004 D1	Tenisha Griggs	Southfield Lathrup	14.37
2005 D1	Chidimma Uche	Ann Arbor Pioneer	14.27
2006 D1	Leslie Aririguzo	West Bloomfield	14.24 (1.0)
2007 D1	Ra'jae Marable	Ann Arbor Pioneer	14.32 (-4.8)
2008 D1	Leslie Aririguzo	West Bloomfield	13.84 (0.7)
2009 D1	Bridgette Owens	Southfield	14.13 (-1.4)
2010 D1	Bridgette Owens	Southfield	14.29 (-3.4)
2011 D1	Laticia Sims	Farmington Hills Harrison	14.11 (0.9)
2012 D1	Cindy Ofili	Ann Arbor Huron	13.78 (-1.7)
2013 D1	Quenee' Dale	Saline	14.79
2014 D1	Allyson Goff	Walled Lake Western	13.80 (0.0)
2015 D1	Maya Roberts	Farmington Hills Harrison	13.95 (0.3)
2016 D1	Britten Bowen	Ann Arbor Pioneer	14.08 (-1.8)
2017 D1	Britten Bowen	Ann Arbor Pioneer	13.40* (-0.2)
2018 D1	Grace Stark	White Lake Lakeland	13.16* (1.7)

100H – Class B/Division 2 Champions

(100m hurdles, 30"; y=110 yards)

1975 B	CIndy Armock	Remus Chippewa Hills	15.3y*
1976 B	Janet Cook	Novi	15.1y*
1977 B	Kim Willis	Southgate Aquinas	14.8y*
1978 B	Kim WIllis	Southgate Aquinas	14.2y*
1979 B	Michelle Priefer	St. Joseph	14.4y
1980 B	Monica Williams	Port Huron	14.6
1981 B	Martha Hans	Tecumseh	14.8
1982 B	Martha Hans	Tecumseh	14.4y
1983 B	Felecia Veal	Saginaw Buena Vista	14.4

(100m hurdles, 33")

1984 B	Paulette Bryant	Southgate Aquinas	14.5*
1985 B	Alana Davis	Jackson Lumen Christi	15.2
1986 B	Alana Davis	Jackson Lumen Christi	14.8
1987 B	Kelly Olszewski	Saline	15.15*
1988 B	Tara Allen	Detroit DePorres	15.33
1989 B	Jennifer Merritt	Grand Rapids West Catholic	15.3
1990 B	Rita Harden	Dearborn Heights Robichaud	15.64
1991 B	Rita Harden	Dearborn Heights Robichaud	15.40
1992 B	Kristy Thorley	Lake Odessa Lakewood	15.97

1993 B	Jennifer Story	Stanton-Central Montcalm	15.27
1994 B	Kenyetta Grigsby	River Rouge	14.71*
1995 B	Kenyetta Grigsby	River Rouge	14.68*
1996 B	Kenyetta Grigsby	River Rouge	14.60*
1997 B	Terresha Derosett	Otisville LakeVille	15.33
1998 B	Kendall Terhune	St. Joseph	15.25
1999 B	April Saxton	Dowagiac	15.39
2000 D2	Arthurene Powell	Ypsilanti	14.59*
2001 D2	Audrey Graham	Battle Creek Lakeview	14.74
2002 D2	Meghan Strachota	Chesaning	14.39*
2003 D2	Stephanie Allers	Coopersville	14.29w
2004 D2	Tiffany Ofili	Ypsilanti	14.34*
2005 D2	Tiffany Ofili	Ypsilanti	14.19*
2006 D2	Katie Hunt	Tecumseh	14.77
2007 D2	Kyra Caldwell	Ypsilanti	14.65
2008 D2	Kyra Caldwell	Ypsilanti	14.26w
2009 D2	Tori Desira	DeWitt	15.22
2010 D2	Megan Yanik	Livonia Ladywood	14.75
2011 D2	Quenee Dale	Romulus	14.49
2012 D2	Tori Desira	DeWitt	14.52

2013 D2	Alexsis Studer	DeWitt	14.69w (3.5)
2014 D2	Alison Rich	Haslett	15.30
2015 D2	Michaiah Thomas	Detroit Country Day	14.65

100H – Class C/Division 3 Champions

(80y hurdles, 30")

1974 C/D	Linda Arnold	Grass Lake	11.2

(100m hurdles, 30"; y=110 yards)

1975 C	Debbie Daschke	East Jackson	15.4y*
1976 C	Janet Hastings	Leroy Pine RIver	14.9y*
1977 C	Debbie Dashke	East Jackson	15.4y
1978 C	Jill Anderson	Haslett	14.7y*
1979 C	Karen Vanstienlandt	St Joseph Lake Mich Catholic	14.8y
1980 C	Karen VanSteinlandt	St Joseph Lake Mich Catholic	15.1y
1981 C	Karice Loveberry	Quincy	14.5*
1982 C	Kristi Jackson	Detroit Country Day	15.0
1983 C	Kristi Jackson	Detroit Country Day	14.3w

(100m hurdles, 33")

1984 C	Kristi Jackson	Detroit Country Day	14.8*
1985 C	Lori Lerch	Haslett	15.21*
1986 C	Dawn Schottenloher	Bronson	14.82*
1987 C	Melanie Chard	Union City	15.07
1988 C	Peggy Evans	Detroit Country Day	15.1
1989 C	Lisa Adams	St Charles	15.75
1990 C	Naheed Irani	Onsted	15.62
1991 C	Naheed Irani	Onsted	15.3
1992 C	Angie Sneider	Morenci	15.8
1993 C	Nancy Gross	New Lothrop	15.53
1994 C	Salina Clark	New Haven	15.68
1995 C	Wendy Feldman	Almont	15.12
1996 C	Jessica Hawkins	Jonesville	15.28
1997 C	Alicia Britton	Olivet	15.57
1998 C	Maria Dereczinski	Muskegon Oakridge	15.54
1999 C	Amber Bright	Benzie Central	14.91
2000 D3	Leah Dixon	Saginaw Swan Valley	15.40*
2001 D3	Leah Dixon	Saginaw Swan Valley	15.23*
2002 D3	Leighann Dowell	Millington	15.00*
2003 D3	Katie Pickette	Hopkins	14.50w
2004 D3	Leighann Dowell	Millington	14.94*
2005 D3	Meghan Strachota	Chesaning	14.36*
2006 D3	Emily Cross	Armada	14.56
2007 D3	Ann Myler	Ann Arbor Gabriel Richard	15.43
2008 D3	Jessi Craun	Hemlock	15.53
2009 D3	Rachel Hoffman	Shelby	15.16 (1.2)
2010 D3	Sami Michell	Reed City	14.73
2011 D3	Sami Michell	Reed City	14.07*
2012 D3	Sami Michell	Reed City	13.84*
2013 D3	Sami Michell	Reed City	14.04
2014 D3	Sydney Bronner	Frankenmuth	15.08 (0.6)
2015 D3	Jessica Gustad	Manistee	14.93 (2.0)
2016 D3	Kaiya Wall	Adrian Madison	15.49
2017 D3	Jaylah Walton	Dearborn Advanced Tech	14.76 (-0.1)
2018 D3	Emily Schaub	Marlette	15.01 (0.2)

100H – Class D/Division 4 Champions

(100m hurdles, 30"; y=110 yards)

1975 D	Debra Hodgson	Colon	15.2y*
1976 D	Jean Schrader	Centreville	15.4y
1977 D	Sharon Beebe	Mendon	15.6y
1978 D	Cindy Arnold	Grass Lake	15.0y*
1979 D	Maria Shoup	Mason County Eastern	14.9*
1980 D	Maria Shoup	Mason County Eastern	14.8*
1981 D	Bradley Nixon	Ann Arbor Greenhills	15.1
1982 D	Bradley Nixon	Ann Arbor Greenhills	14.9
1983 D	Kathy Doane	Marine City Holy Cross	14.6*

(100m hurdles, 33")

1984 D	Elenor Marks	Potterville	15.27*
1985 D	Heather Smalley	Potterville	15.65
1986 D	Lisa Nixon	Ann Arbor Greenhills	16.03
1987 D	Connie Klein	Inland Lakes	15.61
1988 D	Laura Selby	Tekonsha	15.31
1989 D	Sherine Rowell	Fowler	15.7
1990 D	Nicole Robinson	Detroit Lutheran West	16.0
1991 D	Marnie Peplinski	Maple City Glen Lake	15.37
1992 D	Marnie Peplinski	Maple City Glen Lake	15.06*
1993 D	Holly Lamkin	McBain N Michigan Christian	15.5
1994 D	Holly Lamkin	McBain N Michigan Christian	15.57
1995 D	Elycia Hall	Grass Lake	16.15
1996 D	Courtney Huffman	Homer	15.93
1997 D	Courtney Huffman	Homer	15.44
1998 D	Desha Feldpausch	Fowler	15.5
1999 D	Jennifer Wendling	New Lothrop	16.33
2000 D4	Jennifer Wendling	New Lothrop	15.57*
2001 D4	Erica Bechtal	Beal City	16.31
2002 D4	Sarah Ingersoll	Marcellus	15.73
2003 D4	Dana Westover	Maple CIty-Glen Lake	15.71w
2004 D4	Lesly Hale	Detroit Benedictine	15.94
2005 D4	Brooke Robertson	Saginaw Valley Lutheran	15.47*
2006 D4	Jonae Coleman	Flint Hamady	15.54
2007 D4	Audrey McMurry	Pellston	16.10
2008 D4	Whitney Thorp	Reading	15.30*
2009 D4	Liz Sherzer	Battle Creek St. Phillip	15.14* (-1.9)
2010 D4	Brianna Ratchford	Birmingham Roeper	16.18
2011 D4	Brianna Ratchford	Birmingham Roeper	15.72
2012 D4	Chantel Davenport	Athens	15.37
2013 D4	Chantel Davenport	Athens	15.41
2014 D4	Michelle Davis	Reading	15.05* (0.5)
2015 D4	Sierra King	Mesick	15.26 (-1.0)
2016 D4	Mary Leighton	Mendon	14.93* (1.7)
2017 D4	Mary Leighton	Mendon	14.89* (-1.1)
2018 D4	Alyssa Vandegriff	Fowler	15.56w (2.2)

100H – UP Class AB/Division 1 Champions

(50y hurdles, 30")

1972 UP-All	Mary Morin	Iron Mountain	7.6*

(80y hurdles, 30")

1973 UP-All	Mary Morin	Iron Mountain	12.2*
1974 UPAB	Debi Perry	Iron River West Iron Co.	12.2*

(100m hurdles, 30"; y=110 yards)

1975 UPAB	Debi Perry	Iron River West Iron Co.	16.8y*
1976 UPAB	Mary Dulek	Escanaba	16.0y*
1977 UPAB	Jean White	Escanaba	15.4y*
1978 UPAB	Jean White	Escanaba	15.1y*
1979 UPAB	Chris St. Louis	Kingsford	15.4
1980 UPAB	Chris St. Louis	Kingsford	15.1*
1981 UPAB	Liz Hatfield	Sault Ste. Marie	16.1
1982 UPAB	Karen Scott	Escanaba	16.3
1983 UPAB	Carolee Boudreau	Escanaba	16.1

(100m hurdles, 33")

1984 UPAB	Carolee Boudreau	Escanaba	16.5*
1985 UPAB	Shelly Sarasin	Escanaba	16.8
1986 UPAB	Melisa Michewich	Sault Ste. Marie	16.1*
1987 UPAB	Laura Bero	Escanaba	16.0*
1988 UPAB	Lynn Kleiman	Kingsford	15.9*
1989 UPAB	Lisa Corbiere	Sault Ste. Marie	16.0
1990 UPAB	Lisa Corbiere	Sault Ste. Marie	15.7*
1991 UPAB	Lisa Corbiere	Sault Ste. Marie	15.4*
1992 UPAB	Tiffany Hodge	Menominee	15.2w
1993 UPAB	Tiffany Hodge	Menominee	15.4*
1994 UPAB	Tiffany Hodge	Menominee	15.3*
1995 UPAB	Tiffany Hodge	Menominee	15.7
1996 UPAB	Saundra Anderson	Escanaba	16.7
1997 UPAB	Rebecca Johnson	Sault Ste. Marie	16.7
1998 UPAB	Katie Peterson	Marquette	17.0
1999 UPAB	Angie Vandermisson	Escanaba	16.7
2000 UPAB	Sarah Duesing	Sault Ste. Marie	17.2
2001 UPD1	Sarah Ducheny	Gladstone	15.5*
2002 UPD1	Sarah Ducheny	Gladstone	15.9
2003 UPD1	Amanda Holtz	Marquette	16.37*
2004 UPD1	Hayley Ford	Gladstone	16.83
2005 UPD1	Hayley Ford	Gladstone	16.19*
2006 UPD1	Shannon Helminen	Calumet	16.05*
2007 UPD1	Jamie Roberts	Kingsford	16.30
2008 UPD1	Jamie Roberts	Kingsford	16.12
2009 UPD1	Jaimie Roberts	Kingsford	16.06
2010 UPD1	Jamie Roberts	Kingsford	15.68*
2011 UPD1	Selena Meser	Sault Ste. Marie	15.86
2012 UPD1	Ashley Veale	Negaunee	16.34
2013 UPD1	Ashley Veale	Negaunee	16.57
2014 UPD1	Paiton Plutchak	Menominee	16.71
2015 UPD1	Sunny Martineau	Escanaba	16.19
2016 UPD1	Paiton Plutchak	Menominee	15.95
2017 UPD1	Ahnika Puskala	Marquette	16.32
2018 UPD1	Makenzie Wellner	Menominee	16.52

100H – UP Class C/Division 2 Champions

(80y hurdles, 30")

1974 UPC	Mary Seaton	Hancock	11.7

(100m hurdles, 30"; y=110 yards)

1975 UPC	Pam Selden	L'Anse	16.6y*
1976 UPC	Gina Selmo	Iron River West Iron Co	15.7y*
1977 UPC	Gina Selmo	Iron River West Iron Co	15.1y*
1978 UPC	Mary Ricci	Hancock	15.9y
1979 UPC	Ann Edwards	L'Anse	16.1
1980 UPC	Lynn Harris	Iron Mountain	15.7
1981 UPC	Chris St. Louis	Kingsford	16.4
1982 UPC	Lori Jukuri	Calumet	17.0
1983 UPC	Julie Kemppainen	Hancock	15.9

(100m hurdles, 33")

1984 UPC	Bobbi Jo Bergman	Ishpeming	16.8*
1985 UPC	Jackie Mattson	Ishpeming Westwood	16.4*
1986 UPC	Bobbi Jo Bergman	Ishpeming	16.4*
1987 UPC	Bobbi Jo Bergman	Ishpeming	16.0*
1988 UPC	Julie Hanes	Calumet	16.7
1989 UPC	Joanne Weber	Negaunee	16.4
1990 UPC	Becky Wheaton	St. Ignace	17.2
1991 UPC	Amy Brock	Newberry	16.6
1992 UPC	Jessica Hermann	Newberry	16.7
1993 UPC	Betsy Scott	Munising	16.6
1994 UPC	Betsy Scott	Munising	16.5
1995 UPC	Ashley Peffers	Munising	16.2
1996 UPC	Ashley Peffers	Munising	16.6
1997 UPC	Colleen Verrette	Iron Mountain	17.2
1998 UPC	Colleen Verrette	Iron Mountain	16.5
1999 UPC	Katie Wood	Houghton	16.9
2000 UPC	Kaitlyn Wood	Houghton	16.3
2001 UPD2	Brittany Fila	Norway	16.4*
2002 UPD2	Kate Hosking	Iron Mountain	16.3*
2003 UPD2	Brittany Fila	Norway	16.53*
2004 UPD2	Leslie Luehmann	Ishpeming	16.59
2005 UPD2	Natalie Bertucci	Republic Michigamme	16.05*
2006 UPD2	Jessica Wood	Ishpeming	16.28
2007 UPD2	Jessica Wood	Ishpeming	16.29
2008 UPD2	Carlen Smith	Hancock	17.66
2009 UPD2	Tonu Enrietti	Ishpeming Westwood	17.38
2010 UPD2	Brooke Julian	Norway	17.14
2011 UPD2	Megan Kangas	Norway	17.08
2012 UPD2	Megan Kangas	Norway	16.55
2013 UPD2	Mary Jarvis	Hancock	16.85
2014 UPD2	Caitlin Hewitt	Ishpeming Westwood	16.89
2015 UPD2	Mary Jarvis	Hancock	16.76
2016 UPD2	Mary Jarvis	Hancock	16.74
2017 UPD2	Taylor Bryant	Newberry	16.56
2018 UPD2	Katie Loman	Ishpeming	16.55

100H – UP Class D/Division 3 Champions

(80y hurdles, 30")

1974 UPD	Kimberly Izzard	Pickford	11.8

(100m hurdles, 30"; y=110 yards)

1975 UPD	Mary Zelinsky	Watersmeet	17.2y*
1976 UPD	Joyce Kronemeyer	Pickford	16.4y*
1977 UPD	Connie Miettinen	Republic-Michigamme	15.5y*
1978 UPD	Connie Miettinen	Republic-Michigamme	15.7y
1979 UPD	Terri Miron	Republic-Michigamme	15.7
1980 UPD	Terri Miron	Republic-Michigamme	15.8
1981 UPD	Terri Miron	Republic-Michigamme	16.4
1982 UPD	Gwen Wilkie	DeTour	15.6
1983 UPD	Gwen Wilkie	DeTour	15.4*

(100m hurdles, 33")

1984 UPD	Gwen Wilkie	DeTour	15.2*
1985 UPD	Denise Beauchamp	Bark River-Harris	16.5
1986 UPD	Berry Walker	Pickford	16.8
1987 UPD	Amy Wallis	Pickford	16.6
1988 UPD	Julie Eising	Rock-Mid Peninsula	16.8
1989 UPD	Sue Harteau	Felch North Dickinson	17.0
1990 UPD	Jody Erickson	Bessemer	16.6
1991 UPD	Brooke Hine	Bessemer	16.4
1992 UPD	Brooke Hine	Bessemer	15.9
1993 UPD	Brooke Hine	Bessemer	15.8
1994 UPD	Susan Trevarrow	Cedarville	16.3
1995 UPD	Jill Gobert	Rock-Mid Peninsula	17.0
1996 UPD	Jill Gobert	Rock-Mid Peninsula	16.7
1997 UPD	Sara Boyer	Rapid River	16.4
1998 UPD	Sara Boyer	Rapid River	16.9
1999 UPD	Becky Londo	Bessemer	17.0
2000 UPD	Karin Roberts	Bessemer	16.9
2001 UPD3	Ashley Wery	Rock-Mid Penindula	17.0*
2002 UPD3	Cassi Rushford	Rapid River	16.8*
2003 UPD3	Caroline Cochrane	Cedarville	16.90*
2004 UPD3	Cassi Rushford	Rapid River	16.89*
2005 UPD3	Holly Seppala	Lake Linden-Hubbel	16.50*
2006 UPD3	Holly Seppala	Lake Linden-Hubbel	15.97*
2007 UPD3	Kayla Shope	Rapid River	17.40
2008 UPD3	Brooke Granquist	Powers-North Central	17.06
2009 UPD3	Brooke Granquist	Powers-North Central	16.82
2010 UPD3	Tara Cooper	Cooks-Big Bay De Noc	17.26
2011 UPD3	Becca Carruthers	Brimley	16.96
2012 UPD3	Heather Roell	Felch North Dickinson	16.44
2013 UPD3	Kim Cruickshank	Pickford	17.15
2014 UPD3	Kerri Chartrand	Brimley	16.89
2015 UPD3	Valerie Rowe	Bessemer	16.51
2016 UPD3	Taylor Bryant	Newberry	16.73
2017 UPD3	Sienna Anderson	Lake Linden-Hubbell	17.55
2018 UPD3	Taylor Opolka	Pickford	17.91

GIRLS 300m HURDLES

Records

D1	42.64	Kyanna Evans	Wyandotte Roosevelt	2017
D2	42.82	Tiffany Ofili	Ypsilanti	2005
D3	42.23	Sami Michell	Reed City	2012
D4	44.92	Michelle Davis	Reading	2013
UPD1	45.40	Selena Meser	Sault Ste. Marie	2010
UPD2	46.65	Ellary Renier	Norway	2005
UPD3	47.27	Lori Wardynski	Ontonagon	2016

Records by Class (pre-2000 for LP, pre-2001 for UP)

A	42.81	Lashaunta Blander	Pontiac Northern	1997
	(hand42.4	Carolyn Ferguson	Benton Harbor	1984)
B	44.42	Kari Karhoff	Durand	1997
	(hand44.0	Paulette Bryant	Southgate Aquinas	1984)
C	44.49	Naheed Irani	Onsted	1990
D	44.82	Marnie Peplinski	Maple City Glen Lake	1992
UPAB	45.3	Tiffany Hodge	Menominee	1994
UPC	46.2	Lynne Scholie	Hancock	1983
UPD	47.5	Gwen Wilkie	DeTour	1984
	47.5	Sara Boyer	Rapid River	1998

300H – Class A/Division 1 Champions

(200m Low Hurdles; y=220 yards)

1979 A	Jean Delvalle	Trenton	29.1y*
1980 A	Tonya Lowe	Flint Northern	28.0y*
1981 A	Judy Tucker	Flint Northern	28.7y
1982 A	Kelly Graham	Westland Glenn	28.4

(300m Low Hurdles)

1983 A	Carolyn Ferguson	Benton Harbor	43.0*
1984 A	Carolyn Ferguson	Benton Harbor	42.4*
1985 A	Sabrina Jordan	Ann Arbor Pioneer	43.43*
1986 A	Darchelle Ross	Detroit Cass Tech	43.24*
1987 A	Darchelle Ross	Detroit Cass Tech	43.89
1988 A	Dawn Adams	Detroit Cooley	43.10*
1989 A	Nicole Franklin	Ann Arbor Pioneer	44.9
1990 A	Marjona Howard	Flint Northern	43.46
1991 A	Alicia Bernier	Holland West Ottawa	45.68
1992 A	Nikkie Bouyer	Lansing Sexton	44.46
1993 A	Nikki Bouyer	Lansing Sexton	43.35
1994 A	Nikki Bouyer	Lansing Sexton	44.0
1995 A	Shaunetta Smith	Detroit Mumford	45.55
1996 A	Shaunetta Smith	Detroit Mumford	44.54
1997 A	Lashaunta Blander	Pontiac Northern	42.81*
1998 A	Lashaunta Blander	Pontiac Northern	43.34
1999 A	Arthurene Powell	Ypsilanti	43.70
2000 D1	Lindsay Bond	Southfield	44.23*
2001 D1	Lindsay Bond	Southfield	43.79*
2002 D1	Andrea Mosher	Ann Arbor Pioneer	43.19*
2003 D1	Kathleen LaValley	GR Forest Hills Central	42.89*
2004 D1	Osamuede Iyoha	Ann Arbor Pioneer	42.85*
2005 D1	Kathleen LaValley	GR Forest Hills Central	44.22
2006 D1	Chidimma Uche	Ann Arbor Pioneer	43.80
2007 D1	Chidimma Uche	Ann Arbor Pioneer	43.98
2008 D1	Ariel Roberts	Ann Arbor Pioneer	43.96
2009 D1	Christienne Linton	Romulus	42.86
2010 D1	Jaelynn Pryor	Jackson	44.83
2011 D1	Tory Schiller	Grand Ledge	43.63
2012 D1	Cindy Ofili	Ann Arbor Huron	45.02
2013 D1	Breanna Luba	Southgate Anderson	43.91
2014 D1	Ashlynn Schiro	Okemos	43.09
2015 D1	Brianna Holloway	Oak Park	43.50
2016 D1	Brianna Holloway	Oak Park	42.71*
2017 D1	Kyanna Evans	Wyandotte Roosevelt	42.64*
2018 D1	Melissa Symons	Lake Orion	43.02

300H – Class B/Division 2 Champions

(200m Low Hurdles; y=220 yards)

1979 B	Michelle Priefer	St Joseph	29.0y*
1980 B	Monica Williams	Port Huron	29.2
1981 B	Martha Hans	Tecumseh	29.4
1982 B	Martha Hans	Tecumseh	28.8y*

(300m Low Hurdles)

1983 B	Paulette Bryant	Southgate Aquinas	44.7*
1984 B	Paulette Bryant	Southgate Aquinas	44.0*
1985 B	Alana Davis	Jackson Lumen Christi	44.66*
1986 B	Alana Davis	Jackson Lumen Christi	44.6
1987 B	Kelly Olszewski	Saline	45.3
1988 B	Tara Allen	Detroit DePorres	45.10
1989 B	Jennifer Merritt	Grand Rapids West Catholic	46.2
1990 B	Shelly Rennie	Croswell-Lexington	46.1
1991 B	Rita Harden	Dearborn Hts Robichaud	45.20
1992 B	Chanty Allen	Chelsea	47.09
1993 B	Jennifer Story	Stanton-Central Montcalm	45.50
1994 B	Kenyetta Grigsby	River Rouge	45.10
1995 B	Kenyetta Grigsby	River Rouge	45.55
1996 B	Kari Karhoff	Durand	44.70
1997 B	Kari Karhoff	Durand	44.42*
1998 B	Ashley Carroll	Flint Powers	46.0
1999 B	April Saxton	Dowagiac	44.87
2000 D2	Arthurene Powell	Ypsilanti	44.73*
2001 D2	Audrey Graham	Battle Creek Lakeview	44.88
2002 D2	Tiffany Ofili	Ypsilanti	44.04*
2003 D2	Courtney Kersten	Yale	44.35
2004 D2	Tiffany Ofili	Ypsilanti	44.78
2005 D2	Tiffany Ofili	Ypsilanti	42.82*
2006 D2	Stephanie McCarthy	Grand Rapids Kenowa Hills	43.95
2007 D2	Kyra Caldwell	Ypsilanti	44.25
2008 D2	Kyra Caldwell	Ypsilanti	45.31
2009 D2	Tori Desira	DeWitt	45.18
2010 D2	Megan Yanik	Livonia Ladywood	43.85
2011 D2	Tori Desira	DeWitt	44.21
2012 D2	Tori Desira	DeWitt	45.25
2013 D2	Mallory Myler	Dearborn Divine Child	44.82
2014 D2	Hannah Coverdill	Marine City	45.38
2015 D2	Lauren Huebner	Saginaw Swan Valley	44.62
2016 D2	Hannah Coverdill	Marine City	44.01
2017 D2	Mariel Bruxvoort	Grand Rapids South Christian	43.06
2018 D2	Arabia Bacon	Battle Creek Harper Creek	44.74

300H – Class C/Division 3 Champions

(200m Low Hurdles; y=220 yards)

1979 C	Sue Raper	Mt Clemens Lutheran North	30.1y*
1980 C	Karice Loveberry	Quincy	29.4y*
1981 C	Terri Reed	Napoleon	29.2*
1982 C	Kari Agin	Manchester	28.7*

(300m Low Hurdles)

1983 C	Kari Agin	Manchester	44.7*
1984 C	Debbie Bennett	Leroy Pine River	46.3
1985 C	Debbie Barnett	Leroy Pine River	46.05*
1986 C	Stacy Dukes	Morley Stanwood	46.2
1987 C	Melanie Chard	Union City	45.62*
1988 C	Rhonda Bedker	Mason County Central	45.4
1989 C	Naheed Irani	Onsted	45.23*
1990 C	Naheed Irani	Onsted	44.49*
1991 C	Naheed Irani	Onsted	44.90
1992 C	Nancy Gross	New Lothrop	46.4
1993 C	Nancy Gross	New Lothrop	45.14
1994 C	Wendy Feldman	Almont	46.10
1995 C	Wendy Feldman	Almont	45.58
1996 C	Nikki Harrison	Pewamo-Westphalia	45.79
1997 C	Amber Bright	Benzie Central	46.1
1998 C	Amber Bright	Benzie Central	45.1
1999 C	Jennifer Delamater	Blanchard-Montabella	45.60
2000 D3	Kelly Walker	Standish-Sterling	45.90*
2001 D3	Pam Hoyt	Parchment	46.07
2002 D3	Courtney Kersten	Yale	45.38*
2003 D3	Katie Pickette	Hopkins	44.94*
2004 D3	Lindsay Lange	Manistee	46.43
2005 D3	Michelle Elliott	Goodrich	45.90
2006 D3	Alexis Brown	Otisville LakeVille	45.67
2007 D3	Amy Myler	Ann Arbor Gabriel Richard	44.82*
2008 D3	Amy Myler	Ann Arbor Gabriel Richard	46.08
2009 D3	Rachel Hoffman	Shelby	46.09
2010 D3	Emily Wee	Frankenmuth	44.15*
2011 D3	Sami Michell	Reed City	43.83*
2012 D3	Sami Michell	Reed City	42.23*
2013 D3	Sami Michell	Reed City	45.18
2014 D3	Kylie Hicks	Boyne City	44.59
2015 D3	Sydney Bronner	Frankenmuth	46.28
2016 D3	Regan Berg	Parchment	45.74
2017 D3	Megan Rosales	Adrian Madison	45.05
2018 D3	McKena Russell	Onsted	45.15

300H – Class D/Division 4 Champions

(200m Low Hurdles; y=220 yards)

1979 D	Maria Shoup	Mason County Eastern	29.0*
1980 D	Maria Shoup	Mason County Eastern	29.1
1981 D	Maria Shoup	Mason County Eastern	28.9*
1982 D	Bradley Nixon	Ann Arbor Greenhills	30.2

(300m Low Hurdles)

1983 D	Brenda Stewart	Covert	46.1*
1984 D	Sherri Jones	Muskegon West Shore	44.85*
1985 D	Janice Kresge	Fulton-Middleton	46.05
1986 D	Lisa Nixon	Ann Arbor Greenhills	46.6
1987 D	Angela Salvatore	Concord	47.82
1988 D	Laura Selby	Tekonsha	46.70
1989 D	Marcy Sillman	Fowler	47.5
1990 D	Marnie Peplinski	Maple City Glen Lake	46.10
1991 D	Marnie Peplinski	Maple City Glen Lake	45.59
1992 D	Marnie Peplinski	Maple City Glen Lake	44.82*
1993 D	Jessica Cunningham	Manton	46.7
1994 D	Tanya Wilcox	Maple City Glen Lake	47.31
1995 D	Holly Lamkin	McBain Northern Mich Christian	47.15
1996 D	Liz Powers	Homer	46.09
1997 D	Desha Feldpausch	Fowler	45.79
1998 D	Desha Feldpausch	Fowler	45.2

1999 D	Elly Johnson	Bellaire	46.28		2009 D4	Megan Heffner	Kinde-North Huron	46.05
2000 D4	Jenifer Wendling	New Lothrop	45.49*		2010 D4	Megan Heffner	Kinde-North Huron	44.98*
2001 D4	Elly Johnson	Bellaire	45.89		2011 D4	Savannah Feldpausch	Fowler	47.82
2002 D4	Tanya Durian	Gobles	46.87		2012 D4	Brooke Bovee	Morenci	47.55
2003 D4	Kali Briggs	Vandercook Lake	46.57		2013 D4	Michelle Davis	Reading	44.92*
2004 D4	Sarah Thomas	Reading	45.65		2014 D4	Savannah Feldpausch	Fowler	45.42
2005 D4	Shelly Johnnson	Grass Lake	47.04		2015 D4	Allison Hufnagle	Fowler	47.38
2006 D4	Dominique Porter	Merrill	46.24		2016 D4	Balaigh Irelan	Reading	46.25
2007 D4	Valerie Watkins	Detroit Urban Lutheran	46.14		2017 D4	Kaelin Ray	Southfield Christian	45.98
2008 D4	Miranda Iles	Athens	45.84		2018 D4	Baleigh Irelan	Reading	45.85

300H – UP Class AB/Division 1 Champions

(200m Low Hurdles; y=220 yards)

1979 UPAB	Chris St. Louis	Kingsford	32.2*		1998 UPAB	Allison Koskey	Negaunee	48.5
1980 UPAB	Chris St. Louis	Kingsford	30.1*		1999 UPAB	Kristen Press	Sault Ste. Marie	48.4
1981 UPAB	Liz Hatfield	Sault Ste. Marie	30.9		2000 UPAB	Sarah Duesing	Sault Ste. Marie	49.6
1982 UPAB	Karen Scott	Escanaba	32.1		2001 UPD1	Sarah Duesing	Sault Ste. Marie	47.6*

(300m Low Hurdles)

					2002 UPD1	Mallory Nelson	Gladstone	48.90*
1983 UPAB	Carolee Boudreau	Escanaba	48.5*		2003 UPD1	Amanda Holtz	Marquette	48.68*
1984 UPAB	Carolee Boudreau	Escanaba	48.2*		2004 UPD1	Shannon Helminen	Calumet	48.21*
1985 UPAB	Melissa Michewicz	Sault Ste. Marie	49.2		2005 UPD1	Hayley Ford	Gladstone	47.81*
1986 UPAB	Melisa Michewicz	Sault Ste. Marie	49.1		2006 UPD1	Shannon Helminen	Calumet	46.50*
1987 UPAB	Laura Bero	Escanaba	49.3		2007 UPD1	Jordan Kronsage	Calumet	46.75
1988 UPAB	Laura Bero	Escanaba	48.2*		2008 UPD1	Jaime Roberts	Kingsford	48.06
1989 UPAB	Joan Lancour	Escanaba	49.8		2009 UPD1	Selena Meser	Sault Ste. Marie	46.81
1990 UPAB	Lisa Corbiere	Sault Ste. Marie	49.2		2010 UPD1	Selena Meser	Sault Ste. Marie	45.40*
1991 UPAB	Lisa Corbiere	Sault Ste. Marie	47.9		2011 UPD1	Selena Meser	Sault Ste. Marie	47.99
1992 UPAB	Michelle Olds	Marquette	49.8		2012 UPD1	Ashley Veale	Negaunee	48.49
1993 UPAB	Tiffany Hodge	Menominee	47.1		2013 UPD1	Ashley Veale	Negaunee	47.31
1994 UPAB	Tiffany Hodge	Menominee	45.3*		2014 UPD1	Hunter Viitala	Marquette	46.27
1995 UPAB	Tiffany Hodge	Menominee	47.0		2015 UPD1	Hannah Detmers	Marquette	47.57
1996 UPAB	Rebecca Johnson	Sault Ste. Marie	48.6		2016 UPD1	Brenna Jones	Sault Ste. Marie	47.11
1997 UPAB	Nicole Grubb	Ishpeming Westwood	49.2		2017 UPD1	Jacuelin Cammarata	Marquette	48.52
					2018 UPD1	Chloe Norman	Negaunee	47.78

300H – UP Class C/Division 2 Champions

(200m Low Hurdles; y=220 yards)

1979 UPC	Andrea Spiroff	Ishpeming	31.4*		1998 UPC	Casey McGrath	Ironwood	49.0
1980 UPC	Lynn Harris	Iron Mountain	31.4*		1999 UPC	Allison Koskey	Negaunee	48.7
1981 UPC	Mary Nault	Ishpeming Westwood	32.4		2000 UPC	Cacey McGrath	Ironwood	46.4
1982 UPC	Jenifer Domitrovich	Ontonagon	32.5		2001 UPD2	Cacey McGrath	Ironwood	47.6*

(300m Low Hurdles)

					2002 UPD2	Kate Hisking	Iron Mountain	48.24*
1983 UPC	Lynne Scholie	Hancock	46.2*		2003 UPD2	Stephanie Mishica	Hancock	47.93*
1984 UPC	Lori Eatherton	Stephenson	48.0		2004 UPD2	Melissa Girard	Norway	48.43
1985 UPC	Amber Harris	Calumet	47.5		2005 UPD2	Ellary Renier	Norway	46.65*
1986 UPC	Lori Eatherton	Stephenson	47.9		2006 UPD2	Ellary Renier	Norway	47.44
1987 UPC	Jackie Jeschke	Stephenson	49.5		2007 UPD2	Ellary Renier	Norway	47.89
1988 UPC	Traci Jeschke	Stephenson	47.8		2008 UPD2	Ally Markstrom	Rudyard	52.23
1989 UPC	Becky Wheaton	St. Ignace	49.8		2009 UPD2	Megan Kangas	Norway	50.41
1990 UPC	Becky Wheaton	St. Ignace	49.0		2010 UPD2	Joanna Pellizzer	West Iron County	50.24
1991 UPC	Amt Brack	Newberry	48.8		2011 UPD2	Megan Kangas	Norway	49.63
1992 UPC	Kristen Stratton	Iron Mountain	51.4		2012 UPD2	Alexa Thibault	St. Ignace	48.63
1993 UPC	Kelly Klein	Stephenson	47.8		2013 UPD2	Cassilyn Pellizzer	West Iron County	48.7
1994 UPC	Kelly Klein	Stephenson	46.8		2014 UPD2	Cassilyn Pellizzer	West Iron County	48.18
1995 UPC	Ashley Peffers	Munising	48.7		2015 UPD2	Mary Jarvis	Hancock	49.21
1996 UPC	Ashley Peffers	Munising	49.2		2016 UPD2	Mary Jarvis	Hancock	48.85
1997 UPC	Holly Brown	St. Ignace	47.8		2017 UPD2	Taylor Bryant	Newberry	49.18
					2018 UPD2	Katie Loman	Ishpeming	48.88

300H – UP Class D/Division 3 Champions

(200m Low Hurdles; y=220 yards)

1979 UPD	Terri Miron	Republic-Michigamme	31.1*		1998 UPD	Sara Boyer	Rapid River	47.5
1980 UPD	Terri Miron	Republic-Michigamme	30.5*		1999 UPD	Sara Boyer	Rapid River	47.9
1981 UPD	Terri Miron	Republic-Michigamme	31.6		2000 UPD	Karin Roberts	Bessemer	49.1
1982 UPD	Penny Cappaert	Bark River-Harris	32.8		2001 UPD3	Ashley Wery	Rock-Mid Peninsula	50.7*

(300m Low Hurdles)

					2002 UPD3	Tara Amarose	Cedarville	51.00*
1983 UPD	Gwen Wilkie	DeTour	48.5*		2003 UPD3	Cassi Rushford	Rapid River	50.25*
1984 UPD	Gwen Wilkie	DeTour	47.5*		2004 UPD3	Erin VanEnkevort	Bark River-Harris	49.65*
1985 UPD	Denise Beauchamp	Bark River-Harris	49.2		2005 UPD3	Erin VanEnkevort	Bark River-Harris	50.58
1986 UPD	Jeri Hosang	Lake Linden-Hubbell	48.5		2006 UPD3	Erin Tucker	Ontonagon	50.08
1987 UPD	Jeri Hosang	Lake Linden-Hubbell	48.5		2007 UPD3	Brooke Granquist	Powers-North Central	48.98*
1988 UPD	Julie Elsing	Rock-Mid Peninsula	47.7		2008 UPD3	Brooke Granquist	Powers-North Central	48.89*
1989 UPD	Sue Harteau	Felch North Dickinson	50.3		2009 UPD3	Brooke Granquist	Powers-North Central	48.07*
1990 UPD	Jody Erickson	Bessemer	48.7		2010 UPD3	Emily Lehto	Felch North Dickinson	50.11
1991 UPD	Nicole Skinner	Pickford	48.5		2011 UPD3	Becca Carruthers	Brimley	48.56
1992 UPD	Brooke Hine	Bessemer	50.0		2012 UPD3	Aspen Hood	Engadine	48.77
1993 UPD	Brooke Hine	Bessemer	48.1		2013 UPD3	Haillee Brown	St. Ignace	49.41
1994 UPD	Jill Gobert	Rock-Mid Peninsula	49.3		2014 UPD3	Lori Wardynski	Ontonagon	48.75
1995 UPD	Kristen Nichols	Lake Linden-Hubbell	50.5		2015 UPD3	Valerie Rowe	Bessemer	48.09
1996 UPD	Kristen Nichols	Lake Linden-Hubbell	49.8		2016 UPD3	Lori Wardynski	Ontonagon	47.27*
1997 UPD	Sara Boyer	Rapid River	48.8		2017 UPD3	Hailee Demers	Bark River-Harris	49.46
					2018 UPD3	Hailee Demers	Bark River-Harris	50.16

GIRLS HIGH JUMP

Records

D1	5-9¼	Jailah Mason	Sterling Heights Stevenson	2014
D2	5-9	Sara Jane Baker	Mattawan	2001
	5-9	Christine Krellwitz	Big Rapids	2004
D3	5-6	Jasmine Thomas	Flint Hamady	2008
	5-6	Kara Craig	Schoolcraft	2012
	5-6	Sydney Bronner	Frankenmuth	2014
D4	5-7	Jenny Kulchar	Burton Atherton	2001, 2002
UPD1	5-8	Sarah Duesing	Sault Ste. Marie	2001
UPD2	5-4	Nicole Vanderlin	Norway	2011, 2012
	5-4	Linnie Gustafson	St. Ignace	2017
UPD3	5-5	Tabitha Graham	Brimley	2011

Records by Class (pre-2000 for LP, pre-2001 for UP)

A	5-10	Gwen Wentland	Grand Blanc	1990
B	5-9	Beth Brunn	Utica	1976
	5-9	Terri Johnson	Muskegon Catholic	1977
C	5-11¼	Ellie Hayden	Capac	1980
D	5-8¾	Kay Leighton	Northport	1978
UPAB	5-8¼	Brenda Teague	Gwinn	1981
UPC	5-5	Gael Butkovich	Houghton	1995
UPD	5-4	Jill Gobert	Rock-Mid Peninsula	1994, 1996

HJ – Class A/Division 1 Champions

1973 All	Anita Lee	Detroit Cass Tech	5-4*		1996 A	Stacey Thomas	Flint Southwestern	5-8
1974 A/B	Ellen Dempsey	Howell	5-6*		1997 A	Maia Knox	Ypsilanti	5-7
1975 A	Anita Lee	Detroit Cass Tech	5-6*		1998 A	Maia Knox	Ypsilanti	5-8
1976 A	Linnell Jones	Flint Northwestern	5-6*		1999 A	Stephanie Lutz	Okemos	5-7
1977 A	Cathy Ballard	Macomb L'Anse Creuse North	5-8*		2000 D1	Stephanie Linz	Okemos	5-7*
1978 A	Joanna Bullard	Ann Arbor Pioneer	5-6½		2001 D1	Vanessa Maher	Roseville	5-4
1979 A	Rhonda Filius	Muskegon Mona Shores	5-5½		2002 D1	Katie Price	Fraser	5-5
1980 A	Mary Brunn	Utica	5-7		2003 D1	Katherine Johnson	Birmingham Marian	5-7*
1981 A	Judy Tucker	Flint Northern	5-9*		2004 D1	Christina Solomon	Belleville	5-6
1982 A	Angie Hafner	Flushing	5-7		2005 D1	Trinka Boatright	Benton Harbor	5-4
1983 A	Cathy Nash	Saginaw	5-8		2006 D1	Whitney Tremain	East Kentwood	5-4
1984 A	Jeanine Gant	Midland Dow	5-6		2007 D1	Ariel Roberts	Ann Arbor Pioneer	5-7*
1985 A	Laura Wheeler	Ypsilanti	5-8		2008 D1	Ariel Roberts	Ann Arbor Pioneer	5-9*
1986 A	Cheri Johnson	Bishop Borgess	5-8		2009 D1	Emelle McConney	West Bloomfield	5-8
1987 A	Angie Miller	Plymouth Canton	5-5		2010 D1	Nyki Caldwell	Dexter	5-8
1988 A	Angie Miller	Plymouth Canton	5-5		2011 D1	Nyki Caldwell	Dexter	5-8
1989 A	Gwen Wentland	Grand Blanc	5-7		2012 D1	Keinaa Ingram	Southfield Lathrup	5-9*
1990 A	Gwen Wentland	Grand Blanc	5-10*		2013 D1	Kerry McMahan	Novi	5-6
1991 A	Rebecca Willey	Livonia Ladywood	5-5		2014 D1	Jailah Mason	Sterling Heights Stevenson	5-9¼*
1992 A	Alicia Bernier	Holland West Ottawa	5-3		2015 D1	Whitney Mergens	Milford	5-7
1993 A	Stacey Thomas	Flint Southwestern	5-5		2016 D1	Kayla Dobie	Macomb Dakota	5-7
1994 A	Stacey Thomas	Flint Southwestern	5-7		2017 D1	Breanna Perry	Flushing	5-7
1995 A	Jenny Englehardt	Battle Creek Lakeview	5-8		2018 D1	Hannah Hood-Blaxill	Novi	5-4

HJ – Class B/Division 2 Champions

1975 B	Beth Brunn	Utica	5-7*		1997 B	Sara Behnke	Stevensville-Lakeshore	5-5
1976 B	Beth Brunn	Utica	5-9*		1998 B	Crystal White	Mt Clemens	5-5
1977 B	Terri Johnson	Muskegon Catholic	5-9*		1999 B	Kelli Wilson	Durand	5-6
1978 B	Jane Anderson	Saginaw Eisenhower	5-7½		2000 D2	Sara Jane Baker	Mattawan	5-7*
1979 B	Laurie Rogers	Saline	5-7		2001 D2	Sara Jane Baker	Mattawan	5-9*
1980 B	Laurie Rogers	Saline	5-7		2002 D2	Sara Jane Baker	Mattawan	5-8
1981 B	Karla Link	Fruitport	5-6		2003 D2	Chrstine Krellwitz	Big Rapids	5-7
1982 B	Laurie Bennett	Ludington	5-6		2004 D2	Chrstine Krellwitz	Big Rapids	5-9*
1983 B	Kathy McBride	Livonia-Clarenceville	5-6		2005 D2	Katherine Johnson	Birmingham Marian	5-7
1984 B	Sue Bulkema	Hudsonville Unity Christian	5-4		2006 D2	Lesly Hale	Detroit Renaissance	5-6
1985 B	Vicki Oostendorp	Hudsonville Unity Christian	5-5		2007 D2	Lindsey McKnight	Sparta	5-4
1986 B	Molly McCoy	Big Rapids	5-6		2008 D2	Caitlyn Bronczkowski	St. Joseph	5-5
1987 B	Amy Warner	Linden	5-8		2009 D2	Sara Nitz	Zeeland East	5-6
1988 B	Cathie Vos	Grand Rapids Christian	5-5		2010 D2	Kelsey Kuipers	Otsego	5-6
1989 B	Jennifer Merrett	Grand Rapids West Catholic	5-5		2011 D2	Katherine Mills	Eaton Rapids	5-6
1990 B	Linda Stuck	Milan	5-5		2012 D2	Katherine Mills	Eaton Rapids	5-6
1991 B	Linda Stuck	Milan	5-6		2013 D2	Ade Ayoola	Grand Rapids Christian	5-5
1992 B	Linda Stuck	Milan	5-4		2014 D2	Charley Andrews	Battle Creek Harper Creek	5-7
1993 B	Karen Sisung	Monroe St. Mary	5-6		2015 D2	Charley Andrews	Battle Creek Harper Creek	5-4
1994 B	Kelly Etheridge	Eaton Rapids	5-5		2016 D2	Suenomi Norinh	Zeeland East	5-6
1995 B	Terresha Derossett	Otisville LakeVille	5-5		2017 D2	Suenomi Norinh	Zeeland East	5-8
1996 B	Stephanie McIntyre	Haslett	5-4		2018 D2	Suenomi Norinh	Zeeland East	5-8

HJ – Class C/Division 3 Champions

1974 C/D	Sue Bouck	Haslett	5-6*		1976 C	Ami Borelli	Watervliet	5-6*
1975 C	Sue Florip	Rogers City	5-2		1977 C	Kathy Brozowski	Capac	5-4

1978 C	Ellie Hayden	Capac	5-5½
1979 C	Ellie Hayden	Capac	5-8*
1980 C	Ellie Hayden	Capac	5-11¼*
1981 C	Dena Davis	Bronson	5-6
1982 C	Deb Hartline	Cassopolis	5-8
1983 C	Deb Hartline	Cassopolis	5-4
1984 C	Deb Hartline	Cassopolis	5-9
1985 C	Kelly Ward	Kalamazoo Hackett	5-5
1986 C	Cris Vredenburg	Morley Stanwood	5-5
1987 C	Coleen Wruble	Harbor Beach	5-5
1988 C	Clarissa Jones	Flat Rock	5-6
1989 C	Clarissa Jones	Flat Rock	5-5
1990 C	Abbie Schaefer	Onsted	5-7
1991 C	Kelly Oberlin	Grant	5-8
1992 C	Dawn Dziuban	Flat Rock	5-4
1993 C	April Widner	Concord	5-6
1994 C	Susie Lee	Bangor	5-7
1995 C	Jennifer Allen	Lake Fenton	5-5
1996 C	Jennifer Allen	Lake Fenton	5-4
1997 C	Monyka Paul	St Louis	5-5
1998 C	Kristi Pykosz	Capac	5-4
1999 C	Jenny Kulcher	Burton Atherton	5-7
2000 D3	Jessica Kochendorfer	Quincy	5-4*
2001 D3	Rachel Munniksma	Hamilton	5-3
2002 D3	Lauren Colyn	Kalamazoo Christian	5-4*
2003 D3	Jenny Theisen	Saginaw Swan Valley	5-3
2004 D3	Shanna Tamminga	Delton Kelogg	5-5*
2005 D3	Emily Cross	Armada	5-3
2006 D3	Amber Siegel	Macomb Lutheran North	5-5*
2007 D3	Mary Ramsey	Parchment	5-5*
2008 D3	Jasmine Thomas	Flint Hamady	5-6*
2009 D3	Jasmine Thomas	Flint Hamady	5-5
2010 D3	Jordyn Kiser	Reese	5-4
2011 D3	Taylor Penzien	New Haven	5-4
2012 D3	Kara Craig	Schoolcraft	5-6*
2013 D3	Marissa Johnson	Durand	5-5
2014 D3	Sydney Bronner	Frankenmuth	5-6*
2015 D3	Emma Burns	Manistee	5-3
2016 D3	Hannah Hall	Millington	5-4
2017 D3	Rylie Bisbelle	Lake City	5-4
2018 D3	Hannah Hall	Millington	5-3

HJ – Class D/Division 4 Champions

1975 D	Kate Stanton	Mesick	4-11*
1976 D	Pam Brown	Morenci	5-7*
1977 D	Pam Brown	Morenci	5-4
1978 D	Kaye Leighton	Northport	5-8¾*
1979 D	Kaye Leighton	Northport	5-5¼
1980 D	Kaye Leighton	Northport	5-6
1981 D	Dawn Rich	Deckerville	5-6
1982 D	Robin Pavka	Reading	5-3
1983 D	Ledesa Schultz	Saginaw Mi Lutheran Seminary	5-3¼
1984 D	Jenny Campbell	Battle Creek St Phillip	5-3
1985 D	Jane Janusziewski	Springport	5-5
1986 D	Sarah Reed	Springport	5-3
1987 D	Angela Salvatore	Concord	5-5
1988 D	Beth DeMeester	Muskegon Christian	5-2
1989 D	Nicole Whitaker	Genesee	5-1
1990 D	Ronele Lamkin	McBain N Michigan Christian	5-3
1991 D	Ronele Lamkin	McBain N Michigan Christian	5-2
1992 D	Ronele Lamkin	McBain N Michigan Christian	5-2
1993 D	Ronele Lamkin	McBain N Michigan Christian	5-3
1994 D	Elicia Hall	Grass Lake	5-2
1995 D	Elycia Hall	Grass Lake	5-2
1996 D	Courtney Huffman	Homer	5-2
1997 D	Courtney Huffman	Homer	5-6
1998 D	Nicole McCadie	Hale	5-2
1999 D	Nicole Mccadie	Hale	5-4
2000 D4	Jenny Kulchar	Burton Atherton	5-7*
2001 D4	Jenny Kulchar	Burton Atherton	5-7*
2002 D4	Porsha Ellis	Southfield Christian	5-5
2003 D4	Kali Briggs	Vandercook Lake	5-3
2004 D4	Heather McDaniel	Rochester Hills Lutheran NW	5-3
2005 D4	Shelly Mathewson	Bellevue	5-5
2006 D4	Vicky Reyes	Marcellus	5-3
2007 D4	Allyson Karaba	North Muskegon	5-6
2008 D4	Sarah MacCourtney	Rochester Hills Lutheran NW	5-5
2009 D4	Sarah MacCourtney	Rochester Hills Lutheran NW	5-6
2010 D4	Megan Hefner	Kinde-North Huron	5-6
2011 D4	Amanda Lowell	Mendon	5-5
2012 D4	Addie Schumacher	Beal City	5-5
2013 D4	Addie Schumacher	Beal City	5-6
2014 D4	Jessica Tea-Hui	Evart	5-4
2015 D4	Ashley Harrmann	Petersburg-Summerfield	5-3
2016 D4	Ashley Harrmann	Petersburg-Summerfield	5-4
2017 D4	Alyssa Vandegriff	Fowler	5-4
2018 D4	Alyssa Vandegriff	Fowler	5-5

HJ – UP Class AB/Division 1 Champions

1972 UP-All	Mary Parks	Marquette	4-9*
1973 UP-All	Francis Bathos	Pickford	4-10*
1974 UPAB	Anne Eslinger	Iron Mountain	4-7
1975 UPAB	Shelly Chapman	Marquette	4-9
1976 UPAB	Jean White	Escanaba	5-0*
1977 UPAB	Becky Drake	Kingsford	5-3*
1978 UPAB	Jean White	Escanaba	5-2
1979 UPAB	Brenda Teague	Gwinn	5-½
1980 UPAB	Brenda Teague	Gwinn	5-5*
1981 UPAB	Brenda Teague	Gwinn	5-8¼*
1982 UPAB	Karen Nevala	Marquette	5-0
1983 UPAB	Tammy Funke	Escanaba	5-1
1984 UPAB	Candie Miron	Escanaba	5-2
1985 UPAB	Stacey Lewis	Kingsford	5-2
1986 UPAB	Theresa Bernier	Marquette	5-1
1987 UPAB	Laura Bero	Escanaba	5-0
1988 UPAB	Laura Bero	Escanaba	4-11
1989 UPAB	Beth Blake	Marquette	4-11
1990 UPAB	Traci Anderson	Kingsford	5-2
1991 UPAB	Traci Anderson	Kingsford	5-4
1992 UPAB	Amy Lassila	Marquette	5-0
1993 UPAB	Jessica Fugere	Menominee	4-10
1994 UPAB	Lisa Potvin	Escanaba	5-2
1995 UPAB	Lisa Potvin	Escanaba	5-3
1996 UPAB	Michele Scherer	Marquette	5-0
1997 UPAB	Jenny Swanson	Ishpeming Westwood	4-11
1998 UPAB	Sarah Ketvirtis	Marquette	5-1
1999 UPAB	Haley Thomas	Escanaba	5-0
2000 UPAB	Sarah Duesing	Sault Ste. Marie	5-4
2001 UPD1	Sarah Duesing	Sault Ste. Marie	5-8*
2002 UPD1	Tracy Barney	Gwinn	5-2
2003 UPD1	Emily Bailey	Sault Ste. Marie	4-11
2004 UPD1	Ashley Moore	Negaunee	5-2
2005 UPD1	Ashley Moore	Negaunee	5-2
2006 UPD1	Kara Rastello	Calumet	5-0
2007 UPD1	Ashley Moore	Negaunee	5-1
2008 UPD1	Helen Richards	Houghton	5-0
2009 UPD1	Olivia Nash	Escanaba	5-0
2010 UPD1	Olivia Nash	Escanaba	5-2
2011 UPD1	Olivia Nash	Escanaba	5-0
2012 UPD1	Adeline Grier-Welch	Houghton	5-4
2013 UPD1	Hunter Viitala	Marquette	5-1
2014 UPD1	Hailey Wickstron	Calumet	5-0
2015 UPD1	Hailey Wickstron	Calumet	4-10
2016 UPD1	Sydney Mills	Gladstone	5-0
2017 UPD1	Hailey Wickstron	Calumet	4-11
2018 UPD1	Tessa Leese	Ishpeming Westwood	4-9

HJ – UP Class C/Division 2 Champions

1974 UPC	Marcia Jasonowicz	Norway	4-6*
1975 UPC	Marcia Jasonowicz	Norway	5-0*
1976 UPC	Gina Selmo	Iron River West Iron Country	4-11
1977 UPC	Gina Selmo	Iron River West Iron Country	5-3*
1978 UPC	Gino Selmo	Iron River West Iron Country	5-0
1979 UPC	Linnea Laurila	Negaunee	4-11¾
1980 UPC	Trudy Young	St. Ignace	5-2
1981 UPC	Roberta Bucklin	Houghton	5-3*
1982 UPC	Trudy Young	St. Ignace	5-0
1983 UPC	Chris Orr	Calumet	4-11
1984 UPC	Lisa Newman	Munising	5-1
1985 UPC	Allison Bowerman	Munising	5-2
1986 UPC	Tracy Haines	Houghton	5-0
1987 UPC	Allison Bowerman	Munising	5-2½
1988 UPC	Laura Lobhner	Norway	5-0
1989 UPC	Samantha Sullivan	Ontonagon	4-10
1990 UPC	Lisa Broemer	Ontonagon	5-1
1991 UPC	Tyling Simmons	St. Ignace	5-2

1992 UPC	Nicole McMullin	L'Anse	5-2
1993 UPC	Kelly Klein	Stephenson	5-3*
1994 UPC	Kelly Klein	Stephenson	5-3*
1995 UPC	Gael Butkovich	Houghton	5-5*
1996 UPC	Gael Butkovich	Houghton	5-0
1997 UPC	Jenny Witting	Hancock	4-9
1998 UPC	Jenny Swanson	Ishpeming Westwood	5-0
1999 UPC	Heidi Helminen	Calumet	4-11
2000 UPC	Heidi Helminen	Calumet	5-1
2001 UPD2	Kristin Ruppe	Ironwood	5-0*
2002 UPD2	Jessica Hartwig	Iron Mountain	5-0*
2003 UPD2	Kristen Ruppe	Ironwood	5-0*
2004 UPD2	Natalie Bertucci	Ishpeming	5-3*
2005 UPD2	Natalie Bertucci	Ishpeming	5-2

2006 UPD2	Jessica Wood	Ishpeming	4-11
2007 UPD2	Melissa Beauchamp	West Iron County	4-10
2008 UPD2	Ally Markstrom	Rudyard	4-11
2009 UPD2	Melissa Beauchamp	West Iron County	5-0
2010 UPD2	Nicole Vanderlin	Norway	5-2
2011 UPD2	Nicole Vanderlin	Norway	5-4*
2012 UPD2	Nicole Vanderlin	Norway	5-4*
2013 UPD2	Rachel Hudacek	Ironwood	5-0
2014 UPD2	Alexis Kallenbach	Norway	4-11
2015 UPD2	Rachel Hudacek	Ironwood	5-0
2016 UPD2	Linnie Gustafson	St. Ignace	5-0
2017 UPD2	Linnie Gustafson	St. Ignace	5-4*
2018 UPD2	Linnie Gustafson	St. Ignace	4-11

HJ – UP Class D/Division 3 Champions

1974 UPD	Kimberly Izzard	Pickford	4-7*
1975 UPD	Mary Joy Satori	Crystal Falls Forest Park	5-0*
1976 UPD	Linsa Winkelbauer	Rock	5-0*
1977 UPD	Vickie Thomas	Engadine	5-2*
1978 UPD	Vickie Thomas	Engadine	5-0
1979 UPD	Brenda Rogalski	Crystal Falls Forest Park	5-½
1980 UPD	Brenda Rogalski	Crystal Falls Forest Park	5-3*
1981 UPD	Katherine Hannula	Lake Linden-Hubbell	5-2
1982 UPD	Katherine Hannula	Lake Linden-Hubbell	5-2½
1983 UPD	Robin Daniels	Wakefield	4-10
1984 UPD	Gail Keranen	Lake Linden-Hubbell	4-11
1985 UPD	Julie Belinski	Pickford	5-0
1986 UPD	Sheri Thomas	Engadine	5-2
1987 UPD	Julie Belinski	Pickford	5-0
1988 UPD	Jill Keranen	Lake Linden-Hubbell	5-2
1989 UPD	Brenda Nummela	Eben Junction Superior Central	5-0
1990 UPD	Trisha Bailey	Ewen-Trout Creek	4-10
1991 UPD	Heather Applegate	Cedarville	5-3*
1992 UPD	Susan Trevarrow	Cedarville	5-2
1993 UPD	Heather Applegate	Cedarville	5-3*
1994 UPD	Jill Gobert	Rock-Mid Peninsula	5-4*
1995 UPD	Jill Gobert	Rock-Mid Peninsula	5-2
1996 UPD	Jill Gobert	Rock-Mid Peninsula	5-4*

1997 UPD	Kristen Nichols	Lake Linden-Hubbell	4-11
1998 UPD	Ariel Huff	Cedarville	4-11
1999 UPD	Dana Evaou	Brimley	4-10
2000 UPD	Megan Grondin	Power North Central	5-2
2001 UPD3	Megan Grondin	Power North Central	4-10*
2002 UPD3	Megan Grondin	Power North Central	5-2*
2003 UPD3	Nikki Wyers	Ontonagon	5-0
2004 UPD3	Molly McIntyre	Brimley	4-11
2005 UPD3	Jamie VanEnkevort	Bark River Harris	5-1
2006 UPD3	Katelin Domitrovich	Ontonagon	5-1
2007 UPD3	Michelle Jorasz	Bark River-Harris	4-10
2008 UPD3	Jessica Graham	Brimley	5-2*
2009 UPD3	Jessica Graham	Brimley	5-4*
2010 UPD3	Nicole Melcer	DeTour	4-10
2011 UPD3	Tabitha Graham	Brimley	5-5*
2012 UPD3	Tabitha Graham	Brimley	5-3
2013 UPD3	Kelsey Shope	Rock-Mid Peninsula	5-3
2014 UPD3	Kelsey Shope	Rock-Mid Peninsula	5-1
2015 UPD3	Linnie Guftafson	St. Ignace	5-1
2016 UPD3	Lori Wardynski	Ontonagon	4-10
2017 UPD3	Jamie Hendrickson	Lake Linden-Hubbell	5-1
2018 UPD3	Jamie Hendickson	Lake Linden-Hubbell	4-10

GIRLS POLE VAULT

Records

D1	13-4	Landon Kemp	Greenville	2016
D2	12-7	Brianna Bredeweg	Allendale	2018
D3	12-4	Kasey Staley	Clare	2016
D4	12-0	Kirstie Wieber	Pewamo-Westphalia	2010
UPD1	12-0	Jamie Roberts	Kingsford	2010
UPD2	9-1	Kali Jo Marshall	St. Ignace	2010
UPD3	10-¼	Sarah Audette	Munising	2015
	10-¼	Michaela Peramaki	Munising	2015

Records by Class (pre-2000 for LP, pre-2001 for UP)

A	11-0	Jillian Hinds	Traverse City Central	1999
B	11-7	Rachel Zukowski	Grand Rapids Catholic Central	1999
C	10-0	Jamie Foote	Bath	1999
D	8-8	Becky Prielipp	Marion	1999
UPAB	10-0	Angela Abernathy	Marquette	1999
UPC	9-0	Pam Bolduc	Ironwood	1998
UPC	9-0	Deb Palmer	Stephenson	1998
UPC	9-0	Amy Hokenson	Manistique	2000
UPD	8-3	Danielle Richmond	Eben Junction Superior Central	1998

PV – Class A/Division 1 Champions

1998 A	Kellie Kern	South Lyon	9-6*
1999 A	Jillian Hinds	Traverse City Central	11-0*
2000 D1	Missy Smith	Grand Rapids Christian	10-7*
2001 D1	Mellisa Ullenbruch	Port Huron Northern	11-6*
2002 D1	Bethany Hecksel	Rockford	11-0
2003 D1	Jennifer Vandermeer	Holland	11-6*
2004 D1	Stacy Orosz	Rockford	11-6*
2005 D1	Christi Kettelhut	Rockford	11-1½
2006 D1	Amy Morrison	Fenton	12-1*
2007 D1	Abby Shanahan	East Kentwood	12-2*
2008 D1	Sarah Birkmeier	Rockford	11-3

2009 D1	Sarah Birkmeier	Rockford	13-0*
2010 D1	Sarah Birkmeier	Rockford	11-9
2011 D1	Jennifer Schornak	Macomb Dakota	11-6
2012 D1	Katie Rancourt	East Kentwood	12-6
2013 D1	Jane McCurry	Plymouth	11-3
2014 D1	Mackenzie Shell	Port Huron Northern	12-7
2015 D1	Mackenzie Shell	Port Huron Northern	12-0
2016 D1	Landon Kemp	Greenville	13-4*
2017 D1	Landon Kemp	Greenville	13-3
2018 D1	Jessica Mercier	Waterford Kettering	12-10

PV – Class B/Division 2 Champions

1998 B	Stephanie Teeple	Sturgis	10-4¼*		2009 D2	Tori Wesley	Marine City	11-8
1999 B	Rachel Zukowski	Grand Rapids Catholic Central	11-7*		2010 D2	Kristen Hixson	Remus Chippewa Hills	12-4*
2000 D2	Stephanie Teeple	Sturgis	11-10*		2011 D2	Brittany London	Middleville Thornapple-Kellogg	12-1
2001 D2	Stephanie Teeple	Sturgis	11-4		2012 D2	Janica Pollatz	Grand Rapids Christian	11-6
2002 D2	Missy Smith	Grand Rapids Christian	11-5		2013 D2	Janica Pollatz	Grand Rapids Christian	11-8
2003 D2	Angie Maxey	Caledonia	11-0		2014 D2	Allie LeRoux	Spring Lake	11-8
2004 D2	Angie Maxey	Caledonia	11-8		2015 D2	Gabriella LeRoux	Spring Lake	11-8
2005 D2	Lisa Krupp	Sparta	11-3		2016 D2	Gabriella LeRoux	Spring Lake	11-8
2006 D2	Lisa Krupp	Sparta	11-3		2017 D2	Gabriella LeRoux	Spring Lake	12-6*
2007 D2	Amy Morrison	Fenton	12-0*		2018 D2	Brianna Bredeweg	Allendale	12-7*
2008 D2	Becca Pilkerton	Dexter	11-3					

PV – Class C/Division 3 Champions

1998 C	Cindy Roberson	Bath	9-6*		2009 D3	Kassie Powell	Durand	11-0
1999 C	Jamie Foote	Bath	10-0*		2010 D3	Kassie Powell	Durand	11-8
2000 D3	Michele Vanderhyde	Howard City Tri County	9-11*		2011 D3	Kassie Powell	Durand	11-7
2001 D3	Michele Vanderhyde	Howard City Tri County	10-9*		2012 D3	Kirstie Wieber	Pewamo-Westphalia	11-7
2002 D3	Rachel Duthler	Grandville Calvin Christian	10-9*		2013 D3	Kenzie Wieber	Pewamo-Westphalia	11-0
2003 D3	Rachel Duthler	Grandville Calvin Christian	10-9*		2014 D3	Kenzie Wieber	Pewamo-Westphalia	11-6
2004 D3	Katie Martin	Boyne City	10-9*		2015 D3	Stephanie Lambeth	Frankenmuth	12-3*
2005 D3	Katie Shaw	Lakeview	12-0*		2016 D3	Kasey Staley	Clare	12-4*
2006 D3	Carly Schiffer	Ovid-Elsie	11-6		2017 D3	Kasey Staley	Clare	12-0
2007 D3	Kahty Angelova	Adrian Madison	10-6		2018 D3	Anna Harmeling	Boyne City	11-6
2008 D3	Elizabeth Willford	Gladwin	11-3					

PV – Class D/Division 4 Champions

1998 D	Becky Prielipp	Marion	8-3*		2009 D4	Kirstie Wieber	Pewamo-Westphalia	11-3*
1999 D	Becky Prielipp	Marion	8-8*		2010 D4	Kirstie Wieber	Pewamo-Westphalia	12-0*
2000 D4	Jamie Foote	Bath	9-6*		2011 D4	Kirstie Wieber	Pewamo-Westphalia	11-3
2001 D4	Jamie Foote	Bath	10-0*		2012 D4	Jaylee Brown	Onekama	10-0
2002 D4	Jessica Miela	Fife Lake Forest Area	10-3*		2013 D4	Amanda McDonald	Coleman	10-1
2003 D4	Jessica Miela	Fife Lake Forest Area	10-6*		2014 D4	Bethany Kuenzer	Pittsford	11-3
2004 D4	Jessica Miela	Fife Lake Forest Area	10-10½*		2015 D4	Tallison Wilson	Colon	11-0
2005 D4	Amanda Schafer	Pewamo-Westphalia	9-9		2016 D4	Sydnie Avery	Saugatuck	10-3
2006 D4	Karin Diebold	Central Lake	10-0		2017 D4	Katie Clement	Pittsford	10-6
2007 D4	Amanda Schafer	Pewamo-Westphalia	10-7		2018 D4	Ciera Weber	Fowler	10-3
2008 D4	Aubrey Schafer	Pewamo-Westphalia	9-9					

PV – UP Class AB/Division 1 Champions

1998 UPAB	Angela Abernathy	Marquette	8-6*		2009 UPD1	Jordan Kronshage	Calumet	9-6
1999 UPAB	Angela Abernathy	Marquette	10-0*		2010 UPD1	Jaimie Roberts	Kingsford	12-0*
2000 UPAB	Kristin Pearson	Escanaba	8-6		2011 UPD1	Rachel Crane	Houghton	9-0
2001 UPD1	Kristin Pearson	Escanaba	10-1*		2012 UPD1	Laura Alexander	Gladstone	9-0
2002 UPD1	Emily Browning	Sault Ste. Marie	9-2		2013 UPD1	Corina Armstrong	Sault Ste. Marie	8-6
2003 UPD1	Emily Browning	Sault Ste. Marie	9-9¼		2014 UPD1	Jamie Snowaert	Gladstone	9-6
2004 UPD1	Emily Browning	Sault Ste. Marie	9-6		2015 UPD1	Aleda Johnson	Negaunee	9-0
2005 UPD1	Jessica Hongisto	Gladstone	9-0		2016 UPD1	Sophia Sarorelli	Menominee	8-6
2006 UPD1	Brianna Weigele	Iron Mountain	9-0		2017 UPD1	Keirra Mayotte	Calumet	8-6
2007 UPD1	Megan Bunker	Sault Ste. Marie	9-6		2018 UPD1	Lilly Baker	Houghton	8-3
2008 UPD1	Jaime Roberts	Kingsford	9-6					

PV – UP Class C/Division 2 Champions

1998 UPC	Deb Palmer	Stephenson	9-0*\		2008 UPD2	Jamie Bloxsom	St. Ignace	8-6
	(Pam Bolduc/Ironwood also cleared 9-0*)				2009 UPD2	Kali Jo Marshall	St. Ignace	8-6
1999 UPC	Amy Hokenson	Manistique	8-11		2010 UPD2	Kali Jo Marshall	St. Ignace	9-1*
2000 UPC	Amy Hokenson	Manistique	9-0*		2011 UPD2	Nicole Emmblad	St. Ignace	8-6
2001 UPD2	Kate Ruegg	St. Igance	9-0*		2012 UPD2	Sarah Cullip	St. Ignace	8-6
2002 UPD2	Robin Vitton	Hancock	9-0*		2013 UPD2	Breanna Martin	Stephenson	8-6
2003 UPD2	Stephany Mishica	Hancock	9-0*		2014 UPD2	Libbie Doney	Ishpeming	8-6
2004 UPD2	Robin Vitton	Hancock	8-6		2015 UPD2	Katie Davis	Manistique	8-0
2005 UPD2	Robin Vitton	Hancock	8-6		2016 UPD2	Libbie Doney	Manistique	8-6
2006 UPD2	Shelby Bednarz	Norway	8-6		2017 UPD2	Michaela Peramaki	Munising	8-6
2007 UPD2	Jamie Bloxsom	St. Ignace	8-6		2018 UPD2	Ashley McDonald	Manistique	8-0

PV – UP Class C/Division 3 Champions

1998 UPD	Danielle Richmond	Eben Junction Superior Central	7-6*		2009 UPD3	Ashley Branham	Lake Linden-Hubbell	8-6
1999 UPD	Danielle Richmond	Superior Central	8-3*		2010 UPD3	Emily Lehto	Felch North Dickinson	8-6
2000 UPD	Nicole Coleman	Crystal Falls Forest Park	8-0		2011 UPD3	Victoria Cusick	Pickford	7-6
2001 UPD3	Lindsay Anonich	Wakefield	8-6*		2012 UPD3	Sarah Audette	Lake Linden-Hubbell	8-6
2002 UPD3	Lindsay Thome	Cooks Big Bay de Noc	8-6*		2013 UPD3	Sarah Audette	Rock Mid Peninsula	9-6
2003 UPD3	Emily Marsicek	Carney-Nedeau	9-½*		2014 UPD3	Michaela Peramaki	Munising	9-0
2004 UPD3	Lauren Marshall	Rapid River	8-6		2015 UPD3	Sarah Audette	Munising	10-¼*
2005 UPD3	Lauren Marshall	Rapid River	9-6*			(Michaela Peramaki/Munising also cleared 10-¼*)		
2006 UPD3	Lauren Marshall	Rapid River	9-6*		2016 UPD3	Stephanie Harry	Lake Linden-Hubbell	7-6
2007 UPD3	Lauren Marshall	Rapid River	10-0*		2017 UPD3	Clare Cottle	Pickford	8-6
2008 UPD3	Emily Bushie	Bessemer	9-1		2018 UPD3	MacKenzie LePage	Lake Linden-Hubbell	9-0

GIRLS LONG JUMP

Records

D1	19-3¾ (0.2)	Angelica Floyd	Clinton Township Chippewa Valley	2017
D2	18-9¼	Tiffany Ofili	Ypsilanti	2005
	18-9¼	Miasha Blair	Flint Southwestern Academy	2015
D3	18-6½	Sami Michell	Reed City	2012
D4	18-2½	Miranda Johnson	Ottawa Lake Whiteford	2013
UPD1	17-3½	Adeline Grier-Welch	Houghton	2012
UPD2	16-10	Emily McDonald	Gwinn	2016
UPD3	16-7½	Olivia Soumis	Ontonagon	2012

Records by Class (pre-2000 for LP, pre-2001 for UP)

A	19-8	Trinette Johnson	Detroit Cass Tech	1989
B	18-6	Lindsay Mulder	Grandville Calvin Christian	1997
C	18-11½	Kim Pearson	Muskegon Oakridge	1987
D	18-7½	Brittany Hedgepath	St. Joseph Lake Michigan Catholic	1998
UPAB	18-3	Becky Drake	Kingsford	1977
UPC	17-5½	Holly Brown	St. Ignace	1997
UPD	17-3½	DeDe Susterich	White Pine	1991

LJ – Class A/Division 1 Champions

1973 All	Anita Lee	Detroit Cass Tech	17-2¾*
1974 A/B	Anita Lee	Detroit Cass Tech	17-¾
1975 A	Anita Lee	Detroit Cass Tech	17-8*
1976 A	Cynthia Tett	Grand Rapids Ottawa Hills	18-1¾*
1977 A	Cynthia Tett	Grand Rapids Ottawa Hills	19-½*
1978 A	Chris Jones	Benton Harbor	18-10
1979 A	Lorri Thornton	Flint Central	19-7*
1980 A	Kori Gifford	Bloomfield Hills Andover	18-11
1981 A	Leteia Hughley	Flint Northern	18-8
1982 A	Chris Boehmer	Lapeer West	19-6¼
1983 A	Latonja Curry	Grand Rapids Ottawa Hills	17-8¼
1984 A	Latonja Curry	Grand Rapids Ottawa Hills	19-3¼w
1985 A	Susie Frodge	Midland Dow	18-2½
1986 A	Susie Frodge	Midland Dow	17-9
1987 A	Shaun Hawkins	Taylor Truman	18-0
1988 A	Trinette Johnson	Detroit Cass Tech	19-0
1989 A	Trinette Johnson	Detroit Cass Tech	19-8*
1990 A	Katrina Jones	Lansing Eastern	18-2½
1991 A	Nicki Walker	Saginaw Arthur Hill	17-4
1992 A	Colette Carter	Mt Clemens L'Anse Creuse	17-6
1993 A	Mwanza Russell	Southfield	17-7
1994 A	Marla Benford	Detroit Martin Luther King	18-0
1995 A	Mwanza Russell	Southfield	17-6½
1996 A	Marjoriea Hicks	Flint Northern	18-3¼w
1997 A	Charnita Allen	Portage Central	17-11¾
1998 A	Charnita Allen	Portage Central	18-1½
1999 A	Tanasha Williams	Ypsilanti	18-10¾
2000 D1	Joanna Grandas	Dearborn Edsel Ford	17-6½*
2001 D1	Marquita Howard	Ann Arbor Huron	17-10¼*
2002 D1	Janee Beville	Grand Rapids Ottawa Hills	18-0*
2003 D1	Janee Beville	Grand Rapids Ottawa Hills	18-4½*
2004 D1	Jennifer Anderson	Wayne Memorial	17-6½
2005 D1	Bettie Wade	Farmington	17-8½
2006 D1	Brittant Howard	Romulus	18-8½*
2007 D1	Monsherri Hall	Saginaw Arthur Hill	18-9*
2008 D1	Monsherri Hall	Saginaw Arthur Hill	18-1¼
2009 D1	Christienne Linton	Romulus	18-8¼
2010 D1	Ashley Watley	East Detroit	17-3
2011 D1	Tory Schiller	Grand Ledge	18-8
2012 D1	Cierrra Pryor	Jackson	19-0*
2013 D1	Cierrra Pryor	Jackson	19-½* (1.6)
2014 D1	Sekayi Bracey	East Kentwood	18-7¼ (0.7)
2015 D1	Sekayi Bracey	East Kentwood	17-5¾
2016 D1	Sekayi Bracey	East Kentwood	18-10 (1.5)
2017 D1	Angelica Floyd	Clinton Twp Chippewa Valley	19-3¾* (0.2)
2018 D1	Clare McNamara	Northville	18-7½w (3.2)

LJ – Class B/Division 2 Champions

1975 B	Joyce Horne	Three Rivers	17-4*
1976 B	Beth Brunn	Utica	18-5¾*
1977 B	Beth Brunn	Utica	18-4¾
1978 B	Janine Smithson	Flint Powers	18-3¾
1979 B	Lisa Gwuzdala	Bay City Glenn	18-3½
1980 B	Chris Boehmer	Lapeer West	17-7¼
1981 B	Lynn Fisher	Standish Sterling	17-7¾
1982 B	Debbie Baldridge	Monroe Jefferson	17-1½
1983 B	Kathy Kost	Mt Clemens L'Anse Creuse	18-4¼
1984 B	Shenitha Walker	Muskegon Heights	17-3
1985 B	Imelda Ramirez	St Joseph	17-4½
1986 B	Sandy Fleming	Mt Clemens Lutheran North	17-3¼
1987 B	Regina Clark	Saginaw Buena Vista	18-2
1988 B	Regina Clark	Saginaw Buena Vista	17-1¼
1989 B	Carrie Isanhart	Big Rapids	17-7¾
1990 B	Kara Baker	North Branch	17-½
1991 B	Carla Ploeg	Middleville Thornapple	17-10
1992 B	Carla Ploeg	Middleville Thornapple	17-11
1993 B	Carla Ploeg	Middleville Thornapple	17-7¾
1994 B	Carla Ploeg	Middleville Thornapple	18-2¼
1995 B	Amy DeJonge	Hudsonville Unity Christian	17-1
1996 B	Lindsay Mulder	Grandville Calvin Christian	18-2¾
1997 B	Lindsay Mulder	Grandville Calvin Christian	18-6*
1998 B	Brandis O'Neal	Detroit Renaissance	17-5¾
1999 B	Brandis O'Neal	Detroit Renaissance	17-8
2000 D2	Janae Bridges	Ypsilanti	17-8¾*
2001 D2	Alexis Noel	Livonia Ladywood	17-10*
2002 D2	Annie Diener	Pinconning	18-6¼*
2003 D2	Lisa Winkle	Grand Rapids South Christian	17-3
2004 D2	Aleese Heinzman	Auburn Hills Avondale	17-0
2005 D2	Tiffany Ofili	Ypsilanti	18-9¼*
2006 D2	Katie Guikema	Grand Rapids South Christian	18-6¼
2007 D2	Katie Guikema	Grand Rapids South Christian	18-1¾
2008 D2	Katie Guikema	Grand Rapids South Christian	18-3¾
2009 D2	Keyandrea Rohelia	Saginaw	18-6¼
2010 D2	Joylisa Davis	Bloomfield Hills Lahser	18-¼
2011 D2	Michaela Lewis	Flint Northwestern	18-1
2012 D2	Sidney Bisher	Yale	18-1¾
2013 D2	Janina Pollatz	Grand Rapids Christian	18-7
2014 D2	Gabriella Collins	Mt Morris	18-0
2015 D2	Miasha Blair	Flint Southwestern Academy	18-9¼*
2016 D2	Casey Korte	Gaylord	18-¼
2017 D2	Taylor Dziatczak	Macomb Lutheran North	17-11½
2018 D2	Suenomi Norinh	Zeeland East	18-1¾

LJ – Class C/Division 3 Champions

1974 C/D	Sue Bouck	Haslett	17-10½*
1975 C	Debbie Hughes	Fowlerville	17-2¼
1976 C	Valerie Horne	Montrose	17-1¾
1977 C	Judy Dalecki	Memphis	18-3½*
1978 C	Beth Veldhoff	Blissfield	17-8
1979 C	Carrie Butler	Howard City Tri County	17-2½
1980 C	Beth Veldhoff	Blissfield	18-4¾*
1981 C	Julie O'Donnell	Perry	18-1¾
1982 C	Kathy Olson	Byron Center	17-8
1983 C	Chris Tuerk	Harper Woods Lutheran East	17-5¼

1984 C	Chris Wilson	Ann Arbor Richard	17-5¾
1985 C	Kelly McKinley	DeWitt	17-3¾
1986 C	Chris Wilson	Ann Arbor Richard	18-7*
1987 C	Kim Pearson	Muskegon Oakridge	18-11½*
1988 C	Cathy Fromwiller	Marlette	17-9½
1989 C	Cathy Fromwiller	Marlette	18-1½
1990 C	Elizabeth Clark	New Haven	18-4½
1991 C	Angie Sneider	Morenci	17-5¼
1992 C	Kelly Vanschoyck	Blissfield	17-9
1993 C	Kelly Vanschoyck	Blissfield	17-1¼
1994 C	Becky Falkner	Decatur	17-5½
1995 C	Rhonda Cangealose	Dundee	17-2¾
1996 C	Katie Robison	Farwell	17-4¾
1997 C	Sarah Booms	Lake City	17-4
1998 C	Marie Derezinski	Muskegon Oakridge	17-0
1999 C	Erin McFarland	Saginaw Mi Luth Seminary	16-11 /2
2000 D3	Kelly Walker	Standish-Sterling	17-2*
2001 D3	Jenna Gaines	Breckenridge	17-½

2002 D3	Leighann Dowell	Millington	17-11*
2003 D3	Jenna Gaines	Breckenridge	17-2¾
2004 D3	Megan Garvey	Vermontville-Maple Valley	17-4
2005 D3	Chelsea Millen	Evart	17-4
2006 D3	Kortni Elsworth	Goodrich	17-½
2007 D3	Juandretta Oliver	Albion	18-1*
2008 D3	Whitney Rogers	Flint Hamady	16-11¼
2009 D3	Rachel Hoffman	Shelby	17-3¼
2010 D3	Kaisha Martin	Dowagiac	16-11
2011 D3	Sami Michell	Reed City	17-6½
2012 D3	Sami Michell	Reed City	18-6½*
2013 D3	Sami Michell	Reed City	17-3¼
2014 D3	Kaniya Weatherspoon	Napoleon	17-4½ (0.0)
2015 D3	Erica Sheahan	Ithaca	17-7¾
2016 D3	Erica Sheahan	Ithaca	17-10¼ (1.5)
2017 D3	Ella Suliman	Grass Lake	17-2½
2018 D3	Harlie Sweet	Onsted	17-3½

LJ – Class D/Division 4 Champions

1975 D	Linda Arnold	Grass Lake	17-0*
1976 D	Susan Saltzgaber	Tekonsha	16-10½
1977 D	Donna Whitehead	Glen Arbor Leelanau School	17-1¾*
1978 D	Debra Spieth	Camden Frontier	17-5¾*
1979 D	Maria Shoup	Mason County Eastern	17-5½
1980 D	Sue Steeby	Saginaw Mi Luth Seminary	18-3*
1981 D	Maria Shoup	Mason County Eastern	18-5*
1982 D	Jeanine Poritt	Suttons Bay	17-2½
1983 D	Jane Pincombe	Schoolcraft	16-8¼
1984 D	Melanie Lovely	Concord	17-3¼
1985 D	Brenda Stewart	Covert	17-6¼
1986 D	Cheri Swartout	Climax-Scotts	17-3¼
1987 D	Amy Piotter	Deerfield	17-4
1988 D	Angela Frick	Walkerville	17-6
1989 D	Sherine Rowell	Fowler	17-1¼
1990 D	Marnie Peplinski	Maple City Glen Lake	17-2¼
1991 D	Marnie Peplinski	Maple City Glen Lake	17-1
1992 D	Marnie Peplinski	Maple City Glen Lake	17-5
1993 D	Dana Falke	Deerfield	16-6¼
1994 D	Brooke Formsma	Battle Creek St. Phillip	16-¾
1995 D	Brooke Formsma	Battle Creek St Phillip	15-11
1996 D	Heidi Leidy	Galien	16-8¼

1997 D	Brittany Hedgepath	St. Joseph Lake Mich Catholic	17-5½
1998 D	Brittany Hedgepath	St. Joseph Lake Mich Catholic	18-7½*
1999 D	Brittany Hedgepath	St. Joseph Lake Mich Catholic	17-4¾
2000 D4	Erin McFarland	Michigan Lutheran Seminary	16-1*
2001 D4	Amanda Gatzner	Coleman	15-9½
2002 D4	Amanda Weber	Portland St. Patrick	17-2½*
2003 D4	Kyla Crawford	Burton Atherton	16-10
2004 D4	Amanda Weber	Portland St. Patrick	17-11¾*
2005 D4	Melissa Hale	Atlanta	17-0
2006 D4	Melissa Hale	Atlanta	17-0
2007 D4	Valerie Watkins	Detroit Urban Lutheran	16-9¾
2008 D4	Miranda Iles	Athens	17-2½
2009 D4	Amber Arndt	Beal City	17-2
2010 D4	Kelly David	Beal City	16-9
2011 D4	Rita Morris	Gobles	17-6¼
2012 D4	Miranda Johnson	Ottawa Lake Whiteford	17-8¾
2013 D4	Miranda Johnson	Ottawa Lake Whiteford	18-2½*
2014 D4	Miranda Johnson	Ottawa Lake Whiteford	18-6½w
2015 D4	Sarah Rievert	Unionville-Sebewaing	17-11¾
2016 D4	Akwia Tilton	Birmingham Roeper	17-6w (2.2)
2017 D4	Ally McLouth	Addison	17-¼
2018 D4	Katie VanHavel	Hillsdale Academy	17-4¾w (4.6)

LJ – UP Class AB/Division 1 Champions

1972 UP-All	Denise Redding	Gwinn	15-3½*
1973 UP-All	Pat Rector	Gwinn	15-7½*
1974 UPAB	Pat Rector	Gwinn	16-9*
1975 UPAB	Debbi Perry	West Iron County	15-8
1976 UPAB	Becky Drake	Kingsford	16-11½*
1977 UPAB	Becky Drake	Kingsford	18-3*
1978 UPAB	Becky Drake	Kingsford	18-½
1979 UPAB	Becky Drake	Kingsford	17-5
1980 UPAB	Julie Drake	Kingsford	16-10
1981 UPAB	Jean Tolfa	Escanaba	16-10
1982 UPAB	Jean Tolfa	Escanaba	17-½
1983 UPAB	Laura Gidley	Gwinn	16-2
1984 UPAB	Laura Gidley	Gwinn	17-0
1985 UPAB	Laura Gidley	Gwinn	16-6½
1986 UPAB	Laura Bero	Escanaba	15-7¾
1987 UPAB	Laura Bero	Escanaba	15-10
1988 UPAB	Laura Bero	Escanaba	16-11
1989 UPAB	Stacie Wiegman	Menominee	16-6
1990 UPAB	Jackie Sweeney	Gladstone	16-5
1991 UPAB	Mary Scherer	Marquette	15-10¾
1992 UPAB	Tiffany Hodge	Menominee	16-4
1993 UPAB	Tiffany Hodge	Menominee	15-11
1994 UPAB	Brooke Berube	Marquette	15-9
1995 UPAB	Tiffany Hodge	Menominee	17-¾

1996 UPAB	Lisa Potvin	Escanaba	16-2½
1997 UPAB	Nicole Grubb	Ishpeming Westwood	15-10½
1998 UPAB	Alexi WIlkinson	Marquette	16-7
1999 UPAB	Alexi WIlkinson	Marquette	16-5
2000 UPAB	Sarah Duesing	Sault Ste. Marie	15-7
2001 UPD1	Sarah Duesing	Sault Ste. Marie	16-3¾*
2002 UPD1	Hope Yomker	Calumet	14-7¾
2003 UPD1	Amanda Kudwa	Menominee	15-7½
2004 UPD1	Becky Kangas	Calumet	16-7¼*
2005 UPD1	Becky Kangas	Calumet	16-4½
2006 UPD1	Becky Kangas	Calumet	17-½*
2007 UPD1	Erin Gignac	Menominee	16-5¼
2008 UPD1	Melissa Christensen	West Iron County	16-2¾
2009 UPD1	Kristin Nelson	Iron Mountain	16-6½
2010 UPD1	Jaime Roberts	Kingsford	16-8½
2011 UPD1	Adeline Grier-Welch	Houghton	17-¾*
2012 UPD1	Adeline Grier-Welch	Houghton	17-3½
2013 UPD1	Carlee Benzie	Kingsford	15-11¾
2014 UPD1	Allia Stwart	Menominee	15-1¾
2015 UPD1	Chelsea Jacques	Calumet	16-6
2016 UPD1	Kristina Tetzlaff	Menominee	15-4
2017 UPD1	Sydney Mills	Gladstone	15-10½
2018 UPD1	Rachael Hunt	Marquette	15-2½

LJ – UP Class C/Division 2 Champions

1974 UPC	Mary Seaton	Hancock	15-7*
1975 UPC	Pam Selden	L'Anse	15-10½*
1976 UPC	Sharon Ahlberg	Iron River West Iron Country	16-5½*
1977 UPC	Pat Louma	Ironwood	16-6½*
1978 UPC	Jan Merrick	Negaunee	16-10¼*
1979 UPC	Janet Dzarnowski	Iron River West Iron County	15-1½
1980 UPC	Jan Merrick	Negaunee	15-9½
1981 UPC	Betsy Nault	Ishpeming Westwood	16-4
1982 UPC	Marion Walker	St. Ignace	16-1
1983 UPC	Julie Kemppainen	Hancock	16-3
1984 UPC	Shirley Newland	L'Anse	15-11
1985 UPC	Shirley Newland	L'Anse	16-3¼

1986 UPC	Kathy Amos	Ontonagon	16-7
1987 UPC	Shirley Newland	L'Anse	15-6¼
1988 UPC	Mary Hoefferle	Ontonagon	15-3¼
1989 UPC	Nicole McMullin	L'Anse	15-5
1990 UPC	Tyling Simmons	St. Ignace	15-7½
1991 UPC	Nicole McMullin	L'Anse	16-½
1992 UPC	Tyling Simmons	St. Ignace	16-2
1993 UPC	Kelly Klein	Stephenson	15-11½
1994 UPC	Kelly Klein	Stephenson	16-1¼
1995 UPC	Holly Brown	St. Ignace	16-9½
1996 UPC	Holly Brown	St. Ignace	16-6¾
1997 UPC	Holly Brown	St. Ignace	17-5½*

1998 UPC	Allegra Saving	Iron River West Iron County	16-2
1999 UPC	Kylie Anderson	Ishpeming	16-3
2000 UPC	Kylee Anderson	Ishpeming	15-7½
2001 UPD2	Casey McGrath	Ironwood	14-7¾*
2002 UPD2	Leslie Luehmann	Ishpeming	15-9*
2003 UPD2	Leslie Luehmann	Ishpeming	15-1½
2004 UPD2	Leslie Luehmann	Ishpeming	16-2½*
2005 UPD2	Jessica Wood	Republic-Michigamme	16-2¼
2006 UPD2	Tori Nault	Ishpeming Westwood	16-4¼*
2007 UPD2	Jessica Wood	Ishpeming	16-4¼*
2008 UPD2	Carlen Smith	Hancock	15-5¼
2009 UPD2	Samantha Radecki	St. Ignace	14-9
2010 UPD2	Dani Gagne	Norway	15-2¾
2011 UPD2	Dani Gagne	Norway	16-8¼*
2012 UPD2	Dani Gagne	Norway	15-9
2013 UPD2	Alexis Golfis	West Iron County	14-3¾
2014 UPD2	Autumn Orm	St. Ignace	15-3¼
2015 UPD2	Nassi Thomas	Ishpeming	14-10½
2016 UPD2	Emily McDonald	Gwinn	16-10*
2017 UPD2	Michaela Peramaki	Munising	15-8¾
2018 UPD2	Heather Lamb	St Ignace	14-8½

LJ – UP Class C/Division 3 Champions

1974 UPD	Mary Jo Sartori	Crystal Falls Forest Park	16-0*
1975 UPD	Shari Yipe	Brimley	15-10½
1976 UPD	Michelle Davis	Bark River-Harris	15-11½
1977 UPD	Connie Miettinen	Republic-Michigamme	16-10*
1978 UPD	Wendy Darling	Republic-Michigamme	16-5½
1979 UPD	Jennifer Maksym	White Pine	16-2¾
1980 UPD	Debbie Ives	Bark River-Harris	16-1
1981 UPD	Debbie Ives	Bark River-Harris	17-2*
1982 UPD	Debbie Ives	Bark River-Harris	16-6½
1983 UPD	Linda Lefebvre	Lake Linden-Hubbell	15-2½
1984 UPD	Michelle Hatfield	Pickford	15-3
1985 UPD	Gail Keranen	Lake Linden-Hubbell	15-8½
1986 UPD	Theresa Petrick	Bark River-Harris	15-6
1987 UPD	Theresa Petrick	Bark River-Harris	15-11
1988 UPD	Julie Elsing	Rock-Mid Peninsula	15-7¼
1989 UPD	Marie Sawicky	Baraga	16-2
1990 UPD	DeDe Sustraich	White Pine	15-9¾
1991 UPD	DeDe Susterich	White Pine	17-3½*
1992 UPD	Janeen Forslund	Bessemer	15-7½
1993 UPD	Janeen Forslund	Bessemer	15-11
1994 UPD	Tawna Urmon	Mackinac Island	14-10
1995 UPD	Crystal Brunelle	Wakefield	16-½
1996 UPD	Tawna Urmon	Mackinaw Island	16-7
1997 UPD	Jaclyn BeBeau	Bessemer	15-5½
1998 UPD	Holly Brown	St. Ignace	16-10
1999 UPD	Tiffanay Adams	Engadine	15-4½
2000 UPD	Kim McDonald	Felch North Dickinson	15-11¼
2001 UPD3	Stephanie Boyer	Rapid River	15-2¾*
2002 UPD3	Stephanie Boyer	Rapid River	16-1¾*
2003 UPD3	Stephanie Boyer	Rapid River	15-9¼
2004 UPD3	Jamie VanEnkevort	Bark River-Harris	15-3¾
2005 UPD3	Jamie VanEnkevort	Bark River-Harris	15-7¼
2005 UPD3	Jamie VanEnkevort	Bark River-Harris	15-9¾
2007 UPD3	Jesse Ledy	Pickford	15-11¾
2008 UPD3	Emily Leto	Felch North Dickinson	15-5
2009 UPD3	Olivia Soumis	Ontonagon	16-4¾*
2010 UPD3	Olivia Soumis	Ontonagon	16-5½*
2011 UPD3	Olivia Soumis	Ontonagon	16-2
2012 UPD3	Olivia Soumis	Ontonagon	16-7½*
2013 UPD3	Teslyn Tyner	Eben Junction Superior Cent	15-3½
2014 UPD3	Sara Sivula	Carney-Nedeau	14-8¼
2015 UPD3	Paige Blake	Ontonagon	14-11¾
2016 UPD3	Laura Lyons	Lake Linden-Hubbell	15-3
2017 UPD3	Laura Lyons	Lake Linden-Hubbell	15-5
2018 UPD3	Laura Lyons	Lake Linden-Hubbell	16-½

GIRLS SHOT

Records

D1	49-11¾	Corinne Jemison	East Kentwood	2018
D2	48-9¾	Mary Angell	Byron Center	2007
D3	46-9¾	Becky Breisch	Edwardsburg	2001
D4	44-1½	Erica Lechner	Harbor Springs	2016
UPD1	38-1¼	Emily McLean	Sault Ste Marie	2018
UPD2	38-4	Andrea Smith	Ironwood	2001
UPD3	42-½	Ashley Bishop	Pickford	2002

Records by Class (pre-2000 for LP, pre-2001 for UP)

A	45-7	Karen Sapp	Temperence Bedford	1983
B	44-7	Alana Robinson	Grosse Ille	1998
C	44-0	Sara Neely	Bath	1988
D	40-9	Theresa Wright	Marcellus	1986
UPAB	39-5½	Cheryl Jacobson	Escanaba	1989
UPC	38-9½	Lydia Edwards	Gwinn	1999
UPD	37-8	Jill Lewis	Lake Linden-Hubbell	1986

SP – Class A/Division 1 Champions

(3.63k / 8lbs)

1973 All	Jane Pearce	Holt	38-5*	
1974 A/B	Jane Pearce	Holt	41-10¾*	
1975 A	Helen Williams	Detroit Northeastern	40-7	
1976 A	Sharon Upshaw	Mt Clemens	45-½*	
1977 A	Josephine Mask	Lansing Sexton	41-6½	
1978 A	Josephine Mask	Lansing Sexton	43-¾	
1979 A	Pam McGee	Flint Northern	45-¼	

(4k / 8.82lbs)

1980 A	Delores Bennett	Pontiac Central	44-8¼*	
1981 A	Vivian Fisher	Pontiac Central	43-2½	
1982 A	Alice Short	Farmington Hills Harrison	42-7½	
1983 A	Karen Sapp	Temperance Bedford	45-7*	
1984 A	Debbie Duncan	Ann Arbor Huron	40-7¼	
1985 A	Sonya Payne	Ann Arbor Huron	43-¼	
1986 A	Sonya Payne	Ann Arbor Huron	44-10½	
1987 A	Kim Sanford	East Lansing	39-11	
1988 A	LaTonya White	Flint Northern	42-7½	
1989 A	LaTonya White	Flint Northern	44-3	
1990 A	Karyn Quick	Battle Creek Central	44-5¾	
1991 A	Jessica Ballenger	Romeo	41-8¾	
1992 A	Jessica Ballenger	Romeo	42-5	
1993 A	Rafa. Lopez-McKnight	Okemos	41-2¼	
1994 A	Suzie Von Bernuth	Okemos	41-1½	
1995 A	Suzie Von Bernuth	Okemos	42-5	
1996 A	Mellissa Brousseau	Alpena	42-5	
1997 A	Mellissa Brousseau	Alpena	44-9¾	
1998 A	Michelle Fowler	Romeo	42-11½	
1999 A	April Phillips	Fraser	43-8¾	
2000 D1	Tiffany Grubaugh	Salem	41-11½*	
2001 D1	Melissa Ballard	Holt	40-6	
2002 D1	Takara Dunning	Kalamazoo Central	40-11	
2003 D1	Kamitra Carroll	Flint Carman-Ainsworth	45-6¼*	
2004 D1	Takara Dunning	Kalamazoo Central	41-8½	
2005 D1	Takara Dunning	Kalamazoo Central	43-0	
2006 D1	Joy Rolfe	Fraser	43-1	

2007 D1	Norianna Brown	Port Huron	42-3½
2008 D1	Tia Brooks	East Kentwood	48-½*
2009 D1	Alysha Johnson	Walled Lake Western	42-5¾
2010 D1	Alysha Johnson	Walled Lake Western	42-3¼
2011 D1	Angela Bursey	Pontiac	44-0
2012 D1	Sam Pavlika	Novi	40-0
2013 D1	Mariah Davis	East Kentwood	44-10½
2014 D1	Charde Madoula-Bey	Ann Arbor Skyline	42-6¼
2015 D1	Emily Maier	Canton	46-2
2016 D1	Kayli Johnson	Grosse Pointe South	44-7¾
2017 D1	Aniya Davis	Grand Rapids Ottawa Hills	40-10½
2018 D1	Corinne Jemison	East Kentwood	49-11¾*

SP – Class B/Division 2 Champions

(3.63k / 8lbs)

1975 B	Jane Pearce	Holt	43-7*
1976 B	Doni Meier	Richland Gull Lake	38-1
1977 B	Audrey Artz	Grosse Ille	38-8
1978 B	Deana Adams	Jackson Northwest	39-4½
1979 B	Shelly Dagley	Lapeer West	40-3¼

(4k / 8.82lbs)

1980 B	Sue Maceroni	Richmond	40-1½*
1981 B	Shelly Lape	Jackson Northwest	38-5¾
1982 B	Lisa Wesley	Detroit Northern	41-0*
1983 B	Sharon Granberry	Flint Beecher	39-1½
1984 B	Anita Capone	Paw Paw	38-6
1985 B	Sue Breternitz	Hemlock	40-5¾
1986 B	Sue Breternitz	Hemlock	41-11¼*
1987 B	Karen Wood	Ionia	41-8½
1988 B	Alison Fournier	Coloma	39-9½
1989 B	Tamie Gipe	Wyoming Park	40-9¼
1990 B	Karie Kuzma	Otisville LakeVille	38-9¼
1991 B	Karri Kuzma	Otisville LakeVille	41-1 ½
1992 B	Amy Houghton	Paw Paw	41-10½
1993 B	Shahla Bolbolan	Fremont	41-9½
1994 B	Shahla Bolbolan	Fremont	43-3¼
1995 B	Makiba Batten	Detroit Renaissance	41-4½
1996 B	Makeba Batten	Detroit Renaissance	40-9¼
1997 B	Makeba Batten	Detroit Renaissance	42-2*
1998 B	Alana Robinson	Grosse Ille	44-7*
1999 B	Becky Breisch	Edwardsburg	42-8½
2000 D2	Natasha Neal	Wyoming Park	40-11¾
2001 D2	Kari Taylor	Chelsea	41-5¾
2002 D2	Kari Taylor	Chelsea	42-8¾
2003 D2	Tamara Parr	Coloma	39-6¾
2004 D2	Whitney Nevins	Eaton Rapids	41-¼
2005 D2	Mary Angell	Byron Center	39-10¼
2006 D2	Mary Angell	Byron Center	41-9½
2007 D2	Mary Angell	Byron Center	48-9¾*
2008 D2	Kristin Cameron	Algonac	40-8¾
2009 D2	Victoria Buhr	Cheboygan	44-2
2010 D2	Kimmy Schmid	Haslett	41-½
2011 D2	Brittany Mann	Detroit Country Day	41-0
2012 D2	Brittany Mann	Detroit Country Day	41-11
2013 D2	Brittany Casey	Zeeland East	41-9¾
2014 D2	Brittany Casey	Zeeland East	43-1¼
2015 D2	Nikole Sargent	Flint Powers	45-4¾
2016 D2	Nikole Sargent	Flint Powers	47-5½
2017 D2	Elizabeth Pyles	Cadillac	45-4
2018 D2	Brianna Copley	Whitehall	42-5

SP – Class C/Division 3 Champions

(3.63k / 8lbs)

1974 C/D	Sue Carlson	Bath	38-11¼*
1975 C	Pat Stopcsynski	Shelby	37-11
1976 C	Sue Carlson	Bath	36-11¼
1977 C	Annette Bohach	North Muskegon	39-7*
1978 C	Annette Bohach	North Muskegon	46-¾*
1979 C	Annette Bohach	North Muskegon	48-6*

(4k / 8.82lbs)

1980 C	Julie Ravary	Erie-Mason	39-6½*
1981 C	Mendy Matuzak	Lincoln-Alcona	40-2*
1982 C	Marge Albaugh	Bullock Creek	41-10¾*
1983 C	Yvonne Laderach	Erie-Mason	41-9¼
1984 C	Yvonne Laderach	Erie-Mason	42-0*
1985 C	Jeania Stuppia	Clare	42-5*
1986 C	Jami Skuse	Lincoln Alcona	40-10
1987 C	Sarah Neely	Bath	41-3
1988 C	Sarah Neely	Bath	44-0*
1989 C	Connie Claus	Rogers City	40-6½
1990 C	Karen Mann	Quincy	39-2
1991 C	Jenny Groh	Decatur	37-11
1992 C	Tracy Kangas	Vermontville-Maple Valley	38-5
1993 C	Trena Cook	Harper Woods Lutheran East	39-8½
1994 C	Kim Sturm	Elkton-Pigeon-Bayport	40-5
1995 C	Liz Mulvaney	Hemlock	42-6¼
1996 C	Liz Mulvaney	Hemlock	43-¾
1997 C	Jane Ludtke	White Cloud	42-4½
1998 C	Leslie Woodcock	St. Louis	40-2½
1999 C	Amiee Stiverson	Pittsford	39-5½
2000 D3	Becky Breisch	Edwardsburg	46-4¾*
2001 D3	Becky Breisch	Edwardsburg	46-9¾*
2002 D3	Mary Raney	Vassar	44-2
2003 D3	Mary Raney	Vassar	42-½
2004 D3	Lauren Buresh	Morley-Stanwood	43-9¾
2005 D3	Lauren Buresh	Morley-Stanwood	43-11½
2006 D3	Lauren Buresh	Morley-Stanwood	44-4¼
2007 D3	Samantha Cormier	Frankenmuth	41-10
2008 D3	Ashlyn Gulvas	Standish-Sterling	44-6¼
2009 D3	Ashlyn Gulvas	Standish-Sterling	44-5¼
2010 D3	Tonia Pratt	Michigan Center	40-9¾
2011 D3	Tonia Pratt	Michigan Center	40-7
2012 D3	Kayla Deering	Elkton-Pigeon-Bayport	41-8¼
2013 D3	Kayla Deering	Elkton-Pigeon-Bayport	42-11½
2014 D3	Kayla Deering	Elkton-Pigeon-Bayport	44-11
2015 D3	Cali McLean	Watervliet	40-11
2016 D3	Brooklin Klopf	Montrose	40-3¼
2017 D3	Brooklin Klopf	Montrose	45-½
2018 D3	Alicia Aldrich	Beaverton	44-7½

SP – Class D/Division 4 Champions

(3.63k / 8lbs)

1975 D	Abby Currier	Lake City	37-1¼*
1976 D	Abby Currier	Lake City	39-9*
1977 D	Renee Naert	Akron Fairgrove	41-3½*
1978 D	Penny Neer	North Adams	41-1½
1979 D	Jill Treml	Mason County Eastern	41-7¼*

(4k / 8.82lbs)

1980 D	Kay Schmitt	Fowler	37-5*
1981 D	Sheri Stone	Akron Fairgrove	36-8
1982 D	Carla Herwarth	Athens	40-6½*
1983 D	Marcia Holstege	Allendale	38-1¾
1984 D	Rona Westdorp	McBain	37-1¾
1985 D	Theresa Wright	Marcellus	39-11
1986 D	Theresa Wright	Marcellus	40-9*
1987 D	Amy Griffiths	Litchfield	38-2
1988 D	Teresa Green	Colon	36-5
1989 D	Teresa Green	Colon	37-11½
1990 D	Teresa Green	Colon	38-11¼
1991 D	Amy Roe	Athens	37-5
1992 D	Amy Roe	Athens	38-9½
1993 D	Allison Greenman	Central Lake	37-1
1994 D	Toyra Lunzy	Eau Claire	38-8¼
1995 D	Zabina Brock	Central Lake	40-1¼
1996 D	Amanda Kirksey	North Muskegon	39-6½
1997 D	Robin Wiersma	Potterville	36-7¼
1998 D	Sarah Chobot	Mendon	39-6
1999 D	Sarah Chobot	Mendon	39-5½
2000 D4	Sarah Adelaine	Harbor Springs	41-9*
2001 D4	Jeaniae Lawton	Harper Woods Gallagher	39-10
2002 D4	Jeaniae Lawton	Harper Woods Gallagher	39-10
2003 D4	Katie McPhee	Potterville	39-6
2004 D4	Deedee Briggs	Vandercook Lake	39-7½
2005 D4	Deedee Briggs	Vandercook Lake	39-7¼
2006 D4	Cirana Jones	Fulton-Middleton	38-7¾
2007 D4	Hilary England	Marion	36-11¾
2008 D4	Beth Rohl	New Buffalo	39-1
2009 D4	Jasmine Hines	Central Lake	40-2
2010 D4	Jasmine Hines	Central Lake	42-7*
2011 D4	Jasmine Hines	Central Lake	38-9
2012 D4	Elizabeth Herriman	Sand Creek	39-0
2013 D4	Elizabeth Herriman	Sand Creek	40-11
2014 D4	Jade Madison	New Buffalo	43-8¼*
2015 D4	Mara Carter	Lawrence	40-2
2016 D4	Erica Lechner	Harbor Springs	41-11¾
2017 D4	Erica Lechner	Harbor Springs	44-1½*
2018 D4	Allie Vanous	Litchfield	40-4

SP – UP Class AB/Division 1 Champions

(3.63k / 8lbs)

1972	UP-All	Jamie Brebner	Marquette	33-3½*
1973	UP-All	Rhonda Connery	Felch North Dickinson	33-1
1974	UPAB	Anne Eslinger	Iron Mountain	32-5½
1975	UPAB	Ann Van Dyke	Escanaba	35-2½*
1976	UPAB	Dawn LaPine	Escanaba	39-¾*
1977	UPAB	Dawn LaPine	Escanaba	43-10½*
1978	UPAB	Lori Mosca	Kingsford	33-10
1979	UPAB	Lori Hollowell	Gwinn	34-9½

(4k / 8.82lbs)

1980	UPAB	Kelly Berrigen	Escanaba	35-4¼*
1981	UPAB	Julie Bahrman	Gwinn	34-3½
1982	UPAB	Julie Bahrman	Gwinn	35-9¾*
1983	UPAB	April Mecario	Gwinn	32-9½
1984	UPAB	Gaye Wright	Menominee	33-2½
1985	UPAB	Jill Applin	Kingsford	36-1*
1986	UPAB	Jill Applin	Kingsford	35-9
1987	UPAB	Dindy North	Gwinn	38-¾*
1988	UPAB	Dindy North	Gwinn	38-4½*
1989	UPAB	Cheryl Jacobson	Escanaba	39-5½*
1990	UPAB	Lori Creten	Gladstone	32-8¼
1991	UPAB	Shelly LaFave	Marquette	34-9½
1992	UPAB	Shelly LaFave	Marquette	36-8½
1993	UPAB	Missy VanDamme	Gwinn	36-10
1994	UPAB	Nichole Fisher	Escanaba	36-0
1995	UPAB	Jennifer Taylor	Marquette	36-4
1996	UPAB	Jennifer Taylor	Marquette	38-11¼
1997	UPAB	Jennifer Taylor	Marquette	37-0
1998	UPAB	Allison Conaway	Escanaba	34-9½
1999	UPAB	Jacoba Williamson	Marquette	36-4½
2000	UPAB	Allyson Conaway	Escanaba	36-3¼
2001	UPD1	Jobeth Williams	Negaunee	37-1½*
2002	UPD1	Kelly Pavlovich	Ironwood	35-10
2003	UPD1	Jobeth Williams	Negaunee	33-¼
2004	UPD1	Jenna Guay	Escanaba	34-2½
2005	UPD1	Kasey Willis	Calumet	34-2¾
2006	UPD1	Amy Tinkell	Negaunee	35-¼
2007	UPD1	Molly Wiltzius	Kingsford	34-1
2008	UPD1	Molly Wiltzius	Kingsford	35-11½
2009	UPD1	Meredith Buck	Gwinn	34-4¾
2010	UPD1	Natalie Berryman	Houghton	36-¼
2011	UPD1	Keenan Marana	Negaunee	33-5½
2012	UPD1	Savannah Roush	Negaunee	31-10½
2013	UPD1	Kirsten Iwanski	Marquette	31-4
2014	UPD1	Annika Wheeler	Houghton	34-4
2015	UPD1	Kendra Monette	Houghton	31-5½
2016	UPD1	Kendra Monette	Houghton	36-6
2017	UPD1	Kendra Monette	Houghton	35-5½
2018	UPD1	Emily McLean	Sault Ste Marie	38-1¼*

SP – UP Class C/Division 2 Champions

(3.63k / 8lbs)

1974	UPC	Kristine Steen	Ontonagon	31-8*
1975	UPC	Cathy Phillips	L'Anse	33-3½*
1976	UPC	Beth Beaudoin	Manistique	34-2¾*
1977	UPC	Kelly Gorgan	St. Ignace	35-10*
1978	UPC	Connie Erickson	Negaunee	34-7¾
1979	UPC	Brenda Witz	Ishpeming Westwood	35-6½

(4k / 8.82lbs)

1980	UPC	Kelly Grogan	St. Ignace	35-3*
1981	UPC	Brenda Witz	L'Anse	34-2½
1982	UPC	Brenda Witz	L'Anse	34-4½
1983	UPC	Amy Kraft	L'Anse	34-1½
1984	UPC	Amy Kraft	L'Anse	35-8¼*
1985	UPC	Laura Shifflet	Newberry	34-5½
1986	UPC	Ann Hoefferle	Ontonagon	37-10*
1987	UPC	Ann Hoefferle	Ontonagon	37-¾
1988	UPC	Amy Mathias	Stephenson	32-7
1989	UPC	Jennie Hetwick	Newberry	32-3½
1990	UPC	Brandi VanBuren	Ishpeming	37-6¼
1991	UPC	Brandi VanBuren	Ishpeming	35-6½
1992	UPC	Danielle Thiernan	Munising	34-7
1993	UPC	Sandra Brattge	St. Ignace	34-10
1994	UPC	Leslie Jerks	Iron Mountain	35-½
1995	UPC	Mary Lund	Manistique	34-11
1996	UPC	Kim Palovich	Ironwood	34-4¼
1997	UPC	Kelly Evosevich	Iron Mountain	33-4½
1998	UPC	Rosie Aho	Munising	36-10
1999	UPC	Lydia Edwards	Gwinn	38-9½*
2000	UPC	Andrea Smith	Ironwood	34-10
2001	UPD2	Andrea Smith	Ironwood	38-4*
2002	UPD2	Melanie Barker	Manistique	35-2
2003	UPD2	Brittany Reynolds	Ishpeming	34-9
2004	UPD2	Brenda Burby	Rudyard	35-8½
2005	UPD2	Brenda Burby	Rudyard	38-3¼
2006	UPD2	Shelby Bednarz	Norway	32-9½
2007	UPD2	Rachel Ryan	Munising	33-4½
2008	UPD2	Briana Raasio	Hancock	34-3¾
2009	UPD2	Hannah Holma	West Iron County	35-4¾
2010	UPD2	Hannah Holma	West Iron County	36-10
2011	UPD2	Hannah Holma	West Iron County	36-9¼
2012	UPD2	Savannah Dugan	Rudyard	35-1
2013	UPD2	Megan Miatech	West Iron County	34-10
2014	UPD2	Sarah Smith	St. Ignace	35-¼
2015	UPD2	Marissa Maino	Ishpeming	35-1
2016	UPD2	Marissa Maino	Ishpeming	35-0
2017	UPD2	Marissa Maino	Ishpeming	36-6¼
2018	UPD2	Rachael Tefft	West Iron County	36-6½

SP – UP Class C/Division 3 Champions

(3.63k / 8lbs)

1974	UPD	Mary Zelinski	Watersmeet	35-0*
1975	UPD	Mary Zelinski	Watersmeet	33-3½
1976	UPD	Mary Zelinski	Watersmeet	35-10*
1977	UPD	Kathy Matonoch	Bessemer	35-4
1978	UPD	Karen Marcotte	Lake Linden-Hubbell	36-1½*
1979	UPD	Jennifer Maksym	White Pine	36-2*

(4k / 8.82lbs)

1980	UPD	Jennifer Maksym	White Pine	34-5*
1981	UPD	Sally Schroeder	Engadine	33-10½
1982	UPD	Sally Schroeder	Engadine	33-7½
1983	UPD	Laurie Lynn	Pickford	33-9¾
1984	UPD	Mary LaBeske	Hancock	35-5½*
1985	UPD	Jill Lewis	Lake Linden-Hubbell	36-5½*
1986	UPD	Jill Lewis	Lake Linden-Hubbell	37-8*
1987	UPD	Jill Lewis	Lake Linden-Hubbell	37-3
1988	UPD	Giene Cain	Crystal Falls Forest Park	33-4
1989	UPD	Atenai Motu	Carney-Nedeau	34-0
1990	UPD	Giene Cain	Crystal Falls Forest Park	34-8½
1991	UPD	Brooke Hine	Bessemer	35-1½
1992	UPD	Brooke Hine	Bessemer	32-3
1993	UPD	Sarah Hood	Baraga	37-½
1994	UPD	Sarah Hood	Baraga	36-3
1995	UPD	Sarah Greenlund	Rapid River	36-6½
1996	UPD	Sarah Greenlund	Rapid River	35-9½
1997	UPD	Lisa Froberg	Rapid River	34-4¼
1998	UPD	Kristina Peltier	Rapid River	34-3
1999	UPD	Lisa Froberg	Rapid River	35-5
2000	UPD	Ashley Bishop	Pickford	37-6½
2001	UPD3	Ashley Bishop	Pickford	39-8*
2002	UPD3	Ashley Bishop	Pickford	42-½*
2003	UPD3	Emily Marsicek	Carney-Nedeau	38-3¾
2004	UPD3	Angela Leckson	Big Bay de Noc	37-5
2005	UPD3	Angie Leckson	Big Bay de Noc	38-9
2006	UPD3	Angie Leckson	Big Bay de Noc	40-1
2007	UPD3	Karrie Meyers	Bark River-Harris	34-0
2008	UPD3	Karrie Meyers	Bark River-Harris	36-11
2009	UPD3	Karrie Meyers	Bark River-Harris	35-7½
2010	UPD3	Brianna Raasio	Hancock	33-9¼
2011	UPD3	Chelsey Gerou	Rock Mid Peninsula	34-11½
2012	UPD3	Avery Jackson	Bessemer	30-9
2013	UPD3	Savannah Dugan	Rudyard	39-2
2014	UPD3	Savannah Dugan	Rudyard	38-11
2015	UPD3	Alyssa Kyvarinen	Brimley	35-6
2016	UPD3	Ashtyn Buss	Engadine	37-3¾
2017	UPD3	Ashtyn Buss	Engadine	36-3
2018	UPD3	Ashtyn Buss	Engadine	38-4

GIRLS DISCUS

Records

D1	163-9	Malin Smith	Lansing Waverly		2018
D2	159-5	Mary Angell	Byron Center		2007
D3	158-3	Becky Breisch	Edwardsburg		2001
D4	141-6	Caylin Bonser	Harbor Springs		2016
UPD1	126-4	Missy Gurchinoff	Houghton		2005
UPD2	122-10	Hunter Perry	Rudyard		2011
UPD3	116-1	Sydni Petrie	Bark River-Harris		2013

Records by Class (pre-2000 for LP, pre-2001 for UP)

A	146-0	Suzie Von Bernuth	Okemos	1995
B	155-6	Alana Robinson	Grosse Ile	1997
C	150-7	Donna Wright	Parchment	1984
D	130-9	Abby Currier	Lake City	1977
UPAB	123-5	Shelly Chapman	Marquette	1977
UPC	124-8	Rebecca Palmer	Stephenson	1993
UPD	119-5	Jill Rairigh	Pickford	1996

DT – Class A/Division 1 Champions

1976 A	Sheila Warren	Lansing Waverly	108-0*		1998 A	Mese Roberts	Holt	138-9
1977 A	Sheila Warren	Lansing Waverly	123-6*		1999 A	Tiffany Grubaugh	Salem	134-7
1978 A	Josephine Mask	Lansing Sexton	130-3*		2000 D1	Shanna Dubose	Adrian	132-6*
1979 A	Mary Palaszek	Grand Rapids Union	120-4		2001 D1	Tara Kennedy	Woodhaven-Brownstone	134-7*
1980 A	Michelle Pfeiffer	Davison	136-7*		2002 D1	Anna Baker	Saline	135-6*
1981 A	Betsy Smith	Midland	130-10		2003 D1	Astin Steward	Okemos	154-9*
1982 A	Rhonda Morehead	Adrian	132-3		2004 D1	Maggie Dwyer	Grand Haven	137-2
1983 A	Jeannette Long	Kalamazoo Central	134-1		2005 D1	Charity Sunderman	Jackson	132-0
1984 A	Cammie Maki	Warren-Lincoln	115-9		2006 D1	Alexander Hartley	Lake Orion	134-8
1985 A	Starry Hodge	Flint Northwestern	128-0		2007 D1	Lauren Krupsky	Livonia Churchill	129-9
1986 A	Lisa Waite	Ann Arbor Pioneer	132-5		2008 D1	Samantha Lockhart	Lansing Sexton	139-11
1987 A	Lisa Waite	Ann Arbor Pioneer	140-3*		2009 D1	Lindsey Karpowicz	Grandville	136-1
1988 A	LaTonya White	Flint Northern	136-4		2010 D1	Kylie Basarabski	Rockford	125-10
1989 A	LaTonya White	Flint Northern	123-1		2011 D1	Taylor Gunn	West Bloomfield	136-7
1990 A	Erinn Wikaryasz	Milford	125-3		2012 D1	Jae-vyn Wortham	Harrison Twp L'Anse Creuse	136-6
1991 A	Ruth Thawnghmung	Battle Creek Lakeview	128-7		2013 D1	Jae-vyn Wortham	Harrison Twp L'Anse Creuse	144-6
1992 A	Katja Pettinen	Lansing Eastern	144-9*		2014 D1	Jae-vyn Wortham	Harrison Twp L'Anse Creuse	140-5
1993 A	Elizabeth Kluka	Macomb L'Anse Creuse North	134-5		2015 D1	Andrea Sietsema	GR Forest Hills Central	145-5
1994 A	Summer Beydoun	Dearborn Fordson	135-0		2016 D1	Quiara Wheeler	Grand Blanc	136-2
1995 A	Suzie Von Bernuth	Okemos	146-0*		2017 D1	Corrine Jamison	East Kentwood	151-0
1996 A	Karen Chastina	Lake Orion	140-2		2018 D1	Malin Smith	Lansing Waverly	163-9*
1997 A	Mese Roberts	Holt	139-4					

DT – Class B/Division 2 Champions

1976 B	Suzanne Maynard	Fremont	115-4*		1998 B	Alana Robinson	Grosse Ile	154-0
1977 B	Diane Arens	Hastings	126-5*		1999 B	Becky Breisch	Edwardsburg	151-5
1978 B	Diane Arens	Hastings	116-10		2000 D2	Morgan Acre	Otisville LakeVille	133-5*
1979 B	Sue Lang	Warren Woods	131-2*		2001 D2	Kari Taylor	Chelsea	140-3*
1980 B	Diana Mason	Ortonville Brandon	121-0		2002 D2	Kari Taylor	Chelsea	142-3*
1981 B	Sharon Granberry	Flint Beecher	138-11*		2003 D2	Siobhan Martin	Wyoming Park	141-0
1982 B	Sharon Granberry	Flint Beecher	135-4		2004 D2	Sara Camacho	Byron Center	141-5
1983 B	Sharon Granberry	Flint Beecher	129-7		2005 D2	Jessica Rutherford	West Branch Ogemaw Heights	132-8
1985 B	Sue Breternitz	Hemlock	119-7		2006 D2	Jessica Rutherford	West Branch Ogemaw Heights	151-11*
1986 B	Sue Breternitz	Hemlock	130-8		2007 D2	Mary Angell	Byron Center	159-5*
1987 B	D-Ann Hoppa	Fremont	125-3		2008 D2	Jamie Smith	Richland Gull Lake	152-1
1988 B	D-Ann Hoppa	Fremont	135-9		2009 D2	Samantha Lockhart	Lansing Sexton	139-7
1989 B	Tamie Gipe	Wyoming Park	127-8		2010 D2	Kendra Meyers	Grand Rapids West Catholic	132-5
1990 B	Connie Most	Remus-Chippewa Hills	127-7		2011 D2	Brittany Mann	Detroit Country Day	141-10
1991 B	Andrea Balliet	Gaylord	126-9		2012 D2	Brittany Mann	Detroit Country Day	156-8
1992 B	Liz Mast	Caledonia	133-9		2013 D2	Kaylyn Hill	Auburn Hills Avondale	133-8
1993 B	Liz Mast	Caledonia	137-0		2014 D2	Brittany Casey	Zeeland East	138-10
1994 B	Shahla Bobolan	Fremont	142-10*		2015 D2	Mary Hecksel	Eaton Rapids	136-8
1995 B	Alana Robinson	Grosse Ille	139-11		2016 D2	Nicole Sargent	Flint Powers	147-9
1996 B	Makiba Batten	Detroit Renaissance	147-7*		2017 D2	Elizapeth Pyles	Cadillac	146-3
1997 B	Alana Robinson	Grosse Ile	155-6*		2018 D2	Allie Filiatraut	Dearborn Divine Child	136-0

DT – Class C/Division 3 Champions

1976 C	Marylin Kegler	Capac	102-2*		1985 C	Yvonne Laderach	Erie-Mason	129-9
1977 C	Sheri Anderson	Shelby	121-0*		1986 C	Pam Shepherd	Stockbridge	122-4
1978 C	Annette Bohach	North Muskegon	127-0*		1987 C	Kathy Boss	Howard City Tri County	126-1
1979 C	Lisa Clark	Clinton	135-4*		1988 C	Connie Claus	Rogers City	135-8
1980 C	Julie Ravary	Erie Mason	124-1		1989 C	Connie Claus	Rogers City	137-9
1981 C	Julie Ravary	Erie Mason	124-1		1990 C	Theresa Hall	Byron	118-1
1982 C	Donna Wright	Parchment	117-0		1991 C	Theresa Hall	Byron	129-4
1983 C	Donna Wright	Parchment	135-7*		1992 C	Tracy Kangas	Vermontville-Maple Valley	121-10
1984 C	Donna Wright	Parchment	150-7*		1993 C	Judy Pavlik	Whittemore-Prescott	124-5

1994 C	Dasha Yeakey	Union City	140-11
1995 C	Liz Mulvaney	Hemlock	127-8
1996 C	Liz Mulvaney	Hemlock	134-2
1997 C	Jane Ludtke	White Cloud	139-0
1998 C	Jane Ludtke	White Cloud	138-1
1999 C	Rebecca McCann	Freeland	127-4
2000 D3	Becky Breisch	Edwardsburg	156-11*
2001 D3	Becky Breisch	Edwardsburg	158-3*
2002 D3	Bridgette Maynard	Madison Heights Foley	127-5
2003 D3	Mary Raney	Vassar	134-0
2004 D3	Jenn Hawley	Kent City	125-0
2005 D3	Jill Walton	Kingsley	126-9
2006 D3	Katie Christensen	Lakeview	131-6
2007 D3	Stacey Harrington	Lakeview	125-6
2008 D3	Ashlyn Gulvas	Standish-Sterling	130-3
2009 D3	Ashlyn Gulvas	Standish-Sterling	144-9
2010 D3	Andrea Hiler	Watervliet	143-0
2011 D3	Tonia Pratt	Michigan Center	147-10
2012 D3	Rebecca Cousineau	Leslie	124-8
2013 D3	Ashley Bussing	Adrian Madison	135-0
2014 D3	Molly Franke	Kingsley	122-11
2015 D3	Jessica Marvin	Byron	118-6
2016 D3	Keri Frahm	Frankenmuth	138-4
2017 D3	Amanda Schaare	Clinton	145-7
2018 D3	Amanda Schaare	Clinton	128-0

DT – Class D/Division 4 Champions

1976 D	Abby Currier	Lake City	121-6*
1977 D	Abby Currier	Lake City	130-9*
1978 D	Penny Neer	North Adams	126-1
1979 D	Kay Pringle	Peck	124-4
1980 D	Kay Pringle	Peck	122-6
1981 D	Colleen Wiseman	Marine City Holy Cross	118-0
1982 D	Sheri Stone	Akron-Fairgrove	125-6
1983 D	Sheri Stone	Akron-Fairgrove	121-6
1984 D	Stephanie Joseph	Flint Carman	128-6
1984 D	Julie Diedrich	Webberville	119-7
1985 D	Sandra Cook	Mendon	124-7
1986 D	Alisa Swan	Akron-Fairgrove	119-1
1987 D	Doreen Kenney	Athens	122-1
1988 D	Leah Petiprin	Akron-Fairgrove	113-7
1989 D	Deanna Lauchlen	Camden-Frontier	121-9
1990 D	Deanna Lauchlen	Camden-Frontier	121-5
1991 D	Shana Bombrys	Mendon	112-1
1992 D	Ellie Harden	Whitmore Lake	116-4
1993 D	Pam Blonde	Litchfield	125-11
1994 D	Sara Zuiderveen	McBain N. Michigan Christian	116-3
1995 D	Sara Zuiderveen	McBain N. Michigan Christian	111-3
1996 D	Amanda Romel	Posen	117-11
1997 D	Amber June	Pittsford	116-6
1998 D	Lynnea Sibley	Walkerville	128-0
1999 D	Lynnea Sibley	Walkerville	122-1
2000 D4	Jeaniae Lawton	Harper Woods Gallagher	130-6*
2001 D4	Jeaniae Lawton	Harper Woods Gallagher	137-6*
2002 D4	Jeaniae Lawton	Harper Woods Gallagher	135-11
2003 D4	Alica Tanner	Walkerville	124-9
2004 D4	Stephanie Robinson	Walkerville	123-9
2005 D4	Sophie Braden	Birmingham Roeper	127-2
2006 D4	Alyssa Panck	New Haven	117-2
2007 D4	Erica Marsh	Litchfield	123-11
2008 D4	Erica Marsh	Litchfield	125-1
2009 D4	Carly Trieber	Unionville-Sebewaing	127-2
2010 D4	Heather Lantis	Hillsdale Academy	117-3
2011 D4	Lena Madison	New Buffalo	120-5
2012 D4	Alexander Ferguson	Albion	124-3
2013 D4	Jade Madison	New Buffalo	120-7
2014 D4	Jade Madison	New Buffalo	123-0
2015 D4	Maddie Clark	Pittsford	129-7
2016 D4	Caylin Bonser	Harbor Springs	141-6*
2017 D4	Maddie Clark	Pittsford	137-06
2018 D4	Allie Vanous	Litchfield	132-10

DT – UP Class AB/Division 1 Champions

1976 UPAB	Jean White	Escanaba	109-2*
1977 UPAB	Shelly Chapman	Marquette	123-5*
1978 UPAB	Sue Rogers	Escanaba	109-10
1979 UPAB	Lori Hollowell	Gwinn	98-5
1980 UPAB	Sharon Kuivinen	Escanaba	99-7
1981 UPAB	Julie Bahrman	Gwinn	103-2
1982 UPAB	Julie Bahrman	Gwinn	111-10
1983 UPAB	Alvetta Bence	Gwinn	102-4
1984 UPAB	Tori Knispel	Menominee	117-0
1985 UPAB	Tori Knispel	Menominee	107-7
1986 UPAB	Chris Nemacheck	Gladstone	109-1
1987 UPAB	Colleen Ordiway	Sault Ste. Marie	118-3
1988 UPAB	Dindy North	Gwinn	121-0
1989 UPAB	Cheryl Jacobson	Escanaba	105-4
1990 UPAB	Janet Lancour	Escanaba	105-11
1991 UPAB	Cheryl Jacobson	Escanaba	105-4
1992 UPAB	Carly Bourque	Sault Ste. Marie	114-8
1993 UPAB	Missy VanDamme	Gwinn	112-1
1994 UPAB	Jennifer Taylor	Marquette	117-3
1995 UPAB	Jennifer Taylor	Marquette	111-10
1996 UPAB	Beck Hirm	Escanaba	120-8
1997 UPAB	Jessica Donckers	Marquette	105-10
1998 UPAB	Allison Conaway	Escanaba	109-10
1999 UPAB	Shana Watson	Gladstone	112-8
2000 UPAB	Allyson Conaway	Escanaba	113-3
2001 UPD1	Kimberly Kimmes	Marquette	109-7*
2002 UPD1	Jobeth Williams	Negaunee	101-7
2003 UPD1	Julian Plimpton	Gladstone	100-11
2004 UPD1	Missy Gurchinoff	Houghton	119-0*
2005 UPD1	Missy Gurchinoff	Houghton	126-4*
2006 UPD1	Sarah DeShambo	Escanaba	112-2
2007 UPD1	Molly Wiltzius	Kingsford	123-7
2008 UPD1	Molly Wiltzius	Kingsford	113-9
2009 UPD1	Stephanie Bonenfant	Calumet	95-1½
2010 UPD1	Natalie Berryman	Houghton	106-0
2011 UPD1	Emi Tomassucci	Iron Mountain	101-9
2012 UPD1	Jessica Young	Gladstone	106-6
2013 UPD1	Jessica Young	Gladstone	111-6
2014 UPD1	Hailee Richards	Negaunee	111-1
2015 UPD1	Jenny Brandt	Escanaba	112-0
2016 UPD1	Jenny Brandt	Escanaba	108-10
2017 UPD1	Jenny Brandt	Escanaba	123-6
2018 UPD1	Rylee Palmer	Kingsford	101-0

DT – UP Class C/Division 2 Champions

1976 UPC	Shelly Millimaki	Ishpeming	104-8*
1977 UPC	Tammy Huotari	Ontonagon	105-1*
1978 UPC	Connie Erickson	Negaunee	110-5*
1979 UPC	Becky England	Newberry	105-8
1980 UPC	Becky England	Newberry	114-11*
1981 UPC	Cathy Delongchamp	Ishpeming Westwood	102-9
1982 UPC	Tricia Andrews	Stephenson	104-9
1983 UPC	Lisa Annola	Ishpeming Westwood	111-4
1984 UPC	Kathy Hill	L'Anse	110-4
1985 UPC	Darlene Eakin	Houghton	107-4
1986 UPC	Peggy Gasperich	Calumet	103-9
1987 UPC	Kim Mathias	Stephenson	104-10
1988 UPC	Vicky Butchko	Manistique	122-0*
1989 UPC	Pam Havelka	Stephenson	104-0
1990 UPC	Pam Havelka	Stephenson	107-5
1991 UPC	Polly Luoma	Houghton	115-10
1992 UPC	Mandy Palzewicz	Stephenson	106-7
1993 UPC	Rebecca Palmer	Stephenson	124-8*
1994 UPC	Kim Pavlovich	Ironwood	103-4
1995 UPC	Mary Lund	Manistique	106-10
1996 UPC	Mary Lund	Manistique	118-9
1997 UPC	Lydia Edwards	Gwinn	101-11
1998 UPC	Courtney Paananen	Ishpeming	115-7
1999 UPC	Martha Frantti	Calumet	112-1
2000 UPC	Martha Frantti	Calumet	117-1
2001 UPD2	Andrea Smith	Ironwood	115-2
2002 UPD2	Becky Genschow	L'Anse	100-6*
2003 UPD2	LeAnn Gingras	Iron Mountain	98-0
2004 UPD2	Katie Spencer	St. Ignace	112-4*
2005 UPD2	Katie Spencer	St. Ignace	115-9*
2006 UPD2	Sandy Turay	Ishpeming Westwood	110-2
2007 UPD2	Katie Turay	Ishpeming Westwood	99-10
2008 UPD2	Veronica Stone	Ishpeming	98-8
2009 UPD2	Brianna Raasio	Hancock	100-10
2010 UPD2	Desirae Rasmussen	West Iron County	120-4*
2011 UPD2	Hunter Perry	Rudyard	114-10

2012 UPD2	Hunter Perry	Rudyard	122-10*
2013 UPD2	Olivia Rouleau	Hancock	102-5
2014 UPD2	Kelly Wright	St. Ignace	107-2
2015 UPD2	Marissa Maino	Ishpeming	109-4

2016 UPD2	Marissa Maino	Ishpeming	115-5
2017 UPD2	Marissa Maino	Ishpeming	108-9
2018 UPD2	Rachael Tefft	West Iron County	112-7

DT – UP Class C/Division 3 Champions

1976 UPD	Karen Marcotte	Lake Linden-Hubbell	112-8*
1977 UPD	Karen Marcotte	Lake Linden-Hubbell	103-3
1978 UPD	Karen Marcotte	Lake Linden-Hubbell	113-2*
1979 UPD	Michelle Ozzello	Wakefield	107-1
1980 UPD	Karen Rohrer	Cedarville	100-3
1981 UPD	Colleen Ross	Rudyard	95-4
1982 UPD	Lisa Ogren	Ewen-Trout Creek	101-8
1983 UPD	Kris Swartz	Rapid River	103-9
1984 UPD	Vickie McKiddie	Pickford	113-6*
1985 UPD	Vickie McKiddie	Pickford	113-7*
1986 UPD	Vickie McKiddie	Pickford	114-1*
1987 UPD	Michelle Pearson	Wakefield	112-9
1988 UPD	Missy Hatfield	Pickford	105-3
1989 UPD	Annette Brown	Brimley	109-10
1990 UPD	Julie Eddy	Crystal Falls Forest Park	104-6¾
1991 UPD	Maggie Clawson	Pickford	97-0
1992 UPD	Shanell Johnson	Rapid River	102-8
1993 UPD	Sarah Hood	Baraga	118-2*
1994 UPD	Sarah Hood	Baraga	110-2
1995 UPD	Jill Rairigh	Pickford	107-4
1996 UPD	Jill Rairigh	Pickford	119-5*
1997 UPD	Lisa Froberg	Rapid River	108-0

1998 UPD	Mandy Bishop	Pickford	113-5
1999 UPD	Mandy Bishop	Pickford	116-9
2000 UPD	Ashley Bishop	Pickford	112-10
2001 UPD3	Ashley Bishop	Pickford	114-3*
2002 UPD3	Ashley Bishop	Pickford	108-4
2003 UPD3	Anna Stenvig	Baraga	104-2
2004 UPD3	Liz Reno	Cedarville	104-7
2005 UPD3	Juliann Plimpton	Rapid River	112-1
2006 UPD3	Angela Leckson	Cooks-Big Bay de Noc	102-2
2007 UPD3	Karrie Meyers	Bark River-Harris	105-3
2008 UPD3	Karrie Meyers	Bark River-Harris	108-6
2009 UPD3	Karrie Meyers	Bark River-Harris	115-7*
2010 UPD3	Brianna Raasio	Hancock	97-8
2011 UPD3	Jackie Formolo	Engadine	110-6
2012 UPD3	Neena Brockway	Rapid River	105-7
2013 UPD3	Sydni Petrie	Bark River-Harris	116-1*
2014 UPD3	Anne Archambeau	Brimley	108-4
2015 UPD3	Alyssa Hyvarinen	Brimley	104-8
2016 UPD3	Alyssa Hyvarinen	Brimley	103-4
2017 UPD3	Mackenzie Barr	Cedarville	103-10
2018 UPD3	Holly Jo Wardynski	Ontonagon	101-1

GIRLS 4 x 100 RELAY

Records

D1	46.28	Oak Park	Janae Barksdale, Anna Jefferson, Brianna Holloway, Tamea McKelvy	2016
D2	48.40	GR Forest Hills Eastern	Sam Reno, Camron Nelson, Jaclyn Goble, Alli Gutschow	2013
D3	49.57	St Charles	Najiyah Holden, Hope Kushion, Celine Whiren, Mikayla Williams	2018
D4	50.41	Pewamo-Westphalia	Rachel Schmitt, Allison Fedewa, Kara Thelen, Abbey Hengesbach	2010
UPD1	51.22	Gladstone	Sarah Skultety, Miranda Miron, Laura Pfotenhauer, Beth Frazer	2007
UPD2	52.36	Manistque	Jasmine Volk, Natalie Pohlman, Hannah Bryant, Sam Bryant	2010
UPD3	51.92	Crystal Falls Forest Park	Hilary Roose, Ana Cornelia, Kathleen Grandahl, Maria Valesano	2010

Records by Class (pre-2000 for LP, pre-2001 for UP)

A	47.81	Detroit Cass Tech	Stacey Randolph, Angela Jones, Cynthia Merritt, Dana McKeithen	1985
B	48.95	Detroit DePorres	Atemia McClure, Kenyetta Kendrick, Janiene Dickson, Nicole Embry	1990
C	50.42	Detroit Dominican	Nichelle Ewing, Bedria Purifoy, Daminya Allison, Dorothea Game	1994
	(hand 49.9y	Muskegon Catholic	Karen Washington, Jean Dault, Mary Gauthier, Cecelia Terrien	1978)
	(hand 49.9y	North Muskegon	Shelly Guy, Cindy Tjarksen, Julie Panzenhagen, Cindi Guy	1978)
	(hand 49.9y	Detroit Lutheran West	Darlene Fortman, Celeste Allen, Becky Wilson, Donna Smith	1980)
D	50.5	Covert	Betty Wright, Janice Lewis, Lisa Lewis, Meriel Toliver	1982)
UPAB	50.1y	Marquette	Kris Tacculini, Suzanne Patterson, Mary Ottoson, Lisa Wiedenhoefer	1978
UPC	51.8	St Ignace	Anna Pemble, Melanie Sheridan, Holly Brown, Richelle Robinson	1995
UPD	52.7y	Norway	Jan Sandrin, Linda Grodeski, Darlene Allen, Darla Koller	1979

4 x 100 – Class A/Division 1 Champions

(y=4 x 110 yards)

1973	All	Cadillac	51.3y*	Linda Porter, Sandra Oliver, Cheryl Soles, Bonnie Bell
1974	AB	Flint Northern	49.8y*	Kay Turner, Sheila Hopson, Elaine Hamlin, Lucinda Price
1975	A	Detroit Cass Tech	49.5y*	Angela Johnson, Julie Gibson, Cheryl Gilliam, Angela Cumberlander
1976	A	Detroit Cass Tech	48.6y*	Cheryl Gilliam, Angela Johnson, Donna Smitherman, Sharon Sims
1977	A	Mt Clemens	48.2y*	Crystal Thomas, Marcelle Rickman, Roberta Brown, Eileen Rickman
1978	A	Grand Rapids Ottawa Hills	48.8y	Cynthia Tett, Mary Hughes, Rhonda Fleming, Fawn Crosby
1979	A	Detroit Mackenzie	48.8y	Lela Fitten, Alfreda Bronson, Melane Tillman, Myra Jones
1980	A	Flint Northern	49.2y	Yvonne Lee, Lagretta Riley, Edyth Childress, Leteia Hughley
1981	A	Flint Northern	48.5	Joanna Childress, Terri Barber, Yvonne Lee, Leteia Hughley
1982	A	Grand Rapids Ottawa Hills	48.5	Jackie Tyson, Latonja Curry, Sharon Ambrose, Filipa Smith
1983	A	Benton Harbor	48.2*	Chauna Burton, Linda McMillion, Sandra Rice, Jeanan Langston
1984	A	Benton Harbor	47.9*	Marita Rimpson, Chauna Burton, Sandra Rice, Linda McMillion
1985	A	Detroit Cass Tech	47.81*	Stacey Randolph, Angela Jones, Cynthia Merritt, Dana McKeithen
1986	A	Detroit Cass Tech	49.3	Kenya Clement, Benita Jackson, Stacey Randolph, Darchelle Ross
1987	A	Flint Central	48.4	Patrice Verdun, Quita Turner, Kayce Shephard, Sarita Verdun
1988	A	Ann Arbor Pioneer	48.92	Bridgette Thomas, Diane Laurin, Sheila Rowry, Crystal Braddock
1989	A	Detroit Cass Tech	48.82	Chelsea Young, Trinette Johnson, Sonya Knight, Shemeakia Dunwoody
1990	A	Ann Arbor Pioneer	48.96	Dana Newberry, Nicole Franklin, Seena Waters, Heather Brown
1991	A	Ann Arbor Pioneer	48.2	Hayley Wilkins, Heather Brown, Seena Walters, Vania Nelson
1992	A	Ann Arbor Pioneer	49.54	Dana Newberry, Hayley Wilkins, Takiya Jenkins, Vania Nelson
1993	A	Kalamazoo Central	48.86	Terra Joyce, Kendra Worthy, D'Nielle Suhuba-Baruti, Jeannette Robinson

1994	A	Detroit Cass Tech	48.5	Lakesha Snoddy, Tiffany McNair, Emily Higgins, Chantelle Nagbe
1995	A	Detroit Cass Tech	48.38	Kanisa Williams, Lakesha Snoddy, Emily Higgins, Chantelle Nagbe
1996	A	Ann Arbor Pioneer	48.52	Ayesha George, Nyota Pieh, Robyn Woolfolk, Reagen Sidney
1997	A	Ann Arbor Pioneer	48.47	Ayesha George, Joneigh Slaughter, Robyn Woolfolk, Nyota Pieh
1998	A	Ann Arbor Pioneer	47.87	Jamilla Bowman, Joneigh Slaughter, Robyn Woolfolk, Nyota Pieh
1999	A	Ann Arbor Pioneer	49.04	Christine Kutchinski, Matiangela Mosely, Venice Jones, Jamillah Bowman
2000	D1	Ann Arbor Pioneer	48.40*	Cheryl Green, Mariangela Mosley, Venice Jones, Christine Ku
2001	D1	Detroit Cass Tech	48.37*	Crystal Lee, Ariss Seals, Karla Marshall, Crystal Higginbotham
2002	D1	Ann Arbor Pioneer	48.18*	Lauren Fortson, Candice Davis, Keisha Townsend, Cheryl Green
2003	D1	Detroit Mumford	48.34	Stephanie Porter, Dana Hill, Courtney Crosby, Jeannetta Stutts
2004	D1	Detroit Mumford	47.78*	Porsche Ries, Shayla Mahan, Dana Hill, Stephanie Porter
2005	D1	Detroit Mumford	47.15*	Stephanie Porter, Dana Hill, Shayla Mahan, Chanell Wright
2006	D1	Ann Arbor Pioneer	48.36	Ra'jae Marable, Kiara Moore, Brittiney Jones, Stephanie Foster
2007	D1	Ann Arbor Pioneer	48.17	Ra'jae Marable, Kiara Moore, Tiara Sharp, Paige Madison
2008	D1	Southfield Lathrup	48.38	Amber Avery, Tofunmi Akeredolu, Chelsea Gholston, Jordan Clark
2009	D1	Rockford	47.97	Courtney Klawieter, Abby Blanchard, Becky Caywood, Emma Breen
2010	D1	Rochester	48.42	Emily Leppek, Teanna Murray, Lauren Hetrick, Ashley Keyes
2011	D1	Novi	48.35	Jasmine Ward, D'Mya Davis, Janee Hood, Mariah Smith
2012	D1	Saline	48.45	Amanda Luurtsema, Quenee' Dale, Alana Hollis, Samantha Richart
2013	D1	Saline	48.57	Amanda Luurtsema, Aleca Rose, Alana Hollis, Quenee' Dale
2014	D1	Oak Park	47.35	Kailsi Latta-Thompson, Anna Jefferson, Johnyce Powell, Tamea McKelvy
2015	D1	Oak Park	48.17	Kailsi Latta-Thompson, Tamea McKelvy, Carlita Taylor, Anna Jefferson
2016	D1	Oak Park	46.28*	Janae Barksdale, Anna Jefferson, Brianna Holloway, Tamea McKelvy
2017	D1	Oak Park	46.69	Janae Barksdale, Aasia Laurencin, Karin Tate, Tamea McKelvy
2018	D1	Detroit Renaissance	47.42	Imani Jackson, Donae Adams, Paige Chapman, Mizan Thomas

4 x 100 – Class B/Division 2 Champions

(y=4 x 110 yards)

1975	B	Albion	50.8y*	Melanie Ridley, Karen Harris, Dawn Metzler, Charmain Mitchell
1976	B	Muskegon Catholic	50.6y*	Cindy Allore, Sue Bordeaux, Mary Gauthier, Terri Johnson
1977	B	Muskegon Catholic	49.8y*	Cindy Allore, Susan Bordeaux, Mary Gauthier, Terri Johnson
1978	B	Standish-Sterling	51.0y	Nancy Kurtz, Lori Marx, Lynn Fischer, Jennie McAlister
1979	B	St. Joseph	49.1y*	Shawn Watt, Joan Horton, Torre Ranum, Michele Priefer
1980	B	Flint Beecher	49.1*	Sheri Brock, Lajewell Gaston, Diane Wiley, Sandra Harris
1981	B	Auburn Hills Avondale	49.7y	Kay Buckhalter, Paula Buckhalter, Kathy Kaehler, Jean Tingley
1982	B	Muskegon Orchard View	49.8	Patty Wells, Teresa Anderson, Kiesha Fox, Colleen Gajeski
1983	B	Milan	49.8	Rhonda Pope, Karman Killyon, Pat Taylor, Anjer Delaine
1984	B	Muskegon Heights	49.9	Janet Evans, Sherry Kelly, Doris Hardiman, Shenitha Walker
1985	B	Flint Beecher	49.69*	Twynette Wilson, Michelle Westbrook, Jan Washington, Danita Sims
1986	B	Albion	49.9	Shasta Mace, Jessica Gamble, Paula Langston, Leslie Spicer
1987	B	Flint Beecher	49.02*	Daphne Perry, Yolanda Jones, Michelle Westbrook, Twynette Wilson
1988	B	Detroit DePorres	49.94	Kenyetta Kendrick, Tawanda Oree, Janiene Dickson, Nicole Embry
1989	B	Detroit DePorres	50.4	Atemia McClure, Kenyetta Kendrick, Janiene Dickson, Tawanda Oree
1990	B	Detroit DePorres	48.95*	Atemia McClure, Kenyetta Kendrick, Janiene Dickson, Nicole Embry
1991	B	Detroit DePorres	50.61	Jeanie Hill, Janiene Dickson, Chandra Spence, Atemia McClure
1992	B	Flint Beecher	51.13	Nikketa Williams, Carmia Marshall, Theresa Thomas, Rhosa Read
1993	B	Inkster	51.06	Tameka Gibson, Mirah Tatum, Faith Henderson, Charnell Lynn
1994	B	River Rouge	49.85	Kenyetta Grigsby, Kembria Peterson, Marie Edwards, Simby Bonner
1995	B	Cheboygan	51.11	Jessie Wenger, Denise Hesselink, Beca Robiadek, Betina Manzel
1996	B	Parma Western	50.49	Armanda Frank, Jana White, Jenny Leuken, Jessie Leuken
1997	B	Corunna	50.61	Anna Carr, Sarah Walworth, Alesha Caverly, Nicole Johnson
1998	B	Albion	49.2	Jamila Morehead, Alesha Ashley, Tracy Egnatuk, Martine Barbour
1999	B	Detroit Renaissance	49.80	Brandis O'Neal. Erin Anderson, Stephanie Douglas, Veryle Ro
2000	D2	Detroit Renaissance	48.69*	Fallon Jenkins, Erin Anderson, Brandis O'Neal, LaTosha Jollet
2001	D2	Ypsilanti	49.64	Denise Smith, Jennifer Frierson, Megan Hall, Janae Bridges
2002	D2	Romulus	49.61	Chrystal Austin, Marika Wise, Shaepree Lee, Patrice Beasley
2003	D2	Ypsilanti	49.59	Shannon Sanders, Tiffany Ofili, Denise Smith, Zanita Clipper
2004	D2	Saginaw	49.88	Charlea West, Ashley Staffney, Damonica Jackson, Dejuana Bonner
2005	D2	Lansing Waverly	49.40	Michelle Rogers, Tiara Adams, Shanaye Car, Jordan Dunn
2006	D2	Tecumseh	50.12	Katie Hunt, Lauren Prueter, Jessica Bloomer, Samantha Hong
2007	D2	Lansing Waverly	49.13	Shombrieka Williams, Tiara Adams, Jordan Dunn, Shanaye Carr
2008	D2	Lansing Waverly	49.13	Shombrieka Williams, Tiara Adams, Jordan Dunn, Shanaye Carr
2009	D2	Detroit Renaissance	49.13	Adrienne Parnell, Lorreal Jones, Tiara Heard, Ashlee Abraham
2010	D2	Flint Southwestern	48.92	Michaela Lewis, Chistal Wilson, Lashyla Nelson, Ciarra Adams
2011	D2	Flint Southwestern	49.08	Taylor McClain, Michaela Lewis, Lashyla Nelson, Ciarra Adams
2012	D2	Detroit Country Day	49.14	Jonell Nwabueze, Kendall Baisden, Natasha Wood, Sydney Cureton
2013	D2	Grand Rapids Forest Hills Eastern	48.40*	Sam Reno, Camron Nelson, Jaclyn Goble, Alli Gutschow
2014	D2	Flint Southwestern	49.41	Breanna Turner, Miaisha Blair, Diamond Boyd, Mildrenae Young
2015	D2	Lansing Waverly	49.87	Teaghan Thomas, Jabea Morris, Maya Garrett, Tra'chele Roberts
2016	D2	Lansing Waverly	48.70	Teaghan Thomas, Jazlynn Wilson, Maya Garrett, Tra'chele Roberts
2017	D2	Lansing Waverly	48.98	Teaghan Thomas, Priscilla Trainor, Maya Garrett, Tra'chele Roberts
2018	D2	Detroit Country Day	49.14	Jasmine Powell, Taylor Aibana, Ahvon Mitchell, Alexis Officer

4 x 100 – Class C/Division 3 Champions

(y=4 x 110 yards)

1974	CD	Montrose	51.0y*	Valerie Horne, Roni Nogaj, Sabrina Schmidt, Mary Nickoley
1975	C	Williamston	51.9y	Martha Powell, Karen Lockwood, Kelly Monette, Linda Merrifield
1976	C	Williamston	50.4y*	Cindy Clinton, Karen Lockwood, Kelly Monette, Linda Merrifield
1977	C	Detroit Lutheran West	50.2y*	Linda Crawford, Angela Holt, Darlene Fortman, Kristi Barksdale
1978	C	Muskegon Catholic	49.9y*	Karen Washington, Jean Dault, Mary Gauthier, Cecelia Terrien
		(North Muskegon also ran 49.9y*)		
1979	C (tie)	Montrose	50.7y	Pallastean Harris, Alfreda Bragg, Lizjuan Green Almedia Bragg
1979	C (tie)	North Muskegon	50.7y	Dana Precious, Shelly Guy, Cindy Tjarksen, Cindy Guy

1980	C	Detroit Lutheran West	49.9y*	Darlene Fortman, Celeste Allen, Becky Wilson, Donna Smith
1981	C	Whitehall	50.1	Kelly Rankin, Tracy Brandel, Yvette Hunter, Pam Sheesley
1982	C	Detroit Lutheran West	50.6	Lenore Stephen, Becky Wilson, Joya Davis, Donna Smith
1983	C	Detroit DePorres	50.1	Tisha Dias, Felicia Dias, Andrea McKenzie, Dawn Jones
1984	C	Detroit Country Day	50.4	Pam Laker, Natalie Greenspan, Whitney Bell, Kristi Jackson
1985	C	Cassopolis	50.44*	Ronda Lawson, Nicki Butkin, Janice Harp, Marla Mitchell
1986	C	Cassopolis	50.51	Janice Harp, Debbie Edwards, Aretha Glover, Ronda Lawson
1987	C (tie)	Detroit Country Day	51.25	Hameera Newman, Mary Bridges Marie Bridges, Diane Grauer
1987	C (tie)	Detroit DePorres	51.25	Kenyetta Kendrick, Tawanda Oree, Adele Mix, Nicole Embry
1988	C	New Haven	51.0	Sonja Clark, Shantel Crosby, Wendy Goodhue, Sue Veith
1989	C	Onsted	51.01	Jennifer Wood, Kelly Keefe, Kaurie Pantera, Naheed Irani
1990	C	New Haven	51.44	Irene Clark. Alvera Clark, Liz Clark, Donita Sims
1991	C	Cassopolis	50.8	Jean Couyeou, Ketmany Manichanh, Tilyne Christoper, Stacey Turner
1992	C	Cassopolis	51.8	Lisa Glover, Stacey Turner, Ketmany Manichanh, Tilyne Christopher
1993	C	Comstock Park	50.88	April Selka, Stephanie Brown, Renee Pardon, Regina Pardon
1994	C	Detroit Dominican	50.42*	Nichelle Ewing, Bedria Purifoy, Daminya Allison, Dorothea Game
1995	C	Quincy	51.94	Amanda May, Katherine Lynch, Billy Jo Hogle, Tara Montgomery
1996	C	Clare	51.10	Audrey Jelenek, Jill Jelenek, Meghan Smith, Jessica Champine
1997	C	Napoleon	50.77	Michelle Kline, Jessi Rudolph, Jessie Taylor, Jenny Hetu
1998	C	Napoleon	51.51	Jessica Roberts, Kate Decker, Jessi Rudolph, Jenny Hetu
1999	C	Napoleon	50.82	Jessica Roberts, Jenny Hetu, Maggie Clemens, Kate Declan
2000	D3	Albion	51.21*	Tracy Egnatuk, Ariane Payne, Deona Peace, Jamila Mohead
2001	D3	Shepherd	51.53	Jessica Quakenbush, Ashley Neuhaus, Anna Tschetter, Katie Porter
2002	D3	Muskegon Heights	50.28*	Crystal Sain, Brieanna Carter, Tamara Sullivan, Brandi Martin
2003	D3	Albion	50.63	Alpha Clark, Mika Clark, Kate Diedrick, Elyse Lee
2004	D3	Kent City	50.19*	Kristi Boehm, Courtney Zahrt, Sarah Shirey, Amber Holcomb
2005	D3	Albion	50.06*	Juandretta Oliver, Mika Clark, Bara Lovelace, Alpha Clark
2006	D3	Kent City	50.06*	Sarah Shirey, Kristi Boehm, Courtney Zahrt, Amber Holcomb
2007	D3	Albion	49.74*	Marcola Ridley, Juandretta Oliver Alyssa Alvarez, Joranda Chapman
2008	D3	Ann Arbor Gabriel Richard	51.13	Becky Meagher, Susie Pauley, Megan McIntyre, Kristen Gancalves
2009	D3	Albion	50.51	Marcola Ridley, Tre Washington, Amelia Bannister, Carly Moore
2010	D3	Kent City	50.58	Dena Bliss, Hannah Miller, Katie Murphy, Suzy Sticking
2011	D3	Bronson	51.34	Amberly Bercaw, Mariah Roberts. Cecilia Mendez, Lacie Lind
2012	D3	Bridgeport	50.22	Shonrea Matthews, Octavia Myles, Ce'Aira Richardson, Kimberly Balls
2013	D3	Pewamo-Westphalia	50.63	Sasha Platte, Jenna Thelen, Tori Klein, Kenzie Wieber
2014	D3	Pewamo-Westphalia	49.78	Sasha Platte, Jenna Thelen, Gabbie Hummel, Kenzie Wieber
2015	D3	Pewamo-Westphalia	50.86	Sarah Barrett, Claudia Heckman, Gabbie Hummel, Marissa Wirth
2016	D3	Pewamo-Westphalia	50.02	Claudia Heckman, Brenna Wirth, Kelly Thelen, Amelia Thelen
2017	D3	Dearborn Heights Robichaud	49.75	Shaquetta Woods, Kierra Rice, Mariah Harris, Terria Fisher
2018	D3	St Charles	49.57*	Najiyah Holden, Hope Kushion, Celine Whiren, Mikayla Williams

4 x 100 – Class D/Division 4 Champions

(y=4 x 110 yards)

1975	D	Battle Creek St Phillip	51.5y*	Pat Guerra, Sue Behnke, Sue Wzenski, Jane Beck
1976	D	Battle Creek St Phillip	51.1y*	Kathy Green, Lynn Brutsche, Peggy Nemeth, Pat Guerra
1977	D	Camden-Frontier	51.1y*	Denise Forrester, Sara Spieth, Debra Spieth, Brenda Moore
1978	D	Athens	51.2y	Anita Carpenter, Carol Clemence, Mary Miller, Cathy Clemence
1979	D	Athens	50.9*	Carol Clemence, Cathy Clemence, Julie Kinney, Mary Miller
1980	D	Athens	53.5	Mary Miller, Julie Kinney, Becky Carvine, Carrie VanHouten
1981	D	Covert	50.7*	Betty Wright, Vanessa Brice, Annette Perry, Merle Tolliver
1982	D	Covert	50.5*	Betty Wright, Janice Lewis, Lisa Lewis, Meriel Toliver
1983	D	Athens	51.6	Cara Voss, Kim Cousins, Jil Dolbee, Marcy Hinkley
1984	D	Athens	51.65*	Carla Voss, Jill Dilbee, Angie Brown, Marcy Hinkley
1985	D	Athens	51.54*	Cindy Cayo, Jackie Boddy, Angie Brown, Carla Voss
1986	D	New Haven	51.1	Wendy Goodhue, Barbara Bankston, Sue Veith, Kristal Mack
1987	D	Bridgman	51.67	Jeni Maxam, Karen Niemi, Angie Keltner, Ronja Pschigoda
1988	D	Athens	52.4	Ranae Hoskins, Melissa Stemaly, Mari Voss, Amy Miller
1989	D	Detroit Lutheran West	51.1	Toni Hunter, Pamela Ndom, Dwana McKee, Yvonne Hall
1990	D	Detroit Lutheran West	51.52*	Sylvia Edwards, Lasundres Bettis, Yvonne Hall, Pamela Ndon
1991	D	Detroit Lutheran West	51.38*	Sylvia Edwrads, Lasundres Bettis, Pam Ndon, Yvonne Hall
1992	D	Litchfield	52.64	Kammy Bills, Alicia Ochsenrider, Lesley Keeney, Dana Smith
1993	D	Royal Oak Shrine	52.00	Camey Ellis, Desma Johnson, Brandie Henderson, Erica Dunbar
1994	D	Battle Creek St Phillip	51.40	Heidi Curtiss, Stephanie Lantinga, Brecca Formsma, Brooke Formsma
1995	D	Maple City Glen Lake	52.78	Erin Gearhart, Kelly MacMillan, Chris Cyr, Erin Attwood
1996	D	St. Joseph Lake Michigan Catholic	51.77	Brittany Hedgepeth, Becky Dudding, Shelly Nelson, Amy Jovan
1997	D	Carsonville-Port Sanilac	52.4	Becky Slivka, Amber Berrien, Henneka Berrien, Julia Berrien
1998	D	Carsonville-Port Sanilac	51.7	Becky Slivka, Amber Berrien, Henneka Berrien, Julia Berrien
1999	D	St. Joseph Lake Michigan Catholic	51.92	Brittany Hedgepeth, Micehlle Sears, Rebecca Dudding, Naquasha Worsham
2000	D4	Saginaw Michigan Lutheran Seminary	51.45*	Erin McFarland, Jennie Mueller, Megan Falthaut, Faith Shmitz
2001	D4	Detroit Benedictine	51.78	Dessary Cranford, Crystal Young, Alex Thomas, Cynthia Jordan
2002	D4	Detroit Benedictine	51.65	Amy Sshneider, Ashley Weber, Heather Pung, Erika Fedewa
2003	D4	Pewamo-Westphalia	51.48	Amy Schneider, Ashley Weber, Vanessa Thelen, Dawn Pohl
2004	D4	Detroit Benedictine	51.39*	LaCresha Nix, Valerie Watkins, Terri Thomas, Seonetta Belin
2005	D4	Flint Hamady	51.24*	Shameeka Parrish, Jonae Coleman, Quannika Horne, Tara Johnson
2006	D4	Flint Hamady	51.15*	Jasmine Thomas, Jonae Coleman, Quannika Horne, Tara Johnson
2007	D4	Frankfort	51.06*	Keeton Spenceley, Britt Frantz, Abby Gilbert, Kelly Tousley
2008	D4	Pewamo-Westphalia	50.84*	Kristy Bengel, Allison Fedewa, Kyan Thelen, Abbey Hengesbach
2009	D4	Pewamo-Westphalia	50.63*	Rachel Schmitt, Allison Fedewa, Kara Thelen, Abbey Hengesbach
2010	D4	Pewamo-Westphalia	50.41*	Rachel Schmitt, Allison Fedewa, Kara Thelen, Abbey Hengesbach
2011	D4	Pewamo-Westphalia	50.50	Rachel Schmitt, Allison Jegla, Kyan Thelen, Kenzie Wieber
2012	D4	Onekama	51.44	Meredith Hengy, Nisha Collins, Alyson Fink. Breanna Fink
2013	D4	Reading	51.22	Jennifer Davis, Sam Pfeiffer, Teddi Zimmerman, Michelle Davis
2014	D4	Reading	51.60	Kaitlin Seager, Jennifer Davis, Samantha Pfeiffer, Teddi Zimmerman
2015	D4	Onekama	51.00	Medidith Hengy, Kassidy Ward, Alyson Fink, Alycia Peterson

2016	D4	New Lothrop	50.83	Skye Nancarrow, Alex Bedrosian, Syden Pope, Caitlyn Bruff
2017	D4	Fowler	51.49	McKenzie Feldpausch, Ciera Weber, McKenzie Koenigsknecht, Sidney Horak
2018	D4	Fowler	50.61	McKenzie Koenigsknecht, Kaitlyn Langin, Ciera Weber, Sidney Horak

4 x 100 – UP Class AB/Division 1 Champions

(y=4 x 110 yards)

1972	UP-All	Marquette	55.7y*	
1973	UP-All	Marquette	55.0y*	
1974	UPAB	Marquette	55.0y*	
1975	UPAB	Marquette	52.6y*	
1975	UPAB	Marquette	54.1y	
1976	UPAB	Escanaba	nt	
1977	UPAB	Kingsford	51.1y*	
1978	UPAB	Marquette	50.1y*	Kris Tacculini, Suzanne Patterson, Mary Ottoson, Lisa Wiedenhoefer
1979	UPAB	Escanaba	51.9	Jean Aiken, Sandy Davison, Tammy Sovey, Jean Tolfa
1980	UPAB	Escanaba	51.8	Jean Tolfa, Jill Bolm, Jean Aiken, Tammy Sovey
1981	UPAB	Marquette	52.4	Amy Dorais, Cathy Parejko, Jill Frailing, Beth Fisher
1982	UPAB	Marquette	52.7	Amy Dorais, Cathy Parejko, Jill MacDougall, Elizabeth Sarvello
1983	UPAB	Menominee	52.3	Michelle Blake, Karen Englund, Amy Poquette, Coralee Poquette
1984	UPAB	Marquette	52.2	Jill MacDougall, Stephanie Hurley, Jill Frailing, Kathry Richie
1985	UPAB	Escanaba	52.7	Candie Miron, Laurie Raymond, Liz Provo, Tammy Cook
1986	UPAB	Gwinn	52.0	Coleen Walker, Lesley Viitala, Earcella Henderson, Denise Dani
1987	UPAB	Gwinn	52.2	Cheryl French, Lesley Viitala, Shon Henderson, Denise Dani
1988	UPAB	Marquette	52.7	Aimee Waino, Lisa Hawley, Teri Busse, Tammy Busse
1989	UPAB	Marquette	53.1	Aimee Waino, Lisa Hawley, Teri Busse, Tammy Busse
1990	UPAB	Marquette	52.6	Aimee Waino, Amanda Smith, Terri Busse, Tammy Busse
1991	UPAB	Sault Ste. Marie	52.4	Ashley Beacom, Denise Fabry, Tammy Albom, Lisa Corbiere
1992	UPAB	Marquette	53.7	Shelly LaFave, Corinne Bohjanen, Colleen Michelson, Sarah Heikkil
1993	UPAB	Menominee	51.6	Jodi Sunilla, Toni Moucha, Jill Kehoe, Tiffany Hodge
1994	UPAB	Menominee	52.3	Jodi Sunilla, Jessica Fugere, Michelle Menard, Tiffany Hodge
1995	UPAB	Escanaba	52.5	Shaundra Anderson, Carolin School, Laura LaCrosse, Lisa Potvin
1996	UPAB	Marquette	53.2	Maggy Cowell, Margaret Eppinga, Kristine Jentoft, Marja Emblad
1997	UPAB	Escanaba	53.1	Jessica Berube, Angie Vadermissen, Julie McKnight, Laura Lacrosse
1998	UPAB	Marquette	52.8	Elizabeth Chapman, Angela Abernqathy, Erica Helmica, Kristine Jentoft
1999	UPAB	Marquette	53.1	Alexi Wilkinson, Jacoba Williamson, Kristen Poulsen, Maija Embad
2000	UPAB	Kingsford	53.1	Jamie Fornetti, Elissa Brown, Shannon McHugh, Kelly Hicks
2001	UPD1	Escanaba	52.6*	Marilyn Dwyer, Jamie Groos, Gina Pearson, Kristen Pearson
2002	UPD1	Gladstone	52.71*	N Lalonde, Breanne Marshall. Sarah Ducheny, Tiffany Petr
2003	UPD1	Escanaba	52.43*	Cara Groos, Jamie Groos, Gina Pearson, Jami Acker
2004	UPD1	Marquette	52.28*	Mary Storm, Megan Minchess, Brittnee Balbierz, Jenna Robinson
2005	UPD1	Marquette	51.72*	Jackie Saunderrs, Brittnee Balbierz, Megan Mincheff, Jessica Trotochaud
2006	UPD1	Marquette	51.72*	Alyssa Espamer, Hannah Mincheff, Jessica Trotochaud, Jessica Roche
2007	UPD1	Gladstone	51.22*	Sarah Skultety, Miranda Miron, Laura Photenhauer, Beth Frazer
2008	UPD1	Marquette	52.11	Areanna Bennett, Savannah Mallo, Katy Lafayette, Justine Olson
2009	UPD1	Marquette	52.57	Justine Olson, Savannah Mallo, Katy LaFayette, Jessica Roche
2010	UPD1	Marquette	51.51	Justine Olson, Claire Smith, Ashton Guidebeck, Savannah Mallo
2011	UPD1	Marquette	51.72	Justine Olson, Loghyn Davis, Tabitha Graham, Piper Mlsna
2012	UPD1	Menominee	52.6	Jane Enderby, Courtney Conery, Lexi Christian, Allia Stewart
2013	UPD1	Calumet	52.35	Lexee Rowe, Caitlin Klobuchar, Terra Erkkila, Chelsea Jacques
2014	UPD1	Escanaba	51.86	Jayna LeVigne, Sunny Martineau, Hannah Beversluis, Maddy Willis
2015	UPD1	Calumet	52.65	Caitlin Klobuchar, Lea Bjorn, Annie Tervo, Chelsea Jacques
2016	UPD1	Marquette	52.59	Hanna Johnson, Jacquie Cammarata, Izzie Peterson, SydnyWaterman
2017	UPD1	Marquette	51.83	Abby Kroll, Jacquelin Cammarata, Izabelle Peterson, Sierra Carlson
2018	UPD1	Sault Ste Marie	52.69	Lilly Alaspa, Jocelyn McKee, Maddy Blakeslee, Jordan Scott

4 x 100 – UP Class C/Division 2 Champions

(y=4 x 110 yards)

1975	UPC	L'Anse	53.5y*	
1975	UPC	L'Anse	55.1y	
1976	UPC	Newberry	52.5y*	Susan Smith, Lori Bouchard, Laura Bergstrom, Patty Rubick
1977	UPC	Norway	52.9y	
1978	UPC	Norway	52.7y	
1979	UPC	Negaunee	53.1	Joanna Carlson, Becky Filizetti, Jan Merrick, Jill Merrick
1980	UPC	Hancock	52.4*	Lynne Scholie, Mary Lewis, Betsy Julien, Amy Sporalski
1981	UPC	Stephenson	52.8	Becky Mayer, Chris Sullivan, Debbie Hoots, Robin Eick
1982	UPC	Calumet	52.8	Kay Mugford, Lori Jukuri, JayAnn Schneiderhahn, Tina Antilla
1983	UPC	Calumet	52.2*	Chris Orr, Kay Mugford, Amber Harris, Tina Antilla
1984	UPC	Ishpeming Westwood	52.7	Heidi Knutson, Robin Legassa, Jill Reddy, Sue Lahtela
1985	UPC	Ishpeming Westwood	53.4	Heidi Knutson, Jill Reddy, Robin LeGassa, Sue Lahtela
1986	UPC	Stephenson	51.9*	Karen Chaltry, Heidi Birie, Karen Olson, Roberta VanPool
1987	UPC	Ishpeming Westwood	53.2	Sherry Covell, Crystal Luokkala, Krista Knutson, Heidi Knutson
1988	UPC	Iron River West Iron County	52.8	Stacey Marcell, Chris Buhro, Cari Dzanbazoff, Maria Valesano
1989	UPC	Iron River West Iron County	53.8	Stacey Marcell, Chris Buhro, Cari Dzanbazoff, Maria Valesano
1990	UPC	St. Ignace	53.3	Tyling Simmons, Tracey Paquin, Becky Wheaton, Helena Brown
1991	UPC	Calumet	53.4	Brenda Rowe, Dianne Johnson, Martha Sturos, Brenna Plante
1992	UPC	Ironwood	54.2	Angela Jenko, Julie Talaska, Heidi Zieman, Angela Arthur
1993	UPC	Ironwood	53.0	Nicole Berquist, Alicia Jackson, Haley Puotinen Angela Arthur
1994	UPC	Ironwood	52.8	Heidi Zieman, Alicia Jackson, Haley Puotinen, Angeka Arthur
1995	UPC	St. Ignace	51.8*	Anna Pemble, Melanie Sheridan, Holly Brown, Richelle Robinson
1996	UPC	Ironwood	52.6	Amanda Kinnunen, Jamie Bunt, Shannon Puotinen, Kelly Stempihar
1997	UPC	Ironwood	53.0	Jamie Bunt, Pam Cisweski, Jill Cisewski, Hannon Puotinen
1998	UPC	Ironwood	53.3	Shannon Pontinen, Kristin Harma, Jamie Bunt, Pam Balduc
1999	UPC	Houghton	52.8	Alicia Melton, Andrea Hansel, Mary Kay Pietila, Angela Cattelino

2000	UPC	Iron Mountain	53.2	Jeanna Dinnocenzo, Catherine Lundy, Kristen Pedo, Katy Vros
2001	UPD2	Ishpeming	53.4*	Melissa Besola, Jade Jacobson, Susan Tousignant, Jamie Roos
2002	UPD2	Ishpeming	54.09*	Angela Berticci, Leslie Luehmann, Melissa Besola, Susan Tousignant
2003	UPD2	Ishpeming	53.71*	Angela Bertucci, Natalie Bertucci, Katelyn Argall, Leslie Luehmann,
2004	UPD2	Ishpeming	53.28*	Katelyn Argall, Joyce Bussierre, Natalie Bertucci, Leslie Luehmann
2005	UPD2	Republic-Michigamme	52.75*	Katelyn Argall, Lindsey Antilla, Jessica Wood, Natalie Bertucce
2006	UPD2	St. Ignace	53.30	Stacee Schnicke, Casey Brown, Ashley St. Louis, Kelsey Cryderman
2007	UPD2	Manistique	53.30	Kayla Anthony, Samantha Bryant, Katie Lamuth, Robin Vaughn
2008	UPD2	Manistique	54.12	Robin Vaughn, Bree Yurk, Gabbie Kieffer, Sam Bryant
2009	UPD2	West Iron County	54.80	Jesse Schmidt, Latoya Carter-Bartley, Adriana Ceron, Joanna Pellizzer
2010	UPD2	Manistique	52.36*	Jasmine Volk, Natalie Pohlman, Hannah Bryant, Sam Bryant
2011	UPD2	St. Ignace	53.71	
2012	UPD2	St. Ignace	55.42	Margo Brown, Rebecca Brown, Morgan Lavake, Rachel Hetherington
2013	UPD2	Manistique	52.59	Eliza MacGregor, Kyra Lauzon, Chelby Carlson, Hannah Bryant
2014	UPD2	West Iron County	53.38	Cassey Harrington, Ally Jo Polich, Elizabeth Pellizzer, Carli Johnson
2015	UPD2	West Iron County	53.05	Nassi Thomas, Anna Terres, Johanna Harvey, Jessica Spencer
2016	UPD2	Ishpeming	55.64	Anna Terres, Johanna Harvey, Madigan Johns, Hailey Smith
2017	UPD2	Newberry	53.21	Makenna Bryant, Madison Grigg, Megan Grigg, Taylor Bryant,
2018	UPD2	Iron Mountain	52.76	Riley Paupore, Tiana Brooks, Taylor Talerico, Olivia Berutti

4 x 100 – UP Class C/Division 3 Champions

(y=4 x 110 yards)

1976	UPD	Bark River-Harris	53.7y*	
1977	UPD	Republic-Michigamme	53.7y*	Diane Heliste, Wanda Darling, JoAnn Heliste, Kathy Koski
1978	UPD	Republic-Michigamme	52.9y*	Connie Miettenen, Karolyn Skogman, Terri Miron, Wanda Darling
1979	UPD	Norway	52.7*	Jan Sandrin, Linda Grodeski, Darlene Allen, Darla Koller
1980	UPD	Norway	52.9	Darla Koller, Meg Weiland, Mary Biolo, Darlene Allen
1981	UPD	Norway	52.9	Darla Koller, Meg Weiland, Mary Biolo, Darlene Allen
1982	UPD	Baraga	53.8	Julie Mayo, Colleen Swanson, Lisa Michaels, Josie Drennan
1983	UPD	Baraga	53.0	Tammy Ross, Julie Mayo, Colleen Swanson, Lisa Michaels,
1984	UPD	Baraga	53.9	Tammy Ross, Mary Messer, Colleen Swanson, Julie Mayo
1985	UPD	Pickford	54.4	Cindy Schwiderson, Missy Hatfield, Tammy Ball, Michelle Stevenson
1986	UPD	Pickford	53.1	Betty Baker, Michelle Stevenson, Cindy Schwiderson, Missy Hatfield
1987	UPD	Pickford	53.8	Kelly Huyck, Cindy Schwiderson, Missay Hatfield, Betty Baker
1988	UPD	Pickford	54.3	Kelly Huyck, Kris Kyle, Betty Baker, Missy Hatfield
1989	UPD	Pickford	54.1	Nicole Skinner, Gina Weatherly, Kelly Huyck, Maggie Clawson
1990	UPD	Bark River-Harris	54.1	Carol Petrick, Traci Gudwer, Donna Peterson, Janelle Ives
1991	UPD	Pickford	54.0	Chrissy Opperman, Gina Hopkins, Wendy Hartwig, Nicole Skinner
1992	UPD	Powers-North Central	56.2	Missy Sanford, Alicia Cianfarani, Annell Veeser, Becca Malchow
1993	UPD	Engadine	54.1	Christina Bertucci, Jill Barrett, Jennifer LeGault, Janelle LeGault
1994	UPD	Lake Linden-Hubbell	53.1	Missy Gervais, Dawn Savolainen, Sarah Johns, Cristina Koski
1995	UPD	Bark River-Harris	54.1	Beth Ives, Melissa Richer, Chantelle Kleikamp, Jenny Wienckowski
1996	UPD	Wakefield	55.4	Karen Brunelle, Crystal Brunelle, Laura Ritter, Krista Niemi
1997	UPD	Bessemer	55.6	Rachel Pertile, Laura Jacobson, Kari Londo, Heidi Maccani
1998	UPD	Bessemer	54.6	Heidi Maccani, Kari Londo, Rachel Pertile, Jaclyn BeBeau
1999	UPD	Bessemer	54.2	Rachel Pertile, Ashley Barto, Becky Londo, Jacklyn Bebeau
2000	UPD	Rapid River	53.5	Christa Leduc, Val Peterson, Shannon McLaughlin, Stephanie Boyer
2001	UPD3	Big Bay De Noc	53.93*	Jamie Lucas, Kristi Thill, Lindsay Thome, Amber Tatrow
2002	UPD3	Cooks Big Bay de Noc	54.15	Jamie Lucas, Linsay Thome, Randi Ferrebee, Amber Tatrow
2003	UPD3	Rock Mid Peninsula	54.81	Sarah Lepisto, Jenny Stevenson, Renee Kivioja, Becky Baron
2004	UPD3	Rock Mid Peninsula	53.52*	Sarah Lepisto. Lindsay Carlson, Renee Kivioja, Becky Baron
2005	UPD3	Rapid River	54.68	Katie LeDuc, Cassi Rishford, Randi Gustafson, Juliann Plimpton
2006	UPD3	L'Anse	53.8	Lisa Bennett, Lauren Bianco, Jacki Collins, Kellie Collins
2007	UPD3	L'Anse	53.64	Lisa Bennett, Lauren Bianco, Jacki Collins, Kellie Collins
2008	UPD3	Lake Linden-Hubbell	55.56	Jeana Hendrickson, Molly Monette, Siranda Normand, Paige Codere
2009	UPD3	Crystal Falls-Forest Park	53.08*	Hilary Roose, Ana Cornelia, Kathleen Grandahl, Maria Valesano
2010	UPD3	Crystal Falls-Forest Park	51.92*	Hilary Roose, Ana Cornelia, Kathleen Grandahl, Maria Valesano
2011	UPD3	Crystal Falls-Forest Park	53.07	Taylor Taunton, Mary Grandahl, Ana Cornelia, Kathleen Grandahl
2012	UPD3	Brimley	53.92	Mindy Wilson, Alexis Mason, Taylor Wilson, Emily Lounds
2013	UPD3	St. Ignace	53.28	Margo Brown, Kelley Wright, Autumn Orm, Morgan Lavake
2014	UPD3	Eben Junction Superior Central	54.08	
2015	UPD3	Lake Linden-Hubbell	53.96	Rachel Holzberger, Laura Lyons, Lily Kampula, Sarah Audette
2016	UPD3	Newberry	54.40	Karley Honeysette, Megan Grigg, Monika Tomica, Taylor Bryant
2017	UPD3	Lake Linden-Hubbell	54.10	Lily Kampula, Jamie Hendrickson, Kaitlyn Baccus, Joslyn Perala
2018	UPD3	Bark River-Harris	53.63	Ashleigh White, Makena Lockwood, Jaelin Lockwood, Hailee Demers

GIRLS 4 x 200 RELAY

Records

D1	1:36.66	Oak Park	Janae Barksdale, Anna Jefferson, Brianna Holloway, Tamea McKelvy	2016
D2	1:39.92	Detroit Renaissance	Stephanie Douglas, Erin Anderson, Jennifer Lawson, Julia Stevenson	2000
D3	1:41.17	Frankenmuth	Sydney Bonner, Cadi Palreuter, Sarah Buella, Angie Ritter	2014
D4	1:45.38	Potterville	Jill Witaker, Jenna Whipple, Kaila Cool, Kelsey Letson	2009
UPD1	1:46.34	Marquette	Alyssa Espamer, Jessica Trotochaud, Brittnee Balbierz, Catherine Angeli	2006
UPD2	1:48.9	St Ignace	Kate Ruegg, Karolyn Getzen, Marielle Calcatera, Eryn Mercer	2001
UPD3	1:49.6	Norway	Darlene Allen, Meg Wieland, Connie Fuller, Darla Koller	1980

Records by Class (pre-2000 for LP, pre-2001 for UP)

A	1:38.4	Detroit Cass Tech	Chantelle Nagbe, Julia Ford, Emily Higgins, Felicia Baker	1994
B	1:41.82	Flint Beecher	Twynette Wilson, Yolanda Jones, Michelle Westbrook, Pretoria Wilson	1987
C	1:44.3	Whitehall	Yvette Hunter, Michelle Cox, Tracy Brandel, Pam Sheesley	1981
D	1:46.2y	Grass Lake	Brenda Johnson, Cindy Arnold, Kellie Clark, Karen Arnold	1978
UPAB	1:46.6y	Marquette	Kris Tacculini, Suzanne Patterson, Mary Ottoson, Lisa Wiedenhoefer	1978
UPC	1:48.4y	Stephenson	Jane Kuntze, Cindy Schlaack, Connie Swanson, Tammi Revall	1977
UPD	1:50.7	Brimley	Alexis Mason, Becca Carruthers, Taylor Wilson, Tabitha Graham	1980

4 x 200 – Class A/Division 1 Champions

(y=4 x 220 yards)

1973	All	Lincoln Park	1:51.6y*	Nancy Popp, Sandy Brawner, Vicky Slater, Lynn Lovat
1974	A	Detroit Cass Tech	1:49.0y*	Anita Lee, Julie Gibson, Rita Dalton, Cheryl Gilliam
1975	A	Detroit Cass Tech	1:43.1y*	Angela Johnson, Cheryl Gilliam, Julie Gibson, Angela Cumberlander
1976	A	Detroit Cass Tech	1:42.3y*	Cheryl Gilliam, Angela Johnson, Donna Smitherman, Sharon Sims
1977	A	Flint Central	1:41.9y*	Renee Turner, Robin Flynn, Nancy Nard, Demetria Fulgham
1978	A	Detroit Kettering	1:42.7y	Florette McGowan, Felicia Clark, Mona McGowan, Edwina Mason
1979	A	Detroit Mumford	1:41.4y*	Kim Turner, Angela Sibby, Darlene Johnson, Lisa Madison
1980	A	Flint Northern	1:42.1y	Judy Tucker, Lagretta Riley, Tonya Lowe, Leteia Hughley
1981	A	Ann Arbor Pioneer	1:41.5y	Rhonda Latnie, Teresa Arnold, Tara Cope, Barb Ellis
1982	A	Detroit Chadsey	1:40.0*	Vivian McKenzie, Vera Pruitt, Cynthia Dixon, Kari Manns
1983	A	Flint Northern	1:41.1	Terri Barber, Marlene Isabelle, Monica Taylor, Carlene Isabelle
1984	A	Benton Harbor	1:39.2*	Marita Rimpson, Linda McMillion, Sandra Rice, Carolyn Ferguson
1985	A	Ann Arbor Pioneer	1:42.37	Michele Kennedy, Karin Surratt, Rolanda Officer, Victoria Shields
1986	A	Ann Arbor Pioneer	1:42.13	Ratennia Paige, Michele Kennedy, Karin Surratt, Sabrina Jordan
1987	A	Ann Arbor Pioneer	1:41.87	Binti Allen, Michelle Kennedy, Diane Laurin, Crystal Braddock
1988	A	Detroit Cass Tech	1:42.86	Kenya Clement, Benita Jackson, Trinette Johnson, Darchelle Ross
1989	A	Ypsilanti	1:41.6	Nicole Wilson, Moyette Wilson, Shanta Covington, Camay Thurman
1990	A	Ypsilanti	1:41.30	Angela Wilkins, Nicole Wilson, Moyette Wilson, Camay Thurman
1991	A	Ann Arbor Pioneer	1:42.7	Haley Wilkins, Gennifer Bridges, Seena Walters, Vania Nelson
1992	A	Ann Arbor Pioneer	1:43.98	Hayley Wilkins, Takiya Jenkins, Annette Chisolm, Vania Nelson
1993	A	Detroit Cass Tech	1:41.55	Nicole Callaway, Chantelle Nagbe, Emily Higgins, Erica Shepherd
1994	A	Detroit Cass Tech	1:38.4*	Chantelle Nagbe, Julia Ford, Emily Higgins, Felicia Baker
1995	A	Detroit Cass Tech	1:41.0	Lakesha Snoddy, Julia Ford, Chantelle Nagbe, Traci Ball
1996	A	Detroit Cass Tech	1:39.52	Meshia Maton, Julia Ford, Chantelle Nagbe, Traci Ball
1997	A	Detroit Cass Tech	1:39.22	Kanisa Williams, Traci Ball, Julia Ford, Meshia Maton
1998	A	Detroit Cass Tech	1:39.33	Crystal Lee, Tiarra Jones, Traci Ball, Meshia Moton
1999	A	Detroit Cass Tech	1:40.41	Katrice Walton, Eboni Jenkins, Tiarra Jones, Meshia Moton
2000	D1	Detroit Cass Tech	1:40.03*	Tiarra Jones, Katrice Walton, Crystal Lee, Eboni Jenkins
2001	D1	Detroit Cass Tech	1:40.77	Karla Marshall, Katrice Walton, Ariss Seals, Crystal Lee
2002	D1	Ann Arbor Pioneer	1:40.57	Andrea Mosher, Cheryl Green, Keisha Townsend, Lauren Fortson
2003	D1	Detroit Mumford	1:41.59	Sharda Grace, Amina Daniels, Courtney Crosby, Jeanetta Stutts
2004	D1	Detroit Mumford	1:39.12*	Porsche Ries, Charnell Wright, Jessica Jones, Jasmine Webb
2005	D1	Detroit Mumford	1:37.72*	Shayla Mahan, Stephanie Porter, Chanell Wright, Jessica Jones
2006	D1	Detroit Mumford	1:40.40	Shayla Mahan, Dane Hill, Aisha Osborne, Chanell Wright
2007	D1	Detroit Mumford	1:39.19	Aisha Osborne, Dominque Brown, Jasmin Webb, Shayla Mahan
2008	D1	Jackson	1:41.08	DeHara Soto, Brittani Williams, Brenda Gibson, Elise Brown
2009	D1	Flint Southwestern Academy	1:42.29	Dynasty McGee, Christal Wilson, Jillian Sledge, Ciarra Adams
2010	D1	Rockford	1:42.16	Abby Blanchard, Courtney Klaweiter, Rachel Jerrils, Margaret Smiley
2011	D1	East Kentwood	1:42.16	Lameeka Davis, Fiana Comer, Brittany Terry, Rebecca Hall
2012	D1	Ann Arbor Huron	1:41.12	Maya Long, Bria Johnson, Stevi Smith, Cindy Ofili
2013	D1	Detroit Renaissance	1:38.92	Dominique Funchess, Assaundra Dalton, Dominique Taylor, Paros Parnell
2014	D1	Oak Park	1:38.15	Anna Jefferson, Carlita Taylor, Brianna Holloway, Tamea McKelvy
2015	D1	Oak Park	1:39.55	Tamea McKelvy, Carlita Taylor, Anna Jefferson, Brianna Holloway
2016	D1	Oak Park	1:36.66*	Janae Barkdale, Anna Jefferson, Brianna Holloway, Tamea McKelvy
2017	D1	Oak Park	1:38.38	Janae Barksdale, Aasis Laurencin, Carlita Taylor Tamea McKelvy
2018	D1	Detroit Renaissance	1:39.91	Makylah Slappy, Mizan Thomas, Paige Chapman, Donae Adams

4 x 200 – Class B/Division 2 Champions

(y=4 x 220 yards)

1974	B	Montrose	1:53.5y*	Grace Love, Roni Nagaj, Sabrina Schmidt, Brenda Pyrc
1975	B	Holt	1:46.0y*	Johanna Matthyssen, Sue Montgomery, Brenda Walker, Brenda Schroeder
1976	B	Holt	1:45.0y*	Sue Montgomery, Marilyn Barner, Brenda Schroeder, Johanna Matthyssen
1977	B	Muskegon Catholic	1:44.4y*	Ceceila Terrien, Susan Bordeaux, Mary Gauthier, Terri Johnson
1978	B	Grand Rapids Christian	1:45.7y	Sandy VanSpronsen, Lori VanEssen, Amy Boerman, Julie Boerman
1979	B	St. Joseph	1:44.3y*	Shawn Watt, Karrin Kasischke, Torre Ranum, Michelle Prifer
1980	B	Flint Beecher	1:43.8*	Sheri Brock, Lajewell Gaston, Diane Wiley, Sandra Harris
1981	B	Flint Beecher	1:42.7*	Leslie Arder, Geraldine Collier, Diane Wiley, Sandy Harris
1982	B	Oak Park	1:44.8y	Veronica Daffin, Genia Redfern, Lavanda Perry, Michelle Morris
1983	B	Mt Clemens L'Anse Creuse	1:45.2	Nancy Marcetti, Sandy Ary, Christie Ary, Kathy Shacklett
1984	B	Muskegon Heights	1:43.5	Janet Evans, Doris Hardiman, Sherry Kelly, Shenitha Walker
1985	B	Flint Beecher	1:43.67	Twynette Wilson, Pretoria Wilson, Michelle Westbrook, Danita Sims
1986	B	Flint Beecher	1:44.0	Pretoria Wilson, Twynette Wilson, Michele Westbrook, Yolanda Jonees
1987	B	Flint Beecher	1:41.82*	Twynette Wilson, Yolanda Jones, Michelle Westbrook, Pretoria Wilson
1988	B	Detroit DePorres	1:43.71	Tawanda Oree, Tara Allen, Kenyetta Kendrick, Nicole Embry
1989	B	Detroit DePorres	1:44.8	Nicole Embry, Danielle Pierce, Kenyetta Kendrick, Tawanda Oree
1990	B	Detroit DePorres	1:42.72	Atemia McClure, Jelene Boyd, Nicole Embry, Danielle Pierce
1991	B	Flint Beecher	1:45.90	Rhoda Read, Niketa Williams, Renona Childress, Chantella Byrd
1992	B	Flint Beecher	1:46.64	Rhoda Read, Carmia Marshall, Niketa Williams, Chantella Byrd
1993	B	Flint Beecher	1:47.43	Nicole McCarlston, Lashaunda Tipton, Teresa Thomas, Carmia Marshall
1994	B	River Rouge	1:44.62	Kenyetta Grigsby, Kembria Peterson, Maria Edwards, Simby Bonner
1995	B	Tecumseh	1:47.65	Deanna Vogel, Jenny Webb, Jocelyn Morse, Angie Stanifer
1996	B	Parma Western	1:46.99	Jenny Leuken, Brandi Stalhhood, Jessie Leuken, Jana White

1997	B	St. Joseph	1:46.0	Danella Harbison, Kendall Terhune, Amy DeSchaaf, Mellissa Adams
1998	B	Detroit Renaissance	1:42.25	Brandis O'Neal, Julia Redd, Julia Stevenson, Jennifer Lawson
1999	B	Detroit Renaissance	1:42.51	Stephanie Douglas, Erin Anderson, Jennifer Lawson, Julia Stevenson
2000	D2	Detroit Renaissance	1:39.92*	Stephanie Douglas, Erin Anderson, Jennifer Lawson, Julia Stevenson
2001	D2	Detroit Renaissance	1:40.60	Chasity Armstrong, Erin Anderson, Jennifer Lawson, LeTosha Jollet
2002	D2	Detroit Renaissance	1:42.61	Jessica Jones, Fallon Jenkins, Camilla Nelson, LeTosha Jollet
2003	D2	Detroit Renaissance	1:42.85	Jessica Jones, Amber Hay, Fallon Jenkins, Alexandrea Cunningham
2004	D2	Mt Pleasant	1:45.47	Shauna Carrier, Courtney Olson, Jenilee Rathje, Megan Starns
2005	D2	Detroit Renaissance	1:43.17	Elesha Logan, Sharay Hale, Kiara Smith, Amber Hay
2006	D2	Grand Rapids Forest Hills Northern	1:44.07	Kelcie Daniels, Phaebre Colbert, Marieme Mbaye, Darcy Rhoden
2007	D2	Detroit Renaissance	1:42.00	Ashlee Abraham, Autumn Jones, Camille Johnson, Christina Farrow
2008	D2	East Lansing	1:43.73	Karah Robertson, Gabriell Jennings, Hannah Fitzpatrick, Victoria Lipscomb
2009	D2	East Lansing	1:43.48	Milika Glover, Hannah Fitzpatrick, Mercedes Lee, Victoria Lipscomb
2010	D2	Chelsea	1:42.48	Olivia DeTroyer, Christina Coffman, Grace Sauers, Corinne Carpenter
2011	D2	Dearborn Divine Child	1:42.41	Mallory Myler, Carikinne Strasser, Liz Mullen, Paige Patterson
2012	D2	Detroit Country Day	1:42.24	Jonell Nwabueze, Sydney Cureton, Ava Nasrollahzadeh, Kendall Baisden
2013	D2	Dearborn Divine Child	1:41.39	Mallory Myler, Kayla Gandy, Liz Mullen, Paige Patterson
2014	D2	Lansing Waverly	1:42.92	Teaghan Thomas, Erin Pete, Taylor Manson, Chante Roberts
2015	D2	Remus Chippewa Hills	1:43.61	Jennifer McNeal, Jacki Scheaffer, Nicole Snyder, Hannah Todd
2016	D2	Lansing Waverly	1:43.88	Teaghan Thomas, Jazlynn Wilson, Maya Garrett, Tra'chele Roberts
2017	D2	Lansing Waverly	1:43.71	Teaghan Thomas, Maya Garrett, Princella Trainor, Jazlynn Wilcox
2018	D2	Detroit Country Day	1:45.10	Jasmine Powell, Taylor Aibana, Ahvon Mitchell, Alexis Officer

4 x 200 – Class C/Division 3 Champions

(y=4 x 220 yards)

1975	C	Montrose	1:48.9y*	Valerie Horne, Roni Nagaj, Sabrina Schmidt, Mary Nickoley
1976	C	Williamston	1:48.9y*	Cindy Clinton, Kelly Manette, Karen Lockwood, Linda Merrifield
1977	C	North Muskegon	1:47.1y*	Shelly Guy, Cindy Tjarksen, Julie Panzenhagen, Cindi Guy
1978	C	Muskegon Catholic	1:44.8y*	Cindy Allore, Susan Bordeaux, Mary Gauthier, Cecelia Terrien
1979	C	North Muskegon	1:46.2y	Jenny Knowlton, Cindy Guy, Cindy Tjarksen, Shelly Guy
1980	C	Grand Rapids South Christian	1:46.6y	Kathy DeHaan, Brenda Marsman, Karri Lautenbach, Kim Lautenbach
1981	C	Whitehall	1:44.3*	Yvette Hunter, Michelle Cox, Tracy Brandel, Pam Sheesley
1982	C	Detroit Lutheran West	1:45.3	Lenore Stephen, Becky Wilson, Joya Davis, Donna Smith
1983	C	DeWitt	1:46.2	Tami Noyce, Jabe Skoczylas, Sheri Schmitt, Teresa Kirchen
1984	C	Detroit Country Day	1:45.4	Pam Laker, Natalie Greenspan, Whitney Beli, Kristi Jackson
1985	C	Detroit Country Day	1:45.44	Marie Bridges, Natalie Greenspan, Karen Yuille, Shirley Evans
1986	C	Cassopolis	1:45.35	Ronda Lawson, Janice Harp, Aretha Glover, Debbie Edwards
1987	C	Detroit Country Day	1:44.85	Shirley Evans, Peggy Evans, Diane Grauer, Marie Bridges
1988	C	Detroit Country Day	1:45.5	Shannon Curtis, Diane Graves, Peggy Evans, Shirley Evans
1989	C	Onsted	1:44.96	Jennifer Wood, Laurie Pantera, Erin Schaefer, Naheed Irani
1990	C	Erie-Mason	1:46.77	Suzette Bates, Heather Guinn, Heather Stevens, Lynn Beutler
1991	C	Cassopolis	1:48.1	Ketmany Manichanh, Tilyne Christopher, Stacey Turner, Lisa Glover
1992	C	New Lothrop	1:49.1	Kerry Gross, Tracy VanOrder, Nancy Gross, Kellie Gauthier
1993	C	Hemlock	1:47.59	Sherrie Lumsden, Geneve McPhee, Mindy Call, Heidi Goodenough
1994	C	Grandville Calvin Christian	1:45.66	Kristen Karsten, Lindsay Mulder, Ryndee Wilson, Emily Velthouse
1995	C	Clare	1:48.59	Audrey Jelenek, Cora Strouse, Meghan Smith, Jessica Champine
1996	C	Lutheran Westland	1:47.53	Rebekah Hoffmeier, Amy Clark, Hana Hughes, Laura Clark
1997	C	Hemlock	1:46.84	Christy Tedrow, Hillary Allison, Emily Luplow, Lisa Daubert
1998	C	Kingsley	1:48.05	Alaina Olds, Anna Giannda, Berh Summerfield, Amber Hayes
1999	C	Hemlock	1:46.12	Lisa Daubert, Janelle Woida, Colette Puchacz, Hillary Allis
2000	D3	Hemlock	1:46.88*	Hillary Allison, Lisa Daubert, Colette Puchacz, Janette Woid
2001	D3	Cass City	1:47.37	Holli Cooper, Jamie Fluegge, Sara Homakie, Amanda Sullins
2002	D3	Dearborn Heights Robichaud	1:47.37	Whitney Wilson-Renfroe, Marjorie Jackson, Altravese Turner, Cierra Jones
2003	D3	Lansing Catholic	1:45.17*	Jocelyn Marks, Renee Rademacher, Erin Sachau, Allison Strouse
2004	D3	Albion	1:46.53	
2005	D3	Albion	1:44.24*	Alpha Clark, Joranda Chapman, Juandretta Oliver, Mika Clark
2006	D3	Kent City	1:45.45	Sarah Shirey, Kristi Boehm, Courtney Zahrt, Amber Holcomb
2007	D3	Albion	1:43.49*	Marcola Ridley, Chartney Blair, Amelia Bannister, Joranda Chapman
2008	D3	Shepherd	1:46.93	Stephanie Snyder, Alison Jerome, Sarah Frisbey, Cady Sandel
2009	D3	Frankenmuth	1:44.00	Olivia Shelton, Emily Wee, Kelsey Ritter, Chelsea Mertz
2010	D3	Frankenmuth	1:45.63	Lauren Reinbold, Kayla Bender, Chelsea Mertz, Emily Wee
2011	D3	Onsted	1:45.78	Alexis Johnson, Ashlin McNutt, Ashlin Aiken, Kelsey Ross
2012	D3	Frankenmuth	1:44.61	Sydney Bronner, Olivia Shelton, Emily Wee, Angela Ritter
2013	D3	Frankenmuth	1:45.16	Sydney Bonner, Rachel Compton, Sarah Buella, Angie Ritter
2014	D3	Frankenmuth	1:41.17*	Sydney Bonner, Cadi Palreuter, Sarah Buella, Angie Ritter
2015	D3	Pewamo-Westphalia	1:45.19	Brenna Wirth, Kelly Thelen, Gabbie Hummel, Marissa Wirth
2016	D3	Adrian Madison	1:46.06	Megan Rosales, Delaney Stersic, Sierra Hernandez, Benedetta Vianello
2017	D3	Adrian Madison	1:44.11	Megan Rosales, Delaney Stersic, Sierra Hernandez, Chelsea Short
2018	D3	St Charles	1:44.97	Najiyah Holden, Hope Kushion, Erica Garcia, Celine Whiren

4 x 200 – Class D/Division 4 Champions

(y=4 x 220 yards)

1975	D	Grass Lake	1:49.5y*	Kathy Sherwood, LuAnn Yonkin, Karen Arnold, Linda Arnold
1976	D	Colon	1:49.6y	Debbra Decker, Mary Sparks, Peggy Smoker, Barbara King
1977	D	Grass Lake	1:47.4y*	Brenda Johnson, Leonore Zelaney, Karen Arnold, LuAnn Younkin
1978	D	Grass Lake	1:46.2y*	Brenda Johnson, Cindy Arnold, Kellie Clark, Karen Arnold
1979	D	Colon	1:48.0	Vicki Kime, Barb Loudenslager, Cathy Nightingale, Kim Richardson
1980	D	Athens	1:51.2	Mary Miller, Julie Kinney, Becky Carvine, Carrie VanHouten
1981	D	Fowler	1:47.0	Kay Snyder, Lana Hafner, Jan Schmitt, Becky Klein
1982	D	Detroit St Andrew	1:46.5	Marie Przybylski, Sharon Uroda, Kim Estrada, Kim Jonik
1983	D	Fowler	1:46.8	Connie Thelan, Jan Schmidtt, Lana Hafner, Becky Klein
1984	D	Potterville	1:47.82	Heather Smalley, Cheryl Simpson, Shelli Nemeth, Eleanor Marks
1985	D	Athens	1:47.57	Angie Brown, Cindy Cayo, Jackie Boddy, Carla Voss

1986	D	New Haven	1:47.97	Wendy Goodhue, Barbara Bankston, Sue Veith, Kristal Mack
1987	D	Redford St. Mary	1:47.58	Sharon Holloway, Kim Brown, Twane Rigney, Kim Thompson
1988	D	Reading	1:49.71	Carol Clark, J.J. Parker, Teri Coe, Kim Burger
1989	D	Detroit Lutheran West	1:48.2	Nicole Robinson, Ardra Hunter, Cleo Johnson, Dwana McGee
1990	D	Detroit Lutheran West	1:47.78	Nicole Robinson, Yvonne Hall, Sylvia Edwards, Ardra Hunter
1991	D	Detroit Lutheran West	1:47.98	Lasundres Bettis, Tvonne Hall, Pam Ndon, Ardra Hunter
1992	D	Fairview	1:48.69	Rachel Emery, Cambria Handrich, Shanda Panks, Stacy McCallum
1993	D	Royal Oak Shrine	1:49.7	Camey Ellis, Desma Johnson, Brandie Henderson, Erica Dunbar
1994	D	Battle Creek St Phillip	1:47.23	Heidi Curtiss, Stephanie Latinga, Breeka Formsma, Brooke Formsma
1995	D	Maple City Glen Lake	1:50.28	Erin Gearhart, Kelly MacMillan, Tonya Wilcox, Erin Attwood
1996	D	Bellaire	1:49.83	Amy Czajkowski, Sarah Dunson, Courtney Kellner, Jessica Poel
1997	D	Onekema	1:48.50	Christina Hilliard, Wendy Lautner, Sandy Lautner, Sarah Wild
1998	D	Carsonville-Port Sanilac	1:47.7	Becky Slivka, Amber Berrien, Henneka Berrien, Julia Berrien
1999	D	Potterville	1:49.79	Angie Harris, Jessica Howard, Katie Nimphie, Cheyenne Luzynski
2000	D4	Saginaw Michigan Lutheran Seminary	1:46.81*	Erin McFarland, Jenni Mueller, Lisa Mueller, Megan Filthaut
2001	D4	Reading	1:47.66	Summer Stewart, Erica Young, Jessica Mundy, Emily Trott
2002	D4	Lincoln-Alcona	1:47.54	Callie Boik, Charina Stewart, Rosemary Myrick, Stacy Dellar
2003	D4	Pewamo-Westphalia	1:48.56	Amy Schneider, Ashley Weber, Dawn Pohl, Vanessa Thelen
2004	D4	Detroit Benedictine	1:46.64*	Ashley Green, Terri Thomas, Lesly Hale, Seonetta Belin
2005	D4	Flint Hamady	1:46.95	Shameeka Parrish, Jonae Coleman, Quannika Horne, Tara Johnson
2006	D4	Flint Hamady	1:46.48*	Whitney Rodgers, Jonae Coleman, Quannika Home, Tara Johnson
2007	D4	Athens	1:48.19	Miranda Iles, Emily Wickemeyer, Kelsey Harris, Nicole Cripe
2008	D4	Potterville	1:47.18	Kelsey Letson, Jenna Whipple, Kaila Cook, Breann Beck
2009	D4	Potterville	1:45.38*	Jill Witaker, Jenna Whipple, Kaila Cool, Kelsey Letson
2010	D4	Pewamo-Westphalia	1:46.06	Rachel Schmitt, Allison Fedewa, Kyam Thelen, Abbey Hengesbach
2011	D4	Pewamo-Westphalia	1:47.21	Rachel Schmitt, Cammie Noeker, Kyan Thelen, Kenzie Wieber
2012	D4	Fowler	1:47.26	Savannah Feldpausch, Britney Weber, Breann Klein, Elizabeth Thelen
2013	D4	Royal Oak Shrine	1:48.79	Julia Liggett, Irene Peaslee, Autumn Washington, Taylor Kilgore
2014	D4	Reading	1:47.36	Jennifer Davis, Kaitlin Seager, Teddi Zimmerman, Samantha Pfieffer
2015	D4	Fowler	1:48.35	Allison Hufnagel, McKenzie Feldpausch, Madison Koenigsknecht, Sidney Horak
2016	D4	Fowler	1:46.57	Sidney Horak, Madison Koenigsknecht, McKenzie Koenigsknecht, Julie Thelen
2017	D4	Springport	1:48.73	Carrie Creger, Emmy Dyer, Makenzie Patterson, Katelynn Creger
2018	D4	Fowler	1:46.28	Shannon Schmitz, McKenzie Koenigsknecht, Sidney Horak, Kaitlyn Langin

4 x 200 – UP Class AB/Division 1 Champions

(y=4 x 220 yards)

1972	UP-All	Iron Mountain	2:00.6y*	
(medley relay)				
1973	UP-All	Iron Mountain	2:05.1y*	
1974	UPAB	Marquette	2:00.5*	
(4 x 220 yards)				
1975	UPAB	Escanaba	1:49.3y*	
1976	UPAB	Escanaba	1:47.7y*	
1977	UPAB	Marquette	1:47.4y*	
1978	UPAB	Marquette	1:46.6y*	Kris Tacculini, Suzanne Patterson, Mary Ottoson, Lisa Wiedenhoefer
1979	UPAB	Marquette	1:48.5	Mary Ottoson, Suzanne Patterson, Kris Taccolini, Lisa Wiedenhoefer
1980	UPAB	Gwinn	1:49.3	Sherri Reid, Sue Shipley, Barb Nash, Sue Contois
1981	UPAB	Menominee	1:53.0	Michelle Blake, Shelley Lerret, Kristin Swanson, Caralee Poquette
1982	UPAB	Escanaba	1:50.3	Hope Laviolette, Jill Peterson, Sandy Davision, Jean Tolfa
1983	UPAB	Marquette	1:50.5	Jill MacDougall, Stephanie Hurley, Teresa Bernier, Liz Sarvello
1984	UPAB	Escanaba	1:50.4	Carolee Boudreau, Laurie Raymond, Barb Bradley, Liz Provo
1985	UPAB	Escanaba	1:50.5	Jean Ammel, Lauri Raymond, Liz Provo, Tammy Cook
1986	UPAB	Escanaba	1:48.8	Jean Ammel, Jill Green, Liz Provo, Tammy Cook
1987	UPAB	Escanaba	1:49.8	Liz Provo, Kerri Bolm, Jill Green, Tammy Cook
1988	UPAB	Escanaba	1:50.4	Chris Juhl, Jodi Herioux, Lisa Steele, Tammy Cook
1989	UPAB	Kingsford	1:51.6	Lori Glaser, Jennie Drake, Sara Fornetti, Vicki Brown
1990	UPAB	Gladstone	1:50.0	Barb Klodt, Molly Cain, Christa Beaver, Jennifer Ostlund
1991	UPAB	Marquette	1:49.4	Aimee Wainio, Amanda Smith, Michelle Olds, Lori Larson
1992	UPAB	Gladstone	1:53.5	Nicole Kanerva, Molly Cain, Michelle Bolek, Crista Beaver
1993	UPAB	Marquette	1:51.0	Sarah Heikkila, Megan Scherer, Colleen Michelson, Michelle Olds
1994	UPAB	Marquette	1:49.2	Maggie Cowell, Nikki Goodwin, Colleen Michelson, Sarah Heikkila
1995	UPAB	Escanaba	1:50.2	Saundra Anderson, Carolin School, Laura LaCrosse, Lisa Potvin
1996	UPAB	Marquette	1:51.7	Maggy Cowell, Margaret Eppinga, Kristine Jentoft, Maija Emblad
1997	UPAB	Sault Ste. Marie	1:55.0	Rebecca Johnson, Julie McDonald, Alice Duesing, Holly Goetz
1998	UPAB	Marquette	1:50.7	Elizabeth Chapman, Jacoba Williamson, Margaret Eppinga, Jill Kimmes
1999	UPAB	Kingsford	1:51.4	Tracy Wier, Jamie Fornetti, Shannon McHugh, Adrianna Ostwald
2000	UPAB	Kingsford	1:50.4	Jamie Fornetti, Elissa Brown, Shannon McHugh, Kelly Hicks
2001	UPD1	Marquette	1:50.1*	Kelsey McKinney, Amanda Holtz, Emily Knuskern, Danielle Sto
2002	UPD1	Menominee	1:52.0	Jessica Parette, Ash Kostreva, Amanda Kudwa, Ashley Taccolini
2003	UPD1	Escanaba	1:51.71	Jami Acker, Jamie Gross, Gina Pearson, Madelyn Anthony
2004	UPD1	Gladstone	1:49.50*	Sarah Skultety, Kristin Johnson, Hayley Ford, Ashley Nyenhuis
2005	UPD1	Gladstone	1:48.40*	Sarah Skultety, Nikki LaLonde, Hayley Ford, Ashley Nyenhuis
2006	UPD1	Marquette	1:46.34*	Alyssa Espamer, Jessica Trotochaud, Brittnee Balbierz, Catherine Angeli
2007	UPD1	Marquette	1:46.57	Katy LaFayette, Jessica Trotochaud, Brittnee Balbierz, Catherine Angell
2008	UPD1	Iron Mountain	1:50.72	Jacqueline Cowling, Allison Leb, Brittany Newberry, Michaela Newberry
2009	UPD1	Negaunee	1:49.28	Mykka Marana, Faith Rushford, Kristina Mattson, Heather Moore
2010	UPD1	Negaunee	1:48.25	Mykka Moore, Jocelyn Clickner, Kristina Mattson, Heather Moore
2011	UPD1	Sault Ste. Marie	1:48.64	Heather Johnston, Kaitlyn Thomas, Hailey Perron, Megan Jean
2012	UPD1	Menominee	1:50.54	Jane Enderby, Courtney Conery, Lexi Christian, Allia Stewart
2013	UPD1	Marquette	1:49.60	Kathleen Noblet, Cassidy Thomas, Hunter Viitala, Bente Korte
2014	UPD1	Escanaba	1:48.42	Jaynala Levigne, Maddy Willis, Hannah Beversluis, Lynsey Collins
2015	UPD1	Escanaba	1:51.24	Sunny Martineau, Lucy Slivia, Maddy Willis, Lauren Collins
2016	UPD1	Kingsford	1:49.10	Sarah Roell, Kendra Nora, Olivia Allen, Raegan Pratt
2017	UPD1	Marquette	1:50.31	Abby Kroll, Ahnik Puskala, Izabelle Peterson, Sierra Carlson

| 2018 | UPD1 | Marquette | | 1:49.20 | Abby Kroll, Tellena Nystrom, Rachael Hunt, Clarissa Remilard |

4 x 200 – UP Class C/Division 2 Champions

(medley relay)

Year	Class	School		Time	Team
1974	UPC	Ontanagon		2:04.3y*	Mary Sorenson, Virginia Banks, Sheri Store, Sandy Kalunki

(4 x 220 yards)

Year	Class	School	Time	Team
1975	UPC	Iron Mountain	1:52.2y*	
1976	UPC	Ishpeming Westwood	1:50.6y*	
1977	UPC	Stephenson	1:48.4y*	Jane Kuntze, Cindy Schlaack, Connie Swanson, Tammi Revall
1978	UPC	Ishpeming Westwood	1:50.4y	
1979	UPC	Negaunee	1:50.8	
1980	UPC	Hancock	1:50.7	Lynne Scholie, Betsy Julien, Mary Lewis, Amy Sporalski
1981	UPC	Stephenson	1:50.8	Robin Eick, Chris Sullivan, Debbie Hoots, Becky Mayer
1982	UPC	Negaunee	1:51.3	Lesley Coduti, Clare Mendelsohn, Beth Collins, Kathy Kontio
1983	UPC	Calumet	1:50.8	Libby Green, Debbie Butler Amber Harris, Tina Antilla
1984	UPC	Calumet	1:51.4	Chris Orr, Mya Frantti, Sarah Jurmu, Tina Antilla
1985	UPC	Stephenson	1:51.0	Terry Jeschke, Lori Eatherton, Karen Olson, Roberta VanPool
1986	UPC	Stephenson	1:50.2	Lori Eatherton, Heidi Burie, Karen Olson, Roberta VanPool
1987	UPC	Ishpeming Westwood	1:52.0	Sherry Covell, Krista Knutson, Crystal Luokkala, Heidi Knutson
1988	UPC	Stephenson	1:50.5	Jean Wiandt, Lauri Eckert, Traci Jeschke, Karen Steinhoff
1989	UPC	Iron River West Iron County	1:52.4	Stacy Marcell, Kim Bracket, Carl Dzanbozoff, Maria Velesano
1990	UPC	Iron River West Iron County	1:50.6	Stacy Marcell, Roberta Maki, Brenda Buhro, Maria Velesano
1991	UPC	Ironwood	1:50.6	Heidi Zieman, Nicole Bergquist, Anne Borowski, Tina Davis
1992	UPC	Ironwood	1:54.0	Heidi Zieman, Haley Puotinen, Anna Spaete, Angela Arthur
1993	UPC	Stephenson	1:51.4	Erin Koller, Heather Schmidt, Jessica Anders, Sandy Schnell
1994	UPC	Ironwood	1:50.6	Ann Spaete, Jamie Milakovich, Haley Poooutanen, Angela Arthur
1995	UPC	St. Ignace	1:49.5	Anna Pemble, Melanie SHeridan, Holly Brown, Richelle Robinson
1996	UPC	St. Ignace	1:49.7	Anna Pemble, Marion Clement, Melanie Sheridan, Richelle Robinson
1997	UPC	Iron Mountain	1:51.5	Stacy Olson, Kerry Kusz, Erica Cousineau, Megan De Groot
1998	UPC	Ishpeming	1:51.5	
1999	UPC	Ironwood	1:52.2	Ginger Polich, Kelly Finco, Kristin Harina, Pam Balduc
2000	UPC	St. Ignace	1:48.7	Marielle Calcaterra, Karolyn Getzen, Kate Ruegg, Eryn Mercer
2001	UPD2	St. Ignace	1:48.9*	Kate Ruegg, Karolyn Getzen, Marielle Calcatera, Eryn Mercer
2002	UPD2	Ishpeming Westwood	1:51.2	Kaylee Laaskao, M Johnson, Kristin Pellonpaa, Hilary Lucarel
2003	UPD2	Ishpeming Westwood	1:53.40	Kayle Laasko, Kristen Pellonpaa, Molly Johnson, Hillary Lucarelli
2004	UPD2	Ishpeming	1:50.40	Katelyn Argall, Jessica Wood, Natalie Bertucci, Leslie Luehmann
2005	UPD2	Manistique	1:51.76	
2006	UPD2	St. Ignace	1:51.19	Stacee Schnicke, Casey Brown, Ashley St. Louis, Kelsey Cryderman
2007	UPD2	Manistique	1:52.11	Kayla Anthony, Samantha Bryant, Katie Lamuth, Robin Vaughn
2008	UPD2	Ishpeming Westwood	1:56.52	Hannah Hegbloom, Mariah Schultz, Katie Ray, Taylor Watters
2009	UPD2	West Iron County	1:55.92	Jessie Schmidt, Latoya Carter-Bartley, Adri Ceron, Joanna Pellizzer
2010	UPD2	St. Ignace	1:51.68	Kali Jo Marshall, Autumn Huskey, Taylor Becker, Alexa Thiba
2011	UPD2	St. Ignace	1:53.47	
2012	UPD2	Ishpeming	1:52.39	Bella Stocker, Jessica Spencer, Aubrey Millimaki, Kara Dale
2013	UPD2	West Iron County	1:52.19	Casey Harrington, Sarah Penkivech, Elizabeth Pellizer, Carli Johnson
2014	UPD2	St. Ignace	1:53.10	Eileen Law, Morgan Lavake, Margo Brown, Rachel Harrington
2015	UPD2	Ishpeming	1:55.63	Anna Terres, Johanna Harvey, Jessica Spencer, Katie Loman
2016	UPD2	Hancock	1:54.89	Taylor Pertile, Julie Heinonen, Ellie Lucier, Mary Jarvis
2017	UPD2	Ishpeming	1:53.77	Hailey Smith, Mariah Austin, Emma Pourier, Katie Loman
2018	UPD2	Ishpeming	1:53.68	Anna Terres, Kayla Koski, Hailey Smith, Katie Loman

4 x 200 – UP Class C/Division 3 Champions

(y=4 x 220 yards)

Year	Class	School	Time	Team
1975	UPD	Rapid River	1:52.9y*	Sally Stenlund, Kay LaBumbard, Julie Siering, Sharon Kaukola
1976	UPD	Engadine	1:52.9y*	
1977	UPD	Engadine	1:52.4y*	
1978	UPD	Engadine	1:50.8y*	Sherry Ozanich, Robby Roberts, Gloria Bell, Vicki Thomas
1979	UPD	Norway	1:49.7*	Jan Sandrin, Connie Fuller, Darlene Allen, Aoria Koller
1980	UPD	Norway	1:49.6*	Darlene Allen, Meg Wieland, Connie Fuller, Darla Koller
1981	UPD	Norway	1:51.0	Darlene Allen, Meg Wieland, Trisha Priante, Darla Koller
1982	UPD	Lake Linden-Hubbell	1:52.0	Michelle Halperin, Gail Keranen, Chris Beaudoin, Jackie Keranan
1983	UPD	Lake Linden-Hubbell	1:52.2	Michelle Halperin, Gail Keranen, Chris Beaudoin, Jackie Keranan
1984	UPD	Cedarville	1:54.6	Michelle Kasper, Lora Torsky, Michelle Houk, Jill Labinski
1985	UPD	Pickford	1:54.4	Cindy Schwiderson, Missy Hatfield, Michelle Stevenson, Kris Kyle
1986	UPD	Pickford	1:51.8	Cindy Schwiderson, Michelle Stevenson, Tamara Ball, Kris Kyle
1987	UPD	Pickford	1:52.7	Cindy Schwiderson, Missy Hatfield, Betty Baker, Kris Kyle
1988	UPD	Pickford	1:53.2	Gina Weatherly, Denise Fabry, Betty Baker, Kris Kyle
1989	UPD	Felch North Dickinson	1:52.6	Chastity Pool, Jessica Davison, Madge Lucas, Connie Harder
1990	UPD	Pickford	1:51.9	Maggie Clawson, Gina Hopkins, Becky Moore, Nicole Skinner
1991	UPD	Pickford	1:52.4	Wendy Hartwig, Gina Hopkins, Becky Moore, Nicole Skinner
1992	UPD	Lake Linden-Hubbell	1:54.7	Christina Koski, Michelle Gervais, Missi Pini, Missy Gervais
1993	UPD	Engadine	1:53.0	Christina Bertucci, Jill Barrett, Jennifer LeGault, Janelle LeGault
1994	UPD	Lake Linden-Hubbell	1:52.0	Cristina Koski, Missy Gervais Sarah Jones, Dawn Savolainen
1995	UPD	Bark River-Harris	1:53.7	Beth Ives, Melissa Richer, Chantelle Kliecamp, Jenny Wienckowski
1996	UPD	Bark River-Harris	1:55.2	Lori Popeika, Melissa Richer, Chantelle Kliecamp, Jenny Wienckowski
1997	UPD	Bessemer	1:54.7	Rachel Pertile, Laura Jacobson, Kari Londo, Jaclyn Bebeau
1998	UPD	St. Ignace	1:51.7	Karolyn Getzen, Eryn Mercer, Richelle Robinson, Heather Sayles
1999	UPD	Bessemer	1:53.4	Rachel Pertile, Ashley Barto, Karin Roberts, Jacklyn Bebeau
2000	UPD	Pickford	1:51.6*	Yvonne Keith, Ashley Fountain, Gabby Morrison, Rachel Morri
2001	UPD3	Pickford	1:52.6	Kara Waybrant, Rachel Morrison, Gabby Morrison, Yvonne Keith
2002	UPD3	Pickford	1:52.4	Megan Hunter, Gabby Morrison, Kristina Peffers, Rachel Morrison
2003	UPD3	Bessemer	1:55.87	Hannah Kolesar, Corrie Reil. Kaleena Meldrum. Elizabeth Bravatto
2004	UPD3	Rapid River	1:52.43	Lauren Marshall, Cassi Rushford, Kayla McCormick, Breanne Marshall

2005	UPD3	Lake Linden-Hubbell	1:53.83	Paige Cidere, Amy Cloutier, Anela Guisfredi, Holly Seppala
2006	UPD3	Bessemer	1:53.05	Marie Ahnen, Sasha Sprague, Nichole Merten, Kaleena Meldrun
2007	UPD3	L'Anse	1:52.51	Lisa Bennett, Lauren Bianco, Jackie Collins, Kellie Collins
2008	UPD3	Lake Linden-Hubbell	1:55.35	Jeanna Hendrickson, Molly Monette, Jestina Poissant, Paige Codere
2009	UPD3	Crystal Falls Forest Park	1:52.81	Hilary Roose, Ana Cornelia, Kathleen Grandahl, Maria Valesano
2010	UPD3	Crystal Falls Forest Park	1:52.31	Hilary Roose, Ana Cornelia, Taylor Taunton, Maria Valesano
2011	UPD3	Brimley	1:50.61*	Alexis Mason, Becca Carruthers, Taylor Wilson, Tabitha Graham
2012	UPD3	Crystal Falls Forest Park	1:53.56	Audrey Sholander, Sierra Sholander, Ana Cornelia, Mary Grandahl
2013	UPD3	St. Ignace	1:51.48	Hailey Brown, Autumn Orm, Morgan Lavake, Rachel Hetherington
2014	UPD3	Crystal Falls Forest Park	1:53.21	Maria Stankiewicz, Libby Shamion, Mary Grandahl, Abby Nyland
2015	UPD3	Bark River-Harris	1:55.52	Hannah Starnes, Alissa Willa, Jaelin Lockwood, Katie Schultz
2016	UPD3	Pickford	1:55.37	Kayla Rambo, Jade Ledy, Victoria Portice, Heidi Hagen
2017	UPD3	Lake Linden-Hubbell	1:54.99	Erin Seppala, Kaitlyn Baccus, Mariah Wilmer, Joslyn Perala
2018	UPD3	Lake Linden-Hubbell	1:53.22	Erin Seppala, Jamie Hendrickson, Maria Willmer, Joslyn Perala

GIRLS 4 x 400 RELAY

Records

D1	3:46.43	Ann Arbor Pioneer	Melissa Phillips, Osamueda Phillips, Kiara Moore, Lauren Fortson	2004
D2	3:56.07	Battle Creek Lakeview	Jennifer Johnson, Allison Hunt, Audrey Graham, Jennifer Price	2000
D3	3:57.80	Adrian Madison	Chelsea Short, Delaney Stersic, Sierra Hernandez, Megan Rosales	2016
D4	4:04.48	Ubly	Kayla Kubacki, Lyndsay White, Andrea Hill, Jade Kaufman	2007
UPD1	4:00.15	Marquette	Holly Blowers, Shayla Huebner, Lindesy Rudden, Amber Huebner	2015
UPD2	4:14.55	Iron Mountain	Tilica Singh, Christen Alquist, Jessica Hartwig, Hilary Beauchamp	2004
UPD3	4:20.26	Cedarville	Lindsay McLeod, Lauren Izzard, Katie Bowlby, Billie McLeod	2006

Records by Class (pre-2000 for LP, pre-2001 for UP)

A	3:49.5	Flint Northern	Alisha Johnson, Marlene Isabelle, Carlene Isabelle, Pamela Brown	1983
B	3:55.64	Flint Beecher	Twynette Wilson, Pretoria Wilson, Michelle Westbrook, Ayuna Hairston	1987
C	4:03.4	Burton-Bentley	Laurie Diehl, Jennifer Erickson, Beth Cummings, Amanda Aldrich	1984
	4:03.45	Detroit Country Day	Peggy Evans, Ngina Burgette, Shirley Evans, Hameera Newman	1987
	4:03.4	Detroit Country Day	Peggy Evans, Shirley Evans, Ngina Burgette, Hameera Newman	1988
D	4:02.1	Fowler	Jan Schmidt, Kelly Hafner, Lana Hafner, Becky Klein	1983
UPAB	4:07.9y	Marquette	Kay Levandoski, Karen Levandoski, Cyne Cory, Katie Miller	1977
UPC	4:09.9	St Ignace	Holly Brown, Marion Clement, Melanie Sheridan, Richelle Robinson	1996
UPD	4:16.2	White Pine	Lori Kempainen, Charlotte Menghini, Kristin Kroll, Sandra Crocker	1983

4 x 400 – Class A/Division 1 Champions

(y=4 x 440 yards)

1975	A	Walled Lake Western	4:00.1y*	Laurel Taylor, Kathy Samples, Vanessa Parish, Ruth Hubbard
1976	A	Walled Lake Western	3:57.8y*	Vanessa Parrish, Sue Reimer, Karen Ruschak, Ruth Hubbard
1977	A	Walled Lake Western	3:57.5y*	Vanessa Parrish, Karen Abel, Sue Reimer, Ruth Hubbard
1978	A	Detroit Mackenzie	3:55.5y*	Mira Jones, Melanie Tillman, Kimberly Watts, Delisa Walton
1979	A	Flint Northern	3:51.6y*	Paula McGee, Pam McGee, Levy String, Tonya Lowe
1980	A	Flint Northern	3:54.0y	Edyth Childress, Meoachy Proby, Levy String, Tonya Lowe
1981	A	Ann Arbor Pioneer	3:51.3y*	Theresa Arnold, Rhonda Lathie, Tara Cope, Barb Ellis
1982	A	Detroit Chadsey	3:52.7	Vera Pruitt, Vivian McKenzie, Kari Manns, Cynthia DIxon
1983	A	Flint Northern	3:49.5*	Alisha Johnson, Marlene Isabelle, Carlene Isabelle, Pamela Brown
1984	A	Ann Arbor Pioneer	3:49.7	Karin Surratt, Rolanda Officer, Charmaine Byer, Victoria Shields
1985	A	Detroit Cass Tech	3:53.2	Nancy Wheeler, Tracey Harris, Luaneada Moten, Angela Jones
1986	A	Detroit Cass Tech	3:54.99	Paula Lee, Stacey Randolph, Tamiko Powell, Angela Jones
1987	A	Detroit Cass Tech	3:50.6	Paula Lee, Stacey Randolph, Darchelle Ross, Tamiko Powell
1988	A	Detroit Denby	4:00.36	Myrtis Hyman, Nikita Shumake, Deshawn McFarlin. Dawn McFarlin
1989	A	Ann Arbor Pioneer	3:58.4	LaTonya Payne, Heather Brown, Ashanti Harris, Crystal Braddock
1990	A	Detroit Cass Tech	3:56.48	LuRonda Poole, Kim Turnbough, Shameakia Dunwoody, Kemyetta Knox
1991	A	Ann Arbor Pioneer	3:59.86	Hayley Wilkins, Heather Brown, Gennifer Bridges, Seena Walters
1992	A	Detroit Cass Tech	4:00.44	Obiama Alhamisi, Cheryl Omar, Erica Shepherd, Lamika Harper
1993	A	Detroit Cass Tech	3:54.34	Nicole Calloway, Chery Omar, Erica Shepherd, Chantelle Nagbe
1994	A	Detroit Cass Tech	3:56.5	Nicolle Callaway, Obiama Alhamisi, Katie Chapman, Julia Ford
1995	A	Detroit Cass Tech	3:57.45	Janelle Toles, Katie Chapman, Julia Ford, Ayobani Bell
1996	A	Detroit Cass Tech	3:51.17	Ayobani Bell, Katie Chapman, Julia Ford, Traci Ball
1997	A	Detroit Cass Tech	3:53.33	Kanisa Williams, Julia Ford, Traci Ball, Katie Chapman,
1998	A	Detroit Martin Luther King	3:54.75	Sherita Williams, Akilah Washington, Keisha Spight, Shannon Vesey
1999	A	Southfield	3:51.51	Melonie Williams, Imani Williams, Lindsay Bond, Carly Knazze
2000	D1	Ann Arbor Pioneer	3:54.80*	Alexis Evans, Tiffany Hall, Venice Jones, Christine Kutscchinski
2001	D1	Ann Arbor Pioneer	3:55.82	Andrea Mosher, Aja Hunter, Jennifer Harrold, Christine Kutschinski
2002	D1	Ann Arbor Pioneer	3:54.60*	Lauren Fortson, Keisha Townsend, Osameude Iyoha, Andrea Mosher
2003	D1	Rockford	3:54.62	Kylie Freyling, Selina Johnson, Kristie Powers, Lisa Krueger
2004	D1	Ann Arbor Pioneer	3:46.43*	Melissa Phillips, Osamueda Phillips, Kiara Mooe, Lauren Fortson
2005	D1	Ann Arbor Pioneer	3:52.48	Chidimma Uche, Kiara Moore, Saisha Gillard, Brittiney Jones
2006	D1	Milford	3:56.67	Amber Pearsall, Carlie Green, Katherine Carter, Cara Dukes
2007	D1	Ann Arbor Pioneer	3:51.5	Jessica Lee, Chidimma Uche, Tiara Sharp, Kiara Moore
2008	D1	Jackson	3:50.85	Jaelynn Pryor, Elise Brown, Brenda Gibson, Brittani Williams
2009	D1	Romulus	3:52.53	Kanaya Williams, Britnee Bishop, Malita Rutherford, Christienne Linton
2010	D1	Pinckney	3:54.12	Eliza Vandekerkhove, Julia Vanderkkhove, Natalie Nelson, Rachel Clark
2011	D1	Detroit Cass Tech	3:50.25	Ravyn Baxter, Alexie Hull, Kyra Jefferson, Janika King
2012	D1	Grosse Pointe South	3:53.90	Caitlin Moore, Ersula Farrow, Haley Meier, Hannah Meier

2013	D1	Grosse Pointe South	3:52.32	Lily Pendy, Ersula Farrow, Haley Meier, Hannah Meier
2014	D1	Oak Park	3:49.88	Brianna Holloway, Johnyce Powell, Drew Coleman, Jayla Fleming
2015	D1	Oak Park	3:51.50	Johnyce Powell, Drew Coleman, Ersula Farrow, Dorriann Coleman
2016	D1	Northville	3:50.58	Morgan Kloosterman, Yasmine Affes, Lindsey Walters, Chloe Abbott
2017	D1	Oak Park	3:49.73	Carlita Taylor, Drew Cileman, Mayala Gate, Miyala Broolks
2018	D1	Oak Park	3:51.01	Makayla Gates, Jayla Jones, Mariyah Archibald, Dorriann Coleman

4 x 400 – Class B/Division 2 Champions

(y=4 x 440 yards)

1975	B	Alma	4:13.8y*	Jan Almaugher, Dennie Frank, Lisa Fandell, Debbie Bradford
1976	B	Holt	4:03.0y*	Brenda Schroeder Marilyn Barner, Joy Parker, Joanna Matthyssen
1977	B	Fenton	4:05.1y	Katie Anderson, Angie Pitman, Susan Ambler, Sue Hintz
1978	B	Holt	3:56.5y*	Joy Parker, Shannon Grable, Marilyn Barner, Yvonne Matthyssen
1979	B	Flint Beecher	4:01.5y	Vennette Watkins, Shari Brock, Jackie Ferguson, Diane Wiley
1980	B	Grand Rapids Christian	3:59.9	Tanya DeVries, Gayle Heyer, Amy Boerman, Dawn Walstrom
1981	B	Livonia Ladywood	4:02.9	Ronna Greenberg, Leslie Nedeau, Katy Harley, Jennifer Rioux
1982	B (tie)	Grand Rapids Christian	4:05.8y	Tanya DeVries, Kris Honderd, Ann Shannon, Cheryl Bokhoven
1982	B (tie)	Richmond	4:05.8y	Kim Quinn, Monica Lelowicz, Linda Krammer, Kelly Cracchiolo
1983	B	Grand Rapids Christian	4:02.2	Diann Takens, Becky Anderson, Vickie VaanDrager, Kris Honderd
1984	B	Livonia Ladywood	4:04.7	Susan Willey, Angela Ovgas, Julie Camiller, Joan Arndt
1985	B	Flint Beecher	3:59.20	Twynette Wilson, Pretoria Wilson, Danita Sims, Michelle Westbrook
1986	B	Flint Beecher	4:03.0	Pretoria Wilson, Twynette Wilson, Tracy Payton, Michele Westbrook
1987	B	Flint Beecher	3:55.64*	Twynette Wilson, Pretoria Wilson, Michelle Westbrook, Ayuna Hairston
1988	B	Redford Borgess	4:03.72	Angie Ross, Philana Hooper, Shelly Blanding, Kim Mitchell
1989	B	Dexter	4:01.9	Andrea Spurr, Jenny Gilbert, Laura Atkinson, Val Muck
1990	B	Dexter	4:03.2	Sheila Hammons, Amy Hiatt, Jenny Gilbert, Val Muck
1991	B	Flint Beecher	4:00.87	Rhoda Read, Niketa Williams, Renona Childress, Chantella Byrd
1992	B	Flint Beecher	4:05.19	Rhoda Read, Niketa WIlliams, Renona Childress, Chantella Byrd
1993	B	Middleville Thornapple Kellogg	4:04.14	Carla Ploeg, Kim Wohlford, Sarah Kaechele, Tracy Middleton
1994	B	Hamilton	4:02.67	Gina Reuschel, Amy Molenaar, Sarah Peters, Lisa Poll
1995	B	Dearborn Heights Robichaud	4:07.66	Tamika Craig, Lorri Alverson, Juanita McGrew, Andrea McGrew
1996	B	Dearborn Heights Robichaud	3:57.81	Tamika Craig, Stephanie Gray, Juanita McGrew, Andrea McGrew
1997	B	Detroit Renaissance	4:00.0	Adriane Mayes, Julia Stevenson, Rashida Bradley, Julia Redd
1998	B	Detroit Renaissance	3:57.77	Jennifer Lawson, Julia Stevenson, Rashida Bradley, Julia Redd
1999	B	Battle Creek Lakeview	4:02.47	Jennifer Johnson, Holly Gremore, Audrey Graham, Jennifer Price
2000	D2	Battle Creek Lakeview	3:56.07*	Jennifer Johnson, Allison Hunt, Audrey Graham, Jennifer Price
2001	D2	Detroit Renaissance	3:59.30	Camille Nelson, Erin Anderson, Ashley Bright, Chasity Armstrong
2002	D2	Detroit Renaissance	4:00.75	Amber Hay, Camilla Nelson, Jessica Jones, Kelly Sampson
2003	D2	Detroit Renaissance	3:56.64	Alexandrea Cunninghan, Amber Hay, Fallon Jenkins, Jessica Jones
2004	D2	Detroit Renaissance	3:59.34	Elesha Logan, Kelly Sampson, Patricia Gellespe, Amber Hay
2005	D2	Detroit Renaissance	3:56.45	Elesha Logan, Sharay Hale, Selly Sampson, Amber Hay
2006	D2	Middleville Thornapple Kellogg	4:02.83	Emma Ordway, Kersta Gustafson, Rebecca Winchester, Chaney Robinson
2007	D2	Detroit Renaissance	3:56.44	Kiara Smith, Christina Farrow, Camille Johnson, Ramzee Fondren
2008	D2	Ypsilanti	3:57.89	Talecia Francis, Maria Williams, Sha'meka Hamilton, Kyra Caldwell
2009	D2	Middleville Thornapple Kellogg	4:03.93	Hana Hunt, Stephanie Beleher, Cassie Holwerda, Emily Ordway
2010	D2	Chelsea	3:57.56	Corine Carpenter, Danielle Dahl, Grace Sauers, Olivia DeTroyer
2011	D2	Dearborn Divine Child	3:59.67	Mallory Myler, Liz Mullen, Carolinne Strasser, Paige Patterson
2012	D2	Dearborn Divine Child	3:59.05	Mallory Myler, Liz Mullen, Nicole Urbank, Paige Patterson
2013	D2	Dearborn Divine Child	3:58.78	Mallory Myler, Liz Mullen, Erin Drabicki, Paige Patterson
2014	D2	Lansing Waverly	4:02.08	Taylor Manson, Teaghan Thomas, Anaiyah Brewer, Chante Roberts
2015	D2	Battle Creek Harper Creek	4:02.02	Lexus Kerr, Kenzie Callahan, Catie Scott, Charley Andrews
2016	D2	Bloomfield Hills Marian	4:01.21	Morgan Cochran, Emily Below, Maggie DePorre, Jansen Eichenlaub
2017	D2	Grand Rapids Catholic Central	4:01.10	Mary Claire Mckolay, Avery Gill, Tess Ens, Jakarri Alvan
2018	D2	Holland Christian	4:00.09	Michelle Kuipers, Dolly Slenk, Elizabeth Bruxvoort, Madylin VanderZwaag

4 x 400 – Class C/Division 3 Champions

(y=4 x 440 yards)

1975	C	Bath	4:11.6y*	Penny Hull, Sally Carlson, Cindy Torrant, Mary Hull
1976	C	St. Louis	4:09.6y*	Cheryl Cline, Lori Flicik, Tracy Osgood, Mary Diaz
1977	C	St. Louis	4:14.8y	Cheryl Cline, Lorie Flicek, Sheila Cline, Tracy Osgood
1978	C	Portland	4:10.9y	Lynn Sochor, Bonnie Hall, Donna Bennett, Darcy Seal
1979	C	Portland	4:07.0y*	Lynne Sochor, Bonnie Hall, Monica Moyer, Donna Bennett
1980	C	Mt Clemens Lutheran North	4:08.0y	Terri Johns, Debbie Kenjorski, Anne Schmidt, Debbie Webb
1981	C	Stockbridge	4:04.3*	Heidi Withrow, Tammy Bumpus, Lucinda Willsey, Amy Bumpus
1982	C	Burton-Bentley	4:08.1	Laurie Diehl, Carol Nowicki, Bethany Cummings, Amanda Aldrich
1983	C	DeWitt	4:04.1*	Rhonda Davis, Sheri Schmitt, Stacey Ballard, Teresa Kirchen
1984	C	Burton-Bentley	4:03.4*	Laurie Diehl, Jennifer Erickson, Beth Cummings, Amanda Aldrich
1985	C	Bronson	4:07.09	Dawn Schottenloher, Missy Wilbur, Ekizabeth Wilbur, Kim Clover
1986	C	Detroit Country Day	4:08.57	Karen Tuille, Natalie Greenspan, Nginia Burgette, Hameera Newman
1987	C	Detroit Country Day	4:03.45*	Peggy Evans, Ngina Burgette, Shirley Evans, Hameera Newman
1988	C	Detroit Country Day	4:03.4*	Peggy Evans, Shirley Evans, Ngina Burgette, Hameera Newman
1989	C	Center Line St. Clement	4:08.85	Judy Gianino, Ann Pakizer, Amy Pakizer, Cathy Hall
1990	C	Tawas Area	4:11.27	Michelle Mochty, Tracy Suhan, Laurel Hay, Julie Bush
1991	C	Frankenmuth	4:09.4	Jaime Cloutier, Bree Nuechterlein, Michelle Mueller, Kristi Kern
1992	C	Vermontville-Maple Valley	4:09.4	Jennifer Phenix, Stephanie Bouwens, Mindy Shoup, Janet Boldrey
1993	C	Shepherd	4:05.46	Amy McCaul, Andrea Campbell, Jamie White, Jodi Gelina
1994	C	Clare	4:08.09	Katie Cole, Kylie Schultz, Dana Cole, Audrey Jelenek
1995	C	Hemlock	4:10.38	Christy Tedrow, Kelly Taylor, Nikki Schluckebier, Heidi Goodenough
1996	C	Addison	4:07.22	Christina Wolcott, Kristi Davenport, Gina Watson, Tricia Fo
1997	C	Kingsley	4:06.87	Alaina Olds, Amber Hayes, Kate Rieger, Erin Ockut
1998	C	Benzie Central	4:08.55	Keely Bigelow, Sarah Warnke, Caryn Waterson, Amber Bright
1999	C	Benzie Central	4:04.52	Keely Bigelow, Sarah Warnke, Caryn Waterson, Amber Bright
2000	D3	Benzie Central	4:03.80*	Keely Bigelow, Sarah Tarsney, Sarah Warnke, Caryn Waterson

2001	D3	Yale	4:05.74	Taryne Kavanagh, Courtney Kersten, Beth Vinckier, Heather Rejc
2002	D3	Yale	4:07.87	Beth Vinckier, Heather Rejc, Taryne Kavanagh, Courtney Kersten,
2003	D3	Lansing Catholic Central	4:06.04	Amanda Strouse, Erin Scahua, Renee Rademacher, Allison Strouse
2004	D3	Lansing Catholic Central	4:07.27	Liz Watson, Liz Hart, Eric Schau, Allison Strouse
2005	D3	Albion	4:01.89*	Mika Clark, Juandretta Oliver, Joranda Chapman, Alpha Clark
2006	D3	Albion	4:02.89	Jaundretta Oliver, JoRanda Chapman, Sharde Johnson, Amelia Bannister
2007	D3	Ann Arbor Gabriel Richard	3:59.06*	Alex McCoy, Amy Myler, Katie Weishaar, Kristen Goncalves
2008	D3	Stockbridge	4:03.99	Rachel Kurkowski, Christina Watson, Whitney Williams, Zoey Hohman
2009	D3	Frankenmuth	4:00.82	Olivia Shelton, Chelsea Mertz, Emily Wee, Kelsey Ritter
2010	D3	Frankenmuth	4:01.31	Brooke Crandall, Chelsea Mertz, Emily Wee, Kelsey Ritter
2011	D3	Onsted	4:03.12	Ashlin Aiken, Brittany Powell, Kelsey Rose, Allexis Johnson
2012	D3	Frankenmuth	4:03.77	Lauren Peterson, Olivia Shelton, Angela Ritter, Emily Wee
2013	D3	Pewamo-Westphalia	4:03.56	Erica Nurenberg, Cammie Noeker, Betsy Arens, Marissa Wirth
2014	D3	Pewamo-Westphalia	4:01.16	Brenna Wirth, Cammie Noeker, Betsy Arena, Marissa Wirth
2015	D3	Adrian Madison	4:04.24	Rita DeHoyos, Delaney Stersic, Sierra Hernandez, Megan Rosales
2016	D3	Adrian Madison	4:01.51	Chelsea Short, Delaney Stersic, Sierra Hernandez, Megan Rosales
2017	D3	Adrian Madison	3:57.80*	Chelsea Short, Delaney Stersic, Sierra Hernandez, Megan Rosales
2018	D3	Jackson Lumen Christi	4:01.90	Renae Kutcha, Allison Rand, Marilyn Schonhard, Audrey Warriner

4 x 400 – Class D/Division 4 Champions

(y=4 x 440 yards)

1975	D	Centreville	4:20.1y*	Karen Tomicek, Jean Schrader, Pat Buscher, Cheryl Henningsen
1976	D	Battle Creek St Phillip	4:14.5y*	Janet Chappell, Julie Flees, Judy Osterman, Veronica Collins
1977	D	Mt Pleasant Sacred Heart	4:10.7y*	Carol Goenner, Amy Kasprzewa, Barb Pohl, Patty Goenner
1978	D	Battle Creek St Phillip	4:14.7y	Cathy Petrucco, Shannon O'Brien, Sharon Haan, Julie Flees
1979	D	Ann Arbor Greenhills	4:12.0	Renee Cheng, Sue Kerry, Karen Kirk, Bradley Nixon
1980	D	Marion	4:17.0	Renee Dorman, Renee Blackledge, Mary Miller, Lynne Mitchel
1981	D	Fowler	4:05.8*	Lana Hafner, Kay Snyder, Jan Schmitt, Becky Klein
1982	D	Fowler	4:07.3	Jan Schmitt, Jill Armmbrustmacher, Lana Hafner, Becky Klein
1983	D	Fowler	4:02.1*	Jan Schmidtt, Kelly Hafner, Lana Hafner, Becky Klein
1984	D	Fowler	4:09.15	Nancy Sillman, Kelly Hafner, Beth Wirth, Darcy Schmidtt
1985	D	Athens	4:08.06	Carla Voss, Tina Kinney, Cindy Cayo, Cheryl Boddy
1986	D	Grass Lake	4:10.52	Andi Clark, Kim Cook, Janey Sczykutowicz, Cait Spaan
1987	D	Redford St. Mary	4:13.14	Kim Townsend, Cherie Sheldon, Whonda Morris, Twana Ragney
1988	D	Fowler	4:11.4	Marcy Sillman, Beth Wieber, Sherine Rowell, Mindy Sillman
1989	D	Maple City Glen Lake	4:05.5	Jane Derengowski, Marnie Peplinski, Jennifer Plowman, Theresa Proost
1990	D	Maple City Glen Lake	4:11.53	Jennifer Plowman, Theresa Proost, Edie Aylsworth, Marnie Peplinski
1991	D	Maple City-Glen Lake	4:06.75	Sue Hobbins, Marnie Peplinski, Jennifer Plowman, Theresa Proost
1992	D	Maple City Glen Lake	4:03.90	Marnie Peplinski, Theresa Proost, Jennifer Plowman, Erin Attwood
1993	D	Litchfield	4:09.4	Lesley Keeney, Chey Phelps, Pam Blonde, Karen VanNieuwenhuyzen
1994	D	Pittsford	4:11.84	Julie Rigers, Holly Leupp, Lyndsey Burchardt, Stacie Barron
1995	D	Fowler	4:12.69	Kim Hafner, Karmen Epkey, Gwen Thelen, Desha Feldpausch
1996	D	Homer	4:11.66	Mandy Buell, Jennifer Russell, Courtney Huffman, Liz Powers
1997	D	Homer	4:11.52	Sarah Baxter, Courtney Huffman, Marion Crandall, Jennifer Russell,
1998	D	Fowler	4:07.6	Courtney Weber, Jessica Schmitt, Emily Pohl, Desha Feldpausch
1999	D	Bellaire	4:09.57	Elly Johnson, Libby Conkle, Katy Belanger, Kendra Johnson
2000	D4	Saginaw Michigan Lutheran	4:09.17*	Jenny Mueller, Emily Krentz, Mary Kelly, Lisa Mueller
2001	D4	Reading	4:08.17*	Jessica Mundy, Summer Stewart, Erica Young, EMily Trott
2002	D4	Burton Atherton	4:06.26*	Kyla Crawford, Courtney Klagstad, Brooke Crawford, Angela Crawford
2003	D4	Burton Atherton	4:09.25	Elizabeth Christie, Courtney Klagstad, Brooke Crawford, Kyla Crawford
2004	D4	Reading	4:11.53	Sarah Thomas, Tarrah Pifer, Jamie Carver, Erin Dillon
2005	D4	Saginaw Valley Lutheran	4:10.49	Krista Wegener, Angie Soldan, Brooke Robertson, Laura Adams
2006	D4	Ubly	4:08.58	Ashley Romzek, Lyndsay White, Andrea Hill, Jade Kaufman
2007	D4	Ubly	4:04.48*	Kayla Kubacki, Lyndsay White, Andrea Hill, Jade Kaufman
2008	D4	Potterville	4:09.41	Kristina Donley, Kaila Cook, Amy LaDuke, Kelsey Letson
2009	D4	Potterville	4:06.32	Jenna Whipple, Justeen Roe, Kaila Cook, Kelsey Letson
2010	D4	Fowler	4:12.12	Brittany Weber, Elizabeth Thelen, Brianne Feldpausch, Lindsey Hufnagel
2011	D4	Hillsdale Academy	4:05.96	Shena Albaugh, Carly Hubbard, Emily Brady, Shaley Albaugh
2012	D4	Traverse City St. Francis	4:12.47	Kaitlyn Hegewald, Maddy Danz, Erin McDonnell, Lauren Buckel
2013	D4	Reading	4:07.29	Sam Pfeiffer, Terasa Ridenier, Jennifer Davis, Michelle Davis
2014	D4	Reading	4:10.96	Michelle Davis, Samantha Pfeiffer, Terasa Eidenier, Alyssa Kinney
2015	D4	Harbor Springs	4:08.14	Charlotte Cullip, Claire Fleming, Kyra LaRue, Salix Sampson
2016	D4	Fowler	4:08.28	Madison Koenigsknecht, McKenzie Koenigsknecht, Julie Thelen, Taryn Schafer
2017	D4	Southfield Christian	4:07.33	Rebekah Wilson, Kaelin Ray, Chika Amene, Shelby Goodson
2018	D4	Fowler	4:05.99	McKenzie Koenigsknecht, Josie Koenigsknecht, Grace Boak, Morgan George

4 x 400 – UP Class AB/Division 1 Champions

(y=4 x 440 yards)

1972	UP-All	Marquette	4:46.8y*	
1973-4	not held			
1975	UPAB	Marquette	4:18.5y*	
1976	UPAB	Marquette	4:13.8y*	
1977	UPAB	Marquette	4:07.9y*	Kay Levandoski, Karen Levandoski, Cyne Cory, Katie Miller
1978	UPAB	Marquette	4:13.8y	
1979	UPAB	Menominee	4:12.9	Sandy Garbowicz, Sandy Harpt, Leigh Otterley, Linda Eward
1980	UPAB	Menominee	4:14.1	Patti Parpt, Lori Danielson, Linda Ewald, Sandy Farbowicz
1981	UPAB	Escanaba	4:15.8	Michelle Hall, Lisa Phelan, Jeanne Courneene, Sharon Kuivinen
1982	UPAB	Escanaba	4:19.4	Tammy Funke, Laurie Brink, Jeanne Courneene, Sharon Kuivinen
1983	UPAB	Marquette	4:14.3	Kyrin Smith, Dawn Snyder, Theresa Bernier, Liz Sarvello
1984	UPAB	Marquette	4:18.6	Theresa Bernier, Lisa Schwindt, Kathy VanKosky, Joeli Wichar
1985	UPAB	Menominee	4:18.0	Karen Englund, Marlo Blake, Kory Gunderson, Tori Knispel
1986	UPAB	Menominee	4:12.9	Karen Englund, Sally Gentile, Kory Gunderson, Vina Poquette
1987	UPAB	Menominee	4:17.4	Amberly Lake, Sally Gentile, Korry Gunderson, Vina Poquette

1988	UPAB	Marquette	4:16.3	Liz Connor, Wendy Price, Sherrill VanBeynen, Michelle Chause
1989	UPAB	Marquette	4:17.8	Liz Connor, Mary Scherer, Kelly Larson, Amy Lassila
1990	UPAB	Marquette	4:16.9	Mary Scherer, Wendy Price, Lori Larson, Amy Lassila
1991	UPAB	Kingsford	4:12.8	Tracy Anderson, Heather Sparapani, Lori Glaser, Jennie Drake
1992	UPAB	Kingsford	4:21.2	Heather Sparapani, Kris Wozniak, Lori Glaser, Jennie Drake
1993	UPAB	Marquette	4:17.1	Lisa Larson, Carol Anderson, Megan Scherer, Michelle Olds
1994	UPAB	Marquette	4:16.9	Michele Scherer, Lisa Larson, Megan Scherer, Sommer Stesney
1995	UPAB	Marquette	4:12.4	Michele Scherer, Brooke Berube, Sommer Stesney, Sarah Heikkila
1996	UPAB	Sault Ste. Marie	4:10.3	Nicole Pietrangelo, Laura Abrahamson, Rebecca Johnson, Maryea Pike
1997	UPAB	Marquette	4:16.7	Sommer Stesney, Kristine Jentoft, Jessica Taylor, Chrissy Barnes
1998	UPAB	Marquette	4:16.5	Jacoba Williamson, Margaret Epinga, Jill Kimmes, Alex Wilkinson
1999	UPAB	Marquette	4:14.4	Angela Abernathy, Nikki Cowell, Katie Anderson, Erica Helmila
2000	UPAB	Gladstone	4:13.5	Jessie Orhanen, Kari Brodeen, Jamie Lyberg, Tiffany Petr
2001	UPD1	Gladstone	4:14.59*	Jessie Orhanen, Kari Brodeen, Jamie Lyberg, Tiffany Petr
2002	UPD1	Marquette	4:14.75	Kara Patterson, Emily Knickern, Jen Pertile, Christy Griffen
2003	UPD1	Kingsford	4:13.90*	Allyson Caudell, Janelle Schillerstrom, Aimee D'Amour, Larenda Hintz
2004	UPD1	Escanaba	4:10.25*	Jamie Acker, Kali Anderson, Chelsey Guay, Stephanie Ostrenga
2005	UPD1	Marquette	4:10.10*	Jackie Saunders, Brittnee Balbierz, Megan Mincheff, Catherine Angeli
2006	UPD1	Marquette	4:04.92*	Alyssa Espamer, Jessica Trotochaud, Brittnee Balbierz, Catherine Angeli
2007	UPD1	Marquette	4:08.55*	Katy LaFayette, Sara Storm, Jessica Trotochaud, Catherine Angeli
2008	UPD1	Marquette	4:10.90	
2009	UPD1	Negaunee	4:17.93	Mykka Marana, Sarah Tresseder, Heather Moore, Kristina Mattson
2010	UPD1	Negaunee	4:08.98	Jacelyn Clickner, Jayne Alexander, Heather Moore, Kristina Mattson
2011	UPD1	Marquette	4:08.64	Kathleen Noblet, Megan Dickinson, Sheila Flood, Tana Lakene
2012	UPD1	Marquette	4:11.82	Ashton Guidebeck, Hunter Viitala, Shayla Huebner, Jessica Fluette
2013	UPD1	Marquette	4:14.12	Cassidy Thomas, Bente Korte, Hunter Viitala, Shayla Huebner
2014	UPD1	Marquette	4:12.84	Cassidy Thomas, Lindsey Rudden, Hannah Detmers, Hunter Viitala
2015	UPD1	Marquette	4:00.15*	Holly Blowers, Shayla Huebner, Lindesy Rudden, Amber Huebner
2016	UPD1	Kingsford	4:12.67	Sarah Roell, Kendra Nora, Peyton Johnson, Olivia Allen
2016	UPD1	Marquette	4:05.40	Lindsey Rudden, Amber Huebner, Hannah Detmers, Holly Blowers
2017	UPD1	Kingsford	4:12.67	Sarah Roell, Kendra Nora, Peyton Johnson, Olivia Allen
2018	UPD1	Kingsford	4:19.00	Sarah Roell, Emma Allen, Peyton Johnson, Olivia Allen

4 x 400 – UP Class C/Division 2 Champions
(y=4 x 440 yards)

1975	UPC	Hancock	4:27.8y*	Barb Masters, Lori Houle, Mary Kay Ricci, Mary Joe Ricci
1976	UPC	L'Anse	4:18.2y*	
1977	UPC	Stephenson	4:14.1y*	Cheryl Shampo, Connie Swanson, Jane Kuntze, Cindy Schlaack
1978	UPC	Ishpeming Westwood	4:17.1y	
1979	UPC	Stephenson	4:23.2	C. DeMille, F. Kuntze, Connie Swanson, Cheryl Shampo
1980	UPC	Negaunee	4:13.8*	Clare Mendelsohn, Jill Merrick, Kimberly Barb, Carrie Talus
1981	UPC	Munising	4:22.9	Lisa McCollum, Kathy Marshall, Kathy Ghiardi, Beth McNally
1982	UPC	Negaunee	4:14.2	Clare Mendelsohn, Lesley Coduti, Vickie Bengry, Beth Collins
1983	UPC	Ontonagon	4:17.5	Betsy Domitrovich, Cheyl Saaranen, Nicole Morin, Jacki Hickey
1984	UPC	Ishpeming Westwood	4:15.0	Jesse Green, Pam Ostlund, Rhonda Ebner, Lisa Garrett
1985	UPC	Stephenson	4:14.5	Traci Jeschke, Lauri Eatherton, Karen Olson, Terry Jeschke
1986	UPC	Ishpeming Westwood	4:16.4	Krista Knutson, Heidi Knutson, Amy Laitala, Kelly Jandron
1987	UPC	Ishpeming Westwood	4:18.7	Crystal Luokkala, Kelly Jandron, Krista Knutson, Heidi Knutson
1988	UPC	Stephenson	4:17.8	Terri Jeschke, Andrea Frenzel, Lauri Erkert, Traci Jeschke
1989	UPC	Iron River West Iron County	4:18.8	Kim Brackey, Cari Dzanbozoff, Brenda Buhro, Chris Buhro
1990	UPC	Ontonagon	4:23.7	Mary Hoefferle, Lori Muhren, Cheri Rinne, Melllissa Rinne
1991	UPC	Ironwood	4:17.9	Nicole Berquit, Joy Makinen, Anne Borwoski, Jennifer Puotinen
1992	UPC	Munising	4:24.3	Nancy Patterson, Jamie St. Amour, Briggita Castiglione, Kelly Peterson
1993	UPC	Ironwood	4:18.6	Jane Somerville, Jill Pollock, Naomi Baksic, Lisa Kinnunen
1994	UPC	Munising	4:18.9	Betsy Scott, Jamie St. Amour, Jessica Bowerman, Kelly Peterson
1995	UPC	Ironwood	4:14.6	Naomi Baksic, Jill Pollack, Lori Carlson, Ann Somerville
1996	UPC	St. Ignace	4:09.9*	Holly Brown, Marion Clement, Melanie Sheridan, Richelle Robinson
1997	UPC	Ironwood	4:15.7	Chelsea Finco, Kim Yelich, Tara Makinen, Ann Somerville
1998	UPC	Ironwood	4:16.3	
1999	UPC	Ironwood	4:13.2	Chelsea Finco, Kim Yelich, Kelly FInco, Casey McGrath
2000	UPC	St. Ignace	4:14.5	Randi Johnson, Maarielle Calcaterra, Karolyn Getzen, Eryne Me
2001	UPD2	St. Ignace	4:14.9*	Karolyn Getzen, Maarielle Calcaterra, Krista Clement, Eryn Mercer
2002	UPD2	St. Ignace	4:20.6	Marielle Calcaterra, Adria West, Carlie Levi, Krista Clement
2003	UPD2	St. Ignace	4:15.15	Marielle Calcaterra, Carlie Levi, Liz Stempki, Krista Clement
2004	UPD2	Iron Mountain	4:14.55*	Tilica Singh, Christen Alquist, Jessica Hartwig, Hilary Beauchamp
2005	UPD2	Newberry	4:18.86	Andrea Roquist, Laurtn Shaffer, Chelsea Hanert, Cori Glime
2006	UPD2	Norway	4:27.28	Kalee LaCoursier, Miranda Zygiel, Brianna Tickler, Ellary Renier
2007	UPD2	Norway	4:18.93	Kalee Lacoursier, Miranda Zygiel, Hilary Zanoni, Ellary Renier
2008	UPD2	L'Anse	4:31.43	Lauren Bianco, Erin Connor, Jessica Kemppainen, Kellie Collins
2009	UPD2	Ishpeming	4:26.65	Macy Mahoski, Kerrie Myers, Kymber Beltrame, Kara Dale
2010	UPD2	West Iron County	4:24.45	Jaclyn Waara, Alyssa Davis, Shannon Koski, Joanna Pellizzer
2011	UPD2	West Iron County	4:21.51	Alyssa Davis, Shannon Penkivech, Jaclyn Waara, Joanna Pelli
2012	UPD2	West Iron County	4:21.02	Jacyyn Waara, Joanna Pellizzer, Cassilyn Pellizzer, Kylee Erickson
2013	UPD2	West Iron County	4:28.92	Rebekah Serbinski, Elizabeth Pellizer, Kylee Erickson, Cassilyn Pellizer
2014	UPD2	West Iron County	4:18.96	Elizabeth Pellizzer, Emmy Kinner, Brianna Lambert, Cassilyn Pellizzer
2015	UPD2	West Iron County	4:26.18	Erin Angeli, Sydney Mazurek, Elizabeth Pellizzer, Emmy Kinner
2016	UPD2	St. Ignace	4:23.12	Allison Smith, Libby Becker, Calli Kammers, Emily Coveyou
2016	UPD2	St. Ignace	4:27.18	Callie Kammers. Libby Becker, Allison Smith, Emilly Coveyou
2017	UPD2	St Ignace	4:23.12	Allison Smith, Libby Becker, Callie Kammers, Emily Coveyou
2018	UPD2	St Ignace	4:24.82	Allison Smith, Emily Coveyou, Elizabeth Becker, Emmalee Hart

4 x 400 – UP Class C/Division 3 Champions
(y=4 x 440 yards)

1975	UPD	Rapid River	4:28.7y*	Patti Thibault, Becky Martin, Terri Sanchez, Vicky Pearson
1976	UPD	Crystal Falls Forest Park	4:24.4y*	
1977	UPD	Lake Linden-Hubbell	4:25.0y	
1978	UPD	Lake Linden-Hubbell	4:25.6y	Lynn Norcross, Karen Hendrickson, Karen Beaudoin, Lori Moehrke
1979	UPD	Norway	4:23.1*	Jan Sandrin, Linda Grodeski, Joan Casanova, Diana Milligan
1980	UPD	Cedarville	4:18.9*	Jane Haske, Sherri Lee, Davine Carr, Sue Smith
1981	UPD	Norway	4:19.0	Kathy Roberts, Julie Polomis, Trisha Priante, Joan Casanova
1982	UPD	Engadine	4:19.1	Suzanne Beaudoin, Kelly Roberts, Georgette Legault, Cheryl Dementer
1983	UPD	White Pine	4:16.2*	Lori Kempainen, Charlotte Menghini, Kristin Kroll, Sandra Crocker
1984	UPD	DeTour	4:24.4	Missy Manisto, Annette Callaghan, Bebecca Bailey, Marian Lapoint
1985	UPD	White Pine	4:21.1	Kristin Kroll, Schan Kempainen, Wendy Newhouse, Lori Kempainen,
1986	UPD	Wakefield	4:19.3	Lauri Deloria, Cindy Deloria, Kathi Davidson, Cathy Blodgett
1987	UPD	Lake Linden-Hubbell	4:20.4	Sheri Klobucarich, Connie Kuru, Kelly Mills, Jeri Hosang
1988	UPD	Pickford	4:23.0	Lynn Bennin, Kristin Bumback, Gina Weatherly, Stacy Ledy
1989	UPD	Felch North Dickinson	4:24.0	Melody Mashak, Jessica Davidson, Kimberly Harder, Lisa Roell
1990	UPD	Pickford	4:25.7	Lynn Bennin. Jill Wallis, Tracy Thompson, Gina Hopkins
1991	UPD	Felch North Dickinson	4:20.5	Connie Harder, Jessica Davidson, Dana Feak, Melanie Standifer
1992	UPD	Pickford	4:33.4	Amy Rye, Shelly Curtis, Tracy Thompson, Jill Wallis
1993	UPD	Cedarville	4:23.2	Erica Huff, Lindsay Scherer, Jill Clement, Kara Scherer
1994	UPD	Painesdale-Jeffers	4:21.0	Mary Nordstrom, Carrie Iskra, Laura Kilpela, Janie Wesa
1995	UPD	Lake Linden-Hubbell	4:22.6	Betsy Baril, Kristen Nichols, Ramona McDonald, Megan Mikavetz
1996	UPD	Pickford	4:27.3	Stacy Lajoie, Brooke Lofdahl, Tamara Perry, Becky Harrison
1997	UPD	Rapid River	4:24.3	Sharon McLaughlin, Laura McLaughlin, Stacey Boyer, Sarah Boyer
1998	UPD	St. Ignace	4:17.6	Holly Brown, Richelle Robinson, Marion Clement, Randi Johnson
1999	UPD	Rapid River	4:17.4	Crista LeDuc, Shannon Boyer, Molly Bacon, Sara Boyer
2000	UPD	Rapid River	4:16.6	Crista LeDuc, Micehlle Dennis, Val Peterson, Molly Bacon
2001	UPD	Rapid River	4:23.8*	Crista LeDuc, Shannon Boyer, Melissa Hall, Molly Bacon
2002	UPD3	Pickford	4:23.0*	Rosanna Chapman, Megan Hunter, Gariella Morrison, Rachel Morrison
2003	UPD3	Bessemer	4:25.46	Nichole Merten, Becky Roberts, Kaleena Meldrum, Elizabeth Bravatto
2004	UPD3	Rapid River	4:27.62	Lauren Marshall, Ronni Jo Furlong, Julian Plimpton, Cassi Rushford
2005	UPD3	Rapid River	4:32.80	Ronni Jo Furlong, Cassi Rushford, Michelle Giesel, Lauren Marshall
2006	UPD3	Cedarville	4:20.26*	Lindsay McLeod, Lauren Izzard, Katie Bowlby, Billie McLeod
2007	UPD3	Felch North Dickinson	4:21.86	Jessica Roell, Kristin Luedtke, Emily Lehto, Megan Harper
2008	UPD3	Felch North Dickinson	4:27.62	Jessica Roell, Kristin Luedtke, Emily Lehto, Megan Harper
2009	UPD3	Brimley	4:26.23	Rachel Carruthers, Recca Carruthers, Alexis Mason, Jessica Graham
2010	UPD3	Dollar Bay	4:25.85	
2011	UPD3	Crystal Falls Forest Park	4:23.57	Taylor Taunton, Mary Grandahl, Audrey Sholander, Kathleen Grandahl
2012	UPD3	Eben Junction Superior Central	4:20.68	Jamie Seppanen, Vanessa Freberg, Mikayla Barrows, Lauren Spranger
2013	UPD3	St. Ignace	4:29.34	Lillian Calcaterra, Haillee Brown, Margo Brown, Morgan Lavake
2014	UPD3	Ontonagon	4:27.98	Paige Blake, Raquel Jenney, Molly Domitrovich, Brooke Turin
2015	UPD3	Pickford	4:30.02	Jade Ledy, Heidi Hagen, Kayla Rambo, Alyssa McCord
2016	UPD3	Lake Linden-Hubbell	4:23.23	Laura Lyons, Mariah Wilmer, Erin Seppala, Jamie Hendrickson
2016	UPD3	Munising	4:24.02	Madeleine Peramaki, Frankie Mattson, Kelsea Ackerman, Marissa Ackerman
2017	UPD3	Lake Linden-Hubbell	4:23.23	Laura Lyons, Mariah Wilmer, Erin Seppala, Jamie Hendrickson
2018	UPD3	Lake Linden-Hubbell	4:28.95	Jamie Hendrickson, Melissa Wagner, Erin Seppala, Maria Willmer

GIRLS 4 x 800 RELAY

Records

D1	8:48.29	Grosse Pointe South	Kelsie Schwartz, Ersula Farrow, Haley Meier, Hannah Meier	2012
D2	9:09.41	Holland Christian	M. VanderZwaag, Michelle Kuipers, Elizabeth Bruxvoort, Kayla Windemuller	2017
D3	9:18.06	Shepherd	Rachel Mathers, Katelyn Hutchinson, Kylie Hutchinson, Amber Gall	2017
D4	9:28.88	Ubly	Kayla Kubacki, Chelsey Kubacki, Jennifer White, Kylee Kubacki	2007
UPD1	9:30.25	Marquette	Holly Blowers, Shayla Huebner, Amber Huebner, Lindsey Rudden	2015
UPD2	10:02.7	Ishpeming Westwood	Hannah Vissering, Crystal Vivian, Ann Perry, Amber Smith	2001
UPD3	10:20.07	Cedarville	Lindsay McLeod, Ashley Sweeny, Katie Bowlby, Lauren Izzard	2006

Records by Class (pre-2000 for LP, pre-2001 for UP)

A	9:17.46	West Bloomfield	Amira Danforth, Tracy Abbott, Maureen Reed, Stacy Abbott	1988
B	9:22.75	Caledonia	Shannon Houseman, Barb Warner, Sarah Parbel, Karyn Duba	1994
C	9:30.56	Mason County Central	Crystal Fluter, Jenny Irwin, Kristie Lehrbass, Leanna Wolf	1999
D	9:40.0	Mendon	Kasey Culp, Christina Stephenson, Elyssa Vernon, Michelle Klein	1998
UPAB	9:41.3	Marquette	Erica Helmilla, Angela Abernathy, Emily Anderson, Katie Anderson	1999
UPC	9:51.6	Ironwood	Chelsea Finco, Jenny Schull, Tara Makinen, Ann Somerville	1997
UPD	10:15.2	Cedarville	Jessica Torsky, Jill Clement, Tricia St. Onge, Tina Haske	1996

4 x 800 – Class A/Division 1 Champions

1984	A	Dearborn Edsel Ford	9:35.1*	Elizabeth Lehenbauer, Kris Salt, Rose Leanne, Mary Peruski
1985	A	Dearborn Edsel Ford	9:33.94*	Leanne Rose, Elizabeth Lehenbauer, Laura Squibbs, Kris Salt
1986	A	Ann Arbor Pioneer	9:25.44*	Seana Arnold, Kellie Henderson, Karin Surrott, Danielle Harpell
1987	A	Ann Arbor Huron	9:20.4*	Laura Simmering, Mara Matuszak, Amy Bennett, Tracy Boudreau
1988	A	West Bloomfield	9:17.46*	Amira Danforth, Tracy Abbott, Maureen Reed, Stacy Abbott
1989	A	Clarkston	9:22.6	Carrie Roester, Jenny Mahler, Nicole Chinavore, Sonya Schaffer
1990	A	Muskegon Mona Shores	9:31.18	Mary Amy Hornik, Heather Swinburne, Julie Jorgenson, Kristen Crouch
1991	A	Traverse City	9:37.48	Jenny Peters, Steph Walton, Marlo Mata, Karlene Kurtz
1992	A	Detroit Cass Tech	9:43.50	Obiama Alhamisi, Cheryl Omar, Erica Sherpard, Lamika Harper

1993	A	Brighton	9:34.29	Lindsay Towne, Katie Szopo. Hilary Green, Andrea Boyer
1994	A	Brighton	9:31.3	Lindsay Towne, Katie Szopo. Hilary Green, Andrea Boyer
1995	A	Ann Arbor Pioneer	9:30.08	Emily Magner, Christine Richter, Adrienne Hunter, Lisa Timmer
1996	A	Ann Arbor Pioneer	9:21.10	Emily Magner, Ann Richtmyer, Adrienne Hunter, Lisa Timmer
1997	A	Traverse City	9:21.91	Sara Debruyn, Rachel Sturtz, Heather Wilson, Heather Rhoad
1998	A	Ann Arbor Pioneer	9:22.5	Anne Richtmyer, Erin Leonard, Emily Magner, Leah Grassman
1999	A	Rockford	9:22.34	Linsey Blaisdell, Renae Sobie, Nora Colligan, Kristen Podein
2000	D1	Rockford	9:13.83*	Renae Sobie, Aimee Keenan. Nora Colligan, Lindsey Blaisdell
2001	D1	Rockford	9:16.82	Kalin Toedebusch, Lindsey Blaisdell, Aimee Keenan. Brittney Ogden,
2002	D1	Ann Arbor Pioneer	9:14.03	Rachel Eyler, Jennifer Kraus, Alexandra Cassar, Clarissa Codrington
2003	D1	Rockford	9:16.2	Kristie Powers, Lindsay John, Lisa Krueger, Nicki Bohnsack
2004	D1	Rockford	9:17.78	Rachel Wittum, Lindsey John, Nicki Bohnsack, Kristi Boerman-Powers
2005	D1	Clarkston	9:05.49*	Lyndsay Smith, Liz Mengyan, Lisa Sickman, Jenny Morgan
2006	D1	Clarkston	9:13.42	Lyndsay Smith, Jenny Morgan, Lisa Sickman, Stephanie Morgan
2007	D1	Saline	9:14.20	Meagan Creutz, Lindsey Cummings, Alex Leptich, Kate Carter
2008	D1	Detroit Mumford	9:13.19	Dominque Brown, Shariece Painkston, Ajia Olison, Aisha Osborne
2009	D1	Waterford Mott	9:13.03	Alyssa Osika, Shannon Osika, Asia Rawls, Kelsey Chapman
2010	D1	Rochester	9:05.47*	Erin Leppek, Cady Pozola, Megan Goethals, Brook Handler
2011	D1	Ann Arbor Huron	9:09.23	Chinyere Omino, Kennedy Beazley, Annie-Norah Beveridge, Maya Long
2012	D1	Grosse Pointe South	8:48.29*	Kelsie Schwartz, Ersula Farrow, Haley Meier, Hannah Meier
2013	D1	Grosse Pointe South	9:01.98	Christina Firl, Ersula Farrow, Haley Meier, Hannah Meier
2014	D1	Birmingham Seaholm	8:59.08	Rachel DaDamio, Brooke Callaghan, Patty Giradot, Audrey Belf
2015	D1	Oak Park	8:54.29	Jayla Fleming, Lashae Bowens, Ersula Farrow, Dorriann Coleman
2016	D1	Ann Arbor Pioneer	8:56.52	Anne Forsyth, Sydney Dawes, Jacalyn Overdier, Alice Hill
2017	D1	Ann Arbor Pioneer	9:06.13	Anne Forsyth, Elizabeth Kos, Sydney Dawes, Jacalyn Overdier
2018	D1	Oak Park	9:08.75	Dorriann Coleman, Jayla Jones, Makayla Gates, Mariyah Archibald

4 x 800 – Class B/Division 2 Champions

1984	B	Wyoming Park	9:44.3*	Missy VanHeulen, Wendy Vanderarr, Lori VanderHarr, Amy Blok
1985	B	Chelsea	9:45.82	Kasey Anderson, Amy Wolfgang, Sallie Wilson, Laura Damm
1986	B	Grand Rapids Christian	9:39.1*	Betsy Start, Denise Griffioen, Kim Stapert, Sheri Prince
1987	B	Marshall	9:46.6	Lori Edinger, Diane Weaver, Susan Peck, Sara Reichert
1988	B	Wyoming Park	9:33.02*	Kim Blouw, Janice Roberts, Tiffany House, Stephanie Settle
1989	B	Lansing Catholic	9:27.8*	Akua Osei-Bonsu, Kelly Gelino, Marcy Gillespie, Karen Thelen
1990	B	Grand Rapids South Christian	9:40.2	Becky Dykhouse, Jodi Engen, Lisa Kuiper, Jennifer Petroelje
1991	B	Petoskey	9:26.06*	Wendy Johnecheck, Diohariah Stevens, Katy Hollbacher, Kelly Smith
1992	B	Hillsdale	9:40.32	Karen Lagassee, Jennifer Tesch, Krista Coulter, Shannon Dye
1993	B	Hudsonville	9:36.48	Kathy Huffman, Stacey Lenard, Kristin Hulst, Melanie Weidner
1994	B	Caledonia	9:22.75*	Shannon Houseman, Barb Warner, Sarah Parbel, Karyn Duba
1995	B	Caledonia	9:27.83	Shannon Houseman, Keri Bloem, Barb Warner, Sarah Parbel
1996	B	Caledonia	9:25.40	Shannon Houseman, Keri Bloem, Barb Warner, Sarah Parbel
1997	B	Caledonia	9:31.6	Keri Bloom, Jenny Sprague, Brooke Wierenga, Shannon Houseman
1998	B	Coldwater	9:34.9	Melissa Clay, Kathryn Klaver, Amanda Dekmar, Sara Dekmar
1999	B	Corunna	9:36.37	Colleen Lange, Nicole Johnson, Emily Faber, Jamie Krzyminski
2000	D2	Battle Creek Lakeview	9:31.06*	Jennifer Johnson, Abigail Barentt, Rachel Cox, Jennifer Price
2001	D2	Dearborn Divine Child	9:32.12	Kristine Umlauf, Dominique Lewis, Elizabeth Webster, Erin Webster
2002	D2	Dearborn Divine Child	9:34.65	Leanne Velhuis, Dominique Lewis, Elizabeth Webster, Erin Webster
2003	D2	Detroit Renaissance	9:19.83*	Amber Hay, Alexandrea Cunningham, Elisha Logan, Kelly Sampson
2004	D2	Detroit Renaissance	9:32.20	Elesha Logan, Amber Hay, Amber Thomas, Kelly Sampson
2005	D2	Detroit Renaissance	9:22.78	Elesha Logan, Amber Hay, Kiara Smith, Ramzee Fondren
2006	D2	East Grand Rapids	9:30.95	Bianca Stubbs, Erin Cvengros, Jenny Dunten, Raeanne Lohner
2007	D2	East Grand Rapids	9:29.87	Nikki Brown, Randi Brown, Brianna Clifford, Raeanne Lohner
2008	D2	Holland Christian	9:28.98	Brooke Eilers, Breana Verkaik, Carissa Verkaik, Lis Potts
2009	D2	Williamston	9:29.84	Emma Drenth, Lauren Halm, Shelby Guile, Hannah Grischke
2010	D2	East Grand Rapids	9:24.12	Brianna Clifford, Katie Samuelson, Lauren Grunewald, Jessie Baloga
2011	D2	GR Forest Hills Eastern	9:24.98	Alyssa Dyer, Mary Kostielney, Clara Cullen, Ellen Junewick
2012	D2	East Grand Rapids	9:20.94	Kassidy Clark, Becca Solberg, Mckayley Gourley, Jessie Baloga
2013	D2	St. Joseph	9:28.88	Rachel Benewald, Stephanie Mumper, Summer Lennartz, Estkowski Maddy
2014	D2	East Grand Rapids	9:25.69	Emily Converse, Kate Krug, Becca Solberg, Kaela Theut
2015	D2	East Grand Rapids	9:29.66	Anna Laffrey, Becca Solberg, Kaela Theut, Emily Converse
2016	D2	Flint Powers	9:29.01	Lyndsey Braman, Olivia Bennett, Libbie Gleason, Julie Vanivelt
2017	D2	Holland Christian	9:09.41*	M. VanderZwaag, Michelle Kuipers, Elizabeth Bruxvoort, Kayla Windemuller
2018	D2	Holland Christian	9:10.01	Michelle Kuipers, Elizabeth Bruxvoort, Madylin VanderZwaag, Kayla Windemuller

4 x 800 – Class C/Division 3 Champions

1984	C	Burton-Bentley	9:42.9*	Amanda Aldrich, Laurie Diehl, Jackie Rahmon, Beth Cummings
1985	C	Bath	9:46.4	Alicia Witchell, Karen Snyder, Deb Nichols, Laurie Wentzel
1986	C	Detroit Country Day	9:55.69	Kristen Sall. Abigail Warwick, Ngina Burgette, Hameera Newman
1987	C	Detroit Country Day	9:46.25	Kristen Sall, Abigair Warwick, Ngina Burgette, Hameera Newman
1988	C	Detroit Country Day	9:50.3	Kristen Sall, Shannon Curtis, Ngina Burgette, Hameera Newman
1989	C	Mayville	9:48.74	Jamie Freeland, Andrea Foote, Jenny Smith, Gail LaBair
1990	C	Southfield Christian	9:56.90	Anna Kraftson, Tammy Cobb, Joy Wright, Charleen Long
1991	C	Frankenmuth	9:42.5*	Alisa Rummel, Sarah Carnes, Lisa Bauer, Jenny Barber
1992	C	Vermontville-Maple Valley	9:43.7	Janet Bouldrey, Cheri Sessions, Sarah Leep, Mindy Shoup
1993	C	Farwell	9:46.67	Heather Richardson, Andrea Ludlum, Angelea Cusumano, Mich. Richardson
1994	C	Vermontville-Maple Valley	9:43.90	Kathryn Murphy, Sarah Leep, Jasmine Harvath, Rachel Thompson
1995	C	Addison	9:53.47	Kristy Davenport, Stacey Brockway, Gina Watson, Chris Walcott
1996	C	Clare	9:42.58*	Michelle Shepperley, Meghan McNeilly, Beth Wolfe, Kylie Schultz
1997	C	Kalamazoo Hackett	9:42.61	Eiren Delong, Jenny Gerteisen, Sara Seifert, Kerry Schurtz
1998	C	Kalamazoo Christian	9:46.27	Sarah Schripsema, Errin Boot, Kristin Bishop, Michelle Post
1999	C	Mason County Central	9:30.56*	Crystal Fluter, Jenny Irwin, Kristie Lehrbass, Leanna Wolf
2000	D3	Lansing Catholic Central	9:30.24*	Lynne Gratz, Rachel Kirvan, Katie Chenoweth, Stephanie Meke
2001	D3	Mason County Central	9:31.71	Crystal Fluter, Jamie Anderson, Jenny Irwin, Leanne Wolf

2002	D3	Hanover-Horton	9:32.22	Courtney Ingraham, Chris Alcenius, Laura Rainey, Christine Ingraham
2003	D3	Monroe St. Mary	9:49.16	Carlie Holden, Brittany Langdon, Mary Bellino, Alissa Hall
2004	D3	Goodrich	9:24.33*	Samantha Minkler, Kayla O'Mara, Kaitlin O'Mara, Janee Jones
2005	D3	Goodrich	9:35.43	Mary Haiderer, Kelsey Meyers, Kayla O'Mara, Kaitlin O'Mara
2006	D3	Jackson Lumen Christi	9:31.27	Cara Cremeans, Hilary Snyder, Kelly Crowley, Kristine Knapp
2007	D3	Jackson Lumen Christi	9:30.60	Cara Cremeans, Kelly Crowley, Hilary Snyder, Theresa Walsh
2008	D3	Leroy Pine River	9:27.06	Brittany Anderson, Becca Holmquist, Lia Jones, Rachel Whitley
2009	D3	Benzie Central	9:30.27	Devyn Ramsey, Taylor Nye, Theresa Warsecke, Michaela Carnegie
2010	D3	Benzie Central	9:32.19	Theresa Warsecke, Miranda Besey, Taylor Nye, Michaela Carnegie
2011	D3	Benzie Central	9:22.71*	Theresa Warsecke, Bryce Cutler, Taylor Nye, Michaela Carnegie
2012	D3	Benzie Central	9:37.97	Alyssa Bennett, Makayla Huddleston, Bryce Cutler, Theresa Warsecke
2013	D3	Grandville Calvin Christian	9:38.02	Ashley Jourdan, Raechel Broek, Emma Augustyn, Emma Doorn
2014	D3	Shepherd	9:30.22	Rachel Mathers, Kylie Hutchinson, Taylor Thrush, Katelyn Hutchinson
2015	D3	Shepherd	9:33.11	Taylor Thrush, Rachel Mathers, Kylie Hutchinson, Katelyn Hutchinson
2016	D3	Traverse City St. Francis	9:23.95	Emma Fifarek, Katelyn Duffing, Joyana Tarsa, Holly Bullough
2017	D3	Shepherd	9:18.06*	Rachel Mathers, Katelyn Hutchinson, Kylie Hutchinson, Amber Gall
2018	D3	Hart	9:32.67	Alayna Ackley, Brenna Aerts, MacKenzie Stitt, Adelyn Ackley

4 x 800 – Class D/Division 4 Champions3

1984	D	Ann Arbor Greenhills	9:55.40*	Sue Gunn, Jannie Gilliland, Wendi Fegner, Larissa Szporluk
1985	D	Fowler	9:57.35	Kim Epkey, Shari Schneider, Beth Wirth, Cindy Schneider
1986	D	Fowler	9:54.04*	Kim Epkey, Stacie Rowell, Mindy Sillman, Cindy Schneider
1987	D	Akron-Fairgrove	9:52.30*	Michelle Brown, Theresa Bischoff, Yvonne Siler, Robin Aldrich
1988	D	Camden-Frontier	9:55.03	Theresa Padilla, Polly Osting, Michelle Zilch, Jacki Clark
1989	D	Lawton	9:52.5	Beth Happel, Stephanie Connor, Debbie Pio, Dawn Noble
1990	D	Lawton	9:51.03*	Beth Happel, Debbie Pio, Stephanie Conner, Dawn Noble
1991	D	Akron-Fairgrove	9:57.70	Stefanie Miklovik, Julie Kruueger, Danielle Salgat, Farrah Petiprin
1992	D	Fowler	10:05.67	Kim Simmon, Sheri Thelen, Kara Hafner, Laura Tirer
1993	D	Fowler	9:55.5	Laura Irrer, Karmen Epkey, Sheri Thelen, Nadine Hafner
1994	D	Manistee Catholic	9:53.41	Nicole Miehlke, Jane Skiera, Cheryl Fischer, Jayme Riggs
1995	D	Fowler	10:14.59	Kim Hafner, Nadine Hafner, Sarah Wirth, Karmen Epkey
1996	D	Mendon	9:54.9	Kasey Culp, Stephanie Klein, Christina Stephenson, Michelle Klein
1997	D	Mendon	9:44.6*	Kasey Culp, Christina Stephenson, Lena Rice, Michelle Klein
1998	D	Mendon	9:40.0*	Kasey Culp, Christina Stephenson, Elyssa Vernon, Michelle Klein
1999	D	Potterville	9:57.7	Cheyenne Luzynski, Emily Flower, Candi Mason, Angie Harris
2000	D4	Burton Atherton	9:52.58*	Jackie Smith, Jenny Kulchar, Megan Freeman, Angela Crawford
2001	D4	Bath	9:54.93	Carrie Badgley, Melissa Boone, Leah Tarrant, Katie Forsyth
2002	D4	Traverse City St. Francis	9:50.99*	Christine Andres, Vanessa Taylor, Lauren Fewins, Pam Demerle
2003	D4	Traverse City St. Francis	9:58.58	Jena Brown, Vanessa Taylor, Lauren Fewins, Pam Demerle
2004	D4	Rochester Hills Lutheran Northwest	9:54.15	Laura Rolf, Lindsay Looker, Heather McDaniel, Katie Rolf
2005	D4	Rochester Hills Lutheran Northwest	9:43.21*	Laura Rolf, Lindsay Looker, Katie Rolf, Heather McDaniel
2006	D4	Ubly	9:41.18*	Kayla Kubacki, Jennifer Messing, Chelsea Kubacki, Kylee Kubacki
2007	D4	Ubly	9:28.88*	Kayla Kubacki, Chelsey Kubacki, Jennifer White, Kylee Kubacki
2008	D4	Harbor Beach	9:42.1	Alica Erdman, Holly Bucholz, Ali Wessels, Brianne Woycehoski
2009	D4	Fowler	9:44.80	Liz Blackwell, Brianne Feldpausch, Julia Contreras, Brooke Simon
2010	D4	Hillsdale Academy	10:00.10	Shaley Albaugh, Anna Woods, Elyse Lisznyai, Carley Hubbard
2011	D4	Hillsdale Academy	9:38.18	Shena Albaugh, Carly Hubbard, Liz Whalen, Shaley Albaugh
2012	D4	Fowler	9:50.86	Elizabeth Thelen, Rebecca Thelen, Brianna Feldpausch, Kieren Becker
2013	D4	Hillsdale Academy	9:54.59	Elyse Lisznyai, Victoria Beckenlively, Chrissy Craig, Shaley Albaugh
2014	D4	Beal City	9:51.45	Hannah Neyer, Hannah Steffke, Anna Reihl, Emily Steffke
2015	D4	Beal City	9:51.45	Hannah Steffke Grace Schafer, Ashley Reihl, Emily Steffke
2016	D4	Fowler	9:38.00	Kiah Becker, Morgan Goerge, Madison Koenigsknecht, Julia Thalen
2017	D4	Hillsdale Academy	9:47.02	Andrea Jagielski, Makenna Banbury, Taylor Doty, Megan Poole
2018	D4	Fowler	9:51.85	Josie Koenigsknecht, Taryn Schafer, Grace Boak, Morgan George

4 x 800 – UP Class AB/Division 1 Champions

1984	UPAB	Sault Ste. Marie	10:11.0*	Jackie Samek, Mary Kallio, Karen Anderson, Maribeth Anderson
1985	UPAB	Sault Ste. Marie	10:09.3*	Tammie Veum, Karen Anderson, Barb Bumstead, Meribeth Anderson
1986	UPAB	Escanaba	9:50.9*	Lorraine Boucher, Becky Marquineau, Liz Cibula, Jean Ammel
1987	UPAB	Marquette	10:01.7	Cheryl Van Beynan, Lisa Werner Jennifer Smith, Kelly Abramson
1988	UPAB	Marquette	10:04.6	Lisa Werner, Sherrill VanBeynen, Debbie Townsend, Kelly Abramson
1989	UPAB	Marquette	10:07.4	Anne Goodwin, Debbie Townsend, Kristin Davis, Hayley Murphy
1990	UPAB	Marquette	10:04.1	Anne Goodwin, Carol Anderson, Missy Davis, Wendy Price
1991	UPAB	Marquette	10:16.6	Bobie Rodriguez, Carol Anderson, Carla Johnson, Kelly Larson
1992	UPAB	Escanaba	10:37.0	Sara Cowen, Lori Zalaznik, Mary Gustafson, Lisa Hansen
1993	UPAB	Marquette	10:11.6	Carol Anderson, Sarah Racine, Ginger Price, Lisa Larson
1994	UPAB	Marquette	10:10.0	Michele Sherer, Lucy Lea, Sommer Stesney, Lisa Larson
1995	UPAB	Marquette	9:57.4	Jenny Morris, Emily White, Lucy Lea, Michele Scherer
1996	UPAB	Marquette	10:04.6	Jenny Morris, Mel Ball, Jill Kimmes, Chrissy Barnes
1997	UPAB	Ishpeming Westwood	10:06.7	Laura Burnette, Jenny Swanson, Angela Sandretto, Terri Campbell
1998	UPAB	Escanaba	9:54.9	
1999	UPAB	Marquette	9:41.3*	Erica Helmilla, Angela Abernathy, Emily Anderson, Katie Anderson
2000	UPAB	Escanaba	9:47.6	Linsey Olson, Erin Gannon, Kari O'Dell, Krista O'Dell
2001	UPD1	Sault Ste. Marie	9:55.9*	Tara Dougherty, Mary Miller, Chelsea Bryan, Natalie Cahill
2002	UPD1	Sault Ste. Marie	10:09.2	Tara Dougherty, Jen Corbiere, Desiree Payment, Natalie Cahill
2003	UPD1	Escanaba	10:11.0	Mallery Fisher, Annalise Conaway, Chelsea Guay, Stephanie Ostrenga
2004	UPD1	Escanaba	9:51.39*	Allison Harvey, Chelsea Guay, Kali Anderson, Stephanie Ostrenga
2005	UPD1	Iron Mountain	9:46.95*	Hilary Beauchamp, Jessica Hartwig, Kelly McClure, Danielle Mellon
2006	UPD1	Escanaba	10:04.31	Allison Harvey, Jami Acker, Kallie Eisenberger, Erica Beversluis
2007	UPD1	Escanaba	9:59.51	Allison Harvey, Heather Rusch, Kirsten Warstler, Erica Beversluis
2008	UPD1	Marquette	10:07.01	Sydney Johnson, Katie Holway, Colleen Peterson, Tara Dowling
2009	UPD1	Marquette	10.06.65	Liz Tuma, Sydney Johnston, Tara Dowling, Jessica Fluette
2010	UPD1	Calumet	9:47.56	Lindsey Kiilunen, Tara Kiilunen, Julia Lean, Rachel Poyhonen

2011	UPD1	Marquette	10:05.15	Liana Storm, Tara Dowling, Abby Potts, Tana Lakenen
2012	UPD1	Marquette	10:03.70	Liana Storm, Carleigh Hillier, Abby Potts, Jessica Fluette
2013	UPD1	Marquette	9:55.75	Liana Storm. Cassidy Thomas, Shayla Huebner, Lindsey Rudden
2014	UPD1	Negaunee	10:08.12	Wyleen Kniola, Clara Churchill, Alyssa Blake, Aleda Johnson
2015	UPD1	Marquette	9:30.25*	Holly Blowers, Shayla Huebner, Amber Huebner, Lindsey Rudden
2016	UPD1	Marquette	10:12.92	Holly Blowers, Amber Huebner, Rebecca McNamee, Lindsey Rudden
2017	UPD1	Negaunee	10:06.41	Ielee Shiroda, Emily Paupore, Megan Syrjala, Clara Johnson
2018	UPD1	Negaunee	10:04.56	Ielee Shiroda, Chloe Norman, Clara Johnson, Emily Paupore

4 x 800 – UP Class C/Division 2 Champions

1984	UPC	Ishpeming Westwood	10:09.2*	Jesse Green, Kelly Jandron, Kim Skaja, Amy Laitila
1985	UPC	Stephenson	9:55.6*	Virginia Grinsteiner, Karen Olson, Tracie Jeschke, Connie Grinsteiner
1986	UPC	Iron River West Iron County	10:07.7	Dawn Anderson, Becky Rometti, Sherry Hytinen, Shelby Johnson
1987	UPC	Calumet	10:27.5	Karyn O'Connell, Kim Moyle, Loana Perko, Brita Sturos
1988	UPC	Negaunee	10:12.9	Jackie Borlace, Ann Mileski, Jamey Coduti, Kim Trewhella
1989	UPC	Houghton	10:32.2	Debbie Jobst, Tina Holmes, Karen Evensen, Reva Rogers
1990	UPC	Newberry	10:20.6	Chris Nance, Katie Aoy, Stacy Jago, Christie Nutkins
1991	UPC	Munising	10:18.2	Melanie Kueber, Christina Tunteri, Jamie St. Armour, Kelly Peterson
1992	UPC	Stephenson	10:38.9	Jill Schultz, Erin Koller, Tanya Heidam, Casle Paulson
1993	UPC	Calumet	10:19.7	Christine Heikkala, Amy Kangas, Gretchen Sturos, Kelly Johnson
1994	UPC	Calumet	10:23.0	Gretchen Sturos, Carla Johnson, Myra Peterson, Kelly Johnson
1995	UPC	Ironwood	10:05.4	Amy Kinnunen, Amy Somerville, Jenny Routheaux, Tara Makinen
1996	UPC	Ironwood	10:14.6	Amy Kinnunen, Jenny Routheaux, Ann Somerville, Tina Makinen
1997	UPC	Ironwood	9:51.6*	Chelsea Finco, Jenny Schull, Tara Makinen, Ann Somerville
1998	UPC	Ironwood	9:59.6	Tara Makinen, Ashley Busakowski, Chelsea Finco, Anne Sommerville
1999	UPC	Ironwood	10:09.4	Chelsea Finco, Kim Yelich, Anna Hagstorm, Diana Corcoran
2000	UPC	Ishpeming Westwood	10:02.7	Hannah Vissering, Crystal Vivian, Shelly Ruspakka, Jessica Koski
2001	UPD2	Ishpeming Westwood	10:02.7*	Hannah Vissering, Crystal Vivian, Ann Perry, Amber Smith
2002	UPD2	Hancock	10:10.1	Alexandra Tepkasetkul, Sarah Pelto, Robin Vitton, Kate Hagenbuch
2003	UPD2	Iron Mountain	10:29.3	Jessica Hartwig, Margaux Baker, Brianna Olsen, Kelly McClure
2004	UPD2	Iron Mountain	10:09.09	Whitney Boyle, Margaux Baker, Jessica Hartwig, Kelly McClure
2005	UPD2	Munising	10:21.57	Megan Davis, Vicki DesJardins, Kaitlyn Owen, Jillian Dolkey
2006	UPD2	Stephenson	10:49.61	Courtney Swanson, Ellen Dupler, Shayna Zahorik, Amanda Newlin
2007	UPD2	Munising	10:31.22	Mollie Schultz, Abbey Kelto, Hillard Guynn, Emily Cook
2008	UPD2	Munising	10:27.08	Megan Grey, Hillary Guynn, Aliisa Paquette, Abbey Kelto
2009	UPD2	Munising	10:19.62	Megan Grey, Hillary Guynn, Amy Kerst, Abbey Kelto
2010	UPD2	Munising	10:21.74	Megan Grey, Aliisa Paquette, Amy Kerst, Abby Kelto
2011	UPD2	St. Ignace	10:21.45	
2012	UPD2	Iron River West Iron County	10:40.86	Jaclyn Waara, Madeline Waara, Brianna Lambert, Kylee Erickson
2013	UPD2	Iron River West Iron County	10:36.1	Rebekah Serbinski, Mariah Marcell, Kylee Erickson, Victoria Hoogenboom
2014	UPD2	Newberry	10:37.07	Natalie Beaulieu, Alexis Pillon, Maysa Sitar, Bridget Staetzer
2015	UPD2	Ishpeming	10:44.75	Mariah Austin, Chloe Sjoholm, Morgan Skytta, Khora Swanson
2016	UPD2	Ishpeming	11:09.24	Brooke Johnson, Mariah Bertucci, Chloe Sjoholm, Khora Swanson
2017	UPD2	Munising	10:32.63	Mari Ackerman, Kela Ackerman, Frankie Mattson, Dzaryn Johnson
2018	UPD2	St Ignace	11:04.29	Allison Smith, Caiti Dean, Hallie Marshall, Regan Mortensen

4 x 800 – UP Class C/Division 3 Champions

1984	UPD	DeTour	10:37.8*	Annette Callahan, Michelle Mannisto, Denise Fountain, Marian LaPoint
1985	UPD	Rapid River	10:35.8*	Kim Hilgendorf, Holly Harwood, Joni Muffler, Beth Patana
1986	UPD	Rapid River	10:18.9*	Kim Hilgendorf, Holly Harwood, Beth Partana, Joni Muffler
1987	UPD	Rapid River	10:26.4	Jennifer Montgomery, Kim Hilgendorf, Beth Patana, Joni Moffler
1988	UPD	Pickford	10:29.6	Stacy Ledy, Lynn Bennin, Kristin Dumbeck, Julie Wallis
1989	UPD	Pickford	10:41.2	Stacy Ledy, Lynn Bennin, Kristin Dunbeck, Julie Wallis
1990	UPD	Pickford	10:30.1	Jill Wallis, Becky Moore, Tracy Thompson, Lynn Bennin
1991	UPD	Pickford	10:32.2	Jill Wallis, Becky Moore, Tracy Thompson, Lynn Bennin
1992	UPD	Felch North Dickinson	11:02.8	Cristy McGuire, Constance Harder, Dana Feak, Melanie Standifer
1993	UPD	Felch North Dickinson	10:33.5	Heather Anderson, Molly Johnson, Carrie Broeders, Dina Feak
1994	UPD	Felch North Dickinson	10:23.3	Carrie Broeders, Susan Burns, Sarah Holswirth, Molly Johnson
1995	UPD	Ontonagon	10:20.4	Amy Young, Jodi Morin, Jill Marczak, Ambre Veldman
1996	UPD	Cedarville	10:15.2*	Jessica Torsky, Jill Clement, Tricia St. Onge, Tina Haske
1997	UPD	Painesdale-Jeffers	10:37.0	Sara Wesa, Renee Johnson, Mary Daavetilla, Jane Rautiola
1998	UPD	Crystal Falls Forest Park	10:45.8	
1999	UPD	Pickford	10:27.8	Rachel Morrison, Leslie Slater, Katrina Curtis, Gabriele Morrison
2000	UPD	Pickford	10:22.2	Tiffany Campbell, Leslie Slater, Gabby Morrison, Rachel Morrison
2001	UPD3	Pickford	10:35.0*	Rosanna Chapman, Tiffany Campbell, Courtney Brown, Rachel Morrison
2002	UPD3	Pickford	10:35.1	Rosanna Chapman, Courtney Brown, Tiffany Campbell, Rachel Morrison
2003	UPD3	Pickford	10:42.5	Tiffany Campbell, Courtney Brown, Megan Hunter, Rosanna Chapman
2003	UPD3	Rapid River	10:38.32	Melissa Hall, Ronni Jo Furlong, Linzy Monticello, Sarah Boulley
2004	UPD3	Rapid River	10:38.32	Melissa Hall, Ronni Jo Furlong, Linzy Monticello, Sarah Boulley
2005	UPD3	Rapid River	10:30.41*	Michelle Hall, Linzy Monticello, Ronni Jo Furlong, Sarah Boulley
2006	UPD3	Cedarville	10:20.07*	Lindsay McLeod, Ashley Sweeny, Katie Bowlby, Lauren Izzard
2007	UPD3	Powers-North Central	10:21.12	Katie Granquist, Brooke Granquist, Samantha Kleiman, Amber Garnquist
2008	UPD3	Pickford	10:40.11	Jenna Ledy, Callin Smith, Jasmine Ledy, Brandi Kopiitz
2009	UPD3	Brimley	10:38.98	Megan Parish, Kelly Graham, Miranda Reattoir, Lynette Carrisk
2010	UPD3	Carney-Nedeau	10:38.17	Autam Wery, Brittinie Larson, Casey Charlier, Allison Theor
2011	UPD3	Brimley	10:27.62	Taylor Mills, Tabitha Graham, Megan Parish, Lynette Carrick
2012	UPD3	Brimley	10:42.07	Taylor Millls, Megan Parish, Emily Chartrand, Tabitha Graham
2013	UPD3	Pickford	10:29.64	Krysta Wondergem, Heidi Hagen, Alyssa McCord, Olivia Smith
2014	UPD3	Pickford	10:42.37	Krysta Wondergem, Jade Ledy, Heidi Hagen, Alyssa McCord
2015	UPD3	Munising	10:45.15	Alyssa Webber, Frankie Mattson, Marissa Immel, Marissa Ackerman
2016	UPD3	Munising	10:22.90	Alyssa Webber, Frankie Mattson, Marissa Immel, Marissa Ackerman
2017	UPD3	Cedarville	10:31.39	Emma Bohn, Caroline Freel, Lily Freel, Cassidy Barr
2018	UPD3	Chassell	10:59.99	Jenna Pietila, Gwen Kangas, Paige Sleeman, Maelen Warren

DETROIT PUBLIC SCHOOL CHAMPIONS

From 1931 to 1961, athletes from the Detroit Public Schools were not able to participate in the state championships. However, as many of the Detroit athletes were the best in the state, the PSL Championships in those years need to be recognized as being just as important and legitimate as the state championship.

100 YARDS

1931	Frances Krug	Northwestern	10.4*
1932	William Bryant	Hamtramck	10.2*
1933	Joe Pisarski	Hamtramck	10.6
1934	Dorsey Gary	Eastern	10.2*
1935	Morrie Barnes	Miller	10.8
1936	Walter Radzienda	Hamtramck	10.6
1937	Bob Abbott	Redford	10.4
1938	Al Thomas	Cooley	10.2*
1939	Bob Grant	Central	10.4
1940	Leonard Alkon	Northern	9.9*
1941	Adiel Bernard	Southeastern	10.5
1942	Don Wines	Eastern	10.3
1943	David Bernard	Southeastern	10.4
1944	Cleo Caldwell	Miller	10.2
1945	Chester Jenkins	Pershing	10.4
1946	Tom Stewart	Denby	10.3
1947	Tom Stewart	Denby	10.1
1948	Jim Mitchell	Northeastern	10.2
1949	John Keaton	Northeastern	10.2
1950	Dave Mann	Miller	10.1
1951	Bolicar McGowen	Central	10.2
1952	Chuck Sherrill	Northern	10.1
1953	Don Thomas	Miller	10.3
1954	Max Harris	Northwestern	10.2
1955	Bill Stephens	Northwestern	10.2
1956	Bob Manning	Western	10.0
1957	Bob Manning	Western	10.2
1958	Claude Miller	Cass Tech	9.8w (4.5)
1959	Henry Carr	Southwestern	10.1
1960	Henry Carr	Northwestern (9.6* heat)	9.9
1961	Henry Carr	Northwestern	10.1

220 YARDS

1931	Frances Krug	Northwestern	22.8*
1932	William Bryant	Hamtramck	21.8w
1933	Ernest Thomas	Southwestern	23.8
1934	Dorsey Gary	Eastern	23.2
1935	Jack Pflaus	Eastern	23.4
1936 (tie)	Walter Radzienda	Hamtramck	23.4
1936 (tie)	Bob Abbott	Redford	23.4
1937	Bob Abbott	Redford	22.8*
1938	Bob Swayer	Redford	22.4*
1939	Ed Connor	Hamtramck	23.4
1940	Leonard Alkon	Northern	22.1*
1941	Paul Bargowski	Hamtramck	22.8
1942	Don Wines	Eastern	22.7
1943	David Bernard	Southeastern	22.9
1944	Cleo Cladwell	Miller	22.9
1945	Chester Jenkins	Pershing	22.7
1946	Leon Wingo	Hamtramck	22.8
1947	Tom Stewart	Denby	22.5
1948	Jim Mitchell	Northeastern	22.1*
1949	George Reese	Southwestern	23.6
1950	Dave Mann	Miller	22.4
1951	Charles Sherrill	Northern	22.6
1952	Charles Sherrill	Northern	22.3
1953	Don Thomas	Miller	22.5
1954	Marvin Pettway	Miller	21.7*
1955	Bill Stephens	Central	22.2
1956	Bob Manning	Western	21.7*
1957	Bob Manning	Western	22.7
1958	Claude Miller	Cass Tech	21.7w
1959	Henry Carr	Southwestern	21.8
1960	Henry Carr	Northwestern	20.6* (1.7)
1961	Robert Harris	Northwestern	21.9

440 YARDS

1931	Frank Bolog	Southwestern	51.0*
1932	William Perry	Redford	51.6
1933	Lawrence Jeffries	Northwestern	54.2
1934	Sam Swartz	Northwestern	52.0
1935	James McMillan	Hamtramck	51.2
1936	James McMillan	Hamtramck	53.2
1937	Bob WIngo	Hamtramck	52.0
1938	Alan Olds	Central	51.4
1939	Ronald Whetter	Central	51.2
1940	Edward Grant	Cass Tech	52.3
1941	Glen Cato	MacKenzie	52.1
1942	Ed Harris	MacKenzie	51.7
1943	Luther Burnette	Eastern	53.7
1944	Bob Rutila	Cooley	52.4
1945	Bill MacKean	Pershing	52.1
1946	Ed Gruse	Denby	51.7
1947	Julius Jones	Northwestern	52.1
1948	Stan McConnor	Northwestern	49.8*
1949	Jim Shivers	Miller	51.8
1950	Willie Wright	Miller	51.3
1951	Cliff Hatcher	Central	48.8*
1952	Walter Hodo	Northwestern	51.2
1953	Paris Whittington	Cass Tech	51.1
1954	Paris Whittington	Cass Tech	51.1
1955	Campbell Owens	Northwestern	50.7
1956	Bob Herrington	Denby	50.5
1957	Ron Benson	Pershing	51.1
1958	Leonard Cereone	Denby	52.9
1959	Jim Smith	Southwestern	50.6
1960	William Marsh	Pershing	50.8
1961	David Cox	Redford	49.7

880 YARDS

1931	Ray Whitney	Northwestern	2:07.4*
1932	Lawrence Jeffries	Northwestern	2:01.4*
1933	Luther Frederick	Eastern	2:05.0
1934	Nelson Mashatt	Northwestern	2:05.4
1935	Ulysses Amos	Northwestern	2:00.2*
1936	George Young	Cooley	2:01.6
1937	Tait White	Hamtramck	2:06.4
1938	Mac Umstattd	Northwestern	1:58.8*
1939	Mac Umstattd	Northwestern	1:56.6*
1940	Tom Collinson	Cooley	2:00.4
1941	Judson Beckwith	Redford	2:04.8
1942	Art Marx	Cooley	2:05.4
1943	Joe Metz	Redford	2:01.7
1944	Frank Dyson	Cooley	2:02.8
1945	Alex Drabkowski	Western	2:04.5
1946	Stanley McConnor	Northwestern	2:02.2
1947	Jim Henry	Northwestern	2:05.7
1948	Marvin Banks	Northwestern	2:02.0
1949	Marvin Banks	Northwestern	2:02.7
1950	Clifford Hatcher	Central	2:01.6
1951	John Mackenzie	Mackenzie	2:00.1
1952	John Mackenzie	Mackenzie	1:59.0
1953	Jay McKenzie	Pershing	2:03.2
1954	Bob Williams	Pershing	1:58.7
1955	Wilbert Wilson	Miller	2:01.7
1956	Doug Carroll	Redford	1:59.2
1957	Lonnie Sanders	Pershing	2:07.3
1958	Charles Brown	Southeastern	2:04.4
1959	Gerald Henderson	Northeastern	2:00.4
1960	William Stewart	Redford	1:58.7
1961	Terry Moore	Redford	1:55.0*

MILE

1931	Bill Daly	Cass Tech	4:45.5*
1932	Bill Daly	Cass Tech	4:30.8*
1933	John Bush	Hamtramck	4:44.4
1934	John Bush	Hamtramck	4:47.8
1935	Wilfred Spencer	Southeastern	4:37.8
1936	Tate White	Hamtramck	4:40.6
1937	John White	Hamtramck	4:44.0
1938	John White	Hamtramck	4:36.2
1939	Henry Lord	Cooley	4:39.2
1940	Britton Lux	Cooley	4:28.6*
1941	James Earl	Southeastern	4:35.4
1942	Al Pingel	Denby	4:38.9
1943	Fred Stolicker	Redford	4:42.3
1944	Joe Metz	Redford	4:36.6

1945	Ross Smith	Cooley	4:35.2
1946	Ross Smith	Cooley	4:37.4
1947	Bob Hahn	Cooley	4:38.1
1948	Arron Gordon	Miller	4:31.7
1949	Terry Iverson	Redford	4:38.8
1950	Al Williams	Northwestern	4:24.9*
1951	Jim Clark	Mackenzie	4:33.1
1952	Burle Huggins	Northwestern	4:33.0
1953	Ken Santer	Redford	4:38.2
1954	Dick Ehrle	Redford	4:33.6
1955	Jerry Bocci	Denby	4:32.0
1956	Jerry Bocci	Denby	4:27.1
1957	Tom Bleakley	Denby	4:42.2
1958	Louis Molnar	Redford	4:36.9
1959	Terry Moore	Redford	4:23.6*
1960	Frank Carissimi	Denby	4:17.7*
1961	Dick Sharkey	Redford	4:20.2

120-YARD HIGH HURDLES
(42 inches)

1931	Willis Ward	Northwestern	15.1*
1932	Willie Henderson	Southwestern	15.8
1933	Willie Henderson	Southwestern	15.8
1934	Bernard Lucas	Eastern	16.0

(39 inches)

1935	Willie Henderson	Southwestern	16.6*
1936	John Knight	Hamtramck	15.4*
1937	Orville Roberts	Southeastern	15.6
1938	Dave Wall	Cooley	15.0*
1939	Dave Wall	Cooley	15.2
1940	Louis Schmidt	Southeastern	15.7
1941	Elmer Swanson	Northeastern	15.3
1942	Don Davis	Cooley	15.5
1943	Don Davis	Cooley	15.5
1944	Ralph Rowan	Miller	15.5
1945	George Sayles	Miller	15.2
1946	George Sayles	Miller	14.8*
1947	Don Harrower	Cooley	15.4
1948	Bruno Boelstler	Denby	15.3
1949	Bill Smith	Northwestern	15.4
1950	Orlin Jones	Pershing	15.2
1951	Joe Howard	Northwestern	14.4*
1952	Willie Wright	Miller	14.9
1953	Lloyd Swanson	Miller	14.6
1954	John Dowdell	Miller	15.2
1955	Artenus Clover	Pershing	15.3
1956	Paul Jones	Pershing	15.1
1957	Charles Hunter	Mackenzie	15.0
1958	Mike Dinkins	Northeastern	15.0
1959	Lonnie Sanders	Pershing	15.1
1960	Willie Madison	Northern	15.2
1961	Mike Burnley	Mumford	15.2

120-YARD LOW HURDLES (30 inches)

1931	Willis Ward	Northwestern	13.2 (13.0* ht)
1932	Willie Henderson	Southwestern	13.6
1933	Willie Henderson	Southwestern	13.8
1934	Willie Henderson	Southwestern	13.4
1935	Willie Henderson	Southwestern	14.0
1936	Jimmy Knight	Hamtramck	13.2
1937	Al Thomas	Cooley	13.4
1938	Al Thomas	Cooley	13.2
1939	Dave Wall	Cooley	13.4
1940	Ed Conner	Hamtramck	13.4
1941	Elmer Swanson	Northeastern	13.1
1942	Bob Fraser	Mackenzie	13.4
1943	Dan Davis	Cooley	13.6
1944	Adam Haughton	Miller	13.3
1945	Don Harrower	Cooley	13.3
1946	George Sayles	Miller	13.2
1947	Don Harrower	Cooley	13.4
1948	Bruno Boelstler	Denby	13.3
1949	Billy Smith	Northwestern	13.5
1950	Isaac Groves	Miller	13.3
1951	Joe Howard	Northwestern	13.0w
1952	Willie Wright	Miller	13.4
1953	Lloyd Swanson	Miller	13.4
1954	Willie Adkins	Northeastern	13.0*
1955	Narrin Miller	Mackenzie	13.2
1956	Paul Jones	Pershing	13.5
1957	Jim Ruddy	Cody	13.2
1958	Leon Fields	Chadsey	13.1

180-YARD LOW HURDLES (30 inches)

1959	Felton Rogers	Eastern	20.0*
1960	Samuel Davidson	Northern	19.3*
1961	Ralph Wilson	Mumford	19.8

HIGH JUMP

1931	Willis Ward	Northwestern	6-4*
1932 (tie)	Albert King	Pershing	6-2
(tie)	Arnold Deneau	MacKenzie	6-2
1933	Albert King	Pershing	6-2
1934	Bernard Lucas	Eastern	6-4¾*
1935	Bernard Lucas	Eastern	6-3
1936	Randall Pittman	Northwestern	6-1
1937	Charles Moored	Cooley	6-0
1938	Willie Marsh	Pershing	6-2 7/8
1939	Art Jenkins	Southeastern	6-0
1940	Glenn Mathias	Cooley	5-10
1941	Fred Weaver	Southeastern	6-2
1942	Ernest Boyd	Northern	6-2
1943	Adam Houghton	Miller	6-0
1944	Adam Houghton	Miller	5-10
1945	Fred Knack	Northwestern	5-10
1946	Harold Jackson	Northeastern	6-1
1947	Harry Wilson	Southeastern	5-11
1948	Ross Tuttle	Cooley	6-1
1949 (tie)	Jim Johnson	Miller	6-0
(tie)	Don Owens	Northwestern	6-0
(tie)	Ted Kress	Redford	6-0
(tie)	Art Kelsey	Mackenzie	6-0
1950 (tie)	James Johnson	Miller	5-10
(tie)	Charles Gandy	Miller	5-10
1951 (tie)	Doug McFetters	Mackenzie	5-10
(tie)	Paul Domeny	Mackenzie	5-10
1952 (tie)	Louis Turner	Southeastern	5-8
(tie)	Jess Cokley	Northeastern	5-8
(tie)	Chuck Worthington	Redford	5-8
(tie)	Jim Landrum	Northern	5-8
(tie)	Clyde Howard	Northwestern	5-8
(tie)	Zeb Dennard	Northwestern	5-8
(tie)	Bill Maleskie	Western	5-8
1953 (tie)	Rex McLeod	Miller	6-3
(tie)	Jess Cokley	Northeastern	6-3
1954	Jack Vivian	Cooley	5-10
1955 (tie)	Al Clark	Miller	5-10
(tie)	Saul Getson	Southeastern	5-10
1956	Gerald Krolikowski	Cody	5-10
1957 (tie)	Don Byard	Mackenzie	5-8
(tie)	Dan Sowell	Northern	5-8
(tie)	Karl Jackson	Chadsey	5-8
(tie)	Ed Stewart	Miller	5-8
(tie)	Lionel Ashford	Western	5-8
1958	Felton Rogers	Eastern	6-3
1959	Felton Rogers	Eastern	6-3
1960	Tait Malone	Northwestern	6-3
1961	Oliver Darden	Western	6-1

POLE VAULT

1931	Ed Pierce	Northern	10-9*
1932	William Hawthorne	Eastern	11-9¾*
1933	Earl McInnis	Cooley	11-0
1934	William Mechance	Hamtramck	11-0
1935	Willard Simmons	Central	11-4
1936	Merrill Gottschalk	Cooley	11-3
1937	Bob White	Redford	11-0
1938 (tie)	Brennan Clark	Northwestern	11-6½
(tie)	Dick Slevin	Cooley	11-6½
1939	John Watrobski	Hamtramck	11-9
1940	Bruce Thomas	Cooley	11-3
1941 (tie)	Claude Wise	Southeastern	11-0
(tie)	Alphonse Wilssens	Southeastern	11-0
1942	William Rockefeller	Northwestern	10-10
1943	Bernard Archer	Cooley	11-2
1944 (tie)	John Harrower	Cooley	11-7¾
(tie)	Chuck Smith	Cooley	11-7¾
1945	George Sayles	Miller	11-0
1946	Al Foley	Mackenzie	11-6
1947	Bob Smith	Cooley	10-8
1948	Fletcher Gilders	Northwestern	12-7¾*
1949	Fletcher Gilders	Northwestern	12-6
1950 (tie)	Charles Gandy	Miller	10-8
(tie)	Jim Sturdevant	Cooley	10-8
1951	Willie Wright	Miller	11-2
1952	Willie Wright	Miller	11-8
1953 (tie)	Dick Anderson	Redford	11-8
(tie)	Willie Adkins	Northeastern	11-8

1954	Willie Adkins	Northeastern	11-4
1955	Bill Guiness	Redford	12-2
1956 (tie)	Jerry Dehanau	Denby	11-4
(tie)	Jerry Luia	Cody	11-4
(tie)	Bernard LaMarr	Pershing	11-4
1957 (tie)	Jerry Dehenau	Denby	11-4
(tie)	Don Judd	Redford	11-4
(tie)	Don Gilliam	Eastern	11-4
1958	Jerry Dehenau	Denby	11-8
1959 (tie)	Russ Binion	Mumford	11-4
(tie)	Ray WInters	Cass Tech	11-4
1960	Charles Louis	Eastern	11-8
1961 (tie)	James Sande	Henry Ford	11-4
(tie)	John Rowser	Eastern	11-4
(tie)	Mel Martin	Central	11-4
1961 (tie)	Clinton Griffin	Chadsey	11-4
(tie)	Karl Kelpelalen	Cooley	11-4

LONG JUMP

1931	Frank Bolog	Southwestern	22-4½*
1932	Joseph Gordon	Hamtramck	22-10*
1933	Francis Detrick	Highland Park	21-5½
1934	Bernard Lucas	Southeastern	21-8
1935	Bernard Lucas	Southeastern	21-9
1936	Carl Culver	Central	21-3
1937	Ed Petrykowski	Cass Tech	20-11¼
1938	Otto Nichols	Northwestern	22-1 1/8
1939	Bob Ramsey	Cass Tech	21-5¾
1940	Tom Patsalis	Southeastern	22-1¾
1941	William Dunnell	Northwestern	20-11
1942	John Kent	Southwestern	21-6
1943	Tom Clark	Redford	21-11¼
1944	Lorenzo Wright	Miller	20-2¼
1945	Tom Truss	Miller	22-1
1946	Tom Stewart	Denby	21-5¼
1947	Gordon Cronk	Redford	22-0
1948	Ed Whitaker	Miller	20-10
1949	Dave Mahn	Miller	21-4
1950	Harold Dye	Southwestern	22-7½
1951	Tom Hendricks	Northwestern	22-¾
1952	Charles Stewart	Northern	21-11 7/8
1953	Godfrey Little	Miller	22-9½
1954	Fred Hopgood	Eastern	22-7
1955	Jerry Green	Miller	22-6¼
1956	Lane Jenkins	Miller	21-2
1957	Danny Watkins	Central	21-11¼
1958	Claude Chapman	Northwestern	22-0

1959	Jerry Burrell	Northern	23-¾*
1960	Henry Carr	Northwestern	23-1½*
1961	Henry Carr	Northwestern	22-9¼

SHOT

1931	Jack Fundis	Northwestern	46-1½*
1932	Constantine Eizak	Pershing	45-4½
1933	Constantine Eizak	Pershing	48-3*
1934	Walter Kratt	Cooley	44-3½
1935	Robert Herrera	Western	47-4½
1936	Harold Cochrell	Southeastern	48-1½
1937	Mike Kraatz	Cooley	49-9¼*
1938	Eugene Hirsch	Southeastern	50-6*
1939	Eugene Hirsch	Southeastern	51-10½*
1940	Milford Woods	Miller	49-4
1941	Carl Neych	Hamtramck	49-3¼
1942	Frank Senter	Southeastern	49-1
1943	Dick Brown	Redford	45-5½
1944 (tie)	Bob Walls	Redford	46-4¾
(tie)	Tom Krzeminski	Mackenzie	46-4¾
1945	Charles Fonville	Miller	51-8
1946	Ken Wenzel	Western	47-9¼
1947	Percy Smith	Miller	50-11¼
1948	Walter Jenkins	Miller	50-7
1949	Walter Jenkins	Miller	53-5*
1950	Charles McIntosh	Miller	50-6
1951	Bruce Hilty	Redford	49-7
1952	Leo Hadys	Chadsey	46-8 5/8
1953	Bob McClendon	Miller	51-3
1954	Calvin Vinson	Northern	50-7
1955	Ermin Crownley	Miller	53-10½*
1956	Clarence Cheeatham	Eastern	49-9½
1957	Edsel Reid	Chadsey	50-8
1958	Len Cranston	Redford	51-7¾
1959	Martin Tansil	Northeastern	53-9
1960	Fred Hatcher	Northwestern	58-8*
1961	Percy Mun	Eastern	52-10

DISCUS

1931	Jack Fundis	Northwestern	103-1*
1932	Clarence Ehland	Redford	116-0*
1933	Constantine Eizak	Pershing	120-5*
1934 (tie)	John Cole	Northwestern	119-5
(tie)	Bill Skorupski	Hamtramck	119-5
1935	Robert Scott	Cooley	127-4*
1936	Howard Carter	Pershing	123-10
1937	Bob McKenna	Redford	122-10

The 1941 Detroit city championships hurdle final, won by Elmer Swanson of Detroit Northeastern (third from right).

880-YARD RELAY

1931	Northwestern	nt	Coogan, Mroch, Todd, Frank Krug
1932	Hamtramck	1:32.0*	Steve Kubacki, James Scott, Joe Gordon, William Bryant
1933	Hamtramck	1:35.8	Jack Muckle, Joe Pasarski, Jackowski, Bush
1934	Central	1:33.6	Zerbel, Hedgecock, Lachowitz, Sam Swartz
1935	Hamtramck	1:33.8	William Lalewicz, James Knight, James McMillan, Harry Damasko
1936	Redford	1:34.6	Alward Pinncok, William Smith, Bob Abbott, Douglas Pearse
1937	Redford	1:33.6	Bill Atkins, Warren Burrows, Bob Swayer, Bob Abbott
1938	Central	1:33.6	Zerbel, Hedgecock, Lachowitz, Sam Schwartz
1939	Central	1:33.6	Roy Meyers, Lynn Woughter, Bob Grant, Ronald Whetter
1940	Central	1:33.7	Irving Weinstein, Sanford Warshawsky, Bill Davidson, Graham Landau
1941	Mackenzie	1:32.9	Pedler, Fraser, Keegan, Drake
1942	Eastern	1:32.0*	Don Wines, Bob Knoll, Emile Simonel, Arnold Jones
1943	Southeastern	1:34.7	Louis Palmer, Ronald Jenkins, George Mitchell, Davis Bernard
1944	Miller	1:32.2	Lorenzo Wright, Elmer Coleman, Adam Houghton, Cleo Caldwell
1945	Cooley	1:34.7	Bob Quehl, Ron Fedraw, Wes Reynolds, Dick Butcher
1946	Pershing	1:33.8	Jettie Byrd, John Grabowski, Ted Jackson, Chester Jenkins
1947 (tie)	Redford	1:34.2	
(tie)	Denby	1:34.2	
1948	Cooley	1:31.3*	Don Englahder, Jim Doodle, Larry Pickrell, Joe Larue
1949	Cooley	1:33.3	Norton Foley, Larry Dilworth, Tom Witherspoon, Joe Larue
1950	Miller	1:32.8	Hershey Bryant, Howard Gordon, Isaac Groves, David Mann
1951	Northern	1:32.6	Bob Farmer, Charles Dillard, Alvin Jackson, Charles Sherrill
1952	Northwestern	1:32.0	Gene Williams, Bill Swain, Tom Glenn, Walter Hodo
1953	Miller	1:30.6*	Rex McLeod, John Massingille, Godfrey Little, Don Thomas
1954	Eastern	1:37.0	Vern LaFaive, Alonzo Smith, John Mayhen, Fred Hopgood
1955	Miller	1:32.4	Luther Hill, Woodrow Thomas, Johnson Beasley, Fred Freeman
1956	Miller	1:32.3	Tyrone Green, Cecil Thomas, Lane Jenkins, Joe Overall
1957	Pershing	1:30.2*	Ron Benson, Ron Bass, Ron Hale, Don Haley
1958	Mumford	1:32.3	Homer Heard, Jim Hampton, Mel Bishop, Ken Burnley
1959	Mumford	1:28.9*	Dave Shevitz, Jim Hampton, Homer Heard, Ken Burnley
1960	Northwestern	1:28.2*	Robert Harris, Troy Allen, Tait Malone, Henry Carr
1961	Mumford	1:30.5	Tom Bright, Ralph Wilson, David Montgomery, Lou Williams

MILE RELAY

1961	Eastern	3:24.0	George Harris, Roy Mormon, Tilmon Blair, Clanta Wilson

MEDLEY RELAY

1950	Eastern	2:35.5*	Ron Gabel, Tom Dukes, Harold Dukes, Frank Weldon
1951	Southeastern	2:33.9*	Chuck Korpal, Brennan Gillespie, Jerry Smith, Ray Foran
1952	Southwestern	2:32.0*	Lester Sherman, Basil Szabo, Dick Conz, Milton Lewis
1953	Northern	2:29.9*	Dave Benson, Don McCuin, Dennis Gibson, Lee Daniels
1954	Northwestern	2:33.0	Bruce Greenwood, Oliver Harmon, Jim McCarty, Fred Harris
1955	Northern	2:28.8*	Clarence Willis, Joe Collins, Roosevelt Wilson, Dave Benson
1956	Northwestern	2:29.3	Tom Patrick, Maurice Poole, Charles Dunbar, Doug Beard
1957	Pershing	2:31.9	Ed Humphrey, Ron Bass, Ron Hale, Mel Benson
1958	Northwestern	2:32.1	Claude Chapman, Jerry Graham, Tait Malone, Bob Pettway
1959	Mumford	2:28.1 (2:27.1h)	Charles Byrd, Willie Arnold, Harold Miller, Jim Hampton
1960	Mumford	2:27.3	David Montgomery, Clifford Frazier, Leon Linderman, Elvin Roper

Bob Rutila of Cooley won the 1944 city championship in the 440.

BOYS TEAM CHAMPIONS & RUNNERS-UP

BOYS ALL SCHOOLS

Year	Champion	Score	Runner-up	Score
1895	Lansing (no coach)	81	2. Ann Arbor	58
1896	Detroit Central	72	2. Lansing	52
1897	Lansing (Gail Chapman)	76	2. Detroit Central	56
1898	Lansing (Gail Chapman)	49	2. Detroit Central	47
1899	Detroit Central (Jack Collins)	43	2. Ann Arbor	33
1900	tie, Ann Arbor	20		
	& Grand Rapids (Walton)	20		
1901	Detroit Central (Jack Collins)	34	2. Ann Arbor	33
1902	Detroit University (Stewart McComber)	38	2. Detroit Central	34
1903	Detroit University (Stewart McComber)	28.5	2. Ann Arbor	28.5
1904	Detroit University (Stewart McComber)	36	2. Detroit Central	19.5
1905	Detroit University (Stewart McComber)	50	2. Detroit Central	35.5
1906	Detroit University (Eddie Ryan)	33	2. Detroit Central	28
1907	Grand Rapids (Thomas Wanty)	29.5	2. Detroit Central	28 1/3
1908	Detroit Central (Jack Collins)	29.5	2. Muskegon	20.5
1909	Muskegon (Bob Zuppke)	43.5	2. Detroit University	27.5
1910	Muskegon (Bob Zuppke)	28	2. Shelby	22
1911	tie, Alma (coach?)	26.5		
	& Detroit Central (Jack Collins)	26.5		
1912	Bay City Eastern (Percy Pratt)	18	2. Wayne	15
1913	Grand Rapids Central (Dinnie Upton)	19 2/3	2. tie, Coldwater	18
			& Detroit Eastern	18
1914	Detroit Eastern (Ernie Wuesthoff)	25	2. Bay City Eastern	23
1915	Detroit Eastern (Ernie Wuesthoff)	30	2. Muskegon	21.5
1916	Grand Rapids Central (Dinnie Upton)	37	2. St Joseph	15
1917	Grand Rapids Central (Dinnie Upton)	33	2. Detroit Central	25.5
1918	No meet because of war			
1919	Detroit Eastern (Ernie Wuesthoff)	24.5	2. Battle Creek	24
1920	Detroit Northwestern (Bert Maris)	29	2. Grand Rapids Central	27.25

BOYS CLASS A

Year	Champion	Score	Runner-up	Score
1921	Detroit Northwestern (Bert Maris)	36.5	2. Muskegon	18
1922	Detroit Northern (McCrea)	21	2. Detroit Eastern	19
1923	Detroit Northwestern (Bert Maris)	31 1/3	2. Lansing	19
1924	Detroit Northwestern (Bert Maris)	33	2. Kalamazoo Central	24.5
1925	Detroit Northwestern (Bert Maris)	38	2. Detroit Cass Tech	34 2/3
1926	Detroit Cass Tech (Bill Van Orden)	29.5	2. Kalamazoo Central	23
1927	Detroit Northwestern (Malcom Weaver)	29	2. Detroit Northeastern	27
1928	Detroit Northeastern (Alvin Sandall)	32	2. tie, Detroit Cass Tech	17
			& Grand Rapids South	17
1929	Detroit Northwestern (Malcom Weaver)	36.5	2. Detroit Cass Tech	15 1/3
1930	Detroit Northwestern (Malcom Weaver)	37 1/8	2. Detroit Cass Tech	20
1931	Monroe (Dick Waters)	27	2. Grand Rapids Central	26
1932	GR Ottawa Hills (Lowell Palmer)	26	2. Ann Arbor	24
1933	Kalamazoo Central (A.E. Stoddard)	27	2. Saginaw Eastern	17 1/11
1934	GR Ottawa Hills (Lowell Palmer)	35	2. Grand Rapids South	23 7/10
1935	Saginaw (Chester Stackhouse)	43 10/21	2. Monroe	22 1/7
1936	Monroe (Dick Waters)	39.5	2. Grand Rapids South	23
1937	Monroe (Dick Waters)	26	2. Saginaw	25
1938	Saginaw (Chester Stackhouse)	31 2/5	2. Flint Central	30.5
1939	River Rouge (James McDonald)	34.25	2. Lansing Central	26
1940	Battle Creek (Hal Smith)	36.5	2. Grand Rapids South	23 5/6
1941	Benton Harbor (Jack Smith)	30	2. Monroe	25
1942	Kalamazoo Central (A.E. Stoddard)	32	2. Flint Central	22
1943	No meet because of war			
1944	Saginaw Arthur Hill (William Kelly)	36	2. Dearborn Fordson	26 5/8
1945	Saginaw (Carl Nordberg)	29.5	2. Flint Central	28.5
1946	Saginaw (Herb Korf)	36.5	2. Saginaw Arthur Hill	28
1947	Saginaw (Herb Korf)	42 1/3	2. Flint Central	31

Year	Champion	Score	Runner-up	Score
1948	Saginaw (Herb Korf)	37.5	2. Saginaw Arthur Hill	34.5
1949	Saginaw (Herb Korf)	44	2. Saginaw Arthur Hill	25 1/5
1950	Flint Northern (William Cave)	27	2. Kalamazoo Central	25 1/7
1951	GR Ottawa Hills (Clarence Brouwer)	27.75	2. Saginaw	24.75
1952	Saginaw (Herb Korf)	21	2. Pontiac	19
1953	Flint Northern (William Cave)	37	2. Pontiac	24
1954	Saginaw (Herb Korf)	35	2. Flint Northern	32
1955	Pontiac (Wallace Schloerke)	51 13/14	2. Flint Northern	17
1956	Pontiac (Wallace Schloerke)	61	2. Flint Northern	26
1957	Pontiac (Dean Wilson)	33	2. Flint Northern	23 6/11
1958	Pontiac (Dean Wilson)	43.5	2. Flint Northern	41 1/5
1959	Flint Central (James Whittaker)	35	2. Flint Northern	28
1960	Pontiac Central (Dean Wilson)	44	2. Flint Northern	41
1961	Flint Northern (Norb Badar)	32.5	2. Flint Southwestern	24
1962	tie, Grosse Pointe (James Curlett)	30		
	& Muskegon Heights (Rudy Thies)	30		
1963	Flint Northern (Norb Badar)	37.5	2. Flint Central	32
1964	Battle Creek Central (Jack Finn)	28	2. Flint Central	26
1965	Kalamazoo Central (Elf Pedler)	45	2. Flint Central	34
1966	Flint Southwestern (Fred Jackson)	39	2. Flint Central	34
1967	Battle Creek Central (Jack Finn)	48	2. Flint Central	36
1968	Battle Creek Central (Jack Finn)	37.5	2. Flint Central	33
1969	Redford Union (John McKenzie)	29	2. Battle Creek Central	24
1970	Benton Harbor (George McGinnis)	29	2. Highland Park	23
1971	Detroit Northern (Woody Thomas)	54	2. East Lansing	32
1972	Oak Park (Alvin Delidow)	31	2. Saginaw	26.5
1973	Saginaw (Claude Marsh)	41	2. Pontiac Central	35
1974	Pontiac Cental (Roger Shepler)	52	2. Ann Arbor Pioneer	35
1975	Flint Southwestern (Fred Jackson)	39	2. Flint Northwestern	38
1976	Flint Northern (Norb Badar)	44	2. Flint Southwestern	35
1977	Flint Southwestern (Fred Jackson)	35	2. GR Ottawa Hills	30
1978	Detroit Cass Tech (Robert Glenn)	43	2. Flint Southwestern	34
1979	Flint Northern (Norb Badar)	40	2. Detroit Cass Tech	32
1980	Detroit Central (Woody Thomas)	57.5	2. East Lansing	40.75
1981	Detroit Central (Woody Thomas)	61	2. Detroit Cody	32
1982	Detroit Central (Woody Thomas)	78	2. Taylor Center	38
1983	Lansing Everett (Rod Barr)	53	2. Flint Northern	41
1984	Detroit Central (Woody Thomas)	53	2. Detroit Cooley	39
1985	Lansing Everett (Ron Barr)	56	2. Detroit Cooley	28 1/5
1986	Lansing Sexton (Paul Pozega)	43	2. Kalamazoo Norrix	37
1987	Lansing Sexton (Paul Pozega)	64	2. Kalamazoo Norrix	50.5
1988	Southfield (Tom Eschmann)	58	2. Jackson	34
1989	Southfield (Tom Eschmann)	65.5	2. Monroe	44
1990	Pontiac Northern (James Nelson)	48.5	2. Kalamazoo Norrix	37
1991	Detroit Cooley (Gene Ballard)	48	2. Lansing Sexton	42
1992	Traverse City (John Lober)	37.5	2. Flint Kearsley	35
1993	Flint Carman-Ainsworth (Kenn Domerese)	44.5	2. Detroit Mumford	41
1994	Detroit Cass Tech (Thomas Wilcher)	47	2. Ann Arbor Pioneer	53
1995	Detroit Cass Tech (Thomas Wilcher)	47	2. Detroit Chadsey	33
1996	Detroit Cass Tech (Thomas Wilcher)	62	2. Pontiac Northern	44
1997	Pontiac Northern (James Nelson)	74	2. Pontiac Central	52
1998	East Lansing (Jeff Smith)	39.5	2. Rockford	39
1999	Detroit Mumford (Robert Lynch)	65	2. Rockford	42

DIVISION 1

Year	Champion	Score	Runner-up	Score
2000	Portage Northern (Bill Fries)	64	2. Saginaw Heritage	53
2001	Saginaw Heritage (Jeff Rastello)	46	2. Detroit Cass Tech	41
2002	Detroit Mumford (Robert Lynch)	63	2. Detroit Cass Tech	62
2003	Detroit Mumford (Robert Lynch)	44	2. Southfield	31
2004	Detroit Mumford (Robert Lynch)	44	2. Flint Carman-Ainsworth	39
2005	Flint Carman-Ainsworth (Kenn Domerese)	53	2. Detroit Mumford	43
2006	Saline (Brian Boze)	39.5	2. Portage Central	30.5
2007	Ann Arbor Pioneer (Don Sleeman)	63	2. East Kentwood	33

2008	Flint Carman-Ainsworth (Kenn Domerese)	56	2. East Kentwood	55
2009	East Kentwood (Dave Emeott)	79	2. Portage Northern	34
2010	East Kentwood (Dave Emeott)	92	2. Ann Arbor Pioneer	44
2011	East Kentwood (Dave Emeott)	72	2. Ypsilanti	28
2012	Lake Orion (Stan Ford)	50	2. Grand Blanc	44
2013	East Kentwood (Dave Emeott)	43	2. Grand Blanc	32
2014	East Kentwood (Dave Emeott)	71	2. Oak Park	50
2015	Saline (Al Leslie)	71	2. East Kentwood	51.5
2016	Oak Park (Robert Lynch)	81.5	2. Rockford	64
2017	East Kentwood (Dave Emeott)	78.5	2. Rockford	62
2018	East Kentwood (Dave Emeott)	61	2. Ann Arbor Pioneer	39

BOYS DETROIT 1931-1961

1931	Detroit Northwestern (Ernest Wuestoff)	54	2. Detroit Cass Tech	24
1932	Detroit Eastern (Claude Snarey)	28	2. Detroit Northwestern	27
1933	Hamtramck (Floyd Stocum)	41 4/6	2. Detroit Southwestern	21.5
1934	Detroit Eastern (William Arbaugh)	39	2. Hamtramck	31
1935	Hamtramck (Floyd Stocum)	31 1/3	2. Detroit Eastern	26
1936	Hamtramck (Floyd Stocum)	39	2. tie, Detroit Cooley & Redford	17
1937	Hamtramck (Floyd Stocum)	42	2. Detroit Redford	33
1938	Detroit Cooley (Claude Snarey)	29	2. Detroit Redford	23
1939	Detroit Cooley (Claude Snarey)	87 2/3	2. Detroit Southeastern	65
1940	Detroit Cooley (Claude Snarey)	68	2. Detroit Southeastern	63
1941	Detroit Southeastern (Leighton Boyd)	89 2/5	2. Detroit Mackenzie	42
1942	Detroit Southeastern (Leighton Boyd)	52	2. Detroit Eastern	43
1943	Detroit Cooley (Claude Snarey)	102.5	2. Detroit Southeastern	80
1944	Detroit Cooley (Claude Snarey)	98.5	2. Detroit Miller	88
1945	Detroit Miller (Leroy Dues)	105 1/5	2. Detroit Cooley	76
1946	Detroit Cooley (Claude Snarey)	50	2. Detroit Denby	33
1947	Detroit Cooley (Claude Snarey)	53	2. Detroit Northwestern	35.5
1948	Detroit Cooley (George Cairns)	55.5	2. Detroit Miller	45.5
1949	Detroit Northwestern (Jimmy Russell)	49.5	2. Detroit Miller	42.5
1950	Detroit Miller (Leroy Dues)	75	2. Detroit Northwestern	38
1951	Detroit Mackenzie (Leo Grimes)	43	2. Detroit Northwestern	38
1952	Detroit Miller (Leroy Dues)	56.5	2. Detroit Northern	54.5
1953	Detroit Miller (Leroy Dues)	69.5	2. tie, Detroit Northern & Northwestern	35
1954	Detroit Pershing (Carl Holmes)	43.5	2. Detroit Miller	36
1955	Detroit Miller (Leroy Dues)	59	2. Detroit Denby	37
1956	Detroit Denby (Ralph Green)	44	2. Detroit Pershing	43
1957	Detroit Pershing (Carl Holmes)	64	2. Detroit Cody	51 5/6
1958	Detroit Redford (Bruce Waha)	69 1/3	2. Detroit Chadsey	38.75
1959	Detroit Mumford (Stan Mullin)	82 1/3	2. Detroit Redford	54 1/3
1960	Detroit Northwestern (Tom Hendricks)	94	2. Detroit Mumford	87
1961	Detroit Northwestern (Tom Hendricks)	84 1/5	2. Detroit Redford	57

BOYS CLASS B

1921	Allegan (Jack Damoth)	41	2. Petoskey	27 6/7
1922	Allegan (Jack Damoth)	40.75	2. Niles	27 3/20
1923	Coldwater (?)	30.5	2. Allegan	21.5
1924	Petoskey (Fred Doyle)	25	2. Wyandotte	23
1925	Niles (Leland Walker)	47	2. Allegan	28
1926	St Johns (Homer Hanham)	33	2. St Joseph	26
1927	St Joseph (Hank Howe)	28	2. Birmingham	24
1928	Dearborn (Leith Wetzel)	23	2. St Joseph	22
1929	Niles (Claudis Collisi)	27	2. Dearborn	22
1930	Monroe (Dick Waters)	27	2. Allegan	13
1931	South Haven (David Baer)	29	2. Grand Haven	25.5
1932	St Joseph (Hank Howe)	23	2. Dowagiac	18
1933	Birmingham (Frank Whitney)	34	2. Niles	24.5
1934	Dowagiac (James Lewis)	23	2. Dearborn	22
1935	Niles (Chet Davidson)	34	2. Allegan	27
1936	Birmingham (Frank Whitney)	35	2. Niles	28

Year	Champion	Score	Runner-up	Score
1937	Birmingham (Frank Whitney)	35	2. Niles	20.5
1938	Belding (Russel Krooze)	29	2. East Lansing	28
1939	St Joseph (Arnold Karsten)	25	2. Niles	24.5
1940	East Lansing (Lynn Adams)	36 11/12	2. Kalamazoo State High	21
1941	East Lansing (Lynn Adams)	35	2. Three Rivers	32.5
1942	Birmingham (Ernie Engle)	33.5	2. Three Rivers	24 1/7
1943	No meet because of war			
1944	East Grand Rapids (Reed Waterman)	23 1/5	2. Niles	22 43/65
1945	St Joseph (Arnold Karsten)	27	2. East Grand Rapids	22
1946	Charlotte (Malcom Gobel)	37	2. Fremont	22 11/12
1947	Alma (Vic Hicks)	25 1/3	2. Hastings	23 5/12
1948	Ypsilanti (Ralph Deetz)	40 1/10	2. Birmingham	28 7/10
1949	Birmingham (Kermit Ambrose)	49 1/3	2. Ypsilanti	29
1950	Niles (Homer Hatcher)	23	2. Birmingham	17 1/3
1951	Cadillac (Hiram Becker)	33 6/7	2. Mt Pleasant	18.5
1952	Roseville (Jim Gibbert)	33	2. Cadillac	16
1953	Battle Creek Lakeview (Joseph Bogart)	20	2. Roseville	18
1954	Inkster (Khamalaw White)	39	2. Ludington	24
1955	Inkster (Khamalaw White)	27.5	2. Grand Rapids Central	25
1956	Inkster (Khamalaw White)	33	2. St Louis	32
1957	St Joseph (Dick Higgs)	32.5	2. Inkster	27
1958	East Grand Rapids (Reed Waterman)	30 3/8	2. River Rouge	29
1959	Willow Run (Lamar Miller)	34	2. BH Cranbrook	21
1960	Ecorse (Eugene Lacarelli)	48 3/5	2. BH Cranbrook	46 6/11
1961	Detroit Lutheran West (Erv Ruth)	35	2. Ecorse	30
1962	Dowagiac (Paul Watt)	38 7/8	2. Ecorse	35 5/6
1963	River Rouge (Roy Krueger)	52	2. East Grand Rapids	26
1964	Willow Run (Lamar Miller)	38	2. River Rouge	35
1965	River Rouge (Roy Krueger)	61	2. Willow Run	26
1966	Bloomfield Hills Cranbrook (Ben Snyder)	38	2. Ecorse	36.75
1967	Ecorse (Jim Bibbs/Paul Piper)	43	2. Howell	27
1968	Bay City Glenn (Robert Beaumont)	42	2. Detroit East Catholic	36
1969	Ecorse (Lorenzo Croft/Paul Piper)	32	2. Oscoda	23
1970	Ecorse (Lorenzo Croft/Edward Pruett)	41	2. Bloomfield H Cranbrook	20
1971	Holly (Duane Raffin)	38	2. Ecorse	29
1972	Bloomfield Hills Cranbrook (Ben Snyder)	41	2. Mt Morris	36
1973	Ecorse (Lorenzo Croft/Edward Pruett)	43	2. Dearborn Heights Robichaud	29
1974	Dearborn Heights Robichaud (Leit Jones)	45.5	2. Linden	42
1975	Inkster (Mary Mabry)	39.5	2. Wyoming Park	31
1976	Flint Beecher (Marty Crane)	42	2. Dearborn Heights Robichaud	39
1977	Flint Beecher (Marty Crane)	40	2. Wyoming Rogers	39
1978	tie, Flint Beecher (Marty Crane)	29		
	& Muskegon Heights (Theodoro Martinez)	29		
1979	Dearborn Heights Robichaud (Leit Jones)	48	2. Ecorse	32
1980	Flint Beecher (Marty Crane)	57	2. Dexter	42
1981	Ecorse (Ed Pruett)	56	2. Flint Beecher	32
1982	Flint Ainsworth (Kenn Domerese)	45	2. Oak Park	33
1983	Flint Beecher (Marty Crane)	91	2. Ecorse	33.5
1984	Detroit Benedictine (Ted Mac)	56	2. Ypsilanti Lincoln	39
1985	Flint Beecher (Marty Crane)	56	2. Detroit Benedictine	48
1986	Flint Beecher (Marty Crane)	85	2. Detroit Benedictine	58 2/5
1987	Flint Beecher (Marty Crane)	71	2. Dearborn	40
1988	Flint Beecher (Marty Crane)	77	2. Detroit East Catholic	45
1989	Grand Rapids Northview (Al Korytkowski)	48	2. Detroit Benedictine	39
1990	Dearborn Heights Robichaud (Leit Jones)	49	2. Three Rivers	46
1991	Oxford (Elmer Ball)	40	2. Dearborn Heights Robichaud	31
1992	Flint Beecher (Marty Crane)	87	2. Bloomfield Hills Andover	56
1993	Detroit UD Jesuit (Jerry Myszkowski)	59	2. Flint Beecher	53
1994	Comstock (Tim Cashen)	53	2. Ypsilanti Lincoln	51
1995	Comstock (Tim Cashen)	70	2. Fremont	28 1/10
1996	Whitehall (Kurt Mikkleson)	39	2. tie, Dowagiac & Godwin Hts	36
1997	St Joseph (Ron Waldvogel)	47	2. Dowagiac	46

1998	Corunna (Chris Curtiss)	58	2. St Joseph	36
1999	Corunna (Gordin Aldrich)	45	2. Romulus	42

BOYS DIVISION 2

2000	Romulus (Norbert Glover)	47	2. Detroit Renaissance	46
2001	Farmington Hills Harrison (John Reed)	34	2. Stevensville Lakeshore	31.5
2002	Farmington Hills Harrison (John Reed)	39	2. Three Rivers	36.5
2003	Farmington Hills Harrison (John Reed)	44	2. Stevensville Lakeshore	41
2004	Flint Kearsley (Paul Adas)	48	2. Lansing Sexton	42
2005	Lansing Sexton (Daniel Boggan)	70	2. Ypsilanti	49
2006	tie, GR Forest Hills Northern (Joe Circuro)	40		
	& Ypsilanti (Torin Moore)	40		
2007	Dexter (Chris Hanion)	48	2. East Lansing	35
2008	Williamston (Paul Nilsson)	57	2. East Lansing	42
2009	Hamilton (Kevin Spotts)	61	2. Williamston	38
2010	Byron Center (Craig Reinstein)	30	2. Zeeland West	29
2011	East Lansing (Pat Murray)	56	2. Chelsea	48
2012	Auburn Hills Avondale (Wes Harden)	47	2. Lansing Sexton	40
2013	Chelsea (Eric Swager)	64	2. Grand Rapids Ottawa Hills	56
2014	Zeeland West (Phil Hoover)	50	2. Auburn Hills Avondale	40
2015	Orchard Lake St Mary (Sean Clouse)	52	2. Zeeland East	44.5
2016	Orchard Lake St Mary (Sean Clouse)	46	2. Mason	44
2017	Zeeland East (Ralph Neal)	71	2. Coldwater	42
2018	Coldwater (Jeff Schorfhaar)	60	2. Zeeland East	53

BOYS CLASS C

1921	Plainwell (Dwight Harwood)	16 7/10	2. Vassar	15 1/5
1922	Plainwell (Dwight Harwood)	48	2. Dearborn	19
1923	Plainwell (Dwight Harwood)	33	2. Clinton	31
1924	Plainwell (Dwight Harwood)	33	2. Morenci	20
1925	Wayland (Al Vedders)	31	2. Croswell	30
1926	Otsego (Bernard McCann)	24 5/8	2. Marine City	15
1927	Plainwell (Rock Fleming)	24	2. Yale	15
1928	Yale (Paul Smarks)	28	2. Paw Paw	17.5
1929	Lowell (Ronald Finch)	15	2. Kalamazoo State High	13
1930	Kalamazoo St Augustine (Harv Freeman)	14	2. Otsego	13
1931	Algonac (Milford Finch)	23	2. Paw Paw	22
1932	Caro (Don Stamants)	25	2. Boyne City	18
1933	Buchanan (Harold Bradfield)	22 1/6	2. Caro	17.5
1934	Paw Paw (Byran Emmert)	26 1/5	2. East Grand Rapids	25
1935	Paw Paw (Byran Emmert)	36 6/7	2. South Lake	21 6/7
1936	Paw Paw (Byran Emmert)	29	2. Lowell	23
1937	Okemos (Ken Barnhill)	25.5	2. Plainwell	23
1938	Algonac (Milford Finch)	42	2. Charlevoix	19.5
1939	Algonac (Ted Soule)	35.5	2. Paw Paw	17 6/11
1940	East Grand Rapids (Reed Waterman)	23	2. Leelanau School	21 7/8
1941	St Clair Shores South Lake (Jim Touma)	43	2. Imlay City	24
1942	Imlay City (Thurlow H. King)	40 2/3	2/ Grandville	24
1943	No meet because of war			
1944	Fowlerville (John S. Munn)	33 1/9	2. St Clair Shores Lakeshore	28
1945	Romulus (Harold Cass)	33	2. St Clair Shores Lakeshore	31
1946	East Grand Rapids (Reed Waterman)	31	2. Ypsilanti Roosevelt	23
1947	Paw Paw (Wilbert Schank)	30.5	2. Ypsilanti Roosevelt	22
1948	East Grand Rapids (Reed Waterman)	35	2. St Clair Shores South Lake	21
1949	Dundee (Robert Decker)	40 7/10	2. East Grand Rapids	29
1950	East Grand Rapids (Reed Waterman)	43	2. Milan	32
1951	Ann Arbor University (Prentice Ryan)	30	2. Algonac	22
1952	tie, Ann Arbor University (Gene Freed)	24		
	& East Jackson (Howard Loomis)	24		
1953	St Louis (Sherman Olmstead)	30	2. Berrien Springs	23.5
1954	Lansing Everett (Archie Ross)	26 2/3	2. Marlette	20
1955	Reed City (Dale R. Clark)	17.25	2. Cassopolis	17
1956	Lansing Everett (Archie Ross)	45	2. Reed City	23

Year	Champion (Coach)	Score	Runner-up	Score
1957	Boyne City (Robert O'Niell)	27	2. Mt Clemens St Mary	18
1958	Boyne City (Robert O'Niell)	23	2. Grosse Ile	21
1959	Grosse Ile (Jay Tossot)	24	2. Flint Dye	22
1960	Haslett (Ed Townsend)	19	2. East Jackson	17
1961	Saginaw MI Lutheran (Armin Schultz)	27 1/5	2. East Jackson	21
1962	Lansing St Mary (Paul Pozega)	40.5	2. Lansing Boys Training	37
1963	Lansing Boys Training (David Jach)	18 1/6	2. Vandercook Lake	17
1964	Battle Creek St Phillip (Donald Pape)	42	2. Detroit St Theresa	22
1965	tie, Battle Crk St Phillip (Michael Hume)	31		
	& Fowlerville (Bob Mohre)	31		
1966	Haslett (Mike Hart)	36	2. Battle Creek St Phillip	35
1967	Laingsburg (Carl Clarke)	30	2. Hartford	24
1968	DeWitt (W. Gillingham/Thomas Kroner)	41	2. Akron-Fairgrove	32
1969	Reading (James Newell)	44	2. Shepherd	38
1970	tie, Grass Lake (Rod Hall)	37.5		
	& Reading (James Newell)	37.5		
1971	Detroit Country Day (George Brown)	46	2. Muskegon Christian	39
1972	Detroit DePorres (Ted Mac)	58	2. Battle Creek St Phillip	46.5
1973	Detroit DePorres (Fred Wright/Ed Conley)	73	2. St Louis	48
1974	Detroit DePorres (Fred Wright/Ed Conley)	58	2. New Haven	36
1975	Unionville-Sebewaing (Mike McCormick)	72	2. Charlevoix	45.5
1976	Detroit Benedictine (Ted Mac)	52	2. Unionville-Sebewaing	44
1977	Redford St Mary (Darian Keener)	45.5	2. Bronson	37
1978	Detroit Benedictine (Ted Mac)	46	2. Whitehall	45
1979	DeWitt (Barry Kloenhamer)	45.5	2. Detroit Benedictine	44
1980	Ecorse (Ed Pruett)	55	2. Grand Rapids South Christian	28
1981	Detroit Lutheran West (Mike Unger)	44	2. Middleville	24
1982	Detroit Lutheran West (Mike Unger)	110.5	2. Redford St Mary	41.5
1983	Detroit DePorres (Robert Lynch)	64.75	2. Detroit Lutheran West	61
1984	Detroit DePorres (Darryl Jenkins)	56	2. Flint Hamady	46
1985	Ecorse (Ed Pruett)	43	2. Scottville Mason Co Central	36
1986	Scottville Mason Co Central (Bruce Krieger)	46	2. Detroit DePorres	44
1987	Detroit Lutheran West (Mike Unger)	51	2. Ecorse	41
1988	Detroit Lutheran West (Dave Ruth)	67	2. Saginaw Nouvel	50
1989	Saginaw Nouvel (Leo Boyd)	71	2. Constantine	49
1990	Middleton-Fulton (Randall Troub)	41	2. Edwardsburg	39
1991	Cassopolis (Larry Rogers)	50	2. Sandusky	47
1992	Detroit DePorres (Darold Gholston)	41	2. Edwardsburg	37
1993	Eau Claire (Jerry Mitchell)	40	2. tie, Napoleon & New Haven	36
1994	New Haven (Frank Reed)	46	2. Breckenridge	43.5
1995	New Haven (Frank Reed)	70	2. Newaygo	54
1996	New Haven (Frank Reed)	41	2. Buchanan	31.5
1997	Detroit DePorres (Tony Taylor)	42	2. New Haven	33.5
1998	Detroit DePorres (Tony Taylor)	37	2. New Haven	36
1999	Buchanan (Rusty Stitt)	45	2. Clare	42

BOYS DIVISION 3

Year	Champion (Coach)	Score	Runner-up	Score
2000	Clare (Rob Johnson)	45	2. Albion	42
2001	Williamston (Paul Nilsson)	55	2. Benzie Central	27
2002	Yale (Scott Brown)	37	2. Battle Creek Pennfield	36
2003	Williamston (Paul Nilsson)	65	2. Muskegon Oakridge	36.5
2004	Detroit Country Day (David Wilson)	86.5	2. Frankenmuth	44
2005	Frankenmuth (Jerry Sheppard)	51	2. Detroit Country Day	47.5
2006	Williamston (Paul Nilsson)	81	2. Detroit Country Day	65
2007	Detroit Country Day (David Wilson)	70	2. Williamston	69 2/3
2008	Albion (Mike Jurasek)	44	2. Allendale	43
2009	Albion (Mike Jurasek)	61.5	2. Allendale	43
2010	Vassar (Jason Kiss)	40	2. Frankenmuth	33
2011	Frankenmuth (Jerry Drake)	44	2. Union City	38
2012	Lansing Catholic (Tim Simpson)	68	2. Union City	45
2013	Wyoming Kelloggsville (Tom Degannaro)	52	2. Scottville Mason Co Central	31
2014	Sanford-Meridian (Dave Pettyplace)	45	2. Scottville Mason Co Central	39
2015	Jackson Lumen Christi (Mike Woolsey)	44	2. Hillsdale	37

Year	Champion	Score	Runner-up	Score
2016	Sanford-Meridian (Mike Bilina)	39	2. Hillsdale	34
2017	Chesaning (Jason Hemgesberg)	47	2. Hillsdale	42
2018	Clare (Adam Burhans)	44	2. Berrien Springs	42

BOYS CLASS D

Year	Champion	Score	Runner-up	Score
1927	Trenton (Walter Farrar)	46	2. Woodland	23
1928	Okemos (Lyle Allen)	27	2. Lawton	14 1/5
1929	Newaygo (John W. Ferguson)	22	2. Okemos	21 1/8
1930	Okemos (Lyle Allen)	34	2. South Lake	27.5
1931	Centreville (Wayne Smith)	37 9/16	2. South Lake	37
1932	Centreville (Wayne Smith)	24	2. South Lake	19.5
1933	Centreville (Wayne Smith)	23 1/3	2. Portage	19
1934	Centreville (Wayne Smith)	51.5	2. Bergland	34
1935	Bear Lake (Nick Musselman)	33	2. Royal Oak Madison	29 1/5
1936	Onekama (M.C. Wolf)	46	2. St Clair Shores Lakeview	43
1937	Mt Morris St Mary (Vernon Gay)	36.5	2. Bloomfield Hills	34
1938	Bloomfield Hills (Richard J. Speiss)	35	2. Mt Morris St Mary	34
1939	Bloomfield Hills (Richard J. Speiss)	42	2. Michigan School for Deaf	29
1940	Bath (Harold Hoyle)	35.5	2. Michigan School for Deaf	21 13/18
1941	Bear Lake (Willis Johnson)	31 2/3	2. Bath	30
1942	Bear Lake (A.G. McDaniels)	40.5	2. Mt Morris St Mary	29.5
1943	No meet because of war			
1944	Leelanau School (John Evans)	54	2. Bloomfield Hills	52.5
1945	Michigan School for Deaf (Earl Roberts)	60 7/10	2. Leelanau School	56 1/5
1946	Michigan School for Deaf (Earl Roberts)	52	2. Baldwin	47
1947	Baroda (Bob Wisner)	39.5	2. Baldwin	33 9/10
1948	Bloomfield Hills (Richard J. Speiss)	50	2. Michigan School for Deaf	38
1949	Michigan School for Deaf (Earl Roberts)	45.5	2. Bloomfield Hills	33.75
1950	Benton Harbor St John (Ray Null)	43.5	2. Michigan School for Deaf	40
1951	Otisville (Leroy Gunderson)	45	2. Benton Harbor St John	39
1952	Brethren (Bob Dunnavan)	46 2/5	2. Edwardsburg	20 2/5
1953	Brethren (Bub Dunnavan)	67.5	2. Detroit University	27.5
1954	Brethren (Doyle Eckhardt)	58.5	2. Spring Arbor	36.5
1955	Brethren (Doyle Eckhardt)	46.5	2. Spring Arbor	33
1956	Covert (Larry Deschene)	28.5	2. Brethren	25
1957	Covert (Marland Howard)	39	2. Dansville	34
1958	Brethren (Doyle Eckhardt)	37 1/8	2. Beal City	30 2/3
1959	Schoolcraft (Fred Tremblay)	27	2. Covert	23
1960	Covert (Ronald Lazo)	34.5	2. Schoolcraft	24
1961	Michigan School for Deaf (Earl Roberts)	41	2. Centreville	29
1962	Michigan School for Deaf (Earl Roberts)	41	2. Covert	37
1963	Michigan School for Deaf (Earl Roberts)	43	2. Brethren	36
1964	Covert (Ronald Clark)	53	2. Lake City	33
1965	Covert (Ronald Clark)	38	2. Lake City	36
1966	Covert (Ronald Clark)	59 4/5	2. Kalamazoo University	50
1967	Detroit St Charles (Jim Murray)	64.5	2. Ann Arbor University	47
1968	Unionville (Mike McCormick)	43	2. tie, Mendon & Pentwater	29
1969	Grass Lake (Rod Hall)	55	2. Athens	50
1970	Covert (Alfred Hawkins)	35.5	2. Utica St Lawrence	32
1971	Unionville (Mike McCormick)	75	2. Camden-Frontier	46.5
1972	Unionville (Mike McCormick)	83.25	2. Mendon	63.5
1973	Mendon (Bob Critz)	74	2. Grass Lake	42
1974	Mendon (Bob Critz)	60	2. North Muskegon	44.5
1975	Detroit DePorres (Robert Lynch)	48	2. Detroit East Catholic	44
1976	Detroit DePorres (Robert Lynch)	73.5	2. Homer	38
1977	Detroit DePorres (Robert Lynch)	92	2. Potterville	50.5
1978	Akron-Fairgrove (Jerry Lasceski)	70	2. Ann Arbor Richard	44
1979	Detroit DePorres (Robert Lynch)	87	2. Ann Arbor Richard	48
1980	Detroit DePorres (Robert Lynch)	110	2. Covert	30
1981	Detroit DePorres (Robert Lynch)	92	2. Battle Creek St Phillip	50
1982	Detroit East Catholic (Chris Hurley)	64	2. Battle Creek St Phillip	62
1983	Detroit East Catholic (Chris Hurley)	80	2. Akron-Fairgrove	60

Year	Winner	Score	Runner-up	Score
1984	Detroit East Catholic (Chris Hurley)	87	2. Potterville	56
1985	Fowler (Neil Hufnagel)	75	2. Detroit East Catholic	47
1986	Detroit East Catholic (Kent Baker)	75	2. Fowler	45
1987	Detroit East Catholic (Kent Baker)	92	2. Fowler	63
1988	Fowler (Neil Hufnagel)	52 3/10	2. Mendon	43 3/10
1989	Detroit Lutheran West (Dave Ruth)	67.5	2. Fowler	61
1990	Reading (Bob Lutz)	84	2. Detroit Lutheran West	73
1991	Reading (Bob Lutz)	69	2. Detroit Lutheran West	68
1992	Athens (Larry Brown)	53	2. Litchfield	50
1993	Akron-Fairgrove (Jerry Lasceski)	47	2. Litchfield	45
1994	Pittsford (Bruce Caswell)	66	2. Au Gres	58
1995	Pittsford (Bruce Caswell)	57	2. New Buffalo	38
1996	Pittsford (Bruce Caswell)	96	2. Webberville	37
1997	Pittsford (Bruce Caswell)	116	2. Grass Lake	44
1998	Centreville (Bob Critz)	78	2. Frankfort	55.5
1999	Harper Woods Gallagher (Michelle Batten)	68	2. Centreville	48

BOYS DIVISION 4

Year	Winner	Score	Runner-up	Score
2000	Maple City Glen Lake (Tom Christiansen)	45	2. Centreville	37
2001	Lutheran Westland (Mike Unger)	60	2. Detroit Benedictine	42
2002	Detroit Benedictine (Les Hale)	53	2. Redford Borgess	43
2003	Detroit Benedictine (Les Hale)	53	2. Detroit DePorres	45
2004	Detroit DePorres (Tony Taylor)	52	2. Bath	49
2005	Detroit DePorres (Tony Taylor)	55	2. Fowler	47
2006	Potterville (Dan Brunk)	49	2. Ottawa Lake-Whiteford	32
2007	Ottawa Lake-Whiteford (Jamie LaRocca)	55	2. tie, RO Shrine & Springport	30
2008	Pewamo-Westphalia (Scott Werner)	62	2. Jonesville	34
2009	Potterville (Dan Brunk)	64	2. Pewamo-Westphalia	37
2010	Concord (Joyce Grimes)	52	2. Pewamo-Westphalia	39
2011	tie, Albion (Mike Jurasek)	48		
	& Big Rapids Crossroads Acad (Ben Talsma)	48		
2012	Albion (Mike Jurasek)	49	2. Muskegon WM Christian	36
2013	Saugatuck (Rick Bauer)	58	2. Albion	47
2014	Concord (Mike Hersha/David Jordan)	78	2. Saugatuck	46
2015	tie, Concord (Mike Hersha/David Jordan)	40		
	& Saugatuck (Rick Bauer)	40		
2016	Saugatuck (Rick Bauer)	66	2. Evart	32
2017	Whittemore-Prescott (Jeff Erickson)	36	2. Manton	31
2018	Kalamazoo Hackett (Simon Cholometes)	51	2. Sand Creek	36

BOYS UP CLASS B

Year	Winner	Score	Runner-up	Score
1940	Ironwood (Jack Kraemer)	39 3/5	2. Escanaba	37 7/20
1941	Escanaba (Jim Rouman)	46 2/3	2. Ironwood	29
1942	Escanaba (Dick Schram)	47.5	2. Ironwood	39
1943	No meet because of war			
1944	Escanaba (Dick Schram)	57.5	2. Ironwood	36.5
1945	Sault Ste. Marie (Clyde Peterson)	42	2. Escanaba	36.5
1946	Ironwood (Jack Kraemer)	41	2. Escanaba	40 .5
1947	Menominee (Kenneth Radick)	46.5	2. Sault Ste. Marie	36 1/3
1948	Ironwood (Jack Kraemer)	43	2. Menominee	35
1949	Menominee (Kenneth Radick)	4.5	2. Ironwood	35.5
1950	Ironwood (Jack Kraemer)	28	2. Escanaba	27
1951	Ironwood (Jack Kraemer)	39 1/15	2. Sault Ste. Marie	33
1952	Sault Ste. Marie (Ernie Kranz)	56.5	2. Iron Mountain	31
1953	Marquette (Bill Hart)	23.5	2. Sault Ste. Marie	22.5
1954	Sault Ste. Marie (Ernie Kranz)	42	2. Stephenson	34 1/3
1955	Stephenson (Francis Cappaert)	36 9/10	2. Iron River	28
1956	Sault Ste. Marie (Ernie Kranz)	38 11/12	2. Ishpeming	30 3/4
1957	Sault Ste. Marie (Ernie Kranz)	41.5	2. Calumet	25
1958	Sault Ste. Marie (Ernie Kranz)	28	2. Stephenson	26.5
1959	Marquette (Bill Hart)	41	2. Ironwoo24	

BOYS UP CLASS A/B

Year	Winner	Score	Runner-up	Score
1960	Manistique (Rudi Bramstrom)	30	2. Marquette	28

Year	Champion	Score	Runner-up	Score
1961	Newberry (Art Allen)	44 1/3	2. Marquette	23.5
1962	Newberry (Art Allen)	40	2. Kingsford	36.5
1963	Kingsford (Dick McCarthy)	26	2. Rudyard	24
1964	Marquette (Bill Hart)	38	2. Kingsford	28
1965	Sault Ste. Marie (Robert Wallis)	37 1/3	2. Kingsford	36
1966	Sault Ste. Marie (Robert Wallis)	44.5	2. Escanaba	24.5
1967	Ishpeming (Norman Andrew)	47	2. Escanaba	37.5
1968	Menominee (Francis Mellinger)	40	2. Ishpeming	31
1969	Gladstone (Robert Richards)	38	2. Escanaba Holy Name	24
1970	Gwinn (George McCormick)	47	2. Marquette	32
1971	Calumet (Walt Kitti)	49.5	2. Menominee	33
1972	Escanaba (Jim Hirn)	36	2. Ishpeming	34
1973	Escanaba (Jim Hirn)	45.5	2. Iron Mountain	36
1974	Escanaba (Jim Hirn)	64.5	2. Ironwood	43
1975	Calumet (Walt Kitti)	58	2. Escanaba	45
1976	Sault Ste. Marie (Robert McKerroll)	43	2. Calumet	40
1977	Escanaba (Jim Hirn)	53.5	2. Marquette	52
1978	Ironwood (Thomas Doman)	42.5	2. Menominee	35
1979	Kingsford (George Nygaard)	66	2. Escanaba	51
1980	Menominee (Fran Mellinger)	79	2. Escanaba	54
1981	Menominee (Fran Mellinger)	83.5	2. Marquette	62
1982	Escanaba (Jim Hirn)	66	2. Marquette	55.25
1983	Kingsford (George Nygaard)	76	2. Marquette	75
1984	Marquette (Jon Peterson)	72.5	2. Menominee	72
1985	Marquette (Jon Peterson)	64 1/3	2. Escanaba	61
1986	Escanaba (Jim Hirn)	67.5	2. Kingsford	59 1/3
1987	Escanaba (Jim Hirn)	76	2. Gwinn	57
1988	Gwinn (Dick Mettlach)	66.5	2. Marquette	54.5
1989	tie, Gwinn (Dick Mettlach)	61		
	& Kingsford (David Murvich)	61		
1990	Kingsford (David Murvich)	45	2. Ironwood	41
1991	Menominee (David Smith)	46	2. Ishpeming-Westwood	43
1992	Escanaba (Russ Bluse)	68	2. Sault Ste. Marie	60
1993	Escanaba (Russ Bluse)	52	2. Kingsford	37
1994	Menominee (Greg Langlois)	55	2. Marquette	49
1995	Menominee (Greg Langlois)	62	2. Marquette	59.5
1996	Escanaba (Dan Flynn)	81	2. Ishpeming-Westwood	54
1997	Menominee (Greg Langlois)	70	2. Escanaba	50
1998	Negaunee (Kevin Bell)	66.5	2. Menominee	65
1999	Escanaba (Gary Seehafer)	70	2. Menominee	66
2000	Escanaba (Dan Flynn)	70	2. Marquette	72

BOYS UP DIVISION 1

Year	Champion	Score	Runner-up	Score
2001	Sault Ste. Marie (Jim Martin)	55	2. Calumet	42.5
2002	Marquette (Matt Edgell)	82	2. Calumet	79
2003	Marquette (Matt Edgell)	115	2. Menominee	108
2004	Gladstone (Gary Whitmer)	116	2. Marquette	76
2005	Gladstone (Gary Whitmer)	150	2. West Iron County	65
2006	Gladstone (Gary Whitmer)	96	2. Marquette	78
2007	Gladstone (Gary Whitmer)	90	2. Escanaba	74.5
2008	Gladstone (Gary Whitmer)	114	2. Sault Ste. Marie	77
2009	Gladstone (Gary Whitmer)	101	2. Marquette	88
2010	Marquette (Michael Leanes)	112	2. Kingsford	93.5
2011	Marquette (Michael Leanes)	139	2. Menominee	90
2012	Marquette (Michael Leanes)	97	2. Gladstone	82
2013	Gladstone (Gary Whitmer)	112	2. Menominee	80
2014	Kingsford (Doug Roberts)	127	2. Marquette	82
2015	Marquette (Kyle Detmers)	131	2. Kingsford	98
2016	Marquette (Kyle Detmers)	144	2. Houghton	111
2017	Marquette (Kyle Detmers)	128	2. Iron Mountain	76.5
2018	Marquette (Kyle Detmers)	110	2. Houghton	86

BOYS UP CLASS C

1940	L'Anse (Steve Baltic)	32.5	2. Escanaba St. Joseph	31
1941	Stephenson (Robert Decker)	37 2/3	2. Newberry	26
1942	Newberry (A.P. Vescolani)	63	2. Stephenson	46.5
1943	No meet because of war			
1944	Stephenson (Robert Decker)	27 9/10	2. Gladstone	27 1/5
1945	L'Anse (Leo Outinen)	39.5	2. Hancock	39
1946	Munising (Robert Villemure)	43.5	2. Newberry	34.25
1947	L'Anse (Leo Outinen)	48	2. Houghton	38
1948	Houghton (Pete Bugni)	49	2. Wakefield	45 7/10
1949	Munising (Robert Villemure)	59	2. Wakefield	47
1950	Munising (Robert Villemure)	37.5	2. L'Anse	35
1951	Bessemer (Warren Smith)	37	2. L'Anse	30.5
1952	Wakefield (Roman Yatchak)	41 7/10	2. Bessemer	33
1953	Houghton (Pete Bugni/John Gaffney)	46	2. Ontonagon	34
1954	Houghton (Pete Bugni/John Gaffney)	58 2/3	2. Bessemer	38.25
1955	Houghton (Pete Bugni/John Gaffney)	64 8/10	2. Wakefield	39.5
1956	Houghton (Pete Bugni/John Gaffney)	48.5	2. Iron River	47.5
1957	Munising (Walfred Mickelson)	48 2/3	2. St. Ignace	34
1958	Munising (Walfred Mickelson)	54 1/10	2. Wakefield	51 1/10
1959	Wakefield (Roman Yatchak)	56.5	2. Sault Ste. Marie Loretto	35
1960	Wakefield (Roman Yatchak)	52	2. Stephenson	42.5
1961	Wakefield (Roman Yatchak)	53	2. Sault Ste. Marie Loretto	28
1962	tie, Rudyard (Roy Hamilton)	30.5		
	& Wakefield (Roman Yatchak)	30.5		
1963	Ontonagon (Don Lundin)	40	2. Lake Linden	38
1964	Wakefield (Duane Lane)	40 1/5	2. St. Ignace	36 2/5
1965	tie, Gwinn (George McCormick)	27		
	& L'Anse (Jim Mattson)	27		
1966	Stephenson (Guss Ford)	38.5	2. Wakefield	27
1967	L'Anse (Jim Mattson)	40	2. Wakefield	38
1968	L'Anse (Jim Mattson)	43	2. Wakefield	40
1969	tie, Ontonagon (Doug Filpulla)	34.5		
	& Hancock (?)	34.5		
1970	Rudyard (Roy Hamilton)	69	2. Norway	44.5
1971	L'Anse (Jerry Bugni)	50	2. Norway	40
1972	Houghton (Don Swatski)	58	2. Ontonagon	40
1973	Rudyard (Roy Hamilton)	53	2. Houghton	35
1974	Rudyard (Roy Hamilton)	46	2. Munising	34
1975	Ishpeming (R. Norman Andrew)	43	2. Norway	33
1976	Ishpeming Westwood (Gordon Chinn)	45	2. Ishpeming	40
1977	Rudyard (Roy Hamilton)	52	2. Ishpeming	41
1978	Ishpeming Westwood (Gordon Chinn)	32.5	2. St. Ignace	30
1979	Ishpeming Westwood (Gordon Chinn)	43	2. Ironwood	31
1980	Munising (Fran DesArmo)	42	2. Ishpeming-Westwood	42
1981	Iron Mountain (Rick Olds)	57	2. Ironwood	39
1982	Ironwood (Tom Doman)	64	2. Iron Mountain	50
1983	Iron Mountain (Rick Olds)	46	2. Ishpeming-Westwood	37
1984	Ishpeming Westwood (Gordon Chinn)	55	2. Munising	34
1985	Negaunee (Dick Koski)	40	2. Houghton	32
1986	Houghton (Don Sawaski)	50	2. Munising	40
1987	Iron Mountain (Rick Olds)	55	2. Ironwood	42
1988	Ironwood (Tom Doman)	49	2. Iron Mountain	42
1989	Iron Mountain (Rick Olds)	40	2. Ishpeming-Westwood	36
1990	Ishpeming Westwood (Daniel Harrington)	48	2. Ontanagon	40
1991	Ironwood (Tom Doman)	71	2. Stephenson	47.5
1992	Houghton (Don Sawaski)	37	2. St. Ignace	33
1993	St Ignace (Charles Otlewski)	43.5	2. Munising	43
1994	Munising (Fran DesArmo)	73	2. Rudyard	38
1995	Munising (Fran DesArmo)	47	2. Ironwood	45.5
1996	Munising (Fran DesArmo)	41	2. Ironwood	36
1997	Calumet (John Croze)	42	2. Stephenson	38.5
1998	Calumet (John Croze)	56.5	2. Ishpeming-Westwood	42

| 1999 | Calumet (John Croze) | 42 | 2. Manistique | 33 |
| 2000 | Iron Mountain (Tom Wender) | 38 | 2. Manistique | 34 |

BOYS UP DIVISION 2

2001	Newberry (John Carlson)	69	2. Munising	40
2002	tie, Norway (Bob Madigan)	76		
	& Stephenson (Dale Fountain)	76		
2003	Ishpeming (Mark Olgren)	77 1/3	2. Norway	71 1/3
2004	Norway (Bob Madigan)	73	2. Iron Mountain	73
2005	Newberry (Mike Carpenter)	107	2. Norway	102.5
2006	Newberry (Mike Carpenter)	96	2. St. Ignace	90
2007	Stephenson (Jeff Ness)	114	2. Ironwood	73
2008	Ironwood (Chuck Vitton)	101	2. Ishpeming	75
2009	Ironwood (Chuck Vitton)	81	2. Munising	72
2010	St Ignace (Emily Fullerton)	98	2. Rudyard	89
2011	St Ignace (Emily Fullerton)	124	2. Ishpeming	91.5
2012	St Ignace (Emily Fullerton)	112	2. Stephenson	85
2013	Manistque (MaryLou Lund)	102	2. Ishpeming	96
2014	Ishpeming (Scott Syrjala)	115	2. Manistique	76
2015	Ishpeming (Scott Syrjala)	164	2. Ishpeming-Westwood	75
2016	Ishpeming (P.J. Pruett)	134	2. Iron Mountain	94
2017	Newberry (Gene Schroll)	130.5	2. Ishpeming	102
2018	Ishpeming (P.J. Pruett)	100	2. Iron Mountain	92

BOYS UP CLASS D

1940	Rock (Clifford Buckmaster)	39.5	2. Channing	33
1941	Hermansville (Harold Cass)	43	2. Rock	37
1942	Hermansville (Harold Cass)	37	2. Marquette Pierce	34
1943	No meet because of war			
1944	Chassell (?)	46 5/6	2. Hermansville	40.5
1945	Ewen (Lawrence Sain)	41.5	2. Chassell	40
1946	Chassell (Wilmer Savela)	46.5	2. Powers	44.5
1947	Powers (George Hill)	52	2. Eben	47
1948	Eben (Walfred Mickelson)	60	2. Chassell	25.25
1949	Chassell (Wilmer Savela)	34 7/10	2. Hermansville	33 3/5
1950	Hermansville (Robert Tacker)	47	2. Eben	46
1951	Eben (Webster Morrison)	37	2. Hermansville	26.5
1952	Pickford (Webster Morrison)	32	2. Eben	30
1953	Pickford (Webster Morrison)	45	2. Hermansville	29
1954	Pickford (Webster Morrison)	58 4/5	2. Chassell	33
1955	Pickford (Webster Morrison)	59 6/10	2. Rapid River	31 1/10
1956	Pickford (Webster Morrison)	59	2. Rapid River	27 1/5
1957	Pickford (Webster Morrison)	54	2. DeTour	35
1958	Pickford (Webster Morrison)	54.5	2. Chassell	34 9/10
1959	Pickford (Webster Morrison)	57.5	2. Nahma	32
1960	Pickford (Webster Morrison)	62	2. DeTour	27.5
1961	Pickford (Webster Morrison)	44.25	2. DeTour	38.5
1962	Pickford (Webster Morrison)	50 2/3	2. DeTour	27
1963	Pickford (Webster Morrison)	58	2. Rapid River	33
1964	Pickford (Webster Morrison)	66	2. DeTour	36.5
1965	Pickford (Webster Morrison)	85 1/3	2. DeTour	34
1966	Pickford (Webster Morrison)	51	2. Channing	35.5
1967	Pickford (Webster Morrison)	70	2. tie, Ironwood St Ambrose & Rapid River	21
1968	Pickford (Webster Morrison)	50	2. DeTour	33.5
1969	Pickford (Webster Morrison)	47	2. Rapid River	37
1970	Pickford (Webster Morrison)	60.75	2. Channing	21.5
1971	Pickford (Webster Morrison)	50	2. Ewen-Trout Creek	38
1972	Pickford (Webster Morrison)	57	2. Ewen-Trout Creek	30
1973	Pickford (Webster Morrison)	62	2. Crystal Falls Forest Park	46
1974	Pickford (Webster Morrison)	74	2. Crystal Falls	45 7/10
1975	Pickford (Webster Morrison)	53	2. DeTour	26.5
1976	Pickford (Webster Morrison)	35	2. Bessemer	31
1977	Pickford (Richard Johnson)	50.5	2. Crystal Falls Forest Park	42

Year	Champion	Score	Runner-up	Score
1978	Pickford (Robert McHaney)	79	2. White Pine	34
1979	Crystal Falls Forest Park (Stuart Smith)	50.5	2. DeTour	34
1980	Pickford (Robert McHaney)	42	2. Norway	28
1981	Cedarville (Tom Wilson)	38	2. Norway	31
1982	Wakefield (Allan Davidson)	34	2. Cedarville	28
1983	Wakefield (Allan Davidson)	35	2. St Ignace	34
1984	Felch North Dickinson (Miles Ferguson)	44	2. Bessemer	42
1985	Crystal Falls Forest Park (Jim Mocerini)	64	2. Rudyard	42
1986	Rudyard (Roy Hamilton)	47	2. Crystal Falls Forest Park	45.5
1987	Crystal Falls Forest Park (Jim Mocerini)	51	2. Bessemer	36
1988	Crystal Falls Forest Park (Jim Mocerini)	48	2. Wakefield	44
1989	Pickford (Sam Lightfoot)	58	2. Crystal Falls Forest Park	52
1990	Pickford (Sam Lightfoot)	63	2. Lake Linden-Hubbell	29.5
1991	Pickford (Sam Lightfoot)	53	2. Ewen-Trout Creek	33
1992	Pickford (Sam Lightfoot)	48.25	2. Rock-Mid Peninsula	33
1993	Felch North Dickinson (Joe Reddinger)	42	2. Pickford	30
1994	Ontonagon (Mark Bobula)	47	2. Powers North Central	38
1995	Powers North Central (Jerry Root)	44	2. Ontonagon	30.5
1996	Rapid River (Steve Ostrenga)	49	2. Powers North Central	34
1997	Rapid River (Fred Stage)	51	2. Powers North Central	46
1998	St Ignace (Marty Spencer)	57	2. Mohawk Keweenaw	30.5
1999	Felch North Dickinson (Joe Reddinger)	38.5	2. Rapid River	36
2000	Rapid River (Steve Ostrenga)	66.5	2. Felch North DIckinson	26

BOYS UP DIVISION 3

Year	Champion	Score	Runner-up	Score
2001	Rapid River (Steve Ostrenga)	58	2. Wakefield	38
2002	Rapid River (Steve Ostrenga)	117	2. Rock-Mid Peninsula	64
2003	Rapid River (Steve Ostrenga)	117	2. Bark River-Harris	58.5
2004	Pickford (Jerry Rairigh)	62	2. Rapid River	60
2005	Powers North Central (?)	85	2. Bessemer	66
2006	Rock-Mid Peninsula (Gary Brayak)	68	2. Rapid River	55
2007	Rock-Mid Peninsula (Jill VanDamme)	81	2. Felch North Dickinson	74
2008	Felch North Dickinson (Dale Powell)	99	2. Rapid River	65
2009	Crystal Falls Forest Park (Erich Ziegler)	75	2. Felch North Dickinson	72.5
2010	Crystal Falls Forest Park (Erich Ziegler)	83.5	2. Rapid River	73
2011	Cedarville (Ryan Wilson)	85	2. Pickford	78
2012	Pickford (Gerald Rairigh)	89	2. Bark River-Harris	58
2013	Felch Dickinson (Michael Lindholm)	77	2. Pickford	51
2014	Munising (Matt Mattson)	107.5	2. Felch North Dickinson	68
2015	Munising (Matt Mattson)	134	2. Rapid River	65
2016	Rapid River (Steve Ostrenga)	72	2. Powers North Central	68
2017	Rapid River (Steve Ostrenga)	108	2. Bessemer	104
2018	Bessemer (Mark Mazzon)	151	2. Rapid River	104

GIRLS TEAM CHAMPIONS & RUNNERS-UP

GIRLS ALL CLASSES

1972	Marquette (Barb Krill)	67	2. Iron Mountain	46
1973	Lincoln Park (Jeanette Bowman)	34	2. Walled Lake Western	31.5

GIRLS CLASSES A/B

1974	Detroit Cass Tech (Richard Cole)	40	2. Walled Lake Western	26.5

GIRLS CLASSES C/D

1974	Montrose (Cathy Markland)	62	2. Williamston	39

GIRLS CLASS A

1975	Detroit Cass Tech (Richard Cole)	54	2. Walled Lake Western	40.5
1976	Detroit Cass Tech (Sandra Smith)	35	2. Detroit Pershing	34
1977	Flint Central (Clinton Turner)	33	2. Walled Lake Western	30
1978	Detroit Mackenzie (Barbara Halanski)	41	2. Flint Northern	24.5
1979	Flint Northern (George Dedrick)	53	2. Detroit Mumford	38
1980	Flint Northern (Al Sigman)	82	2. Pontiac Central	39
1981	Flint Northern (George Dedrick)	67	2. Detroit Chadsey	35
1982	Detroit Chadsey (Charles Span)	56	2. Flint Northern	39
1983	Flint Northern (George Dedrick)	59	2. Benton Harbor	52
1984	Benton Harbor (Eddie Watson)	64	2. Dearborn Edsel Ford	36
1985	Ann Arbor Pioneer (Bryan Westfield)	56	2. Detroit Cass Tech	50
1986	Ann Arbor Pioneer (Bryan Westfield)	85	2. Detroit Cass Tech	63
1987	Ann Arbor Pioneer (Bryan Westfield)	90	2. Detroit Cass Tech	64
1988	Ann Arbor Pioneer (Bryan Westfield)	82	2. Detroit Cass Tech	60
1989	Ann Arbor Pioneer (Bryan Westfield)	70.5	2. Detroit Cass Tech	58
1990	Ann Arbor Pioneer (Bryan Westfield)	64	2. Ypsilanti	56
1991	Ann Arbor Pioneer (Bryan Westfield)	95	2. Detroit Cass Tech	52
1992	Detroit Cass Tech (Bertha Smiley)	62	2. Ann Arbor Pioneer	51
1993	Detroit Cass Tech (Bertha Smiley)	65	2. Plymouth Salem	36
1994	Detroit Cass Tech (Bertha Smiley)	65	2. Detroit M.L. King	42
1995	Detroit Cass Tech (Bertha Smiley)	71	2. Ann Arbor Pioneer	55
1996	Ann Arbor Pioneer (Bryan Westfield)	93	2. Detroit Cass Tech	71
1997	Ann Arbor Pioneer (Bryan Westfield)	87	2. Detroit Cass Tech	54
1998	Ann Arbor Pioneer (Bryan Westfield)	82	2. Detroit Cass Tech	48
1999	Ann Arbor Pioneer (Bryan Westfield)	76	2. Rockford	60

GIRLS DIVISION 1

2000	Rockford (Randy Vanderveen)	76	2. Ann Arbor Pioneer	70
2001	Ann Arbor Pioneer (Bryan Westfield)	81	2. Rockford	80
2002	Ann Arbor Pioneer (Bryan Westfield)	97	2. Rockford	76
2003	Rockford (Randy Vanderveen)	77.5	2. Ann Arbor Pioneer	60
2004	Detroit Mumford (Marc Parker)	81	2. Ann Arbor Pioneer	69
2005	Detroit Mumford (Marc Parker)	74	2. Ann Arbor Pioneer	56
2006	Ann Arbor Pioneer (Bryan Westfield)	80	2. Clarkston	50
2007	Ann Arbor Pioneer (Bryan Westfield)	104	2. Detroit Mumford	57
2008	Ann Arbor Pioneer (Bryan Westfield)	59	2. Jackson	54
2009	Romulus (Wade Cook)	38	2. Rockford	37
2010	Rochester (Larry Adams)	65	2. Rockford	58
2011	Grosse Pointe South (Steve Zaranek)	54	2. tie, Ann Arbor Huron & Detroit Cass T	50
2012	Grosse Pointe South (Steve Zaranek)	77.5	2. Ann Arbor Huron	64
2013	Grosse Pointe South (Steve Zaranek)	76	2. Saline	55
2014	Oak Park (Brandon Jiles)	92	2. Northville	50
2015	Oak Park (Brandon Jiles)	93	2. East Kentwood	54.5
2016	Oak Park (Brandon Jiles)	81.5	2. Ann Arbor Pioneer	64
2017	Ann Arbor Pioneer (Nancy Boudreau)	69	2. Oak Park	65
2018	Oak Park (Brandon Jiles)	66	2. Rockford	59.5

GIRLS CLASS B

1975	tie, Ionia (Kay Breining) & Muskegon Catholic (Dorothy Chiaverini)	35		
1976	Holt (Lila Guenther)	40	2. Muskegon Catholic	32
1977	Muskegon Catholic (Dorothy Chiaverini)	36	2. tie, Fenton & Hastings	25

Year	Champion	Score	Runner-up	Score
1978	Detroit Immaculata (Jan Greenwell)	33	2. Holt	32
1979	St Joseph (Joe Collins)	41	2. Flint Beecher	38
1980	Grand Rapids Christian (Ken Bokhoven)	30	2. Flint Beecher	28
1981	Flint Beecher (Tyrone Armstrong)	50	2. Livonia Ladywood	36
1982	tie, Mt Clemens L'Anse Creuse (Ken Hoover)	32		
	& Oak Park (Bernard Wells)	32		
1983	Mt Clemens L'Anse Creuse (Ken Hoover)	42	2. St Joseph	39
1984	Muskegon Heights (Edgar Watson)	40	2. Hudsonville Unity Christian	35
1985	Hemlock (Lori Griffing)	51	2. Flint Beecher	50
1986	Flint Beecher (Tyrone Armstrong)	42	2. Grand Rapids Christian	29
1987	Flint Beecher (Tyrone Armstrong)	58	2. Grand Rapids Christian	36
1988	Detroit DePorres (Pat Gerraghty)	47	2. Redford Borgess	38
1989	Detroit DePorres (Pat Gerraghty)	66	2. Wyoming Park	53
1990	Detroit DePorres (Pat Gerraghty)	54	2. Corunna	38
1991	Otisville-LakeVille (Dale Hammond)	54	2. Detroit DePorres	38
1992	Flint Beecher (Joe Wilkerson)	87	2. Bloomfield Hills Andover	36
1993	Inkster (Jenny Madison)	40	2. River Rouge	34
1994	River Rouge (Robert Washington)	58	2. Caledonia	48
1995	Caledonia (Joe Zomerlei)	41	2. Otisville-LakeVille	32
1996	Dearborn Heights Robichaud (Francis McCauley)	58	2. Flint Powers	28
1997	Detroit Renaissance (Rick Miotke)	46	2. Corunna	42
1998	Detroit Renaissance (Rick Miotke)	66	2. Grosse Ile	38
1999	Detroit Renaissance (Rick Miotke)	75	2. Corunna	57.5

GIRLS DIVISION 2

Year	Champion	Score	Runner-up	Score
2000	Detroit Renaissance (Rick Miotke)	84	2. Battle Creek Lakeview	61
2001	Detroit Renaissance (Rick Miotke)	53	2. Battle Creek Lakeview	49.5
2002	Detroit Renaissance (Rick Miotke)	52	2. Ypsilanti	43
2003	Detroit Renaissance (Rick Miotke)	67	2. Coopersville	50
2004	Ypsilanti (Tom Micallef)	57	2. Detroit Renaissance	49
2005	Detroit Renaissance (Rick Miotke)	80	2. Ypsilanti	38
2006	Detroit Renaissance (Rick Miotke)	68	2. Grand Rapids Forest Hills Northern	47
2007	Detroit Renaissance (Rick Miotke)	76	2. Grand Rapids Forest Hills Northern	45
2008	Grand Rapids Forest Hills Northern (Keith Boeve)	54	2. Ypsilanti	40
2009	East Lansing (Charles Pollard)	36	2. DeWitt	34
2010	Dearborn Divine Child (Tony Mifsud)	61	2. Detroit Country Day	49
2011	Detroit Country Day (David Wilson)	58	2. Dearborn Divine Child	44
2012	tie, Dearborn Divine Child (Tony Mifsud)	60		
	& Detroit Country Day (David Wilson)	40		
2013	Dearborn Divine Child (Tony Mifsud)	81	2. Ada Forest Hills Eastern	53
2014	Remus Chippewa Hills (Sally Schafer)	34	2. Lansing Waverly	31
2015	St Johns (Neil Feldpausch)	36	2. Flint Southwestern	34
2016	Lansing Waverly (Rex Wilkes)	42	2. Flint Powers	40
2017	Lansing Waverly (Rex Wilkes)	47	2. Zeeland East	46
2018	Zeeland East (Josh Vork)	64	2. Holland Christian	62

GIRLS CLASS C

Year	Champion	Score	Runner-up	Score
1975	Bath (Nancy Roberson)	55	2. Montrose	50
1976	Williamston (Paul Nilsson)	63	2. Montrose	50.5
1977	North Muskegon (Carol McCollough)	44	2. Detroit Lutheran West	36
1978	Muskegon Catholic (Dorothy Chiaverini)	56	2. Montrose	50
1979	North Muskegon (Karel Bailey)	45	2. Shepherd	38
1980	North Muskegon (Karel Bailey)	48	2. Detroit Lutheran West	38
1981	St Louis (Kathy Hutfilz)	53	2. Detroit Lutheran West	40.5
1982	Detroit Lutheran West (Phyllis Luedders)	45	2. Cassopolis	27
1983	Carson City-Crystal (Ted Galbraith)	39	2. Burton Bentley	35
1984	Detroit Country Day (George Prosperi)	45	2. Burton Bentley	38
1985	Detroit Country Day (George Prosperi)	46	2. Haslett	40
1986	Detroit Country Day (George Prosperi)	71	2. Cassopolis	39
1987	Detroit Country Day (George Prosperi)	85	2. Hart	34
1988	Detroit Country Day (George Prosperi)	65	2. New Haven	45
1989	Onsted (Jim Hill)	44	2. Redford St Mary	35
1990	Onsted (Jim Hill)	52	2. Buchanan	31

Year	Winner	Score	Runner-up	Score
1991	Frankenmuth (Bruce Barber)	64	2. Onsted	52
1992	Vermontville Maple Valley (Gary Hamilton)	59	2. Morenci	34
1993	Shepherd (David Burke)	45	2. Comstock Park	30
1994	Clare (Judy Johynson)	48	2. Reading	29
1995	Hemlock (William Agresta)	63	2. Clare	53
1996	Clare (Judy Johnson)	58	2. Hemlock	43
1997	Kingsley (Rob Glover)	38	2. Napoleon	35
1998	Kingsley (Rob Glover)	55	2. Benzie Central	46
1999	Benzie Central (Andy Herman)	52	2. Mason County Central	41

GIRLS DIVISION 3

Year	Winner	Score	Runner-up	Score
2000	Yale (Rich Dams)	44	2. Benzie Central	43
2001	Cass City (Scott Cuthrell)	39	2. Laingsburg	30
2002	Yale (Rich Dams)	33.25	2. Hanover-Horton	31
2003	tie, Laingsburg (Chris Lantis)	36		
	& Monroe St Mary (Chuck Byron)	36		
2004	Goodrich (John Shaw)	47	2. Lansing Catholic	45
2005	Goodrich (John Shaw)	93	2. Albion	44
2006	Kent City (Jill Evers)	42	2. Goodrich	40
2007	Albion (Brad Shedd)	66	2. Ann Arbor Richard	43
2008	Ann Arbor Richard (Carl Brock)	50	2. Leroy Pine River	42
2009	Frankenmuth (Jamie Engel)	58	2. Benzie Central	48
2010	Frankenmuth (Jamie Engel)	89	2. Benzie Central	39
2011	Benzie Central (Tracie Jelly)	54	2. Frankenmuth	53
2012	Frankenmuth (Mike Snyder)	63	2. Benzie Central	52
2013	Pewamo-Westphalia (Scott Werner)	54	2. Reed City	40
2014	Frankenmuth (Mike Snyder)	96	2. Pewamo-Westphalia	72
2015	Pewamo-Westphalia (Scott Werner)	62	2. Frankenmuth	59.5
2016	Ithaca (Gene Lebron)	57.5	2. Adrian Madison	54
2017	Adrian Madison (Josh Powers)	56.5	2. Lansing Catholic	41 3/5
2018	tie, Hart (Mindy Whitney)	46		
	& St Charles (Andre Williams)	46		

GIRLS CLASS D

Year	Winner	Score	Runner-up	Score
1975	Battle Creek St Phillip (Sheila Guerra)	67	2. Centreville	42
1976	Morenci (Kay Johnson)	50	2. Battle Creek St Phillip	48.5
1977	Grass Lake (Rod Hall)	50	2. Indian River Inland Lakes	44.5
1978	Grass Lake (Rod Hall)	58	2. Indian River Inland Lakes	42
1979	Indian River Inland Lakes (Terri Lee Smith)	64	2. Custer Mason County Eastern	52
1980	Ann Arbor Greenhills (Dave McDowell)	42	2. Athens	41
1981	Ann Arbor Greenhills (Dave McDowell)	48	2. Fowler	41 3/5
1982	Fowler (Kim Spalsbury)	53	2. Detroit St Andrew	39
1983	Fowler (Kim Spalsbury)	58.5	2. Ann Arbor Greenhills	58
1984	Potterville (Joe Wood)	71	2. Ann Arbor Greenhills	58
1985	Athens (Walt Schalau)	65	2. Akron-Fairgrove	61
1986	Athens (Walt Schalau)	75	2. Akron-Fairgrove	58
1987	Akron-Fairgrove (Gordon Aldrich)	63	2. Fowler	44
1988	Akron-Fairgrove (Gordon Aldrich)	54	2. Fowler	51
1989	Fowler (Kim Spalsbury)	82	2. Detroit Lutheran West	75
1990	Fowler (Kim Spalsbury)	65	2. Detroit Lutheran West	57
1991	Maple City Glen Lake (Bill Brendel)	65	2. Fowler	49.5
1992	Maple City Glen Lake (Bill Brendel)	86	2. Litchfield	58
1993	Litchfield (Randy Brinks)	68	2. McBain Northern Michigan Christian	57
1994	Maple City Glen Lake (Bill Greer)	37.5	2. Pittsford	46
1995	Maple City Glen Lake (Bill Greer)	60	2. Grass Lake	52
1996	Homer (Rick Cooley)	77	2. Bellaire	46
1997	Mendon (Sue Bombrys)	58	2. St Joseph Lake Michigan Catholic	52
1998	Fowler (Mark Ulman)	85	2. Mendon	64.5
1999	North Muskegon (Doug Clark)	61	2. Potterville	59

GIRLS DIVISION 4

Year	Winner	Score	Runner-up	Score
2000	Saginaw Michigan Lutheran Seminary (Daryl Weber)	58	2. Detroit DePorres	40
2001	Reading (Deb Price)	74	2. Burton Atherton	33
2002	Maple City Glen Lake (Paul Christiansen)	42	2. Lincoln-Alcona	35

2003	Detroit Benedictine (Fermon Tate)	53	2. Pewamo-Westphalia	44
2004	Detroit Benedictine (Fermon Tate)	75	2. Reading	48
2005	Saginaw Valley Lutheran (Jon Frank)	46	2. tie, Rochester H Lutheran NW & Ubly	44
2006	Ubly (Pat Bolda)	64	2. Flint Hamady	61
2007	Ubly (Pat Bolda)	61.5	2. Southfield Christian	39
2008	Potterville (Mike Kuyers)	49	2. Reading	38
2009	Potterville (Mike Kuyers)	51	2. Fowler	43
2010	Pewamo-Westphalia (Scott Werner)	65	2. Fowler	61
2011	Fowler (Jill Feldpausch)	89	2. Pewamo-Westphalia	81.5
2012	Fowler (Jill Feldpausch)	54	2. Traverse City St Francis	50
2013	Traverse City St Francis (Julie Duffing)	66	2. Reading	52
2014	Reading (Deb Price)	81	2. Traverse City St Francis	56
2015	Harbor Springs (Emily Kloss)	57	2. Fowler	53.5
2016	Fowler (Jill Feldpausch)	56	2. Concord	44
2017	Southfield Christian (Todd Crouch)	62	2. Fowler	52
2018	Fowler (Jill Feldpausch)	87	2. Pittsford	55.5

GIRLS UP ALL CLASSES

1973	Marquette (Barb Crill)	66	2. Pickford	41

GIRLS UP CLASS A/B

1974	Escanaba (Gary Seehafer)	42	2. Marquette	41.5
1975	Escanaba (Gary Seehafer)	62	2. Marquette	51
1976	Escanaba (Gary Seehafer)	91	2. Marquette	53
1977	Marquette (Barb Crill)	73	2. Marquette	66
1978	Escanaba (Gary Seehafer)	68	2. Marquette	51
1979	Kingsford (Marilyn Phillips)	59	2. Escanaba	55
1980	Escanaba (Gary Seehafer)	57	2. Kingsford	49
1981	Escanaba (Gary Seehafer)	72	2. Menominee	46
1982	Escanaba (Gary Seehafer)	74	2. Marquette	65
1983	Escanaba (Gary Seehafer)	60	2. Marquette	57
1984	Escanaba (Gary Seehafer)	73	2. Menominee	47
1985	Escanaba (Gary Seehafer)	79.5	2. Sault Ste. Marie	45
1986	Escanaba (Gary Seehafer)	89.5	2. Sault Ste. Marie	46
1987	Escanaba (Gary Seehafer)	79	2. Gwinn	66
1988	Escanaba (Gary Seehafer)	85	2. Marquette	61
1989	Marquette (Dale Phillips)	88	2. Escanaba	54
1990	Marquette (Dale Phillips)	70	2. Gladstone	45
1991	Marquette (Dale Phillips)	102	2. Sault Ste. Marie	41
1992	Escanaba (Gary Seehafer)	55	2. Marquette	47
1993	Marquette (Dale Phillips)	52.5	2. Menominee	51
1994	Marquette (Dale Phillips)	84	2. Menominee	58
1995	Marquette (Dale Phillips)	97	2. Escanaba	58
1996	Marquette (Dale Phillips)	88	2. Escanaba	56
1997	Marquette (Dale Phillips)	82	2. Ishpeming-Westwood	48
1998	Marquette (Dale Phillips)	102	2. Escanaba	84
1999	Marquette (Dale Phillips)	88.5	2. Escanaba	47.5
2000	Marquette (Jeff Stevenson)	70	2. Escanaba	49.5

GIRLS UP DIVISION 1

2001	Sault Ste. Marie (Scott Menard)	62	2. Marquette	52.5
2002	Gladstone (Jim Murtha)	125	2. Marquette	69
2003	Escanaba (Dan DeLong)	94	2. Marquette	90
2004	Escanaba (Dan DeLong)	96	2. Marquette	87
2005	Escanaba (Dan DeLong)	102	2. Iron Mountain	88
2006	Calumet (Steve Parks)	117	2. Marquette	114
2007	tie, Escanaba (Dan DeLong)	101		
	& Marquette (John Peterson)	101		
2008	Marquette (John Peterson)	124	2. Kingsford	81
2009	Marquette (John Peterson)	92	2. Calumet	83
2010	Negaunee (Victoria Paupore)	95	2. Marquette	92
2011	Marquette (John Peterson)	90	2. Sault Ste. Marie	82
2012	Marquette (John Peterson)	106	2. Negaunee	99
2013	Marquette (John Peterson)	145	2. Negaunee	62.5

Year	Champion	Score	Runner-up	Score
2014	Marquette (John Peterson)	145	2. Escanaba	86
2015	Marquette (John Peterson)	154	2. Calumet	71
2016	Marquette (Natalie Messano)	169	2. Escanaba	61
2017	Marquette (Natalie Messano)	118	2. Negaunee	91
2018	Negaunee (Victoria Paupore)	115	2. Marquette	89.5

GIRLS UP CLASS C

Year	Champion	Score	Runner-up	Score
1974	Ontonagon (Dorothy Phillips)	46	2. L'Anse	43
1975	L'Anse (Carol Seavoy)	54	2. Ishpeming Westwood	39
1976	Ishpeming Westwood (Patricia Phillips)	39	2. Iron River West Iron Co.	26
1977	Rudyard (Judy Hamilton)	35	2. St. Ignace	26
1978	Negaunee (Karen Clements)	47	2. Ishpeming	27
1979	Negaunee (Karen Clements)	72	2. Ishpeming	44.5
1980	Negaunee (Karen Clements)	56	2. St. Ignace	39
1981	Kingsford (Marilyn Phillips)	40	2. Ishpeming-Westwood	34
1982	Negaunee (Karen Clements)	40	2. Houghton	24
1983	Hancock (Richard Miller)	38	2. Negaunee	36
1984	Ishpeming Westwood (Gordon Chinn)	38.5	2. Negaunee	35.5
1985	Ishpeming Westwood (Gordon Chinn)	51	2. Stephenson	41
1986	Stephenson (Greg Dausey)	42 1/3	2. Calumet	34
1987	Ishpeming Westwood (Gordon Chinn)	35	2. Stephenson	33
1988	Calumet (Mary Joosten)	52 1/3	2. Stephenson	44
1989	Newberry (Lori Fair)	33	2. Iron River West Iron Co.	30
1990	Newberry (Ken Haggart)	51.5	2. St. Ignace	39
1991	Newberry (Lori Fair)	41	2. Ironwood	37
1992	Munising (Dee Jay Paquette)	49	2. Stephenson	39
1993	Stephenson (Greg Dausey)	70	2. Ironwood	59
1994	Ironwood (Dale Davis)	69	2. Munising	48
1995	Ironwood (Dale Davis)	75	2. Munising	36
1996	Ironwood (Dale Davis)	66	2. St. Ignace	59.5
1997	Ironwood (Dale Davis)	56	2. St. Ignace	52
1998	Ironwood (Dale Davis)	63.5	2. Ishpeming-Westwood	53
1999	Ironwood (Dale Davis)	49	2. St. Ignace	46
2000	Ishpeming Westwood (Scott Jette)	60	2. St. Ignace	50

UP GIRLS DIVISION 2

Year	Champion	Score	Runner-up	Score
2001	Ironwood (Charles Vitton)	62	2. St. Ignace	56
2002	Ishpeming Westwood (Jon Beckman)	96	2. Iron Mountain	85
2003	Ishpeming Westwood (Jon Beckman)	93	2. Iron Mountain	91
2004	Iron Mountain (Rex Terwilliger)	103	2. Ishpeming	78
2005	Ishpeming/Republic-Michigamme (Scott Syrjala)	94	2. Norway	77
2006	Ishpeming Westwood (Jon Beckman)	82	2. Norway	79
2007	Ishpeming (Scott Syrjala)	73	2. St. Ignace	69
2008	St Ignace (Diane Huskey)	89	2. Ishpeming Westwood	79
2009	Munising (Fran DesArmo)	81	2. Ishpeming Westwood	71
2010	St Ignace (Trudy Olsen)	131	2. West Iron County	78
2011	St Ignace (Trudy Olsen)	132	2. West Iron County	110
2012	St Ignace (Trudy Olsen)	142	2. Norway	96
2013	West Iron County (Kristi Beruttin)	144	2. Manistique	97
2014	St Ignace (Trudy Olsen)	116	2. West Iron County	107
2015	Ishpeming (Scott Syrjala)	151	2. West Iron County	126
2016	Ishpeming (Scott Syrjala)	127	2. Hancock	104
2017	St Ignace (Trudy Olsen)	110	2. Munising	102
2018	St Ignace (Trudy Olsen)	160	2. Iron Mountian	90

GIRLS UP CLASS D

Year	Champion	Score	Runner-up	Score
1974	Crystal Falls Forest Park (Nancy Anderson)	39	2. Pickford	28
1975	Crystal Falls Forest Park (Nancy Anderson)	50	2. Rapid River	38
1976	Pickford (Sharon Beacom)	36	2. tie, Engadine & Lake Linden	25
1977	Republic-Michigamme (Greg Johnson)	44.75	2. Engadine	34
1978	Engadine (Kathy Konie)	41	2. Republic-Michigamme	33
1979	Norway (Robert Giannunzio)	58	2. Engadine	29
1980	Norway (Robert Giannunzio)	58	2. Cedarville	45

Year	Winner	Score	Runner-up	Score
1981	tie, Norway (Robert Giannunzio)	45		
	& Cedarville (Jim Cousineau)	45		
1982	Cedarville (Randy Nellis)	40	2. Lake Linden-Hubbell	26
1983	Lake Linden-Hubbell (Barbara Sickler)	38	2. DeTour	35
1984	Pickford (John Bennin)	63	2. DeTour	47
1985	Pickford (John Bennin)	52	2. Lake Linden-Hubbell	33
1986	Pickford (John Bennin)	92	2. Rapid River	33
1987	Pickford (John Bennin)	70	2. Wakefield	34
1988	Pickford (John Bennin)	65	2. Rock-Mid Peninsula	35
1989	Felch North Dickinson (Paul Feak)	64	2. Pickford	58
1990	Pickford (John Bennin)	48.5	2. Bark River-Harris	31.5
1991	Pickford (John Bennin)	51	2. tie, Cedarville & Detour	46
1992	Cedarville (Gil Trevarrow & Tom Wilson)	51	2. Felch North DIckinson	46
1993	Cedarville (Gil Trevarrow & Tom Wilson)	56	2. Bessemer	44
1994	tie, Felch North Dickinson (Paul Feak)	38		
	& Lake Linden-Hubbell (Craig Sundblad)	38		
1995	Rock-Mid Peninsula (Kathy Paul)	36	2. Rapid River	35
1996	Rapid River (Fred Stage)	35	2. Pickford	33
1997	Rapid River (Fred Stage)	43	2. Lake Linden-Hubbell	39
1998	St Ignace (Lynwood Leightner)	79	2. Rapid River	49
1999	Pickford (John Bennin)	57.5	2. Rapid River	55
2000	Pickford (John Bennin)	67	2. Rapid River	64.5

UP GIRLS DIVISION 3

Year	Winner	Score	Runner-up	Score
2001	Pickford (John Bennin)	64	2. Rapid River	59
2002	Pickford (John Bennin)	105.5	2. Rapid River	102.5
2003	Rapid River (Greg Rubick)	131	2. Rock-Mid Peninsula	60
2004	Rapid River (Greg Rubick)	144.5	2. Rock-Mid Peninsula	45
2005	Rapid River (Greg Rubick)	135	2. Bark River-Harris	54
2006	Pickford (John Bennin)	80.5	2. Rapid River	69
2007	Pickford (John Bennin)	73	2. Rapid River	67 1/3
2008	Brimley (Joyel Hyvarinen)	68	2. Powers North Central	64
2009	Brimley (Joyel Hyvarinen)	84	2. Powers North Central	68
2010	Cooks-Big Bay deNoc (Dave Partyka)	67	2. Ontonagon	60
2011	Brimley (Joyel Hyvarinen)	96	2. Crystall Falls Forest Park	61
2012	Brimley (Joyel Hyvarinen)	78	2. Eben Junction Superior Central	66
2013	St Ignace (Trudy Olsen)	121	2. Brimley	57
2014	Brimley (Joyel Hyvarinen)	84	2. Bessemer	67
2015	Newberry (Lori Fair)	64	2. Brimley	58
2016	Ontonagon (Brian Amos)	72	2. Newberry	65
2017	Lake Linden-Hubbell (Gary Guisfredi)	110	2. Pickford	58
2018	Lake Linden-Hubbell (Gary Guisfredi)	96	2. North Dickinson	63

STATE FINALS – SITES & DATES

For 9 years, from 1923-31, the state finals was a 2-day event.

Prior to 1972 ('73 in the Lower Peninsula), all meets are boys. After that point, where boys and girls meets were at different sites, they are denoted by (b) for boys and (g) for girls.

All SCHOOLS

Year	Class	Date	Site
1895	all	5/30-31	County Fairgrounds, Jackson
1896	all	5/30, 6/6	State Fairgrounds, Lansing
1897	all	6/4-5	Regents Field, Univ. Michigan, Ann Arbor
1898	all	5/28	Regents Field, Univ. Michigan, Ann Arbor
1899	all	5/26	Regents Field, Univ. Michigan, Ann Arbor
1900	all	5/26	Regents Field, Univ. Michigan, Ann Arbor
1901	all	5/25	Regents Field, Univ. Michigan, Ann Arbor
1902	all	5/17	Regents Field, Univ. Michigan, Ann Arbor
1903	all	5/23	Ferry Field, Univ. Michigan, Ann Arbor
1904	all	5/27	Ferry Field, Univ. Michigan, Ann Arbor
1905	all	5/27	Ferry Field, Univ. Michigan, Ann Arbor
1906	all	5/25	Ferry Field, Univ. Michigan, Ann Arbor
1907	all	5/24	Ferry Field, Univ. Michigan, Ann Arbor
1908	all	5/16	Mich. Agricultural Coll., East Lansing
1909	all	5/14	Mich. Agricultural Coll., East Lansing
1910	all	5/14	Mich. Agricultural Coll., East Lansing
1911	all	5/13	Mich. Agricultural Coll., East Lansing
1912	all	6/8	Bois Blanc Island, Amherstburg, Ontario
1913	all	6/6	Mich. Agricultural Coll., East Lansing
1914	all	6/6	Mich. Agricultural Coll., East Lansing
1915	all	6/5	Mich. Agricultural Coll., East Lansing
1916	all	6/10	Mich. Agricultural Coll., East Lansing
1917	all	5/26	Mich. Agricultural Coll., East Lansing
1918	-	Meet not held because of war	
1919	all	5/31	Mich. Agricultural Coll., East Lansing
1920	all	5/29	Mich. Agricultural Coll., East Lansing
1921	ABC	6/5	Mich. Agricultural Coll., East Lansing
1922	ABC	6/4	Mich. Agricultural Coll., East Lansing
1923	A	6/8-9	Michigan State Coll., East Lansing
	BC	6/1-2	Michigan State Coll., East Lansing
1924	A	6/6-7	Michigan State Coll., East Lansing
	BC	5/30-31	Michigan State Coll., East Lansing
1925	A	5/29-30	Michigan State Coll., East Lansing
	BC	6/5-6	Michigan State Coll., East Lansing
1926	A	5/28-29	Michigan State Coll., East Lansing
	BC	6/4-5	Michigan State Coll., East Lansing
1927	ABCD	5/27-28	Michigan State Coll., East Lansing
1928	ABCD	5/25-26	Michigan State Coll., East Lansing
1929	ABCD	5/24-25	Michigan State Coll., East Lansing
1930	ABCD	5/23-24	Michigan State Coll., East Lansing
1931	ABCD	5/22-23	Michigan State Coll., East Lansing
1932	ABCD	5/28	Michigan State Coll., East Lansing
1933	ABCD	5/27	Michigan State Coll., East Lansing
1934	ABCD	5/26	Michigan State Coll., East Lansing
1935	ABCD	5/25	Michigan State Coll., East Lansing
1936	ABCD	5/23	Michigan State Coll., East Lansing
1937	ABCD	5/22	Michigan State Coll., East Lansing
1938	ABCD	5/21	Michigan State Coll., East Lansing
1939	ABCD	5/26	Michigan State Coll., East Lansing
1940	ABCD	5/25	Michigan State Coll., East Lansing
	UP	5/25	Michigan Tech Univ., Houghton
1941	ABCD	5/24	Michigan State Coll., East Lansing
	UP	5/24	Michigan Tech Univ., Houghton
1942	ABCD	5/23	Michigan State Coll., East Lansing
	UP	5/23	Michigan Tech Univ., Houghton
1943	-	Meet not held because of war	
1944	ABCD	5/20	Michigan State Coll., East Lansing
	UP	5/20	Michigan Tech Univ., Houghton
1945	ABCD	5/26	Michigan State Coll., East Lansing
	UP	5/26	Michigan Tech Univ., Houghton
1946	ABCD	5/25	Michigan State Coll., East Lansing
	UP	5/25	Michigan Tech Univ., Houghton
1947	ABCD	5/24	Michigan State Coll., East Lansing
	UP	5/24	Escanaba HS, Escanaba
1948	ABCD	5/29	Michigan State Coll., East Lansing
	UP	5/29	Escanaba HS, Escanaba
1950	ABCD	5/27	Michigan State Coll., East Lansing
	UP	5/27	Michigan Tech Univ., Houghton
1951	ABCD	5/26	Michigan State Coll., East Lansing
	UP	5/26	Escanaba HS, Escanaba
1952	AC	5/24	Michigan State Coll., East Lansing
	BD	5/24	Ferry Field, Univ. Michigan, Ann Arbor
	UP	5/24	Michigan Tech Univ., Houghton
1953	AC	5/23	Michigan State Univ., East Lansing
	BD	5/23	Ferry Field, Univ. Michigan, Ann Arbor
	UP	5/23	Marquette HS, Marquette
1954	AC	5/22	Ferry Field, Univ. Michigan, Ann Arbor
	BD	5/22	Michigan State Univ., East Lansing
	UP	5/22	Michigan Tech Univ., Houghton
1955	AC	5/21	Michigan State Univ., East Lansing
	BD	5/21	Ferry Field, Univ. Michigan, Ann Arbor
	UP	5/21	Escanaba HS, Escanaba
1956	AC	5/19	Ferry Field, Univ. Michigan, Ann Arbor
	BD	5/19	Michigan State Univ., East Lansing
	UP	5/19	Marquette HS, Marquette
1957	AC	5/18	Michigan State Univ., East Lansing
	BD	5/18	Ferry Field, Univ. Michigan, Ann Arbor
	UP	5/18	Michigan Tech Univ., Houghton
1958	A	5/24	Ferry Field, Univ. Michigan, Ann Arbor
	B	5/24	Michigan State Univ., East Lansing
	CD	5/24	Central Michigan Univ., Mt Pleasant
	UP	5/24	Marquette HS, Marquette
1959	AB	5/23	Michigan State Univ., East Lansing
	CD	5/23	Central Michigan Univ., Mt Pleasant
	UP	5/23	Marquette HS, Marquette
1960	A	5/21	Ferry Field, Univ. Michigan, Ann Arbor
	B	5/21	Houseman Field, Grand Rapids
	CD	5/21	Central Michigan Univ., Mt Pleasant
	UP	5/27	Kingsford HS, Kingsford
1961	A	5/20	Michigan State Univ., East Lansing
	B	5/20	Ferry Field, Univ. Michigan, Ann Arbor
	CD	5/20	Central Michigan Univ., Mt Pleasant
	UP	5/27	Michigan Tech Univ., Houghton
1962	A	5/26	Ferry Field, Univ. Michigan, Ann Arbor
	B	5/26	Michigan State Univ., East Lansing
	CD	5/26	Central Michigan Univ., Mt Pleasant
	UP	5/26	Marquette HS, Marquette
1963	A	5/25	Michigan State Univ., East Lansing
	B	5/25	Ferry Field, Univ. Michigan, Ann Arbor
	CD	5/25	Central Michigan Univ., Mt Pleasant
	UP	5/25	Marquette HS, Marquette
1964	A	5/23	Ferry Field, Univ. Michigan, Ann Arbor
	B	5/23	Michigan State Univ., East Lansing
	CD	5/23	Central Michigan Univ., Mt Pleasant
	UP	5/23	Marquette HS, Marquette
1965	A	5/22	Michigan State Univ., East Lansing
	B	5/22	Ferry Field, Univ. Michigan, Ann Arbor
	CD	5/22	Central Michigan Univ., Mt Pleasant
	UP	5/22	Michigan Tech Univ., Houghton
1966	A	5/21	Ferry Field, Univ. Michigan, Ann Arbor
	B	5/21	Michigan State Univ., East Lansing
	CD	5/21	Central Michigan Univ., Mt Pleasant
	UP	5/21	Marquette HS, Marquette
1967	A	5/26	Michigan State Univ., East Lansing
	B	5/26	Ferry Field, Univ. Michigan, Ann Arbor
	CD	5/26	Central Michigan Univ., Mt Pleasant
	UP	5/27?	Marquette HS, Marquette
1968	A	5/22	Ferry Field, Univ. Michigan, Ann Arbor
	B	5/25	Michigan State Univ., East Lansing

	CD	5/25	Central Michigan Univ., Mt Pleasant
	UP	5/25	Marquette HS, Marquette
1969	A	5/24	Michigan State Univ., East Lansing
	B	5/24	Ferry Field, Univ. Michigan, Ann Arbor
	CD	5/24	Central Michigan Univ., Mt Pleasant
	UP	5/24	Marquette HS, Marquette
1970	A	5/23	Ferry Field, Univ. Michigan, Ann Arbor
	B	5/23	Michigan State Univ., East Lansing
	CD	5/23	Central Michigan Univ., Mt Pleasant
	UP	5/23	Marquette HS, Marquette
1971	A	5/22	Michigan State Univ., East Lansing
	B	5/22	Ferry Field, Univ. Michigan, Ann Arbor
	CD	5/22	Central Michigan Univ., Mt Pleasant
	UP	5/22	Marquette HS, Marquette
1972	A	5/20	Guy Houston Stadium, Flint
	B	5/20	Michigan State Univ., East Lansing
	C	5/20	Central Michigan Univ., Mt Pleasant
	D	5/20	Caro HS, Caro
	UP (b)	5/20	Marquette HS, Marquette
	UP (g)	6/2	Marquette HS, Marquette
1973	A (b)	5/19	Michigan State Univ., East Lansing
	All (g)	5/19	East Lansing HS, East Lansing
	B (b)	5/19	Guy Houston Stadium, Flint
	C (b)	5/19	Central Michigan Univ., Mt Pleasant
	D (b)	5/19	Caro HS, Caro
	UP (b)	5/26	Marquette HS, Marquette
	UP (g)	5/19	Iron Mountain HS, Iron Mountain
1974	A (b)	6/1	Guy Houston Stadium, Flint
	B (b)	6/1	Michigan State Univ., East Lansing
	AB (g)	6/1	Houseman Field, Grand Rapids
	C (b)	6/1	Central Michigan Univ., Mt Pleasant
	D (b)	6/1	Caro HS, Caro
	CD (g)	6/1	Alma HS, Alma
	UP (b)	5/25	Marquette HS, Marquette
	UP (g)	5/25	Gwinn HS, Gwinn
1975	A (b)	5/31	Guy Houston Stadium, Flint
	A (g)	5/31	Franklin HS, Livonia
	B (b)	5/31	Michigan State Univ., East Lansing
	B (g)	5/31	Houseman Field, Grand Rapids
	C (b)	5/31	Central Michigan Univ., Mt Pleasant
	C (g)	5/31	Central HS, Kalamazoo
	D (b)	5/31	Caro HS, Caro
	D (g)	5/31	Kearsley HS, Flint
	UP	5/24	Marquette HS, Marquette
1976	A (b)	6/5	Houseman Field, Grand Rapids
	A (g)	6/5	Lahser HS, Bloomfield Hills
	B (b)	6/5	Harper Creek HS, Battle Creek
	B (g)	6/5	Comstock HS, Comstock
	C (b)	6/5	Ithaca HS, Ithaca
	C (g)	6/5	St Louis HS, St Louis
	D (b)	6/5	Waverly HS, Lansing
	D (g)	6/5	Sexton HS, Lansing
	UP	5/29	Marquette HS, Marquette
1977	A (b)	6/4	Guy Houston Stadium, Flint
	A (g)	6/4	Lahser HS, Bloomfield Hills
	B (b)	6/4	Harper Creek HS, Battle Creek
	B (g)	6/4	Comstock HS, Comstock
	C (b)	6/4	Ithaca HS, Ithaca
	C (g)	6/4	St Louis HS, St Louis
	D (b)	6/4	Waverly HS, Lansing
	D (g)	6/4	Sexton HS, Lansing
	UP	5/28	Marquette HS, Marquette
1978	A (b)	6/3	Guy Houston Stadium, Flint
	A (g)	6/3	Brighton HS, Brighton
	B (b)	6/3	Marysville HS, Marysville
	B (g)	6/3	Otsego HS, Otsego
	C (b)	6/3	Michigan Center HS, Michigan Center
	C (g)	6/3	Haslett HS, Haslett
	D (b)	6/3	Waverly HS, Lansing

	D (g)	6/3	Sexton HS, Lansing
	UP	5/27	Marquette HS, Marquette
1979	A (b)	6/2	Guy Houston Stadium, Flint
	A (g)	6/2	Brighton HS, Brighton
	B	6/2	Houseman Field, Grand Rapids
	C (b)	6/2	Michigan Center HS, Michigan Center
	C (g)	6/2	Cassopolis HS, Cassopolis
	D	6/2	Grand Blanc HS, Grand Blanc
	UP	5/26	Marquette HS, Marquette
1980	A	5/31	Houseman Field, Grand Rapids
	B	5/31	Sturgis HS, Sturgis
	C (b)	5/31	Middleville HS, Middleville
	C (g)	5/31	Cassopolis HS, Cassopolis
	D	5/31	Grand Blanc HS, Grand Blanc
	UP	5/24	Marquette HS, Marquette
1981	A	5/30	Guy Houston Stadium, Flint
	B	5/30	Sturgis HS, Sturgis
	C	5/30	Clare HS, Clare
	D	5/30	Caro HS, Caro
	UP	5/23	Marquette HS, Marquette
1982	A	6/5	Guy Houston Stadium, Flint
	B	6/5	Houseman Field, Grand Rapids
	C	6/5	Bangor HS, Bangor
	D	6/5	Caro HS, Caro
	UP	5/29	Marquette HS, Marquette
1983	A	6/4	Withington Stadium, Jackson
	B	6/4	Caro HS, Caro
	C	6/4	Bangor HS, Bangor
	D	6/4	Central HS, Traverse City
	UP	5/28	Marquette HS, Marquette
1984	A	6/2	Withington Stadium, Jackson
	B	6/2	Caro HS, Caro
	C	6/2	Clare HS, Clare
	D	6/2	Central HS, Traverse City
	UP	5/26	Marquette HS, Marquette
1985	A	6/1	Guy Houston Stadium, Flint
	B	6/1	Northwest HS, Jackson
	C	6/1	Clare HS, Clare
	D	6/1	Hillsdale Coll., Hillsdale
	UP	5/25	Marquette HS, Marquette
1986	A	5/31	Guy Houston Stadium, Flint
	B	5/31	Northwest HS, Jackson
	C	5/31	Bangor HS, Bangor
	D	5/31	Hillsdale Coll., Hillsdale
	UP	5/24	Marquette HS, Marquette
1987	A	5/30	Alma Coll., Alma
	B	5/30	Sturgis HS, Sturgis
	C	5/30	Bangor HS, Bangor
	D	5/30	Central HS, Traverse City
	UP	5/23	Marquette HS, Marquette
1988	A	6/4	Eastern Michigan Univ., Ypsilanti
	B	6/4	Sturgis HS, Sturgis
	C	6/4	Alma Coll., Alma
	D	6/4	Central HS, Traverse City
	UP	5/28	Marquette HS, Marquette
1989	A	6/3	Eastern Michigan Univ., Ypsilanti
	B	6/3	Northwest HS, Jackson
	C	6/3	Alma Coll., Alma
	D	6/3	Hillsdale Coll., Hillsdale
	UP	5/27	Marquette HS, Marquette
1990	A	6/2	Midland HS, Midland
	B	6/2	Northwest HS, Jackson
	C	6/2	Wyoming Park HS, Wyoming
	D	6/2	Hillsdale Coll., Hillsdale
	UP	5/26	Marquette HS, Marquette
1991	A	6/1	Houseman Field, Grand Rapids
	B	6/1	Wyoming Park HS, Wyoming
	C	6/1	Byron Center HS, Byron Center
	D	6/1	Forest Hills Northern HS, Grand Rapids

	UP	5/25	Marquette HS, Marquette
1992	A	5/30	Houseman Field, Grand Rapids
	B	5/30	Wyoming Park HS, Wyoming
	C	5/30	Byron Center HS, Byron Center
	D	5/30	Forest Hills Northern HS, Grand Rapids
	UP	5/23	Marquette HS, Marquette
1993	A	6/5	Houseman Field, Grand Rapids
	B	6/5	Wyoming Park HS, Wyoming
	C	6/5	Byron Center HS, Byron Center
	D	6/5	Forest Hills Northern HS, Grand Rapids
	UP	5/29	Marquette HS, Marquette
1994	A	6/4	Midland HS, Midland
	B	6/4	Saginaw HS, Saginaw
	C	6/4	Western HS, Auburn
	D	6/4	Glenn HS, Bay City
	UP	5/28	Marquette HS, Marquette
1995	A	6/3	Saginaw HS, Saginaw
	B	6/3	Dow HS, Midland
	C	6/3	Western HS, Auburn
	D	6/3	Glenn HS, Bay City
	UP	5/27	Marquette HS, Marquette
1996	A	6/1	Rockford HS, Rockford
	B	6/1	Lowell HS, Lowell
	C	6/1	Comstock Park HS, Comstock Park
	D	6/1	Forest Hills Northern HS, Grand Rapids
	UP	5/25	Kingsford HS, Kingsford
1997	A	5/31	Rockford HS, Rockford
	B	5/31	Lowell HS, Lowell
	C	5/31	Comstock Park HS, Comstock Park
	D	5/31	Forest Hills Northern HS, Grand Rapids
	UP	5/24	Kingsford HS, Kingsford
1998	A	5/30	Western HS, Auburn
	B	5/30	Saginaw HS, Saginaw
	C	5/30	Midland HS, Midland
	D	5/30	Frankenmuth HS, Frankenmuth
	UP	5/30	Marquette HS, Marquette
1999	A	6/5	Midland HS, Midland
	B	6/5	Western HS, Auburn
	C	6/5	Saginaw HS, Saginaw
	D	6/5	Frankenmuth HS, Frankenmuth
	UP	6/5	Marquette HS, Marquette
2000	D1	6/3	Rockford HS, Rockford
	D2	6/3	Grandville HS, Grandville
	D3	6/3	Comstock Park HS, Comstock Park
	D4	6/3	Forest Hills Northern HS, Grand Rapids
	UP	6/3	Kingsford HS, Kingsford
2001	D1	6/2	Rockford HS, Rockford
	D2	6/2	Forest Hills Northern HS, Grand Rapids
	D3	6/2	Comstock Park HS, Comstock Park
	D4	6/2	Lowell HS, Lowell
	UP	6/2	Kingsford HS, Kingsford
2002	D1	6/1	Rockford HS, Rockford
	D2	6/1	Houseman Field, Grand Rapids
	D3	6/1	Comstock Park HS, Comstock Park
	D4	6/1	Forest Hills Northern HS, Grand Rapids
	UP	6/1	Kingsford HS, Kingsford
2003	D1	5/31	Rockford HS, Rockford
	D2	5/31	Houseman Field, Grand Rapids
	D3	5/31	Comstock Park HS, Comstock Park
	D4	5/31	Forest Hills Northern HS, Grand Rapids
	UP	5/31	Kingsford HS, Kingsford
2004	D1	6/5	Rockford HS, Rockford
	D2	6/5	Caledonia HS, Caledonia
	D3	6/5	Comstock Park HS, Comstock Park
	D4	6/5	Houseman Field, Grand Rapids
	UP	6/5	Kingsford HS, Kingsford
2005	D1	6/4	Rockford HS, Rockford
	D2	6/4	Caledonia HS, Caledonia

	D3	6/4	Comstock Park HS, Comstock Park
	D4	6/4	Houseman Field, Grand Rapids
	UP	6/4	Kingsford HS, Kingsford
2006	D1	6/3	East Kentwood HS, Kentwood
	D2	6/3	Forest Hills Northern HS, Grand Rapids
	D3	6/3	Comstock Park HS, Comstock Park
	D4	6/3	Forest Hills Eastern HS, Ada
	UP	6/3	Kingsford HS, Kingsford
2007	D1	6/2	East Kentwood HS, Kentwood
	D2	6/2	Zeeland Stadium, Zeeland
	D3	6/2	Comstock Park HS, Comstock Park
	D4	6/2	Forest Hills Eastern HS, Ada
	UP	6/2	Kingsford HS, Kingsford
2008	D1	5/31	Rockford HS, Rockford
	D2	5/31	Zeeland Stadium, Zeeland
	D3	5/31	Comstock Park HS, Comstock Park
	D4	5/31	Forest Hills Eastern HS, Ada
	UP	5/31	Kingsford HS, Kingsford
2009	D1	5/30	East Kentwood HS, Kentwood
	D2	5/30	Zeeland Stadium, Zeeland
	D3	5/30	Comstock Park HS, Comstock Park
	D4	5/30	Forest Hills Eastern HS, Ada
	UP	5/30	Kingsford HS, Kingsford
2010	D1	6/5	Rockford HS, Rockford
	D2	6/5	Zeeland Stadium, Zeeland
	D3	6/5	Comstock Park HS, Comstock Park
	D4	6/5	Jenison HS, Jenison
	UP	6/5	Kingsford HS, Kingsford
2011	D1	6/4	Rockford HS, Rockford
	D2	6/4	Houseman Field, Grand Rapids
	D3	6/4	Comstock Park HS, Comstock Park
	D4	6/4	Jenison HS, Jenison
	UP	6/4	Kingsford HS, Kingsford
2012	D1	6/2	East Kentwood HS, Kentwood
	D2	6/2	Houseman Field, Grand Rapids
	D3	6/2	Comstock Park HS, Comstock Park
	D4	6/2	Jenison HS, Jenison
	UP	6/2	Kingsford HS, Kingsford
2013	D1	6/1	East Kentwood HS, Kentwood
	D2	6/1	Forest Hills Eastern HS, Ada
	D3	6/1	Comstock Park HS, Comstock Park
	D4	6/1	Hudsonville HS, Hudsonville
	UP	6/1	Kingsford HS, Kingsford
2014	D1	5/31	Rockford HS, Rockford
	D2	5/31	Houseman Field, Grand Rapids
	D3	5/31	Comstock Park HS, Comstock Park
	D4	5/31	Hudsonville HS, Hudsonville
	UP	5/31	Kingsford HS, Kingsford
2015	D1	5/30	Rockford HS, Rockford
	D2	5/30	Zeeland Stadium, Zeeland
	D3	5/30	Comstock Park HS, Comstock Park
	D4	5/30	Hudsonville HS, Hudsonville
	UP	5/30	Kingsford HS, Kingsford
2016	D1	6/4	Hudsonville HS, Hudsonville
	D2	6/4	Zeeland Stadium, Zeeland
	D3	6/4	Comstock Park HS, Comstock Park
	D4	6/4	Houseman Field, Grand Rapids
	UP	6/4	Kingsford HS, Kingsford
2017	D1	6/4	East Kentwood HS, Kentwood
	D2	6/4	Zeeland Stadium, Zeeland
	D3	6/4	Comstock Park HS, Comstock Park
	D4	6/4	Houseman Field, Grand Rapids
	UP	6/4	Kingsford HS, Kingsford
2018	D1	6/2	East Kentwood HS, Kentwood
	D2	6/2	Zeeland Stadium, Zeeland
	D3	6/2	Comstock Park HS, Comstock Park
	D4	6/2	Hudsonville HS, Hudsonville
	UP	6/2	Kingsford HS, Kingsford

The State Finals by the Numbers

Since the first state meet in Jackson in 1895, thousands of young people have competed in what for many would be the most memorable track & field experience of their lives. For us numbers buffs, there are probably thousands of different ways to make sense out of these numbers. Below are just a few, and now that for the first time a complete list of champions is available, our readers are welcome to sort out the numbers any way they want, if for no other reason than the fun of the inevitable debates.

For these compilations, we have included the Detroit city meet from 1931-61 as being equivalent to the state finals (and usually better).

The nature of these compilations favors smaller divisions. Frankly, it's easier to win a state title in the smaller divisions, and much easier in the Upper Peninsula. The smaller the pond, the easier the wins come. For instance, for instance, in the listing of which schools have won the most individual/relay titles, if we combine the peninsulas into one listing, no Lower Peninsula teams would even make the top 10

Number of state individual champions:
Boys: 8720 (LP 5343, UP 2960, Detroit 382, outmoded events 35)
Girls: 3882 (LP 2204, UP 1678)

State champion relays:
Boys: 1769 (LP 1030, UP 695, Detroit 44)
Girls: 1192 (LP 678, UP 514)
Total number of relay spots: 11,844

Which means that, ignoring multiple winners, there are 24,446 state champions in Michigan history.

MOST TEAM TITLES

Lower Peninsula Boys
1. Detroit DePorres 16; 2. tie, Flint Beecher & Saginaw 10; 4. Detroit Central 9; 5. Tie, Detroit Northwestern & Ecorse 8; 7. Tie, Covert & East Kentwood 7; 9. Tie, Detroit Lutheran West, East Grand Rapids, Michigan School For The Deaf, Pontiac Central & St Joseph 6; 14. Tie, Birmingham, Brethren, Centreville, Detroit Benedictine, Detroit Cass Tech, Detroit East Catholic, Detroit University, Grand Rapids Central & Plainwell 5.

Lower Peninsula Girls
1. Ann Arbor Pioneer 17; 2. Detroit Renaissance 10; 3. Fowler 9; 4. Tie, Detroit Cass Tech & Detroit Country Day 7; 6. Tie, Frankenmuth, Maple City Glen Lake & Oak Park 5; 9. Tie, Flint Beecher, Flint Northern & North Muskegon 4; 12. Tie, Dearborn Divine Child, Grosse Pointe South, Muskegon Catholic, Pewamo-Westphalia & Potterville 3.

Upper Peninsula Boys
1. Pickford 34; 2. Escanaba 15; 3. Marquette 14; 4. Tie, Ironwood & Munising 11; 6. Sault Ste. Marie 10; 7. Menominee 9; 8. Tie, Houghton, Rapid River & Wakefield 8.

Upper Peninsula Girls
1. Marquette 24; 2. Escanaba 18; 3. Pickford 14; 4. St Ignace 9; 5. Ishpeming Westwood 8; 6. Ironwood 7; 7. Negaunee 6; 8. Tie, Brimley & Rapid River 5.

MOST STATE CHAMPIONS BY SCHOOL

These are not team titles, but individual/relay crowns.

Lower Peninsula Boys
1. Detroit Central 98; 2. Detroit Northwestern 88; 3. Detroit DePorres 75; 4. Detroit Cass Tech 66; 5. Saginaw 64; 6. Pontiac/Pontiac Central 62; 7. Ann Arbor/Ann Arbor Pioneer 59; 8. Detroit Miller 55; 9. tie, Grand Rapids Central & Michigan School for the Deaf 54; 11. tie, Detroit Cooley & Detroit Eastern 53; 13. Flint Central & Flint Northern 50; 15. tie, Lansing Central & Monroe 48; 17. tie, Kalamazoo Central & Muskegon 47; 19. Detroit Lutheran West 46; 20. tie, Centreville, Ecorse & River Rouge 44; 23. tie, Detroit Country Day & Detroit Redford 43; 25. East Grand Rapids 42; 26. Detroit Mumford 41; 27. Tie, Birmingham, Detroit East Catholic & St. Joseph 40; 30. Brethren 39; 31. tie, Allegan, Detroit University & Litchfield 38; 34. Flint Beecher 37; 35 tie, East Kentwood & Paw Paw 36; 37. Battle Creek Central & East Lansing 35; 39. tie, Detroit Southwestern, Jackson, Niles & Ypsilanti 33.

Lower Peninsula Girls
1. Ann Arbor Pioneer 75; 2. Detroit Cass Tech 69; 3. Fowler 54; 4. Detroit Renaissance 47; 5. Detroit Country Day 45; 6. Maple City Glen Lake 37; 7. tie, Flint Beecher & Ypsilanti 30; 9. Frankenmuth 29; 10. tie, Oak Park & Pewamo-Westphalia 27; 12. Rockford 26; 13. tie, Albion, Detroit Mumford, Flint Northern & Reading 24; 17. Athens 23; 18. tie, Ann Arbor Greenhills, Battle Creek St. Phillip & Detroit DePorres 20; 21. Grass Lake 19; 22. tie, Benzie Central & East Kentwood 18; 24. tie, Concord & Detroit Lutheran West 17; 26. tie, Ann Arbor Huron, Grand Rapids Christian, Hemlock, Onsted & Richland 16; 31. tie, Bath & DeWitt 15; 33. tie, Grosse Pointe South & Lansing Waverly 14; 35. tie, Battle Creek Lakeview, Cadillac, Camden-Frontier, Mason County Eastern, Mendon, Potterville, Southfield Christian, St. Joseph Lake Michigan Catholic & Traverse City St. Francis 13.

Lower Peninsula Combined Boys & Girls
1. Detroit Cass Tech 135; 2. Ann Arbor Pioneer 134; 3. Detroit Central 105; 4. Detroit DePorres 95; 5. Detroit Northwestern 90; 6. Detroit Country Day 88; 7. Fowler 78; 8. Flint Northern 74; 9. tie, Flint Beecher, Pontiac/Pontiac Central & Saginaw 67; 12. Detroit Mumford 65; 13. tie, Ypsilanti & Detroit Lutheran West 63; 15. Flint

Central 57; 16. tie, Detroit Cooley & Detroit Miller 55; 18. tie, East Kentwood, East Grand Rapids, Grand Rapids Central & Michigan School for the Deaf 54; 22. Detroit Eastern 53; 23. tie, Detroit Renaissance, Kalamazoo Central & River Rouge 52; 26. Albion 51; 27. St. Joseph 50; 28. tie, Lansing Central, Litchfield & Monroe 48; 31. tie, Centreville & Muskegon 47; 33. tie, Frankenmuth & Reading 45; 35. tie, Ecorse & Rockford 44; 37. tie, Detroit Redford, Lansing Sexton, Oak Park & Pewamo-Westphalia 43.

Upper Peninsula Boys

1. Pickford 215; 2. Escanaba 188; 3. Marquette 178; 4. Menominee 142; 5. Munising 138; 6. Kingsford 125; 7. Sault Ste Marie 116; 8. Wakefield 115; 9. Ironwood 114; 10. Houghton 110.

Upper Peninsula Girls

1. Marquette 207; 2. Escanaba 146; 3. St. Ignace 107; 4. Pickford 101; 5. Rapid River 78; 6. tie, Hancock & Ishpeming 69; 8. Negaunee 68; 9. Lake Linden-Hubbell 67; 10. Ishpeming Westwood 64.

Upper Peninsula Combined Boys & Girls

1. Marquette 385; 2. Escanaba 334; 3. Pickford 316; 4. St. Ignace 208; 5. Menominee 194; 6. Munising 191; 7. Kingsford 187; 8. Sault Ste. Marie 175; 9. Ironwood 173; 10. Rapid River 168.

MOST INDIVIDUAL TITLES - BOYS

With the four-event limit, obviously the maximum number of state individual titles that any current high schooler could win would be 16, which means that Clarence Christopher's record of 18 wins is safe for all time. His record will be easy for many to dismiss—it came in the first four years of the championships. However, he had athletic skills that would still shine today: a 21-6 long jump and a 43-5½ triple jump speak to that. But his record does include one event that basically was a non-scoring exhibition, the 40-yard hurdles, as well as one that wasn't the forerunner of any modern event, the standing hop-step-jump. So if any of our readers would rather consider someone else the "real" recordholder, the authors have no objection.

(*=one or more of the titles came in a higher division)

Class A/Division 1

18 – Clarence Christopher (Lansing) 1-40H, 1-100, 1-220, 1-440, 1-120LH, 1-120H, 1-220H, 2-HJ, 4-PV, 2-LJ, 2-TJ, 1-standingHSJ
7 – Roy Ellis (Detroit Central) 2-100, 2-220, 1-HJ, 2-LJ
7 – Ralph Keeler (Detroit Central/University) 3-100, 3-220, 1-440
6 – Art Kohler (Lansing Central) 2-SP, 1DT, 3-HT
6 – George Widman (Detroit Central) 3-100, 3-220
6 – George Hester (Detroit Northern) 3-100, 3-220
6 – Eugene Beatty (Detroit Northeastern) 2-120H, 2-220H, 2-LJ
6 – Joe Horner (Grand Rapids Central) 2-PV, 2-SP, 1-DT, 1-HT
6 – Willis Ward (Detroit Northwestern) 2-120H, 1-120LH, 1-220H, 2-HJ

Detroit 1931-1961

7 – Henry Carr (Detroit Southwestern/Northwestern) 3-100, 2-220, 2-LJ
7 – Willie Henderson (Detroit Southwestern) 3-120HH, 4-120LH
5 – Bernard Lucas (Detroit Pershing) 1-120HH, 2-HJ, 2-LJ
5 – Willie Wright (Detroit Miller) 1-440, 1-120HH, 1-120LH, 2-PV

Class B/Division 2

9 – Tyrone Wheatley (Dearborn H Robichaud) 3-100, 1-200, 2-110H, 3-LJ
6 – Ron Mead (East Lansing) 3-100, 3-220
6 – John Palmer (St Louis) 4-180H, 2-LJ

Class C/Division 3

7 – John Mack (New Haven) 3-200, 4-400
6 – Alan Smith (Paw Paw) 2-100, 2-220, 2-LJ
6 – Ham White (Boyne City) 3-100, 2-220, 1-LJ

Class D/Division 4

7 – Juson Johnson (Baldwin) 4-100, 3-200
7 – Ryan Shay (Central Lake) 1-800, 3-1600, 3-3200
6 – Ken Beane (Brethren) 4-100, 2-220
6 – Cory Noeker (Pewamo-Westphalia) 1-100, 1-200, 2-110H, 2-300H
6 – Thomas Robinson* (Wyoming Lee) 3-100, 3-200
6 – Ancel Rodgers (Benton Harbor) 3-100, 3-220
6 – Lester Walters (Centreville) 2-120H, 3-220H, 1-LJ
6 – William Weise (Bear Lake) 1-100, 1-220, 4-HJ

UP Class AB/Division 1

9 – Justin Wiles (Escanaba) 2-100, 3-200, 3-400, 1-LJ
8 – Matt Wise (Calumet) 1-100, 2-200, 3-110H, 2-300H
7 – Dick Berlinski (Kingsford) 2-100, 2-220, 3-LJ
7 – Clayton Sayen (Houghton) 1-100, 2-200, 3-400, 1-800

UP Class C/Division 2

8 – Peter Remien* (Ishpeming Westwood) 2-800, 3-1600, 3-3200
7 – Chris Lett (Houghton) 1-800, 3-1600, 3-3200

UP Class D/Division 3

9 – Brett Hannah (Munising) 2-800, 3-1600, 4-3200
7 – Joe Baker (Pickford) 1-100, 2-110H, 2-300H, 2-LJ
7 – Brock Bower (Bark River-Harris) 2-110H, 3-HJ, 2_LJ
7 – Andy Cooper (Munising) 1-200, 2-110H, 2-300H, 2-HJ
7 – Tyler Crossman (Rapid River) 3-1600, 4-3200
7 – Ryan Holm (Wakefield) 2-800, 2-1600, 3-3200
7 – Mike Schmaus (Ontonagon) 1-100, 3-200, 2-300H, 1-HJ

MOST INDIVIDUAL TITLES – GIRLS

Class A/Division 1

10 – Sekayi Bracey (East Kentwood) 4-100, 3-200, 3-LJ
7 – Hannah Meier (Grosse Pointe South) 4-800, 3-1600
7 – Sharon Van Tuyl (Portage Northern) 4-1600, 3-3200
6 – Josephine Hobbs (Detroit Central) 3-100, 3-200
6 – Anita Lee (Detroit Cass Tech) 1-100H, 2-HJ, 3-LJ
5 – Elaine Jones (Detroit Chadsey) 2-100, 2-200, 1-400
5 – Shayla Mahan (Detroit Mumford) 3-100, 2-200
5 – Delisa Walton (Detroit Mackenzie) 3-400, 2-800

Class B/Division 2

8 – Kendall Baisden (Detroit Country Day) 2-100, 2-200, 4-400
7 – Rochelle Collins (Detroit Immaculata) 3-400, 4-800
6 – Charnell Lynn (Inkster/Ypsilanti Willow Run) 2-100, 2-200, 2-400
6 – Tiffany Ofili (Ypsilanti) 2-100H, 3-300H, 1-LJ
6 – Kelly Smith (Petoskey) 3-800, 3-1600
5 – Sara Jane Baker (Mattawan) 2-400, 3-HJ
5 – Tori Desira (DeWitt) 2-100H, 3-300H
5 – Zoe Eby (Carleton Airport) 1-100, 3-200, 1-400
5 – Kenyetta Grigsby (River Rouge) 3-100H, 2-300H
5 – Kathy Kost (Mt Clemens L'Anse Creuse) 2-100, 2-400, 1-LJ
5 – Jamie Kryzminski (Corunna) 3-1600, 2-3200
5 – Suenomi Norinh (Zeeland East) 1-100H, 1-HJ, 3-LJ
5 – Heather Slay (East Grand Rapids) 3-1600, 2-3200
5 – Kayla Windemuller (Holland Christian) 3-1600, 2-3200

Class C/Division 3

12 – Sami Michell (Reed City) 2-200, 4-100H, 3-300H, 3-LJ
9 – Shirley Evans (Detroit Country Day) 4-100, 4-200, 1-400
9 – Naheed Irani (Onsted) 3-200, 1-800, 2-100H, 3-300H
9 – Julie Johnson (Laingsburg) 3-100, 3-200, 3-400
8 – Bethany Brewster (Saginaw Valley Lutheran) 1-800, 3-1600, 4-3200
7 – Amelia Bannister (Albion) 2-100, 2-400, 3-800
7 – Nicole Bush (Wyoming Kelloggsville) 3-1600, 4-3200
7 – Annie Fuller (Manistee) 4-800, 3-1600
6 – Becky Breisch* (Edwardsburg) 3-SP, 3-DT
5 – Cathy Ackley (Hart) 3-800, 2-1600
5 – Kelsey Ritter (Frankenmuth) 3-200, 2-400
5 – Jeanne Spitler (Montague) 2-1600, 3-3200
5 – Ali Wiersma (Allendale) 1-1600, 4-3200

Class D/Division 4
10 – Maria Shoup (Mason Co Eastern) 1-400, 2-800, 2-100H, 3-300H, 2-LJ
8 – Brittany Hedgepeth (SJ Lake Michigan Catholic) 3-100, 2-200, 3-LJ
8 – Marnie Peplinski (Maple City Glen Lake) 2-100H, 3-300H, 3-LJ
7 – Lindsey Hufnagel (Fowler) 1-100, 3-200, 3-400
7 – Marissa Treece (Maple City Glen Lake) 1-800, 3-1600, 3-3200
6 – Holly Bullough* (Traverse City St Francis) 3-800, 3-1600
6 – Andrea Kincannon (GP University Liggett) 2-100, 3-200, 1-400
6 – Erin Dillon (Reading) 3-200, 3-400
6 – Theresa Proost (Maple City Glen Lake) 1-100, 1-200, 4-400
5 – Chika Amene (Southfield Christian) 2-100, 2-200, 1-400
5 – Miranda Johnson (Ottawa Lake-Whiteford) 2-200, 3-LJ
5 – Jenny Kulchar (Burton Atherton) 2-800, 3-HJ
5 – Jeaniae Lawton (Harper Woods Gallagher) 2-SP, 3-DT
5 – Robin Magee (Ann Arbor Greenhills) 1-800, 2-1600, 2-3200
5 – Kirsten Olling (Breckenridge) 1-1600, 4-3200
5 – Samantha Saenz (Concord) 1-800, 3-1600, 1-3200

UP Class AB/Division 1
10 – Tiffany Hodge (Menominee) 4-100H, 3-300H, 3-LJ
9 – Becky Drake (Kingsford) 3-100, 1-400, 1-HJ, 4-LJ
9 – Chelsea Jacques (Calumet) 4-100, 4-200, 1-LJ

UP Class C/Division 2
12 – Amber Smith (Ishpeming Westwood) 4-800, 4-1600, 4-3200
10 – Dani Gagne (Norway) 3-100, 3-200, 1-400, 3-LJ
10 – Erin Holmberg (Cooks-Big Bay de Noc) 2-400, 1-800, 4-1600, 3-3200

UP Class D/Division 3
12 – Gwen Wilkie (DeTour) 3-100, 4-200, 3-100H, 2-300H
10 – Dana Feak (Felch North Dickinson) 1-400, 3-800, 4-1600, 2-3200
10 – Kara Scherer (Cedarville) 3-100, 4-200, 3-400

MOST INDIVIDUAL/RELAY TITLES – BOYS

Class A/Division 1
18 – Clarence Christopher (Lansing) 1-40H, 1-100, 1-220, 1-440, 1-120LH, 1-120H, 1-220H, 2-HJ, 4-PV, 2-LJ, 2-TJ, 1-standing HSJ
8 – Eugene Beatty (Detroit Northeastern) 2-120H, 2-220H, 2-LJ, 2-4x2
7 – Roy Ellis (Detroit Central) 2-100, 2-220, 1-HJ, 2-LJ
7 – Ralph Keeler (Detroit Central/University) 3-100, 3-220, 1-440
7 – George Hester (Detroit Northern) 3-100, 3-220, 1-4x2
7 – George Widman (Detroit Central) 3-100, 3-220, 1-4x2
7 – Thomas Wilcher (Detroit Central) 2-110H, 1-300H, 2-4x1, 2-4x4

Detroit 1931-1961
8 – Henry Carr (Detroit SW/Northwestern) 3-100, 2-220, 2-LJ, 1-4x2
7 – Willie Henderson (Detroit Southwestern) 3-120HH, 4-120LH
5 – Bob Abbott (Detroit Redford) 1-100, 2-220, 2-4x2
5 – Bernard Lucas (Detroit Pershing) 1-120HH, 2-HJ, 2-LJ
5 – Willie Wright (Detroit Miller) 1-440, 1-120HH, 1-120LH, 2-PV

Class B/Division 2

9 – Tyrone Wheatley (Dearborn H Robichaud) 3-100, 1-200, 2-110H, 3-LJ
7 – Willie Betts (River Rouge) 2-120H, 2-180H, 2-4x2, 1-4x4
7 – Ron Mead (East Lansing) 3-100, 3-220, 1-4x2
7 – Kent Pritchard (Allegan) 1-100, 2-HJ, 2-LJ, 2-4x2

Class C/Division 3
13 – John Mack (New Haven) 3-200, 4-400, 3-4x2, 3-4x4
11 – Chris Rucker (Detroit Country Day) 2-100, 1-400, 2-4x1, 4-4x2, 2-4x4
8 – Alan Smith (Paw Paw) 2-100, 2-220, 2-LJ, 2-4x2
7 – Joe Corbett (Detroit Lutheran West) 2-100, 2-110H, 2-4x1, 1-4x2

Class D/Division 4
9 – Richard Beane (Brethren) 1-120HH, 1-120LH, 2-180H, 1-HJ, 4-4x2
9 – Anthony Bowman* (Det DePorres/OL St Mary) 2-200, 4-4x1, 3-4x2
9 – Juson Johnson (Baldwin) 4-100, 3-200, 2-4x1
8 – Ken Beane (Brethren) 4-100, 2-220, 2-4x2
8 – Lawson Bright-Mitchell (Albion/Concord) 2-100, 3-200, 2-4x2, 1-4x4
7 – Arlon Davison (Michigan School / Deaf) 2-100, 2-220, 1-SP, 2-4x2
7 – Vernon Lynch (Detroit DePorres) 2-110H, 1-300H, 1-4x1, 2-4x2, 1-4x4
7 – Ed Robinson (Michigan School for the Deaf) 3-100, 2-220, 2-4x2
7 – Willy Scott (Detroit East Catholic) 2-110H, 2-300H, 1-LJ, 1-4x2, 1-4x4
7 – Ryan Shay (Central Lake) 1-800, 3-1600, 3-3200
7 – Kelvin Singleton* (Centreville) 1-200, 2-400, 2-LJ, 1-4x2, 1-4x4
7 – Lester Walters (Centreville) 2-120H, 3-220H, 1-LJ, 1-4x2
7 – Robert Willhight (Detroit East Catholic) 2-100, 2-200, 2-4x1, 1-4x2

UP Class AB/Division 1
10 – Justin Wiles (Escanaba) 2-100, 3-200, 3-400, 1-LJ, X
9 – Matt Wise (Calumet) 1-100, 2-200, 3-110H, 2-300H, X

UP Class C/Division 2
9 – Nate Meyer (Ishpeming) 1-100, 1-200, 2-400, 1-4x2, 3-4x4, 1-4x8
9 – Peter Remien* (Ishpeming Westwood) 2-800, 3-1600, 3-3200, X
9 – Nick Zweifel (Norway) 3-400, 1-HJ, 2-4x2, 2-4x4, 1-4x8

UP Class D/Division 3
9 – Brock Bower (Bark River-Harris) 2-110H, 3-HJ, 2-LJ, 2X
9 – Brett Hannah (Munising) 2-800, 3-1600, 4-3200
9 – Ryan Holm (Wakefield) 2-800, 2-1600, 3-3200, 2X

MOST INDIVIDUAL/RELAY TITLES – GIRLS

Class A/Division 1
11 – Hannah Meier (Grosse Pointe South) 4-800, 3-1600, 2-4x4, 2-4x8
10 – Sekayi Bracey (East Kentwood) 4-100, 3-200, 3-LJ
10 – Shayla Mahan (Detroit Mumford) 3-100, 2-200, 2-4x1, 3-4x2

Class B/Division 2
10 – Kendall Baisden (Det Country Day) 2-100, 2-200, 4-400, 1-4x1, 1-4x2
10 – Jessica Jones* (Det Renaissance/Mumford) 1-200, 3-400, 4-4x2, 2-4x4
10 – Twynette Wilson (Flint Beecher) 1-400, 1-800, 2-4x1, 3-4x2, 3-4x4

Class C/Division 3
14 – Shirley Evans (Det Country Day) 4-100, 4-200, 1-400, 3-4x2, 2-4x4
12 – Sami Michell (Reed City) 2-200, 4-100H, 3-300H, 3-LJ
11 – Naheed Irani (Onsted) 3-200, 1-800, 2-100H, 3-300H, 1-4x1, 1-4x2
10 – Amelia Bannister (Albion) 2-100, 2-400, 3-800, 1-4x1, 1-4x2, 1-4x4

Class D/Division 4
12 – Marnie Peplinski (Maple City Glen Lake) 2-100H, 3-300H, 3-LJ, 4-4x4
10 – Brittany Hedgepeth (SJ Lake Mich Catholic) 3-100, 2-200, 3-LJ, 2-4x1
10 – Maria Shoup (Mason Co Eastern) 1-400, 2-800, 2-100H, 3-300H, 2-LJ
10 – Theresa Proost (MC Glen Lake) 1-100, 1-200, 4-400, 4-4x4

UP Class AB/Division 1
12 – Tammy Cook (Escanaba) 4-100, 2-200, 1-400, 1-4x1, 4-4x2
12 – Tiffany Hodge (Menominee) 4-100H, 3-300H, 3-LJ, 2-4x1

UP Class C/Division 2
13 – Amber Smith (Ishpeming Westwood) 4-800, 4-1600, 4-3200, 1-4x8

12 – Abbey Kelto (Munising) 1-800, 3-1600, 4-3200, 4-4x8
UP Class D/Division 3
12 – Richelle Robinson* (St Ignace) 3-200, 3-400, 1-4x1, 3-4x2, 2-4x4
12 – Gwen Wilkie (DeTour) 3-100, 4-200, 3-100H, 2-300H

FOUR STRAIGHT IN INDIVIDUAL EVENT - BOYS

Class A/Division 1
Clarence Christopher (Lansing) PV – 1895-98
Harold Stein (Monroe) PV – 1931-34
Detroit 1931-1961
Willie Henderson (Detroit Southwestern) 120LH – 1932-35
Class C/Division 3
John Mack (New Haven) 400 – 1993-96
John Palmer (St Louis) 180H – 1953-56
Class D/Division 4
Ken Beane (Brethren) 100 – 1955-58
Juson Johnson (Baldwin) 100 – 1994-97
William Weise (Bear Lake) HJ – 1932-35
Jim Herendeen (Grass Lake) PV – 1973-76
UP Class AB/Division 1
none
UP Class C/Division 2
Austin St Louis (St Ignace) HJ – 2008-11
UC Class D/Division 3
Tyler Crossman (Rapid River) 3200 – 2005-08
Mark Oberlin (Crystal Falls Forest Park) 800 – 1974-77

FOUR STRAIGHT IN INDIVIDUAL EVENT - GIRLS

Class A/Division 1
Sekayi Bracey (East Kentwood) 100 – 2013-16
Hannah Meier (Grosse Pointe South) 800 – 2011-14
Sharon Van Tuyl (Portage Northern) 1600 – 1995-98
Class B/Division 2
Kendall Baisden (Detroit Country Day) 400 – 2010-13
Rochelle Collins (Detroit Immaculata) 800 – 1975-78
Carla Ploeg (Middleville Thornapple Kellogg) LJ – 1990-94
Class C/Division 3
Bethany Brewster (Saginaw Valley Lutheran) 3200 – 1995-98

Nicole Bush (Wyoming Kelloggsville) 3200 – 2001-04
Shirley Evans (Detroit Country Day) 100 – 1985-88
Shirley Evans (Detroit Country Day) 200 – 1985-88
Annie Fuller (Manistee) 800 – 2012-15
Sami Michell (Reed City) 100H – 2011-14
Ali Wiersma (Allendale) 3200 – 2009-12
Class D/Division 4
Ronele Lamkin (McBain Northern Michigan Christian) HJ – 1990-94
Kirsten Olling (Breckenridge) 3200 – 2011-14
Theresa Proost (Maple City Glen Lake) 400 – 1989-92
Kristie Wieber* (Pewamo-Westphalia) PV 2008-11
UP Class AB/Division 1
Tammy Cook (Escanaba) 100 – 1985-88
Becky Drake (Kingsford) LJ – 1976-79
Tiffany Hodge (Menominee) 100H – 1992-95
Jamie Roberts (Kingsford) 100H – 2007-10
UP Class C/Division 2
Angela Arthur (Ironwood) 200 – 1992-95
Tracy Holappa (Ishpeming) 100 – 1987-90
Tracy Holappa (Ishpeming) 200 – 1987-90
Abbey Kelto (Munising) 3200 – 2007-10
Jill Merrick (Negaunee) 1600 – 1977-80
Christie Nutkins (Newberry) 3200 – 1988-91
Amber Smith (Ishpeming Westwood) 800 – 2001-04
Amber Smith (Ishpeming Westwood) 1600 – 2001-04
Amber Smith (Ishpeming Westwood) 3200 – 2001-04
UC Class D/Division 3
Dana Feak (Felch North Dickinson) 1600 – 1991-94
Erin Holmberg (Cooks-Big Bay de Noc) 1600 – 2007-10
Erin Holmberg (Cooks-Big Bay de Noc) 3200 – 2007-10
Danielle Holmgren (Rapid River) 1600 – 2002-05
Danielle Holmgren (Rapid River) 3200 – 2002-05
Lauren Marshall (Rapid River) PV – 2004-07
Kara Scherer (Cedarville) 200 – 1990-93
Olivia Soumis (Ontonagon) LJ – 2009-12
Lauren Sprangler (Eben Superior Junction) 400 – 2009-12
Gwen Wilkie (DeTour) 200 – 1981-84

State Titles By School

A complete alphabetical listing of schools that have won state individual and relay titles. The first column is boys titles, the second is girls, and the third is boys/girls combined.

Schools (with divisions they have won in)	BOYS	GIRLS	TOTAL
Addison (C, D3, D4)	5	3	8
Adrian (A, B, D1, D2)	17	2	19
Adrian Madison (D, D3, D4)	6	11	17
Airport (B)	2	0	3
Akron (D)	1	0	1
Akron-Fairgrove (C, D, D4)	20	12	32
Alba (D)	1	0	1
Albion (B, C, D3, D4)	27	24	51
Albion Starr Commonwealth (D)	4	0	4
Algonac (B, C, D2)	18	1	19
Allegan (B, C, D2)	38	0	38
Allen Park (A, D2)	2	1	3
Allendale (D, D2, D3)	18	12	30
Alma (B, D2)	19	2	21
Almont (C, D, D3)	10	3	13
Alpena (A, B)	10	2	12
Alpena Catholic (C)	1	0	1
Alpha (UPD)	12	0	12
Ann Arbor/Ann Arbor Pioneer (A, D1)	59	75	134
Ann Arbor Greenhills (C, D, D4)	8	20	28
Ann Arbor Huron (A, D1)	9	16	25
Ann Arbor Richard (D, D3)	5	8	13
Ann Arbor Skyline (D1)	1	1	2
Ann Arbor St Thomas (D)	7	0	7
Ann Arbor University (C, D)	19	0	19
Arenac-Eastern (D)	3	0	3
Armada (C, D3)	2	2	4
Ashley (D)	1	0	1
Athens (C, D, D4)	8	23	31
Atlanta (D4)	0	2	2
Auburn Hills Avondale (B, D1, D2)	16	3	19
Au Gres (D)	3	0	3
Au Gres-Sims (D4)	1	0	1
Augusta (C)	1	0	1

Schools (with divisions they have won in)	BOYS	GIRLS	TOTAL
Bad Axe (B, C, D3)	7	1	8
Baldwin (C, D, D4)	24	2	26
Bangor (B, C, D3)	11	1	12
Baraga (UPC, UPD, UPD3)	23	13	36
Bark River (UPD)	2	0	2
Bark River-Harris (UPD, UPD2, UPD3)	25	36	61
Baroda (D)	6	0	6
Bath (C, D, D3, D4)	22	15	37
Battle Creek / Battle Creek Central (A, D1)	35	4	39
Battle Creek Harper Creek (B, D2)	2	4	6
Battle Creek Lakeview (A, B, C, D1, D2)	8	13	21
Battle Creek Pennfield (B, C, D3)	10	2	12
Battle Creek Springfield (C)	1	0	1
Battle Creek St Phillip (C, D, D4)	21	20	41
Bay City Central (A, D1)	14	0	14

School	BOYS	GIRLS	TOTAL
Bay City Eastern (A)	7	0	7
Bay City Handy (B)	2	0	2
Bay City Glenn (B)	1	2	3
Bay City St Mary (D)	1	0	1
Bay City Western (B, D1)	2	0	2
Bayport (D)	2	0	2
Beal City (D, D4)	7	8	15
Bear Lake (D)	15	0	15
Beaverton (B, D3)	5	1	6
Belding (B, C)	11	0	11
Bellaire (D, D4)	11	4	15
Belleville (A, B, D1)	8	1	9
Bellevue (C, D4)	2	1	3
Benton Harbor (A, D1, D2)	16	12	28
Benton Harbor St John (D)	17	0	17
Benzie Central (C, D3)	8	18	36
Bergland (D, UPD)	4	0	4
Berkley (A, B, C, D1)	6	0	6
Berrien Springs (C, D3)	16	1	17
Bessemer (UPC, UPD, UPD3)	89	33	122
Big Rapids (B, D2)	10	6	16
Big Rapids Crossroads (D4)	8	0	8
Birch Run (D3)	1	0	1
Birmingham (A, B)	40	0	40
Birmingham Brother Rice (A, D1)	6	0	6
Birmingham Groves (D1)	1	0	1
Birmingham Roeper (D4)	0	4	4
Birmingham Seaholm (A, D1)	3	6	9
Blanchard (D)	1	0	1
Blanchard-Montabella (C, D3, D4)	1	3	4
Blissfield (C)	2	7	9
Bloomfield Hills (D)	22	0	22
Bloomfield Hills Andover (A, B)	5	7	12
Bloomfield Hills Lahser (A, D2)	5	5	10
Bloomfield Hills Marian (D1, D2)	0	3	3
Boyne City (C, D3)	14	3	17
Breckenridge (C, D3, D4)	11	8	19
Brethren (D)	39	0	39
Bridgeport (D2, D3)	0	6	6
Bridgman (C, D, D3)	13	1	14
Brighton (A)	2	3	5
Brimley (UPD, UPD3)	21	24	45
Bronson (C, D3)	5	4	9
Brooklyn (B)	1	0	1
Brooklyn Columbia Central (D3)	4	0	4
Brown City (D4)	4	1	5
Buchanan (B, C, D3)	10	3	13
Burr Oak (D)	1	0	1
Burton Atherton (C, D4)	1	9	10
Burton Bentley (B, C, D4)	7	5	12
Byron (C, D, D3)	5	3	8
Byron Center (C, D2)	7	6	13

Detroit Southwestern (A, D2) .... 33 ..... 0 33
Detroit St Ambrose (C) .... 1 .... 0 1
Detroit St Andrew (D) .... 0 .... 1 1
Detroit St Anthony (B) .... 1 .... 0 1
Detroit St Charles (B, D) .... 2 .... 0 2
Detroit St Joseph (B) .... 1 .... 0 1
Detroit St Rita (C) .... 1 .... 0 1
Detroit St Theresa (C) .... 2 .... 0 2
Detroit UD Jesuit (A, B) .... 7 ..... 0 7
Detroit University (all, C, D) .... 38 ..... 0 38
Detroit Urban Lutheran (D4) .... 0 ..... 2 2
Detroit Western (A) .... 17 ..... 0 17
DeWitt (C, D, D2) .... 6 .... 15 21
Dexter (B, D1, D2) .... 12 ..... 7 19
Dimondale (D) .... 13 ..... 0 13
Doelle (UPD) .... 1 .... 0 1
Dollar Bay (UPD, UPD3) .... 7 .... 6 13
Dowagiac (all, B, D2, D3) .... 31 ..... 4 35
Dryden (D) .... 1 .... 0 1
Dundee (C, D3) .... 11 ..... 1 12
Durand (B, D3) .... 4 .... 9 13

Schools (with divisions they have won in)   BOYS GIRLS TOTAL
East Detroit (A, B, D1) .... 7 .... 3 10
East Grand Rapids (A, B, C, D2) .... 42 ..... 12 54
East Jackson (C, D3) .... 19 ..... 3 22
East Jordan (C, D3) .... 1 .... 1 2
East Kentwood (A, D1) .... 36 ..... 18 54
East Lansing (A, B, C, D1, D2) .... 35 ..... 6 41
Eaton Rapids (B, C, D2) .... 5 .... 5 10
Eau Claire (C, D, D4) .... 12 ..... 2 14
Eben (UPC, UPD) .... 37 ..... 1 38
Eben Junction Superior Central (UPD, UPD3) 13 ..... 15 28
Ecorse (B, C) .... 44 ..... 0 44
Ecorse St Francis (D) .... 2 .... 0 2
Edwardsburg (B, C, D, D3) .... 3 .... 8 11
Elberta (D) .... 3 .... 0 3
Elk Rapids (C, D) .... 2 .... 0 2
Elkton-Pigeon-Bayport (B, C, D3) .... 3 .... 4 7
Ellsworth (D) .... 6 .... 0 6
Elsie (C) .... 2 .... 0 2
Engadine (UPD, UPD3) .... 29 ..... 21 50
Erie Mason (B, C, D3) .... 4 .... 8 12
Escanaba (A, B, UPAB, UPB, UPD1) .... 188 ... 146 334
Escanaba Holy Name (UPAB, UPB) .... 11 ..... 0 11
Escanaba St Joseph UPC) .... 4 .... 0 4
Essexville Garber (B, D2, D3) .... 8 .... 0 8
Evart (C, D3, D4) .... 5 .... 2 7
Ewen UPC, UPD) .... 14 ..... 0 14
Ewen-Trout Creek (UPD, UPD3) .... 10 ..... 3 13

Schools (with divisions they have won in)   BOYS GIRLS TOTAL
Fairgrove (D) .... 2 .... 0 2
Fairview (D, D4) .... 6 .... 3 9
Farmington (A, B, C, D1) .... 15 ..... 2 17
Farmington Hills Harrison (A, D1, D2) .... 10 ..... 3 13
Farmington Our Lady-Sorrows (C) .... 1 .... 0 1
Farwell (C, D3) .... 3 .... 3 6
Felch North Dickinson (UPD, UPD3) .... 51 ..... 34 85
Fennville (C) .... 3 .... 1 4
Fenton (B, D1, D2) .... 13 ..... 5 18

Ferndale (A, B, D2) .... 13 ...... 0 13
Fife Lake Forest Area (D4) .... 1 ...... 4 5
Flat Rock (C) .... 0 ...... 3 3
Flint Academy (C, D) .... 2 ...... 0 2
Flint Ainsworth (B) .... 4 ...... 0 4
Flint Atherton (C) .... 2 ...... 0 2
Flint Beecher (B, D3) .... 37 ..... 30 67
Flint Bendle (B, C) .... 7 ...... 2 9
Flint Carman (A) .... 1 ...... 1 2
Flint Carman-Ainsworth (A, D1) .... 15 ..... 1 16
Flint Central (A, D1) .... 50 ..... 7 57
Flint Dye (C) .... 3 .... 0 3
Flint Hamady (C, D3, D4) .... 6 ...... 8 14
Flint Holy Redeemer (C) .... 1 ...... 0 1
Flint Holy Rosary (D) .... 5 ...... 0 5
Flint Hoover (C) .... 3 ...... 0 3
Flint Kearsley (A, B, D2) .... 14 ..... 0 14
Flint Northern (A) .... 50 ..... 24 74
Flint Northwestern (A, D2) .... 6 ...... 5 11
Flint Powers (A, B, D2) .... 11 ..... 9 20
Flint Southwestern (A, D1, D2) .... 20 ..... 9 29
Flint St Agnes (C) .... 1 ...... 0 1
Flint St Matthew (D) .... 3 ...... 0 3
Flint St John (C) .... 1 ...... 0 1
Flint Utley (D) .... 1 ...... 0 1
Flushing (A, D1) .... 4 .... 3 7
Fowler (D, D4) .... 24 ..... 54 78
Fowlerville (B, C, D2) .... 9 .... 3 12
Frankenmuth (B, C, D3) .... 16 ..... 29 45
Frankfort (C, D, D4) .... 9 .... 1 10
Fraser (A, D1) .... 1 .... 3 4
Freeland (C, D, D2) .... 12 ..... 2 14
Freesoil (D) .... 8 .... 0 8
Fremont (B, C) .... 22 ..... 7 29
Fremont Providence Christian (D4) .... 1 ...... 0 1
Fruitport (B, D, D2) .... 7 .... 1 8
Fulton-Middleton (C, D, D4) .... 11 ..... 3 14

Schools (with divisions they have won in)   BOYS GIRLS TOTAL
Galesburg (C) .... 1 .... 0 1
Galesburg-Augusta (C) .... 5 .... 1 6
Galien (D) .... 15 ..... 1 16
Garden (UPD) .... 4 .... 0 4
Garden City (A) .... 2 .... 0 2
Gaylord (B, D2) .... 2 .... 2 4
Gaylord St Mary (D) .... 2 .... 0 2
Genessee (D, D4) .... 5 .... 2 7
Gladstone (UPAB, UPC, UPD1) .... 84 ..... 48 132
Gladwin (D3) .... 0 .... 1 1
Glen Arbor Leelanau School (C, D) .... 15 ..... 1 16
Gobles/Gobleville (all, C, D) .... 6 .... 2 8
Goodrich (C, D, D3) .... 5 .... 8 13
GR Forest Hills Central (A, B, D1) .... 3 .... 4 7
GR Forest Hills Eastern (D2) .... 2 .... 3 5
GR Forest Hills Northern (C, D2) .... 5 .... 4 9
Grand Blanc (A, B, D1) .... 17 ..... 6 23
Grand Haven (A, B, D1) .... 8 .... 6 14
Grand Ledge (D1) .... 7 .... 2 9
Grand Marais (UPD) .... 1 .... 0 1
Grand Rapids Catholic (A, B, D2) .... 19 ..... 5 24
Grand Rapids Central (all) .... 54 ..... 0 54

Grand Rapids Christian (B) .... 4 .... 16 20

Grand Rapids Creston (A, D1) .... 8 .... 0 8

Grand Rapids Davis Tech (A) .... 5 .... 0 5

Grand Rapid Kenowa Hills (D1) .... 5 .... 4 9

Grand Rapids Lee (B, C) .... 7 .... 0 7

Grand Rapids Northview (B) .... 9 .... 1 10

Grand Rapids Ottawa Hills (A, D2) .... 22 ..... 9 31

Grand Rapids South (A) .... 18 ..... 0 18

Grand Rapids South Christian (B, C, D2) .... 5 ..... 10 15

Grand Rapids Union (A, D1) .... 7 .... 1 8

Grand Rapids West Catholic (B, D3) .... 10 ..... 6 16

Grand Rapids Wyoming Park (C) .... 5 .... 0 5

Grandville (A, C, D1) .... 13 ..... 1 14

Grandville Calvin Christian (B, C, D3) .... 10 ..... 7 17

Grant (C) .... 4 .... 1 5

Grass Lake (D, D3, D4) .... 22 ..... 19 41

Grayling (D2) .... 1 .... 0 1

Greenland (UPD) .... 1 .... 0 1

Greenville (A, B, C, D1) .... 7 .... 4 11

Grosse Ile (B, C, D, D2) .... 15 ..... 5 20

Grosse Pointe (A) .... 9 .... 0 9

Grosse Pointe Liggett (C, D) .... 4 .... 0 4

Grosse Pointe North (A) .... 10 ..... 1 11

Grosse Pointe South (D1) .... 0 .... 14 14

Grosse Pointe St Paul (C) .... 1 .... 0 1

Grosse Pointe University (D) .... 4 .... 0 4

Grosse Pointe University Liggett (C, D) .... 8 .... 7 15

Gwinn (UPAB, UPC, UPD, UPD1, UPD2) .... 68 ..... 48 116

Holt (A, B, C, D1) .... 4 .... 12 16

Homer (C, D, D4) .... 9 .... 11 20

Honor (C) .... 1 .... 0 1

Hopkins (D3) .... 2 .... 2 4

Houghton (UPC, UPD1) .... 110 ... 36 146

Houghton Lake (C, D3) .... 5 .... 0 5

Howard City (C, D) .... 2 .... 0 2

Howard City Tri County (C) .... 3 .... 4 7

Howell (B) .... 6 .... 1 7

Hudson (C, D3) .... 6 .... 0 6

Hudsonville (D1) .... 1 .... 1 2

Hudsonville Unity Christian (B) .... 4 .... 5 9

Lake Linden-Hubbell (UPC, UPD, UPD3)........ 21 ..... 67......88
Lake Odessa Lakewood (D2) .... 6 .... 1........7
Lake Orion (A, B, D1)................................... 7 .... 6.......13
Lakeview (C, D3) .... 4 .... 3........7
Lambertville (C) .... 2 .... 0.......2
Lansing/Lansing Central (A) .... 48 ..... 0........48
Lansing Blind School (D)............................. 1 ...... 0.......1
Lansing Boys Training/Vocational (C, D) .... 7 ...... 0.......7
Lansing Catholic (B, C, D2, D3) .... 12 ..... 11......23
Lansing Eastern (A) .... 16 ..... 2......18
Lansing Everett (A, C, D1)........................... 28 ..... 0.......28
Lansing Hill (A) .... 1 ...... 0.......1
Lansing Sexton (A, D1, D2) .... 31 ..... 12......43
Lansing St Mary (C) .... 5 .... 0.......5
Lansing Waverly (D1, D2) .... 7 ..... 14......21
Lapeer West (A, B) .... 0 .... 3........3
Lawrence (D, D4)....................................... 2 ..... 1........3
Lawton (C, D, D4) .... 11 .... 3.........14
Leroy Pine River (C) .... 3 ...... 6.........9
Leslie (C, D3) .... 6 ...... 1........7
Lincoln Alcona (C) .... 1 ...... 6........7
Lincoln Park (A, D1) .... 2 ...... 2........4
Linden (B, D2) .... 6 ...... 1........7
Litchfield (D, D4) .... 38 ..... 10......48
Littlefield (D) .... 1 ...... 0.......1
Livingston Christian (D4) .... 3 ...... 0.......3
Livonia Bentley (A) .... 4 ...... 0........4
Livonia Churchill (A) .... 2 ...... 1........3
Livonia Clarenceville (B, D2, D3) .... 3 ...... 1........4
Livonia Franklin (A) .... 1 ...... 0.......1
Livonia Ladywood (A, B, D2) .... 0 ..... 11......11
Livonia Stevenson (A, D1) .... 3 ...... 1........4
Lowell (B, C) .... 12 ..... 0........12
Ludington (B, D2) .... 16 ..... 4........20
Luther (D) .... 2 ...... 0.......2
Lutheran Westland (C, D4)........................... 4 .... 1........5

Marquette Baraga (UPC) .... 4........0 4
Marquette Pierce (UPD) .... 13......0 13
Marshall (all, B) .... 7........1 8
Martin (D) .... 5........0 5
Marysville (B, C) .... 4........0 4
Mason (B, D2) .... 10......1 11
Mason County Central (C, D3) .... 14......6 20
Mason County Eastern (D)............................ 7......13 20
Mass (UPD) .... 1........0 1
Mattawan (C) .... 2......5 7
Mayville (C) .... 2.......1 3
McBain (D, D4).. 6.......1 7
McBain Northern Michigan Christian (D4) ... 1........9 10
Melvindale (B, D2).................................... 5.......1 6
Melvindale ABT (D4).................................. 2........0 2
Memphis (C, D) .... 1.......1 2
Mendon (D, D4) .... 24......13 37
Menominee (UPAB, UPB, UPD1) .... 142...52 194
Merrill (C, D, D4) .... 6........1 7
Merritt (D) .... 1........0 1
Mesick (C, D, D3, D4) .... 10......4 14
Michigan Center (C, D3) .... 3........3 6
Michigan Military Academy (all) .... 7........0 7
Michigan School For The Deaf (D) .... 54......0 54
Middleton (D) .... 7........0 7
Middleville Thornapple Kellogg (B, C, D2) .... 5........9 14
Midland (A) .... 10......4 14
Midland Bullock Creek (B, C) .... 4........1 5
Midland Dow (A)...................................... 1........3 4
Milan (B, C, D2)....................................... 15......7 22
Milford (A, B, C, D1).................................. 9........4 13
Millington (B, C) .... 2........5 7
Mio (D4) .... 1........0 1
Mohawk Keweenaw (UPD) .... 7........0 7
Monroe (A, D1).. 48......0 48
Monroe Jefferson (B, D2) .... 0......5 5
Monroe St Mary (B, D3)............................. 2........2 4
Montague (C)... 2........5 7
Montgomery (D) .... 1........0 1
Montrose (B, C, D3).................................. 7......10 17
Morenci (all, C, D, D4) .... 16......8 24
Morley-Stanwood (C, D3) .... 4........5 9
Morrice (D, D4) .... 6........1 7
Mt Clemens (A, B)..................................... 13......1 14
Mt Clemens L'Anse Creuse (B)...................... 0........6 6
Mt Clemens Lutheran North (C) .... 1........2 3
Mt Clemens St Mary (D) .... 7........0 7
Mt Morris (B, D2)..................................... 11......1 12
Mt Morris St Mary (D) .... 6........0 6
Mt Pleasant (A, B, D2)............................... 14......1 15
Mt Pleasant Sacred Heart (C, D, D4) .... 11......8 19
Muir (D) .... 2........0 2
Munising (UPAB, UPB, UPD2, UPD3) .... 138...53 191
Muskegon (A) .... 47......0 47
Muskegon Catholic (A, B, C, D4) .... 11......9 20
Muskegon Christian (C, D) .... 3........1 4
Muskegon Heights (A, B, D3) .... 13......6 19
Muskegon Mona Shores (A, D1) .... 3........3 6
Muskegon Oakridge (C, D3)......................... 10......3 13
Muskegon Orchard View (B, D2) .... 4........1 5
Muskegon Reeths Puffer (B, C) .... 2........0 2

Muskegon West Shore (D) .... 0 .... 1 1
Muskegon Western Mich. Christian (C, D4) .. 3 .... 0 3

Schools (with divisions they have won in)   BOYS GIRLS TOTAL
Nahma (D, UPD) .... 16 ..... 0 16
Napoleon (C, D, D3) .... 7 ..... 8 15
Nashville (C) .... 6 ..... 0 6
National Mine (UPD) .... 2 ..... 0 2
Negaunee (UPAB, UPB, UPC, UPD1) .... 73 ..... 68 141
Negaunee St Paul (UPD) .... 2 ..... 0 2
New Boston (C) .... 1 ..... 0 1
New Boston Huron (D2) .... 0 ..... 1 1
New Buffalo (D, D4) .... 7 ..... 5 12
New Haven (C, D3, D4) .... 29 ..... 11 40
New Lothrop (C) .... 1 ..... 8 9
New Troy (D) .... 1 ..... 0 1
Newaygo (C, D) .... 6 ..... 0 6
Newberry (UPAB, UPB, UPC, UPD2) .... 99 ..... 36 135
Niles (A, B, D2) .... 33 ..... 2 35
Niles Brandywine (B, C, D3) .... 10 ..... 0 10
North Adams (D) .... 0 ..... 2 2
North Branch (B, C, D2) .... 3 ..... 1 4
North Central (UPD3) .... 3 ..... 0 3
North Farmington (A) .... 2 ..... 0 2
North Muskegon (B, D, D4) .... 9 ..... 11 20
Northport (D) .... 0 ..... 3 3
Northville (B, C, D1) .... 9 ..... 5 14
Norway (UPC, UPD, UPD2) .... 43 ..... 54 98
Novi (D1) .... 2 ..... 5 7

Schools (with divisions they have won in)   BOYS GIRLS TOTAL
Oak Park (A, B, D1) .... 16 ..... 27 43
Oak Ridge (C) .... 1 ..... 0 1
Oakland Christian (D) .... 1 ..... 0 1
Okemos (A, B, C, D, D1) .... 21 ..... 10 31
Olivet (C, D3) .... 4 ..... 1 5
Onekama (D, D4) .... 21 ..... 7 28
Onsted (B) .... 2 ..... 16 18
Ontonagon (C, UPC, UPD, UPD3) .... 63 ..... 37 100
Orchard Lake (all) .... 1 ..... 0 1
Orchard Lake St Mary (C, D2) .... 16 ..... 0 16
Ortonville Brandon (B, C) .... 2 ..... 1 3
Oscoda (all, B) .... 3 ..... 0 3
Osseo (D) .... 1 ..... 0 1
Otisville (D) .... 4 ..... 0 4
Otisville LakeVille (B, D2, D3) .... 2 ..... 8 10
Otsego (all, B, C, D2) .... 20 ..... 1 21
Ottawa Lake Whiteford (C, D, D4) .... 6 ..... 8 14
Ovid (D) .... 1 ..... 0 1
Ovid-Elsie (D3) .... 8 ..... 1 9
Owendale-Gagetown (D) .... 2 ..... 0 2
Owosso (A, B) .... 6 ..... 0 6
Oxford (B, C, D1) .... 20 ..... 1 21

Schools (with divisions they have won in)   BOYS GIRLS TOTAL
Painesdale (UPC, UPD) .... 6 ..... 0 6
Painesdale-Jeffers (UPD, UPD3) .... 6 ..... 4 10
Parchment (B, C, D3) .... 6 ..... 9 15
Parma Western (B, C, D2) .... 6 ..... 3 9
Paw Paw (B, C) .... 36 ..... 2 38
Peck (D) .... 1 ..... 2 3

Pellston (D, D4) .... 1 .... 1 2
Pentwater (D) .... 6 .... 0 6
Perkins (UPD) .... 4 .... 0 4
Perry (C, D3) .... 5 .... 1 6
Petersburg-Summerfield (C, D4) .... 2 .... 2 4
Petoskey (B, D2) .... 21 ..... 8 29
Petoskey St Francis (D) .... 3 .... 0 3
Pewamo-Westphalia (C, D3, D4) .... 16 ..... 27 43
Pickford (UPD, UPD3) .... 215 .... 101 ... 316
Pinckney (D1) .... 4 .... 1 5
Pinconning (D2) .... 0 .... 1 1
Pittsford (C, D, D4) .... 27 ..... 9 36
Plainwell (all, B, C, D2) .... 23 ..... 1 24
Plymouth (B, C, D1) .... 13 ..... 1 14
Pontiac/Pontiac Central (A, D1) .... 62 ..... 5 67
Pontiac Catholic (C, D) .... 2 .... 1 3
Pontiac Northern (A, D1) .... 21 ..... 2 23
Pontiac Notre Dame (D2) .... 1 .... 4 5
Port Hope (D) .... 1 .... 0 1
Port Huron (A, B, D1) .... 1 .... 9 10
Port Huron Central (B) .... 4 .... 0 4
Port Huron Northern (A, D1) .... 4 .... 3 7
Portage/Portage Central (A, B, C, D) .... 5 .... 2 7
Portage Northern (A, D1) .... 16 ..... 7 23
Portland (B, C, D3) .... 4 .... 3 7
Portland St Patrick (D, D4) .... 2 .... 2 4
Posen (D) .... 0 .... 1 1
Potterville (D, D4) .... 16 ..... 13 29
Powers (UPD) .... 15 ..... 0 15
Powers-North Central (UPD, UPD3) .... 46 ..... 12 58
Prattville (D) .... 1 .... 0 1

Schools (with divisions they have won in)   BOYS GIRLS TOTAL
Quincy (C, D3) .... 8 .... 5 13

Schools (with divisions they have won in)   BOYS GIRLS TOTAL
Rapid River (UPD, UPD3) .... 90 ..... 78 168
Ravenna (C) .... 3 .... 0 3
Reading (C, D, D4) .... 21 ..... 24 45
Redford Borgess (A, B, C, D4) .... 16 ..... 5 21
Redford St Mary (C, D) .... 6 .... 3 9
Redford Thurston (B, D2) .... 3 .... 0 3
Redford Union (A, B, D1) .... 11 ..... 1 12
Reed City (B, C, D3) .... 10 ..... 12 22
Reese (C, D3) .... 12 ..... 1 13
Remus Chippewa Hills (B, D2) .... 3 .... 6 9
Republic (UPD) .... 2 .... 0 2
Republic-Michigamme (UPD, UPD2) .... 8 .... 2 10
Richland (C) .... 5 .... 16 21
Richland Gull Lake (B, D2) .... 10 ..... 3 13
Richmond (all, B) .... 2 .... 2 4
River Rouge (A, B. D2) .... 44 ..... 8 52
Riverview (B, D2) .... 4 .... 0 4
Riverview Gabriel Richard (B, C, D3) .... 4 .... 1 5
Rochester (A, C, D1) .... 4 .... 8 12
Rochester Adams (A, D1) .... 3 .... 3 6
Rochester Hills Lutheran Northwest (D, D4) . 0 .... 7 7
Rock (UPD) .... 10 ..... 1 11
Rock Mid Peninsula (UPD3) .... 32 ..... 24 56
Rockford (A, C, D1) .... 18 ..... 26 44
Rogers City (C, D4) .... 1 .... 7 8

Romeo (C, D1)..3 ...... 4........7
Romulus (A, B, C, D1, D2)...................21 ..... 7........28
Roscommon (C)....................................0 .... 1........1
Roseville (A, B, D1)..............................8 ...... 2........10
Roseville Eastern (C) ....1 ...... 0........1
Royal Oak (A) ....5 ...... 0........5
Royal Oak Dondero (A) ....3 ...... 0........3
Royal Oak Kimball (A).............................1 ...... 0........1
Royal Oak Madison (D) ....2 .... 0........2
Royal Oak Shrine (B, C, D, D4)..............9 ...... 8........17
Rudyard (UPAB, UPC, UPD, UPD2)......67 ..... 18......85

Schools (with divisions they have won in) BOYS GIRLS TOTAL

Saginaw (A, D1, D2)............................64 ..... 3........67
Saginaw Arthur Hill (A, D1) ....20 ..... 3........23
Saginaw Buena Vista (B, D4) ....9 ..... 7........16
Saginaw Carrollton (B) ....1 ...... 0........1
Saginaw Eastern (A) ....2 ...... 0........2
Saginaw Eisenhower (B)..........................1 ...... 2........3
Saginaw Heritage (A, D1) ....5 ...... 0........5
Saginaw MacArthur (B) ....0 ...... 5........5
Saginaw Michigan Lutheran (C, D, D4)..........7 ...... 9........16
Saginaw Nouvel (C) ....10 ..... 0........10
Saginaw SS Peter & Paul (C)..................7 ...... 0........7
Saginaw Swan Valley (D2, D3)................4 ...... 4........8
Saginaw Valley Lutheran C, D3, D4) ....3 ...... 10......13
Salem (A, D1) ....2 ...... 4........6
Saline (C, D1)......................................14 ..... 9........23
Sand Creek (D, D4) ....9 ...... 2........11
Sandusky (C) ....5 ...... 0........5
Sanford Meridian (C, D3) ....8 ...... 4........12
Saranac (C, D, D3) ....6 ...... 0........6
Saugatuck (D, D3, D4) ....13 ..... 2........15
Sault Ste Marie (UPAB, UPB, UPD1)..............116 ... 59......175
Sault Ste Marie Loretto (UPC) ....4 ...... 0........4
Schoolcraft (D, D3) ....7 ...... 3........10
Scottville (C) ....1 ...... 0........1
Scottville Mason County Central (C) ....4 ...... 2........6
Shelby (all, B, C, D3) ....17 .... 5........22
Shepherd (C, D3) ....7 ...... 12......19
South Haven (B) ....12 ..... 1........13
South Lyon (B, C, D, D1) ....7 ...... 4........11
Southfield (A, D1)...............................10 ..... 12......22
Southfield Bradford Academy (D3) ....1 ...... 0........1
Southfield Christian (C, D, D4) ....3 ...... 13......16
Southfield Lathrup (A, D1) ....3 ...... 6........9
Southgate/Southgate Anderson (A, D1) ...... 1 ...... 1........2
Southgate Aquinas (B, C, D) ....2 ...... 8........10
Southgate Schaffer (B) ....1 ...... 0........1
Sparta (all, B, D2) ....8 ...... 4........12
Spring Arbor (D) ....10 ..... 0........10
Spring Lake (D2) ....0 ...... 6........6
Springport (C, D, D4)............................4 ...... 3........7
St Charles (C, D3) ....4 ...... 4........8
St Clair (C) ....2 ...... 0........2
St Clair Shores Lakeview (B, D)..............6 ...... 0........6
St Clair Shores Lake Shore (C, D) ....11 ..... 0........11
St Clair Shores South Lake (B, C, D) ....24 ..... 2........26
St Ignace (UPC, UPD2, UPD3)....................101 ... 107....208
St Johns (all, B)...................................19 ..... 2........21
St Joseph (A, B) ....40 .... 10......50

St Joseph Catholic (D) ....4.........0 4
St Joseph Lake Michigan Catholic (C, D, D4) . 11......13 24
St Louis (B, C) ....26......10 36
Stambaugh (UPC) ....1.........0 1
Standish-Sterling (B, D3) ....4.........8 12
Stanton (C, D) ....2.........0 2
Stanton-Central Montcalm (B, D3) ....1.........2 3
Stephenson (UPB, UPC) ....105....29 134
Sterling Heights Ford (A).............................2.........0 2
Sterling Heights Stevenson (A, D1) ....4.........6 10
Stevensville (D) ....4.........0 4
Stevensville-Lakeshore (B, D2) ....16.......4 20
Stockbridge (all, B, C, D3) ....8.........3 11
Sturgis (B, C, D2) ....11.......3 14
Suttons Bay (D, D3) ....7.........6 13
Swartz Creek (A, D1)..................................5.........0 5

Schools (with divisions they have won in)   BOYS GIRLS TOTAL

Tawas (B, C, D3) ....4.........3 7
Taylor Center (A) ....5.........0 5
Taylor Kennedy (D1) ....0.........1 1
Taylor Truman (A, D1) ....2.........1 3
Tecumseh (B, C, D2)...................................6.........7 13
Tekonsha (D)...1.........3 4
Temperance (B) ....2.........0 2
Temperance Bedford (A, D1) ....7.......1 8
Three Oaks (C, D) ....3.........0 3
Three Oaks River Valley (C)..........................1.........0 1
Three Rivers (B, D2) ....14......2 16
Traverse City/TC Central (A, B, D1) ....16......6 22
Traverse City Pathfinder (D) ....0.......1 1
Traverse City St Francis (C, D, D3, D4) .... 4........13 17
Traverse City West (D1) ....2.........0 2
Trenary (UPD) ....4.........0 4
Trenton (B, D, D2) ....9.........1 10
Trout Creek (UPD) ....1.........0 1
Troy (A, B, D1) ....10......0 10
Troy Athens (A) ....0.........1 1

Schools (with divisions they have won in)   BOYS GIRLS TOTAL

Ubly (D4)..4........7 11
Union City (C, D3, D4) ....16......3 19
Unionville (D)..14......0 14
Unionville-Sebewaing (C, D3, D4) ....13......4 17
Utica (B, D1)...4........5 9

Schools (with divisions they have won in)   BOYS GIRLS TOTAL

Vandercook Lake (C, D4)..............................3........4 7
Vassar (B, C, D3) ....16......3 19
Vermontville (D) ....2.........0 2
Vermontville Maple Valley (D3)......................3.........8 11
Vestaburg (D)..5.........0 5
Vicksburg (B, D2) ....10......1 11
Vulcan (D, UPD) ....3.........0 3

Schools (with divisions they have won in)   BOYS GIRLS TOTAL

Wakefield (UPB, UPC, UPD3) ....115....12 127
Waldron (D4)...1........0 1
Walkerville (D, D4).....................................0........12 12
Walled Lake / Walled Lake Central (A, B, D1) 6.........1 7
Walled Lake Western (A, D1).........................3........7 10

Warren (B) .... 1 .... 0 1
Warren Bethesda Christian (D) .... 2 .... 2 4
Warren Cousino (A) .... 1 .... 0 1
Warren DeLaSalle / Det DeLaSalle (A, B, D1) 8 .... 0 8
Warren Fitzgerald (B, D2) .... 5 .... 0 5
Warren Lincoln (A) .... 0 .... 1 1
Warren Michigan Collegiate (D3) .... 1 .... 0 1
Warren Mott (A) .... 1 .... 0 1
Warren Tower (A) .... 1 .... 1 2
Warren Wood (B) .... 0 .... 1 1
Washington Eisenhower (A) .... 2 .... 0 2
Waterford Kettering (A, D1) .... 4 .... 1 5
Waterford Mott (A, D1) .... 1 .... 4 5
Waterford Our Lady (D4) .... 0 .... 1 1
Waterford Township (A) .... 2 .... 0 2
Watersmeet (UPD, UPD3) .... 2 .... 4 6
Watervliet (C, D3) .... 2 .... 3 5
Wayland (C, D2) .... 6 .... 2 8
Wayne/Wayne Memorial (A, D1) .... 5 .... 2 7
Webberville (D, D4) .... 7 .... 1 8
Weidman (D) .... 2 .... 0 2
West Bloomfield (A, D1) .... 7 .... 9 16
West Branch/Ogemaw Heights (all, B, D2) ... 11 ..... 5 16
Westland Glenn (A, D1) .... 2 .... 3 5
White Cloud (C, D4) .... 5 .... 3 8
White Lake Lakeland (A, D1) .... 6 .... 2 8
White Pigeon (C, D, D4) .... 6 .... 6 12
White Pine (UPD) .... 12 ..... 14 26

Whitehall (B, C, D, D2) .... 20 ..... 4 24
Whitmore Lake (D, D3) .... 3 .... 3 6
Whittemore-Prescott (C, D, D3) .... 4 .... 1 5
Williamston (B, C, D2, D3) .... 23 ..... 10 33
Willow Run (B) .... 16 ..... 0 16
Wolverine (D) .... 10 ..... 0 10
Woodhaven (D1) .... 0 .... 1 1
Woodland (C, D) .... 7 .... 0 7
Wyandotte Roosevelt (A, B, D1) .... 13 ..... 1 14
Wyandotte Smith (C, D) .... 4 .... 0 4
Wyoming Godwin Heights (B, C, D, D2, D3) .. 11 ..... 1 12
Wyoming Kelloggsville (D3) .... 3 .... 7 10
Wyoming Lee (C, D, D2, D3, D4) .... 12 ..... 1 13
Wyoming Park (B) .... 9 .... 6 15
Wyoming Potter's House (D4) .... 1 .... 0 1
Wyoming Rogers (B) .... 8 .... 0 8

Schools (with divisions they have won in)	BOYS	GIRLS	TOTAL
Yale (C, D2)	7	8	15
Ypsilanti /Ypsilanti Central (A, B, D1, D2)	33	29	62
Ypsilanti Lincoln (B, C, D1)	21	2	23
Ypsilanti Roosevelt (B, C, D)	22	0	22
Ypsilanti Willow Run (B)	1	3	4
Ypsilanti St John (D)	4	0	4

Schools (with divisions they have won in)	BOYS	GIRLS	TOTAL
Zeeland East (D2)	10	9	19
Zeeland West (D2)	6	2	8

Trevor Stephenson's winning D1 vault of 16-9½ at the
2018 D1 Finals was an outdoor state record.
(Peter Draugalis photo)

Jim Moyes

Jeff Hollobaugh

Jim Moyes began his career in the media back in 1956 as a 15-year-old sophomore covering sports for the *Muskegon Chronicle*. Following a stint in the Army that included a tour of duty in Vietnam in 1965, Moyes began his career in broadcasting by announcing high school sports in Traverse City in 1967.

Later taking over as the owner of the Bear Lake Tavern in his native North Muskegon, Moyes continued broadcasting high school sports for the Greater Muskegon Area. He served as the voice of high school sports in Muskegon from 1976 through 2009, before retiring to Florida.

Moyes called 45 state championship games in football and basketball but always kept an active interest in track & field. He worked as the PA announcer for more than 30 years for the Greater Muskegon City Meet while also announcing a number of conference, regional and state meets.

He still remains active on the sports scene in Florida broadcasting high school football and basketball games for Ponte Vedra High School and is currently in his 7th year as the PA announcer for the University of North Florida baseball team.

Inducted into the Michigan Basketball Coaches Hall of Fame as an announcer in 2003, and the Muskegon Area Sports Hall of Fame in 2013, Moyes is married to Mary and is the proud father of 5 children and 8 grandchildren and currently resides in Ponte Vedra, Florida.

Jeff Hollobaugh began creating all-time lists for Michigan high school track & field when he was a 15-year-old distance runner in Allen Park. After going to Western Michigan University, he was hired as statistician by *Track & Field News*, the Bible of the Sport.

That started his career as a writer and editor in the sport. In his first stint with *T&FN*, he stayed for 7 years and after several years as managing editor returned to Michigan.

He taught for 15-plus years at the community college and high school level and has coached everything from munchkins to national champions. Along the way, he covered 7 Olympic Games and 13 World Championships for *T&FN*. He has worked as an information specialist for the World Championships and the 1996 Olympic Games. In 2016 he returned to *T&FN* as associate editor.

Hollobaugh's writing has also been published by ESPN.com, the Detroit Free Press, RunMichigan, Michigan Runner, USATF and the IAAF.

In 1996 Hollobaugh founded www.michtrack.org to share his enthusiasm for Michigan track history and records. A longtime announcer of the MHSAA Finals in cross country and Div. I track, he also announces for the University of Michigan and Aquinas College, as well as many major high school events.

A resident of Dexter, Hollobaugh and his wife Karen have two daughters and a dog named Huckleberry.